Marriages and Families
Diversity and Change

SEVENTH EDITION

Mary Ann Schwartz

Northeastern Illinois University

BarBara Marliene Scott

Northeastern Illinois University

PEARSON

Boston   Columbus   Indianapolis   New York   San Francisco   Upper Saddle River
Amsterdam   Cape Town   Dubai   London   Madrid   Milan   Munich   Paris   Montréal   Toronto
Delhi   Mexico City   São Paulo   Sydney   Hong Kong   Seoul   Singapore   Taipei   Tokyo

Editorial Director: Craig Campanella
Editor in Chief: Dickson Musslewhite
Acquisitions Editor: Karen Hanson
Editorial Assistant: Joseph Jantas
Director of Marketing: Brandy Dawson
Senior Marketing Manager: Kelly May
Marketing Assistant: Diana Griffin
Managing Editor: Denise Forlow
Inhouse Liaison: Barbara Reilly'
Senior Manufacturing and Operations Manager for Arts & Sciences: Mary Fischer
Operations Specialist: Alan Fischer
Creative Director: Blair Brown
Design Manager: John Christiana
Art Director: Anne Bonanno Nieglos
Interior and Cover Designer: Karen Quigley
Cover Images: *Tablet background:* Oleksiy Mark/Shutterstock Images; *Top row, left to right:*
    Blend Images/Alamy, Blue Jean Images/Alamy, Blend Images/Alamy, Sonia Etchison/
    Shutterstock Images, Paul Prescott/Shutterstock Images; *Middle row:* Images Bazaar/Alamy,
    Myrleen Pearson/Alamy, Galina Barsakaya/Shutterstock Images, Absolut/Fotolia, Noam
    Armonn/Shutterstock Images; *Bottom row:* Tim Gainey/Alamy, Upper Cut Images/Alamy,
    Supri Suharjoto/Shutterstock Images, Blend Images/Alamy, Gulfimages/Alamy
Media Director: Brian Hyland
Digital Media Editor: Thomas Scalzo
Digital Media Project Manager: Nikhil Bramhavar
Full-Service Project Management/Composition: Integra
Printer/Binder: Quad/Graphics
Cover Printer: Lehigh-Phoenix Color
Text Font: 9.5/12 Minion Pro

Credits and acknowledgments borrowed from other sources and reproduced, with permission, in this textbook appear on appropriate page within text (or on page 581).

Library of Congress Cataloging-in-Publication Data

Schwartz, Mary Ann.
    Marriages and families : diversity and change / Mary Ann Schwartz,
BarBara Marliene Scott. — 7th ed.
        p. cm.
    Includes bibliographical references and index.
    ISBN 978-0-205-84530-9
1. Marriage—United States.   I. Scott, BarBara Marliene.   II. Title.
    HQ536.S39 2013
    306.80973—dc23
                                            2011053411

10 9 8 7 6 5 4 3 2 1

Student Edition ISBN 10:   0-205-84530-4
                ISBN 13: 978-0-205-84530-9
Instructor's Review Copy ISBN 10:   0-205-87904-7
                ISBN 13: 978-0-205-87904-5
À la Carte ISBN 10:   0-205-86750-2
                ISBN 13: 978-0-205-86750-9

To our husbands,
Richard and Roger,
who share with us
the joy and value of family life

Brief Contents

Contents

13 REMARRIAGE AND REMARRIED FAMILIES 419

14 MARRIAGES AND FAMILIES IN LATER LIFE 447

15 ISSUES CONFRONTING FAMILIES AT HOME AND ABROAD 478

Boxes

Preface

Today, many marriages and families are buffeted by global economic and political forces. Increasing unemployment rates, record home foreclosures and personal bankruptcies, and corporate bailouts, as well as ongoing violence at home and abroad, are taking a toll on the health and stability of family life. In this context, a sociological approach to studying marriages and families is especially helpful. Such an approach enables us to understand the constraints and opportunities that affect our lives and those of other people, thereby positioning us to make more discriminating and successful decisions and to exercise greater control over our lives.

In this seventh edition of *Marriages and Families: Diversity and Change*, there is a conscious effort to present a continuity of major issues, concerns, and themes on contemporary marriages, families, and intimate relationships. Our initial resolve when writing the first edition of this textbook has not changed, and it informs this seventh edition as well. The subtitle of this book, *Diversity and Change*, continues to be the major thematic framework that runs through all 15 chapters and is informed by the scholarship of a wide variety of scholars, most notably scholars of color and feminist scholars in sociology and from across a number of other academic disciplines. The emphasis on diversity helps students to understand that many different forms of intimate relationships exist beyond the traditional heterosexual, two-parent, White, middle-class family and the legally sanctioned heterosexual marriage. As we show throughout this textbook, marriages and families more generally include single-parent families, headed by women or men; lesbian or gay families with or without children and with or without a live-in partner; adoptive and foster families; biracial and multiracial families; cohabiting couples involving heterosexual or same-sex partners; and blended families that emerge following divorce, remarriage, or simply when people bring to a new relationship children from a previous intimate relationship. In this context, we treat marriages and families as social constructs whose meanings have changed over time and from place to place.

Consistent with this position, we continue to give high priority to framing our discussions of marriages and families in historical context. Most, if not all, aspects of our lives are shaped by larger historical circumstances. To be born during a particular historical period is to experience intimacy, marriage, family life, childbearing and child rearing, family decision making, household labor, and marital and family satisfaction (to name a few) in particular ways germane to the time, place, and social structure within which we find ourselves. For example, the economic growth and prosperity of the 1950s, a period during which the nuclear family was idealized, encouraged or made possible this particular family structure. During this period, both women and men married at early ages, had children within a relatively short interval from the wedding, and generally stayed married until the death of one spouse. For many families, a husband's income was sufficient to support the family. Thus, wives and mothers typically remained at home fulfilling domestic and child-care roles. Although economic conditions have changed, now often requiring multiple wage earners, this 1950s "idealized" image continues to dominate popular discourse on marriages and families. However, in the 1990s and continuing today, most children grow up in single-parent families, in remarried families, and/or in families where both parents work outside the home. Framing our discussion of marriages and families in historical context not only provides students with knowledge about marriages and families in earlier periods of U.S. history but also enables them to understand and interpret the changes occurring around them in marriages and families today.

Our objectives in this seventh edition are simple yet significant:

- to help students recognize and understand the dynamic nature of marriages, families, and intimate relationships;
- to enable students to recognize, confront, and dispel prominent myths about marriages, families, and intimate relationships;
- to help students see the interactive relationships of race, class, gender, and sexual orientation;
- to encourage an informed openness in student attitudes that will empower them to make informed choices and decisions in their own marriage, family, and intimate relationships;
- to enable students to see how marriages, families, and intimate relationships around the world are increasingly affected by global events, particularly economic upheavals, armed conflicts, and acts of terrorism and war; and
- to provide students with a comprehensive introduction to a number of key issues facing marriages and families today.

In this age of rapid communication and technological changes, not only does the evening news bring into our homes stories about marriages and families in distant places, but, more importantly, the news also calls attention to how political and economic decisions, both national and international, affect families in the United States as well as those in other countries of the world. For example, decisions of multinational corporations to relocate from one country to another in pursuit of lower labor costs and less regulation impact families in both countries. On the one hand, family budgets and patterns of living are often seriously disrupted when a family member loses a job because a business moves offshore. On the other hand, family patterns are also affected when members must work for subsistence-level wages, often in an unhealthy environment. In this example, the experiences of these families are globally interdependent.

In addition, issues of violence and the massive abuse of human beings both nationally and internationally crowd our psyches. In the United States, racism, homophobia, hate crimes, street violence, the escalation of violence in schools, and threats of terrorist attacks are indeed very troubling issues faced by all families. Elsewhere, the violence and atrocities related to political, cultural, religious, and ethnic conflicts in Afghanistan, Iraq, Israel, the Congo, Sudan, and some parts of North Africa have had devastating consequences for millions of families. These global incidents are not unrelated to life in the United States. In turn, both human and financial resources must be reallocated from domestic agendas to help meet humanitarian commitments around the world. By examining the process of globalization and its consequences or, as C. Wright Mills (1959) suggested, by grasping history and biography and the connections between the two, students should be better able to understand their personal life experiences and prepare themselves for meeting the challenges of living in a global world.

Rapid changes in the racial and ethnic composition of the U.S. population, due to immigration and differential fertility rates, have focused our nation's attention on diversity. Although some dimensions of this issue are new, a historical review quickly shows that throughout U.S. history, marriages and families have taken many diverse forms. A focus on structured relationships such as race, class, gender, and sexual orientation allows us to see how marriages and families are experienced differently by different categories of people. In this seventh edition, we continue to make a special effort to treat this diversity in an integrative manner. Thus, we have no separate chapters on class or families of color. Instead, when marriage and family experiences are differentiated by race, class, or gender, these differences are integrated into the discussion of specific experiences. Two examples will illustrate this point. First, although the vast majority of all Americans will eventually marry, the marriage rate is lower for some groups than others. White females are more likely to marry than African American females, who are confronted with an increasing shortage of African American males of comparable age and education. Second, although both women and men suffer from the dissolution of their marriages through divorce or death, gender also differentiates those experiences in important ways. The most striking difference is an economic one: The standard of living declines for women and children, but it is stable or improves for men.

It is not always easy to discuss diversity, partly because our thinking about diversity is itself diverse. One of the first issues we face in discussing diversity is language—what are the appropriate designations to use in reference to different groups at this point in time? Names are often controversial and reflect a power struggle over who has the right or authority to name. Not surprisingly, those in positions of power historically have assumed that right and authority. As the "named" groups themselves become more powerful and vocal, however, they often challenge the naming process and insist on designations they believe more clearly express their sense of their own identity. For example, as a result of pressure from people with mixed ancestry, the U.S. Census Bureau gave official recognition to a biracial or multiracial category on its year 2000 census forms. However, even this is not without problems. The multiracial category has yielded significant changes in the number of reported members in various racial and ethnic groups of color. This fact has political and economic significance in terms of the distribution of governmental resources and services.

Although there is no unanimity on these matters even among members of the same group, some terms have emerged as the preferred ones. Thus, for example, Latina/o is preferred to Hispanic, Native American is preferred to American Indian, lesbian and gay are preferred to homosexual, and African American is preferred to Black. Throughout this text, we try to be consistent in using the preferred terms. When we make specific comparisons by race, however, we use the terms *Black* and *White* for ease of presentation. In addition, we have consciously avoided using the term *minority group* to refer to racial and ethnic groups in our society. Instead, we use the term *people of color*. Although this term is not problem-free, it avoids an implicit assumption in the term *minority* that groups so designated are not part of the dominant culture in terms of shared values and aspirations.

NEW TO THIS EDITION

- New MyFamilyLab is a state-of-the-art interactive and instructive solution for the Marriage and Family course, designed to be used as a supplement to a traditional lecture course, or to completely administer an online course.
- New learning objectives open each chapter to help students focus their reading and expand their analytical and critical-thinking skills.
- Coverage of contemporary topics—such as changing immigration patterns, same-sex marriage, adoption laws, divorce laws, the growing income gap in the United States and the recent recession, and the xenophobia, isolationist tendencies, and religious intolerance that result from increasing globalization—has been updated and expanded in this edition.
- New photos have been added, and line art, tables, and maps have been updated throughout the book.
- Hundreds of new research studies have been added to this edition and are highlighted in blue in the references section at the end of this book.
- The black/white format of previous editions has been replaced with a striking color design.

EXPANDED FEATURES

Marriages and Families: Diversity and Change continues to be distinguished from other textbooks in a number of important ways, including the expanded features of the seventh edition.

IN THE NEWS

The In the News chapter opener has been a popular feature in past editions of this textbook. In this edition, we continue the trend of beginning each chapter with this feature. These chapter openers continue to be contemporary, true stories of people caught up in the web of marriage, family, and other intimate relationships or issues either directly or indirectly related to marriage, family, and intimacy. Following each In the News feature is a series of questions under the heading "What Would You Do?" This feature helps students to see the relevance of many political, economic, and cultural issues of the day to ordinary people's lives and invites them to reflect on the topics covered in that chapter in light of their own value expectations and experiences.

STRENGTHENING MARRIAGES AND FAMILIES BOX

As in previous editions of this textbook, this box appears in several key chapters and continues to use a question-and-answer format with family therapist Joan Zientek. The purpose of this box is to introduce students to the concept of family therapy and show them how such therapy can help family members confront some of the many issues and problems that today's families might encounter. For example, in Chapter 8, Joan Zientek describes how couples can improve communication and resolve conflicts, and in Chapter 15, she discusses how deployment and war affects military families and how therapy might help these families recover.

APPLYING THE SOCIOLOGICAL IMAGINATION BOX

Each box provides: 1) Web site(s) where students can find up-to-date data on relevant topics discussed in the chapter and 2) questions to help them develop a sociological perspective in analyzing aspects of marriages and families. The questions are designed to help students see the relationship between personal behavior and how society is organized and structured. For example, in Chapter 2, students can learn at a glance from statistics presented about the characteristics of the welfare population, helping to dispel many of the myths about this population while at the same time learning about the diversity among American families. In Chapter 9, students are directed to Web sites that provide historical data about Father's Day as well as factual information about today's fathers who are often overlooked in discussions of parenting.

FAMILY PROFILE BOX

This popular feature, first introduced in the second edition, continues to provide photos and profiles of real people, including updated information about what these families view as major challenges in the current stage in their family life cycle and the philosophy that guides their behavior in their marriage and family relationships. These family profiles allow students to read about and understand how diverse individuals and families navigate their everyday lives as members of marriages, families, domestic partnerships, and/or other intimate relationships. For example, in Chapter 10, the Parkinson family is profiled, providing students with a glance of the challenges parents face when the older child is in school and the younger one is at home coupled with their concerns about the economy. And, the profile of the Willis family in Chapter 15 shows us how parents who adopted a child from another country help their child develop an identity that reflects the values and accomplishments of both their culture of origin and the culture in which she is raised. At the same time, these parents are adjusting to their new role as grandparents. These family profiles serve as a good basis for students to examine their own attitudes and values regarding where they are in their family's life cycle.

IN OTHER PLACES BOX

Students remain interested in learning about diverse forms of marriages and families. Therefore, this box continues to offer students insights into the diverse structures and functions of marriages and families, both global and local. For example, in Chapter 11, they can learn about global and local responses to violence and sexual assault against women. And in Chapter 12, students can see how more liberal divorce laws and changing social and economic conditions have contributed to an increase in divorce and remarriage in countries like Korea and China. Each In Other Places box includes a series of questions under the heading "What do you think?" These questions require students to reflect on cultural similarities and differences. It also helps students understand that culture is relative.

DEBATING SOCIAL ISSUES BOX

In recent years, considerable controversy has surrounded numerous policy issues regarding marriages, families, and intimate relationships. Students often hear media stories designed to grab headlines rather than inform the public about the different perspectives people have on these difficult and often emotionally laden issues such as same-sex marriage (Chapter 7) and immigration reform (Chapter 1). Thus, we have included a Debating Social Issues box in every chapter to help students understand the pro and con arguments that surround a given policy issue and then use the related questions to help them clarify their own views on the subject.

WRITING YOUR OWN SCRIPT BOX

These exercises again can be found at the end of each chapter. Students and instructors have told us that this focused approach makes it easy for students to reflect on their own life choices and in writing their own marital or relationship scripts. In this way, students are encouraged to think sociologically about their personal decision making in light of the relevant research presented in that chapter.

EXPANDED THEMES

One of the criticisms students sometimes make about marriage and family courses and their related textbooks is that they are pessimistic in tone and content. They use as examples the high divorce rate, individual and family violence, poverty, inequality, and sexual problems. Students realize these patterns of behavior are real and must be addressed, but they also want to know more about how to strengthen marriages, families, and intimate relationships. Therefore, in addition to our featured Strengthening Marriages and Families box, we have retained the section at the end of each chapter, Supporting Marriages and Families, that discusses various initiatives being carried out or proposed to help individuals, couples, and families in their relationships and, where appropriate, suggests areas in which resources and support for families are still needed.

In addition, we have enriched each chapter by incorporating hundreds of new research studies. We have also included new photos, examples, tables, and figures to illustrate contemporary marriage and family concepts, events, trends, and themes.

- Changing immigration patterns have resulted in greater racial, ethnic, and racial diversity among families in the United States and throughout the world (Chapters 1 and 15).
- Just as families are changing, so too is the discipline of sociology. Although in the past women and people of color were involved in research and theorizing about marriages and families, their

contributions were largely ignored. But today, women and people of color are gaining much deserved recognition as researchers and theorists (Chapter 2).

- Although gender roles are less limiting than in the past, women (and men, too) continue to confront gender stereotyping at work and in their personal, political, and family lives (Chapter 3).
- Most often when we think about love, we think about people who love each other as being close in age. But an increasing number of people are falling in love and establishing intimate relationships with people much older or younger than themselves, raising questions about whether or not society should put age constraints on love (Chapter 4).
- Although interracial dating has become more acceptable to Americans in recent years, there is a generation gap in terms of acceptance. For example, the generations born before 1946 are the least accepting, and those born since 1977 are the most accepting (Chapter 5).
- For most American teens, oral sex is not "really" sex; real sex, they believe, is vaginal intercourse. This perspective puts young people in jeopardy of contracting sexually transmitted infections, including HIV/AIDS. The incidence of AIDS continues to increase dramatically around the globe (Chapter 6).
- Despite great controversy, same-sex marriages are now legal in Massachusetts, New York, Connecticut, New Hampshire, Vermont, Iowa, and the District of Columbia. The lifestyles of the unmarried population continue to take many diverse forms (Chapter 7).
- Although some people think of premarital agreements as cold, unromantic, and businesslike, an increasing number of couples are making them part of their marriage preparation. Additionally, because conflict is now recognized as a normal part of intimate relationships, many couples are participating in marriage preparation classes that teach conflict resolution skills (Chapter 8).
- Polls show that an increasing number of fathers desire to spend more time and develop a closer relationship with their children. New research documents the importance of fathers in the lives of children, indicating that when fathers provide strong emotional, financial, and other support, their children are likely to be healthier physically and psychologically (Chapter 9).
- In recent years, the income gap between wealthy and other families widened dramatically. Unemployment rates, home foreclosures, and poverty have all increased since the recession of 2007–2009 (Chapter 10).
- Power, abuse, and gender-based violence within families and other intimate relationships continue to be a major human rights violation in the United States and around the world. The most vulnerable victims of gender-based violence are women and young girls (Chapter 11).
- Although the overall divorce rate has decreased slightly over the past several years, the rate remains high and varies among different groups and in different geographic regions. Several states are trying to reverse this trend by reforming divorce laws (Chapter 12).
- Greater numbers of children are living in stepfamilies. Although no precise figures exist on the number of children being raised in lesbian and gay stepfamilies, the increasing use of reproductive technology (Chapter 9) and changes in adoption laws (Chapter 15) suggest that more children will live in lesbian and gay stepfamilies in the future (Chapter 13).
- People are living longer. Expectations are that by 2050, one in five Americans will be 65 or older in the United States. Contrary to popular stereotypes, the majority of older people maintain their independence and enjoy an active social life (Chapter 14).
- As globalization expands, so, too, does the inequality that accompanies it, leaving many children and families behind. Rising inequality can result in an increase in racial bias, xenophobia, isolationist tendencies, and religious intolerance. In this process, individuals and societies who are among the most disadvantaged sometimes respond with violence and acts of terrorism (Chapter 15).

PEDAGOGY: READER INVOLVEMENT

Marriages and Families: Diversity and Change is intended as a text that challenges students to become involved in a direct way by examining their personal belief systems as well as societal views of the many forms that marriages and families have taken in the past and are taking in the present. Based on more than 50 years of combined teaching experiences, we have found that a course on the sociology of marriages and families almost always invokes concern and interest among students regarding how the general principles and descriptions of marriages and families in a given textbook apply to and are similar to or different from their own personal experiences. Thus, throughout the process of revising this book, we continued to use an innovative, sensitive, and inclusive approach to writing about marriages and families. We use a sociological and feminist–womanist perspective, encouraging the application of the sociological imagination to everyday life. In this context, we focus on the link between social structure and our personal experiences of marriages, families, and intimate relationships. That is, we examine how cultural values, historical context, economic and political changes, and structured relationships of race, class, gender, sexual orientation, and age interact and affect individuals and groups as they create, sustain, and change their various intimate relationships.

The positive response of students as well as instructors to the pedagogical strategies included in the first six editions encouraged us to continue them in this edition. It has been gratifying to hear how these strategies have facilitated students' involvement in understanding marriages and families and empowered them to make more informed lifestyle decisions.

LEARNING OBJECTIVES

New to this edition, each chapter begins with a series of objectives designed to help students focus their reading and expand their analytical and critical thinking skills.

KEY TERMS

The important terms and concepts that help us to understand and analyze marriages and families are boldfaced and defined in the text. The key terms are also listed at the end of each chapter and defined in the glossary at the end of the book as a way of facilitating the study and review process.

CHAPTER QUESTIONS

Throughout this edition, students will find a shaded question mark that asks them to apply the material in the chapter to their own experiences and to critically evaluate aspects of interpersonal relationships.

END-OF-CHAPTER STUDY AIDS

At the end of each chapter, students will find a summary of the chapter's main points, a list of key terms, and a set of questions for study and reflection. The chapter summary and key terms are designed to facilitate a quick review of the material in the text. The study questions are designed to help students stretch their understanding of marriages and families beyond the contents of this textbook. Finally, we provide suggestions for additional resources, which include traditional sociological materials as well as relevant literary works pertaining to a topic or general theme of the chapter. The use of literature is intended to enrich the study of sociology and provide yet another springboard from which students can develop a more in-depth understanding of various sociological concepts. Because of its popularity, we have continued the suggested popular films and documentaries feature that adds a visual dimension to a subject that can provide insights into people's feelings and experiences. In addition, we include a number of Internet sites where students can explore and do independent research on marriage and family issues. Given the fluidity of many Web sites, we have listed only those that have proven to be relatively stable over time, well documented, and updated as needed.

APPENDICES

The appendices included at the back of the book supplement the text's sociological discussion of key aspects of relationships by providing technical information on sexual dysfunctions and sexually transmitted infections (Appendix A), human anatomy and reproduction (Appendix B), abortion techniques (Appendix C), and methods of birth control (Appendix D).

SUPPLEMENTS

This book is accompanied by an extensive learning package to enhance the experience of both instructors and students.

Instructor's Manual and Test Bank (0-205-86753-7) For each chapter in the text, this valuable resource provides a chapter overview, list of objectives, lecture suggestions, discussion questions, student assignments and projects, and multimedia resources. In addition, test questions in multiple-choice, short answer, and essay formats are available for each chapter; the answers to all questions are page-referenced to the text. For easy access, this manual is available within the instructor section of MyFamilyLab for *Marriages and Families, Seventh Edition,* or at www.pearsonhighered.com.

MyTest (0-205-84547-9) This computerized software allows instructors to create their own personalized exams, to edit any or all of the existing test questions, and to add new questions. Other special features of this program include random generation of test questions, creation of alternate versions of the same test, scrambling question sequence, and test preview before printing. For easy access, this software is available within the instructor section of MyFamilyLab for *Marriages and Families, Seventh Edition,* or at www.pearsonhighered.com.

PowerPoint Presentations (0-205-86755-3) The Lecture PowerPoint slides follow the chapter outline and feature images from the textbook integrated with the text. The Special Topics PowerPoint slides allow you to integrate rich supplementary material into your course with minimal preparation time. They are available to adopters at www.pearsonhighered.com.

MyFamilyLab (0-205-85672-1) is an interactive and instructive multimedia site designed to help students and instructors save time and improve results. It offers access to a wealth of resources geared to meet the individual teaching and learning needs of every instructor and student. Combining an e-book, video, audio, multimedia simulations, research support, and assessment, MyFamilyLab engages students and gives them the tools they need to enhance their performance in the course. Tools include

- an e-book that matches the exact layout of the printed text
- a wealth of hands-on activities to help students in their study of marriages and families
- a gradebook that automatically tracks student progress and reports this information to instructors.

ACKNOWLEDGMENTS

Although we continue to refer to this book as ours, we recognize that such an endeavor can never singularly be attributed to the authors. As with any such project, its success required the assistance of many people from many different parts of our lives. Our interaction with students, both within and outside the classroom, continues to have a significant impact on our thinking and writing about marriages and families, and that impact is quite visible in this seventh edition. Our decisions to retain and, in some cases, update, certain pedagogical aids, such as the boxed features and the examples used in the text, were made in response to student questions, reactions, and discussions. Student feedback was also instrumental in the development of the applied exercises, which we have found to be most effective in teaching about marriage and family issues and concerns.

We wish to acknowledge the skilled professionals at Pearson Education—the editors, artists, designers, and researchers who saw this edition through the process, from its inception through the many stages of development and production. We owe a particular debt of gratitude to Karen Hanson whose support, patience, and perseverance were major factors in our completing this project. We are grateful to the entire team at Integra for their assistance during the production process. Our thanks also go to permission editors and all others whose tasks were so essential to this book.

The timely, thoughtful, and extensive reactions, suggestions, and critical reviews of the previous editions of this textbook were greatly appreciated and, in each case, they have helped us avoid major mistakes and weaknesses while enhancing our ability to draw on the strengths of the book. We are also grateful to the reviewers of this edition:

Stacey Allen, Seaport Coastline College

Brad van Eeden-Moorefield, Central Michigan University

Margaret Preble, Thomas Nelson Community College

Beverly Stiles, Midwestern State University

Meifang Zhang, Midlands Technical College

We again wish to acknowledge and thank our marriages and families (nuclear, extended, blended, and fictive) for continuing to love, understand, and support us as we undertook, for yet another time, the demands and responsibilities involved in researching, writing, and revising this seventh edition. As in the past, when our time, attention, and behavior were dedicated to this endeavor, often at the expense of our time, attention, and activities with them, they remained steadfast in their support and encouragement. Now that we have finished this edition, they are as proud as we are and rightfully so, for this book, too, is as much theirs as ours. Its completion is due in large part to their understanding and the sacrifices they made to facilitate our ability to revise this book. We acknowledge our parents, Helen and Charles Schwartz and Lillian Johnson, for their love and support throughout our lives. As always, our partners, Richard and Roger, gave us their unconditional support and contributed to partnerships that were significantly critical to our meeting the various demands and deadlines that revising this book engendered. In addition, we continue to acknowledge our children, Jason, Roger Jr., Dionne, and Angella, granddaughters Courtney and Mariah, and grandson Roger III (Trey) for their unwavering love, patience, and understanding when our work forced us to miss family gatherings and events. We thank them all, especially for providing us with continuing opportunities for the exploration and understanding of marriage and family life.

Last, but certainly not least, we wish to acknowledge and thank each other. As with the previous editions, this book has been a joint effort in every sense of the word. Time has not diminished our appreciation of each other's skills, perspective, humor, and experiences, and our collaborative effort continues to deepen our appreciation and respect for one another. We continue to learn from one another about diversity and the differential impact of race on various intimate relationships. In the process, we continue to learn more about a particular type of intimate relationship, one based on love, respect, commitment, understanding, tolerance, and compassion: namely, friendship.

KEEPING IN TOUCH

Just as we appreciate all of the comments, suggestions, and ideas that we received on the first six editions of this textbook, we would like to hear your reactions, suggestions, questions, and comments on this new edition. We invite you to share your reactions and constructive advice with us. You can contact us at: m-schwartz@neiu.edu or b-scott1@neiu.edu.

Mary Ann Schwartz
BarBara Marliene Scott

Dr. Mary Ann Schwartz has been married for 35 years. She earned her bachelor of arts degree in sociology and history from Alverno College in Milwaukee, Wisconsin; her master's degree in sociology from the Illinois Institute of Technology in Chicago; and her doctorate in sociology from Northwestern University in Evanston, Illinois. She is Professor Emerita of Sociology and Women's Studies and former chair of the Sociology Department at Northeastern Illinois University, where she cofounded and was actively involved in the Women's Studies Program. She also served as a faculty consultant to the Network for the Dissemination of Curriculum Infusion, an organization that presents workshops nationally on how to integrate substance abuse prevention strategies into the college curriculum.

Throughout her educational experiences, Professor Schwartz has been concerned with improving the academic climate for women, improving student access to higher education, and improving the quality of undergraduate education. As a union activist, Professor Schwartz worked to win collective bargaining for higher education faculty in Illinois. She served as union president at Northeastern and spent more than 8 years as the legislative director for the University Professionals of Illinois, where she lobbied for bills of interest to higher education faculty and students. She edited the union's newsletter, *Universities 21*, which focused on academic issues. She continues to be active in the labor movement and serves as an officer in the retirees' chapter. Professor Schwartz is the Board Secretary of Lincoln Park Village whose mission is to help older people age well in their homes and communities.

Professor Schwartz's research continues to focus on marriages and families, socialization, nonmarital lifestyles, work, aging, and the structured relationships of race, class, and gender. Although she found teaching all courses thought-provoking and enjoyable, her favorites were Marriages and Families; Women, Men, and Social Change; Sociology of Aging; and Introductory Sociology. In her teaching she employed interactive learning strategies and encouraged students to apply sociological insights in their everyday lives. Seeing students make connections between their individual lives and the larger social forces that influence them remains one of the most rewarding and exciting aspects of her teaching career.

Dr. BarBara M. Scott has been married for 46 years and is the proud mother of two sons and proud grandmother of three grandchildren: two granddaughters and one grandson. As a wife and mother of two small children, she returned to school, earning a bachelor of arts degree in sociology and two different master's degrees: a master of arts degree in sociology and a master of philosophy from Roosevelt University in Chicago, and later a doctorate in sociology from Northwestern University in Evanston, Illinois. Dr. Scott is Professor Emerita of Sociology, African and African American Studies, and Women's Studies, and was the first coordinator of the African and African American Studies Program at Northeastern Illinois University. She has served as president of the Association of Black Sociologists, a national organization, and she is currently its interim executive officer. Dr. Scott is also a former chair of the Sociology, Justice Studies, Social Work, and Women's Studies departments at Northeastern Illinois University. She is a strong advocate for curriculum transformation and the integration of race, class, gender, and sexual orientation into the college curriculum, as well as a social activist who has been in the forefront of organizing among national and international women of color, both within and outside academia.

Professor Scott has received meritorious recognition for her work and has served for over 35 years as an educational and human resource consultant. She has coordinated the Women's Studies Program and was a founding member of the university's Black Women's Caucus. Her research and teaching interests include marriages and families, particularly African American families; the structured relationships of race, class, gender, and sexual orientation; institutionalized racism and inequality; cultural images and the social construction of knowledge in the mass media; and Africana (aka Black) women's studies. She finds teaching challenging and invigorating; among her favorite courses are Marriages and Families, Sociology of Black Women, Sociology of Racism, and Introductory Sociology. She is an enthusiastic advocate of applying sociology to the everyday worlds in which we live and routinely engages her students in field research in the communities in which they live and work. After years of teaching, she still gets excited about the varied insights that sociology offers into both the simplest and the most complex questions and issues of human social life.

Marriages and Families over Time

What Will You Learn?

- Define and understand the sociological meaning of key terms.
- Describe the various forces which have affected the structure and functioning of families over time.
- Apply the sociological imagination to compare how the composition of households have changed from your parents' generation and your own.
- Assess the pros and cons of passing the DREAM Act to help children of undocumented immigrants have a pathway to citizenship.
- Increase your awareness and understanding of the diversity of marriages and families today and in the past.
- Question how myths and contrasting views of marriages and families shape current social policies.

IN THE NEWS

Delhi, India

In June 2010, in a community on the northwestern outskirts of Delhi, a young woman and her boyfriend, both 19, were badly beaten and then electrocuted. The girl's father and uncle were later arrested in what police suspect was a case of "honor killing" (Pandey, 2010). The girl's family disapproved of the couple's relationship because they were from different castes. Aisha Sainin's and Yogesh Kumar's story is not uncommon, but rather a reflection of centuries-old

(continued on next page)

(continued from previous page)

beliefs that if a woman's and, in this case, a man's behavior violates or is even perceived to violate cultural norms that bring shame to the family, it is expected that male family members redeem that honor by killing the offender(s). The United Nations estimates that more than 5,000 women and girls die each year as a result of these "honor killings;" many women's groups in the Middle East and Southwest Asia put the figure at four times that amount (Fisk, 2010).

Although "honor killings" occur more frequently in Asian and Middle Eastern countries, such killings are increasing in other parts of the world, particularly in countries where there are large, close-knit immigrant communities. The London Metropolitan Police recorded 211 such incidents in 2009 ("Honour Killing…," 2010). Two recent trials in the United States involved suspected cases of honor killings (Adelman, 2011).

WHAT DO YOU THINK?

Suppose your family forbids you to marry someone you love. Would you marry anyway, knowing that both of your lives might be in danger? What causes some groups to feel so strongly about who their children marry?

((•─┤Listen to the Chapter Audio on myfamilylab.com

The family, and marriage as a process that can generate it, exists in some form in all societies. Families are created by human beings in an attempt to meet certain basic individual and social needs, such as survival and growth. Marriage and family are among the oldest human social institutions. An institution consists of patterns of ideas, beliefs, values, and behaviors built around the basic needs of individuals and society and that tend to persist over time. **Institutions** represent the organized aspects of human social existence that are established and reinforced over time by the various norms and values of a particular group or society. The family as an institution organizes, directs, and executes the essential tasks of living for its members. Although, historically, marriage and family have been considered the most important institutions in human society, humans have created many other important institutions—for example, education, government, the economy, religion, and law. Throughout this textbook, we will examine how these other institutions affect marriages and families.

Families encompass cultural patterns as well as social structure. For example, as the story of Aisha Sainin and Yogesh Kumar illustrate, the cultural recognition of mating is intimately bound up with familial and societal norms and customs about appropriate mates. As we discuss in detail in Chapter 5, two of the most common ways in which families regulate who their members can mate with is through rules of **exogamy,** the requirement that marriage must occur outside a group, and **endogamy,** the requirement that marriage occur within a group. Clearly, Aisha's and Yogesh's romantic relationship was deemed unacceptable to their families. In many societies, marital endogamy is so important that an infraction of the rule is not only considered a violation of group customs but also cause for violent retribution. Although both political and religious leaders have spoken out against this practice, it remains rampant in a number of Middle Eastern communities where the perpetrators, mostly male family members, often go unpunished. Opponents of attempts to outlaw honor killings argue that without such controls on women, families would disintegrate.

Do you think it is necessary for a society to put controls on women to ensure the stability of families? On men? Explain. What controls, if any, do you experience as you think about dating and possibly marriage?

Contemporary Definitions of Marriages and Families

Because all of us belong to some sort of family and have observed marriages (including our parents—and perhaps our own), we probably think we know exactly what the terms "marriage" and "family" mean. Although marriage and family go hand in hand, they are not one and the same. You might ask, then, exactly what are they? Take a few minutes to jot down your perceptions, definitions, and ideas about each of these institutions. How did you define them? Not surprisingly, many of your definitions and images of marriages and families are probably tied to ideas about a "traditional" family that consists of a husband, wife, and their children—an image often portrayed in both popular and academic literature and transmitted throughout American popular culture. This family pattern is an institution of the past, if indeed it ever really existed at all. To be sure, it is far from typical today. Many people reading this textbook, for example, come from single-parent families or families that include a stepparent and stepsiblings or half-siblings. Some of you perhaps moved between your parents' separate households as you were growing up or lived under the guardianship of a grandmother, a great-grandmother, or some other relative. And still others grew up in families where their parents were of different races or of the same sex. Clearly then, families are not static but dynamic—they change over time.

Throughout history, the definition of what constitutes a family has changed. For example, at one time a family consisted of servants and slaves and everyone else in the household who were under the authority of the head of household. At a later historical time, the term "family" referred only to a man's offspring. Moreover, ethnically as well as globally, definitions of what constitutes a family vary; for example, in some African cultures as well as some Native American cultures, the concept of family includes everyone in the community as family. It was not until the nineteenth century that the idea of the traditional American family—a married couple and their children in which the male is the breadwinner and the female stays at home to care for the home and the children—gained popular usage (Arnold, 2007). Today, however, this traditional family structure is all but disappearing; for example, the traditional American family structure has declined from 60 percent of all U.S. families in 1972 to 20 percent in 2010 (U.S. Census, 2010c). Therefore, more accurate definitions of marriages and families must take into account the many different forms of marriages and families that have existed historically and still exist today, both in the United States and in other countries and cultures.

WHAT IS MARRIAGE?

Marriage has been defined in the United States as a legal contract between a woman and a man who are at or above a specified age and who are not already legally married to someone else. Although some people still regard this definition as adequate, increasing numbers of scholars and laypersons alike consider it too narrow. By focusing on heterosexuality and the legal aspect of marriage alone, it excludes a variety of relationships, such as some heterosexual and homosexual cohabitive relationships that function in much the same way as legally sanctioned marriages—albeit without the same legal protection. Thus, in this book, we utilize a more encompassing and reality-based definition of **marriage** as a union between people (whether widely or legally recognized or not) that unites partners sexually, socially, and economically; that is relatively consistent over time; and that accords each member certain agreed-upon rights.

Read the **Document**
What Is Marriage For?
on **myfamilylab.com**

Types of Marriages Marriages across cultures generally have been either monogamous or polygamous. **Monogamy** involves one person married to another person of the other sex. Although, legally, monogamy refers to heterosexual relationships, any couple can be monogamous if they are committed exclusively to each other sexually and otherwise during the course of the relationship. Monogamy is the legally recognized marital structure in the United

States. Although demographers project that somewhere between 40 to 50 percent of marriages starting out today will end in divorce, the vast majority of divorced people remarry; thus, the U.S. marriage pattern is more accurately classified as **serial monogamy.** Individuals may marry as many times as they like as long as each prior marriage was ended by death or divorce.

In some societies, polygamy is the accepted marriage structure. **Polygamy** is a broad category that generally refers to heterosexual marriage in which one person of one sex is married to several people of the other sex. It can take one of two forms: **polygyny,** in which one male has two or more wives, and **polyandry,** in which one female has two or more husbands. Even though the practice of polyandry is rare, polygyny is legally practiced or recognized civilly in nearly 50 countries around the world such as the Middle East, South America, Asia, and in parts of Africa (see Figure 1.1 on page 4). In Saudi Arabia, for instance, men are allowed to marry up to four wives; however, some wealthy men have as many as 11 wives and 50 or more children (Dickey and McGinn, 2001). In 2005, one wealthy 64-year-old Saudi businessman reported that in 50 years he had married 58 women and fathered 10 sons and somewhere between 22 and 25 daughters (he's not sure of the exact number). Reportedly, his polygamous marriages have cost him more than $1.6 million in wedding expenses and settlements for divorced wives (FoxNews.com, 2005). Societies that allow polygyny maintain that allowing men to have more than one wife is a more equitable way of organizing relationships. Critics of polygamy, however, disagree. They argue that polygamy is an unequal relationship where men have more rights than women; it is demeaning to women; it places women in a subordinate child-like role; and it can be a source of violence and abuse (Hamilton, 2008).

Although polygamy is illegal in almost all Western countries, small pockets of polygamous groups can be found in Western countries such as the United States, Canada, and Europe. Nonetheless, many Americans tend to view polygamy as an exotic relationship that occurs in societies far remote from the United States. However, although both forms of polygamy are illegal in the United States, some religious and parareligious groups here routinely practice polygyny. The Church of Jesus Christ of Latter Day Saints renounced polygamy more than 100 years ago and excommunicates its practitioners, but Mormons participating in plural marriages defend polygamy as a fulfilment of their religion as prescribed by their ancestors (Janofsky, 2001). Splintered from the Mormon church, the Fundamentalist Church of Jesus Christ of Latter Day Saints (FLDS) is one of the largest Mormon fundamentalist denominations and one of United States' largest practitioners of polygamy. Perhaps the largest group overall of FLDS live in British Columbia where they are left to practice polygamy because of the government's concerns about religious freedom. In addition, although polygamy has been illegal in France for almost 2 decades, an estimated 20,000 or more polygamous families (primarily immigrant families from African and Middle Eastern countries where polygamy is legal) live within French borders (Hamilton, 2008; Renout, 2005).

There are widely varying estimates of how many people practice polygamy in the United States, ranging anywhere from 30,000 to 60,000 or more, but the secrecy of such groups makes a definitive number elusive. Despite the illegality of polygamy, it thrives in states such as Utah and Arizona where the twin headquarters of FLDS are located, but also in Texas, Colorado, and South Dakota. For example, among a polygamous Mormon sect in Colorado City,

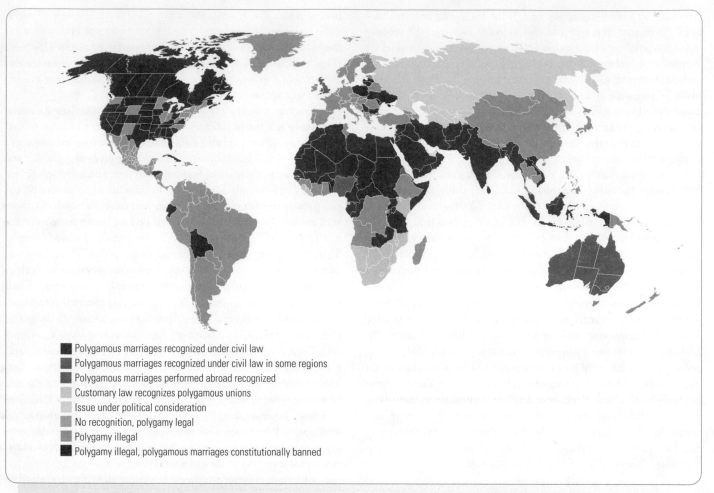

FIGURE 1.1 Map of Polygamy Around the World

Source: "The Legal Status of Polygamy." 2011. Wikipedia: http://en.wikipedia.org/wiki/Legal_status_of_polygamy.

Arizona, a typical household reportedly consists of a husband, three or more wives, and as many as twelve children (Townsend, 2007). Although this form of marriage is illegal, few of its practitioners are ever prosecuted. However, in 2007, FLDS polygamous sect leader Warren Jeffs was convicted of two counts of rape as an accomplice for his role in the marriage of a 14-year-old to her 19-year-old cousin in 2001 (Riccardi, 2007). And in 2008, after allegations of physical abuse, being forced to marry a 50-year-old man, and having a baby at age 15 was called in to Texas authorities by a 16-year-old living in a polygamous compound, Texas authorities raided a 1,700-acre polygamist compound in Eldorado, Texas, and removed 400 children and 133 women "who wanted to leave" (Koch, 2008:1) in order to protect them from alleged abuse. This response to polygamy in the United States was the largest such response/removal from a polygamist compound in nearly 55 years. However, shortly thereafter, the Texas Supreme Court ruled that the state overreached in its massive custody of the FLDS children by taking all of the children from the ranch when evidence of sexual abuse was limited to a few teenage girls. Although the children were returned to their parents, it is not known how many families returned to the polygamous Eldorado ranch (Koch, 2008; Fox News.com, 2008).

For years now, the practice of polygamy by some in these communities—and the Church of Jesus Christ of Latter Day Saints more generally—has raised serious issues concerning the physical abuse of children; child sexual molestation and abuse by some religious high priests, bishops, and others in the polygamous community; felony rape; and statutory rape (some of the plural brides become wives as young as age 11 to men sometimes as old as in their 50s and 60s) (Janofsky, 2003).

As we indicated, polyandry is rare, but it can be found in the Himalayan areas of South Asia; in parts of Africa, China, Sri Lanka, northern India, Oceania, the Suruí of northwestern Brazil; and among some Native Americans. Anthropologists have recorded two forms of polyandry: fraternal polyandry, in which a group of brothers share one wife, and nonfraternal polyandry, in which a woman's husbands are not related. Fraternal polyandry is common in the mountainous areas of Nepal and Tibet. For example, among the Tibetan Nyinba, brothers live together throughout their lives in large patrilineal households where they share a common estate, common domestic responsibilities, and a common wife with whom each maintains a sexual relationship. This type of polyandry can be understood, in part, as a response to a shortage of women due to a lower survival rate in comparison to men and/or in response to severe environmental conditions, limited land, and widespread poverty. Today, polyandry is almost exclusively practiced by the Toda of India where the practice is intended to keep land—a precious resource in a populous country like India—from being split up amongst male heirs. In Tibet (once considered the world's most polyandrous society), under the political control of the People's Republic of China, polyandry has been outlawed, making it difficult to document its occurrence. It is worth noting that unlike polygyny, polyandry is not sanctioned in the United States by any religious groups and, in fact, many U.S. groups that support polygyny denounce the practice of polyandry.

> Why do you think polygyny is more acceptable than polyandry to some Americans? As you read further in this chapter, think about what this suggests about the structure of American families and about patriarchy.

A third form of marriage is **cenogamy,** or **group marriage,** in which all of the women and men in a group are simultaneously married to one another and may exist in a number of forms such as where more than one man and more than one woman form a single family unit, and all members of the marriage share parental responsibility for any children arising from the marriage. Like polygamy, this form of marriage is also illegal in the United States. In the mid-1800s, however, the Oneida Community, a communal group living in New York, practiced cenogamy until they were forced to disband.

WHAT IS A FAMILY?

What is a family? This question is not to be taken lightly. Over the last decade, questions and issues relating to family, marriage, and intimacy have become highly publicized, causing many of us to question what family, family values, marriage, and intimacy mean and how these terms relate to our lives. Social definitions of what constitutes a family have varied historically. It is worth noting, for example, according to family historian Stephanie Coontz (2000), the word *family* originally meant a band of slaves. Even after the word came to apply to people affiliated by blood and marriage, for many centuries the notion of family referred to authority relations rather than love relations. The sentimentalization of family life and female nurturing was historically and functionally linked to the emergence of competitive individualism and formal egalitarianism for men. As the stories of Aisha and Yogesh and other "honor killings" suggest, social definitions of families raise important public policy issues. These issues are related to issues of power and control and the ability of individuals and institutions to exert their will over others. An important question in this regard is: Who defines or who has the right to define family? Power gives one the leverage not only to define but also to set public policy based on a particular set of beliefs, in turn impacting the ways in which various individuals are treated. One thing that seems clear from the opening vignette is that static images and definitions of families from the past do not provide us with an accurate picture of families today.

Like marriage, family has been defined historically in rigid and restrictive language. For example, the U.S. Census Bureau defines a family as two or more persons (one of whom is the householder) living together and related by blood, marriage, or adoption. As with the popular definition of marriage, this definition of family

is limiting in that it does not take into account the considerable diversity found in families. Thus, we define **family** as any relatively stable group of people bound by ties of blood, marriage, adoption; or by any sexually expressive relationship; or who simply live together, and who are committed to and provide each other with economic and emotional support. According to this more inclusive definition, a family can be any group of people who simply define themselves as family based on feelings of love, respect, commitment, and responsibility to and identification with one another. This concept of family has a subjective element in that it takes into account people's feelings of belonging to a particular group. Thus, communes, children living in foster care, and cohabiting individuals either of the same or other sex who identify themselves as a family meet these criteria and thus are indeed families.

Most Americans, it seems, agree with this broader definition. Recent research, government reports, and public opinion polls, for example, find that while Americans continue to place a high value on family life, they do so today with a vastly expanded concept of family to include much more than the stereotypical traditional family of married Mom, Dad, and children. For example, one of the most comprehensive surveys to date on Americans' attitudes toward family conducted by the Pew Research Center in Washington, suggests that Americans no longer believe that marriage and/or children constitute the only paths to family formation, although both play a role in how Americans define family. According to the Pew Survey, for example, 86 percent of Americans say a single parent and child constitute a family; nearly as many (80 percent) say an unmarried couple living together with a child is a family; and 63 percent say a gay or lesbian couple raising a child is a family. On the other hand, if a cohabiting couple has no children, a majority of the public says they are not a family. The presence of children clearly matters in these definitions. Likewise, as with children, marriage plays an important role in how the American public defines a family. For example, if a childless couple is married, 88 percent of Americans consider them to be a family (Pew Research Center, 2010b). So, while both marriage and children figure prominently in today's definitions of family, they do not go hand in hand (see Figure 1.2 on page 6).

Stephanie Coontz, professor of history and family studies and a member of the Pew Research team for this survey, says that people think today of "family as a relationship rather than an institution. If you are in a close relationship and act committed, they count you as family. If you're making obligations to partners and kids, you get counted as a family as opposed to older ways of thinking when it was purely the legal definition." (Quoted in Jayson, 2010)

Types of Families As we have seen, American families are diverse; thus, several types are worth noting. The **family of orientation** is the family into which a person is born and raised. This includes, for example, you, your parents, and any siblings. In contrast, when we marry or have an intimate relationship with someone or have children, we create what sociologists call the **family of procreation.** Some of us were born into a **nuclear family,** consisting of a mother, father, and siblings. Others were born into an **extended,** or **multigenerational family,** consisting of one or both parents, siblings, if any, and other relatives, including grandparents. In both urban and rural areas of the United States, a form of the traditional extended family is often evident. That is, in many neighborhoods, especially

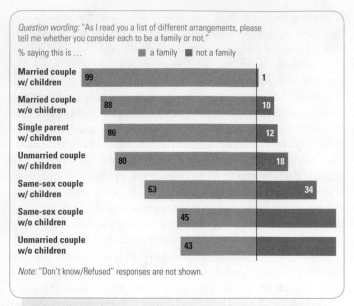

Question wording: "As I read you a list of different arrangements, please tell me whether you consider each to be a family or not."

% saying this is ...   ■ a family ■ not a family

	a family	not a family
Married couple w/ children	99	1
Married couple w/o children	88	10
Single parent w/ children	86	12
Unmarried couple w/ children	80	18
Same-sex couple w/ children	63	34
Same-sex couple w/o children	45	
Unmarried couple w/o children	43	

Note: "Don't know/Refused" responses are not shown.

FIGURE 1.2 What Is a Family?

Source: Pew Research Center: A Social and Demographic Trends Report. 2010. "The Decline of Marriage and Rise of New Families." Washington, DC: http://pewsocialtrends, p. 48.

those with ethnic or poor and working-class groups, a variety of relatives live, not necessarily in the same household but in very close proximity to one another (upstairs, next door, down the block, around the corner); interact on a frequent basis; and provide emotional and economic support for one another. Some sociologists have labeled this family form the **modified extended family.**

As you read this book, you will discover repeatedly that the family mosaic in the United States is not limited to nuclear and extended families. As our definition and discussion earlier implies, there is a wide variety of families and thus a wide variety of terms to identify them. For example, voluntarily child-free families consist of couples who make a conscious decision not to have children. Single-parent families (resulting either from divorce, unmarried parenthood, or death of a parent) consist of one parent and her or his children. Sometimes these families are specifically described as female- or male-headed families. In either case, legal marriage is not a criterion for family status, as the parent may or may not have been legally married. Reconstituted, blended, or stepfamilies are formed when a widowed or divorced person remarries, creating a new family that includes the children of one or both spouses. Over the last several decades, racially and ethnically mixed families have become an ever-growing part of the American national landscape. America's mixed-race population is up 25 percent since it was first calculated in the 2000 Census, while the nation's overall population has grown only 7 percent in that same time.

Lesbian and gay families are composed of individuals of the same sex who are legally married and/or simply live together and identify themselves as a family; these relationships may or may not include natural-born or adopted children. An increasing number of people living in the United States, especially children, live in foster families. A foster family consists of one or two parents and one or more children who have been taken away from their biological families (parents) and become wards of the state. In 2008, 463,000

children were living in foster families (Child Welfare Information Gateway, 2010). Foster parents typically raise these children as their own. Other contemporary forms of the family include two families living in the same household and what some social scientists call the "surrogate, or chosen, family"—set of "roommates" or group of people either of different or the same sex who choose to share the same household and who define themselves as a family. Traditionally, families in the United States have had a patriarchal structure. A **patriarchal family** is a family in which the norm is the male (husband or father) is the head of the family and exercises authority and decision-making power over his wife and children. This family structure is much more than simply a man controlling women and children in the household. More importantly, the ideological foundation of this family structure is manifested and upheld in most American institutions, including educational, religious, economic, and legal institutions.

RACE, CLASS, GENDER, AND SEXUAL ORIENTATION

Race, class, gender, and sexual orientation are four of the most important social categories of experience for individuals and families in the United States, primarily because these categories also represent significant, comprehensive, and structured systems of oppression for some individuals and groups and privilege for others. Historically, some families in the United States have experienced social, political, and economic inequalities vis-à-vis other families, principally as a consequence of their race, ethnicity, ancestry, social class, sex or gender, their sexual orientation, or other characteristics defined as inferior.

◉—Watch the **Video**
Is Marriage For White People? on **myfamilylab.com**

At a very elementary level, we can say that family experiences are shaped by the choices that individual members make. However, the options that families have available to them and thus the choices they make are either limited or expanded by the ways in which race, class, gender, and sexuality are organized. To fully understand families and how they function, then, we must examine the influence of race, class, gender, and sexual orientation on family resources and processes and explore how these factors have shaped and continue to shape the experiences of families throughout the world.

Race, class, gender, and sexual orientation are interrelated or interactive categories of social experience that affect all aspects of human life—shaping all social institutions and systems of meaning—including the institutions of marriage and family as well as family values. By "interrelated," we mean that complex interconnections exist among race, class, gender, and sexual orientation such that families are not separately affected because of the racial composition of their members, to which is added the influence of their economic situation, then the gender of their members, after which comes the impact of the sexual orientation of its members. In other words, race, class, gender, and sexual orientation are not independent variables that can be tacked onto each other or separated at will. They are concrete social relations interconnected with one another, and their various intersections produce specific effects. Thus, any concrete analysis of marriages

The growing visibility of multiracial families calls attention to the diversity of American families. It also makes it even more critical that policies relating to marriages and families address the impact of intersections of race, class, and gender on family functioning.

and families must take this into account. As sociologists Margaret Andersen and Patricia Hill Collins (1992) have observed, race, class, and gender (to which we add sexual orientation) are part of the total fabric of experience for *all* families. Although these categories are different aspects of social structure, individual families experience them simultaneously. The meaning of the concepts of race, class, gender and sexual orientation as interrelated or interactive categories of experience refers not only to the simultaneity of oppression or privilege but also to the multiplicative relationships among these experiences (for example, see King, 1990).

Understanding race, class, gender, and sexual orientation in this way also allows us to see the interrelationship of other important categories of social experiences such as ethnicity, age, religion, geographic location, historical context, and physical and mental abilities. Later in this chapter, we will see that many of these categories of experience have been interwoven in family form and functioning throughout U.S. history.

Family Functions and the Debate over Family Values

Historians and the lay public alike have often discussed families in terms of the vital social functions they serve for individuals and the society at large. These functions have included regulation of sexual behavior, reproduction, social placement, socialization, economic cooperation, and the provision of care, protection, and intimacy for family members.

SOCIAL FUNCTIONS OF FAMILIES

Regulation of Sexual Behavior Every society is concerned about the sexual behavior of its members. In most societies, sexual behavior is regulated and enforced within the context of families. Although the **norms**—cultural guidelines or rules of conduct that direct people to behave in particular ways—governing sexual behavior vary among societies, no known society allows its members to have sexual relations with whomever they please. For example, all societies prohibit sexual relations between blood or close relatives; this is known as the incest taboo. Forcing people to have sexual relations outside the family unit promotes alliances between families, reinforces their social independence, and prevents or minimizes sexual jealousies and conflicts within families. The set of relatives subject to the taboo varies across societies, however. Whereas in most societies parents and siblings are subject to the incest taboo, in ancient Egyptian and Hawaiian societies, siblings in the royal families were permitted to mate with and marry each other; in some cases, father–daughter marriages were also permitted. This system preserved the purity of royalty, enabled the royal family to maintain its power and property, and prevented the splintering of its estate through inheritance.

Moreover, in most contemporary societies, sexual relations are linked with marriage. Even in those societies where it is not, their members' sexual behavior is nonetheless regulated so that it reinforces the social order. For example, among the Masai (a polygynous pastoral group in Kenya, Africa), where men dominate in the family, young wives of older men are allowed to take lovers discreetly from the unmarried warrior class. If the wife becomes pregnant from such a relationship, family stability is not disrupted. The children from these unions simply belong to the husband and further increase his wealth and prestige.

Reproduction To perpetuate itself, a society must produce new members to replace those who die or move away. The reproductive function of families is considered so important that many societies employ a variety of practices to motivate married couples to have children. For example, in the United States, couples typically receive tax exemptions and other tax breaks for each child they produce. Couples who cannot or consciously choose not to have children are penalized by tax laws and are sometimes stigmatized by society's members. In contrast, other societies, like India and China, concerned with overpopulation, develop policies to limit population growth. India's central government establishes population targets but allows its state governments to develop their own policies for controlling the birthrate. Some state policies are coercive, denying certain benefits to workers with large families; other states use a softer approach by leading campaigns to curb teenage weddings, promoting the use of contraceptives, and providing a "honeymoon package of cash bonuses to couples willing to wait to begin a family" (Yardley, 2010). China, on the other hand, has established a restrictive one-child policy that has been in place for more than 30 years (see the In Other Places box on page 8).

THE CHINESE 4-2-1 PHENOMENON

Imagine that your family and most other families in your neighborhood consisted of four grandparents, two parents and one child, a 4-2-1 phenomenon. This is the reality in much of China today as a result of a government fertility policy adopted in 1979 in an effort to slow its population growth and to encourage economic development. From its very beginning, controversy surrounded this policy—popularly known as the one-child policy. Proponents argued that such a policy was necessary to prevent uncontrolled population growth that threatened to deplete natural resources, harm the environment, and impoverish an ever-increasing percentage of Chinese society. Opponents feared that enforcement of such an unprecedented policy would lead to human rights violations, especially for women who could be coerced into having abortions and/or face sterilization. They also worried that limiting a couple's reproduction to only one child would change China's traditional family structure, create gender imbalances

due to the ongoing preferences for sons, and, as a consequence, increase the number of elderly citizens who would lack traditional family support.

The initial implementation of the policy met with strong resistance, especially in rural areas where children were economic assets to their farming parents. Thus, from about 1984 on, policymakers adjusted the one-child nationwide policy to accommodate a variety of circumstances. Exemptions were allowed under various circumstances in rural areas where more hands were needed; for couples who themselves were only children; for urban residents whose first child was physically handicapped; for remarried couples without children from previous marriages; and among ethnic minorities.

More than 30 years later, scholars and policymakers are again debating the wisdom, necessity, and consequences of this fertility policy. Although there is widespread agreement that China's fertility rate has dropped to a level below replacement—resulting in a population of about 1.3 billion rather than the anticipated 1.6 billion—and that its economic growth has increased the per capita standard of living of its citizens by more than fourfold, there is no consensus as to whether the one-child policy was necessary to achieve these results. Dissenters point out that China's fertility levels were already declining rapidly in the 1970s before the onset of the one-child policy as young couples, like couples elsewhere in the world, were restricting their childbearing out of economic concerns. They also argue that changes in China's economic system, such as the break-up of collective farming and a greater emphasis on education and improving people's job skills, contributed more to achieving economic gains

than that particular fertility policy. Others point to the challenges China will face because of its skewed sex ratio. Worldwide, the norm seems to be about 105–107 boys born for every 100 girls. China's sex ratio is now 120 boys for every 100 girls, resulting in an estimated 20–30 million surplus men (Wang and Yong, 2011). Some social scientists fear that this demographic trend will lead to a situation where over the next two decades, millions of Chinese males will be unable to find brides. They predict that many of these unmarried men, lacking the stability that family life traditionally provides, will engage in violent activities such as trafficking in women and social rebellion. However, not all social scientists accept a causal relationship between an imbalanced sex ratio and male violence, citing a variety of possible alternative explanatory variables for male violence such as economic status, cultural norms, and type of governmental controls.

A further problem confronting China is the rapid increase in an aging population at the same time there are fewer children to care for them. Estimates are that there are 150 million families with only one child, accounting for a third of all Chinese households (Wang and Yong, 2011). Predictions are that by 2050, one in four Chinese will be 65 or older. Adult children often leave their parental homes to pursue economic opportunities, resulting in the isolation of many elderly. To deal with this issue, the Civil Affairs Ministry proposed that adult children be required by law to regularly visit their elderly parents. If they fail to do so, parents would be allowed to sue them (LaFraniere, 2011). Despite all of these concerns, the Chinese National Family Planning Commission said it will continue the one-child policy until at least 2015 (Moore, 2010).

Social Placement When new members are born into society, they must be placed within the social structure with a minimum of confusion and in a way that preserves order and stability. The **social structure** of society refers to the recurrent, patterned ways people relate to one another. It consists of an intricate web of social **statuses**—a position in a group or society—and **roles**—a set of behaviors associated with a particular status. Members of society must be placed within these statuses and motivated to play the appropriate roles. One of the ways in which families function is to assign social status to individuals on the basis of their membership within that particular family. The status placement function of families occurs at a number of levels. On one level, families confer statuses that orient members to a variety of interpersonal relationships involving parents, siblings, and a variety of relatives. In addition, simply by being born into or raised in a particular family we automatically inherit membership in—and the status of—certain basic groups, including racial, ethnic, religious, class, and nationality. Social status influences almost every aspect of our lives. It influences the way we see the world as well as how the world sees us. Much of what we consider as our unique values and preferences are really the results of our assignment to certain statuses through our families. As you will learn in later chapters, statuses such as race and class impact families differentially, depending on where families fall within these status hierarchies. Lower- and working-class families as well as certain racial and ethnic families, for example, face greater risks of experiencing poverty, welfare dependency, low academic achievement, being the victims of crime, being victimized by unscrupulous business people, violence, and higher infant and adult mortality rates.

Socialization Human babies are born with no knowledge of the norms, values, and role expectations of their society; however, they soon learn what their society considers appropriate ways of acting, thinking, and feeling. Children's social development, as well as the continuation of society, depends on the **socialization** process—a lifetime of social interaction through which people learn those elements of culture essential for effective participation in social life. Today, as in the past, families are the primary transmitters of culture to each new generation of the young. Through the socialization process, children learn the language of their culture and the accumulated knowledge, attitudes, beliefs, and values not only of the larger culture but also of their family group and the social and interpersonal skills necessary to function effectively in both the family and society. Many people in our society believe that because parents are more likely than others to be deeply committed to their own offspring, they are thus the best or most appropriate socializing agents. Compulsory education, however, has placed a significant amount of the socialization function in the hands of the state and schools. In addition, the increasing need for mothers to work outside the home has placed part of this function in the hands of child-care workers; and the mass media, especially television, have become important agents of socialization.

Economic Cooperation Children have physical and economic needs as well as social needs. They must be fed, clothed, and sheltered. Providing for these needs is the basic economic function of families. Families are responsible for the physical and economic well-being not only of their children but also of all members of their family. In the past, families consumed primarily the goods they produced. Although this is no longer true, families are still productive economic units, although the value of what they produce is less recognized today. The goods and services produced by families today are delivered primarily by women (for example, child care and housework). Because the majority of men work outside the home for wages and, women, whether or not they work outside the home for wages, perform the majority of the work within the family—work that is unpaid—the productive and essential nature of families achieved through the work that women (and some stay-at-home husbands) do has been overlooked, downplayed, and often trivialized. Nevertheless, in every society and every household, women provide critical economic support to their families, whether in agriculture or by earning income in the informal or formal labor market. When all of women's work—paid and unpaid—is taken into account, their economic contribution is generally greater than that of men. The changing structures of families notwithstanding, most continue to divide essential tasks among their members and cooperate economically to meet each one's physical, social, and economic needs.

Care, Protection, and Intimacy During infancy and early childhood, humans cannot take care of themselves and thus are totally dependent on their caretakers. A large amount of sociological and psychological research indicates that, in addition to the necessities of life, human infants also need warmth and affection. Furthermore, even as adults, humans need intimacy and often need other human beings for care and protection during periods of illness, disability, or other dependencies. Ideally, families function to provide an intimate atmosphere and an economic unit in which these needs can be met. As the center of emotional life, families can provide the love, caring, and emotional support that we need to lead happy, healthy, and secure lives that most people believe cannot easily be obtained outside the family context. For many of us, our families will be our most important source of comfort and emotional support throughout life.

Any given family may or may not perform any or all of these functions. The family as an institution is so diverse that not all families fulfill all of these functions; those who do fulfill them, do not always fulfill them well. That we live in a time of transition and change is unquestionable. Thus, many of the activities previously identified by social scientists as family functions have been taken over by or are shared with other societal institutions such as schools, religious organizations, mass media, and government agencies. The socialization of children and stabilization for adult family members, however, remain one of the primary functions of families.

Thinking about your own family, how do each of these functions operate in your family? Do they all operate equally and all of time, or are some more important than others?

CONTRASTING VIEWS OF FAMILIES

Some people see the loss of family function as a contributing factor to a variety of social ills that beset modern families. A proponent of this point of view, the late social scientist Christopher Lasch (1977, 1978), contended that the encroachment of outside institutions, especially the state, has left modern families with too few functions to perform. Even the socialization function, which had been a primary function of families, has been largely taken over by an educational system that increasingly communicates a set of values and behaviors that may conflict with the realities of some families. A number of other people—including a long line of politicians today and the religious right—believe that contemporary families are in grave danger, perhaps even in a state of crisis and moral decay. Many of these people consider the family seriously flawed and its breakdown the major source of most societal ills (illegitimacy, divorce, declining educational standards, drug addiction, delinquency, violence, HIV/AIDS). Others view the family as the foundation of society, albeit one undergoing massive changes that are connected to other large-scale societal transformations.

Blaming various societal ills and problems on the breakdown of the family and targeting various victims of America's inequality system as the perpetrators of this breakdown is not new. Throughout American history, for example, public policies have stigmatized and penalized unmarried parents and often their children and made divorce difficult to obtain. Although there was a period of tolerance expressed in public opinions during the 1960s and 1970s, there was a return to a new case for the *old* (or traditional) family in the early 1990s when sparked by the so-called conservative revolution.

These contrasting views of the family, and many gradations of them, are as prevalent today as they were in the 1990s. Today, marriages and families continue to be in a state of transformation and to be political issues. Some political conservatives, for example, want to put fathers back at the head of families as the breadwinners and protectors of women and children. Some liberals (among them some feminists), on the other hand, have long argued that the patriarchal family is the major source of women's oppression and inequality.

Some people have seen evidence of the decline and moral decay of families in terms of a number of contemporary patterns of marriage and family life today: the transformation of women's roles both inside the home and in the world at large, the increasing number of children and families beset by serious stresses and troubles, the high divorce rates, lower marriage and birth rates, the increase in single-parent families, the high rate of welfare dependency, sexual permissiveness, the increasing number of public disclosures of incest and sexual and mental abuse of children, the increasing number of unmarried couples living together openly, unmarried mothers keeping their babies, and the legalization of abortion and gay unions. Moreover, recent events such as the legalization of same-sex marriage in five U.S. states and Washington, D.C. have fueled the debate and caused many people, from social scientists to public officials to ordinary people, to take the position that the tradition of human family life is being replaced by an alien and destructive set of relationships that is detrimental to children and tearing at the very heart of U.S. society.

Although not as salient as a political issue today, protracted public discourse about family values continues to polarize Americans. The issue of family values still shapes public discourse and debate on a variety of social issues such as sex and violence on television, abortion, the ideal of the traditional family as heterosexual consisting of two parents, the role of women in society, the role of women within marriages and families, the place of motherhood, what constitutes pornography, sex education and prayer in schools, censorship, the place of religion in politics, and whether society should be allowed to impose structures that protect "traditional values" (Supporting Family Values, 2005). Although staunch political and religious conservatives carried the pro-family campaign in the 1980s, academicians—most of them also political conservatives—became the chief pro-family spokespersons in the 1990s. The religious right, conservative politicians, and other conservatives carry the banner today and have broadened the debate about family to include traditional values and moral values.

On the other side of these ongoing debates are those who are equally concerned about the problems of modern families but who view current events and trends in marriage and family life as indicative of the redefinition of marriages and families in the context of the massive transformation that took place worldwide over the last several decades. They concede that marriages and families may perform fewer direct functions for individual members than they did in the past and that there are serious problems associated with marriage and family life today. They argue, however, that marriage and family life are still extremely important to most people in the United States. They cite census data indicating that the United States has perhaps the highest marriage rate in the industrial world. And although the United States also has one of the highest divorce rates in the world, the overwhelming majority of divorced Americans remarry.

Many of those on this side of the debate refute the idealized version of families of the past and give us instead a picture of a traditional family that was often rigid and oppressive. They remind us that members of traditional families were often expected to fit into roles based on a clear division of labor along age and gender lines. Frequently, this resulted in a very restrictive life, especially for women and children. They also question the premise that family values and traditional family structure are one and the same and that both are synonymous with stability. Rather than debate something called "family values" they say, the focus should be on "valuing families."

How does the polarization of the public discussion about family and family values into a two-sided debate affect our understanding of what is happening in American families today? Is there only one accurate family form? Do you think families of the past were really the way they have been portrayed in the media and how many Americans, including politicians, describe them today? If there were "good old days," do you think they were good for all marriages and families? Why is valuing families regardless of their form considered to be antifamily by some individuals and groups? Explain.

Debunking Myths about Marriages and Families

Take another few minutes to think about the "traditional family." Again, if you are like most people, your vision of the traditional family is similar to or the same as your more general view of families. Therefore, you probably describe the traditional family in terms of some combination of the following traits:

- Members loved and respected one another and worked together for the good of the family.
- Grandparents were an integral and respected part of the family.
- Mothers stayed home and were happy, nurturing, and always available to their children.
- Fathers worked and brought home the paycheck.
- Children were seen and not heard, were mischievous but not "bad," and were responsible and learned a work ethic.

These images of past family life are still widely held and have a powerful influence on people's perceptions and evaluations of today's families. The problem, however, is that these are mostly mythical images of the past based on many different kinds of marriages and families that never coexisted in the same time and place. A leading authority on U.S. family history, Stephanie Coontz (2000), argues that much of today's political and social debate about family values and the "real" family is based on an idealized vision of a past that never actually existed. Coontz further argues that this idealized and selective set of remembrances of families of yesteryear in turn determines much of our contemporary view of traditional family life. A look at some statistics and facts from our historical past supports her argument.

- We bemoan the increasingly violent nature of families (and rightfully so). As you will see in Chapter 11, however, the United States has a long and brutal history of child and

woman abuse. Therefore, we cannot blame domestic violence on recent changes in family life or on the disappearance of family values and morals.
- We think that contemporary high school dropout rates are shockingly high. As late as the 1940s, however, less than one-half of all young people entering high school managed to finish, producing a dropout rate that was much higher than today's.
- Violence in all aspects of society is high today, but before the Civil War, New York City was already considered the most dangerous place in the world to live. As a matter of fact, the United States has had the highest homicide rates in the industrial world for almost 150 years. And, among all the relationships between murderers and their victims, the family relationship is most common.
- Although alcohol and drug abuse are at alarmingly high rates today, they were widespread well before modern rearrangements of gender roles and family life. In 1820, for example, alcohol consumption was three times higher than today. There was also a major epidemic of opium and cocaine addiction in the late nineteenth century. Over time, these and other problems led to the emergence of a new field called *family therapy*, designed to help families cope with and resolve problems (see the Strengthening Marriages and Families box on page 12).
- Although the United States has the highest teen pregnancy rate in the industrialized world, this fact cannot be blamed on the diversity of contemporary family structures and declining family values. For example, the teen pregnancy rate in the United States has declined substantially over the past two decades, hitting its lowest in 2009 since tracking began over 70 years ago.

As these facts demonstrate, our memory of past family life is often clouded by myths. A **myth** is a false, fictitious, imaginary, or exaggerated belief about someone or something. Myths are generally assumed true and often provide the justification or rationale for social behaviors, beliefs, and institutions. In fact, most myths do contain some elements of truth. As we will see, however, different myths contain different degrees of truth.

Some family myths have a positive effect in the sense that they often bond individual family members together in familial solidarity. When they create unrealistic expectations about what families can or should be and do, however, myths can be dysfunctional or dangerous. Many of the myths that most Americans hold today about traditional families or families of the past are White middle-class myths. This is true because the mass media, controlled primarily by White middle-class men, tend to project a primarily White middle-class experience as a universal trend or fact. Such myths, then, distort the diverse experiences of other familial groups in this country, both presently and in the past, and they do not even describe most White middle-class families accurately.

We now take a closer look at four of the most popular myths and stereotypes about the family that are directly applicable to current debates and beliefs about family life and gender roles in the United States: (1) the universal nuclear family, (2) the self-reliant traditional family, (3) the naturalness of different spheres for wives and husbands, and (4) the unstable African American family.

TALKS WITH FAMILY THERAPIST JOAN ZIENTEK

Introducing Family Therapy

In various chapters throughout this textbook, we will call on Joan Zientek, a marital and family therapist, to answer questions about how families cope with major problems and what they can do to strengthen family relationships. Ms. Zientek is a graduate of the Family Institute, Institute of Psychiatry of Northwestern Memorial Hospital Medical School. She has been in private practice for more than 25 years. In addition, she has presented seminars on various family and human relations topics to school faculties, parent groups, and service organizations. In addition, she has served as a consultant to many school districts. Ms. Zientek has developed and conducted a program entitled *FOCUS ON E.Q.: A Social Skills Training Program for Kids* and is the author of *Mrs. Ruby's Life Lessons for Kids*, a storybook and workbook on emotional intelligence.

What Is Family Therapy? Family therapy is a systems approach to helping families function more effectively. It views the family as a web of interlocking relationships within which every member is intimately linked in a powerful way with every other person in the family. Family therapy starts with the assumption that an individual's problems are an overt manifestation of a larger, less obvious family systems problem. Thus, problems are seen as existing between people, rather than solely within them. Unlike psychoanalysis, which delves into the origin of problems, family therapy focuses on the circular interaction between and among individuals

Joan Zientek

that keeps the problem going. The desired outcome is change rather than insight.

Who Can Benefit from Family Therapy? All individuals and families experience problems from time to time and, for the most part, many of these can be resolved without therapy. However, when a couple marries, the intensity of that bond, its reminiscent impact of each person's family of origin experiences, along with the demands of negotiating life as a dyad, often cause latent unresolved issues from childhood to emerge. These are acted out in the marriage relationship and can be disruptive and confusing to the couple. Also, as families move from one life stage to another, from the birth of children to the retirement years, some individuals and

families may need special support to make the required adaptations in family patterns and relationships. At other times, situational difficulties may be caused by divorce, remarriage, illness, death, unemployment, or relocation. The family therapist also works with individuals and subsystems of the family, treating problems that stem from emotional and biochemical issues such as depression, attention deficit disorder, or addictions. Nonetheless, the family therapist always maintains a systems framework, knowing that changes any individual(s) make influence—and are influenced by—the system in which they live.

Do Myths about Family Life Have Any Relationship to How Families Function? They can. At times, a young person uses marriage as a ticket out of their dysfunctional family of origin hoping to create a blissful life. Failing to realize that this is a myth, they and their spouse bring those unresolved issues to the marriage, only to compound the problems that they now face in the marriage. Also, we live in a culture of high expectations, prosperity, and a cultural mandate to have it all: monetary success, a wonderful family, and above all, great sex. This myth that the perfect life is possible for all leads to feelings of dissatisfaction that become intolerable when the standards are sky high. Believing in this myth can lead to skewed priorities placing monetary gain above all else. According to Joshua Coleman (2003), author of *Imperfect Harmony*, "There is an enormous amount of pressure on marriage to live up to an unrealistic ideal."

MYTH 1: THE UNIVERSAL NUCLEAR FAMILY

Although some form of marriage and family is found in all human societies, the idea that there is a universal, or single, marriage and family pattern of mother, father, children, or husband, wife, and children blinds us to the historical reality and legitimacy of diverse marriage and family arrangements. The reality is that marriages and families vary in organization, membership, life cycles, emotional environments, ideologies, social and kinship networks, and economic and other functions. Although it is certainly true that a female and male (egg and sperm) must unite to produce a child, social kinship ties or living arrangements do not automatically flow

from such biological unions. For example, in some cultures, mating and childbirth occur outside legal marriage and sometimes without couples living together. In other cultures, wives, husbands, and children live in separate residences.

During the 1950s, 1960s, and early 1970s, the idea of the nuclear family was idealized as millions of Americans came to accept a media version of the American family as a White, traditional, middle-class nuclear family consisting of a wise father

✳ Explore the Concept
Social Explorer Activity: Trends in Marriage Rates on **myfamilylab.com**

who worked outside the home; a homemaker mother whose major responsibility was to take care of her husband, home, and two or three children who were well-behaved and obedient. They all got along happily dealing with bland crises that barely caused a ripple in their ideal lives. This image, depicted in a number of 1950s and 1960s family sitcoms, such as *Leave It to Beaver*, *Father Knows Best*, *The Donna Reed Show*, and *The Adventures of Ozzie and Harriet*, and 1970s family sitcoms, such as *The Partridge Family*, *The Brady Bunch*, and poor but strong and loving nuclear families in *Little House on the Prairie* and *The Waltons*, was believed to represent the epitome of traditional family structure and values. Although family sitcoms over the last two decades have presented some diversity in family structures and lifestyles,[1] critics of today's families continue to define families in terms of the 1950s and 1960s traditional model and see the movement away from this model as evidence of the decline in the viability of the family as well as a source of many family problems.

It is true that, compared with today, the 1950s were characterized by younger ages at marriage, higher birth rates, and lower divorce and premarital pregnancy rates. To present the 1950s as representing "typical" or "normal" family patterns, however, is misleading. Indeed, the divorce rates have increased since the 1950s, but this trend started in the nineteenth century, with more marital breakups in each succeeding generation. Today's trends of low marriage, high divorce, and low fertility are actually consistent with long-term historical trends in marriage and family life. Recent changes in marriage and family life are considered deviant only because the marriage rates for the postwar generation represented an all-time high for the United States. This generation married young, moved to the suburbs, and had three or more children. The fact is that this pattern was deviant in that it departed significantly from earlier twentieth-century trends in marriage and family life. According to some, if the 1940s and 1950s had not happened, marriage and family life today would appear normal (Skolnick and Skolnick, 1999). Although some people worry that young people today are delaying marriage to unusually late ages, Figure 1.3 shows that the median age at first marriage in 2010—26.1 for women and 28.2 for men—the highest levels since these data were first recorded in 1890, more closely approximates the 1890 average than it does the 1950s average of 20.3 for women

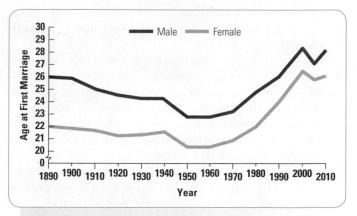

FIGURE 1.3 Estimated Median Age at First Marriage, by Sex: 1890 to 2010

Source: U.S. Census Bureau, Current Population Survey, March, and Annual Social and Economic Supplements, 2010 and earlier.

and 22.8 for men. The earlier age at marriage in the 1950s was a reaction to the hardships and sacrifices brought about by the depression and World War II. Thus, marriage and family life became synonymous with the "good life." Although there is growing acceptance of diverse family forms, many people today still think of the 1950s and 1960s as the epitome of traditional marriage and family life.

MYTH 2: THE SELF-RELIANT TRADITIONAL FAMILY

The myth of the self-reliant family assumes that families in the past were held together by hard work, family loyalty, and a fierce determination not to be beholden to anyone—especially the state. It is popularly believed that such families never asked for handouts; rather, they stood on their own feet even in times of crisis. Unlike some families today, who are welfare dependent or rely on some other form of state subsidy, families of yesteryear did not accept or expect "charity." Any help they may have received came from other family members.

This tendency to overestimate the self-reliance of earlier families ignores the fact that external support for families has been the rule—and not the exception—in U.S. family history. Although public assistance has become less local and more impersonal over the past two centuries, U.S. families have always depended to some degree on other institutions. For example, colonial families made extensive use of the collective work of others, such as African American slaves and Native Americans, whose husbandry and collective land use provided for the abundant game and plant life colonial families consumed to survive. Early families were also dependent on a large network of neighbors, churches, courts, government officials, and legislative bodies for their sustenance. For example, the elderly, ill, and orphaned dependents were often taken care of by people who were not family members, and public officials often gave money to facilitate such care. Immigrant, African American, and native-born White workers could not have survived in the past without sharing and receiving assistance beyond family

---

[1]For example, during the 1980s, 1990s, and 2000s, although television still portrayed families overwhelmingly as traditional and nuclear, there were a number of programs that showed families with different structures reflecting the reality of marriages and families in American society. Such programs included *Roseanne*: working-class married couple, children, dual earners; *King of Queens*: married couple, no children; *Family Matters*: middle-class African American family, married couple, children, extended family; *Gilmore Girls*: female head of household, children; *One on One*: male head of household, children; *Colors*: married couple, blended family; *Murphy Brown*: unmarried mother; *Grace Under Fire*: divorced mother with a sister and mother-in-law as key extended family members; *Who's the Boss?*: two single parents living together with reversed roles, he is the housekeeper and she is the breadwinner; *Kate and Allie*: two divorced mothers live together, one taking the role of breadwinner and the other the homemaker; *My Two Dads*: two men share parenting roles because of the undetermined paternity of their shared daughter; and *Modern Family*: an exploration of several different types of modern families through the stories of a gay couple who have adopted a Vietnamese baby, a traditional nuclear family in which the dad works and the mother stays home caring for their three children, and a divorced 60-year-old man remarried to a thirtysomething Latina with a preteen child.

networks. Moreover, middle-class as well as working-class families were dependent on fraternal and mutual aid organizations to assist them in times of need.

Today, no less than in the past, families need help at one time or another. The changing economy, high unemployment and underemployment rates, home foreclosures and recessions, especially the late-2000s "Great Recession," have led to increasing rates of poverty with one in seven people living in poverty today. This is the largest number of Americans living in poverty in the 51 years that such data has been available (*The Washington Informer*, 2010). Poor and working-class families have little access to major societal resources and thus often need some sort of assistance in order to survive. It is not always so easy for middle-class families, either. According to some observers, a middle-class lifestyle is becoming increasingly out of reach for middle-class families, many of whose middle-class status depends entirely on one or more wage earners. Because of recessions, unemployment, outsourced jobs, increasing medical costs, and, of late, the subprime lending crisis and the attendant massive number of home foreclosures each year, many individuals and families—across economic and social class—need assistance at some time.

MYTH 3: THE NATURALNESS OF DIFFERENT SPHERES FOR WIVES AND HUSBANDS

This myth dates to the mid-nineteenth century, when economic changes led to the development of separate spheres for women and men. Prior to this, men shared in childrearing. They were expected to be at least as involved in childrearing as mothers. Fatherhood meant much more than simply inseminating. It was understood as a well-defined set of domestic skills, including provisioning, hospitality, and childrearing (Gillis, 1999). With industrialization, wives and mothers became the caregivers and moral guardians of the family, while husbands and fathers provided economic support and protection and represented their families to the outside world. Thereafter, this arrangement was viewed as natural, and alternative forms were believed destructive to family harmony. Thus, today's family problems are seen by some as stemming from a self-defeating attempt to equalize women's and men's roles in the family. It is assumed that the move away from a traditional gendered division of labor to a more egalitarian ideal denies women's and men's differing needs and abilities and thus destabilizes family relations. Those who hold to this myth advocate a return to traditional gender roles in the family and a clear and firm boundary between the family and the outside world. As we shall see later on, however, the notions of separate spheres and ideal family form are far from natural and have not always existed.

MYTH 4: THE UNSTABLE AFRICAN AMERICAN FAMILY

Although many critics of today's families believe the collapse of the family affects all racial and ethnic groups, they frequently single out African American families as the least stable and functional. According to sociologist Ronald Taylor (2002), myths and misconceptions about the nature and quality of African American family life are pervasive and deeply entrenched in American popular thought. Although there are far fewer systematic studies of Black families than

of White families, African American families have been the subject of far more sweeping generalizations and myths. The most pervasive myth—the myth of the collapse of the African American family—is fueled by racist stereotypes and media exaggerations and distortions that overlook the diversity of African American family life. No more is there one Black family type than there is one White family type.

Nonetheless, this myth draws on some very real trends that affect a segment of the African American community. In the 1960s, social historian Andrew Billingsley (1968) called attention to the division of the African American community along class lines and demonstrated the importance of social class in any analysis of African American families. Today, most contemporary scholars agree that significant class differences exist in African American communities today. This fact notwithstanding, it is generally from multiproblem poor families (which some contemporary sociologists refer to as an "underclass") that stereotypes and generalizations are made about all African American families. Welfare debates, discussions of crime, violence and safety, urban policy initiatives, promiscuousness, teen pregnancy, and even the cultural criticism of things like rap music are focused on the situation of African Americans and their families.

This segment of African American families experiences a pattern of chronic and persistent poverty. Some of the most visible manifestations of this pattern are high levels of unemployment, welfare dependency, low marriage rates, high rates of teenage pregnancy, mother-focused families composed of a mother and her dependent children, and an escalating level of violence. Although these trends have occurred among White and other nonwhite families as well, their impact on Black families has been much more substantial, resulting in increasingly different marital and family experiences for these groups (Taylor, 2002).

Based on ideal middle-class standards, these trends seem to support the myth of an unstable, disorganized family structure in one segment of the African American community. And, indeed, among some individuals and families, long-term and concentrated poverty and despair, racism, social contempt, police brutality, and political and governmental neglect have taken their toll and are often manifested in the behaviors just described. To generalize these behaviors to the entire African American community, however, is inaccurate and misleading. Moreover, to attribute these behaviors, when they do occur, to a deteriorating, immoral family lifestyle and a lack of middle-class family values ignores historical, social, and political factors such as a history of servitude, legal discrimination, enforced segregation and exclusion, **institutional racism**—the systematic discrimination against a racial group by the institutions within society—and structural shifts in the economy and related trends that have created new and deeper disparities in the structure and quality of family life between Blacks and Whites. In addition, such claims serve to perpetuate the myth that one particular family arrangement is a workable model for all families in modern society. They also serve to cover the fact that many of the variations found in African American families have produced healthy individuals with a strong group consciousness that has helped them cope with widespread racism, violence, and poverty and—more often than not—to rise above these limitations (Coontz, 2000). (These variations are examined in later chapters of this text.)

Most sociologists today take the position that there is no one family type; African American families, like other families, should be viewed as unique and essential subcultural family forms and not simply as deviant departures from White middle-class family forms. Assuredly, the lack of adequate resources, access to stable employment, quality education, racism, discrimination, and inequalities are the problems impacting these families—not some mysterious, self-perpetuating pathology in African American families.

This discussion of mythical versus real families underscores the fact that not all families are the same; there is not now and never has been a single model of the family. Families and their experiences are indeed different; however, difference does not connote better or worse. Families are products of their historical context and, at any given historical period, families occupy different territories and have varied experiences, given the differential influence of the society's race, class, and gender systems.

Families in Early America

When the first English and Dutch settlers arrived on the eastern seaboard of North America in the early seventeenth century, between 1 and 2 million people were already living here, composing more than 240 distinct groups, each with its own history, culture, family, and patterns of **kinship**—people who are related by blood, marriage, or adoption, or who consider one another family (Mintz and Kellogg, 1988). By the end of that century, a variety of immigrants, primarily from Scotland, Ireland, Germany, and France, had arrived in North America. In addition, large numbers of Africans were forcibly brought to the colonies and sold into slavery. Thus, from the very beginning, the United States was economically, racially, ethnically, religiously, and familially diverse. One chapter in a textbook cannot possibly convey how all these different groups struggled to adapt to a new and often hostile environment and at the same time to create and maintain a stable family structure. Thus, our depiction of family life in the seventeenth and eighteenth centuries is limited to three groups: White colonial families, African American families, and Native American families.

COLONIAL FAMILIES

Our knowledge of family life among the first immigrants to this country comes primarily from three sources: (1) physical objects such as furniture, tools, and utensils; (2) personal diaries, letters, sermons, literary works, and wills that contain references to the relationships that existed among different family and community members; and (3) census data and other public records. Given that these materials represent only fragmentary remains of that period, our understanding of family life in colonial America is somewhat impressionistic. We do know, however, that there was considerable variation in family organization among the colonists, reflecting the differences in cultural backgrounds that they brought with them as well as differences in the local conditions they encountered in the areas in which they settled. Limitations of space prevent a full discussion of this diversity; hence, our discussion focuses primarily on family life in the northern colonies and incorporates some examples from the other colonies.

Household Composition A popular belief about colonial America is that most people lived in extended families. Research,

however, shows that the opposite was true. With few exceptions, early colonial families were nuclear families, consisting of wife, husband, and children (Greven, 1970; Laslett, 1971). Immediately after marriage, the couple was expected to establish their own household. About the only exception to this pattern was when elderly parents were unable to care for themselves and, out of necessity, had to live with their adult children. Nevertheless, colonial families differed in at least three major respects from the modern nuclear family. First, nonkin—such as orphans, apprentices, hired laborers, unmarried individuals, and children from other families—could and often did join colonial households. These "servants," as they were referred to, lived and worked as regular members of the household. Additionally, at times, local authorities would place criminals and poor people with families. These people were to provide service to the household in return for care and rehabilitation.

Second, the family formed the basic economic unit of colonial society. Women, men, and children combined their labor to meet the subsistence needs of the family. Until approximately the middle of the eighteenth century, relatively little was produced to sell. Calling this pattern the "family-based economy," social historians Louise Tilly and Joan Scott (1978:12) observed, "Production and family life were inseparably intertwined, and the household was the center around which resources, labor, and consumption were balanced."[2] Hence, as the basic economic unit of life, the family was synonymous with whoever lived and worked within the household, rather than strictly defined by blood and marital ties.

Finally, unlike today, the functions of the colonial family and the larger community were deeply intertwined. In his book, *A Little Commonwealth,* historian John Demos (1970:183–84) describes how the family in Plymouth colony functioned as a business, a school, a vocational institute, a church, a house of corrections, and at times a hospital, an orphanage, and a poorhouse. Although the family was involved in these tasks, public authorities determined how the tasks were to be met. Social life was highly regulated. Individuals were told where to live, how to dress, and what strangers to take in and for how long. Unlike today, there was little privacy within or among households.

Marital Roles The colonial family was a patriarchy. Fathers were regarded as the head of the family, and they exercised authority over wives, children, and servants. Men represented their households in the public sphere and held positions of leadership in the community. However, not all fathers were in this position. Those without property came under the rule of the propertied class. The ownership of property gave men considerable power in their families, and their decisions to distribute property to their offspring had a profound effect on their children's choice of careers and on when and who their children married. This practice often kept children economically dependent on their parents for much of their adult lives.

Legally, a father had the right to determine who could court his daughters, and it was up to him to give consent to a child's marriage or withhold it. His decision was based largely on whether

---
[2]This pattern was not unique to Europe and colonial America. The family-based economy can still be found in rural areas around the world, especially in developing countries.

the marriage would maintain or enhance the economic and political status of the family. Although romantic love may have existed between courting couples, marriage was viewed first and foremost as an economic arrangement, with the assumption that affection would develop after marriage (Mintz and Kellogg, 1988).

Under these patriarchal arrangements, wives were expected to be submissive and obedient to their husbands. Although unmarried women had the right to own property, enter into contracts, and represent themselves in court, after marriage the English concept of coverture was evoked, whereby the wife's legal identity was subsumed in that of her husband, giving him the authority to make decisions for her. This doctrine was often ignored in practice, however. Records show that some colonial women, especially widows, entered into contracts and operated stores; ran taverns; and worked as millers, tanners, blacksmiths, silversmiths, shoemakers, and printers—occupations usually held by men.

Although both wives and husbands contributed their skills and resources to the household, the actual division of labor was based on sex. For the most part, husbands did the planting, harvesting, bookkeeping, and supervisory tasks. Wives were responsible for cooking, sewing, milking, cleaning, and gardening. In addition, they produced many products for home consumption and traded surplus goods with other families. A wife sometimes served as a "deputy husband," assuming her husband's responsibilities when he was away on business or military duty. Thus, women often performed traditional male tasks. Men, however, only infrequently reciprocated by performing women's domestic chores (Riley, 1987:13). Today, our culture views childrearing as predominantly women's work. Yet, according to historian Carl Degler (1980), childrearing in the colonial period was mainly the task of fathers who were responsible for transmitting religious values and for instilling discipline in their offspring. As we shall see, economic changes in the nineteenth century caused a major shift in family roles.

Childhood The social experiences of colonial children differed in several major ways from those of children today. First, survival to adulthood was less likely. Death rates among children were higher than among other age groups. In the more prosperous and healthier communities in seventeenth-century New England, 1 out of 10 children died in infancy; in other communities, the rate was 1 out of 3 (Mintz and Kellogg, 1988:14).

Second, childrearing did not occupy the same place it does today. For example, well-to-do families often employed wet nurses to breastfeed and care for infants so that mothers could concentrate their attention on household duties. Children were not viewed as "innocent beings"—rather, they were seen as possessing original sin and stubborn willfulness. Thus, childrearing practices were designed to break down a child's willful nature. Religious instruction, threats, and even physical beatings were frequently used to discipline wayward children.

Third, childhood itself was quite short. Around the age of 6 or 7, both girls and boys assumed productive roles. Girls were taught domestic skills such as sewing, spinning, and caring for domestic animals. Like their mothers, they also assisted their fathers in the fields or in the shops. Young boys worked small looms, weeded fields, and were taught a craft. Finally, around the age of 14, many colonial children from all social classes were "put out" to other families to learn a trade, to work as servants, or to receive the proper discipline their natural parents could not be expected to deliver (Mintz and Kellogg, 1988).

Thus far, the family patterns we have been discussing applied primarily to the White settlers. People of color had very different experiences. In the process of adapting to their environment, they created some distinct patterns of family life.

AFRICAN AMERICAN FAMILIES UNDER SLAVERY

Andrew Billingsley (1968) points out three important elements that distinguish the experience of African Americans from that of other groups in the United States.

1. Unlike most of their colonial contemporaries, African Americans came to America from Africa and not Europe.
2. They were uprooted from their cultural and family moorings and brought to the United States as slaves.
3. From the beginning, and continuing even today, they were systematically excluded from participation in the major institutions of U.S. society.

Slaveholders often prohibited legal marriages among slaves, sold family members away from one another, and sexually exploited African American women. Nonetheless, a growing body of research shows that many slaves established strong marital and family arrangements that endured for long periods of time—even under conditions of separation.

Slave Marriages Although southern laws prohibited slaves from contracting legal marriages, some slaveholders granted permission for their slaves to marry, and a few even provided separate living quarters or household goods for the new couple. For many slaves, the solemnity of the occasion was marked by a religious ceremony at which either a Black or White minister officiated. Other marriage rituals were used as well, the most common of which involved the couple's jumping over a broomstick. These rituals, however, did not guarantee that a couple could live together. Slave spouses often had different owners and lived on different plantations; thus, they could see each other only when their masters permitted visits or when, risking severe punishment, they went off on their own.

Although many slave marriages were stable, slave couples lived under the constant fear of forced separation. The reality of these fears was expressed in some of the vows these couples took, "Until death or distance do you part" (quoted in Finkelman, 1989: xii). This fear became a reality for many slave couples, as evidenced by numerous accounts of ex-slaves who referred to earlier marriages terminated by sale to new owners. Some slaves, however, fought back against this separation. Historian Eugene Genovese (1974) found considerable evidence that when couples were separated by their masters, they often ran away in an attempt to be together.

According to Genovese, slave communities exhibited a high degree of sexual equality. This pattern has been linked to the slaves' African heritage and to the similar work roles they had on the plantations, where women worked alongside men in the fields and in the master's house. Although slave parents did not have legal authority over their own children, considerable evidence shows that both women and men had ongoing involvement with their families and that both sexes participated in childrearing.

Childhood Despite the abuses of slavery, African Americans succeeded in forming and maintaining families. Nineteenth-century census data show that both before and after slavery, most African Americans lived in two-parent households. According to plantation records examined by social historian Herbert Gutman (1976), slave women frequently bore their first child in their late teens. Because of harsh living conditions, more than one-third of the babies born to slave women died before the age of 10, a rate double that for White infants (Mintz and Kellogg, 1988:72, 73). As soon as they were able, slave children worked in the barnyards or in the master's house and soon followed their parents into the fields. Between the ages of 7 and 10, children had to leave their parents' cabin and move into quarters occupied by other unmarried youth.

Slave parents had to overcome many obstacles to hold their families together. Many succeeded in asserting some small measure of independence by securing additional food for their families by hunting small game and cultivating small gardens. Like other parents, they instructed their children in religious and cultural beliefs and trained them in various crafts. They also developed networks of extended kin that helped family members survive the material privations and harsh treatment under slavery and the chaotic economic conditions that followed them into freedom after the Civil War.

FREE AFRICAN AMERICAN FAMILIES

Prior to the Civil War, there were approximately 250,000 free African Americans in the United States. About 150,000 lived in the South, and the remaining 100,000 lived in the North (Mintz and Kellogg, 1988). Many slaves freed themselves by running away; others were freed by slaveholders after the American Revolution. A few managed to buy their own freedom. Freedom, however, did not mean full integration into the larger society. In many communities, both in the North and South, free African Americans were not allowed to vote, hold public meetings, purchase liquor, marry Whites, or attend White churches and schools.

Most free African American families were structured around two-parent households. Nevertheless, as today, inadequate family income, high levels of unemployment, illness, and early death put considerable strain on these families. One study found, for example, that in Philadelphia during the nineteenth century, between one-fourth and one-third of the city's African Americans lived in female-headed households, a figure two to three times higher than that for other groups in the city. This differential is explained by two factors. First, slaveholders tended to free women rather than men. Employment opportunities were better for women than men in urban areas, as Whites sought Black women to be domestic servants, cooks, nurses, and seamstresses. Many fathers remained slaves and could not migrate with their families. Consequently, free African American women outnumbered men in urban areas. Second, then as now, life expectancy was lower for African Americans, especially for men, leaving many women widowed by their 40s. When property holdings are held constant, however, the higher incidence of one-parent families among African Americans largely disappears, revealing the significant impact of economic factors on family stability (Mintz and Kellogg, 1988:78–79).

Slavery's Hidden Legacy: Racial Mixing

Rumors about a sexual liaison between Thomas Jefferson, the third president of the United States, and his young slave, Sally Hemings, circulated during his lifetime but were not responded to by Jefferson. Hemings, who was born in 1772 or 1773, was the illegitimate half-sister of Jefferson's wife Martha—the offspring of a relationship between Martha's father, John Wayles, and a slave, Elizabeth Hemings. For almost two centuries, most White historians debunked the notion of Jefferson's fathering a child with

Racial mixing has a long history in the United States. As a result, many Whites and African Americans, whether or not they are aware of it, have a common biological heritage. Recently evidence surfaced showing that President Barack Obama is distantly related to both former Vice President Dick Cheney and former President George W. Bush.

a slave, citing his negative views on racial mixing and his moral stature. As a result of their own cultural biases, some of these historians ignored corroborating evidence and discredited the strong oral tradition attesting to the relationship that was passed down through Hemings's descendants. However, recent DNA tests performed on the descendants of the families of Thomas Jefferson and Sally Hemings have illuminated a hidden legacy of slavery—the common biological heritage of many Whites and African Americans. These test results, reported in the prestigious journal *Nature* (1998), offer compelling new evidence that Jefferson fathered at least one of Hemings's children, her last son, known as Eston Hemings Jefferson. Eston, who was said to have borne a striking resemblance to Thomas Jefferson, was freed by Jefferson in his will and moved first to Ohio, where he worked as a professional musician, and then to Madison, Wisconsin, where he lived his life as a member of the White community. Three other surviving Hemings children were allowed to leave the plantation, and at least two of them, like Eston, are believed to have blended into White society, leaving behind numerous descendants who even today are unlikely to suspect that their ancestry is either African or presidential (Murray and Duffy, 1998).

As more historians trace African American and White families across time, the more likely we are to discover common biological roots. Barack Obama, an African American and now the 44th President of the United States, is said to be distantly related to both former President Bush and former Vice President Dick Cheney. According to reports, President Obama is related to former President Bush through Samuel Hinckley and Sarah Soole Hinckley of seventeenth-century Massachusetts, and he is related to former Vice President Cheney through Mareen Duvall, a seventeenth-century French immigrant (Fornek, 2007).

In an effort to deepen conversations about race, Pennsylvania State University sociology professor Samuel Richards gave his students the opportunity to take a DNA test to determine their genetic ancestry. Many of the students were surprised by the results. A 20-year-old, light-skinned student who always thought of himself as Black discovered he was 52 percent African and 48 percent European. He then recalled a great-grandfather who was so fair, he could pass as White. A 21-year-old public relations major said, "Some people think it's funny that I consider myself Irish and celebrate St. Patrick's Day because no matter how you cut it, when you look at me you don't think, there goes a White girl." Her test results showed her to be 58 percent European and 42 percent African American; her mother is Irish–Lithuanian and her father West Indian (Daly, 2005). In a similar fashion, a group of students at the University of Maryland played a game called, "What Are You?" in an effort to guess each other's race. Their answers were many and varied—Ghanaian/Scottish-Norwegian, Japanese/Spanish, Black/German, Asia/White. Today's college population includes the largest group of mixed-race people to come of age in the United States. These students are increasingly rejecting the old racial categories that have defined Americans for decades in favor of a much more fluid and inclusive sense of identity (Saulny, 2011b).

What the DNA tests cannot answer, and what is frequently missing from narratives of biological mixing, is the nature of the intimate relationship between the races. It was certainly true that slaveholders legally could, and frequently did, sexually assault and rape their slaves. However, evidence in the Jefferson–Hemings case points more in the direction of a caring and loving relationship than an openly abusive or exploitive one. That members of different racial and ethnic groups can and do have happy and successful marital relationships can be seen by examining current interracial marriages, a subject we will discuss in more detail in Chapter 8.

> How would you answer the question of "What Are You?" Are you comfortable asking and answering this question? Explain. Why has this become such an important question to many people today?

NATIVE AMERICAN FAMILIES

A review of the literature on family life among early Native American peoples reveals that no one description adequately covers all Native American families. Prior to European settlement of North America, Native American peoples were widely dispersed geographically. As a result, each group developed an economic system, a style of housing, and a kinship system that fit the demands of its particular environment. Even those groups living in the same region of the country were likely to develop different organizational patterns (Mintz and Kellogg, 1988). For example, there were two basic language groups among the Woodland groups living in the Northeast: the Algonquin and the Iroquois. The social and economic unit of the Algonquins was a dome-shaped structure called a wigwam, usually occupied by one or two families. In contrast, the basic social unit of the Iroquois was the longhouse, a large, rectangular structure containing about 10 families.

Among groups living in the Southeast, social life centered around the extended family. After marriage, the new husband went to live in his wife's family's household. For many tribes living in what is now California, however, that pattern was reversed, and the

Grandparents play a significant role in the lives of Native American children. This grandparent shares stories of Native American culture with the younger generation.

wife moved in with her husband's family after marriage. The basic economic unit for the Eskimos who inhabited the Arctic regions was either a family composed simply of wife, husband, and children or a household containing two such families.

Rules of Marriage and Descent Native American women married early, many between the ages of 12 and 15. Men were usually several years older than women when they married, and there was considerable variation in mate selection among different groups. Some permitted free choice, whereas others practiced arranged marriages. The rules of marriage also varied from one group to another. Although most Native American peoples practiced monogamy, some were polygamous. Unhappy marriages were easily dissolved in some groups, with either spouse able to divorce the other. Among some peoples, special practices governed widowhood. In the sororate, a widower married a sister of his deceased wife; in the levirate, a widow married one of her dead husband's brothers.

Rules of descent also varied among Native American societies. Some societies, like that of the Cheyenne, were **patrilineal,** whereby kinship or family lineage (descent) and inheritance come through the father and his blood relatives. Others, like that of the Pueblos, were **matrilineal,** whereby kinship or family lineage (descent) and inheritance come through the mother and her blood relatives. Historical records indicate that Native American families were generally small. Infant and child mortality were high. Additionally, mothers nursed their children for two or more years and refrained from sexual intercourse until the child was weaned. In contrast to early European families, Native American parents rarely used physical punishment to discipline their children. Instead, they relied on praise, ridicule, and public rewards to instill desired behavior. Among some groups, child care was in the hands of mothers; among others, fathers and maternal uncles played a more significant role. From early on, children worked alongside their parents and other adults to learn the skills that would be required of them as adults.

Families in the Nineteenth Century

Major changes occurred in the United States at the beginning of the nineteenth century, radically transforming family life. New technology brought about the creation of the factory system, which required a concentrated supply of labor away from the home. Wage labor took the place of working private family farms or shops as the main means of earning a living. The patriarchal preindustrial household no longer functioned as a unit of economic production. Consequently, it grew smaller in size as apprentices and other live-in laborers gradually left to find work in the new factories. Over time, the nuclear family of only parents and children became the new family form, which has lasted well into the twentieth century. Work and family became separated, leading to the development of a division of family labor that divided the sexes and the generations from each other in new and far-reaching ways. These changes did not affect all families in the same way, however. There were significant variations across race and class.

EMERGENCE OF THE GOOD PROVIDER ROLE

In the opening stages of industrialization, women and children worked in the factories. After that period, however, men became the predominant workers in the factories, mines, and businesses of the nation. According to sociologist Jessie Bernard (1984), a specialized male role known as the good provider emerged around 1830. The essence of this role was that a man's major contribution to his family is economic, that is, as primary (and often sole) wage earner. Masculinity became identified with being a successful breadwinner (Demos, 1974). To be a success in the breadwinning role, men had to concentrate their energies on work, and other roles, such as husband, father, and community member, became less important. Consequently, husbands and fathers were often emotionally as well as physically distant from their families. More and more, a man's status and therefore that of his family, depended on his occupation. A man's success was measured by whether he could afford to keep his wife and children out of the labor force.

THE CULT OF DOMESTICITY

The movement of production out of the household affected the roles of women, too. Although from the beginning of U.S. history, women were encouraged to think of themselves primarily in a domestic role, as industrialization advanced this ideology became even more prevalent. Now women were expected to stay at home, have children, and be the moral guardians of the family. This cult of domesticity, or as historian Barbara Welter (1978) called it, the "cult of true womanhood," was the counterpart to the good provider role. If men were to spend long hours working away from home, then women would offer men emotional support, provide for their daily needs, raise the children, and, in short, create for men a "haven in a heartless world" (Lasch, 1977). Aspects of this domestic role were oppressive and limiting for women, who by and large were excluded from most institutional life outside the family.

CHANGING VIEWS OF CHILDHOOD

The economic transformation that took place in the early nineteenth century altered not only marital roles but also children's roles. Childhood came to be seen as a distinct period, a time of innocence and play without much responsibility. Children no longer had to begin productive work at an early age. Instead, they became economic dependents. During this time, children's birthdays became occasions to celebrate, and the first specialty toy stores for children were opened. For the first time, books written especially for children were published, and other books were targeted for mothers to give them guidance on childrearing.

THE IMPACT OF CLASS AND ETHNICITY

The family lifestyle just described applied primarily to White middle- and upper-class families in which the father made a "family wage" that enabled him to support his entire family. In contrast, large numbers of African American, immigrant, and native-born White working-class men found it impossible to support their families on their income alone. Thus, the working-class family did not embrace the ideal of privacy and separate spheres of a nuclear unit to the same degree as the middle class. Working-class family boundaries were more fluid. Between 1850 and 1880, the number of extended families among the urban, industrial, immigrant working class increased (Coontz, 1988:306).

Additionally, working-class family life, both for Blacks and Whites, did not develop in isolation from the community. Alleys, stoops, gangways, and streets functioned as common areas where adults could socialize, exchange information, and observe their children at play. Contrary to many stereotypes of working-class families, there was no simple or rigid gender differentiation in these activities. In fact, "in the 1880s, when the first modern investigations of working-class family life were undertaken by the Massachusetts Bureau of Labor Statistics, one of the findings that most shocked and dismayed the middle-class male investigators was that working-class men would cook, clean, and care for the children while their wives were at work and they were not" (quoted in Coontz, 1988:306).

IMMIGRATION AND FAMILY LIFE

Many working-class families in the nineteenth century were immigrants. Between 1830 and 1930, more than 30 million immigrants left their homes to come to the United States. The first wave of immigrants was predominantly from Northern and Western Europe—England, Germany, Ireland, and Scandinavia. Beginning in the early 1880s, immigration patterns shifted to Southern and Eastern Europe—Italy, Greece, Austria, Hungary, and Russia. Historians refer to the Slavs, Italians, Greeks, and Eastern European Jews who came to the United States at this time as the "new" immigrants. Frequently, the decision to emigrate followed economic or political upheavals. At the same time, immigrants were attracted to the United States by the promise of land and jobs.

The manner of emigration varied. Some immigrants, especially the Italians, Poles, and Slavs, came without families, planning to return home after making their fortunes. A Polish folk song conveys the enormity of disruption such families experienced when the father returned after several years: "There my wife was waiting for me. And my children did not know me. For they fled from me, a stranger. My dear children I'm your papa; three long years I have not seen you" (quoted in Daniels, 1990:219). Other unaccompanied immigrants hoped to earn enough to send for their families. Still others came with their families and planned to settle permanently in the United States. To help ease their problems of adjustment, these new arrivals—whether alone or with families—sought out family, friends, or neighbors from their native country who were already settled here.

All immigrant groups faced a common set of problems: language barriers, periodic unemployment, difficulties in finding shelter, inadequate income, and often hostility from native-born workers, who feared the immigrants would take their jobs and lower the overall wage scale. Each group of immigrants developed distinct family and work patterns in response to these problems. At the same time, immigrants shared many common experiences with native-born members of the working class. Among the most serious of these was the need to have more than one breadwinner so that they could make ends meet.

THE ECONOMIC ROLES OF WOMEN AND CHILDREN

Women and children in the working class contributed to the material support of the family in a variety of ways. Overall, a working-class wife did not work outside the home unless her spouse lost his job or was unable to work because of illness or injury. Maintaining a household was a full-time job. Working-class wives grew some of their own food, baked bread, carried water and wood for cooking and heating, managed the family finances, and coordinated the schedules of working members. Additionally, wives often supplemented family income by taking in boarders or by doing laundry or sewing in their homes. Working outside the home was more common among first-generation immigrant women whose husbands earned less than their native-born counterparts. The choice of occupation varied among ethnic groups. For example, Polish women chose domestic work over factory work, whereas the opposite pattern was true for Jewish women (Coontz, 1988).

Working-class children did not experience the luxury of a playful childhood. Children were employed in factories by age 8. Even though children and women worked as hard and as long as men, often in unhealthful and unsafe environments, they were paid considerably lower wages than men.

ETHNIC AND RACIAL FAMILY PATTERNS

Racism and discrimination also made a profound difference in how work and family roles were constructed. For example, although immigrant Chinese males were recruited to build the railroads of America, they were not allowed to build families. The Chinese Exclusion Act of 1882 restricted Chinese immigration and thus restricted Chinese women from joining the men already here. "From 1860 to 1890 the sex ratio fluctuated from 1284 to 2679 Chinese men per 100 Chinese women" (Wong, 1988:235). Faced with this unbalanced sex ratio and prevented by law from marrying Whites, single Chinese laborers were destined to remain bachelors if they stayed in the United States. Married Chinese laborers, who were required to leave their families behind, could play the good provider role only minimally by sending money home to China. Sociologist Evelyn Nakano Glenn (1983) called this pattern of maintenance the "split-household family system."

With the end of slavery, Black men, like White men, preferred that their wives remain at home. African American men had difficulties finding jobs, however, and the jobs they did find tended to pay very poorly. Thus, these men could not afford to keep their wives and daughters from working. "In 1900 approximately 41 percent of Black women were in the labor force, compared with 16 percent of White women" (quoted in Staples, 1988:307). Sojourner Truth, a former slave, speaking as far back as 1851 at a women's rights convention in Akron, Ohio, eloquently addressed the exclusion of African American women from the "cult of true womanhood."

> That man over there says that women need to be helped into carriages, and lifted over ditches, and to have the best place everywhere. Nobody ever helps me into carriages, or over mud puddles, or gives me any best place! And ain't I a woman? Look at me! Look at my arm! I have ploughed and planted, and gathered into barns and no man could head me! And ain't I a woman? I could work as

much as a man—when I could get it—and bear the lash as well! And ain't I a woman? I have borne thirteen children, and seen them most all sold off to slavery, and when I cried out with my mother's grief, none but Jesus hear me! And ain't I a woman?

(Quoted in Schneir, 1972:94–95)

MEXICAN AMERICAN FAMILIES

Similarly, Chicanos (Mexican Americans) were rarely able to exercise the good provider or domestic roles exclusively either. After the Mexican–American War in 1848, the United States annexed a considerable amount of Mexico's territory, an area that encompasses present-day Texas, New Mexico, Arizona, and California. The Mexicans who lived within this new region were granted U.S. citizenship and the right to retain ownership of their land by the Treaty of Guadalupe Hidalgo. Through the unscrupulous practices of some Anglos, however, many of the original Chicano landowners soon lost their land. The erosion of the Chicano agrarian economic base had a profound impact on Mexican–American family life.

Family and Kinship One of the most distinctive features of the Chicano family was its emphasis on familism, "a constellation of values which give overriding importance to the family and the needs of the collective as opposed to individual and personal needs" (Bean, Curtis, and Marcum, 1977:760). Although the primary family unit was nuclear and patriarchal in form, there was heavy reliance on extended kinship networks for emotional and economic support. Another centuries-old source of support was

Sojourner Truth, born a slave in Ulster County, New York, was sold four times before she was 30 years old. She obtained her freedom in 1827. An electrifying public speaker, she became a forceful advocate for human rights for all people.

the ritual kinship of compadrazgo, which linked two families together. Within this system, madrinas, or godmothers, and padrinos, or godfathers, were carefully chosen from outside the kinship circle to become members of the extended family, participating in all the major events of their godchildren's lives. In effect, they assumed the role of compadres, or coparents, providing discipline, companionship for both parents and godchildren, emotional support, and, when needed, financial aid (Griswold del Castillo, 1984).

Marital Roles Chicano households practiced a fairly rigid division of labor based on gender. Wives were expected to stay home and take responsibility for domestic chores and child rearing. They were also expected to be the carriers of cultural traditions and to organize celebrations of important rituals such as baptisms, weddings, saints' days, and funerals.

In contrast, men were expected to protect and control their families and to perform productive work outside the household. The traditional male role is sometimes referred to as *machismo*. Although some writers have called attention to the negative aspects of this role, such as male infidelity and oppression of women (Madsen, 1964), most contemporary social scientists believe these aspects have been exaggerated and tend to focus on what has come to be viewed as a more "genuine machismo," characterized by bravery, courage, and generosity (Mirande, 1985).

Signs of Change White settlers bought up large tracts of land in the Southwest and instituted commercial agricultural production. The displaced Chicanos became a source of cheap labor. Much of this work was seasonal, and men experienced periodic unemployment. At times, men migrated in search of jobs in the mines or on the railroads. As a result, their wives became heads of families—sometimes on a permanent basis—as a result of prolonged separation, divorce, or more frequently, desertion. Even when men worked full time, their wages were often insufficient to support their families. Consequently, wives and mothers were drawn into the labor force, most frequently in low-paying domestic or agriculture-related work such as canning and packing and housework. Kinship structures were weakened as entire families left the area to find work. With the entrance of wives into the labor force and the frequent migration of families outside their familiar cultural area, the foundation of the patriarchal family structure began to erode.

Families in the Twentieth Century

Although applicable only to certain groups, these idealized images of men as providers and women as homemakers continued to influence popular thought about the family well into the twentieth century. However, economic and political changes were already at work to undermine these roles. Technological innovations led to the mass production of goods and to the development of large-scale corporations.

In this new work environment, the demand for child labor declined, and schools assumed more of the responsibility for the socialization of children. Young working-class women increasingly left domestic service for better opportunities in industry and in the expanding clerical fields. As a result, social contacts increasingly took place outside the family as women and men worked in proximity to each other. New products, such as movies, amusement parks, and the automobile, changed family recreation patterns. Young adults dated without chaperones and placed more emphasis on personal and sexual attractiveness. Women, dissatisfied with the restrictions of their domestic role, became activists for women's rights, particularly the right to vote.

THE EMERGENCE OF THE COMPANIONATE FAMILY

These changes gradually led to a shift away from the nineteenth-century ideal of the family. In its place emerged the idea of a more personal and companionate model for heterosexual relationships, based on mutual affection, sexual fulfillment, and sharing of domestic tasks and child rearing. Personal happiness came to be viewed as the primary goal of marriage. New symbols—the observance of Mother's Day, for example—were created to celebrate family life. Although economic and social inequalities persisted across groups, this new model of the family took hold, and many of the distinct cultural differences among families began to disappear.

Other changes were helping reshape families. Medical advances reduced the rate of infant mortality so that couples felt less pressure to have large families to ensure the survival of some children. Life expectancy had increased. Thus, families were less likely to be disrupted by the premature death of spouses. In the short span of 40 years, from 1900 to 1940, the chances of a marriage lasting 40 or more years increased from one in three to one in two (Mintz and Kellogg, 1988:131).

There was another side to these changes in family life, however. As more people came to expect companionship and emotional fulfilment in marriage, they also became more willing to terminate an unhappy relationship. Some saw the increase in the divorce rate, the decline in the birth rate, the increase in the number of married-women workers, and the change in sexual behavior as a sign of family disintegration and a breakdown of moral values. Others, however, interpreted these same patterns as signs of greater freedom of choice and as a continuing response to changing economic and social conditions in the larger society.

THE GREAT DEPRESSION

In the 1930s, families were rocked by an economic crisis of staggering proportions. Millions of workers throughout the country were unemployed for periods of one to three years or longer. The consequences of joblessness were enormous. Some families became homeless and wandered from city to city in hopes of finding food and shelter; other families were forced to share living quarters. Young adults delayed marriage, couples postponed having children, and the number of desertions increased. The depression affected all members of the family, but it undermined the male breadwinner role in particular. This inability to support their families eroded the self-esteem of many fathers. Growing numbers of women became the major source of family income. Although all groups suffered economic hardships during the depression, the elderly, the poor, and those in low-paying, unskilled jobs—predominantly people of color—were hardest hit. Family stability was often a casualty of economic instability.

The severe problems confronting millions of families led to a shift in thinking about the family. No longer could the myth of the self-reliant family be sustained. Clearly, outside support was necessary if families were to weather the economic upheavals. The government responded to the depression by creating a series of social programs, known collectively as the New Deal, to aid distressed workers and their families.

WORLD WAR II AND ITS AFTERMATH

No sooner was the depression over than another major upheaval confronted families. World War II brought about numerous changes—primary among them was the dramatic increase in the marriage rate. Between 1940 and 1946, it is estimated that 3 million more Americans married than would have been expected had rates remained at prewar levels (Bailey, 1978:51). There were many reasons for this upsurge. Some couples had postponed marriage because of the depression and were now financially able to marry. Others feared that if they did not marry now, it might prove too late later on. Some servicemen, fearing death in battle, asked women to marry them "to give them some happiness before going off to fight." Similarly, there was a dramatic increase in the birthrate as many couples decided to have a child right away.

During World War II, the image of Rosie the Riveter became popular. However, the ideology of women as men's helpmates had not changed, as evidenced in the language of this poster.

Millions of families were disrupted by wartime migration to find work and by long-term separations for military service. These disruptions resulted in changes in family roles and functioning. With husbands and fathers off to war, wives, mothers, and teenagers went to work in war-related industries. "Rosie the Riveter" became a popular image of the woman factory worker who built planes and ships. These changes made conditions difficult for families. Although some preschool children were cared for in government-sponsored daycare centers, many mothers had to find child care on their own. As raw materials were diverted to support the war effort, many families faced shortages in housing and other consumer goods.

Although the majority of families experienced some dislocation during the war years, this experience was most intense for Japanese Americans on the West Coast, who were forcibly relocated from their homes to detention centers in isolated regions of several western states. This massive relocation was inspired by fear, prejudice, and economic jealousy and resulted in depression, deprivation, and often family conflicts among the detainees.

Problems did not end with the cessation of hostilities. Families that had been separated for several years had enormous adjustments to make. Wives who had assumed both the financial and the economic responsibilities for their families had experienced a sense of independence, self-confidence, and self-sufficiency that was often at odds with their husbands' desire to return to a traditional family arrangement. Postwar housing shortages contributed to family strain as newly reunited couples found themselves living with other relatives in overcrowded conditions. Children who spent some of the war years as "latchkey" kids, taking care of themselves while their mothers worked, resented the new imposition of parental discipline. These problems were exacerbated in families whose returning loved ones were physically, psychologically, or emotionally impaired. Many families were unable to survive the tensions and hardships created by the war and its aftermath. Divorce rates soared. In 1940, one marriage in six had ended in divorce; by 1946, the figure stood at one in four (cited in Mintz and Kellogg, 1988:171).

Other transformations were also underway. In the immediate aftermath of the war, many women were forced to give up their higher paid factory jobs so that returning veterans could resume the role of the family breadwinner. Once again, the popular culture extolled the virtues of domesticity. Women were encouraged to be stay-at-home moms. The age at first marriage fell and birth rates climbed to a new high. At the same time, governmental initiatives, aimed at bolstering the economy, fueled the construction of new homes and highways, thus giving rise to what has come to be called suburban sprawl. Although many families prospered during this period, other families—especially families of color and the working poor—experienced discrimination in housing, employment, and education. Many women felt isolated and limited in their domestic roles. These restrictions and tensions eventually led to the civil rights and women's liberation movements of the 1960s and 1970s.

Ongoing Wars and Today's Military Families WW II did not end America's involvement in armed conflict. In the latter half of the twentieth century, Americans fought in the Korean War, the Vietnam War, and in Desert Storm (Kuwait and Iraq). However, with the end of the draft in 1973, the burden of fighting shifted dramatically as America turned to an all-volunteer army to defend its interests. Consequently, the physical, emotional, psychological, and economic costs of wartime military deployment are now borne by a small percentage of the population. Prior to 1973, the military was composed primarily of single young men who postponed marriage and fatherhood until after completing military service. Today's volunteer army is more family oriented. Over half of all military personnel are married. Twelve percent are married to another service member; nearly three-quarters are parents; 13 percent of army women and 6 percent of army men are single parents (Kelty, Kleykamp, and Segal, 2010).

Like all other families, military families must balance work and family, parenting issues, and maintain healthy relationships. However, unlike other families, they experience unique stressors of frequent separation and then subsequent reintegration. This is especially true during wartime. After the September 11, 2001 attack on the World Trade Centers and the Pentagon, America became involved in two wars—in Afghanistan and Iraq. These ongoing wars, involving multiple deployments for active service personnel, have put enormous stress on military families. Too often, the fears of the loss of a loved one become a reality. Additionally, loved ones may return from war with altered personalities as a result of their experiences. Estimates are that more than 300,000 troops have returned from Iraq or Afghanistan with post-traumatic stress disorders, depression, severe brain injury, or some combination of those (Dao, 2011). A recent study found that a greater percentage of children from military families suffer from emotional difficulty and anxiety symptoms compared to other children their age. Military spouses cite growing household workloads, changing marital roles, and family communication challenges as among the major stressors they experienced during their spouses' deployment (Chandra, et al., 2010).

CHANGING PATTERNS OF IMMIGRATION

After World War II, political and economic turmoil around the world led many other groups to leave their homelands in search of

"THEY SAY THEY'RE BUILDING A WALL BECAUSE TOO MANY OF US ENTER ILLEGALLY AND WON'T LEARN THEIR LANGUAGE OR ASSIMILATE INTO THEIR CULTURE..."

Does the language of this cartoon sound familiar? Given today's controversy over immigration reform, it is good to remember that the United States has always had a significant immigrant population, both documented and undocumented.

a better life. The number of foreign-born people in the United States jumped from 10.3 million in 1950 to 38.5 million in 2009, increasing from nearly 7 percent of the population to 12.5 percent, nearing the all-time high of nearly 15 percent reached in the late 1800s (U.S. Census, 2007; Greico and Trevelyan, 2010). Although historically, most immigrants to the United States came from Europe, today more than 80 percent come from Latin America and Asia. Each new group of immigrants arrived under different social and economic conditions, and each group brought some distinct family and kinship patterns. Overcoming language and other cultural barriers forced many immigrants to adopt new survival strategies, often necessitating changes in their traditional patterns of family life. Current trends in immigration and differential patterns of fertility continue to change the composition of our population, adding to the rich diversity of family life in the United States. At the same time, however, the increase in the number of immigrants, especially of undocumented immigrants, has created its own set of problems. For example, there are now upwards of two million or more foreign-born children and young adults living in the United States—approximately 65,000 of them graduate from high school each year.

Many young people like Tam, whose parents escaped Vietnam as boat people, find that despite putting herself through college, she is unable to be employed legally. Thousands of students declared their illegal status during a nationwide campaign in support of the Development, Relief, and Education for Alien Minors (DREAM) Act that would have put them on a path to legal residence and then citizenship. Now those same students, who publicly revealed their illegal status, fear they will be deported. Tam said, "Without the DREAM Act, I have no prospect of overcoming my immigration status limbo. I'll forever be a perpetual foreigner in a country I've always considered my home" (UCLA Center for Labor Research and Education, 2007) (see the Debating Social Issues box).

LESSONS FROM HISTORY

What lessons can we draw from this historical review? Five points seem relevant:

1. Although families have changed continuously over time, this change has not been in any single direction.
2. We cannot say with any certainty which changes have been good or bad. Rather, each change brings with it gains and losses. For example, the creation of childhood as a separate and distinct period created many opportunities for children's growth and development, but it also kept children dependent on parents for longer periods of time.
3. Throughout history, there has never been a perfect family form that has protected its members from poverty or social disruption, nor has any one structure provided a workable model for how all families might organize their relations in the modern world.
4. Understanding the source of our idealized view of the "traditional" family can lead us to develop a more realistic sense of families, both in the past and in the present. Studying families in the past can help us see how they endured and adapted to historical changes. It also helps us realize that many of the changes we observe in contemporary families and that cause us concern are not a result of changing family values, per se. Rather, they are more frequently reactions to rapid economic and social transformations taking place on an unprecedented scale.

5. Given the past, it is likely that additional changes in family life will continue to occur as families continue to adapt to changing economic, social, and political forces. The more we understand these changes and their impact on families, the more likely we can develop social policies to assist families in adapting to these changes.

Contemporary Patterns in Marriages and Families

Given this review of the history of families in the United States, today's patterns may seem more a continuation of trends rather than a startling new phenomenon. For example, over the last hundred years, there has been a steady increase in the number of mothers of small children who are in the labor force (see Chapter 10) and in the percentage of couples who divorce before their children reach adulthood (Chapter 12).

In tracking these and other changes, the U.S. Census Bureau identifies and counts households. A **household** contains one or more persons living in a housing unit. One of the people who owns or rents the residence is designated as the householder. The Census Bureau distinguishes between family households and nonfamily households. A **family household** has at least two members related by birth, marriage, and adoption—one of whom is the householder. A **nonfamily household** can be either a person living alone or a householder who shares the housing unit only with nonrelatives (Kreider and Elliott, 2009). Figure 1.4 on page 26 reveals some of the changes in U.S. households between 1970 and 2009. One of the most significant changes is the increase in nonfamily households, which grew from 19 percent of all households in 1970 to 33.5 percent in 2009. According to the U.S. Census Bureau, nonfamily households are made up of individuals living alone; people of the same sex who share living quarters, often for financial reasons; cohabiting couples; adults who delay or forgo marriage; or those who are "between marriages."

Additional information on households and other marriage and family patterns can easily be accessed by visiting the U.S. Census Bureau Web site (www.census.gov). As the Applying the Sociological Imagination box on page 26 shows, households are getting smaller, and the proportion of households consisting of one person living alone is increasing. Individuals are delaying marriage for longer periods of time. In addition, the number of single parents has increased dramatically while the percentage of households headed by married couples who had children under age 18 living with them declined. Each of these patterns will be examined in detail in subsequent chapters.

Looking Ahead: Marriages and Families in the Future

As we discussed earlier, many changes occurred in the composition of families over the last three decades. Nevertheless, the concerns that many people raised about the viability and future of families remain on the public agenda. Much of the debate

Debating Social Issues

SHOULD CONGRESS PASS THE DREAM ACT?

Senators Orrin Hatch (R-UT) and Richard Durbin (D-IL) first introduced the Development, Relief, and Education for Alien Minors (DREAM) Act in 2001. Since then, the bill has been introduced regularly both as a stand-alone bill and as part of major comprehensive immigration reform bills. Although the bill has had some bipartisan support and passed in the House of Representatives in 2010, it lost in the Senate on a vote of 55–41.

The DREAM Act would extend conditional legal status to undocumented youth who meet the following criteria: entered the United States before the age of 16, lived in the United States for at least the last five years prior to the law's enactment, obtained a high school diploma or its equivalent, and are under age 35. The conditional basis of their status would be removed in six years if they successfully complete at least two years of postsecondary education or military service and if they maintain good moral character during that time year period (Batalova and McHugh, 2010).

Proponents of the bill argue that passing the Act is the moral and compassionate thing to do and that children, who had no choice about coming to the United States, should not be punished for the actions of their parents. Although undocumented children can attend school through the grade 12, at the age of 18 they cannot legally work, receive financial aid, or even drive a car in most states. The threat of deportation is a constant in their lives; they fear being forced to leave the only home they have known and move to a "foreign" country. Children who have lived in America long enough to graduate from high school most likely see themselves as Americans in much the same way as native-born children do. They have learned the same values, listened to the same music, played the same video games, and share similar aspirations—go to college, join the military, get married, and raise a family. Supporters of the DREAM Act believe easing the path to citizenship for these young people has tangible benefits for the country as a whole. Many of these young men and women are willing to serve in the military at a time when America is involved in two wars. Their pursuit of a college education and establishment of a career would help the economy by infusing it with needed skills, talents, and tax revenue.

Opponents of the DREAM Act say they are sympathetic to the plight of these children but that their parents broke the law and are the ones responsible for their situation. Allowing these children a path to citizenship would encourage continued illegal emigration and would put more strain on the country's already limited resources if these children were later allowed to petition for their parents' and other family members' residency. Opponents also fear that implementation of this legislation would take education spots away from native-born children and deprive them of much-needed financial aid. Those who favor more restrictive immigration legislation believe passage of the DREAM Act would divert attention and resources away from the larger problem of protecting the borders.

Although the debate about immigration and immigration reform continues, it is unlikely that the DREAM Act or any comprehensive legislation will be considered before the 2012 presidential elections. In the meantime, many immigrant families find themselves at risk of family separation, economic hardship, and psychological trauma as the U.S. Immigration and Customs Enforcement—the federal agency charged with enforcing immigration laws—has dramatically increased the number of worksite raids to apprehend and deport undocumented immigrants. When parents are suddenly arrested and/or deported, children are often separated from their parents and suffer both emotionally and physically. Nationally, about half of all working-age undocumented adults have at least one child. There were 9.3 million undocumented working-age adults and 4.9 million children living with those adults in 2005. The majority of children in undocumented families are U.S. citizens by birth (Capps, R. et al., 2007).

What do you think? Do you know anyone who came to the United States as a child and is still undocumented? How have they adjusted to the United States? What problems do they face? What do you think of the DREAM Act? Is it a fair piece of legislation? Explain.

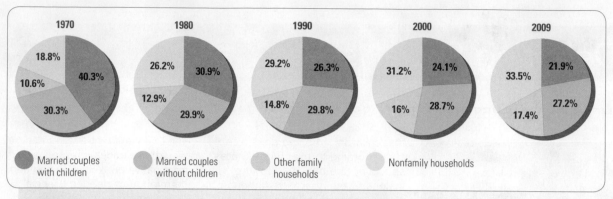

FIGURE 1.4 Households by Type, 1970–2009 (in percent)

Source: Adapted from Kreider, Rose M. and Diana B. Elliot. 2009. *America's Families and Living Arrangements: 2009.* U.S. Census Bureau, Current Population Reports, P20–561. Washington, DC: Figure 1, p. 4. J. Fields, 2004, "America's Families and Living Arrangements: March 2003," U.S. Census Bureau, 2009 (1-Year Estimates), 2009 ACS Report. (Washington, DC: U.S. Government Printing Office): 4, Figure 2.

centers on questions regarding the form that families should take, the degree to which divorce harms children, and the degree to which same-sex marriages would undermine the meaning of families when the real challenge ahead is how to help all people construct and maintain marriages and families that provide personal satisfaction and that contribute to the general welfare of society. Meeting this challenge requires solving several structural problems: insufficient well-paying jobs, lack of health insurance, inadequate educational opportunities, poor health care, inadequate and costly day care for working parents, lack of resources to care for elderly relatives, inadequate housing, discrimination, and unrealistic expectations about marriages and families. Additionally, millions of families throughout the world have and are experiencing enormous suffering, loss, and deprivations because of terrorist acts and racial, ethnic, and religious conflicts. We will discuss how these structural factors and widespread violence both on local and

international levels impact marriages and families throughout the remainder of this textbook.

The Sociological Imagination

This brief review of the history of the family in the United States reveals an ongoing pattern of diversity and change. Sociologist C. Wright Mills (1959) observed that in an age of rapid change, ordinary people often feel overwhelmed by the events confronting them, feeling that their private lives are a series of traps over which they have little control. They feel that cherished values are being replaced with ambiguity and uncertainty. Mills argued that people

APPLYING THE SOCIOLOGICAL IMAGINATION

AMERICAN HOUSEHOLDS SHRINKING

In 2010:

- The average household size declined to 2.59 from 2.62 people in 2000. However, in households where the householder had less than a high school degree, the average size increased to 2.87 up from 2.67 in 2000.
- The percentage of households headed by a married couple who had children under age 18 living with them declined to

21 percent down from 24 percent in 2000.
- The percentage of children under age 18 living with two married parents declined to 66 percent down from 69 percent in 2000.
- The percentage of one-person households rose to 27 percent up from 25 percent in 2000.

Begin with this Web page, and then connect to other links on the Census

Bureau Web site. Using your birth year and your parents' birth years, find comparable data on the composition of households in the United State for those years. Do you see any trends occurring across those decades? If so, what political, economic, or social factors do you think contributed to those trends?

Source: http://www.census.gov/newsroom/releases/archives/families_households/cb10-174.html

can counter this sense of frustration and powerlessness and come to understand their own experiences by locating themselves within their historical period. By this, he meant that we can understand our own life chances by becoming aware of those of all individuals in our same circumstances. Thus, Mills called on us to develop a **sociological imagination** to grasp history and biography and the relations between the two within our society. To do this requires asking three questions: (1) What is the structure of a particular society, and how does it differ from other varieties of social order? (2) Where does this society stand in human history, and what are its essential features? (3) What varieties of women and men live in this society and in this period, and what is happening to them?

The sociological imagination allows us to distinguish between what Mills called "personal troubles of milieu" and the "public issues of social structure." A "trouble" is a private matter, occurring within the character of the individual and within the range of her or his immediate relationship with others. An "issue," however, is a public matter that transcends the local environment of the individual. For example, any couple may experience personal troubles in their marriage, but the fact that in recent years approximately 1 million divorces occurred annually is an indication of a structural issue having to do with the institution of marriage and the family and with the other societal institutions that affect them. Mills argued that many of the events we experience are caused by structural changes. Thus, to understand the changes that affect our personal lives, we must look beyond our private experiences to examine the larger political, social, and economic issues that affect our lives and the lives of others in our society.

Although applying the sociological perspective offers many benefits, four general ones stand out: (1) It allows us to take a new and critical look at what we have always taken for granted or assumed to be true; (2) it allows us to see the vast range of human diversity; (3) it allows us to understand the constraints and opportunities that affect our lives and those of other people; and (4) it enables us to participate more actively in society (Macionis, 1991). Throughout the remainder of this textbook, we will stress the application of the sociological imagination in everyday life, focusing on social structure: how cultural values, historical context, economic and political changes, and various social-structural variables and social systems—such as race, class, gender, sexual orientation, and age—interact and affect the personal experiences of individuals and groups as they create, sustain, and change their marriages and families.

Writing Your Own Script

A course on the sociology of marriages and families usually invokes concern and interest among students about how the general principles and descriptions in the textbook apply to their own lives. As you have seen in the discussion of the sociological imagination, a guiding theme in the discipline of sociology is that individual lives are influenced, patterned, and shaped by large and powerful social forces beyond the control of any one individual. At the same time, individuals are not passive in this process. Individuals act in ways that influence these larger social forces. Therefore, a connection exists between our own personal and private experiences and the culture, society, groups, marriages, and families to which we belong. In this textbook, we stress the application of the sociological imagination in everyday life. That is, we stress the personal relevance of the topics, issues, and concerns

addressed in this book with the goal of helping you, the reader, fully appreciate the connection between yourself (the individual) and society. In this context, we present in each chapter a box entitled "Writing Your Own Script" (see page 28) to reinforce your knowledge of the sociological imagination and your ability to apply it.

Writing Your Own Script is simply an exercise that utilizes an everyday life approach to the study of marriages and families. It encourages you to become directly involved in the learning process by using your own personal experiences (and those of others you know) as a way of understanding and critically examining or evaluating both the commonly shared elements as well as the uniqueness of your own personal life. Throughout our lives, all of us are confronted with life events, living arrangements, and other activities about which we must make decisions. Some of the most important of these decisions concern marriage and family living. One way of doing this is to keep a personal journal of your thoughts and reactions to the material presented in the text.

In the Writing Your Own Script exercises, you are provided with a more formalized process for reflecting on and planning your own life script. As you complete each chapter of the book, you are in a good position to reflect, examine, and evaluate your feelings and desires regarding the life choices you have made or will be making over the course of your lifetime. You can select only those exercises or marriage and family issues that are of immediate concern to you, or you can do them all. The exercises correspond to key topics discussed in each chapter; therefore, it is important that you understand and refer back to the chapter, if necessary, as you think about your own life. Even if you have already made some decisions, such as getting married and having children, these exercises can give you added or new insight into how well your decision making worked and can perhaps suggest other areas where improvements can be made. The exercises can also simply help you understand your life experiences and those of others within the sociohistorical and political contexts in which they occur.

Supporting Marriages and Families

Over the centuries, marriages and families have undergone many changes. For most of human history, marriage was a way of ensuring economic and political stability. The belief that young people could choose their own mates and should choose them on the basis of something like love—which had formerly been considered a tremendous threat to marriage—is only about 200 years old. Historian Stephanie Coontz (2005) argues that once this belief took hold, it created new demands—demand for divorce, the right to refuse marriage, even recognition of same-sex relations. The view that the old rules for marriage are not working has led some social critics to argue that marriages are in crisis. Although Coontz agrees that marriage has been weakened as an institution in that it has lost its former monopoly over organizing sexuality; male–female relationships; legitimacy; and political, social, and economic rights, she disagrees with those who think we can return to some idealized image of marriages and families. Instead, she argues that the main things that have weakened marriage as an institution are the same things that have strengthened marriage as a relationship. Marriage is now

Writing Your Own Script

DEFINE IT, AND KNOWLEDGE FOLLOWS*

As you have seen in this chapter, the structure and lifestyles of marriages and families are diverse. However, for many people in the United States today, family is still defined in very narrow terms. According to Joan Ferrante (1995), narrow social definitions enable narrow legal definitions to persist, and both such definitions can cause pain and deprivation, or simply discomfort. Thinking about popular cultural definitions of the family, as well as narrow legal definitions, where do you and your family fit?

Write a brief sociological description of your family. Some questions or issues to pay particular attention to are the following: How do you define family? Think about your own family and the individual members. What or who constitutes family for you? Does your idea of family

*The title of this box is borrowed from the ideas of Joan Ferrante (1992) concerning the power to define.

include distant cousins (third and beyond) and great-great-aunts and uncles? Does it include people not related to you by blood, adoption, or ancestry? Is your definition of family consistent with that of other family members? If not, how does it differ? Do you make a distinction between the notion of "family" and that of "kinship"? If yes, how so? What are the typical marriage types in your family? Marriage eligibility customs? Residential patterns? Family power patterns? You might want to make a family tree, starting with yourself and going back as far as you can.

To be sure, what you do now (how you write your own script) is not written in stone. The Writing Your Own Script exercises are simply one method among many that allow you to understand your life and begin making informed choices by applying the sociological imagination. Some of these choices, like becoming a parent, are permanent; others, such as

entering into or dissolving a relationship, can be altered. In addition, we should realize that the choices we make at various stages of our lives may affect later options. For example, a decision to delay marriage or childbearing into our 30s or 40s may result in fewer, if any, options to engage in these behaviors at a later date.

To best utilize the Writing Your Own Script exercises, consider the following: (1) the factual information presented in each chapter; (2) the key life events and activities around which the Writing Your Own Script exercises are built; (3) the options available to you in each area of decision making; (4) the larger social forces that may affect the range of options available to you; (5) the possible positive and negative consequences (advantages or disadvantages) of each option; and (6) how social forces and your own personal values may interact to influence your choices and those of others.

more optional because women and men now have equal rights in marriage and more equal economic opportunities. Thus, on the one hand, people can negotiate a marriage, making it more flexible and individualized and giving it the potential to be fairer, happier, more satisfying, and more fulfilling than ever before. On the other hand, these same forces allow people to choose to stay single or to leave an unsatisfactory marriage. Coontz believes the marriage revolution, like the Industrial Revolution, is irreversible and that we have to learn from both the opportunities and the problems this raises

for us. We would add one more thing: If we are serious in our belief that marriages and families are the foundations of our society, then it is all of our responsibilities to see that couples and families have the tools and societal supports to help them build and sustain satisfying and meaningful relationships and family lifestyles. At the end of each of the remaining chapters, we will briefly consider some of the possible ways to support marriages and families. These can range from governmental action, professional advice, community organizations, individual activists, and even commercial products.

SUMMARY

Marriage and family are among the oldest human social institutions. Each society develops its own patterns of marriage and family life, and these patterns vary considerably across and within cultures. In recent years, family values have become a topic for debate in the United States. Such debates are often clouded by

mythology about the way families used to be. Myths are false, fictitious, imaginary, or exaggerated beliefs that can create unrealistic expectations about what families can or should be. Four of the most popular myths and stereotypes directly applicable to current debates about family life and gender roles are (1) the universal nuclear family, (2) the self-reliant traditional family, (3) the naturalness of the separate spheres of wives and husbands, and (4) the unstable African American family.

The discussion of mythical versus real families underscores the fact that not all families are the same; there is not now and never has been a single model of the family. Families are a product of their historical context, and, at any given historical period, families occupy different territories and have varied experiences. Race, class, and gender are three interlocking categories of social experience that affect all aspects of human life; they shape all social institutions and systems of meaning, including the institutions of marriage and family, and the discussion of family values.

From the very beginning, the United States was economically, racially, religiously, and familially diverse. Native Americans, White ethnic settlers, Africans forcibly brought to this country as slaves, and Chicanos whose land was annexed by the United States all struggled to create and maintain a stable family structure in a new and often hostile environment. Over time, these and other immigrant groups confronted powerful economic and political forces, such as industrialization, depressions, and wars, which led to major transformations in family life.

A course on the sociology of marriages and families can help us develop a sociological imagination and facilitate our understanding of how many of the concepts and issues pertaining to marriage and family lifestyles apply in our own lives and at the same time are linked to social structure and historical circumstance. One way to appreciate fully the connection between our own personal and private experiences and the culture, society, groups, marriages, and families to which we belong is to engage in "writing your own script"—a process for utilizing the sociological imagination to reflect on and plan your own life script.

KEY TERMS

institution	polygyny	nuclear family	norms	kinship
exogamy	polyandry	extended	social structure	patrilineal
endogamy	cenogamy (group	(multigenerational)	status	matrilineal
marriage	marriage)	family	role	household
monogamy	family	modified extended	socialization	family household
serial monogamy	family of orientation	family	myth	nonfamily household
polygamy	family of procreation	patriarchal family	institutional racism	sociological imagination

QUESTIONS FOR STUDY AND REFLECTION

1. In this chapter, we have described some of the major functions of families, historically and presently. Do any of these functions apply to your family experiences? Describe how you have experienced these functions within your family. Be specific. What other social institutions (e.g., schools, government, religion) have served as vital social functions for you or your family members? What conflicts, if any, have arisen as a result of your or your family's participation in these social institutions?

2. What is meant by the idea that race, class, and gender are interactive systems rather than individual variables? Think about your own family of orientation, and take one particular aspect of your family life as an example. Discuss briefly how race, class, and gender act simultaneously to shape that aspect of your family life.

3. Given the tremendous number of immigrants this country has had, it is likely that you, a relative, classmate, neighbor, or someone else you know has migrated to the United States. Interview that person, focusing on the reasons for coming and the ways in which that experience has affected her or his life. To what extent, if any, have that person's family patterns and structures been changed as she or he adjusted to life in the United States?

4. Most people agree that marriages and families underwent major changes during the last half of the twentieth century; however, few people link these changes to larger societal changes that have taken place. Identify some of the major changes that have taken place during the past 50 years (for example, in transportation, technology, and social welfare policies), and discuss their impact on contemporary marriages and families. Reflect on your own family and consider how one such change has affected your family and/or families like yours.

ADDITIONAL RESOURCES

SOCIOLOGICAL STUDIES

CHILDS, ERICA C. 2005. *Navigating Interracial Borders: Black-White Couples and Their Social Worlds*. Piscataway, NJ: Rutgers University Press. Using a variety of research methodologies, including personal accounts, in-depth interviews, and focus groups, Professor Childs explores the social world of Black-White interracial couples and examines the way that collective attitudes shape private relationships.

COONTZ, STEPHANIE. 2005. *Marriage, a History*. New York: Viking. Stephanie Coontz explores the concept of marriage and its history in Western society. Among her many revelations, she finds that "traditional marriage" is a remarkably recent innovation in marriage—the love-based male-breadwinner marriage is younger than the United States of America. Starting with why marriage cropped up in the first place and ending with marriage in modern day, Coontz's history of Western marriage is revealing and an excellent supplement for discussions of the myths about American marriages and families.

FONER, NANCY, RUBEN G. RUMBAUT, AND STEVEN J. GOLD. 2000. *Immigration Research for a New Century: Multidisciplinary Perspectives*. New York: Russell Sage Foundation. This collection of essays explores the rich variety of the immigrant experience, ranging from itinerant farm workers to Silicon Valley engineers. It also provides the fresh insights of a new generation of immigration researchers.

HAWES, JOSEPH M., AND ELIZABETH I. NYBAKKEN, EDS. 2001. *Family and Society in American History*. Urbana and Champaign: University of Illinois Press. An illuminating range of articles examines the changes that have occurred in American families from the eighteenth to the twentieth century that accompanied evolving social, political, and economic changes.

FILM

David and Layla. 2006. This modern day Romeo and Juliet tale was inspired by the true story of a Kurdish-Jewish couple whose families were dead set against their marriage.

The Visitor. 2008. A widowed college professor becomes embroiled in the lives of a young immigrant couple he finds living in his New York apartment. All of their lives are thrown in turmoil when the young Tarek is arrested and told he would be deported.

LITERARY WORKS

FORD, JAMIE. 2009. *Hotel on the Corner of Bitter and Sweet*. New York: Ballantine Books. Set during one of the most conflicted and volatile times in American history, this novel explores the age-old conflicts between father and son, the damage that is caused by war—not on the battlefield, but to the humanity of individual people—and the depths and longing of deep-rooted love. The novel is set in 1940s Seattle, Washington during the interment of Japanese Americans during World War II and at a time when races and ethnicities did not mix. Whites, Blacks, Chinese, and Japanese all lived in separate communities. This novel is an excellent source for students to explore issues of intimacy on a number of levels, for example, father-son, and how intimate relationships are shaped by culture, historical time, and social structure. Other issues students might explore from this novel are commitment, devotion, conflicted loyalties, forgiveness, and enduring hope and love.

NAZARIO, SONIA. 2007. *Enrique's Journey: The Story of a Boy's Dangerous Odyssey to Reunite with his Mother*. New York: Random House. Left in Honduras when he was 5 by a mother who came to the United States out of desperation to feed her children, Enrique, now 17, journeys to America to find her. On the way through Mexico, he is preyed upon by bandits and is nearly knocked off the roof of a freight train.

INTERNET

www.cdc.gov/nchs/nvss.htm The National Vital Statistics System provides data on births, marriages, divorces, and deaths in the United States.

www.census.gov/ipc/www/idb/ This international database offers a variety of country-level data, including data on marital status, ethnicity, religion, employment, and family planning.

www.migrationinformation.org The Migration Information Source provides data from numerous global organizations and governments, including the United States, and analyzes international migration and refugee trends.

www.mayflowerfamilies.com On this Web site, you can find information on early colonial and Native American families and links to historical records and documents as well as resources to help you build your own family tree.

Succeed with MyFamilyLab®
www.myfamilylab.com

Watch. Explore. Read. The New MyFamilyLab is designed just for you. Each chapter features a pre-test and post-test to help you learn and review key concepts and terms. Experience Marriages and Families in action with dynamic visual activities, videos, and readings to enhance your learning experience.

Here are a few activities you will find for this chapter.

Watch on **myfamilylab.com**

Video clips feature important concepts in the study of Marriages and Families. Watch:
- Is Marriage For White People?

Explore on **myfamilylab.com**

Social Explorer is an interactive application that allows you to explore Census data through interactive maps. Explore the Social Explorer Activity:
- Trends in Marriage Rates

Read on **myfamilylab.com**

MyFamilyLab includes primary source readings from classic and contemporary sociologists from around the world. Read:
- Graff, "What Is Marriage For?"

Ways of Studying and Explaining Marriages and Families

What Will You Learn?

- Define and understand the sociological meaning of key terms.
- Describe the various ways social scientists study and explain marriages and families.
- Apply the sociological imagination to examine the impact the Internet has on marriage and family relationships.
- Assess the pros and cons of gun control legislation for the safety and security of families.
- Increase your awareness and understanding of the link between theory and research in studying and explaining marriages and families.
- Question the applicability of traditional research methods and family theories for understanding and explaining contemporary marriages and families.

IN THE NEWS

Washington, DC

Recent survey data indicate that the Internet has become a mainstream information tool for Americans. A majority of Americans (84 percent) now use the Internet to satisfy their information needs. They look to the Internet to provide all kinds of information from services from government agencies; news about what is happening locally, nationally, and internationally;

information about business and commerce to medical and health care information. Internet users and nonusers report having high expectations of online information sources, with many users stating that they use the Internet as their first or primary source of information. Moreover, 75 percent of Internet users say that the Internet actually succeeds in meeting their information needs. Not only do the majority of Internet users expect a business to have a Web site that provides information about a product they are considering buying and expect to be able to find reliable, up-to-date news online, but they also expect to find reliable information about health, diseases, or medical conditions online (Horrigan and Rainie, 2002).

People seeking answers to problems consult the Internet the most, followed by professional advisers, friends, and family members. The Internet is a great resource, but it is also a public forum, where anyone can make a claim or an assertion and post an article, book, or opinion online without any checks for accuracy as is the custom in scientific research, publishing, and journalism (Clemmitt, 2008). This fact notwithstanding, the Internet, rather than healthcare professionals, is the main source for healthcare information in U.S. households, and women more than men seek such information online. In 2010, for example, 175 million Americans searched the Internet looking for information about serious issues of health, illness, and diseases—up from 117 million 5 years earlier. And, for approximately one half of these users, the Internet is their primary source of health information. Some of these users, or e-patients (health consumers who use the Internet to gather information about a medical condition of interest to them), have actively contributed medical comments, reviews, and updates. In addition, in this age of growing technology, a small but increasing number of Americans are using social networking sites such as Facebook and Twitter to access testimonials and advice about drugs or herbal remedies for a variety of maladies (Harris Poll, 2010; Burst Media, 2007).

As millions of people and organizations around the world post information on the Internet, it is not always readily apparent what is—and is not—accurate and reliable information. Nonetheless, the majority of those seeking medical or health care advice on the Internet say that the health information they find online influences their decisions about their own treatment or that for someone they care for, and a small but growing number feel they can act on what they find on the Web without physician guidance. Interestingly, only a small percentage of these users say they always check the accuracy, source, or date of the health information they find online (Madden and Fox, 2006).

The popularity of the Internet as a source of health information has raised considerable concern and questions about the accuracy of the information provided by various health and medical Web sites. In this context, some medical experts have found that many of these sites contain information that is misleading, incomplete, contradictory, out-of-date, erroneous, or pure quackery. While this plethora of Web site medical information can be a good thing, the challenge these days for consumers is to find trustworthy information or advice amid the enormous amount of profit-driven, misleading, or plain inaccurate information on the Web (Berland et al., 2001; Foreman, 2005).

WHAT DO YOU THINK?

Do you use the Internet for health information? If yes, for what types of health information and what sites do you use? Have you used social networking sites such as Facebook or Twitter for health care information? Do you trust these Web sites to transmit accurate and complete health information? Do you investigate the reliability of the information presented? Do you think the health information transmitted via the Internet is representative of the U.S. population? If you have not used these Web sites, why not?

The Sociology of Marriages and Families

Sociologists have conducted thousands of studies on a variety of marital and family behaviors, relationships, characteristics, and problems, ranging from the sexual behavior of members of marriages, families, and other intimate relationships; fathers' involvement in childrearing and child care; the long-term effects of television viewing on the behavior of children to the use of technology in American family households. Studies such as these have yielded a tremendous amount of data that have contributed significantly to what we thought we knew about marriages and families. For example, despite the cultural and religious controversy and debate about the value of abstinence-only programs versus comprehensive sex education, sociologists and other social scientists have well established through their scientific research findings that comprehensive sex education programs that teach both abstinence and birth control do not increase adolescent sexual activity. In fact, this research has found that such programs can help delay the start of sexual activity in teenagers and increase condom use among sexually active teens (see, for example, Centers for Disease Control and Prevention, 2002; Hauser, 2004; McKeon, 2006). Similarly, some research findings have suggested that sex education about birth control can significantly reduce teenage pregnancy and infection rates. For example, comprehensive studies of teenage pregnancy have found that the teenage birth rate has declined steadily over the past two decades. Approximately one-fourth of the decline is attributed to delayed sexual activity among teens, and three-fourths is due to the increased use of long-term contraceptives (see, for example, Manlove et al., 2000; Science Daily, 2007).

Furthermore, sociologists have generated a number of theories from their research that help explain issues like why and how marriages and families emerged, how they are sustained over time, how people involved in these relationships interact with and relate to each other, what effect children have on marriages, what significance marriages and families have for U.S. society, and how and why marriages and families change over time. In this chapter, we examine the ways in which sociologists discover facts—do research—about marriage and family behaviors and devise theories or explanations of these behaviors.

The Link between Research and Theory

Sociology involves observing human behavior and society and then making sense out of what we observe. Thus, both research and theory are involved. However, as controversies and debates surrounding various research findings indicate, the social and political climate, as well as the ideological viewpoint of the researcher, has an impact on what is researched, how it is interpreted, and whether or not it is widely shared—or for that matter, how it is shared—with the public (such as which findings are stressed and which are omitted or downplayed). Politics aside, the link between research and theory is obvious. For example, research about marriages and families provides us with important observations about these intimate relationships. Various marriage and family theories and perspectives provide us with basic points of view or frameworks that help us analyze and understand these observations.

A **theory** is an explanation of some phenomenon. Theories relate ideas and observations to each other as well as help explain them. They contain certain assumptions about the world and about the nature of society and human behavior. In addition, most theories include stated or unstated value judgments concerning the topic or issues related to the topic. For example, if we use a theory that assumes that the family is a system held together through a basic harmony of values and interests and that consensus and stability are desirable in the family (a value judgment) because they facilitate this cooperation, then we are most likely to ask questions concerned with order, stability, and balance, such as how families function in an orderly and consensual way to maintain or preserve their families over time.

Actually, if you think about it, no theory or perspective on human society and behavior is unbiased or completely value-free. Because they contain assumptions about the nature of human beings and their societies, all such theories implicitly or explicitly suggest that certain arrangements are desirable, good, or better than others.

How do we know, then, if a particular theoretical perspective provides a viable explanation of its subject matter? The answer to this question lies in an understanding of the relationship between theory and scientific research. Theories are important sources of ideas for researchers to test. **Scientific research** provides us with empirical evidence as a basis for knowledge or theories. By **empirical evidence,** we mean data or evidence that can be confirmed by the use of one or more of the human senses. Scientific research also allows us to test **hypotheses,** statements of relationships between two or more **variables**—factors that can have two or more values—to determine what is, as opposed to what we think should be.

All scientific research is guided by the **scientific method,** a set of procedures intended to ensure accuracy and honesty throughout the research process. The scientific method involves making systematic and objective observations (collecting information), making precise measurements, and reporting the research techniques and results to other interested parties. If followed, these procedures generally lead researchers to the facts of a situation or event, regardless of what we might hope or believe to be the facts. These procedures also permit others to repeat research studies to validate or invalidate previous findings, thereby allowing us to expose researcher biases where they might appear. In addition, unlike the mass media generally or the Internet specifically, whose claims are often immune to criticism and validation of their reliability even when they are contradictory, biased, or wrong, scientific research on marriages and families and other topics typically undergo peer review before it is published and made available to a wide audience. This fact notwithstanding, scientific research is sometimes influenced by practical matters such as the availability of funding, who funds the research (and publishes it), access to subjects, and time constraints. Research is also sometimes influenced by politics. Consequently, biases, compromises, selectivity, and other nonscientific issues can creep into the scientific research process and can have an effect from the beginning to the end of the process.

How exactly are theory and research related? Theory provides insights—often in the form of abstract ideas—into the nature of individuals and society, and research provides the objective observations on which theories are verified. It is a reciprocal, or back-and-forth, relationship. For example, theories that cannot be confirmed by evidence gathered through scientific research mean nothing. Similarly, facts have meaning only when we interpret them and give them meaning based on some theoretical perspective. Contrary to popular belief, facts do not speak for themselves. This belief is often at the heart of public and political controversies

or debates. For example, in the debate over gun control, opposing groups in the debate have different interpretations of the facts surrounding the relationship between gun ownership among the citizenry and protection from crime versus the proliferation of crime and firearm deaths (see the Debating Social Issues box).

Debating Social Issues

GUN VIOLENCE IN AMERICA AND THE GUN CONTROL DEBATE

In 2010, the U.S. Supreme Court made two landmark rulings: (1) it upheld the right of individuals to bear arms for hunting and self-defense and (2) it expanded the right to bear arms in cities and states. On the heels of these rulings, on January 8, 2011, a mass shooting occurred near Tucson, Arizona. Thirteen people were shot, including a U.S. Representative from Arizona, Gabrielle Gifford, and six, including a U.S. District Court Chief Judge, were killed. This tragic incident fueled an already heated and protracted debate in this country over gun control.

Although gun violence is not new in the United States, it is currently an intensely debated political issue. With over 280 million guns in civilian hands, there are few places to hide from gun violence. Every day in America, guns claim 84 lives and wound nearly 200; every year 30,000 people die—more than 3,000 of them children and teens: one child or teen every three hours, eight every day, 58 every week, and more than 70,000 are injured. The firearms death rate in the United States is eight times higher than in other high-income countries, and the rate among children under age 15 is nearly 12 times higher in the United States than in 25 other industrialized countries combined. The Centers for Disease Control and Prevention estimates that almost 2 million children live in homes with loaded and unlocked guns (Children's Defense Fund, 2010; Gun Violence in America, 2008).

Gun violence plagues every community in America. It does not discriminate; it is an increasingly real

The gun control debate in this country has heightened since the 2008 election of President Barack Obama. Pro-gun advocates such as David McElroy, pictured here, have shown up at protest rallies against President Obama's health care and spending policies wearing holstered guns in plain view to show their support of Second Amendment rights.

problem in American cities, suburbs, and rural areas. While tragedies like the 2011 Arizona shooting and mass school shootings such as those that occurred at Virginia Tech in 2007 and Northern Illinois University in 2008 receive significant media attention, gun deaths and injuries in the United States usually occur quietly, every day, without national press coverage. Such violence increases the probability of deaths in incidents of domestic violence, raises the likelihood

of fatalities by those who intend to injure others and among those who attempt suicide, places children and young people at special risk, and disproportionately affects poor and communities of color. The epidemic of gun violence is particularly acute among Black males and Latinos. For example, in 2007, for the first time, more Black than White children and teens were killed by gun violence. Black males ages 15 to 19 are more than five times as likely as White males of the same age and more than twice as likely as Hispanic males to be killed by firearms. They also are at substantially greater risk of being injured by gun violence than their White and Hispanic peers. Currently, firearm homicide is the leading cause of death for Black men ages 15 to 34, and it is the leading cause of death for all African Americans ages 15 to 24. Additionally, homicide represents the second-leading cause of death for Latinas/os between the ages of 15 and 24, 76 percent of which are firearm related (Legal Communities Against Violence, 2011; Children's Defense Fund, 2010; Child Trends, 2011).

The cost of gun violence to Americans and their families as well as whole communities is staggering both in terms of lost life and the cost to the economy. Estimates of direct medical costs for firearm injuries, for example, range from $2.3 to $4 billion, with additional annual indirect costs estimated at $19 billion. The average cost for treating each unintentional shooting is $22,400 and the average cost for treating each gun-related

(continued on next page)

(continued from previous page)

injury is $18,400. Because most victims of gun violence in America are uninsured, the public ends up footing the bill for their treatment. Overall, the costs of gun violence in the United States have been estimated at between $100 billion and $126 billion. In addition, the economic and emotional cost of gun violence to individual families is noteworthy. For example, for every person who gets shot and dies, it is estimated that another four people get shot and survive. For many of these survivors, although their physical injuries may heal, the emotional trauma and scars often go untreated leaving them traumatized in much the same way as soldiers returning from combat and placing them at increased risk for future injury, substance abuse, and death (Children's Defense Fund, 2010; Gun Violence in America, 2008).

The Debate

According to some observers, the gun control debate may be one of the most heated issues of our time. On both sides of the debate, gun control activists and pro-gun advocates are extremely passionate about their position on the subject. While most Americans seem to have some sort of opinion about guns, violence and control and a myriad of groups are involved in the debate, the most visible and vocal groups in the debate are the National Rifle Association (NRA), which is against more federal regulation of guns, and the Brady Center, along with its affiliate organization, the Center to Prevent Handgun Violence, which are for more firearms regulation.

The NRA argues that the Second Amendment of the U.S. Constitution guarantees individuals the right to own and carry guns. They are against federal regulations because they believe that it will continue to increase until owning a handgun will be difficult to achieve, infringing on their Constitutional rights. In addition, they argue that if law-abiding citizens have guns, they are safer from criminals, bringing crime rates down. Although critics question the research findings provided by the NRA to support its position that gun ownership results

in protection from crime, the NRA counters by arguing that research results provided by the Brady Center and others in favor of gun controls are false or overstated. While advocates for gun control support the efforts of gun manufacturers such as Smith and Wesson to add safety features to various firearms, the NRA has come out strongly against adding such features to guns. They argue that if gun manufacturers build guns with safety features, then the federal government will start requiring those safety features. If the federal government require safety features, that will, in turn, provide momentum to the federal government for passing more regulations (Adams, 2011).

The Brady Center, on the other hand, disagrees with the NRA interpretation of the Second Amendment to the U.S. Constitution. The Center takes the position that the Second Amendment does not guarantee individuals the right to own and carry guns. Further, they argue that when more people have guns, deaths and injuries from guns increase, in particular, more teens and children die from gun wounds. For example, during a year when more than 5,000 teens and children died from gun wounds in the United States, in Great Britain, where gun ownership is very restricted, 19 teens and children died from gun wounds. They argue that the NRA's argument that restricting access to guns causes more crime (because then only criminals will have guns), is not supported by evidence at a national or international level. For example, in countries where guns are greatly restricted, such as Great Britain or Japan, deaths from guns are rare compared to the United States. In fact, the United States is a world leader in the rate of homicides from guns. Although there are a few federal gun laws currently, the Brady Center argues that these laws have important loopholes which lead to senseless gun deaths and injuries affecting thousands each year. Thus, they advocate stronger laws and policies that will protect American marriages, families, and communities from gun violence by making it harder for

convicted felons, the dangerously mentally ill, and other prohibited persons to obtain guns. Furthermore, they argue that preventing gun owners from buying especially dangerous weapons such as assault rifles is not unconstitutional. Neither is using the law to ensure that only law abiding citizens are able to attain guns. In arguing for laws that promote gun safety, such as requiring child-proof locks on gun triggers, the Center has praised Smith and Wesson for starting to make guns with safety features. They believe that the public good is served by enacting laws that more carefully protect children from access to guns (Adams, 2011).

The staggering statistics on gun violence in America and the national debate about gun control notwithstanding, average Americans are fairly split on the issue of gun control. According to a recent CBS News/ *New York Times* Poll (2011a), 46 percent of Americans believe that gun laws should be made stricter, while 38 percent believe they should remain the same. Thirteen percent said they thought gun control laws should be made less strict. However, since the Tucson massacre, residents of Arizona, a national leader in the gun-rights movement, seem to believe that there is a need for change. For example, a survey by Public Policy Polling (2011) found that after the mass shootings in Arizona, 55 percent of Arizonians said they favored more gun control (stricter laws concerning who can buy guns or not), a higher percentage than national surveys have shown. Thirty eight percent were against stricter laws.

What do you think? Which side of the debate are you on? Do you think gun control should be stepped up or restricted in the United States? Do you favor or oppose: (1) more control over the manufacture, sale, and possession of guns; (2) making it mandatory that *all* firearms must be registered; (3) the banning of all handguns; (4) legislation that would outlaw the manufacture of assault weapons; and (5) making it illegal for civilians to own a gun of any type?

Methodological Techniques in the Study of Marriages and Families

People today are bombarded with information about marriages and families. We hear, for instance, that old-fashioned family moral values have disappeared, that children are having babies, that family and intimate violence are increasing, and that entire families are living on the streets. We must therefore learn how to separate what is factual from what is not. As previously explained, scientific research enables us to see what is, as opposed to what might be or what we hoped or thought would be. Most research, like theory, begins with the questions of why and how. Ultimately, the answers to these questions form explanations or theories about some aspect of human behavior and human society.

A potential problem for all scientific research is objectivity. It is not possible, even when using the scientific method, to measure or observe social phenomena without committing to some theoretical perspective. Therefore, we should be aware that researchers bring theoretical biases to the research process: the problems selected for study, the methods chosen to study those problems, the unique and individual observations made, and general assumptions about the world and about human behavior. Although the scientific method minimizes research bias, no one has found a way to eliminate it totally. Therefore, we must carefully examine the information we receive and be prepared for the possibility that what is presented as reality is not impartial. A good example in this regard is the controversy surrounding how one of the lead investigators of a 2001 National Institute of Child Health and Human Development study of early child care reported the study's findings. The investigator was accused by several of his fellow investigators of monopolizing the press and making negative pronouncements about child care that were not based on "conclusive data." Some critics said the investigator had a personal agenda that he had been pushing for some time; for years, he had emphasized the negative aspects of child care to the exclusion of the positive aspects.

Consider another example. Popular views of welfare say women who receive welfare have baby after baby as a way to collect higher payments. The findings of scientific research, however, tell a very different story (see the Applying the Sociological Imagination box). A profile of the welfare population shows that the fertility behavior of women on welfare does not differ from that of women in the general population. The majority of welfare recipients (74 percent) have only one or two children. And like the general population, the average number of children in a welfare family is less than two (O'Malley, 2011; General Characteristics, 2005; The Urban Institute, 2001). Past research has shown that the longer a woman receives welfare, the less likely she is to have additional children.

APPLYING THE SOCIOLOGICAL IMAGINATION

SOME CHARACTERISTICS OF THE WELFARE POPULATION

- Ten percent of welfare adults are married; 36 percent are separated, divorced, or widowed; and the remaining 54 percent have never married.
- Seventy-four percent of welfare mothers are in their 20s and 30s, 7 percent are under the age of 20, and 19 percent are 40 or older.
- The racial composition of welfare families is fairly evenly distributed across racial and ethnic groups: 30 percent are White, 36 percent African American, 26 percent Latina/o, 1 percent Native American, and 2 percent Asian.
- The average number of children in welfare families is two, which is consistent with the fertility patterns of the general public. Two in five welfare families have only one child.
- The majority of children receiving welfare stipends live with one or both parents; only 8 percent live with a grandparent.
- According to some research, women on welfare are more conscientious about using contraceptives while on welfare; they are less likely to want an additional pregnancy, and they are less likely to become pregnant while on welfare.
- Fifty-four percent of all welfare recipients have at least a high school education, including some who have attended college; 25 percent have a college degree.
- Over two-thirds of women who are on welfare had some recent work experience before applying for public assistance.

www.mothersmovement.org/resources/welfare.htm
patomalley.wordpress.com/2011/05/23/welfare-in-america

www.associatecontent.com/shared/print.shtml?content_type=article&content

Use these three Web sites as starting points and find other Web sites or links that provide information about people who receive welfare benefits. Find the typical monthly welfare allotment for a person with two children living in your state. Imagine that this person is you and the welfare payment is all that you and your children have to live on. Using prices from the geographical area in which you live, develop a monthly budget to account for everything you have to spend to get by (day-to-day). What do you think your life and that of your children would be like? What does an exercise like this teach you about popular images of and attitudes about people who receive welfare benefits?

Much of the research on welfare families to date reflects a White middle-class bias. Based on a mythical model of White middle-class families as a measuring rod, welfare families have been described as pathological, disorganized, lacking a work ethic, and locked into a way of life that perpetuates an endless cycle of so-called illegitimate births. However, before we accept such viewpoints as factual, we must carefully analyze the evidence presented to support the conclusions. This analytical process includes asking questions such as: Are the conclusions actually supported by the empirical evidence? Are the findings presented in such a way that they can be tested by others? What are the biases of the research, and does the researcher state them up front? We should also keep in mind that conclusions are not final, but are always open to question and reinvestigation.

In the remainder of this section, we examine some of the primary methods used in marriage and family research: surveys, observation, case studies, and ethnographies. Researchers using each of these methods analyze the data they collect using either or both quantitative or qualitative analysis. **Quantitative analysis** is a process in which data can be analyzed using numerical categories and statistical techniques (for example, determining the percentage of respondents who report certain attitudes or behaviors). **Qualitative analysis** focuses on specific or distinct qualities within the data that show patterns of similarity or difference among the research subjects. Although each represents a different technique for analyzing data, quantitative and qualitative data are not necessarily at odds. Researchers often use both qualitative and quantitative methods to maximize our understanding of their research. Finally, we end this section with a look at who and what does and does not get studied by researchers, and why. In this regard, we pay close attention to issues of ethics and conscious and unconscious biases in the conduct of research on marriages and families.

◉ **Watch** the **Video**
Qualitative vs. Quantitative Research on **myfamilylab.com**

SURVEYS

One of the quickest ways to find out what we want to know about people is to ask them. **Surveys** do just that: They enable us to gather information by asking people questions. Surveys are particularly useful when what we want to know about people is not easily observable, such as the private lives of married or cohabiting couples. The two basic methods by which researchers ask their questions and receive answers are interviews and questionnaires. The **interview** usually involves one person, the interviewer, asking another person questions, with the interviewer recording the answers. The **questionnaire,** in contrast, usually provides autonomy to the person answering the questions. It is typically a set of printed questions that people read on their own and then record their answers. The survey is the most widely used method of studying marriages and families.

▣ **Read** the **Document**
Sense and Nonsense About Surveys on **myfamilylab.com**

A good example of the use of the survey in research related to marriages and families is Marcela Raffaelli and Lenna Ontai's (2004) study of gender socialization in Latina/o families. Using survey data collected from two groups—in-depth interviews completed by 22 adult Latinas, ages 20–45, and 166 self-report surveys completed by Latina/o college students (58 percent women; median age 21)—the researchers found that among the first group, many Latina/o parents socialize their daughters in ways marked by "traditional" gender-related expectations and messages. Findings from the group of college students supported and expanded the findings from the first group. The female and male college student respondents in the second group described different experiences of household activities, socialization of gender-typed behavior, and freedom to pursue social activities or gain access to privileges. The researchers found three overarching themes related to gender socialization: differential treatment of girls and boys and privileging of boys in families with both daughters and sons, enforcement of stereotypically feminine behavior among daughters, and curtailment of girls' activities outside the home. For instance, daughters and sons were given different household chores, with girls expected to help around the house whereas boys were not. In addition, sons were typically granted more freedom than daughters to come and go without as much supervision. Girls' freedom was curtailed far more than boys, with one female respondent describing growing up feeling as if she lived in a "little circle" delineated by her parents. Raffaelli and Ontai also found that Latina/o parental characteristics, particularly gender role attitudes, were linked to gender-related socialization. For example, mothers who held traditional gender role attitudes were more likely to encourage femininity in daughters and "manly" behavior in sons. And fathers who encouraged their sons to do chores and limited their sons' freedom regarding social activities tended to hold more egalitarian gender role attitudes.

Millions of viewers tune in to programs such as *American Idol* and choose their favorite singer by "voting" via their cell or landline phones or on the Internet. Singers who receive the fewest votes are dismissed from the program regardless of how well they can sing. This was the case in 2011 when singer Pia Toscano (shown in black) received the fewest votes and was sent home; her fellow contestants and all three *Idol* judges were visibly shaken. Are such results representative of all those who view this program? Or are they really the results of a self-selection opinion poll?

"How would you rate the treatment you received from your HMO? Poor, fair, good, excellent?"

According to some observers there has been an outrageous proliferation of surveys in contemporary American life—nearly every company we deal with asks us to participate in a follow-up survey. As surveys proliferate, many Americans are feeling overwhelmed by the abundance of questions they are asked and find most surveys to be not only time-consuming but also an intrusion into their already very busy lives.

One of the major advantages of interviews and questionnaires is that they allow researchers to gather large amounts of information at a relatively low cost. On the negative side, the questionnaire method imposes the researcher's point of view on the people being studied by forcing them to respond to questions in terms of pre-established categories of answers. Another disadvantage is that survey methods must rely on people's ability and willingness to give accurate information, especially when the survey involves information about behavior typically considered private, such as sexual relationships or family violence. Thus, survey results are sometimes distorted because the respondents say what they think the researcher wants to hear. However, overall, surveys are useful in describing the characteristics of a large population. No other method of observation can provide this general capability.

OBSERVATION

Surveys are good for telling us what people say they do. What people say they do and what they actually do are not always the same, however. An alternative to asking people questions is to observe their behavior systematically. Observational studies are useful when researchers have only a vague idea of the behavior they want to study, when they want to study people or situations not accessible to the general public, or when there is no other way to get the information. Researchers may observe behavior in a manner that does not intrude on the situation under study, or they may participate in or become a part of the interaction they are studying. This latter approach is referred to as participant observation. Regardless of the approach, observational studies require the researcher to develop a specific set of questions in advance of the study as a way to guide the collection of data.

An interesting example of an observational study relevant to the study of marriages and families is one conducted by researchers Maureen O'Dougherty, Mary Story, and Jamie Stang (2006) to determine the decision-making processes of adult shoppers around food purchases when they have young children with them. Given the dramatic increase in childhood obesity, the researchers' goal was to provide a better understanding of the environmental and behavioral factors that affect children's food preferences. The researchers knew from previous research that food advertising targeted to children shape children's food preferences; parents are central in the formation of young children's food preferences—they mediate the food selection process and ultimately determine what to purchase or not; and parents yield to children's food purchase requests 45–65 percent of the time.

During weekend visits, the lead researcher of the study unobtrusively observed adult and child shoppers as they stopped to consider an item in any food aisle. Based on 133 observations of 142 adult–child grocery shoppers in 11 supermarkets located in diverse urban and suburban areas, the researchers registered adult-child interactions over food selections, including parental yielding or refusal strategies and child engagement in shopping. Characteristics of the sample observed included 33 African American, 33 Latina/o, 60 White, 16 other, 86 female only adults, 22 male only adults, 27 female-male duo, 6 female duo, and 1 male duo; in 85 of the 142 adult-child shoppers, only one child was present; in 48 cases, two children were present; and in 9 cases, three or more children were present. Of the total number of children present among the adult-child shoppers, 128 were girls and 82 were boys.

The researchers found that in one-half of the 133 observations, a child initiated a request and a little more than half of the requests offered and granted across adult–child shoppers were for sweets or snacks. Parents collectively responded affirmatively to children's requests for food items almost half the time and rejected their requests slightly more than half the time. In almost one-third of the selections, brands and marketing techniques appeared to be a factor. However, when refusing the child(ren)'s request, many of the adults used what the researchers defined as effective refusal strategies. The most frequent adult refusals consisted of adults either softly saying "no" (explaining in a nonconfrontational way) and a nonverbal "no," ignoring or walking away. Based on their observations, the researchers concluded that children are clearly engaged in grocery shopping when with an adult, thus affording learning opportunities about nutritious and healthy food preferences which parents should take advantage of. Their findings underscore that parents can be either a strong or a weak link in the food selection process for children.

A major advantage of observation is that it is by far the best method for collecting data on nonverbal behavior. Observation is less restrictive or artificial than some other data collection methods, but the presence of the observer makes bias a real possibility. When people are aware that they are being observed, they frequently modify their behavior, either deliberately or subconsciously. This phenomenon is referred to by social scientists as the **Hawthorne effect.** To avoid this problem in the observational study described above, once a selection or rejection occurred (or no more than 2 minutes had passed), the researcher always moved out of the viewing range of those shoppers to record the event.

Other problems with observational studies include the following: (1) They usually take a long time and thus can be expensive, (2) they generally involve only a limited number of subjects, and (3) they offer the researcher little control over the research situation. However, the depth of understanding gained through observation research compensates for the disadvantages.

CASE STUDIES

Sociologists who study a particular category of people or a particular situation typically do so as a **case study.** The case study is a detailed, in-depth examination of a single unit. Case studies use newly collected and preexisting data, such as those from interviews and participant observation, or existing records, for in-depth examination of a particular individual, group, or organization. Used in research on issues pertaining to marriages and families, case studies can provide a comprehensive and holistic understanding of behaviors within a single setting. Researcher John Bartkowski's 1999 study of how gender, domestic labor (that is, the allocation of financial provision, household tasks, and child-care responsibilities), and family power operate as processes within three White, relatively privileged, conservative Evangelical households is an example of the case study method applied to marriage and family issues. Bartkowski used the case study approach to trace how domestic labor issues emerged, were negotiated, and (at times) resolved through gender strategies employed by these couples. He found that contrary to the stereotypical view of conservative Evangelicals as rigid conformers to a traditional division of labor by gender, these couples exhibited both traditional and progressive gender practices.

Although the couples embraced the Evangelical ideology of wife–husband roles in the family, they sometimes reconfigured or reversed their beliefs about gender, if only temporarily. For example, one husband whose wife worked outside the home indicated that he greatly appreciated the support that his wife provided both financially and emotionally, yet he also clearly believed that the financial provision for his family was his primary responsibility. Equality, per se, was not the guiding principle in the decision for his wife to work.

According to Bartkowski, employed Evangelical wives and mothers may find themselves doubly burdened from shouldering both their traditional homemaking responsibilities and their newly found co-provider role. For example, despite her best efforts, one wife in the study was unable to parlay her extensive labor force commitments into a lightened domestic workload in the home. The study found that, in dealing with their deviation from the prevailing definitions of Evangelical wifehood or motherhood, the women used a "both/and gender strategy" that entailed working two full-time jobs, as both co-provider and homemaker, during the family workday. This gender strategy seemed religiously motivated because it enabled these women to retain for themselves the "homemaker" label. Bartkowski's findings underscore the importance of viewing gender and domestic labor as a product of interpersonal negotiation, while at the same time they highlight how gender relations are mediated by cultural forces such as conservative religious ideologies.

One of the advantages of a study like Bartkowski's is that it provides a great deal of detail about the research subject. In addition, the case study approach offers long-term, in-depth analysis of various aspects of the phenomenon being studied. A disadvantage is that each case study focuses on a very specific case and thus cannot be generalized to the larger population. For example, the Bartkowski findings apply to the specific conservative Evangelical families that he studied and not to all conservative Evangelical families. Furthermore, as with observation, the presence of the researcher may change how people act or interact. Overall, however, case studies have provided some significant insights into marriage and family processes.

ETHNOGRAPHY

In general, **ethnography** is a research technique for describing a social group from the group's point of view. Ethnography is not about pursuing or uncovering an objective reality (which is typically the focus of quantitative analyses). Rather, it is a technique for examining the many different versions of reality from the point of view, or through the eyes, of the researched. Therefore, by necessity, ethnographers use qualitative methods that, by design, allow the researcher to study conditions or processes that are hard to measure numerically. In essence, the ethnographer attempts to gain cultural knowledge from the people she or he is studying. Ethnographic research is particularly useful and relevant in areas of study where researchers have historically studied and measured groups from the perspective of their own cultural, racial, or class biases. In this context, ethnography has special relevance as a technique for studying marriages and families that heretofore have been studied primarily from the cultural perspective of White middle-class male researchers.

An interesting example of ethnographic research in this regard is a study undertaken by Alford A. Young, Jr. and Pamela Holcomb (2007) of how young low-income men view and experience fatherhood. The popular view of these men typically cast them as deadbeat dads; uninterested and uninvolved in their children's lives and uninterested in supporting them financially or emotionally. In recent years, the role of noncustodial fathers in the lives of low-income families has received considerable attention from policymakers and programs. Although child support enforcement efforts have increased in recent years, according to some observers, there is evidence that many low-income fathers cannot afford to support their children financially without impoverishing themselves or their families. In response to this issue, a number of initiatives have focused on developing services to help low-income fathers become more financially and emotionally involved with their families and to help young low-income families become stable. One such initiative, Partners for Fragile Families (PFF) demonstration project, focused on promoting the voluntary establishment of paternity; connecting young fathers with the child support system and encouraging the payment of child support; improving parenting and relationship skills of young fathers; helping young fathers secure and retain employment; and strengthening family ties, commitments, and other types of father involvement when parents do not live together (Young and Holcomb, 2007).

Young and Holcomb present ethnographic case studies of eight young, unmarried, low-income fathers (five Black, two Hispanic, and one biracial) who participated in PFF demonstration projects in Boston and Indianapolis. The authors examined the interplay among their life histories before becoming fathers, their relationships with their children and partners, their work experiences, and their involvement with the child support system. Relying heavily on the actual words of these young fathers, several key themes and findings emerged in this research, including (1) the men generally lacked a strong concept of the meaning of fatherhood, and all were reared in environments where absentee fatherhood was common, leaving them with little understanding of life in a two-parent family structure; (2) some of the men fathered children by more than one woman, and all reported conflict with the mother of the child primarily stemming from their lack of a stable income and inability to contribute to their child's care; (3) given their experience of inconsistent or absent fathers, the men wanted to be a consistent part of their children's lives; and (4) the men hoped and aspired to achieve basic family-centered goals—they wanted to be married and living with their children, and they wanted secure and stable jobs in order to provide the resources that would ensure their children's education. All the men expressed hope that their children would live in a safe community, attain an education, and be happy and well prepared for successful adult lives. This hope was tempered by the awareness that their children might face some of the same hurdles and temptations they had experienced. Nonetheless, the men expressed a strong desire that their children would not have to grow up the way they did.

The men had positive views of the PFF project, and some indicated that as a result of their participation in the program, they have reconsidered the traditional roles of father and mother, view parenting as a shared endeavour, and have greater acceptance of mothers as breadwinners and fathers as caretakers. One of the most important and powerful new ideas about fatherhood that the men said they learned through their participation in the PFF program was that fatherhood is a process rather than a discrete skill or task that can be mastered with finality. They said that they acquired a richer understanding of the responsibilities, expectations, and challenges related to fatherhood and family life and, most important, a better sense of how they should approach them. For these men, the most significant idea was that fathers needed to be a visible presence in the lives of their children, irrespective of their ability to provide material support.

An advantage of ethnographic studies such as that of Young and Holcomb is that they provide firsthand accounts of those whose lives we are studying. Critics, on the other hand, contend that methodological biases limit the reliability and validity of qualitative data. They suggest, for example, that retrospective interviews can elicit idealized accounts of behavior or that the data may be compromised by memory lapses or the respondent's need to present a particular picture of self or the situation. The fact is, however, that all research methods are inherently limited; therefore, to circumvent some of these biases, researchers should use a variety of research strategies.

SCIENTIFIC METHODOLOGIES USED BY FEMINIST RESEARCHERS

Feminist scholars are interested in whom researchers study and how they study them, how conclusions are drawn, and what evidence those conclusions are based on. They are particularly concerned with how women have either been omitted from scientific research or have been studied according to male models of attitudes and behavior. Much of their work is a corrective to these problems.

No method of research is of itself a feminist method. According to feminist sociologist and researcher Marjorie DeVault (1990), what distinguishes feminist methods is what feminist researchers do—how they use the methodologies available to them. For example, feminist researchers rely heavily on qualitative methods. A person using quantitative methods to study rape might measure the rate of rape among various groups of women. On the other hand, one using qualitative methods might measure the reaction to rape or coping strategies devised by rape victims as recounted by the victims. In particular, feminist researchers often use field methods such as the in-depth, face-to-face interview; participant observation; and ethnography. Although other researchers also use these methods, feminist researchers differ in how they define their research goals and how they view their own role as researcher.

A basic goal of feminist research is to present information that has previously been ignored or suppressed, and thus to make visible both the experiences of the people they study (particularly women) in all their diversity and the **ideologies,** or systems of beliefs, that have kept these experiences invisible. In this respect, gender is at the forefront of the analysis, with special attention paid to how race, class, gender, and sexuality interact and affect the lives of women and men. A major advantage to how feminists do their research is the way they define their role as researcher. As researchers, they are conscious of the need to be respectful of the people they are studying, to be personal, collaborative, inclusive, and empowering.

These qualities characterize feminist methods because researchers consciously use techniques of data gathering that allow them to use the perspectives of their subjects. Instead of imposing their personal interpretations on the experiences of the people they study, feminist researchers develop theories and explanations that reflect the real-life experiences of their subjects, as reported by the subjects themselves. Ideally, feminist research is inclusive of the experiences of all women, not just a few, and it is empowering to the extent that it seeks to avoid defining women solely as victims. For instance, as we will see in Chapter 11, although women are often victims of violence and abuse, they are also survivors. So feminist researchers view women as actively involved in the worlds in which they live.

An example of the feminist methodology applied to the people that researchers study can be found in Mary Romero's (1992/2002) classic study of Mexican domestic service workers in the United States. Through interviewing and analyzing the daily lives and activities of 25 Chicana private household workers, Romero provides a narrative of their working conditions and the social constraints that shape their personal lives from their perspective. Based on these women's narratives, Romero argues that these workers struggled to control the work process and alter the employee–employer relationship to a client-tradesperson relationship in which labor services, rather than labor power, was sold. This struggle was aimed at developing new interactions with employers that eliminated aspects of hierarchy along the lines of gender, race, and class. Romero found that while employers in domestic service engage in similar self-interests as other employers—increasing the amount of labor and decreasing its value—they resist other dimensions of employment, such as acknowledging that when a private household worker or caretaker is hired, their home becomes the employee's workplace; accepting the worker as an employee rather than as an extension of the employer's roles as housewife or mother; and actively resisting practices of modern work culture. According to Romero, domestic labor may be priceless, but employers are unwilling to pay very much for it.

These women's self-reports of their day-to-day working conditions as they experienced them have greatly added to our knowledge about those invisible people—often immigrants and people of color—who clean the homes of the middle and upper classes. It also provides insight into how women who hire other women to perform their domestic tasks do not escape the cycle of patriarchy and exploitation of women socioeconomically beneath them. Romero's research reflects a central assumption of the feminist researcher that behavior can best be understood from the perspective of the persons involved. Romero assumed that her subjects understood their experiences better than other people did, and she respected their way of reporting and interpreting those experiences.

The very features that feminist researchers consider advantageous and confirming have been singled out by critics as an important limitation of this research. Because this research is intentionally personal and collaborative, for example, critics immediately raise the question of objectivity. Many feminist researchers agree that their work is subjective in that it is research on people like themselves—other women. But, they argue, it is also objective in that women's experiences are explained in terms of the forces that shape their lives. Thus, like most other research, which to date has been male-centered, feminist research clearly has a point of view and views social change as an important goal. They not only believe that their research and scholarship should be tied to social change, but also that they have a responsibility to critique problems in the content and method of traditional research and scholarship. Sociologist Howard Becker (1967) long ago addressed the role of values in sociological research and why researchers are sometimes accused of bias in their work. According to Becker, we can never avoid taking sides, but we can use research methodologies impartially enough so that the beliefs we hold can be proved or disproved.

A Critical Look at Traditional Research on Marriages and Families

Historically, sociology as a discipline has claimed as one of its major goals the improvement of social life. Today, most sociologists operate from this premise and believe the purpose of their research is to affect social policy and provide the impetus for social change. Some critics, such as feminist scholars, have argued that in practice sociology has not always lived up to this goal. Until the upsurge of feminist research and scholarship over the past few decades, women, their experiences, and their consciousness were largely absent from traditional sociological research and the theoretical paradigms that guide sociological thinking (Andersen, 2005). The same can be said for people of color. In addition, sociological researchers historically have failed to recognize groups other than the White middle class, that is, White middle-class marriages and families have been used as

the norm against which other families are measured. When lower-class and working-class families differ from the White middle-class model, they are defined as deviant. At the other end of the class continuum, the upper classes have been the subject of little scientific research. Thus, although new and exciting research on families across race and class is currently being produced, much of what we know today continues to be based on a model of the family that represents only a small proportion of today's marriages and families.

A MORE INCLUSIVE SOCIOLOGY

Today, researchers are more cognizant of the intersections of social constructions such as race, class, gender, and sexual orientation and are moving beyond conventional topics and traditional research methods to develop a more inclusive base of knowledge about marriages and families. Although traditional sociological research has provided important insights into marriages and families, there are important limitations. Because of the tremendous impact of this research for our ongoing understanding of marriage and family life, it is worth noting some of these past limitations. One way of exploring the limitations of traditional sociological research on marriages and families is to examine who does (did) and does not (did not) get studied.

Conventional topics studied by sociologists lead us to ignore issues that would illuminate women's lives. When women have been studied in traditional marriage and family research, for example, it has usually been in terms of a one-dimensional stereotypical model of women as nurturant caregivers and caretakers confined to the home.

Although we are sometimes afforded a glimpse into the social world of the wealthy through the mass media, there is little systematic research on the daily lives of upper-class families, particularly if they are not White Anglo-Saxon Protestant.

Most of this research has been conducted by men who use themselves as the standard. Gender is seldom considered a significant factor that influences behavior. Evidence of this trend recurs in traditional sociological studies that draw conclusions about marriage and family life based on investigations in which all the research subjects are male. This approach is particularly evident in traditional research concerning issues of individual and family mobility. Most of this research was male-specific, measuring mobility strictly by comparing men occupationally with their fathers. When women's mobility was addressed, it was primarily that of White women, and it was measured by comparing the husband's occupational standing with that of the woman's father. In general, women's mobility was seen as a function of male status, that of either a father or a husband. This model of social mobility is particularly problematic for some women, including a large percentage of African American women, who historically have been required to work outside the home to help support their families.

Like feminist scholars, African American and other scholars of color have long criticized social science research for the negative and stereotypical ways in which African Americans, various people of color, women, and poor and working-class individuals and families have been portrayed. African American women scholars have been particularly vocal in their critiques concerning many myths and half-truths about African American women and their role in their families.

The longest lasting of these seems to be the myth of the "Black matriarchy." One of the most widely publicized documents on African American family life, sociologist and government researcher Daniel Moynihan's 1965 study entitled "The Negro Family: The Case for National Action," dramatically illustrates the use of social science methodology to promote ideas based on questionable data and oversimplification. Based on U.S. census data, Moynihan found that almost 25 percent of African American families were female-headed, a statistic he cited as evidence of a "matriarchy." Moynihan then explained problems in the African American community in terms of this alleged structural feature of African American families. Although Moynihan recognized the historical fact of slavery and its impact on African American family life, he essentially placed the burden of an alleged family pathology squarely on the shoulders of African American women. However, even if one accepts Moynihan's notion of a Black matriarchy, he failed to explain what is innately problematic or detrimental about matriarchies.

In addition to women and African Americans, various groups of color are often overrepresented, misrepresented, or not represented at all in traditional marriage and family research. For instance, compared with research about other groups in U.S. society, very little research has been done on Native American families; thus, little is known about these families. Because Native Americans are small in number and often live in remote areas of the country, they are, perhaps, the most invisible group of color. When they are studied, it is often either within erroneous or outdated models of family life that are generalized to a very diverse group of people or within a pathology/deviance model. According to the U.S. Census Bureau, an estimated 5 million people identify as Native American and Alaska Native, including those of more than one race (U.S. Census, 2010e). These diverse peoples include Cherokee, Sioux, Chippewa, Navajo, Seminole, Lakota, and more than 500 other nations representing over 150 languages. Yet, traditional research continues to refer to Native Americans as if they were a homogeneous group. Thus, although we know much about

the rates of alcoholism and suicide (alleged pathologies in response to oppression) in some of these families (though we are not exactly sure which families because these data too are often generalized), we know very little about their family relations or process.

On the other hand, although there is increasing attention to and research on Latinas/os (currently one of the fastest-growing groups of color in the United States), the family patterns of these groups are also often misunderstood or misrepresented. A major problem in this regard is that very often Latina/o groups are lumped together under the hybrid label *Hispanic*, which has the effect of obscuring important differences among various Latina/o groups. Although most Latinas/os share a common language and cultural ancestry, the diversity among Latinas/os makes generalizations about their family lifestyles exceedingly difficult.

Like other groups of color, Asian Americans are a diverse group with diverse family lifestyles. Yet researchers, especially since the 1970s, have focused almost entirely on the economic and educational achievements of some Asian American families, with the result being a rather widespread depiction or generalization of "success"—strong family ties, strong work ethic, academic excellence, self-sufficiency, and a low level of welfare dependency—to all Asian American families. This is not to say that such characterizations do not describe the realities of some Asian American families; however, the tendency, both in American popular culture and in scholarly research, is to put forth the notion of a monolithic "model minority" model of Asian American families. If nothing else, such a lumping of all Asian American families together obscures the legacy of racism and the difficulties associated with acculturation these families have experienced, with the result that not all Asian American families have been successful.

Although African American families are perhaps the most frequently researched of all families of color, much of the research on them focuses primarily on lower- and working-class families. As critics have pointed out, not only are most of the subjects of marriage and family research on African American families from the lower class, but they are frequently from the most deprived segment of the lower class. Little systematic research exists focusing on middle-class families of color, especially the upper middle class.

Even less is known about wealthy and upper-class families across race. Power is an issue here. Because women, people of color, and the lower classes generally lack power, they are either largely ignored by researchers or they are easily accessible to researchers. Individuals and families with considerable wealth and power can control researchers' access to them. Because there is so little information on the marriage and family lifestyles of the upper classes, Americans—hungry for a glimpse of such lifestyles—are fascinated with media portrayals of how such families live. Whether or not these portrayals reflect the real world of upper-class marriages and families is not readily known because there is so little scientific information against which to compare.

Estimates vary, but somewhere between 4 and 10 percent of the U.S. population is homosexual. Despite popular stereotypes and the increasing visibility of lesbians and gays, we are only just beginning to learn about some aspects of their family lifestyles such as their reproductive choices and ways of parenting. Traditionally, if lesbians and gay couples were referred to at all in research or textbooks, they were treated at best as an aberration of the "real" family and at worst denied family status overall.

Lesbians and gays are similar in their behavior, but they are not a monolithic group. They vary across race, class, age, and other important social characteristics. Yet the lesbians and gays that are studied are most often young, White, and middle class. Few studies focus on lesbians and gays of color or older lesbians and gays across race and class. Indeed, over the past decade, as we (the authors of this textbook) conducted research for each of the previous editions of this book, a major obstacle in our quest to be inclusive was the lack of research on diverse family groupings such as lesbian and gay families. When we did find research on lesbians and gays, for example, much of the traditional research was narrowly focused or concerned with their sexual behavior. Like others in the population, lesbians and gays are ongoing, active members of marriages, families, and intimate relationships. Thus, such narrowly focused research perpetuates many popular myths about homosexuality and is misrepresentative of the diversity of family lifestyles in the United States.

CONTEMPORARY MARRIAGE AND FAMILY SCHOLARSHIP

Although sociology as a discipline has not always made good on its claim to give accurate accounts of the social world and its social problems, sociologists and interdisciplinary scholars are using the perspectives that the discipline offers, including a feminist perspective, to develop and transmit more complete and accurate understandings of marriages, families, and intimate relationships. Unfortunately, shoddy research methodologies; faulty generalizations; and researcher biases, myths, stereotypes, oversimplifications, and misrepresentations continue to affect some research on marriages and families. Much of this research continues to be heterosexist as well as sex-, race-, and class-specific, even though it is generalized as applicable to the largest possible population.

Scientific research on marriages and families does not exist in a vacuum. Its theory and practice reflect the structure and values of U.S. society. In a society where massive inequalities in power, wealth, and prestige exist among classes and racial groups, as well as between

women and men, scientific research—its methods, content, and conclusions—reflects these inequalities. Given this reality, social research must be evaluated by who is or is not the researcher, who does and does not get studied, which theoretical paradigms and underlying assumptions are accepted, which methods are used and how, and what the research actually says and does not say about the subjects.

To their credit, contemporary family researchers exhibit a growing recognition of race, class, gender, and sexual diversity in marriage and family lifestyles. Although no research techniques are specific to people of color, women, poor and working-class people, or lesbians and gays, some existing methods seem more productive than others. For example, as we have already pointed out, various field methods—such as face-to-face interviews, participant observation, and case studies—enable the research subjects to tell their stories from their own point of view. In this context, contemporary scholarship has opened up a new and healthy discourse in the area of marriage and family research. This continuing discourse has greatly enhanced our knowledge of marriages and families. In addition, any attempt to understand marriage, family, and intimate relationships within U.S. society must necessarily be informed by the implications of the globalization of the world's societies. Thus, a new and increasing emphasis on cross-cultural and global research has increased our awareness of how global connections profoundly impact our lives and has provided further insights about marriages and families in the multicultural worlds in which humans live. In the In Other Places box, we take a look, as an example, at a Kenyan-born sociologist, Wamucii Njogu, and her marriage and family research conducted in her native Kenya.

Now let us turn our attention to the other half of the scientific enterprise—namely, theories pertaining to marriages and families.

Theoretical Perspectives

Try as we may, we cannot separate theory from real life. The way we look at and understand society and human behavior depends on our theoretical perspective. In sociology, there is no single theory

In Other Places

MARRIAGE AND FAMILY PATTERNS IN KENYA

As family sociologists, one of our continuing messages is that there are diverse ways in which marriages and families are structured. Cross-cultural research is important in that it allows us to learn and understand cultures different from our own while at the same time appreciate how much all humans have in common. Comparisons and contrasts of

diverse marriage and family lifestyles allow us to apply concepts and theories that broaden our understanding of their meaning. They also challenge ideas of a single model of marriage and family life and highlight the flexibility of humans in creating diverse cultures.

It is often said that social research interests are sparked by

personal biography. Dr. Wamucii Njogu is a classic example. An associate professor of sociology, former chair of the Department of Sociology, African and African American Studies, Latino and Latin American Studies, and Women's Studies and currently Dean of the College of Arts and Sciences at Northeastern Illinois University in

Chicago, Dr. Njogu is an internationally known scholar and a member of the Union for African Population Studies, the International Union for the Scientific Study of Population, and the Population Association of America. Born and raised in Kenya, she speaks three languages fluently and received her Ph.D. at the University of Wisconsin at Madison. As a bilingual bicultural sociologist, she has been able to move back and forth between her native country and the United States and examine both cultures as an "outsider from within." Sociologically, this has had important implications for her research interests, the kinds of questions she asks, the issues that she finds problematic, and the nature of her analyses and contributions to marriage and family theory and research. Some examples from her biography reflect this connection.

Dr. Njogu was first attracted to the study of sociology when, as an undergraduate student at the University of Nairobi, she was assigned to write a sociological research paper. Coming from a background in which her parents owned a large farm and employed a large number of poor rural workers, Dr. Njogu decided to focus on poverty among these workers and the question of how these people came to be where they were in the stratification structure. Her findings—namely, that these workers typically came from generations of such workers, that within these families some members (primarily women) were worse off than others, and that these families generally had a large number of children whom they could not adequately support economically—led her to her long-standing interests in stratification, gender inequality, fertility, family formation, and child fostering and informal adoption.

Her interest in gender inequality is also tied to the fact that she comes from a long line of female-headed households (which defies tradition in the patriarchal society into which

Dr. Wamucii Njogu

she was born), including a paternal grandmother who, after the death of her husband, defied cultural tradition by refusing to marry her dead husband's brother. Remaining single, this woman raised her children alone and instilled in them egalitarian values. Consequently, Dr. Njogu's father raised her and her male siblings as equals. Her research on female law students' participation in the classroom was shaped by her own experiences as a female student in high school and college in Kenya. Because of the preference for males in her culture, monies for school go first and foremost for boys' education. Dr. Njogu was thus one of a small percentage of Kenyan women who attended high school and of an even smaller percentage attending college. She was an extremely bright student, which "was not the thing to do" in Kenya, she says. As a result, the boys called her names, such as "girl/boy," because only boys were supposed to be in school and be smart. This helped her understand what sexism and gender inequality meant, not just in abstract terms but in terms of her actual personal experiences.

Most recently, Dr. Njogu has conducted research and written a series of papers on HIV/AIDS

in Kenya. For example, Dr. Njogu studied the relationship between HIV/AIDS knowledge and risk prevention or safe sexual behavior. Although HIV/AIDS has killed individual family members and sometimes whole families, this deadly reality has not translated into safe sexual behavior, particularly for young women. In a report of her findings at the International Union for the Scientific Study of Population in Salvador, Brazil, Dr. Njogu indicated that the gender gap is one of the greatest barriers to sexual behavior change in Kenya. For example, young Kenyan women are less likely than their male counterparts to know that AIDS can be transmitted through sexual intercourse or that condoms can protect them against infection. The difficulty experienced by women in implementing prevention strategies is another reason why AIDS knowledge may not necessarily lead to behavior change. Young women in Kenya consider their risk of contracting HIV/AIDS to be high, not because of their own behavior but because of their partners' past and current sexual behavior. This knowledge notwithstanding, unequal gender relations and other cultural traditions prevent women from protecting themselves against HIV infection.

According to Dr. Njogu, cross-cultural research not only fosters a better understanding and appreciation for cultural diversity but also often serves to debunk some of the myths created by research that uses Western culture as the model of marriage and family life.

What do you think? Is there a similar gender gap in HIV/AIDS knowledge in the United States? What role does gender play in risk prevention behavior among young American adults? What can we learn from cross-cultural research about the differential impact on family members of diseases such as HIV/AIDS?

of marriages and families. Many different perspectives exist. By **perspective,** we simply mean a broad explanation of social reality from a particular point of view. These perspectives provide us with a basic image of society and human behavior. They define what we should study, what questions we should ask, how we should ask them, what methods we should use to gather information, and how we should interpret the answers or information we obtain.

Sociologists approach the study of human behavior and society with a particular set of theoretical assumptions. Although there is some debate over how many sociological perspectives exist, there is general agreement that three basic perspectives form the backbone of what has been called mainstream sociology: structural functionalism, conflict theory, and symbolic interaction. In addition, we examine the social-constructionist, social-exchange, developmental family life cycle, and feminist theoretical perspectives.

In the remainder of this chapter, we examine and critique these theoretical approaches and perspectives. As you study these different approaches, pay particular attention to how the choice of a theoretical perspective will influence not only the way data are interpreted, but also the very nature of the questions asked. Consider how a different theoretical perspective would lead to a different set of questions and conclusions about marriages and families.

STRUCTURAL FUNCTIONALISM

In the history of the sociology of marriages and families, structural functionalism has been one of the leading theoretical perspectives used to explain how families work and how they relate to the larger society. Basically, **structural functionalism** views society as an organized and stable system, analogous to the human system—that is made up of a variety of interrelated parts or structures. Each structure performs one or several functions or meets vital social needs. These structures, sometimes called subsystems, are the major social institutions in society and include marriages and families, the economy, government, and religion. Each of these structures has a function for maintaining society. Families, for example, through reproduction, provide society with new members, ensuring that society is ongoing. At least in theory, all institutions in society work in harmony for the good of society and themselves. Thus, a functional analysis examines the ways in which each part of a system (society or any one of its parts) contributes to the functioning of society as a whole.

People who believe families must be structured in a certain way (for example, two heterosexual parents) to fulfill important family tasks and who see single-parent or female-headed families, lesbian and gay families, stepfamilies, and the changing role of women in marriages and families as threats to marriage and family life or as indicative of the demise of the family share a common view with structural functionalists. Are you a structural functionalist? Do you share these views?

The Family from a Functionalist Perspective In analyzing the family, a person using the functionalist perspective would ask general questions such as: What do families contribute to the maintenance of society? How does the structure of society affect families? How do families mesh with other institutions in society? Not only does this perspective view society as a system, but it also regards families themselves as systems. Therefore, a functional analysis would examine such issues as how families organize

Married men perform little more than a third of household labor, whether or not their wives are in the paid labor force. Some research has found that having a husband actually creates an extra seven hours of housework a week for women. When men do not participate in the household work and child care tasks of the family, it can be an important source of marital tension.

themselves for survival and what functions families perform for society and for their individual members.

According to functionalists, family functions historically have been divided along gender and age lines. Women and men must perform different tasks, as must younger and older people. Particularly since the Industrial Revolution, an important family task has been to provide economic support for family members. If the family is to survive, someone has to earn money by working for wages outside the home—an instrumental role. At the same time, someone must work inside the home to maintain it for the wage earner as well as for other family members—an expressive role. This division of labor along gender lines is said to make women and men interdependent and characterizes what sociologists call the traditional family, a family form that many conservatives believe to be the one and only true family form.

Functionalists are interested not only in the intended, overt, or **manifest functions** of social institutions such as the family, but in the unintended, unrecognized, or **latent functions** as well. Thus, a manifest function of having children might be to continue the family lineage or to add to marital satisfaction. Because children can add stress to a relationship, however, the introduction of children in the early years of family life often has the latent function of decreasing marital satisfaction. In addition, not all features of a social system are **functional**—performing a positive service by helping to maintain the system in a balanced state or promoting the achievement of group goals. Some features of the system might actually hamper the achievement of group goals and disrupt the system's balance. Such features are said to be **dysfunctional**. A single feature can be functional and dysfunctional at the same time. For example, the movement of married women into the labor force might be defined as functional in that their salaries contribute to the family income but defined as dysfunctional in that their time with their families is limited. A classic example of the use of the structural-functional perspective to explain how marriages and families work is embedded in the "nuclear family model" popularized in the mid 1950s by the late sociologist Talcott Parsons.

The Nuclear Family Model Recall from Chapter 1 that as Western societies became industrialized and urbanized in the late nineteenth and early twentieth centuries, the nuclear family emerged as the dominant family type to meet the needs of an industrial economy. Talcott Parsons (1955, 1964) agreed with the structural-functional assumption that the family is an adaptive system that performs essential functions for its individual members as well as for society as a whole. He argued, however, that in modern society the functional importance of the nuclear family has declined as many of its functions have been taken over and performed by other social institutions. According to Parsons, the two major functions of the modern family are now socialization of the young and personality stabilization of adults. Personality stabilization is the process whereby individuals internalize society's values and expectations concerning gender-appropriate behavior to the point where these values and cultural expectations become a consistent part of the individual's identity throughout her or his lifetime.

The nuclear family model places great emphasis on the differentiation of gender roles within the family as a functional necessity for the solidarity of the marriage relationship. Parsons described the male role in this regard as instrumental and the female role as expressive. The personality traits needed to carry out these roles are quite different. **Instrumental traits** encourage self-confidence, rationality, competition, and coolness—qualities that facilitate male success in the world of work. In contrast, **expressive traits** encourage nurturance, emotionality, sensitivity, and warmth—qualities that help women succeed in caring for a husband, children, and a home.

Critique Parsons's nuclear family model has often been at the center of controversy. Some of the major criticisms of this model are the same as those directed against functionalism generally: The model is specific to a particular time and place, does not use a historical context, and does not deal with the diversity of experiences that has always characterized U.S. families. As we have seen, what seemed true about marriages and families in the 1950s is less true today. The latest census data confirm that fewer and fewer families fit the Parsonian nuclear family model.

In addition, married-couple families often exhibit a diversity of structures and roles that the Parsonian model does not account for. Using this model, for instance, how can we explain the growing number of men today who are openly nurturant, caring, and sensitive—traits that Parsons describes as exclusively expressive and female? The nuclear family model is especially criticized for its rigid, exaggerated, and oversimplified view of marital interaction generally and of women's experiences specifically. It is also criticized for defining the family narrowly, through a White, male middle-class perspective (Andersen, 2005). For example, how does the nuclear family model apply to African American families under slavery, where legal marriage was prohibited and women's and men's roles were interchanged? Similarly, can it explain the diversity in Native American families, particularly those in which women exercised economic power in subsistence residential units that were the basis of their tribal economy?

Although functionalism has provided important insights, such as how marriages and families work and presumably why they exist, several important criticisms have been raised about this perspective generally. For example, although functionalism may be a useful framework for identifying a society's structural parts and the alleged functions of these parts, what function a particular structure serves, and why, are not always clear. What, for example, is the function of the division of labor in the family along gender lines? Is it efficiency and survival, as the functionalists maintain, or is it the perpetuation of the social dominance of certain categories of people—namely, men—and the subordination of others—namely, women? Another important criticism is the conservative bias of functional analysis. Critics argue that by assuming consensus lies at the basis of any social order, functionalists tend to promote and rationalize the status quo and to understate disharmony and conflict. Thus, they do not consider that something might be wrong with the system itself.

Although structural functionalism was the dominant theory in the field for more than 30 years, the changing political consciousness of the 1960s brought about increasing criticism of this perspective. Today, there is widespread recognition that structural functionalism generally and the nuclear family model specifically are limited when used to analyze families in the United States and are therefore no longer representative of "mainstream" sociological thought on families. Consequently, functionalism has greatly declined in importance as a viable frame of reference for understanding society, its institutions, and its members. However, its impact, especially on the public, can still be detected. For many people, the nuclear family remains the ideal form, even though such families are less prevalent today than they were in the past.

CONFLICT THEORY

Since the 1960s, the conflict perspective has become increasingly popular and important in modern sociology and in the works of feminist scholars across academic disciplines. There are several different approaches to conflict theory; however, all of them have their roots in the nineteenth-century pioneering writings of Karl Marx. Thus, our discussion here is of a very general nature and combines various strands of thought on conflict theory today. First, however, we take a brief look at Marxian theory.

Karl Marx Karl Marx (1818–1883) was an economist, political agitator, and social theorist who did much to revolutionize social and philosophical thinking about human society. Appalled by the brutal treatment of workers and their families during the nineteenth-century Industrial Revolution in Europe, Marx sought to understand the causes of this condition, in hopes of changing it. Basically, he believed the problem lay in the social organization of industrial societies. Such societies were capitalistic: The means of production were privately owned and were used to maximize profits.

For Marx, every aspect of social life is based on economic relationships. For example, he believed all industrialized societies are characterized by competition and conflict between two main groups: the capitalists (owners of the land and factories) and the proletariat (workers). These two groups have fundamentally opposing interests as well as unequal power. Conflict arises because the capitalists can maximize their profit only by exploiting the proletariat. At the same time, it is in the interest of the proletariat to revolt and overthrow the capitalist system and to establish a classless society in which wealth and power would be distributed evenly. Thus, meaningful social change comes about only as a result of the struggle between competing groups. In essence, for Marx, economic power explains the structure of societies and social relationships. Order and balance are always tenuous in capitalist societies. Such societies are held together by the power of capitalists to dominate the workers.

Relative to the fundamental sociological question—What is the relationship between the individual and society?—Marxian theory addresses both structure and action. It deals with structural factors in that it stresses that the historical circumstances of capitalism limit most of the choices open to people. At the same time, it stresses the action element in that it recognizes the capacity of workers to join together as a class-conscious group to collectively change existing economic and social conditions (Light, Keller, and Calhoun, 2000).

Themes of Conflict Theory Like functionalism, **conflict theory** focuses on social structures and institutions in society. The basic assumption of the conflict perspective, and perhaps the one that most sets it apart from functionalism, however, is the notion that conflict is natural and inevitable in all human interaction, including family systems. Therefore, a complete understanding of society and social structures such as marriages and families is possible only through a critical examination of competition, coercion, and conflict in society, especially those processes that lead some people to have great power and control and others to have little or no power and control. Thus, of major concern are the inequalities built into social structures or systems. Rather than focusing on interdependence, unity, and consensus, conflict theorists focus on society as an arena in which individuals and groups compete over limited resources and fight for power and control. A key assumption here is that certain groups and individuals have much greater power and access to key resources than others.

For the purposes of our discussion, we can reduce conflict theory to three central themes: (1) humans have basic interests or things they want and attempt to acquire; (2) power is at the base of all social relationships, and it is always scarce, unequally distributed, and coercive; and (3) values and ideas are weapons used by different groups to advance their own ends rather than to define society's identity and goals (Wallace and Wolf, 2005). Given these assumptions, the conflict perspective leads us to ask questions about the sources of tension among individuals and groups with different amounts of power; the techniques of conflict control in society; and the ways in which those with power perpetuate, maintain, and extend that power. In short, a major underlying question of conflict analysis is: Who benefits from and who is systematically deprived by any given social arrangement?

The Family from a Conflict Perspective Whereas functionalists focus on the tasks that serve the interests of the family as a whole, conflict theorists see families, like all societal institutions, as a set of social relationships that benefit some members more than others. Thus, a conflict theorist might ask general questions, such as the following: How is social inequality built into the structure of marriages and families? What is the role of a marital partner or family member in promoting family disintegration or change? When conflict occurs in the family, who wins? Who loses? How are racial, ethnic, gender, class, and other inequalities perpetuated through the operation of the family?

From this perspective, marriages and families can be viewed as smaller versions of the larger class system, where the well-being of one class (men) is the result of the exploitation and oppression of another class (women). The family exploits women specifically by encouraging them to perform unpaid housework and child care so that men can devote their time to capitalist endeavors. Historically, men who had the power to do so defined marriages and families in such a way that women were the sexual property of men. In consequence, marriage became a legally and socially enforced contract of sexual property. Although women in the United States are no longer legally defined as the property of men, other examples of male domination of women within marriages and families abound.

In essence, then, the basic source of male dominance and women's subordination is the home and family. Although functionalists may view the family as a refuge, for the conflict theorist the question is: What kind of refuge is it, for whom is it a refuge, and whom does it benefit?

Critique For many people, especially those who experience oppression, the conflict perspective offers a concrete set of propositions that explain unequal access to resources in terms of institutional structure rather than personal deficiencies. A major strength of this perspective is the way in which it relates social and organizational structure to group interests and the distribution of resources. Furthermore, it provides a historical framework within which to identify social change: the major shifts in the distribution of societal resources and social and political power. By tracing social behavior back to individuals' interests and the purposeful way they pursue them, it suggests a model to explain social and political change. And finally, unlike functionalism, the conflict perspective does not treat norms, values, and ideas as external to, and constraints on, individual behavior. Rather, the conflict perspective views human beings as very much involved in using the system of norms, values, and ideas as much as being used by it. Those who have the power use these systems to further their individual or group interests.

Conflict theory is not without its criticisms. One major criticism is that the underlying assumptions that power is people's main objective and conflict is the major feature of social life are too narrow. Some critics argue, for example, that within the family, societal norms encourage certain behaviors that either prevent conflict or keep it under control. Thus, for example, disagreements among family members usually can be resolved without the use of physical force.

In addition, the conflict perspective is often criticized for explicitly advocating social change, thereby giving up some of its claim to scientific objectivity. Furthermore, conflict theory, like functionalism, raises the issue of value neutrality. Whereas structural functionalists evaluate social patterns in a system in terms of whether they are positive or negative, conflict theorists are purposely critical of society. Both of these positions pose a dilemma for value-free sociology. Most conflict theorists try to separate their value judgments from their analysis of society. However, when they focus on inequalities in society and claim, for instance, that a more equitable distribution of tasks and resources between the sexes is desirable, the inherent value judgment is quite clear. These problems notwithstanding, the conflict perspective is a useful framework for analyzing how factors such as race, class, gender, age, and ethnicity are linked to the unequal distribution of valuable resources in marriages and families, including power, property, money, prestige, and education.

SYMBOLIC INTERACTIONISM

Functionalism and the conflict perspective both concern themselves with macro patterns (large-scale patterns) that characterize society or groups like families as a whole. In contrast, the **symbolic interaction** perspective focuses on micro patterns (small-scale patterns) of face-to-face interaction among people in specific settings such as within marriages and families. This perspective is based on the notion that society is made up of interacting individuals who communicate primarily through the use of shared **symbols**—objects, words, sounds, and events that are given meaning by members of a culture—and construct reality as they go about the business of their daily lives. The most important set of symbols that humans use is language. People interact with one another based on their understandings of the meanings of words and social situations as well as their perceptions of what others expect of them within those situations. Thus, a major emphasis is on individuals and their social relationships, the subjective meanings of human behavior, and the various processes through which people come to construct and agree on various definitions of reality.

The Family from a Symbolic Interaction Perspective

When using the symbolic interaction perspective as a frame of reference for analyzing marriages and families, one might ask questions such as the following: How are marriages and families experienced? How do individual family members interact to create, sustain, and change marriages and families? How do family members attempt to shape the reality perceived by other family members? How do the behaviors of family members change from one situation to another?

According to the late sociologist Ernest Burgess (1926), the family represents a unified set of interacting individuals, that is, unity in family life comes about as a result of interactions among various family members. In this sense, the concern is with marriages and families as social processes rather than with their structure. Thus, a symbolic interactionist would argue that the reality of marriage and family life is not fixed but is *socially constructed* and is constructed differently by various family members with different roles, privileges, and responsibilities. The **social construction of reality** is the process whereby people assign meanings to social phenomena—objects, events, and characteristics—that almost always cause those who draw on these meanings to emphasize some aspect of a phenomenon and to ignore others. These assigned meanings have tremendous consequences for the individuals involved, depending on how they

interact with each other, what decisions they make, and what actions they take (Ferrante, 2007).

SOCIAL CONSTRUCTIONISM

As the limitations of an objectivist explanation of social life have become more and more evident in postmodern society, many social scientists and other scholars (not only sociologists but also social workers, political scientists, lawyers, and historians) increasingly have sought to explain social life in terms of a subjectivist approach. These scholars use what is referred to as a social constructionist perspective. **Social constructionism** is an extension of symbolic interaction theory in which the analysis is framed entirely in terms of a conceptualization of the social construction of reality. A guiding principle is that human experience is developed through a complex process of human interaction in which we learn both the attitudes and the behaviors appropriate to our culture and attempt to modify these scripted behaviors and attitudes to make them more palatable. Some fundamental assumptions of this perspective and symbolic interactionism generally are as follows:

- Reality is invented, constructed largely out of the meanings and values of the observer.
- Language is a mediating influence on all constructions; we bring forth realities through our interactions with other human beings.
- We cannot know an objective reality apart from our subjective views of it.
- Culture, history, politics, and economic conditions all influence individual experiences of social reality.

Social Constructionism and the Family Almost any subject related to marriage and family life can be analyzed within the context of the social constructionist paradigm. One example of the application of the constructivist perspective especially relevant to the sociology of marriages and families can be seen in terms of the concept of gender. Gender is a socially constructed system for classifying people as girl or boy, woman or man, feminine or masculine. Take masculinity, for instance: Men are not born to follow a predetermined biological imperative encoded somewhere in their physical make-up. Rather, to be a man is to participate in the social life of a culture as it defines manhood and masculinity. In this sense, men are not born but made by culture. Men also make themselves, actively constructing their masculinities within a social and historical context. Therefore, the reality of being a male in twenty-first-century U.S. society and its impact on marriage, family, and intimate relationships is quite different from that experienced by individual men, marriages, and families 100 years ago. It is also very different from being a male in South Africa, Sri Lanka, Southeast Asia, Bosnia, Kosovo, Albania, Israel, Palestine, or the former Soviet Union. In this same context, the social construction of masculinity in the United States defines men's roles in the family as economic provider and protector of women and children. In New Guinea, among the Tchambuli, however, men are expected to be submissive, emotional, delicate, and dependent.

The social constructionist perspective is both historical and comparative. In the case of marriages, families, and intimate relationships, such a perspective allows us to explore the ways in which the meanings of social reality and of social experiences vary across marriages, families, and cultures as well as how they change over historical time. This perspective enables us to better understand concepts such as gender and their relationship in marriages and families.

Critique The symbolic interaction perspective brings people back into our analyses. Rather than seeing humans as passive beings who simply respond to society's rules, interactionists give us a view of humans as actively involved in constructing, shaping, sustaining, and changing the social world. It is a useful framework for examining the complexities of relationships and the daily workings of marriages and families, complexities that functionalism and the conflict perspective miss. One of the major advantages of this perspective is that it helps us understand how the roles we play are so important in our social constructions of reality.

Likewise, social constructionism is a useful approach for studying human social life and offers a viable alternative to traditional static, ahistoric, and deterministic theoretical perspectives. According to some scholars (for example, Rosenblum and Travis, 1996), an important advantage of a constructionist approach is that it enables us to understand that certain categories of human experience—such as race, sex, sexual orientation, and class—have social significance, that is, these categories are socially created and arbitrary. Instead of viewing people as essentially different by virtue of these labels, social constructionism leads us to question not the essential difference between categories, but rather the origin and consequence of the labeling or categorization system itself.

Neither symbolic interactionism nor social constructionism are without limitations or critics. In focusing attention on the subjective aspects of human experiences and the situations in which they occur, both perspectives ignore the objective realities of inequality, racism, sexism, and the differential distribution of wealth, status, and power among various groups; they also minimize the impact of these phenomena on individuals and families. Criticisms directed specifically at social constructionism include the claim that it is inherently inconsistent, that its theoretical assumptions are contradictory. Some critics argue that there is no clear agreement about what constitutes constructionism. Most often, those who criticize constructionism are objectivists who argue that (1) social constructionism springs from a particular set of moral and political values or biases, and (2) social constructionism is simply an exercise in debunking previously held truths (Best, 1995). These criticisms notwithstanding, a social-constructionist perspective provides a framework by which to make sense of what categories, such as marriage, family, race, ethnicity, class, and sexual orientation, mean in both historical and contemporary context; in addition, it heightens our awareness of the socially constructed nature of everyday life.

SOCIAL EXCHANGE THEORY

Probably the theoretical perspective most often used in the discipline to study marriages and families is **social exchange theory.** This theory adopts an economic model of human behavior based on costs, benefits, and the expectation of reciprocity; for this reason, it is sometimes referred to as the rational-choice perspective. It tends to be very close to the way many of us see and explain behavior in our everyday lives.

Have you ever wondered why some person you know or heard about remained in an unhappy relationship? Did you try to analyze this behavior by asking what the person might be getting out of the relationship versus whatever makes her or him unhappy (in other words, the pluses, or benefits, and minuses, or costs, of the relationship)? Did the person eventually leave the relationship? Did you wonder what finally made her or him end it? Was your answer that the costs finally became too great or outweighed the benefits? If you have ever engaged in this type of cost–benefit analysis to explain your own or other people's actions and relationships, you were using a basic social exchange perspective. Social exchange theory shares many of the assumptions of symbolic-interaction theory and thus in broad terms is another extension of interaction theory. Social exchange theory is so named because its underlying premise is that social exchange forms the basis of all social interaction. Exchange theorists view social interaction as an exchange of tangible or intangible goods and services, ranging from money or physical labor to social recognition, love, and respect. Humans are thought to be rational beings who, in making decisions, weigh the profits to be gained from a particular action against the costs it will incur. Only when people feel that the gains of their interactions outweigh the costs do they adopt the behavior. People, then, engage in those actions that bring them the greatest benefits at the least cost. They will continue to engage in these actions as long as they perceive them to be profitable.

The two best known proponents of social exchange theory are George Homans and Peter Blau. Homans (1961) focused on actual behavior that is rewarded or punished by the behavior of others. According to Homans, humans react to stimuli based on need, reward, and reinforcement. Thus, in the various exchange relationships in which humans engage, the rewards will usually be proportional to the costs. Blau (1964), on the other hand, was more concerned with explaining large-scale social structures. According to Blau, not all exchange can be explained in terms of actual behavior. Rather, exchange, like other interactions, is a subjective and interpretative process. Blau agrees with Homans that humans want rewards, and in exchange interactions each person receives something perceived as equivalent to that which is given. Blau refers to this as "fair exchange." He contends, however, that our relationship choices and decisions are not made purely on the basis of the perceived rewards but are affected by various social influences such as family and friends.

The Family from a Social Exchange Perspective Most exchange analyses of marriage and family behavior focus on relations between couples. Typically, a person using an exchange perspective is concerned with questions like those previously asked of you. In the language of exchange theory, for example, we might explain the observation that when women work they gain power in

Amid rumors of Prince Albert II of Monaco's increasing need for a legitimate heir (one born within a legal marriage), in 2011, the 53-year-old lifetime bachelor married 33-year-old Charlene Wittstock, a former Olympic swimmer from South Africa who was said to have made three attempts to flee Monaco in advance of her wedding. When the Prince offered his new bride not love but a tepid thank you in his wedding speech, it fueled suspicions that the marriage was a classic exchange in which Wittstock will produce a legitimate heir for Prince Albert in return for a lavish royal lifestyle. Is this what Peter Blau would define as a "fair exchange?" Is each person receiving something she or he perceives to be equivalent to that which she or he is giving?

some value to the person involved, whether or not this is really the case. Furthermore, the notion of rational choice is limiting in that humans do not always act rationally, nor do we always agree on what rational behavior is. We do not always choose relationships or interactions simply because the rewards outweigh the costs. In fact, sometimes the reverse is true. One way of analyzing the "battered woman syndrome" (discussed in Chapter 11) is to assume that women stay in abusive relationships not because the rewards outweigh the costs but because other factors, such as fear of physical violence if they leave, override all other considerations.

These criticisms notwithstanding, an exchange perspective provides us with a unique framework for explaining many face-to-face relationships. It provides insight into people's values, goals, and perceptions of reality. Exchange theory is probably most valuable for explaining people's actions when we want to know and understand the details of individual behavior.

THE DEVELOPMENTAL FAMILY LIFE CYCLE MODEL

Developmental family life cycle theory pays close attention to changes in families over time and attempts to explain family life in terms of a process that unfolds over the life course of families. Sociologist Paul Glick (Glick and Parke, 1965) was the first to analyze families in terms of a life cycle. According to Glick, families pass through a series of stages: (1) family formation (first marriage); (2) start of childbearing (birth of first child); (3) end of childbearing (birth of last child); (4) "empty nest" (when the last child leaves home); and (5) "family dissolution" (death of one spouse). Other life cycle theories identify somewhat similar stages.

According to such developmental theories, families change over time in terms of family members and the roles they play. At various stages in the family life cycle, the family has different developmental tasks to perform. Each new stage in the family life cycle is brought on by a change in the composition of the family. These changes, in turn, affect various aspects of the family's well-being, including its economic viability. At each stage of development, the family is confronted with a distinct set of tasks whose completion is considered essential both for individual development and success at the next stage. One of the most widely used developmental theories in family sociology is an eight-stage model developed by Evelyn Duvall (1977).

As you study this model of family development, think about your own family and other families you know. How do these families fit into such a model? How do they differ? If they differ, does this mean that these families are abnormal or dysfunctional? (To pursue this activity, see the Writing Your Own Script box at the end of this chapter.)

the family (see Chapter 10) with the reasoning that in exchange for their economic contribution, working women share more equitably in decision making. Many sociologists use exchange theory to explain how people in the United States choose whom to date and marry. They contend that Americans search for the best possible mate (product) given their own resources (physical attractiveness, intelligence, youth, status, and money). People in this situation weigh a range of costs and benefits before choosing a mate. As you read this textbook, think about the value of different types of resources and the exchange processes at work in understanding a variety of marriage and family behaviors and relationships.

Critique Exchange theory assumes that humans are rational, calculating beings who consciously weigh the costs versus the benefits of their relationships. A major problem with this notion of human behavior is that it cannot be disproved. Almost any behavior can be explained simply by saying that it must have had

Stage 1: Beginning families. At this first stage of development, the married couple does not have children and is just beginning married life and adjusting to it.

Stage 2: Childbearing families. The family is still forming in this stage. The first child is born, and women are deeply involved in childbearing and childrearing.

Stage 3: Families with preschool children. The family's oldest child is somewhere between 2½ and 6 years of age. The mother is still deeply involved in childrearing. This stage lasts about 3 to 4 years.

Stage 4: Families with schoolchildren. The oldest child (or children) in the family is school-aged. With children in school, the mother is free to pursue other options such as work outside the home.

Stage 5: Families with teenagers. In this stage, the oldest child is between 13 and 20 years old. The family must adjust to having adolescents in the home and adapt to their growing independence. This stage may last up to 7 years.

Stage 6: Families as launching centers. At this stage, the oldest child has been launched into adulthood. Families must develop adult relationships with grown children as they adjust to children leaving the family "nest." This stage lasts until the last child leaves home, usually a period of about 8 years.

Stage 7: Families in the middle years. This stage is sometimes called the "empty nest" stage. It is a distinct new stage in the developmental cycle of the family and spans the time from when the last child leaves home to retirement or old age.

Stage 8: Aging families. Members of the family who work outside the home have retired at this stage. In this stage, families must cope with events related to aging, such as chronic illnesses and the eventual death of one of the spouses. The remaining spouse must then deal with the factors and experiences associated with widowhood.

Critique Although developmental family life cycle theory generally calls attention to the changing nature of family relationships over time, distinguishing a "typical" family life cycle is difficult, if not impossible. As family norms change, the stages of family development also vary. In fact, some scholars believe the stages of the family life cycle have become increasingly useful as indicators of change rather than as stages that all or even most families can be expected to experience. Although life cycle theories give us important insights into the complexities of family life, a shortcoming is that they assume most families are nuclear families with children. Thus, such theories present a "typical" family life cycle descriptive of the "conventional" family. As with structural functionalism, for example, most family life cycle theories do not incorporate the diversity of family lifestyles prevalent in U.S. society. Where, for example, do families without children, single-parent families, same-sex families, and remarried families fit in these models?

Moreover, families within various racial and ethnic groups develop through stages not recognized in these models. For example, due in part to their general disadvantaged economic position, many families of color and poor families across race take in relatives at some time in the family life cycle. In addition, a growing number of families in all classes are taking in and caring for aging parents. What does a developmental family life cycle model tell us about these families? Not only does such a theory omit these arrangements, but it generally implies a linear, or straight-line, progression in family life that few families actually experience. Families, for example, may progress through several of the early stages only to go back and repeat earlier stages, particularly if children are involved.

Furthermore, developmental theories such as Duvall's generally assume that developmental tasks, particularly those in the early stages, are gender-specific. Consider, for example, Duvall's first four stages. Each stage is defined entirely in terms of the presence of

An important critique of the developmental family life cycle theory is that it fails to incorporate the diversity of family lifestyles prevalent in U.S. society today. For example, a growing number of families across race and class are taking in and caring for aging parents (such as this woman sitting on the steps of her daughter's home). Where, if at all, do these families fit in developmental family life cycle models? What do these theories tell us about these families?

children and the role of women as caretakers and caregivers. Men and their parenting roles are totally omitted.

FEMINIST THEORIES AND PERSPECTIVES

Feminist theory is not a single unified view. Rather, there are many types of feminist theory, just as there are many types of sociological theory. In general, feminist theories present a generalized set of ideas about the basic features of society and human experience from a woman-centered perspective. It is woman-centered in three ways: (1) the starting point of all its investigations is the situations and experiences of women; (2) it treats women as the main subjects in the research process, that is, it attempts to view the world from the distinctive vantage points of women; and (3) it is critical and activist on behalf of women (Lengermann and Brantley, 2004).

A word of caution: Not all theories that deal with women or gender issues are feminist theories. To be considered feminist, a theory must reflect a feminist consciousness—an awareness rooted in a commitment to activist goals. In addition, it should adopt three basic philosophical approaches: (1) gender is the central focus; (2) status quo gender relations are viewed as problematic in that women are defined as subordinate to men; and (3) gender relations are viewed as the result of social, not natural, factors (Chafetz, 1988).

Basically, all feminist theories attempt to answer two fundamental questions. The first is, Where are women? The second is, Why is this situation as it is? In addressing these questions, feminist theories typically focus on the ways in which specific definitions of gender affect the organization of social institutions and patterns of gender inequality. Feminists have encouraged us to make the personal political. This helps us understand that individual behavior and experiences within marriages, families, and intimate relationships are part of and impacted by larger societal institutions and other social, political, and historical factors. Finally, a major objective of feminist theories is social change. Perhaps more than most theories, feminist theories are explicitly and self-consciously political in their advocacy of social change.

In general, feminist theories and perspectives demonstrate how traditional ideas and theories have been derived from the particular experiences of some men and then have been used as universal standards against which all others have been viewed and judged. Asking sociological questions and studying marriages and families from a feminist perspective transforms traditional models of inquiry. No matter the discipline, however, when men's experiences are the standard, women and other subordinated groups (including many men) appear incomplete, inadequate, or invisible. On the other hand, when women's experiences are taken seriously, new methods and theoretical perspectives must be established (Andersen, 2005). For example, feminist theories and scholarship make central considerations of the ways that race, ethnicity, sexuality, and class influence our marriage and family experiences. Feminist scholars, for instance, have revised our thinking about motherhood as a static universal category of experience. Scholarship such as Denise Segura's study (1994) of how heterosexual Chicana and Mexicana immigrant women balance work and family roles shows not only how the meaning and practice of motherhood are culturally constructed, and thus vary among different groups of women, but also that a White middle-class model of motherhood has been taken by some scholars to be a universal standard by which all other mothers are evaluated.

The Family from a Feminist Perspective

A feminist investigation of marriages and families asks both macro- and micro level questions. Macro level questions include: What are the causes of women's inequality in marriages and families? How does the structure of marriages and families maintain gender inequality? How can change toward greater equality in marriages and families be brought about? Micro level questions include: What social and interpersonal processes occur in families to generate gender differences and inequality? What roles do various family members play in perpetuating gender inequality? What kind of power structures exist within marriages and families, and how do they affect the distribution of tasks and resources?

Taking the position that women's subordination is based in the social relationships within marriages and families, the objective of an analysis of marriages and families is to explain the ways in which gender inequality is reinforced and maintained in these relationships. On a macro level, for example, a vast Marxist feminist literature asserts that women's oppression is built into and sustained by the patriarchal family structure. On a micro level, a body of feminist theory exists that, by focusing on what these theorists refer to as the "reproduction of gender" in families, explains how gender inequality and oppression are reinforced and maintained.

Critique

There are many critiques of feminist theory. That feminist theory is woman-centered is the most frequent criticism, especially from mainstream sociologists. Basically, the criticism is that feminist theory is biased and excludes male experiences and perspectives. Feminist theorists respond to this criticism by asserting that the partiality to women in their work is necessary given the history of devaluation or exclusion of female experiences and perspectives in traditional social theories. They argue that the inclusion of female experiences and perspectives does not exclude men and male perspectives.

In addition, some critiques have come from feminist scholars themselves, who differ in their conceptualizations of the causes of women's oppression and the goals of feminist theory. For example, radical feminists criticize the liberal feminist notion that the major political goal for feminists should be equal opportunity for women and men. Critics contend that because this approach does not address such structural issues as class and race inequality, it would help only some women but would not help many others, particularly poor women and women of color. Marxist feminist theory is often criticized for its focus on women's oppression as a reflection of the more fundamental class oppression in society. This single focus on economic production largely ignores the importance of social and cultural factors such as race and ethnicity.

One very important criticism of most feminist theories is that they are biased toward the experiences of White, middle-class, heterosexual women. In particular, feminist theory is criticized for not including an adequate analysis of race. Even when such theories deal with issues of race, class, and heterosexuality, they often focus primarily on the life experiences of the poor or working class, women of color, or lesbians. Such analyses cloud the fact that all women experience race, class, gender, and sexual orientation, albeit in different ways. In some cases, for example, women are economically disadvantaged and denied access to power and privilege because of their skin color, sexual orientation, or social class. In other cases, these same factors can enhance access to social and economic resources. No matter the specific critique, various feminist theories have contributed significantly to our current understanding of marriages and families and have made fundamental contributions to social change.

✳ Explore the **Concept**
Social Explorer Activity: Patterns of Inequality Among Women on **myfamilylab.com**

According to recent statistics, the rate of marriage is decreasing while the rate of cohabitation has increased. Thinking about the issue of cohabitation as it pertains to or impacts marriages and families, develop three questions about cohabitation that reflect the focus of each of the theoretical approaches discussed in this chapter. How might you apply these same theoretical approaches to the issue of the current decline in marriage?

Men's Studies and Marriage and Family Research

As we have seen throughout this chapter, there are many critical social and political issues related to explanations of marriage and family life in the United States. Whether or not we accept the feminist claim that their theories and research do not exclude the experiences or perspectives of men, since the 1980s a parallel movement

Traditionally, male socialization and social conditioning discouraged men from developing and expressing a wide range of personality traits or skills, thereby limiting experiences in their marriage and family relationships. However, today, men are becoming more nurturing and developing parenting skills that we routinely assign to or expect from women. They are participating more fully in parenting their children, including performing routine tasks such as teaching their children how to bake.

has developed among some male activists and scholars who call for a larger, visible place in feminist analyses—one that pays attention to the oppression that males experience as a result of social conditioning and learning. They argue that the same values that have restricted women have also restricted men to their roles as aggressors. Not surprisingly, the ongoing inclusive work on women has given rise to men's studies or masculinity studies as it is sometimes called, the academic arm of this movement. That men's studies has gained momentum over the last several decades is evidenced by the fact that more than 500 colleges now offer courses on men and masculinity. Since the 1990s, there has been an explosion of scholarship on men, the contemporary masculine psyche, as well as the ways in which cultures shape or construct definitions and ideas about masculinity and how individual men embody it. And in 2008, *The Men's Bibliography*, a comprehensive bibliography of writings on men, masculinities, gender, and sexualities, first published in 1992, was updated listing over 16,700 works, a vast amount of which

examines men in various intimate relationships and their roles and experiences in marriages and families (see Flood, 2008).

The growth of the movement to explore men's concerns can be seen in the progression from the establishment of men's studies organizations and scientific journals devoted to research and theory on men's lives and issues in the 1980s to the most recent development of Male Studies as a disciplinary focus and the establishment of the Foundation for Male Studies, which debuted in 2010 at Wagner College in New York. This newest discipline is said to have developed in response to what some scholars saw as an anti-male bias and a bias toward feminism in men's studies that gets in the way of the study of men. A stated goal of male studies is to understand men and boys—physically, biologically, and psychologically. The field takes its cues from the belief that females and males are biologically different and that a person's biology, in large part, determines her or his behavior. This point of view, they believe, is not being addressed in most contemporary scholarship on men and boys.

One might say that we have always had "men's studies" because, historically, men have been at the center of most scientific analyses of human behavior and human societies. However, most of men's studies today is not just about men and centering men in research and theory. The major focus of men's studies is men, masculinities, gender, sexualities, and politics. It specifically challenges the patriarchal male bias in traditional scholarship, the existing sexist and homophobic norms in society, and, like women's studies, it combines theory and practice to create a more just society. Men's studies programs and courses often include contemporary discussions of men's rights, masculism, feminist theory, queer theory, matriarchy, patriarchy, and, more generally, the social, historical, and cultural constructions of men and virility. They often discuss the issues surrounding male privilege, seen as evolving into more subtle forms rather than disappearing in the modern era.

The line between men's studies and the men's rights movement is often blurred. However, men's studies looks primarily at the question long asked in feminist analysis: Why are men the way they are? Recognizing that gender and sexism impact men's as well as women's lives, men's studies encompasses a critical examination of the functional and dysfunctional aspects of the traditional male gender role for men, women, children, and society at large. It begins with the basic premise that there is no hierarchy of oppression. Men, like women, are oppressed by a social conditioning that makes them incapable of developing and expressing a wide range of personality traits or skills and limits their experiences.

As with feminist theory, the network of men's studies consists of not one but several diverse perspectives. In fact, the theories and perspectives of much of men's studies parallel feminist theories and perspectives, so much so that some feminist scholars have declared that men's studies is explicitly feminist. Like feminist perspectives, then, perspectives in men's studies consider gender to be a central feature of social life—one of the chief organizing principles around which our lives revolve—examining how gender, specifically the social construction of masculinities, shapes men's ideas, opportunities, and experiences. Too often, there is the tendency for the public and some in academic settings to assume that only women are gendered beings, as if men had no gender. We know, however, from women's and men's studies that this is not the case. Rather, gender affects the experiences of both women and men, albeit in different ways. Thus, as in feminist theories and perspectives, the perspectives of men's studies frame their analyses within the context of the diversity among men, recognizing, on the one hand, that not all men experience their masculinity in the same way or are sexist in their attitudes, beliefs, and behaviors and yet, on the other hand, that as a group, men benefit from gender privilege but this privilege varies according to race, class, and sexual orientation.

MEN IN FAMILIES

What does it really mean to be a man, a father, a friend, a lover in contemporary U.S. society? One of the most important issues for U.S. marriages and families over the past decade has been that of fatherhood. Debates have centered around questions such as: Are men becoming more nurturing and caring fathers and developing parenting skills such as those we routinely expect from women? Men's studies scholarship on this issue has caused us to broaden our perspective about fatherhood. For example, in his study of the lifestyles of gay husbands and fathers, Brian Miller (2001) reported among his findings that although these husbands and fathers perceived their gayness as incompatible with traditional marriage, they perceived their gayness as compatible with fathering. Gays in heterosexual marriages who leave their spouses and enter the gay world report that gay relationships are more harmonious than heterosexual marital relationships. They also report that fathering is more salient once they have left their heterosexual marriages. As more alternatives for fathering have become available within the gay community, fewer gays have become involved in heterosexual marriages and divorce. Adoption, surrogate parenting, and alternative fertilization are some of the methods that have expanded the opportunities for fatherhood regardless of sexual orientation.

On some levels, since the 1990s, a "new father" has emerged. An increasing number of young husbands have joined their wives in birthing courses, have donned empathy bellies, have taken part in the actual delivery of their children, and an increasing number are stay-at-home dads or single parent dads. These developments notwithstanding, there is little evidence, however, that these experiences by themselves produce a strong father–child (or wife–husband) bond or lead to greater participation by fathers with their children. As we shall see in Chapters 9 and 10, few new fathers assume a major role in child care and child rearing. According to the politics-of-masculinity perspective, for most men, no matter how much they would like to be more active in parenting, the demands of outside employment and the continuing definition of men and masculinity in terms of "work" and "family provider" preclude such participation.

Critique In general, men's studies as a discipline offers a useful critique of patriarchal and homosocial relations in American institutions such as marriages and families. However, a major criticism of the more general perspectives of the politics of masculinity such as that of the new discipline of male studies concerns the focus on biology as destiny and the view of men as primary victims. Some critics, for example, claim that such perspectives are not only theoretically underdeveloped but also antifeminist, reactionary, and sexist, depicting men as innocent victims of conniving and selfish women or of social structures and institutions that in fact they control. Another criticism is that although many of these analyses focus on the structural and institutional nature of men's exploitation and oppression, they have

not clearly identified the alleged oppression or oppressors in society. Some scholars argue that these perspectives as well as the men's rights movement, in general, are simply strategies for reaffirming men's authority in the face of the challenge presented by feminism.

Although recognizing the pervasive victimization of women, many proponents of masculinity theory nonetheless caution against the view of some feminists that being a male in and of itself—and not the systems of social control and production—is responsible for the exploitation of women. Although this point is well taken, according to critics, it neglects to emphasize that the systems of social control and production in the United States are owned and controlled by men (albeit primarily White middle- and upper-class men). Thus, the issues of gender and the exercise of power cannot be separated.

In conclusion, we have seen that sociology offers a variety of theories and perspectives that can be used to study marriages and families. Although each framework is somewhat distinct, the various frameworks are not completely incompatible with each other. Rather, they can and often do offer complementary insights.

Supporting Marriages and Families

Few people would disagree that marriages and families are key components of American society and that our future depends on the health and stability of marriages and families. However, contemporary families are under considerable stress and strain due to a number of social and political factors such as war, economic downturns, the home mortgage loan crisis and home foreclosures, job outsourcing, unemployment, natural disasters, violence, and racism. If individual well-being depends on the well-being of our marriages and families, then we must be ever vigilant in seeking practical support to families so that they can survive such hardships and thrive. Support for marriages and families is needed perhaps now more than ever before as families and the country as a whole attempt to recover from both the ongoing pain and loss of family members as a result of the "war on terror" and the horror, mass devastation, separation, and dissolution of thousands of families in the aftermath of natural disasters such as Hurricane Katrina in 2005 and the super outbreak of tornadoes in 2011 that killed more than 500 people in the East, South, and Midwest by midyear.

According to sociologists, the impact of natural disasters on families depends on what the family was like before the storm. Strong families tend to go through such disasters together and come out stronger at the end. But for families that might have been having problems, even within their household or with other relatives, such disasters can make things worse. Thus, families (some more than others) need serious help and support both before and after events such as hurricanes and tornadoes. Government policies and programs as well as community-based initiatives and programs should be implemented and supported to assist families in or responding to a particular crisis.

Scientifically sound research can play an important role in helping to identify marriage and family issues and suggest methods for assisting and supporting families. For example, sociological research on previous hurricanes has provided insights not only about the types of support families need after such a catastrophe occurs, but also before such events happen. For example, some research has shown that the disruption of families as a result of hurricanes or tornadoes can take many different forms, including household and job loss or dislocation because of the total or near total destruction of their home; extended commuting patterns; living in crowded and often deteriorated structures; the maze of paperwork and tasks associated with loss recovery and household reconstruction; as well as the lack of community infrastructure, including parks and recreation facilities and neighborhood stores and services. Daily living conditions make it extremely difficult for many families to regain domestic stability, and it could be expected that within the privacy of the home and its intimate relationships that stress and frustration are most likely to be openly expressed. Such research also suggests that many of the problems in the aftermath of natural disasters were visible prior to the disaster. For example, after Hurricane Andrew in 1992, researchers found strong evidence of racial differentials in insurance settlements and clear evidence of insurance redlining of Black areas in the South Dade County of Florida (IHC Research Activities, 2005). Similar research has shown that before Hurricane Katrina, many in the New Orleans area faced significant health care challenges, and Louisiana consistently reported some of the poorest health statistics in the country (Kaiser Family Foundation, 2007).

Research such as this is important because it highlights the issues and areas in which families impacted by disasters need support, and it can be used to develop concrete proposals for action by the government, communities, and individuals in support of marriages and families. Issues of long-term, pent-up frustration, marginalization, institutional racism, alienation, hopelessness, anger, and lack of social control as surfaced in the aftermath of Hurricane Katrina as well as the mass dispersal and separation of individuals and families should be faced and dealt with in terms of proactive and supportive government policies and programs that address pre- and post-disaster impacts on marriages and families such as individual and family poverty, poor educational systems, long-term chronic unemployment, racism and discrimination in housing, jobs, education, and other sectors of American life. Family and parenting bodies such as the National Council on Family Relations, which provides a forum for family researchers, educators, and practitioners to share in the development and dissemination of knowledge about families and to work to promote family well-being, should be fully employed in the development of policies and programs that will support marriages and families.

Writing Your Own Script

THE FAMILY LIFE CYCLE: LOCATING YOUR FAMILY

Think about the developmental family life cycle theory model discussed in this chapter. Develop a life cycle model of your own family. Which stages of the model discussed in the chapter are applicable to your immediate family? Has it progressed directly through these stages? Have some stages been revisited? Which stages are not covered by the model? Why not? Describe some of the major roles, responsibilities, and adjustments that have been necessary at each stage of your family's life cycle.

SUMMARY

Sociology involves observing human behavior and then making sense out of what we observe. Therefore, both research and theory are involved. Theory is an explanation of some phenomenon, and scientific research includes a set of methods that allow us to collect data to test hypotheses and develop theories. The two are linked in that theory provides insights into the nature of human behavior and society, and research provides the empirical observations from which the theories are verified. Sociologists studying marriages and families have used a variety of research methodologies: surveys, observation, case studies, and ethnographies. Each of these methods has both advantages and limitations.

Although sociology as a discipline claims that the improvement of social life is a major goal, some feminist scholars have argued that in practice sociology has not lived up to this goal. A telling sign is who gets studied and how compared to who is left out and why. Until recent times, conventional topics studied by sociologists and their theoretical perspectives had either ignored issues relevant to the lives of women, poor people, lesbians, gays, and people of color or studied them within White and male middle-class models. Given this history, new scholarship on marriages and families has emerged that recognizes race, class, and gender diversity in marriages and families.

Just as there is no single method for studying marriages and families, there is no single theory to explain these institutions. There are four mainstream theoretical perspectives that, while not specifically family theories, can be used to explain marriages and families. Structural functionalism and conflict theory provide frameworks for analyzing the determinants of large-scale social structure. Symbolic interaction theory allows us to focus on individuals within marriages and families and the interaction between couples or among family members. Social exchange theory is guided by the assumption that people are rational and logical and that they base their actions on what they think is the most effective way to meet their goals.

Moreover, a number of sociological theories designed specially to address issues concerning marriage and family life are also being used. The most common are the nuclear family and the developmental family life cycle theories. Each is an extension of the larger, more encompassing functional perspective and thus provides both the advantages and limitations of a functional analysis. The nuclear family theory, popularized by Talcott Parsons, suggests that the family is an adaptive system that performs essential functions for its individual members as well as for society as a whole. In contrast, the developmental life cycle theoretical perspective focuses on changes in families over time and offers an explanation of family life in terms of a process that unfolds over the life course of marriages and families. Other theories that have important theoretical implications for studying marriages and families include social constructionism and feminist theories. Social constructionists speak of reality as invented or constructed out of the interactions between individuals in face-to-face interactions. It suggests that gender relationships within marriages,

families, and intimate relationships are not uniform and universally generalizable to all people. Rather, they are social productions that have no meaning outside that understood and agreed on by the actors. On the other hand, feminist theory is not a single unified view; rather, there are many types of feminist theory. A basic premise of all feminist theories is that women are oppressed and their lives are shaped by a number of important experiences such as race, class, gender, and culture. However, different theories pay primary attention to different sets of women's experiences as causing or contributing to their inequality and oppression.

Over the last two decades, we have witnessed a growing number of male voices advocating a larger and more visible place in feminist analyses, one that pays attention to the oppression that men experience as a result of gender role socialization. To date, however, very little effort has been made to extend these ideas into a practical agenda for social and political change.

Finally, in recent years, American marriages and families have experienced considerable stress and strain due to a number of social and political factors such as war, home foreclosures, natural disasters, job outsourcing, unemployment, violence, and racism. If individual well-being depends on the well-being of our marriages and families, then we must be ever vigilant in seeking practical support to families so that they can survive such hardships and thrive.

KEY TERMS

theory	qualitative	ethnography	dysfunctional	social construction of
scientific research	analysis	ideologies	instrumental	reality
empirical evidence	survey	perspective	traits	social constructionism
hypotheses	interview	structural functionalism	expressive traits	social exchange
variables	questionnaire	manifest functions	conflict theory	theory
scientific method	Hawthorne effect	latent functions	symbolic interactionism	developmental family life
quantitative analysis	case study	functional	symbols	cycle theory

QUESTIONS FOR STUDY AND REFLECTION

1. Why do sociologists need different theoretical perspectives to explain marriage and family behavior? Why isn't one perspective sufficient?

2. Virtually every practical decision you make and every practical opinion you hold has some theory behind it. Consider any marriage and family behavior or event of interest to you. Develop a "mini theory" to explain the behavior or event. What are some of the major assumptions you make about human beings, society, marriages, families, women, and men? Is your theory a micro or macro level explanation? Which one of the theoretical perspectives or theory models does your theory most resemble? After you have developed your mini theory, consider that you or some researcher wants to test it. What kinds of questions might you ask? Which research methodology would be most appropriate to test your theory? Why?

3. Identify a family from a culture other than the United States. Interview family members in terms of a range of issues, including family values, norms, customs, and rituals relative to marriage, childbearing, and childrearing. Compare your findings to families born and raised in the United States. How does your research help you to understand these sociological concepts, and what does it tell us about the diversity of marriages and families?

4. As discussed in this chapter, marriages and families today are faced with a myriad of challenges such as home foreclosures, unemployment, violence, poverty, and racism. If you were a member of a team charged with developing social policy pertaining to American families, what aspect of family life would you focus on, how might you research the topic, and what kind of policy(ies) might you suggest to policy makers?

ADDITIONAL RESOURCES

SOCIOLOGICAL STUDIES

KIMMEL, MICHAEL, AND MICHAEL MESSNER, EDS. 2010. *Men's Lives*, 8th ed. Boston: Allyn & Bacon. This reader on men and masculinity contains the most current articles on masculinity available. Organized around specific themes that define masculinity and the issues that men confront over the life course, the authors incorporate a social constructionist perspective that examines how men actively construct their masculinity within a social and historical context. Related to this construction and integrated throughout the book are the variations that exist among men across race, class, and sexual orientation.

PETERS, ELIZABETH, AND CLAIRE KAMP DUSH, EDS. 2009. *Marriage and Family: Perspectives and Complexities*. New York: Columbia University Press. The editors of this book explore a range of topics related to contemporary marriages and families, including the motivation to marry and the role of marriage in a diverse group of women and men. They compare empirical data from several family types (single, co-parent, lesbian, and gay, among others) to studies of traditional nuclear families and consider the effect of public policy and recent economic developments on the practice of marriage and the stabilization—or destabilization—of marriages and families. Topics in this book are presented from a variety of theoretical perspectives, including historical, cross-cultural, gendered, demographic, sociobiological, and social-psychological. The book provides a good variety of readings to help students understand the complexity of modern American marriages and families and the growing indeterminacy of their boundaries.

MARSHALL, CATHERINE, AND GRETCHEN B. ROSSMAN. 2006. *Designing Qualitative Research*, 4th ed. Thousand Oaks, CA: Sage. An excellent user-friendly guide for qualitative researchers that walks readers through the crafting of a research project from start to finish in a step-by-step fashion. It includes a number of vignettes from the educational fields studied by the authors and other researchers as well as discussions about ethics and distance-based research such as e-mail interviews and online discussion groups.

BUTTERFIELD JOHNSON, ALICE K., CYNTHIA J. ROCHA, AND WILLIAM H. BUTTERFIELD. 2010. *The Dynamics of Family Policy*. Chicago: Lyceum Books, Inc. The authors of this book outline the current state of family trends, the diversity of family forms in the United States, and underlying relationships to race, gender, class, and sexual orientation. They cover the effects of social problems and the policies designed to combat them in major areas such as welfare, food, and housing; work and employment; health care; the care and support of children; family violence; domestic partnerships and marriage; and aging. The book includes theoretical frameworks for conceptualizing poverty and outlines the policy practice roles that professionals play in developing, implementing, and monitoring family policy. The combination of real family histories and the analysis of government interventions included in this book are an added plus. This book is an excellent resource for offering students conceptual tools for analyzing family problems, policies, and consequences.

FILM

Kinsey. 2004. An excellent film biography of the life of Alfred Kinsey, the man who revolutionized our understanding of human sexuality. For years, Kinsey, an Indiana University professor and researcher, and his research assistants traveled across the country, interviewing and studying thousands of people about their sexual attitudes and behavior. According to this film portrayal, Kinsey was so consumed by statistical measurements of human sexual activity that he almost completely overlooked the substantial role of emotions and their effect on human behavior. This made him an ideal researcher and science celebrity whose scientific research revealed that sexual behaviors previously considered deviant and even harmful (homosexuality, oral sex, and so on) are in fact common and essentially normal in the realm of human experience, but whose obsession with the scientific method frequently placed him at odds with his research assistants as well as his understanding wife.

Bowling for Columbine. 2002. This documentary film—written, directed and narrated by activist filmmaker Michael Moore—explores the nature and causes for the Columbine High School massacre and other acts of violence in the United States. Moore seeks to explain why the Columbine massacre occurred and why the United States has a high violent crime rate (especially crimes involving guns). In search of the reason for what he calls the United States' trigger mania, Moore links the violence at Columbine and in the United States generally to the acceptance of institutionalized violence as a solution to conflict. He examines American bigotry and a culture of fear that he suggests has been created by the government and the media. According to Moore, this fear leads Americans to arm themselves, to gun making-companies' advantage. Moore also seeks to investigate and confront the powerful elite political and corporate interests fanning this culture for their own unscrupulous gain. This is a provocative film that can be a useful companion to the Debating Social Issues Box in this chapter.

LITERARY WORKS

GERRITSEN, TESS. 1996. *Harvest*. New York: Simon & Schuster. An interesting novel about an "organs for cash" ring, run by an elite cardiac transplant team of doctors operating out of a prestigious New England hospital. Although this novel does not pertain to sociological research specifically, it does raise a number of important ethical issues that researchers and other professionals responsible for the well-being of human research subjects must consider.

MCDERMOTT, ALICE. *Charming Billy*. 2009. New York: Picador. This novel chronicles the life of Billy Lynch, an alcoholic who was much loved, as his friends and family gather to mourn his death. After Billy was told that the one true love of his life had died, he spent the next 30 years mourning that loss and drinking. The stories of Billy's life and charm are told from the point of view of many different friends and relatives. The readers of this novel see the good, the bad, and the ugly of Billy's life through the eyes of those who loved him. Issues of love, the devastation of alcoholism, secrets, lies, loyalty, and the redeeming unity of family and friendship are explored. It is left up to the reader to decide right from wrong. Whether it was Billy's angst over losing Eva that caused his alcoholism or whether it was Billy's choice to drink too much are debated and ultimately left up to the reader to decide. Professors might use the telling of events from different points of view (the different perspectives of Billy life as seen through the eyes of his friends) as a springboard for discussions about how the theoretical perspectives discussed in this chapter can look at the same phenomena but do so from different points of view.

INTERNET

www.census.gov U.S. Census Bureau. An excellent resource for the latest statistical data on marriages and families. Pick a letter of the alphabet for a topic of interest to you (for example, fatherhood, motherhood, or parenting), and find the latest statistics on the topic.

www.NCFR.com National Council on Family Relations. The NCFR is the major scientific organization devoted to the study of marriages, families, intimate relationships, and children.

http://socserv.mcmaster.ca/w3virtsoclib/ WWW Virtual Library: Sociology. A comprehensive Web site that provides a myriad of links to particular areas of interest, including many sociology resources, research, and chat rooms that discuss marriage and family issues.

www.aecf.org The Annie E. Casey Foundation. This site features the Annie E. Casey Foundation's *Kids Count* data project. This project compiles data on children, the social conditions in which they live, and indicators of their well-being. Students may explore these data state-by-state.

Succeed with MyFamilyLab®
www.myfamilylab.com

Watch. Explore. Read. The New MyFamilyLab is designed just for you. Each chapter features a pre-test and post-test to help you learn and review key concepts and terms. Experience Marriages and Families in action with dynamic visual activities, videos, and readings to enhance your learning experience.

Here are a few activities you will find for this chapter.

Watch on **myfamilylab.com**

Video clips feature important concepts in the study of Marriages and Families. Watch:
- Qualitative vs. Quantitative Research

Explore on **myfamilylab.com**

Social Explorer is an interactive application that allows you to explore Census data through interactive maps. Explore the Social Explorer Activity:
- Patterns of Inequality Among Women

Read on **myfamilylab.com**

MyFamilyLab includes primary source readings from classic and contemporary sociologists from around the world. Read:
- Schuman, "Sense and Nonsense About Surveys"

Understanding Gender: Its Influence in Intimate Relationships

What Will You Learn?

- Define and understand the sociological meaning of key terms.
- Describe the myriad of ways in which gender role learning occurs.
- Apply the sociological imagination to analyze and to create media guidelines for children and adolescents.
- Assess the pro and con arguments for allowing women to serve in combat positions.
- Increase your awareness and understanding of gender roles in other cultures.
- Question the consequences of gender stereotyping.

IN THE NEWS

Bennington, VT

On February 26, 2011, in a crowded gym, Rachel Hale became the first girl in Vermont and the third girl in the nation ever to win a state wrestling championship while competing against boys. A week earlier, Joel Northrup forfeited a match to Cassy Herkelman in the Iowa state tournament because he refused to compete against her. In explaining his decision, Northrup, the son of a minister, said, "Wrestling is a combat sport and it can get violent at times. As a matter of conscience and my faith, I do not beleve that it is appropriate for a boy to engage a girl in this manner. It is unfortunate that I have been placed in a situation not seen in most high schools in Iowa" (Longman, 2011). After this story broke, an Internet survey asked, should girls be allowed to wrestle boys? Seventy-eight percent of respondents said no; 22 percent said yes (NBC Sports, 2011).

Although wrestling matches featuring women were known to have occurred in Sparta in ancient Greece, it was only in 2004 that women's freestyle wrestling became a medal event at the summer Olympics. According to the National Federation of State High School Associations, more than 6,000 girls competed in wrestling in 2009–2010 compared to 275,000 boys. Texas, California, Washington, Tennessee, and Hawaii have sanctioned gender-specific girls' wrestling. However, in the remaining states, if a female wants to compete in wrestling, she has to fight the boys ("Is High School. . .," 2011)

WHAT WOULD YOU DO?

If you were interested in wrestling as a sport, would you compete in gender-mixed matches? Explain. Do you think boys should be required to compete with girls in wrestling matches, or forfeit a match? Explain.

((•—[Listen to the **Chapter Audio** on **myfamilylab.com**

What are little girls made of?
Sugar and spice
And all that's nice,
That's what little girls are made of.
What are little boys made of?
Snips and snails
And puppy dogs' tails,
That's what little boys are made of.

Anonymous nursery rhyme

Who has not, at one time or another, smiled on hearing this nursery rhyme? On one level, we do not take it seriously, believing it just a cute and harmless caricature of girls and boys. Yet on another level, it suggests that there are differences between females and males and that both sexes must therefore be treated differently. On the basis of this belief system, society constructs an elaborate sex–gender system that has serious ramifications for every facet of our lives, as the experiences of Rachel Hale, Cassy Herkelman, and Joel Northrup so clearly revealed. This chapter explores the meaning of sex and gender, the process by which we acquire gender identity, and the role gender plays in marital and family relationships.

Distinguishing Sex and Gender Roles

If you were asked, "Who are you?" chances are you would reply by saying, "I am a male, female, Latina/o, African American, Asian American, Native American; or a student, parent, daughter, son, wife, husband, mother, father, friend." Such responses reflect the statuses we have and the roles we play in the social order. Sociologists use the term "role" to refer to a set of expected behaviors associated with a specific status, the position we hold in society. These positions, by and large, determine how we are defined and treated by others and provide us with an organizing framework for how we should relate to others. We are born into some of these statuses—for example, female, male, daughter, son, White, Black—and therefore have little control over them. These are called **ascribed statuses.** Others are **achieved statuses,** acquired by virtue of our own efforts. These include spouse, parent, referee, student, teacher. Every status, whether ascribed or achieved, carries with it a set of role expectations for how we are to behave.

Role expectations are defined and structured around the privileges and obligations the status is believed to possess. For example, our society has traditionally expected males, especially fathers, to be strong, independent, and good providers. In return, they expect to be admired, respected, and obeyed. Females, especially mothers, are expected to be nurturing, caring, and self-sacrificing. In return, they expect to be loved and provided for. Such shared role expectations serve an important function in society. By making our behavior fairly predictable, they make social order possible.

Role expectations can be dysfunctional as well, however. They can be defined so rigidly that behavior and expression are seriously curtailed, to the detriment of the individual and the society at large. For example, because U.S. society so often fails to encourage or support fathers as primary-care providers for their offspring, many father–child relationships remain emotionally distant. Rigid role definitions often lead to the development of stereotypes, in which certain qualities are assigned to an individual solely on the basis of her or his social category. **Gender role stereotypes** refer to the oversimplified expectations of what it means to be a woman or a man. Stereotyping is used to justify unequal treatment of members of a specific group. For example, until recently, women serving in the military were believed unfit for combat and thus were denied the opportunity for career mobility associated with combat experience. Although today's military offers more opportunities to women, a good number of people still question the appropriateness of their full participation (see the Debating Social Issues box). Similarly, in the past, men were not hired as flight attendants, telephone operators, or receptionists because these occupations were seen as feminine.

The status of being female or male in our society affects all aspects of our lives; thus, sociologists regard it as a **master,** or **key, status.** For this reason, it is important to understand the dynamics associated with gender status and to distinguish between the concepts of sex and gender.

Debating Social Issues

SHOULD WOMEN BE WARRIORS?

This question became a major issue with the introduction of the all-volunteer service in 1973 and the eventual demise of the separate female units in favor of integration into regular military units. Initially, women were barred from many positions, including combat. Over time, different branches of the military opened up more opportunities for women. For example, the Air Force began training women as pilots in 1976, as navigators in 1977, and as fighter pilots in 1993. Today, women constitute almost 15 percent of all active duty personnel.

In recent years, more than 200,000 women have been deployed to war zones serving as military police, medics, helicopter pilots, truck drivers, and gunners in military convoys; 132 of these women have been killed in Iraq and Afghanistan since 2001, and another 721 have been wounded (Harding, 2011). These deployments led some to believe that the Army was violating the 1994 Department of Defense's (DOD) regulations

exempting female soldiers from combat assignments and reignited the debate. Representative Duncan Hunter (R-CA), then chair of the House Armed Services Committee, sponsored an amendment to the 2006 Defense Authorization Bill that would have prohibited female soldiers from serving in smaller forward support companies that operate 100 percent of the time with land combat battalions such as the infantry. After congressional hearings at which top-level officers argued against this amendment, citing the potential loss of at least 21,000 combat support-related jobs, Duncan withdrew it in favor of a broader measure that strengthened reporting requirements on women in combat and on any changes that open or close positions to women.

Like Representative Duncan, people who oppose having women in combat positions believe that male soldiers would see them as a distraction and that their presence would lower a unit's morale. They further argue that woman's physical characteristics (shorter height, less muscle mass and weight than men) put them at a disadvantage when performing tasks requiring a high level of muscular strength and aerobic capacity. Additionally, they believe that it is not practical for women and men to serve together for long stretches at a time as women may get pregnant and then need to be evacuated. And, if captured, there is the added risk that women POWs may be sexually abused.

On the other hand, those who favor allowing women to serve in combat maintain that women who are properly trained have proven to be as capable as men. They point to the fact that mixed units in Panama in 1989, in the Persian Gulf conflict in 1991, and in Iraq and in Afghanistan in recent years performed as cohesive and effective teams when under fire. Moreover, serving in combat positions is the way to promotion and higher pay. Therefore, proponents argue, to exclude women from combat roles is discriminatory. The Military Leadership Diversity Commission comprised of senior military officers and civilians spent 18 months studying ethnic, gender, and cultural problems hindering career advancement in the military. "Being ineligible for the infantry may be perceived to make a female soldier 'less Army,'" the commission stressed, adding that research has not born out shibboleths that women are too weak for combat, can harm a unit's cohesion or be more prone to mental health disorder than men in combat ("The Reality...," 2011:A22). The Commission recommended to Congress and the President that the military should eliminate the ban in order to create a "level playing field for all qualified service members" (Harding, 2011).

What do you think? Do you favor or oppose allowing women to serve in combat positions? What advantages and disadvantages would such a policy have for women, men, and the society at large?

Sex refers to the biological aspects of a person—the physiological characteristics that differentiate females from males. These include external genitalia (vulva and penis), gonads (ovaries and testes), sex chromosomes, and hormones. These characteristics are the source of sex role differences—women menstruate, become pregnant, and lactate; men have erections and ejaculate seminal fluid. In contrast, **gender** refers to the socially learned behaviors, attitudes, and expectations associated with being female or male, what we call *femininity* and *masculinity*. Whereas a person's sex is biologically determined, gender behaviors and expectations are culturally constructed categories and, as such, change over time. Thus, gender is learned; we acquire gender through interacting with others and the social world (Wood, 1996). **Gender identity** is a person's awareness of being female or male. It sounds simple, doesn't it? We are either female/feminine or male/masculine, are we not? In fact, as we shall see, human development is not as simple as it first appears.

GENDER DIFFERENCES: THE NATURE–NURTURE DEBATE

Because chromosomes and hormones play a critical role in sex differentiation, it is logical to ask whether they also play a role in the physical, behavioral, and personality differences that have been observed between women and men. For example, women, on the average, live longer and score higher than men on tests of verbal ability. Men, on the average, are taller, heavier, more aggressive, and have better spatial skills than women. As Figure 3.1 shows, however, the differences within each sex are often greater than the differences between the two sexes. Thus, more variation in height occurs within a group of women (or men) than between the average female and the average male. This figure also shows that although most women are shorter than most men, some women are taller than some men. Most of the traits identified as masculine or feminine fit this pattern. According to psychologist Janet Hyde (2005), females and males are similar on most, but not all psychological variables; that is, girls and boys and women and men are more alike than different. She refers to this as the **gender similarities hypothesis.**

Despite the fact that an extensive body of research supports the conclusion that gender differences are few in number and relatively small in degree, how much of our development and behavior is biologically based (nature) and how much is culturally based (nurture) remains controversial. On the one hand, sociobiologists, such as Edward Wilson (1975), believe genetic inheritance is responsible for many forms of social behavior such as competition,

aggression, cooperation, and nurturance. Most social scientists, on the other hand, believe the sociobiological approach is too simplistic. For example, studies show that when females are rewarded for behaving aggressively or when they experience certain environmental stresses, they can become just as aggressive as males (Zuger, 1998). Similarly, researchers have found that differences in math and verbal ability based on sex do not manifest themselves much before adolescence and are not found in all societies (Harmatz and Novak, 1983; Fausto-Sterling, 1985). These latter findings suggest that the biological and the cultural are not mutually exclusive categories; rather, they are two essential parts of an interconnected system. Biologist Ruth Hubbard vividly describes the way that biology and environment work together to transform the organism so that it responds differently to other concurrent or subsequent biological or environmental influences.

> If a society puts half its children in dresses and skirts but warns them not to move in ways that reveal their underpants, while putting the other half in jeans and overalls and encouraging them to climb trees and play ball and other outdoor games; if later, during adolescence, the half that has worn trousers is exhorted to "eat like a growing boy," while the half in skirts is warned to watch its weight and not get fat; if the half in jeans trots around in sneakers or boots, while the half in skirts totters about on spike heels, then these two groups of people will be biologically as well as socially different. Their muscles will be different, as will their reflexes, posture, arms, legs, and feet, hand-eye coordination, spatial perception, and so on. . . . There is no way to sort out the biological and social components that produce these differences, therefore, no way to sort nature from nurture. (1990:115–16)

This interconnectedness between biology and culture can be seen by examining a few of the sex/gender variations that exist in the human population—intersexuality, transsexuals, and multiple genders. These variations are generally included under the umbrella term **transgender.** According to sociologist Sarah Wilcox, "transgender refers to the spectrum of gender ambiguity—the various ways in which our gendered behavior, activities, dress and identities do not match up neatly with the assumption that there are two biological categories-'male' and 'female" (quoted in Rankin, 2004).

SEX/GENDER VARIATIONS

Although for the most part, the endocrine and hormonal systems mature and correlate with each other, occasionally a developing fetus is exposed to feminizing or masculinizing hormones at inappropriate times. As a result, an estimated 2 percent of babies are born with anomalous or unusual features; at times, this makes it difficult to classify the infant as either female or male (Blackless et al., 2000). In the past, people with ambiguous genitalia were labeled *hermaphrodites;* scientists now refer to these individuals as **intersexed.** Although intersexuality occurs in every society, until recently it was standard medical practice in the United States to correct the ambiguity through sex reassignment using surgery and hormonal treatments. Although relatively few in number, these cases suggest that biological sex alone does not determine gender identity; the sex in which a child is reared also plays a crucial role, as can be seen in the case of a genetic male (chromosomally XY) who was born with a tiny penis (1 centimeter long) and a urinary

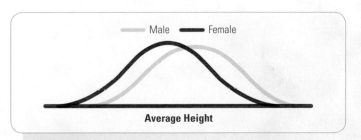

FIGURE 3.1 Overlapping Normal Curves

Male — Female

Average Height

opening similar to that of a genetic female. The child's sex was surgically reassigned. The parents changed the child's name and reared the child as a girl. By age 3, the child showed "feminine" interests, playing with dolls and other toys considered girls' toys.

However, the case of an 8-month-old twin boy whose penis was accidentally burned off during a routine repair surgery shows that sex reassignment does not always work in the person's best interest. The physicians recommended that the child be raised as a female on the assumption that healthy psychosexual development depends on the appearance of the genitals. Over time, with the parents' agreement, they constructed female genitals to replace the lost penis. However, Joan, as she was called, realized she was different and preferred her twin brother's clothing and toys. Despite hormonal treatments and attempts at female role modeling, Joan was convinced she was a boy. Finally, realizing the depth of "her" despair, Joan's father told his son the full story of his life. After a double mastectomy, the construction of a phallus, and male hormone treatments, John, as he was now referred to, felt he had his identity back. As an adult, he married a woman with young children, whom he eventually adopted (Diamond and Sigmundson, 1997). After John Colapinto (2000) chronicled the John/Joan story in his book, *As Nature Made Him,* other individuals with similar experiences came forward to tell their stories. Although some people reported satisfaction with their sex reassignment, many others, like John, rejected theirs. As a result of these reports, an increasing number of scientists and physicians now criticize the practice of infant sex reassignment for putting cultural factors above medical ones and for failing to accept the fluidity of sex and gender as a normal part of the human condition, as do many other societies (Kessler, 1996). Today, an increasing number of medical experts favor treatments centered more on psychological counseling rather than surgery for cases of intersexuality (Dreger, 1998; Fausto-Sterling, 2000). This approach came too late for David Reimer, the Joan/John subject of Colapinto's book. He committed suicide on May 4, 2004, at the age

of 38. According to Colapinto, David suffered bouts of depression related to his childhood experiences (Colapinto, 2004).

If you were born intersexed or with unusual genitalia, what treatment would you want to receive? Why? What do you see as the advantages and disadvantages of infant sex reassignment? What do you see as the advantages and disadvantages of psychological counseling? Who should make the decisions in these cases—medical personnel, parents, or the persons themselves when they are older? Explain.

Another variation in the sex/gender linkage occurs in the case of **transsexuals,** persons who believe they were born with the body of the wrong sex. These individuals cannot accept their assigned gender even though it is congruent with their biological sex. This dissonance between one's body and one's sexual identity is described as "gender dysphoria" or "gender identity disorder" (Kogan, 2004). Some of these individuals undergo surgery and take hormone treatments to achieve a body congruent with their own sense of gender identity. Englishwoman Laura Dillion (Michael) was the first person on record to undergo surgery (13 operations between 1946 and 1949) to change her gender. Michael became a doctor. After meeting Robert Cowell (Roberta), who sought him out for advice and help, Michael removed his testicles even though such surgery of a man who would otherwise be fit for military service was then illegal in Britain. Another surgeon constructed a vagina for Roberta (Kennedy, 2007). In 2011, Chaz Bono, born Chastity Bono to singer Cher and the late Sonny Bono, premiered a documentary, *Becoming Chaz,* about his female-to-male transition. Earlier, he told ABC News that his gender reassignment was "the best decision I've ever made" (Cuomo and Netter, 2009).

Chastity Bono (left image) underwent female to male gender transition between 2008 and 2010 and became Chaz Bono (right image). Chaz, a writer, actor, musician, and transgender activist, competed on *Dancing with the Stars* with Lacey Schwimmer in 2011.

To date, little is known about why transsexualism occurs, but evidence suggests that the majority of postoperative transsexuals who have been surveyed are happy with the results of their sex reassignment surgery and report that it had improved the quality of their lives (Lawrence, 2003). This does not mean, however, that everyone accepts these changes. Many transgendered people experience discrimination in housing, jobs, and in other social situations. Many of these discriminatory practices are becoming more visible and are being challenged across the globe. For example, in Nepal, a country that only recently decriminalized homosexual relationships, its Central Bureau of Statistics is giving official recognition to transgender people by counting a third gender. Thirty-five-year-old Dilu Buduja—who said, "I was born as a girl, but as I grew up I felt I was a boy. Today, I totally feel like a man"—is among those to be counted in the third-gender category ("Nepal May Be…," 2011).

Yet another variation of the sex/gender linkage occurs in societies with multiple genders. Most of us are accustomed to thinking of sex/gender as consisting of only two categories: female/feminine and male/masculine. Yet, as sociologists Claire Renzetti and Daniel Curran (1995: 71–72) point out, anthropologists have found evidence of multiple genders in other cultures. Certain Asian, South Pacific, and North American Indian societies recognized a third gender called the *berdache,* individuals who adopted the gender ascribed to members of the other sex.

Although both females and males could become berdaches, it was more common for men to do so. Generally, men who chose to become berdaches did so at puberty, as an alternative to becoming warriors. These individuals lived, worked, and dressed as members of the other sex and were frequently thought to possess supernatural power. In none of these societies were these individuals thought of as abnormal or deviant. Instead, these possibilities represent alternative ways for people to construct a gender identity. In other societies, like northern Albania and surrounding areas, where traditionally women had few rights, women were allowed to live as men if they took an oath of lifelong virginity (see the In Other Places box). In sum, all of the above variations illustrate the fluidity of gender.

Although the nature–nurture debate has been framed as an either–or proposition, these data suggest that differences between females and males develop out of a complex interaction of biological and cultural factors and take a variety of forms. Before examining **gender role socialization,** a process by which people acquire the gender roles that their culture defines as appropriate for them, let us look at the content of these gender roles.

In Other Places

"SWORN VIRGINS"

For centuries, the role of women in northern Albania, particularly in the remote mountainous areas, has been severely limited. Men held the positions of power and influence. Women could not vote or buy land, marriages were arranged, and male heirs were necessary to perpetuate the family name and fortunes. Thus, when a father died without sons or when a woman did not wish to marry the man chosen for her, she had only one option—to become a man. She could do this by taking an oath of lifelong celibacy. In exchange for this oath, she could cut her hair short, wear men's clothes, adopt men's mannerisms and customs, perform men's work, and become the protector and guardian of "his" family. Known as "sworn virgins," these biological women are accepted and treated as men for the rest of their lives (Young,

2000). The practice is not an issue of changing sexual identity as is the case with transsexuals; rather, it is a change in social roles. Without a male leader, a family is economically vulnerable. Therefore, allowing women to transform into men solved that problem. The practice of "sworn virgins" derives from the ancient traditional law of the Kanun of Lek Dukagjin, which said women belonged to their fathers until marriage when they became the property of their husbands.

According to Elvira Dones, an Albanian now living in Rockville, Maryland, who interviewed 12 "sworn virgins" from twentysomethings to elderly women for a documentary for Swiss television, only 30 to 40 sworn virgins remain in Albania with perhaps a few in the neighboring mountains of Kosovo, Serbia,

and Montenegro (Zumbrun, 2007). Life is becoming easier in Albania; more young people are moving from the mountains to cities, and modern ideas are filtering in to what were formerly isolated villages. As women are gaining more rights, there is less pressure and need for them to give up their womanhood to protect themselves and/or their families.

What do you think? Under similar circumstances, can you imagine becoming a "sworn virgin"? Explain. What do you see as the benefits and costs of such a practice? How does the existence of "sworn virgins" inform the nature–nurture argument regarding gender roles and gender relationships? What alternative ways could be employed to alter traditional gender roles that endanger the welfare of individuals and/or families?

Traditional Meanings of Femininity and Masculinity

In Chapter 2, we discussed the theory of structural functionalism and the Parsonian dichotomy of expressive (female) and instrumental (male) roles. The assignment of these roles is based on the assumption that females and males are fundamentally different from each other and that the content of these roles reflects the biological differences between the sexes. Beginning in the 1960s and continuing to the present day, a number of studies have found a broad consensus among different groups of people regarding the existence of different personality traits associated with each sex. For example, a Gallup poll in which adults were read a list of 10 personality traits and asked which were generally more true of women or men found that women were most often described as emotional, talkative, affectionate, patient, and creative. In contrast, aggressive, courageous, ambitious, and easygoing led the list of traits attributed to men (Newport, 2001). Women and men were in general agreement about the assignment of these traits but with the exception of only one trait—aggressive—women were more likely than men to say that all the traits apply to their gender. In all cases, only a minority of respondents said that the traits described both genders equally. However, 40 percent of the women and 40 percent of the men said that one trait—intelligence—described both genders equally. An analysis of data from 26 cultures found similar patterns in people's perceptions of gender traits (Costa, Jr., Terracciano, and McCrae, 2001).

In the United States, however, traditional views of femininity and masculinity have routinely been associated with White, middle-class heterosexuals. Although only a limited amount of research on gender beliefs across race and class lines is available, from this research it does appear that people perceive different gender traits in other groups. For example, as a group, African American women are perceived as strong, angry, and less deferential than White women (Halberstadr and Saitta, 1987; Anderson and Collins, 2007), whereas Black men are often thought of as more aggressive and emotional than White males (Collins, 2004). Latinas tend to be viewed as more submissive and dependent, hence more feminine, than White women (Vazquez-Nuttall, Romero-Garcia, and DeLeon, 1987; Anderson and Collins, 2007), whereas Latinos are seen as exhibiting machismo or extreme male dominance (Hondagneu-Sotelo, 1996; Ramos-Sanchez and Atkinson, 2009)). Similarly, Asian American women have been described as submissive (Ramos, 2009) and ultra feminine (Ligutom-Kimura, 1995) and as making desirable brides because "they are quiet rather than militant, and unassuming rather than assertive. In a word, non-threatening" (Lai, 1992:168).

Keep in mind that this type of research describes only the extent to which people possess an awareness of **gender stereotypes**—the overgeneralized beliefs about the characteristics associated with being female or male. It does not indicate whether or not they accept these stereotypes as true or, for that matter, whether or not the stereotypes are actually true. Nevertheless, gender stereotypes are widely shared within a society and become a part of the rationale for the different treatment accorded women and men. Critics point out that the acceptance of these images can be problematic. For example, Tamara Beauboeuf-Lafontant (2009) argues that the dominant image of the "strong Black woman" is a limiting rather than empowering construction of Black femininity in that it rewards women for a stoicism that draws attention away from the inequalities they face in their communities and the larger society. Stephanie Covington Armstrong's 2009 memoir tells the story of her struggle to overcome bulimia and her reluctance to reveal her eating disorder for fear of not living up to the Black female archetype.

TRADITIONAL GENDER ROLES: FEMALE AND MALE

Historically, the female gender role clustered around family relationships and was patterned after the belief that a woman's place is in the home. Based on this belief, women are expected to marry; have children; and be nurturing, emotional, caring, and attractive. They should not be aggressive, loud, competitive, or

People often experience stress and anxiety when they don't live up to the gender stereotypes for their sex.
Source: Tribune Media Services, Inc. All Rights Reserved. Reprinted with permission.

independent; rather, they should be passive, submissive, and dependent on their husbands. If women are employed, their work must not interfere with family obligations. To ensure that women can be homemakers, men are to be providers and protectors. Thus, they are expected to be achievement-oriented, competitive, strong, aggressive, logical, and independent. They should not be emotional, expressive, or weak, and must be in control at all times.

GENDER VARIATIONS: A CROSS-CULTURAL PERSPECTIVE

Anthropologist Margaret Mead (1935) was among the first to explore how concepts of masculinity and femininity vary across cultures. In studying three tribal groups, she found that both Mundugumor women and men behaved ruthlessly and aggressively, behaviors usually identified as "masculine." Among the Tchambuli, women were dominant and impersonal, whereas the men were more emotionally dependent—just the reverse of the patterns typically found in our culture. Arapesh women and men usually exhibited traits often described as "feminine"—caring, cooperative, and nonaggressive.

Similarly, other anthropologists have observed societies in which gender relations are not rigidly defined. For example, in Nepal, both women and men are expected to be nurturing, and both sexes provide care for children and the elderly (Wood, 1996). Shared child care is also characteristic of the Mbuti Pygmies of Zaire, a society in which both women and men hunt cooperatively. Among the Agta of the Philippines, both women and men hunt, fish, and gather vegetation (Estioko-Griffin, 1986). Tahitian women and men of the South Pacific are expected to be passive and cooperative (Gilmore, 1990). What are we to make of these findings? As Susan Basow points out:

Gender is not the only variable by which people are stereotyped. Each one of us is situated in sociological space at the intersection of numerous categories—for example, gender, race or ethnicity, class, sexual orientation, and able-bodiedness. These social categories interact with each other in complex ways. A woman who is White, working-class, lesbian, and differently abled will be viewed very differently from a Black, middle-class, heterosexual, able-bodied woman. (1992:4–5)

In sum, humankind is not composed of two homogeneous groupings—one feminine and one masculine. Rather, a rich diversity exists within each gender. To encompass this diversity, Harry Brod (1987), a pioneer in the field of men's studies, has suggested substituting the term *masculinities* for *masculinity*. The same argument could be made regarding the diverse forms of femininity. Although research has shown that Americans tend to adhere to a fairly consistent grouping of gender stereotypes, increasing evidence shows that some people are challenging these stereotypes and creating more flexible gender roles for themselves.

Gender Roles In Transition

Perhaps you find it difficult to identify with the traditional gender roles described in the previous section. Given the many changes that have occurred during your lifetime, that would not be surprising. Of special significance are key demographic changes:

- The majority of the population (51 percent) is now female.
- Both women and men are delaying marriage. The percentage of women who are married declined from 72 percent to 62 percent between 1970 and 2009; the comparable decline for men was from 84 percent to 66 percent.
- Women are having their first child at later ages and more women than in the past have never had a child. In 2008, about

In any historical period, some people are likely to reject their society's definitions of appropriate gender role behavior. During the Civil War, a number of women, eager to fight for a cause they believed in, disguised themselves as men to enlist in the Union and Confederate armies. One such soldier was Frances Clalin, pictured here in nineteenth-century female attire and in her cavalry uniform.

18 percent of women 40–44 has never had a child, almost double that in 1976 (10 percent).

- Younger women are now more likely than younger men to have a college or a master's degree. In 2008, women accounted for 59 percent of graduate school enrollment.
- The number of women and men in the labor force has nearly equalized in recent years (U.S. Department of Commerce, 2010).

These changes, along with the women's, men's, and gay liberation movements have challenged traditional gender roles. Thus, as we shall see throughout this book, there has been a definite shift from traditional to more egalitarian gender roles, at least ideologically if not always behaviorally in both the United States across most racial and ethnic groups as well as in many other countries (Inglehart and Norris, 2003; Bhalla, 2008; Pinto and Coltrane, 2008; Cowdery et al., 2009).

This shift in the United States is reflected in polling data. For the first time since Gallup asked the question, a majority of Americans (53 percent) say that women have equal job opportunities with men, up from 46 percent in 1976. However, men are more likely to believe that women have achieved equality of opportunity in the work force than are women (61 to 45 percent) (Jones, 2005). Although it is true that women have more economic opportunities than before, women, on average, still earn considerably less than men regardless of levels of education or experience (see Figure 3.2). Race and ethnicity disparities also continue to exist. Compared to the earnings of all men, of all race and ethnic groups, Black women earned 71 percent and Latinas earned 62 percent as much. White and Asian women earned 82 percent and 95 percent, respectively. Compared to their direct male counterparts, however, White women earned 79 percent as much as White men while Asian women earned 82 percent as much as Asian men. For Blacks and Latinas, the figures were 94 percent and 90 percent, respectively (U. S. Department of Commerce, 2010). At the current pace, equal pay won't be a reality until 2057 ("The Wage Gap…," 2007). Although the majority of adults believe women should have equal

work opportunities, that increased gender equity has enriched both sexes, and that there should be gender equality in the home, there is also a widespread belief, as we shall see later, that social and economic changes that altered traditional gender roles have made building successful marriages, raising children, and leading satisfying lives more challenging than in the past (Morin and Rosenfeld, 1998).

Some of these challenges are suggested by current attitudes about who should take primary responsibility for childrearing. One study found that although 41 percent of Americans believe it is ideal for one parent to stay at home solely to raise the children, with men slightly more supportive of that position than women (45 to 38 percent), 55 percent of those respondents feel it does not make any difference which parent stays home. Nevertheless, another 43 percent prefer that mothers stay home while only 1 percent prefer that fathers should stay home. Still, this is a noticeable shift from 1991, when 63 percent of the public believed that the mother should stay home to raise the children (Robison, 2002). However, when asked if you were free to do either, would you prefer to have a job outside the home, or would you prefer to stay at home and take care of the house and family, 58 percent of Americans, both women and men, would prefer to have a job outside the home. Only 37 percent would rather do what is often considered traditional homemaking. More men than women (68 percent to 50 percent) would prefer to have a job outside the home; however, nearly one in three men, up from one in four in 2001, now say they would prefer to stay home (Saad, 2007).

In sum, today many women around the world have considerably more options in the workplace and exercise more control over their private lives. Men, too, are experiencing changes in their roles. For many men, this means deemphasizing their work role and emphasizing their family role. Overall, both women and men

Explore the **Concept**
*Social Explorer Activity:
Income Inequality by Gender*
on **myfamilylab.com**

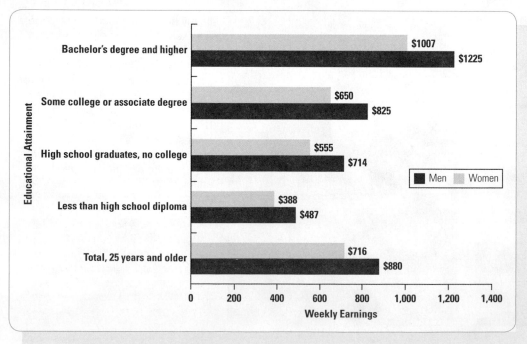

FIGURE 3.2 Earnings by Educational Attainment (Median Weekly Earnings of Full-Time Workers Age 25 and Older by Sex, First Quarter 2011)

Source: Adapted from Bureau of Labor Statistics. 2011. "Usual Weekly Earnings of Wage and Salary Workers, First Quarter 2011". (April 19), Table 5. www.bls.gov/news .release/pdf/wkyeng.pdf (2011, June 14).

feel freer to express a much wider range of personality traits than the traditional gender roles would allow. Because changes in women's roles have been more open to public view than those in men's roles, we are more likely to be aware of assertive and strong women than of gentle and nurturing men. One noticeable exception to this is in the area of familial caregiving situations. Family caregiving is no longer predominantly a woman's issue. Men now make up 34 percent of the family caregiving population (National Alliance for Caregiving, 2009).

Nevertheless, considerable controversy about these changes remains. Not all people are happy with their direction. Some find them confusing, and others prefer a return to a more traditional world. A 24-year-old medical student finds that some men feel threatened by changes in gender roles. "Jim and I dated in college. I thought he was a liberated male, but I found out differently when he took me to meet some of his friends. On the way, he told me not to tell them I was going to be a doctor. He said he didn't want them to think his girlfriend was smarter than he was." A young truck driver complained, "My girlfriend drives me crazy at times. She wants to be paid the same as a man and to have every opportunity a man does. But she still wants to be treated like a woman. She doesn't believe women should be drafted, and if I don't open the door for her or help her with her coat, she gets upset."

Although many people support the movement toward gender equality in theory, they have trouble implementing the idea in their everyday lives. Several factors combine to make change difficult. First, people who hold privileged positions have a vested interest in keeping them. Thus, some men may resist sharing power and authority with women at work and at home, whereas some women may resist sharing with men the aspects they most enjoy about the traditional role, such as nurturing children. Second, existing social arrangements tend to reinforce traditional gender roles. To take just one example, on average, women are still paid less than men. Thus, even if a couple should prefer an arrangement in which the husband is the primary parent and the wife the primary breadwinner, simple household economics might make this impossible. Third, political conflicts and change in some countries undermine the movement for gender equality. For example, according to the United Nations Children's Fund (2006), violence in Iraq is eroding women's rights. Only 14 percent of Iraqi women between ages 16 and 60 are currently employed compared with 68 percent of men. Girls make up 74 percent of the 600,000 school-aged children unable to attend school because of violence and repression.

Finally, as we will see in the next section, gender identities develop early in life, and much of what we learn from parents and other role models is still based on traditional gender norms. Although many women and men manage to challenge these norms successfully, gender socialization remains a powerful force in shaping gender identity. As family therapist Joan Zientek points out in the Strengthening Marriages and Families box, gender issues are often deeply embedded in the problems that families experience. When this occurs, family members must recognize and resolve those gender issues if the family is to function effectively.

STRENGTHENING MARRIAGES AND FAMILIES

TALKS WITH FAMILY THERAPIST JOAN ZIENTEK

Resolving Gender Issues

Do Gender Issues Affect Family Functioning? Indeed, they do. During the span of the twentieth century, our American culture, owing to evolving technology and a growing economy, has moved up Maslow's hierarchy of needs. Emphasis has shifted from physical survival to self-actualization. These changes have brought about economic independence for women, the necessity for many of a dual family income, and the lengthening of the work week for both women and men. These changes have had an extraordinary effect on gender roles in the family. Although there have been some gains in sharing household tasks and child care, the primary responsibility still falls on the shoulders of women even if they work outside the home. Now because of the unstable economic situation of the past several years, many men have lost their jobs, forcing them not only to learn new skills

as they take on the "Mr. Mom" role, but also to come to terms with not being the main provider for their family. In those families where the mom stays at home, when dad returns at the end of the day tired from the stress of the workday and mother is exhausted from the endless demands of clinging toddlers, tensions over household chores and child care can be intense.

In addition, women are no longer compelled to stay in unsatisfying or violent marriages. Economic independence can be a great bargaining chip when negotiating a more equal distribution of family tasks, thus forcing men to step up to the plate to take more responsibility.

One of the most salient gender issues occurs around the expression of affect in the relationship. The work of psychologist William Pollack suggests that by age 5, boys, unlike their female counterparts, have learned to mask their feelings and have come to view feelings as internal states rather than as a

dynamic that exists between people. Later in life, this pattern sets up a dynamic game of pursuit and withdrawal between a couple. In a stereotypical fashion, the woman pursues the man and demands that he speak and reveal his inner life. The man, who many times does not have a clue as to how he should respond, withdraws and the game is set in motion, leaving both parties feeling isolated and dissatisfied.

Further, parents may become concerned about their son's behavior if the exhibited behavior tends to fall on what society considers the feminine side of the behavior continuum. While we as a culture may be less homophobic, many still struggle to determine if a boy's desire to wear a dress or polish his nails is just child's play or a sign that he may be gay. (This debate came to the forefront when J. Crew ran an ad showing one of their designers spending time with her son by

(continued on next page)

(continued from previous page)

painting his toenails pink). On the other hand, if daughters act too "tomboyish" or too "sexy," anxiety and arguments between parents about how the child should be raised can also ensue, but perhaps not as intensely. These issues can be of more concern if these behaviors persist through the teen years. Fears of having raised a gay or lesbian child can dash the parents' ideals how life should be along with their hopes of being grandparents—at least in the way they expected.

How Can Family Therapy Help People in Such Situations? Some issues can be resolved merely through an educational process. The work of Yale psychologist Peter Salovey on emotional intelligence coupled with the emerging neurobiological research have given us a new paradigm for helping couples manage conflict. Couples can be taught to prevent the limbic brain's "emotional hijacking" of rational thought. They can learn how to identify and shift brain-mediated emotional states, thus activating changes that pull them to greater intimacy.

The more difficult dynamic to change is the one in which couples are polarized relative to an issue. In this case, each party needs to identify their part in keeping the polarization alive and make the needed changes in their behavior instead of waiting for the other to change. At other times, work has to be done to help the couple create appropriate boundaries between the generations without alienating extended family members. Other issues may necessitate changing expectations, setting priorities, and/or negotiating commitments regarding the household division of labor. Marital problems that stem from unresolved issues from childhood are more difficult to resolve. For example, a man who has been raised by a controlling father may exhibit controlling behavior toward his wife. The family therapist helps the individual or couple navigate back and forth through the generations, looking both at unresolved issues from their family of origin as well as current dysfunctional marital patterns.

Theories of Gender Role Socialization

Although socialization is a lifelong process, it is especially significant in our formative years. Social scientists have developed several theories to explain the socialization process with respect to the acquisition of gender roles.

SOCIAL-LEARNING THEORY

The perspective known as social-learning theory has its roots in behaviorism, the theory that human behavior is the result of a reaction to objective stimuli or situations. **Social-learning theory** asserts that gender roles and gender identity are learned directly through a system of positive reinforcement (rewards) and negative reinforcement (punishments) and indirectly through observation

One of the ways children learn what is expected of them as they grow up is through imitating adults, as this young boy is doing.

and **modeling,** learning through imitation (Bandura and Walters, 1963). In direct learning, for example, parents reward their daughters with encouragement and approval for engaging in gender-appropriate behavior such as playing with dolls and dressing up in mother's jewelry and high heels. If boys engage in this same behavior, however, they are punished and told, "Boys don't act that way." A girl can be a "tomboy," but a boy who engages in cross-gender behavior risks being labeled a "sissy." Sociologist David Lynn (1966) suggests that this harsher treatment of boys for acting "girl-like" leads boys to develop a dislike and contempt for females and femininity, which may explain their later hostility toward females (see Chapter 11).

Social-learning theory maintains that behavior that is regularly followed by a reward is more likely to be repeated, whereas behavior that brings forth punishment is more likely to be discontinued. Thus, children quickly develop an awareness that females and males are different and that separate gender roles are appropriate for each sex.

Children also learn which behaviors are appropriate for their gender by observing and imitating their parents and other adults, their peers, and media personalities. Social-learning theorists believe children initially model themselves after those who are readily available and perceived as powerful (who control rewards and punishment), warm and friendly (nurturing), and similar to the self (same sex). For example, a longitudinal study of 5,000 preschoolers found that girls with older sisters and boys with older brothers were more sex-typed than children with other sex siblings. Clearly, same-sex older siblings exert significant influence on gender-role development of younger sisters and brothers (Rust, et al., 2000). However, social-learning theorists do not accept the notion that behavior is fixed according to early learning patterns. Rather, they believe behavior and attitudes change as situations and expectations in the social environment change. As children grow older, the range of role models expands, and the work of crafting a gender identity continues.

Although a considerable amount of research supports social-learning theory, it alone cannot fully explain gender role acquisition. For one, modeling is more complex than the theory suggests.

Children do not always model themselves after same-sex individuals. In addition, subcultural differences as well as differences in family structures may affect the variety and choice of available role models. Moreover, learning theory treats children as passive learners. In reality, parent–child interaction is two-directional, in that a child's behavior may have a significant influence on parental behavior as well.

COGNITIVE-DEVELOPMENT THEORY

Fundamental to **cognitive-development theory** is the belief that the child's mind matures through interaction with the surrounding environment. In contrast to social-learning theory, cognitive-development theory asserts that children take an active role in organizing their world. They manage this by creating schemas, or mental categories, that emerge through interaction with their social environment. Subsequently, as new information is encountered, it is processed and assimilated into these categories, or the categories are adjusted to fit the new information. Psychologist Lawrence Kohlberg (1966) adapted cognitive-development theory to explain the emergence of children's gender identities. Early on (about age 2 to 3) children become aware that two sexes exist; they can identify and label themselves and others as girls or boys. This labeling process, however, is based not on anatomical differences but on superficial characteristics such as clothes—girls wear dresses and pastel colors, whereas boys wear pants and bold colors. According to Kohlberg, at this stage children have not yet developed gender identity. This does not develop until children are 6 or 7 and have the mental ability to grasp the concept of constancy or permanency. Prior to this time, they are too young to realize that all people can be so classified and that sex is a permanent characteristic that cannot be changed simply by changing clothes or hairstyles.

Cognitive-development theory maintains that once gender identity is developed, children are able to organize their behavior around it. That is, they strive to behave in a way consistent with their own sex, and they attach value to their behavior. Children come to view gender-appropriate behavior in a positive manner and gender-inappropriate behavior as negative behavior that should be avoided.

A considerable body of research gives support to cognitive-development theory. Early research found evidence that children become more accurate at gender differentiation and labeling as they get older (Coker, 1984). More recent research found that higher male-typical behavior in early childhood is associated with higher physical activity in early adolescence, particularly in boys (Mattocks, et al., 2010). In addition, cognitive-development theory helps explain children's, especially boys', strong preferences for sex-typed toys and for playing with same-sex peers (Zuckerman and Sayre, 1982) as well as the finding that both genders value same-gender traits significantly more than other-gender traits (Robnett and Susskind, 2010).

The most serious criticism of cognitive-development theory is that it overemphasizes gender learning as something children do themselves and minimizes the role culture plays in gender socialization. Hence, as psychologist Sandra Bem (1983:609) writes, "The typical American child cannot help observing, for example, that what parents, teachers, and peers consider to be appropriate behavior varies as a function of sex; that toys, clothing, occupations, hobbies, the domestic division of labor—even pronouns—all vary as a function of sex." In a later work, Bem (1993) criticizes cognitive-development theory for minimizing the role of culture in gender role socialization and offers an alternative theory, the enculturated-lens theory, to explain gender role acquisition.

ENCULTURATED-LENS THEORY

In her **enculturated-lens theory** of gender role acquisition, Bem argues that hidden cultural assumptions about how societal members should look, behave, and feel are so deeply embedded in social institutions and cultural discourse and hence, individual psyches, that these behaviors and ways of thinking are systematically reproduced from one generation to the next. Although every culture contains a wide array of such assumptions, or *lenses*, as Bem calls them, her analysis focuses on three gender lenses: (1) *gender polarization,* whereby females and males are perceived as fundamentally different from each other—these differences, in turn, constitute a central organizing principle for social interaction; (2) *androcentrism*, which encompasses the beliefs that males are superior to females and that males and male experiences are the normative standard against which women should be judged; and (3) *biological essentialism,* which views the first two as natural and inevitable results of the inherent biological differences between females and males.

Bem argues that gender acquisition is a special case of socialization, or what she calls *enculturation*. Accordingly, individuals are constantly receiving *metamessages,* lessons about what is valued and important in their culture. For example, a metamessage about gender is sent when children observe only mothers doing household tasks. As we will see in the next section, from birth on, children quickly learn these social constructions and come to see them as natural—unaware that other constructions are possible. However, Bem does not consider individuals passive in this process. Rather, she sees them as active, pattern-seeking individuals who evaluate themselves in response to these patterns and decide whether or not to conform to them.

Much of the empirical testing of this theory involves the study of parent–child play and children's formation of gender schema (Lindsey, Cremeens, and Caldera, 2010; Grusee and Davidov, 2007; and McHale, Crouter, and Whiteman, 2003) as well as of children's gender stereoypes. For example, researchers have found that younger children are more likely than adolescents to hold more rigid views of gender roles (Signorella and Frieze, 2008). Although some social scientists remain skeptical of the gender schema theory, an examination of the various **agents of socialization**—individuals, groups, and organizations that help form an individual's attitudes, behaviors, and self-concept—provides us with insight into the content of gender messages and how they are communicated in our society.

Agents of Socialization

Gender role socialization begins at birth and continues throughout an individual's lifetime. In our interaction with parents, teachers, and peers and through books, television, and movies, we are constantly taught values, attitudes, and behaviors that our culture sees as appropriate for each sex.

PARENTS

Parents provide children with their first exposure to gender learning and play a key role in helping children develop a sense of themselves as females and males. An extensive body of research indicates that parents think of and treat their daughters and sons differently, even though they frequently are not aware of doing so. This process begins early. Researchers have found that parents' gender influences the types of interaction they have with their children, particularly with infants. For example, across cultures, fathers spend less time with their infants (Parke, 2002). Although mothers spend more time with infants and young children than do fathers, they talk more to daughters and hug them more often. Mothers allow sons to move more more freely and independently than daughters (Clearfield and Nelson, 2006). Other researchers comparing mother's and father's behavior during different caregiving and play situations found both parents behaved similarly in caregiving situations regardless of their child's gender; however, gender differences emerged during play situations. Fathers modeled higher levels of instrumental and assertive behavior, whereas mothers modeled higher levels of facilitative or cooperative behavior (Lindsy, Cremeen, and Caldera, 2010). Similar behavior was observed in other studies of parent–child play interactions. Fathers tend to engage in more rough-and-tumble play whereas mothers tend to be more containing and rhythmic in their behavior (Scher and Sharabany, 2005; Parke, 2002). Fathers also play more interactive games with young sons, promoting visual, fine-motor, and locomotor exploration with them, whereas they have more verbal interaction with daughters and appear to encourage closer physical proximity with them. The consequence of this differential play activity may be that boys learn to be more independent and aggressive than girls (Lindsey, Cremeen, And Caldera, 2010). In fact, traits of dependence and helplessness may be encouraged in girls as a result of parents acting on the belief that daughters need more help than sons (Burns, Mitchell, and Obradovich, 1989).

Not only do parents play differently with their children, they also communicate differently with them. Stories told to daughters tend to contain more emotion words than stories told to sons. By the time they are 6, girls typically use more specialized emotion words and explanations than boys (Tenenbaum, Ford, and Alkhedairy, 2010; Fischer, 2000). Such findings may help explain the difficulty some men experience in expressing their feelings in intimate relationships. Researchers have found that mothers tend to speak to sons more explicitly, ask them more questions, and use more action verbs in conversing with them than they do with daughters. Thus, sons seem to receive more of the kind of verbal stimulation associated with reasoning skills (Weitzman, Birns, and Friend, 1985), whereas the interactions with daughters encourage the development of emotional sensitivity to people's feelings and expressions (Fivush, et al, 2003; Goleman, 1996). As children get older, these patterns are likely to continue. For example, a study of middle-class parents and their sixth- and eighth-grade children found that parents, especially fathers, used less scientific language with their daughters than with their sons, regardless of their childrens' interest in science or the grades they received. In general, parents assumed their sons were more interested in science than their daughters (Tenenbaum and Leaper, 2003). In an innovative study of family behavior in science museums, researchers found that both parents, but especially fathers, explained the content of interactive science exhibits three times more to sons than to daughters, while parents were twice as likely to explain the content of interactive music exhibits to daughters than to sons (Crowley, et al., 2001).

Other research shows that when parents give unsolicited help with math homework to girls, they may be communicating a gender stereotype that suggests that math is a male domain (Bhanot and Jovanovic, 2005). Similarly, researchers at the University of Michigan (2007) found that girls' interest in math decreases as their fathers' gender stereotypes increase, whereas boys' interest in math increases as their fathers' gender stereotypes increase. These findings may help to explain why, even though achievement tests and class performance show that girls have the same math ability as boys, girls tend to express less confidence than boys in their abilities.

Today more parents are aware of the limitations placed on children by the existence of gender stereotypes and are actively taking steps to try to lessen their impact. Some of these efforts are disconcerting to others and generate considerable controversy. A Toronto couple refused to tell people the gender of their newborn, allowing only their other two children and one friend to know. According to the parents, they believe their decision is giving their children the freedom to choose who they want to be, unconstrained by social norms about females and males (Poisson, 2011). Other parents, recognizing their toddlers and children's interest in unconventional gender behavior, are supporting them. For example, a father gave his son a sparkly princess Barbie doll and a mother allowed her 4-year-old daughter who likes to be called "Handsome Prince" to get a Mohawk hair cut. Because these efforts are not in the mainstream, parents often seek out like-minded playgroups, schools, and communities where they believe their children will be more accepted. Some enter family therapy and rely on children's books such as "My Princess Boy" and "10,000 Dresses" and adult books like *Gender Born, Gender Made: Raising Healthy Gender-Nonconforming Children* by Diane Ehrensaft (2011) for help (Hoffman, 2011b).

> How effective do you think these parental strategies are? What are the problems that these parents and their children are likely to face because of their unconventional approach? Should such efforts be encouraged and/or tolerated by others? Explain.

Children's Toys Have you ever noticed how parents decorate their children's rooms? Frequently, the decor reflects traditional gender stereotypes—florals and pastels for girls, animals and action figures in bold colors for boys. As infants grow into toddlers and young children, their rooms contain a marked difference in toys. Boys typically have a wide range of toys (educational, science, sports, tools, objects, large and small vehicles), many of which promote active and outdoor play, whereas girls' toys are less varied in type (dolls, stuffed animals, housekeeping objects, and crafts) and promote mainly indoor activities. These gender stereotypical toys and play also impact children's skill development.

Nerobiologist Lise Eliot (2009) in her book, *Pink Brain, Blue Brain: How Small Differences Grow into Troublesome Gaps and*

What We Can Do About It, argues that certain play activities and toys help to create neural pathways that magnify minute biological differences between girls and boys and lead to gender stereotypes. For example, encouraging boys to play with building blocks and science and sports equipment improves visual-spatial skills linked to math and science performance, whereas encouraging girls to read, color, and play with dolls develops skills more commonly defined as feminine (Francis, 2010, Eliot, 2009).

Although today's parents view more toys as gender-neutral than did their parents, seeing soccer balls and doctor kits as appropriate for both girls and boys, for instance, they still don't want their sons playing with Barbie dolls even though their daughters can play with action dolls like GI Joe. Fathers are more traditional than mothers in their enforcement of gender roles and hence are still more likely to give their children gender-specific toys and occupational costumes (Abrahamy et al., 2003; Kulik, 2002).

Toy companies and their advertising departments are well aware of consumer-gendered preferences and market their products accordingly. Recently, a group of Swedish sixth-graders analyzed a 2008 Christmas catalogue from Toys "R" Us and concluded that the portrayal of boys and girls reflected what they saw as outmoded gender constructions. A 13-year-old reacted to what she found, "Small girls in princess stuff…and here are boys dressed as super heroes. It's obvious that you get affected by this" (Hangum, 2009).

> Have you visited a toy store recently or shopped online for any children's toys? If so, did you find any evidence of gender stereotyping? Were there separate sections for girls' toys? Boys' toys? How were toys displayed? Packaged? Were there different colors used for different toys? What messages were used? Who was depicted on the box or product? How do your findings compare with those of the Swedish students? Can you make any generalizations about gender, marketing, and the packaging of toys today?

Computers and Video Games Studies in the last decade found that boys had more access to computers and the Internet in their homes and used them in more diverse ways than did girls. Even when girls had access to a home computer, male family members were likely to dominate its use (Gunn, 2003). A review of the literature on computer use found that although preschool girls and boys show equal interest in computer games, girls' interest and time investments in computer games declined significantly by their teen years, (Agosto, 2004). This trend was true of older students as well. A study of college students found that men were significantly more likely than women to play video games two or more hours a week and to indicate that video game playing interfered with sleeping and with class preparation. This difference affected interpersonal relationships. A greater proportion of women than men complained about the amount of time their significant other played video games (Ogletree and Drake, 2007).

More recent studies suggest these patterns may be changing. According to the Entertainment Software Association (2010), 40 percent of players on the biggest online games, like World of Warcraft and the Sims Online, are now female, up from 36 percent

in 2006. One of the explanations given for this upward trend is known as the "Lara Croft phenomenon," the introduction of a tough and competent female character in a dominant position in a number of video games (Jansz and Martis, 2007). However, major problems are still apparent in this industry that have implications for gender socialization. Many games still adhere to traditional gender stereotypes. Content analyses of how characters are portrayed in video games find that males are more likely to be heroes and main characters, have more abilities and power whereas females are more often supplemental characters, physically attractive, sexy, and wear more revealing clothing. (Miller and Summers, 2007). Accompanying the overrepresentation of males, Whites, and adults is a systematic underrepresentation of females, Latinos, Native Americans, children, and the elderly (Williams, et al, 2009).

This underrepresenation of women and people of color take on significance when we consider the way video games function in later life choices. According to Emma Westeott, a games research fellow at the Newport School of Art, Media and Design, "The lack of opportunity for identification through role models leads to self-censorship. Many young girls simply don't see gaming as being a feasible career choice" ("We Need More Women…," 2009). The same is true for people of color. The fact that women make up 40 percent of game players but only 11 percent of developers is indicative of this lack of representation. The problem is that young girls who like video games don't connect their leisure activity with a potential career path (Wong, 2010). Thus, relatively few women enroll in university games courses or computer science courses (Davison, 2010). This gender imbalance won't be corrected by simply helping girls develop greater spatial skills. Research shows that differences between women and men on some tasks that require spatial skills are largely eliminated after both groups play a video game for only a few hours. What is needed is game development that is more representative of who they are as girls and women and a message that lets girls know from a young age that there is a place for them in the computer and game industries.

> Are you a game player? If so, have you ever considered taking courses in game development or investigating what kind of careers exist in the industry? Who in your family plays video games? What have you noticed about the representation of the characters in the games you play? Are you satisfied with this representation? What, if anything, would you like to see changed in computer and video games?

Chores Earlier, we saw that toys tend to facilitate either inside or outside play activities. This distinction is also apparent in the chores assigned to children. Girls are expected to do inside work (wash dishes and clean the house), whereas boys are given activities outside the home (yard work and emptying the trash). Further, girls are assigned these chores at earlier ages than boys (Leaper, 2002). Because girls' chores are daily ones whereas a great deal of what boys do is sporadic, girls spend more time than boys doing chores. A nationwide study by the University of Michigan found that not only did boys spend an average 30 percent less time doing chores, they were 10 to 15 percentage points more likely than girls at various ages to receive money for doing these chores (Shellenbarger, 2006). A study in Britain found similar patterns. Nearly 33 percent of girls under 16 compared to 25 percent of boys that age were asked to do household chores, and the boys received 10 percent more pocket money than girls ("Gender Pay Gap..," 2009).

Patterns for a division of labor based on gender are formed early and, thus, it is not surprising that they often carry over into adult marital roles. A recent survey by the Bureau of Labor Statistics (2010b) found that on an average day, women not only did more household work compared to men (85 percent to 67 percent), but they spend more time on inside activities such as cleaning, laundry, and food preparation (51 percent to 20 percent). Men spent more time on outside activities such as lawn and garden care (12 percent to 7 percent).

In later chapters, we will see that class, race/ethnicity, and sexual orientation can affect the household division of labor. For example, middle- and upper-income parents are less likely to assign gender-linked chores than parents from lower-income backgrounds. The assignment of gender-linked chores occurs less frequently in African American homes, where both daughters and sons often are socialized toward independent and nurturing behaviors (Penha-Lopes, 2006; P. H. Collins, 1991; Lips, 1993).

LANGUAGE

There is growing agreement among social scientists that children's acquisition of gender identity and their perception of gender roles are strongly influenced by language. Research shows that the English language contains a number of gender biases. For example, the words *man* and *he* can be used to exclude females—"It's a man's world," "The best man for the job"—or they can be used generically to refer to both women and men, such as in *mankind*. In fact, the use of male terms frequently serves to exclude females. Think of the words *policeman, fireman, postman, chairman, spokesman, congressman, workman*. For example, when the masculine pronoun "he" is used, as it frequently is, in books to refer to doctors, lawyers, and public officials, readers tend to associate those roles with males (Gershaw, 1997; Hyde, 1984). Scientist Susan Niebur (2011) fears that when girls read about manned missions to the moon, manned spacecraft, or a man-made crater on a comet, they are not likely to imagine themselves in the role of one of those scientists and engineers. To counter this restrictive influence, many educators, writers, publishers, and government agencies, have moved to a more gender-neutral language, using *they, he or she, police officer, firefighter,* and *mail carrier.*

PEERS

The games children play and the people with whom they play also influence the acquisition of gender identity. Social scientists studying children's play activities found that as early as age 3, a process of same-sex preference begins and accelerates during the school years (McIntyre and Edwards, 2009). Psychologists Eleanor Maccoby and Carol Jacklin (1987) explain girls' same-sex preference as stemming from unrewarding mixed-sex play activities. Because boys play more roughly than girls and use physical assertion to resolve differences, they tend to dominate and bully girls in mixed-sex play groups. In contrast, girls enjoy more cooperation and mutuality in same-sex groups (Munroe and Romney, 2006)

Boys also prefer same-sex groups, but their motivation is different. Aware of men's higher status, boys attempt to disassociate themselves from girls and anything that suggests femininity (Whiting and Edwards, 1988). Thus, girls and boys grow up in different peer subcultures that reinforce both real and perceived gender differences. That such behavior exists and is reinforced by social approval is substantiated by a large body of research showing that from preschool to high school, children who engage in traditional gender role behavior are more socially acceptable to their peers than children who engage in nontraditional roles (Martin and Fabes, 2001). Peers may play an even more significant role in the lives of African American males. Distinct bodily movements, athletic prowess, sexual competence, and street smarts—including how to fight and defend oneself—are lessons learned in the context of the male African American peer group (Hale-Benson, 1986; Majors, 1995). Additionally, in a study of young African Americans, peer influence was the best predictor of high school completion (Guillory, 2007). Similarly, peer support was a major factor in African American male college achievement (Harper, 2006).

ORGANIZED SPORTS

Rarely has anyone questioned the physical, psychological, and social benefits that active play and organized sports contribute to boys' and men's lives. Only in the last decades, however, have researchers documented the enormous benefits of sport participation for girls and women: physical (lower risks of obesity, heart disease, and osteoporosis); psychological (higher self-esteem, better body image, enhanced sense of competence and control, reduced stress and depression); and academic (better grades, higher standardized test scores, and lower risk of dropping out) (President's Council on Physical Fitness and Sports, 1997; Zimmerman and Reavill, 1998). Since the passage of the Education Amendment Act

Amy Le Peilbet of the United States (6) battles with Shinoba Ohno of Japan (11) during the 2011 Women's World Cup final. Although a growing number of women are playing professional soccer, it remains a largely male-dominated sport.

of 1972 and its Title IX provision, more money went into athletic programs for girls and women. The results of this investment are readily seen in the growing number of professional women athletes like Serena and Venus Williams (tennis), Laila Ali (boxing), Annika Sorenstam (golf), Lisa Leslie (basketball), Jackie Joyner-Kersee (track and field), Zoe Cadman (jockey), and the numerous athletes in the Olympic Games. Nevertheless, the athletic playing field is far from level. A gender gap remains in the media coverage and dollars devoted to women's and men's sports. Top women tennis players earn 59 cents for every dollar earned by their male counterparts; the gap is even wider in golf where women earn only 36 cents for every dollar men earn (Women's Sports Foundation, 2004). And, although women make up 53 percent of the student body at Division I institutions, they get only 41 percent of the opportunities to play sports, 36 percent of overall operating budgets, and 32 percent of recruiting dollars. Women's sports opportunities at the high school level follow a similar pattern (National Association for Girls and Women in Sport, 2005).

Gender stereotypes and socialization experiences contribute to the gender gap in sports' participation rates. Boys and men may take more of an interest in sports to avoid the label of "sissy" and being viewed as unmanly. Some girls may avoid sports out of a fear of being thought unfeminine or labeled "lesbian."

Research has shown that playing with "masculine" (rather than "feminine") toys and games, playing in predominantly male or mixed-gender groups, and being considered a tomboy distinguished between women who later became college athletes and those who did not (Giuliano and Popp, 2000). In a similar vein, earlier research found that women in nontraditional occupations (for example, lawyers and physicians) were, as children, more likely to have played with boys and to have engaged in more competitive male activities than women in more traditional occupations (for example, teachers and librarians) (Coats and Overman, 1992). Thus, breaking down gender-prescribed play in early childhood would most likely lead to more widespread female participation in sport and physical activity, providing them not only myriad physical and psychological benefits but wider career choices as well. This seems to be the case for organized sports as well. Economist Betsey Stevenson (2010) found that increasing girls' high school sports participation led to increases in women's college attendance as well as greater female participation in previously male-dominated occupations, particularly in high-skill occupations.

TEACHERS AND SCHOOL ORGANIZATION

Teachers play a major role in the socialization of children. Over the last three decades, a great deal of research focused on how girls and boys are treated differently in our schools and how this impacts both genders. Studies at all educational levels found that teachers provided more assistance to and challenges for boys than for girls (Sadker and Sadker, 1994) and that males received more attention and tended to dominate the learning environment (Jones and Dindia, 2004; Lips, 1995). Other studies show that boys receive more praise for creative behavior, whereas girls receive more praise for conforming behavior (Grossman and Grossman, 1994). Girls are encouraged to be quiet and neat, whereas boys are rewarded for being boisterous and competitive (Orenstein, 1994). In fact, girls' misbehaviors are attributed to

character defects while boys' misbehaviors are viewed as boys asserting themselves (Reay, 2001).

Gender is not the only variable affecting student–teacher interaction. The race and class of the student may trigger different attitudes and behaviors on the part of teachers. Overall, Asian American students are often perceived as the best students who therefore need little help or encouragement (Chang and Sue, 2003; Basow, 1992). Similarly, Latinas, especially those experiencing language difficulties, are often ignored or seen as less competent than other students (Edl, Jones, and Estell, 2008; Orenstein, 1994). African American girls, compared with White girls, receive less in the way of teacher feedback and academic encouragement, and African American boys receive the most frequent teacher referrals to special education programs (Eiland, 2008; Mead, 2006). A study of teacher perceptions in a predominately racial/ethnic minority school in Texas found that Black teachers and White teachers had different perceptions of their low-income White students. The Black teachers typically saw the White students as middle class and good students, whereas the White teachers tended to view these same students as low income and unremarkable students (Morris, 2005).

The curricular materials used in the classroom often reinforce messages like these. Researchers Piper Purcell and Lara Stewart (1990), for instance, found many examples of gender stereotyping in children's readers. Although both sexes are depicted in a wider range of activities than had previously been the case, certain basic trends remain. Boys and men are featured more often than girls and women, and they tend to be portrayed in more active and powerful positions (Hamilton, et al, 2007; Evans, 2000; Sapiro, 1999). Another gender bias exists. An important male role, that of father, is underrepresented in comparison to the female role of mothers and when fathers are represented, they are portrayed as relatively stoic actors who take little part in the lives of their children (Anderson and Hamilton, 2005)

At the college level, there is growing concern that the percentage of male students is declining, and although females are now enrolled in greater numbers, researchers have found that gender-stereotypical behavior is still quite common in some areas. For example, in many classes, professors call on male students more often than female students, they interrupt female students more than male students, and they are more likely to refer to female students as "girls" or "gals" while referring to male students as "men." Female students are not always taken as seriously as male students, particularly in fields traditionally dominated by males, such as math, science, and information and computer technologies (ICT) (Sanders, 2005; Myers and Dugan, 1996). A 22-year-old female student complained of discriminatory treatment by a math professor: "There were only two other women in the advanced calculus class I was taking. The professor didn't want us there. He made jokes about women not being able to balance their checking accounts, and he always seemed surprised when one of us solved his math challenges. I was going to drop his course because he made me feel like a freak for liking math, but my advisor encouraged me to stay with it." Her experience is not unusual. Female retention in ICT courses is positively related to their professors' positive attitude to female students and negatively related to their professors' belief that female students are not well suited to these majors (Cohoon, 2001). Other research shows that teachers often stereotype computer science as a male domain (Huber and Schofield, 1998). Such attitudes likely contribute to the fact that young women underestimate their computer skills as compared to their male counterparts. Studies have found a gender gap in computer confidence with females rating their computer skills lower than their male counterparts (McCoy and Heafner, 2004). These patterns contribute to the fact that, as we will see in Chapter 10, women are significantly underrepresented in ICT occupations in the United States and in most countries around the world; this is a cause of concern among educators and public officials as well (Charles and Bradley, 2005).

These findings led to many curriculum and educational changes, and the results have been impressive—girls improved their grades, expressed higher educational and career goals, enrolled in advanced placement courses more often, and undertook more and varied leadership positions.

School Organization A major shift has occurred in the organizational structure of our public schools. In 1982, although 66 percent of all public school employees were women, men held the highest positions—76 percent of administrators and officials and 79 percent of principals were male, whereas 84 percent of elementary school teachers and 49 percent of secondary teachers were women (U.S. Census Bureau, 2005b). Although men occupied the highest administrative positions, in the elementary classroom boys had few male role models to emulate. This pattern is even more pronounced today. By 2008, women's share of public school employment had increased to 75 percent and they accounted for 53 percent of administrative and official positions and 55 percent of principals. Secondary school teaching is now the domain of women (61 percent female; 39 percent male), and the percentage of male elementary school teachers declined to 12 percent (U.S. Census Bureau, 2011e). Many researchers see this "feminization of schools" as detrimental to boys and argue that the lack of male teachers has a negative effect on male student behavior and achievement, especially among male students of lower income, single-parent families (Gamory, 2010). This attitude is not unique to the United States. Efforts are being made in Great Britain to recruit more male primary and nursery school teachers to redress the gender imbalance in its schools and to provide boys with male role models (BBC News, 2009, 2005). The teaching profession in Sweden is also female dominated, and research there shows a gender performance gap with girls outperforming boys in school. Research in these and other countries tested the hypothesis that having a same-sex teacher would improve student outcomes. To date, the results of these studies are mixed. Some researchers have found evidence that male role models improve the behavior and achievement of boys and that girls have better educational outcomes when taught by women (Marsh, Martin, and Cheng, 2008; Brichero and Thorton, 2007; Dee, 2006). However, other studies have failed to find this relationship (Driessen, 2007; Holmlund and Sund, 2005). A similar problem exists when we examine race. Some studies point to educational benefits for students with same-race teachers and others have found no relationships (Gamory, 2010; Dee, 2004). Thus, further research in understanding gender and racial dynamics in the classroom are necessary to develop policies and practices that would improve overall levels of educational achievement for all students regardless of class, race, or gender.

ARE BOYS IN CRISIS?

At the same time studies were pointing to girls' gains, researchers found that boys were experiencing a number of problems—they are more likely than girls to (1) fall behind grade level, (2) have poorer reading and writing skills, (3) be diagnosed with emotional and learning disorders, (4) use alcohol and drugs, and (5) be suspended. They are also less likely to go on to college. These patterns are especially evident for African American males (WHITE PAPER, 2011; National Assessment of Educational Progress, 2009; Kleinfeld and Reyes, 2007; Corbett, Hill, & St. Rose, 2008; Barnett and Rivers, 2006; Kimmel, 2001). These findings have led some observers to proclaim the "myth of girls in crisis" and to suggest that there is a "war against boys" going on (Sommers, 2000). Similarly, researchers in Great Britain have warned that schools inadvertently discriminated against boys by failing to improve their literacy skills at an early age and, thus, fueling an "anti-education culture" among boys which, in turn, is likely to contribute to unemployment in adulthood (Paton, 2007). These patterns have also been found in other countries in Western Europe and in Canada.

Geoffrey Canada (1998) sees the problem largely in cultural terms. He argues that existing cultural images of men often give boys mixed messages. For instance, strength is confused with violence; virility is confused with promiscuity; adventurousness is confused with recklessness; and intelligence is confused with arrogance, racism, and sexism. Adherents of this view argue that our institutions are not preparing boys to survive in a world in which traditional masculine strategies that rely on physical strength and dominance are becoming outmoded. For example, Richard Whitmire (2010) argues that the world has become more verbal but boys haven't. Whitmire believes that current institutional trends favor female students. Similarly, Barney Brawer, director of the boys' segment of the Harvard Project on Women's Psychology, Boys' Development, and the Culture of Manhood, believes that a crisis in masculinity is occurring because, while society has become clear about what it wants for girls, it has not for boys (Rosenfeld, 1998).

However, not all analysts share these views and see them as an oversimplification of what the statistics show. They argue that when race, ethnicity, and family income are examined, it turns out that a lot of boys are doing just fine. Thus, it seems, if there is a "war against boys" it is against inner-city and rural boys. On average, White, middle-class boys are not dropping out of school, avoiding college, or lacking in verbal skills (Watson, Kehler, and Martino, 2010; Barnett and Rivers, 2006). Further, in states where girls do well on tests, boys also do well, and states with low-test sores among boys tend to also have low-test scores among girls. Average test scores have risen or remained stable for both girls and boys in recent decades (Corbett, Hill, and St. Rose, 2008). Nevertheless, studies of 8th-grade achievement level shows that gaps have widened between lower- and higher-achieving subgroups of students. Overall, Asian American students outperformed all subgroups in reading and math at the proficient and advanced levels and achievement gaps at the advanced level widened for African American, Latino, and Native American students (Chudowsky and Chudowsky, 2011). Achievement gaps between students of different races and classes are greater than those for students of different genders (Mead, 2006). Nevertheless, there is cause for concern when any students—regardless of gender, race, ethnicity, or class—fail to do well in school. The answer to these problems is not to pit one group against another but to examine the causes of these problems and to develop meaningful ways of addressing them.

In 2005, Harvard University President Lawrence Summers ignited a firestorm when he suggested the possibility that biological differences or differences in personal choices between women and men could be more important than either early socialization or some form of gender discrimination in explaining why there are fewer women than men in math and science professions. Recall your early and later school experiences. Did girls or boys do better in math and science? Who took advanced math and science courses in your school? Do you agree or disagree with President Summers? How can this question be studied scientifically?

TABLE 3.1 Average Daily Media Use Among 8- to 18-year-olds

	2009	2004
TV Content	4:29	3:51
Music/Audio	2:31	1:44
Computer	1:29	1:02
Video Games	1:13	0:49
Print	0:38	0:43
Movies	0:25	0:25
Total Media Exposure	10:45	8:33
Multitasking Proportion	29%	26%
Total Media Use	7:38	6:21

Source: Adapted from Rideout, Foehr, and Roberts, 2010, p. 2.

THE MASS MEDIA

That the mass media play an important part in shaping the values, beliefs, and behaviors of modern societies is difficult to dispute. Table 3.1 shows us just how pervasive media use is among young people. In 2004, children ages 8 to 18 spent an average of 6½ hours a day with media—and managed to include more than 8 ½ hours of media content into that time by multitasking (using more than one medium at the same time). By 2009, they packed a total of 10 hours and 45 minutes of media content into a daily 7½ hours, an increase of almost 2¼ hours of media exposure per day over the last five years. The increase in media use is driven in large part by ready access to mobile devices like cell phones and iPods. Consider:

- More than 70 percent of these young people have a TV in their bedroom.
- Half (50 percent) have a console video game player in their room.
- Sixty-six percent have cell phones.
- Seventy-six percent have iPods and other MP3 players (Rideout, Foehr, and Robertzs, 2010).

Today, young people spend more time listening to music, playing games, and watching TV on their cell phones (49 minutes) than they spend talking on them (33 minutes). Black and Latino children watch more television than their White peers.

What gender messages do these children (and adults) get when they watch television? To answer this question, researchers employ a technique called **content analysis,** whereby they examine the actual content of programs. They do this by counting particular items within specific categories, such as the number of males and females featured in the program. As we shall see, most programming, from children's shows to prime time, casts its major characters in traditional roles.

Children's Shows Content analysis reveals that children's shows are predominantly oriented to the White male, featuring more than twice as many male as female roles. This discrepancy implies that boys are more significant than girls—an image reinforced by the way in which female and male characters are

portrayed. In an early study of commercial children's television programs, researcher Earle Barcus (1983) found that the sexes are presented in a biased and somewhat unrealistic way. Females were more likely found in minor roles with little responsibility for the outcome of the story and were rarely shown working outside the home. In contrast, male characters were depicted in a variety of occupations to which many boys realistically could aspire.

Many of these patterns were still evident 20 years later, but they took more subtle forms. For example, an analysis of 10 episodes of *Teletubbies* and *Barney & Friends* found that, although there was an equal number of female and male characters in each show who

Media use among children has increased dramatically in recent years. When studying, children are often distracted by a call or text message.

TABLE 3.2 Guest Appearances on Political Talk Shows by Network, November 2004–July 2005 and January 2011–March 2011

Network	2004–2005		2011	
	Total Guests	Number/(%) Women	Total Guests	Number/(%) Women
ABC	145	21 (14%)	74	15 (20%)
CBS	115	21 (18%)	41	8 (20%)
CNN	288	31 (11%)	59	6 (10 %)
FOX	93	11 (12%)	91	25 (26%)
NBC	146	23 (16%)	82	23 (28%)
Total	787	107 (14%)	347	77 (22%)

Source: Based on *Who's Talking Now? A Follow-up Analysis of Guest Appearances on the Sunday Morning Talk Shows.* 2005. New York: The White House Project, Appendix A; Sunday Morning Shows Monitor Archive, Women and Politics Institute, School of Public Affairs, American University, www.american.edu/spa/wpi/Sunday-Morning-Shows-Monitor-Archieve.cfm (2011, April 14).

often engaged in cooperative play, they still conformed to gender stereotypes. Female characters were followers a majority of the time and played feminine roles (cooking, cleaning, and caretaking) while the male characters were the leaders and engaged in traditional masculine roles and occupations (Powell and Abels, 2002). This is not to say there hasn't been any progress in portraying girls and boys in more egalitarian ways. The popular and highly acclaimed *Sesame Street* avoids traditional gender, race, ethnic, and class stereotypes. For example, Maria, a Latina, is handy with electronics and anything mechanical. Similarly, the *Electric Company*, aimed at older children, uses many elements of pop culture (music, technology, comedy, and real-life celebrities) to portray its characters in a wide variety of ways (The Community Board, 2010). Nevertheless, in a study of superheroes in children's cartoons, although few instances were found of traditional gender-role stereotyping, the analysis revealed a trend toward defining "superheroics" in strictly traditional masculine terms (Baker and Raney, 2007).

Prime-Time Television and Other Media The situation is not much different on prime-time television. Although there has been an increase in the number of female roles, as well as more programming that deals with issues of gender equality (Dow, 1996), much of prime-time television still adheres to gender stereotypes (Signorielli, 2001). Besides appearing more frequently and having most of the major roles, male characters are older, more mature, and more authoritative than female characters. An analysis of all Sunday political talk shows illustrates this pattern. As Table 3.2 reveals, in 2004–2005, women constituted only 14 percent of all guests, up from 11 percent in 2001. By the first three months of 2011, the percentage of women increased to 22 percent but well under their representation in the general population (51 percent). Women make only rare appearances as experts or leaders on shows that play an important role in shaping people's perceptions of authority and leadership figures. Thus, the public gets a skewed view of who has the knowledge and ability to address political issues. Further, many of the guests are politicians who are trying to connect with a constituency. By their

absence from such shows, women are at a disadvantage in terms of the opportunity to be viewed as leaders and candidates.

Analysis of other prime time programs and films reveal other gender differences. Besides being younger, female characters are typically thin, physically attractive, and scantily attired. One study analyzing 1,018 major television characters found that only 14 percent of females and 24 percent of males were overweight. These female characters were less likely to be considered attractive, to interact with romantic partners, or to display physical affection. Similarly, overweight male characters were less likely to interact with romantic partners and friends or to talk about dating (Greenberg, et al, 2003). An analysis of theatrically-released family films between 2006 and 2009 found similar patterns. Only 29.2 percent of all speaking characters were female, and those who made it to the screen were more likely than their male counterparts to be young, scantily clad, and attractive (Smith and Choueiti, 2010). Such findings may help explain reports of eating disorders in girls as young as 9. A survey of 6,728 adolescents in grades 5–12 found that almost half (45 percent) the girls and 20 percent of the boys reported that they had dieted at some point. Additionally, 13 percent of the girls and 7 percent of the boys reported disordered eating behaviors (Neumark-Sztainer and Hannan, 2000). This gender differential reflects patterns observed in adults as well. According to a recent Gallup poll, a majority of women (57 percent) worry about their weight, while only 39 percent of men do. Age is a factor for women but not for men. Sixty-two percent of younger women (18–49) compared to 51 percent of older women (those 50 and older say they worry about their weight all or some of the time). Among men, 40 percent of younger men and 38 percent of older men say they worry about this often (Carroll, 2005b).

For women in particular, weight is perceived as a crucial indicator of their social acceptability. Although this perception seems to hold across all racial and ethnic groups, social classes, and sexual orientations, African American women appear less obsessed than White women about how much they weigh and about dieting (Celio, Zabinski, and Wilfley, 2002; Levine and Smolak, 2002). The most likely explanation for this difference is that African Americans

For Better or For Worse®   by Lynn Johnston

TOO FAT?!! CANDACE, YOU COULD PUT **ON** WEIGHT AND **STILL** BE PERFECT!!

ARE YOU CRAZY?

MY WAIST IS NON-EXISTENT, MY ARMS ARE FLAB, MY BUTT IS ENORMOUS—WHEN I LOOK IN THE MIRROR, ALL I SEE IS THIS **BLIMP!**

I EAT TOO MUCH. I WISH I COULD THROW OUT EVERY FATTENING THING WE HAVE IN THE HOUSE!

MAYBE YOU SHOULD JUST THROW OUT YOUR MIRRORS!

© 1992 Lynn Johnston/Distributed by Universal Press Syndicate

By the time children are in their teens, they have internalized images of the ideal body form for their sex.

have less restrictive definitions of female beauty, including how much a woman weighs along with support for the cultural image of strong Black women. However, as Tamara Beauboeuf-Lafontant (2005) suggests, the stereotype of strong Black women might also lead to problems of obesity, with eating as a coping mechanism for having to care for others' needs while neglecting their own.

Although we cannot assume a direct cause-and-effect relationship between television images and behavior such as eating disorders, mounting evidence suggests that such a relationship does exist. In one study, for example, 15 percent of the girls and 8 percent of the boys reported that they had dieted or exercised to look like a TV character (Moore, 1995). Other studies of adolescent girls found that they frequently compare themselves to the thin-ideal images routinely provided in television and the print media. Many respondents in these studies reported that these comparisons led them to feel dissatisfied with their bodies, increased their desire to be thin, and, in some cases, motivated them to engage in eating disordered behaviors (Levine and Smolak, 2002; Thomsen, Weber, and Brown, 2001).

The public has long been aware of eating disorders in women, but it is only recently that attention has focused on boys and men. Increasingly, males are bombarded with media images of muscular, half-naked men and getting the message that muscles equal masculinity. Health officials are concerned that increasing numbers of adolescent and young adult males are suffering from muscle dysmorphia, an excessive preoccupation with body size and muscularity. However, because of this limited awareness, fewer treatment options are available for boys and men (Bernstein, 2007). This has led many males, not only athletes, to engage in strategies to increase muscles (McCabe and Ricciardelli, 2003), often risking their health through the use of body-altering steroids. Girls, too, in increasing numbers and some as young as 9, are using steroids. Like boys, some steroid use is to enhance their athletic performance, but for a significant number of others, the purpose is weight control (Johnson, 2005).

Gender role stereotyping is also evident in the content of programs and their television characters. Although there are some notable exceptions (The Good Wife, Harry's Law, and Grey's Anatomy), the vast majority of programs depict women in a limited range of roles—mostly in home or family situations, regardless of whether they are employed; male characters are more likely to enact work-related roles (Lauzen, Dozier, and Horan, 2008). When women characters are employed, their occupations are generally high-status ones, for example, lawyers, doctors, or business executives—a pattern not typical of the majority of working women. Thus, television distorts the reality of the working lives of most women and perhaps gives viewers an erroneous notion that gender barriers have disappeared. In contrast, male characters are shown as powerful individuals, interacting in a wide variety of settings. Just as in children's readers, males are depicted as the problem solvers, whereas females generally are characterized as needing male help in solving their problems. However, there is also a strong tendency to depict men as "macho"males, that is, exaggerating narrowly defined masculine qualities such as aggression. Men are often depicted as extremely violent and antisocial, especially in law and order dramas. At the same time, virtually every media studied provides evidence of the sexualization of girls and women. Women are shown in revealing clothing with bodily postures or facial expressions that imply sexual readiness (American Psychological Association, 2010). These images can be problematic for girls and women and boys and men as they struggle to develop a self-identity and satisfying interpersonal relationships.

Stereotyping in the mass media is not limited to gender. Although racial and ethnic groups are more visible in programming today than in the past, they continue to be underrepresented both on and off camera. This is especially true for Asian Americans, Latinas/os, and Native Americans. And, despite increased Latino visibility, their characters are more likely to hold low-status occupations than other groups, while Arab/Middle Eastern characters are more likely to be portrayed as criminals than members of other groups (Children Now, 2005; Coltrane and Messineo, 2000). Researchers found similar patterns in Canadian programming. Minorities made up 12 percent of characters—not far below their actual percentage in the national population, but they tended to be cast in secondary roles, low or unskilled occupations, and unstable domestic situations (Media Awareness Network, 2005). Because TV and other media are so ubiquitous, pediatricians recommend that parents exert more control over when and what their children watch (see the Applying the Sociological Imagination box).

RELIGION

Religion is another key agent of socialization. Not only is it a transmitter of core personal and societal values, but organized religion also plays a significant role in the development of gender role ideology for many of its adherents. This, in turn, affects many aspects of female/male relationships as well as family organization and functioning. The sacred writings of many of the major religions project traditional gender roles, with men having a dominant status compared to women. For example, the Qur'an states that "Men are in charge of woman because God has made one to excel over the other . . ." (quoted in Haddad, 1985, p. 294). Similarly, the Bible makes many references to male dominance such as "Wives, be subject to your husbands, as to the Lord. For the husband is the head of the wife as Christ is the head of the church . . ." (Eph. 5:22-23). A daily prayer for male Orthodox Jews includes the words "Blessed are thou, O Lord our God, King of the Universe that I was not born a woman." The literal reading and interpretation of these sacred writings are not embraced by all members of these faiths. Nevertheless, they do seem to have an impact on many adherents. An extensive body of research has found that people who belong to and participate in conservative denominations are typically more traditional in gender role orientation than those with weaker religious ties (Bartkowski and Read, 2003; Sherkat, 2000).

Spousal Roles and Division of Household Labor Most religious fundamentalist teaching calls on men to be heads of their families and for wives to be submissive. In general, this has implied that men should be the breadwinners and disciplinarians and women should stay at home to care for the children and their households. For example, Dough Phillips, a San Antonio evangelical minister, founded Vision Forum that promotes "biblical patriarchy." The group shares with more mainline Protestant groups, such as the Southern Baptist Covenant, the belief that wives should be subject to husbands but it goes further to encourage daughters to forgo a college education and employment in favor of early marriage and childbearing. This movement goes by the name of "Stay at Home Daughters" (McGalliard, 2010; Joyce, 2009).

In theologically conservative households, wives perform significantly higher levels of household labor than husbands (Wilcox and Gonsoulin, 2003). However, in-depth interviews with evangelical women and men across the country and across the denominational spectrum found a more nuanced view. Economic pressures have led many of these women into the workforce, with the result that father involvement in parenting and domestic chores has increased. Nevertheless, many of these spouses continue to believe in the concept of male headship but make their day-to-day decisions through a process of negotiation, mutual submission, and consensus. Sally Gallagher (2003) calls this mix of traditional beliefs and practical behaviors "symbolic headship" and "pragmatic egalitarianism." W. Bradford Wilcox (2004) refers to men involved in such relationships as *Soft Patriarchs*.

In sum, gender stereotypes are presented in various degrees by all the agents of socialization. Even when parents make efforts to treat their daughters and sons equally, other socializing forces may undermine those efforts. As we have seen, rarely are either women or men portrayed in terms of the rich diversity and complexity that constitutes the human condition. Thus, it is not surprising that many children develop a stereotypic gender schema in the process of acquiring their gender identity.

Consequences of Gender Stereotyping

That women and men are socialized differently has major consequences for individuals, families, and society at large. This is particularly true when existing social arrangements reinforce these differences, for example, institutionalized patterns of inequities in pay and job opportunities that disregard individual abilities. The scope of this book allows us to consider only a few of these consequences, so we will focus on career and lifestyle choices, mental health, female–male friendships, and patterns of communication.

CAREER AND LIFESTYLE CHOICES

Although women have made major advances in a wide range of fields, from construction work to executive business positions, this progress is still more the exception than the norm. Current gender expectations continue to limit women's and men's career and lifestyle choices. For instance, the choice of a single lifestyle by a growing number of women is still viewed as second best. Women who wish to combine career and family often must do so without much societal support. High-profile women who challenge the status quo are often suspected of undermining "family values." In 2001, when acting Governor Jane Swift of Massachusetts gave birth to twin girls and her husband became a stay-at-home dad, she was immediately criticized for putting her political ambitions ahead of her family. Male office holders, who become fathers, do not experience such pressures. Until relatively recently, women's options in the political sphere were severely limited.

Politics Table 3.3 on page 82 illustrates the slow rate with which the United States has integrated women into its political structures. Although women won the right to vote in 1920, in 2011, women hold only 17 percent of the 535 seats in the 112th Congress, 17 women serve in the Senate, and 72 women are in the House of Representatives. The United States fares poorly in comparison to other countries in the percentage of women serving in legislative bodies—nearly 42 percent in Nordic countries and 20 percent in European parliaments. The world average is 19 percent.

In 2008, for the first time in U.S. history, a woman, Senator Hillary Clinton, was a serious contender for becoming the presidential nominee of the Democratic party. This historic moment was not without controversy. Incidences of sexism and racism received considerable public discussion and debate during the presidential campaign. Prior to the 2008 election, polling data found 92 percent of adults said they would vote for an African American candidate; slightly fewer adults (86 percent) said they would vote for a woman candidate. However, only 59 percent of those adults thought the country was ready for an African American president, and only 58 percent believed the country was ready for a woman president (Newsweek poll, 2007). According to political scientist Matthew Streb and his colleagues (2007), the positive responses people give to controversial questions such as these may suffer from social desirability effects. People may give false answers so as not to be seen as violating social norms. Their research data shows that approximately 26 percent of the public is "angry or upset" about the prospect of a female president. Their finding seems to indicate that for a significant number of people, gender remains a critical social category for deciding the appropriateness of career and lifestyle choices.

Similarly, a recent survey by the Pew Research Center (2008) shows that on seven of eight leadership traits measured in the study, the public rates women either better than or equal to men. On only one trait, decisiveness, did men rate higher than women (44% to 33%). Nevertheless, only 6 percent of survey respondents say that overall women make better political leaders than men. About one-in-five (21 percent) say that men make better leaders. The good news is that the majority (69 percent) say women and men make equally good leaders. When asked what accounts for the slow movement toward gender parity in top political position, 51 percent of the respondents say many Americans simply aren't ready to elect a woman to high office and 38 percent say it is because women are discriminated against. Nevertheless, the election of Barack Obama as the 44th President of the United States indicates that race, as a barrier to the highest political office in the land, has been overcome. Time will tell whether the gender barrier will give way as well.

Religion and the Economy The political sphere is not the only institutional arena in which males dominate. An examination of our religious and economic institutions reveals that gender stereotypes also constrain opportunities and choice for both women and men. In both institutions, women experience a glass ceiling that denies them important leadership positions, whereas men are expected not only to hold these positions but to desire them. Not all men can or want to achieve "success" as defined by having a meaningful career or a high-paying job. Yet they are pressured to assume the role of the major breadwinner in the family, and, as a result, they may experience a serious conflict between their work and family roles.

As Figure 3.3 shows, women outnumber men as participants in religious communities, but they remain a minority not only in leadership positions but in the clergy as a whole. According to an Internet report by CBS News, only 25 percent of pastors in the United Church of Christ are female. Less than 20 percent of clergy in other major denominations are women (19 percent of Presbyterians, 15 percent of Methodists, 12 percent Episcopalians, 11 percent of Lutherans, and fewer than 5 percent among Southern Baptists (Ford-Mitchell. 2008)). The Unitarian Universalists is the only denomination to have a majority of women leaders (53 percent) (Paulson, 2007).The Roman Catholic Church as well

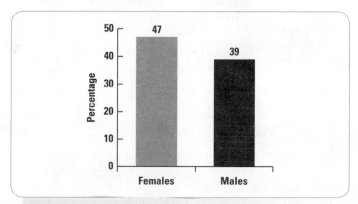

FIGURE 3.3 Average Adult Attendance in U.S. Churches by Sex

Source: "Where Are All the Men?" *Church for Men.* http://www.churchformen.com/allmen.php (2008, March 20). Reprinted with permission of David Murrow.

TABLE 3.3 Firsts for Women in U. S. Politics

Year	Achievement	Year	Achievement
1866	Elizabeth Cady Stanton (NY) was the first woman to run for the U. S. House of Representatives, even though she was not eligible to vote. She received 24 out of the 12,000 votes cast.	1972	Congresswoman Shirley Chisholm ran for president in the Democratic primaries.
1872	Victoria Woodhull, a stockbroker and publisher, ran for president of the United States on the Equal Rights Party ticket.	1981	Sandra Day O'Connor was appointed to the U.S. Supreme Court by President Ronald Reagan.
1887	Susanna Salter was elected mayor of Argonia, Kansas, the first woman mayor in the country.	1984	Congresswoman Geraldine Ferraro (D-NY) was selected by Democratic Presidential nominee Walter Mondale as his vice-presidential running mate.
1896	Martha Hughes Cannon was elected to the Utah State Senate, becoming the first woman state senator.	1989	Ileana Ros-Lehtinen, a Florida Republican, became the first Hispanic woman and first Cuban American to be elected to Congress.
1900	Frances Warren of Wyoming became the first woman delegate to a Republican National Convention; Elizabeth Cohen of Utah was chosen as an alternate to the Democratic National Convention and became the first woman delegate when another delegate became ill.	1993	Janet Reno became the first woman to serve as U.S. Attorney General.
		1997	Madeleine K. Albright became the first woman to serve as U.S. Secretary of State.
1917	Jeannette Rankin, a Montana Republican, became the first women elected to the U.S. House of Representatives.	2001	Elaine Chao became the first Asian American woman to serve in a presidential cabinet when she was appointed Secretary of Labor by President George Bush.
1920	After 72 years of struggle, the 19th Amendment to the Constitution was ratified, giving women the right to vote.	2002	Representative Nancy Pelosi (D-CA) became the first woman to head her party in Congress when she was elected House Democratic Leader. In 2007, she became the first woman to serve as Speaker of the House.
1925	Nellie Taylor Ross, a Wyoming Democrat, became the nation's first woman governor, elected to replace her deceased husband.		
1933	President Franklin D. Roosevelt appointed Frances Perkins as Secretary of Labor, the first woman to serve in a presidential cabinet.	2005	Dr. Condoleezza Rice became the first Republican woman and the first African American woman to serve as United States Secretary of State.
1963	Justice Lorna Lockwood became the first woman to serve as Chief Justice of a state supreme court.	2008	Senator Hillary Clinton's name is placed in nomination for President of the United States at the Democratic national convention.
1968	Shirley Chisholm, a New York Democrat, became the first Black woman to serve in Congress.	2009	Sonia Sotomayor became the first Latina and the third woman to serve on the Supreme Court.
		2011	Major General Margaret Woodward became the first woman to lead a combat air campaign when she was ordered to set up the United Nations–sanctioned no-fly zone over Libya.

Source: Adapted from *Firsts for Women in U.S. Politics,* 2008. http://www.cawp.rutgers.edu/Facts/Ffirst.html (March 20).

as the some Evangelical, Eastern Orthodox, Mormon, Muslim, and Orthodox Jewish faiths continue to reject women as clergy. Additionally, clergy women of all faiths experience difficulty in finding jobs and, when they do, the positions are often in smaller and/or remote congregations. Women clergy are paid less and enjoy fewer benefits than their male counterparts (Lampman, 2006).

However, recent developments indicate that the stained glass ceiling is cracking, albeit slowly. According to the Association of Theological Schools in the United States and Canada, 36 percent of seminary students are now women (Paulson, 2007). In 1972, enrollment was only 4.7 percent. In most denominations today, groups of women (and some men, too) are working to gain equal

Bishop Katharine Jefferts Schori is the first female presiding bishop for the Episcopal Church in the United States and took office amid considerable controversy over the ordination of lesbians and gay men.

Although a statistical minority, some men enjoy teaching young children. This male elementary school teacher helps his young charges learn computer skills.

rights for women at all levels of participation. These efforts were given a boost and more visibility in 2006 with the election of Katharine Jefferts Schori as the first female to become the presiding bishop of the Episcopal Church.

Similar gender inequities exist in the economy. Although we have all heard or read stories about female astronauts, coal miners, and constructions workers as well as stories about male nannies and nurses, many occupations are still perceived as either women's work or men's work. Conversely, a nontraditional job is defined as any occupation in which women or men comprise less than 25 percent of the workforce. For example, women make up less than 25 percent of architects, computer programmers and software engineers, clergy, dentists, firefighters, police and correctional officers, construction workers, machinists, carpenters, and truck drivers. Men comprise less than 25 percent of preschool and kindergarten teachers, social workers, librarians, dietitians, registered nurses, occupational therapists, dental hygienists, housekeeping cleaners, hairdressers, child care workers, travel agents, tellers, and receptionists (U.S. Census Bureau, 2011e).

When either gender crosses into nontraditional jobs, they often experience challenges to their feminine or masculine identities from other workers. This can be extremely stressful, and it often limits their social interactions with their colleagues. One qualitative study of men who have crossed into what are generally defined as "women's jobs," found that these men either attempted to maintain a traditional masculinity by distancing themselves from female colleagues and/or partially reconstructed a different masculinity by identifying with their nontraditional occupations. In both cases, these strategies worked to maintain the men as the dominant gender, even in jobs traditionally considered "women's work" (Cross and Bagilhole, 2002).

MENTAL HEALTH

Given what we now know about the construction of gender role ideology and some of its consequences, it would be surprising if there were no relationship between gender and mental health. In fact, the World Health Organization (WHO) (2008) maintains that gender is a critical determinant of mental health and mental illness. Gender differences occur particularly in the rates of common mental disorders—depression, anxiety, and somatic complaints. At all ages, women tend to have higher rates of these disorders than men. For example, in any two-week period, 8 percent of women and girls report experiencing clinically significant depression compared to 5 percent for men and boys. Race and class are important factors. African American women and girls (11 percent) report higher rates of depression than White women and girls (8 percent), and females living below the poverty level are almost three times as likely to report experiencing depression as females living above the poverty line (U.S. Department of Commerce Economics and Statistics Administration, 2010). However, some researchers see such statistics more as a reflection of women's greater willingness to seek help than real differences in rates (Chandra and Minkovitz, 2006). A recent study in Great Britain confirms this observation. In their analysis of good practice in male mental health, David Wilkins and Marian Kemple (2011) write that the cultural expectations of men, particularly the belief that men and boys should not express vulnerability, militate against men's willingness to admit to themselves or others that they have a mental health problem. Whereas women suffer more from internalizing problems, men predominate in externalizing problems and have higher rates for antisocial personality disorders, including delinquency, aggression, and substance abuse (Wilkins and Kemple, 2011; Rosenfield, Phillips, and White, 2006). According to the WHO, gender specific risk factors for the common mental disorders disproportionately affect women. Among them are violence against women, socioeconomic disadvantage, low or subordinate social status and rank, and the ongoing responsibility for caring for others. Risk factors for men include the stress of unemployment or low and/or inadequate wages and the difficulties involved in trying to live up to internalized notions of what it means to be a man, including stereotypes of always needing to be strong, independent, successful, and aggressive (Artazcoz, et al., 2004).

The attitudes and behaviors of mental health professionals are also important in understanding gender differences in mental health. Historically, the mental health field has frequently reflected gender-related stereotypes. In one study, for example, researchers asked a number of clinicians to define a healthy woman, a healthy man, and a healthy, mature adult of no specified sex. Clinicians described a healthy woman as more emotional, more submissive, less independent, less aggressive and competitive, more easily excitable, more easily hurt, and more concerned with her appearance than a healthy male. Significantly, when describing a healthy adult of no specified sex, clinicians listed a number of traits traditionally associated with the male stereotype, such as independence and assertiveness. Thus, women were viewed as possessing characteristics less positive and less healthy than those of a typical healthy adult (Broverman et al., 1970). Such an association implies that women who conform to the traditional feminine role do not measure up to the mental health standards of the general adult population.

Clinicians today are more sensitive to gender bias and are unlikely to list different characteristics for healthy adult females and healthy adult males. Nevertheless, some clinicians still hold an adjustment standard of mental health. Thus, women and men who conform to traditional gender roles are likely to be seen as healthier than those who deviate from these roles. Assertive and independent women and gentle and nurturing men may therefore be viewed as maladjusted (Gilbert and Scher, 1999).

Thus, it seems rigid adherence to traditional gender norms may interfere with the development of good mental health for both women and men. This latter point raises an interesting question. Can both women and men benefit from becoming **androgynous,** that is, sharing masculine and feminine traits? Research shows that masculine-oriented individuals (high on instrumental traits), both female and male, experience less anxiety, strain, depression, neuroticism, work impairment, achievement conflicts, and dissatisfaction in their lives than feminine-oriented individuals. Similarly, traits traditionally defined as feminine can be beneficial to both women and men. The ability to express feelings and show sensitivity to others enhances interpersonal adjustment and the ability to form intimate relationships (Maheshwari, and Kumar, 2008; Lefkowitz and Zedlow, 2006; Basow, 1992). With this in mind, let us examine the meaning that friendship has in the lives of women and men.

WOMEN, MEN, AND FRIENDS

According to Lillian Rubin (1985:59), throughout most of the history of Western civilization, "men's friendships have been taken to be the model of what friendship is and how it ought to be. … Women's friendships didn't count, indeed were not even noticed." As recently as 1969, anthropologist Lionel Tiger hypothesized that men have a genetically based tendency to form nonerotic bonds with other males, and that these male bonds are stronger and more stable than those formed between women. An impressive array of research studies over the past 25 years, focusing on the similarities and differences between female and male friendship patterns, has not substantiated Tiger's hypothesis. Conversely, much of this research is consistent with Rubin's assessment: "The results of my own research are unequivocal: At every life stage between twenty-five and fifty-five, women have more friendships, as distinct from collegial relationships or workmates, than men, and the differences in the content and quality of their friendships are marked and unmistakable (Rubin, 1985:60–61).

Overall, women's friendships tend to be characterized by intimacy, self-disclosure, nurturance, and emotional support. Conversation is a central part of women's friendships (Karbo, 2009; Johnson, 1996). Men's friendships, in contrast, focus more on shared activities such as sports, politics, and business and tend to be less intimate, but not necessarily less important, than women's friendships (Zaslo, 2010; Inman, 1996). Definitive reasons for these gender differences have not yet been substantiated, but several explanations appear plausible. In contrast to men, women are more likely to be socialized to be more relationship oriented. The emphasis on male competitiveness may make it difficult for men to self-disclose to one another, thereby making men feel vulnerable. Finally, the fear of being labeled homosexual may prevent men from developing emotional attachments to other men. However, there are indications that some of these patterns may be changing. Men-only gatherings and male only vacations seem to be on the increase. The rationale given for these activities is summed up by Jamie Monberg who meets with the same group of nine guys every Wednesday night, to "talk about anything" without the company of their wives, girlfriends, or young children (quoted in Edwards, 2008).

Despite these differences, both females and males report about the same level of satisfaction with their friendship activities (Mazur, 1989). Thus, although they may connect with others in different ways, both women and men share a common need for meaningful relationships with others of their sex. Although difficult to achieve, this need for connectedness sometimes manifests itself in cross-sex friendships.

Cross-Sex Friendships A single parent who lives with her mother and her 9-year-old daughter told this story:

> Recently Jane had a male school chum over to the house. The grandmother was home and the mother was at work. The two

It is not unusual to see all-female gatherings, be it luncheons, book clubs, or just getting together to talk. Today, more and more men are organizing guys-only gatherings to enjoy male companionship in much the same way.

children went up to Jane's room to play computer games. Upon realizing they went upstairs, the grandmother became excited and sent the boy home, telling her granddaughter that it was inappropriate for him to be there.

What do you think motivated the grandmother's behavior? No doubt you have observed mixed-sex groups of preschool children at play. However, this pattern begins to change in elementary school. Like this grandmother, adults become fearful that cross-sex friendships can become sexual. Thus, whether consciously or not, from early on society erects barriers to cross-sex friendships. Some of these barriers are reflected in the organization of elementary schools, with their frequent gender-segregated activities; others are embedded in the belief that women and men have opposite characteristics. As noted earlier, however, as children age, they exhibit more gender flexibility. One consequence of this is the tendency for cross-sex friendships to increase during adolescence and early adulthood. However, heterosexual marriage or a serious involvement frequently acts against maintaining cross-sex friendships. Lillian Rubin (1985) sees this response as keeping with the cultural expectation that romantic commitment and commitment to family must come before friendships. Until relatively recently our culture provided few models of enduring cross-sex friendships contributing to the difficulty in forming and maintaining such relationships. Some of these difficulties are easing. In today's environment, women and men study together on college campuses and share the workplace. Thus, a new cultural message is evolving—women and men can become close friends (Monsour, 2002). This doesn't mean it is easier, however. Cross-sex friends must negotiate this relationship on a number of fronts—physical and sexual attraction, gender role orientation, and other people's

response to this friendship (Lapidos, 2010). Gendered patterns of communication can also exaggerate both the perceived and the real differences between women and men and thus hinder the formation of cross-sex friendships.

PATTERNS OF COMMUNICATION

Linguistic scholars from Robin Lakoff (1975) to Deborah Tannen (2002, 1994, 1990) report that women and men often speak essentially different languages and have different communication goals and behaviors. These patterns begin early and have major consequences both for the society at large and in our interpersonal relationships. Let us take one example of the former context, the political arena. A study of adolescents and young adults, composed roughly of equal numbers of females and males with similar qualifications participating in a Model United Nations Program, found that male delegates spoke more, interrupted other speakers more frequently, and engaged in more aggressive and challenging behavior than female delegates (Rosenthal, Jones, and Rosenthal, 2003). The presence of a female chair and a larger percentage of female committees made only slight differences in these patterns. These norms of male dominance have been found in a wide range of studies and suggest that politics is a masculine domain. Such findings may help explain the low percentage of women in public office and the difficulty women face in getting some of their needs on the political agenda. Gender differences in speaking styles can also affect workplace behavior, including who gets heard, who gets credit, and how work gets done.

Similarly, gender differences in communication styles affect interpersonal relationships. According to Tannen, women speak and hear a language of intimacy and connectedness, whereas men speak and hear a language of status and independence. She calls women's conversational style "rapport talk," the goal of which is to signal support, to confirm solidarity, or to indicate they are following the conversation. In contrast, Tannen sees men's conversational style as "report talk," intended to preserve independence and to negotiate and maintain status in a hierarchical order.

There are also differences in nonverbal communication. Compared to men, women tend to smile more, exhibit more facial expression, and make stronger eye contact when engaged in conversation. Men, on the other hand, maintain more reservation and control over their facial expression, often don't make eye contact, and use more personal space. These differences can lead to misunderstandings. Women may think men aren't paying attention to them because they aren't making eye contact, and men may think women are agreeing because of their smile (Langford, 2011).

These contrasting styles can be problematic in intimate relationships, especially in the realm of self-disclosure. As we will see in other sections of this text, men often find self-disclosure difficult, even to their wives. Nevertheless, these contrasting communication styles need not be problematic. Being aware of such differences and making subtle adjustments can lead to a more effective context for productive working and interpersonal relationships (Langford, 2011).

Imagine for a moment that you had to spend the next year of your life as a member of the other sex. How would your life be different? What advantages and disadvantages would you experience as a female? As a male?

Changing Realities, Changing Roles

Whether we like it or not, the world we inhabit today is quite different from that of our parents and grandparents. Consider two examples that will be discussed in detail in later chapters: (1) More married mothers are working than ever before, many of them in sexually integrated work settings; and (2) increasing numbers of women (and some men) are finding themselves solely responsible for their family's economic and social welfare. Yet, as we have seen throughout this chapter, some of the agents of socialization continue to perpetuate traditional views of White middle-class femininity and masculinity, often in ways that have negative consequences for women's and men's development. Many of these patterns of socialization are not sufficient to provide solutions to the psychological and economic strains experienced by many people today. Thus, it is necessary to seek new ways to socialize children to enable them to make satisfying personal choices and to live full and satisfying human lives.

Given her early socialization experiences, learning carpentry skills from her father, this little girl is likely to grow up with expanded job opportunities and nontraditional gender attitudes.

Writing Your Own Script

REFLECTIONS ON GENDER

As this chapter illustrates, gender is a significant factor in our lives. Social expectations about gender are so deeply woven into the fabric of our society that they often seem natural. Even when we are unhappy about some aspect of our lives, we often fail to see the connections between existing cultural assumptions and social arrangements and our own experiences. Take time to reflect on the role of gender in your experiences.

Questions to Consider

1. How has being a male or a female affected your life to this point? Do you feel you missed out on anything because of your gender? What, if anything, would you change about being a woman or a man in today's society?

2. How satisfied are you with your physical appearance? If you could change any aspect of your appearance, what would it be? Why?

3. What are your friendship patterns like? Are you satisfied with the number of same-sex and cross-sex friendships you have? What are some of the social barriers to developing and maintaining cross-sex friendships? What might you do to increase the likelihood of having more cross-sex friendships?

Supporting Marriages and Families

A growing body of literature documents the fact that gender-stereotyped roles are bad for relationship stability and satisfaction (Johnson, 2003) and that establishing relationship equality provides a critical building block for balancing work and family life (Knudson-Martin and Mahoney, 2005; Haddock, et al., 2001), resulting in higher levels of emotional well-being and satisfaction with interpersonal relationships. Psychologist Sandra Bem (1983:613) offers two strategies that parents and other agents of socialization can employ to modify gender socialization patterns that lead to gender-stereotyped roles. The first strategy is to teach children that the only definitive gender differences are anatomical and reproductive. The second strategy is to help children substitute an "individual differences" schema that emphasizes the "remarkable variability of individuals within groups" for the gender schema they currently use for organizing and processing information. Classroom teachers can institute mechanisms for building gender equity inside and outside their classrooms. One quick example—two science teachers at a middle school created Science Chicks, an after-school club for seventh-grade girls to encourage girls' scientific interests (Cromer, 2005). The media can effectively assist in a move toward gender equality by featuring characters of both genders in substantial numbers in major roles that offer positive and competent role content. When children see females and males in nontraditional ways, they are less likely to see careers and personal options as gendered based. In the same manner, when people of color are portrayed in a diverse range of occupations, including those that are highly valued and respected, it helps erode racial and ethnic stereotypes and creates higher aspirations among children of color.

SUMMARY

Each of us occupies a number of statuses that carry with them expectations for behavior. Some of these are ascribed statuses such as sex and race. Others are achieved by our own efforts, for example, becoming a parent or a teacher. Role expectations serve an important function in society in that they make behavior predictable. However, expectations can be defined so rigidly that they become dysfunctional for individuals and for society as a whole.

The status of being female or male in our society affects all aspects of our lives. Thus, it is important to distinguish between the concepts of sex (being female or male) and gender (the socially learned behaviors, attitudes, and the expectations associated with being female or male).

Social-learning theory, cognitive-development theory, and enculturated-lens theory have been advanced by social scientists to explain how we acquire our gender identity. The traditional notions of femininity and masculinity are based on White middle-class definitions, and they do not accurately reflect the race and class variations in gender role perceptions. From early on, we are socialized to behave in gender-appropriate ways by parents, peers, teachers, the mass media, and religion.

Traditional gender role stereotypes limit the career and life-style options of both females and males and can lead to mental health problems. Gender also influences the type and quality of friendships we have. Although they connect with others in different ways, both females and males have a common need for meaningful relationships with others of the same sex. Women's friendships are characterized by intimacy and self-disclosure, whereas men's friendships focus more on shared activities. Gendered patterns of communication exaggerate both the perceived and real differences between women and men and hinder the formation of cross-sex friendships.

Many efforts are underway to modify gender socialization patterns that lead to gender-stereotyped roles in an effort to create more options for all individuals.

KEY TERMS

ascribed status	sex	intersexuality	modeling	agents of socialization
achieved status	gender	transsexuals	cognitive-development	content analysis
gender role	gender identity	gender role	theory	androgynous
stereotypes	gender similarity	socialization	enculturated-lens	
master (key) status	hypothesis	social-learning theory	theory	

QUESTIONS FOR STUDY AND REFLECTION

1. Distinguish between sex and gender. Why is it important to make this distinction? Many scientists today argue that sex and gender are fluid rather than dichotomous. What do they mean by this? What evidence is there to support this position?

2. Think back to your childhood as far as you can go. When is the first time you can recall that you were aware of being a girl or a boy? (Hint: Sometimes these are painful events, for instance, when we asked for a toy and were told it wasn't appropriate for our gender or when we were criticized "for behaving like a member of the other gender.") How did you feel at the time? How would your life be different today if you were the other gender? Compare and contrast the theories advanced by social scientists to explain the process of gender acquisition. Using yourself as an example, which theory do you think explains how you acquired your gender identity? Is any one of these theories, or are all of them combined, sufficient to explain the content of gender roles in our society? Explain your position.

3. Assume that you are entertaining visitors from another culture who are unfamiliar with the patterns of female–male relationships in the United States today and who do not want to make any major mistakes in their interactions during their visit. What would you tell them? What problems might they run into without this knowledge?

4. Consider the following proposition: Young girls and boys should be raised alike, with similar toys, play activities, and the same expectations regarding their education and future careers. Do you agree or disagree with this proposition? Explain and provide evidence to support your position.

ADDITIONAL RESOURCES

SOCIOLOGICAL

ANDERSON, MARGARET, AND PATRICIA HILL COLLINS, EDS. 2006. *Race, Class, and Gender: An Anthology.* Belmont, CA: Wadsworth. This anthology contains a collection of articles on gender along with the intersections of race and class.

EHRENSAFT, DIANE. 2011. *Gender Born, Gender Made: Raising Healthy Gender-Nonconforming Children.* New York: The Experiment. Drawing on case histories of several children, each "gender creative" in her or his own way, Dr. Ehrensaft provides concrete strategies to parents, teachers, and other adults who want to understand and support gender-variant children as they explore their gender identities.

GRIEF, GEOFFREY L. 2009. *Buddy System: Understanding Male Friendships.* New York: Oxford University Press. Drawing on interviews with nearly 400 men, Geoffrey Greif takes readers on a guided tour of male friendships, showing that men have a variety of friends: *must, trust, just,* and *rust* friends. Each of these types of friends contribute to the health and happiness of men.

ZASLOW, JEFF. 2009. *The Girls from Ames: A Story of Women and a Forty-Year Relationship.* New York: Gotham. Growing up in Ames, Iowa, 11 childhood friends formed a special bond. Although they moved to eight different states, they managed to maintain an enduring friendship that carried them through college, careers, marriage, motherhood, divorce, a child's illness, and the mysterious death of one member of their group.

FILM

Bend It Like Beckham. 2002. A touching story about a teenage girl named Jess who lives in London and who must make a choice between following the traditions of her Indian family or pursuing her dream of playing soccer.

Billy Elliot. 2000. The protagonist is a poor, rural English boy whose traditional father insists he take boxing lessons. While at the gym, Billy observes a girls' ballet class and accepts their invitation to join them. From then on, he is hooked, and despite existing cultural norms and his father's objections, he continues to dance. Great moves.

LITERARY

These two novels powerfully illustrate the intersection of gender, ethnicity, and social class. Both stories are set against a backdrop of political turmoil in Afghanistan over the last three to four decades.

HOSSEINI, KHALED. 2007. *A Thousand Splendid Suns.* New York: Riverhead Books. This tale of two women provides a nuanced portrait of a society where women are agonizingly dependent on fathers, husbands, and sons.

HOSSEINI, KHALED. 2004. *The Kite Runner.* New York: Riverhead Trade. This story focuses on the friendship between two boys and the struggles each encounters in growing up as well as the relationship between fathers and sons.

INTERNET

http://www.thewhitehouseproject.org This national nonpartisan organization works to advance a richly diverse critical mass of woman into leadership positions, up to and including the U.S. presidency. It features information about political and civic leadership programs for young women.

http://www.supportingoursons.org Supporting Our Sons is a national nonprofit membership organization dedicated to helping boys achieve their full potential. Its Web site contains research on boys and provides information and guidelines for parents whose sons want to pursue nontraditional gender roles.

http://www.un.org/womenwatch WomenWatch is the UN Internet gateway on the advancement and empowerment of women; it includes links to other UN Web sites on gender issues.

http://users.ox.ac.uk/~cccrw/ The International Gender Studies Center features research and teaching materials relating to women and gender in Africa, South and Southeast Asia, China, Latin America, the Middle East, and Europe.

Succeed with MyFamilyLab®
www.myfamilylab.com

Watch. Explore. Read. The New MyFamilyLab is designed just for you. Each chapter features a pre-test and post-test to help you learn and review key concepts and terms. Experience Marriages and Families in action with dynamic visual activities, videos, and readings to enhance your learning experience.

Here are a few activities you will find for this chapter.

Watch on **myfamilylab.com**

Video clips feature important concepts in the study of Marriages and Families. Watch:
- Gender Socialization

Explore on **myfamilylab.com**

Social Explorer is an interactive application that allows you to explore Census data through interactive maps. Explore the Social Explorer Activity:
- Income Inequality by Gender

Read on **myfamilylab.com**

MyFamilyLab includes primary source readings from classic and contemporary sociologists from around the world. Read:
- Lorber, "Night to His Day: The Social Construction of Gender"

4

The Many Faces of Love

What Will You Learn?

- Define and understand the sociological meaning of key terms.
- Describe the historical underpinnings and contemporary trends in the expression of romantic love across cultures.
- Apply the sociological imagination to analyze and explain both implicit and explicit messages about love found in popular culture.
- Assess the pros and cons of major theories of love.
- Increase your awareness and understanding of the intersection of race, class, gender and sexual orientation in romantic love relationships.
- Question how myths and metaphors about love shape our ideas about love.

IN THE NEWS

UK: BBC News

In a remarkable story that attests to the power and longevity of love, just before Valentines Day, 2011, the British Library featured an exhibit titled: "First Valentine: Lasting Legacy of 500-year-old Love." On exhibit was a love letter written from a young woman to her love 534 years ago. The letter is said to be the first Valentine in the English language.

In 1477, Margery Brews wrote a letter to her love, John Paston, begging him not to give her up, despite her parents' refusal to increase her dowry. In the letter, she addresses her "right welebeloued Voluntyne" (right well-beloved Valentine) and continues in similar English and spelling, promising to be a good wife to him, saying that if he loves her, she trusts that he will not leave her. She goes on to promise him her undying love, saying that she bids her heart to forever love him truly and she speaks about her ailing body and heart because he has not responded to her pleas. It is not known what her lover was thinking—perhaps he had his mind on business and was trying to drive a hard bargain for her hand in marriage—but it seems clear from her letter that Margery had her sights on love and romance (Browning, 2011).

According to the British Library Curator, it is not necessarily the case that no one had ever used a Valentine in that or any other context before Margery, but hers was probably one of the first times it was written down, thus securing Margery's place in English history. And, according to other historians, Margery's letter is of great importance because it sheds light on relationships of those in the gentry class in the Middle Ages; it reveals a genuine sense of the relationship between a young woman and young man wanting to marry. An added significance of Margery's letter is that most documentation that survives from medieval times are legal and governmental documents, financial records, and property deeds. Few personal letters exist, and even fewer are written by women (Browning, 2011).

Without the letter, we would not know that love matches occurred even within arranged matches so long ago. The general assumption most people hold is that that marriages in the gentry class were arranged for dynastic reasons, but as Margery's letters show, everything was slotted in around the fact that she and John were a couple that loved each other. Thus, while some 534 years later, romantics in several cultures celebrate Valentine's Day with romantic cards with wording designed by a stranger, fine dining, chocolates, flowers, and various gifts, Margery is left pleading with her love not to leave her while pledging her heart to him over all earthly things. For her sixteenth and seventeenth generation descendants, traced via the family history Web site MyHeritage, her letter is a link to the past that they relish (Browning, 2011).

In a somewhat fairytale romance of the heart ending, the heart did win out and despite Margery's father's stubbornness over her dowry, she did marry her great love. The couple had a son, William, born in 1479. Margery died in 1495 and John in 1503 (Browning, 2011).

WHAT WOULD YOU DO?

Although romantic relationships and marriage are not overtly arranged by parents in the United States, what would you do if your parents forbade you to date and/or marry someone you loved dearly? Would you continue the relationship despite their feelings or would you end the relationship? Have you ever written a love letter or personal Valentine message to someone? What, if any, was the person's response? What do such messages tell us about romantic love today?

(◦•—[Listen to the **Chapter Audio** on **myfamilylab.com**

"Love is blind." "Love makes the world go 'round." "Love is a many-splendored thing." "True love never dies." "Love at first sight." "Love conquers all." How many sayings like these can you think of? In Western societies, probably more than in any others, love is a central feature of life. Most Westerners believe that love gives life meaning, that it is essential to a healthy and satisfying life. In the United States, as exemplified in the In the News section opening this chapter, people of all ages devote much thought about and considerable time and effort to love and intimate relationships. Love is referred to or appears as a central theme throughout American popular culture, in the lyrics of all types of music, poems, sonnets, short stories, novels, films, plays, television, and art. The love affairs and love scandals of movie stars and other well-known people are mainstays in the popular media, and we hunger for more and more of this "love" news. The advice columns of daily newspapers, daytime television talk shows and soap operas, as well as a popular literature and even academic courses on how to attract, impress, satisfy, keep, and even dump the lover of our choice all exemplify the extent to which love and intimacy occupy our thoughts and actions.

Humans express many kinds of love, probably as many as there are types of people who love and are loved. Love encompasses a wide variety of feelings and behaviors, ranging from those we feel for our parents, friends, siblings, and children to those we feel for our spouses or partners. However, the type of love dominant in most of our lives, at one time or another, is romantic love. Although a common thread of caring is woven through all love relationships, the major difference between these feelings of love and romantic love is the element of **eroticism**—concerning or intending to arouse sexual desire. Although all types of love are important and merit discussion, our primary concern in this chapter is with romantic or erotic love.

What Is This Thing Called Love?

If we asked 100 people to define love, we would probably get 100 different responses. Love, it seems, is an elusive emotion. Most of us insist that we experience it at some time in our lives, but sometimes we have extreme difficulty explaining it. Other times, adults and even children define love in very powerful and explicit language (see, for example, Table 4.1). This fact notwithstanding, love is often surrounded by myths and metaphors; we dream and hope of finding the love of a lifetime who will love us no matter what and who will transform an otherwise ordinary life into one of bliss. People have been known to do all sorts of things in the name of love: wage wars, forsake family and friends, sign away fortunes, or give up royal standing. We claim that love is blind, and so, blindly, we subject ourselves to a wide range of emotions from ecstasy to torment—all in the name of love.

Because each of us expresses and experiences love differently, there are a variety of definitions and types of love. Some writers, for example, view love as an emotion that causes us to act irrationally. Other writers believe it to be an emotion that is much more centered on self than on another person; or a giving of the heart

---

TABLE 4.1 What Is Love?

It is interesting to look at how various individuals and groups define love. For example, a recent poll asked American adults to define love. Below is a sample from among the top 150 responses (Institute of Human Thermodynamics, 2004). Children, on the other hand, see life and love in simpler terms than adults. For example, a group of professionals asked a group of 4- to 8-year-olds: "What does love mean?" A sample of their answers appears below (Healthy Happy Love Relationships, 2008).

What Is Love—According to Adults	What Is Love—According to Children
When you care about someone more than you care about yourself	When someone loves you the way they say your name is different. You just know that your name is safe in their mouth (4-year-old)
The perfect union of two souls; the home you find in someone	Love is when a girl puts on perfume and a boy puts on shaving cream and they go out and smell each other (5-year-old)
When you can't live without the other person	Love is when you go out to eat and give somebody most of your french fries without making them give you any of theirs (6-year-old)
A state of perpetual bliss	
An energy so pure it makes life want to happen	Love is like a little old woman and a little old man who are still friends even after they know each other so well (6-year-old)
Insanity	
Sincere loyalty, affection, and care bestowed without obligation	Love is when Mommy sees Daddy on the toilet and she doesn't think it's gross (6-year-old)
Total self-sacrifice	Love is when you tell a guy you like his shirt, then he wears it everyday (7-year-old)
When time stands still	
A feeling of intense sexual desire and attraction toward another	When you love somebody, your eyelashes go up and down and little stars come out of you (7-year-old)
Lifelong monogamy	

Source: Reprinted with permission of the Institute of Human Thermodynamics.

and soul, the giving of a person's total self; or an ideology that narrows people's perception of the world; or an innate undeniable aspect of what makes us human. Still other writers have defined love as a contrivance, a fantasy concocted by human beings over the centuries, a cultural delusion that originated in the twelfth century with wandering troubadours and knights in shining armor (Marriott, 2001). Some writers have even argued that love is a male invention used to exploit women. Although many social scientists steer clear of singular definitions of love because in their view love varies in degree, intensity, over time, and across social contexts, William Goode's definition of love is still perhaps the most widely cited in the scientific literature: "A strong emotional attachment, a cathexis, between adolescents or adults of opposite sexes, with at least the components of sex, desire, and tenderness" (1959:49). Although we agree that love defies a single definition, to facilitate a broader understanding of the concept, we will nonetheless use a more general and inclusive definition than that of Goode. In this context, we use the term **romantic love** to refer to, very generally, the intense feelings, emotions, and thoughts coupled with sexual passion and erotic expression that a person directs toward another, as well as the ideology—the set of beliefs—that upholds it.

Although romantic love is often considered unique to Western and modern cultures, anthropologists have found that it does exist in some "traditional" societies. For example, anthropologists William Jankowiak and Edward Fischer (1992) examined 166 traditional cultures and found evidence of romantic love in 88 percent of them. Individuals within these cultures sang love songs and even eloped; the folklore of many of these societies portrayed various types of romantic entanglements. Jankowiak and Fischer concluded that romantic love, which they equate with passionate love, constitutes a human universal, or at the least, a "near-universal."

> How do you define love? Is your definition of love consistent with that of your friends? Your parents and others around you? How many times have you been in love? How do you know when you are in love? Have you ever fallen out of love? How does one fall out of love?

LOVE AS A SOCIAL CONSTRUCTION

People tend to think of love as an individual choice fired by our biological engines. Although research from the biological sciences shows that biochemistry underlies our emotional behavior throughout every stage of human love, of interest to sociologists is how love is conditioned by the cultural context, historical period, and institutional structures in which it occurs. In this context, love emerges out of the unique context in which individuals encounter one another, but the feelings that develop between people are love only when they define it as such. And the criteria that people use to arrive at the conclusion that they are in love are social in origin.

Culture plays an essential role in this process, particularly in terms of whom we choose to love. In early childhood, we develop specific likes and dislikes in response to family, peers, experiences, cultural prescriptions, and definitions of love, beauty, and worthiness, so that by the time we are teenagers, we have developed a mental picture of whom we will find attractive and

Modern technology—text and instant messaging—has revolutionized the way we communicate in our personal lives. One effect of this new technology has been the depersonalization of love and intimacy. Can you imagine what Margery Brew's message to her lover might have said and how he might have responded had today's technology been available 534 years ago?

fall in love with. Anthropologist Helen Fisher (1999) refers to this mental image that we carry around as an unconscious mental template, or **love map**—a group of physical, psychological, and behavioral traits that one finds attractive in a mate.

According to a social constructionist point of view, love can only be understood as symbolic or as a social construction that by itself has no intrinsic meaning. Feelings of romantic love and passion have a physiological component, but neither is based solely on our body reactions. Rather, they are also based on the way in which we interpret and label our feelings and reactions. Take this classic example: You walk into a crowded room; your eyes lock on those of a stranger across the room; after a brief moment of staring, you smile at each other; a short time later, you find a reason to approach each other, and as you do so your heart begins to beat rapidly, you experience a shortness of breath, and you feel the blood rush to your face. What do these physiological responses signify? How do you interpret them? Do you have the flu? Have you had too much to drink? Or is the room's thermostat simply out of control?

If you have grown up in the United States, you have learned from family, peers, and the mass media that what you are feeling can be interpreted in terms of love. These feelings do not have to be interpreted in terms of love, however. It is the context in which they occur (in a room where we have just locked eyes with a stranger) that leads us to that interpretation. The point here is that our emotional states are symbolic states and as such require interpretation and naming to give them meaning (Karp, Yoels, and Vann, 2003). That is, the meanings of objects, emotions, and situations reside in our responses to and interpretations of them. See the Writing Your Own Script box on page 94 and examine and reflect on the social construction of love in your life or the life of someone you know.

Writing Your Own Script

A SOCIAL CONSTRUCTION OF LOVE

Consider how you learned about romantic love and how you learned to behave in culturally appropriate ways within romantic love relationships. Think back to your earliest memories of cultural influences on your views. What did you learn about romantic love from your family? From popular culture? If you have siblings of a different sex, were they given the same messages about romantic love and the appropriate organization of such relationships in your family? In the larger culture? How does your economic class, race, sex/gender, sexual orientation, age, and historical location affect your attitude about and experience of romantic love? Do you agree that romantic love is a meaningless construct outside a cultural context? If not, why not? Write a brief analysis of a specific romantic love relationship you are currently in (if you are not presently in one, consider a previous relationship or that of someone you know) and critically reflect on it, using the following questions as a guide:

- How would you describe each partner in the relationship in terms of gender role ideology: feminine, masculine, androgynous?
- What, if any, impact does the organization of gender have on the way in which you and your partner relate to and love each other? Contribute to the success of the relationship?
- Are there conflicts regarding intimacy (for example, over sharing intimacy)? Is one partner more self-disclosing than the other? Can this be related in any way to gender/gender role socialization? If so, how?

- Think of, at minimum, two factors that contribute to one partner having more power in the relationship than the other.
- If you are part of a same-sex romantic love relationship, relate two examples of how myths about same-sex love relationships impact your specific relationship. What effects does homophobia have on your relationship?
- Is jealousy present in the relationship? If so, identify and evaluate the source of the jealousy.
- Is the jealousy destructive to the relationship? What steps have you taken (or will you take) to change the situation? Think of, at minimum, two ways in which androgyny or egalitarian gender roles might result in increased intimacy and mutual satisfaction in the relationship.

Although no one has quite figured out why we fall in love, approximately 60 percent of American adults believe it can happen and more than 50 percent say they have experienced it. Men are slightly more likely than women to say they have fallen in love at first sight and are more likely than women to say "I love you" during the first week of dating. Interestingly, a small number of Americans believe you can fall in love at first sight more than once. Moreover, according to various polls, somewhere between 75 percent and 90 percent of Americans believe in true love—that there is only "one true love out there" that they are destined to fall in love with (Daily News Brief, 2011; Buri, 2010).

Psychologists say that love at first sight depends on our psychological state at the very moment. They also say we need approximately 30 seconds to fall in love or, to be more precise, to establish whether the person is attractive and a potential mate. As with the belief in love at first sight, men fall in love faster than women. Some theories say that we fall in love not from the first sight but from the first smell. Scientists claim that we pay attention to what our eyes and ears tell us, but on a subconscious level, the way a person smells plays a big part in our impression of them ("Love at First Sight," 2011). Moreover, a recent study conducted by a psychology professor at Syracuse University reports that

falling in love only takes about one-fifth of a second and can elicit the same euphoric feeling as using the drug cocaine. According to this research, falling in love affects various intellectual areas of the brain. That is, different parts of the brain fall in love. For instance, unconditional love, such as that between a parent and child, is sparked by different areas of the brain, including the middle of the brain. On the other hand, passionate love is sparked by the reward part of the brain as well as associative cognitive areas of the brain that have higher-order functions, such as body image (Ortigue, et al., 2010).

In the harsh cold light of reality, however, sociological research shows that our "destiny" is tempered by formal and informal cultural norms and values concerning partner eligibility that filter out millions of potential lovers, one of whom just might have been "our destiny" or "one true love." This research helps us understand and supports the constructionist point of view of love as a social and historical construction. As we stress throughout this textbook, systems of race, class, gender, and sexual orientation shape all intimate relationships. Thus, even something as abstract and hard to define as the concept of love illustrates the significance of historical context and the social construction of love in shaping intimacy.

LOVE IN WESTERN SOCIETY: A HISTORICAL PERSPECTIVE

Romantic love has been portrayed in a variety of ways in Western cultures for centuries. Many of today's myths and legends about romantic love come from antiquity (Fisher, 1999). The love story of Isis and Osiris was recorded in Egypt more than 3,000 years ago. Ovid composed poems to romantic love in the first century B.C. in ancient Rome. And the *Kama Sutra* (Hindu words for "love" and for "pleasure and sensual gratification," respectively), a Hindu treatise on the art of love, including explicit sexual instructions, was composed sometime between the first and fourth centuries A.D.

As we have discussed, today romantic love is almost always linked to sex and marriage. It has not always been this way, however. For much of human history, although marriage and sex were related, there was no conception of love as a necessary part of either. In most societies throughout history, and in many societies in the world today, people marry not out of romantic love, but out of obligation to parents and family. In the typical case, a strong sense of family duty and obligation to parents is symbolically transferred onto marriage to a spouse chosen by one's parents or grandparents (Coltrane, 1998). The linking of love with sex and marriage is a unique feature of romantic love, a type of love relatively new in human social history. It slowly developed in Western societies over many centuries, and its roots can be traced to ancient Greece and Rome.

Love in Ancient Greece Most writers trace contemporary notions of romantic love to Greek society of the fifth century B.C. and the writings of the philosopher Plato who defined love as the highest expression of human virtue because of its ability to inspire people to be kind, honorable, and wise. Plato distinguished several types of love: *Agape* is a selfless love; it is spontaneous and altruistic and requires nothing in return. *Eros* is a selfish love, with an emphasis on physical pleasure. It is based on sexual attraction and can be either homosexual or heterosexual. *Philos* is a deep friendship or brotherly love and includes a love for humanity.

The erotic love that Plato and other Greek philosophers idealized was a combination of the purely physical and the extremely spiritual. Although sex and beauty were its goals, it was not focused, however, on one's marriage partner. Marriages were arranged by families, and men married primarily to reproduce a line of male heirs. The primary role of women was to bear and care for children. Greek men often kept their wives locked up in their homes while entertaining themselves with cultivated prostitutes. Women were considered inferior to men and thus were generally uneducated and accorded low social status. Because the ancient Greeks believed high status made people attractive, and given that the emphasis of love was on mind and heart, women were considered unattractive and thus unfit for *agape*. As a result, ancient Greeks downplayed the significance of heterosexual love. Because only males were considered attractive and good or worthy companions, the highest form of love in ancient Greece typically involved an older man's infatuation with a beautiful adolescent boy. Male homosexual love was considered as natural as heterosexual love.

The Greek influence on modern ideas and practices of love can be found throughout our society. For example, we often hear people refer to relationships as "platonic." The idea of platonic love is rooted in the Greek emphasis that love is of mind and heart, and even today the term continues to mean essentially love without sex. The idea of platonic love is most often attributed to Plato; it thus, bears his name. Some contemporary researchers, however, have claimed that this attribution is misleading, as some of Plato's writings indicate that he recognized a connection between love and sex.

Love in Ancient Rome Female and male relationships in ancient Rome were considerably different from those in ancient Greece. They therefore gave rise to a very different form of love from that described by Plato. Upper-class Roman women were more educated and worldly and more socially and intellectually equal to Roman men than their counterparts in Greek society. Thus, in contrast to ancient Greece, love in Roman society was oriented primarily toward heterosexual love. Love still was not connected to marriage, however. Marriages continued to be arranged by families and took place for the economic, social, and political advantages they accorded.

Love most often occurred in secret, outside these arranged marriages. It consisted primarily of meaningless flirtation and brief encounters between couples. The most important part of a love relationship was the seduction of a desirable person. To be desirable, potential lovers, especially women, had to be physically attractive. Love in this context had to be secretive: If exposed, men could be severely fined by the offended husband; women, however, could lose their lives.

The Early Christian Idea of Love The arrival of Christianity promoted the idea of the love of God, a spiritual love that was different from Plato's ideal forms of love. The Christian church considered the overt sexuality and eroticism of the Greeks, Romans, and pagans as an immoral abomination. The early Christian idea of love was one of a nonsexual, nonerotic relationship, and the ideal person was expected to deny all desires of the flesh to attain holiness. If people could not control their desires of the flesh (that is, remain celibate), they could marry, but even between married couples, sexual desire and attraction were frowned upon. As Christianity spread throughout the Western world, so too did the ideals of celibacy and virginity. From the Christian ideas about love and sexuality grew the notion that priests and nuns should live a celibate life, an ideal that is still part of the Roman Catholic faith but one that often has been not only challenged in recent times but also violated by some Roman Catholic clergy.

Although not the same, the Christian idea of love emphasized aspects of *agape*, especially the idea of honor and devotion to be directed to the spiritual community rather than to individuals. At the very least, the downplaying of eroticism in Christian love weakened the relationship between married couples, making it relatively easy for people to forsake personal relationships and devote themselves instead to the Christian community.

Courtly Love Not everyone accepted the Christian definition of love. In particular, many among the powerful nobility challenged the Christian notion and espoused a new idea of love—referred to as courtly love—that combined two basic ideas of the time period: male chivalry and the idealization of women. Courtly love, which emerged sometime between A.D. 1000 and 1300, involved flirtatious and romantic overtones that marked the beginning of chivalry and was the precursor to our modern version of romance—aptly called courtship (Coltrane, 1998).

The ideas and messages of courtly love were first heard during this period in the love songs and romantic poetry of French troubadours, a unique class of minstrel knights who traveled from one manor to another singing and reciting poetry and later sonnets in exchange for food and shelter. Their songs and poetry were directed toward aristocratic noblewomen whom they idealized in their lyrics and tales about beautiful and superior ladies who were inaccessible to their suitors. Courtly love was a break from earlier idealizations of love because in courtly love noblewomen were exalted, albeit in a spiritual sense. As it is commonly described today, they were placed on a pedestal. One could flirt with a noblewoman and even have sex with her, but she remained unattainable as a permanent love object. Adultery, however, was common. Because noblewomen and their lords had not usually married out of love or developed a close personal relationship, erotic courtly romances frequently developed between ladies and visiting knights (or troubadours) (Coltrane, 1998).

Although this form of chivalrous love was confined to a small segment of the population and was not associated with marriage, the courtly love rituals of the nobility laid the groundwork for more popular ideas about love and romance among the general population. In its popular manifestation, courtly love was often nonsexual. Sex was considered animalistic, dishonorable, and degrading, so courtly love required that there be no sexual relations between lovers. Couples could, however, and sometimes did, lie nude in bed together and caress each other, but they could not have intercourse. Sex was primarily for reproduction and thus generally reserved for marital relationships.

The emergence and development of romantic love was greatly influenced by a number of features of heterosexual relations during this period, most notably the idea that love should be reciprocal or mutual. With the emergence of courtly love, for the first time, women were considered an important part of the love relationship, worthy of the love and passion of men. Most researchers of the subject contend that a major contribution of courtly love was to raise women's status from that of a despised person to one worthy of being worshiped and loved. Many women today, however, insist that setting women apart to be worshiped and protected by men keeps women dependent on men for definitions of self and love and for care and protection.

Whatever we might think of courtly love, its impact on Western thought and romantic behavior cannot be overstated. In fact, a number of the romantic ideas of courtly love are still apparent in contemporary notions of love. For example, the ideas today that you cannot love two people at the same time, that love makes your heart beat wildly, and that love can occur at first sight emerged from the period of courtly love. From these beginnings, romantic love became an institutionalized component of upper-class and then middle-class marriage and family life. Eventually, as Western societies became industrialized and urbanized, romantic love became institutionalized among the lower and working classes as well.

The Institutionalization of Love in Marriage As the market economy developed and capitalism spread, the roles and functions of individuals and societal institutions changed, and the ideal of the family as a separate domestic sphere began to develop. Industrialism created new demands, roles, and responsibilities for families and their members. The most relevant of these new responsibilities for the continued development and spread of romantic love was the responsibility of the family to provide emotional strength and support to its members.

Changing patterns of production and consumption encouraged within the family the development of both economic cooperation and marital love between wives and husbands. Although strongly influenced by the upper- (or noble-) class notion of courtly love, the emerging industrial middle class rejected the central idea that love is to be found outside marriage. Rather, love began to be viewed as a mutual caring that should occur before and continue to develop throughout the course of a marriage; it was supposed to last a lifetime. In many respects, love became a kind of emotional insurance that kept wives and husbands tied together "until death do us part." For this to work effectively, however, it was necessary to develop a new cultural attitude toward sex, one that connected it to love and kept it confined to marriage (Coltrane, 1998).

By the late nineteenth century in the United States, as the middle classes enjoyed more leisure time, courtship came to be extended over a longer period, and the idea of love and romance in such relationships had become widespread among all classes. By the early twentieth century, this concept of love was an essential part of the courtship process (see Chapter 5). Although love was now blended with marriage, it was not yet blended with sex. Romantic love and sex were considered almost polar opposites. For example, romantic love was thought of as tender, warm, and caring, whereas sex was thought of as crude and vulgar. The blending of love and sex ultimately grew out of the sexual revolution of the 1920s, an era that witnessed a marked increase in premarital sexual behavior. In addition, attitudes about sex changed noticeably as people began to tie it to love, intimacy, and marriage.

Today, romance, love, and sex are inseparably intertwined, and some people believe that the intimacy generated by one may actually enhance the others. Whether or not this is true, today many people believe that romantic love without sex is incomplete and sex without love is emotionally shallow and exploitative. However, although most Americans believe that love is an important basis for beginning and maintaining a marriage and that sex should be a part of a loving relationship, recent national polls indicate that they do not believe that sex should be necessarily reserved for marriage—60 percent of Americans believe that premarital sex is morally acceptable. In fact, one recent study found that premarital sex is normal behavior for the vast majority of Americans. However, while Americans do not see premarital sex as wrong, they do see extramarital and casual sex as wrong. On the other hand, roughly about one-fourth of Americans find sexual activity recreational and do not need love or commitment as a prerequisite (Saad, 2011a; Finer, 2007; *Washington Post*–ABC News Poll, 2003). Such attitudes highlight the degree to which our ideas about love, marriage, and sex have changed over time. They also alert us to the fact that the Western sequence of "love, marriage, and then comes the baby carriage" reflects several culturally based assumptions about the nature of intimate heterosexual relationships. These assumptions are by no means universally shared, particularly in non-Western cultures; even in Western societies, this sequence of love, intimacy, and marriage has not always prevailed. And as the discussion in the In Other Places box demonstrates, it is important to take into account the cultural context and cultural and historical factors that contribute to the development of love and intimacy in a particular society.

In Other Places

THE MEANING OF LOVE ACROSS CULTURES

Because romantic love figures so importantly in the culture and lives of people in many Western societies today, we tend to think of it as the only proper basis for forming intimate relationships. However, the concept of romantic love is not found in all cultures and, when it is, it is not necessarily the basis for establishing intimate relationships. Studies across cultures reveal very different attitudes toward romantic love and the ways in which it is channeled into long-term relationships. Among the !Kung of southern Africa, love is an important commodity for women, and it is intimately connected to their sexuality. A !Kung woman's sexuality is her primary means for negotiating the conditions of her relationships with men, and it is also believed to be an important source for the mental well-being of women. According to the !Kung, if a girl grows up not learning to enjoy sex, her mind will not develop normally and, once she is an adult, if she does not have sex, her thoughts are ruined and she is forever angry. In terms of loving relationships, a woman's sexuality attracts lovers and a loving relationship and maximizes her independence. By taking lovers, a !Kung woman proclaims her control over her social life, because in !Kung culture, women's sexuality is believed to be a major source of vitality and life for men; without it, they would die (Robbins, 2005).

In contrast, in traditional Chinese culture, romantic love and sexuality are far less important than other factors as a basis for intimate relations between women and men. Whereas !Kung women use their sexuality to attract lovers, the sexuality of Chinese women figures very little in their relationships with men, both before and after marriage. Unions between Chinese women and men are arranged by the heads of their families, and female virginity is both valued and necessary for a successful match. A Chinese woman's sexuality is not negotiable; rather, her value is in her potential to become a mother of a male child. In fact, becoming a mother cements her relationship with her husband (Robbins, 2005). The concept of romantic love does not fit very well in traditional Chinese society, where the individual is expected to take into account the wishes of others and the primary ties of love and intimacy are linked to family relationships—with parents, siblings, other relatives, and one's children. Romantic love, however, is not a totally foreign concept to the Chinese. In ancient feudal China, falling in love before marriage was not unusual, although parental consent was necessary before the marriage could occur. However, over the 2,000-year period in which the traditional Chinese family flourished, romantic love was considered dangerous and harmful to the development of a "good" marriage, in which women and men took on the proper roles of subservient daughter-in-law and respectful son (Queen, Habenstein, and Quadagno, 1985).

It is interesting to note that among recent cohorts of young adults in China and other Asian countries, there are signs of change toward greater valuing of love as a basis for marriage. In Japan, for example, the number of "love marriages" has increased significantly over the past four decades. Although the older generation of Japanese still holds on to traditional values, survey data indicate a strong desire among young Japanese women for "love" or "love-based" marriage. Similarly, after the revolution in 1949 in the People's Republic of China, and as a result of the increasing wage labor in mainland China's towns and cities as well as the growing Western influence, "love-marriages" have become the norm. Chinese women's roles are changing from passive compliance and obedience to their husbands and in-laws to a more active role in family and intimate relationships (Dion and Dion, 1998; Leeder, 2004).

What do you think? How might intimate relationships be different if the U.S. view of love was similar to that of the !Kung? To that of the traditional Chinese? Explain. Which of the two views of love and intimacy presented here comes closer to approximating your personal viewpoint? Explain. Do you believe individuals in the United States have "free choice" in whom they fall in love with? Whom they date? Whom they "decide" to marry? If you do not believe Americans have free choice, then what do you think stands in the way of free choice?

THE IMPORTANCE OF LOVE

Researchers have found that in U.S. society, love is extremely important both in terms of our physical as well as our emotional health and well-being. Numerous studies demonstrate that being in love romantically and/or being loved are positively related to good physical and emotional health. In a now classic statement on love, medical expert Joseph Nowinski (1980, 1989) asserts that a satisfying love affair is one of the best medicines for fighting off physical diseases. He says that a variety of studies show that married couples or those in a satisfying relationship have fewer psychological problems; single women, on the other hand, have the most. Many experts in the field today agree with Nowinski

Attachment Theory The importance of love in general can also be viewed within the larger context of human social development. According to human attachment theory, love is essential to the survival of human infants and the social, psychological, and emotional well-being of adults. From infancy through adulthood, humans have a need for love and attachment with other human beings. Early interactions with parents lead children to form attachments that reflect children's perceptions of their self-worth and their expectations about intimate relationships. These ideas about attachment are carried forward into later intimate relationships. Sociological studies of children who have experienced extended isolation from other humans have found that the lack of bonding, attachment, and love with at least one other human being has a detrimental effect on the physical, psychological, and emotional development of the child. Later in their life cycle, these children are often unable to develop intimate love relationships because they did not experience such relationships when they were young. For adults, the experience of extended isolation often causes deep feelings of depression, anxiety, and nervousness. This research suggests that a person's attachment style is related to aspects of her or his childhood and remembered relationships with parents or other caregivers and is a predictor of the quality of her or his dating and marital relationships (Moore and Leung, 2002; Hetherington, Parke, and Locke, 2006).

Self-Love The experience of self-love or what some social scientists refer to as self-esteem, the personal judgments individuals make regarding their own self-worth, seems an important prerequisite for loving others. It has been suggested repeatedly in the literature that the ability to feel love, to express it, and to accept it from others is a learned behavior, acquired through our early experiences in infancy and childhood. Infants must be loved so that they can learn how to love. Like romantic love, self-love is tied to an individual's social situation. For example, several studies show that one's self-esteem is directly linked to the love expressed toward that individual by her or his significant others. When significant others give positive feedback, self-esteem increases; conversely, when feedback is consistently negative from significant others, it lowers self-esteem. Thus, infants who are held, touched, caressed, and otherwise shown love develop a self-love—that is, they come to see themselves as important and worthy of love. In adulthood, the people most likely to succeed in their intimate relationships are those who have been socialized in childhood to develop their potential to love (Kennedy, 1999; Ornish, 2005).

Love not only dominates our everyday consciousness, it is also a yardstick against which we evaluate the quality of our everyday lives (Karp, Yoels, and Vann, 2003). The level of love we perceive as existing in our intimate relationships affects how we feel about ourselves and others. It seems, then, that those of us who are most happy with our lives define that happiness in terms of a loving relationship. We typically define a satisfying relationship as one in which there is an intense commitment to love. Attachment theory as well as research and theories about self-love are important frameworks for a sociological understanding of love because they remind us that love is a learned emotion. The importance of love in American lives has fueled a "love industry," making love great for a variety of businesses (see the Applying the Sociological Imagination box).

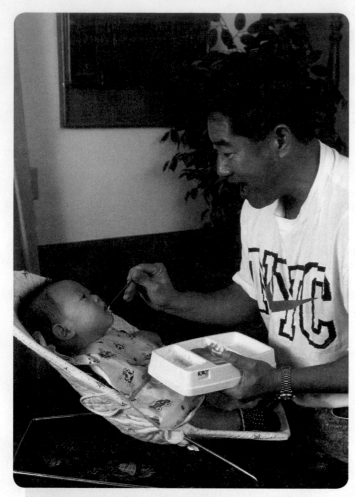

Loving bonds that develop during infancy are essential to the survival of human infants and for the social, psychological, and emotional well-being of adults. Parents, such as this father with his son, often exhibit an agape love style that emphasizes nurturing and an unselfish concern for their children's needs.

and contend as well that long-term love relationships (even if no longer passionate) appear to have a positive effect on the health of those involved. Newer research confirms the health-improving and life-affirming effects of love on the human body. For example, by studying the heart's rhythms, researchers have discovered that when we feel love or any positive emotion such as compassion, caring, or gratitude, the heart sends messages to the brain and secretes hormones that positively affect our health. Love and intimacy may also help protect against infectious diseases. When we feel loved, nurtured, cared for, supported, and intimate, we are much more likely to be happier and healthier. We have a much lower risk of getting sick and, if we do, a much greater chance of surviving (Ornish, 1998, 2005). Conversely, being unloved has been shown to be related to heart disease and early death among unmarried people. Not being loved or the loss of love has also been linked to depression and can even lead some people to commit suicide (McGrath, 2002).

APPLYING THE SOCIOLOGICAL IMAGINATION

LOVE AS BIG BUSINESS

In Western society, especially the United States, love is great for business. For instance, every February, long considered a month of romance, across the country, candy, flowers, and gifts are exchanged between loved ones, all in the name of St. Valentine. On Valentine's Day, the most romantic holiday of the year, Americans spend billions of dollars on valentine cards, roses, candy, jewelry, clothing and dining out.

Did You Know?

- There are at least three legends about the origins of Valentine's Day. One legend, for example, has it that Valentine's Day originated to commemorate the anniversary of the death of St. Valentine, a Roman clergyman who was executed on February 14, about 270 A.D., for secretly marrying couples in defiance of the emperor.
- Americans began exchanging hand-made valentines in the early 1700s. In the 1840s, Esther Howland, a native of Massachusetts, began selling the nation's first mass-produced valentine cards. Today, more than 200 million valentine cards are exchanged each year, and that does not include valentine cards exchanged by millions of school children each year.
- Valentine's Day is the third-largest retail holiday of the year. In 2011, Valentine's Day spending topped $15 billion. The average consumer spent approximately $116 on Valentine's Day. Men spent an average of $159, whereas women spent an average of $76.
- There are more than 29,000 jewelry stores in the United States. Jewelry stores sell engagement, wedding, and other rings to lovers of all ages. In February 2011, these stores sold $3.5 billion worth of merchandise. Close behind spending on jewelry, Americans spent $3.4 billion on dining out, $1.7 billion on flowers (73 percent bought by men, 27 percent bought by women), and $1.5 billion on candy (75 percent of that is spent on chocolates).
- 190 million Valentine's Day cards are exchanged in the United States each year.
- Women purchase more than 80 percent of Valentine's Day cards, but men aren't exactly slackers. When men do buy Valentine's Day cards, they typically choose more overtly romantic cards than their female counterparts.
- According to the condom company Durex, condom sales are highest around Valentine's Day.

Valentine's Day Cross-Culturally

- On Valentine's Day, Japanese women buy gifts for their men. Japanese men reciprocate on March 14, a day commonly known as *White Day*.
- In 2008, a northeastern province in Thailand decided to turn away any couple who wanted to file for divorce on Valentine's Day. On this side of the world, a Charleston, West Virginia, classic rock radio station gave away a free divorce.
- The National Fatwa Council in Malaysia decreed that Valentines Day is not appropriate for Muslims and they should refrain from celebrating it because it is not part of Islamic teachings.
- A Hindu political party had members patrol the central Indian city of Indore to ensure that couples did not engage in any display of their love on February 14.
- Gift shops and florists in Saudi Arabia remove red items from their inventory until after Valentine's Day because the country considers the celebration of such a holiday a sin.

www.historychannel.com/exhibits/valentine
www.wisebread.com/weird-things-you-didn't-know-about-valentines-day
www.cnnmoney.printthis.clickability.com/pt/cpt?action=cpt&title=Valentine%27s+Day=s

Using the Web sites listed above as a beginning point, search the Internet for facts and figures about love. Pay attention to the reliability of the source and the validity of the data and figures. How do the facts and figures you gather fit what you thought you knew about love before you read this chapter and gathered additional information?

How Do People Express Love?

In his now classic book, *The Art of Loving* (1956), psychoanalyst Erich Fromm popularized the notion that many different kinds of love exist, only one of which is erotic or romantic love. Other kinds of love Fromm identified include brotherly, maternal, paternal, infantile, immature, and mature love. According to Fromm, love has four essential components: (1) care (we want the best for the people we love); (2) responsibility (we are willingly sensitive and responsive to their needs); (3) respect (we accept them for what they are); and (4) knowledge (we have an awareness of their needs, values, goals, and feelings). When people share these components, they then become a couple or a pair. Fromm cautioned, however, that contrary to popular belief, love is not a simple process. Finding

In what was called a Valentine's Day gift to Italy, on February 13, 2007, archaeologists excavated two interlocked Stone Age skeletons not far from Verona, the setting of *Romeo and Juliet.* Leaving their "eternal embrace" intact, the 5,000-year-old couple has become an icon of enduring love for many.

the right person is difficult and requires a lot of work and practice. Fromm suggested that falling in love is very different from being in love, which involves facing the realities of living together. He further suggested that being a loving person is the best way to be loved.

Consider the following discussion of styles of loving and think about your own style of loving. Where does your definition of love and style of loving fit, if at all, in Lee's typology of styles of loving? Do you express only one style of loving or some combination of styles? Explain. What would be the best pairing of love styles? The worst? Why? Does Lee's discussion of romantic love help or hinder your understanding of love in general?

LEE'S SIX STYLES OF LOVING

Whenever the subject of styles of loving comes up in the scientific literature, it is the research of Canadian sociologist John Alan Lee that is most often referred to. Using data from more than 4,000 published accounts of love in conjunction with 112 personal interviews,

Lee (1974) concluded that there are many types of love relationships. Half of Lee's respondents were females and half were males. All were White, heterosexual, and under the age of 35. Based on findings from this group, Lee proposed six basic styles of loving. Using the analogy of a color wheel, he identified three primary styles of love relationships (analogous to the three primary colors of red, yellow, and blue): eros, ludus, and storge. In the same way that all other colors are a mixture or combination of the three primary colors, Lee contends that all other styles of love represent a combination of these three primary styles. The three most important compounds or mixtures of the three primary styles of love are mania, pragma, and agape. The six styles of loving are described here.

Primary Styles of Love

- **Eros** is characterized by an immediate, powerful attraction to the physical appearance of another ("love at first sight"). Erotic lovers are often preoccupied with pleasing their lover, and sexual intimacy is strongly desired. In fact, they often engage in sexual relations soon after they meet a partner. Nothing is more problematic for an eros lover than to have a partner who lacks her or his sexual enthusiasm. If the partner is not openly erotic, the relationship will usually be of short duration.
- **Ludus** is a carefree, playful, casual, and nonpossessive love, without a deep commitment or lasting emotional involvement. A ludus lover often has several partners simultaneously or encourages her or his partner to have other relationships to prevent the partner from becoming too attached. The ludus lover engages in sex simply for the fun of it and not as a means to a deep emotional relationship. Thus, this style of loving seldom leads to a long-term relationship or marriage.
- **Storge** (pronounced "stor-gay") is an unexciting and uneventful style of loving. An affectionate style of love with an emphasis on companionship, it usually develops slowly, beginning as a friendship and gradually developing into love. Storge is long-lasting, but it is not passionate. Sexual intimacy occurs late in the relationship and often results in marriage or cohabitation. Even if the relationship ends, storgic lovers often remain good friends.

Derived Styles of Love

- **Mania** combines eros and ludus. Manic love is characterized by obsession and possessiveness. It is a jealous and stressful love that demands constant displays of attention, caring, and affection from the partner. According to Lee, this type of love seldom, if ever, develops into a long-lasting, committed relationship.
- **Pragma,** which combines ludus and storge, is logical, sensible, and practical. Compatibility is a must. A pragmatic lover rationally chooses a partner who shares her or his background, interests, concerns, and values. Not surprisingly, computer dating and matching services are based on a pragmatic viewpoint.
- **Agape** (pronounced "ah-GAH pay"), which combines eros and storge, is selfless and giving, expecting nothing in return. It represents the classical Christian idea of love as altruistic, undemanding, and chaste. Agape lovers tend to advocate and adhere to sexual abstinence. It is a kind of love that is characteristic of saints.

According to Lee, although people generally prefer one particular style of loving, they often express more than one style. For example, a relationship might begin with an erotic style of loving, but as the relationship matures, it might change to a friendship or companionate (storge) style. Lee also observed that the compatibility of styles of loving between two people is important to the success of a love relationship. The greater the differences between a couple in their style of loving, the harder it is for them to relate to each other.

Gender Differences

Interestingly, in over a quarter of a century of research on romantic love, social scientists Susan and Clyde Hendrick (1983, 1987, 1995, 1996, 2002) found a number of gender differences in styles of loving. Although women and men do not differ significantly on eros or agape, gender differences on other love attitudes or styles consistently show up. For example, their research repeatedly shows that men are more ludic in orientation than women, and women are typically more storgic and pragmatic than men. In addition, women report a more manic orientation than men. A national poll found that 1 in 3 Americans think about former lovers at least once a week, and approximately 1 in 6 think about the one that got away almost every single day. Although the gender difference is small, 17 percent of men compared to 14 percent of women think about a former lover every day. And 24 percent of men say that they have been in love five or more times in their adult life, compared with only 11 percent of women who say the same (Covel, 2003b).

On the other hand, although gender differences are apparent, the genders were more similar than different. For example, women and men are similar in rating the typical features of love, and they are similarly passionate and altruistic in their love styles. Women and men are also similarly likely to believe that true love lasts forever and that there is that one person out there who is meant for them. And both women and men tend to link love and sex in their romantic relationships (Hendrick and Hendrick, 1996, 2002; Sprecher and Toro-Morn, 2002).

Moreover, Hendrick and Hendrick (2002) have also found that among many contemporary college students, lovers are also best friends. In written accounts of their love as well as their ratings on the Love Attitude Scale, they described their relationship most often in terms of storge, or friendship love. In one study, almost one-half of the respondents identified their romantic partner as their closest friend. These results certainly indicate the importance of storge or friendship in ongoing, contemporary heterosexual romantic relationships. The Hendricks have found very few differences between male heterosexuals and male homosexuals in their love attitudes leading them to conclude that gay and straight men are similar in love styles.

Although Lee's typology is ideal (in the real world, no one's love style matches any of Lee's styles perfectly) and based on a sample of White heterosexuals under the age of 35, were you able to identify your style of loving in one or more of Lee's six styles? How close or how different are you and your partner's style of loving? Are you more similar than different or more different than similar?

A philosopher once said that we know the taste of love but few of us can distinguish the many flavors of love. Given the various types and styles of love it is possible to experience, how do we distinguish what we feel from true love, puppy love, friendship or infatuation? Perhaps the next section will help you answer this question.

Love versus Friendship and Infatuation

How do we know when we are in love? When we were young, we were told our feelings of love were not really true love, that they were either "puppy love" or infatuation. Furthermore, we were told not to fret because we would know when it was true love. Such responses imply that there is a "fake love" or that some other emotion can very easily be confused with love, but that love is some special feeling that we will recognize the minute we experience it. If this is the case, how do we tell the difference? How do we know if what we feel is not simply friendship or infatuation?

CLOSE FRIENDSHIP VERSUS LOVE

Over the last several decades, a number of researchers have attempted to distinguish love from friendship and infatuation. Researchers Keith Davis and Michael Todd (Davis and Todd, 1985; Davis, 2004) compared close friendship and love and found that although the two are alike in many ways, there are crucial differences between them that make love relationships both more rewarding and, at the same time, more volatile. Davis and Todd's prototype of friendship includes the following eight characteristics:

- *Enjoyment:* For the most part, close friends enjoy being in each other's company.

It is not always easy to distinguish love from close friendship because they share so many of the same characteristics. Couples in love, as well as close friends, often enjoy just being in each other's company.

- *Acceptance:* They accept each other for what they are; they do not try to change each other.
- *Trust:* They share the feeling that the other will act in her or his best interest.
- *Respect:* Each assumes that the other exercises good judgment in making life choices.
- *Mutual Assistance:* They are willing to aid and support each other; they can count on each other when needed.
- *Confiding:* They share feelings and experiences with each other.
- *Understanding:* Each has a sense of what is important to the other and why the other behaves in the manner that she or he does.
- *Spontaneity:* Both feel free to be themselves rather than pretend to be something that they are not.

Love, in contrast, is friendship and more: It is passion, caring, and sexual desire. But it is also instability and mutual criticism. Some social scientists (Tennov, 1979; Davis and Todd, 1985; Davis, 2004) have described romantic love as unstable in that it involves an almost endless series of emotional highs (joys or positive emotions) and lows (despair or negative emotions). It includes all the characteristics of friendship as well as two broad clusters of characteristics not found in friendship: a passion cluster and a caring cluster. The passion cluster includes fascination, preoccupation with each other, and desire to be together all of the time; exclusiveness, with top priority given to the love relationship, making another such relationship with someone new unthinkable; and sexual desire, the desire to be physically intimate with each other. The caring cluster consists of giving the utmost, caring so much for each other that each gives her or his all to the relationship; and being a champion or advocate, helping and supporting each other in all types of situations (adults' and children's definitions of love illustrated in Table 4.1 fall into each of these clusters).

Social scientists have suggested that, like romantic love, friendship is important to our emotional and even physical well-being. It helps us maintain a sense of social reality and staves off feelings of isolation in a largely anonymous world. According to psychotherapist James Grotstein, "Friendship governs all intimate relationships and it is more profound than sex and love" (quoted in Sheehy, 2000). Like romantic love, the development and expression of platonic love or friendship are also heavily influenced by social factors. Research shows that friendship formation is largely a product of our daily interaction patterns rather than of chance or "good chemistry." Friendships tend to develop with the people we see most often. Like romantic love, friendship grows best out of similarity. We tend to build the strongest friendships with those who hold attitudes similar to our own. We also tend to connect with those who share our physical and social characteristics—appearance, income, educational level, race, and so on.

On the level of experience, various research studies show that the way in which we define and express friendship differs in terms of important social characteristics, such as race, gender, sexual orientation, and social class.

Race In the past, most of the research on friendship has been conducted using White middle-class heterosexual females and males (usually college students). However, recent researchers have noted that women and men who are other than White, middle class, and heterosexual may have different types of friendships from those cited in much of the friendship literature. For instance, for people of color, particularly women, "ethnic empathy" is a key factor in choosing friends. Although they often have cross-race friendships, their shared experiences with friends of their own race or ethnicity allow them to do what they feel they cannot do with friends of a different race—namely, share the experience of dealing with racism, the intersections of race, class, and gender, and the impact of these factors in their daily lives. This issue of ethnic empathy is compounded for people whose backgrounds are racially mixed (Sheehy, 2000).

Class Friendship studies focusing on social class show that working-class Americans conceive of friendship as an exchange of goods and services; gifts and favors indicate the strength of a friendship bond. In contrast, this kind of material exchange is not part of the middle-class definition of friendship. Middle-class individuals tend to view friendship as an emotional or intellectual exchange; they also frequently conceive of friendship simply as the sharing of leisure activities. Who our friends actually are also varies by class. Friends among the working classes are highly likely to be relatives—siblings, cousins, parents—whereas friends among the middle classes are typically nonblood relations. Further, among working-class individuals, friendships are overwhelmingly same sex, most often local; friends have known each other for much longer periods of time than is typical of middle-class friends. Interaction among working-class friends is said to be more frequent than among middle-class friends, with some researchers suggesting that working-class friends interact, on average, once a week or more. In contrast, members of the middle classes are more open to cross-gender friendships and, because middle-class lifestyles often involve a high degree of geographic mobility, middle-class friendships are as often long distance as they are local. Not only are middle-class friendships often maintained after individuals move out of the immediate geographic area, but also, because of geographic mobility, friendships among middle-class individuals often develop when people meet as they travel to different locales. As a result of this distance factor, middle-class friends typically report less frequent contact than their working-class counterparts (Walker, 1995; Ruane and Cerulo, 1997). Such findings illustrate the significance of sociological factors in the formation of intimate relationships and illustrate that friendship, like love, is socially and culturally mediated.

Gender plays an important role in structuring intimate relationships—whether in same-sex or heterosexual relationships. For example, some research indicates that the number of close friends that men have increases from adolescence until around age 30, falling off thereafter. In contrast, the research for women is mixed. Some research shows that for women, the number of important friendships rises gradually over the life span, whereas other research suggests that there is a slump in early adulthood followed by an increase beginning somewhere between the late 30s and 40s. Additionally, men are more likely to be intimate with women than they are with other men. Intimacy between men seems strongly influenced by the restrictive attitudes and sanctions in U.S. society generated by homophobia. Thus, for instance, fear of being seen as *gay* causes some men to distance themselves from friendships (at least close ones) with other men. In general, however, from middle to late life, a man is less likely to have a close friend the older he gets, whereas a woman's chance of having at least one such friendship does not change with age.

Contrary to past assumptions that women's primary identity is attached to men, current research shows the important role that friendship between women have, including women who live within heterosexual relationships (Andersen, 2005). Although there are documented gender differences in friendship development and patterns, recent research indicates that women and men share many patterns and styles of friendship. Like women, for example, men rely on their male friends for emotional support and intimacy. In addition, many friendship activities such as seeing friends for dinner, sharing ritual events, and visiting are things that both women and men friends do (Walker, 1994, 2001). In fact, according to Barry Wellman (1992), there has been a widespread *domestication* of male friendship, with men seeing friends in their home in much the same way that women do (quoted in Walker, 2001).

Sexual Orientation Friends are of crucial importance in the lives of both lesbians and gays. In his research on gay friendships, sociologist Peter Nardi (1999) stresses how powerfully supportive and influential friends are in the lives of gays and how their network of friends often become a surrogate family. Likewise, research on lesbian friendships have found the same familial connection. For many lesbians and gays, friends mean more and last longer than romantic relationships. In addition, when asked about their friendships, lesbians and gays often count lovers and ex-lovers among their close friends (Clunis & Green, 2010; Rose and Zand, 2000; Nardi, 1999, 2001). Similar to people of color, an important dimension of lesbian and gay friendships is a sense of shared history, a sense of sister/brotherhood, and a sense of shared marginal identity. And, like for many people of color, forming friendships with people with whom they can be themselves is important to lesbians and gays, given a cultural context that typically does not approve of that "self" (Nardi, 2001).

Infatuation versus Love

That warm and wonderful feeling that we are experiencing, is it love or merely infatuation? All too often we confuse these two emotions. **Infatuation** involves a strong attraction to another person based on an idealized picture of that person. It usually focuses on a specific characteristic of the person and has a strong physical (sexual) element. Some social scientists have defined infatuation as passion without commitment. In contrast to love, infatuation is generally superficial and of short duration. It can, however, bring people together and develop into love (Lewis, Amini, and Lannon, 2000). The differences between infatuation and love are outlined in Table 4.2.

What do you think of the assessment of love and infatuation presented in Table 4.2? The author implies that love is a mature emotion whereas infatuation is a very immature emotion. Do you agree or disagree? Does it seem to you to be an overly biased conception of love? How would you define the difference between love and infatuation? Is there really a difference?

As this discussion of love, friendship, and infatuation reveals, much of the literature and research in this area of intimacy is somewhat dated. Not much research in this area has been conducted since the 1980s. Does this mean that Americans are less concerned with love and intimacy today than in the past and thus researchers no longer find it a hot topic for their research? What do you think? What factors might account for the diminished interest in romantic love among social scientists even though the public continues to be fascinated with the topic? Regardless of how we answer this question, a number of theoretical explanations (now considered classics) of why and how people fall in love are worth noting.

TABLE 4.2 Is There a Difference between Love and Infatuation?

Is there a difference between love and infatuation? According to a wide variety of sources, there is definitely a difference. Everyone from popular culture writers to medical doctors, therapists, and psychologists has weighed in on the subject. Below are just a few of the ways writers characterize love versus infatuation:

- *Love* takes root slowly and grows over time whereas *Infatuation* happens quickly; it leaps into your blood (*Chicago Sun-Times*, 1980).

- *Love* is a feeling that comes from the heart and soul whereas *Infatuation* is a feeling or emotion that has hormonal triggers (Ianceaksh, 2009).

- *Love* is based on reality and founded on respect, trust, and admiration whereas *Infatuation* is based on fantasy and founded on passion and pleasure (WomanSavers, 2011).

- *Love* is strong, mature, and long-lasting whereas *Infatuation* is obsessive, in the moment, and marked by insecurity (S. Jones, 2009).

- *Love* encompasses intimacy, passion, and commitment whereas *Infatuation* encompasses passionate arousal in the absence of intimacy and commitment (R. Sternberg, 2004).

- *Love* is a deep emotion based on long-term friendship, common interests, and effective communication whereas *Infatuation* is a form of self-love that stems from a person's need for self-gratification (H. Hendrix, 1993).

Some Theories of Love

In recent decades, the works of several social scientists and researchers have provided us with significant insights into the nature of love. Some of the more insightful theories or explanations of love today include the wheel theory of love, love as a story, love as a social exchange, and limerence theory.

THE WHEEL THEORY OF LOVE

According to sociologist Ira Reiss (1960, 1971), love emerges and develops over time as we interact with the other person. Although there are more recent theories of love, Reiss's theory of love as a developmental process remains a classic. Stressing our need for intimacy, Reiss focuses on what he sees as the circular progression of love as a couple interacts over time. Describing this progression in terms of a wheel—the **wheel theory of love**—Reiss proposes that love involves four major interpersonal processes: rapport, self-revelation, mutual dependence, and need fulfillment. Each of these processes can be thought of as individual spokes on a wheel (see Figure 4.1).

Rapport To become lovers, partners must develop a sense of *rapport*—feeling at ease or relaxed with one another. A key factor here is social/cultural background. In general, we seem to feel rapport with people with whom we share a common upbringing, social class, religion, educational level, and values. Although similarity is important in the development of rapport, two people who are different are not necessarily precluded from developing rapport and later, a love relationship. For example, love relationships can and do develop between people from different racial, ethnic, religious, and age groups. It seems that if a couple share basic social values, then other differences are not as difficult to overcome.

FIGURE 4.1 The Wheel Theory of Love

Source: Adapted from Ira Reiss, 1971, "Toward a Sociology of the Heterosexual Love Relationship," *Marriage and Family Living* 22 (May): 139–145. Reprinted with permission of Abbey Press, St. Meinrad, Indiana.

However, without rapport, a couple does not have enough in common to establish an initial interest.

Self-Revelation Ease of communication/rapport leads to self-revelation—the disclosure of intimate and personal feelings. People who feel at ease are more likely to open up and share their hopes, dreams, fears, desires, and ambitions. As with the development of rapport, a person's background is critical to self-revelation, determining in large part what and how much she or he will reveal about her- or himself. Often, factors like race, ethnicity, social class, gender, and age are important determinants of how willing people are to disclose personal feelings. These characteristics act as filters when two people first come into contact and they tend to make snap judgments about another person's potential as a lover on the basis of them. If a relationship endures beyond rapport and self-revelation, the participants tend to grow closer and begin to think about the longevity of their relationship and making a commitment to one another.

Mutual Dependence As two people develop a sense of rapport and feel comfortable enough with each other to self-disclose, they develop a mutual dependence—a reliance on each other for fulfillment. At this stage, two people become a couple. They come to need and depend on each other to share their lives, their happiness, their fears, their hopes and dreams, and their sexual intimacies. They develop interdependent habit systems; ways of acting, thinking, and feeling that are no longer fun or fulfilling when done alone. The social and cultural background of the couple continues to play an important role in this stage of love. Mutual dependence leads to the fourth and final stage in Reiss's wheel theory: the fulfillment of personality needs.

Fulfillment of Personality Needs This is the ability of each partner to satisfy the needs of the other. For instance, as the couple confides in each other, make mutual decisions, support each other's ambitions, bolster each other's ambitions, and satisfies each other's basic needs, their sense of rapport increases, which leads to greater self-disclosure and more mutually dependent behaviors, which in turn lead to still greater needs fulfillment.

In his wheel analogy, Reiss captures this circular process of the development of love. All four processes are interdependent. Thus, a reduction in any one of them affects the development or continuation of a love relationship. As long as the wheel moves forward (the processes flow into each other), love develops and increases. However, when the wheel turns in the reverse direction—when there is a reduction in one of the processes—love may not develop, or if it has already developed, it may diminish. For example, if the partners in a couple are forced to spend less time with each other and they eventually develop divergent interests, their mutual dependence could weaken, which in turn could lower self-disclosure, which could lead to a reduced sense of rapport.

Reiss's pioneering theory of love as a process has sparked other researchers to extend or modify his theory using other metaphors besides the wheel. For instance, social scientist Delores M. Borland (1975) uses the analogy of a clock spring such as that in a watch to explain how love develops in a series of windings and unwindings as love intensifies and ebbs. These windings and unwindings occur as each new event takes place in the couple's relationship and can lead toward a closer, more intimate, and mutually understanding relationship, or they may cause tensions that weaken the relationship. Critics of these theories (for example, Albas and Albas, 1987) note that one of their shortcomings is that they ignore the variation in intensity among the different stages of a love relationship.

The Theory of Love as a Story[1]

Love is often as unpredictable as the climax of a suspense novel. We might wonder from time to time why we or someone we know seem destined to make the same mistakes in love over and over, as if the fate of our intimate relationships were a written script. According to social scientist Robert J. Sternberg, in essence it is a script. Sternberg believes that love between two people follows a story. Thus, if we are to understand romantic love, we have to understand the stories that dictate our beliefs and expectations of love. We begin writing these stories as children, and they predict the patterns of our later romantic experiences.

STERNBERG'S TRIANGULAR THEORY OF LOVE

Sternberg is not new to the field of "love theories." His initial work on love, *The Triangular Theory of Love* (1986, 1988), which continues to be cited in most textbooks on marriages and families, suggested that love is composed of three interlocking components in a triangle-like relationship: intimacy, passion, and commitment (each component can be represented as one point on a triangle), with different loving relationships having different combinations of these elements. *Intimacy,* which rests at the top of the triangle, refers to the bonding and emotional closeness or connectedness that the partners in a couple feel for each other. *Passion* refers to the romantic feelings, desires, and arousal that partners feel for each other. And *commitment* refers to a person's attachment to another person. It develops over time and represents a couple's desire to be faithful to one another and to stay together. Love is not static, however. All love relationships undergo some change over time; thus, each vertex of the love triangle will not be equal. If, however, vertexes are very unequal—if there is too much mismatch among the components—the relationship will fail. When gender role socialization is added to the mix, there is increased difficulty in maintaining equal vertexes (Lindsey, 2005). For example, according to this theory, women attach greater importance to the commitment vertex, and men attach greater importance to the passion vertex. Complete love requires all three components. The absence of all three components represents nonlove.

Although interesting, Sternberg's triangular theory of love has some limitations. Indeed, in recent years, Sternberg himself has indicated some dissatisfaction with this theory. For example, he now believes his theory leaves important questions about love unanswered such as, What makes people the kind of lovers they are? And what attracts us to other lovers? Based on research he conducted over the past decade with hundreds of couples in Connecticut, as well as ongoing research on the subject, Sternberg says that he found answers to these and other questions about romantic love in stories. He found that people describe love in many ways but their descriptions reveal their love story.

STERNBERG'S THEORY OF LOVE STORIES

Sternberg identified 25 love stories that people tell, for example: the sacrifice, police, travel, pornography, horror, recovery, gardening, business, fantasy, war, humor, and collection stories (for the other story types, see Sternberg, 1998). Sternberg developed this love story classification scheme after analyzing research subjects' ratings on a scale of 1 to 7 of the extent to which a group of statements characterized their intimate relationships. Their highest ranked statements indicated their personal love story. According to Sternberg, the most common love stories people tell are the *travel love story* ("I believe that beginning a relationship is like starting a new journey that promises to be both exciting and challenging"), the *gardening love story* ("I believe any relationship that is left unattended will not survive"), and the *humor love story* ("I think taking a relationship too seriously can spoil it"). The least popular or least common love stories include the *horror* ("I find it exciting when I feel that my partner is somewhat frightened of me"), *collectibles* ("I like dating different partners simultaneously"), and *autocratic government* ("I think it is more efficient if one person takes control of the important decisions in a relationship") stories.

In essence, Sternberg's love story theory suggests that our love stories begin soon after birth as we start to form our ideas about love based on our individual personality, our early socialization experiences, our observations of our parents' relationships, as well

It is often assumed that romantic love and feelings of sexuality diminish as we age. However, many later-age adults defy this myth as they participate in ongoing powerful love stories throughout their lifetimes. The recent film *The Notebook,* starring James Garner and Gena Rowlands (pictured), captures aging and the power of love as Garner, a devoted husband, reads to his ailing wife from a notebook recounting their love story and how it has endured over the years.

[1] This description of Robert Sternberg's "love story theory" draws heavily from Sternberg's works on the subject (1998, 2001).

as popular culture descriptions of love and romance in the mass media. We eventually seek to live out these notions of love in our personal lives. Sternberg posits that the course of love typically begins with a physical attraction and similar interests and values. Eventually, however, the couple may notice that something is missing in the relationship. Usually, the missing something is story compatibility. If a couple's stories do not match, there is an underlying lack of coordination to their interaction and their love relationship may not go very far. In contrast, when two people's love stories match, this is what keeps their love alive—it is the key to compatibility with a romantic partner.

Although no one story guarantees a successful love relationship, some stories seem to predict failure more than others (for example, the police, recovery, science fiction, and theater stories).[2] The key to a happy healthy love relationship is that both partners have compatible love stories, that is, compatible relationship expectations. Stories are compatible if they include complementary roles in a single story, such as audience–comedian in the humor love story, or if the stories are similar enough so that they can be merged into a new, unified story. According to Sternberg, we end up with the same kind of bad partners in love relationships not because of bad luck, but because we subconsciously find people to play out our love stories or we force our stories on the people we meet (see the Writing Your Own Script box).

LOVE AS A SOCIAL EXCHANGE

Whatever our love story or style, it seems that it can be described in the language of social exchange theory (recall the discussion of social-exchange theory in Chapter 2). While Reiss's theory identifies the stages in the process of love and relationship development and

Sternberg suggests that our love stories determine the patterns of our romantic experiences, family sociologist John Scanzoni (1980) uses some basic principles of economics to explain why we are attracted to and fall in love with some people and not with others and why we pursue and remain in some relationships and avoid or break off others.

Basically, Scanzoni argues that love, like any other commodity, involves an exchange of rewards between two interested parties. The process of rewarding each other and gratifying each other's needs is continuous and forms the basis on which the relationship rests. Some of the more obvious rewards of intimate relationships include love, caring, sensitivity, sexual gratification, companionship, liking, friendship, warmth, protection, and emotional and financial support. Some costs might be jealousy and conflict, the time and effort required to keep the other partner satisfied, and undesirable personal or social characteristics. Although these types of exchanges are not always acknowledged and usually do not seem as cold and calculating as the market metaphor makes them sound, according to social exchange theory, virtually every romantic encounter involves an implicit, if not explicit, exchange of sexual and emotional goods. As long as the love relationship is mutually rewarding, it will continue, but when it ceases to be rewarding, it will end. Thus, although people in love clearly care about each other, love is not totally altruistic. Research indicates that people who are happiest in their intimate relationships are typically couples who provide one another with far more rewarding experiences than costly ones.

LOVE AS LIMERENCE

Another pioneering theory of love comes to us from the discipline of psychology. Limerence theory, advanced by psychologist Dorothy Tennov ([1979] 1999), provides important insights into the distinction between being in love and other types of loving. Tennov uses the term **limerence** to refer to a style of love characterized by an extreme attraction, a complete absorption or obsessive preoccupation of one person with another. She defines this emotion as being "in love" as opposed to "love," which she defines as caring and concern for another person.

---

[2]Police ("I believe it is necessary to watch your partner's every move"), recovery ("I often find myself helping people get their life back in order"), science fiction ("I often find myself attracted to individuals who have unusual and strange characteristics"), theater ("I think my relationships are like plays").

The obsessive compulsion with another person could develop into a full-fledged obsession that has been immortalized in films, novels, and other aspects of popular culture as a "fatal attraction" that is all too often a reality, particularly for celebrities. For example, in 2011, James Rainford, pictured, was arrested outside the Malibu home of Paris Hilton. He had previously been on probation stemming from an incident at another of Ms. Hilton's homes the previous year.

these characteristics show, there is no typical limerent experience. Tennov's description of limerent feelings encompasses a wide spectrum including incessant or continuous thoughts about the lover, mood swings depending on the lover's actions, being completely closed to the possibility of someone else as a lover, a fear of rejection, a preoccupation or obsession with the lover to the neglect of other interests and concerns, and idealizing the lover.

Tennov's concept of limerence is very similar to that of infatuation. Both stress emotional intensity in romantic relationships, especially in the early stages and particularly for some people. In addition, Tennov's discussion of limerence shares many similarities with Davis and Todd's findings concerning romantic love. In fact, many of the features she identifies with limerence parallel those identified by Davis and Todd as characteristic of the passion cluster.

Tennov's discussion of limerence calls to mind what could happen when limerence is taken to an unhealthy extreme. The almost obsessive compulsion with another person could develop into a full-fledged obsession that has been immortalized in films, novels, and other aspects of popular culture as a "fatal attraction" that is all too often a reality. Such full-fledged obsessions in the real world have had fatal consequences not only for the parties involved, but often for intimates involved with the couple as well. Most people's limerence, however, does not go to this extreme. In fact, according to Tennov, if limerence is mutual, it can lead to a love affair, a commitment, and ultimately to marriage.

Love Across Gender, Sexuality, and Race

Romantic love is often considered a universal feeling. As we have noted, however, not everyone experiences romantic love. Furthermore, when we do experience such love, a number of other important life experiences come into play, making love different for each of us. Probably the most powerful individual differences that affect how we experience love are gender, sexual orientation, and race.

ARE WOMEN OR MEN MORE ROMANTIC? GENDER DIFFERENCES IN LOVE RELATIONSHIPS

Although both women and men experience love and consider it an important experience and relationship, a large body of research shows, as we have already seen with styles of love, that females and males construct their realities of love generally in very different terms. We should bear in mind, however, that, like friendship research, much of this research is also based on survey responses of White, middle-class, heterosexual couples.

The widespread notion that contemporary men are hopelessly unromantic is a misconception. Contrary to American cultural stereotypes, men are more romantic and give greater importance than women to the desire to fall in love. According to a recent study of the timing and meaning of "I love you," although women have a reputation for being the first to say "I love you" in romantic relationships, men actually are more likely to say these three words first and men admit thinking about confessing love six weeks earlier

Based on the findings from her study of the love experiences of more than 500 people, Tennov concluded that limerence is a state of mind—that its most important features lie in the fantasies and ideas that one person has about another. Thus, the focus of limerence theory is on the experience of falling or being in love rather than on the relationship itself. Although some people never experience limerence, Tennov suggests that the majority do.

Limerence theory underscores the high level of intensity associated with romantic love; it describes and explains the extreme highs and lows that many people experience in their love relationships. Positive limerence can bring an elated feeling, whereas negative limerence can bring feelings of despondency, despair, pain, and depression. Limerence can be characterized by (1) its speed of occurrence at the onset, (2) its intensity, (3) whether or not the feeling is reciprocated, and (4) the length of time it lasts. As than their female partners. Taking an evolutionary economics perspective, the study's authors theorize that gender differences in the timing and function of saying "I love you" are related to whether a couple has had sex. For example, they found that men are happier than women to hear "I love you" one month into the relationship if they have not yet had sex, while women feel happier than men when they hear "I love you" after the onset of sex in the relationship (*Chicago Tribune*, 2011). While women tend to be affected by emotionally moving moments and long for relationship milestones marked by feelings of deep intimacy, men express romantic thoughts and feelings through everyday action. Although they don't routinely talk about romantic things, they do remember their first kiss as vividly as women. In addition, men tend to hold highly romantic views of love—true love conquers all, love at first sight does exist, couples are destined for each other—while women take a more pragmatic approach to such matters (Marketwire, 2007).

Another popular misconception about women, men, and love relationships is that of women in endless pursuit of men who are unready or unwilling to commit to a relationship. However, in contrast to this popular view of women chasing reluctant men and coyly maneuvering them into an unwanted relationship, it seems that males are more likely to be looking for a committed relationship and they tend to start a relationship with a much more romantic perspective than females. Although both women and men seem to enjoy the chase and are often stimulated by someone they find somewhat mysterious, men tend to fall in love more quickly and earlier in their relationships, fall in love with more people, stay in love longer, have crushes, and fall in love with someone who does not love them in return more often than women. Men are also more preoccupied with love relationships (Covel, 2003b; Madden and Lehnart, 2006; Miller, Perlman, and Brehm, 2007).

Furthermore, women distinguish much more sharply between liking and loving than males. Researchers believe this to be the case because women are much more in tune with their feelings than men. Given that men are socialized to be task-oriented as opposed to social-emotional, they are often unable to make the fine distinctions in their feelings that women are. Yet when men are in love, they tend to describe their love in slightly more passionate terms than women (Covel, 2003a, 2003b)

While women and men fall in love for many of the same reasons—similar values, emotional maturity, dependability—men are more likely than women to fall in love for reasons related to physical attractiveness. Women are more cautious about love using a variety of factors in deciding if they are in love. These factors include physical attractiveness and similarity in values and other traits, but also ambition, industriousness, and financial prospects (Eastwick and Finkel, 2008). When they do fall in love, women tend to be more expressive than men, fall in love harder and more intensely, they are more likely to idealize the love object, and prefer emotional closeness, whereas men prefer giving instrumental help and sex. Women generally regard intimacy, self-growth, self-understanding, and positive self-esteem as important benefits of romantic love, and loss of identity and innocence about relationships as important costs. Men, on the other hand, regard sexual satisfaction as an important

Watch the **Video** *Busting Out* on **myfamilylab.com**

benefit and monetary losses from dates as an important cost. Thus, women's love is more likely than men's to develop incrementally or practically. Once a relationship develops, women tend to form a more intense and lasting love bond and are willing to sacrifice more than men for love (Knox, Kaluzny, and Cooper, 2000; Tavris, 2000; Wood, 2004).

Although women tend to spend more time than men trying to cultivate and maintain love relationships, women are also the ones more likely to decide when to break off a relationship. They tend to initiate a break-up more often than men and they seem better able than men to put aside feelings of rejection and to redefine their relationship as friendship. In contrast, men (gay and straight) are more resistant to breaking up and have a harder time recovering after a break-up, taking significantly longer to get over their lost loves than women. For example, once a relationship is over, men, more often than women, tend to feel sad, lonely, depressed, and unwilling to give up on the relationship. Men are also more violent and possessive when romantic relationships end (Knox, Kaluzny, and Cooper, 2000; Tavris, 2000; Wood, 2004).

Interestingly, it seems that even before adulthood, adolescent boys and girls report similar feelings of love in a relationship and those feelings don't hinge on having sex. Contrary to the popular culture stereotype of adolescent boys as shallow with little interest in the opposite sex beyond meaningless hook-ups, boys place as much importance on romance as girls, though they are often reluctant to talk about or share their feelings for fear of being ridiculed by their male peers. In addition, although adolescent boys have lower levels of confidence navigating romantic relationships than girls, they have similar levels of emotional investment in their relationships. On the other hand, like their adult counterparts, boys generally fall in love sooner than girls, they are in love more often than girls, and they fall in love harder than girls (Giordano, Longmore and Manning, 2006; Stephens, 2011).

These findings seem consistent with female and male socialization in U.S. society. Females are taught almost from birth to be loving, caring, and nurturing. Men, in contrast, are taught to be detached, independent, and unemotional. Obviously, these basic differences do not hold for every woman or man. Rather, they are general tendencies that are subject to change and have sometimes changed over time. The gender gap in the ways that women and men approach romantic love relationships, for instance, seems to be closing as women's and men's lives become more similar.

The Feminization of Love Discussions and investigations of gender differences in love relationships have led some sociologists, such as Francesca Cancian (1993), to call attention to how heavily gendered our ways of thinking about love are. According to Cancian, part of the reason that men seem so much less loving than women is because men's love behavior is measured with a feminine ruler. She describes the social organization of love in the United States in terms of the concept of the feminization of love—love as a central aspect of the female domain and experience and defined purely in female terms. Cancian's research demonstrates that social scientists generally use a "feminized definition of love" in their research, that is, only women's style of loving is recognized as love. At least since the nineteenth century, love has been defined primarily in terms of characteristics that women are thought to be particularly skilled in, such as emotional expression, self-disclosure, and affection. Such a definition typically ignores aspects of love that men prefer, such as providing instrumental help or sharing physical activities. It also presumes that men lack feelings and emotional depth and that relationships and feelings are unimportant in men's lives. Men are thought of as incompetent at loving because the common view of romantic love overlooks the instrumental, pragmatic aspect of loving and stresses primarily the expressive aspect. And based on the myth that women both need love more than men do and are more skilled at loving than men are, love has become a preoccupation with women.

One of several problems with this incomplete and overly feminized view of love, says Cancian, is that it contributes to male dominance of women because it leads women to focus on interpersonal relationships while encouraging men to achieve independence from women and to specialize in the occupational activities that are more highly regarded in this society. She argues that ideally love should be **androgynous**—that is, it should include a wide range of attitudes and behaviors with no gender role differentiation. An androgynous view of love validates both feminine and masculine styles of loving and considers both necessary parts of a good love relationship.

What do you think? Do you agree with Cancian, or do you think that differentiation along gender lines in terms of love has disappeared? What evidence can you give to support your position? Try applying a sociological analysis to this issue. How close are your findings to what you already knew or have experienced?

LESBIAN AND GAY LOVE RELATIONSHIPS

Just as there is no distinct heterosexual style of loving, there is also no distinct same-sex value orientation toward love relationships. Instead, what appears to be more important than sexual orientation is one's sex—being female or male—and one's background. Women's goals in intimate partnerships are similar whether the partner is male or female. The same is true of men. Regardless of the sexual orientation of the two partners, research indicates that most partners want to love and be loved, want to be emotionally close, expect fidelity in the relationship, and expect the relationship to be long-term. In general, patterns of lesbian and gay love are very similar to heterosexual love. Unlike heterosexual couples, however, lesbian and gay couples often feel compelled to hide their feelings of love because many people do not approve of such relationships. Although Americans tend to prize romantic love, they are generally hostile to love and intimacy between people of the same sex. Because of societal disapproval, gay lovers frequently look to each other to satisfy all their needs. Thus, gay love is often intense and sometimes possessive. In this sense, it is often both highly emotional and highly physical.

Social science research has traditionally been heterosexist and homophobic. Much of what was written about lesbians and gays before the 1960s was written by heterosexuals and discussed from a psychoanalytic and/or pathology perspective, which until recently focused almost exclusively on lesbian and gay sexual behavior. Although specific information and research on love among lesbians and gays continue to be limited, an emerging literature on lesbian and gay relationships across a wider span of social behavior is now being conducted by lesbian and gay social scientists, and their findings refute many of the common myths about lesbian and gay intimacy.

For example, one of the most long-standing stereotypes of lesbian and gay relationships is that they are fleeting, uncommitted, and primarily sexual. However, although gays do have more partners on average than heterosexual men, most establish enduring intimate relationships. And research indicates that lesbian couples generally have more stable and longer-lasting love relationships than either heterosexual couples or gay male couples. In the few studies that have included older lesbians and gays, researchers have found that relationships lasting 20 years or more are not uncommon. The long-term nature of these relationships often persists even after the couple is no longer "in love." For instance, research shows that when lesbian and gay partners break up, they frequently maintain a close relationship with one another by making a transition from being lovers to being friends (Weston, 1997; Clark, 1999; Kelly, 2007).

Another popular myth about lesbian and gay relationships is that they are unhappy, abnormal, and dysfunctional. However, a study of matched sets of lesbians, gays, and heterosexual women and men involved in a current romantic/sexual relationship found no significant differences among the three sets of couples in terms of love and relationship satisfaction. Like the heterosexual couples, lesbians and gays reported very positive feelings for their partners and generally reported that their relationships were highly satisfying and very close. Findings such as these negate the persistent negative cultural images of lesbians and gays as unhappy individuals who are unsuccessful in developing enduring relationships, who drift from one sexual partner to another, and end up old and alone. This is not to imply, however, that all lesbian and gay couples are euphorically happy and problem free. Rather, the point is that lesbian and gay couples are no more unhappy, abnormal, or dysfunctional than heterosexual couples.

It is important to keep in mind that lesbian and gay relationships are not monolithic; there is no typical lesbian or gay couple or relationship. Rather, as with heterosexual couples, enormous variation exists among lesbian and gay couples. The emerging scholarship on lesbian and gay couples emphasizes this diversity. It also expands our existing knowledge base about love and intimate relationships by increasing the diversity of types of relationships studied to include same-sex partnerships and close relations. In the future, perhaps this will extend to bisexual and transgendered couples as well.

FEMALE–MALE RELATIONSHIPS ACROSS RACE AND ETHNICITY

As with research on lesbians and gays, there is little systematic data on love and the organization of romantic relationships across race. To the extent that the American public is informed about such relationships among various racial and ethnic groups, often we have had to rely on a popular literature that may or may not accurately capture the essence and real-life experiences of these relationships, given that their bottom line is the selling of their product and profit. And to the extent that we hear about female–male love and intimacy other than among Whites, it is most often about African Americans and it is most often in the context of pathology or crisis. This is perhaps not surprising given that there is little profit to be made by

To the extent that the American public is informed about loving and intimate relationships between women and men among various groups of color, often we have had to rely on mass media portrayals. Although these portrayals of love and intimacy may or may not capture the essence and real-life experiences of such relationships, some programs serve a useful purpose by counteracting popular stereotypes about African American families and female/male relationships as pathological or in crisis. One example is *Are We There Yet?*, which centers on a loving newlywed African American couple facing the challenges of everyday life and the trials of a newly-blended family (the wife brings two children to the marriage) trying to adjust to one another.

noting that the reality of African American intimate relationships are overwhelmingly nonpathological and stable; that African Americans overwhelmingly choose and marry each other and in most cases form stable, satisfying relationships (Hill, 2005). Thus, for example, over the past several decades, popular literature has repeatedly reported a crisis in African American female–male love relationships. According to several popular and scholarly writers on the subject, African American women and men have experienced some difficulty in developing and maintaining meaningful love relationships. This is said to be due, in part, to the suspicions and mistrust generated by years of racism and exploitation, and the pitting of one sex against the other by forces outside their control. Contention over the strong Black woman is a central theme in Black popular culture and literature, with many African Americans embracing and idealizing patriarchal models of love and intimacy that is being abandoned by other races. While African American women are applauded for the active, strong, vital roles they play in their families and communities, they are contradictorily told that such roles are improper in their intimate relationships with men (Hill, 2005).

In turn, some African American women argue that it is difficult for them to develop a committed relationship based on equity because although the roles of women in society have changed, the attitudes of some African American men have not kept pace. Because racism has made achievement of a position of power in the larger society difficult if not impossible for many African American men, many of these men continue to hold on to the one venue where they have been able to exert power: their intimate relationships with African American women. They are said to hold on

tenaciously to the ideology of male dominance and see controlling African American women as crucial to their claim to masculinity.

Contrary to this talk of a crisis, however, African American romantic relationships are no more or no less characterized by crisis than are such relationships for other racial and ethnic groups. In addition, African American females and males fall in love as often and confront the same kinds of obstacles to their relationships as individuals in other racial and ethnic groups. For example, like women in other racial and ethnic groups, African American women perceive a lack of male commitment as a key obstacle to love and romance. In a poll conducted by *Ebony* magazine (cited in Hughes, 2001), African American women respondents reported that what they want in an intimate relationship is a supportive, romantic man who openly expresses his deepest love and feelings and listens attentively to theirs. Above all, they said, they want a lover who is not afraid of commitment. Some experts on African American love and intimate relationships refute the stereotype of African American men as noncommittal, nonpassionate, and afraid of responsibility. Instead, they argue convincingly that when they are in love, African American men are committed to the relationship and passionate about pleasing the women they love. On the other hand, they find that for African American men, as for men of other races, *romance* is a term they hardly think about and they sometimes get it mixed up with "sex."

Although little scientific research has been conducted on differences in styles of loving across race in the United States, evidence suggests a difference in the way various groups of color and Whites view love. Research indicates, for example, that African Americans tend to have a more romantic view of love (Hughes, 2001). As with African Americans, the literature on Latinas/os and romantic relationships is practically nonexistent. According to some of the popular Latina/o literature, Latinas/os are more openly passionate about love and less afraid of falling in love and loving than most Whites. On the other hand, like other groups, Latinas/os say that in love relationships, they look for someone who respects and treats them well; someone who is sensitive, affectionate, exciting and who can be a companion in life. According to some of these sources, the stereotypical macho Latino in Latina/o intimate relationships is passé (Sigler, 2005). A search for data on love relationships among Asian/Asian Americans was equally sparse. Although beset by the limitations of popular literature, an insight into Asian/Asian American views about love can be gleaned from this literature. For example, in an Asian poem written by Mai Van Trang entitled "An Asian View of Cultural Differences" (cited in Selvaraj, 2005), the poet compares, among other issues, Asian/Asian American views of love with those of Western society, citing some of the following examples: (Asians) marry first, then love. (Westerners) love first then marry. (For Asians) marriage is the beginning of a love affair. (For Westerners) marriage is the happy end of a romance. (For Asians) love is mute. (For Westerners) love is vocal.

In any case, continuing racism and discrimination in U.S. society, coupled with the changing social roles of women and men, will no doubt continue to exert pressure on the development and maintenance of love relationships between African American women and men. As for other groups of color, the need for scientific research on love and intimacy is even greater than that for African Americans. Indeed, this is an area of research sorely in need of the skills and insights of scholars across academic disciplines.

Obstacles to Love and Loving Relationships

Few people thrive in an environment of social isolation, so we desire and pursue meaningful love relationships. Unfortunately, a number of individual and cultural factors serve as obstacles to the development and maintenance of love. Some of the most troublesome of these factors are demographic factors and social and cultural change, traditional gender role socialization, patriarchy, lack of trust, and jealousy.

DEMOGRAPHIC FACTORS AND SOCIAL AND CULTURAL CHANGE

As we have pointed out, race, class, gender, and sexual orientation are key factors that impact love and intimacy. A number of other demographic factors—such as age, income, occupation—are also key in shaping our love and intimacy experiences. For example, as you will find in Chapter 5, in the United States, age is a significant demographic factor that impacts whom we fall in love with, date, and eventually marry (if we marry) or cohabit with. In heterosexual relationships, for instance, women are expected to love, date, and marry men who are somewhere between 2 and 5 years older. Conversely, men are expected to love, date, and/or marry women 2 to 5 years younger. Although there are no laws that require us to fall in love with, date, and/or marry people within this age range, informal norms and personal and public pressures operate to keep us typically within this age-related range.

On the other hand, formal norms or laws define when we are considered old enough to marry, thereby defining (even if indirectly) when we are old enough and mature enough to fall in love. In all but one state, the legal age at which marriage can be contracted without the consent of a parent is 18 for both women and men. In some states, couples under age 18 may marry with parental consent. Such restriction is waived, however, if the female applicant is pregnant. In actual practice, age norms and laws around love, intimacy, sex, and marriage are not always followed. When such laws are violated, the consequences for the offending party can be grave, including long jail sentences.

Recently, the relationships of older men and younger women captured the attention of Americans across the country. Examples include the engagement of Hugh Hefner to Crystal Harris (60 years his junior) and the marriage of Doug Hutchinson to Courtney Stodden (35 years his junior). The seemingly increasing phenomenon of love knowing no age boundaries raises interesting and important questions about whether or not or to what extent love between minors and adults should be regulated (see the Debating Social Issues box on page 112).

Social and cultural change also shape our love and intimacy experiences. For example, as you will see in Chapter 5, with increasing technologies—such as electronic mail; answering machines and voice mail; text messaging; social networking sites such as Myspace, Facebook, and Twitter; Skype; Internet chat rooms; and computerized matchmaking services—a burgeoning love industry has developed that has had the effect of decreasing the incidence of face-to-face interactions and thereby depersonalizing love and intimacy.

Economic or financial stress can also be an obstacle to love and intimate relationships. One of the greatest felt needs in our culture today is financial. It has often been reported that money or financial stress reduces intimacy and is the number one cause of marital and intimate conflict; money or financial stress often leads to couple break-ups or divorce. For example, it can cause romantic partners to react angrily toward each other, which can lead to violence and/or break-ups. According to some research, individuals struggling with money problems sometimes tend to drink more alcohol, abuse drugs, and/or smoke more.

Given that today, Americans are said to be drowning in debt, how do couples keep their love alive in spite of financial stress? Interestingly, at the same time that Americans are deeply in debt, we are saturated with financial advice on love, money, and intimacy from a variety of "experts," including some who now offer conferences to help couples eliminate the financial stress in their relationship in order to enjoy greater intimacy with one another.

If you are in an intimate romantic relationship, do issues of money have an impact on your intimacy and love life? How so? Have you bought advice books on how to manage financial stress in your love relationship? Would you attend a conference dedicated to this issue?

TRADITIONAL GENDER ROLE SOCIALIZATION

As the discussions in Chapter 3 and throughout this chapter reveal, differential gender role socialization often creates very different attitudes and behaviors in females and males. Nowhere is this more evident than in the ways in which the two genders view love relationships. Research has shown that women and men seem to have different priorities when it comes to love relationships. Several researchers have found considerable evidence of an emotional division of labor within heterosexual love relationships, with one partner (usually the woman) more oriented toward the relationship than the other is. That is, the relationship and what it should consist of is more familiar to and central in the life and behavior of one partner than it is in that of the other. Likewise, homosexual couples tend to consist of one partner who is more oriented toward the relationship than the other.

Men get much more out of love relationships than they give. Women, because of the way they have been socialized, are able to be compassionate, to give support, and generally to be there for their partners. Men, in contrast, require emotional understanding and tenderness but have not been taught to give it. Thus, they often have less access to their feelings than women. Consequently, it is often the woman who reaches out and makes emotional contact. Feeling this emotional inequality, some women console themselves with the belief that they can rely on their inner strength to make up for what they do not get from their partners. This emotional imbalance between women and men can be an obstacle to either the development or the maintenance of a loving relationship.

PATRIARCHY AS AN OBSTACLE TO LESBIAN LOVE

A number of scholars have identified the patriarchal structure of Western society as an obstacle to same-sex love. Focusing on lesbian

Debating Social Issues

SHOULD SOCIETY PUT AN AGE LIMIT ON LOVE?

Hugh Hefner and Crystal Harris before their wedding was called off.

Although in popular culture the notions that love conquers all, that age is nothing but a number, and that older women and men make great life partners and loyal companions, in the face of both legal and cultural prescriptions about the appropriate age for love, sex, and marriage these adages do not hold up. In the twenty-first century, a person under age 18 is still legally and socially defined as a child. And in most states, sexual relationships between someone age 19 and older and someone younger than 16 is legally classified as statutory rape. In some states, such relationships are illegal even if the couple is married at the time. Furthermore, adults who engage in sexual relationships with a minor are considered sexual abusers and pedophiles. Nonetheless, adults romancing minors seems to have come of age in the United States.

In 2011, amid a myriad of tabloid headlines, 25-year-old Crystal Harris, a former *Playboy* Playmate of the Month, model, singer, and television personality, was dubbed a "runaway bride"

by the media after she called off her wedding to 85-year-old Hugh Hefner of *Playboy* magazine fame just five days before the planned nuptials. Although there was a 60-year age difference, the would-be bride said that the age difference had nothing to do with her decision to call off the wedding.

In the same year, but with a bit less fanfare, reports of the marriage of 51-year-old actor Doug Hutchinson (of the film *The Green Mile* and TV series *Lost*) to 16-year-old aspiring country singer Courtney Stodden in Las Vegas raised anew public reaction and commentary on social networks concerning a large age disparity between engaged and/or married older men and younger women (in this case, a 35-year age difference). However, unlike Crystal Harris, who was 25, Courtney Stodden, at 16 years of age at the time of the wedding, was legally a minor. According to the Clark County, Nevada Marriage Bureau, both marriage license applicants must be at least 18. But minors (below age 18) are able to obtain a license with the consent of a parent or legal guardian. Although not verified, it is assumed that one or both of Courtney's parents approved of the wedding. Nevertheless, in response to the widespread media coverage of their marriage, the couple said they are aware that their vast age difference is controversial but they are very much in love and want to get the message out that true love can be ageless (Mulick, 2011).

In 2005, however, Matthew Koso, a 22-year-old Nebraskan male who married his 14-year-old pregnant lover, was charged with statutory rape even though their parents gave the marriage their blessing. The two became a romantic couple when she was 12 and he was 20. Unable to wed in their home state of Nebraska, which prohibits marriages of people under 17, the couple traveled to Kansas to

marry, one of the few states that allow people as young as 12 to marry. Back home in Nebraska, the Nebraskan attorney general accused Mr. Koso of being a pedophile but Koso said that what he and his bride have is *true love*. Outrage over the Koso case included a deluge of letters to the attorney general's office that opposed the prosecution and angrily urged the attorney general to leave the couple alone and spend more time putting "real criminals" in jail. Nonetheless, if convicted, Mr. Koso could face up to 50 years in prison (Wilgoren, 2005).

In a similar case but where the age of the couple was the reverse of the Nebraska couple, a 37-year-old pregnant Georgia woman, Lisa Lynette Clark, who married her 15-year-old lover in 2005, was charged with child molestation and jailed. The two were wed under a Georgia law that allows pregnant couples to marry regardless of age and without parental consent. Geared toward preventing out-of-wedlock births, the law dates back to at least the early 1960s (Dunwald, 2005).

Cases such as those of Koso and Clark, along with a number of studies that show most babies born to teenage mothers are fathered by adults, have prompted many states to dust off seldom-used statutory rape laws that prohibit sex between adults and minors and to crack down on the older men. These studies of teenage pregnancy indicate that in two out of three births to teenage mothers, the father is 20 or older, often much older than the mother; the younger the mother, the wider the age gap. Although such studies provide revealing data on the incidence of intimacy between underage girls who get pregnant and their adult male lovers, they do not, however, indicate how many older men are sexual partners of teenage girls who do not have babies. Thus, the incidence of female minors and adult male lovers could be much higher. In any event, state legislators face more questions than answers as they debate what is exploitative and what is appropriate in love and intimacy.

Historically, pedophilia, sexual abuse, and statutory rape have generally been thought of by most Americans as a male phenomenon. In the past, the most often publicized relationships between an adult and a minor have been those between an adult male and a minor female. However, in recent years there have been several cases nationwide involving alleged or proven love and sexual relations between adult females and male minors, particularly female teachers and male students. In recent memory, a flood of such cases seems to have begun with Mary Kay Letourneau, a Seattle teacher, who served 7 years in jail stemming from her relationship with a sixth-grade student. That relationship eventually produced two children and, in 2005, after her second release from prison, Letourneau and her by then 22-year-old lover were married. One writer on the subject listed 50 recent cases in the United States involving women as old as 50 and minors as young as 11 (Kovacs, 2005).

Some people claim that the pairing of an older and younger partner is not new—it has always been around. They suggest that the increase in such romantic relationships is a result of today's increasing permissiveness and more relaxed social norms and that we should change the age of consent to accommodate these cultural changes. Others suggest that in the increasingly sexualized American culture, the lines seem to be increasingly blurred between what is appropriate and what is not relative to intimacy and the choice of partners. On one side of the issue of intimacy between adults and minors are those who argue that adults should not have romantic relationships, including sexual intercourse, with minors—those under age 18— who they believe know nothing about the complicated consequences of romantic love and involvement with an adult. On the other side of the issue are those who argue that not all adult–minor relationships are abusive, that, in fact, most are consensual and should not be classified as criminal. For example, a British professor who has been studying such relationships for the past three decades concludes that sexual contact between an

adult and a minor is not necessarily criminal and, in fact, can be a positive experience (Kovacs, 2005).

As older and younger people seek each other out at an increasing rate, centuries-old traditions about what is or is not an appropriate age for love, sex, and/or marriage might have to be reexamined and rethought. In an interview at a public school for teenage parents, a 14-year-old, 7-months-pregnant female who met her husband when she was 12 and he was 23 said that "it's nobody's business whom you love and date" (Navarro, 1996).

What do you think? Are individuals under age 18 who are involved in romantic sexual relationships with adults victims of abuse, or are they capable of entering a consensual relationship that should be recognized by the state? Are such relationships problematic solely because of the age difference between the two partners? Should such relationships be criminalized? Explain. How old is too old or too young for romantic involvements? Does it matter how old lovers are if they are happy? Explain. How much control should the state or federal government have over our personal lives?

love, some of these scholars contend that romantic love between women is outlawed and repressed because it is viewed by men as a threat to the patriarchal structure of intimate relationships and to heterosexuality generally. To these scholars, heterosexuality includes not only sex between women and men, but also patriarchal culture, male dominance, and female subordination, all of which benefit men (Faderman, 1989). The centrality of patriarchy in mate selection is evidenced in the concept of heterosexuality and the notion that women are dependent on men for emotional as well as social and economic well-being. Some of the more common assumptions of patriarchy and heterosexualism are that women's primary love and sexual orientation are naturally directed toward men and that heterosexuality is ordained by nature. Thus, heterosexuals have seldom questioned these assumptions, even though there is ample evidence that lesbian love has existed throughout history and has been accepted at different times by various societies.

From a lesbian perspective, such assumptions not only legitimate heterosexuality as the norm but also denigrate women's romantic relationships with other women, defining these relationships as deviant or pathological. We need only look at the social sanctions

brought against women who love women (as well as men who love men) to understand how, through social control, heterosexuality is maintained as the norm and same-sex love and intimacy is defined as deviant. For example, society subverts any public expression of same-sex consciousness or behavior, defining it with terms such as evil, sick, sinful, and a crime against nature (Andersen, 2005). Such ideas and attitudes are detrimental both to lesbians' sense of self-worth and their ability to establish romantic relationships with other women.

LACK OF TRUST

Do you trust your partner? Does your partner trust you? Is it important to your relationship that each of you trusts the other? Why?

Trust is probably important to your relationship because with it you and your partner can relax; you can feel secure about the relationship and not worry about whether it will continue. Social researchers John Rempel and John Holmes (1986) designed a trust inventory scale to address these questions. According to Rempel and Holmes, **trust**—the degree of confidence a person feels when she or he thinks about a relationship—is one of the most important and necessary aspects of any close or intimate relationship. Because trust can mean something different depending on what aspect of the relationship we are focusing on, Rempel and Holmes identified three basic elements of trust: predictability, dependability, and faith.

Predictability is the ability to foretell our partner's behavior, the knowledge that she or he will consistently act in our best interests. For confidence to grow and trust to develop, it is not enough simply to know in advance how our partner will behave. A sense of predictability must be based on the knowledge that our partner will act in positive ways. As the relationship progresses, however, we begin to focus more on our partner's specific qualities, such as dependability and trustworthiness, and less in terms of predictable behavior. This leads to the second element of trust—dependability—which can be defined as the knowledge that our partner can be relied on when we need her or him. Both predictability and dependability are based on the assumption that people will behave in a fairly consistent manner (the same in the present as they did in the past). But because human behavior is changing, there is no guarantee that this will be so. Therefore, we often remain committed to a relationship based on sheer faith. Faith allows people to go beyond previously observed behaviors to feel assured that the partner will continue to be loving and caring.

THE NATURE AND PATTERNS OF JEALOUSY

Although love can provide us with wonderful feelings and experiences, it often has a dark side as well: jealousy. Most researchers on the subject define **jealousy** as an emotional reaction aroused by a perceived threat to a valued relationship or position and motivates behavior aimed at countering the threat. It is the fear of losing someone whom you love or who is very important to you and is usually an unhealthy manifestation of insecurity, low self-confidence, and possessiveness. To precipitate feelings of jealousy, the perceived threat of loss does not have to be real; instead, it can be potential or even completely imaginary. The key is that we believe the relationship is threatened (Farrell, 1997; Cano and O'Leary, 1997).

Most of us have experienced jealousy at one time or another. Some of the most important relationships have been destroyed by it. What is this powerful emotion, what causes it, who is most likely to exhibit it, and what consequences does it have for our relationships?

Researchers have found that jealousy involves not one but a number of interrelated emotions, including anger, anxiety, uncertainty, fear of loss, vulnerability, hatred, shame, sorrow, humiliation, abandonment, betrayal, loneliness, hopelessness, suspicion, insecurity, and pain. Although jealousy often brings about damage (psychological or physical), it is seldom the case that jealous persons actually mean to do harm. Rather, they usually are simply reacting to one or more of the emotions associated with jealousy, believing they are protecting either their relationship and/or the ego of the threatened partner. However, carried to the extreme, jealousy can lead to the greater probability of abuse and violence in an intimate relationship or even death. For example, recently a woman was convicted of killing the pregnant girlfriend of a former NFL football player and sentenced to life in prison. The victim was shot six times, and two of the bullets struck the baby. Prosecutors accused the woman of carefully planning the execution of someone she viewed as a rival for the football player's affection ("Woman Convicted of Killing ex-Bear's Girlfriend...," 2011).

Jealousy, like love, can be thought of as a social construction, an emotion shaped by a person's culture. It is not biologically determined. Thus, what makes people feel jealous will vary from one culture to another and change over time even within a culture.

Patterns of Jealousy Researchers have found that those who are most likely to be jealous are women, people in open or multiple relationships, people who are unhappy with their lives overall or with their love relationship, less-educated people, younger people, and people who are unfaithful themselves (Salovey and Rodin, 1989; Buss, 2000). Jealousy also varies from one historical period to another and from culture to culture. Examining research studies and records spanning a 200-year period, social psychologist Ralph Hupka (1991) found consistent differences across cultures in both the degree to which jealousy is present in a society and the ways in which it is expressed. This finding led him to classify societies as either high-jealousy or low-jealousy cultures.

Highly stratified societies and those in which heavy emphasis is placed on sexual exclusiveness, such as in the United States, exhibit a high level of jealousy, whereas societies with little or no stratification, where individual property rights are discouraged and sexual gratification and companionship are easily accessible to all people, exhibit a low level of jealousy. A Native American group, the Apaches of North America, is an example of a high-jealousy culture. Among the Apaches, great emphasis is placed on female virginity and on male sexual gratification. Male sexual pleasure must be earned after a prolonged period of deprivation, and it must be judiciously protected from all intruders. Apache wives and children are so important to the status of Apache men that when the men are away from their families, they engage close relatives to watch their wives secretly and report their wives' behavior to them when they return home. In contrast, the Toda of southern India are an example of a low-jealousy culture. Jealousy in this culture is rare because there is little of which to be jealous. The Todas take a sharing attitude toward people and things; neither are defined as personal property. In addition, the Todas place few restrictions on sexual pleasure, and neither marriage nor heirs are prerequisites for social honor and prestige.

Based on his findings of high- and low-jealousy cultures, Hupka concluded that jealousy is not biologically determined; rather, it is a learned emotion. We learn what our particular culture defines as valuable and in need of protection. Hupka's findings are consistent with sociological research suggesting that jealousy is a social emotion learned through the socialization process. The existence and expression of jealousy depend very much on how love and love relationships are defined—which people, things, and relationships are valued in a particular society. In other words, jealousy is rooted in the social structure of a society insofar as cultural norms provide the cues that will or will not trigger it.

An interesting example of the influence of socialization and cultural definitions of intimate relationships (i.e., monogamy versus nonexclusivity) and the incongruence that sometimes occurs between ideological viewpoints and personal feelings about a valued relationship is provided in Candace Falk's (1990) examination of the life and ideology of Emma Goldman. Goldman, an early feminist (from the early twentieth century) known for her so-called radical political and social views, espoused, among other things, the notion of free love and freedom from sexual jealousy. Nonetheless, Falk

Speed Bump

SOMEONE ELSE? HOW COULD I BE SEEING SOMEONE ELSE?

There are probably as many definitions of jealousy as there are people who experience this emotion. As with love, women and men differ in terms of how they view and experience jealousy.

Source: Speed Bump © 2007 Dave Coverly. Used with permission of Dave Coverly and the Cartoonist Group. All rights reserved.

reports that although Goldman spoke and wrote extensively about the perils and negative impact of jealousy, and the pettiness and small-mindedness of jealous people, Goldman herself was beset by jealousy of her lover, who, although he professed his love for Goldman, had a number of sexual liaisons with other women.

On the other hand, if you were born and raised in a culture such as ancient Japan, where extramarital sexual relationships (or nonexclusivity) was the norm for both women and men and acknowledged publicly, such relationships would not provoke sexual jealousy from either gender. In contemporary Japan, while extramarital sexual liaisons are prohibited for both women and men, Japanese men (especially businessmen) nonetheless often seek out and utilize the services of prostitutes. Japanese wives seldom if ever react to this behavior with jealousy. Rather, they tend to define such behavior as harmless because it does not involve love. In essence, Japanese women have learned within the cultural framework and constructs of their society that they should not be jealous of their husbands' indiscretions with prostitutes because such sex is "casual" and not a threat to their marriage. On the other hand, if the husband has a mistress, Japanese wives become extremely jealous. In this cultural context, a mistress is viewed as very threatening to a marriage in that Japanese men who have mistresses often have a second set of children as well (Cherry, 2002).

Gender Differences in Jealousy Are women or men more jealous? There is no set answer to this question. However,

although researchers have found that both women and men experience jealousy when their partners become emotionally or sexually involved with other people and that there is no gender difference in the frequency, duration, or intensity of this jealousy, some have found a gender difference in the causes of jealousy. For example, those taking an evolutionary perspective report that women are more likely to become jealous if the partner is emotionally involved with another person, whereas men are more likely to become jealous if the partner becomes sexually involved with someone else. Critics of this perspective, however, question the validity of both the sample and the type of questions used in evolutionary studies and suggest that both women and men—whether heterosexual or gay—are more jealous of emotional than sexual infidelity. Some of the more prevalent research findings concerning the differences between women and men in the United States in terms of the ways that they feel and act when they are jealous include the following:

- Women feel jealousy more intensely than men.
- Jealousy causes women greater suffering and distress than it does men.
- Men are less likely than women to stay in a relationship that makes them jealous.
- Women are more likely than men to fight to win back a lost lover rather than give up the relationship. When men feel jealous, they try to repair their self-esteem, whereas women try to repair the relationship.
- Women's feelings of personal inadequacy lead to jealousy, whereas men feel jealousy first, which then leads to feelings of inadequacy that something is wrong with them.
- Men are more likely than women to express their jealousy in the form of violence. They are also more likely to shift the blame for both their jealousy and their violent response from themselves to a third party.
- Women more often consciously attempt to make their partner jealous as a way of testing the relationship (see if he still cares), of increasing rewards (get their partner to give them more attention or spend more time with them), of bolstering their self-esteem, of getting revenge, or of punishing their partner for some perceived transgression.

Are any of these gendered patterns of jealousy familiar to you? Are they consistent with your personal experiences with love and jealousy? If not, how do you account for any differences?

Destructive Jealousy Jealousy can be destructive in terms of the toll it takes on the individual psyche, in the form of deep depression, fear, anxiety, self-doubt, and low self-esteem. It can also be physically damaging and life-threatening when it is expressed in terms of anger, violence, and the desire for revenge. For example, recently, as a Minnesota couple watched United States Congressman Anthony Weiner confess on television that he had tweeted a sexually suggestive photo of himself to several women other than his wife, the wife turned to her husband and said, "You'd be dead" (Noveck, 2011). While this wife may or may not have been serious, in the backdrop of Internet relationships: sexting, tweeting lewd photos, Facebook, e-mailing, Skyping, many couples today are grappling with the question: If it is virtual, does it constitute infidelity? Clearly, while social media web sites and the Internet can help relationships, they can also harm them. For example, in 2010, a 37-year-old man got so angry over a message posted on his live-in girlfriend's Facebook page that he beat her, tied her up, jabbed her with a baseball bat, threatened to kill her, and wouldn't let her leave their home for four days (Hopper, 2010).

There are mixed opinions about whether or not digital flirting and various virtual sexual behaviors constitute cheating if you are in a committed relationship. The bottom line, however, is that regardless of whether or not such behaviors are conscious acts of cheating or that there is a consensus about what these behaviors represent, if such behaviors stimulate feelings of jealousy in an individual, they can precipitate a range of responses from outrage to violence.

> Do you consider flirting through texting a form of cheating? When is it harmless, and when does it cross the line?

Managing Destructive Jealousy If jealousy is such a damaging emotion, what can we do either to prevent it or to deal with it in a constructive manner? The options suggested by social researchers Lynn Smith and Gordon Clanton (1987) for dealing with jealousy continue to have relevance in today's intimate relationships. They suggest the following: (1) get out of the relationship, (2) ignore or tolerate those behaviors that make you jealous, (3) attempt to change your partner's behavior, and (4) work on your own jealousy. How we manage jealousy depends on the type of jealousy we feel and our commitment to the relationship. If we are interested in maintaining our relationship, we must bring jealousy out in the open. This process involves self-examination: How does jealousy make me feel? How would I prefer to feel? Which actions cause me to feel jealous? Which behaviors or thoughts can I modify to reduce or eliminate my feelings of jealousy?

As we answer these questions, we must look beyond the specific incidents that disturb us to the underlying causes of our jealousy. For example, Is my jealousy caused by my partner's behavior, or is it rooted in my own feelings of inadequacy and low self-esteem? If the latter, perhaps I should try to discover ways to bolster my self-concept and develop self-confidence. We must also evaluate our situation realistically. For example, Is this situation the best for me? Does my partner return my love? If I decide the relationship is worth saving, perhaps I could move beyond my self-analysis of jealousy and share my feelings with my partner. We can share our goals for our relationship and reiterate or redefine what we expect from each other—the kinds of behaviors that are and are not acceptable. In this way, we can work together to change some of the behaviors and attitudes that spark jealous episodes. If these actions fail, both partners might consider counseling or therapy.

Romantic Love Today

Heterosexual love and romance today reflect the changes that have been evident in the roles of women and men since the emergence of the contemporary women's movement. In the past, female and male roles in love and romance were clearly, if not rigidly, defined, usually as a power relationship characterized by male dominance and female submission. Today, however, dramatic changes have taken place in the relationships between heterosexual lovers, especially among the middle classes. But at the same time, many traditional aspects of love, dating, intimacy, and mate selection remain firmly entrenched in U.S. society. The result is a great deal of anxiety and uncertainty as couples try to balance traditional norms with current developments in the absence of clear-cut rules and guidelines.

📖 **Read** the **Document**
The Balance of Power in Dating on **myfamilylab.com**

The changing nature of female and male roles in intimate relationships has left some couples confused about how to relate to each other and has presented a number of problems that hamper the development or maintenance of love relationships. For other lovers or potential lovers, the challenge to traditional male-dominated intimate relations has set the stage for the development of a new, more equitable type of relationship. Many women and men are confronting the conflicts generated by changing gender roles by changing themselves. In general, women and men have accelerated the trend identified by social researchers in the 1980s and 1990s of dealing with each other in a new way, not as one-dimensional entities who fit into narrow and rigid roles but as whole and complete human beings. If this trend continues as we progress through the twenty-first century, love relationships might be closer to the androgynous love ideal, and lovers may overcome many of the barriers currently caused by gender role stereotypes.

Supporting Marriages and Families

According to some policymakers and various experts, marriages and families have become perhaps *the* most important domestic political issues of the twenty-first century. Whether or not this is the case, as we have already indicated, there is an ongoing need for social policies, principles, initiatives, and programs that support these primary and important institutions. As we have discussed in this chapter, love and intimacy bind society together; they are extremely important in providing both emotional support and a buffer against stress and thus, figure importantly in the preservation of our physical and psychological health as well. Therefore, it is important that there be a focus on the implementation

✴ **Explore** the **Concept**
Social Explorer Activity: Decline in Marriage Rates in the U.S. on **myfamilylab.com**

of policies, principles, programs, and/or initiatives that allow love, loving, and intimate relationships to thrive as well as targeted measures that support these relationships in their variations and diversity.

Increasingly since the election of George W. Bush in 2000, this country has focused on and implemented policies and initiatives said to promote marriages and families. In 2003, for example, the United States Congress passed the *Personal Responsibility, Work, and Family Promotion Act*, the goal of which was to promote and support healthy marriages and families through such provisions as the awarding of grants to states for marriage promotion activities, the initiation of family self-sufficiency plans, the award of grants to public and nonprofit community entities for demonstration projects to test the effectiveness of various approaches to create a fatherhood program as well as a host of other provisions defined as promoting and supporting marriages and families. Such initiatives may have merit, but it is well to keep in mind that healthy love and intimate relationships, including marriages and families, require more than a one size-fits-all approach. Policies that sustain rather than demonize and/or deem inappropriate love, loving relationships, and intimacy that do not fit the "one size" model is what is needed.

Love, respect, and commitment are critical factors in marriages and families; thus, to affirm love and intimacy and promote healthy love relationships is, in essence, the promotion of a wide variety of healthy, intimate relationships including same sex marriages and families. Social policies and programs are only one among many factors that impact the health and well-being of loving and intimate relationships. Such policies and programs are limited in what they can do to strengthen loving relationships and marriages and families but such policies should place these relationships as a critical component of public policy dialogue so as to support all opportunities to strengthen and support these relationships.

SUMMARY

Love is a central feature of life in Western societies. References to love can be found throughout popular culture. Because each of us expresses and experiences love differently, there is a variety of definitions of love and many different kinds of love. However, romantic love can be distinguished from other kinds by its erotic component. It can be defined as the intense feelings, emotions, and thoughts coupled with sexual passion and erotic expression that one person directs toward another, as well as the ideology that upholds it. According to a social-constructionist perspective, love can be understood only as symbolic or as a social construction of a particular historical time, location, culture, and people, having by itself no intrinsic meaning. Romantic love is relatively new in human social history. Its developmental roots in Western societies can be traced to ancient Greek and Roman cultures.

Researchers have found that love is extremely important to our physical and emotional health and well-being. Studies of children and adults who have suffered extended isolation from other humans indicate the learned nature of love and our dependence on other people to provide us with the experiences of love. There is great diversity in the ways in which people express romantic love. Some researchers have attempted to define love by isolating its various components, whereas others have defined it in terms of several styles of loving. Still other researchers have distinguished love from friendship, infatuation, and liking.

Ira Reiss uses a wheel analogy to explain love as a developmental process, whereas Robert Sternberg theorizes that love is a story that dictates our beliefs and expectations of love. A popular sociological framework for examining love is social exchange theory. Using basic economic concepts such as reward, costs, and profits, social exchange theory explains why people are attracted to and fall in love with one another. Psychologist Dorothy Tennov uses the concept of limerence to refer to a style of love characterized by extreme attraction, complete absorption, or obsessive preoccupation of one person with another. Researchers have noted a variety of ways in which women and men differ in terms of how they feel and express love. For example, men fall in love more quickly than women and remain in love longer.

The experience of love is not limited to heterosexuals. In gay couple relationships, but even more so in lesbian relationships, equality between partners is highly valued, and couples work hard to maintain an egalitarian relationship. Because many lesbians and gays do not allow themselves to be constrained by many of the conventional ways of organizing romantic relationships, they have created egalitarian schemes for dividing up responsibilities and rights within their relationships. Regarding race, little research has been conducted that focuses exclusively on love and the organization of romantic relationships across race. According to the research that exists on African Americans' love relationships, African American women, like most other women, want a lover who is supportive, romantic, openly expressive of his deepest love and feelings, listens attentively to theirs, and above all, is not afraid of commitment. Likewise, Latinas/os say that in love relationships, they look for someone who respects and treats them well; someone who is sensitive, affectionate, exciting, and who can be a companion in life.

A number of social and political obstacles hamper the development or maintenance of a loving relationship. These include demographic factors and social and cultural change, traditional gender role socialization, patriarchy, the lack of trust, and jealousy. For example, age norms and laws regulate the age at which love, sex, and/or marriage are acceptable. Jealousy is the dark side of love and can be detrimental to the development or maintenance of a long-term love relationship. As with love, jealousy can best be understood as a social construction, that is, as an emotion largely shaped by a given culture. In addition, as with love, there are gender differences in the expression of jealousy. We can manage or eliminate jealousy by looking inward and working out the problems that make us susceptible to jealousy, and we can talk to our partner. We can also share with her or him our feelings and expectations for the future of the relationship while coming to an agreement about what behaviors are and are not acceptable within the relationship.

Heterosexual romance today reflects the changes evident in the roles of women and men since the contemporary women's movement. In general, women and men in the 1990s accelerated earlier trends toward dealing with each other on a more equitable basis. If this trend continues into the future, romantic love relationships might be increasingly androgynous or egalitarian in nature. Affirming love and supporting healthy loving relationships and intimacy is, in essence, promoting and supporting strong and healthy marriages and families (heterosexual and same sex). Thus, there is an ongoing need for public policies, initiatives, and programs that recognize and support the diversity of loving relationships.

KEY TERMS

eroticism	ludus	pragma	wheel theory	androgynous
romantic love	storge	agape	of love	trust
eros	mania	infatuation	limerence	jealousy

QUESTIONS FOR STUDY AND REFLECTION

1. What does being in love mean to you? Are love and romance necessary for a satisfying intimate relationship? Explain. Parents and grandparents can be an excellent source of information about changes in love and romance. Ask them at what age they fell in love, whom they fell in love with, did they marry their first love, did their parents object to their choice of lover, and what changes in love and romance stand out to them today. Compare their responses with people of several different generations and with your own views on love and romance for differences and similarities.

2. Messages about love and intimate relationships are deeply embedded in American popular culture. Consider greeting cards, for example, and the cultural messages and assumptions they contain about love, sex, intimacy, and appropriate intimate partners. Conduct a content analysis of romantic greeting cards such as valentine, engagement, wedding, and anniversary cards that express love and, using a sociological perspective, analyze the messages and images they contain in terms of some or all of the following points: Do the cards contain the same or different messages for women and men about love and/or being in love? Can you tell if they are intended for a woman or a man, or is the language neutral? How is love described in the cards? Do the cards make assumptions about sexual orientation? Do the cards' messages and images presume heterosexuality? Are there specific cards and/or messages for same-sex couples? What cultural assumptions do the cards make about love and intimacy between women and men of color? Are there specific cards and/or messages for couples of color? Do they differ from those for Whites? What about interracial love? Are there cards that address interracial intimate relationships? If yes, how is the issue addressed? In your assessment, does the greeting card industry promote and maintain patriarchy, racism, sexism, and heterosexism? What changes would you suggest to those who create and promote greeting cards about love and intimacy?

3. Research indicates that our ability to establish and maintain love relationships is profoundly impacted by our childhood experiences and the development of self-love. In some families, children are given positive feedback and are often told verbally that they are important and that they are loved, while in others the expression of love is more subtle, or absent altogether. When you were growing up, did you receive positive feedback? Were you verbally told that you were loved? How were you shown that you were loved? Do you think these early childhood experiences have had an impact on your self-esteem? On how you show love today? Explain.

4. What do sociologists mean when they say that love, romance, and jealousy are socially constructed? What evidence do you see of this process in popular culture, particularly the media that you watch, hear, or read? If love is a social construction, what can heterosexual couples learn from lesbian and gay couples' organization of love relationships? Explain.

ADDITIONAL RESOURCES

SOCIOLOGICAL STUDIES

Aido, Ama Ata, Ed. 2006. *African Love Stories: An Anthology*. Banbury, Ghana: Ayebia Clarke Publishing Ltd. This anthology, edited by one of Africa's most respected writers of today, is a comprehensive collection of 21 contemporary love stories written by African women stretching from Sudan to South Africa, with Ghana, Nigeria, Kenya, Zimbabwe, and much of Africa in-between. Presenting love in the most diverse ways imaginable, the stories deal with the full gamut of love and loving; the process of falling in love—the joys and the pain, the illusions, the betrayals, the forbidden and the consequences. Themes such as unrequited love, rivalry, familial love, religion, extramarital affairs, and sexual love as well as challenging themes including taboo subjects such as same-sex relationships, interracial love, domestic violence, female circumcision, and ageism illustrate the multifaceted complexity of African women's lives and relationships. This anthology is an excellent source of materials for inside- and outside-the-classroom examinations and discussions of love generally and more specifically, love cross-culturally with notable attention paid to the fact that the theme of love in this anthology debunks preconceived notions about African women as impoverished victims who do not experience or enjoy love like others in the world while showing their strength, complexity and diversity.

Clark, Donald H. 2009. *Loving Someone Gay*, 5th ed. Maple Shade, NJ: Lethe Press. A very good examination and discussion of lesbian and gay relationships.

Nardi, Peter M., ed. 1992. *Men's Friendships*. Newbury Park, CA: Sage. An excellent collection of articles and research pertaining to men's friendships, intimacy, sexual boundaries, and gender roles.

Pines, Ayala. 1998. *Romantic Jealousy: Causes, Symptoms, Cures*. New York: Routledge. A compelling discussion of and practical guide for dealing with the psychology of jealousy through a series of real life vignettes. The author suggests that jealousy is a natural, universal, and positive trait—indeed, the "shadow of love." There is no real jealousy where there is no love.

FILM

The Notebook. 2004. This film is a delicate love story about aging and the power of love. It follows the lives of two teenagers from opposite sides of the tracks who fall madly in love during one summer together but are forced apart by family and the social class order. When the couple reunites several years later, their passionate romance is rekindled, forcing one of them to choose between true love and the class order. Decades later, when the wife is drifting into the memory loss of senile dementia, the devoted husband recounts their love story and how it endured, which is preserved in a titular notebook from which he reads to her.

Definitely Maybe. 2008. A 30-something Manhattan dad is in the midst of a divorce when his 10-year-old daughter begins to question him about his life before marriage. His daughter wants to know how her parents met and fell in love. The father relives his past and recounts the history of his romantic relationships with three very different women. He carefully attempts a gentler version of his romances for his daughter and changes the names of his three romantic interests, creating a romantic puzzle that highlights both the joys and hardship of true love. The daughter comes to understand that love is not so simple or easy.

LITERARY WORKS

Canfield, Jack, Mark Hansen, Mark Donnelly, Chrissy Donnelly, and Barbara Deangells. 2003. *Chicken Soup for The Romantic Soul: Inspirational Stories About Love and Romance*. Deerfield Beach, FL: HCI Publishers. This addition to the popular Chicken Soup series of books consists of a variety of stories about love ranging from humorous and poignant to emotional stories dealing with the loss of love and a loved one to discovering and renewing an old love relationship. It contains stories from both celebrities and ordinary people who share their experiences of love.

Hooks, bell. 2000. *All About Love*. New York: HarperCollins. A feminist theorist known for her penetrating and eloquent critiques of racism and sexism takes on the elusive subject of love in today's society and culture. hooks uniquely weaves her childhood search for love with society's misuse and dire need of it. The author provides an excellent analysis of love and sex and details the problems that arise from the confusion between the two.

INTERNET

www.lovingyou.com This site provides a library of love stories, poetry, cards, and dedications. It also includes a collection of other resources such as relationship advice, chat groups, horoscopes, message boards, free postcards, love games, romantic recipes, date night ideas, and a variety of links to other romantic-oriented sites.

www.heartchoice.com This Web site deals with matters of the heart that affect our choices in love and love-related issues. It is divided into six rooms, including "Right Mate," "Marriage Room," and "Divorce Room." In each room, visitors can find articles by professionals, resources, and links to other helpful sites on the Internet.

www.electpress.com/loveandromance/lrlinks.htm The Love and Romance Express Web site provides tips, techniques, and ready-to-use material with which to express your love and affection to someone special in your life. On this site, visitors will find a mountain of romantic information that will help one communicate her or his innermost feelings. Some of the resources provided on the site include love letters and poems, word expressions, a gift emporium, a love and romance book shop, a relationship gallery, love and romance connection, love and romance links, and 89 ways to say "I love you."

www.dataguru.org/love/lovetest/findings This Web site contains a 68-item questionnaire designed to assess love and its dimensions. With Robert Sternberg's and John Lee's theories of love in mind, students can elect to take either one or both versions of The Love Test: The Concept version, designed to assess what people think love is and/or the Experience version, designed to assess people's experience of love. You will receive an analysis of your (and your partner's) love styles after the test is completed.

Succeed with MyFamilyLab®
www.myfamilylab.com

Watch. Explore. Read. The New MyFamilyLab is designed just for you. Each chapter features a pre-test and post-test to help you learn and review key concepts and terms. Experience Marriages and Families in action with dynamic visual activities, videos, and readings to enhance your learning experience.

Here are a few activities you will find for this chapter.

Watch on **myfamilylab.com**

Video clips feature important concepts in the study of Marriages and Families. Watch:
- Busting Out

Explore on **myfamilylab.com**

Social Explorer is an interactive application that allows you to explore Census data through interactive maps. Explore the Social Explorer Activity:
- Decline in Marriage Rates in the U.S.

Read on **myfamilylab.com**

MyFamilyLab includes primary source readings from classic and contemporary sociologists from around the world. Read:
- Peplau and Campbell: "The Balance of Power in Dating"

5

Dating, Coupling, and Mate Selection

What Will You Learn?

- Define and understand the sociological meaning of key terms.
- Describe the historical and contemporary trends in the mate selection process.
- Apply the sociological imagination to analyze and explain the global nature of mate selection.
- Assess the pros and cons of various methods that people typically use to meet an intimate partner.
- Increase your understanding of the social and structural barriers to choosing a mate in the United States.
- Question the consequences of dating violence and sexual assault.

IN THE NEWS

New York, NY

The opening phrase of a new online dating site begins: "The best way to get a ..." with various completions of this phrase flashing across the screen for the user to click such as "study buddy," "girl friend," "friend," "husband," "wife," "free dinner," and "eternal love." While this is not atypical of the language found on many online dating sites, this particular site is unique in that it is designed specifically and only for college students.

The site, DateMySchool.com, was founded by Columbia University students Balazs Alexa and Jean Meyer, shown here. According to the creators, they came up with the idea after one

(continued on next page)

121

(continued from previous page)

of them dated a young woman who complained that in the university's School of Social Work, there were few men enrolled in the program and, for women interested in dating, it was hard to meet people from other departments. At the same time, men in the College of Business were complaining about the dearth of women in their departments. Alexa and Meyer said they thought about it and looked around to see if anyone had provided a solution for this problem but what they found was that many online or offline services had some limitations and none of them addressed these specific issues in a complex way. So the two young men created DateMySchool.com with the goal of facilitating the meeting of students from different departments within the same school and between different universities. Within one week of its launching, the site had attracted close to 1,300 users, approximately 5 percent of Columbia's student population.

While the site was initially meant to generate same-school dates, today students using the site can meet students from other schools. For example, the site, which received $500,000 from private investors in 2011, also launched at 140 more schools nationwide the same year, including the Fashion Institute of Technology. According to Meyer, a friend convinced him that there were a lot of attractive women at the Fashion Institute who specifically wanted to date men at Columbia. Today, the site boasts more than 20,000 registered users. Both Alexa and Meyer believe the site's appeal is its exclusivity. In order to use this dating Web site, one must be a college student with an active college e-mail address. Offered at some of the nation's leading elite colleges and universities, the site offers a highly selective shortcut to love for students who are fluent in social media but too entrenched in their studies for much of

an actual social life (Dittman, 2011; Miet, 2011) One NYU student who became a registered user of the site after her failed attempts with traditional dating sites is quoted as saying: "I am interested in dating people who will not feel threatened by my schedule. I rarely have any free time. The site is elitist and all the better for it." (Miet, 2011:2).

Despite the fact that the site's launch was similar to that of Facebook, the creators insist that their site is unlike Facebook in that the user's profile is not accessible by anybody that they know. Users choose which schools and programs can view their online profiles, which remains invisible to all others. To date someone already known to them, students are advised to use the phone; in contrast, the Web site gives students plenty of opportunities to date people they would not have the chance to meet otherwise. Moreover, the creators contend that the Web site will continue to be different in that they will never go public.

WHAT WOULD YOU DO?

Would you use DateMySchool.com or any other dating site specifically designed for college students? If yes, why? If no, why not? According to one DateMySchool.com user, the selectivity of the site can sound a bit shallow in that it allows you to meet primarily those who are elite and upwardly mobile with the prospects of a lucrative future ahead of them. Do you agree that such dating sites are shallow? Does your college or university have a dating site? If yes, is it part of the DateMySchool.com dating site? If not, do you think it would be a good idea to launch one at your school?

((•—Listen to the **Chapter Audio** on **myfamilylab.com**

Dating, coupling, and mating—these concepts call up a variety of images. Close your eyes. What images come to mind when you think about dating in U.S. society today? Do you think of youth, "swinging," sex, "singles," fun, marriage, or love? Do you think of college campuses where hundreds of young women and men rub elbows, and do you think of couples hooking up and hanging out? Do you think of endless online Web sites where people spend endless hours trying to hook up? Many of these are familiar images associated with dating and mate selection in the United States—images that are relentlessly transmitted through the media. Do these images match the reality of your life? Do they match the reality of the lives of most unmarried people? Do they match the reality of mate selection for your parents?

Traditionally, we have assumed that attraction leads to dating, dating to love, and love to marriage. Indeed, we have assumed that the major function of dating is to teach people to form intimate heterosexual relationships and to prepare people for marriage. However, today an increasing number of Americans are skipping parts or all of this sequence. This is particularly true for teens and college women and men, for many of whom marriage is not necessarily an immediate goal. For example, according to the two young men who created DateMySchool. com, discussed in the In The News vignette opening this chapter, dating itself may be a lower priority to those using his site than professional networking. Almost two-thirds (63 percent) of the site's users answering a question module on the site said that they would prefer "having the most amazing career" to "meeting the love of your life." (Miet, 2011:3).

Indeed, an increasing number of people across age categories are either delaying marriage or not marrying at all. Some are pursuing alternatives to marriage (see Chapter 7). Others simply hook up and/or hang out with little hope that it will lead to marriage, if that is their goal. For still others, age is an important factor that impacts the dating experience. For many later-life individuals who are dating—especially older women—love, marriage, and/or a long-term relationship is not necessarily the goal of dating. (See section on "Dating in Later Life" later in this chapter.) In addition, not all dating is heterosexual. As we discuss more fully later in this chapter, lesbian, gay, bisexual, and transgendered couples, like heterosexual couples, date for recreational and entertainment purposes, but the development of love and long-term relationships are most often the goal. And finally, many dating relationships are based solely on material or sexual interests—not on notions of romantic love.

THE FUNCTIONS OF DATING: PAST AND PRESENT

Of all the stages in the mate selection process, dating is the one that carries the least commitment to continuing the relationship. So why do people date? The reasons are many and varied; however, researchers have identified some specific functions dating has traditionally fulfilled for the individual and, ultimately, for society's continuity. The meaning and functions of dating, of course, depend in large part on the person's age, sex, gender,

social class, and the particular stage in the dating process. One researcher, G.N. Ramu (1989), summarizes the functions of dating in terms of socialization, recreation, status grading and achievement, and mate selection leading to marriage. As you consider these functions of dating, bear in mind that they often overlap and they have been formulated primarily with young heterosexual couples in mind.

Socialization Through dating, people learn the norms, roles, and values that govern heterosexual relationships. One impact of the women's movement has been to change the ways in which some women and men define their roles in intimate relationships. Thus, for example, if a man finds he cannot accept an aggressive, self-confident, and self-reliant partner, or a woman finds that she will not accept a passive role, dating helps them to discover this and to realize what kind of roles they are willing to play in an intimate relationship. This type of learning enables individuals to test and refine a number of interactive skills with respect to the opposite sex. For young people, dating provides an opportunity to test and refine their communication skills and it also provides them an opportunity for sexual experimentation and growth. Obviously, the socialization function of dating is not limited to heterosexual or young couples, nor does it end in our youth. Therefore, socialization continues to be an important function of dating in both heterosexual and same-sex relations and as we grow older. In addition, the socialization function of dating can serve to enhance the ego or sense of self. If a positive self-concept is attributable in part to successful experiences with others, then an important stage in an individual's personality development can occur during successful dating experiences.

Recreation For most people, regardless of age, gender, and sexual orientation, dating provides an opportunity to relax, have fun, and enjoy themselves in the company of someone they like. However, in the past, social scientists have distinguished between adolescent and adult patterns when discussing the recreational function of dating. The assumption is that dating in adolescence serves a recreational function (the seeking of fun and thrills): It is often an end in itself. In contrast, in adulthood, traditional dating involves courtship, often directed toward finding a marriage partner. Today, however, this distinction is less than clear. And as more and more adults are postponing marriage (see Chapter 8), dating has become an increasingly important recreational activity for people across the age spectrum.

Status Grading and Achievement Most Americans view dating in positive terms. Thus, the more one dates, the more likely one's status and popularity will increase. Status grading and achievement in dating is a process whereby women and men are classified according to their desirability as dating partners. For example, very often on college campuses, people try to date those people who are rated as the most desirable on campus—females seeking to date the most popular athletes on campus and males seeking to date the most attractive females—to boost their own status and prestige.

Mate Selection Although dating initially brings people together simply for recreational and romantic purposes, over time it can become a means of socialization for marriage. An accumulation of dating experiences helps those who want to marry in their efforts to find a marriage partner. Given the longer dating period today, dating continues to fulfill the function of **anticipatory socialization**—socialization directed toward learning future roles; in this case, marriage roles. A person's primary reason for dating will influence that person's behavior in the dating relationship. Some researchers have suggested that a person's motivation for dating can be placed on a continuum ranging from completely expressive (dating as an end in itself) to completely instrumental (dating as a means to some larger goal). In addition, a person's emotional involvement in the dating experience may also be placed on a continuum ranging from no emotional involvement to complete emotional involvement. A person's place on these two continua is determined by her or his motive. If the primary motive is mate selection, the person will probably have strong instrumental orientation (dating should lead to marriage) and strong emotional involvement. In contrast, if the motivation is either recreation or status achievement, the individual is likely to have both low instrumental orientation and low emotional involvement. This research suggests that dating couples will seek to continue their relationship if either the emotional involvement or the instrumental orientation is high.

So what does this all mean for current relationships among both heterosexual and same-sex couples? Is today's pattern of mate selection a continuation of trends of the past? Does dating serve the same functions today as in the past? Are dating relationships and mate selection really that different today than they were 50 years ago? A century ago? Are they the same around the world? In the next section, we explore some of these questions focusing on historical, contemporary, and cross-cultural trends in courtship, dating, and mate selection.

Mate Selection in Cross-Cultural and Historical Perspective

Did you know that dating is not a common practice in most countries? In general, when we speak of **dating,** we are referring to a process of pairing off that involves the open choice of mates and engagement in activities that allow people to get to know each other and progress toward coupling and mate selection. In places such as China, India, South America, and most countries in Africa, dating in this sense is very rare. In addition, it is forbidden in most Muslim countries, including Iraq, Egypt, Iran, and Saudi Arabia. Only in Western countries such as the United States, Great Britain, Australia, and Canada is dating a common form of mate selection.

Sociologists use the term **mate selection** to refer loosely to the wide range of behaviors and social relationships individuals engage in prior to marriage and that lead to long- or short-term pairing or coupling whether or not they culminate in legal marriage. An essential element in mate selection is **courtship,** a period of time in which two people spend intentional time together in order to get to know each other with the expressed purpose of evaluating each other as a potential marriage partner. Dating is simply one stage in the courtship process—a process that involves an increasing level of commitment that might culminate with the ultimate commitment, marriage. Whatever its end, mate selection is an institutionalized feature of social life. All known societies exhibit some form of courtship, marriage, and family that ensures the production and nurturing of young people.

DATING DIVERSITY: MATE SELECTION CROSS-CULTURALLY

How do people around the world select a marriage or life partner? Many of the world's societies do not have the "open" courtship and dating system common in the United States and other Western nations. Rather, mate selection varies across a continuum of practices around the world. These customs range from agreements and arrangements among religious or community leaders or the families of prospective partners, arranged matches by village shamans, to contractual arrangements between families (usually fathers); from the outright purchase of a mate to the seemingly free choice of individuals with only limited consultation with parents or other relatives based on criteria ranging from notions of love to physical attractiveness to economic considerations. In some cultures, mate selection begins as early as infancy; in others, the process begins at age 8 or 9, and in still others, it begins in late adulthood.

Read the **Document**
Mate Selection and Marriage Around the World on
on **myfamilylab.com**

Traditional Dating and Mate Selection Much of the literature on mate selection cross-culturally differentiates methods of mate

In Sudan, Africa, members of a Dinka Clan perform a wedding dance around cattle to be given as a dowry.

selection according to a traditional/nontraditional or industrialized/nonindustrialized dichotomy. In most traditional (nonindustrialized) societies, for example, family and/or religious groups try to preserve cultural consistency, family unity, friendship, and religious ties through arranged marriages. For instance, among the Hopi, ancient Chinese, Hebrews, and Romans, mating was arranged by the head of the kinship group who continued to exercise some degree of control over young people even after they married. Although these practices continue in many traditional cultures today, there are a variety of new forms of mate selection as well as some combination of traditional and nontraditional patterns of mate selection that can be found.

Arranged Marriage In arranged marriages, parents and relatives exert considerable influence in the mate selection process. Loyalty of the individual to the family is a most important ideal. Thus, to preserve family loyalty, marriages are carefully arranged, with brides and grooms rarely choosing their own mate. Although in some traditional cultures, the system of mate selection has adjusted somewhat to modernization, in others such as India, the custom of arranged marriages has survived migration and modernization, remaining central to the fabric of Indian society. For millions of Indian women, arranged marriage remains the norm. For example, an estimated 9 out of 10 marriages in India today are arranged, even among those in the educated middle class. And almost three-fourths of the population believes that arranged marriages are more successful than marriages in the West, particularly given the latter's staggering divorce rates. Family elders routinely search out and investigate potential mates, sometimes, in today's age of technology, posting matrimonial ads in newspapers and online. In this mate selection process, there is little or no opportunity for the couple to interact with one another, or freely decide to be a couple, or to marry. It discourages sexual experimentation and serial dating before marriage since the interests of the family are considered more important than the romantic needs of the two individuals. It is expected that the couple's love for one another will grow over time. Arranged marriages serve other important social functions as well. For example, they serve to extend existing family units, and they reinforce ties with other families in the community, thereby strengthening the social order and organization of

the community (Melwani, 2007; Cullen and Masters, 2008; Singh, 2005).

Arranged marriages, complete with ostentatious receptions and large dowries provided by the bride's family, continue to dominate the mate selection process. Families negotiate issues of money, status, health, and even physical appearance so as to make the best or most profitable match. In cities such as New Delhi, families routinely place ads calling for Indian women who are university graduates, who are tall, and who have a fair complexion. Thus, parents with dark-skinned daughters have a harder task getting their daughters married (Lessinger, 2002; Mathur, 2006).

There are indications that the institution of arranged marriages is changing, with marriages increasingly being arranged by unknown, unfamiliar sources and less based on local families who know each other. This is particularly true for Indians who move to Western countries where they often follow the cultural patterns of their new country. Global factors such as increased affluence, the need for longer education, and greater mobility have lessened the appeal for arranged marriages, and these trends have affected criteria for which possible partners are acceptable, making it more likely that pairings will cross previously impenetrable barriers such as caste or ethnic background. In some cities in India today, mate selection combines the traditional aspects of arranged marriages with various nontraditional methods. This modern method of arranged marriages can also be found in the United States. It involves Indian-American parents introducing suitable, prescreened potential mates to their offspring, who are then allowed a courtship period to decide if they like each other well enough to marry. This method allows parents to retain some control in the mate selection process while accommodating their children's desires for a "love relationship," fueled by both the Indian and American media. Some Indian-Americans even participate in Singles Meets organized by Internet Web sites (Lessinger, 2002; Singh, 2005; Melwani, 2007).

Mate selection by negotiation between parents is often time-consuming and can take many directions before the couple is finally united. For example, among Philippine Muslims on Jolo Island, the process of mate selection usually begins when the parents of a young man decide that a particular young woman is a desirable mate for their son. Most often, the parents will consult with their son prior to the beginning of negotiations with the young woman's family. In some cases, a young man will privately suggest the name of a likely mate to his parents. If the parents dislike his choice, he can threaten to abduct her. If they insist that he marry a young woman not of his liking, he can threaten to run away from home, run amuck, or become an outlaw. In general, however, it is considered quite inappropriate for parents to insist that a young man marry against his wishes. Approximately one-half of all arranged marriages on the island are contracted between close kin, usually first or second cousins. Often a very high bridewealth is publicly announced, even if the families have privately agreed on a lesser sum. Islamic marriage custom is framed as a contract between the young man and the young woman's father; this masculine emphasis runs throughout all phases of the mate selection process leading up to marriage. While it is nearly impossible for parents to arrange a marriage completely against the will of their son, daughters are often persuaded into undesired unions (Tausug Marriages, 2008).

Not everyone within Islamic and other societies subscribes to the system of arranged marriages. For example, today, a small but growing group of Islamic women in Saudi Arabia and other Middle Eastern countries are challenging Islamic male guardianship laws, which severely restrict women's freedom. Under such laws, women must obtain permission to work, travel, study, marry, or even access certain types of health care (Lee, 2011).

Mixing Traditional and Non-traditional Approaches to Mate Selection

As we have said, not all traditional societies subscribe to a pattern of arranged mate selection. Some traditional societies now mix traditional approaches with more contemporary approaches as we saw in the case of India. And increasingly, in some nontraditional societies, some form of arranged marriage might be found as in the United States and Britain. Political, social, and/or economic change, especially industrialization, in cultures around the world have brought about some significant changes in mate selection customs cross-culturally.

China today is a good example of modernization mixing with traditional approaches to mate selection. Although mate selection customs in traditional Chinese society consisted of parent-arranged marriages in which the bride's parents received a "bride price," the mating process changed considerably during the 1990s when there was a dramatic decrease in the number of marriageable women. Although in the past the majority of Chinese adults were married by age 30, in the mid-1990s more than 8 million Chinese in their 30s had not yet married, and the ratio of men to women in this age group was a staggering 10 to 1. Among other things, this shortage of women in the pool of potential mates led to a shift from traditional means of mate selection to new and unconventional means (by Chinese standards) of finding a mate. For example, some Chinese men began placing ads in major newspapers begging women to respond (Murphy, 2002; McCurry and Allison, 2004). And, as in many parts of the world, technology has become increasingly important in the Chinese mate selection process. For example, in some parts of China, chat rooms are gaining ground against traditional dating agencies; Internet dating, with computer-assisted matchmaking is becoming more prevalent, and speed dating has come to Shanghai and several other cities (Haili, 2004; China Daily, 2007; Mason, 2010). Even the government has gotten into the mate selection process with several government-sponsored computer dating and matchmaking services, and November 11 is now an unofficial holiday known as Single's Day. Each year, on this day, single women and men are encouraged to make an extra effort to find a partner, and parents of single children often arrange dates for their children on this day (Shanshan, 2006; China Daily, 2005).

Dating for educated Chinese women is particularly difficult because they have to try to balance personal achievement against traditional Chinese relationships. Educated Chinese women have high standards for men, but they also worry that their education might scare away more traditional Chinese men. Ironically, the scarcity of Chinese women has given them a newly found edge in a mate-selection process that historically treated them as chattel. However, the down side of their leverage in mate selection, and a jolting reminder of their continued oppression, is the fact that while the continuing disparity in the ratio of women to men has resulted in an increased demand for women by unmarried males seeking a wife, it has also resulted in an increase in prostitution, forced prostitution, and domestic and international sex trafficking (Tiefenbrun and Edwards, 2008). In addition, as a result of the shortage of Chinese women, there also has been a significant rise in the numbers of bounty hunters who kidnap city women and deliver them to rural farmers desperate for brides and the increasing reliance of many rural Chinese men on the booming trade in kidnapped women in Vietnam and Korea for a source of brides.

Mate Selection in Nontraditional Industrialized Societies

In most nontraditional industrialized societies, dating is a common form of mate selection. Although love is seen as the basis for dating and marriage, the increasing new technology has brought with it some changes or modifications in both the reasons for and approaches to dating and mate selection in these societies. For example, in Australia today, technology is having an important impact on intimacy and intimate relationships such that a growing number of Australian men are abandoning face-to-face contact and resorting to texting a woman of their choice to request or arrange a date. These men sometimes even add a little flirting to the request (called flirtext). While Aussie men are more likely than women to flirtext, once a dating relationship develops, women are more likely to engage in flirtexting. According to a study conducted by an Australian telecommunications and information services company, one in two Australians think it is okay to request a first date by text message, but the majority do not believe that break-ups should be handled through texting, e-mail, or phone. The study also found that given women's growing earning power, many Australians believe it is time to abandon the old-fashioned rule of men paying for the first date (Fuchs, 2010)

MATE SELECTION IN THE UNITED STATES: A HISTORICAL PERSPECTIVE

Historically, mate selection in the United States has been based on notions of romantic love, a sentiment shared by both women and men. For most contemporary Americans, choosing a mate is the culmination of the process of dating, although not necessarily its goal. Although dating, by definition, is supposed to be separate from selecting a marriage partner, many Americans nonetheless expect that dating will provide them with valuable experience that will help them make an informed choice of a marriage partner ("Hooking Up, Hanging Out," 2001; Whyte, 2001). For others, dating is simply about fun and recreation and is not tied in any way to the goal of marriage. However, courtship and dating are about much more than simply leading one to a marital partner. They are also about economic relationships, family control (or the lack thereof), power dynamics, competition, popularity, having sex, recreation, and consumption patterns (Ferguson, 2005). Over time, changing gender norms and power dynamics have contributed to adjustments, adaptations, and/or modifications in the rules and expectations of mate selection, culminating in the process we recognize today. Thus, contemporary patterns of mate selection are linked to our past.

Early U.S. Courtship and the Development of Dating

As in many other societies around the world, mate selection in the United States has always centered on heterosexual pairing or coupling. Because the process was meant to lead to legal marriage, historical descriptions and early mate selection research focused only on heterosexual couples. Thus, the discussion that follows is based on historical and research data for heterosexual mate selection.

In the early history of the United States, mate selection was characterized by community, family, or parental control over the process. It included an array of activities, almost all of which involved couples keeping company under family or community supervision. In colonial times, marriage was considered of the utmost importance in bringing order and stability to daily family living. Thus, there was a stress on coupling and mate selection. During this period, couples came together through a variety of means, including matrimonial advertisements and third-party go-betweens. Demographic considerations as well as very precise cultural norms often dictated the ways in which couples came together. For example, due to a severe shortage of women in the American colonies, different patterns of mate selection evolved. Some men cohabited with Native American women; others imported brides from across the Atlantic. Moreover, the requirement of parental approval of a mate, especially among the prosperous classes, put further constraints on the mate selection process for young people. For instance, throughout this period, young people tended to marry in birth order, and marriage to cousins was not uncommon (Ferguson, 2005).

Courtship Although American parents could not legally choose a partner for their offspring, they exercised considerable power over mate selection well into the eighteenth century. During this historical period, courtship was the typical pattern of mate selection. Traditionally, it was considered the role of a male to actively court a female, thus encouraging her interest in him and her receptiveness to a proposal of marriage. Couples were usually members of the same community and courting was usually carried out under the watchful eyes of family members. Under this process, daughters, in particular, were strictly supervised. If a young man wanted to court a young woman, he had to meet her family, get the family's permission to court her, and be formally introduced to her. In fact, colonial law required a man to secure the permission of a woman's father before he could court her. Even after a man gained permission to court a particular woman and the two people were formally introduced, they were often chaperoned (especially upper-class women) at social events. These distinct gender roles lost some of their importance and rigidity in courtship over time and today courtship involves many private activities (as opposed to family supervised activities) such as talking by telephone or other electronic means such as text messages or e-mail.

Calling The process of mate selection eventually assumed a formal pattern referred to as "calling." In this form of mate selection, the initiative and control were in the hands of women. For example, a male suitor would be invited to call on a female at her home. He was expected to come "calling" only if he was invited to do so. The invitation usually came from the mother of the woman, but eventually the woman herself extended the invitation. When the young man came calling, he was entertained in the woman's parlor. Calling was overseen by adults—parents, kin, church members, and others in the community and often took place in mixed-aged settings. If a woman had several suitors at one time, a man might be told that the woman was not at home to receive him. In this instance, he was expected to leave his calling card. If this happened many times, it was meant to give the man the message that the woman was no longer interested in him. If a serious relationship developed between a couple, they advanced from calling to "keeping company" ("Courtship in America…," 2011; Whyte, 2001).

Keeping Company Keeping company was a very formal and upright relationship that developed only after people had become attracted to or felt romantic about each other and is a precursor of the twentieth-century custom of "going steady." Unlike in calling, couples who kept company were expected to be monogamous—in practice, this meant that a woman was expected to keep company with only one man (Whyte, 2001).

Keeping company involved a variety of activities, and couples kept company in some unique and interesting ways. For example, in colonial New England, unmarried couples practiced bundling, in which they spent the night in bed together, wrapped in bundling blankets or separated only by a long wooden bundling board down the middle of the bed. Only the outer garments could be removed, and the woman sometimes was placed in a sack sealed at the neck. This arrangement evolved in response to harsh winters and the difficulty of traveling, both of which made it difficult for a young man to return home after an evening of keeping company. Although such a practice would seem to discourage sexual contact, it apparently did not. Researchers on the topic estimate that approximately one-third of all eighteenth-century brides were pregnant at the time of their wedding.

Getting Together Significant for the evolving pattern of dating in the United States were industrialization; the rise of free, public, coeducational, and mandatory schooling; and the mass movement of women (predominantly working-class women) into the mills and factories, allowing them increased contact with men. These events helped loosen parents' hold on their children. However, the mass production of the automobile probably had the most profound impact on the course of mate selection in North America. The automobile increased the mobility of young people and made a number of activities and places accessible to them. It also gave young people a new and private place for **getting together,** a pattern of dating that involves women and men meeting in groups, playing similar roles in initiating dates, and sharing equally in the cost of activities. Initiative and control in the mate selection process shifted from women to men. Men now asked women out, instead of waiting to be invited to call on women. And courting moved from the parlor to the front seats and backseats of cars, resulting in the emergence and institutionalization of dating. Some social scientists have gone so far as to suggest that the automobile became, in some sense, a "bundling bed on wheels."

Nine Decades of American Dating: The 1910s through the 1990s The term "dating" entered the American language during the **1910s** and was connected to the emergence of new kinds of commercial amusements such as amusement parks, ice cream parlors, and especially the movies and the rise of the automobile. During this time, young people in rapidly growing cities had begun to spend more of their leisure time in commercial settings such as amusement parks, dance halls, and nickelodeons and a growing number of young boys began to ask girls out. The term dating originally referred to a specific date, time, and place of meeting. Thus, to speak of "dating" simply meant that two people of the opposite sex met at a mutually agreed-on place and time and engaged in conversation. Unlike calling, dating in the early twentieth century was not about finding a mate. Rather, it was about having fun with someone of the opposite sex. In addition, unlike calling, which was monitored by adults, dating was overseen primarily by young people themselves. Young people set the rules for dating; youthful gossiping and teasing served to help determine who went out with whom and how much intimacy was involved ("Courtship in America…," 2011).

During the **1920s** and **1930s**, the affluence and leisure of the White middle class gave rise to a youth culture whose members were relatively free to pursue their personal interests and social life. The rigid Victorian sex ethic (see Chapter 6) of the past was replaced with a new sexual intimacy as part of the courtship process. Couples took the initiative to get to know each other; they dated for fun, pleasure, relaxation, and recreation rather than with marriage as the primary goal. Dating was a highly gendered process where a male was expected to ask a female out on a date, pay for the date, and provide transportation. In return, he expected repayment in the form of physical intimacy—for example, a goodnight kiss or petting. The young woman was responsible for resisting any inappropriate sexual advances ("Courtship in America…," 2011).

Dating became especially visible on college campuses. Although college students represented only a small and select portion of America's youth—primarily White and middle class—their activities and behavior became the model for other youth. Dating for fun was a cultural expectation, and it was assumed that any popular young person would have lots of dates. In fact, in a now classic study conducted during this period, social scientist Willard Waller (1937) described dating, especially on college campuses, as a competitive system that included rating prospective partners on the basis of popularity and prosperity such as owning an automobile, having the right clothing, belonging to the right sorority or fraternity, and of course having money. An individual's popularity, especially for women, was measured by how often she or he dated. Thus, it was not uncommon for urban middle-class young women to go out on dates three or more times a week. According to some later sociological research, young women who dated the most were the least likely to pursue an advanced education and were especially likely to marry at a young age. By the 1930s, a new dating vocabulary appeared that included terms such as girlfriend, boyfriend, and crush. Dating had also become highly ritualized, giving rise to a new phrase: **going steady**—an exclusive relationship with one person—which was a clear and entrenched part of the mate selection process. It was an intermediate stage between casual dating and engagement.

During the **1940s and 1950s**, dating spread from college campuses to most cultural groups in the United States. During this period, dating became essentially a filtering process in the sense that a person dated many people before settling down with one person. Only then did serious dating or courtship begin, with the ultimate goal being marriage. Acceptance of the idea that dating should culminate in marriage seems to be reflected in the fact that the 1950s had the highest percentage of married adults on record. During this period, researcher Ersel LeMasters (1957) suggested that dating involved six stages of progressively deeper commitment from the first date in the junior high school years to marriage in the late teens or early 20s. Going steady, the third stage, occurred somewhere in the late high school years and involved a transition from the first two stages, the noncommitment of casual dating in junior high school and the random dating in the early high school years. The fourth stage occurred in college,

when the couple entered into an informal agreement to date each other exclusively. The final two stages were engagement and marriage. This sequential model of dating tended to be more common among the middle classes than among other classes. According to researchers, lower-income and working-class youth tended to speed up the process, generally marrying at an earlier age.

Like other cultural patterns, dating patterns incorporate many of the values of the larger society. Thus, dating in the 1940s and 1950s continued to illuminate U.S. society's emphasis on traditional gender roles, marriage, and the sexual double standard, with the male being the aggressor and the female playing a submissive role. Males continued to be the initiators of dates and females continued to wait to be picked or asked out. The sexual double standard was also evident in the desired outcomes of dating. For males, a primary expected outcome of dating was sex, whereas for females it was commitment and marriage. Although women exercised some degree of control through their ability to give or withhold their affection and their bodies, the absence of parental control and pressure to respond to a man's initiatives put women in a weaker position than they had been under the earlier system of "calling."

During the **1960s and 1970s**, changing sexual norms, the increasing availability of contraceptives, the continuing decline in parental authority, and the increasing activism of young people helped reverse the conservative dating trends of the 1940s and 1950s. Dating was transformed into a casual and spontaneous form of courtship. Greatly influenced by the women's movement, women no longer waited to be asked out but instead began to initiate dates and intimate relationships. There was an increasing emphasis on each person paying her or his own way. This was particularly common among middle-class youth, who were financially more independent than poor and working-class youths (Guess, 2008; Gwartney-Gibbs, 1986). Cohabitation is discussed in detail in Chapter 7.

In the **1980s and 1990s**, dating started at an earlier age and lasted longer than it had in previous generations. Adolescents as young as age 13 participated in some form of dating or pairing off. If we consider the fact that the average age at first marriage in the 1980s was somewhere around 25, then the average person in

Dating begins at an earlier age and lasts much longer than it did in the past. It is no longer necessarily the means to the end of marriage. Getting together, hanging out, or generally sharing fun activities on a date is now an end in itself.

the United States was dating and courting for more than 10 years before getting married. As the age at first marriage continued to increase slightly in the 1990s, more people were spending more time in a number of dating relationships with a variety of people before marrying, if they married at all. The longer period of dating for most people contributed to a change in the ways dating in the last two decades of the twentieth century was structured and perceived. Dating as a system with clearly defined rules and expectations had broken down and was replaced by a far more casual and less formally structured dating system of "hooking up" and "hanging out." By the mid-1980s, these casual rather unstructured methods of getting together were commonplace. The terms *dating* and *going steady* became passé, replaced with terms such as *seeing, being with, going with someone, hooking up,* and *hanging out.* Although some people continued to date in the traditional pattern, in which each person has specific roles to play, most people preferred to say they were "going out" with someone. According to some researchers, dating itself became passé, replaced by informal pairing off in larger groups, often without the prearrangement of asking someone out (Whyte, 2001; Peterson, 2001).

Contemporary Trends in Dating Although the term "dating" was less commonly used in the 1980s and 1990s, the practice nonetheless continues today, albeit in different forms. For example, almost

two-thirds of American adults were engaged in some form of dating or, at the very least, were interested in dating at the beginning of this century. Nevertheless, according to some observers, by the year 2000, the term dating—as it referred to the practice in which a young man asked a girl or woman out and took her to the movies or dinner—was dead (see the Debating Social Issues box). Today, a large number of single Americans are not actively looking for romantic partners, long-term commitments, or to date in the traditional sense. Instead, especially among 20- and 30-somethings, they are preoccupied with friends, getting an education, establishing a career path, their jobs or professions, and establishing themselves—so they don't make time for relationships. The goal today is to have fun, not serious long-term commitments or marriage. This is particularly true for young women, professionals, those who have been widowed or divorced, and for older singles. On the other hand, some of those who say they are looking for or are interested in traditional dating and having a committed relationship are not very active on the dating scene (Rainie and Madden, 2006; Wilson, 2009).

Today, dating is based far more on mutuality and sharing than on traditional gender roles. Dating for many people has become very time-contained, sometimes existing only for the moment for sexual or recreational purposes, with no pretense that it is a prelude to courtship or marriage. Describing contemporary mate selection in the United States, a colleague of ours commented, with

Debating Social Issues

IS DATING DEAD?

Not everyone is lamenting the *death* of dating. While there has been a paradigm shift in thinking and behavior relative to dating, many people continue to follow a traditional pattern of dating.

Many Americans are lamenting the changed nature of the dating scene today. One can find a number of articles and discussions about contemporary dating and mate selection with pretty much the same titles: "Is Dating Dead?" "The Demise of Dating!" "Dating: An Endangered Species" As with most issues, there are pros and cons to the idea that dating in American society today is dead.

On the pro side, there are those who argue that yes, indeed dating is dead or at the very least, there is very little dating going on in American society—at least not in the traditional sense. Among those who take this position, some say that traditional dating is pretty much dead, particularly when it comes to commitment and long-term relationships as a goal of dating. Hooking up and hanging out is the new normal. Traditional dating has become a

dated concept as women and men increasingly "hook up" simply for sex. Dating, they say, involves commitments, if only for a few hours, days, or weeks. Hooking up and hanging out requires no commitments. Today, singles, especially young singles, are much more likely to define the first interactions of their relationships as hookups or hanging out instead of dates. But hook-ups produce awkwardness afterward, once the alcohol wears off. There is little substance to that. Some who believe that dating is dead cite recent research that indicates that college students hook up almost twice as much as they go out on dates, that hook-ups have replaced casual dating and that most people are rarely asked out on dates today. Or they cite the fact that more of today's high

(continued on next page)

(continued from previous page)

school seniors say that they never date than seniors who say that they date frequently. It's all about the hook-up today (Blow, 2008; *Baltimore Sun*, 2011).

Still others who hold this view blame the leveling effect of the women's movement which they say has contributed to discourage dating. Accordingly, they argue that as women's options have increased and some women have become more aggressive, some men have become reluctant to take traditional initiatives such as asking women out on dates. In addition, dating has become increasingly expensive and often quite elaborate. The more expensive and elaborate a date, the fewer the dates. Expensive and elaborate dates create an expectation that a date is part of a serious long-term commitment which discourages dating even more. Gone are the days of the clumsy or awkward phone call or face-to-face question: Are you busy tonight? Would you like to go to dinner or to a movie? Instead, much communication today is impersonal and carried out through electronic media outlets such as texting, e-mail, Twitter, and online dating services. Most people today are sitting at home alone, on their computer searching for a date rather than courting and going out on dates (*Baltimore Sun*, 2011)

On the con side of the debate are those who are not sitting around lamenting the death of dating. On this side of the issue are those who

agree that dating is definitely different today than it was in our parents and grandparents day but disagree that as a concept, dating is not dead. While there has been a paradigm shift in thinking and behavior relative to dating, many people continue to date in the traditional sense. On the other hand, for many people such as busy, upwardly mobile, career-oriented people, there is not much of a place anymore for old-fashioned dating. It is much easier to take someone to your favorite hangout or to hook up. Conversely, many people today do not do one or the other. Rather, they combine intimate dates with hooking up and hanging out.

In any case, some on the con side criticize those who wring their hands and moan about hooking up as a no strings relations in which bonds between women and men are increasingly brief and sexual. First, they cite data that indicate that oftentimes hook-ups and hangouts can and do lead to formal dates and then a serious relationship. They also point out that hooking up is not synonymous with having sex. In fact, a recent report from the National Center for Health Statistics supports this position. Among its findings it is reported that the percentages of women and men ages 18 to 24 who say they are virgins are increasing. Other research such as that of sociologist Paula England has found that just about one in four college seniors say they are virgins (cited in Jayson, 2011). This may or may not be the result of new ways that young people define "having sex."

Nevertheless, many young people see hooking up as an easier way to act on their sexual desires (whatever those might be) with or without a commitment. Even so, according to England, some people are hooking up many times with the same person but they do not call it a relationship. Others are never doing what is called a hook-up. Some argue that young people today, especially women, have a lot of things going on in their lives such as school and career goals. Thus, hooking up as an alternative to long-term commitment early in life can be a positive. Finally, some on this side of the debate argue that many people today, especially women, still expect the male to initiate a date. Moreover, those on this side of the debate argue that despite the current dating trends, most females and males still seek romantic relationships and long-term commitments (Jayson, 2011; *Baltimore Sun*, 2011).

What do you think? Is dating dead, or is what is happening with dating and mate selection simply a natural evolution of intimacy and mating? Do you think that the primary or only goal of dating is mate selection and ultimately marriage? Or do you think that given the world today, the changing roles of women and men, the increasing number of women pursuing higher education and a career that casual dating and even casual sex is understandable and acceptable? Can you draw up an argument pro or con on this subject?

some degree of frustration: "People don't date anymore: they just get together; they just have sex, live together, and then go their separate ways." Although this was a nonscientific observation, it is nonetheless fairly consistent with scientific research that reports that contemporary dating patterns include considerably more casual sexual involvements and fewer committed relationships than in the past. New dating trends have led some observers to suggest dating is no longer the self-evident activity that it was in the past (Lehman, 2004; Wolcott, 2004).

In a major shift in the mate selection process, **hooking up**—a meeting and mating ritual that started among high school and college students—is the latest rung on the evolutionary ladder of mate

selection and can be found in some form in many Western societies today. While there are varied definitions of hooking up (for example, in Australia, it just means kissing with tongues), most people generally agree that it is a casual sexual encounter that can range from meeting with a friend, kissing, making out, touching, and oral stimulation to sexual intercourse, with no expectation of future emotional commitment. In the past, people dated, and it might lead to something sexual occurring. Today, in the hook-up era, something sexual happens between two people, and it may or may not lead to dating. Some observers refer to hooking up as comparable to a "one-night stand." Others describe it as "friends with benefits"—they are a bit more than casual acquaintances, but a lot less than girlfriend or boyfriend. However hooking up is defined, social scientists have traced the hook up phenomena back to the 1960s and 1970s on college campuses, where female and male college students were thrown together in dormitories and revolted against the strict rules on having a person of the opposite sex in your dormitory room. Throw in the phenomena of heavy drinking that occurred on most college campuses, and there were no inhibitions to stand in the way of students hooking up (Wilson, 2009). However, today, hooking up is no longer primarily a college campus mating phenomenon. It is evident not only on college campuses (religious and secular), but also in high schools and middle schools, in the workplace among young workers, and even among later life adults (see Chapter 6).

This dating pattern notwithstanding, in general, young adults believe current patterns of dating are more natural and healthier than they were in the past. Although, as in every generation, some couples still follow a traditional pattern, for many couples dating, sexual intimacy, living together, becoming engaged, and sometimes having a child have become a common part of heterosexual relationships that may or may not culminate in marriage. While some people are fed up with the direction of contemporary dating and yearn for dating patterns of old, most social demographers predict a continuation of current trends (Popenoe and Whitehead, 2002). For those wishing for a relationship (committed, long-term, or one leading to marriage), it seems that the challenges of traditional dating notwithstanding, it is still easier to get a date than to find a relationship with someone who is a good match for you. Moreover, today people are ever more aware that mate selection is not just a heterosexual phenomenon, nor is dating just for the young at heart. Dating (or whatever term we choose to use) involves lesbians, gays, bisexuals, and transgendered people, the very young, as well as an increasing number of older people who either have never married or are divorced or widowed. Dating among older adults differs somewhat from dating among high school and college students, but many similarities exist. This is especially the case in terms of the purpose of dating.

Many scholars who study contemporary American dating patterns suggest that today's changed patterns of dating may be due to the reduced pressure to marry. Dating today, they say, is not oriented to marriage as it was in the past. Others contend that current dating patterns have been significantly impacted by online matchmaking activity. Still others point out that geography and the lack of proximity to desirable partners can complicate the search for a dating partner. For example, in a recent survey, when people who were actively seeking dates were asked about the dating scene where they lived, a majority said it was difficult to meet people. When asked to describe the dating possibilities where they live, almost one-half said there were very few single people in their town they would be interested in dating. Not surprisingly, the difficulty of finding a dating partner varies depending on where one lives (Madden and Lenhart, 2006). For instance, as shown in Table 5.1, urban dwellers report that it is easier to find a dating partner than those living in suburban and in rural areas.

The changing rules of dating or lack thereof have left many people confused about dating as the various studies of dating on college campuses suggest. However, this confusion is not limited to the young on college campuses nor is it limited to fast-track young people in corporate America who are dating. As more older adults

TABLE 5.1 Availability of Dating Partners by Community Types

Percentage of Those Who Are Actively Seeking Dates Who Say	Urban	Suburban	Rural
There are a lot of singles in my community that I would be interested in dating.	57%	38%	21%
It is easy to meet people in the place where I live.	58%	34%	36%

Source: Lee Rainie and Mary Madden, 2006, "Not Looking for Love: The State of Romance in America," Pew Internet & American Life Project, www.pewinternet.org, p. 4. Reprinted with permission of the Pew Research Center.

return to the dating scene, they are confronted with a different (sometimes radically different), oftentimes confusing set of rules and expectations about dating in today's society. However, despite the challenges of dating in contemporary society, a majority of American adults date at some time in their lives and find marriage partners or long-term relationships.

DATING AMONG LATER-LIFE ADULTS

According to a growing body of research and popular articles on dating, the dating game changes significantly after the age of 40. In a dating world that has changed tremendously over the last several decades, the standard parameters of dating from your teens to your mid-20s are no longer the norm. Not only are Americans living longer and healthier lives, as they age they are more actively engaged in or looking for meaningful intimate relationships. Today, more than 45 million Americans over age 40 are separated, divorced, widowed, or never married. Not that all of them are seeking mates, but many are. Of these singles, more than one-half are women, many of whom are more fit and health-conscious than their parents' generation, have a younger mind-set, and are seeking dating partners at record numbers. Traditionally, young women dated with the ultimate goal of getting married and having children. However, as women age, these are no longer the primary focus and reason for dating. But reentering the dating scene when one is older is not an easy matter, particularly since the rules of the game have changed since the time they might have initially been involved in the dating process. Paula England, a 55-year-old Stanford University sociology professor and divorcée, for example, says that what she experienced after her divorce was the feeling of being back in high school again, but the rules and conventions of dating had changed and she didn't know them (quoted in Jayson, 2005:4).

Older people, like their younger counterparts, date, fall in love, and behave romantically. Older adults tend to view romance similarly to younger people—consisting, for instance, of intimate activities such as candlelit dinners, flowers, candy, and other gifts.

For many older men, as for many younger men, sex and romance are closely linked. Also, like their younger counterparts, some older adults are embracing their sexuality and hooking up. Many older singles, some of whom have already been married at least once, are not looking to get married. Rather, they are looking for companionship and fulfillment in who they are today. Some may be looking for a new soul mate—to date one person exclusively; a long-term commitment leading to marriage or remarriage. Others may absolutely want—or not want—sex as part of their dating experience. Whatever the preference, recent studies indicate that at least one-third of later life singles are either in a relationship or dating one person exclusively. But of those who are dating, only a very few (8 percent) say they are dating in order to find a marriage partner. Most (49 percent) indicate that they are dating simply to have someone to talk to and to do things with (Voo, 2007).

As we have indicated, dating today is not always easy. For older people, particularly those who have lost partners, negotiating the dating world can present an unsettling conflict between long-ago experiences and the present-day dating reality. There are unique challenges that older adults face that distinguish their dating experiences from those of younger people. Women, it seems, especially later-life women, face unique relationship challenges in today's dating scene. For example, in a recent study of the dating and courtship experiences of 15 women ages 60 to 75, the researchers found three major themes: the need for independence, the need for companionship, and gender role conflict between dating partners. The women in this study clearly wanted, desired, and enjoyed the companionship of their male dates, but they also prided themselves on their independence and did not want to give it up (Walker, Dickson, and Hughes, 2005).

In general, the women in the study said they wanted to date; they enjoyed dating, but they did not see marriage as a viable option. Unfortunately, this created relational problems for them because most of the later-life men they met wanted to get married. Some of them reported losing good dating partners and losing very satisfying relationships due to their refusal to get married or cohabit. Interestingly, these women chose their desire to remain independent over their need for companionship. They were willing to be lonely rather than give up their independence or become a caretaker for an older partner. The paradox is that the women also wanted to maintain the relationship at its present level of intimacy while not committing to a long-term relationship. For older women and some older men as well, remarriage, in their view, is fraught with complications such as the eventual inheritances of children and risks to pensions and alimony of widows and divorcées. For these older adults, then, rather than mingle assets, they choose not to marry (Walker, Dickson, and Hughes, 2005; Kilborn, 2004).

Although women across age groups are setting relationship boundaries (for example, whether a date will open the door, whether to kiss on the first date, or whether to marry or not) and although many older women are very often confident about what they want in an intimate relationship, not all are necessarily secure in the dating realm. Some are not even sure of what they want. Whatever the case, for those older women wishing to date, a significant barrier to dating and romance is the rather short supply of older men to date. According to recent U.S. Census Data, there are approximately 10 women age 65 and older for every 7 men age 65 and older. This means that many women are removed from the

dating equation, not by choice, but by chance. However, whether by choice or by chance, a good number of older women are finding that they can readily do without men. Some say they are simply looking for a date or for friends, but not a commitment. Some older women are looking for marriage, others want a relationship without legal entanglements, and still others just want companionship (Kilborn, 2004; Jayson, 2005; U.S. Census Bureau, 2011e).

To be sure, for later life singles of both genders, the dating game is more complex once you mature. Potential matches tend to have a past—children, former spouses, maybe old flames that have not quite died out. The need for understanding and compromise may be greater. With women outliving men, and given that many older men often seek younger women to date and marry, there is a growing trend for older women to date younger men. In a recent survey, 56 percent of women and 51 percent of men said it is acceptable for a potential date to be up to 10 years younger. Consistent with these reported attitudes, an AARP (American Association of Retired Persons) study found that 34 percent of the women over age 40 in their survey were dating younger men, and 35 percent said they preferred it to dating older men. And, in a recent survey conducted by *Cosmopolitan* magazine, 29 percent of the men said they would date an older woman (Demasi, 2007; Jayson, 2005).

Older men dating younger women is not new. It is common around the world; however, today, older women are getting into this mix. Older women are becoming bolder, and because women's life expectancy is increasing, they feel younger and a whole lot sexier than their mothers and grandmothers did at similar ages. The modern term for an older woman who dates a younger man is *cougar*. These women date younger men for a variety of reasons, including not being ready to give up on dating just because of their age. Even when men their own age are available, some older women report that older men are less exciting, less romantic, or les spontaneous than their younger counterparts. And, younger men who date older women say that these women are more mature and less demanding, and they often report that they learn quite a bit about love, life, and physical intimacy from their older partner ("Cougars on the Hunt for the Younger Man," 2010). As societal views continue to change as to what are acceptable age partnerships, older women will have an increasingly larger pool of eligible males to date.

The Intersections of Race, Gender, Class, and Sexual Orientation

If we are to move away from an analysis of dating that stems only from the experiences of the White middle and upper classes, we must consider how race, class, gender, and sexual orientation influence dating and mate selection patterns.

We cannot provide a comprehensive picture of dating and mate selection for all groups, but we can provide some insight into these processes for some groups. Unfortunately, the literature in this area continues to be highly limited. Most of the literature on dating among groups of color deals with African Americans. Little work has been done on courtship among Native Americans, Asian Americans, and Latinas/Latinos. For example, although we know

Dating in the twenty-first century takes many forms and crosses all age lines. Today, it is not unusual to see interracial, older, same-sex as well as opposite sex couples enjoying each other's company.

that family networks continue to make up the fabric of contemporary Native American social organization and are central to the day-to-day functioning of Native Americans, we do not know how these families are formed vis-à-vis courtship and mate selection. Nor do we know whether Native Americans have been affected by the larger cultural and changing patterns of dating and courtship. And despite the existence of a growing body of data on lesbian and gay relationships, most studies focus specifically on sexual behavior rather than more generally on the whole process of mate selection. For other groups, such as Asian Americans and Latinas/os, the sparse literature on dating for these groups consists almost entirely of research, discussions, and data on interracial marriage among these groups with little or no discussion of patterns of dating and mate selection that may or may not lead, for instance, to marriage—interracial or otherwise.

DATING PATTERNS AMONG AFRICAN AMERICANS

The practice of dating among African Americans varies by region, historical period, social class, and age. In the past, when African Americans lived in small, cohesive communities in the rural and urban South, what might be called dating behavior centered on the neighborhood, church, and school. As African Americans began to move to urban areas outside the South, however, the

greater anonymity associated with urban life modified their dating patterns. The school and house party became major centers for heterosexual fraternizing, particularly among the lower class. Dating patterns among the middle class did not differ significantly from those of the larger society and included activities like movies, dances, and bowling. In the past few decades, African American singles relied on the use of personal ads in African American and general singles magazines, meeting potential dating partners at singles clubs and through dating services aimed at African American urban professionals. While the Black church was, and remains today, an important place for Black singles to meet a dating partner, Blacks are increasingly utilizing various social networking sites, especially online dating sites designed specifically for African Americans, to meet and negotiate dates with partners of their choice.

According to most research, traditional dating patterns among Blacks, as among other groups, is more prevalent among the middle and upper class than the lower class. For the African American middle class, dating is typically sequential, occurring over the course of several stages: getting together in the teen years; keeping company on the porch and eventually in the house under family supervision; group dating; and finally, individual one-on-one dating, engagement, and often marriage. Past research comparing Black and White dating attitudes and expectations found Blacks to be less flexible and more traditional than Whites in several aspects

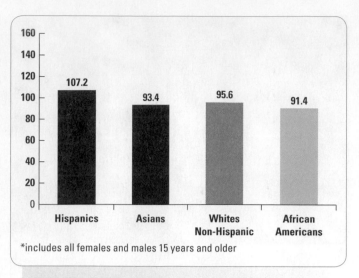

FIGURE 5.1 Sex Ratios by Race and Ethnicity

Source: U.S. Census Bureau, Statistical Abstract of the United States, 2011. Resident Population by Sex, Race and Hispanic-Origin Status: 2000–2009. Table 6, p. 10.

of dating-related attitudes and expectations. For example, Whites typically endorse more flexible role patterns in dating and seem less concerned with a traditional dating protocol (such as the expectation that males will bear the costs of dating) than Blacks.

The historically low **sex ratio**—the number of men to every 100 women—in the African American community has traditionally limited the dating and mate selection options of African American women. Some researchers have suggested that the numerical scarcity inflates male value, giving them a decided advantage in the dating–mating game. The consequence is that many African American women who want to date may find themselves either left out of the game completely or having to settle for far less than their ideal (see Figure 5.1). The famed Oprah Winfrey as well as several major news media has reminded us in recent times of this continued and increasing imbalance of Black women to Black men. They variously site statistics such as 70 percent of professional Black women are single or that 42 percent are unmarried. Some cite the fact that there are 1.8 million more Black women than Black men today. And if you consider how many Black men are dating outside of their race, the number of Black men who are incarcerated or otherwise not considered educated or successful enough to be suitable mates by many Black women, the number of eligible Black single men for Black single women in the dating pool dwindles even more. This situation is even more dire for successful Black women (professionals and/or the highly educated) who far outnumber successful Black men (Jenkins, 2005).

This topic of the lack of eligible Black men is a constant source of conversation today. Everyone—from everyday Black women and men to Black and White scholars on race to self-proclaimed Black relationship experts to celebrities and news and social commentators across race—has an opinion on the dating and mating situation of Black women and men. Increasingly, given the low Black sex ratio, a variety of these sources are advising Black women to expand their dating options by expanding their dating pool outside the circle in which they previously confined themselves.

This means to expand their options beyond Black men as dating partners and mates (Brown, 2010). This advice has met with mixed reactions among Blacks, ranging from those who espouse the idea and view interracial dating generally as a positive step toward smoother race relations to those who see it as "sell-out" behavior and a denial of racial heritage (Walker, 2007). Black men are already exercising this option at increasing rates—statistically, they are twice as likely as Black women to date outside of their race. However, regardless of one's position on the issue of dating across race, most people seem to agree that the Black sex ratio, particularly the gender disparity in education and business among African Americans, is having an adverse effect on dating and intimate relationships for African American women. In response, some successful African American women are dating blue-collar or less affluent men. Others are dating across race. And still others have quit the dating game altogether.

As with women generally, as African American women age, the already small pool of eligible males available to date shrinks even further. At the other end of the age continuum, research has found that African American high school students who date place more emphasis on materialistic factors than personality factors when choosing a partner, whereas White students rank personality traits more highly. At the college level, there does not appear to be a specific pattern of traits that African American students look for in a dating partner. (Wolcott, 2004; Walker, 2007). On many college campuses, Blacks, as well as members of other racial groups, are increasingly dating interracially. For African Americans, this phenomenon is attributable in part to the fact that many middle-class and high-status African Americans go to school, live, and/or work in worlds that tend to be racially mixed or where there are few other African Americans. This has important implications for whom they meet and with whom they socialize, which, in turn, are important factors in the formation of dating and intimate relationships. It is probably also due, in some part, to the low rate of African American men in college, a place where women of all races often meet dating partners. Some people believe that it might also be attributable to the liberation of many White youth from parental control and the rejection of racist values conveyed throughout society (Walker, 2007).

THE IMPACT OF GENDER

Perhaps more than most relationships, dating is affected by gender roles and stereotypes. Society has traditionally conveyed certain messages concerning dating: We should mate with the opposite sex; women are supposed to want a masculine man; men are supposed to want a feminine woman; men should initiate the relationship and sexual behavior, although women may guide them by flirting; men should be dominant and women submissive; and sexuality is supposed to be more important to men, and love or commitment to women. As we shall see later in this chapter, although these messages are still widespread, they frequently do not reflect the realities of contemporary relationships.

Social scientists contend that men's dating scripts focus on planning and paying for the date as well as initiating sexual behavior, whereas women's scripts focus on enhancing their appearance, making conversation, and controlling sexual behavior. However, more women today reject a passive role in their intimate relationships and seek to equalize the dating relationship by initiating and paying for dates. On the other hand, many of us have apparently learned traditional sexual scripts well. For example, as you read in Chapter 4, researchers have documented that women and men have different orientations to romantic love and that this difference continues when they consider a prospective mate. Women and men have also differed in terms of the characteristics they look for in a mate. Women tend to put less emphasis on aesthetic concerns and place greater value on qualities of a prospective mate such as working, saving, and paying bills. Women tend to prefer men who grew up in affluent neighborhoods. They also put greater weight on the intelligence and the race of a dating partner, while men, especially upwardly mobile men, emphasize physical and sexual attractiveness. Moreover, men do not value women's intelligence or ambition when it exceeds their own (Fisman et al., 2006; Clark, Shaver, and Abrahams, 1999).

Other gender differences in dating and courtship behavior include differences in how women/girls and men/boys signal their interest in each other and initiate relationships. For instance, eye contact is the most frequently used initiation tactic for both genders, but women use indirect or subtle tactics more often than men, while men engage in direct verbal tactics more often than women. Men are also more confident in initiating a relationship and a greater percentage of men than women seek sexual intimacy in the beginning stage of their romantic relationships. On the other hand, because of a fear of being rejected, women take a more tentative approach to initiating relationships and are more likely to rely on the man to initiate the relationship. However, today's high-tech dating environment reflects some blurring of gender boundaries. Women want more independence in their relationships than their mothers did; and, for them, hooking up and one-night stands aren't necessarily meaningless sexual encounters. Men, on the other hand, are feeling more empowered today to acknowledge their desires for commitment and their desires for connection in their relationships. And both women and men are looking for similar assets and are not judging a potential dating partner on the basis of gender-related traits. But some dating attitudes and behaviors do not reflect changing gender beliefs, especially among women. For example, a recent national survey found that although the vast majority of women (9 out of 10) surveyed said they would pick up the tab on a date under some circumstances, the same number said they had not asked someone out, and almost half said they typically wait for the other person to call after a first date (Jayson, 2011; Clark, Shavers, and Abrahams, 1999).

Americans are not the only people who display gender differences in dating and courtship attitudes and behavior. For instance, a survey of university students in China and the United Kingdom found that both women and men highly valued personality, appearance, interests, and intelligence. However, British men placed greater value on appearance and health than British women, while British women were more concerned about income and morality than British men. The traits that Chinese men valued most were personality, morality, health, and appearance, whereas the traits that Chinese women valued most were morality, intelligence, personality, and health. In addition, Chinese women were more concerned than Chinese men about income, education, occupation, and family background (Higgins et al., 2002).

THE IMPACT OF SOCIAL CLASS ON THE DATING PROCESS

Social class, like race and gender, profoundly impacts whom we meet, to whom we are attracted, and who is available to date. Although social classes are not sharply delineated in the United States, people's location in the class structure vis-à-vis factors such as race, education, income, and occupational status is related to differences in attitudes, values, approach to life, behavior, and access to the means necessary to realize one's goals in life. So, how does social class affect dating and mating behavior? Individuals from similar social class backgrounds share similar interests and goals, which are the bases for dating and mate selection choices. Thus, most people in the United States date and marry within their social class.

Upper Class Dating within the upper strata of U.S. society tends to be far more regulated than it is for other classes. According to various research studies, children in upper- and middle-class families are more likely than children from working-class and poor families to be socialized to delay gratification and focus on education and career preparation rather than romance and sex. Thus, upper- and middle-class women and men tend to start dating later, delay intimacy, and marry later. This appears true across race. For instance, upwardly mobile African American women, more often than not, are consciously socialized to delay dating and serious relationships until after they have completed a college education.

Moreover, social class is related to dating and mate selection in a number of other ways. Individuals from the middle and upper classes, for example, are generally viewed as more attractive dating partners and potential marital partners than those from the lower classes. Furthermore, upper-class families still exert considerable influence over mate selection. They tend to use their considerable resources to influence their offspring either to delay dating and marriage or to marry someone they consider a suitable mate and match for the family. Dates are sometimes arranged by parents, and dating partners are almost always selected from within their own ranks. Although dating and mate selection can move us up or down the social class ladder, seldom do upper-class members date someone from the middle or lower classes. Adults also exercise more control over the sexuality of young people than is true of other classes. When upper-class women reach age 18, they are formally presented to society. After this "coming out," they engage in a number of activities, during which they encounter a number of eligible men. If the couple becomes engaged, the man presents the woman with an expensive ring, and the engagement is announced in the society pages of the print media. The wedding, which is generally a very formal and often lavish affair, is attended by the rich and famous and is usually announced in the newspapers and the electronic media. For example, when Melissa Rivers, daughter of comedienne Joan Rivers, married several years ago, the wedding is said to have cost her mother over $1 million and was attended by a long list of the "Who's Who" among this country's elite and celebrities.

Middle Class Dating behaviors among middle-class youths, at least traditionally, are fundamentally no different from those of the upper classes. Middle-class dating behaviors are likewise generally supervised by adults, although not to the same degree as are those of their wealthier counterparts. Dating activities among middle-class couples include going to sports events and engaging in sporting activities such as ice skating and tennis, going to the beach, going out to dinner, and entertaining at home. On the one hand, going steady remains common among some segments of the middle classes and usually leads to an engagement. Engagements of middle-class couples, like those of wealthy couples, are usually announced in the print media. Weddings are fairly elaborate, expensive, and often performed in a church or synagogue. However, the custom of parents paying for the wedding is dying out (Barton, 2010). On the other hand, contemporary dating and mate selection patterns among middle-class youth include increasing freedom from parents' watchful eyes and supervision. For example, proms and homecoming parties often include a continuation of the celebration in rented hotel rooms and suites, where both same-sex groups as well as mixed-sex groups spend the rest of the night together, presumably under the watchful eyes of adults, although very often they are unsupervised.

Lower Class   Most research on dating suggests that lower-class families tend to exercise the least control over mate selection. However, this does not mean that these parents are any less concerned with and supervisory of their children's dating behavior. Dating among this group is most often very informal and often includes hanging out—getting out of often small and cramped living quarters in favor of such places as bowling alleys and local bars. Serious, unsupervised dating usually begins in the mid-teens and is most often exclusive or monogamous. Lower-class couples often skip the engagement phase and progress directly to marriage. When engagements occur, they are not usually announced in the press, and weddings are often small, inexpensive, and informal. Sometimes they are conducted in the home of one of the partners.

It should be noted that just as the lines separating various social classes are often blurred, so too are methods of dating and mate selection across class. Thus, methods of dating and mate selection are similar and sometimes overlap across social classes. For example, formal rites of passage such as coming out parties can be found among both the middle and upper classes. Many middle-class groups present their daughters to the community and society by means of coming-out parties to signal the daughters' readiness to date and assume other adult responsibilities. In some middle-class African American communities, for example, this coming out party is often in the form of a cotillion—a fairly elaborate formal affair and a very significant event in the life of a young, middle-class African American female. Such an event involves family and friends and can cost parents several thousand dollars as their daughters make this very public and symbolic transition to adulthood. Likewise, in some Latina/o communities, the *quinceañera* represents a social and religious coming out celebration for Latinas. It includes a religious mass followed by a reception for the young woman, who may begin dating after her *quinceañera*. Traditionally, these rites of passage activities have focused exclusively on females. However, recently, among some middle-class African Americans, the *beautillion* has emerged as a rite of passage for African American males. As with the cotillion, parents present their offspring—in this case, their sons—to the community and society to signal their readiness to date and assume more adult responsibilities.

Several African American organizations, such as the Jack & Jills of San Francisco, sponsor a type of coming out celebration for young African American males called a Beautillion, which follows 12 weeks of mentoring, leadership, and character-building experiences. Selected African American high school male juniors and seniors are chosen for their achievements in academics, sports, the arts, community, church, leadership, and overall commitment to the advancement of African Americans. Young female high school juniors and seniors (belles) who share the same complimentary attributes as the young men (beauxs) are selected as escorts for the young men and as partners during the waltz presentation at the Beautillion.

LESBIAN, GAY, BISEXUAL, AND TRANSGENDERED DATING

We know very little about the dating and mating behavior of lesbians, gays, bisexuals, and transgendered people because relatively little research has been done specifically in this area. Moreover, since the first edition of this textbook in the early 1990s, the research that exists continues to deal primarily with lesbian and gay sexual behavior and lifestyles. This is an even more compelling problem for data on the dating and mating behavior of lesbian, gay, bisexual, and transgender (LGBT) youths. Unlike for heterosexuals, LGBT dating and romance across age categories are seldom recognized and rarely supported or celebrated. Because society continues to stigmatize same-sex behavior, much mate selection behavior is carried out in the privacy of homes and recreational establishments frequented only or predominately by LGBT individuals and couples. Like heterosexual couples, most of these couples date for recreational and entertainment purposes, but the development of love relationships is also an important goal. In this regard, the function of dating for some LGBT couples is to find a mate with whom they can share love, psychological and economic support, and perhaps children. Because lesbians and gays are legally prohibited from marrying in all but six states (and the District of Columbia) in the United States, for some lesbians and gays, the ultimate goal of mate selection is a type of symbolic marriage, such as a domestic partnership, in which cohabiting lesbians and gays officially register as a couple. (Chapter 7 contains a more detailed discussion of these topics.)

In a society where being lesbian, gay, bisexual, or transgendered has challenges all its own, finding a partner and love can sometimes be a daunting task. For instance, in isolated, rural, and some urban areas, lesbian and gay meeting places are nonexistent. Even in urban areas where there are large LGBT populations, meeting a potential partner is not always easy. A large number of lesbians and gays remain "closeted"; thus, finding potential partners in gay bars and other gay-oriented meeting places limits the field of eligibles and potential partners to those lesbians and gays who feel comfortable in such settings. Because the dating experience increases the likelihood that an intimate relationship will develop, the absence of this opportunity may have long-term repercussions. On the other hand, lesbians themselves report a fairly wide range of ways that they meet potential partners. These include coffee shops, blind dates, group and community events, including places such as church and coming out groups, LGBT student unions, 12-step programs, Dyke Marches, meetings through mutual friends, chance meetings, and online (Teeple and Craig, 2011).

As with heterosexuals, there appear to be some fundamental gender differences in the dating and mate selection attitudes and behaviors of lesbians and gays. For instance, lesbians, like their heterosexual counterparts, are less competitive and more relationship oriented than gay and heterosexual men, and both lesbians and heterosexual women are more likely than gays and heterosexual men to value their relationships more than their jobs. In addition, lesbian bars are not nearly as common as gay bars; therefore, women cannot always count on them as a place to meet potential partners. Lesbians tend to meet their partners through lesbian friendship networks, mutual acquaintances, and participation in various lesbian and women's political and activist groups, with the period of courtship lasting on average 2 to 3 years (Alice, 2009; Stacey, 2003; Huston and Schwartz, 1996). Their partners tend to be women they have known for a while and with whom they have had no prior sexual relationship. Lesbians tend to practice a kind of serial monogamy in that they may have several partners over the course of their lifetime but are involved in only one intimate relationship at a time. In contrast, as we noted in Chapter 4, the courtship period for gays—as for heterosexual men—is often relatively short and is most often preceded by sexual relations.

The subculture of gay bars has been a prime place for gays to meet potential sexual partners but it has also acted to inhibit long-term partnerships. For example, research indicates that a major characteristic that gays look for in a potential partner is physical attractiveness; they prefer a partner who is very handsome—a trait that does not necessarily ensure a long-lasting relationship. Until recent times, the subculture of gay bars did not encourage gay men to form long-term relationships. In many places, singlehood rather than couplehood is still the norm.

In general, there is no one-size-fits-all set of dating and mating patterns among lesbians, gays, bisexual, and transgendered couples any more than there are among heterosexual couples. Lesbians and gays, like heterosexuals, are a diverse group representing many races, ethnicities, ages, religions, having diverse resources, values, attitudes, and dating and mate selection practices. Indeed, based on what we know about the patterns of lesbian and gay dating and mate selection, they do not appear to differ significantly from those found among heterosexual women and men. Thus, these patterns seem much more reflective of female and male socialization patterns than of patterns specific to lesbians and gays.

African American Lesbian and Gay Dating Unfortunately, research pertaining to lesbian, gay, bisexual, and transgendered mate selection across race is especially scarce. One of the few and earliest studies is of African American lesbians. This study found that African American lesbians were first attracted to a woman at around age 16 but did not have their first lesbian experience until age 19. Interestingly, two-thirds had at least one such relationship with an Anglo woman and over one-third reported having a lesbian relationship with some other woman of color. The median number of sexual partners they had was nine, which is similar to that reported by research on White lesbians. Dating and mate selection among lesbians and gays of color may be influenced by sociocultural factors such as the unavailability of same-race, same-sex partners; residential immobility; fewer social and financial resources than Whites generally and White gays specifically; and a general lack of employment opportunities. In addition, as in heterosexual relationships and White lesbian and gay relationships generally, there are gender differences in dating and mating attitudes and behaviors among African American lesbians and gays. For example, African American lesbians are more likely than African American gays to report exclusively same-sex relationships. In a recent Black gay pride survey, 82 percent of the women surveyed reported having sex exclusively with women, while only 66 percent of the men reported having sex exclusively with men (Battle et al., 2002).

For African American gays, some research and popular literature report that many of these gay men live an alternative secret sexual life referred to as "down low." African American men living on the down low date and/or have sex with other men and also date and/or have sex with women, but they do not identify themselves as gay or bisexual (we present a more detailed discussion of this behavior in Chapter 6). By way of comparison, a now classic study of Black and White gays found the following: Black and White gays reported equivalent numbers of sexual partners, both lifetime and over a 12-month period; Black gays were significantly less likely than White gays to engage in brief relationships with anonymous partners; over two-thirds of Black gays reported that more than half of their partners were White men. This last finding is in stark contrast to White gays in the same study, none of whom reported that more than half of their partners were Black. Over a quarter of a century after this study, recent research statistics show that 21 percent of all African American same-sex couples are interracial compared to only 10 percent of White same-sex couples (Dang and Frazer, 2005). Thus, it seems that similar to heterosexual African American women who date, a shortage of eligible potential mates may encourage African American lesbians and gays to couple with people of other races and ethnicities far more often than for Whites.

Theories of Mate Selection

Thus far, we have discussed mate selection cross-culturally, historically, and within the context of U.S. society. We have also paid particular attention to issues of race, class, gender, and sexual orientation in dating behavior. A complete understanding of why and how we choose each other within these contexts requires a theoretical framework that shows how these and other social, economic, and political factors are variously related and influence our mate selection. In the next section, we present some of the most frequently used theoretical explanations of mate selection.

EXCHANGE THEORIES

Within the discipline of sociology, exchange theories are perhaps the most often used explanations of interpersonal attraction and mate selection. Applied specifically to mate selection, various exchange theories hold that people looking for mates try to maximize their chances for a rewarding relationship. In other words, we enter into and remain in an intimate relationship as long as we perceive that the rewards outweigh the costs. When our relationships are no longer rewarding, we discontinue them. If each person maximizes outcomes, then stable relationships will develop between people who have very similar levels of resources because they will exchange comparable resources.

This principle is explained in the exchange theory of homogamous mating. According to this theory—sometimes referred to as the "principle of least interest"—within any pool of eligibles, a person looking to get married will seek out a person who she or he thinks will maximize her or his rewards. We therefore enter or do not enter into a romantic relationship depending on whether the other person possesses both tangible resources, such as money, and intangible resources, such as physical appearance. People with equivalent resources are most likely to maximize each other's rewards. Because couples with equivalent resources are most likely to have homogamous characteristics, mate selection is homogamous with respect to a given set of characteristics. As the relationship progresses, a couple engages in many other exchanges, including those involving power, sex, companionship, and love. Seldom are both parties equally interested in continuing the relationship. Thus, the one who is least interested has an advantage and is in a position to dominate.

In traditional mate selection, men maximized their rewards because they generally had a range of rewards to offer such as social status, economic support, power, and protection. In contrast, women generally had a limited set of resources, primarily involving their physical appearance and their ability to bear and care for children. Today, however, women have many more rewards to offer, including many of the same ones that men have traditionally had to offer, thus women can be more selective in choosing a mate. Instead of the traditional male trade-off of economic security, many women today are looking for men who are expressive, sensitive, and caring and who are willing to share housework and child-rearing responsibilities. Men who do not possess these characteristics are finding themselves less desirable and sought out as a potential mate. On the other hand, however, many men seem to be flipping the gender script and are acknowledging their desire for commitment and connection, intrinsic characteristics that some women are looking for in a partner. Along the same lines, instead of the traditional female trade-off of physical attractiveness and nurturance, many men today are looking for women who are assertive, creative, and self-confident and who can contribute to the economic support of a family. Basically, women and men are looking for similar assets and both bring similar assets to the exchange relationship. So exchange theories help us understand how people develop a close relationship through an exchange of rewards. But why is it that some people develop an intimate relationship while others do not?

Stimulus-Value-Role Theory A popular variation of the general exchange theory of mate selection is Bernard Murstein's (1980, 1987) stimulus-value-role theory of interpersonal attraction. According to Murstein, in a situation of relatively free choice, attraction and interaction depend on the exchange value of the assets and liabilities that each person brings to the situation. In the mate selection process, couples move through three stages: stimulus, value, and role. They are first attracted to each other by an initial *stimulus* such as good looks, the way one walks, money, power, or notoriety. Whatever the stimulus, it draws the two people together initially and tends to energize the relationship past the boundaries of simple friendship. If both feel the situation is equal concerning the exchange of resources they move to the *value* stage where they test their suitability for establishing a permanent relationship with each other by comparing their value orientations on such things as family, religion, politics, and lifestyle preferences. The more similar the two people's values, the stronger their attraction becomes and the more likely they will progress toward a long-lasting relationship and move on to the *role* stage. Here, each partner has the opportunity to see how the other acts out her or his roles in real-life situations. If mutual benefits at this stage are positive and fairly equal—if their feelings and behaviors about issues such as power and authority in the relationship, the division of labor, and other expectations that they have for each other are the same or similar—then the couple might proceed to marriage. The key here is that these three stages act as filtering devices for evaluating a dating relationship to determine if it will continue or end. The three stages are not mutually exclusive but rather work together to move a couple toward a committed relationship.

Equity Theory is yet another variation of exchange theory used to explain mate selection. When used in this sense, the term *equity* signifies "fairness." An intimate relationship is stable and satisfying if both parties believe that it is "fair"—equitable and mutually beneficial. Equity theory proposes that a person is attracted to another by a fair deal rather than by a profitable exchange. It argues that most people believe they should benefit from a relationship in proportion to what they give to the relationship. People are attracted to those from whom they get as much as they give. Two people do not usually seek the exact same things in a relationship; however, they are attracted by a deal that is fair to them. Values involved in judging equity range from physical attractiveness to family background to anything that a given person might value. If the relationship is inequitable, people will try to move the relationship to an equitable level. However, the greater the inequity, the harder it will be to move the relationship to an equitable level.

FILTER THEORIES

As our discussion thus far indicates, mate selection involves a complex process of making choices within the context of a range of factors that can restrict or enhance our ability to choose. Some

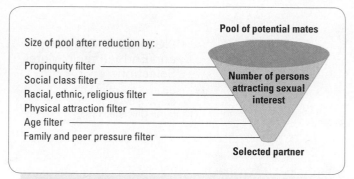

FIGURE 5.2 The Filter Theory of Mate Selection

Source: Based on David Klimek, 1979, *Beneath Mate Selection and Marriage: The Unconscious Motives in Human Pairing* (New York: Van Nostrand Reinhold), p. 13.

years ago, David Klimek (1979) described this process in terms of a series of filterings. As Figure 5.2 suggests, individuals use a series of filters to sort through a large number of potential mates to arrive at the final choice. Each filter, in descending order, reduces the pool of eligible mates until relatively few eligibles are left. We then choose a mate from among this group. Filter theories, or process theories as they are sometimes called, suggest that many factors are involved in the marital choice. In the next section we discuss some of the most prevalent of these factors. After reading this section, you should be more conscious of the fact that contrary to popular belief, Americans do not have complete freedom of choice in mate selection.

Mate Selection: Finding and Meeting Partners

"There's supposed to be more women than men, so where are they?" "I know there are a lot of good men out there—you just have to know where to find them." Do these comments sound familiar to you? Increasingly, over the last couple of decades, single women and men looking for "Ms. Right" or "Mr. Right" have lamented the mounting problem of finding someone to date or marry. How people meet and where, how, or why they are attracted to each other and not someone else are some of the most basic questions surrounding mate selection. As you will see in the following discussion, finding a mate has become almost a national pastime in the United States.

THE MARRIAGE MARKET AND THE POOL OF ELIGIBLES

Throughout our history, various romantic theories of love and mate selection have suggested that when the time is right we will meet a "Fair Maiden" or "Prince Charming" without much effort on our part. Most such notions imply that mate selection is a rather unsystematic and random event determined by the "luck of the draw" or by a power higher than ourselves. In reality, meeting prospective mates, choosing partners, developing a dating relationship, and falling in love are not random activities but

are predictable and structured by a number of social and demographic factors. For example, if you are a female college student in a heterosexual dating relationship, without meeting you or your partner we could predict fairly accurately many things about your partner. For instance, he is probably a college student like you (or he has already completed college or attended college previously), he is probably of the same racial or ethnic background and social class as you, he is probably a little taller than you, a few years older, and as religious or spiritual as you are. We might even predict that you both are similarly attractive and intelligent. Likewise, if you are a male student in a heterosexual dating relationship the same predictions apply, with a few differences: Your partner is probably your age or 1 to 5 years younger, and she is probably your height or shorter. The point here is that we have not randomly guessed about the characteristics of people who date and marry. Rather, we have used the knowledge that sociologists have provided us about the principles of homogamy, endogamy, and exogamy in mate selection.

Marriage Market Historically, sociologists have described mate selection in terms of a **marriage market.** That is, they use the analogy of the commercial marketplace to explain how we choose the people we date, mate, live with, and marry. The marriage market concept implies that we enter the mate selection process with certain resources and we trade these resources for the best offer we can get. In this sense, the marriage market is not a real place but a process.

Regardless of how we choose mates, as exchange theory suggests, some sort of bargaining and exchange probably takes place. Although the idea of swapping or exchanging resources in matters of love and intimacy may seem distant and applicable only to those cultures in which marriages are arranged, this process is also very much a part of mate selection in the United States. Although the nature of the marital exchange has changed, the market has not been eliminated. Despite important improvements in their bargaining position, women remain at a disadvantage vis-à-vis men in the mate selection marketplace. Although women have entered the labor force in record numbers and have become increasingly independent, their actual earnings are still well below those of their male counterparts, as is their ability to earn. Furthermore, many of the traditional resources that women could offer, such as child care, housework, and sexuality, can be obtained by men outside marriage and thus have less value in the marriage market today. Women are further disadvantaged in the dating and marriage market by the sexual double standard attached to aging: As women age, they are considered unattractive and undesirable by men.

Does this description of the marital marketplace sound cold, calculating, and unromantic? Even if we are uncomfortable with the idea, most of us engage in the exchange of various personality and social characteristics (consciously or unconsciously) in our quest for a mate.

Pool of Eligibles Theoretically, every unmarried person in the United States is a potential eligible mate for every other unmarried person. Realistically, however, not every unmarried person is equally available or accessible to every other unmarried person. The people whom our society has defined as acceptable

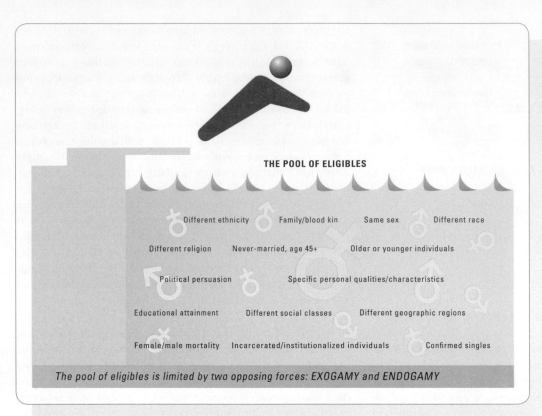

FIGURE 5.3 Exogamy and Endogamy in Mate Selection

Source: Adapted from a drawing by John Chauncey Byrd, Chicago, 1993.

THE POOL OF ELIGIBLES

Different ethnicity   Family/blood kin   Same sex   Different race

Different religion   Never-married, age 45+   Older or younger individuals

Political persuasion   Specific personal qualities/characteristics

Educational attainment   Different social classes   Different geographic regions

Female/male mortality   Incarcerated/institutionalized individuals   Confirmed singles

The pool of eligibles is limited by two opposing forces: EXOGAMY and ENDOGAMY

marriage partners for us form what sociologists call a **pool of eligibles.** For almost all of us, the pool of eligibles consists of people of the same race, class, and educational level as ourselves. With amazing consistency, we are very much like the people we meet, date, fall in love with, and marry—far more so than can be attributed simply to chance. Sociologists refer to this phenomenon as **homogamy:** the tendency to meet, date, and marry someone very similar to ourselves in terms of important or desirable characteristics.

As we learned in Chapter 1, two of the most common sets of social rules governing mate selection and the pool of eligibles are exogamy and endogamy (see Figure 5.3). Our pool of eligibles is first narrowed by society's exogamous norms. The most common exogamous norms in the United States are those that prohibit us from dating or marrying someone who is a family member or who is of the same sex. (These norms can be formal or informal). As you know from Chapter 1, the incest taboo is a universal exogamous norm that narrows our pool of eligibles by eliminating close blood relatives. Regarding same-sex partners, people of the same sex are considered socially unacceptable mates and are also excluded, at least theoretically. Endogamy is the opposite of exogamy. Endogamous norms can be formal, such as the laws in many U.S. states prior to 1967 that prohibited interracial marriage thus forcing people to marry within their racial or ethnic group. Most, however, are informal. For example, social convention, not formal laws, dictates that we marry someone near our own age. Although our pool of eligibles is loosely or closely organized around a number of factors such as these, perhaps two of the most important of these factors are the marriage squeeze and the marriage gradient.

Do you know how your parents met? Was it love at first sight? How alike are they? What about you? Are you looking for a mate or partner? What characteristics do you look for in a mate? Character? Social conscience? A strong religious conviction? Money? Is it difficult to find someone who meets your standards? Think about your own dating and mate selection experiences and priorities as you continue reading this chapter. At the end of this chapter, you may find that your thinking has shifted, or perhaps you have become aware of priorities and feelings that you never realized you had.

The Marriage Squeeze Why do you think some people who want a mate and are actively looking cannot connect? Why do women complain more often than men about having difficulty finding a mate? Is there someone out there for all of us, no matter what resources we have to offer? Or will some of us not find a mate no matter how hard we look? In reality, there is not someone out there for everyone. If those people being advised to "sit tight and wait" are women born after World War II, they may be waiting for a very long time. Demographic data reveal that at any given time in the United States since World War II, there has been a greater number of women than men who are eligible for marriage and looking for a partner. Sociologists have defined this imbalance in the ratio of marriage-aged men to marriage-aged women as a **marriage squeeze,** whereby one sex has a more limited pool of eligibles than the other.

Demographic data indicate that the marriage squeeze reversed itself in the 1990s such that by the year 2000, never-married men outnumbered never-married women. As the number of never-married women compared to never-married men fluctuated over the next several years, by 2009, the number of never-married men again outnumbered never-married women. For example, when we consider the total population of unmarried adults (never-married, separated, divorced, and widowed), age 15 and older in 2009, as Table 5.2 shows, there was a greater percentage of unmarried men (32.4) than unmarried women (26.7). However, not surprisingly, although never-married men outnumbered never-married women in 2009, as women and men age, the marriage squeeze shows up again for women 45 years of age and older. By the time women reach 55 years of age there is almost twice as many unmarried women (48.4 percent) as there are unmarried men (25.6 percent). It should also be noted that these percentages alone do not tell the whole story. Many women continue to find their options for dating and mate selection limited even though theoretically there are more eligible men than women in a particular same-age category. This might be accounted for, in part, by the fact that women tend to date and marry men who are 3 to 5 years older than themselves. Given this, when we look again at the data in Table 5.2, we can see, for example, that although unmarried men outnumber unmarried women within their respective age categories, when we look at the percentage of unmarried women in a particular age category and compare it with the next highest age category of unmarried men, there is a noticeable decrease in the pool of eligibles for women (for instance, women ages 20 to 24 theoretically would date men in the 25 to 29 age category). Although the causes are different, as we noted earlier, countries like India, China, and Japan are experiencing a similar marriage squeeze, with high percentages of single men and a scarcity of single women.

Moreover, as we indicated earlier, African American women are more vulnerable to the marriage squeeze than any other racial or ethnic group of women. Women in other countries have experienced this marriage squeeze as well. For example, women in Australia faced a similar marriage squeeze in the 1980s and 1990s when there were only 97 men for every 100 women. Today, the pattern of in-migration into New Zealand is causing a similar marriage squeeze as women of "marriageable age" are moving to New Zealand at rates of up to one-third higher than men. This is especially true for Asian migrants, with 53,000 more women than men in the age group 20 to 49. A recent study found that as a result of this gendered immigration, New Zealand has a higher ratio of women to men in the peak childbearing ages of 30 to 34 than any other industrialized country, with 9 percent more women than men. The ratio of women to men in this age group is as high as 32 percent for Asian women and even higher among certain Asian nationalities such as Thais and Filipinas/os. Although experts do not know the exact reasons for the influx of women into New Zealand, they think it may be one of the factors that has contributed to New Zealand having the second-highest rate of single-parent families in the world. There is some speculation that New Zealand's changing economy calling for more nurse aides, child-care workers, cleaners, and even prostitutes has brought in a predominantly female labor pool, particularly since the 1990s ("New Zealand Attracting Young Female Immigrants," 2005).

The Marriage Gradient Another factor that affects the availability of eligible mates in the marriage market is the marriage gradient. In general, the **marriage gradient** suggests that men marry women who are slightly lower down the social class continuum (younger, a little poorer, less educated). Accordingly, the pool of eligible mates for men increases as they get older, richer, and more educated while the pool of eligible mates decreases for women as they get older, richer, and more educated. For men, getting older, achieving more schooling, and becoming occupationally successful increases the number of women who consider them acceptable marriage partners. However, older, well-educated, successful women find that their choices are reduced because fewer men consider them acceptable partners.

The marriage gradient certainly shapes dating and marital choices for women and men, but it does so within culturally accepted limits. For example, in most cultures, including the United States, informal norms encourage women to marry men of equal or higher social status. When men marry outside their social class level, they more often marry downward than upward. Conversely, when women marry outside their social class, they most often marry upward. The tendency to marry upward in social status is referred to as **hypergamy;** marriage downward is known as **hypogamy.** Thus, in most cultures, women practice hypergamy, and men practice hypogamy. Because women marry upward and men marry downward, men at the top have a much larger field of eligibles than do men at the bottom. The reverse is true for women: Those at the top have a very small pool of eligibles, whereas those on the bottom have a much wider range of men from which to choose. This pattern therefore works to keep some of the highest status women and lowest status men from marrying.

Although the marriage gradient traditionally provided most women with upward mobility, this is not necessarily the case today.

TABLE 5.2 Percentage of Unmarried Women and Men by Selected Age Categories, 2009

	Females (%)	Males (%)
Never-married 15 years and older	26.7	32.4
Unmarried (overall)* for selected ages		
20–24	79.2	87.8
25–29	51.7	64.2
30–34	34.9	41.0
35–44	28.5	31.6
45–54	31.1	30.2
55 and older	48.4	25.6

*Includes all categories of singles: never-married, separated, divorced, and widow/widower.

Source: U.S. Census Bureau Statistical Abstract, 2011, Table 57, P. 53, Marital Status of the Population by Sex and Age: 2009.

The increasing economic independence of some women has made marriage less of a mobility mechanism. In particular, the growing gender gaps in college enrollment and degree attainment in the United States have led many popular writers and others among the lay public to ask, as the title of one article suggests, if "The College Gender Gap Could Mean Women Lose in the Mating Game" (see, for example, Sealey, 2002). Thus, whether or not the shrinking pool of eligibles for women at the top of the education hierarchy is real or perceived, many of these women, across racial categories, are dating and marrying men who are less educated and earn less money. For instance, a woman with a college degree was heard to say, "If I could find a kind plumber with a sense of humor, I'd marry him." Other women, although interested in dating and/or marriage, are not willing to settle for less than their ideal, so they neither date nor marry.

Race Perhaps the most important norms in mate selection in the United States revolve around race and ethnicity. Because interracial dating and interracial marriage were outlawed or ostracized throughout much of American history, many sociologists today, as well as those among the lay public, consider interracial dating and marriage to be key indicators of the state of American race relations. Certainly one of the most public manifestations of race (along with gender and sexual orientation) is the choice of one's dating and/or marital partner. Citing the results of their respective surveys, many researchers today report that Americans have become much more racially tolerant. For example, the idea of African Americans and Whites dating, once a highly divisive issue, is said to be broadly accepted in the population at large today, at least in terms of attitude if not in terms of behavior (see Table 5.3).

Changes in attitude over the last several decades about interracial dating and people of other races are reflected in several major demographic and political groups. However, age is a major factor in American's racial attitudes. For example, although attitudes across generations have changed about interracial dating, there remains a persistent generation gap. According to researchers at the Pew Research Center for the People and the Press, succeeding generations of young people are moving into adulthood with more tolerant attitudes toward interracial dating than the age cohorts that preceded them. For example, the highest acceptance of interracial dating occurs among people born since 1977. For example, 93 percent of what researchers have variously dubbed "Generation Y," "Millennials," and "Generation Next" accepts interracial dating. Not surprising, people born before 1946 (sometimes dubbed the "Greatest Generation") express the least tolerance for interracial dating (only 67 percent are supportive of interracial dating). According to one survey, more than one-half of Generation Y teenagers who date say they have dated someone of another race or ethnic group and another one-third say they would have no objection to doing so. Moreover, most of these teens think that interracial dating is "no big deal;" it is no different than any other kind of dating; it is here to stay, and in most cases, their parents are not a major obstacle (Jayson, 2006; Wellner, 2005).

Social Explorer Activity: Increases in the Multiracial Population on **myfamilylab.com**

✳ **Explore** the **Concept**

TABLE 5.3 The Racial Landscape: Attitudes about Interracial Dating

Approve of Interracial Dating

Population at Large	1987	2007	2009
Public approval of interracial dating	48%	83%	83%
All right for Blacks and Whites to date			
Blacks	74%	97%	94%
Whites	44%	81%	79%

Approve of African Americans and Whites Dating

Generations	1987–1988	2007	2009
Generation Y (1977–)	-----	94%	93%
Generation X (1965–1976)	64%	87%	86%
Baby Boomers (1946–1964)	59%	84%	83%
Born prior to 1946	36%	65%	67%

Source: The Pew Center for the People and the Press 2007, "Trends in Political Values and Core Attitudes: 1987–2007," (March 22). Washington, DC: The Pew Research Center for the People and the Press: www.people-press.org. The Pew Research Center Publication, 2009 (December 11), Scott Keeter and Paul Taylor. "The Millennials." The Pew Research Center for the People and the Press: www.pewresearch.org/pubs/1437/millennials-profile. Reprinted with permission of the Pew Research Center.

Differences in attitudes also fall along the lines of geographic location. Although the South remains a more conservative region on racial issues, the differences between the South and the rest of the country appear to be narrowing. Compared to the 1980s, when roughly around 3 in 10 Southern Whites were open to African Americans and Whites dating, today the number has doubled to 7 in 10 (69 percent). In comparison, 84 percent or roughly 8 in 10 Whites living outside of the South hold such attitudes. These regional differences in racial attitudes are not confined to Whites. African Americans in the South, for example, tend to hold a more conservative view on the subject than their counterparts in other regions of the country. While Whites generally and southern Whites specifically are far more tolerant of interracial dating today than in the past, a recent poll gauging Mississippi Republicans' preferences revealed that almost one-half (46 percent) of GOP voters in the state think interracial marriage should be illegal (The Pew Center for the People and the Press, 2009, 2010; McShane, 2011).

Clearly, racial attitudes have changed, at least as they are reported to researchers and surveyers. However, the changing attitudes on interracial dating notwithstanding, we must be ever cautious in interpreting these surveys and other related data as evidence of more people dating across race lines. Despite such survey reports and the increasing depiction of interracial intimacy in the media, interracial dating and romance continue to be a significant taboo in American society. More importantly, attitudes (racial or otherwise) do not always translate into behavior. Although most surveys query the public about their attitudes, a recent survey asked respondents about their actual dating practices and found that Whites had the lowest rate of interracial dating (35.7 percent) and Asian Americans had the highest, with 57 percent of Asians reporting that they had dated someone outside of their race. Falling in the middle, 56.5 percent of African Americans and 55.4 percent of Latinas/os had dated interracially. The gap between dating attitudes and behavior also can be seen, for example, in a study of the online dating preferences of Whites, which showed that one-half of White women and more than three-fourths of White men declare no racial preference in searching for a date. However, in practice, almost all (97 percent) of the women and men (90 percent) send e-mail queries to members of their same race/ethnicity (Tagorda, 2005). Even on college campuses where dating attitudes and behaviors are often more progressive and open to interracial dating, research on interracial dating on college campuses reveal that student attitudes about the topic are not necessarily consistent with their behavior. Thus, for example, despite the diversity of some university populations, students are more likely to date individuals from their own racial group than people from outside their racial group (Wellner, 2005; Lee, 2008). Overall, men and African Americans are more open to dating and marrying someone of a different race than are women and Whites.

According to some observers of interracial dating trends, as Americans struggle with racially charged issues from affirmative action to record-breaking immigration, the emerging dating attitudes and behavior among high school students specifically and millennials generally could signal a shift in the way the nation will come to look at race. Others say the notion of a generation that ignores race paints too rosy a picture. They contend that decades devoted to ending racial segregation and creating a colorblind society may have created a new problem: a generation so unconcerned about race that it ignores racial disparities that still exist (Jayson, 2006). In any case, although attitudes are changing and interracial dating is more common than ever before, as we have seen, interracial dating is still not accepted everywhere and by everyone, and it continues to be controversial in many areas of the country. Interracial couples still upset families, inspire stares and comments, and are often targets of hostility and violence. Interracial couples are having a particularly hard time in the midst of rising racial and ethnic tensions in this country today. Since the 1980s, race relations have been particularly strained. Racial slurs, race riots, bigotry, the dramatic increase in the number of reported hate crimes during the 1990s, the continued racially motivated violence, including widely publicized cases of African American men being killed or beaten for associating with White women, as well as the highly racially charged environment since the 2008 election of President Barack Obama have given many observers cause for translating survey data on interracial dating and marriage with extreme caution.

Think about your own dating history and that of people you know such as family members. Use the exercise in the Writing Your Own Script box to analyze some of your own attitudes and those

Writing Your Own Script

PERSONAL BIOGRAPHY AND SOCIAL STRUCTURE

Selecting a Mate

Think about the structure of mate selection in U.S. society generally and in the various social groups to which you belong. Write a short essay that includes an analysis of your mate selection in terms of the following framework.

First, think about what initially attracts you to another person. Consider this question within the context of some or all of the following possibilities: physical attractiveness, race, age, sexual orientation, religion, residence, occupational status, popularity, social status, personality, character. Are you attracted to people very much like you, or the opposite?

Next, ask your parents or others with whom you are close and whose opinions you value, whom among the following they would object to if you dated or married:

Race: African American, White American, Asian American, Native American, Puerto Rican, Mexican American, other Latino, other race.

Age: 15, 20, 25, 30, 35, 40, 45, 55, 65, 75, 76 or older.

Educational level: Fifth grade or below, eighth grade only, some high school, high school graduate, some college, college graduate, graduate or professional school.

Religion: Catholic, Baptist, Methodist, Muslim, Buddhist, Mormon, Lutheran, Unification Church, Orthodox Jew, Jehovah's Witness, Atheist, other.

Bood relatives: First cousin, second cousin, third or more removed cousin.

Gender: Same sex.

Also think about the following questions, and incorporate your responses in the essay. How do you feel about interracial dating and marriages? Do you know anyone who is dating or married to a person of a different racial group? What problems, if any, have they encountered? Have you ever been involved in an interracial relationship? If not, would you consider such a relationship? What barriers do you think you would encounter if you were a partner in such a relationship? Are any members of your immediate family dating or married interracially? If yes, how do you feel about these relationships? To what extent do parents, relatives, and friends' attitudes about interracial dating and marriage affect your dating and marital choices?

of people you know concerning the issue of race and intimate relationships. See the In Other Places box to see how interracial dating and marriage in South Africa—a formerly colonized country that prohibited interracial pairings until the 1980s—compares to the United States, which banned prohibitions to interracial marriage in the 1960s.

Social Class Sociologists typically measure class using a composite scale consisting of level of educational attainment, occupation, and level of income. As we have seen, much of our behavior is affected by our location in the status hierarchy. People who share a similar social class background tend to share common interests, goals, lifestyles, and general behavior. These kinds of compatibility of interest and general homogamy are the bases of intimate relationships. As with race, Americans mate with people from their own socioeconomic class with far greater frequency than could

be expected simply by chance. As you learned earlier, this is especially true among the upper classes of all races. Because social researchers disagree on the nature and number of social classes in U.S. society, it is difficult to determine accurate statistics on class endogamy. We know, however, that courtships and marriages tend to be highly endogamous for such class-related factors as education and occupation. Educational homogamy is most observable for women with four or more years of college, who tend to marry men with comparable or higher levels of education, and for men who have never attended college.

Age When you see a much younger woman with an older man do you think, "Gee, she must be looking for a father figure," or "My God, he's robbing the cradle"? As we learned from our discussion of love in Chapter 4, age norms represent yet another important constraint on our freedom to fall in love and choose a mate.

In Other Places

INTERRACIAL DATING IN SOUTH AFRICA

Since the transition to democracy in South Africa in the 1990s, what are race relations there like today? Is there more interracial dating in the "new" democratic postapartheid South Africa? According to a 2001 news item on interracial dating in South Africa, such relationships, particularly public interracial relationships, are still unimaginable to some in South Africa. This is not surprising, given that the "new" South Africa, even after more than a decade, is still in its infancy and given the history of race, racism, and the legal bans prohibiting the intermingling of the races in South Africa. For decades, under the apartheid government, love, dating, and marriage across the color line were strictly forbidden.

Although the ban on interracial dating was lifted in 1985, Blacks and Whites were still required by law to live in separate areas. Thus, couples who dated or married across race experienced harassment as well as other negative sanctions. Interestingly, the statistics on interracial marriage under apartheid in South Africa were strikingly similar to those in the United States today, where the ban against interracial marriage

was lifted almost 50 years ago. For instance, in 1987, the South African government reported that about 2 percent of all marriages that year were interracial. The latest figures on interracial marriage in the United States indicate that about 4 percent of all marriages are interracial, and they include interracial marriages across all groups (not just Blacks and Whites).

True, the races are mingling more than ever before in South Africa. Black and White South Africans increasingly share public spaces, as well as office cubicles, suburban neighborhoods, and books in integrated classrooms. Indeed, some prominent Blacks, including a former South African political prisoner, are married to Whites, and one of South Africa's most popular soap operas, *Isidingo*, features an interracial couple. However, the reality of the "new" South Africa is that it is still largely a country of two nations—of wealthy Whites and poor Blacks—and interracial dating and marriage are still rare. Black-White marriages are the rarest and get the most attention. Some such couples are called "Top Decks," (an insult) after a candy bar that's both white and

milk chocolate. Moreover, there's a big gap between Blacks and Whites on the issue of interracial marriage. For example, 27 percent of Blacks and fully 75 percent of Whites say they'd be bothered if their child married across race lines (McLaughlin, 2004). Not only interracial dating and marriage but also interracial friendships remain rare. And although interracial couples are no longer oddities in big cities, they are seldom visible in restaurants, shopping malls, or movie theaters. It seems that the new democracy and intimate relationships across race have not yet caught up with each other.

What do you think? Although there are no longer laws in South Africa that prohibit interracial dating and marriage, why do you think it is still uncommon? Why do you think that the United States and South Africa have similar interracial marriage rates? Explain.

Source: "Sunday Q&A: Interracial Dating in South Africa," *New York Times* (May 27, 2001): 16; McLaughlin, A. 2004. "South African Couples Bridge Racial Divide." *The Christian Science Monitor* (May 7): www .csmonitor.com.

Although no laws require us to date, live with, or marry people within our age group, informal norms and pressures operate to keep mate selection fairly homogamous in terms of age. Most Americans mate with people from a closely related age group. For most of us, this means that we date and marry people roughly within two to five years of our own age. Although the sanctions for dating or marrying someone very much older or younger (within the law) than oneself are mild; most people adhere to the age custom in selecting a mate. However, as we have pointed out, older women are deviating from this informal norm, dating younger men with increasing frequency. When people deviate, however, it usually goes unnoticed for the most part, unless, of course, the principals are wealthy or high-profile celebrities.

Religion Historically, religion has played a significant role in mate selection in the United States. Some religious groups forbid all inter-faith marriage, and while others allow it, most restrict it. Others, like Islam, typically enforce a limited form of endogamy—Muslim men can take chaste wives from neighboring non-Muslim populations but Muslim women are normally forbidden to marry outside of the Muslim community. According to recent surveys of religiously mixed marriages in the United States, although some groups remain highly religiously homogeneous in marriage, a growing number of marriages today are interfaith or religiously heterogamous. For example, 27 percent of all married Americans are in religiously mixed marriages. And if we consider marriages between people of different Protestant denominations, the percentage rises to 37 percent, or nearly 4 in 10. A breakdown of interfaith marriage among various religious traditions reveal that Hindus (90 percent) and Mormons (83 percent) are the most likely to have a spouse with the same religion. Following these two religious traditions, nearly 4 in 5 Catholics (78 percent) and 7 in 10 Jews (69 percent) are also married to someone of the same faith. Additionally, in total, 81 percent of married Protestants are married to other Protestants: about 6 in 10 (63 percent) are married to a person of the same Protestant denomination and an additional 18 percent have a spouse who belongs to a Protestant domination different from their own (Lemmons, 2011; The Pew Forum on Religion and Public Life, 2008).

Although religious traditions have traditionally opposed interfaith marriage based on the belief that such marriages weaken one's commitment to the faith, some of them have responded to the challenges and the realities of increasing interfaith marriages. For example, according to the Catholic faith, of all of the challenges an interfaith couple will face, the most challenging might likely revolve around their children. In response to this issue, non-Catholic spouses are no longer required to promise to raise their children in the Catholic faith. However, they are encouraged to do all in their power to have their children baptized and raised in the Catholic faith. On the other hand, the trend toward interfaith marriages among Jews (up 20 percent since 1965) has led some observers to predict the disappearance of the American Jewish community within a few decades. This perceived threat to Jewish identity and culture has prompted some Jewish parents to actually arrange marriages for their children. Moreover, some synagogues have started dating services and singles programs to discourage interfaith marriages. And since 1980, there has been a growing trend for interfaith married couples and their children

From left, Sarah and Nora Ismail apply makeup in their Fremont, California home in 2003, as they prepare for their special all-girl Muslim prom. The prom is a spirited response to Muslim religious and cultural beliefs in which dating, dancing with or touching boys or appearing without wearing a hijab is not permitted. The all-girl Muslim prom was the idea of Fatima Haque and her friends in Fremont California and just may be a new American ritual.

to embrace Judaism and identify themselves as Jewish (Bukhari, 2004; Berkofsky, 2001).

Sex and Gender When discussing factors that limit our pool of eligible mates, we cannot overlook sex. As we have indicated repeatedly, heterosexuality is the norm in mating, dating, and mate selection in the United States. Most Americans are so socialized into a heterosexual frame of reference that it is outside their scope of reality even to consider a same-sex relationship as an option. So important is the value of heterosexuality to many Americans that exogamous norms regulating this behavior have been encoded into law to ensure that people mate heterosexually. The stigma attached to same-sex relationships, legal constraints, and the physical abuse ("gay bashing") that such couples frequently experience can act as deterrents for some people who might otherwise choose a partner of the same sex.

OTHER FACTORS THAT NARROW THE DATING AND MARRIAGE MARKET

As we have seen, mate selection in the United States is an individual decision, yet many social and structural barriers and limitations act to constrain our freedom to choose a partner. Besides race, class, age, religion, and sex, these barriers can also include propinquity and family and peer pressure.

Propinquity We have already touched on the subject of propinquity and its role in mate selection, particularly as we discussed racial and ethnic homogamy. The term **propinquity** is used by sociologists to denote proximity or closeness in place and space. Traditionally, Americans met, were attracted to, dated, and married people who lived in the same community. Although we are no longer tied to our local communities in the way we were before mass transportation and the mass production of the automobile, residential propinquity continues to contribute to homogamy in mate selection. Residential propinquity is closely tied to many of the factors we have already discussed: race, social class, sexual orientation, and to a lesser degree, religion. Historically, people of the same general social characteristics, for any number of reasons, have lived close together. For example, most U.S. cities are racially and ethnically segregated, and many are class segregated as well. It is not unusual to go to a city and find very distinct racial or ethnic communities: the African American community, Little Italy, Chinatown, Greektown, Little Cuba. In addition, many cities have neighborhoods with predominantly lesbian and gay inhabitants (in Chicago, for example, there is a neighborhood called *Boystown*) where women and men in close proximity can meet potential partners. These residential patterns increase the likelihood that we will meet, date, and marry people of similar racial and social backgrounds. However, propinquity is not limited to place of residence. In a mobile society such as ours, propinquity operates as much, if not more, in schools, the workplace, entertainment venues, and other institutions as we increasingly move out of our communities for a good portion of each day. Today, when Americans are working longer hours and multiple jobs, some observers of the dating scene consider the workplace the "new tavern" for striking up relationships. One recent survey, for example, found that 30 percent of working adults have dated a co-worker (CareerBuilder.com, 2011). Whatever the case, the probability of meeting someone and establishing an intimate relationship still depends on the likelihood of interacting with that person. And the likelihood of interacting with someone is a function of their nearness or close proximity to us.

Family and Peer Pressure Consider the following scenario:

> I am a female working on a doctorate; my boyfriend has never attended college. We love each other, but my family and friends insist that I should break off with him because he is not on my level. I think they might be right because sometimes even I am embarrassed by the way he speaks and carries himself. I feel so pressured by them. Can love overcome the prejudices of society?

Stated another way, this woman's question could well be: Can love overcome the pressures of family, friends, or peers? Who is or is not acceptable to parents and other relatives is of importance to most Americans. Parents in particular exercise direct and indirect influence on whom we meet and develop relationships with. Parents influence our choice of mate from the moment we are born through their teaching, their example, where they choose to live, which schools they send us to, and so forth. How, where, and when we are brought up has a profound impact on our views and decisions concerning dating, marriage, and family. Additionally, the closer we are to our parents and kin, the more likely we will consider their views.

Peers, too, can be powerful forces affecting both whom we meet and whom we decide to date or pair with. If our peer relationships are significant and close, we are far more likely to consider our friends' views and feelings about the people we date and marry. When you have completed the Writing Your Own Script exercise, you will probably have a greater awareness of just how influential parents, other family members, and peers can be in choosing a mate.

PERSONAL QUALITIES AND MATE SELECTION

As we saw in Figure 5.2, social factors such as those we have just discussed act as an initial screening. Once our pool of eligibles is determined, other factors come into play, such as the personal qualities or characteristics of the people we meet and consider as potential mates. The personal qualities we consider cover a wide range that includes physical appearance, lifestyle, ability to communicate, values and attitudes, personality, and family background, to name but a few. Probably the most important, at least initially, is physical appearance, because first impressions are often based on whether or not we find a person attractive. In addition, first impressions are often lasting impressions.

Attraction What does "Ms. Right" or "Mr. Right" look like? All of us have some image, vague though it may be, of who our ideal mate will be. Usually this image includes both physical and personality features, and we consciously or unconsciously rate or compare potential mates in accordance with these images. These ideas and images do not develop in a vacuum; rather, they are shaped in large part by the society in which we live. For most Americans, physical appearance is one of the most important ingredients in mate selection. Whether we admit it or not, how someone looks has a considerable impact on whether we choose that person as a friend or lover.

Researchers and pollsters have found a number of interesting points about physical attractiveness and its influence on mate selection. For example, attractiveness of a potential partner is critical, followed by ambition and earnings. Americans overwhelmingly agree that being physically attractive is a strong asset in the dating–mate selection game. Seven out of 10 Americans believe that physical attractiveness is important in society today in terms of social life, happiness, and the ability to get ahead. In addition, dating and marriage relationships tend to be endogamous for physical attractiveness. Various studies have documented our general tendency to look for and end up with partners whose attractiveness is roughly equivalent to our own. University of Wisconsin professor Linda Roberts (2009) says the folk wisdom that birds of a feather flock together is really true when it comes to dating and mate selection. For example, according to Roberts, people choose mates who have the same ear-lobe length or nose width. While it seems we do so unconsciously, nevertheless we seem to have a propensity to choose people who look similar to ourselves. Both women and men tend to choose partners having the same general level of attractiveness. Roberts' research is consistent with other studies of physical attractiveness in dating and mate selection, which suggests that statistically, beautiful people marry beautiful people and less beautiful people marry less beautiful people. People who lack looks place more emphasis on nonphysical features, such as sense of humor, than in physical beauty. Men tend to be less concerned with their own looks when deciding whom to date. That is, while men generally might not have any qualms about going after someone much better looking than they are, women, however, tend more often to choose partners with compatible looks.

In any event, once people meet and dating begins, personality characteristics become important considerations, although attractiveness does not decline in importance. Attractiveness can impact the depth and duration of our relationships. For example, some researcher have found that couples who are similarly attractive are more likely to progress deeper into the relationship than couples in which one partner is relatively more attractive than the other. In the dating game, people tend to shop around for an attractive partner. The greater our level of attractiveness, the greater our bargaining ability in the marriage market.

Companionship Some demographers have predicted that many people who have married in recent times will likely stay married to the same person for the next 50 years or more unless death or divorce intervenes. If they are correct, then qualities such as compatibility and companionship are critically important in mate selection. It is essential to choose a mate with whom we can communicate; enjoy sexually and socially; and depend on for friendship, support, and understanding. The presence or absence of these attributes can have a tremendous impact on the quality and longevity of the relationship. Researchers have identified communication and sexual adjustment as the two most crucial personal attributes that contribute to companionship in an intimate relationship. On a personal level, one of the authors of this textbook has been married 46 years, the other 34 years. Both authors agree that communication, trust, and respect for one another are key to the quality and longevity of an intimate relationship. These attributes are complex and depend on a number of factors: the partners' intellectual compatibility, their sensitivity and empathy toward each other, each partner's ideas about the other's sexual behavior, similarity in social class and other important social characteristics, and the importance to both partners of sexual relations in marriage.

Meeting Partners: Where and How

"Looking for Mr. Right." "Suffering from a Man Shortage? Try Honey Hunting in the Boondocks." "Single Men from Coast to Coast Seek Sensible, Sensitive, Athletic and Sophisticated Mates." "A Few Good Men: Where?" "Where Are the Men?" "Where Are the Men for the Women at the Top?" "How to Meet Someone on the College Campus."

These quotes represent but a handful of the many titles that have appeared in recent popular and scientific literature. What do these titles suggest about contemporary mate selection? First, they suggest that single people in the dating market today face a great challenge, namely, finding a significant other. Moreover, they indicate that women more often than men express difficulty in finding a mate. Given what we already know about the marriage gradient and the sex ratios in some groups, this is not surprising. There are, however, many facts and figures that we probably do not know about dating or notions about dating we take as givens. Because most of the literature on dating continues to focus on college students, it perpetuates the myth that dating is still primarily a White, middle-class, college-aged phenomenon. The fact is, today people who date come from all walks of life, represent a wide range of ages, and are increasing in number. This fact has not gone unnoticed by an increasingly competitive service industry that has recognized and capitalized on this phenomenon. Dating is big business. One of the most significant additions to contemporary dating and mate

selection is the highly developed dating technology that provides singles with increased opportunities to meet prospective partners by using a variety of new technologies. In this section, we present a brief discussion of some of the traditional as well as new ways that those who want to date look for a partner.

SCHOOL, CHURCH, AND WORK

The high school or college campus is a traditional place where pairing and dating take place. Most high schools and colleges that used to be segregated by sex are now coeducational. Many campus dormitories are now desegregated, and even some fraternities have gone coed. These changes have increased the opportunities for heterosexual interaction and coupling. Students meet each other in the dormitories, in classes, or through friends. In addition, various groups sponsor activities such as dances, beach parties, and retreats to bring people together. Obviously, high school and college campuses are insufficient places in and of themselves for meeting possible mates. Even on campuses, we find those who want to date using a variety of other methods to meet people, such as being introduced by roommates, relatives, or friends; advertising in the college or local newspaper; and using computerized dating services. And as we saw in the vignette opening this chapter, some colleges now have online dating sites where students interested in dating can hook up with each other on a particular campus or across several campuses. Interestingly, on many college campuses today, by the time students graduate, a growing number are either engaged or married. This has prompted some people to refer to the college campus as an incubator for marriage (Essley, 2011).

In the past, the church or synagogue frequently brought people together. Today, however, as church attendance has generally declined, particularly among young adults, religious institutions and services less frequently serve this purpose. Although the world of work at the turn of the century provided women with new and increased opportunities to meet and establish intimate relationships with the opposite sex in the sense that it got them out of the house and away from their parents' supervision, it no longer provides the same level of opportunities for pairing. As in the past, the work women do is often sex-segregated or predominantly female, such as elementary school teachers. Thus, it offers only limited contact with eligible males. In general, workplace dating is less taboo than it was in the past however it is still discouraged by many employers. Nevertheless, a recent poll found that 40 percent of workers have dated a co-worker at some point in their career, 18 percent have done it twice or more, and 31 percent went on to marry the person they dated at work ("The Dos and Don'ts of Office Romance," 2011).

On your campus, what kinds of activities are generally conducted that seem specifically aimed at getting people of the opposite sex together? People of the same sex? If you have a significant other, did you meet her or him in high school or college? Is it difficult or easy to meet and establish relationships with people of your choosing on your campus? Do you know how many people on your campus met on campus and became engaged or married?

SINGLES' BARS AND GAY BARS

Singles' bars reached their peak in popularity during the 1970s and early 1980s. Once symbolic of the singles' scene and a significant means of meeting potential mates, singles' bars today are rejected by many people who see them as nothing but "meat (not meet) markets." In the past and to some degree today, singles' bars have provided a space where people could feel comfortable and meet other single people. Studies of why people go to singles' bars indicate that the major reason is for companionship. Gay bars are similarly rejected by some lesbians and gays as meat markets. The motivations for attending gay bars are basically the same as those for attending heterosexual bars. Because of homophobia and discrimination against lesbians and gays, and because many lesbians and gays feel uncomfortable expressing or being themselves in a predominantly heterosexual environment, gay bars continue to serve a significant mate selection function. In general, dating bars are still popular as sites to meet potential dating partners, particularly those that are linked to speed-dating services that match like-minded people by arranging dates in the most suitable environments.

SELF-ADVERTISING: PERSONAL ADS

Are you Italian? Petite, attrac. DIF 40+, degreed, seeking S/DIM 40+, must be finan/emot secure. No drugs/alcohol/smoking. Must like music, din out and travel.

Attractive Aquarian. Gay, SWF, 33, tired of bar scenes. 59; 50, 142 lbs., very romantic, honest, open-minded. Seeks honest open-minded gay SF, 30 to 40, nondrug user, for a long-lasting relat. Only serious need reply.

Sexy and Cute. SWF, 23, wants the best and won't settle for less! If you're attra., ambitious, prof. S/D White/Hispanic, fin secure please respond. Photo please.

SWM, 70, attract., very active, outgoing & sincere, looking for a SWF who desires companionship & romance.

Although fictitious, these ads are typical of real ads found in many local newspapers around the country. Personal ads as an approach for finding mates is not a new phenomenon. For example, in the 1800s, settlers in the Northwest used a mail-order system in which they advertised for a bride (Steinfirst and Moran, 1989). This type of advertising for a bride continues today in some circles. For instance, some American men use this approach to advertise for Asian brides. Some researchers and others have criticized these men, suggesting that they are looking to Asia for brides out of a stereotypical view of them as subordinate, subservient, and easier to control than American women

Not until the 1980s, however, did the use of personals become widespread and public. Since the 1980s, it seems that using personal ads has become not only acceptable but also a fashionable way to meet people, especially among educated people. Today, people who use the personals are no longer considered either perverted or desperate. In fact, some experts consider the use of personal ads to be a healthy and creative adaptation to societal change.

Content analyses of personal ads indicate that men are twice as likely as women to place an ad seeking a partner. Such analyses also consistently report gender differences in these ads. For example, women define or offer themselves as attractive more often than men, and men seek attractiveness and request photographs far more often than women. Men offer financial security much more than women, while women seek financial security and more permanent relationships than men. In addition, personality or character (for instance, intelligent, kind, honest, warm, sense of humor) is most frequently cited by both sexes although it seems to be more important to women than men. For women, the second and third most frequently mentioned characteristics were nonsmoking and a professional job based on a college degree. For men, the second and third most frequently mentioned characteristics sought in a potential partner were good looks and nonsmoking. Believing that they know what women want, men describe themselves in terms of their success, professional status, or as "caring" or "sensitive" or "loving." Women, on the other hand, emphasize their femininity (Fischer and Heesacker, 1995; Raybeck et al., 2000).

Do any of these findings surprise you? Can you determine the principles of endogamy and exogamy in the sample ads presented at the beginning of this section? Check your local or school newspaper. What do personals tell us about mate selection in the United States? In your city? On your campus? About the qualities that people look for in a mate? If you were to write such an ad, what would you say?

DATING CLUBS AND DATING SERVICES

Dating clubs and services advertise and hope to attract those individuals who have difficulty meeting people through conventional routes or who are simply fed up with the commercialized nature of the singles' scene. A wide variety of dating clubs exist across the country that, for a fee, sort out compatible couples and bring them together. Rather than go the route of advertising in a newspaper or magazine, many people join or use the services of specialized dating clubs. A primary appeal of these clubs is they provide immediate visual stimuli (which is important to those concerned with physical attributes and appearance). They also save people from having to sort through pages of personals to find a person who fits what they are looking for in a mate and then, sometimes through trial and error, having to arrange to meet. Many of these clubs are open to anyone interested in joining, but some are specialized and tailored to the interests of a particular group. Specialized dating clubs can be especially appealing because they cater to a specific clientele. A number of such clubs around the country specialize in attracting members of a specific group, for example, professionals, vegetarians, bisexuals, Catholics, Jews, African Americans, single parents, lesbians, gays, and people who like to travel. There is even a dating club for the wealthy that charges its members a fee as high as $100,000 to match them with a marriage partner.

Although dating and/or singles' clubs are common in the United States, they do not exist in some cultures, and in others they are a relatively new and unique phenomenon. For instance, until 1998 there was no such thing as a singles' club in the East African nation of Kenya. In that year, a Kenyan advice columnist opened the country's first singles' club. As definitions of women's and men's roles in marriages and families continue to undergo changes globally, traditional ways of mate selection in other non-Western countries may follow Kenya's lead and give way to Western trends, such as singles' or dating clubs, and even the widespread use of online dating.

COMPUTER DATING AND THE INTERNET

Before the Internet, dating and mate selection was both simple and complicated. To meet a potential date, one actually had to see her or him. To get a date, you had to have chemistry. Today, millions of people can and do manage their social lives, including dating and mate selection, sitting at their computers. Millions of singles have joined computerized matching services that sell their members information on other members. This information is fed into a computer, which matches it with other clients who have similar profiles. Such services do not guarantee a match; even if there is a match, some of the same risks one encounters in meeting potential mates in bars or other places are present such as noncompatibility or sexual aggression and violence.

▶ Watch the **Video** *Online Dating* on **myfamilylab.com**

Other people, who want more control over the mate selection process, use their personal computer to get in touch with prospective partners through dating networks called "dial-your-mate." People using these networks dial into a central computer and provide information similar to that contained in the questionnaires of the computerized matching services. Dial-your-mate services are geared toward heterosexual couples in that the information provided is compared with that of all opposite-sex participants and then ranked in terms of percentage of agreement.

DATING IN CYBERSPACE

Regardless of whether or not one is engaged in the dating process, there is little doubt that the dating industry has changed dramatically as a result of new and increasing computer technology. Some observers say that a quiet revolution has overtaken the world of romance as the increasingly popular electronic bulletin boards have transformed into what some call "online pickup joints." According to some sources, there are 1,400 online dating sites in North America alone with new ones emerging almost daily. Among the largest in 2011, Match.com boasted more than 26 million members followed by Chemistry.com (13.5 million) and Zoosk, (10.5 million). Worldwide, this industry is now worth more than $4 billion. Online dating has now reached an all-time high. In 2010, Internet users of online dating sites surpassed 1 billion. There are all kinds of dating Web sites catering to a wide range of singles. For instance, broad categories include international sites, dating sites for marriage, adult sites, niche sites, and mail bride sites. The most numerous sites are niche sites, which run the gamut from sites specifically for Seventh Day Adventists; big, beautiful women; Christians; interracial couples; singles who are deaf; military singles and their admirers; and singles over 40 to single parents; single and widowed seniors; lesbians; gays; bi-sexuals; and one for every possible racial/ethnic and religious group. Interestingly, Prescription4Love.com has become a popular site where single people who happen to have diseases from hepatitis to herpes to irritable bowel syndrome can find love and companionship without having to worry about being revealed (Scott, 2009; "Latest Dating Trends...," 2011; DatingSitesReviews.com, 2011; "Top Ten Dating Sites for 2011," 2011).

One thing for sure, there is broad public contact with the online dating world. There are 96 million people in the United

Texting has become a centerpiece in the social lives of most Americans today. While texting has revolutionized the dating scene and the ways and the speed in which we communicate, it has also introduced some problems for lovers or would-be lovers. On the one hand, the Internet increases the possibility of interacting with and dating multiple partners. On the other hand, it has had the effect of decreasing face-to-face verbal communication between couples, even when they are in each other's company.

States who are not married. This means that 43 percent of all Americans over age 18 are single. While not all of these people are actively looking for a date or a mate, many are. Over 40 million U.S. singles use online dating and social networking sites like Facebook and Myspace to meet new people and find a date. Three-fourths of these singles have done at least one dating-related activity online ranging from using dating Web sites to searching for information about prospective dates to flirting via e-mail and instant messaging to browsing for information about the local singles scene (see Table 5.4). The digital age of dating has given rise to a newfound ability for singles to gather information on a potential mate beyond that provided by an individual her or himself. For instance, many online dating users Google each other or search online for information relating to a potential date before they meet or even agree to meet. One in five of those Internet users who are single and looking for a romantic partner have searched for information about someone they were currently dating or were about to meet for a first date. Ironically, it is the same technology that some people feel isolates us and is too invasive that is also responsible for bringing people together.

Singles who are more likely to use dating sites are those who are more sociable and have high self-esteem. Reportedly, they also put more value on romantic relationships. Of those singles using online dating sites, 43 percent of them have gone on offline dates with people they met on dating sites, and 17 percent of these individuals have gone on to have long-term relationships or marriages with partners they met online. Furthermore, some 31 percent of American adults say they know someone who has used a dating Web site and 15 percent of American adults—about 30 million people—say they know someone who has been in a long-term relationship or married someone she or he met online. According to some reports, more than 120,000 marriages occur each year as a result of online dating. It is predicted that Americans will spend $1.7 billion on dating services in 2013 (Madden & Lenhart, 2006; "Online Dating Statistics," 2010; U.S. Census Bureau, 2011e).

At both ends of the dating age spectrum, an increasing number of teenagers and people age 50 and older are growing segments of online daters. In fact, one of the biggest rise in users of the top dating sites are Baby Boomers. Around 30 percent of the nation's 77 million people dubbed Baby Boomers are single and, according to a recent poll, three-fourths of them consider themselves middle-aged or younger. Many Baby Boomers have money and are spending it online searching for a date (Associated Press, 2011).

Moreover, not only are singles flocking to the Internet to find "relationship partners," but they are also using a variety of other—often unique—methods of hooking up. In the fast-paced digital age, electronic matchmaking services are shifting their focus to an even larger market, cell-phone user singles. More people today are accessing the Internet worldwide through the use of their cell phone and several online dating services offer "mobile" versions of their Web service through most of the major cellular services providers in the United States. Text messaging via cellular phones has become an increasingly popular method of flirting or asking someone out on a date. This method of flirting and hooking up is particularly popular among the younger generation. Both women and men indicate that they feel more comfortable sending text messages than speaking on their mobile phones ("Online Dating Industry...," 2010; Eng, 2005; Telecomworldwire, 2001).

Online dating has advantages as well as pitfalls. Some of the advantages of online dating are its accessibility, autonomy, and increasingly low cost. Subscribers can sit in the privacy of their homes and access tens of thousands of eligible mates, sifting through them as often as they like by specific "niche" characteristics such as age, race/ethnicity, religion, or body type. They can also remain anonymous as long as they like, thus allowing people to portray the persona they choose until they are ready to get involved. This can lead to more open expression because people do not have to worry about seeing or running into each other if the online relationship does not work. It also saves the time and expense that might be spent on a bad blind or fix-up date, and it cuts out the need for barhopping. A pitfall is that the world of Internet romance is fraught with peril, from those who are dishonest to harassment, sexual predators and even murderers who hide their identity and motives behind seemingly innocuous virtual identities. Examples of this danger to online users of dating and other such sites abound. One recent example involved Myspace, which was forced to cancel 90,000 accounts on its site that authorities said were linked to registered sex offenders. That same year, a Boston medical student, dubbed the Craigslist killer by the media, was arrested and charged with the murder of a masseuse who had

TABLE 5.4 Dating-Related Activities Online

Approximately 10 million Internet users say they are single and looking for a romantic partner. Some of the ways they have used the Internet include	Single and looking Internet users (%)
Flirt with someone	40
Go to an online dating Web site	37
Ask someone out on a date	28
Find a place offline, like a nightclub or singles event, where you might meet someone to date	27
Been introduced to a potential date by a third party using e-mail or instant messaging	21
Participate in an online group where you hope to meet people to date	19
Search for information about someone you dated in the past	18
Maintain a long-distance relationship	18
Search for information about someone you were currently dating or were about to meet for a first date	17
Break up with someone you were dating	9

Source: Mary Madden and Amanda Lenhart, Pew Internet and American Life Project Survey, September–December 2005: Online Dating (March 5) (Washington, DC: www.pewinternet.org). Reprinted with permission of the Pew Research Center.

Although the exception and not the norm, Boston University medical student Philip H. Markoff, pictured here at his arraignment at Boston Municipal Court in 2009, represents the dark side or the danger to online users of dating and other such sites. Dubbed the "Craigslist Killer," Markoff was charged with the robbery and murder of masseuse Julissa Brisman who he allegedly lured to his hotel room through an ad she posted on Craigslist—a centralized network of online communities with sections devoted to jobs, housing, and personals—offering erotic services. A year later, while in custody and awaiting trial, Markoff committed suicide. In 2011, the events surrounding the killings were dramatized in the made-for TV movie *The Craigslist Killer*.

advertised on the popular Web site's erotic services section (Peters, 2009; Madden & Lenhart, 2006; Nichcolas and Milewski, 1999). However, when it does work, as we have indicated, it can lead a couple to the altar.

SPEED DATING

A unique matchmaking strategy in the speed dating industry and which has become increasingly popular is "8minuteDating," a matchmaking event popularized on such TV shows as *Frasier* and *Sex and the City*. The purpose of this dating system is to encourage people to meet a large number of new people. According to some sources, speed dating was invented by a Los Angeles Rabbi as a way to help Jewish singles meet and marry (NPR, 2005). The concept is rather simple. At the beginning of an 8minuteDating event, an equal number of women and men are given eight computer-generated dating combinations listed on a card. The participants then move from one table to another, revealing only a first name as they spend 8 minutes in pairs, getting to know each other, which amounts to a date. An 8-minute conversation may be all it takes to find true love, or at least a second date. Afterward, when the mini-dates are over, the singles decide who they would like to see again and submit the information to the organizer, who feeds it into a computer. If there is a match, the computer acts as a go-between, providing full names and contact information to the pair. Because the participants stick to first names only and meet for brief conversations, the 8minuteDating events take much of the anxiety and pressure out of the dating process and avoids the awkwardness of a bad blind date (The 8 Minute Matchmaker, 2002).

Organizers of 8minuteDating events pride themselves on providing a comfortable social atmosphere in venues such as trendy bars and restaurants for people to see if there is chemistry with anyone they meet. Many speed dating organizers now offer niche events such as specific events for gays, lesbians, later life adults, older men with younger women and vice versa, graduates only, single ethnic groups, and specific religious affiliations such as Christian speed dating. Not surprising, with the success of speed dating in bars and restaurants, several online dating sites now offer online speed dating where users meet online for video, audio, or text chats without leaving their homes. Facebook, for example, has an application with almost 5,000 participants who can chat for five minutes and then move on to the next date. There are even services for iPhone and Skype users. A recent online trend allows people to set up quick blind dates in their areas. These dates occur in public places where the person has 20 minutes to decide whether or not she or he wants to stick with that person for the rest of the evening (Miller, 2011).

It seems that such events are not only popular, but also many of the participants seem to have found that chemistry with someone they met on an 8-minute date. For example, 99 percent of singles say they enjoy the speed dating events, 90 percent of those who participate in such events say they met someone they would like to see again, and approximately one-half of all participants come away with a potential match. While some people may be uncomfortable with the idea of speed dating, advocates of this form of dating believe that its success lies in simple chemistry. And this chemistry is often detected very early in the process. For example, several studies have found that people make a decision within three to thirty seconds after meeting (The 8 Minute Matchmaker, 2002; DiscoveryHealth.com, 2011).

The Future of Dating

What is the future of dating? We cannot be sure. Some people lament the decrease in traditional dating forms and the rise of the hook-up culture suggesting that dating is dead. Others take the position that dating is not dead rather there has simply been a paradigm shift in how people meet, date and/or marry (see the Debating Social Issues box on page 129). Whatever one's position on the subject, it is a safe bet that dating will be around for some time to come, albeit in an increasingly modified form. It is also a safe bet that single people looking for that "right" partner will continue to use traditional as well as creative new ways to facilitate their search. Whatever methods single people use to meet partners, as computer technology continues to advance, people will continue to find creative ways to use the technology to meet potential partners. And whatever the future of dating, no doubt we as parents and grandparents some day will reminisce about the "good old days" when we were dating.

Violence in Dating and Intimate Relationships

Although dating is often fun and can be a very positive experience in our lives, it can, and often does, involve negative experiences such as violence and abuse, and breaking up. Because of the seriousness and high incidence of violence, abuse, and rape in marriages and families, we devote a full chapter (Chapter 11) to its discussion. Here we are concerned specifically with dating violence and assault.

PHYSICAL ABUSE

Dating violence, the perpetration or threat of an act of violence by at least one member of an unmarried couple on the other member within the context of dating or courtship, encompasses any form of sexual assault, physical violence, and verbal or emotional abuse. Dating violence is a subject that few people like to discuss. Most people are reluctant to admit that it occurs. However, violent behavior that takes place in the context of dating or courtship is quite prevalent in U.S. society. Estimates vary because studies and surveys use different methods and definitions of dating violence. A review of dating violence research statistics, for example, shows that the rate of nonsexual courtship violence ranges from 9 to 65 percent, depending on how dating violence is defined—that is, whether threats and emotional or verbal aggression are included in the definition. This also includes dating between same-sex couples, although most statistics have been gathered from heterosexual couples. Same-sex couples often have the additional threat and fear of being outed by their partner.

However dating violence is defined, intimate partner violence is widespread in the United States and around the world. Intimate partner violence affects all cultures, races, classes, occupations, income levels, and ages in society. However, victims of dating violence are most often women and teenage girls. For instance, nearly 1 in 4 women in the United States reports experiencing violence by a current or former boyfriend or spouse in her life. And approximately one in three adolescent girls in the United States is a victim of physical, emotional, or verbal abuse from a dating partner—a figure that far exceeds victimization rates for other types of violence affecting youth. Some experts have suggested that violence among intimates is an epidemic whose casualties outnumber the Vietnam War in the number of people killed (Family Violence Prevention Fund, 2009; Kong, 1998).

College campuses are prevalent sites where dating violence occurs. College students experience dating violence at staggering rates and face unique obstacles in accessing services to escape an abusive relationship. According to a variety of sources, the prevalence rate for nonsexual dating violence is between 32 and 53 percent among college students. Three in five college students at campuses across the United States indicate that they personally know friends, relatives, or someone else close to them who is or has been affected by intimate partner violence.

As in all cases of intimate partner violence, the gendered nature of such violence is apparent on college campuses, where one of every five females will experience some form of dating violence during their campus lifetime ("College Dating Violence," 2009; U.S. Department of Justice, 2009b).

In addition, teen dating violence is particularly troubling. Consider the following statistics:

- One-fourth of teens in a relationship report having been threatened with violence or experienced verbal abuse, one-half have been personally victimized by controlling behaviors, and 1 in 3 have experienced the most serious forms of intimate partner violence, including physical abuse, sexual abuse and/or threats of physical harm to self or partner (Liz Claiborne, Inc., 2009; Family Violence Prevention Fund, 2009).
- One in three teens reports knowing a friend or peer who has been hit, punched, kicked, slapped, or physically hurt by a partner, and 45 percent of girls know a friend or peer who has been pressured into having either intercourse or oral sex (Family Violence Prevention Fund, 2009).
- One in four teen relationships usually begin at 14 years of age or younger. Seventy-two percent of eighth-and ninth-graders reportedly "date; by the time they are in high school" (Liz Claiborne, Inc., 2008; Centers for Disease Control and Prevention, 2008a).
- Among tweens (ages 11 to 14), one in five have friends who are victims of dating violence and among the youngest tweens, ages 11 and 12, two in five report the same.
- Forty-two percent of boys and 43 percent of girls say the abuse occurs in a school building or on school grounds; more than 30 percent of teenagers do not tell anyone about being victimized by their partner; less than 3 percent report the abuse to police or another authority figure, and only 3 percent tell a family member about the violence (National Coalition Against Domestic Violence, 2007a).
- Rates of drug, alcohol, and tobacco use are more than twice as high in girls who report physical or sexual dating abuse than in girls who report no abuse (Family Violence Prevention Fund, 2009; Centers for Disease Control and Prevention, 2008a).

As if these facts are not serious enough, in today's digital age, reports of dating abuse via technology is a particularly serious problem, especially for teens. For example, two out of five teens know friends who have been verbally abused, called names, put down, or insulted via cell phone, IM, and/or social networking sites such as Myspace and Facebook.

In addition, 68 percent say girlfriends/boyfriends sharing private or embarrassing pictures or videos on cell phones and computers is a serious problem. The frequency with which teens use electronic methods to communicate and what or how they communicate messages is astounding. For instance, about one in four teens in a relationship communicate with their partner via cellphone or texting hourly between midnight and 5:00 a.m., and one in three say they are text messaged 10, 20, 30 times an hour by a partner inquiring where they are, what they are doing, or who they are with. This frequency of cell phone calls and texting means constant control day or night by one or the other partner (Liz Claiborne, Inc., 2008; T.E.A.R., 2007).

Some studies of teenage violence suggest that both females and males inflict and receive dating violence in equal proportion, but the motivation for violence by women is most often for defensive purposes. Other studies have found that girls and women are victims of dating violence twice as often as boys and men, and females suffer significantly more injuries than males. Additionally, more than 70 percent of pregnant or parenting teens are beaten by their boyfriends; about half of these teens say that the battering began or intensified after their male partner learned of the pregnancy (Family Violence Prevention Fund, 2009). Family therapists say that the pattern in these relationships is typically one in which male jealousy escalates into controlling and restricting behavior, accusations, and suspicions that ultimately escalate into violence. Furthermore, it is rarely the case that violence in courtship is a one-time occurrence. Only about one-half of all couples in violent relationships end the relationship after the first act of violence. Nearly 80 percent of girls who have been victims of physical abuse in their dating relationships continue to date the abuser.

Control and jealousy are often confused with love by both the victims and the offenders, who believe that the violence in their relationship is an indication of their love for one another and that it helps to improve the relationship. However, violence is not love (see the Applying the Sociological Imagination box). Victims who hold this "romantic" view of violence frequently blame themselves for their mistreatment, rationalizing that because their partners love them, they must have done something to "deserve" the abuse. Traditionally, females are taught to take responsibility for whatever goes wrong in a relationship. Thus, the abuser often convinces her that the abuse is her fault; that the violence used to control her is brought on by her less than perfect behavior; that she needs to be disciplined for her lack of consideration; that the discipline is for her own good; and that the abuser has a right to chastise her.

Statistics on violence in same-sex relationships do not specifically target dating relationships; however, the data show that intimate partner violence among same-sex couples occurs at about the same rate as with heterosexual couples. Although most people do not think of dating abuse outside of a heterosexual model, the fact is that dating abuse is also a problem in LGBT communities, especially among the young. Reportedly, up to one in three same-sex relationships are abusive. However, despite the high rates of partner abuse in young LGBT relationships, the abuse is rarely reported ("LGBQ Teens and Dating Abuse," 2011).

> In your opinion, what factors of life in the United States might account for the high incidence of dating violence? Why do you think that females are most often the victims of intimate violence? Are there battered males? What legal remedies could be enacted to deal effectively with dating violence? If you were asked to testify before the U.S. Congress on the subject of intimate violence, what would you say? How would you prepare for your testimony? What recommendations would you make?

APPLYING THE SOCIOLOGICAL IMAGINATION

LOVE IS NOT ABUSE

Since 1991, Liz Claiborne Inc. has been working to end domestic violence, including date violence and date and acquaintance rape. Through its Love Is Not Abuse Program, the company provides information and tools that women, men, children, teachers, teens, and corporate executives can use to learn more about the issue and find out how they can help end this epidemic (see the Love Is Not Abuse Web site).

Using your sociological imagination and what you have learned reading this chapter, go to the Liz Claiborne "Love Is Not Abuse" Web page (http://loveisnotabuse.com/web/guest) and test your knowledge about teen dating violence by taking the short quiz there. Afterward, examine some of the several tools the company provides to deal with dating and intimate violence. The company has produced a college edition of Dating Violence and Abuse Curriculum. Can this or any of the other tools offered be used on your campus? Would you be willing to bring them to your campus? Finally, the Love Is Not Abuse Coalition is a grassroots partnership of parents, teachers, and anyone who advocates for teen dating abuse education in every middle and high school in the nation. In the tradition of the activism of sociology and sociologists, would you be willing to take action and get involved at some level with this coalition? As a member, you would be able to download various resources to contact your city's schools and state legislators. You would also receive monthly e-mail updates of your state's progress and member achievements. In this digital age, you could stay connected to the coalition on Facebook and Twitter. If you choose to do this, consider reporting it back to your class or design a short seminar on the topic.

Celebrities and other public figures are increasingly calling attention to sexual assault, rape, physical battering, and verbal abuse in their intimate relationships. For example, Fantasia Barrino, pictured, became the winner of the popular television reality show *American Idol* in 2004 after overcoming sexual abuse, illiteracy, and other setbacks in her life. According to Barrino, she was also physically, verbally, and emotionally abused by her ex-boyfriend Brandel Shouse, who is the father of her daughter Zion Quari Barrino.

DATE AND ACQUAINTANCE RAPE

Sexual assault is one of the most serious and fastest-growing violent crimes in the United States. **Rape**—unwanted, forced, or coerced sexual intercourse—is the most extreme form of sexual abuse, although sexual assault includes (but is not limited to) treating a partner like a sex object, forcing someone to go further sexually than she/he wants to, and unwanted or uncomfortable touching. The Bureau of Justice Statistics reports that 94 percent of the reported incidents of sexual assaults in intimate relationships are committed by males, and 71 percent of these assaults are planned. According to the National Criminal Victim Center, one woman is raped every minute (Rand, 2009; National Crime Victimization Survey, 2009).

The problem received national attention in the early 1990s when William Kennedy Smith, nephew of the late president John Kennedy, and Mike Tyson, former heavyweight boxing champion, were accused of sexual assault. In widely publicized trials, Smith was acquitted, and Tyson was convicted and sentenced to prison. The public debate surrounding these cases made many people aware that the majority of rapes are not committed by strangers. Rather, current estimates are that over 85 percent of all sexual assaults involve acquaintances or friends. Rape of a person who simply knows or is familiar with the rapist is called **acquaintance rape.** And rape of a victim who is actually "going out with" the rapist is known as **date rape.** Acquaintance and date rape can be with someone a person has just met, or dated a few times, or even with someone to whom the victim is engaged. The force can come from threats or tone of voice as well as from physical force or weapons. These terms are so closely interrelated that they often are used interchangeably. Although most rapes are date or acquaintance rapes, most reported rapes are stranger rapes. The reason that most acquaintance and date rapes go unreported is because many people still believe that a sexual encounter between two people who know each other cannot be rape.

Like physical assault, date rape and acquaintance rape cut across race, social class, and sexual orientation and can be found in all geographic regions, and women and girls are most often the victim. And like physical assault, high school and college-age women are most vulnerable to date and acquaintance rape. Date and acquaintance rape are probably most commonplace on college campuses; rape is the most common violent crime reported on American college campuses today. According to some reports, every 21 hours there is a rape on a college campus in the United States. In 2010, nearly 5 percent of college women were sexually assaulted in their campus community. Furthermore, over an entire academic career, approximately 1 in 4 college women will be the victim of some form of sexual assault and the perpetrator is seldom a stranger. Rather, in approximately 90 percent of rapes of college women involved a perpetrator she knew. Most often they are classmates, followed in frequency by friends, boyfriends, ex-boyfriends, or acquaintances. Only a very small percentage of these crimes are perpetrated by someone other. On a dark side of the growing world of girls' sports, 159 coaches have been reprimanded or fired for sexual misconduct in the past decade. And 98 continued to coach or teach as schools, the state, and even some parents have turned their heads. In addition, historically, fraternities and sports team members have been disproportionately involved in campus rapes. This said, it should be noted that to date, there is no clearly identifiable acquaintance rapist (Willmsen and O'Hagan, 2003; UIC Campus Advocacy Network, 2008; Carbon, 2010).

Date and acquaintance rape happen in dorm rooms with invited guests, at parties with friends in the next room, in seemingly safe and well-lit places. Alarmingly, almost 60 percent of on-campus sexual assaults take place in what one would think is the safest of all locations: in the victim's living quarters. Although most cases of date and acquaintance rape go unreported (only 5 percent are reported to police), it is estimated that one in four college women have either been raped or suffered an attempted rape at least once since age 14. And almost one in four female students are victims of multiple rapes. However, less than one in 10 college women report to law enforcement that they have been raped or that someone attempted rape to them. Although by and large, these crimes go unreported to law enforcement, in two-thirds of completed or attempted rape cases, the victim told another person, usually a friend but not the campus police. (Carbon, 2010).

The incidence and prevalence of rape and sexual assault vary across types of college campuses. For instance, private colleges and major universities have higher than the national average rates of rape, while religiously affiliated institutions have lower than average rates. Also, students at two-year institutions are significantly more likely than those at four-year institutions to report having been forced during their lifetime to have sexual intercourse. Although the majority of the victims of campus rape and sexual assault are women, college men also report incidents of rape. However, college men who are raped are usually raped by other men and because so few men report their rape, statistical data are limited relative to the extent of the problem. Even current national data collection systems such as the FBI's Uniform Crime Report fail to provide data on male rape victims. The limited research that does provide such information is provided by recent surveys that suggest up to 10 percent of acquaintance rape victims on college campuses are men (Sampson, 2003).

The statistics for teens and tweens are equally alarming. For example, recent data indicate that nearly 4,000 reported incidents of sexual battery and more than 800 reported rapes and attempted rapes occur in American public high schools. By the time girls graduate from high school, more that one in 10 will have been physically forced to have sexual intercourse in or out of school. About 50 percent of rape victims are under age 18 when they are victimized. Youths 12–17 are two to three times more likely to be sexually assaulted than adults. Dating relationships and dating violence and abuse start by age 11. According to recent statistics, one in three sexually active adolescent girls in ninth to twelfth grade report ever experiencing sexual or physical violence from a dating partner. And as with college-age women, teens and tweens who are raped or sexually assaulted are most often victimized by someone they know; four out of five teenage victims know their rapist before the assault takes place. Early dating with sexual activity appears to fuel extremely high levels of dating violence and abuse (Liz Claiborne, Inc., 2008; Family Violence Prevention Fund, 2009; "Date Rape and Dating Violence," 2011; U.S. Department of Education Office for Civil Rights, 2011).

Most females as well as males hold the attitude that the male use of force and aggression to have sexual intercourse is acceptable among acquaintances or dates, at least under certain circumstances, such as if the female arouses the male. Although it is sometimes hard for some victims to recognize date rape as a crime because the rapist is someone they know and often trust, it is important to remember that date rape is still a crime of power and control, and not of a sexual nature.

What Are Contributing Factors to Date Violence and Date Rape? Teen battering and date and acquaintance rape should not come as a surprise to us. Sociologically speaking, it is a reflection of the violence within relationships that is accepted socially and reflected in virtually every aspect of our mass culture—from movies to print and electronic advertisements to fiction as well as nonfiction to video games to MTV, BET Music Videos, and other popular music to daily talk shows to soap operas and most other forms of everyday television. Date rape can be considered an outgrowth of a cultural socialization into masculinity. Male socialization sets the stage for rape in that being aggressive is considered normal masculine behavior, being sexually aggressive is masculine, and rape is sexually aggressive behavior; therefore, rape is masculine behavior. Because American culture still supports female and male relationships that are stereotypically masculine and feminine—passive-aggressive and submissive-dominant—notions

of masculinity are often associated with violence and force. Other factors that contribute (not cause) to date violence and date rape include but are not limited to:

- Alcohol and drugs—for instance, one in 10 women who have been sexually assaulted were incapacitated after voluntarily consuming drugs, alcohol or both and a smaller percentage were sexually assaulted when they were incapacitated after having been given a drug such as Rohypnol without their knowledge. Rohypnol, sometimes called the "date rape drug," is a pill that is typically slipped unnoticed into a female's drink. The combined effect of the drug and the alcohol produces intoxication in which, upon awakening from the drug-induced sleep, the victim is unable to remember what has happened. Problem drinking is also a factor in dating violence. Severe drinking problems increase the risk for violence and victimization in dating and other intimate relationships (Krebs, Lindquist, Warner, Fisher, and Martin, 2007).
- Family violence—while it is not a cause, growing up in a family where sibling, parent, or others are perpetrators and victims of violence has been found to be related to being either a perpetrator or a victim of dating violence.
- Poverty, early pregnancy, and unemployment are also factors in date and intimate partner violence as are romanticized notions of love and intimacy and peer pressure. New research even links the troubled economy to high levels of teen dating violence and abuse (see, for example, Liz Claiborne, Inc., 2009).

What Are the Consequences? There is a link between dating violence and poor health. Both girls and boys experience physical and emotional harm as a consequence of dating violence. However, dating violence against adolescent girls is associated with increased risk of substance abuse, unhealthy weight-control behaviors (taking diet pills or laxatives and vomiting to lose weight), sexual risk behaviors, pregnancy, and suicidal thinking. In addition, rates of drug, alcohol, and tobacco use are more than twice as high in girls who report physical or sexual dating violence than in girls who report no violence. Moreover, victims of dating violence are not only at greater risk for injury, they are also more likely to suffer from depression and anxiety, engage in binge drinking, physical fights, attempt or consider suicide, and engage in sexual activities that can lead to sexually transmitted diseases and HIV infections. Studies of lesbian, gay, and bisexual adolescents indicate that youths involved in same-sex dating are just as likely to experience dating violence as youths involved in opposite sex dating and the consequences are the same. Finally, unhealthy violent relationships often carry over into future relationships (Doyle, 2009; Centers for Disease Control and Prevention, 2010a).

What Are Some Possible Solutions? Many things can be done to reduce or eradicate courtship violence. Given that rape is learned behavior within the context of a masculine self-concept, it can be unlearned. We can teach future generations of males new roles that do not emphasize and exaggerate domination, aggression, and sexual prowess. On college and high school campuses, administrators must deal with sexual aggression swiftly and punitively without blaming the victim. In addition, campus security police must work cooperatively with local police officials to expedite the prosecution of offenders. Furthermore, colleges and other school officials should provide counseling and other referral services for both the perpetrators and the victims of both physical and sexual assault. They should also provide sexual assault and prevention training to every student. In the final analysis, it will take each and every member of the national community, both on and off campuses, to stop intimate partner violence. Finally, boys and men must be part of the solution.

Breaking Up

It sounds very pessimistic, but some researchers claim that nearly all romances fail. Some end before they get off the ground and others sputter out early. Furthermore, breaking up can be viewed as a logical consequence of the courtship filtering process, whereby those who are incompatible eventually break up before they make the "ultimate" commitment: marriage. According to one survey, American adults have experienced a break-up of a romantic relationship at least twice during their lifetime, and almost one in four say that they have been "dumped" six or more times by a romantic partner. Most serious dating relationships end after 2 or so years, and even if a relationship succeeds and the couple marries, the relationship still faces a 50–50 chance of breaking up (divorce) (Buss 2008; Manis, 2001). Breaking up a relationship can take many forms: The partners drift apart or stop calling or coming by; they have a fight over a minor incident or something said in anger; or, in rare cases, both agree to terminate the relationship. Breaking up can be very painful, especially if the break-up is not mutually agreed on. However, some social scientists claim that breaking up before marriage is less stressful than breaking up after marriage, when the couple has to deal with legally ending the relationship and with possible custody issues.

On the other hand, some so-called experts and other social commentators claim that breaking up can be healthy. Ending a relationship can be difficult they say, but staying in a relationship for all the wrong reasons can be unhealthy. Breaking up or ending the relationship can be healthy in the sense that it can relieve one or both partners of the stress, guilt, or pain that is sometimes part of a failing or failed relationship. A study of 92 students conducted at the University of Minnesota found that the subjects reported several types of personal growth after a break-up, including more self-confidence and knowing better what they want in a future partner. Once the relationship ends, the parties involved no longer necessarily need to justify why she or he should be with the person, and that allows her or him to see some things with more clarity (reported in Beckman, 2010).

In today's digital age, the Internet is full of pop culture ideas about and rules for breaking up—how to, when, and for what reasons; the right way versus the wrong way. Many of these writers claim that there may be 50 ways to leave your lover, but not all of them are good. And of course they have the answer—they know the best ways for a healthy break-up. The explosion of Internet dating has muddied the waters in terms of advice about when and how to break up an online relationship versus a face-to-face relationship. Technology and social media like texting, e-mail, Facebook, and Twitter have upped the ante in terms of how to end

a relationship. The tabloids widely reported that pop star Britney Spears broke up with her now-ex-husband Kevin Federline via a text message. But almost everyone agrees that it is a bad idea to break up via e-mail, text messages, Twitter, or other high-tech message delivery systems.

As in other aspects of dating and courtship behavior, some researchers have found gender differences related to break-ups before marriage. For example, most break-ups are initiated by women; however, the chances of the break-up being amiable is far greater if the male initiates the break-up. As we pointed out in Chapter 4, men are more likely than women to report feeling depressed, lonely, unhappy, and less free after a break-up. However, men get over break-ups more quickly than women. For example, men resume dating after a break-up much sooner than women; and women, more often than men, call friends and family members for consolation and comfort after a break-up (Fetto, 2003). No matter the gender, however, it is easier on a person when she or he is the leaver than the person being left. Whether or not this is true, breaking up can have substantial consequences, no matter what the relationship or who makes the break. Unlike in marriage, there is no institutionalized means, such as divorce, to handle the break-up of a dating relationship; however, as our expert (family therapist Joan Zientek) tells us, like married couples, dating couples interested in strengthening and preserving their relationships and sorting through and dealing with anger and hurt, misunderstandings, and miscommunications can avail themselves of the counseling and advice of family therapists.

Supporting Marriages and Families

Dating, hooking up, going out, getting together—or whatever term one uses to describe the process of meeting and socializing with someone for possible long-term intimacy—is a common feature of American society. It may lead to marriage. It may not. But, whether or not one is on the way to the altar, dating is supposed to have a romantic, light, and fun quality. It is a form of recreation where couples go out to relax, enjoy themselves, and have fun. Dating and mate selection, however, is far more complex than merely two or more people engaging in recreational behavior or just "having fun." People who date and mate are members of families, and thus the impact of what they do and how they do it during the process of mate selection goes beyond the specific individuals involved.

Our ideas and feelings about love, intimacy, dating, and mate selection are influenced by cultural stereotypes about gender, race, and sexual identity. Unfortunately, many of the norms and values associated with dating and intimacy can, and often do, lead to unhealthy, addictive, and even lethal behavior. We spent some time at the end of this chapter discussing intimate partner violence, particularly that which occurs within dating relationships. Such violence has significant psychological, economic, health, and social consequences. The psychological harm to victims of violence includes shock, humiliation, anxiety, depression, substance abuse, posttraumatic stress syndrome, suicidal thoughts and behavior, loss of self-esteem, social isolation, anger, distrust of others, guilt, and sexual dysfunction. Economic consequences include the costs of providing health care and other services, increased absenteeism, decreased productivity, and lower earnings. Thus, it seems clear that intimate partner violence generally and that against women and girls specifically places a significant burden on individuals, families, and society at large. It contributes to reduced quality of life of families and communities and decreased participation by women in democratic processes (Sampson, 2003).

Given that dating and other intimate partner violence exacts an enormous toll on individuals, families, and society, national policymakers, civil society, and communities must be galvanized to address the pervasive violence in society to protect individuals and strengthen American marriages and families. We must strengthen existing policies that pertain to intimate partner violence, ensure that there are ample resources available to respond to such violence, and increase ongoing efforts in this regard. It is important to explore cultural and societal policies and initiatives that will assist people, especially teens, in making and engaging in healthy love and dating relationships. For example, many of the issues that surround and contribute to teen dating violence include the fact that teens are often inexperienced with dating relationships, have romanticized views about love and intimacy, and are often pressured by their peers to have dating relationships. Moreover, teen dating violence is influenced by how teenagers view themselves and others. On the one hand, many young male teens believe that they have the right to "control" their female partners in any way necessary, that masculinity is physical aggressiveness, that their partner is their property, that they can and should demand—be in control—and that they might lose respect if they are attentive and supportive toward their girlfriends. Girls, on the other hand, believe that their boyfriend's jealousy, possessiveness, and even his physical and/or sexual abuse is "romantic," that abuse in intimate relationships is "normal" because their friends are also being abused, that they can change their abusive boyfriend, and that most often there is no one to ask for help (Cool Nurse, 2005). Policies, initiatives, and community programs are needed that will support teaching teens that they are valuable people and that will teach them how to choose healthy relationships.

Although increased resources are needed for effective responses to intimate partner violence, some of the most effective solutions for preventing intimate partner violence and methods for strengthening marriages and families lie in mobilizing communities to transform norms on the acceptability of violence within dating and other intimate relationships—transforming norms within families and at the cultural level that define women and girls as subordinate to men and boys and that narrowly define masculinity and femininity and how women and men should relate to each other.

SUMMARY

Mate selection refers loosely to the wide range of behaviors and social relationships that individuals engage in prior to marriage that lead to short- or long-term pairing. It is an institutionalized feature of social life and can be found in some form in all human societies, although the exact processes vary widely from one society to another. In the United States, the mate selection process, particularly for first marriages, is highly youth-centered and competitive.

Mate selection customs vary widely across cultures. Most researchers have divided mate selection customs along a traditional/nonindustrialized and nontraditional/industrialized society continuum. A review of mate selection cross-culturally reveals that many traditional societies now combine traditional and contemporary methods of selecting mates. Dating, an American invention that first appeared in the 1920s, is the focus of our courtship system today and incorporates a wide range of social relationships prior to marriage. The history of mate selection in this country has ranged from highly visible parental involvement during the colonial and preindustrial periods to the informal, indirect involvement of parents today. Dating became a widespread phenomenon in the 1920s and 1930s; in the 1940s and 1950s, it filtered down to high school students, who started to go steady; in the 1960s, 1970s, and 1980s, it became a more casual process; during the 1990s, dating underwent many changes that reflect contemporary social and gender roles. Today, dating is based far more on mutuality and sharing than on traditional gender roles. Hooking up and hanging out today as methods of getting together or mate selection represent a generational shift in the idea of how to begin an intimate relationship. Given today's extended life expectancy, an increasing number of later-life Americans are entering and reentering the dating scene. Because dating and mate selection has changed considerably since some later-life adults have been in the dating game, many have to learn anew the rules of the dating game.

The functions of dating include socialization, development of self-image, recreation, and status grading and achievement. Like all other social behavior and organization, dating is deeply rooted in the social and historical conditions of life. Race, gender, class, and sexual orientation are basic and central categories in American life and thus must be considered in any analysis of mate selection.

A wide range of theories exists that attempt to explain who selects whom and under what circumstances. These theories include explanations in terms of social exchanges and rewards, stimulus-value-role theories, and filtering theories. The process of mate selection can be viewed sociologically as a sequential or filtering process that stresses homogamy and endogamy. Mate selection in U.S. society is mediated by a range of structural and social factors: the nature of the marriage market, the marriage squeeze and marriage gradient, race, class, age, sex, religion, education, propinquity, family and peers, and cultural ideals about beauty and worth. Due to the impact of these factors, we are very much like the people we meet, fall in love with, and marry—far more so than can simply be attributed to chance. Computer technology has had a dramatic impact on the nature of mate selection around the world. Increasingly, couples are using cyberspace not only for recreation but also for serious mate selection. Many of these matches lead to matrimony.

However, not all intimate relationships lead to marriage or long-term commitment. Couples often break up under the pressure of a variety of sociopolitical factors. Moreover, a large number of dating couples are involved in physically or sexually abusive relationships. Battering and abuse among young couples as early as elementary and junior high school has reached epidemic proportions. The same can be said for date and acquaintance rape. In both cases, the victims are overwhelmingly girls and women. Most

intimate relationships, however, survive the problems of human frailty. Couples wishing to strengthen and preserve their dating and intimate relationships can and do seek family counseling. Given that dating and other intimate partner violence exacts an enormous toll on individuals, families, and society, national policymakers, civil society, and communities must be galvanized to address the pervasive violence in society to protect individuals and strengthen American marriages and families.

KEY TERMS

anticipatory socialization	getting together	marriage market	marriage gradient	dating violence
dating	going steady	pool of eligibles	hypergamy	rape
mate selection	hooking up	homogamy	hypogamy	acquaintance rape
courtship	sex ratio	marriage squeeze	propinquity	date rape

QUESTIONS FOR STUDY AND REFLECTION

1. As you have read in this chapter, dating patterns in the United States have changed dramatically over the years. What are the current norms of dating in your community? On your college campus? Are these norms different or the same for each gender? Explain. What do you consider the advantages and disadvantages of such norms? What, if any, changes would you like to see in today's dating norms?

2. "Cupid's arrow does not strike at random." Explain this statement. Discuss the predictable factors that influence who meets, falls in love with, and marries whom in the United States.

3. Define the concepts of marriage squeeze and marriage gradient. How are the two related? How would the marriage squeeze and marriage gradient be significant in the lives of a 35-year-old female with a Ph.D. and a 35-year-old male who

is a high school dropout? Why is the marriage squeeze so significant for African American women? Find information about the marriage squeeze for other groups of women.

4. Think about the discussion in this chapter of violence in dating relationships. How prevalent is date rape and other intimate violence on your college or university campus? What are some of the attitudes, behaviors, and activities on your campus that encourage male physical and sexual aggressiveness and contribute to a climate that is conducive to abuse? Is there any information about male victims of rape on your campus? Have you ever experienced relationship violence? If yes, how did you handle it? What institutional supports and services on your campus are there for victims of dating violence? In your community, city, and state?

ADDITIONAL RESOURCES

SOCIOLOGICAL STUDIES

BECKER, CAROL S. 1988. *Unbroken Ties: Lesbian Ex-Lovers*. Boston: Alyson. An interesting case study approach to lesbian interpersonal relations, including separation.

KAUFMAN, MICHAEL. 1995. "The Construction of Masculinity and the Triad of Men's Violence." In Michael Kimmel and Michael Messner, eds., *Men's Lives*, pp. 13–25. New York: Macmillan. A provocative article that examines male violence in the social context of the construction of masculinity and the institutionalization of violence in the operation of most aspects of social, economic, and political life in the United States.

KIRKWOOD, CATHERINE. 1993. *Leaving Abusive Partners*. Newbury Park, CA: Sage. A compelling collection of stories by 30 formerly abused women told in their own voices.

WOOD, JULIA T., ED. 1996. *Gendered Relationships*. Mountain View, CA: Mayfield. An excellent set of readings on gendered relationships, focusing specifically on the reciprocal influence between gender and intimacy. The readings cover issues of communication, friendship, heterosexual love, lesbian and gay romantic relationships, sexuality and AIDS, intimate violence, sexual harassment, and gender issues in the workplace.

FILM

Must Love Dogs. 2005. A romantic comedy centered around the comic potential of Internet dating. After a recent divorce, a fortysomething woman, who is hesitant to get back into the dating scene, is pressured by her overly involved family to find a man by placing an ad for her in an online dating site. The movie touches on issues such as finding *the* love of one's life, the problems of online dating, a love triangle, the search for love and companionship after the death of a loved one, and the not so pretty side of love.

Friends With Benefits. 2011. A romantic comedy starring Justin Timberlake and Mila Kunis that mirrors today's youthful "Hooking Up" generation. It is a story about two young professionals, one of whom (Mila Kunis) is trying to recruit the other (Justin Timberlake) to take a job at a magazine in New York. After a fun night together exploring the city, Timberlake agrees to take the job. Not knowing anyone else in the city, he and Kunis quickly develop a friendship. One night while hanging out at Kunis' apartment watching a romantic comedy, they get on the topic of sex and relationships. They come to the conclusion that sex should not come with so many emotional attachments. Both feeling the need for a physical connection, they agree to have sex without emotion or commitment involved. After several trysts together, Kunis comes to the realization that this isn't really what she wants, and she would like to start dating again and informs Timberlake that they need to stop. This is a very contemporary film that can provoke a lively class discussion around the topics of "hooking up" and "hanging out" and whether or not adding sex to a friendship brings complications or love.

LITERARY WORKS

Gibson, Rachael. 2006. *Sex, Lies, and Online Dating*. Avon. This book is an entertaining and funny romantic suspense novel that examines the world of Internet dating. Mystery writer Lucy is on assignment, a date to gather info on guys that she can use in her latest novel. She's been hooking up with men online and going to Starbucks for mini dates in the hopes that one of these guys will inspire a character. Unfortunately, a serial killer is also using the Internet to snare dates/murder victims and Lucy gets caught up in the intrigue. A simple but good starting point to discuss and reinforce various issues raised in this textbook about online dating.

McMillan, Terry. 1997. *How Stella Got Her Groove Back*. New York: Signet Books. This novel is a chronicle of the dating and mate selection experiences of an African American divorced superwoman who has everything—except an intimate relationship with a man, something she is convinced she can well do without. However, much to her dismay, when she meets a man half her age while on vacation in Jamaica, she soon realizes that she must make some difficult decisions about her passions, desires, and dating, mating, and marital expectations. This novel is a good jumping-off point for a discussion of age differences in heterosexual intimate relationships, particularly when the woman is older than the man (what is called today a cougar relationship).

INTERNET

www.CollegeClub.com This Web site, part of the Student Advantage Network, allows students to connect with each other; it provides them with a variety of information and services from academics to love, dating relationships, and much more. For example, through its MatchU engine, it allows students to meet and match up online.

www.meetmeonline.com Powered by AmericanSingles.com, this site is advertised as the best place on the Internet to meet someone. It boasts of a membership of 3 million high-quality singles.

www.agelesslove.com The first Web site exclusively devoted to older women and younger men/older men and younger women relationship support and intergenerational dating. A wide range of subjects is discussed in a number of forums regarding age-gap relationships.

www.match.com The world's largest online dating, relationships, singles, and personals service, offering its members a range of services including an online advice magazine, local personals, match international, and match mobile, a feature that will connect members anonymously with singles near them on their mobile.

Succeed with MyFamilyLab®
www.myfamilylab.com

Watch. Explore. Read. The New MyFamilyLab is designed just for you. Each chapter features a pre-test and post-test to help you learn and review key concepts and terms. Experience Marriages and Families in action with dynamic visual activities, videos, and readings to enhance your learning experience.

Here are a few activities you will find for this chapter.

Watch on **myfamilylab.com**

Video clips feature important concepts in the study of Marriages and Families. Watch:
- Online Dating

Explore on **myfamilylab.com**

Social Explorer is an interactive application that allows you to explore Census data through interactive maps. Explore the Social Explorer Activity:
- Increases in the Multiracial Population

Read on **myfamilylab.com**

MyFamilyLab includes primary source readings from classic and contemporary sociologists from around the world. Read:
- Ingoldsby: "Mate Selection and Marriage Around the World"

6

Sexuality and Intimate Relationships

What Will You Learn?

- Define and understand the sociological meaning of key terms.
- Describe the nature and scope of human sexuality.
- Apply the sociological imagination to examine and analyze the media as a source of sexual learning.
- Assess the pros and cons of the abstinence only until marriage approach to safe sex.
- Increase your awareness and understanding of sexually transmitted infections and sexual responsibility.
- Question the sexual double standard.

IN THE NEWS

Lacey, WA

Recently, a 14-year-old eighth grade student in the state of Washington, posed naked in front of her bathroom mirror, held up her cell phone and took a picture. Afterward, she sent the full-length frontal photo to her new boyfriend, who was also an eighth grader. Not long after this, the two students broke up. A few weeks after the break-up, the now ex-boyfriend forwarded the young girl's photo to another eighth-grade girl who was once a friend of his ex-girlfriend. Later that night, that girl typed a text message on the photo: "Ho Alert! If you think this girl is a whore, then text this to all your friends" (Hoffman, 2011a). She then sent the photo and her message to the long list of contacts on her phone. In less than 24 hours, the effect was as if the young 14-year-old had walked

(continued on next page)

(continued from previous page)

naked down the hallways of the four middle schools in the racially and economically diverse suburb of Lacey, Washington, where she lived. Who knows how many students received the photo: hundreds or quite possibly thousands of students received her photo and forwarded it to others (Hoffman, 2011a).

Three teens identified as being responsible for the viral outbreak (the ex-boyfriend and the two girls who initially forwarded the nude photo) were arrested and spent the night in juvenile detention. They were charged with dissemination of child pornography, a Class C felony, and arraigned before a judge the next day. At juvenile detention, the young man who initiated this event was forced to take off his clothes and shoes and change into regulation white briefs and a blue jumpsuit. Reportedly, he was miserable and terrified and complained that his socks got wet in the shower. Eventually, a deal was brokered for the three teens, and the offense was amended to a gross misdemeanor of telephone harassment. These charges were later dropped with the stipulation that the teens participate in a community service program. If the teens had been convicted of dissemination of child pornography, they could have faced a sentence of up to 36 weeks in a juvenile detention center. They would also have been registered as sex offenders. However, because they were under the age of 15, after two years they would have been able to petition the court to remove their names from the sex offender registry, if they could prove they no longer posed a threat to the public (Hoffman, 2011a; Gray, 2011).

Unfortunately, this scenario is not a rarity today. It is a real-life drama playing out all across the country. What this drama describes is a case of *sexting*—a combination of the words sex and texting—which usually involves sending nude or sexually explicit images or text messages primarily between cell phones. The term was first popularized around 2005; since then, it has been reported as taking place worldwide.

The role of technology, particularly cell phones, in the sex lives of American teens and young adults has become increasingly an issue of grave concern among parents, educators, and advocates. It seems that at the same time that the age at which American teens acquire their first cell phone has grown younger (in 2009, 58 percent of 12-year-olds owned a cell phone compared to 18 percent five years earlier), the capacity of cell phones has changed dramatically. Texting has become a centerpiece in the social lives of today's teens. Teens use their phones not only for calling but also to access the Internet and to take and share photos and videos (Lenhart, 2009).

According to the *New York Times*, the prevalence of teen sexting is unclear and can often depend on the culture of a particular school or circle of students. A nationally representative survey of cell-owning young people ages 12–17 conducted by the Pew Research Center found that among these teens, 4 percent said they have sent sexually suggestive, nude, or nearly nude images of themselves to someone else via text messaging, and 15 percent said they have received the same type of images of someone they know via text messaging on their cell phone. In addition, older cell-owning teens are much more likely to send and receive these images. For example, 8 percent of 17-year-olds said they have sent a sexually provocative image by text, and 30 percent have received a nude or nearly nude image on their phone. Furthermore, teens who pay their own cell phone bills are more likely to send "sexts"—17 percent compared to only 3 percent among those teens who do not pay for, or only pay a portion of, the cost for their cell phone. Focus groups conducted by the Pew Researchers revealed three main scenarios for sexting: 1) exchange of images solely between two romantic partners, 2) exchanges between partners that are shared with others outside of the relationship, and 3) exchanges between people who are not yet in a relationship but where at least one person hopes to be (Hoffman, 2011a; Lenhart, 2009).

WHERE SHOULD WE DRAW THE LINE? This is a question that law enforcement officials, adults in various positions of authority, parents, and educators are debating in terms of how to respond to minors who "sext." A number of school districts around the country have banned sexting and now authorize principals to search students' cell phones. And, at least 26 states have tried to pass some sort of sexting legislation since 2009. According to Justin Fitzsimmons, an attorney at the National District Attorneys Association who specializes in Internet crimes against children, the majority of states are trying to put something in place to educate kids before and after an event such as that described above happens. "We have to protect kids from themselves sometimes.

We're on the cusp of teaching them how to manage their electronic reputations" (Justin Fitzsimmons quoted in Hoffman, 2011a).

WHAT WOULD YOU DO?

Would you ever send, or have you ever sent, a sext to anyone? Have you ever received nude or nearly nude photos of someone you knew? Someone you didn't know? If so, would you ever forward such photos to others? If you are a parent, would you allow your 12- or 13-year-old to have a cell phone? Would (do) you monitor your teens' cell phone usage? Would you agree that sending nude photos by sexting should be considered as a distribution of child pornography and thus warrant criminal charges? If yes, why; if no, why not?

((•—[Listen to the **Chapter Audio** on **myfamilylab.com**

Sex continues to be the topic "du jour" in the twenty-first century. Continuing a pattern that emerged in the late twentieth century, sex and talk of sex, images of sex, sex scandals, and media and popular culture hype about sex are pervasive in the United States today. And no one is exempt from sexual scrutiny. For example, in the last decade of the twentieth century, a sitting president was involved in a highly publicized sex scandal with a young White House intern, in which he claimed, not unlike many teenagers today, that oral sex was not having sex. And by 2011, approximately 19 politicians, at least five of whom were U.S. senators and a governor of the state of New York, and 14 others holding an assortment of political offices, each had resigned their elected positions after being linked with one type of sex scandal or another.

Sex is on television (prime time, soap operas, talk shows, comedians' dialogue), in advertisements, newspapers, films, music, books and magazines, and increasingly in cyberspace. We are indeed talking about sex today more than at any other time in our history, and this makes sex more accessible than it has ever been.

Because sexuality figures so prominently in marriage and family life, as well as in other intimate relationships, this chapter, in conjunction with the supplementary materials presented in Appendix A, concentrates on sexual attitudes and behaviors before, during, and after marriage or a committed relationship as

well as throughout the life cycle. We begin with a brief discussion of sexuality and human development: sexual orientations. We then consider the historical roots of Western sexuality, from the Judeo–Christian tradition to U.S. sexual codes in the early twenty-first century. This discussion is followed by a consideration of the social basis of human sexuality through an examination of sexual learning and how sexual learning varies across gender and other social categories as well as trends in sexual attitudes and behavior. In addition, we discuss physiological aspects of sexuality such as human sexual response and expression. We also examine various codes of sexual conduct and patterns of sexual relationships across the life cycle. Finally, we examine human sexuality within the context of sexual responsibility and protecting yourself and your partners from AIDS and other sexually transmitted infections such as HPV.

Human Sexuality

Often people use the terms *sex* and *sexuality* interchangeably. Thus, when someone talks about sexuality, we often assume that she or he is referring to sexual intercourse. On the other hand, when we speak of sex, it is not always immediately clear whether we are speaking of sexual activity such as intercourse or whether we mean a person's genetic sex (that is, biologically female or male). Although neither usage is incorrect, for the purposes of clarification and consistency, we try to use the term *sexual activity* or *sexuality* to refer to a wide range of sexual behaviors, including intercourse. However, it is not always so simple a choice. In those cases, we use the term *sex*—not to refer to biological females or males but to refer to sexual intercourse or other sexual activities. We use the term gender when we are referring to the attitudes and behaviors females and males have learned and enact according to a set of culturally prescribed norms and expectations.

As you will find, human sexuality is far more complex than simply who we have sexual relations with. It comprises a broad range of attitudes and behaviors and is a product of sociological, psychological, biological, and physiological factors. Because human sexuality is so broad, no one all-encompassing definition is appropriate. In general terms, however, **human sexuality** refers to the feelings, thoughts, attitudes, values, and behaviors of humans who have learned a set of cues that evoke a sexual or an erotic response. It includes behaviors well known to us, such as sexual intercourse and masturbation, as well as behaviors we do not readily identify as sexual, such as breast-feeding, giving birth, and talking affectionately with someone. Furthermore, human sexuality involves issues of power, authority, and emotional and physical vulnerability in relationships. Thus, it is not just one thing; it includes sociological, psychological, and biological components (Boston Women's Health Book Collective, 2011).

Sexual Identity

It is impossible to discuss human sexuality without discussing sexual identity and sexual orientation. Contrary to popular belief, sexual identity and sexual orientation—whether heterosexual, homosexual, or bisexual—are not synonymous with each other nor are either synonymous with sexual behavior. How we identify sexually includes more than simply who we have sex with and/ or the kinds of sex we participate in. Rather, **sexual identity** is a broad idea referring not only to the ways we define ourselves sexually, but also how we define ourselves in terms of the biological categories of female and male and all of the ways in which we think about and express ourselves in terms of our beliefs, attitudes, and values. Sexual identity is something we define for ourselves not based solely on sexual desires, but on how we understand ourselves in relation to others and the world. It involves identifying our sexual selves within the socially constructed categories our society creates for female, male, femininity, masculinity, heterosexual, homosexual, bisexual, and so on. Our sexual identity also may incorporate who we look to for emotional and intimate love and support and who we identify with in terms of desire, lifestyle, politics, and more. Sexual identity is the cognitive aspect of sexual orientation.

Sexual Orientations

Like sexual identity, **sexual orientation** involves not only whom one chooses as a sexual partner, but, more fundamentally, the ways in which people understand and identify themselves. Although Americans tend to think of sexual orientation in terms of clear-cut categories—for example, heterosexual versus homosexual—various sex researchers have concluded that fundamental

categories of sexual desire are nonexistent for most of us. Rather, sexual desire is constructed in the context of social relationships and identities (Andersen, 2005). Cultural historian and sex researcher Shere Hite (1976) believes we are born with a natural desire to relate to people of the same as well as the other sex. Society, however, teaches us to inhibit all of our sexual desires except those for partners with whom we can procreate. Regardless of whether we accept Hite's hypothesis, it is clear that the multiplicity of desires, pleasures, and sexual acts themselves assures that sexuality becomes an experience so highly personal that no one term can come to represent sexualities. It is also clear that U.S. culture historically has espoused **heterosexism,** the belief that heterosexuality is the only right, natural, and acceptable sexual orientation and that any other orientation is pathological.

Heterosexism is so strong in U.S. society that most sex research is based on the assumption of heterosexuality. This assumption overlooks the fact that many people have a homosexual orientation and even more people have engaged in homosexual behavior at least once in their life. Furthermore, some research suggests that sexual orientation forms a continuum with at least four recognizable levels of orientation. According to this research, at the two extremes are exclusively heterosexual and exclusively homosexual orientations, with bisexuality and asexuality falling somewhere in the middle.

HETEROSEXUALITY

Heterosexuality refers to the preference for sexual activities with a person of the other sex. In a more sociological and political sense, heterosexuality also includes an individual's community, lifestyle, and core identity. It is difficult to know precisely how many people in the U.S. population are heterosexual. Research during the mid-1990s reported that 97 percent of Americans identify themselves as exclusively heterosexual (for example, Laumann et al., 1994). Recent data indicate little change reporting that 96 percent of American women and men identify themselves as exclusively heterosexual (Chandra, Mosher, Copen, and Sionean, 2011; Gates, 2011). In describing a person's sexual orientation, most social scientists view sexual orientation, like other aspects of our identity, as an ongoing process that can vary considerably over the life course. Thus, they question whether it is more meaningful to emphasize a person's perceived attractions, her or his current sexual partners, her or his lifetime partners, or the description the person prefers for her- or himself. This fact notwithstanding, most people think of sexual orientation, sexual identity, and sexual behavior as all one and the same.

Although sexual identity will typically include an expression of a person's underlying sexual orientation and both will often correspond with sexual behavior, they do not always match. For example, one can have a homosexual orientation but choose to have a heterosexual identity. In addition, for any number of reasons, people sometimes change their sexual preference. Phillip Blumstein and Pepper Schwartz (1983), in their now classic study of American sexuality, for example, found that people often became homosexual after satisfactory heterosexual lives or became heterosexual after many years of homosexual identity and behavior. Moreover, some people who would prefer partners of their same sex might restrict themselves to heterosexual relationships because of religious, family, professional, or other social or political reasons or pressures. Conversely, in restrictive environments such as prison, people who are more attracted to members of the other sex might sometimes engage in sexual and other intimacy with members of the same sex (Shriver et al., 2002). This situational aspect of sexual orientation is exemplified in Claire Farrer's discussion of institutional homosexuality in the edited book: *Two Spirit People: Native American Gender Identity, Sexuality, and Spirituality* (Jacobs, Thomas and Lang, 1997). While discussing Apache institutionalized homosexuality, Farrer relates a story about Apache men who engage in same sex relations while on hunting trips. According to Farrer, these same-sex relations did not mean either or both men were homosexual. Rather, it was situational homosexuality.

Social scientists using a feminist perspective maintain that in the United States, sexuality generally and sexual activities specifically that are associated with a heterosexual orientation are *phallocentric,* male-centered, and are defined almost exclusively in terms of genital intercourse and male orgasm (which might explain why so many people do not view oral sex as having sex). According to this point of view, the ideology of heterosexuality assumes that women exist for men, that their bodies and services are men's property. If a woman rejects this definition of "normal sexuality," she is stigmatized no matter whom she chooses as a sexual partner. For men, the notion of heterosexual intercourse, with its assumptions of male power and control; male lust, passion, and aggression; and the male as the initiator of sexual activity is the proving ground for acceptable male sexuality and identity in this society. It also provides the script that most men adopt, with some individual modification, as the foundation of both their masculinity and sexual activity. Some feminist social scientists such as Adrienne Rich (1980) have argued that making heterosexuality compulsory stymies or restricts the sexuality of males as well as females. Rich suggests that both heterosexism and **homophobia**—an extreme and irrational fear or hatred of homosexuals—act to inhibit the possibility of some women and men finding emotional and sexual satisfaction with same-sex partners.

Clearly, sexual orientation is much more complicated than simply identifying with whom one sleeps or even the label people use to identify themselves sexually. Although heterosexuality is the predominant sexual orientation, homosexuality exists in all known societies.

HOMOSEXUALITY

Like heterosexuality, **homosexuality** refers to both identity and behavior. It is part of a person's core identity and includes whom she or he defines as an acceptable sexual partner, but it does not consist solely of sexual preference. To label homosexuality entirely in terms of choice of sexual partner distorts our perception of lesbians and gays. We certainly do not define heterosexuals entirely or even primarily in terms of their choice of sexual partner. But what if we did? If you are heterosexual, how would you feel if people defined you entirely in terms of whom you slept with? What if people routinely asked you questions such as, "When or how did you first realize that you were a heterosexual?" "Do your parents know?" "What do you think caused your heterosexuality? Is it possible that it is just a phase that you are going through?" "If you choose to have children, would you want them to be heterosexual, knowing

Jesse Tyler Ferguson and Eric Stonestreet, pictured here, play one of the most famous and high-profile same-sex couples on prime time television in ABC's Emmy Award–winning sitcom *Modern Family.* The show takes a satirical look at three different family types: a traditional heterosexual family with three children, a gay couple with an adopted Vietnamese baby daughter, and an older White man recently married to a Latina woman who has a young son from a previous marriage. In the sitcom, Ferguson and Stonestreet's sexuality is secondary to their story lines, which include issues like how to behave at a kiddie gym class with their adopted daughter.

the problems they would face?" "Why do heterosexuals put so much emphasis on sex?" "If you have never slept with a person of the same sex, is it possible that all you need is a good gay lover?" (see, for example, Rochlin, 1992). Would you find such questions offensive? Can you see and understand the indignity engendered when we routinely ask such questions of lesbians and gays?

As we will see, some scientists explain both homosexuality and heterosexuality in terms of social learning, social experiences, and role models. However, no specific social experience or type of social relationship has been found to be significant in the development of human sexual preference. At the same time, there is no conclusive evidence to support the argument that sexual orientation is determined entirely by biology. Nonetheless, the debate over the relative roles of social environment and biology in determining sexual orientation continues to spark controversy among a number of groups in society, including scientists, gay activists, and religious and political leaders. In recent years, those who take a biological stance in this debate have received a boost from research results suggesting that sexual orientation (at least in men) is determined in large part by genetic factors. If it turns out that sexual orientation is genetically determined, then can we continue to define either homosexuality or heterosexuality as sexual preference?

How Widespread Is Homosexuality? Because homosexuality is still so stigmatized, the exact determination of homosexuality at any given time is difficult to know. Moreover, self-reports as lesbian or gay vary across time and type of sexual survey and responses are not always consistent with respondents' reported sexual behaviors. In the mid-1990s, 1.4 percent of women and 2.8 percent of men identified themselves as homosexual or bisexual. However, the number who reported having had same-sex experiences or same-sex attractions was considerably higher (8.6 percent for women and 10.1 percent for men) (Laumann, Gagnon, Michael, and Michaels, 1994). More recently, some researchers estimate that about 4 percent of adults in the United States identify as lesbian, gay, bisexual, or transgender, 1.7 percent of whom identify as lesbian or gay. However, as in the 1990s, a disparity between how people identify sexually and their sexual behavior is evident. For example, in a recent National Health Statistic Report on American sexual behavior, 2.8 percent of survey respondents ages 18–44 identified themselves as lesbian or gay. However, 12.5 percent of females and 5.2 percent of males indicated that they have had same-sex contact in their lifetimes. Similarly, although 93 percent of the women identified as heterosexual, only 82 percent said they were sexually attracted only to the opposite sex. For men who identified as heterosexual (95 percent), only 92 percent reported being sexually attracted to the opposite sex only (Chandra, Mosher, Copen, and Sionean, 2011). In any event, as these statistics indicate, a definition of homosexuality is complicated by the fact that sexual preference, sexual attraction, and/or actual sexual behavior are not always consistent with one's sexual identity or sexual orientation.

An increasing amount of public focus, discourse, and debate around this very issue has permeated the media and scholarly writings and discussions over the last decade or so. For example, in the late 1990s and early 2000s, it was claimed that many African American men who have sex with other men nevertheless think of themselves as heterosexual. Whites and Latinas/os are far more likely to report being gay than African American women and men. According to some analysts, machismo has always been a strong component of African American masculinity. The concept of being gay is seen as the antithesis of manhood. Thus, many African American men who have sex with other men do not consider themselves gay. While attempting to present a heterosexual image to the outer world, these men frequently engage in sexual behavior with men while engaged in ongoing sexual relationships with one or more women. Experts in the field have dubbed this tendency the "down-low syndrome" (Emory Health Sciences Press Release, 2004; Herbert, 2001; Muwakkil, 2001).

The same discrepancy between how one self-identifies and what one actually does is also observable for women: 1.7 percent of White women and 1.1 percent of Latinas identified themselves as homosexual or bisexual, compared with less than 1 percent (0.6 percent) of the African American women in the sample. Findings such as these raise questions regarding the accuracy of statistics that purport to tell us the prevalence of homosexuality, heterosexuality, bisexuality, and transgendered orientations.

BISEXUALITY

Although bisexuality is difficult to define, some researchers have suggested that it is more prevalent in American society than homosexuality. On the one hand, as with other sexual orientations, bisexuality is subject to a variety of definitions, based on perceived attractions, current partnerships, past partnerships, or how a person self-identifies. On the other hand, **bisexuality** refers generally to individuals who do not have an exclusive sexual preference for one sex over the other. Rather, a bisexual has partners of both sexes, either simultaneously or at different times. It does not

necessarily mean being equally attracted to both. Bisexuality also represents an identity and a lifestyle. As we have already noted, an important aspect of sexual orientation is how one defines oneself. Similar to homosexuality, it is difficult to know exactly how many people are bisexual. Some researchers suggest that this is so because bisexual is not a very well-defined social category. This fact notwithstanding, recent surveys report that a little less than 2 percent (1.8 percent) of the American population is bisexual. Women are far more likely than men to identify as bisexual. For instance, 3.5 percent of women and 1.1 percent of men ages 18–44 identify as bisexual. According to some research, more men are bisexual based on their behavior than based on their self-identity (Gates, 2011; Chandra, Mosher, Copen and Sionean, 2011).

One of the difficulties in attempting to estimate the bisexual population is that many researchers and laypersons alike view bisexuals exclusively as homosexuals. Thus, in some studies, statistics on bisexuals and homosexuals are collapsed into one category. Although some people who engage in both same-sex and heterosexual relationships categorize themselves as either heterosexual or homosexual, many bisexuals do not see themselves in this either/or dichotomy; they do not see themselves as gay or straight, and their behavior does not necessarily correspond to either (Shriver et al., 2002).

Like homosexuality, bisexuality is stigmatized in the larger society. In addition, bisexuals are often rejected by the homosexual community as well. Some lesbians and gays, for instance, view bisexuals with suspicion or hostility, perceiving their heterosexual behavior as indicative of a lack of commitment to the lesbian and gay community (Shriver et al., 2002). Many people who hold to society's rigid sexual binary do not believe people can really be bisexual; they have to be one thing (heterosexual) or another (homosexual). The suggestion that the terms homosexual and heterosexual should not be used as nouns but as adjectives is noteworthy. Perhaps *bisexual* should also be used as an adjective to describe people's activities and not people themselves, particularly given that few people are completely bisexual.

TRANSGENDER

Defining the transgender population can also be challenging. There is not exact agreement on the details of what exactly it means to be transgender. In the very broadest sense, a **transgender** person is anyone who transgresses traditional gender norms in terms of identity, appearance, or behavior, either intentionally or unintentionally, on a regular basis. However, not everyone whose appearance or behavior is gender-atypical will identify as a transgender person. At the core, transgender people's gender identity (sense of themselves as female or male) or gender expression differs from that usually associated with their birth sex. Many transgender people live part-time or full-time as members of the other gender. However, the term "transgender" does not necessarily imply any particular sexual orientation. Transgender people may identify as lesbian, gay, straight, bisexual, or anywhere in between (for instance, pansexual, polysexual, asexual, agender, bigender, genderqueer, third gender, and so forth). For many transgender people, conventional sexual orientation labels are inadequate or inapplicable to them.

There are no concrete statistics on the number of transgender people in the United States, and it is difficult to estimate their prevalence. Complicating our ability to determine just how many people are transgendered is the fact that this group is not static. That is, transgender is an umbrella term used to describe many types of gender diverse behaviors, people, and groups who are not satisfied with society's strict definitions of gender and who do not accept a simple two-gender categorization. While people identify as transgender, as we have indicated, transgender identity includes heterosexual, homosexual, lesbian, gay, and bisexual. In addition, transgender identity includes many overlapping categories. For example, some transgendered people are transsexuals (people who have undergone sex change surgery); some are transvestites (people who dress in the clothing of the opposite sex); and some are masculine-appearing women and feminine-appearing men. Others are trans women or trans men, people who have adopted a social and personal identity that corresponds to their own sense of the gendered self and may or may not include those who have transitioned from one sex to another through medical interventions such as hormone treatment or surgery. The term trans woman refers to male-to-female (MtF or M2F) transgender people, and trans man refers to female-to-male (FtM or F2M) transgender people, although some transgender people identify only slightly with the gender not assigned at birth. Even those who feel they are the opposite sex, but do not express it outwardly, are considered transgendered.

Still other transgendered people are cross dressers (These are people who dress occasionally in the clothing of the opposite gender, specifically for sexual pleasure. Cross dressers may or may not identify with or want to be the opposite gender. In fact, the majority of cross dressers self-identify as heterosexual.); androgynies (people who lack a clear or specified singular gender trait but rather identify as both genders—feminine and masculine—or neither, or as beyond gender, between genders, moving across genders, entirely genderless, or any or all of these); genderqueer (a recently developed concept to describe people whose gendered experiences that do not fit into rigid binary definitions of sex and gender and refers to a combination of gender identities and sexual orientations); people who live cross-gender (people who always or mostly live as the gender other than that assigned at birth); drag kings and drag queens (people who cross-dress for the effect or for entertainment); and intersexed (people born with full or partial genitalia of both genders, or with underdeveloped genitalia), to name but a few. Current estimates of the prevalence of transsexualism are about 1 in 10,000 for biological males and 1 in 30,000 for biological females. The number of people in other transgender categories is unknown (American Psychological Association, 2011; National Transgender Advocacy Center, 2011; Larson, 2010.).

Like any other sexual orientation, transgender is also about identity, about expression—how a person feels about her- or himself and how she or he wants to identify or present her- or himself to other people. Given the general difficulty of defining sexual orientation, what criteria, if any, should we use to classify people in terms of their sexual orientation? Do we use their behavior? Their attitudes? Both? How many female and male partners does a person need to have to be classified as heterosexual, homosexual, or bisexual? Do we classify someone who has had 2 partners of the same sex and 15 of the other sex as heterosexual, homosexual, or bisexual? Or do we simply rely on self-labeling and what people feel rather than what they do?

Clearly from our discussion thus far, it seems that the traditional sexual orientation dichotomy of heterosexual versus homosexual is misleading. Over six decades ago, sexuality researcher Alfred Kinsey and his colleagues (1948) suggested that few of us are completely and exclusively heterosexual or homosexual. Rather, although many people would prefer not to entertain the thought, there are some aspects of both orientations in all of us. As with heterosexuality, we cannot speak of homosexuality or any other sex or gender category as if they are monolithic behavioral and attitudinal patterns. Like heterosexuality, other sex/gender categories vary in terms of importance, organization, and actualization in people's lives. It is sufficient to say here that, except for the sex or gender of one's partner, the sexual attitudes, behaviors, and relationships of lesbians and gays do not differ significantly from those of heterosexual couples. Although we provide a more in-depth discussion of lesbian and gay lifestyles in Chapter 7, lesbian and gay lifestyles, issues, and concerns can be found throughout the text.

Human Sexuality: Past and Present

We are sexual beings, and a large proportion of our lives consists of sexual daydreaming, fantasy, and desire; reading about sexual activities or viewing a wide range of sexual behaviors; sexual pleasure, activity, joy, and pain. Given the fact that sexuality is such an important dimension of human experience, all societies are involved, in some way, in controlling the sexual behavior of their members. Although the ways in which sexual behavior are controlled have varied over time and from culture to culture, all societies have a set of rules or codes that define appropriate sexual behavior. Throughout U.S. history, Americans have been subject to one set of sexual codes or another. The codes we adhere to today have their roots in sexual attitudes and practices that existed hundreds, if not thousands, of years ago. Before we discuss the history of human sexuality in Western society, two points must be made:

1. Although the historical descriptions emphasize the sexual codes that were most prevalent during a given historical period, it is not our intention to imply that sexual ideas and behavior have progressed directly from very strict and repressive codes of sexual conduct to more liberal sexual norms. Rather, sexual ideas and behavior change according to cyclical patterns, with periods of extremely or moderately repressive norms followed by periods of more liberal norms. In addition, at any given time, many different sexual codes, ideas, and behaviors coexist.
2. Generalizations about human behavior are always risky. Human attitudes and behavior are so flexible that they are never the same for all people or all groups. Thus, there are many variations in sexual attitudes and behavior. The historical period in which people live; the political and economic climate; the social organization of race, class, and gender; and factors such as sexual orientation, age, and religion all affect human attitudes and behavior.

Consider, for example, the effects of gender on sexual behavior. Women historically have experienced sexuality in terms of reproduction, oppression (powerlessness), and vulnerability (victims of sexual assault). In contrast, men have experienced sexuality primarily in terms of power and control, passion and emotions, and freedom of sexual choice and behavior. Furthermore, sex and sexuality have traditionally been defined in terms of heterosexuality and monogamy, with homosexuality considered a form of deviance. Thus, for lesbians and gays, the experience of sexuality has been far more repressive and has involved a high degree of public concern and social control by outside forces such as the state.

Similarly, the sexuality of various racial groups (African Americans, Latinas/os, Native Americans, and Asian Americans) as well as poor people of all races has been defined primarily by outsiders. Thus, these groups have often been defined in scientific research or the popular culture as sexually promiscuous and uncontrolled. These definitions of sexuality have often been used in conjunction with other ideologies of racial or cultural inferiority to rationalize oppression and unequal treatment. These examples illustrate how human sexuality involves issues of power and authority and emotional and physical vulnerability. As you read this chapter, keep this point in mind.

JEWISH TRADITIONS AND HUMAN SEXUALITY

Ancient Jewish tradition placed great emphasis on marriage and reproduction. Women and men who did not marry and have children were considered sinful. Marriage was the only appropriate context for sexual intercourse, the sole purpose of which was reproduction. Although in principle the norm of premarital chastity applied to both sexes, it was more rigidly applied to women. A woman was supposed to be a virgin at the time of marriage. If she was not, she could be put to death. Moreover, women could not own property, nor could they obtain a divorce without their husband's consent. A further restriction placed on women's sexuality can be seen in the rules surrounding menstruation. Because menstruation was considered unclean, menstruating women were isolated from their husbands and other family members and were forbidden to engage in sexual activities. Strongly forbidden by Jewish custom were nakedness, masturbation, and homosexuality. Although homosexuality was not mentioned in earlier Hebrew codes, it was made punishable by death in later Hebrew documents.

The two ancient Jewish notions about human sexuality—reproduction as a married couple's obligation and male dominance over women in sexual relations—became a part of Christian as well as non-Christian doctrine and to some degree can still be found in contemporary U.S. sexual codes.

CHRISTIAN TRADITIONS AND HUMAN SEXUALITY

Although in the Gospels Jesus refers to marriage as a sacred union, values pertaining to women, marriage, and sexuality decreased as Christian ideas of chastity took hold. The early Christian sexual tradition seems to have been influenced most by St. Paul, who believed that celibacy is superior to marriage and that all humans should strive for a chaste life. A person who could not resist sexual temptation could engage in sexual intercourse, but only within marriage. In the fifth century, Christian scholar St. Augustine continued Paul's tradition of condemning sexuality, and his influence lasted throughout the Middle Ages. St. Augustine believed that all sexual experience was lustful and shameful and would lead one to burn in Hell for eternity. He saw intercourse as animal lust to be tolerated for the sake of procreation. Celibacy, however, was the ideal, but for the weak-willed it was better that they marry than burn in Hell. Church documents of the eighth century specified that only the male-superior, or "missionary," position was to be used because any other position might cause some enjoyment. People who engaged in other than the male-superior position faced a range of penalties. During the thirteenth century, the church, through the writings of St. Thomas Aquinas, renewed its position on sexuality. Sexual intercourse continued to be viewed as an activity to be avoided except for reproduction. Celibacy and virginity were the ideals; masturbation, engaging in intercourse while unclothed, during the daylight, or in forbidden postures became sexual crimes that had to be confessed. In addition, nakedness, looking at parts of the body, dancing, singing, and touching other people were also considered sinful (Shriver et al., 2002).

The Protestant Reformation of the sixteenth century ushered in a diversity of views and attitudes concerning human sexuality. Religious reformer Martin Luther, for example, renounced celibacy as an unnatural and unrealistic goal for human beings. Leaving the priesthood to marry, he considered sex a natural and appropriate act when carried out within the context of marriage. Likewise, other theologians, such as John Calvin, argued against celibacy, believing sex was a holy act when it occurred within marriage. Although Christianity exerted considerable influence, not everyone adhered to its teachings concerning human sexuality. For instance, it has been noted that during most historical periods, sexual behavior varies according to social class. Often the middle classes followed the prevailing sexual mores more closely than did the aristocrats (upper classes) or the peasants (lower classes).

SEXUALITY IN THE UNITED STATES: AN OVERVIEW

Puritan Sexuality In the seventeenth century, Puritan immigrants from England brought their Calvinist sexual traditions to the United States. The Puritans defined marriage as a covenant of God and thus the only legitimate mechanism for sex and procreation. Inside marriage, sex was an act that brought a wife and husband together morally and physically. The Puritans also believed that a husband was obliged to satisfy his wife physically. Outside marriage, sex was considered a sin and a threat to the institutions of marriage and the family. Sanctions against premarital and extramarital sex thus were very rigidly enforced. As in earlier historical periods, sexual codes of conduct were especially restrictive and rigid regarding female sexuality. Some of the Puritan views on sexuality can still be found in contemporary U.S. sexual attitudes and behavior. As late as the 1980s, many of the sex laws still on the books in various states throughout the country were a legacy of the Puritan forefathers. For example, in some communities it was still illegal to kiss on Sundays (a law rarely enforced). In general, the Puritan codes of conduct continued to dominate U.S. sexual norms well into the nineteenth century, when the Victorians introduced a new and, according to some researchers, even more rigid set of sexual taboos.

The Scarlett Letter by Nathaniel Hawthorne relates a fictional account of life in seventeenth-century Boston where Puritan codes of sexual conduct were strictly enforced. Sexual behaviors were confined to acts between a wife and husband within a legal marriage, and sex outside of marriage was considered a sin. Along with her public shaming, the book's protagonist, pictured, a young woman whose adulterous relationship produced a daughter, is forced to wear a huge red letter A (meant to be a symbol of shame for committing adultery) as punishment for her sin.

Victorian Sexuality At the base of the Victorian view of sexuality was the notion that any kind of sexual stimulation, especially orgasm, sapped a person's "vital forces." Both women and men were fully clothed in several layers during sexual intercourse so that nudity and human flesh would not provide them with excessive stimulation.

According to the Victorian codes, sexuality was basically a male phenomenon. In contrast, women (specifically middle- and upper-class White women) were idealized and considered morally superior to men in matters of sexuality. The prevailing belief was that decent women did not experience sexual desire; decent women were delicate, passive, asexual, and passionless. A woman who dared to express sexual feeling or enjoy sexual intercourse was considered to have loose morals. In contrast, males were considered sexual animals driven by their lust and desires whether inside or outside marriage. Because men were perceived this way, their sexuality, including premarital and extramarital affairs, was accepted (although not necessarily approved of), whereas similar behaviors by women were condemned (Shriver et al., 2002). Although single women were to refrain from sex altogether, married women were taught that sex with their husbands was their wifely duty. Given men's alleged greater sexual appetite and needs, wives were taught to look the other way when their husbands had extramarital affairs or engaged in sexual activities with prostitutes. Many of these Victorian ideas persist in some form in American society today. This differing set of norms based on gender is referred to as the **sexual double standard.**

According to some scholars, human sexuality during the Victorian era was characterized by contradiction, hypocrisy, and ambivalence. For example, sexual pleasuring activities such as masturbation were considered the cause of various maladies such as blindness and insanity. Given the Victorian views of sexuality, the Social Purity Movement in the United States began a campaign of sexual abstinence. Moreover, during this period there was an extreme ambivalence regarding homosexuality. Although in previous historical periods homosexuality had been considered sinful, in the Victorian era it became criminalized. Some writers have pointed out the contradictory nature of the Victorian view of sexuality and the norms regulating it—despite the strict Victorian position regarding sexual virtue and restraint, prostitution flourished in the United States (for example, authorities counted 20,000 prostitutes in Manhattan, New York, alone in 1830) (Shriver et al., 2002).

The degree to which people adhered to the Victorian sexual codes varied from one social group to another. As in earlier periods, the rich and ruling elites basically ignored the restrictions and enjoyed considerable freedom in their sexual behavior. At the other end of the class structure, the poor were also exempted from the prevailing codes. As we indicated earlier, sexual purity was reserved for middle-class White women. Working-class, immigrant, and nonwhite women, on the other hand, were viewed as strongly sexual; in fact, they were defined as depraved and loose. This stereotype functioned as a rationalization for the continued mistreatment of these groups, especially the repeated rapes of African American women by White men.

Sexuality and Slavery If Victorian norms regarding sexuality applied only to certain groups of Whites, they did not apply at all to Blacks. The lives and bodies of slaves were completely controlled by slave owners. Whereas for middle-class Whites sex was considered sacred and ideally restricted to marriage, Black female and male slaves were prohibited from legally marrying (although as we saw in Chapter 1 there were some exceptions), and they were routinely forced to mate with each other to reproduce and increase the slave population. Norms of White female purity were based on the need to establish the paternity of heirs to property; however, slaves did not and could not own property. Thus, such norms made little sense in the lives of slaves. The control and manipulation of slave sexuality, although oppressive for both sexes, was experienced differently by slave women and men. For men, it took the form of being used as studs or being castrated to render them even more powerless and helpless. For women, it included the experiences of concubine, mistress, and rape victim as well as the bearer of new generations of slaves. Slave women were robbed of sexual choice and had no legal protection from the rape of any White male who so chose to exploit them. In fact, laws made it legitimate for slave owners to "work out" their sexual desires with slave women (Shriver et al., 2002:11).

SEXUAL ATTITUDES AND BEHAVIOR IN THE TWENTIETH CENTURY AND BEYOND

In the twentieth century, sexual attitudes and behavior continued to change. Researcher Carol Darling and her associates (1989) have divided the century into three major eras in terms of sexual behavior. The first era lasted from 1900 to the early 1950s. Despite moral standards that defined sex as acceptable only in the context of marriage, this period witnessed an increase in the number of single women and men reporting sexual involvement before marriage. The sexual double standard, however, remained largely in force.

For example, women were to be pure; men had sexual appetites, women did not. The second major era, from the 1950s to 1970, was characterized by greater sexual permissiveness. Darling refers to this period as an "era of permissiveness with affection" because sex outside marriage was acceptable as long as it occurred within a love relationship and the couple expected to marry each other. The prosperity of this era coupled with the ground-breaking work of sex researchers such as Alfred Kinsey, as well as William Masters and Virginia Johnson, sparked an exploration of alternative lifestyles and a new openness about sex, leading into the third era.

Since 1970, technological advances leading to greater travel and increased job opportunities for women and men resulted in a decreasing emphasis on the nuclear family and an increasing view that sexuality could be recreational as well as an expression of love. Women as a group became less sexually inhibited as they became more independent in other areas of their lives. As in the previous era, many people during this era viewed sexual intercourse as natural and expected for both women and men in love relationships. The difference in this era is that the couple did not have to plan marriage to justify their sexual conduct. Sex before marriage was no longer defined as deviant; rather, it became somewhat the norm.

What about human sexuality and attitudes about sexual activities today? Should this be a fourth historical period? How or what would you add to Darling's three eras to account for today's sexuality? When would this era begin, and how would you describe it? Would your description agree with or parallel that which we describe below?

These changes in attitudes and behavior did not happen by chance. Not only did the mass movement of women into the labor force influence sexual attitudes and standards, but other major changes during the twentieth century such as advances in birth control technology (especially the Pill), the contemporary women's movement, the 1973 Supreme Court decision (*Roe* v. *Wade*) legalizing abortion, innovative lifestyles on college campuses, the delay in marriage and childbirth, and the lesbian and gay liberation movements all helped move U.S. society toward less rigid sexual standards. These changes exerted a tremendous influence on sexuality. For example, improved birth control technology enabled women to spend less time bearing and raising children. This had the effect of separating sexual intercourse from reproduction, which in turn contributed to a wider acceptance of sex outside of marriage.

However, the discovery of Acquired Immunodeficiency Deficiency Syndrome (AIDS) in the 1980s led to a change in sexual attitudes and practices for many. A growing awareness, concern, and fear of contracting a sexually transmitted infection, especially AIDS, led many people to rediscover traditional values of fidelity, obligation, and marriage. For the next two decades at least, the era of casual and spontaneous sex was replaced by more cautious and committed sexual behavior. During this period, American sexual attitudes and practices became much more subdued. Some researchers reported either a decrease in unmarried sexual activity and a renewed emphasis on monogamous sexual relationships or a limiting of the number of sexual partners, if not

both. However, for many people, the question of casual and spontaneous sex remained open.

A Sexual Revolution? Do fundamental changes in the sexuality of Americans represent a sexual revolution? Some people say yes, given the broad scope of the changes. Others contend that there has been no revolution, just the continued evolution of sexual norms. Those who claim that America has undergone a sexual revolution often base their claims on what they perceive to have been profound societal change in American sexual behavior, particularly during the 1960s. However, those who say not argue that the term revolution implies radical and widespread change; while some sexual attitudes and behavior changed, sometimes radically, this was not necessarily the case for most Americans. They argue that even in the liberal sixties, conservative, traditionalist views continued to be widely held and many modern sociologists and historians think that the revolution described in that period is an overstatement. There is little doubt that attitudes and behavior have moved toward more liberal and permissive standards, but many individuals and groups still hold securely to traditional sexual norms and values.

Understanding America's Changing Sexuality: Contemporary Patterns Sexuality in the United States today is as diverse as the American population. Indeed, major changes have occurred in American sexual attitudes and behaviors since the public became increasingly more aware of the spread of sexually transmitted infections, the types of sex education that is now available to young people, the growing legalization of same-sex marriage, and the increasing use of the Internet as a tool for social interaction, including sex.

As we learned in Chapter 4 and in the opening vignette of this chapter, hooking up and hanging out, surfing the Internet for dates and sex, and sexting are all very much a part of the dating and sex lives of Americans today. First, we heard that hooking up was the latest dating and mating trend among young college women and men. Then came word that thousands of Americans of all ages and from all walks of life are hooking up—not just on college campuses, but also in cyberspace with one thing in mind: hooking up with their sex-mate. Although the exact number of people using the Internet to hook up solely for sex is hard to determine, some Web sites are claiming to have millions of registered users and hundreds of posts per day from people looking for sexual encounters. Some surveys support this claim reporting that about 70 percent of time online is spent in chat rooms or sending emails, of these interactions, the vast majority are romantic or sexual in nature. Moreover, although pornography is banned on cell phones, a number of sex-related applications (apps) have been created for some cell phones such as the iPhone. Some of these apps are designed specifically to help people attract a mate or simply find a one-night stand. There is even an app for phone sex (Manolith Team, 2010).

And we cannot ignore the significant role of social networks, including cell phones, Facebook, YouTube, and Twitter, in people's sex lives today. For example, sexting, a practice typically associated with teenagers, extends far beyond young people. Today's reality is that an increasing number of adults 50 years and older (and even their elder parents), both single and married, as well as those in long-term relationships, routinely use text messaging to send tantalizing pictures and provocative words to their partner (Infidelity Statistics, 2011; Leshnoff, 2011).

Although sex is everywhere in American society and everyone seems to be doing it, comprehensive and reliable research on American sexuality has been sparse to non-existent for the last almost two decades. However, recently, several sex surveys, some claiming to be the most comprehensive since the 1990s, present an array of statistics on American sexuality and some of what they indicate is that what we once thought was abnormal is really normal in our sex lives today. For example, contrary to the traditionalist view that back in the good old days, the only sex was married sex, most Americans did not in the past nor do they today enter marriage as virgins. Youth as young as 14 are engaging in some sort of sexual behavior, including sexual intercourse. For instance, Indiana University reports in its National Survey of Sexual Health and Behavior (Reece, et al., 2010), that among 14–15-year-olds, 9 percent of males and 11 percent of females reported having vaginal intercourse in the previous year. And, by age 17, 40 percent of the males had engaged in sexual intercourse in the past year. These teens' other reported sexual activities included masturbation, both alone and with a partner; oral sex, heterosexual and from/to a same-sex partner; and penis/anus insertion both heterosexual and same-sex. This versatility in sexual behavior occurs across the age spectrum. While vaginal intercourse is still the most common sexual behavior among adults, much of their sexual behavior does not involve intercourse. For example, oral sex is the second most common sexual activity for both women and men (80 percent and 83 percent, respectively). And as much as 40 percent have had anal sex. In addition, people across all ages, report 41 different combinations of sexual acts they engage in.

Speaking about premarital sex and virginity, 95 percent of Americans have had premarital sex, yet almost 4 in 10 (36 percent) believe that premarital sex is morally wrong. Looking at premarital sex in terms of age, 99 percent of women and men age 25 and older have had vaginal intercourse. In addition, about 89 percent of women and 90 percent of men in this same age group have had heterosexual oral sex, and 36 percent of women and 44 percent of men have had anal sex with an opposite-sex partner. For those younger, ages 15 to 24, 28 percent say they are virgins, reporting no sexual contact with another person ever (Chandra, et al., 2011; Gallup, 2011). Although these data indicate that teens and young adults are waiting longer before engaging in sexual activities than they have in the past (up from 22 percent in 2002), these data are not always consistent with the reality of what people actually do. For example, a recent study of the sexuality of young adults whose average age was 22, reported that about 10 percent of those in the study who tested positive for a sexually transmitted infection (STI) reported that they had been abstinent for the past year, and one half of them said that they had never had sex at all (DiClemente, et al., 2011). Reporting not having had sex/abstinence or being a virgin seems inconsistent with the fact of the respondents' STI diagnosis, but it might be very consistent with how many Americans (young and old) define sex or being sexually active today. For instance, an overwhelming majority of teens and young adults do not define oral sex as having sex; if they have engaged in oral sex only, they consider themselves to be a virgin.

According to several sex experts, Americans continue to be curious about the sex lives of others. They want to know how often people have sex, the types of sex they engage in, and whether or not they enjoy it or experience sexual difficulties. Sociologists and other social scientist have long ago shown that there is often a big difference between what people say in surveys and what they actually think or do. Keeping this fact in mind, consider the following facts from recent studies and surveys about contemporary American sexuality.

Why Do We Have Sex? Let Me Count the Ways Although there have been many scholastic attempts to count and describe the positions in which humans have sex, few have systematically counted and catalogued the many reasons that individuals give for getting into those positions. For some people, the motivations for having sex may seem obvious. For others, particularly those who are interested in knowing what is going on in people's minds that leads them to engage in one or another sexual activity, two psychologists at the University of Texas at Austin have provided us with a window into "The Whys of Mating." Based on data collected from a survey of nearly 2,000 college students, the researchers came up with 237 reasons why people have sex from wanting to feel closer to God, to help them fall asleep, keep warm, and burn calories to hurt an enemy, someone dared me, or to change the topic of conversation. Women and men were pretty similar in their responses, but regardless of the reason, men cited it more often than women with the notable exception: Women were more likely than men to say they had sex because they were in love with the person and wanted to express their love for the person (Meston and Buss, 2007). (See Table 6.1 on page 172 for a list of the top 15 reasons and a snapshot of gender differences.)

Are You Having Enough Sex? The average American, age 18 and older, has sex 120 times a year—2.3 times a week and report very high levels of sexual satisfaction. This result notwithstanding, almost two-thirds (63 percent) still wish they were having sex more frequently. Additionally, Americans report a high comfort level in exploring with and learning from their partners. Moreover, single people clearly report having sex more frequently than married people, 130 and 109 times a year, respectively (Trojan U.S. Sex Census, 2010).

If You Want More Sex—Consider Moving It seems that how often we have sex depends on where we live. For instance, people living in the Northeast report the highest frequency of having sex, averaging about 130 times a year, or 2.5 times a week. At the other end of the spectrum, people living in the South have sex the least often (114 times a year, or 2.1 times a week). In the middle, people in the Midwest have sex 125 times a year, and those living in the West, 120 times a year. Metropolitan centers such as Los Angeles and Houston have the most sex, 135 and 125 times, respectively, while people living in cities such as Philadelphia and Dallas have the least amount of sex—99 and 104 times, respectively (Trojan U.S. Sex Census, 2010).

Sex by the Numbers—Good Sex or Simply by the Numbers? Although 11 percent of women and men ages 15 to 44 say that they have had no sexual contact with another person ever, many of the remaining individuals in this age group are actively sexually engaged. For example, the median number of opposite sex partners in a lifetime is 3 for females and 5 for males.

TABLE 6.1 The Whys of Having Sex: The Top 15 Reasons and Counting . . . by Gender

Why people have sex is important but an understudied topic. Historically it has been assumed that humans have sex for simple reasons such as reproduction. However, as it turns out our motivations to engage in sex are far richer than we might have imagined. Is your motivation(s) to have sex listed?

Women

1. I was attracted to the person.
2. I wanted to experience the physical pleasure.
3. It feels good.
4. I wanted to show my affection to the person.
5. I wanted to express my love for the person.
6. I was sexually aroused and wanted the release.
7. I was "horny."
8. It's fun.
9. I realized I was in love.
10. It was "in the heat of the moment."
11. I wanted to please my partner.
12. I desired emotional closeness (i.e., intimacy).
13. I wanted the pure pleasure.
14. I wanted to achieve an orgasm.
15. It's exciting, adventurous.

Men

1. I was attracted to the person.
2. It feels good.
3. I wanted to experience the physical pleasure.
4. It's fun.
5. I wanted to show my affection to the person.
6. I was sexually aroused and wanted the release.
7. I was "horny."
8. I wanted to express my love for the person.
9. I wanted to achieve an orgasm.
10. I wanted to please my partner.
11. The person's physical appearance turned me on.
12. I wanted the pure pleasure.
13. It was "in the heat of the moment."
14. I desired emotional closeness (i.e., intimacy).
15. It's exciting, adventurous.

Source: Cindy M. Meston and David M. Buss. 2007. "Why Humans Have Sex." *Archives of Sexual Behavior,* (August). New York: Springer. 36, 477–507.

At each end of the numbers scale, after abstinence, 22 percent of women and 15 percent of men report having only one sexual partner in their lifetime. At the high end of the scale, 8 percent of women and 21 percent of men report having 15 or more sexual partners over their lifetime. Interestingly, among the 94 percent of women who identify as exclusively heterosexual, 9 percent say that they have had some same-sex contact. Similarly, among the 96 percent of men who identify as exclusively heterosexual, 3 percent say they have had some same-sex contact.

A look at sex by the numbers in terms of race and gender, 11 percent of African American women and Latinas and 12 percent of White women say that they have had no sexual contact with another person ever, compared to 10 percent of African American men, 8 percent of Latinos, and 12 percent of White men. At the other end of the numbers scale, 4 percent of African American females, 2 percent of Latinas, and 4 percent of White women report having 15 or more sexual partners in their lifetime. For men, 7 percent of African American men, 5 percent of Latinos, and 5 percent of White males have had 15 or more sexual partners in their lifetime (Chandra, et al., 2011). (See Table 6.2 for more Sex by the Numbers.)

I Can('t) Get (No) Satisfaction While most Americans have sex frequently, frequency is not synonymous with satisfaction.

TABLE 6.2 Sex by the Numbers

3	Percentage married but abstinent
12	Percentage of married people who sleep alone
20	Percentage of Americans who have had sex with a coworker.
20	Number of minutes an average couple spends on foreplay
29	Percentage of people who had sex on their first date
41	Percentage of teens 18–19 years old who know little or nothing about condoms
44	Percentage of college students who masturbate
48	Percentage of women who have faked an orgasm at least once in their life
60	Percentage of people who find sex to be fun, enjoyable and an important part of life
63	Percentage of people who say sex is better on vacation
75	Percentage of teens 18–19 years old who know little or nothing about the contraceptive pill
80	Percentage of sexually active teenage boys who say they use a condom
84	Percentage of women who say they have sex to get their man to help out around the house
90	Percentage of women who crave more tenderness from their sexual partner
200	Number of calories the average person burns during 30 minutes of sexual intercourse

Sources: Sarah Jio. 2010. "Sex By The Numbers," *Woman's Day.* www.womansday.com/Articles/Sex-Relationships/Sex/Sex-by-the-Numbers.html. Accessed October 7, 2011. Manolith Team. Feb. 15, 2010. "Sex: By the Numbers," *Manolith Men's Magazine.* www.manolith.com/2010/02/15/sex-by-the-numbers/. Accessed July 23, 2011.

For instance, only about one half (48 percent) of sexually active adults say they are satisfied with their sex lives. Sexual satisfaction, it seems, is based on one's relationship status. Contrary to the popular myth, our sex lives do not necessarily diminish once we say, "I do." For instance, married couples report much higher levels of satisfaction compared to singles, although singles report having sex more often. If orgasm is in any way related to good sex or sexual satisfaction, the ways in which this pinnacle is achieved varies by gender. For instance, men are more likely to experience orgasm when vaginal intercourse is involved whereas women are more likely to experience orgasm when they engage in a variety of sexual acts including oral sex (Reece, et al., 2010).

Kinky Sex? While many people favor having sex in a bed (theirs or someone else's), clearly the bed isn't the only place people enjoy and/or prefer to have sex. While there is probably varying agreement on what constitutes kinky sex, three-fourths of the population admits to experimenting in order to enhance their sex lives. Even those who describe themselves as traditional desire a more adventurous sex life and are open to experimenting to make this happen. From sexual fantasies to vibrators, they embrace and use a variety of methods to enhance the sexual experience for themselves as well as their partners. While it might not seem so romantic, for almost one-half of the population, having sex in a car is the most sexually exciting place they have had sex. Another one-third cite someone else's bed as the most sexually exciting place they have had sex. Women and men differ on the question of having sex in a place they have not yet tried. One in four women, for instance, say the beach or by the sea is a place they would like to have sex but have not yet tried, whereas one in three men say on an airplane (Trojan U.S. Sex Census, 2010) .

S-E-X-Y Talk Americans spend a tremendous amount of time talking about sex both on- and off-line. Not only are they sexting (19 percent), one in five also say that they have engaged in cyber sex; one-fifth have had sex with someone they met over the Internet, 10 percent have discussed sex on Facebook and/or Twitter; and almost one-half of Americans talk about sex with friends of the same gender and 28 percent talk about sex to friends of the opposite gender. Moreover, 15 percent of adults say they have received a sexually suggestive nude or nearly nude photo or video on their cell phone, and 6 percent say they have sent such a text. Among those ages 18 to 29, the prevalence rises to 32 and 23 percent, respectively. Interestingly, women are more likely than men to send nude photographs and sexually explicit text messages than men. Women are also more likely than men to meet people in real life after meeting them online (Trojan U.S. Sex Census, 2010; Pew Internet and American Life Project, 2010; Paul, 2011).

Your Cheating Heart Monogamy is something most people say they believe in and want for themselves. Most surveys, past and present, show that a high percentage of people think monogamy is important to marriage, saying when they marry they intend to be monogamous, and that cheating or having an affair is morally wrong. In a 2011 Gallup Poll, for example, 91 percent of Americans said that married women and men having an affair is morally wrong. However, the belief in monogamy as an ideal does not necessarily translate into monogamy as a reality. Because of the inherent secrecy of "cheating," it is difficult to determine with precise accuracy just

how many people have an affair outside of a committed relationship or marriage. The statistics on the subject vary reflecting this difficulty. In general, it is estimated that roughly 30 to 60 percent of married adults will engage in infidelity at some time during their marriage. Men are found to cheat more often than women; however, women under age 30 are just as likely as men under the age of 30 to cheat (Marcotte, 2011; "Facts and Statistics About Infidelity," 2011).

According to some experts, technology has also contributed to the rising incidence of infidelity. It seems that the Internet has created a whole new way for people to cheat. For example, there are Web Sites specifically designed to help married people cheat on their partners. A variety of studies report that around 6 in 10 people have used the Internet to flirt, 4 in 10 people have engaged in explicit online sexual conversation, and 5 in 10 have made phone contact with someone they chatted with online. In addition, about 10 percent of Internet users are addicted to cybersex, and 31 percent of people have had an online sexual conversation that led to real-time sex. Research has shown that hypersexual online behavior has led to increasing infidelity. However, while it is easy to find sexual interests online, some people do not consider online affairs to be cheating. This is particularly so for men, 54 percent of whom do not believe that online affairs are cheating. Others, especially women, believe that flirting online demonstrates unfaithfulness and that just because cybersex is virtual does not mean that it isn't infidelity. For those who take this position, they believe that cheating does not have to be physical; it can also come in the form of emotional betrayal (CBS News, 2011; "Infidelity Statistics," 2011).

In general, the lower the marital satisfaction and the lower the frequency and quality of marital intercourse, the greater the likelihood of extramarital sexual relationships. Most people indicate that they became involved in an extramarital relationship because they felt that something was missing in their marriage or that their marital sexual life was boring. Early and later studies of marital infidelity, however, have noted important attitudinal differences between husbands and wives who engage in extramarital relationships. Most wives indicated that they were dissatisfied with some aspect of their marriage, most often the expressive area. Some wives reported that loneliness was the primary reason for engaging in an extramarital relationship. They also reported an improvement in their marital relationship, which they believed to be a direct result of their participation in an extramarital relationship. Husbands, on the other hand, more often said that they participated in extramarital relationships because of the sexual excitement of such a liaison or the sheer availability of another woman. In addition, women tend to justify extramarital affairs when they are in love, whereas men do when the affair is not for love (Covel, 2003a; Rathus, Nevid, and Fichner-Rathus, 2008).

The frequency and nature of an extramarital relationship will vary not only with age, race, class, and other structural factors, but also in terms of sexual orientation. Extramarital relationships are not just about physical sex. Nor are they always of short duration or meaningless. However, they are always about the violation of commitment, trust, and intimacy unless, of course, the couple has an *open* marriage in which they agree to have openly acknowledged and independent sexual relationships with persons other than each other. What constitutes infidelity varies across gender, but both women and men agree that infidelity can include a range of behaviors, sexual intercourse being only one. For some people, lustfully thinking about another person also constitutes infidelity (Covel, 2003a).

What is ironic about the incidence of marital infidelity is that, as a nation, we say that such behavior is improper and unacceptable. Yet, a significant number of women and men admit that they have cheated on a partner, either physically or in cyberspace. One-half or more of adults surveyed on the subject say that they know someone who has had an extramarital relationship, and even more believe that half or more of all married men have had an affair (Saad, 2008). In a sense, contrary to the morality of infidelity in the minds of Americans, those who engage in it seem to normalize or, at the very least, rationalize it when it comes to their own personal behavior. However, when high profile celebrities and politicians' assorted infidelities are exposed, the public is appalled and even outraged at their "cheating." As we have discussed in an earlier chapter, there is no short supply of such exposés. One recent example is former New York U.S. Representative Anthony Weiner, a married man with a wife expecting their first child. In 2011, after steadfastly denying for over one week that he had sexted (sent a nude frontal image of himself over Twitter) to a young female college student whom he had met in cyberspace, he finally admitted to the deed. In fact, he went on to admit that he had engaged in a number of "inappropriate" electronic relationships with six different women over the past three years. The outrage over his infidelity was loud, vocal, widespread, and persistent. In its wake, Weiner resigned his seat in Congress. Clearly, then, despite the stigma of marital infidelity, there is an inherent conflict between Americans' moral ideals about marriage and sexual fidelity, what they say about their sexual behavior, and what they actually do.

Although infidelity can be found in every segment of society, we are most aware of it when celebrities, politicians, and other notable people engage in extramarital or relationship affairs. For example, in a highly publicized reveal of infidelity in 2011, California Governor Arnold Schwarzenegger (shown here with his wife Maria Shriver after his election in 2005), admitted to having an extramarital affair over a decade ago with a household staff member (Mildred Patricia Baena) who worked in the family's home for more than 20 years. The affair produced a child, born less than a week apart from Schwarzenegger and Shriver's fourth child, whom Schwarzenegger has been supporting since birth.

More than two decades ago, researcher Lynn Atwater (1982) suggested that a primary reason for extramarital relationships is society's continued unrealistic views on love and the belief in the ability of one person to satisfy all the sexual needs of another person. Can one person totally satisfy another? Why do you think married people today enter into extramarital relationships? Are such relationships ever justified? Why or why not?

Sources: Crary, D. 2010. "Sex Study By National Survey of Sexual Health and Behavior is Biggest Since 1994." (October 4). www.huffingtonpost .com/2010/10/04/sex-study-by-national-sur_n_748751.html (2011, August 2). Fisher, T., Moore, Z., and Pittenger, M. J. 2011. "Sex on the Brain?: An Examination of Frequency of Sexual Cognitions as a Function of Gender, Erotophiloia, and Social Desirability." *Journal of Sex Research, Online,* (April 19). www.tandfonline.com/doi/abs/10.1080/00224499.2011.565429 (2011, August 5). Reece, M., Herbenick, D., Schick, V., Sanders, S., Dodge, B., and Fortenberry, D. 2010. Findings From the National Survey of Sexual Health and Behavior, *The Journal of Sexual Medicine.* Plymouth, MA: Wiley-Blackwell, Vol. 7, Supplement 5. Sex By The Numbers." 2010. *Manolith.com.* (February 15). www.manolith.com/2010/02/15/Sex-by-the-numbers/. Trojan. 2010. U.S. Sex Census. 2010. *Trojan Condoms.com.* www.trojancondoms.com/ ArticleDetails. aspx?ArticleId=25 (2011, July 31).

Gender Differences Not surprisingly, as in other areas of life, women and men diverge on some issues of sex and sexuality.

- Men (50 percent) are much more likely than women (32 percent) to say that they enjoy both oral and penetrative sex equally;
- Seven in ten men compared with five in ten women indicate that they would like to have more sex;
- Women and men differ on their favorite sex position: the missionary position is the favorite for both genders but after that they diverge; the next favorite for women is the reverse missionary position and for men it is doggy style;
- Men are much more likely than women to discuss their sex life on Facebook or Twitter;
- Forty percent of women compared to only 22 percent of men are against hooking up;
- Thirty one percent of men describe themselves as sexually liberal compared to 16 percent of women;
- Men tend to think more often about sex than women, and women overwhelmingly (9 in 10 women) care more about love and intimacy than orgasm.

Clearly, today sex plays a much bigger role in some people's lives than others. Not everyone is actively engaged in sexual behavior. Some people are publicly and actively disengaging in sex. Although there is some debate about who is a virgin and how we define virginity as well as the impact of abstinence versus sex education in the nation's schools on our sexual behavior, the fact is that today there is still a visible movement to promote sexual chastity directed particularly at the nation's teenagers and young adults. For those in this movement, there is no debate; chastity and virginity means refraining from *all* sexual activity before marriage and being faithful to one's spouse after marriage. A leading spokesperson for this movement today is Bristol Palin (daughter of former Republican Governor of Alaska, Sarah Palin). Although she fell short of the movement's goals and proclamations about abstinence, after becoming a single mother at age 18, Bristol became a public advocate for sexual abstinence for unmarried teens and is a paid speaker on the subject of teen pregnancy (Kotz, 2009).

The movement for sexual abstinence is not limited to a focus on youth. In a contemporary culture saturated with sexual messages and innuendo, a small minority of older adults live sex-free lives (practice celibacy). Calling themselves "born-again virgins," they embrace abstinence not so much on moral or religious grounds but to cleanse themselves, recharge their spirit, and reassert self-control. There are no figures for how many Americans are born-again virgins. However, the bulk of them are women, with only a small number of men among the ranks (La Ferla, 2000).

A growing number of women today are becoming, in a sense, born-again virgins not as a result of abstinence but as a result of getting cosmetic surgery on the most private part of their anatomy—their genitals. Genital cosmetic surgery—hymenoplasty specifically (re-creating the intact hymen)—is not new. Historically, it has been a big business for sexually active girls who come from families who place a high value on being a virgin at marriage. It is said to be especially prevalent among first-generation immigrants, especially Muslims. According to a Texas female board-certified obstetrician (Hailparn, 2005), there are typically three groups of women interested in hymenoplasty: (1) women who must be certified virgins before getting married or they may face being ostracized by their family or even death; (2) women who are raped or abused and stripped unwillingly of their virginity and now want to give it willingly to a partner of their choice; and (3) women who simply want a "prettier look" or to give their significant other that "virgin-again" experience.

Joining the ranks of the millions of American women today who inject Botox, reshape noses, augment breasts, lift buttocks, and suck away unwanted fat, close to 30,000 American women are exploring and getting genital plastic surgery to tighten vaginal muscles, plump up or shorten the labia, remove fat from the pubic area, and most notably, to restore the hymen (to regain their virginity), often against doctor's suggestions that such cosmetic surgery is unnecessary. The majority, if not all, of these women fall into category number three above which is a classic example of the sexual double standard. Procedures that were once reserved to address medical problems such as incontinence, congenital malformations, or injuries related to childbirth are now being marketed by some gynecologists and plastic surgeons as "vaginal rejuvenation" and designed solely to enhance sexual satisfaction and improve the look of the genitals. Some physicians as well as others believe that the cultural emphasis on a youthful look, fashions such as flimsier, more revealing swimsuits, the Brazilian bikini wax, and more exposure to nudity in magazines, movies, and on the Internet are key factors driving women to pay anywhere from $3,500 to $8,000 dollars for this surgery, the most popular of which is the tightening of the vaginal muscles, or vaginoplasty, and reduction of the labia minor, called labiaplasty.

Although many women are motivated to undergo vaginal cosmetic surgery to improve or increase their sex lives, there is no scientific evidence to suggest that such surgery will actually produce these women's desired results. To the contrary, after such surgery, for instance, the tightening of the vaginal muscles, sexual intercourse could be painful if the vaginal muscles are too snug. Other possible risks from genital cosmetic surgery are painful scarring or nerve damage that could result in loss of sensation or hypersensitivity. What about men? According to some doctors, men probably would be flocking to their offices for their own genital surgery if such procedures as penile enlargement were not fraught with complications and unintended outcomes.

Bristol Palin (daughter of former Governor of Alaska Sarah Palin), became a single mother at age 18. Despite intense public scrutiny and strong criticism for falling short of the goal of abstinence for which her mother advocated, Bristol, shown here with her son Tripp, has gone on to become a leading public advocate and paid speaker on the subject of abstinence.

What do you think? Do you know women or men who have had genital cosmetic surgery? If yes, what reasons do they give for having such surgery? Would you consider such surgery for nonmedical reasons? If yes, why would you? If no, why not?

Contemporary Sexuality in a Global Context What is people's sexual behavior like around the globe? How does it compare to what Americans say and do sexually? At what age do people have their first sexual experience? Over the last decade, global sex surveys have reported on the sexual well-being—a balance of physical, emotional, and sociological factors; getting the most from one's sex life and feeling confident and happy about oneself (Durex, 2011)—of individuals in countries across the world. For instance, globally, the average age at which virginity is lost is 17. This statistic varies across countries with Iceland and Germany reporting the youngest age (15) and India and Vietnam reporting the oldest age at 19. In the United States, the average age at which virginity is lost is 16 (Manolith, 2010). Like Americans, people around the world are adventurous when it comes to their sex lives, which include a range of sexual behaviors from vaginal sex and massage to oral and anal sex. Over one-half of people believe it is beneficial to bring experimentation into their sex lives. Globally, there is a high incidence of oral sex across all age groups, and there is also a high degree of anal sex among people other than gay men. Australia and Brazil lead the way with the most people who engage in oral sex, while Switzerland leads the way with the most people having sexual fantasies and Thailand has the greatest percentage of people who are most likely to prefer using erotic materials to enhance their sexual activities. However, the range and number of sexual activities people engage in varies significantly by country. Greece, for example, is identified as the sexiest country in the world, with Greeks reporting engaging in the widest range and number of sexual activities and Nigerians engaging in the least on both counts. Not only are some people globally willing to experiment to enhance their sex lives, almost half of them expect that people will become increasingly more experimental in their sex lives over the next decade, and Mexicans and Thais are the most optimistic in this regard (Durex, 2011).

On average, 67 percent of adults have sex weekly. Greeks are the most sexually active with almost one-fourth having sex five or more times a week compared to only 10 percent of people globally. Although the number of sexual partners varies considerably from individual to individual, the global averages for heterosexual females and males are 7 and 13, respectively. For gays, the average number of male sexual partners is a whopping 108, whereas for lesbians the average number of female partners is 11. And for bisexual women, the average number of female partners is 3 and male sexual partners is 13 compared to 14 and 21, respectively, for bisexual men. Looking specifically at heterosexual women and men in various countries around the world, men have more sexual partners over their lifetime than women. A notable exception is New Zealand women who average 20 sexual partners compared to 17 for New Zealand men. Otherwise, Austrians are the most sexually experienced topping the numbers scale with 17 and 29 sexual partners for women and men, respectively. At the other end, Chinese have had the fewest sexual partners with an average of 2 for Chinese women and 4 for men (Durex, 2010).

As we have already learned, a little better than one-half of Americans are not completely satisfied with their sex lives. But what about globally—are people around the world as satisfied with their sex lives as they could be or want to be? Not so, says some global surveys that describe global sexual satisfaction as mediocre. It seems that although people around the world are experimenting and trying different ways to make their sex lives better and more satisfying, sex could be a lot better. While 60 percent of those surveyed think that sex is fun and enjoyable and a significant part of their lives, only 44 percent report being fully satisfied with their sex lives. At one end of the scale, Nigeria is the most sexually satisfied nation in the world followed by Mexico, India, and Poland. The least sexually satisfied people in the world are Japanese, with only 15 percent of those surveyed describing their sexual lives as satisfying. (See the In Other Places Box.) Two-thirds of people worldwide feel that they don't have sex often enough and one-half say their sex lives lack excitement. However, as with sexual satisfaction generally, people in Nigeria and Mexico say their sex life is as exciting as it could be, whereas only 10 percent of Japanese and 36 percent of the French say the same (Durex, 2011).

Given the level of global dissatisfaction people experience relative to their sex lives, the questions arises: Do partners talk to one another about their dissatisfaction or about what it would take to make the relationship more satisfying? Here again, according to survey data, the answer seems to be no. For example, less than 6 in 10 people say they are comfortable telling their partner what they like sexually. The most confident in this respect are Mexicans, Greeks, Indians, and Spaniards with the British being the least comfortable and least sharing of all people in Europe. There are many factors that contribute to sexual satisfaction, one of the most important of

In Other Places

NO SEX, PLEASE . . .

In 2005, the number of deaths in Japan exceeded births. With a record low birth rate, coupled with policies that virtually forbid immigration, the population shrank for the first time since Japan began compiling data in 1899 (Pesek, 2006). It seems, however, that the birth rate is not the only thing spiraling downward in Japan. Marriage and sexual intimacy are also on the decline. In a 2007 survey, condom maker Durex found that the Japanese have the least active sex lives. Japan ranked last among 41 countries in terms of frequency of sex: The average Japanese had sex only 48 times a year. Ranking number 37 out of 41, people in Hong Kong had sex only a bit more often—78 times a year (Durex, 2005, 2007). In addition, according to some reports, condom shipments are down 40 percent in Japan since the early 1990s and love-hotel check-ins are down at least 20 percent since the end of the 1990s (Wiseman, 2004).

Japanese women and men are finding relationships today to be too messy, tiring, and potentially humiliating to bother with them anymore. According to some analysts, this downward trend in marriages, births, and "hanky-panky" has important implications for the country's future. For instance, in 2000, 54 percent of women and almost 70 percent of men between 25 and 29 years of age were unmarried. This behavioral pattern could have a devastating impact on the birth rate as conservative Japanese society frowns on having children outside marriage. The declining birth rate means that fewer working-age Japanese will be around to support a growing population of elderly. In addition, Japan's faltering sex drive and record low birth rates do not bode well for the country's economy. A declining workforce will reduce tax revenue, making it harder to pay the country's national debt. Things have gotten so bad that a popular weekly Japanese newsmagazine exhorted Japanese youth to abstain, not from sexual activity, but from abstinence. That is, they were encouraged to have more sex (Pesek, 2006; McCurry, 2005; Wiseman, 2004).

The gender divide appears to be growing among Japan's young 20- and 30-somethings—women and men in their 20s and 30s are increasingly going their separate ways. Women, for instance, are off to designer boutiques and chic restaurants with their mothers or girlfriends while men are socializing with their buddies from work or spending their time in front of their computer screens romancing virtual women. Better educated, more widely traveled, and raised in more affluence than their mothers, Japanese women no longer feel bound by the cultural tradition that encourages marriage by age 25. A growing number of these women are either postponing marriage or deciding to not marry at all. They are weighing marriage against what they see as important shortcomings of love and marriage Japanese style: The husband works long hours and afterwards, instead of coming home, he parties late into the night with his buddies from work. The wife, on the other hand, is expected to stay home, do the domestic chores, and nurture the young. If the children are unruly, it is her fault—she is a "bad" mother. If her husband has an affair, she is a "bad" wife (Wiseman, 2004).

Although Japanese society still thinks there is something wrong with women who are not married by age 25 or 30, the increasingly well-educated and career-oriented Japanese woman, seeking a career or already firmly established in one, is unwilling to give it up and lead the traditional life of a Japanese housewife. For their part, Japanese men seem bewildered by the rising assertiveness of Japanese women. Rather than risk rejection or expend the energy necessary to maintain a modern intimate relationship, many Japanese men simply pay for affection and sex in the country's massive sex trade—hostess bars and brothels. Others prefer virtual women online. Cybersex affords these men a quick way to get sexual satisfaction (Wiseman, 2004).

The Japanese gendered sexual disconnect is most telling in the following statistics: (1) The rate of marriage is declining—54 percent of Japanese women in their late 20s are still single, a 74 percent increase since 1985. In a 2004 survey, one-half of single Japanese women between ages 35 and 54 said they had no intention of ever marrying. (2) The number of births in Japan have steadily declined since 2000—Japan's birth rate hit a record low of 1.29 in 2003 and remained unchanged in 2004—one of the lowest rates in the world. This rate is well below the minimum 2.08 needed to compensate for deaths. As a consequence of the declining birth rate, Japan's population is expected to peak soon and then decline rapidly. (3) The divorce rate has nearly doubled over the past decade, with some divorcing women blaming sexually inactive husbands for the breakup (McCurry, 2005; Foreign Press Center Japan, 2005).

Sexless marriages—a phenomenon that some experts describe as one of the factors pushing Japan toward a demographic disaster—have greatly exacerbated the problem between the sexes. For instance, a survey of Japanese women found that more than one-fourth had not had sex with their husbands in the past year. Each year, 200 women seek clinical help because they have not had sex with their husbands in up to 20 years, and some have never had sex with their husbands. They love their husbands but the problem, it seems, is that their husbands have either lost interest in sex or did not want sex from the start. According to Kim Myong-gan, who runs a clinic for women in sexless marriages, "Many men think of their wives as substitute mothers, not as women with emotional and sexual needs" (quoted in McCurry, 2005:1). In response to these women's needs, the clinic head offers them a short-term unconventional solution: After an initial, rather costly counseling session, he shows them photos of 45 men, the majority of whom are professionals in their 40s. The women are invited to go on dates with these men, and then, in almost all cases, can arrange regularly assigned meetings in hotel rooms. Accused of running nothing short of a male prostitution ring, the head of the clinic dismisses such charges, saying that the men are sex volunteers who pay half the hotel and restaurant bills, therefore there is absolutely nothing wrong with this arrangement (McCurry, 2005).

There are a variety of Web sites and links that claim to provide "facts" and "figures" concerning human sexuality. Based on the topics covered in this chapter, choose one and explore it in more depth. Write a brief paper outlining what you have found about human sexuality. Using your sociological imagination, explain the issue by placing it in the broader social context of American sexual norms and values, and ask your professor if you can present it to your class. Pay particular attention to the reliability of the source and the validity of the data and figures. How does the information you gather fit what is presented in this chapter?

which is achieving orgasm. Globally, only 48 percent of people say they usually reach orgasm during sex. Of those reaching orgasm, twice as many men (64 percent) as women regularly have orgasms. Sexual satisfaction appears to peak between the ages of 20 and 34; however, it continues to be important to most people throughout the life cycle with people age 65 and older still having sex more than once a week. Achieving sexual satisfaction begins with one's very first sexual experience, according to almost 4 in 10 people (37 percent). Having a positive first sexual experience is linked to having an effect on satisfaction levels later in life (Durex, 2011).

One recent global sexual survey found a high level of agreement among people across a number of countries about the desire to be in a monogamous relationship and the difficulty of forgiving a cheating partner. Forgiveness for infidelity, for instance, does not seem to come easy for most people no matter what their culture. For example, on average, only 28 percent of singles around the world say they could forgive a cheating partner. Similarly, only 31 percent of American singles say they would forgive a cheating partner, while the remaining singles say "no way." Germans are the most forgiving (35 percent), and Danish singles are the least forgiving (23 percent). On the other hand, the majority of singles in the United States, Sweden, France, Denmark, and Germany think that a cheater can change; however, the majority of singles in Italy, the UK, and Australia say "once a cheater, always a cheater" (Zoosk, 2011).

Given so much talk about sex, we should bear in mind that most people do not engage in sexual activities and behaviors simply for the sake of it. Rather, most people today both in the United States as well as globally are looking for the softer side of sex, more quality time with their partners, more romance, respect, and a sense of security in their sexual relationships (Durex, 2011). On a lighter side, it is interesting to learn the facts and figures of sexual expression (see Applying the Sociological Imagination box).

Sexuality as Social Learning

How do we become sexual beings? Anthropologists have long shown that human sexuality is defined and learned within a particular cultural context. What constitutes sexuality, then, will vary from one culture to another. In this section, we consider sexual behavior as a learned social product.

Since the late nineteenth century, when Sigmund Freud first introduced his beliefs about the nature of human sexuality, the general public as well as professionals such as psychologists, social workers, and sex therapists have been influenced by his theories of human sexuality. According to Freud, the sex drive, which he viewed as a biologically determined force, is the motivator for all human behavior. Humans have innate sexual desires that require gratification. Such desires cannot go unchecked in a society, however, or they would lead to uncontrolled sexual activity, which in turn would generate social chaos. Thus, through its sexual codes, society forces the individual to repress these desires or channel them into sexually appropriate behaviors.

Even if we could confirm that an innate sexual drive exists in human beings, it seems clear from research across academic disciplines that this drive is given shape and direction by culture. The sexual feelings and desires we experience may seem innate, natural, and beyond our control, but we are not born knowing how to think, feel, or behave sexually. Cultural norms prescribe (tell us what we should do) and proscribe (tell us what we should not do) our sexual behavior. They determine what is or is not sexually attractive and stimulating, why we should or should not engage in sexual behavior, and how we should or should not feel sexually.

Human sexual behavior is not unlike other behavior. It does not come naturally; rather, it is socially constructed. From this point of view, then, what Freud commonly referred to as the *sex drive* is really something we have learned in a particular social environment. Like other behaviors, our sexual behavior is guided by cultural scripts similar to those that guide the actions of actors. These **sexual scripts** are simply our society's guidelines or blueprints for defining and engaging in sexual behaviors. We begin learning these scripts very early in life through the process of socialization. In learning our culture's sexual guidelines, we in effect create or invent our capacity for sexual behavior.

SOURCES OF SEXUAL LEARNING

In earliest childhood, as we are learning other important norms of our culture, we are also learning about our sexuality, first from **significant others,** such as parents, friends, relatives, and religious figures, who play an important role in our lives, and later from the point of view of **generalized others,** that is, the viewpoint of society at large. We also learn about our sexuality in school and from the mass media.

Some of the cultural information about our sexuality is consciously presented and learned; much of it, however, we learn unconsciously.

Learning Sexuality in the Family Many authorities on early childhood behavior believe the family is the first and most significant agent of socialization. Where sexuality is concerned, however, survey data during the last decade suggested that children learn very little from their parents. Although parents overwhelmingly (98 percent) believe that they should be the ones to teach their children about sex, only 24 percent believe that they are actually the ones to do so. Rather, they think that the major source of their children's knowledge about sex comes from peers and/or the media. Previous research, however, indicate that most young people rank their parents as their most preferred source of information about sex and sexuality and a key influence in their learning about sex. This fact notwithstanding, only 40 percent of teens today say they talk with their parents about sex on a regular basis. Some researchers suggest that these may be the children of parents who grew up during the sexually liberal era of the 1960s and 1970s and thus are better able to communicate with their children about sex based on their own values and experiences (Fogarty and Wyatt, 2009).

Although almost all teens and adults agree that it would be easier for teens to delay sex and prevent teen pregnancy if teens were able to have more open, honest conversations about these topics with their parents, many parents still feel ashamed, intimidated, and fearful of broaching the subject with their teens. In addition, many parents think their children know more about sex than they actually know and some even think their children know more about sex than they, as parents, do. Other parents report that they do not know what to say to their children about sexuality, how to say it, or when to start the conversation so they either say nothing or their conversations involve a brief discussion of rudimentary information about reproduction concerning "where babies come from" or the acknowledgment that females have a vagina and males have a penis. Many other parents simply don't have enough knowledge or information about important sexual issues such as contraception and sexually transmitted infections. Still other parents wait until their children reach puberty and then give them scant information on bodily changes, sometimes discussing menstruation with girls but rarely, if ever, mentioning things like *wet dreams* to boys. In one study, in response to an interview question about when she would discuss sex with her teenage son, the mother responded that she had no plans to discuss sex with her son until he was ready to go to college.

Because some parents feel uncomfortable discussing sex with their children, they sometimes talk about sexuality in negative terms—sex is evil, nasty, dirty—or in the form of prohibitions (such as a negative response when a child touches her or his genitals). Although research indicates that sexual play during late infancy and early childhood is both normal and positive preparation for adult sexuality and harms children only if reacted to negatively, many children are prohibited from engaging in such activities. Some parents also give children a negative feeling about their sexuality by using euphemisms or silly names for the sexual organs (for example, *kitty cat, wiener, pocket book, ding-a-ling*). Children often do not learn the proper name for female and male sexual organs until they are taught by others outside the family. A recent survey report, however, indicate that more and more parents are moving away from such euphemisms and using the actual names to refer to female and male genitals (Center for Advancing Health, 2011).

Researchers have also found that some parents go to great lengths to desexualize their children's lives. They stop touching each other or showing any signs of intimacy when the children are around. They do not discuss sexuality around children except in hushed tones, and they often become embarrassed and speechless when their children ask them a frank question about some aspect of sexuality. Parents who avoid answering their children's questions concerning sexuality may teach their children that sex is something to be ashamed of. At the other end of this continuum, parents can be negative sexual role models if they are sexually promiscuous themselves; initiate sexual activities with youth; have children outside legal marriage; do not supervise their children's coed activities; and overemphasize the sexuality and physical appearance of their daughters.

◉—Watch the **Video** *Sexuality Education Debate* on **myfamilylab.com**

There are many parents who have little problem talking with their children and sharing factual sexuality information with them. They are open and nonjudgmental, putting the sex education of their children into a perspective that encourages asking questions, feeling good about themselves, embracing sexual feelings as a joyful part of life, and developing self-control and good judgment in sexual matters. Indeed, research indicates that when it comes to decisions about sex, parents are more influential than they think. When parents are open and encourage dialogue about sex, contraception, morals, expectations, risks, and responsibilities, adolescents can make better-informed decisions. Teens whose parents communicate with them are more likely than teens of noncommunicative parents to postpone sex and to have sex less often and act more responsibly (use birth control) when they do become sexually active. When teens are given misinformation, no information, or threats about sex, they are far less likely to behave reasonably and responsibly (Sexualityandu.ca, 2010; Rodriguez, 2006). Other

Historically, parents have gone to great lengths to desexualize their children's lives, including presenting themselves as asexual. However, some parents model healthy aspects of love and intimacy whereby they openly touch and show one another affection.

research has indicated that teens of divorced parents are much more likely than those from families with two parents present to engage in premarital sexual intercourse; teens, especially younger teens, who feel close to their mothers are less likely to begin having sex early; and teens whose parents value education are less likely to have sex. Conversely, teens whose mothers are highly religious are no less likely than other teens to start having sex. Similarly, parents who oppose sex education in the schools are less likely to talk openly and honestly with their children about sex (Byers, et al., 2008; *Science Daily*, 2002; Palo Alto Medical Foundation, 2001).

Interestingly, two new trends seem to be emerging among parents with teenagers regarding their children's sexuality: (1) an increasing number of parents are putting their teenage daughters on the pill for a number of reasons, the most prominent of which is to prevent pregnancy; and (2) some parents are encouraging their children to have safe sex by permitting them to have sex at home. Both of these trends have stirred loud and intense debate among the general public (see the Debating Social Issues box).

> What did you learn about sexuality from your parents? Did they discuss the issue with you in an open and honest manner? What information did they leave out? What happened when or if you explored your body? What euphemisms did they use for the genitals?

Gender Differences in Sexual Scripts Parents tend to communicate the content of sexual behavior to their children differently, depending on the sex of the child. Despite changes in attitudes about gender-specific behavior, certain aspects of the double standard remain, and parents continue to pass these on to their children. For instance, girls and boys are given different sexual scripts for understanding how a sexual experience is supposed to proceed and be interpreted. Girls are more likely to have scripts that include romance, whereas for boys sexual attraction tends to outweigh emotional factors. Furthermore, parents tend to be more open with daughters than with sons about reproduction and its relationship to sexual activities as well as the morality of sex. In fact, because females can become pregnant, the sexual scripts they learn tie sexual activity almost exclusively to reproduction and family life. Boys, on the other hand, learn that their sexuality is connected to society's notion of masculinity and their ability to achieve in different areas of life (Arnett, 2003). Many parents also practice a sexual double standard whereby they place more restrictions on their daughters' sexuality than on that of their sons. Thus, female movements, social activities, and friendships are far more guarded and chaperoned than male activities. Researchers have identified several areas of gender difference in traditional sexual scripting including an emphasis on achievement and frequency of sexual activities for males and an emphasis on monogamy and exclusiveness for females (for example, a woman saving herself for marriage or for the one right man in her life).

Despite the liberalization of sexual attitudes over the last several decades and the so-called sexual liberation of women, sexual scripts and gender socialization relative to human sexuality have changed very little. For example, women's bodies continue to be treated differently than men's in advertisements and other areas of popular culture (such as the exploitation of women's bodies in terms of nudity to sell products). Although there is increasing emphasis on and exploitation of male sexuality as well, women remain the primary objects of sexual exploitation.

The gender-based differential sexual script is rooted in the cultural belief that male sexual needs are stronger and more important than female sexual needs. This represents a classic example of the greater power and status given males in American and most other cultures of the world. These messages and scripts continue to shape our sexual behavior. Research continues to show that both women and men accept this double standard. For instance, recently, researchers found that males who engaged in premarital sex were viewed with a higher level of respect than females. Furthermore, males who engaged in premarital sex were perceived to be more assertive than females. Thus, as the old adage goes, the more things change, the more they remain the same (Pichierri and Corcoran, 2005).

Peer Influence Many psychologists and others believe that no influence in a teenager's life is as powerful as peer pressure. When it comes to sex, next to physiological readiness, peer pressure is probably the single most important factor that determines when adolescents become sexually active. For instance, perhaps the strongest predictor of adolescent sexual behavior is the perceived or actual sexual behavior of friends or peers. Adolescents who have close friends who are sexually active are much more likely to become sexually active as well. Some teens feel that they must keep up with their friends, that they have to have sex in order to be popular, more accepted and to gain respect from their peers, or that sex will make their girlfriend or boyfriend happy. Peer pressure to engage in sexual activity is especially strong among young males. For instance, when it comes to the first time they had sexual intercourse, more boys than girls say they were pressured by their friends to have sex. At the same time, almost one-half of sexually active teens say they have done something sexual or felt pressure to do something they weren't ready to do. In this case, female teenagers were more likely than male teenagers to have had these experiences. Although they are not always the most accurate source of information, peers are often helpful to each other. They are typically less judgmental and more open to listening to each other's questions and concerns about their sexuality (Real Sex Education Facts, 2010; Genuis and Genuis, 2006; Kaiser Family Foundation, 2005). Until around age 15, young people report learning about sex equally from parents, peers, and school. After this age, they learn almost twice as much about sex from peers than family; they get an increasing amount of their information about sex from the media and a decreasing amount from school.

The Mass Media Although there are a variety of factors that impact how we view ourselves and others sexually and that contribute to early sexual activity, popular culture and the mass media play a key role in constructing, shaping, and transforming our views and knowledge about sexuality. The changes in media representations of sexuality over the last 50 years are astonishing. No longer do scenes of intimacy involve only married couples who occupy separated beds, where sexual activity is only subtly implied. The media-saturated world in which we live today is one in which sexual behavior is frequent and increasingly explicit as many advertisers have capitalized on the knowledge that "sex sells."

Debating Social Issues

SHOULD PARENTS ALLOW THEIR TEENAGERS TO HAVE SEX IN THEIR HOMES?

In 2011, Elizabeth Hasselbeck (pictured), a part-time contributor to ABC's *Good Morning America*, participated in a televised discussion with parents and teens about an emerging trend where a small but growing number of American parents are allowing their teenage children to have sex at home. While several of the parents said the family home provided their already sexually active teens a "safe" environment to have sex, in a separate discussion with a panel of teens, most of the teens expressed horror and/or discomfort at the thought of having sex with their parents in the other room.

In America today, it seems that everyone has an opinion about sexual behavior, especially adolescent sexuality. An ongoing debate, in this regard, centers on whether or not young people should be taught about sexuality in school-based sex education courses or taught abstinence. The debate over school-based sexuality education centers on one crucial question: whether providing young people with full and accurate information makes them more or less likely to engage in sexual activity. Whereas, proponents of abstinence-only sexuality education believe that youngsters need time-tested principles to live by; that if children are taught about sexuality in school, teachers should teach and reinforce premarital abstinence—that unmarried teens should not be having sex.

When it comes to parents of teens, some do not want to know about their children's sex lives and others do not believe that their children are sexually active. Some parents insist on abstinence. Still other parents believe that their children's sex education should take place at home and some of these parents appear to be pushing the envelope. According to ABC News, an increasing number of parents are beginning to relax their rules about their children's sexuality, especially when it comes to their having sex. At first, it might sound shocking, but some parents are permitting their teens to have sex in the family home, stirring a new debate about adolescent sexuality. They say that if their children are going to have sex, then why not at home? They defend their decision to allow their children to have sex under the home roof by insisting that it is a way to ensure that their teens are having safe sex. On a nationally televised program in 2011, several parents discussed their position saying that if their children wanted to have sex, they should do it at home rather than somewhere else. This, they said, was being a responsible parent. By allowing their adolescents to have sex at home, it gives them access to a cleaner, safer, and more familiar environment than a motel, a parked car, in the park, or wherever they can find. Further, they are better protected, and it can be done without secrecy and guilt (Pflum, 2011).

Critics of these parents argue that teens are not able to handle the emotions and responsibilities that come with being sexually active. Allowing them to have sex in their own bedrooms encourages them to do things that they should wait to do when they are older and more mature. Further, they argue, having sex at home is no safer than the backseat of a car or a hotel room. Others say that it sends the wrong message about responsibility; parents should be promoting abstinence, not encouraging their teens to have sex. Having sex, especially at a young age, opens the door to pregnancy and sexually transmitted infections. These critics argue that programs such as True Love Waits and similar abstinence movements prove that many teens are waiting until marriage to have sex, either out of religious conviction or as a way of protecting themselves from pregnancy and sexually transmitted infections ("There's No Place Like Home . . .," 2011).

What do you think? If you have teenagers, would you encourage/allow your teen daughter or son to engage in sexual activity with their significant others behind closed doors in your house? Even if you don't have teenagers, weigh in on this debate; would you allow your teen or any teen to engage in sexual activity in your house? Conversely, did you grow up or do you currently live in a house where parents allow teens (or at least do not attempt to stop) to have sex? Do you think this is a good idea? Does allowing teens to have sex at home promote safe sex? In your opinion, do the benefits of safe sex and less secrecy and guilt outweigh the costs of allowing teens to have sex at home? Do you think your parents would have allowed you and/or your siblings to have sex in your house? Would you have wanted this privilege? Why? Why not?

Today, we can hear and see sexual talk and portrayals in every form of media. Unfortunately, much of this social construction is inaccurate, distorted, inflated, misleading, or outright false. It is most often a far cry from the ways in which average Americans experience sexuality. According to some analyses, the American media is the most sexually suggestive in the world (Strasburger, 2005). Print and electronic advertising, television, films, music, and increasing graphic sexuality throughout American popular culture are extremely powerful sources of information about sex and human sexuality more generally, some positive and accurate, some negative or incorrect.

Advertisers Advertisers routinely use sexuality—particularly female sexuality—in their advertising copy. Nudity or near nudity is now found in even the more established magazines today. It is commonplace to see undressed or scantily dressed women selling a variety of products, from heavy construction equipment to designer jeans, from candy and watches to cars, boats, and guns. Although it is the female body that is most often sexualized and exploited in ads, increasingly men are shown in print ads and other media as sex objects with super attractive hard and muscular bodies that are unattainable for most men (Lindsey, 2005). Moreover, advertisers are targeting increasingly younger consumers (some as young as age 7) with sexually explicit and mature products—items that in the past were reserved for adult consumers, such as rhinestone bras and sexy, skimpy thong underwear. For instance, Abercrombie and Fitch, who claims to target college students, sexualizes its clothing and advertising for kids (ages 7–14) as well as adults. Many detractors have accused the company of not only selling sex but also promiscuity. Whatever the intention, the ramifications of such sexualized marketing are great, especially for families with young children. Even when teens are not the intended target of advertisers' and retailers' sexualized messages, the ubiquity of such messages influences both the degree to which such advertising and marketing to increasingly younger audiences is acceptable and teenagers' and others' receptivity to and demand for such products (Escobar-Chaves et al., 2004; Ramos, 2002).

Television Similarly, television, considered by some media scholars to be the most influential medium shaping our views of sexuality, routinely depicts sexual situations and behaviors. Sexual content is overt in the content of day- and-nighttime soap operas and talk shows, evening shows and movies, and perhaps most overt on cable channels devoted to sexual movies and shows. They present a never-ending stream of sexual liaisons between family members, friends, and strangers (anybody is fair game); explicit petting; references made to sex and actual simulations of sexual intercourse that are often so realistic that it is difficult to tell that it is just acting. By and large, these images are limited, stereotypical, and one-dimensional, depicting sex as an activity that is only acceptable for the young, single, beautiful, slim, and White heterosexuals. Some researchers, for instance, report that 70 percent of all television shows include some sexual content; over one-fourth (28 percent) of these include explicit sexual content—they average five sexual scenes an hour—and most of the sexual portrayals involve youthful characters from the ages of 18 to 24, with 1 in 10 involving characters under age 18. In addition, most of the sexual action and language occurs between unmarried heterosexual characters.

One study found that unmarried heterosexual characters engage in sexual intercourse four to eight times as much as married characters (Sexinfo, 2006).

On soap operas in particular, sex is romanticized, and few characters are sexually responsible, use condoms, or seem concerned about pregnancy and sexually transmitted infections. On average, there is only one representation of a married couple engaging in sex for every 24 portrayals of unmarried characters engaged in sexual acts (Sexinfo, 2006). These images and messages about the sexuality of single people is grossly exaggerated based on what single people report in various sex surveys and research studies of American sexuality. In addition, when lesbian and gay characters are presented in television programming, they are presented at each of two extremes: either asexual or consumed with sex. The sexual lessons of the media are particularly influential in shaping the sexual views and behaviors of America's youth. For example, adolescents consistently cite the mass media as important sources of sexual information. On average, American teenagers spend more time watching television than any other activity besides sleeping. The average teen watches nearly 22 hours of television per week, mostly without parental oversight. Within this television viewing, the number of sexual messages that young people are given is an estimated 15,000 references per year. Today, more than 75 percent of shows have sexual content, yet less than 15 percent provide responsible sexual information about abstinence, birth control, or the risks of pregnancy or sexually transmitted infections and how they can be prevented, and when sexual activity is appropriate. Rather, the sexual messages that teens receive suggest that sex is a casual pastime with few, if any, consequences (The Media Project, 2011; Sexualityandu.ca, 2010; Strasburger, 2005).

Soap opera portrayals of sex have been found to be particularly influential for teenage girls, who are heavy viewers of soaps and who develop their expectations of what their sex lives might or should be like from watching such programs. Although we do not know the exact influence of the media on young people's sexuality, a large body of evidence indicates that exposure to sexual content in the media accelerates young people's sexual activity and increases their risk of engaging in early sexual intercourse. For example, adolescents whose TV viewing includes a heavy amount of sexual content are twice as likely as others to have had sex by the time they reach their sixteenth birthday. One study found that as many as 8 out of 10 teens say that one reason that they have sex is because TV shows and movies make it seem normal for teens (The Media Project, 2011). Some experts on teen sexuality and the media suggest that the media functions essentially as a "sexual super peer group," and as such, it encourages and pressures teens to have sex by making them believe that everyone is having sex but them, that sex is without risks or consequences, and that birth control is completely unnecessary. Current television programming, especially reality programs such as MTV's *Teen Moms* and *16 and Pregnant*, is criticized by some who suggest that such programs promote rather than discourage early sexual behavior. They cite as evidence, the fact that some industry insiders have said that some teenage girls are so eager to be on reality TV that they are actually getting pregnant just to land an audition (Huff Post, 2011; Luscombe, 2008; Jones, 2006; Brody, 2006).

Despite increasing public concern about the potential health risks of early, unprotected sexual activity, sexually transmitted

The sexual double standard pervades our culture almost to the extent of being unrecognizable. Yet it is apparent in most American institutions as well as throughout popular media such as films where men who have multiple sexual liaisons (like James Bond, portrayed here by Daniel Craig) are depicted as virile, macho, masculine, and powerful—every woman's dream man—while the females they have sexual liaisons with (like Vesper Lynd, portrayed by Eva Green) are depicted as women who are promiscuous or enjoy being sexually dominated.

infections other than HIV and AIDS are almost never discussed, and unintended pregnancies are rarely shown as the outcome of unprotected sex. Abortion is a taboo topic, and same-sex, bisexual, and transgendered youth rarely find themselves represented in the mainstream media. Although a growing number of programs are either devoted entirely to lesbian and gay lifestyles or have incorporated lesbian or gay characters into their plots (for example, *Modern Family*), what Adrienne Rich calls *compulsory heterosexuality* prevails. Despite V-chips, movie ratings, and televised warnings of appropriateness for young people, American teenagers have no trouble getting access to graphic sexual representations and messages. Most have a television in their bedrooms; more than two-thirds live in homes with cable television; and all have access to music, movies, and the Internet (Sexinfo, 2006; Brown and Keller, 2000).

Talk Shows Added to this mix is the influx of daytime talk shows that have deteriorated to a forum for a series of sexually dysfunctional people to air their dysfunctionalities publicly for hours upon hours every day on programs hosted by people such as Jerry Springer and Maury Povich who air salacious episodes about sleaze and sex. Like soap operas, these talk shows attract a very large and youthful audience. Many of the young females in the live audience expose their breasts on camera and on cue to the wild applause of the audience. Many teens indicate that by the time their parents get around to talking to them about sex (if at all), they have already been indoctrinated by the sexual fare on television programs. Critics of these programs argue that the presentation of human sexuality in a sleazy and sensational manner makes the abnormal seem normal and provides audiences with distorted notions of sexuality and perverse role models for the young.

Pressured by critics and lobbies to present more sexually responsible media, some of the people responsible for television

programming have begun adding more depth and accuracy to stories involving sex, ranging from stories about teenage pregnancy, coming to terms with being lesbian or gay, to sensitive portrayals of homosexual youth, lessons in how to put on a condom, and portrayals of teenagers postponing sexual intercourse (Brown and Keller, 2000). In 2008, the Gay and Lesbian Alliance Against Defamation (GLAAD) gave recognition to prime-time television programs such as *Brothers and Sisters*, *Ugly Betty*, and *Desperate Housewives* for "gay-affirming" television programming. In addition, several soap opera executives have explored ways to make "love in the afternoon" more responsible as well. This would include showing that the use of contraceptives is essential, avoiding the linkage of sex with violence, and showing that not all encounters or even relationships result in sex (CitizenLink, 2008).

Films Increasingly since the 1970s, sex and sexual violence have become so explicit in films that a rating system is used to determine the degree of suitability for audiences under a certain age. James Bond films, which were highly popular among the young, routinely depicted women being raped and enjoying it, rather than as an act of criminal violence, especially if the rapist was every woman's assumed dream man—James Bond himself. The sexual double standard is as apparent in the media as it is in other cultural institutions in American society. For instance, though films are full of nudity, women's and men's nude bodies are not shown in the same way. Women are often completely nude, and the view is almost always a frontal view, whereas men are generally semiclad as opposed to completely nude, or their backside is shown. Seldom, if ever, is the penis visible. Moreover, an entire genre of teenage films over the last two to three decades present sex in crude and vulgar detail for teenagers to emulate. These films, like much television programming, typically emphasize casual sex and deemphasize sexual responsibility, sending a message that there is little or no connection between sex, responsibility, and commitment. As with television and music producers, a number of groups are working with Hollywood scriptwriters to encourage more sexually responsible film content.

Music Contemporary music, from popular ballads to rock, heavy metal, rhythm and blues, rap, and hip hop is full of lyrics that are either sexually explicit or convey messages about sexuality that are mixed with messages about love, hate, rejection, loneliness, and violence. Popular music is produced and marketed increasingly to younger teens and preteens while becoming more sexualized. Music videos are full of men grabbing or holding their crotch and gyrating women and men in sexually suggestive clothing, positions, and situations. For example, one of the most popular female singers today, Beyonce, is known as much for her flimsy sexually alluring dress and gyrating hip movements on stage as she is for her singing.

Sex has always been in music. But the increasing concern today is not so much that music artists are singing about sex, but rather what they are saying about sex and how they are saying it. Much of this music is misogynistic, defining women as sex objects, "whores" and "bitches," and appropriate targets for male fantasy, hatred, and violence. Teenagers and other viewers are fed a constant diet of women asking, sometimes begging, to be raped and sodomized. The message, especially to young people, is that "everyone is doing it" so "let yourself go sexually." The increasing link of sex and violence in contemporary music makes sex seem like an act that should be done violently and to degrade women (Brown et al., 2006).

Moreover, a new wave of women's voices and lyrics have been added to the sexually charged music mix. Women rappers are articulating sexual desire and activity in a manner that voices their irreverence for decorum as defined through cultural expectations of the proper behavior for "respectable" women and male expectations of female subordination. Female artists such as Lil' Kim, almost always nearly nude, and with no respect for sexual taboos, holds her crotch, grinds, gyrates, and speaks sexual language that seriously transgresses cultural boundaries of polite respectability and convention. Although some analysts have described this music as libratory, as a deconstruction of the phallocentric male rap and hip-hop lyrics and as an inversion of the sexual gaze to make males the sexual object (Perry, 1995), the fact is, like their male counterparts, female rappers never give the slightest attention to sexual responsibility or safe sex while they are calling for every kind of sex act from cunnilingus to "buck wild" sex. The lack of a caveat concerning the sexual responsibility and protection of self that should accompany this new sexual liberation is problematic for those who emulate this behavior.

Teenagers who listen to sexually explicit music with degrading lyrics are more than twice as likely to be having sex. Such music offers sexual scripts that some adolescents may feel compelled to play out, regardless of whether they are in the female or male role. An alarming set of statistics reported recently comes from a study that found that middle-school-aged boys who watch music videos or pro-wrestling one day a week are 10 percent more likely to have a higher acceptance rate for rape than boys who do not watch any. And boys who watch music videos four days a week and pro wrestling approximately 2 days a week have 70 percent higher odds of endorsing a greater level of rape acceptance. Both music videos and pro wrestling shows are extremely popular with youth, combine violent and sexual content, and glorify individuals who behave violently. Some research, looking at the media's impact on teens across race, has found that although African American teens watch more television than their other racial counterparts, the relationship between exposure to sexual contact in the media and increased sexual activity among adolescents is more pronounced in White youths than Black youths. Black teens are more likely to be influenced by their friends' sexual experiences and their parents' expectations than by what they see in the media (Primack, Douglas, Fine, and Dalton, 2009; Kaestle, Halpern, and Brown, 2007; Brown, et al., 2006).

When we add the popularity and preponderance of ownership of cell phones, smartphones, and iPods to the mix, the potential exposure of teens to sexually explicit music and other sexually explicit content increases even more. While 85 percent of American adults own a cell phone, almost all 18- to 29-year-olds (96 percent) and fully three-fourths (75 percent) of teenagers own cell phones or iPods. Teens whose iPods are full of music with sexual lyrics begin having sex at an earlier age than those who listen primarily to other types of music. The impact these lyrics have on their behavior seems to depend on the way in which the sex is portrayed. For instance, music that depicts women as sex objects and men as sex-driven studs and with explicit references to sex acts is more likely to trigger early sexual behavior than music where the sexual

references and innuendos are veiled and sex is presented as part of a committed relationship.

Internet The diffusion of computer and Internet use has had a phenomenal impact, in a variety of ways, on contemporary sexuality. There is little disagreement that the Internet has dramatically increased the availability of sexually explicit messages and content. Some researchers estimate that there are currently more than 1 million exotic Web sites with chat rooms, video feeds, and cascading porn pop-ups on the Internet (Jerome et al., 2004). In fact, the word *sex* is said to be the most popular search term used on the Internet today. The selling of sex (in a variety of manifestations) via the Internet is particularly troublesome when it comes to today's youth, who are spending a growing amount of time surfing the Internet. Through the Internet, young people (as well as older adults) have access to almost any sexual information there is, in one place, and at any time they want it. To date, it is far easier to find sexually explicit, unhealthy sites on the Internet than it is to locate those that promote sexually responsible behavior in an equally compelling way. Many Internet users, some as young as age 10, report that they have been exposed to unwanted sexual solicitations while online. Others say they inadvertently encountered explicit sexual content. This is particularly compelling given that today, most homes with children in the United States have access to the Internet. Although the Internet generally has many positive features, and cybersex specifically can be used positively to expand our ideas about sex and sexuality and to promote sexually responsible behavior, the dark side of cybersex is the increasing violence and victimization associated with it as a result of the increasing phenomena of online predation, cyberstalking, sexual harassment, pornography, pedophilia, and virtual rape.

Knowledge of children's heavy involvement with computers has led some child pornographers and child molesters to use the Internet as a primary source for contacting children. One in five young people ages 10 to 17 who is on the Internet is exposed to unwanted sexual solicitations and approaches. It is estimated that between the third and tenth grades, 9 out of every 10 children will be exposed to pornography. The majority of adolescents who consciously seek out pornography, both over the Internet and off, are males. According to some reports, the average American male will first view pornography when he is age 11. It is said to be a major form of sex education for boys today and a significant force in shaping the sexual attitudes of an entire generation (Sullivan, 2008; Ybarra and Mitchell, 2005). In 2000, Congress enacted the Children's Internet Protection Act; however, young people remain quite vulnerable and primary targets and victims of the cybersex stalkers and the cybersex industry. This is particularly problematic given that about three in five parents of adolescents and teens do not use controls to block their children's access to (and thus predators access to them) age inappropriate Web sites. The bad news is that according to the small amount of research that currently exists on the subject, the constant exposure to pornography and other sexually explicit materials on the Internet may have the effect of distorting adolescent views about sex (Jerome et al., 2004). The good news is that there is a growing number of Internet sites that promote healthy sexual behavior and provide sound advice on a wide range of intimate and sexuality issues

Human Sexual Expression

Human sexuality is a universal human experience that is the result of a complex interaction of our biology and culture that is evidenced, first, in the fact that regardless of how we choose to express our sexuality, our bodies experience a physiological response pattern when we are sexually stimulated. Next, research is full of testimony that suggests that despite the universality of human sexuality, sexual norms, values, attitudes, and behaviors vary considerably across subgroups with cultures as well as across cultures around the world. The point is that many people view human sexuality simply in terms of sex—sexual intercourse—and, thus a physiological or biological phenomena that compels our sexual thoughts and behaviors and over which we have little or no control. However, the reality is that from the point of view of physical pleasure that one might derive from various sexual activities, we can relate erotically to either sex depending on our feelings (Hite, 1976). Heterosexual intercourse is simply one of many ways to express human sexuality. Human sexual expression covers a wide variety of behaviors ranging from activities involving only the self—**autoeroticism**—to activities involving one or more other individuals, such as "swapping" or group sex.

AUTOEROTICISM

Some of the most common and recognizable forms of autoeroticism are masturbation, sexual fantasy, and erotic dreams. Until recent times, U.S. society placed particularly heavy restrictions on autoeroticism. Today, however, it seems that Americans as well as people around the globe are engaging in a wide variety of sexual behaviors both with a partner and alone.

Masturbation Masturbation involves gaining sexual pleasure from the erotic stimulation of oneself through caressing or otherwise stimulating the genitals. Most people's first experience with sexual pleasure and orgasm is through masturbation. Masturbatory behavior is said to begin in infancy, when children accidentally discover the pleasure to be derived from rubbing, squeezing, caressing, or otherwise stimulating their genitals. For many people, this is the beginning of a lifelong way of expressing their sexuality. Some people describe masturbation as the best sex they have ever had. An old joke observes that 98 percent of people masturbate and the other 2 percent are lying (Castleman, 2009). Joke or not, it seems that almost everyone masturbates. In one national study, for example, 89 percent of females and 95 percent of males reported that they have masturbated (WebMD, 2010). This fact notwithstanding, our culture is remarkably ambivalent about masturbation and other autoerotic behaviors. Some readers of this text might recall that Jocelyn Elders lost her position as U.S. Surgeon General in 1994 because she dared to publicly advocate that masturbation be discussed, and even promoted as "safe sex," as a part of sex education for young people. The outrage, anger, and loathing leveled at her for her position on masturbation cost Elders her job, but it also demonstrated how much we as a society deny the legitimacy of safe sexual expressions such as masturbation for teens and our difficulty accepting sexual feelings and behaviors outside of a spiritual, religious, relational or reproductive context (Risman and Schwartz, 2002). Although masturbation was once regarded as a perversion and a sign of mental illness or something not to speak publicly about, masturbation is now regarded as a normal, healthy sexual activity that is pleasant, fulfilling, acceptable, and safe.

Although most people masturbate, some racial groups seem to do so more than others. For instance, White people report masturbating more than any other racial group, while Blacks, Asian Americans, and Pacific Islanders report masturbating the least. And, contrary to the popular stereotype that masturbation is the sexual province of singles who use it as a way to compensate for the lack of a sexual relationship, even people who are in a sexual relationship with a partner report masturbating. In fact, research shows that people who masturbate the most are usually involved in a sexual relationship (Castleman, 2009).

Masturbation is not limited to the self-stimulation of the genitals; it can also include the self-stimulation of other parts of the body such as the breast, the inner thighs, and the anus. Although masturbation is becoming more common among women, boys and adult men still tend to masturbate more often than girls and women; 1 man in 4 and 1 woman in 10 report masturbating once or more a week. Some studies have found that many women and men in their 70s and older masturbate (Pinkerton et al., 2002). As in other areas of our lives, women and men tend to differ in a number of ways relative to masturbation. For example, women and men differ in terms of their attitudes toward masturbation. For men, masturbation functions more as a supplement to sexual life, whereas for women it functions more as a substitute for intercourse. Females tend to begin masturbation at much later ages than males, sometimes for the first time in their 20s or 30s, whereas males typically begin to masturbate during early adolescence (Lindsey, 2005). Interestingly, Shere Hite (1976) found that most women have more intense and quicker orgasms with masturbation than with intercourse. Other researchers report that women who masturbate have significantly more single and multiple orgasms, greater sexual desire, higher self-esteem, and greater marital and sexual satisfaction; they become sexually aroused faster than women who do not masturbate (Shriver et al., 2002).

Frequently, people continue to masturbate after marriage. Husbands tend to masturbate more often than wives. The majority of wives who masturbate rate their marriage as unsatisfactory. Many married and nonmarried couples participate in mutual masturbatory activities rather than have intercourse. Others find that manual stimulation of the genitals during intercourse heightens the likelihood that both partners will reach orgasm. It is interesting that so many people engage in a behavior that not long ago was thought to cause blindness, dementia (insanity), and a host of other mental and physical ills. So intense were feelings about masturbation in our early history that children's hands and feet were often tied to bedposts to prevent them from masturbating during the night. Various "experts" in the late nineteenth and early twentieth centuries as well as a variety of others blamed masturbation for every kind of human malady from brain damage to blindness, deafness, heart murmurs, and destroying the genitals to acne and bad breath (Wade and Cirese, 1991).

Although many people still consider masturbation to be wrong, sex therapists have found that it serves some important positive functions, such as providing a means for people (especially women) to explore and determine in private what is most sexually stimulating for them. It is also considered to be a good way to experience sexual pleasure and can be done throughout life. Masturbation is only considered a problem when it inhibits sexual activity with a partner, is done in public, or causes significant distress (Castleman, 2009). Despite the benefits of masturbation and the more liberal attitudes toward it today, many people find that their emotional needs are not met through self-stimulation.

Sexual Fantasy and Erotic Dreams Sexual fantasy and erotic dreams, like masturbation, are common methods of auto-eroticism. People use these activities to supplement or enhance a reality that is less exciting than the images they can construct in their minds. Some researchers have suggested that sexual fantasies might help prepare women for experiences that are erotically satisfying. Others suggest that they provide a harmless way for people to release pent-up sexual feelings or escape a boring sexual life. Whatever their particular function, fantasies help maintain emotional balance in the individual. More males than females engage in sexual fantasy and erotic dreaming, and they do so more often. Over one-half of men (54 percent) report that they fantasize about sex several times a day. Another 43 percent fantasize about sex several times a week. In comparison, only 19 percent of women have sexual fantasies several times a day, while more than two-thirds (67 percent) do so a few times a week (Langer, Arnedt, and Sussman, 2004).

Male fantasies appear to differ from female fantasies in that males tend to fantasize situations in which they are strong and aggressive and in which the sexual activity itself is basically impersonal. Women, on the other hand, tend to have more romantic, passive, and submissive fantasies. The most frequent fantasies for both women and men involve oral sex and sex with a famous person (Patterson and Kim, 1991). Men also frequently fantasize about having sex as part of a threesome. Beyond the two similarities between the genders, there are some interesting differences in the frequency of different types of sexual fantasies (see Table 6.3).

Erotic dreams, often referred to as nocturnal dreams with sexual content, frequently lead to orgasm during sleep. This phenomenon is referred to as **nocturnal emissions** or **wet dreams.** Kinsey and his colleagues found that almost all men and the majority of women have nocturnal dreams with sexual content. Men tend to have more wet dreams than women: Four-fifths of all men, as opposed to one-third of all females, have nocturnal dreams that lead to orgasm. Between 2 and 3 percent of a woman's orgasms may be achieved during nocturnal dreaming. In contrast, for men that number may be as high as 8 percent. The content of such dreams can cover a wide variety of erotic or sexual possibilities, including any one or all of the items listed in Table 6.3. The dream need not be overtly sexual, but it is usually accompanied by sexual sensations (Strong et al., 2004).

INTERPERSONAL SEXUAL BEHAVIOR

In contrast to autoerotic behavior, which involves an individual acting alone, interpersonal sexual activity involves two or more people acting in concert for the purpose of giving each other pleasure.

TABLE 6.3 Common Sexual Fantasies for American Women and Men

Contrary to the popular notion of sexual fantasizing as only the province of "dirty old men," according to many experts in the field of sexuality and sexual health, sexual fantasizing is a natural, normal, universal phenomenon similar to dreaming. Although there are gender differences in sexual fantasies, women and men are surprisingly similar. Some of the most common sexual fantasies for women and men cited in an array of literature are listed below in no particular order.

WOMEN	MEN
Fantasies involving romantic sex	Anal sex
Sex on the beach	Oral sex (both giving and receiving)
Oral sex (giving and receiving)	Sex with a celebrity
Sex with a man other than her partner (typically a celebrity)	Sex with another man
Sex with a woman	Sex with two women
Sex with two men	Bisexual sex (e.g. sex with women willing to perform bisexual acts)
Sex with an ex lover	Sex with a threesome or a harem of women
Sex with a stranger	Sex with a stranger
Having sex in a public place	A sexual orgy
Voyeuristic sex (having sex in front of an audience)	Watching girlfriend/spouse/partner have sex with another man
Group sex	Watching two women have sex
Sexual submission: sexual ravaging	Fantasizing about a current partner
Kinky sex	Domination/submission: sexual ravaging
Taking on the role of a male (strapping on a penis)	Kinky sex
Working as a prostitute or stripper	Watching partner masturbate

Sources: Berman, L. 2011. "10 Sexual Fantasies for Women." *Everyday Health.* www.everydayhealth.com/sexual-health/better-sex/10-sexual-fantasies-for-women.aspx. Hutcherson, H. 2010. "Women's Top 5 Sexual Fantasies—and What They Mean." *Redbook.* www.redbookmag.com/love-sex/advice/erotic-fantasy-meaning. *Men's Health.* 2008. "Make Her 5 Fantasies Come True." www.menshealth.com/sex-women/her-sexual-fantasies. "Women's Top 10 Sexual Fantasies." 2009. www.healthyplace.com/sex/psychology-of-sex/womens-top-ten-sexual-fantasies/menu-id-1482/.

Sources: Curezone. 2009. "Top 10 Sex Fantasies for Men." www.curezone.com/forums/fm.asp?i=1418020. Conner, S. 2009. "The Fantasy Sex Lives of Men and Women." www.lifewise.canoe.ca/SexRomance/Lovewise/2009/03/10/8697436.html. Parker, B. 2009. "Top 10 Male Sexual Fantasies." www.foreverpleasure.com/catalog/male-sexual-fantasies-a-105.html. Lamm, S. 2008. "Threesomes are Every Man's Fantasy." *Psychology Today.* www.psychologytoday.com/blog/great-sex/200806/threesomes-are-every-mans-fantasy.

Pleasuring As far back as the mid-nineteenth century, women were describing what to them was sexually pleasurable. Elizabeth Blackwell, the first woman to earn a medical degree in the United States, suggested that both women and men could experience sexual pleasure from each other without penile–vaginal intercourse. This idea of giving and receiving pleasure without intercourse was described over a century later by Masters and Johnson as **pleasuring.**

Pleasuring involves a couple exploring each other's bodies. It is erotic behavior that involves one person touching, exploring, and caressing nongenital areas of her or his partner's body for the purpose of giving erotic pleasure. After a while, the partners exchange roles. This exchange can continue until orgasm, or it can function as foreplay followed by genital intercourse. However pleasuring is conducted, it seems that a large number of women find touching and caressing to be a natural eroticism and the most important part of sexual activity. More than three decades ago, women reported that one of the most basic changes that they wished for in their sexual relationships was touching and closeness for their own sake rather than only as a prelude to intercourse. Although traditional sexual scripts define women as the passive recipients of pleasuring, they are now acting and reciprocating more during this phase of sexual activity than in the past.

Petting and Oral Sex **Petting,** which involves various forms of physical contact for the purpose of sexual arousal, is a common activity among adolescent girls and boys. Petting includes kissing, oral contact with the body, finger insertion, and fondling. Kinsey once said that petting was one of the most significant factors in the sexual lives of high school and college females and males. If that was true in the past, it is even more so today. The great majority of young people today have experienced some type of petting behavior before they reach adulthood. Whereas in the past these behaviors were used most often as a substitute for copulation, for many couples today they are a prelude to copulation (Christopher and Sprecher, 2000).

In many parts of society, oral–genital sex is an unmentionable subject and a taboo behavior. As late as the 1970s, social researcher Morton Hunt (1974) reported that oral–genital sex was still classified as a punishable crime against nature in the statutes of most states. By this time, however, **cunnilingus,** the oral stimulation of the female genitals, and **fellatio,** the oral stimulation of the male genitals, had become standard practices for a majority of White people of all social classes, single or married. Today, an overwhelming majority of women and men engage in oral sex, both giving and receiving. Although the percent of Americans engaging in oral sex increases with age, at the other end of the age spectrum an increasing number of adolescents and teens also engage in oral sex. Such behavior has been evident to a lesser degree among comparable samples of Latinas/os and African Americans. The practice of oral sex is particularly prevalent among married and cohabiting couples and White, college-educated men (Chandra, and Jones, 2005). Although oral–genital sex has gained acceptance over the years, it may well be on the decline among some groups given the heightened sensitivity to various sexually transmitted infections, especially herpes and AIDS. For other groups, especially teens, the risk of sexually transmitted infections does not appear to have lessened the practice in any significant way.

Coitus **Coitus** refers only to penile–vaginal intercourse. Other forms of intercourse such as anal intercourse are not included in

As with other aspects of behavior, there is often little difference in heterosexual and same-sex family behavior. In the 2010 film *The Kids Are All Right,* Annette Bening and Julianne Moore, pictured, play a long-term married lesbian couple who enjoys a lively family life with their two children (portrayed by Josh Hutcherson and Mia Wasikowska, pictured) conceived by artificial insemination. Although many Americans have not exactly embraced same-sex marriage, this film family is portrayed as a typical American family that happens to be gay dealing with marriage and family challenges that are universal.

this term. The U.S. patriarchal structure of heterosexual relations assumes that coitus is the most satisfying sexual activity for women and men. In this context, coitus is the primary method through which heterosexuals seek erotic pleasure. In every sex survey that the authors reviewed, both heterosexual women and men overwhelmingly identify coitus as the most appealing sexual practice. Coitus can occur with the partners in any number of positions. The most common is the "missionary position," in which the female lies on her back and the male faces her, lying on top of her. Some couples also adopt a position popularly called "69," in which the couple lie down with their heads in opposite directions and simultaneously perform oral–genital sex on each other. Because sexual intercourse is personal and private, people usually employ whatever positions they find mutually satisfying. Defining coitus as the sexual norm is problematic in that it is a limited viewpoint and it does not take into account sexual behaviors enjoyed and preferred by non-heterosexuals such as lesbians and gays.

SEXUAL EXPRESSION AMONG LESBIANS AND GAYS

As with other aspects of behavior, there is little difference in same-sex and heterosexual sexual expression and physiological response. Like heterosexuals, same sex couples engage in kissing, caressing, sexual arousal, and orgasm. Because lesbians and gays are socialized with the same gendered sexual scripts as their heterosexual counterparts, their approach to sexual activity and intimacy reflects our culture's heavily gendered prescriptions for women and men. For instance, lesbians are more emotionally involved with their partners and are more likely than gays to connect sex with love. They express affection before actual sexual activity begins, and they often reach orgasm through mutual masturbation and cunnilingus. Gays often kiss, caress each other's penises, and reach orgasm through anal intercourse or through fellatio (Strong et al., 2004). As indicated in Chapter 5, gays tend to have sex with more partners and in shorter-term relationships than lesbians. Gays also tend to act on their sexuality earlier than lesbians, just as heterosexual males act earlier than heterosexual females. Some research indicates that these behaviors have changed in recent years because of the spread of AIDS. However, many gays have been, and some continue to be, sexually active with multiple partners. For some gays and lesbians as well, monogamy and fidelity are not central features of their relationships. Gays and lesbians in "open" relationships (a couple in a long-term committed relationship with lovers on the side) argue that, as a result of the openness of their relationship, they have stronger, longer-lasting and more honest relationships (James, 2010).

While same-sex couple's sexual behavior is not much different from that of heterosexuals, there are some distinctive features of same-sex intimacy as well. For instance, researchers have found that same-sex couples, especially lesbians but gays as well, take much more time in their sexual relationships, holding and kissing each other. In addition, lesbians are less genitally oriented and less fixated on orgasm, compared to men. Romance and other emotional aspects of sexual intimacy are more central in their sexual activities. Contrary to popular belief, lesbians seldom use dildos or other objects in an attempt to simulate heterosexual intercourse, nor do they engage in rigid role playing that imitates heterosexual sexual behavior. Rather, both lesbian and gay couples typically alternate active and receptive roles (Shriver et al., 2002).

We know that an increasing number of heterosexual teenagers are engaging in some form of sexual activity, but we know very little about lesbian, gay, bisexual and transgendered teens' sexual behavior. Almost all survey studies of teenage sexuality presume that "sex" means heterosexual sex. Thus, there is little trend data available on teenage same-sex behavior, bisexuality, transgender behavior or gay identity. Somewhere around 10 percent of teens in some sex surveys report being confused about their sexual identities. Researchers are unsure as to the cause of this uncertainty—whether it reflects typical adolescent struggles with identity or the decreased stigma attached to being gay, reflected in the mass media (Risman and Schwartz, 2002). Past research on lesbian and gay teenagers focused narrowly on self-identifying lesbian and gay teens who were routinely characterized as less emotionally healthy—as suicidal—than their non-identifying, same-sex-attracted and heterosexual peers. However, contrary to such popular negative stereotypes about young lesbians and gays, most same-sex-attracted teens are healthy, resilient, and mature, able to integrate their same-sex attractions into their emerging personalities as merely one aspect of who they are. In other words, lesbian and gay teens are not unlike other teens. As with adults, many teenagers today, despite having sex and relationships with same-sex partners, do not feel particularly "gay" (Earls, 2005).

Sexuality Across the Life Cycle

As we have indicated repeatedly throughout this chapter, sexual behavior for most people begins earlier and lasts longer over the life cycle today than at any other period in U.S. history.

Adolescents at increasingly younger ages report being involved in some sort of sexual behavior. At the other end of the age spectrum, many people continue to enjoy sex well into old age. In addition, one's marital status seems to be connected in some important ways to our sexuality. The following discussion is a brief examination of sexuality within and outside of legal marriage and during several key periods of the life cycle.

NON-MARRIED SEXUALITY AND PREGNANCY

Although the terms premarital sex and premarital intercourse are commonly used in research studies of human sexuality, for a number of reasons they are outdated and inadequate for discussing contemporary sexuality. For example, an increasing number of adults are delaying marriage and many (an estimated 10 percent) will never marry (only 52 percent of American adults are married), therefore, their sexual relationships cannot be categorized with any reliability and validity as "premarital." In addition, given that lesbians and gays are denied the legal right to marry in all but six states and the District of Columbia, their sexual relationships certainly cannot be legitimately categorized as "premarital" either. Thus, whenever possible, we use the term single or unmarried whenever we refer to a non-married status.

The incidence of intercourse among singles has increased considerably over the past decade. In addition, gender is no longer a distinguishing factor in unmarried sexual behavior. The behavior of White females dramatically illustrates both of these points. Over the last three decades, intercourse among single White females increased significantly, considerably narrowing the gap between them and their male peers. Among single African American women, a significant change also occurred, although it came primarily in terms of the earlier age at which coitus begins. At the end of the twentieth century, three-fourths of unmarried women had had sexual intercourse by the age of 19 and more than four-fifths by the age of 29. Today, the median age at first sexual intercourse for women is 17.4 and among men coming to maturity, the median age at first sexual intercourse is 16.9. However, with most women and men delaying marriage to a later age than in the past or not marrying at all, this means that a growing number of young adults are at increased risk of unwanted pregnancy and sexually transmitted infections (Guttmacher Institute, 2011; Lindberg and Singh, 2008; Kaiser Family Foundation, 2006).

The increased sexuality among the singles population is fairly consistent with the sexual attitudes and morals of the general population about sex outside a legal married relationship. For instance, as we have already indicated, in answer to a 2011 Gallup poll question about whether or not it is morally wrong for a woman and man to have sexual relations before marriage, 60 percent said it was morally acceptable and 36 percent said it was morally unacceptable. Over the years, the percent of Americans who view sex outside marriage as morally acceptable has grown but continues to vary by age. Seventy one percent of young adults ages 18 to 34 think sex before marriage is morally acceptable whereas older adults are much less liberal, with adults age 55 and older the least liberal on this question (only 53 percent think it is morally acceptable) (Gallup Poll, 2011).

Added to the singles' mix are adolescents whom we have already discussed in terms of the increase in their sexual behavior. Some observers have suggested that many teens have had sexual intercourse before they have learned to drive a car. According to recent surveys, by the age of 15, 13 percent of teens have never had sex. However, sexual activity becomes quite common after this with 42 percent of teens ages 15 to 19 having had sex at least once. And by the time they reach age 19, 7 in 10 teens have engaged in sexual intercourse (Guttmacher Institute, 2011; Chandra, et al., 2010). As a result, some sex researchers are suggesting that American youth are in the midst of their own sexual revolution. These researchers claim that television, entertainment, and even the news and children's cartoons have contributed to this sexual revolution. Teens today not only seem nonchalant about sex, but also they seem to know more of the mechanics of sex than many adults.

Interestingly, most parents don't think their teens are interested in or having sex but they believe that everyone else's children are (Elliot, 2010). However, as we learned in the Debating Social Issues box, not all parents think that their children are sexually innocent; some parents suspect that their teens are either interested in or actually having sex and they are taking precautions to ensure that their teen's sexual activity is safe and will not result in an early and/or unwanted pregnancy.

The statistics on adolescent sexual behavior should not lead us to assume that unmarried sexual activity (adolescent or adult) is synonymous with casual sex. According to most sex surveys and research, the majority of unmarried intercourse among adolescents as well as adults occurs within an affectionate, serious, monogamous, and steady relationship. For example, among sexually active teens, 72 percent of females and 56 percent of males report that their first sexual experience was with a steady partner, while only 14 percent of females and 25 percent of males report that their first sexual experience was with someone whom they had just met or who was just a friend. However, the other side of this is that a small but nonetheless important group of young women ages 18 to 24 who had sex before age 20 (7 percent) report that their first sexual experience was involuntary. What's more, those whose first sexual partner was three or more years their senior were more likely to report this than other women in their age group (Guttmacher, 2011).

Pregnancy and Single Motherhood A major practical issue associated with early coitus and declining and delayed marriage is an increase in childbirth among unmarried women. Although unmarried pregnancy is not a new phenomenon resulting from the so-called sexually liberated years of the 1960s and 1970s, births to unmarried individuals and couples have increased significantly over the decades. In 2009, 41 percent of children born in the United States were born to unmarried women, an eightfold increase over the past half-century. And in comparison to some of the other industrialized countries, the percentage of American children born outside of legal marriage is roughly 20 times higher than for Japan (2.1 percent), 8 times higher than Greece (5.0 percent), and double that of Italy (20.7 percent). Relative to race, 72 percent of non-Hispanic Black children, 53 percent of Hispanic children, and 29 percent of non-Hispanic White children are born outside of legal marriage. For young women, the birth rate for unmarried teens ages 15 to 19 has declined steadily from a high of 61.8 in 1991 to an

✳ **Explore** the **Concept**
Social Explorer Activity: The Increase of Single Women with Children on **myfamilylab.com**

all-time record low of 39.1 in 2009, the lowest level ever reported for the nation. Declines were evident for all racial and ethnic groups. However, the most dramatic decrease in teenage unmarried childbearing over the last decade occurred among African American teens. The decline in the teen birth rate generally is attributed to a number of factors including a decrease in the number of teens who have had sexual intercourse, a growing number of teens choosing to delay having sexual intercourse, and the increased use of contraceptives among sexually active teens. Still, almost all teens who give birth are unmarried. In 2009, 87 percent of teens ages 15 to 19 who gave birth were unmarried. Furthermore, despite the decline, the U.S. teen pregnancy rate continues to be one of the highest in the developed world—twice that of Canada and Sweden (Child Trends, 2010b; Hamilton, Martin, and Ventura, 2010).

Although the proportion of births to single women typically decreases with age, interestingly, there has been a significant increase in the number of births to single women over age 40. Considering that just three decades ago, almost no one in that age group had babies at all, let alone without being married, the current generation of these women is turning that paradigm on its head (U.S. Census Bureau, 2011e; Hamilton, Martin, and Ventura, 2010). The percentage of births to single women also varies across race and nativity as well as level of education (see Figure 6.1 on page 190). For instance, 17 percent of all births to Asian and Pacific Islanders were to single women, compared with 73 percent for African American women; 53 percent for Latinas; 65 percent for Native Americans, Eskimos, and Aleuts; and 29 percent for White non-Hispanic women. The proportion of births among foreign-born and native-born single women are quite similar, 36 percent and 39 percent, respectively. And the least educated single women had the highest rate of births (52 percent) compared to college-educated women (11 percent) ("Quick Facts on Single Moms and Educational Attainment," 2011; Hamilton, Martin, and Ventura, 2006; Dye, 2005).

Some observers have suggested that the increase in childbearing among single women is due to welfare benefits. Others have linked the rise in the number of births to single women to an increase in unmarried cohabitation, later-in-life marriage, and an increase in childbearing by older, unmarried women. Still others have concluded that economic factors, along with significant changes in societal attitudes about marriage, sex, and childbearing, are what explain increases in unmarried childbearing. Most agree, however, that more research is needed to determine whether efforts to strengthen families; to remove barriers to adoption, abortion, and marriage; to enforce child support orders; and to remove the marriage penalty in various tax and public assistance programs would substantially reduce out-of-wedlock childbearing.

Although most American teenagers do not have sex initially to reproduce, 1 in 10 Whites and 2 in 10 Blacks say that during their first sexual intercourse they neither thought about nor cared if they got pregnant. However, the majority of teenagers who are sexually active today report using some form of birth control, most often the Pill followed by condoms. And as they become more sexually active, the more consistently they use birth control methods. So what explains the higher teenage pregnancy rate in the United States? Some experts argue that insufficient knowledge as well as our general discomfort with sex and sexuality may help explain why the United States has a higher rate of teenage pregnancy and childbirth than any other industrialized country. Discussions of sexuality and

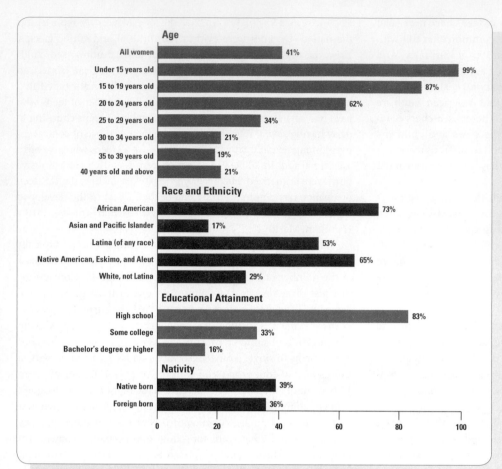

FIGURE 6.1 Births to Single Women: 2008–2009 (Percent of all births to single women in specified categories)

Sources: Hamilton B., J. Martin, and S. Ventura. 2010. "Births: Preliminary Data for 2009." National Vital Statistics Report (December 21): Volume 59, Number 3. Hyattsville, MD: U.S. Department of Health and Human Services, Centers for Disease Control and Prevention, National Center for Health. U.S. Census Bureau, 2011 Statistical Abstract. Project Working Mom. 2011. "Quick Facts on Single Moms and Educational Attainment." http://www.elearners.com/projectworkingmom/quick-facts-on-single-moms-and-education.

childbirth and the dispensation of condoms and other forms of birth control in American schools are at the heart of a major divide in the United States today. On one side of the divide are those who believe that American youth deserve to have an accurate and comprehensive education about sexuality. On the other side are those who believe that abstinence only until marriage is the only strategy appropriate to teach young people about their sexuality.

No matter which side of the debate one is on, teenage pregnancy is a particularly unsettling issue given that the majority of teen mothers lives in or will live in poverty. Most teenaged parents, regardless of race, have low academic skills and high unemployment rates. They tend to come from poor families, most do not marry (at least not immediately), and they are likely to drop out of school, although Black teenaged mothers are more likely than their White or Latina counterparts to continue attending school during and after pregnancy. According to sociologist Margaret Andersen (2008), regardless of their race and social class status, teenage mothers value marriage as an ideal, but they do not see it as a viable option given expectant parents' general lack of economic resources. Unfortunately, far more attention is focused on teenage mothers, even though teenage fathers are equally responsible for teenage pregnancies. Teenage mothers tend to fare better when they have the support of the father of the child, but most teenage fathers cannot support themselves, let alone a family (Bunting and McAuley, 2004a).

In the final analysis, we should be very careful not to perpetuate myths about unmarried pregnancy or to lump single teenage and adult pregnancy together. As we have discussed, the majority of unmarried births are not to teenagers, nor are they to teenagers of color. The fact is that the majority of births to unmarried women occur among women who are age 20 or older. Equally important, we cannot assume that unmarried pregnancies are always unwanted, nor can we assume that the custodial parent or parents are incapable of providing for the newborn simply because of age or marital status. Indeed, contrary to popular stereotypes, as it turns out, most children born to unmarried mothers are not the result of casual sexual encounters. Rather, more than one-half of unmarried parents were living together at the time their child was born, and almost one-third of them were romantically involved though not living together (Luscombe, 2010). In other words, we cannot assume that single parenting in and of itself is "problematic" and damaging.

MARITAL SEXUALITY: DOES GOOD SEX MAKE GOOD MARRIAGES?

Because marital sex is considered the norm, scholars have not paid much attention to this subject. However, based on some of the most recent data in this regard, the changes in sexuality we have discussed in this chapter have affected married as well as unmarried people. As with single relationships, most marriages today have moved toward greater variety in sexual behavior, more frequent intercourse, and higher levels of sexual satisfaction. Major surveys of women's sexuality during the 1970s and 1980s pointed out major shifts among heterosexual couples from penile–vaginal intercourse and simultaneous orgasm to a variety of sexual practices directed toward the needs and desires of women. These changes have increased over the last several decades and have weakened what some researchers have described as the male monopoly over the nature of sex.

Married couples are not only engaging in a variety of sexual behavior more frequently but also enjoying it more. How often married couples have intercourse varies depending on age, social class, how long they have been married, if there are children, as well as a number of other factors. For example, factors such as job demands, household chores and demands, monetary issues and concerns, number of adults living in the household—all may conspire to limit a couple's sexual life of spontaneity and frequency. However, for the majority of married couples, the rate ranges from two to three times a week to several times a month. Married couples are more likely to have more sex, and more varied sex, than single people. For instance, oral sex is more common in married couples than among single couples. However, frequency of marital sexual intercourse typically decreases over time, with a sharp reduction after age 50 (Durex, 2010; "Love and Marriage," 2006; Waite and Joyner, 2001).

Sexual satisfaction is important to both wives and husbands, the majority of whom report both emotional and physical satisfaction in their sexual relationships. Most research indicates that how a couple gets along sexually is an indication of how their marriage is going in general. Although most married people consider sexual activity important to their marriage, both wives and husbands report that the quality of the marriage relationship is more important than sex per se. Accordingly, most surveys show that approximately three of four people who are married are happy with their marital status compared with two of four single people. In most of these surveys, men generally report being more content with their marital status than women and singles. Likewise, husbands also report greater sexual satisfaction than wives. When couples define their sexual activities as satisfying, they generally define their overall relationship as satisfying as well (Niolon, 2010).

POSTMARITAL SEXUALITY

As divorce and separation rates have increased and a growing number of widowed people—particularly women—are living into old age without a partner, a larger number of adults than in the past are confronted with the task of adjusting to a postmarital life. Popular cultural images have these individuals living either a life of great excitement, entertainment, and sexual activity, or conversely, feeling depressed, devastated, and lonely, with no sex life. As we shall see, neither of these images is completely accurate.

Divorced People Most divorced people become sexually active within a year following their divorce, although older people are somewhat slower in this regard than people under age 40 (Shriver et al., 2002). Although divorced people appear to have a fairly active sex life and find postmarital sex more pleasurable and fulfilling than married sex, when people across marital statuses are asked whether intercourse is occurring frequently enough for their desire, divorced people are the most dissatisfied with the frequency (74 percent), compared to cohabitants and married couples (38 and 49 percent dissatisfied, respectively). In addition, next to single people (65 percent), more than half (60 percent) of widowed people also report that they are dissatisfied with the frequency of sexual intercourse

in their lives (Dunn, Croft, and Hackett, 2000). Such findings, however, should not cloud the fact that divorce often involves adjustments of many sorts, such as transition and recuperation, ending some relationships and developing new ones, and adjusting to nonmarital sex and a nonmarital lifestyle generally. Loneliness and anxiety sometimes accompany this transition, as do financial strains and concerns. Some people find the world of postmarital sex to be anxiety producing, particularly in terms of relearning the rules of dating and mate selection. Nonetheless, most divorced people manage to reintegrate their sexuality with their emotional needs.

Widows and Widowers Widowed women and men sometimes choose to abstain from sex after their spouse's death, but almost one-half of widows and widowers eventually engage in postmarital coitus. The death of a partner is a great emotional and social loss. Far less so than in the past, today's widows and widowers are not willing to resign themselves to a life without partner companionship and sexual activity. As we discussed in Chapter 5, for older heterosexual women who are also widowed, the problem becomes finding a suitable single man. Given the toll that HIV/AIDS has taken in the gay male community, many gays go through a similar mourning period and then a reentering or reintegration into a single's lifestyle. This might include dating, companionship, sexual activity, and even cohabitation. Because there is little or no specific research on the sexuality of separated and widowed people, much of the information about them is speculative. The prevailing view at this time is that their sexual behavior does not differ much from that of the divorced population.

SEX IN LATER LIFE

Not only is there a gender gap in American sexual behavior, but also there is a generation gap. On the one hand, for example, although most later-life adults lead sexually active lives, they continue to be far more conservative than younger Americans in their attitudes about sex. Only 53 percent of people age 55 and older, for instance, approve of sex before marriage compared to 71 percent of people ages 18 to 34 who think it is okay. Yet when it comes to the issue of infidelity or cheating, more older than younger adults report having cheated in a relationship. Overall, however, young adults, whether single or in a committed relationship, are more progressive sexually; they are more likely to talk with their partners about their sexual fantasies, more likely to describe themselves and their partners as sexually adventurous, more likely to say that same-sex relationships are okay, and more likely than older people to look at sexually explicit Web sites (*Senior Journal*, 2005; Gallup, 2011).

On the other hand, according to recent reports, single baby boomers are changing the way older people look at sex, romance, marriage, and relationships and how younger people view older people relative to their sexuality. If we use baby boomers as a gauge, it seems sex is no longer the exclusive territory of the young, but a quality of life issue that continues well after age 50. Unlike earlier generations of older single Americans, baby boomers (who are now turning 65) are flaunting their sexuality. They desire fun, excitement, passion, and sex in their relationships. Boomer women in particular are increasingly more sexually confident, an observation consistent with research findings that report women's sexual confidence and self-knowledge increase as they go through life.

Contrary to popular stereotypes about the sexuality of later-life adults, many women and men in their later years (like the couple pictured) continue to enjoy healthy, loving, and sexual relationships. Baby Boomers, in particular, are changing the way that later-life adults think about and act out their sexuality. Like their younger counterparts, they are sexually confident and routinely incorporate fun, excitement, and sex in their intimate relationships.

Boomer sexuality notwithstanding, the common stereotype of older women and men is that they are asexual—that is, as they age, they lose interest in and the ability to engage in meaningful sexual activities—is still accepted by many people. In addition, those elderly who remain sexually active are frequently dismissed as "dirty old women" or "dirty old men." Given our views concerning aging and the elderly, many people in the United States believe women and men must give up sex as they age. Research on sexuality and aging, however, indicates that, in fact, sexuality is one of the last functions to be affected by age. In reality, people who are healthy and happy with their lives can continue to be sexually active well into their advanced years (Shriver et al., 2002).

It is true that as people become older, they experience biological and psychological changes that can affect their sexual functioning. For instance, some older adults take longer to become aroused, are less sensitive to stimulation, and experience less intense orgasms than younger people; however, the capacity to enjoy sex is not altered with age. Indeed, sexuality remains an essential factor in the lives of many older Americans. Later-life adults can be, and many often are, highly sexual beings with sexual thoughts and desires that continue into advanced age. Most report that they like sex, and a majority report that orgasm is important to their sexual fulfillment. Although two in three believe that too much emphasis is placed on sex in today's society, almost two-thirds believe that sexual activity is critical to a good relationship and fewer than one in 20 believe sex is only for young people (Fisher, 2010).

Older people may be sensual as well as sexual. As with younger people, older women and men rank hugging and kissing as top sexual pleasures. Moreover, many older adults, like their younger counterparts, engage in and enjoy a range of sexual behaviors, including hooking up and hanging, self-stimulation, and sexual thoughts and fantasies, including engaging in such fantasizing while having sex with a partner and while masturbating. Men over age 50, like their younger counterparts, think about sex more often

than older women. They also see sex as more important to the quality of life, engage in sexual activities more often, are less satisfied if without a partner, and are twice as likely as older women to admit to sexual activity outside their relationships. Although less than half of older adults report being satisfied with their sex lives, for most, the presence of a sexual partner seems to be a prerequisite for satisfaction. Although condom use and protection is fairly normative among certain groups, especially among sexually active adolescents, women and men over age 50 are far less responsible in their sexual activities. For example, recent research indicates that nine out of 10 men over age 50 did not use a condom when they had sex with a date or casual acquaintance, and seven out of 10 did not do so even when they had sex with someone they just met. While women over age 50 are somewhat more careful than their male counterparts, a majority of them have sex without a condom. Some even had sex without a condom when they knew they or their partner had a sexually transmitted infection (Fisher, 2010; Luscombe, 2010).

All too often, unfortunately, society does not deal well with later-life people and their sexuality. Families, senior care facilities, and other caretakers often ignore or disregard the sexual needs and desires of older people. Sadly, some older adults accept cultural prescriptions about their sexuality and either discontinue their sexual activities or experience guilt, doubt, and shame about their desire for and engagement in sexual activity (Rathus, Nevid, and Fichner, 2008). Aging can necessitate some adjustments in a couple's sexual activity. Illness, for instance, might bring about a temporary loss of sexual interest or ability; however, it usually does not mean the end of people's sex lives. Rather, it might require different ways of giving and receiving sexual pleasure. Most importantly, as people age, open and effective communication grows in importance. To maintain a comfortable and successful sexual relationship, the couple must communicate their sexual desires—what makes them feel good and what does not. In any event, the years of middle age and beyond can be a time for exploring sex at a deeper, more confident, and more satisfying level.

Women, Aging, and Sexuality As women age, their reproductive ability declines gradually. Somewhere around age 50, the menstrual cycle stops completely, marking **menopause.** Experts disagree on the impact of menopause on female sexuality. Some studies suggest a decline in sexual interest and possibly the loss of female orgasmic response in the immediate postmenopausal years. Other research, however, suggests that despite these physiological changes, menopausal women are still capable of experiencing orgasm, their sexual interest may increase, and for many of these women, the quality of their sexual experience seems higher than when they were younger.

Because of the sexual double standard, regardless of age, women are more likely than men to feel physically undesirable. Likewise, with society's double standard with regard to aging, we often have difficulty thinking of older people as sexually active and uninhibited, especially older women. For instance, men retain their sexual eligibility as they age, whereas older women are generally considered less desirable than their younger counterparts. This perception, we should note, extends beyond sexuality to many other ways in which women and men are valued or devalued.

Men, Aging, and Sexuality Unlike women, men do not have a typical pattern of reproductive aging because there is no definite end to male fertility. Although the production of sperm abates after age 40, it continues into the 80s and 90s. Likewise, although the production of testosterone decreases after age 55, there is usually no major decrease in levels of sex hormones in men as there is in women. A very small percentage of men (approximately 5 percent) over age 60 experience what some sex researchers have labeled a *male climacteric,* which is similar in some ways to female menopause. However, unlike women, some men father children when well into their 70s. For example, the late U.S. Senator, Strom Thurmond, and global media baron Rupert Murdock both fathered children when they were in their 70s. For those who experience it, the male climacteric is generally characterized by some of the following: weakness, tiredness, decreased sexual desire, reduced or loss of potency, and irritability (Masters, Johnson, and Kolodny, 1992).

In general, males typically reach their peak of sexual function in their late teens or early twenties. Thereafter, their sexual function begins a gradual, progressive decline. Although sex continues to be important, as men age the urgency of the sex drive decreases and a reduced frequency of sexual activity is typical. Normal physical changes include a decline in the sensitivity of the penis, and some men experience an enlargement of the prostate gland. In older men, erections are also slower in developing, less precoital mucus is produced, the amount of semen is reduced, the intensity of the ejaculation is lessened, orgasmic reflex is shorter, and sensitivity to distractions increases (Masters, Johnson, and Kolodny, 1992). On the other hand, they tend to experience an increased capacity to delay ejaculation, which some men (and women) find satisfying. In general, men tend to stay sexually active longer than women.

Women and men who were sexually active in their younger years typically remain sexually active into their 80s and 90s, although the frequency of intercourse is limited by their physical health and social circumstances, such as having an available partner. Although older people generally can and do remain sexually active, the existing evidence suggests that most forms of sexual behavior decline significantly for women and men after age 75. In any event, as we learned in Chapter 5, a rising number of older adults are romantically and sexually involved in relationships, and some choose to carry out their relationships in cohabitation with their partner. (Issues related to the elderly are examined in more detail in Chapter 14.)

Sexual Dysfunctions

Like other aspects of human experience, sex is not always smooth and problem-free. The fact is that almost everyone who is sexually active, even couples who are very satisfied with their relationship, experiences occasional sexual problems. These problems can range anywhere from lack of interest in sexual activities to an actual **sexual dysfunction,** the inability to engage in or enjoy sexual activities. Approximately one-third of the general population (not including the geriatric subgroup) experiences some type of sexual dysfunction. This fact notwithstanding, it is important to note that what is considered a sexual dysfunction is relative to time, place, and the individuals involved. That is, "a sexual dysfunction may be said to exist only if the person or couple is distressed by a particular aspect of their sexual response, rather than on the basis of some objective criteria" (Shriver et al., 2002:217). Although a few cases of sexual dysfunction can be traced to physical problems, the majority

of cases are the result of social-psychological factors that interfere with or impair people's ability to respond as ordinarily expected to sexual stimuli. These factors range from anxiety about sexual performance to general life stress. Sexual dysfunctions can be distinguished along gender lines. The most common sexual dysfunctions for women are related to penetration and orgasm: inhibited sexual desire, inhibited sexual excitement, inhibited female orgasm or anorgasmia, vaginismus, rapid orgasm, and dyspareunia. The most common sexual dysfunctions for men are related to erection and ejaculation: erectile dysfunction, premature ejaculation, inhibited male orgasm, priapism, dyspareunia, and inhibited sexual desire.

In American society, a great deal of emphasis is placed on performance as a measure of people's personal worth. Sexual performance, like other performance, becomes a measure of our personal adequacy and value to others. Thus, when people do not perform sexually as expected, they often feel embarrassed, guilty, frustrated, confused, and depressed. This can often cause problems in personal relationships as well as in other aspects of people's lives. We will not go into detail here regarding the specifics of these sexual dysfunctions. Rather, they are presented in some detail in Appendix A. Suffice it to say here that whenever people recognize that they have a sexual dysfunction, they should seek the help of a qualified physician, psychiatrist, or marriage or sex therapist, depending on the problem (see the Strengthening Marriages and Families box).

In an interesting article about sexual dysfunction, it seems that a few sex therapists and counselors are prescribing sex surrogates to some of their clients. Pioneered in the 1970s by sex therapy giants Masters and Johnson, sex surrogates teach people (mostly men) the methods and pleasures of a range of sexual activities. Between 1970 and 1980, it was estimated that there were somewhere between 400 and 500 sex surrogates working in the United States in conjunction with sex therapists and counselors. Today, that number has dwindled to approximately 40. Despite the dubious legality of sex surrogacy (for instance, paying for sex), some therapists and counselors continue to prescribe sex surrogacy to some of their clients (Alexander, 2009).

Sexual Responsibility: Protecting Yourself and Your Partner(s) from AIDS and Other STIs

Sexually transmitted infections (STIs), infections acquired primarily through sexual contact—although some can also be transmitted in other ways—are fairly common in today's society. They were formerly called sexually transmitted diseases (STDs) and before that venereal diseases. Such infections can be caused by viruses (AIDS, herpes, hepatitis B, and genital warts); bacteria (syphilis, gonorrhea, and chlamydia infections); and tiny insects or parasites (pubic lice). The United States has the highest rates of STIs in the industrialized world. Globally, it is estimated that about 448 million new infections of curable sexually transmitted infections occur yearly. This does not include HIV/AIDS, which continues to adversely affect the lives of millions of people around

TALKS WITH FAMILY THERAPIST JOAN ZIENTEK

Talking Frankly about Our Sexual Needs

What Kinds of Sexual Issues Do People Bring to Therapy? A couple's sexual relationship holds a very special place in the context of the total relationship. When sexual issues arise, then, tensions can permeate the entire relationship. These problems can result from sexual dysfunctions, such as impotence and premature ejaculation for the male, or vaginismus or orgasmic difficulties for the female. Issues such as these are usually addressed by a sex therapist or a medical doctor. More than likely, couples who come to marital therapy have sexual issues that stem from boredom, differing sexual needs and preferences, childhood sexual abuse, or affairs (either physical or emotional). For some struggling with these issues, the Internet and Craig's List invite an easy, quick, and superficial solution to their problems. Usually all of these sexual issues are interwoven with other marital problems, and the therapist needs to carefully evaluate how best to treat the couple or individual.

It is only natural that the novelty and passion that was once part of marriage wears off over time. Even with all the self-help books, starting with Masters and Johnson in the 1970s, followed by Dr. Ruth, and now the work of Dr. Drew Pinsky, author and TV and radio personality, couples still struggle with issues of sexual intimacy. At the heart of the struggle lies the misguided notion that sexual intimacy has more to do with mastering sexual skills and achieving orgasm than it does with deeply knowing and being known by one's partner. The latter requires that each partner in the marriage has a solid personal identity and is able to reveal him- or herself while risking the possibility that the other may not respond with empathy, validation, or delight.

What Are Some Strategies That Therapists Use to Help People with These Issues? The therapist generally begins by working in the here and now. This can sometimes be accomplished simply through education, problem solving, and/or compromise. If the presenting problem is one of a difference in sexual desire, the therapist can normalize the couple's experience, conveying that these differences are normal and natural and may be due to each person's biochemical makeup. These differences are initially disguised because, according to some scientists, the euphoria of new love produces a hefty dose of PEA (phenylethylamine, a neurotransmitter), which elevates sexual desire. However, research also shows that the rapture of this infatuation burns out after 18 to 36 months, and couples then experience the natural differences in their need for sex. Understanding and accepting this natural phenomenon takes the sting out of worrying about the loss of desirability and the shame of refusal and places the couple in a better position to problem-solve and compromise in meeting their divergent sexual needs. Issues of sexual boredom or the use of sex as blackmail can often be resolved with these same techniques, along with enhancing the couple's communication skills.

Couples who come to therapy because of an affair, regardless of which person was unfaithful, need to explore the behavior of both parties that contributed to the marital context that made the affair possible, as well as working toward restoring trust in the relationship.

With the guidance of the therapist, both parties either discover that they cannot recoup the marriage and need to work toward an amicable divorce or work through the marital crisis to achieve an even healthier and satisfying relationship.

If these interventions do not work, the therapist then turns to exploring the interpsychic blocks originating from past experiences, perhaps stemming back to childhood and early insecurities. Looking back to early experiences and working through the feelings and messages that accompany them, along with adapting new behaviors, is part of the long-term psychotherapy needed for issues of a deeper nature such as childhood sexual abuse and sexual addiction.

What Influences How Successful People Are in Solving These Issues? Different couples bring different strengths and resources for resolving their issues. One of the main issues is the strength of the love they have for one another. Some couples marry in a hurry and for the wrong reasons, only to wake up years later to discover they have grown apart. Other couples ignore the tensions in their relationship for years, gathering resentment and living parallel lives until a crisis such as an affair brings them to therapy. Also, if each person gets caught in blaming the other and refuses to examine her or his own part in the problem, success can be stymied. On the other hand, if couples seek help when they first realize that their own efforts have not resolved the conflicts or when their own efforts only exacerbate the problem, there is a greater chance at success. When this is coupled with love, goodwill, and personal responsibility, most problems can be resolved.

---

the world (World Health Organization, 2011d). The Centers for Disease Control and Prevention (CDC) estimates that about 65 million Americans are currently living with a sexually transmitted infection. Around 19 million (including 2.5 million adolescents) new cases of STIs are reported to the CDC each year, which cost the U.S. healthcare system more than $16 billion annually and costs individuals and their families even more in terms of acute and long-term health consequences. In addition, about one-fourth of Americans will contract an STI in their lifetime, two-thirds of whom will be under age 25 when they contract an STI.

Women suffer more frequent and more serious complications from STIs than men (Centers for Disease Control and Prevention, 2007, 2009b; Banis, 2006; National Women's Health Information Center, 2005). Some experts are claiming that the United States is in the throes of an STI epidemic in poor, underserved areas of the country that rivals that of some developing countries. However,

"How do I know you don't have herpes?"

Increasing public awareness and individual concern about sexually transmitted diseases have sparked a rise in humor about human sexuality. However, the contraction and transmission of STIs is a serious matter that should be discussed before having sexual relations.

Source: Reprinted with permission of V. G. Myers. © *Cosmopolitan,* 1982.

the risk is not limited to this population. Recent data show that STIs are becoming increasingly common among teenagers, including those from middle- and upper-class families as well as older adults. It is estimated that one-fourth of sexually active teenagers will contract an STI within one year after becoming sexually active. There are also large disparities in the rates of STIs among various racial and ethnic groups. There are more than 30 identified STIs; the most common are chlamydia, genital herpes, genital warts, gonorrhea, hepatitis B, human papillomavirus, syphilis, and AIDS. Many cases of STIs go undiagnosed, and some highly prevalent viral infections, such as human papillomavirus and genital herpes, are not reported at all. For instance, it is estimated that as many as one in four Americans have genital herpes, and up to 90 percent are unaware that they have it. Because of the risks to physical and mental health, we must become more knowledgeable about STIs, and more responsible to ourselves and others in our sexual behaviors. With the exception of AIDS, which we discuss next, STIs are examined in Appendix A.

AIDS

Over the last few decades, women and men living in the United States have been perhaps more challenged in their exploration and enjoyment of sexuality than at any other time in our history. Protracted media, public attention, and information about responsible sexual behavior—abstinence, safe sex, and the use of condoms—reflect the contemporary era of sexuality and sexual choices in America. In this new era of sexuality, HIV/AIDS continues to be a serious and deadly threat to women and men, the young and old, rich and poor, heterosexual, homosexual, bisexual, and transgendered, and across race and ethnicity. Identified in 1981, **acquired immunodeficiency syndrome (AIDS)** is a viral

syndrome, or group of infectious diseases that destroys the body's immune system, thereby rendering the victim susceptible to all kinds of infections and diseases. People may have HIV without knowing it, given that the incubation period can be as long as 10 years and given symptoms of AIDS usually do not appear for a year or longer. Because the body is unable to fight off HIV/AIDS infections and diseases, they eventually kill the person.

More than 1 million people in the United States are living with HIV, almost one-half of whom are living with AIDS; more than one in five of those living with the virus are unaware of their infection. Every 9.5 minutes, someone in the U.S. is infected with HIV—believed to be the main cause of AIDS—and more than half a million have died after developing AIDS, the equivalent of the entire population of Las Vegas. Although the total number of new HIV infections has remained fairly stable, new infections continue to be high. An estimated 56,300 Americans become infected with HIV each year—a person who tests positive for HIV is regarded as infected and capable of transmitting the virus to others. Although people living with AIDS are now surviving longer, more than 18,000 people living with AIDS still die each year in the United States (Centers for Disease Control and Prevention, 2010b, 2011a, 2011b). Figure 6.2 illustrates the number of AIDS cases diagnosed and the number of AIDS deaths that occurred in selective years through December 2008.

The Transmission of AIDS HIV/AIDS is transmitted through blood, semen, vaginal fluid, breast milk, and other body fluids containing blood. It can enter the body through a vein (such as intravenous drug use), the anus or rectum, vagina, penis, mouth,

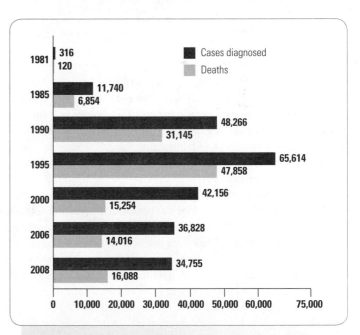

FIGURE 6.2 AIDS Cases and Deaths in the United States, 1981–2008

Source: Adapted from Centers for Disease Control and Prevention. 2009. *HIV/AIDS Surveillance Report, 2009,* Vol. 21 (Atlanta: U.S. Department of Health and Human Services, Centers for Disease Control and Prevention): pp. 21–22; 42–43, Table 2a, 12a: www.cdc.gov/hiv/topics/surveillance/resources/reports/. Published February 2011.

TABLE 6.4 Adult and Adolescent Reported AIDS Cases, by Exposure Category and Sex, Through December 2009*

	Females (%)	Males (%)
Adults and Adolescents		
Male-to-Male Sexual Contact	—	60.3
Injection Drug Use	39.5	21.2
Male-to-Male Sexual Contact and Injection Drug Use	—	9
Heterosexual Contact	57.4	8.1
Other	3.1	1.4
Totals	100%	100%
Child (<13 years at diagnosis)	**Both Sexes**	
Perinatal	91.5	
Other or undetermined	8.5	
Totals	100%	

*The Centers for Disease Control and Prevention tracks diagnosis of AIDS in terms of two basic age groups: adult/adolescents (age 13 and older) and pediatric (children under 13).

Source: Adapted from Centers for Disease Control and Prevention. 2009. *HIV/AIDS Surveillance Report, 2009,* Vol. 21, pp. 21–22, Table 2a. Atlanta: U.S. Department of Health and Human Services, Centers for Disease Control and Prevention. www.cdc.gov/hiv/topics/surveillance/resources/reports/. Published February 2011.

mucous membranes (such as eyes or inside of the nose), or cuts and sores. To date, the most common means of transmission is through sexual contact, as indicated in Table 6.4. For children under age 13, the most common means of contracting the AIDS virus is from a mother either with or at risk for HIV infection (Centers for Disease Control and Prevention, 2010b).

Contrary to what some people continue to believe, according to current evidence, HIV cannot be transmitted by casual contact. That is, AIDS cannot be transmitted through touching, coughing, sneezing, breathing, handshakes, or socializing, nor can it be spread through toilet seats, food, eating utensils, drinking out of the same glass, water fountains, or insects. And the risk of contracting AIDS through saliva (as in kissing) is said to be extremely low.

HIV/AIDS and Risk Most observers of HIV/AIDS agree that certain kinds of behavior place people at greater risk of infection than other kinds of behavior. There is little dispute that oral and genital sex are the most risky for the transmission of HIV and AIDS. And given the high rate of oral sex not only among gays, heterosexuals—young and old, but also adolescents, the potential risks of Americans contracting HIV and/or AIDS is quite high. While research indicates that HIV transmission can occur through oral sex, it is considered a rare occurrence. However, the risk, no matter how small, can be reduced by making

sure one's mouth and gums are in good condition before engaging in oral sex as well as not allowing a sexual partner to ejaculate in her/his mouth ("Safe Sex," 2011; Centers for Disease Control and Prevention, 2009). Other risk factors include, but are not limited to, engaging in sexual activities (anal, oral, or vaginal) without protection, with multiple partners and, if one currently has another STI or vaginal infection. Right now, the most basic ways to control the spread of both viruses are believed to be through avoiding high-risk sex (either through abstinence, exclusive relationships, latex condoms) and through careful monitoring of transfusions of blood and other body fluids.

Who Gets AIDS? The Intersections of Race, Class, Gender, Sexual Orientation, and Age The intersections of race, class, gender, age, and sexual orientation are clearly revealed in various HIV/AIDS statistics (see Figure 6.3). People most frequently affected by HIV continue to be men generally and gay men more specifically, but increasingly there is a new face of AIDS: It is an epidemic among heterosexuals, especially heterosexual women. It is also an epidemic of the poor, which means it is increasingly an epidemic of some groups of color that are found disproportionately among the poor. For example, an increasingly high percentage of new HIV infections is occurring in African American women, particularly poor rural women. And although the number of new AIDS cases among White gays has declined in several major cities since 1990, the rate of infection among gay men of color, especially African Americans, has surged significantly. No longer confined to gay men and intravenous drug abusers, AIDS in the United States is increasingly an epidemic of the heterosexual population as well (see Table 6.4).

Race/Ethnicity and HIV/AIDS Among racial/ethnic groups in the United States, African Americans face the most severe burden of HIV and AIDS. More African Americans are living with HIV or are already dead from AIDS than any other single racial or ethnic group in the United States—a crisis one African American AIDS activist calls a state of emergency for the African American community. Although African Americans represent only about 13 percent of the U.S. population, in 2009, they accounted for more than one-half (52 percent) of all diagnoses of HIV infection, and the rate of AIDS diagnosis was 44.4. Although new HIV infections among African Americans overall have been fairly stable since the early 1990s, compared with members of other races and ethnicities, they continue to account for a higher proportion of cases at all stages of HIV—from new infections to deaths. Researchers at the CDC estimate that about 1 in 50 African American men and 1 in 160 African American women are infected with HIV. By comparison, 1 in 250 White men and 1 in every 3,000 White women are infected. To date, 230,000 African Americans have died from HIV-related illnesses representing almost one-half (40 percent) of the total such deaths in the United States (Avert, 2011; Centers for Disease Control and Prevention, 2010b).

Latinas/os are also disproportionately impacted by HIV/AIDS. In 2009, Latinas/os accounted for an estimated 20 percent of all persons living with HIV/AIDS, 20 percent of all new diagnoses, and 16 percent of deaths of persons with AIDS in that year. From 1992 through the end of December 2009, 89,297 Latinas/os with an AIDS diagnosis had died. Although the incidence of new cases among Latinas/os is lower than that for African Americans, it is more than three times the rate for Whites. The rates and percentages of HIV and AIDS infections as well as deaths for other groups of color are

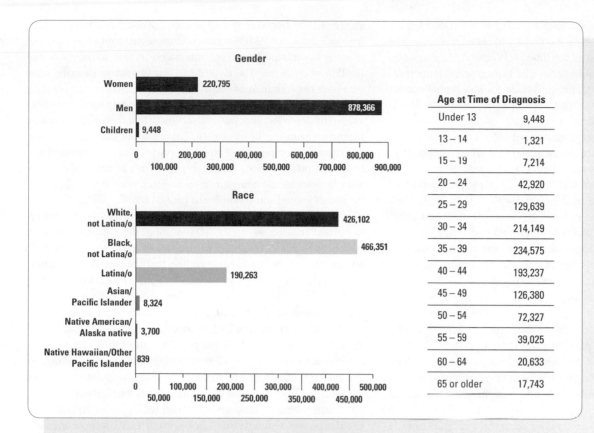

FIGURE 6.3
Cumulative AIDS Cases in the United States by Gender, Race, and Age through December 2009

Source: Adapted from Centers for Disease Control and Prevention. 2009. *HIV/AIDS Surveillance Report, 2009,* Vol. 21 (Atlanta: U.S. Department of Health and Human Services, Centers for Disease Control and Prevention): pp. 21–22, Table 2a: www.cdc.gov/hiv/topics/surveillance/resources/reports/. Published February 2011.

considerably smaller. For example, Native Hawaiians and other Pacific Islanders and Native Americans and Alaskan Natives had the lowest percentage of all persons living with AIDS in 2008—0.09 and 0.36 percent, respectively. Likewise, in 2009, these two groups also had the lowest percentage of new diagnoses of AIDS—0.15 and 0.16 percent, respectively. In addition, only about 1 percent of Asian Americans were living with AIDS in 2008. In raw numbers, next to African Americans, the most people living with AIDS in 2008 were White Americans, an estimated 163,238 representing 34 percent of the AIDS infected population. Thirty percent of those who died from AIDS in 2008 were White, and Whites represented more than two-fifths (43 percent) of all HIV/AIDS-related deaths from 1992 through 2008. Some of the most important HIV/AIDS prevention challenges faced by African American and Latinas/os have to do with culture and the fact that members of both groups may face greater barriers to accessing HIV/AIDS information, resources, and medical care than their White counterparts (Centers for Disease Control and Prevention, 2011a, 2011b).

Socioeconomic Class and HIV/AIDS Not only is race a significant and very visible factor in the HIV/AIDS epidemic but also socio-economic class and geographic regions in the United States have emerged as key factors in the nations HIV/AIDS epidemic. According to a *USA Today* analysis of HIV infection from 43 states, there is a strong link between poverty and HIV, with the strongest link in the South. According to this analysis, there has been a tremendous shift in percentages of HIV/AIDS diagnoses from large cities across the United States to the South, becoming heavily concentrated in poor counties in southern states. Southern counties with the highest rates of HIV infection are among the

poorest in the country. Moreover, the South's HIV infection rates in general are statistically higher than the rest of the country. That there is a strong interconnection between HIV, poverty, and the South is evidenced in the fact that of 175 counties in the United States that rank among the top 20 percent for both HIV and poverty, all but six are located in the South. Elsewhere in the country, counties with the highest rates of HIV-infected people have on average about one in seven people living in poverty, compared to one in five people in the South's most heavily infected counties. Some experts point out that southern states generally suffer from a myriad of health issues, including HIV/AIDS because of poverty, a low-level of academic achievement, fragile families, insufficient sex education for children, misinformation about HIV/AIDS among adults, and the stigma associated with being gay. Other factors include the rising rate of drug addiction and the disproportionate rate of poverty compared to cities and counties outside the South. Furthermore, the age at which children first become sexually active is fairly young, especially in the Deep South.

The HIV/AIDS epidemic has become particularly heavily entrenched among African American women and men living in pockets of poverty in the South. On average, they are poorer than Whites in 96 percent of the 175 counties with high HIV and poverty rates. In some of these counties, more than 40 percent of African Americans live below the poverty level. These counties are also those with the highest rates of HIV-infection. The rate of HIV infection in Mississippi is particularly acute for African Americans where they account for 37 percent of the population but twice that (76 percent) of new cases of HIV. In the highest-ranking counties, only 11 had higher rates of HIV infection among Whites than Blacks (Sternberg and Gillum, 2011).

Gender, Age, Sexual Orientation, and HIV/AIDS Men are more affected by HIV/AIDS in the United States than women. For example, in 2009, three out of four new HIV and AIDS diagnoses were for male adults or adolescents. The transmission route leading to HIV diagnoses for this group is male-to-male sexual contact followed by heterosexual contact and injection drug use. This is true for males and adolescents across racial and ethnic categories. However, the lifetime risk of becoming infected with the HIV infection is much greater for some racial and ethnic groups than others. For example, it is estimated that at some point in their lifetimes, 1 in 16 Black men and 1 in 36 Hispanic men compared to 1 in 104 White men will be diagnosed with HIV. In 2009, Black males accounted for almost one-half (47 percent) of all new infections, followed by White males (32 percent) and Hispanic males (19 percent). Relative to sexual orientation, gay and bisexual men account for the greatest number of new HIV infections as well as those living with HIV/AIDS (59 percent).

On the other hand, although more men than women are infected with HIV/AIDS, the viruses are taking an increasing toll on women. Women now account for an estimated 24 percent of new HIV infections as well as an increasing share of new AIDS cases. Women of color, especially African American women, as we have seen, have been very hard hit and represent 66 percent of all women diagnosed and living with the HIV infection. In addition, African American women and Latinas together represent about one-fourth of all U.S. women, yet they account for 80 percent of AIDS cases to date among women. Women and adolescent girls are most vulnerable to the infection as a result of heterosexual sexual contact. In 2009, for example, 73 percent of adult females and adolescents living with an HIV diagnosis were infected through heterosexual contact; the remaining females were infected through injecting drug use (Centers for Disease Control and Prevention, 2011b).

As with males, the main transmission route leading to HIV diagnoses for females is consistent across racial and ethnic groups. However, African American women have not only the highest prevalence of HIV diagnosis among women but also a much higher risk for contracting HIV/AIDS through heterosexual contact. According to many experts on the subject, this is due, in part, to the *down low* (or DL) phenomena. The term down low is used to describe men who have sex with men as well as with women. However, these men do not call themselves gay or bisexual. Female partners of men who are on the down low generally do not know that their partner is also having sex with one or more men. These women have a higher risk of getting HIV, especially if the male partner had unprotected sex with HIV-positive men. Although this term has most often been used to describe the behavior of some Black men, it also describes the sexual lives of some White and Latino men.

Some observers believe this down-low behavior may be an important source of HIV/AIDS among heterosexual African American women. Because the incidence of AIDS remains highest among gays, there is still some feeling that the rest of the population is relatively safe from exposure to the virus. However, this could not be farther from the truth. For example, estimates are that roughly one-fifth of gays marry heterosexually. Thus, heterosexual wives of gay men stand a high probability of being exposed to the virus. This does not include the possible exposure of women who are married to or have sexual relationships with bisexual males. In this context, of concern in African American communities is the increasing number of new HIV/AIDS cases that involve African American men who have sex with men (MSM) who do not identify themselves as homosexual or bisexual. Some of these men are former prison inmates who may have been raped or started engaging in sex with men while incarcerated.

Women who only have sex with other women might think they are safe from HIV, given that to date, female-to-female transmission of HIV/AIDS is rare. However, these women are not necessarily safe from the possibility of contracting HIV or AIDS, particularly if other risk factors are present. For example, of those who report having had sex only with women, 98 percent also had another risk—intravenous drug use in most cases (Centers for Disease Control

The AIDS gap between the sexes is one gap that women are not fighting to close. Unfortunately, although an increasingly high number of newly infected adults have been women, some health specialists warn that AIDS prevention is still too focused on men.
Source: Reprinted by permission of William Costello for *USA Today*.

and Prevention, 2011a; Kaiser Family Foundation, 2008). Overall, the estimated lifetime risk of contracting the HIV virus is 1 in 32 for Black women and 1 in 106 for Latinas compared to 1 in 588 for White females. Many women with HIV are low income or poor and most of them have important family and other responsibilities, face limited access to the health care system, and experience deep disparities in receipt of care and treatment compared to men. All of these factors complicate the management of their illness (Centers for Disease Control and Prevention, 2010b, 2011a, 2011b).

As we already know, age is also an important factor in contracting AIDS. Through the end of 2008, 99 percent of children with AIDS contracted the disease from their mothers before, during, or after birth (for example, during breast-feeding). Of the remaining 1 percent of children with AIDS, 7 percent contracted the disease from blood transfusions or are hemophiliacs. Today, AIDS is the sixth leading cause of death in children under age 5 (Centers for Disease Control and Prevention, 2008b, 2011b). Often these children, across race, have mothers who are poor, are intravenous drug abusers, or have partners who are. These women also have little or no access to drug treatment programs or health care facilities.

At the other end of the age spectrum, elderly people are seldom thought of as HIV- or AIDS-infected. However, the number of people age 50 and older living with HIV/AIDS has been increasing in recent years. Women and men age 50 and older account for 14 percent of all AIDS cases, and the rates of diagnosis has increased faster than for those under age 50. According to the Centers for Disease Control and Prevention (2008b), this increase is due in part to highly active anti-retroviral therapy, which has made it possible for many HIV-infected persons to live longer, and partly due to newly diagnosed infections in persons over age 50. HIV among adults over age 50 is not new. What has changed over the years is the mode of transmission. In the early years of the HIV epidemic, blood transfusion was the major

Although no country is untouched by HIV/AIDS, countries in sub-Saharan Africa, such as Tanzania (with 1,400,000 people living with HIV/AIDS), are the hardest-hit. In its wake, AIDS is responsible for leaving vast numbers of children across Africa without one or both parents. For example, the young orphan pictured here at the Nkoaranga Orphanage near Arusha in Tanzania is one of 1,300,000 AIDS orphans alive in Tanzania in 2009.

transmission mode among the senior population. Today, however, heterosexual contact and needle sharing among IV drug users older than age 50 are the main causes of HIV infection in older Americans.

The figures are staggering. Heterosexual transmission in men over age 50 is up 94 percent, and the rate has doubled in women since 1991. And while prevention and education dollars are concentrated toward young adult populations, seniors are not getting safer sex education and continue to get infected with HIV (Centers for Disease Control and Prevention, 2011b; Cichocki, 2007). Statistics such as these illustrate how our misconceptions about various social and cultural groups have ramifications for various other aspects of our lives, including medical diagnoses for certain diseases and illnesses. Because the majority of people who are at the highest risk of contracting the virus are members of categories that this society values least (gays, poor people, people of color, women, the elderly), AIDS is a deeply divisive social and political issue. However, AIDS is first and foremost a critical public health issue that represents not one but multiple epidemics: an inner-city epidemic, a rural epidemic, an epidemic of the poor, and an epidemic among women, among the elderly, among intravenous drug users, among gay men, among African Americans, among Latinas/os, among non-Latina/o Whites, and heterosexual women.

AIDS as a National and International Issue As bleak and disturbing as the discussion of HIV/AIDS and the accompanying statistics are for the United States, the AIDS epidemic is not merely a U.S. problem. It is a global pandemic and disaster. Since the beginning of the HIV/AIDS epidemic, 60 million people have contracted HIV, and 25 million have died of AIDS-related causes. An estimated 33.3 million people are living with HIV/AIDS today. Every day, more than 7,200 persons become infected with HIV and more than 5,700 persons die from AIDS, primarily because of inadequate access to HIV prevention and treatment services. About half of all new adult HIV infections occur among 15–24-year-olds. AIDS is the leading cause of death in sub-Saharan Africa and the fourth leading cause of death globally. In 2009, an estimated 2.6 million people in the world were newly infected with HIV—370,000 of whom were children, bringing the total number of children living with HIV to 2.1 million. And, as of 2009, 16.6 million children had lost one or both parents to HIV/AIDS, the overwhelming majority of whom are children living in sub-Saharan Africa.

Globally, women are disproportionately affected with HIV/AIDS, accounting for half of all adults living with HIV worldwide, the majority of whom are believed to be between ages 15 and 35; and they account for 76 percent of those infected in sub-Saharan Africa. Young women and girls make up a growing proportion of those infected in Asia, Eastern Europe, and Latin America and 50 percent of those living with HIV/AIDS in the Caribbean. There are several reasons that women and girls are at increased risk, including (1) gender-related norms related to masculinity and power: for example, women often are powerless in decisions to have sex or use a condom; they are also often forced into sexual slavery; (2) women and girls have greater biological susceptibility to HIV infection; (3) gender-related barriers: for instance, in many countries women are denied equal access to information, education, training, health care, and other social services, which makes it difficult to achieve effective preventive programs; (4) in some poor countries where there are limited job opportunities, many women are forced to labor as sex workers (prostitutes); because of their poor economic situations they are unlikely to refuse clients who do not wear condoms. In many countries (such as South Africa, China, Thailand) large numbers of prostitutes have been infected with HIV and are blamed for its spread; and (5) violence against women, which is experienced by 10 to 60 percent of women worldwide (UN Women, 2011; USAID, 2011; Global Health Council, 2008).

Approximately 97 percent of people living with HIV/AIDS live in low- and middle-income countries. Although no country is untouched by HIV infection and AIDS, sub-Saharan Africa continues to be the hardest-hit region and is home to 68 percent of all people living with HIV worldwide, with North Africa and the Middle East and the Caribbean are a close second and third, respectively. Seven countries in sub-Saharan Africa each have more than one million people living with HIV/AIDS, with South Africa leading the way with 5,600,000 followed by Nigeria with 3,400,000. The other five countries include Kenya (1,500,000), Mozambique and Tanzania (each with 1,400,000), and Uganda and Zimbabwe (each with 1,200,000). According to some health experts and AIDS activists, AIDS is Africa's greatest social disaster since the transatlantic slave trade (Avert, 2011; Ritter, 2001b).

Parts of Asia (especially the South and Southeast) and Latin America also continue to experience severe epidemics at the national or local level. Moreover, Eastern Europe and Central Asia continue to be the regions with the fastest-growing HIV/AIDS epidemic in the world (UN Women, 2011; USAID, 2011). The HIV infection rate in South and Southeast Asia is also at epidemic proportions. It is estimated that there are close to 6 million adults and children living with HIV or AIDS in this region, more than the total number of people elsewhere in the entire industrialized world. The spread of HIV infection and AIDS in China, India, Thailand, and Cambodia, to name only a few, has been fueled by an extensive sex trade and the use of illicit drugs. In China, for instance, it is estimated that close to three-quarters of 1 million people were infected with HIV in 2007, the majority of whom are intravenous drug abusers (UNAIDS/WHO, 2008; UNAIDS, 2008).

The social and economic consequences of AIDS are tremendous. AIDS has not only impacted the health of people around the world, but also education, industry, agriculture, transportation, human resources, and economies in general. AIDS has widened the gulf between rich and poor nations, and the United States and other wealthy nations have been criticized for completely ignoring or, at best, doing little to help fight the spread of the devastating virus in Africa. Critics say that rich countries could go a long way in helping the peoples of Africa by funding prevention programs and drug treatments. And drug companies could help by selling drugs to Africa at cost (AIDS in Africa, 2001; Ritter, 2001).

AIDS Prevention and Sexual Responsibility The AIDS pandemic has focused the spotlight on sexuality and sexual responsibility. A variety of groups have campaigned for **safe sex.** Such campaigns are geared toward informing people of how to protect themselves from AIDS and other sexually transmitted infections through abstinence or by engaging in responsible sex. The major underlying theme is that abstinence is desirable and the only sure method of prevention, but that people who cannot or will not abstain should use protective methods, most notably condoms. Not all people agree with the premise of the safe-sex

Sparked by the AIDS crisis, posters, advertisements, and warning signs like these amusing condoms encourage the practice of safer sex.

philosophy, however. Critics contend that the premise of safe sex promotes sexual promiscuity and does little, if anything, to promote abstinence. They argue that abstinence, not safe sex, should be the official public policy. The evidence on the effectiveness of campaigns for safe sex or complete abstinence is mixed. Although there was some evidence in the mid-1990s that casual sex was on the decrease and sexual partners (from teenagers to the elderly) were practicing safe sex, primarily through the increased use of condoms, today there is some indication that, at least among some groups, casual sex or sex with risky partners without the use of condoms or other protective measures is on the rise again.

In the final analysis, each one of us has a responsibility to engage in sex in a manner that is protective of both our own and our partners' health and well-being. In addition, the AIDS prevention agenda today and in the future must be global and must not focus exclusively on effecting changes in individuals' sexual behavior. More broadly, it must promote improvements in the overall status and quality of life of women, people of color, children, poor people, and people living in developing countries so that they have more control over when and how sex takes place. The AIDS prevention agenda must also work toward providing individuals and families with better medical care, regardless of whether or not they are impacted by HIV/AIDS or other sexually transmitted infections. And it must encourage continued and improved funding for research on an AIDS vaccine that would be appropriate for use in developing countries.

Having read this chapter, now think about your own sexuality and write your personal sexual script (see the Writing Your Own Script box).

Supporting Marriages and Families

People are engaging in sexual activities at earlier ages and remaining sexually active for much longer periods into old age. Although individuals, marital partners, and families bear responsibility in

Writing Your Own Script

IDENTIFYING YOUR SEXUAL VALUES

Thinking about your own sexuality, write a short essay outlining your values with respect to sexuality. What have been the major sources of sexual information for you? Consider major periods in your life, for example, childhood, adolescence, young adulthood, middle age, and older. Who or what has been the major influence on your sexual values? Are your sexual values the same as those of your parents? If not, how do they differ? How tolerant are you of sexual lifestyles different from your own? If you have children, what will you teach them about sexuality? Will you be supportive of sex education in your child's school? Why or why not?

promoting and living safe sexual lifestyles, the need for policies and programs that support marriages and families is nowhere more glaring than in the area of human sexuality. Whatever values and beliefs we hold individually about human sexuality, it is clear that as a nation, we cannot bury our heads in the sand and pretend that celibacy is the only answer to many of the pressing issues and problems that surround the sexual practices and behaviors of many Americans. Research, for instance, clearly demonstrates that the majority of both younger and older people no longer tie sexuality to long-term personal or institutional commitment. Teens and adults have sex before, during, and after marriage with a variety of partners over their life course. Therefore, in order to contribute to the strength of intimate partnered relationships, marriages, and families, there is a need for federal, state, and local policies that recognize these realities and that provide access to quality medical and social education that promotes responsibility and safety in terms of sexual practices and behaviors.

The overwhelming majority of Americans agree that preventing HIV/AIDS and other sexually transmitted infections as well as unintended teenage pregnancies are public health issues that should rely on scientific evidence and not political or religious ideology. Although sexual abstinence is a desirable objective, especially for youth, programs and policies must also include education and support for those who are already sexually active, including later-life adults. Policies that (1) are ideologically motivated rather than empirically driven, (2) do not support access for all Americans to quality and affordable health care, as well as (3) support the investment of hundreds of millions of federal and state funds to programs that have little or no evidence of effectiveness, all constitute poor fiscal and public health initiatives and contribute to the weakening rather than the strengthening of American marriages and families. The bottom line must be the efficacy in educating and modifying unsafe and risky sexuality behaviors and strengthening American marriages, families, and intimate partnered relationships.

SUMMARY

We are all sexual beings, and we spend a large amount of our time engaged in a variety of sexual behaviors. Although some people still believe the Freudian notion that our sexuality is biologically driven, sociologists stress the social basis of human sexuality. A sociological perspective of human sexuality focuses on the tremendous role that culture plays in creating and shaping the content of our sexuality. Like other behaviors, sexual behavior is guided by cultural scripts. In learning society's sexual guidelines, we in effect create or invent our capacity for sexual behavior. As we learn other important norms of our culture, we also simultaneously learn about our sexuality from a variety of sources including family, peers, and mass media.

There is some debate over whether a sexual revolution has occurred. Whatever the verdict, it is clear that significant changes occurred in the approach to sexuality in twentieth-century United States. The most dramatic changes occurred among women, across race, class, and the age cohort. Americans have continued many of the sexual patterns and behaviors noted in the closing decades of the twentieth century. However, in the wake of increasingly new ways of communicating through technology, new ways of engaging with others sexually have emerged in the twenty-first century and become popular among growing segments of the American population. Moreover, over the last decade, global sex surveys have reported on a range of sexual behaviors in countries across the world indicating that as with Americans, people worldwide are more sexually active and engage in a wider variety of sexual practices than in the past. However, Americans sexual behavior in general seems often to fall somewhere is the middle of the average sexual practices of adults worldwide.

Although historically U.S. society has classified heterosexuality as the only acceptable form of human sexuality, humans actually express a range of sexual orientations or preferences. According to Alfred Kinsey, these orientations fall along a continuum, with heterosexuality and homosexuality at each extreme, and bisexuality falling somewhere in the middle. As with sexual orientation, sexual expression incorporates a variety of behaviors, ranging from activities involving only the self to those that involve two or more individuals. Masturbation and sexual fantasies and dreams are autoerotic activities in which the majority of people engage at some point in their lives. Petting and oral–genital sex are the most common sexual behaviors in which humans engage.

There have been dramatic changes in human sexuality in every phase of the lifecycle. Many unmarried people are engaging in sexual activities with little expectation that such relationships will lead to marriage. Teenagers in particular are increasingly sexually active. Within marriages, wives and husbands are experiencing a wider range of sexuality and are more satisfied with their sexual relationships than in the past. In addition, a growing number of married people are engaging in extramarital relationships. And

although physiological changes cause changes in the sexual response of older adults, most enjoy satisfying romantic and sexual relationships well into old age.

The devastating effect of HIV/AIDS for individuals, families, communities, and nations cannot be overstated. The spread of HIV/AIDS is not just a concern in the United States. HIV/AIDS is a global pandemic affecting peoples in almost every country of the world. The hardest hit, however, are the peoples of Africa and South and Southeast Asia. In the final analysis, on a national and structural level, government, social, political, and economic policies must address not only the viruses of HIV and AIDS but also all of the factors associated with it including poverty, unemployment, racism, and discrimination. On an individual or personal level, each one of us has a responsibility to engage in sex in a manner that is protective of both our own and our partners' health and well-being.

KEY TERMS

human sexuality	homophobia	nocturnal emissions	coitus	acquired
sexual double standard	homosexuality	wet dreams	menopause	immunodeficiency
sexual identity	bisexuality	pleasuring	sexual dysfunction	syndrome (AIDS)
sexual orientation	transgender	petting	sexually transmitted	safe sex
heterosexism	autoeroticism	cunnilingus	infections (STIs)	
heterosexuality	masturbation	fellatio		

QUESTIONS FOR STUDY AND REFLECTION

1. For the most part, the media and mass advertising flaunt sexuality and define its content for all of us, including children. Consider how sexuality is presented in ads for popular products (cars, perfume, and alcoholic beverages) as well as in rock and hip-hop videos. How have these images and definitions of sexuality affected your behavior? How closely do they resemble your everyday life? Is it possible to ignore the sexual messages of the media? Do you think there is a relationship between media emphasis on sexuality and the high rate of unmarried pregnancies? Explain.

2. What kind of AIDS awareness, if any, takes place on your college campus? Has awareness of the disease affected sexual behavior on your campus? Conduct a brief survey of students on your campus about their knowledge of HIV/AIDS and other STIs and their sexual behavior relative to HIV/AIDS and other STIs. Do you think that people who have AIDS should be isolated from those who do not? What do

you think about mandatory AIDS testing in schools and in the workplace?

3. How do your views differ from those of people you know in your own generation and those of your parents and your grandparents concerning sexual activity or pregnancy outside of legal marriage, oral–genital sexual activity, extramarital sexual behavior, homosexuality, bisexuality, and sexual behavior among older adults? How do you feel about your body? Are your feelings different from those of people of younger or older generations? Explain.

4. What were your feelings when reading this chapter? Did some subjects or topics make you uncomfortable? How comfortable are you discussing topics such as masturbation, wet dreams, sexual fantasies, and positions in sexual intercourse with a significant other? Parents? In a classroom? Your answers to these questions can be used as a way of getting in touch with your own orientation toward sexuality.

ADDITIONAL RESOURCES

SOCIOLOGICAL STUDIES

CARBADO, DEVON W. 1999. *Black Men on Race, Gender, and Sexuality*. New York: New York University Press. A collection of essays covering such topics as the legal construction of Black male identity and sexuality, the role of Black men in Black women's quest for racial equality, and the heterosexist nature of Black political engagement. It features the work of diverse African American males. It is an excellent source for discussions about the intersections of race, class, gender, and sexuality.

REINISCH, JUNE, AND RUTH BEASLEY. 1990. *The Kinsey Institute New Report on Sex: What You Must Know to Be Sexually Literate*. New York: St. Martin's Press. Over the years, the Kinsey Institute has received hundreds of questions concerning human sexuality. This book attempts to address some of the most commonly asked questions surrounding topics such as AIDS, other sexually transmitted infections, and sexuality and aging.

RICH, ADRIENNE. 1980. "Compulsory Heterosexuality and Lesbian Existence." *Signs* 5:631–660. A classic and influential essay on the sociopolitical nature of female sexuality generally and lesbianism specifically.

ROSE, TRICIA. 2004. *Longing to Tell*. New York: Picador. A set of revealing and inspiring narratives from a variety of women of color—of various ages and economic and educational backgrounds—who talk about sexuality, race, their sexual relationships, first sexual encounters with women and men, intimate clichés, and their coming of age as a woman. Tricia Rose sums up well the overall dynamics of the sexual ramifications that women of color encounter today.

FILM

Brokeback Mountain. 2005. This film presents an epic love story about a forbidden and secretive relationship between two young men—a ranch hand and a rodeo cowboy—who meet in the summer of 1963 herding sheep in the high grasslands of contemporary Wyoming and unexpectedly form a lifelong bond. The complications, joys, and tragedies of their relationship provide excellent text for a sociological analysis of same-sex love, heterosexual marriage, family, and American cultural confines, definitions, and expectations of masculinity—what it is to be a man.

Sex and the City. 2008. A romantic comedy, this film is an adaptation of the hit cable television series of the same title. A little time has passed, and in keeping with the TV series' melancholy tone that fairy-tale endings don't necessarily mean happily ever after, the major characters in this film are: Carrie is still involved with the on-off-and-finally-on-again relationship with Mr. Big; Miranda is adjusting to marriage and overscheduled motherhood; Charlotte remains a wide-eyed dreamer; and Samantha chafes at monogamy. Each woman, inevitably, faces her own obstacles in her respective relationships. The film demythologizes love and presents sexual relationship issues without the silver lining. It undermines many of the American myths about romantic love and sex as issues of ambivalence, regret, and hope as well as singlehood, childbearing and childrearing, and

female professionalism are explored within the context of various types of sexual relationships. The movie (as does the series) presents an excellent cultural paradigm through which classroom discussions of female sexuality, femininity, sexual relationships, singlehood, and urban life can be carried out.

LITERARY WORKS

KUDAKA, GERALDINE, ED. 1995. *On a Bed of Rice: An Asian American Erotic Feast*. New York: Anchor. An interesting anthology of contemporary erotic prose and poetry by established and up-and-coming writers of Chinese, Filipino, Japanese, Korean, Vietnamese, and Indian descent explores the themes of sexual awakening, marriage, and interracial love. The stories range from haunting to humorous; some deal with the way that race and sex are intertwined in America; others with the myths about Asian American sexuality. This anthology is proof that sex and eroticism need not be taboo subjects for college students.

WILSON, BARBARA. 1990. *Gaudi Afternoon*. Seattle, WA: Seal Press. The author of this novel uses the mystery genre to explore a feminist perspective on sociologically relevant topics such as sexual orientation and identity, gender identity, and gender roles. It is an interesting lesbian crime novel that raises questions such as what makes a person straight or queer, femme or butch, lesbian or dyke, transgendered or translated. This novel provides professors and students with a rich narrative to examine, analyze, and critique the shifting debates that view gender and sexual identities as, in the words of gender theorist Judith Butler, "performative strategies of insubordination."

INTERNET

www.indiana.edu/~kinsey/index.html The Kinsey Institute, founded by noted sociologist Alfred Kinsey, sponsors this site, which is dedicated to supporting interdisciplinary research in the study of human sexuality. The site contains descriptions of the center's latest published research on human sexuality.

www.thebody.com This site, The Body, is a comprehensive multimedia HIV and AIDS health Internet site and information resource center. It provides information on more than 250 topics. Its stated mission is to lower barriers between patients and clinicians, demystify HIV/AIDS and its treatment, improve patients' quality of life, and foster community through human connection.

www.goaskalice.columbia.edu/ This site, Go Ask Alice!, is a health question-and-answer Internet service produced by Columbia University's Health Education Program. Its mission is to increase access to, and use of, health information by providing factual, in-depth, straightforward, and nonjudgmental information to assist users' decision making about their physical, sexual, emotional, and spiritual health.

www.guttmacher.org This site of the Alan Guttmacher Institute is committed to understanding issues of family planning, contraception, and social issues such as teenage pregnancy. Those who visit this Web site can search for a variety of information in the form of fact sheets as well as information about current research and family planning services.

Succeed with MyFamilyLab®
www.myfamilylab.com

Watch. Explore. Read. The New MyFamilyLab is designed just for you. Each chapter features a pre-test and post-test to help you learn and review key concepts and terms. Experience Marriages and Families in action with dynamic visual activities, videos, and readings to enhance your learning experience.

Here are a few activities you will find for this chapter.

Watch on **myfamilylab.com**

Video clips feature important concepts in the study of Marriages and Families. Watch:
- Sexuality Education Debate

Explore on **myfamilylab.com**

Social Explorer is an interactive application that allows you to explore Census data through interactive maps. Explore the Social Explorer Activity:
- The Increase of Single Women with Children

Read on **myfamilylab.com**

MyFamilyLab includes primary source readings from classic and contemporary sociologists from around the world. Read:
- Fausto-Sterling: "The Five Sexes: Why Male and Female Are Not Enough"

7

Living Single, Living with Others: Nonmarital Lifestyles

What Will You Learn?

- Define and understand the sociological meaning of key terms.
- Describe the major nonmarital lifestyles in the United States today.
- Apply the sociological imagination to examine the types of intentional communities around the world and the motivations people have for being members.
- Assess the pro and con arguments for legalizing same sex marriages.
- Increase your awareness and understanding of changing marriage norms in the United States and around the world.
- Question how and why the experience of cohabitation can affect marital stability.

IN THE NEWS

United States: New York Times

On March 22, 2011, an article appeared in the *New York Times* that set off a heated debate in many evangelical churches across the country. The article documented the frustrations of a single 37-year-old man, Mark Almlie, an ordained evangelical minister, as he searched for a new clerical position. Mr. Almlie lost his church position because of downsizing. In his search for a new position, Mr. Almlie replied to more than 500 job postings without success. He discovered

(continued on next page)

(continued from previous page)

that despite his seminary degree and years of experience, the fact that he was not married worked against him. He believes that he is being unfairly discriminated against because he is a single pastor (Eckholm, 2011). Similarly, Amy Mark, also ordained by the Evangelical Covenant Church, is seeking a permanent position but has only been able to find some temporary pastoral positions.

Both candidates have been questioned about whether they could counsel congregations composed of mostly married couple with children. Many of the postings they applied to specifically request "a family man." When they obtained interviews, they found that their singleness was seen as problematic. The interviewers seem to be concerned that a single person might be lesbian or gay, that children might not be safe with a single male or that

there could be something wrong because she or he isn't married. On the other hand, the economics of having a married pastor could work to the detriment of single candidates. There is often an expectation that a pastor's wife will provide unpaid labor, perhaps teaching Sunday school or doing volunteer work in the congregation.

WHAT WOULD YOU DO?

If you were to serve on a pastoral search committee, would a candidate's marital status be one of the criteria you would consider in your decision-making? Explain. Do you think that Mark Almlie and Amy Mark are correct when they assert that their singleness is a factor in their failure to find a church position?

((•─ Listen to the **Chapter Audio** on **myfamilylab.com**

lthough most Americans will marry at some point in their lives, increasing numbers of people are choosing to remain single into their 30s or even permanently. Many adults are forming relationships that differ in significant ways from traditional family structures. Others are living alone or remaining in their parental home well into their 20s and beyond. As is true of marriages and families today, nonmarital lifestyles make up a diverse range of social forms. Among the most common forms are singlehood, heterosexual cohabitation, lesbian and gay relationships, communal living, and group marriages. In this chapter, each of these lifestyles is examined from both a historical and a contemporary perspective.

Before we examine what it was like to be single in America's early years, we must clarify exactly what we mean by "single." The term is frequently used to describe anyone who is not currently married—the divorced, widowed, separated, and those who have never married. Including all of these diverse groups under one heading obscures the unique aspects of the lifestyles associated with each group. Thus, in this chapter we apply the concept of "single" to never-married people only.

📖● Read the **Document** *The Way We Weren't: The Myth and Reality of the "Traditional" Family* on **myfamilylab.com**

Historical Perspectives

Most of the data available on singles in colonial America refer primarily to White settlers. The marital status and lifestyles of Native Americans and African Americans, both free and enslaved, went largely unrecorded during this time. Therefore, we do not know how many individuals in these groups remained unmarried or what such a lifestyle might have been like for them. In addition, although there is a growing body of literature on single women in the eighteenth and nineteenth centuries, particularly middle-and upper-class women, scant information exists on the role of single men during this time. It is not that single men were nonexistent; in fact, quite the opposite was true. Single men made up a large proportion of immigrants to the United States at this time. But then as now, men's economic and political roles rather than their marital status were emphasized. Thus, the conclusions we can draw about the lifestyles of singles in America's past are indeed limited and cannot be assumed to apply to all of the diverse groups living here at that time.

A survey of America's past reveals that for much of this country's history marriage was the cultural ideal and the norm. In fact, positive views concerning the permanently single were rarely articulated. Instead, a social climate evolved that tended to devalue singlehood and to discriminate against individuals who remained unmarried. That some of this climate still prevails can be seen in the experiences of Mark Almlie and Amy Mark who we met at the opening of this chapter.

SINGLEHOOD IN EARLY AMERICA

Being single in early America was not easy—unmarried people often faced personal restrictions. For example, N. B. Shurtleff's (1853/1854) examination of the Massachusetts Bay Company's public records found that the authorities mandated "every town to dispose of all single persons and inmates within their town to service or otherwise" (quoted in Schwartz and Wolf, 1976:18). This "disposal" took the form of placing single people in the home of a responsible family, the belief being that all people need to be associated with a family to ensure that they live a proper life.

Unmarried women and men were commonly seen as defective or incomplete and were often the subject of ridicule. After studying this period, one investigator concluded that "bachelors were rare and were viewed with disapproval. They were in the class of suspected criminals" (Calhoun, 1917, 1:67). Single women were not spared derogatory labels either. Those women not married by age 20 were referred to as "stale maids." Unmarried women 5 years older became known as "ancient maids." Even today, terms such as old maid and spinster convey negative connotations.

Why were single people treated this way? The devaluation of singlehood was in large measure a result of the high value attached to marriage, a value strongly associated with religious beliefs. The Bible stressed the importance of marriage and family life. For example, in the book of Genesis (2:24), men are enjoined "to leave father and mother and cleave to a wife." There were also practical considerations. The early settlers were concerned with economic and personal survival. Hence, there was an imperative to increase the population and to share the burdens of earning a livelihood in this new land. Writer Alice Earle (1893:36) took note of this in her reflection on New England customs: "What could he do, how could he live in that new land without a wife? There were no housekeepers and he would scarcely have been allowed to have one if there were. What could a woman do in that new settlement among unbroken forests, uncultivated lands, without a husband?"

In sum, marriage was seen as a practical necessity, and singlehood was not considered an acceptable alternative because "the man without a family was evading a civic duty…and the husbandless woman had no purpose in life" (Spruill, 1938:137). Despite the negative ways in which single people were viewed and treated in colonial America, their numbers in the general population gradually increased as political, social, and economic changes combined to create new opportunities for them, especially for women.

SINGLEHOOD IN THE NINETEENTH AND EARLY TWENTIETH CENTURIES

The percentage of single women began to increase in the last decades of the eighteenth century and continued to do so into the nineteenth century. At its height, the trend represented some 11 percent of American women, those born between 1865 and 1875 (cited in Chambers-Schiller, 1984:3). This historical increase is important to recognize, because we tend to think of developments in our own period as unique rather than as a continuation of long-term trends. In 1890, 15 percent of women and 27 percent of men aged 30 to 34 had never married. In

1940, the comparable figures for this age group were 15 and 21 percent, respectively; by 1970, they had dropped to 6 and 9 percent (Kain, 1990:75). By 2009, however, the rates had increased to 26.3 percent for women and 34.9 percent for men (U.S. Census Bureau, 2011e).

What accounted for the increase in the single population in the nation's early years? As we saw in Chapter 5, marriage rates are related to changing demographic, economic, political, and cultural factors. So, too, are changing rates of singlehood. In the early 1800s, industrialization created new jobs for both women and men, allowing them a measure of financial independence. Furthermore, some occupations were considered incompatible with marriage. For example, it was common for communities to have rules requiring teachers to resign when they got married (Punke, 1940).

The Industrial Revolution was not the only event contributing to the growth of the single population. Earlier, the American Revolution gave rise to a new cultural ethos that emphasized individualism, self-reliance, and freedom of choice in pursuing one's goals. According to historian Lee Chambers-Schiller (1984), society's views of the unmarried woman moderated somewhat in this climate. Most Americans no longer thought of singlehood as a sin, even though to many it still seemed unnatural. An analysis of the professional and popular literature of the late nineteenth and early twentieth centuries reveals a changing attitude toward both singlehood and marriage (Freeman and Klaus, 1984).

The very title of Chambers-Schiller's (1984) study, *Liberty, a Better Husband*, provides insight into the decision to remain single.

Like many women in her day, Susan B. Anthony (1820–1906) received several proposals of marriage. She refused them all, preferring her independence to being a wife and homemaker. She devoted her life to the pursuit of equal rights for women.

Marriage could now be viewed as an option, and more women chose not to marry; some even proclaimed their decision publicly. As one nineteenth-century woman explained: "I've chosen my life as deliberately as my sisters and brothers have chosen theirs…I want to be a spinster, and I want to be a good one" (quoted in Freeman and Klaus, 1984:396). Other women saw their singlehood as a form of protest against the demands and restrictions of middle-class marriage and became advocates for women's rights. Thus, there emerged a new ideology, called "the cult of single blessedness," which proved beneficial to families and the community at large. It became socially acceptable for unmarried women to care for aging parents, the orphaned, the sick, and the indigent members of the community. Over time, such work came to be seen as appropriate vocations for women.

SINGLEHOOD TODAY: CURRENT DEMOGRAPHIC TRENDS

Although marriage remains the most common living arrangement for Americans today, significant numbers of people are choosing to be unmarried for all or at least part lives. In 2009, 26.1 percent of all people age 18 and over had never married, up from 15.6 percent in 1970 (Saluter, 1994; U.S. Census Bureau, 2011e). Most Americans who eventually marry do so by their mid-30s. Thus, as age increases, the proportion that have never married declines. This can readily be seen in Table 7.1, which compares the percentages of both sexes remaining single beyond the usual ages of marriage. At

✳ Explore the Concept
Social Explorer Activity:
Single Americans
on **myfamilylab.com**

TABLE 7.1 Never-Married by Age and Sex, 2009

	Sex	
Age	Males	Females
Total	29.5%	22.8%
18–19	98.1%	95.7%
20–24	87.0%	77.4%
25–29	61.1%	46.3%
30–34	34.9%	26.3%
35–39	22.5%	16.4%
40–44	18.4%	13.1%
45–54	14.8%	10.8%
55–64	7.9%	7.1%
65–74	4.8%	4.2%
75 and over	3.8%	3.9%

Source: Adapted from U.S. Census Bureau, *2011, Statistical Abstract of the United States: 2011.* Washington, DC: Government Printing Office: Table 57, p. 53.

all ages, the percentage of never-married men exceeds that of never-married women.

Among both sexes, African Americans and Latinos have higher rates of singlehood than their Asian and White counterparts: 43.3 percent of African American males, 37.5 percent of Latinos, 28.4 percent of Asian males, and 27.4 percent of White males were single compared to 40.7 percent of African American females, 27.1 percent of Latinas, 19.4 percent Asian females, and 19.9 percent of White females (U.S. Census Bureau, 2011e). Some social scientists attribute the higher rates among Blacks and Latinos to the economic disadvantages and higher unemployment rates experienced by these groups, especially among men (Ooms, 2002). Demographic trends play an especially crucial role in the lower marriage rate of African Americans, especially of African American women. High incarceration and mortality rates among young African American men have dramatically decreased the pool of marriageable men (Davis and Karar, 2009). Furthermore, African American parents often encourage their daughters to put education before marriage (Packer-Williams, 2009). Many of these women may place a higher value on academic achievement and consequently may forgo marriage if they do not find a partner who meets their expectations (Perry, Steele, and Hillard, 2003).

Comparable census data on the marital status of Native American women reveal a similar pattern of delayed marriage. For example, in 1980, 21 percent of Native American women ages 25 to 29 had never been married. By 2000, the corresponding rates had increased to 42 percent (Lichter and Qian, 2004). Nevertheless, as Table 7.1 shows, relatively few women and men remain unmarried after age 64.

The United States is not the only country to experience a growth in the never-married segment of the population. In fact, Britain is predicting that if present trends continue, married people will soon be in the minority. According to the government's Office for National Statistics, the percentage of married men is expected to fall from 53 percent in 2003 to 42 percent in 2031, while the percentage of married women will decline from 50 to 40 percent. The proportion of women who have never married is expected to rise from 28 to 39 percent between 2003 and 2031. The change in the percentage of never-married men is expected to be even more dramatic, increasing from 35 percent to almost 50 percent during that same period ("Marriage on the Rocks in Britain," 2005). Similarly, even in Asian countries where marriage has been considered almost compulsory for most adults, statistical trends indicate that the incidence of delayed marriage is increasing rapidly (see the In Other Places box).

Demystifying Singlehood

In his analysis of the lifestyles of singles, sociologist Peter Stein (1976) observed that for many years most Americans, including social scientists, thought of single people as "those who fail to marry," believing that no one would want to remain single by choice. Stein's work has helped dispel this myth and shows that the decision of whether to marry or stay single is conditioned by psychological, social, cultural, and economic factors. He characterizes these factors as a series of **pushes,** or negative factors in a current situation, and **pulls,** or attractions to a potential situation.

In Other Places

STAYING SINGLE IN ASIA: CHANGING NORMS

A major demographic change is sweeping the Asian continent. Recent census data reveal dramatic increases in the proportions of never-married women in their 30s and 40s. Near-universal marriage had been the norm in most Asian countries until quite recently. Only three decades ago, half of all women in many Asian countries were married before their 18th birthday. Then, the proportion of women ages 45–49 who had never married exceeded 2 percent only in Sri Lanka, Myanmar, and the Philippines. Today, however, delayed marriages and permanent singlehood are becoming common, especially in East and South East Asia. In Hong Kong, Singapore, and Myanmar, the proportion of women reaching their late 40s never married exceeds 10 percent and, if current trends continue, this rate will grow dramatically. For example, in Hong Kong, 20 percent of women ages 35–39 has never married. Other countries have similar figures—Myanmar (19 percent), Japan (18 percent), Taiwan (16 percent), and Singapore (15 percent) (Jones, 2010).

Several factors account for this rapid change. First, more women have expanded opportunities for higher education and careers. This, in turn, frees many women from having to rely on men for their financial well-being and provides women with the option of being more selective in finding a partner. An end result of this process can be delayed marriage or permanent singlehood, especially if they have found a career that is fulfilling to them. Second, cultural preferences for men to marry younger and less educated women and for women not to "marry down" have created a marriage squeeze for certain segments of the population. As education levels have increased, notions of individual choice have become more prevalent, leading some parents and families to forgo the practice of arranged marriages, thus taking pressure off women to marry. With the decline of arranged marriages, many young people have lost a means of finding suitable marriage prospects. Further, many young people migrate to urban areas for employment where services once provided by families such as food preparation, laundry, entertainment, and transportation are readily available. What many also find in large cities is greater toleration for nontraditional intimate relationships. Interviews with never-married women in Indonesia found that although many still retain a positive view of marriage and had expected to marry whey they were younger, they now realize that they may have postponed marriage too long and are now unable to find suitable mates. However, they also have a positive view of singlehood, believing that remaining single can also result in a satisfied and happy life (Ibrahim and Hassan, 2009; Situmorang, 2007).

Not all people see this demographic trend in a positive light. There is considerable tension about the role of singles in societies where marriage and family norms are still dominant. Sociologist Masahiro Yamada of Tokyo's Chuo University coined the term *parasite singles* to describe unmarried adults who still live with their parents and rely on them for taking care of many of their daily needs (Harney, 2010). It is too early to say whether these new rates of singlehood are temporary or long term. However, the governments of many of these Asian countries are sounding some alarms. What does a growing proportion of never marrieds mean for future fertility rates? What impact will this have on family structure and functioning? The government of Singapore is concerned enough about these trends that it sponsors Internet dating services for its unmarried adults (Jones and Gubhaju, 2009).

What do you think? Should a government be concerned about the marital status of its population? Should governments institute policies to encourage marriage and/or singlehood? If so, what should those policies look like? Explain.

INDIVIDUAL DECISION MAKING

On the one hand, people are pushed toward marriage by pressures from parents, cultural expectations, loneliness, a fear of independence, and a feeling of guilt about staying single. On the other hand, parental approval, the marriages of friends, physical attraction, and emotional attachment to another person and a desire for security, social status, and children pull people toward marriage. In a similar vein, the perception of relationships as suffocating and as obstacles to self-development as well as an awareness of the high divorce rate may push people toward singlehood. Career opportunities, a sense of self-sufficiency, freedom, and the desire for psychological and social autonomy may pull people toward singlehood.

Although Stein's data represent common patterns of experiences, pressures, and desires, these are not necessarily experienced in the same way by everyone or even by the same person at different times in the life cycle. For example, some parents exert great pressure on their children to marry; others do not. Some people are self-sufficient in young adulthood but as they get older feel a greater need to be involved with someone else on a daily basis, as voiced by a 34-year-old male: "I've liked being single. It allowed me to travel to exotic places, change jobs several times, and really get to know who I am as a person, but now that I've done all that, I'm ready to share my life with someone."

THE INFLUENCE OF SOCIAL AND ECONOMIC FORCES

Many Americans no longer view marriage as an economic or social necessity. The stigma attached to singlehood has lessened in recent years, and there has been a corresponding reduction in the perceived benefits associated with marriage. Indeed, changes in gender role expectations (see Chapters 3 and 10) may make marriage seem more unattractive to both women and men. On the one hand, some women are putting careers before marriage, not wishing to undertake the conflict involved in balancing work and family. On the other hand, some men delay or forgo marriage because they are reluctant to share in household tasks and childcare, now expected by increasing numbers of working women.

Economic factors play a critical role in the decision to stay single. In 2009, the number of young adults who have never married surpassed, for the first time in more than a century, the number of adults who were married. Many experts attribute this decline in marriage to the severe recession of the last several years. Will McElroy, 26, who lost his job as a computer programmer explains why he and his girlfriend of three years aren't getting married. "Yeah, it definitely takes money to get married and being married probably means eventually buying a house and having kids..." However, he said he would start thinking about a wedding once he gets a new job and the economy picks up (Eckholm, 2010). So, too, it seems will a majority of his peers. According to a recent survey, among 18- to 29-year-olds who are not currently married, 70 percent say they want to marry. Only a small minority (5 percent) say they do not want to marry (Wang and Taylor, 2011). Slightly younger adults tended to put a higher value on marriage. In a longitudinal study of 11,988 young adults between the ages of 20 and 24, 83 percent of unmarried respondents reported that they thought it was important or very important to be married

someday. This attitude varied somewhat by race and ethnicity. Asian young adults were most likely to report that marriage in the future was important to them (88 percent), followed by White young adults (84 percent), Latino young adults (83 percent), and Black young adults (78 percent) (Scott, et al, 2009). This study found that women were somewhat more likely to report that marriage was very important (53 percent than were men (47 percent). However, a recent study of 5,200 unmarried people ages 21 to 65 suggests that age is a factor. Overall, researchers found that as many men as women wanted to marry but younger ages (21 to 24) and older men (50 and up) were more favorably disposed to marriage than their female peers. In the between years, when women's biological clock is ticking, the ratio shifts the other way.

Studies of teenagers (ages 15–19) reveal that their attitudes toward marriage and intimate relationships are complex and changing. In a recent study, 91 percent of teen respondents indicated that having a good marriage and family life was either "quite important" or "extremely important" to them. A slightly lower percentage (81 percent) said they expected to marry some day. A still lower percentage (72 percent) said that they felt well prepared for marriage (Wood, Avellar, and Goesling, 2008). Although data from an earlier study found strong support for marriage, it also found considerable support for singlehood. Thirty-six percent of teen respondents strongly disagreed or disagreed with the statement, "It is better for a person to get married than to go through life being single." Teen boys were more likely than teen girls to hold this view (68.9 to 54.2 percent). Although teen girls of different racial/ethnic groups favor marriage nearly equally (55.4 percent of Latinas, 54.4 percent of Whites and 52.1 percent of Blacks), the picture is different for teen boys. Black teens are less likely than White teens and young Latinos to favor marriage, 59.8 percent, 70.3 percent, and 74.7 percent respectively (Flanigan, Huffman, and Smith, 2005). Perhaps at this early age, girls already perceive that expanding economic opportunities have provided more women with the means to be financially independent outside of marriage. Research has shown that women in labor markets with favorable economic opportunities have lower rates of marriage than do other women (White, 1981). Interviews with single women show that career aspirations and increased occupational opportunities factor into their decision to forgo marriage either temporarily or permanently (Ferguson, 2000; Rollins,1986) Data collected by the U.S. Department of Labor (2006) show that never married women earn more than married counterparts. Similarly, as we saw earlier, increasing numbers of women in Southeast Asia are giving priority to their careers and a newly found sense of independence.

Men may also delay marriage for the same reasons as women, choosing to devote their energy to finishing their education and establishing their careers. Declining economic fortunes, however, may contribute to an increase in the single population, especially for men. Women may perceive men who are unemployed or who earn low wages as less attractive candidates for marriage (Teachman, Tedrow, and Crowder, 2000; Hacker, 2003), or such men may not want to undertake additional responsibilities until their job situation improves. Some people face other obstacles in finding a suitable marriage partner. People who have a physical or mental disability may find that their intimacy and sexual needs go unfilled because others may perceive them as unattractive or sexless (Wilson, 2002).

Other factors that affect the decision to remain single include the media's more positive images of this lifestyle. For example, TV programs increasingly depict attractive, stylish 30-ish singles on hit shows like *Sex and the City, Friends,* and *Will and Grace,* conveying the notion that being single is fun and exciting. And, the increasing visibility of older unmarried people leading satisfying and meaningful lives such as talk show host Oprah Winfrey, former Secretary of State Condoleeza Rice, social activist Ralph Nader, and actor Al Pacino has enabled younger adults to find a greater number of role models to emulate. A study of attitudes toward never-married women over forty found this to be the case. Female college students saw these women in a positive light—independent, competent, goal-oriented, and single by choice (Croskey, 2007). Finally, over the last several decades, the liberalization of sexual norms and the availability of contraceptive devices have freed women and men to pursue an active social and sexual life outside of marriage. Despite increased opportunities to choose singlehood, not everyone who remains single does so by choice. As discussed in Chapter 5, some people find their desire for marriage frustrated by a marriage squeeze. The influence of these social and economic factors is reflected in Stein's typology of singlehood.

TYPES OF SINGLES

Using the reasons that respondents gave for being single, Stein (1981) developed a typology of singlehood that places singles, including those who have never married and those who were formerly married, into four different categories based on the likelihood of their remaining unmarried:

- *Voluntary temporary singles* are currently unmarried and are not seeking mates. They remain open to the possibility of marrying someday, perhaps after completing their education or becoming established in a career.
- *Voluntary stable singles* choose to remain single and see themselves doing so on a permanent basis. Priests and nuns are included in this category.
- *Involuntary temporary singles* want to marry and are actively seeking mates.
- *Involuntary stable singles* desire marriage but have not yet found a mate. They tend to be older singles who have more or less accepted the probability of remaining single for life.

Similarly, Robert Staples (1981) developed a fivefold typology describing the variations among African American single men:

- The *free-floating single* dates a variety of people and is unattached.
- The *single in an open-couple relationship* dates others, but has a steady partner.
- The *single in a closed-couple relationship* expects her or his partner to be faithful.
- The *committed single* thinks of the relationship as permanent and may be engaged or cohabiting.
- The *accommodationist* is generally an older single who lives alone and who does not date.

Each of these typologies calls attention to the special characteristics of the single state: its heterogeneity and its fluidness. At any given time the population of singles is composed of individuals who either choose or hope to be single for only a limited period of time as well as those who plan to be or who will find themselves single for the rest of their lives. Perhaps not surprisingly, research indicates that individuals who are voluntarily single tend to have a better sense of well-being than the involuntarily single (Shostak, 1987).

Regardless of which category of singlehood never-married people find themselves in, they enjoy certain advantages and cope with some disadvantages resulting from this lifestyle. Before reading the next section, reflect on your perceptions of a single lifestyle.

> Using either Stein's or Staples' typology, can you place yourself (if single) and/or your nonmarried friends in distinct categories? On what basis did you make those decisions? What do you see as the advantages/disadvantages of being single?

ADVANTAGES AND DISADVANTAGES OF SINGLEHOOD

Studies have found a general agreement among single people regarding both the advantages and disadvantages of a single lifestyle. Among the most frequently cited advantages are personal freedom, financial independence, privacy, greater opportunities to pursue careers and other activities, and more time to develop a variety of friendships, including sexual relationships (DeMont, 2000). As we saw earlier, these perceived advantages have contributed to the growing numbers of women remaining single in many Asian countries today.

According to Bella DePaulo and Wendy Morris (2006), one of the major disadvantages of not being married is that single adults are the targets of **singlism,** the negative stereotypes and discrimination faced by singles. Their research found that single people were viewed more negatively than married people. Compared to married or coupled people, who are often described in very positive terms, singles are assumed to be immature, maladjusted, and self-centered. Loneliness, lack of companionship, being excluded from couples' events, or feeling uncomfortable in social settings involving mostly couples, not having children, and social disapproval of their lifestyle are among the other frequently reported disadvantages of being single (Barker, 2005). Another disadvantage of living alone is more gender-specific. Women living alone confront safety issues in deciding where to live, what mode of transportation to use, and which leisure activities to attend. A recent survey indicated that 50 percent of women respondents said there was an area within a mile of their homes where they would be afraid to walk alone at night. Only 19 percent of male respondents said there is such an area near their homes (Saad, 2003).

These advantages and disadvantages are general categories and do not necessarily apply in every individual case or at all times in the life cycle. For example, not all singles are uncomfortable in social settings involving couples; some mix easily in such situations. Economic status also affects how singlehood is experienced, as singles with low incomes or singles who lose their jobs may not be able to implement the freedoms associated with being single.

Additionally, changing family circumstances may alter a lifestyle in the direction of less freedom and more responsibility for others, as is often the case for single adult children who find themselves caring for sick or elderly relatives.

Single Lifestyles

The major challenge facing single people through the ages has been building a satisfying life in a society highly geared toward marriage. Until recently, the general tendency in U.S. popular culture has been to portray singles as belonging in one of two stereotypical groups. On the one side is the "swinging single"—the partygoer who is carefree, uncommitted, sexually adventuresome, and the subject of envy by married friends. Poles apart from this image is the "lonely loser"—the unhappy, frustrated, depressed single who lives alone and survives on TV dinners, a fate few people would envy.

How accurate are these images? Research on the lives of single women and men contradicts these stereotypes and reveals a wide variety of patterns. For example, one in-depth study of 73 White, never-married, college-educated women and men over age 30 found significant variation in how these singles went about organizing their lives. Although there was some overlapping of activities, six different lifestyle patterns were observed, each having a central focus:

- *Supportive:* These singles spend much of their time helping and supporting others and have careers in the teaching and nursing professions.
- *Passive:* These singles spend much of their time alone, have low levels of social participation and more negative outlooks on life, and show little initiative in shaping their lives.
- *Activists:* These singles center their lives around political or community involvement. They derive a great deal of satisfaction from working for social causes.
- *Individualistic:* These singles strive for autonomy and self-growth. They see their independence, freedom, and privacy as an environment in which to grow and develop as a whole person. They enjoy reading, hobbies, and other solitary pursuits.
- *Social:* These singles have extensive personal relationships and spend little time alone. Friends and social activities have a high priority in their lives. They are deeply involved in hobbies, organizations, and family activities.
- *Professional:* These singles organize their lives around work and identify with their occupational roles. Most of their time and energy is spent on their careers (Schwartz, 1976).

Another study of a representative sample of never-married women and men, including both Whites and Blacks, also revealed a rich diversity among this population. However, this research also found that, compared with married persons, persons who never marry are overrepresented in both extremes of social interaction. Singles had higher rates of never interacting with relatives, friends, and neighbors as well as higher rates of seeing these support networks several times a week. Similar patterns were found among never-married women in urban centers in Southeast Asia (Situmorang, 2007). Thus, the single population, like their married peer group, is not a homogeneous group. Singles differ not only in lifestyle orientation but also in the type of living arrangements they select.

Student loan debt and limited economic opportunities have led many recent college graduates, like this young woman, to return to the parental home to live.

THE BOOMERANG PHENOMENA

Only a generation ago, parents whose children were becoming young adults, worried about how they would adjust to having an "empty nest" when the kids left home to be on their own. Today's parents are more likely to worry about how to get them to leave. In today's economy, with its tight job market, low starting salaries, high rents, and large student-loan debts, many young adults find achieving financial independence difficult. Some 37 percent of 18- to 29-year-olds are unemployed or out of the workforce entirely, the highest share among this age group in more than three decades (Pew Research Center Publications, 2010). Only 29 percent of recent college graduates reported a starting salary greater than $36,000 well below the 51 percent who reported that starting salary in 2009. Forty percent of their classmates reported starting salaries of less than $25,000 (Monster.com, 2010). According to an AFL-CIO (2009) report, 34 percent of workers under age 35 live with their parents for financial reasons. The majority of this group has never married, although included in this group are some separated, divorced, and even some widowed children. An online survey found that 52 percent of recent college graduates are living with their parents up from 40 percent in 2009 (Monster.com, 2010). Some social scientists have dubbed this group the "boomerang generation." This pattern is not unique to the United States, but is raising concerns in Canada and many European countries as well. In England, almost one in five college graduates in their late twenties now live with their parents (Bingham, 2009). Recent research suggests that compared to their parents, today's young adults are taking longer to complete their education, to find steady employment, to acquire health insurance, and to get married and have children (Wang and Morin, 2009). This decline in independent living is sometimes referred to as delayed adulthood or extended adolescence.

Intergenerational living arrangements can be stressful. Higher parental household bills and conflicts of lifestyles and values are common. Both generations complain about a lack of privacy. Regression is a likely result. Parents may want to know where their children are going and what they are doing, and adult children may revert to a high school mode, expecting their parents to cook and clean for them. Personal satisfaction and self-esteem can erode under such circumstances. One 23-year-old returnee expressed it this way, "I sort of felt like a loser. Everyone I graduated with was moving away to pursue careers or getting an apartment with friends, and I couldn't afford to do anything. I was pretty depressed about moving home, at least initially" (cited in Eng, 2005). However, according to Jason Eckert, Director of Career Services at the University of Dayton, today the idea of moving home after graduation has lost much of its negative connotation among young adults. And, given the economic contraction of the last several years, parents are willing to help out (Wedell, 2010). Nevertheless, some parents express ambivalence about these relationships. They do not want to be bad parents so they agree to the arrangement but sometimes feel trapped. As one parent said, "Once your kids are out of the house, you establish a schedule for yourself eating, sleeping, etc. You have your own household rhythms. When the kids come home, they are not interested in your schedules. They see no problem with coming and going at all hours of the day and night…You worry if they don't come home, and they're shocked that you worry" (cited in Levine, 2005).

Despite these difficulties, however, many parent report spending enjoyable time with their co-resident adult children. To minimize difficulties, all parties must remember that they are now a collection of adults living together. Boomerangers Elina Furman (2005), author of *Boomerang Nation,* and Christiana Newberry (2010), author of *The Hands–On Guide to Surviving Adult Children Living at Home,* suggest that parents and returning adult children discuss mutual expectations, house rules, chores, time limit for the stay, and shared financial responsibilities before the move to help all members of the family sort out the wrinkles of redefined relationships.

Do you or any of your friends plan to live at home after graduation? If not, under what conditions would you consider returning to or continuing to stay in your parental home? If you are a parent with adult children, would you entertain their returning home to live? What do you see as the advantages and disadvantages of adult intergenerational living?

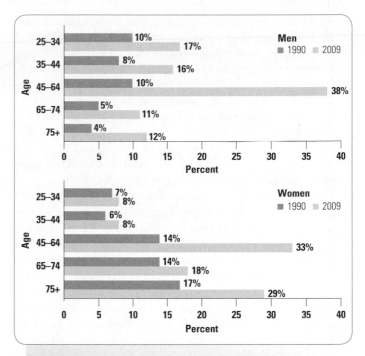

FIGURE 7.1 Living Alone by Sex and Age, 1990 and 2009

Source: Adapted from the U.S. Census Bureau. 2004–2005. *Statistical Abstract of the United States, 2004–2005.* Washington, DC, Table 66, p.54; *Statistical Abstract of the United States, 2011,* Table 72, p. 60.

LIVING ALONE

Overall, however, as adult children age, they are more likely to live alone. This pattern is more pronounced for women, especially in the later years when 29 percent of women live alone compared to 12 percent of men (see Figure 7.1). This is due in large measure to two factors: women live, on average, 5 to 7 years longer than men and divorced men are more likely to remarry than divorced women—and hence are more likely to be living with a spouse in their later years.

A number of unmarried people live in specially designed singles areas—apartments or condominiums developed to meet the perceived needs of this population. These areas offer access to swimming pools, health facilities, restaurants, and singles bars. Although these complexes have attracted a number of singles, especially younger ones, the majority of the never-married are dispersed throughout the general population. Some singles prefer the excitement of city living; others desire the less dense suburban areas or the openness of the countryside. With the changes in credit regulations beginning in the 1970s, more singles were able to get mortgages and become homeowners. The ability to buy a house, however, is dependent on income and, as we will see, as a category, single people do not fare quite as well as do their married peers.

INCOME

Earlier, we noted that one of the perceived advantages of being single is financial independence. How well off are single people? Are they better off economically than married people? These questions are difficult to answer because the needs of these populations may vary significantly. On the one hand, married people with children may need a larger living space than a single person does. On the other hand, singles may find that they spend more on food and traveling, as their married counterparts benefit from buying in quantity and sharing double-occupancy rates. We can, however, gain some insight into the relative status of single people by comparing their median income with that of their married peers. As Table 7.2 reveals, in 2008, nonfamily households made less than family households with a median income of $30,078 compared to a median income of $62,621 for family households and $73,010 for married-couple families. Additionally, female householders made less their male counterparts, $25,014 compared to $36,006.

What factors explain these differences between the married and single populations? One possible explanation is that singles, as a whole, are younger and less experienced than are the married. This argument fails to hold up, however, when age differences are controlled. At the same age levels, singles still earn less than their married peers. Two factors are particularly significant in this regard. First, many married households have more than one wage earner, thus enhancing household earnings. Second, these earning differences may reflect a systematic bias against singles in the workplace. For example, studies show that marital status and sexual orientation affect men's wages. Married men have higher incomes and are more likely to be promoted across a broad range of occupations and professions than are single men even when controlling for relevant factors such as performance or seniority (Antonovics and Town, 2004; Chun and Lee, 2001). Research on wages among German workers found similar patterns (Pollmann-Schult, 2011). Economists Bruce Elmslie and Edinaldo Tebaldi (2007) found that gay men working in management and traditional blue-collar, male-dominated jobs make less than their heterosexual counterparts.

What accounts for this wage difference? Economist Robert Nakosteen and his colleagues (2004) found evidence to support a selection hypothesis, that is, men with higher earning potential are more likely to get married. However, British academics Elena Bardasi and Mark Taylor (2005) analyzed the hourly wages of men who have been interviewed annually since 1991 and concluded it was not selection but a specialization effect that explained the male marriage premium, that is, as long as wives stayed home taking care of household tasks, husbands were free to concentrate on work and increase their productivity, and hence their wages. The researchers found that when wives went to work, the wage premium decreased or disappeared altogether. Still other research suggests yet another factor at work—employer attitudes. According to this view, some employers assume that married men have greater financial needs than single men and reward them accordingly, while other employers believe married men are more stable, more dedicated to their careers, better able to get along with others, and less likely to cost the company money by changing jobs. Thus, they are more eager to hire married men and reward them more (Loh, 1996). An earlier survey of top executives found some support for that view. Although half of the top executive women were single, less than a tenth of the men were (Bradsher, 1989). In a similar vein, a 30-year-old graduate student told the authors about an experience he had looking for a job in public relations when he was 27: "When I was being interviewed, he [the personnel manager] kept referring to the social requirements of the job—entertaining, attending fundraisers and such. I could tell by his attitude that he wanted someone who was married, so I said I was engaged. The funny thing was, I didn't get the job, but I did get married a year later." Given the high percentage of men postponing marriage until their late 20s and early 30s, employer attitudes and behaviors, much like those of the larger society, are becoming more accepting of single lifestyles.

Support Networks

As we saw in Chapter 4, everyone, regardless of marital status, has intimacy needs and must work at developing intimate and supportive relationships. A growing body of literature reveals that singles, especially women, create their own "family," a support group of friends who function in much the same way as families do—exchanging services, traveling together, giving and receiving advice, celebrating birthdays and holidays, and creating shared rituals and meanings (McDill, Sharon, and Turell. 2006; Johnson, 1996). Ethan Watters (2003) refers to these relationships as "urban tribes." Both women and men value friends, but in somewhat different ways. Women concentrate on establishing close, emotional bonds, whereas men focus more on sharing their interests and their values.

Another key intimacy need experienced by many people regardless of marital status is the bond that exists between parent and child. This need can present special problems for single people. Historically, great stigma has been attached to having children out of wedlock, and single women and men were denied the right to adopt children. However, changing attitudes as well as new reproductive technologies have made it possible for single people to bear and raise children and laws now permit single adults to adopt children.

HAPPINESS AND LIFE SATISFACTION

How satisfied with their lives are never-married people? In the past, studies in the United States consistently found that married people reported higher levels of happiness and satisfaction than their never-married counterparts (Lee, Seccombe, and Shehan, 1991; Mastekaasa, 1992). Similar findings were reported in a large number of studies for different countries and time periods (see, for example Diener et al., 2000). The two most commonly reported explanations for the difference in happiness between married and

TABLE 7.2 Median Income by Household Types, 2008	
Household Types	**Median Income**
All households	50,303
Family households	62,621
Married-couple families	73,010
Nonfamily households	30,078
Female householder	25,014
Male householder	36,006

Source: Adapted from "Median Income of Households by Selected Characteristics, 2008." http://www.infoplease.com/business/economy/median-income-households-characteristics.html (2011, April 27).

Many older singles lead active lifestyles enjoying social outings with friends, like these swimmers sharing the hot tub.

never-married individuals relate to the benefits associated with marriage and a selection factor. In the first case, marriage is credited with providing financial security, ongoing companionship, psychological support, and increased self-esteem, in large part because marital status is positively valued in the larger society (Waite and Gallagher, 2000). In the second case, longitudinal data suggest that individuals who get married are happier than individuals who stay single (Stutzer and Frey, 2003). Nevertheless, these data must be interpreted with some caution. Questions of happiness and life satisfaction are not always easy to answer for several reasons. First, happiness and life satisfaction depend on a number of factors other than marital status per se, such as good health, satisfying work, personal growth, financial security, love, family, and friends. For example, research has found that the more time spent socializing with friends, the happier the person regardless of his or her gender, age group, income group, and marital status (Powdthavee, 2005). Other research has found that physical health was the best single predictor of self-reports of happiness, followed by income, education, and marital status (Firebaugh and Tach, 2005).

Second, every living arrangement contains advantages and disadvantages. Some people may experience more of the advantages, whereas others with different life circumstances may endure more disadvantages. Third, life satisfaction is not static; perceptions of satisfaction may vary over time depending on the changes occurring in an individual's life and in the society at large. There is a relationship between the way society evaluates a lifestyle and the perceived desirability of that status. Historian Stephanie Coontz (2005:258) points out, "By 1978 only 25 percent of Americans still believed that people who remained single by choice were 'sick,' 'neurotic,' or 'immoral,' as most had thought it was in the 1950s. By 1978, 75 percent of the population thought that it was morally okay to be single and have children." As attitudes toward singlehood became more positive, never-married individuals were freer to think more positively about themselves and to express high levels of satisfaction and happiness with their lifestyle.

THE NEVER-MARRIED IN LATER LIFE

In 2008, an estimated 39 million Americans were 65 years of age and older. Of that number, approximately 1.3 million had never married. Table 7.3 shows men are slightly more likely to have remained unmarried than women, except for those between ages 75 and 84. Just as with younger singles, numerous factors account for the marital status of older people. Although some older people are unmarried by choice, for those who want to marry, gender plays a role. A longer life expectancy and a marriage gradient that favors men mean that older women find a limited pool of eligible males in their age categories, and those males who are eligible often have few resources with which to attract a prospective mate. Older women are also more likely than older men to have responsibilities for caring for elderly parents, which limit their marital prospects.

Our examination of the lifestyles of elderly singles is hampered by the fact that relatively little systematic research has been done on this population. Three decades ago gerontologist Jaber

TABLE 7.3 Never Married Elderly by Age and Sex, 2008

Age	Both Sexes	Men	Women
65 and Over	4.1	4.2	4.0
65–74	4.3	4.4	4.2
75–84	3.6	3.6	3.7
85+	4.3	4.7	4.1

Source: Federal Interagency Forum on Ageing Related Statistics, 2010, *Older Americans 2008: Key Indicators of Well-Being.* www.agingstats.gov/agingstatsdotnet/Main_Site/Data/2010_Documents/Docs/OA_2010.pdf (2011, May 2).

Gubrium (1975, 1976) reviewed what research had been done on elderly singles and concluded that (1) they tend to be lifelong isolates, (2) they are not particularly lonely, (3) they evaluate everyday life in much the same way that their married peers do (both groups are more positive than the widowed or divorced), and (4) due to their single status, they avoid the desolation of bereavement that follows the death of a spouse.

The "Lifelong Isolate" Reconsidered Later research has challenged some of these findings. For example, in his study of older men who live alone, Robert Rubinstein (1986) points out that the majority of the never-married men in his study spent many years living with other family members, particularly parents, and therefore could hardly be classified as isolates. These respondents did experience loneliness, but much less so than many of the widowers in his sample did. Although acknowledging that the married elderly may experience a unique form of desolation at the death of a spouse, Rubinstein argues that the death of a parent or sibling (and we would add friends) can be equally devastating to single people.

Other research indicates that there may be two distinct patterns among the older unmarried population. Some elderly people do experience a degree of isolation. Pat Keith (1986:392), in his analysis of census data, reported that about 33 percent of the elderly never see neighbors, about 30 percent never see friends, and 21 percent of the men and 14 percent of the women never see relatives. These findings must be interpreted carefully, however. Older singles with health problems, lower levels of education, and low-status occupations tend to be the most isolated. A second pattern appears more frequently: Many elderly singles lead active social lives. For instance, Keith found that more than 50 percent of all older singles interact with family, friends, and neighbors. More recent research also suggests that memberships in different types of social organizations help augment an older person's social network, reduces social isolation, and provides sources of identity and self-esteem (Arber, Perren, and Davidson, 2002).

Although a small sample, Katherine Allen's (1989) study of working-class women born in 1910 also shows the importance of family of origin in the lives of the elderly unmarried. Allen found that, like Rubinstein's respondents, the majority of the never-married women in her sample lived with one or both of their parents until their parents died. When this happened, however, they tended to replace the deceased parents with friends or other family members. Single women often have a more extensive social support system than single men. Allen also found that the majority of her respondents were pleased with their living arrangements, valued their independence, and had no regrets about not marrying. Later research has also found that never-marred women are more involved in social organizations (Arber, 2004), enjoy more practical and emotional support from family and friends than their male counterparts (Davidson, Daly, and Aber, 2003) and believe their life experiences and opportunities have prepared them for a successful and productive old age (Cwikel, Gramotnev, and Lee, 2006). A study involving subjects in six countries found that the majority of women and men who had always been single have significant supportive social networks (Wenger, Dykstra, and Melkas, 2007).

Other researchers (for example, DePaulo, 2006; Kalata, 2006) have examined heterosexual relationships and activities among older singles. She discovered that older singles, like their younger counterparts, enjoy movies, dances, travel, camping, plays, and romance. Like their younger counterparts, older singles take advantage of Internet Web sites designed to help them meet other people who share their interests.

Heterosexual Cohabitation

People who are not married choose a variety of living arrangements. Some singles are opting to share their life with an adopted child. These singles have much in common with other parents (see Chapter 9). Another arrangement that is increasingly popular among both the never-married and the formerly married is cohabitation, popularly referred to as "living together."

HISTORICAL PERSPECTIVES

In the past, the people most likely to live together outside of legal marriage were the poor or those individuals involved in unpopular relationships, for example, couples with mixed racial, religious, or ethnic backgrounds. Because of the prohibition against lesbian and gay marriages, homosexual couples have often lived together as well. As frequently occurs, however, when living together became widespread among the White middle class, researchers and other social commentators "discovered" it and gave it a new label, one not associated with poor, working-class, and nonwhite groups.

One form of living together that was visible in America's past is **common-law marriage,** "a cohabiting relationship that is based on the mutual consent of the persons involved, is not solemnized by a ceremony, and is recognized as valid by the state" (Stinnet and Birdsong, 1978:84). In sparsely populated areas of the country, clergy or judges often were not readily available to officiate at marriages. Thus, couples intending to wed established a home together without any official ceremony. Later on, if the couple wanted legal recognition of their relationship, they had to prove that they had lived together for a significant period of time, viewed themselves as a married couple, and were legally eligible to be married. By the 1920s, most states had abandoned the concept of common-law marriage. Today, only 10 of the 50 states (Alabama, Colorado, Iowa, Kansas, Montana, Oklahoma, Rhode Island, South Carolina, Texas, and Utah) and the District of Columbia continue to recognize such marriages; other states (Georgia, Idaho, Ohio, and Pennsylvania) have established a cut-off date whereby only relationships existing before that date can be so recognized. New Hampshire recognizes common-law marriage only for inheritance purposes.

THE MEANING OF COHABITATION TODAY

The U.S. Census Bureau first began to collect data on unmarried-couple households, or what the Bureau calls POSSLQS, "persons of the opposite sex sharing living quarters," in 1960. There are some problems with this definition—it may miss cohabiting couples in households with more than two adults, and it may include noncohabiting adults who may be boarders, roommates, or employees living in the household. Thus, although this definition is useful for measuring the number of nonrelated adults sharing living space, it does not convey the full meaning of the concept of cohabitation. The 1990 census attempted to improve the estimate of the number of cohabiting households by adding the relationship category "unmarried partner" to the 1990 census questionnaire, defining it as "a person who is not related to the householder, who shares living quarters, and who has a close personal relationship with the householder."

Cohabitation is similar to marriage in that couples create emotional and physical relationships with each other, and in some cases they also bear or rear children. It differs from marriage, however, in that it lacks formal legal, cultural, and religious support. People's attitudes toward cohabitation have changed over the years. In a 1981 ABCNews/*Washington Post* poll only 40 percent of adults approved of women and men living together without being married; 45 percent disapproved. The comparable figures in 2007 were 55 percent and 27 percent (Taylor, 2010). Fifty-seven percent of young adults between ages 20 and 24 agree that it is okay for unmarried couples to live together even if marriage is not being considered (Scott et al, 2009), but there are differences within this age group. Young women are less likely than young men to agree that cohabitation was all right (52 percent to 62 percent). Black young adults were least favorably disposed to cohabitation (43 percent) compared to 54 percent for Asians, 58 percent for Latinos, and 61 percent for Whites. People age 65 and older are most likely to disapprove of cohabitation. Similar age discrepancies exist elsewhere as well. For example, a 2008 survey in Korea found that 60 percent of respondents ages 20 to 29 supported cohabiting, whereas more than half of the respondents age 50 and older disapproved of cohabiting (Min-seok, 2009).

Although approval ratings have increased, it is still likely that perceived parental or societal disapproval may still lead some couples to keep their relationship secret and describe themselves as simply roommates sharing expenses. Thus, our interpretation of past and current numbers of cohabiting couples must be somewhat tentative. In all probability, the census data underestimate the total number of cases.

Current Demographic Trends Figure 7.2 traces the growth in numbers of unmarried-partner households since 1960, when they totaled only about 439,000. By 2010, this number had jumped to over 8 million, consisting of slightly more than 7.5 million (92 percent) heterosexual partners and 620 million (8 percent) same-sex partners. Between 2009 and 2010, there was a 13 percent increase in the number of opposite-sex couples who were cohabiting and a 30 percent increase in the number of same-sex cohabitors. Rose Kreider (2010) and her colleagues at the Census Bureau were so surprised at such a high yearly increase that they double-checked their data. Kreider concluded the data were accurate and attributed this dramatic change in living arrangements of couples to the worsening of the economy. Newly formed heterosexual couples in 2010 had a higher proportion of men who did not work the previous year than newly formed couples in 2009, and a higher proportion of new couples in 2010 did not have both partners employed, compared with coupes who had already been together at least a year.

Because these census data capture living arrangements only at a given point in time, they do not reveal the full extent of the cohabitation experience in the United States. However, when we consider the cohabitation experiences of women over time, a much stronger pattern emerges. More than half of all women ages 19–44 have cohabited (Reinhold, 2007). Sociologists Wendy Manning and Pamela Smock (2005) believe that current measurement

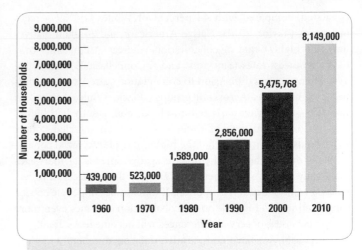

FIGURE 7.2 Unmarried-Partner Households, 1960–2010

U.S. Census Bureau. 2002. *Statistical Abstract of the United States, 2002*, p. 48, Table 49; Kreider, Rose. 2010. Housing and Household Economic Statistics Division Working paper (September 15) www.census.gov/population/www/socdemo/Inc-Opp-Sex-2009-to-2010.pdf (2011, May 8).

strategies probably underestimate the extent of cohabitation. Their interviews with a sample of young women and men with recent cohabitation experience suggest that there is considerable fluidity between singlehood and cohabitation and that many people "slide" or "drift" into (and out of) cohabitation. For some people today, especially among the younger population, cohabitation has become an extension of the courtship process. In a recent study, about two-thirds of all teens ages 15 to 19 said it is okay for a young couple to live together while unmarried. Those who were sexually experienced were more likely to approve of cohabitation than those who were virgins, and those who grew up in two biological or adoptive parent households were more likely to disapprove of cohabitation than were their peers who grew up in other types of households (Flanigan, Huffman, and Smith, 2005). More than 60 percent of first marriages are now preceded by living together, compared to virtually none 50 years ago (Kennedy and Bumpass, 2008). Remarriages are even more likely to be preceded by cohabitation.

Cohabitants: An Increasingly Diverse Population
Contrary to popular belief, college-age individuals make up only a small portion of cohabitants. The age group most likely to cohabit is 30- to 49-year-olds, more than half of whom (57 percent) report they have done so whereas only 18 percent of adults age 65 and older report having lived with an unmarried partner. Women (41 percent) are somewhat less likely than men (46 percent) to say they cohabit (Taylor, 2010). In general, cohabitants tend to be less educated, less likely to identify with an organized religion and/or to attend religious services, and more likely to be politically liberal, unemployed, live in large urban areas, have been divorced, have divorced or remarried parents, experienced fatherlessness, and became sexually active at younger ages than their noncohabiting peers (Taylor, 2010; Houseknecht and Lewis, 2005; Simmons and O'Connell, 2003).

Although cohabitants are found among all classes, ages, and racial and ethnic groups, cohabitation is not uniformly distributed across these groups. Some 47 percent of Blacks say they have cohabited, compared with 44 percent of Whites and 39 percent of Latinos (Taylor, 2010). Native Americans and Alaskan Natives have the highest rate of cohabitation whereas Asian Americans have the lowest rates (Simmons and O'Connell, 2003). Race also adds an interesting dimension to cohabitation patterns when compared to marriage. Across all groups—Black, White, Asian, and Latina/o—unmarried-partner households consistently had higher percentages of partners of different races than married couple households. It is probable that the higher rate of interracial cohabitation is due to the social pressure against interracial marriages that many people still experience. Despite these observed differences, a word of caution is in order. If the number of people cohabiting continues to increase and if cohabitation becomes even more acceptable, these observed differences will become less salient.

Although we have comparative data on numbers and rates of cohabitation of these racial and ethnic groups, no systematic research on the cohabiting experiences of people of color has been done. Thus, we do not know if people of color attach the same meaning to this experience as do their White counterparts. We do know, however, that cohabitation is less likely to lead to legal marriage among Black women than among White women (Oppenheimer, 2003). Additionally, Black women and Latinas are more likely than their White counterparts to give birth in a cohabiting relationship. Thirty-five percent of White cohabitors, 54 percent of Black cohabitors, and nearly 60 percent of Hispanic cohabitors have children present in the household (cited in Smock and Manning, 2004). These different patterns may reflect the fact that rates of cohabitation are higher among educationally and economically disadvantaged groups, including relatively disadvantaged White women (Bumpass and Lu, 2000). Thus, among poor women cohabitation is more likely than that among nonpoor women to be a long-term alternative or substitute for traditional marriage (Lichter, Qian, and Mellott, 2006).

COHABITATION IN OTHER COUNTRIES

Although cohabitation is increasing in the United States, the rate remains relatively low in comparison with some other countries, particularly those in northern Europe (see Table 7.4). In contrast, the lowest rates of cohabitation are found in the southern European countries of Spain and Italy. Both of these countries have a heavily Roman Catholic tradition that emphasizes marriage and traditional family structures.

Cohabitation as an Alternative to Marriage: The Scandinanvian Experience In the early twentieth century, many Swedish couples protested against the institution of church marriage and openly entered into "marriages of conscience." In response to this practice, the government created civil marriages in 1909 (Kiernan, 2002). Today approximately 30 percent of all couples in Sweden cohabit and it is generally within this cohabitation that first-born children enter the world. Although the majority of these cohabiting couples eventually marry, for a significant number of couples, cohabitation is replacing marriage. This is especially the pattern when cohabitation follows a divorce. Similarly, cohabitation and extramarital childbirth are also becoming more of a norm in Norway and Denmark, where 50 and 46 percent of births were outside of marriage (cited in Popenoe, 2008).

TABLE 7.4 Percentage of Couples Who Cohabit by Country and Year

Country	Year	Percent of All Couples
Sweden	2005	28.4
Denmark	2006	24.4
Norway	2007	21.8
New Zealand	2006	23.7
Canada	2006	18.4
France	2001	17.2
United Kingdom	2004	15.4
United States	2005	7.6
Italy	2003	3.8
Spain	2002	2.7

Source: Adapted from Popenoe, D. 2008. *Cohabitation, Marriage and Child Wellbeing: A Cross-National Perspective.* New Brunswick, NJ: The National Marriage Project at Rutgers University, Table 1, p. 2.

Scandinavian patterns of cohabitation are longstanding and seem to represent a substitute for marriage for many of these couples who tend to see marriage as either having little value or as a huge commitment for which they are not yet ready. Government policies in these countries may also contribute to people's willingness to cohabit. For example, in Sweden and Norway, all parents, regardless of marital status, are eligible to receive a children's allowance from their respective governments. Further, many of these countries now provide benefits, such as insurance or pension rights, to cohabiting couples and some have laws regulating the distribution of property in the event of a breakup.

What do you think? Is the United States likely to follow the pattern of cohabitation that emerged in the Scandinavian countries? Why or why not?

WHY DO PEOPLE COHABIT?

In an earlier section of this chapter, we discussed Stein's model of pushes and pulls to analyze the decision to marry or to remain single. These conceptual categories are also appropriate for understanding the reasons people give for cohabiting.

Push Factors Among the negative factors in their environment that lead people to consider living with someone are unemployment, feelings of loneliness, high costs of living alone, disenchantment with traditional dating and courtship, fear of marital commitment, awareness of the high divorce rate (and for the formerly married, fear of making another mistake), sexual frustration, and education or career demands that preclude early marriage (Dougherty, 2010; Kreider, 2010).

For many people cohabitation has become a stage in the dating process. This couple enjoys doing household chores together.

Pull Factors There are also many positive forces that people experience that draws them into a cohabiting relationship. Among the pull factors are a strong physical attraction toward someone, being in a strong emotional relationship, desire for intimacy and sex on a regular basis, desire to experiment with a new living arrangement, desire for personal growth, example of peers, desire to test compatibility for marriage, and the sense that it is a socially acceptable lifestyle (Taylor, 2010; Willetts, 2006; Wilson, 2002).

Once again we can see the complexity of lifestyle choices. Cohabitation, like other options, is explained by a number of factors, both positive and negative. The meaning and experience of cohabitation varies considerably and reflects the different needs of individuals. For example, for some couples, living together is a new stage in a dating relationship, a "going steady" but with a live-in twist. A common pattern found among college students in the 1960s and 1970s was a gradual drifting into staying together, first spending the night, then the weekend, and then moving in (Macklin, 1972). For many, living together was a logical step in getting to know and share their lives with another person.

For other couples, cohabitation may represent a cheaper way to live. For example, sharing expenses might enable younger cohabitants to commit more time and energy to education or career development. For older divorced or widowed people with grown children, cohabitation is sometimes chosen over marriage to avoid possible complications with social security or inheritance issues. Because there are many different motivations for cohabitation, partners should never assume agreement about where a relationship is heading. Like people entering into any relationship, the partners need to discuss and understand each other's expectations.

Types of Cohabiting Couples Just as many reasons are given for cohabitation, the relationships established by cohabiting couples vary in terms of individual needs and degree of commitment. According to a study by the Pew Research Center (2007), for some respondents, the relationship is simply a utilitarian arrangement motivated by the desire to share expenses, convenience or a simple desire to live together. The motivation for some elderly couples is also financial—to avoid loss of financial benefits such as alimony, welfare, or pension checks. In such utilitarian arrangements, intimacy may or may not be present. For others, there is intimate involvement with emotional commitment. However, they have no plans for marriage. In contrast, some cohabiting partners create a trial marriage to test their compatibility for a possible future marital commitment. This, however, carries the risk that they may stay for years in what turns out to be an unsuitable relationship and risk not finding new partners after a break-up (Weston and Qu, 2006). Others go a step further. They have already decided to marry in the future and see no reason to live apart prior to that event, so for them cohabitation is a precursor to marriage. The Pew Research study mentioned earlier found 8 percent of their respondents gave this as a reason for deciding to live together. Despite these latter expectations, Sharon Sassler and James McNally (2003) found that of the cohabiting couples they studied, only about 40 percent ended up marrying within 4 to 7 years. Other researchers found that cohabitation is more likely to turn to marriage if the woman comes from a two-parent home, values religion, and comes from a higher family education and income. Marriage following cohabitation was more likely for White women and Latinas than for Black women (Bramlett and Mosher, 2002). These differences are most frequently attributed to economic factors, such as low earnings and periodic unemployment, which inhibit marriage. Further, because more cohabiting couples of color have greater rates of childbearing than their White counterparts, some social scientists are coming to see them as another family form, an alternative rather than a prelude to marriage.

Given these reasons for and types of cohabitation, what, then, is gained or risked by living together?

Gains Among the most commonly reported advantages of living together are better understanding of self; greater knowledge of what is involved in living with another person; increased interpersonal skills, especially communication and problem-solving skills; increased emotional maturity; better understanding of marital expectations; companionship; and the sharing of economic and domestic responsibilities. Although expenses may be shared, cohabitating couples are less likely than married couples to pool all their financial resources, preferring to maintain more independence (Heimdal and Houseknecht, 2003).

Risks Cohabitation is not without its problems, however. Among the disadvantages, cohabitants report are lack of social support for their relationship, which for some contributes to a sense of guilt about their lifestyle; conflict with their partner over domestic tasks; the potential instability of the relationship; loss or curtailment of other relationships; differing expectations with partner; the emotional trauma of breaking up; and legal ambiguity—a point we will return to shortly. In addition, research shows that there is often less sexual fidelity between cohabiting couples than between married couples, and cohabiting couples report less sexual fidelity and lower levels of happiness and sexual satisfaction than their married peers (Amato and Booth, 1997; Treas and Giesen, 2000).

Gender role expectations may also play a role in the degree of satisfaction with the cohabiting experience. In contrast to their married counterparts, cohabiting men are more likely to be unemployed, whereas cohabiting women are more likely to be employed (Fields and Casper, 2001). Furthermore, both women and men in cohabitating relationships may feel used when their partner gives no indication of making a marital commitment. Sharon Sassler and Jim McNally (2003) found that 42 percent of the cohabiting couples in their study disagreed about the future of their relationship. Conversely, some couples, rather than making a definite decision may slide into a marital relationship, that is, marrying somebody they might not otherwise have married (Stanley and Rhoades, 2009). Scott Stanley (2005) refers to this process as relationship "inertia."

Finally, spouses who cohabit before marriage exhibit a higher rate of verbal abuse and violent behavior than spouses who did not cohabit (Cohan and Kleinbaum, 2002; Kenney and McLanahan, 2006). Similarly, a study comparing 21-year-old females and males in dating and cohabiting relationships found that cohabitants were almost twice as likely as daters to be abusive toward their partners (Magdol, Moffitt, and Caspi, 1998). Additionally, children living with cohabiting couples are more likely to be victims than children living with married parents. If the mother is living with a man who is not the father, the child's risk of abuse is even higher (Crouse, 2004; Spohn, 2004). Several factors contribute to the higher rate of violence among cohabiting couples: economic difficulties, isolation from family and friends, and differing levels of emotional involvement in the relationship. Additionally, researchers have found differences in selection out of cohabitation and marriage, including selection of the least-violent cohabiting couples into marriage and the most-violent married couples into divorce. These patterns lead to higher observed rates of violence among cohabiting couples in cross-sectional samples (Kenney and McLanahan, 2006).

The data on cohabitation seem to suggest that regardless of the outcome, most individuals feel they learned something from the experience. Furthermore, because cohabitation has become more widespread, it is likely that fewer individuals now experience a sense of guilt about their living arrangement. For some couples, however, living together may go counter to their religious upbringing or to parental values; thus, their adoption of this lifestyle may trouble them.

COHABITATION AND THE DIVISION OF HOUSEHOLD LABOR

How do cohabitants go about the daily tasks of living? Do they behave differently from their married peers? Data from more than 17,000 respondents across 28 countries suggest they do. Cohabiting couples tend to be more egalitarian in sharing household chores and more gender neutral in task assignments than married couples. For example, cohabiting men perform more indoor tasks than married men and cohabiting women do more outdoor tasks than married women. Although cohabiting women spend more time on housework than cohabiting men, they spend less time than married women. Cohabiting men and married men spend approximately the same amount of time in housework but cohabiting men do more indoor household tasks (Davis, Greenstein, and Marks, 2007). One likely explanation for these findings is the respective institutional contexts of marriage and cohabitation. Within the institution of marriage, there are definite role expectations of what wives and husbands should do. Society

has fewer role expectations for cohabitation so couples are able to ignore traditional gender allocations of household labor and to negotiate their own (Baxter, 2001). Further evidence of this contextual relationship is suggested by the fact that many cohabitating couples who hold egalitarian views on gender and who shared domestic tasks while cohabiting experienced a behavioral shift to more traditional roles after getting married.

COHABITATION AND MARITAL STABILITY

Is cohabitation a good predictor of marital success? According to a recent USAToday/Gallup Poll, almost half (49 percent) believe living together makes divorce less likely; another 13 percent said it makes no difference. Only 31 percent think living together before marriage makes divorce more likely (Jayson, 2008). To date the research in this regard has yielded some contradictory findings. Some early research found that cohabitants who married are more likely to remain together than couples who did not cohabit (White, 1987) while other researchers concluded that cohabitation has no clear effect on marital success or satisfaction (Watson and DeMeo, 1987). Despite these contradictory findings, the weight of the evidence seemed to be that couples who engage in premarital cohabitation run a greater risk of divorce than do couples who do not cohabit prior to marriage. Depending on the specific statistical methods used, a wide range of studies found that couples who marry after a period of cohabitation are at a 35 to 50 percent greater risk of separating and/or divorcing than marriages without prior cohabitation (Seltzer, 2000; Teachman, 2002; VanGoethem, 2005). Research needs to continue in this area, but several explanations for the higher divorce risk of premarital cohabitants seem likely. Some cohabitants engage in behavior that in the long run is detrimental to marriage. For example, in the cohabitive situation they may put their best foot forward and share household responsibilities on an equitable basis. After exchanging marriage vows, however, one or both partners may, without consciously realizing it, change role expectations and fall back on traditional patterns in the division of household labor. There may be outside pressure as well. Parents and friends may be tolerant of a "live-in lover" because they do not want to jeopardize the possibility of marriage. After marriage, they may feel free to say or do things that could cause conflict between the now-married couple. Self-selection may also play a role. Cohabitants may hold more nontraditional views on marriage and therefore be more accepting of divorce. Finally, people who cohabit may be less concerned about homogamous factors (see Chapter 5) in partner choice, factors that may increase the risk of divorce for couples.

However, several caveats are in order when we consider the relationship between cohabitation and the risk of marital dissolution. The situation of the cohabitants may make a difference. For example, research found that women who were serial cohabitants (cohabited with more than one partner and then married) were more likely to divorce than those who cohabited only with their eventual husbands (Jose, O'Leary, and Moyer, 2010; Lichter and Qian, 2008) and women who cohabited only with their future husband did not have a higher risk of divorce than women who did not cohabit before marriage (Teachman, 2003). Similarly a study of a national representative sample of more than 1,000 married women and men concluded that premarital cohabitation when limited to a period after an engagement was not associated with an elevated risk of marital problems (Rhoades, Stanley, and Markman, 2009). Another study, comparing patterns in 16 European countries found that former cohabitants run a higher risk of union dissolution than people who married without prior cohabitation only in societies in which cohabitation is a small minority or a large majority phenomenon (Liefbroer and Dourleijn, 2006). In a similar vein, researchers in Australia have found that as premarital cohabitation has become normative, the higher risk of marital dissolution among those who cohabited before marriage has declined substantially (de Vaus, Qu, and Weston, 2005). A recent study using U.S. data from 1988 to 2002 also found that the positive relationship between premarital cohabitation and marital instability has weakened over time and suggested that the two may no longer be associated with each other (Reinhold, 2007). In order to arrive at a more definitive conclusion regarding the relationship of cohabitation to marital stability requires research into what cohabitation means to those involved as well as the diverse characteristics and timing of the cohabiting experience.

COHABITATION AND THE LAW

If you are part of an unmarried couple currently living in Virginia, West Virginia, Florida, Michigan, Mississippi, North Dakota, and until recently, North Carolina, you are a lawbreaker and could be subject to fines and imprisonment. Such was the reality for 40-year-old Debora Hobbs, an unmarried woman living in North Carolina who lost her job as a 911 dispatcher with the Pendar County Sheriff's office because she chose to live with her unmarried boyfriend in violation of a 200-year-old law that states, "If any man and woman, not being married to each other, shall lewdly and lasciviously associate, bed and cohabitate together they shall be guilty of a class 2 misdemeanor." The American Civil Liberties Union (2006) filed a lawsuit on her behalf and was successful in having the law declared unconstitutional.

Although living together is not illegal in the other 44 states, serious legal issues need to be considered by anyone choosing to cohabit. Cohabitation, like singlehood, can be temporary and fluid. Many cohabitants are together for only short periods of time. Approximately half break up in a year or less and over 90 percent end by the fifth year; only about 44 percent end in marriage (Lichter, Qian, and Mellot, 2006). Like their married peers, cohabitants end their relationship for many reasons: growing apart, loss of interest, unequal commitment, value conflicts, outside pressures, or the need to relocate because of work or other family commitments. However, unlike their married peers, cohabitants have fewer legal protections to guide them through their break-ups.

What happens when cohabitants terminate a relationship? Who gets the apartment? The stereo? The children? Even though you do not need a court decree to stop living together, there may be legal ramifications to ending a cohabitive relationship. Former live-in partners may file suit for what has come to be called **palimony,** a payment similar to alimony and based on the existence of a contract (written or implied) between the partners regarding aspects of their relationship. For example, if there were a promise of future marriage, of an economic partnership, or of support for a child, courts may hold a partner responsible for legally fulfilling these obligations or, conversely, may deny that such a claim has

any merit. Twenty percent of court cases dealing with relationship dissolutions involve cohabiting couples, many with children (Hymowitz, 2003). People who cohabit are well advised to put their financial and other agreements in writing. Similarly, it is a good idea to keep ownership of possessions separate and to maintain separate bank accounts and credit cards. Cohabitants seem to be heeding some of this advice as cohabitors are far less likely to pool their finances than are married couples (Heimdal and Houseknecht, 2003).

A Legal Response: Domestic Partnerships and Civil Unions So far, we have been talking about what happens when cohabitants break up. However, a number of other areas to consider when living together also have legal implications. For example, you cannot assume that because you live with someone you will be covered by her or his car or renter's insurance. Sometimes insurance companies require the insured to have a conventional family tie. Health benefits are problematic as well. Without legal recognition both heterosexual and homosexual cohabiting partners may have little to say in the medical treatment or other affairs of their partner. In case of death, who is to inherit property? Without a properly executed will, the state makes this determination, and the decision will likely favor family members over live-in partners. You cannot automatically claim ownership to any property that does not bear your name even if you helped pay for it. The status of children can be ambiguous in cohabiting relationships as well. If the biological parent dies and there is no provision for naming the live-in partner the legal guardian, again the court may decide the matter. Often, it does so contrary to the wishes of the cohabitants. These are just a few of the items that cohabitants need to consider as they establish their living arrangements.

In an attempt to address these problems some organizations, businesses and communities make provisions for extending benefits generally reserved for married employees to other employees involved in what have come to be known as **domestic partnerships,** a term referring to unmarried couples who live together and share housing and financial responsibilities. Although still relatively modest in number, a growing list of nonprofit organizations and private sector employers now recognize some form of domestic partnership, although the rights and benefits involved in these arrangements vary from place to place. Some benefits are minor, a membership in a gym or museum; others are substantial—including health insurance, family and funeral leave, family membership rates, and inheritance protection. To receive these benefits, couples are required to register their partnership. Such registration provides public recognition of the union, thereby granting it a degree of legitimacy. Some agencies, however, restrict partnership benefits to those of the same sex, arguing that heterosexual partners can marry if they wish to receive such benefits.

Several states (Vermont, Connecticut, New Jersey, Illinois, New Hampshire, Hawaii, and Delaware) passed legislation granting same-sex couples the same rights, privileges, and responsibilities as married spouses under state law. This legally recognized status, similar to marriage, is known as a **civil union.**

The movement to grant same-sex couples the right to marry, although still controversial, is gaining ground around the world. Canada, Sweden, Norway, the Netherlands, Belgium, Spain, Portugal, Iceland, and South Africa give same-sex couples the right to marry. In the United States, Massachusetts was the first state to grant same-sex civil marriages. It has now been joined by New York, Connecticut, New Hampshire, Vermont, Iowa, the District of Columbia, and the Coquille Indian Tribe in Oregon. Rhode Island, and Maryland recognize same-sex marriage, but do not grant same-sex marriage. However, the action of these states confers no federal recognition or federal tax and other benefits to these unions nor are these uions portable—recognized in other states. In 1996, Congress passsed the Defense of Marriage Act (DOMA) whereby no state may be required to recognize as a marriage a same-sex relationship considered a marriage in another state. The lack of legal recognition of their union is particularly difficult for lesbian and gay couples whose partner is not a citizen. Laws governing residence of a partner from another country most frequently require a blood or marital relationship, thus excluding homosexual couples. However, in February 2011, the Obama administration announced it would no longer defend DOMA in the courts but it would continue to enforce the law until the courts reached a decision on whether it was constitutional. As a result of this action, Judge Alberto Riefkohl of immigration court in Newark postponed the deportation hearing of Venezulan Henry Velandia who was married to American Josh Vandiver in Connecticut in 2010 to allow time for the appeals cout to work out whether a gay partner might be eligible for residency under some circumstances (Preston, 2011).

The granting of civil unions or same-sex marriage in a state is not always the end of the story. Same sex marriages could be legally performed in California between June 16, 2008 and November 4, 2008, when a slim majority of voters passed Proposition 8 prohibiting same-sex marriage (Liptak, 2008). Proponents of same-sex marriage went to court to argue the constitutionality of the measure. In August 2010, Federal Judge Vaughn Walker ruled that Proposition 8 violated the constitutional rights of gay citizens. After his ruling, it emerged that Judge Walker was gay and living in a committed relationship. Supporters of Proposition 8 went back to court to argue that his ruling should be overturned because of a conflict of interest. Judge James Ware, Walker's successor, upheld Walker's ruling and ruled that his sexuality did not in itself constitute a conflict of interest. Black and mixed race justices are not prevented from hearing race-relations cases nor are female judges denied the opportunity to rule in sex-discrimination cases (Adams, 2011). It is likely this issue will go to the U.S. Supreme Court, and the Court's decision will likely impact every state. See the Debating Social Issues box for a discussion of some of the controversy surrounding same-sex marriages.

Lesbian and Gay Relationships

Many of the legal issues we have just discussed concerning cohabitants apply to lesbian and gay relationships as well. As with our discussion of heterosexual cohabitants, our focus here is primarily on social relationships constructed by lesbian and gay couples.

In U.S. society, homosexuality historically has been considered a form of deviant behavior. Medical research into this "dis-

order" focused on its causes, with the emphasis on discovering a "cure." Various treatments were used to affect a "cure," including castration, hysterectomy, electric shock treatment, lobotomy, and estrogen and testosterone injections (Harvey, 1992). During the latter half of the twentieth century, some of these negative attitudes began to change as lesbians and gays began to organize to challenge laws and customs discriminating against them and condemning their behaviors. Although initially these groups were predominantly White, several African American, Asian American, and Latina/o organizations emerged in the 1970s and gave visibility to the ethnic and racial diversity that exists within the homosexual population. In 1973, an important step in the redefinition of homosexual behavior occurred when the American Psychiatric Association (APA) removed homosexuality from its list of psychiatric disorders. Experiencing prejudice and/or discrimination based on sexual orientation may cause lesbians and gays considerable stress (Mays and Cochran, 2001; Meyer, 2003); nevertheless, there is no reliable data to show that homosexual orientation per se impairs psychological functioning. Despite such findings, some psychotherapists and religious counselors still see homosexuality as an inherently deficient or sinful lifestyle and try to change lesbians and gays, especially teens, into heterosexuals through what is called reparative therapy or sexual conversion therapy. Although some therapists report having successfully changed the sexual orientation of numerous clients, the APA remains highly critical of this approach, citing its potential to do psychological harm and the fact that to date there are no systematic studies in peer-reviewed scientific journals that attest to the success of reparative or conversion therapy (American Psychological Association, 2008a).

METHODOLOGICAL ISSUES

Earlier in the chapter, we noted the methodological problems surrounding the study of singlehood and heterosexual cohabitation. Similar problems of small, unrepresentative samples have also limited the study of homosexual behavior. Additionally, the long tradition of homophobia in the United States has kept many homosexual people from revealing their sexual orientation and from participating in research studies. Earlier studies with small samples of Asian Americans (Liu and Chan, 1996), Latinas/os (Morales, 1996), and African Americans (Green and Boyd-Franklin, 1996) suggested that people of color were even more reluctant to identify themselves as lesbian or gay because of the intense cultural disapproval of homosexuality in their respective communities. Thus, they found themselves caught between two communities, facing double or even triple stigmatization with the potential for losing support in both the lesbian/gay community and in their gender/ethnic/racial community.

Even today among many of these cultures, homosexuality is still viewed as a White, Western phenomenon. This view may be changing, however, as countries like China now admit to having a sizeable homosexual population of their own. In 2001, China published a third version of its classification and diagnosis criteria of mental disorders and, for the first time, excluded homosexuality from the list ("Lesbians, Gays…," 2005). Although official statistics suggest there are approximately 30 million homosexuals in mainland China, that figure is probably an undercount. Many lesbians and gays in China are still likely to be reluctant to publicly

Debating Social Issues

SHOULD LESBIANS AND GAYS BE ALLOWED TO MARRY?

New York City Mayor Michael Bloomberg officiated over one of the first same-sex weddings in the state of New York—this one between two of his top aides.

The question of whether people of the same sex should be allowed to marry is an emotionally charged issue in public and popular discourse, debate, and legal actions across the country. Marriage is a critical issue because it touches all at once on questions of love and sex, religion and politics, access to legal and economic benefits, and the role of government in our personal lives. There are literally hundreds of rights, benefits, and protections that accompany civil marriage in the United States. Because they are so automatic, most heterosexuals take these rights for granted. However, even with civil unions, lesbian and gay couples do not enjoy the full range of these benefits. The national debate surrounding the rights of same-sex couples to marry intensified in 2004 after the state of Massachusetts became the first state in the country to legalize same-sex marriage. Since that time the U.S. Census Bureau has estimated that there are 20,000 lesbian and gay couples living in cities and suburbs across the state (Schworm and Carroll, 2011).

There is a range of complex issues reflected in the marriage debate, some normative, some moral, and others legal. Figure 7.3 on page 224 shows that although there has been a significant decline in opposition to same-sex marriage, the country remains divided over the issue. As many adults (45 percent) favor as oppose (46 percent) allowing lesbians and gays to marry. One of the most common arguments against same-sex marriage is that it would subvert the stability and integrity of heterosexual marriages and families and, in turn, would further weaken the traditional family values that are seen as essential to society. Most opponents of same-sex marriage view marriage as an institution between one woman and one man only. People who oppose same-sex marriage observe that most religions of the world consider homosexuality unacceptable and sinful. People who attend religious services on a regular basis are the most opposed to same-sex marriage (Masci, 2008). Opponents further argue that to legalize same-sex marriage would create a slippery slope that would ultimately destroy the whole idea of marriage, leading to granting people in polygamous and other nontraditional relationships the right to marry as well (Masci, 2008). They also believe that same-sex marriage is an oxymoron, an ideological invention that is designed to force societal acceptance of homosexuality. Some opponents fear that legalizing same-sex marriage will somehow influence young people to perhaps try out same-sex relationships. This is perhaps most evident in the bans that many schools and libraries have instituted with regard to books and materials that depict same-sex relationships. The opposition to same-sex marriages at the state level is reflected in the fact that 41 states have passed Defense of Marriage Acts, allowing these states to refuse to recognize a same-sex marriage obtained in another state (National Conference of State Legislatures, 2008). Finally, some opponents, including former President George W. Bush, favor a constitutional amendment that would define marriage as being between a man and a woman, thus barring same-sex marriages in all states.

On the other side of the debate, those who support same-sex marriage argue that marriage is a civil right and the denial of marriage as an option for lesbians and gays not only violates their civil rights but also it is a violation of their religious freedom. Marriage, they say, is a secular activity and should not be governed by religious ideology. Lesbian and gay couples ought to be allowed the option of civil marriage which does not entail any religious ceremonies and ought to be acceptable to those who object to same-sex marriages on the grounds of their religious beliefs. In fact, they

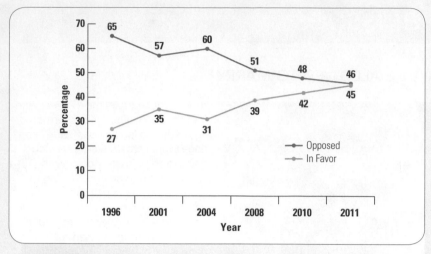

FIGURE 7.3 Attitudes toward Same-Sex Marriage, 1996–2011

Source: Adapted from Pew Research Center. 2010. "Support for Same-Sex Marriage Edges Upwaard." (October 6). http://people-press.org/2010/10/06/support-for-same-sex-marriage-edges-upward/ (2011, May 10); Pew Research Center. 2011. "Fewer Are Angry at Government, But Discontent Remains High" (March 3) http://peple-press.org/2011/03/03/section-3-attitudes-toward-social-issues/ (2011, May 10).

decision in 1967 that mixed race couples could marry anywhere in the United States; but, until recently, same-sex couples could not marry anywhere in the world. Rather than weakening marriages and families, proponents of same-sex marriage argue that expanding the definition of marriage will strengthen it, not destroy it. Giving lesbians and gays the same rights to marry as heterosexuals would reinforce the commitment of many same-sex couples to live within long-term, committed relationships and encourage others who might not otherwise do so; it would encourage people to have strong family values, discourage high-risk sexual lifestyles, and encourage monogamy.

What do you think? On which side of the debate do you fall? Explain your position using sociological insights, concepts, and a theoretical paradigm (see Chapter 2). Why do you think it is important to lesbians and gays that they have a legal right to marry? Is it a fundamental civil right or a special privilege? Explain. In your opinion, would same-sex marriage require a redefinition of marriage? If so, how might we redefine marriage?

argue, many religious views are outdated and should be modified to reflect the changes in society. Legalizing same-sex marriage would provide lesbians and gays with the fundamental American freedom of having the right to choose whether and whom to marry. Proponents argue further that same-sex marriage does not threaten the institution of marriage—an institution that has been in a state of flux for centuries: for example, it was only after the Civil War that African-Americans were allowed to marry in all areas of the United States; it was only after a U.S. Supreme Court

---

Watch the **Video** *Alternative Sexual Orientation* on **myfamilylab.com**

---

acknowledge their sexuality for fear of being stigmatized despite some of these changing attitudes.

Finally, there are many variations in lesbian and gay lifestyles that have yet to be systematically studied. Nevertheless, data from the 2000 Census provides demographic and socio-economic information about same-sex couples in the United States.

- Same-sex couples live in every state and virtually every county in the United States. The states with the highest percentage of same-sex couple households are Vermont, California, Washington, Massachusetts, and Oregon. The urban areas of San Francisco, Ft. Lauderdale, and Seattle have the highest percentage of same-sex couple households. Individuals living in same-sex couples include every race and ethnicity.
- Seventy-one percent of individuals in same-sex couples are employed compared with 65 percent of individuals in married couples.
- Fifteen percent of individuals in same-sex couples are veterans compared with 19 percent of individuals in married couples.

- Members of same-sex couples are more likely than married couples to have obtained a college degree.
- More than 39 percent of same-sex couples ages 22–55 are raising children; they are raising more than 250,000 children under age 18. Some had their children when they were part of a heterosexual union; others elected to have children outside of a biological relationship through artificial insemination; and still others have adopted children. Lesbian and gay parenting is discussed in Chapter 9.
- The median household income for same-sex parents is $10,000 lower than the median household income for different-sex parents. The rate of home ownership for same-sex parents is 15 percent lower than for different-sex parents (Sears, Gates, and Rubenstein, 2005).
- Lesbian couples have a poverty rate of 6.9 percent compred to 5.4 percent for different sex-married couples and 4.0 percent for gay male couples. African Americans in same-sex couples and same-sex couples living in rural areas have particularly high poverty rates (Albelda, et al., 2009).

DEMYSTIFYING LESBIAN AND GAY RELATIONSHIPS

What images do you have of lesbian and gay cohabitants? No doubt you are aware of some of the many stereotypes about lesbians and gays. Among the most prevalent images are those depicting lesbians as masculine or "butch" and gay men as effeminate. The major stereotypes involving cohabiting same-sex couples assume that these couples imitate heterosexual patterns, with one partner acting as "wife" (submissive female) and the other playing the "husband" (dominant male). Earlier research, however, shows that these stereotypes apply to only a small minority of same-sex relationships, those in which partners tend to be older, male, and from lower socioeconomic and educational levels (Peplau and Gordon, 1983; Harry, 1984). Later research confirmed that partners in same-sex couples are less likely than those in heterosexual couples to assume gender-typed roles (Herek, 2000).

What, then, are lesbian and gay relationships like? First, it is important to recognize that just as there is tremendous diversity among heterosexuals who cohabit, there is rich diversity across race, ethnicity, religion, and social class among homosexual cohabitants (Stacey, 2003). Second, research comparing lesbian, gay, and heterosexual relationships shows that they are quite similar and operate essentially on the same principles, seek the same kind of mutually supportive, romantic, and emotionally intimate bonds, and confront the same issues in living together—division of household labor, finances, communication, and decision making (Herek, 2000; Kurdek, 2006; Roisman, et al, 2008). Lesbians and gays, like their heterosexual counterparts, experience the same fears of rejection, the same relationship problems, and the same problems with sexual functioning. However, compared to heterosexuals, lesbian and gay partners report fewer barriers to leaving a relationship (Kurdek, 1998). This finding is likely related to the lack of legal recognition and social acceptance of homosexual relationships.

LIVING TOGETHER: DOMESTIC TASKS, FINANCES, AND DECISION MAKING

Because traditional gender distinctions are irrelevant to same-sex relationships, lesbian and gay couples are in a unique position to create living arrangements tailored to their needs and interests. How, then, do same-sex couples resolve the day-to-day requirements of living? Research shows that there is considerable discussion and conscious joint decision making in these areas. An early study found that over half of both lesbians and gays in the sample reported sharing housework equally (Bell and Weinberg, 1978). In one of the earliest studies comparing heterosexual and homosexual couples, sociologists Philip Blumstein and Pepper Schwartz (1983) found several factors that affect the division of household tasks. Among gay couples the number of hours spent at work determines the relative contribution of each partner—the one with the fewer outside hours does more of the household tasks. There were some constraints on this pattern, however. For example, these authors found that "both heterosexual and homosexual men feel that a successful partner should not have to do housework" (1983:151). More recent research shows that although lesbian couples work harder than either gay or heterosexual couples to create an equitable distribution of tasks, overall for same-sex partners, individual interests in household labor is related to the frequency of performing specific household tasks (Kurdek, 2007).

Decision making, like housework, is often related to income—that is, the partner with the highest income tends to have the most power. In a comparative study of heterosexual and same-sex couples, Blumstein and Schwartz (1983) found this to be true for gay and heterosexual couples but not for lesbian couples. In this same study, lesbian respondents reported less conflict over finances than did other couples. Among both heterosexual and gay couples, partners who feel they have equal control over how money is spent have a more tranquil relationship. An intriguing observational study of how lesbian, gay, and heterosexual couples behave in conflict interactions found that homosexual partners were less belligerent, less domineering, and exhibited less fear/tension and less whining than did heterosexual partners. Additionally, the data showed that the homosexual initiators of the conflict also demonstrated more positive emotions, more affection, more humor, and more joy/excitement when compared with the heterosexual initiators. The researchers speculate that the reasons for these observed differences is that homosexual couples value equality far more than do heterosexual couples and that because there are fewer barriers to leaving homosexual than heterosexual relationships, homosexual couples may be more careful in how they communicate with their partners (Gottman et al., 2003). However, these findings do not mean that conflict and violence are absent in lesbian and gay relationships. In fact, domestic violence occurs with about the same frequency as in heterosexual communities (Sorenson and Thomas, 2009) and takes many of the same forms (see Chapter 11). However, until relatively recently this behavior has been ignored both in the lesbian and gay communities and in the larger society as well.

THE SOCIAL AND LEGAL CONTEXT OF LESBIAN AND GAY RELATIONSHIPS

Although there has been a positive shift in public attitudes toward lesbians and gays with growing numbers of the population opposed to discrimination in areas such as housing and employment, many people in the United States still consider homosexuality to be abnormal or sinful. Prejudice against lesbians and gays is particularly strong among men, the less educated, older adults, rural

Tammy Baldwin (D-WI), an openly lesbian member of Congress, helps celebrate the passage of the Affordable Care Act at the U.S. capital.

residents, those who hold traditional beliefs about gender roles and who have conservative religious beliefs. They are also less likely to have had any close relationships with an openly gay person. Conversely, heterosexuals with close friends who have acknowledged their sexual orientation are among those most likely to have positive and supportive attitudes toward lesbians and gays (Herek, 2000; Religious Tolerance.Org, 2003).

Many work environments have improved considerably for people who are open about their sexual orientation, nevertheless, discrimination still exits. Despite the fact that lesbians and gays have long served in the U.S. armed forces, any open acknowledgment of (or even suspicion of) one's homosexuality could result in a dishonorable discharge. In 1993, in an attempt to end discrimination against lesbians and gays in the military, the United States adopted a "don't ask, don't tell" policy, intended to be less punitive than the past policy of an outright ban, but it still denied gays and lesbians equal treatment with their heterosexual counterparts. Things that heterosexuals take for granted when they enter the military—help in keeping contact and communication with family and friends, establishing insurance beneficiaries, and completing wills—became dangerous minefields for lesbians, gays, and their partners. Under the "don't ask, don't tell" policy, thousands of lesbians and gays were discharged once their sexual orientation was known. After heated debate in Congress, a bill to end the policy was passed and signed into law in 2010 by President Barack Obama. With this action the United States joined the majority of Western industrialized countries that allow lesbians and gays to serve openly in their military.

Lesbians and gays also confront other problems because of their sexual orientation. They are often the victims of name-calling, ridicule, and even violence. Such "gay bashing" behavior has long been a problem in the United States but recently collected data have shown a slight decline in the number of reported incidents. According to the National Coalition of Anti-Violence Programs (2007), there were 1,393 incidents in 2006, down 3 percent from 2005. Violence against homosexuals is not confined to the United States. A report by Amnesty International documents abuses in 30 countries throughout Latin America, Eastern Europe, Africa, Asia, the Caribbean, and the Middle East. A recent United Nations report documents increased persecution, torture, and killing of lesbians and gays in Iraq (Buckley, 2007). In Jamaica, violence against gays has become common, forcing many gays to go into hiding or to leave the island (Lacey, 2008). In Chechnya, under the Muslim Shari'a code, men can be executed for homosexual acts (Leland, 2001). Because of the extreme prejudice and violence directed against homosexuals in their native countries, the United States grants asylum to individuals when their sexual orientation poses a serious threat to their lives. All too often, however, the asylum seekers face further rejection from their fellow countrymen who have migrated to the United States, bringing homophobic attitudes with them.

In such a climate, it is easy to understand why many lesbians and gays keep their sexual orientation hidden. Individuals who "come out of the closet" and acknowledge their homosexuality risk discrimination and alienating their family and friends. Given this context, lesbians and gays often create kinship structures of friends and lovers who provide the social and emotional support traditionally expected of biological kin. Even with this support,

the issue of closeting or "coming out" has implications for the kind of personal relationships that lesbians and gays establish. For example, a study of 124 lesbians involved in a couple relationship found that closeting often has a negative impact on the couple's relationship quality. If couples can be open with family and friends, the quality of their relationship is likely to be higher.

Research on "coming out" suggests that patterns of disclosure and subsequent family reactions vary considerably (Merighi and Grimes, 2000). For example, mothers are more often told than fathers (D'Augelli et al., 1998). Lesbians and gays perceived more rejection and disapproval from families in conservative rural regions. Parents with strong convictions that homosexuality is always wrong find it difficult to accept their child's homosexuality (Elias, 2007). Although some parents react negatively and distance themselves from their children, others are very supportive. A number of supportive parents formed Parents and Friends of Lesbians and Gays (PFLAG), a nonprofit organization with 200,000 members and supporters and local affiliates in more than 500 communities across the United States and abroad. A recent survey conducted via social networking sites suggest that this increased support and greater visibility in the larger community has given lesbian, gays, and bisexuals confidence to come out earlier. The average age at which people come out as lesbian, gay, or bisexual has fallen steadily over the last four decades (Williams, 2010).

ELDERLY LESBIANS, GAYS, AND BISEXUALS

No one can say with certainty how many lesbian and gay adults there are. Few national surveys ask about sexual orientation, and even when they do, older respondents are not likely to disclose their sexual orientation given the negative attitudes to homosexuality that they experienced over their lifetime. Estimates put the number of the LGB population 65 and older at about 1.5 million with the number expected to increase to 3 million by 2030 ("Improving the Lives...", 2011). The research that does exist on elderly LGBs suggests that they face the same challenges of aging as do elderly heterosexuals. At the same time, however, LGBs have unique life experiences stemming from their homosexual and bisexual identity that create specific issues and needs. A first of its kind statewide study on aging lesbian, gay, and bisexual adults in California found:

- Gay and bisexual men have more chronic conditions (high blood pressure, diabetes, physical disability, and poor self-rated health) than their heterosexual counterparts.
- Aging LGBs report greater symptoms of psychological distress than their heterosexual peers, 1.45 times higher for gay and bisexual men and 1.35 times higher for lesbian and bisexual women (Wallace, et al., 2011).

Many closeted elderly LGBs are afraid to tell their doctors about their sexual orientation for fear their doctor will treat them differently or discriminate against them. Similarly, when elderly LGBs enter long-term care facilities, they may face hostility from other residents and/or if they enter a retirement facility with a partner, existing policies may require them to have separate rooms.

LGBs are more likely than their heterosexual peers to be alone. The California study found that

- Half of aging gay and bisexual adult men live alone compared to 13.4 percent of heterosexual men. About one-third of aging gay and bisexual adult men are married or living with a partner while more than three-fourths of heterosexual men are married or living with a partner.
- More than one in four aging lesbian and bisexual women live alone compared to one in five heterosexual women. More than one-half of aging lesbian and bisexual adult women are married or living with a partner as are almost two-thirds of aging heterosexual women (Wallace, et al., 2011).

Two factors are at work here. First the majority of lesbians and gays have never had children. Second, many others are estranged from their families because of disapproval of their lifestyle. These factors can lead to isolation and loneliness. To address these problems, many health care facilities are developing Lesbian, Gay, Bisexual, and Transgender Aging Projects to train long-term care providers (Domrose, 2008). Some in the LGB community are building retirement communities of their own to support and nurture one another. Approximately 25 of theses are now open, primarily in Arizona, New Mexico, and Florida. Other communities have been proposed but have been stalled by the recession.

Israeli children from Kibbutz Harel (in blue) play soccer with Palestinian children from a West Bank village. Adults in this communal organization share many of the tasks of daily living, including child care.

Communal Living and Group Marriage

Thus far, this chapter has focused primarily on single people who live alone or cohabit. Not everyone, however, is content to live alone or to cohabit with just one other person. Some people join a commune to satisfy their needs for intimacy and companionship.

A **commune** refers to a group of people (single or married, with or without children) who live together, sharing many aspects of their lives. Communes have existed from earliest times. In particular, they are likely to develop or expand in periods of political and social unrest (Mead, 1970). The communal movement in the United States originated around the end of the eighteenth century. Most of the early communes were religious in origin. Some, like the Shakers, named for the way they moved during prayer and song, believed monogamous marriage and the nuclear family were detrimental to the spiritual health of the community. Thus, they required all members, whether married or not, to live celibate lives. Eighteen Shaker communes were established in Maine, New Hampshire, Massachusetts, Connecticut, New York, Kentucky, Ohio, Indiana, Georgia, and Florida. Membership reached its numerical high of around 5,000 souls during the 1850s. The only remaining active Shaker community, located in Sabbathday Lake, Maine, consists of a small group of women and men who care for the commune's 18 buildings, orchards, fields, and gardens. Besides spending their days in prayer and work, members often travel throughout the country, visiting museums and art galleries to tell the Shaker story as well as hosting visitors and students.

Marriage and sexual relationships took other forms in other of the early communes. The Mormons, for example, practiced polygyny. Still others engaged in free love whereby members could engage in sexual relationships with any other member of the group. The political instability in the years immediately preceding and following the Civil War produced about a hundred new communes. One of them, the Hutterites, a commune with a religious origin, still has members in the United States today. The economic turmoil of the 1930s and the political activism of the 1960s also led to new waves of communal development (Zablocki, 1980). It is estimated that today there are over 3,000 functioning communes worldwide ("The World Communal Scene," 2005). Among the better-known communes surviving in the United States are Sandhill Farm in Missouri, Twin Oaks in Virginia, and The Farm in Tennessee. To learn more about the variety of modern communes, see the Applying the Sociological Imagination box on page 228.

ADVANTAGES AND DISADVANTAGES OF THE COMMUNAL LIFESTYLE

Have you ever wondered what motivates someone to adopt a communal lifestyle? Studies of communes suggest that their members are motivated by a desire for egalitarian, personalized, cooperative, and satisfying intimate relationships—qualities they perceive are not readily available in the traditional nuclear family structure.

Among the advantages most frequently reported by members of communes are close intimate relationships with a variety of people; personal growth through group experiences; the sharing of economic resources, domestic tasks, and child care; companionship; social support; spiritual rebirth or strengthening; and a respect and reverence for nature (Alford, 2009; Nichols, 2008). These advantages also create some disadvantages, including limitations on privacy, restrictions on personal freedom, limitations on parental influence and control, lack of stability, legal ambiguity, financial problems, and the possibility of sexual jealousy (Weale, 2010; Thies, 2000; Cornfield, 1983).

Intentional communities take diverse form. Among the most common are:

- Ecovillages—communities with a strong ecological focus.
- Cohousing—communities that incorporate both private homes and shared common facilities and support neighborly connections.
- Communes—income sharing communities.

- Co-ops—expense sharing, often urban, shared housing communities. Many of those listed are focused on college students.
- Christian communities—communities that include prayer and Christian practices and values in their daily routines.

Go to http://directory.ic.org/iclist/community_type.php, part of the Intentional Communities Web site. Click on each type and then select at least two communes from each list. Examine their organizational structure and functioning. What kinds of people join these communities? How do residents earn their living? How do they raise their children? What kind of governance structures do these communities have? Would you consider joining any of these communities? Are age and marital status factors in your consideration? Explain.

Most communes last for only short periods of time. Many of the problems encountered in communes center on conflicts over power, authority, and ideology. Those communes that survive the longest share certain characteristics: religious orientation, strict admission requirements, strong member commitment, controls on sexuality, adequate financing, time and space for privacy, and clearly defined authority and distribution of tasks (Cornfield, 1983; Kantor, 2005).

COMMUNES, SHARED HOUSING, AND THE FUTURE

As with other lifestyles, communes are not for everyone, and we can only speculate on their future viability. It is likely that as the economy worsens or if new political turmoil develops, the number of communes and new communal arrangements will grow. For example, in Japan, a country with a stagnant economy over the last decade, a firm called Tulip Estates has created communal rental units for young women migrating to Tokyo to work. By sharing rent and space, these newcomers avoid loneliness, save money, and learn survival strategies from their peers ("Women-only Communal Housing…," 2010). Earlier predictions that as populations age, some form of communal or group living will become a viable option for the elderly who otherwise might be forced to live alone seem to be coming true (Dressel and Hess, 1983). For example, cohousing for older people is now a valued housing niche in the Netherlands and in Denmark (Bramford, 2005). Here in the United States, one organization, the National Shared Housing Resource Center in Baltimore, a clearinghouse that helps people find ways to maintain their independence by living interdependently with others, keeps tabs on hundreds of shared-housing programs across the country. Shared housing usually takes one of two forms: group homes, in which several people share a residence, or match-ups, where a homeowner and a home seeker agree to live together. Some programs are open only to the elderly; others are intergenerational.

New patterns of cooperative living arrangements are emerging in the United States. Some involve individuals and multigenerational families living in their own private self-sufficient units but also sharing common space where they can gather for social and recreational activities, as these three generations of women are doing.

Other experiments in cooperative living are also emerging. Two architects, Katie McCamant and Chuck Durret, intrigued by community developments in Denmark, founded the CoHousing Company in Berkeley, California, to introduce the idea in the United States. The concept of cohousing, or as some call it, "intentional neighborhood," is characterized by individuals or families living in their own private, self-sufficient units, but also sharing common spaces—a large dining room and kitchen, a garden, workshops, and a children's play area. Thus, members can share responsibilities like cooking and child care. Other benefits include ongoing support and companionship. Since their inception, over 230 cohousing communities have been completed in the United States.

GROUP MARRIAGES

Group marriages represent a variation of communal living. Sociologists Larry and Joan Constantine (1973:29) define **group marriage** as "a marriage of at least four people, two female and two male, in which each partner is married to all partners of the opposite sex." The actual number of documented group marriages has been small. One of the best-known experiments with group marriage was the Oneida Community in New York, founded by the Protestant minister John Noyes. It lasted from 1849 to 1881 and had about 300 adult members. Monogamous marriage and sexual exclusivity were not permitted. Children were reared in a communal nursery by specialized caretakers, and they were taught to consider all adults in the community as parents. Thus, the entire community was to be viewed as a single family. Hostile outside pressure contributed to the demise of this experiment in group marriage (Kephart, 1988).

No one knows for sure how many group marriages currently exist in the United States. Because group marriages are neither legal nor socially acceptable to most Americans, locating them is a difficult task. For an account of one son's story of his parents' group marriage, see, for example, Laird Harrison (2008). Extensive research on alternative lifestyles, including communes and group marriage, took place in the 1960s and 1970s, a period of social turmoil that included the Vietnam War, and various political and social movements (women's liberation, civil rights, and lesbian and gay rights). During this period, many people were publicly criticizing the institutions of marriage and the family as well as traditional gender roles and experimenting with alternative lifestyles. This climate provided a fertile ground for social scientists such as the Constantines, whose research on group marriages found that the most commonly reported reason respondents gave for their involvement was their dissatisfaction with traditional monogamous marriage. However, many of these relationships were short-lived, lasting on average only 16 months. Beginning in the 1980s, interest in and research on alternative lifestyles diminished dramatically.

Supporting Nonmarried Adults

Changes in social customs and social policy could alleviate some of the problems encountered by the never-married as they grow older. For example, we are all familiar with the rituals, showers, and gift giving that accompanies the marriage ceremony. Rarely, however, do we formally assist single people or cohabiting couples to establish their homes or symbolically, through a ritual celebration, recognize and give support to their lifestyle. Tax laws tend to favor homeowners (mostly marrieds), heads of households, and parents. Singles are often at a financial disadvantage, especially today when homeownership and material goods require more than one income. As single people age, they may experience other disadvantages. If they are without children of their own, they may find themselves relatively isolated due to the age-graded character of our society, or they may feel some regret at not having children to carry on their legacy. More opportunities for intergenerational contact and perhaps even intergenerational or some other form of communal living arrangements could minimize these difficulties.

Writing Your Own Script

CONSIDERING LIFESTYLE OPTIONS

Do I want to marry? The answer to this question represents one of the most fundamental choices we will make in our lifetime. As we saw in this chapter, people are more likely today than in the past to consider alternatives to traditional marriage. Nevertheless, pressure to marry remains intense, especially for young adults. The United States is still one of the most marrying societies in the world. Although increasing numbers of individuals are not marrying at all, delaying marriage to a later age, and divorcing at high rates, demographers predict that nine out of ten people born in the United States in recent years will marry at least once in their lifetime. Thus, one must weigh the merits of alternative lifestyles.

Questions to Consider

If I decide not to marry, is this a permanent decision, or will I reevaluate this decision at some later time? What lifestyle will I choose? Will I cohabit with a partner or live alone? What are the advantages and disadvantages of a single or nonmarried lifestyle? If I choose not to marry, will I be sexually active or remain celibate?

SUMMARY

Over the last several decades, the number of never-married people in the United States has grown. This increase is not a new phenomenon. Rather, it represents a return to historically higher levels of singlehood, which began to decline markedly only after 1940. In the past, singlehood was a devalued status, and single people were often the objects of ridicule. Today, there is greater acceptance of single people. Singlehood can be voluntary or involuntary, temporary or permanent. Singles engage in a variety of lifestyles. Some live alone, others live with relatives or friends, and some choose to cohabit.

In the past, cohabitation, or "living together," was more common among the poor. Today's cohabitants include people of all ages, races, and classes. Cohabitation, like living alone, can be temporary and fluid. For many, cohabitation has become an extension of the dating process. The number of unmarried-couple households has increased from 439,000 in 1960 to more than 8 million in 2010. Cohabitation is similar to marriage in that couples create emotional and physical relationships with each other, and in some cases they also bear or rear children. It differs from marriage, however, in that it lacks formal legal, cultural, and religious support. Some couples choose to cohabit prior to marriage. The weight of research findings on the relationship of cohabitation to marital stability indicates that it increases the risk of divorce although this relationship may be weakening as cohabitation becomes more widespread.

An increasing number of communities now allow lesbian, gay, and heterosexual cohabitants to register as domestic partners and enter into civil unions and receive some of the same benefits that married couples do. Lesbians and gays deal with the same issues of living together as heterosexuals: household division of labor, decision making, and finances. Additionally, however, they confront discrimination and social disapproval of their lifestyle.

Some individuals, seeking an alternative to traditional marriage, join a commune or participate in a group marriage.

KEY TERMS

push/pull factors

singlism

common-law marriage

palimony

domestic partnership

commune

group marriage

QUESTIONS FOR STUDY AND REFLECTION

1. Identify and discuss the structural changes that have led to the increase in nonmarital lifestyles. What are some of the problems people face when they live a nontraditional lifestyle? What advice would you give to someone whose lifestyle meets with social disapproval?

2. Increasing numbers of people are delaying marriages into their late 20s and early 30s, and some never marry at all. What social, demographic, and economic factors are responsible for this trend? What consequences, if any, exist for the larger society if a growing percentage of the population does not marry? Do women and men experience being single in similar or different ways? Explain. Do younger and older adults experience being single in similar or different ways? Explain.

3. Compare and contrast the legal status of married couples with that of cohabitants. What do you see as the advantages or disadvantages of the concepts of domestic partnership and civil unions? Do you favor or oppose granting domestic partnership or civil union status to heterosexual cohabitants? To homosexual cohabitants? What impact, if any, would this have on our understanding of marriages and families? Explain your position.

4. As noted earlier in this chapter, gay bashing, or attacks that are now called hate crimes, appear to be decreasing but remain a serious problem. Has there been any such behavior on your campus, in your workplace, neighborhood, or city? What causes or triggers this behavior? What steps can be taken to minimize the likelihood of such incidents from taking place in your immediate environments?

ADDITIONAL RESOURCES

SOCIOLOGICAL

ARNETT, JEFFREY JENSEN. 2004. *Emerging Adulthood: The Winding Road from the Late Teens Through the Twenties.* New York: Oxford University Press (USA). The author's interviews with young adults leads him to conclude that the majority of those coresiding with parents are not spoiled or self-indulgent as so often portrayed in the media but are trying to establish themselves in difficult economic times.

DEPAULO, BELLA M. 2006. *Singled Out: How Singles Are Stereotyped, Stigmatized, and Ignored, and Still Live Happily Ever After.* New York: St. Martin's Press. In her well-researched book, the author argues that the place of singles in society and the significance of getting married have change dramatically over the past decades but society's views of single and married people have not yet caught up. She debunks many of the myths and stereotypes about single people and suggests changes in government policies and business practices that discriminate against them.

FAIRFIELD, RICHARD. 2010. *The Modern Utopian: Alternative Communes of the 60s and 70s.* Port Townsend, WA: Process Publishers. Fairfield examines alternative communities of the 60s and 70s with documentation by those who lived the experience and explores how current economic and political developments are reviving interest in collective living.

POLIKOFF, NANCY D. 2008. *Beyond (Straight and Gay) Marriage: Valuing All Families Under the Law.* New York: Beacon Press. Given the increase in the number of households following untraditional family models, law professor Polikoff argues that we need to look at ways the law can change to value all families beyond those created by marriage, including same-sex and different-sexed, married and unmarried couples.

FILM

Brokeback Mountain. 2005. Ang Lee's epic western tells the story of two young cowboys who fall in love while working as sheepherders in the Wyoming high country. When their summer employment ends, they break up, both going their separate ways. Both marry and have children. Four years later, they meet again and their romance is rekindled. They spend the remainder of their otherwise straight lives concealing their love with tragic consequences for themselves and others they care about.

Failure to Launch. 2006. This romantic comedy focuses on a young man who is affable, intelligent, good-looking, and still living at home. He seems to have no ambitions beyond playing video games and hanging out. In desperation, his parents hire a professional motivation consultant who pretends to fall in love with him in the hope that a romantic relationship will motivate him to move out of his parents' home and get a life.

LITERARY

KINGSOLVER, BARBARA. 1993. *Pigs in Heaven.* New York: HarperCollins. A single woman finds and then adopts (perhaps illegally) a Cherokee child called Turtle and is faced with the possibility of losing her when a Native American lawyer enters the case.

BINCHY, MAEVE. 1992. *The Lilac Bus.* New York: Dell. Eight intriguing, never-married women's and men's lives unfold as they ride the special Lilac Bus from Dublin to their families' homes for the weekend.

INTERNET

http://www.thetasksforce.org The National Gay and Lesbian Task Force provides data on lesbian and gay issues and links to other resources.

http://ilrg.com/forms/cohab-agreement.html The Internet Legal Research Group provides a nonmarital cohabitation/living together agreement form that can help couples address many of the issues they will face when living as an unmarried couple.

http://www.unmarried.org The Alternatives to Marriage Project advocates for equality and fairness for unmarried people and provides support and information for people who are single, choose not to marry, cannot marry, or choose to cohabit.

http://www.cohousing.org The Cohousing Association of the United States provides information about collaborative housing in which residents actively participate in the design and operation of their own neighborhoods.

Succeed with MyFamilyLab®
www.myfamilylab.com

Watch. Explore. Read. The New MyFamilyLab is designed just for you. Each chapter features a pre-test and post-test to help you learn and review key concepts and terms. Experience Marriages and Families in action with dynamic visual activities, videos, and readings to enhance your learning experience.

Here are a few activities you will find for this chapter.

Watch on **myfamilylab.com**

Video clips feature important concepts in the study of Marriages and Families. Watch:
- Alternative Sexual Orientation

Explore on **myfamilylab.com**

Social Explorer is an interactive application that allows you to explore Census data through interactive maps. Explore the Social Explorer Activity:
- Single Americans

Read on **myfamilylab.com**

MyFamilyLab includes primary source readings from classic and contemporary sociologists from around the world. Read:
- Coontz: "The Way We Weren't: The Myth and Reality of the "Traditional" Family"

8

The Marriage Experience

What Will You Learn?

- Define and understand the sociological meaning of key terms.
- Describe major aspects of the marriage experience.
- Apply the sociological imagination to examine various social policies that reward some types of marriages and families and discourage other types.
- Assess the pros and cons of marriage or relationship contracts.
- Increase your awareness and understanding of the changes and continuities in the meaning of marriage over time and across cultures.
- Question how and why effective communication is related to marital or intimate partner satisfaction.

IN THE NEWS

James City, NC

At a time when marriages begin and end with relative ease, when major national surveys are reporting a significant decline in the number of Americans entering into legal marital unions, and when one-half or more of all marriages will end in divorce, Herbert and Zelmyra Fisher (105 and 103 years of age, respectively) are a rarity. The Fishers hold the Guinness World Record of being the world's longest married living couple, having been married 87 years. The couple got married on May 23, 1924, when a dozen eggs cost

(continued on next page)

(continued from previous page)

25 cents, Calvin Coolidge was president, and Americans were enjoying a pre–Wall Street crash economic boom (Hawkins, 2010).

The Fishers, who are African-American, were poor when they got married, but they worked hard to create a good life for their family, despite the difficulties caused by racism, segregation, and discrimination. The early years of their marriage included the lean years of the Great Depression when Herbert worked for as little as a nickel a day. The couple had to raise their own food and ration it for their young children. A retired Coca-Cola Bottling Company mechanic, revered for his hard-working demeanor and behavior and for being a good provider, Herbert built the family home in 1942, and he and Zelmyra still reside there. His diligence and aggressive saving paid for the college educations of their five children. They also have 10 grandchildren, 9 great-grandchildren, and 4 great-great grandchildren (Hendricks, 2011). Remembering what Herbert was like when she first married him, Zelmyra says that he was her first and only boyfriend and that it was his sweetness that pulled her toward him. Zelmyra is quoted as saying: "He was not mean; he was not a fighter. He was quiet and kind. He was not much to look at, but he was sweet" (quoted in Hawkins, 2010).

The Fishers say there is no secret to the longevity of their marriage. Rather, love, respect, honesty, and support are among the most important factors that have kept them together. They also credit their marital success to faith in God, family, a close-knit and supportive community, and a few big fusses over their long marriage. Herbert says that he had no idea that he would be married this long. As for Zelmyra, while she too did not know that her marriage would last so long, she says that she did know that she wouldn't be looking for another husband. Although the couple is unfazed by the public fanfare over their accomplishment, they nonetheless captured the attention of newspapers, magazines, and Web sites throughout the world. And recently, they received a signed commendation from President Barack Obama with a promise of an official invitation to the White House to meet him (Hendricks, 2011).

Although the Fishers have been together for many decades, they claim to never fight. They have a simple understanding of each other and enjoy a simple life. They consciously take care to give each other space: they attend separate churches and, Zelmyra, who is not fond of baseball, is always happy to turn over the TV to Herbert when baseball comes on. And they each have their own bedroom so that Herbert can stay up late watching baseball. Herbert also gets pleasure from playing golf. Otherwise, they enjoy doing most everything else together. For instance, they are fond of television news programs, and they enjoy hanging out together on the front porch in their rocking chairs, watching trains pass by, counting cars, and talking to their neighbors. Despite separate church memberships, their hearts stay connected. Through the ups and downs of marriage, neither has ever considered divorce. In fact, Zelmyra says that she is adamantly opposed to the idea of divorce and remarriage (Hendricks, 2011).

Both Herbert and Zelmyra still have sharp minds and on Valentine's Day 2010, the couple went high tech taking to the popular online social network Twitter to answer relationship questions and give relationship advice. Referred to by many as America's "tweethearts," the couple also has a Facebook page. When asked if fighting was important in a marriage, the couple responded that physical fighting was absolutely unacceptable but that it is okay to disagree and fight for what really matters; that in marriage you have to learn to bend but not break. Their greatest marriage advice is that love has no limits; marriage is not a contest, never keep a score. The couple still possesses a fondness, affection, and respect for each other. To this day, they still depend on each other for protection, supervision, and warmth (Twitter.com, 2010).

WHAT DO YOU THINK?

Do you think that marriage is becoming obsolete? How do you think the Fishers have maintained a more or less traditional marriage for 87 years given all of the social, political and economic changes in American society over the past century? How has the structure of and thinking about marriage and family changed in America since the Fishers got married in 1924 and how have these changes shaped the institutions of marriages and families of today? What are some of the major historical events that have impacted the structure of marriages and families in your generation? In your parents' generation? What do these events tell us about where we are today in terms of our thinking about and behavior relative to marriage and family life?

((•—Listen to the Chapter Audio on myfamilylab.com

For those of us who have the choice, deciding whether to marry or not is one of the most important decisions we will make in our lifetime. This decision has implications for almost every aspect of an individual's life. Regardless of one's gender and sexual orientation, Americans continue to search for love and the "right" partner, to move in together, to vow to love each other, and, when legally allowed, to enter into marriages and often remarriages. And despite dramatic changes in marriages, families, and intimate relationships over the past half century, most people in the United States marry at least once in their lifetime. Approximately one-half of those marriages will last until one of the partners dies. Sociologists note that Americans have a rate of marriage and remarriage among the highest in the Western world. Additionally, among those who do not marry, partnering with the expectation of a long-term or even lifetime commitment is still widespread. However anxious we may be as a society in the face of charges that the institutions of marriages and families are dissolving and dysfunctional, surveys and other research consistently reveal that most Americans continue to view a happy marriage as either the most important goal or one of the most important goals in their lives. Most rank a good marriage at the top of their list of sources of satisfaction—above wealth, fame, good health, and a good job (Luscombe, 2010; Glenn, 2005; Waite and Gallagher, 2000).

These facts notwithstanding, as pointed out in Chapter 7, people in the United States today have more options with regard to marital roles than they did in the past. Shifts in gender roles and the growing demand for the right to marry among same-sex couples have altered not only how we view marriages and families, but also how we experience them. In this chapter, we focus on the ties between two people who commit to a long-term union, primarily, but not exclusively, within marriage. We examine the meaning of marriage in the United States in both traditional and contemporary terms, paying particular attention to the legal aspects of marriage and their effect on marital relationships. In addition, we examine the nature of marriage and other long-term relationships in the United States and the processes by which couples meet some of the many challenges of married life.

Why Do People Marry?

What is so attractive about marriage? What, if anything, does it offer that other lifestyles do not? Recall the discussion of love in Chapter 4, where we indicated that most people in the United States believe that romantic love and marriage naturally go together—that marriage naturally follows falling in love. Given this notion about the interrelationship of love and marriage, it should not be surprising that the single most important reason people give for getting married is that they are in love. For example, 93 percent of married people and 84 percent of singles cite love as the most important reason to get married. After love comes making a lifelong commitment, followed by companionship, a desire to have children, financial stability, happiness, convenience, dependence, and the fear of contracting AIDS. Although most teens are just beginning to explore the complex world of dating and relationships, the majority, like their adult counterparts, also rate love as the most important reason to marry, followed by finances, compatibility, and common interests. For many Americans, marriage is a lifelong commitment—a formal way for a couple to express their love, devotion, and commitment to each other and share their lives with the person of their choice. In this respect, marriage represents both a private and a public statement of commitment, trust, sharing, stability, intimacy, and the expectation of a permanent relationship (Luscombe, 2010; Kiefer, 2004).

However, love and commitment are not key aspects of a durable and long-lasting marriage in all cultures. In Japan, for example, although marriages, on average, are long lasting, many married couples live without love. Based on interviews with Japanese couples living in a small community 200 miles southeast of Tokyo, *New York Times* writer Nicholas Kristof found that happiness and love are not key aspects of a durable marriage in Japan. Japanese couples are often perplexed when asked about love in marriage. For example, when asked if he loved his wife, a Japanese man who had been married 33 years furrowed his brow and looked perplexed, then responded, "Yeah, so-so, I guess. She's like air or water. You couldn't live without it, but most of the time, you're not conscious of its existence" (Kristof, 1996:6).

This is a common theme in the narratives of the people Kristof spoke with. According to Kristof, it does not seem that Japanese marriages survive because wives and husbands love each other more than American couples, but rather because they perhaps love each other less. Many Japanese couples believe love marriages are more fragile than arranged marriages. In love marriages, when something happens or if the couple falls out of love, they split up. Although the divorce rate in Japan is at a record high, it is still less than half that of the United States, and Japan is said to have one of the strongest marriage and family structures in the industrialized world.

Although the traditional married couple household is disappearing throughout most of the world, Japan is a prominent exception. Yet couples neither marry for love nor live with it during much of their marital life. In fact, based on answers to survey questions about politics, sex, social issues, religion, and ethics, a Japanese research institute found Japanese couples to have the lowest level of compatibility than couples in 20 other countries. The example of Japan raises the obvious questions about what love is, as defined by whom, and its relevance or relationship to marital longevity. In short, it directs our attention to the socially constructed nature of love.

In addition to love and commitment, particularly in the United States, a number of social and economic reasons motivate people to marry. For example, many people believe being single inevitably leads to loneliness, even though there is no scientific evidence to support this view. In fact, some evidence suggests that people can be married and lonely; nonetheless, many people believe marriage offers the best opportunity for steady companionship.

Some people marry for personal fulfillment while some marry purely for financial reasons, although this is less true in the United States today than in the past. For some individuals, the acquisition, maintenance, or extension of wealth, power, and status are strong motivations to marry. Financial marital arrangements sometimes occur among the upper classes, who build their lives around highly selective social encounters and relationships. It is also relatively common among many recently arrived ethnic groups, whose subcultural norms may include arranged marriages, dowries, and bride prices.

Because social norms, values, and ideologies often equate adulthood with marriage, for some people, achieving adulthood means getting married. People whose religious beliefs prohibit sexual intercourse and living together outside of legal marriage marry to legitimize and sanctify their relationship. And some people marry because of peer or family pressure. Women in particular are often pressured to marry by well-meaning relatives and friends who do not want to see them end up as "lonely old maids." Finally, some people marry for reproductive reasons—they want to have children or heirs who are recognized as legitimate by the state. Although an increasing number of people are having children outside legal marriage and a very few believe that children are the most important reason to get married, 75 percent of Americans indicate that having children is best done within the context of marriage (Luscombe, 2010).

SOCIOLOGICAL PERSPECTIVE

On a theoretical level, there are several ways to explain why people marry. A dominant point of view in the field of sociology has been a structural–functional analysis that ignores individual motivation, and instead explains why people marry in terms of society's need or demand for legitimate children. The **principle of legitimacy,** the notion that all children ought to have a socially and legally recognized father, was first put forth by anthropologist Bronislaw Malinowski (1929).

● ──Watch the **Video** *PBS FRONTLINE: Let's Get Married* on **myfamilylab.com**

According to Malinowski, although many societies allow individuals the freedom to be sexually active whether or not they are married, only a very few societies allow their members the freedom to conceive children outside of marriage. Almost universally, marriage is based on the official control of childbearing. Because women give birth, there is no doubt who is the mother of a child. There is, however, no visible means of identifying paternity. Thus, society must develop some means whereby men can be publicly (socially) and legally connected with their offspring. All societies, then, require that every child must have a man (a legitimately married father) who will assume the social role of father and protector and who will link the child to society. In essence, such an explanation implies that people marry solely to have children. We know, however, that this is not the case for most people. As we have already indicated, currently 4 out of 10 babies in the United States are born to unmarried mothers. And the United States is not alone when it comes to unmarried births. For instance, in Sweden, 55 percent of all children born are to unmarried mothers (see Figure 8.1). Statistics such as these gives us cause alone to question the viability of this principle to explain why people marry.

In contrast, a feminist perspective challenges theories such as the principle of legitimacy, maintaining that they place far more importance on the role of social father than mother in giving children social and legal status. Instead, a feminist perspective focuses on traditional gender role socialization, in which girls are taught to consider love, marriage, and children the ultimate goals for women and the most fulfilling roles they can play in society (see Chapter 3). Thus, a woman's decision to marry can represent, in part, a response to social pressures and expectations. Whatever reasons people have for marrying, and whatever theories we use to explain why people marry, the fact remains that an overwhelming majority of us will marry at some time in our lives. The probability of an adult getting married at some point during their lifetime is still nearly 90 percent and demographers predict that this trend will continue into the future. Only 4 percent have ruled out marriage, while 5 percent are unsure or refuse to designate their marital status or intentions. But Americans' relationship with marriage is complex. For example, although married people consistently report being happier and healthier than unmarried people, an

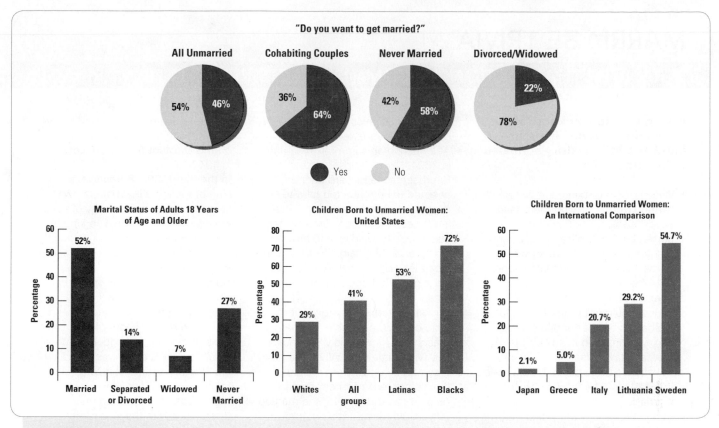

FIGURE 8.1 Current Trends in American Marriages and Families

Source: Belinda Luscombe. 2010. "Marriage: What's it Good For?" *Time* magazine. Vol. 176, No. 22, pp. 48–56.

increasing number of adults are spending more of their lives single or living unmarried with partners than ever in the past (Mather and Lavery, 2010; Bergman, 2006; Roberts, 2006; Saad, 2006).

In the next section of this chapter, we discuss the current state of marriage in the United States, who is and is not marrying and why or why not. Before moving to the next section, however, think about what you know about marriage in the United States. Although most Americans agree (and rightfully so) that marriage is not what it used to be, most of what "everyone knows" about marriage—what it used to be and just how it has changed—is not correct (Coontz, 2006). Before continuing to the next section, go to the Marriage Trivia box on page 238 and test yourself on how many of the facts you are familiar with.

Who Needs Marriage? The Changing Shape of American Marriages and Families

We asked the question: Why do people marry? Let's now consider the converse of that question: Why don't people marry? Consider the following: In 1960, almost 70 percent of American adults were married; today only about one-half are. Back then, two-thirds of

adults in their twenties were married; in 2008 only 16 percent were. And in a reversal of past trends, college graduates are now far more likely to marry (64 percent) than those without a college education (48 percent). In addition, eight times as many children are born to unmarried mothers today than in 1960 (see Figure 8.1) (Luscombe, 2010).

✳ **Explore** the **Concept**
Social Explorer Activity: Patterns Within the Married Population on **myfamilylab.com**

So, what is going on with America's marriages and families? According to Belinda Luscombe of the Pew Research Center (2010), when institutions such as these that are so very vital to human experience shift and change shape in the course of a couple of generations it is noteworthy. It is so noteworthy that *Time* magazine devoted its November 29, 2010 cover to the topic under the heading: Who Needs Marriage? Inside, the results of a 2010 nationwide poll conducted by the Pew Research Center in association with *Time* magazine[1] revealed the contours of modern American marriages and new American families.

What do people want and expect out of marriage and family life today? Whatever the appeal and the reasons why people

---

[1] Much of the discussion in this section relies heavily on the Pew Research Center/*Time* magazine National Poll: Luscombe, Belinda. 2010. "Marriage: What's It Good For?" *Time*, Vol. 176, No. 22, pp. 48–56.

MARRIAGE TRIVIA

STRANGER THAN FICTION: UNCOMMON FACTS RELATED TO MARRIAGE

How much do you know about the wedded world? Try your hand at a little history sprinkled with humor.

- Widowers in Britain once were banned from marrying their dead wives' sisters. The law was supported by the Anglican Church and many politicians to protect what Prime Minister William Gladstone call "the purity of sister love." Even after that ban was lifted in 1907, a widow could not marry her dead husband's brother until a similar ban was dropped in 1921. Britain's marriage laws also extended into the classroom: Until 1944, a female teacher could be fired if she got married.

- Beatle Paul McCartney said that when he was considering whether to pursue a relationship with Heather Mills, he heard the sound of an owl and took it as a sign from his late wife, Linda, that she approved. After a much publicized and bitter divorce, the owl still has not been brought to justice.

- Approximately 3 percent of Americans marry three times or more.

- The Mosuo ethnic group in the Himalayan foothills of Southwestern China follows a custom called "walking marriage." The man visits the woman at night for sex but does not live with her and has no legal commitment to her. The woman is free to entertain a variety of men in her bedroom, and the children from

these relationships are raised by the mother and her extended family.

- At a hearing on same-sex marriage in 2004, New Hampshire state Representative Richard Kennedy seemed to be trying too hard to express his heterosexuality. "There are times when I see some comely young lady I would love to have as a house pet," he said. "But my wife won't let me, damn it. And I bought her a gun! That shows you how smart I am."

- An Associated Press story out of Ohio began memorably: "James Mason had known his wife since she was a little boy." When the boy grew up, he underwent male-to-female sex-reassignment surgery. As a 30 year-old female, she married 70-year-old Mason. Their marital relations were perfectly legal except when she forced him to exercise for more than two hours in a pool despite his heart condition. She was caught on videotape blocking his path 43 times as he tried to get out of the water. After Mason collapsed and died, his wife pleaded guilty to reckless homicide.

- Why is it okay for Fred and Wilma Flintstone to sleep in the same bed in the "Flintstones" but not Rob and Laura Petrie on the "Dick Van Dyke Show?" Did cartoon characters have sex in the early 1960s but real people did not? Some people say that "The Brady Bunch" or "The Munsters" was the first TV show to depict married couples sharing a bed, but in fact

the first such program was "Mary Kay and Johnny," which began on the DuMont Television Network in 1947.

- In the mid-1800s, Rumanika, the king of Karagwe in what is now Tanzania, had a special way of keeping his wives at home. The king fed them a steady diet of milk through straws and if they resisted, a man with a whip forced them to keep sipping. As a result, the wives became so obese that they could not stand up on their own and instead wallowed on the floors of their huts.

- Less than a century ago, boys could legally marry at age 14 and girls could marry at age 12 in Virginia, Louisiana, and Kentucky.

- LaRae Lundeen Fjellman was threatened with the loss of her massage therapist license for violating a Minnesota law banning people in her profession from having sex with former clients for two years. The man she had sex with was her husband, whom she married more than a year after he stopped being her client and started being her date. The state health department relented in the case in 2007 after three years of wrangling and agreed to pay $5,800 of Fjellman's more than $13,000 in legal fees and expenses, which meant that the state fined Fjellman at least $7,200 for having sex with her own husband.

Source: Mark Jacob. 2009. "History Lesson: 10 Things You Might Not Know About Marriage," *Chicago Tribune.* (April 19): Section 1, p. 25.

married in the past, in purely practical terms, for many people, marriage is not as necessary as it used to be. In the overall population, only 52 percent of adults 18 years old and older are married; 27 percent have never married and the remaining 21 percent have been married but are now either separated, divorced or widowed. As we learned in Chapter 6, American women and men are increasingly sexually active at younger ages and outside of marital relationships, an increasing number of children are born outside of legal marriage, and both of these are occurring across class levels, indicating that women and men do not have to be married to have

sex, have children or attain educational success. That an increasing number of Americans are less and less wedded to the idea of marriage is evidenced in the fact that 39 percent of Americans today believe that marriage is becoming obsolete compared to only 28 percent who thought so in 1978. Women and men are close in agreement on this issue with 36 percent of men and 41 percent of women saying that they believe that marriage is becoming obsolete. This does not, however, mean that marriage is dead. For example, fully 7 in 10 Americans today have been married at least once. In addition, although 44 percent of people under the age of 30 believe that marriage is becoming obsolete, only 5 percent of them do not want to get married. So, it seems that it is not the case that marriage in America is heading for extinction. Rather, it is that it is no longer obligatory or even, in some cases, helpful.

So, who is marriage for, what are its benefits, and for whom? Increasingly today, women and men who marry tend to be older and more similar to one another than different. That is, those who marry are typically on the same socioeconomic and educational level. In fact, perhaps the most profound change in who marries and who does not is in terms of the rich versus the poor. While the median household income of married adults has always been higher than that of single adults after adjusting for household size, today that gap has increased from 12 percent in 1960 to 41 percent today. Put another way, the richer and more educated one is, the more likely one is to get married or to already be married. In other words, if you are married today, you are more likely to be well off.

This trend is related to other broader issues and trends (see Table 8.1). For example, almost two-thirds (62 percent) of Americans (compared to less than one-half in 1978) think that the ideal marriage is one in which both the wife and the husband work outside of the home. This should not come as a surprise given that in the early 1970s only about 40 percent of wives worked compared to 61 percent today. In the past, some researchers have suggested that when women work, they are more likely to meet eligible men, and their economic independence might be an attraction in the marriage market (Jones, 2006; Kinnon, 2003). In addition, this trend is related to what people look for in a marital mate. Beginning with economic support, two-thirds of all people think that a man should be a good provider while about one-third think that it is important for women to be good providers as well. This might well explain the delay in marriage especially among the 20-somethings. If people are expecting a partner who is equally educated and economically stable, then it would make sense that they are delaying marriage at least until they finish college. This fact notwithstanding, curiously, high school educated couples who, in the past, made it to the altar sooner that college graduates, are now lagging behind, marrying even later than college graduates. According to sociologist Andrew Cherlin (2009), college-educated

couples delay marriage until they have completed their education and established themselves in a career whereas less educated couples delay marriage until they feel comfortable financially.

Social scientists have long known that economic factors are often key considerations in decisions to marry or not. While low income and economic marginality do not appear to affect men's development and formation of intimate romantic relationships, however, they do become factors in the decision regarding marriage. A variety of studies, for example, have indicated that during depressions and periods of high unemployment, men tend to put off getting married. However, when men have relatively good access to economic opportunities and resources; when there is economic prosperity (for example, a high availability of jobs or access to good-paying jobs) they are more likely to make the decision to marry (Whitehead and Popenoe, 2004). In this regard, race is an important sociopolitical construction that has a major impact on a person's decision of whether to marry. Several writers have suggested that the lack of employment opportunities, which hits poor people and people of color disproportionately, and the unlikeliness of a livable guaranteed minimum income often act as a deterrent to marriage. For example, the increasing economic marginality of many African American men has meant that marriage is often not a viable option. Given that men are still expected (consciously or unconsciously) to be the family "breadwinner," the disproportionately higher rates of African American male unemployment, sporadic or seasonal employment, and underemployment make marriage an unattractive proposition for many African American women and men (Jones, 2006; Kinnon, 2003). In this context, it appears that among low-income African American men, many men tend to postpone marriage until they feel they can support a family (fulfill the traditional "good provider" role). On the other hand, during times of economic prosperity African American women and men are far more likely to marry and start a family and the chances of staying married increase dramatically (Hill, 2005; Kinnon, 2003).

In any event, in today's crumbling economic climate, with the increasing loss of decent paying jobs and high unemployment rates, it is increasingly more difficult for people to get and stay married. However, that does not mean that they are not coupling and

TABLE 8.1 Trends That Are Good or Bad for Society

What do you think of these trends?

	Bad for Society	Good for Society
More women never having children	29%	11%
More unmarried couples raising children	43%	10%
More single women having children without a male partner	69%	4%
More lesbian and gay couples raising children	43%	12%
More people living together without getting married	43%	9%
More mothers of young children working outside the home	37%	21%

Source: Belinda Luscombe. 2010. "Marriage: What's it Good For?" *Time* magazine. Vol. 176, No. 22, pp. 48–56.

committing to long-term relationships. For example, as the percentage of people marrying has decreased, there has been a dramatic increase in couples living together. This increase has been attributed to the economic recession that began in 2008; people are cohabiting because they don't have enough economic resources to go it alone and they are not marrying until they do. But it is not just those who are economically strapped that are cohabiting. Well-off couples are also increasingly choosing to cohabit before marrying, if they marry at all. Beyond educational and economic success, other qualities that Americans look for in a mate include someone who will be a good mother or father, who will put family before anything else, who is good at household chores, and who is a good sexual partner.

Finally, although most people believe that raising children is best done within marriage, the new face of American families increasingly includes single-parent, unmarried mother families. The number of children living in a single-parent home has almost tripled since 1960. However, contrary to the conservative view that these children are "fatherless" or without a man in their lives, most of the children born to unwed mothers (more than one-half) were the product of a loving and committed relationship where both parents were living together at the time of their birth. Another 30 percent of these children were born to parents who were romantically committed and involved though not married nor living together.

The Meaning of Marriage

As we have seen, marriage means different things to different people and different people do or do not marry for different reasons. Virtually everyone, however, regards marriage as a relatively permanent and committed relationship. In addition, given the fact that most marriages take place within some religious context, we can surmise that most people also view marriage as a sacrament. How many of us, however, think of marriage in terms of a legal contract?

Marriage is not an isolated event. Rather, it joins together both the couple involved and their respective families. The relationships formed by marriage sometimes become complex and can require some regulation. For example, to prevent conflict, the issue of inheritance and property rights requires a stable and consistent set of rules that prevails over time and applies fairly consistently across marriages and families. Thus, in the interest of order and stability, the state has set certain legal standards to which marriages and families must conform. Although the specific laws regulating marriages and families may vary from state to state, in all states marriage is a legal contract with specified rights and obligations.

MARRIAGE AS A COMMITMENT

According to some social scientists, human beings have a deep-seated need for secure, stable, and long-term relationships. Marriage is typically the type of relationship with which most people seek to fulfill this need. In studies examining marital quality and longevity among couples who had been married 30 or more years, various researchers and writers found commitment to be a key factor in a long-term, enduring marriage. Couples who were highly committed to each other were usually also strongly committed to the institution of marriage. This is evidenced, for example, in the Fishers' (discussed in the opening vignette) 87 years of marriage.

Researchers have also found that when couples are equal in terms of power in the relationship, there is a high rate of exchange and commitment to each other. Other factors found to contribute to marriage longevity include compatibility, mutual trust, friendship, honesty, faithfulness, and open and effective communication (Kalajian, 2006). Although important, commitment is not a single expectation or action. There are many aspects to commitment, some of which include the personal commitment between partners to each other, commitment to the relationship itself, commitment to the overall family unit, and long-term commitment.

MARRIAGE AS A SACRAMENT

If you have not yet married but plan to in the future, what type of wedding will you have, and who will officiate at the ceremony? From a religious perspective, marriage is regarded as a **sacrament**— a sacred union or rite. In the past, the majority of people in this country who married for the first time did so under the auspices of some religious figure, such as a priest, rabbi, or minister. Although for economic and other considerations many people chose to bypass a religious ceremony, most first-time marriages and remarriages among divorced people take place within the context of some type of religious ceremony.

However, according to a *USA Today* analysis of marriage license statistics, it appears that this trend is changing as fewer American couples who marry today see the need for religion's approval. Although there are no national data on how many marriages in this country are performed by a religious figure versus a civil authority such as a notary, judge, or justice of the peace, statistics from those states that have tracked data for any significant period of time since 1980 suggest that the rate of civil marriage is on the rise across the United States. According to sociologist Pepper Schwartz, this trend toward civil versus religious marriage ceremonies might be attributable to high divorce and remarriage rates, more interfaith marriages, and more personalized ideas about spirituality. Other experts suggest that this trend could influence the larger debate in this country over same-sex unions—as fewer Americans feel a need for religious blessings on their marriage, they may be more inclined to support same-sex marriages (Grossman and Yoo, 2003). Is your choice of wedding ceremony consistent with these data or with past trends?

The trend toward civil marriages notwithstanding, most people in this country continue to at least regard marriage as a significant religious or holy institution based on a sacred commitment to each other and their God. In the Christian tradition, for example, the sacredness and joyfulness of marriage is often voiced in the story of Christ's first public miracle, which was said to have been the act of turning water into wine for a wedding celebration. In addition, marriage is considered a holy state ("holy matrimony") conducted under the direct authority of God ("What God has joined together let no man put asunder"). Marriage in the religious context is also considered a lifelong commitment. Recognizing that not all marriages will last a lifetime, however, some Protestant and Jewish denominations allow for the termination of marriage through divorce and sanctify remarriage based on the same principles of the sacrament. Some religions, however, most notably Catholicism, are quite literal in their interpretation of marriage as a holy union sanctioned by God. Thus, the Catholic Church does not recognize divorce as a valid means of terminating a marriage. Under certain circumstances, however, the Catholic Church may annul a marriage, declaring that the marriage never actually occurred.

MARRIAGE AS A LEGAL CONTRACT

Some marriage and family researchers have distinguished between what they call legal and social marriage. **Legal marriage** is a legally binding agreement or contractual relationship between two people and is defined and regulated by the state. In contrast, **social marriage** is a relationship between people who cohabit and engage in behavior that is essentially the same as that within a legal marriage, but without engaging in a marriage ceremony that is validated by the state. Thus, the relationship is not, under most circumstances, legally binding.

Marriage in the United States is a legal and financial contractual agreement that, like most other contractual agreements, is regulated by certain legal requirements. When two people marry, they agree to abide by the terms of the marriage contract. Although the marriage contract is very similar to an ordinary private contract, there are some very important differences. Unlike an ordinary private contract, the marriage contract is either unwritten or is not written in any one place. In addition, the terms and penalties of the contract are usually unspecified, that is, they are scattered throughout marriage and family laws and court decisions handed down over the years, or they are not very well known by the parties involved. Furthermore, the state, and not the married couple, specifies the conditions of the marriage contract. Therefore, unlike a private contract, where the parties involved may break, modify, change, or restrict the contract by some mutual action, a married couple cannot on their own change or break the marriage contract.

The most important marriage laws are state laws. The U.S. government has both created and defined marriage, giving the individual states the responsibility for ruling marriages. Each state defines the rights and obligations of married couples through a myriad of marriage and family laws, and only representatives of the state may marry people and terminate marriages. Even when people choose to be married by a member of the clergy, only those clergy that the state has granted the right to officiate at marriages may do so. In addition, state marriage laws cover only the residents of the particular state. Thus, if a couple marries in one state and later move to another state, their marriage is covered by the laws of the new state as soon as they become residents. In a sense, then, the marriage contract is much less an expression of love for one's chosen partner and much more realistically a pact with the state. In this context, it is well worth noting that historically states have maintained social and legal control over women and children, defined women as property, and legitimized a gender-based division of paid and unpaid labor within society—women's labor is unpaid, men's labor is paid (Brownsworth, 1996).

Most people probably do not think of marriage in this way—as a legally binding contract ruled by individual states and that disadvantages one partner to the advantage of the other. Most of us are not aware of marriage laws and the extent of the state's role in marriage until separation, divorce, or death occurs, or when inheritance or property rights are at issue.

SOME LEGAL ASPECTS OF THE MARRIAGE CONTRACT

Some of the more apparent legal aspects of the marriage contract specify who can marry whom and when. Every state in this country has laws that specify who can marry whom in terms of age and sex. In addition, until 1967, some states continued to specify who could marry whom in terms of race.

Sexual Orientation Marriage is a civil right that most heterosexuals take for granted. By and large, however, lesbian and gay couples do not enjoy this same civil right. This is not surprising given that most states define marriage as a commitment by two people to carry on their lineage through conceiving and rearing children. The topic of same-sex marriages, almost unimaginable a few decades ago, is so potent a topic today that it is a major issue in many political campaigns and debates, public and popular discourse, and legal actions across the country. As an increasing number of lesbian and gay couples openly cohabit in long-term relationships and are progressively more militant and litigious in their demand for the right to express their love and commitment to one another as do heterosexual couples, they have placed greater and greater pressure on business, government, religious institutions, the workplace, and lawmakers to extend to them the same rights and privileges as heterosexual married couples. Although marriage between same-sex couples is legal in six states and the District of Columbia, and several states allow same-sex couples the rights and benefits of marriage in civil unions and/or domestic partnerships that provide similar benefits, same-sex couples are still a long way from enjoying all the benefits and institutional privileges accorded heterosexual married couples (see Figure 8.2 on page 242).

Because marriages performed in one state are typically recognized by the others, the U.S. Congress passed the Defense of Marriage Act in 1996, which stipulates that no state can be forced to recognize another state's same-sex marriage, defines marriage in all federal policies, laws, and acts of Congress as a legal union of one woman and one man, and withholds federal marriage benefits from lesbian and gay married couples (104th Congress, HR 3396). Currently, 41 states have statutory Defense of Marriage Acts or amendments to the state's constitution. Essentially, in four-fifths of the United States while the law sanctions heterosexual marriage, it denies same-sex couples the same legal standing and undermines progress on same-sex marriage (see Figure 8.3 on page 243). As a consequence, defense of marriage laws, which rank with the most overtly discriminatory laws in this country's history, are currently being challenged as a violation of the equal protection clause of the U.S. Constitution.

Lesbian and Gay Coupledom and Marriage According to recent census data, there are well over a half million (581,300) cohabiting same-sex couples in the United States and, while many of these couples have taken advantage of laws that allow them to marry, many others would like to be married if marriage were an option in the states in which they reside. In this regard, an estimated 80,000 same-sex couples have married, 50,000 of whom were married in the United States. The remaining couples might have married in other countries such as Canada (The Williams Institute, 2011). Given that most Americans view marriage as a

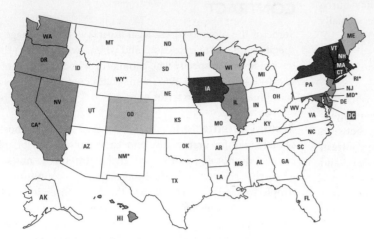

FIGURE 8.2 The Status of Same-Sex Marriage in the United States

Source: Human Rights Campaign, 2011. (July 6). "Marriage Equality and Other Relationship Recognition Laws." www.hrc.org/state_laws. Reprinted with permission of the Human Rights Campaign.

State issues marriage licenses to same-sex couples (six states and the District of Columbia): *Connecticut (2008), District of Columbia (2010), Iowa (2009), Massachusetts (2004), New Hampshire (2010), New York (2011), and Vermont (2009).*

State recognizes marriages by same-sex couples legally entered into in another jurisdiction (one state): *Maryland (2010).*

Statewide law providing the equivalent of state-level spousal rights to same-sex couples within the state (nine states and Washington, DC): *California* (domestic partnerships, 1999, expanded in 2005), Delaware (civil unions, effective Jan. 1, 2012), Hawaii (civil unions, effective Jan. 1, 2012) Illinois (civil unions, 2011), Nevada (domestic partnerships, 2009), New Jersey (civil unions, 2007), Oregon (domestic partnerships, 2008), Rhode Island (civil unions, 2011), and Washington (domestic partnerships, 2007/2009).*

Statewide law providing some statewide spousal rights to same-sex couples within the state (two states): *Colorado (designated beneficiaries, 2009), Maine (2004), and Wisconsin (domestic partership, 2009).*

* California: Same-sex marriages that took place between June 16, 2008 and Nov. 4, 2008 continue to be defined as marriages. On Oct. 12, 2009, Gov. Schwartzenegger signed into law a bill that recognizes out-of-jurisdiction same-sex marriages that occurred between the June to Nov. 2008 time frame as marriages in California and all other out-of-jurisdiction same-sex marriages as domestic parterships.

* Maine: Gov. John Baldacci signed marriage equality legislation May 6, 2009. However, the new law was repealed by a ballot measure in November 2009.

* Maryland: Does not have a registry but does provide certain benefits to statutorily defined domestic partners. Also, in 2010, the Maryland Attorney General issued an advisory opinion declaring that the state can recognize out-of-jurisdiction same-sex marriages.

* New Mexico: In Jan. 2011, the New Mexico Attorney General issued an advisory opinion declaring that the state can recognize out-of-jurisdiction same-sex marriages. At this time, it is unclear what effect this opinion will have.

* Wyoming: On June 6, 2011, the Wyoming Supreme Court decided *Christensen v. Christensen*, ruling that Wyoming trial courts have the ability to hear divorce proceedings terminating same-sex marriages created in other jurisdictions.

significant religious and holy institution, it is not surprising that many lesbians and gays, like heterosexuals, want to sanctify their commitment to each other and their God. The desire to make a public commitment to one another in the church or synagogue of their choice is not only controversial, but also a divisive issue within religious institutions. Today, Presbyterians, Catholics, Jews, and members of other religions have been forced increasingly to grapple with whether to sanction same-sex unions and ceremonies within their faith, whether or not they are legally recognized by state and federal governments.

Some people feel that the legal prohibition of same-sex marriage prevents lesbian and gay couples from forming legal, religious, and public marital bonds that would secure their relationship rights, and it deprives them of a litany of benefits and protections, rights, and responsibilities. And this is certainly true. Although marriage has its drawbacks, some of its most striking benefits include the right of a surviving marital partner to inherit property, the right to file a joint income tax return (married couples filing jointly are taxed at a lower rate than single people and married couples who file separately), and the right to share pension, social security and health care insurance benefits offered

by many employers to their employees. *Civil unions* for same-sex couples give them almost all of the rights and privileges of married couples (for example, joint property rights, inheritance rights, shared health care benefits, hospital visitation rights, and immunity from being compelled to testify against a partner) (Goldberg, 2001), but a major caveat is that, unlike traditional marriage unions, civil unions are only recognized in five states. Likewise, in states that recognize same-sex domestic partnerships, such recognition does not include the same legal rights that come automatically with marriage.

What do you think? Should same-sex couples be allowed to marry in their respective churches and synagogues, even if such unions are not legal in the state in which they reside? Do you think that same-sex marriage requires a redefinition of marriage? If so, how might we redefine marriage? Should American children be taught to accept same-sex marriage as a "normal" marital lifestyle?

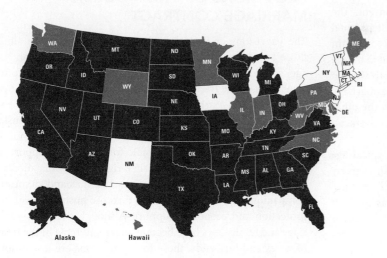

FIGURE 8.3 In Defense of Marriage: State Prohibitions on Marriage for Same-Sex Couples

Source: Human Rights Campaign, 2010. (January 13). "Statewide Marriage Prohibitions." http://www.hrc.org/state_laws. Reprinted with permission of the Human Rights Campaign.

Statewide prohibitions against marriage for same-sex couples are in place in most states—either in the form of statutory law or amendment to the state's constitution. States that explicitly bar same-sex couples from marriage are as follows.

■ States with constitutional amendments restricting marriage to one man and one woman. (29 States)
Alabama (2006), Alaska (1998), Arizona (2008), Arkansas (2004), California (2008), Colorado (2004), Florida (2008), Georgia (2004), Kansas (2005), Idaho (2006), Kentucky (2004), Louisiana (2004), Michigan (2004), Mississippi (2004), Missouri (2004), Montana (2004), Nebraska (2000), Nevada (2002), North Dakota (2004), Ohio (2004), Oklahoma (2004), Oregon (2004), South Carolina (2006), South Dakota (2006), Tennessee (2006), Texas (2005), Utah (2004), Virginia (2006) and Wisconsin (2006).

■ States with law restricting marriage to one man and one woman. (12 States)
In addition to those listed above, *Delaware, Hawaii, Illinois, Indiana, Maine, Maryland, Minnesota, North Carolina, Pennsylvania, Washington, West Virginia and Wyoming.*

*Broader Consequences: States where the law or amendment has language that does, or may, affect other legal relationships, such as civil unions or domestic partnerships. (18 states): *Alabama, Arkansas, Florida, Georgia, Kentucky, Idaho, Louisiana, Michigan, Nebraska, North Dakota, Ohio, Oklahoma, South Carolina, South Dakota, Texas, Utah, Virginia and Wisconsin.*

As homosexuality generally and same-sex marriage specifically have become more and more visible components of U.S. culture, same-sex domestic partners are gaining some legitimacy and protections. For instance, many states and cities, as well as many major corporations, offer medical and other benefits to the partners of lesbian and gay employees, but not to unmarried heterosexual couples. According to a survey of same-sex benefits in the workplace, more than 3,500 private and public employers in the United States now provide domestic-partner benefits for lesbian and gay employees.

In addition to requiring heterosexuality in marital relationships, marriage law also requires monogamy. Under legal statutes, people cannot have more than one spouse at a time. If an individual does, he or she can be prosecuted for **bigamy**—marrying one person while still being legally married to another. Although seldom enforced, many states have laws that prohibit **adultery,** extramarital sexual intercourse, and **fornication**—sexual intercourse outside legal marriage.

The Incest Taboo Not only does the traditional marriage contract prohibit marriage between persons of the same sex, but it also prohibits marriage or sexual relations between a variety of relatives ranging from parents and siblings to non-blood-related in-laws. Although the specific set of blood relatives whom we cannot legally marry or have sex with differs from state to state,

no state allows us to marry a parent, a sibling, an uncle or aunt, a niece or nephew, a grandparent, or a grandchild. The majority of states even prohibit marriage between half-siblings and first cousins. Some states also exclude second cousins and, in a few cases, third cousins. In addition, some states go so far as to prohibit marriage between **affinal relatives,** people related by marriage, such as a brother- or sister-in-law, even though they are not related by blood.

As we discussed in Chapter 1, although the range of relatives covered by the incest taboo has varied over human history, some theorists maintain that this taboo serves an important social and political function for families and society. By forcing families to mate and reproduce outside the immediate family network, marriage helps create political and economic relationships vital to society's structure and survival.

Age Restrictions Marriage rules also define when we are considered mature enough to marry. In the past, the legal age at which people could marry was tied to puberty and the ages at which women and men could reproduce. If a person was old enough to reproduce, she or he was considered old enough to marry. Often the legal age for marriage was different for women and men. Today, however, the concern is whether a person is mature enough to marry, regardless of the ability to reproduce. To ensure that a person is both old enough and mature enough, each state has set a legal age for marriage. That age varies, however, according to whether the couple has obtained their parents' consent. The marriageable age for women and men, with or without parental consent, is the same in most states. For example, as discussed in Chapter 5, in every state except one the legal age at which marriage can be contracted without parental consent is 18 for both women and men. In Georgia, a female or male may contract a marriage without parental consent as early as 16 years of age. On the other hand, on the island of Puerto Rico, individuals cannot contract a marriage on their own until age 21.

With parental consent the picture changes. The typical age requirement for marriage with parental consent is 16. In as many as five states (Alabama, New Hampshire, New York, Texas, and Utah), however, females and males may marry as early as age 14 if their parents consent. Moreover, in a few states, parental consent is not required if a minor was previously married. And two states (California and Mississippi) have no age limits. In some states, minors may obtain a marriage license if the female is pregnant, if a child has already been born to the couple, or under what some states define as "special circumstances." In other states, a minor wishing to marry must not only have parental consent but must also get the permission of a judge.

Change and Continuity in the Meaning of Marriage

One of the most fundamental and significant premises on which U.S. marriage and family laws have been based is the historical notion that the family is the property of the husband, and therefore he is the head of the household. The other side of this premise is the belief that women are the weaker sex and need the care and protection of men. This belief reflects the common-law concept of **coverture,** the idea that a wife is under the protection and influence of her husband—that the two become one at the time of marriage, and that one is the husband. From these assumptions flow many rights, obligations, and expectations about how a married couple should behave and relate to each other. Therefore, not surprisingly, we find that over the course of time many of the rules and laws surrounding marriage have treated women and men differently based solely on their biological sex. For example, the symbolic loss of a woman's identity once she marries is still evident today in the common practice of a married woman legally taking her husband's name when she marries, whereas the man's legal identity remains the same as it was before marriage. Many of the marriage traditions and rituals practiced around the world (see the In Other Places box) are also rooted in this premise.

Historically, marriage has extended the rights of men vis-à-vis women and children. Women, in contrast, lost many legal rights when they married, because their marital obligations and rights were defined primarily in terms of their service to husbands and children. Under this arrangement, for example, women have suffered a long history of violence at the hands of their husbands, who, until the late 1800s, could legally beat their wives if they did not fulfill their wifely duties. (Chapter 11 contains a detailed discussion of this issue.)

PROVISIONS OF THE MODERN MARRIAGE CONTRACT

The provisions of the modern marriage contract are similar to those based on the old principle of coverture. More than 30 years ago, social scientist Lenore Weitzman (1977) identified four basic provisions of the traditional marriage contract that have been incorporated into marriage laws in the United States: (1) the wife is responsible for caring for the home, (2) the wife is responsible for caring for any children, (3) the husband is head of the household, and (4) the husband is responsible for providing support for the family. In the language of marital rights and obligations, these provisions assert that the wife owes her husband domestic and companionship services, and in return the husband owes his wife protection and economic support. Although over the years marriage and family laws have become more equitable in the treatment of wives and husbands, these four provisions are not simply old-fashioned ideas that are no longer relevant. In many states, women continue to lose legal rights when they marry, and they continue to be treated as the property of their husbands. And among fundamentalist Christians and other Christian groups, women continue to be subjugated in marriage. Although as we have seen, a declining percentage of Americans believe that the ideal marriage is based on a division of traditional gender roles, still many individuals and groups continue to buy into the essence of the traditional marriage contract where men work outside the home and provide for a wife and children while women stay home and perform domestic work.

Today, the specific conditions of the marriage contract vary from one state to another, but some common assumptions are evident. In the following discussion, we examine some specific beliefs and practices from the past in terms of their impact on current marital patterns, noting both continuity and changes where they have occurred.

Residence In the past, a woman was expected to take her husband's surname and move into his domicile (place of residence). Although a wife is no longer required to take her husband's name, a husband retains the legal right to decide where the couple will live, and marriage law imposes an obligation on the wife to live in her husband's choice of residence. Therefore, when a woman marries, if her place of residence is different from her husband's, his place of residence automatically supersedes hers. If a woman lives in a different state from her husband and she does not take her husband's place of residence as her own, the legal ramifications are many. For instance, she must reregister to vote; she could lose the right to attend a university in her hometown as a resident student; and she could lose the privilege of running for public office in her home state (Renzetti and Curran, 2002). Laws pertaining to the marital domicile reflect traditional gender inequalities in other ways. For example, if a husband gets a job in another city and his wife refuses to relocate with him, she is assumed by law to have abandoned him. If, on the other hand, a wife gets a job in another city and her husband refuses to relocate with her, she is still defined by law as having abandoned him.

In this sense, men are still assumed to be the head of the household and can therefore determine where the family will live. Over the years, however, some equalizing of marital roles and

MARRIAGE TRADITIONS AND RITUALS IN THE UNITED STATES

Marriage is a critical rite of passage in most cultures and includes a wide range of rituals and customs. For example, in the United States, following the wedding ceremony, the couple typically leaves the marriage site in a vehicle decorated by friends and relatives that signals to the public that the couple has just married.

Today, most Americans take the customs and rituals associated with marriage as givens and view them primarily within the context of love and romantic intrigue. However, in many ways the traditional marriage contract and the various rituals associated with "getting married" underscore the subordinate position of women in marriage and can be viewed as a transference of property among males, that is, from father to husband. Indicative of the property status of women was the practice in the past whereby a prospective husband had to receive the father's permission to marry his daughter. At the time of the wedding, the father gave his daughter to the groom, usually for a price. Today, fathers still *give their daughters away* in marriage; however, they do not consider it a transference of property but rather a symbol of their blessing of the marriage.

If you are a married male, did you carry the bride over the threshold on your wedding night? It seems that the custom of *carrying the bride over the threshold* originally symbolized the abduction of a daughter who was reluctant to leave her father's home. Further, in ancient times, men sometimes captured or kidnapped women to make them their brides. A man would take along his strongest and most trusted friend to help him fight resistance from the woman's family and kidnap the woman he desired. This warrior friend was considered the best man among his friends and became the *best man* at his wedding, accompanying the groom up the aisle to help defend the bride (Kvale, 2006; Lemmon, 2006). These are only a few of many marriage traditions that in some way reflect the unequal status of women and men.

How much do you know about rituals and traditions surrounding marriage in the United States? For example, do you know why brides today need "something old, something new, something borrowed, and something blue"? This tradition apparently dates back to ancient Hebrew society, when brides wore blue ribbons on their wedding day to signify love, purity, and fidelity. In addition, the ancient Hebrews believed that if a bride wore an item borrowed from a married woman, the married woman's wedded happiness would transfer to the bride-to-be. There are, of course, multiple explanations for many of these traditions and some cannot be definitively traced back to their roots. The following are some of the most common and popular wedding traditions practiced by Americans and the stories about their origins.

The Bridal Shower

The first bridal shower is believed to have been held in Holland, when a father denied his daughter permission to marry a poor man with whom she had fallen in love. When the man's friends heard this, they gave the bride-to-be numerous gifts so that the couple could be married.

The Bachelor Party

The ritual of the bachelor party dates back to ancient Greece. The night before the wedding, a lavish dinner, called the "men's mess," was held for the groom-to-be.

The Ring

The first wedding ring might have been worn by the Romans, who believed a small artery, or "vein of love," ran from the third finger of the left hand to the heart. Thus, wearing a ring on this finger symbolized the joining of two hearts in destiny and the ring itself is a never-ending circle that symbolizes everlasting love.

Why are engagement and wedding rings typically diamond? Medieval Italians used diamonds because they

(continued on next page)

(continued from previous page)

believed diamonds were created from the eternal flames of love.

The Wedding Veil

The tradition of the wedding veil cannot be traced to one single country; rather, it has its origins in many cultures. In general, to protect the bride from the evil wishes of her rivals, her face was covered on her wedding day. In ancient Rome and Greece, wedding veils were brightly colored, whereas the early Christian bride wore a white or purple veil to symbolize purity and virginity. After the marital vows were exchanged, the veil was pulled back from the bride's face to symbolize her new status as wife.

Standing Arrangements at the Wedding Ceremony

It is said that the custom that the bride stand to the left of the groom at the altar dates back to a time when men carried swords to protect themselves and their loved ones. The groom had to keep his right hand (his sword hand) free to be able to defend himself and his bride from his enemies or disgruntled in-laws.

Throwing the Bouquet

This ritual is said to have originated in England and has its basis in a bride's desire to save herself from an onslaught of wedding guests. In times past, it was the custom for guests to reach for the bride's garter. Moreover, women guests would try to rip pieces of the brides dress and flowers in order to obtain some of her good luck. One bride, tiring of the practice, decided that throwing the bouquet would be safer. Today, single women line up as the bride tosses her bouquet with the belief that the unmarried woman who catches the bouquet will be the next one to get married.

The Wedding Cake

The origin of the wedding cake is attributed to ancient Romans, who actually broke a specially baked cake over the head of the bride as a symbol of luck and fruitfulness. Wedding guests scrambled to catch pieces of the cake to share some of the couple's good luck. The story of the tiered-wedding cake has its origins in Anglo-Saxon times when guests would bring small cakes to the wedding and stack them on top of each other. Later, a clever French baker created a cake in the shape of the small cakes and covered it in frosting (Olson, 2006). The wedding cake continues to be an important part of traditional weddings today because it is a symbol of oneness through sharing. The bride and groom sharing the first piece of the cake is seen as a gesture of goodwill for the happy couple. (Does this include smashing the cake in each other's face?)

The Honeymoon

Did you ever wonder why newlyweds keep their honeymoon a secret? In fact, sometimes even the bride-to-be does not know where she is going for the honeymoon. It is probably not surprising that the honeymoon originated in France, a country synonymous with love and romance. Several hundred years ago, to escape relatives who opposed their marriage, the newlywed couple would seclude themselves in some secret place for a month until the opposition gave up and stopped looking for them. During this time of seclusion, the couple drank a special wine made with honey while watching the moon go through all of its phases. Thus, the term honeymoon literally means "moon of honey" ("Wedding Traditions," 1988).

…And Around the World

Sometimes, we get so caught up in our own traditions we think that they are the same for all people. However, people studying different cultures have discovered interesting marriage practices that demonstrate the uniqueness of each culture.

China

The Chinese have a perfect solution for individuals who do not marry in their lifetime: a posthumous wedding. The "spirit wedding" is an ancient custom that is being revived in the Chinese countryside today. It is supposed to ensure that people who die unmarried will have a partner in the afterlife. In this custom, an aging unmarried person buys a corpse in preparation for the "spirit wedding" when she or he dies. Upon death, the two will be "married" with a full ceremony and will be buried together (*Chicago Tribune*, 1991).

Iraq

In the 1950s, Elizabeth and Robert Fernea lived in an Iraqi peasant village and studied the women's lives in detail. In this culture, parents arranged their children's marriages, and a couple could not meet before their wedding. For women, virginity was essential and had to be maintained at all costs until the wedding day, when the couple consummated their marriage while their mothers, friends, and other relatives waited outside the couple's bedroom. When they finished, the mothers inspected the wedding sheets for blood from the young bride's broken hymen (a membranous fold of tissue partly closing the external opening of the vagina) and publicly announced the proof of the bride's virginity. If there was no blood, it was assumed the bride was not a virgin, and her family suffered great humiliation. The bride herself was often put to death as a ruined woman (Fernea, 1965).

The Tiwi of Australia

Among the Tiwi, an aboriginal people on the islands off the coast of Australia, there is no such thing as an unmarried female. Females are betrothed by their fathers before they are born into a system of reciprocity among males. Tiwi males gain prestige through the number of marriage contracts they make. Thus, marriage contracts are highly valued, even if some are with brides who are not yet born or who are not yet old enough to join the husband's household. In this system of polygyny for males and serial marriage for females, because the husband must be an adult before an infant female can be married to him, females are likely to outlive their husbands.

obligations has occurred. Thus, in many states today a woman can establish a separate household for a specific purpose. In addition, at least one state court has ruled that a wife who is the primary breadwinner can decide where the couple will live (Renzetti and Curran, 2002).

Property Rights In the past, a woman's property rights also came under the control and management of her husband once she married. Not only did a husband gain control of his wife's property on marriage, but he could also do with it as he pleased, with or without her knowledge or consent. Today, however, women have considerable property rights, although the specifics differ across states.

Most U.S. states recognize the individual ownership of property. Whoever has proof of ownership of property owns it in the eyes of the law. If neither the wife nor husband has proof of ownership, however, most courts determine that the husband is the owner, particularly if the wife has remained in the home as a homemaker during the marriage. The court's rationale is that because the wife had no income with which to acquire the assets, they belong to the husband, who has simply allowed her use of them over the years. Thus, for example, in some cases a joint bank account has been deemed by the court to belong to the husband if the wife did not earn an income.

As this discussion makes clear, common-law property states, as they are called, give quite an advantage to husbands. It is ironic that those women who conform most closely to the patriarchal norms that surround marital roles are the ones who are hurt most by marriage laws and regulations pertaining to property ownership. Women who have spent their lives in service to their husbands (and children) end up with few assets of their own. Moreover, because of their dependency on their husbands, they are the most vulnerable during and after marriage. On the other hand, in the community property system, practiced in only a few states, wives and husbands own all assets jointly and equally whether or not the wife earns an income. This system does not penalize women for choosing to be full-time homemakers, although it does present other problems for wives, as discussed in more detail in Chapter 12.

As disadvantaged as married women were in the past and are today under the principle of coverture, men also were and still are restricted in several important ways as well. For instance, it has been argued that because marriage awarded a wife a right of inheritance, the husband's estate was reduced. In addition, marriage obligated a husband to support his wife and family, an obligation that poor and working-class men often found difficult to meet solely on their own. The continuation of this idea and the inequities it engenders for men are reflected in the fact that husbands today are still legally obliged to support their wives even if the wife works and earns a higher wage than the husband. However, in some cases, the amount of support that husbands are required to pay has been reduced by the courts if the wife has a higher income.

Given our discussion of marital rights and obligations thus far, are you wondering about the degree to which these principles are enforceable by law? We turn our attention next to an examination of this question.

The Law According to some experts on the subject, a husband's right to his wife's services is basically unenforceable by law in a direct sense. There are, however, some very important consequences of this provision of the marriage contract. One such consequence is a result that can be attributed to a husband's **conjugal rights**—rights pertaining to the marriage relationship. Because of this right and because, until recent times, rape statutes read that rape was forced sexual intercourse with a woman not your wife, husbands had license to rape their wives. It was not until the 1970s, when some members of the women's movement argued for the elimination of this spousal exemption from charges of rape, that a married woman could charge her husband with rape. Although it took the next 20 years, marital rape is now a crime in all 50 states, under at least one section of the sexual offense codes (National Clearinghouse on Marital and Date Rape, 2005). (We will discuss this issue in more detail in Chapter 11.) Furthermore, because the marriage contract obliges a wife to perform domestic labor for her husband, she cannot be directly compensated for her work; until recent times, her economic contribution to the marriage was not considered in the division of property at the time of divorce. Interestingly, although the husband has no legal obligation to compensate his wife for domestic services, if a third party injures the wife, the husband can legally sue the party for the value of the domestic services he lost.

Although a wife has a legal right to be supported by her husband, she has little control over the nature or amount of that support. Based on an accumulation of findings in various court cases, it seems that as long as a wife and husband live together the husband has a right to support his wife in whatever manner he chooses. If a wife feels she is not being adequately supported, she has little legal recourse.

THE MARRIAGE CONTRACT TODAY

Since the 1970s, marriage and family law in the United States has changed substantially, although certain traditions and legal restrictions continue to leave women at a disadvantage. As pointed out, women no longer have to take their husband's surname. In some states, however, a wife who takes her husband's surname must seek his permission to return to using her birth name. In the past, the decision not to adopt the husband's surname often created legal problems and unnecessary difficulties for the couple. Today, however, legal and business establishments have caught up with this practice, and a woman's decision to retain her family name does not appear to cause as many difficulties.

Rather than give up their family name upon marrying, some women choose to hyphenate their name after marriage (for example, Lillian Brown-Johnson). This practice, however, is not without problems. For instance, how will the couple name their children? Will their children carry the father's surname only? Will they carry the hyphenated name? If so, when the children become adults, will they hyphenate their already-hyphenated name?

Other ways in which contemporary couples attack gender-stereotypic wedding rituals and traditions include brides having "best women" or best men, grooms having "men of honor" or women (rather than best men) stand up for them, both parents (as opposed to the father alone) giving away a daughter, one or both parents giving away the groom, or completely eliminating the ritual of someone "giving away" a human being.

MARRIAGE TRADITIONS IN THE UNITED STATES

Marriage is a critical rite of passage in most cultures, and, as demonstrated in the In Other Places box, in most cultures it is steeped with tradition and rituals. In the traditional sense, marriage in the United States is a culmination of the mate selection process: courtship, dating, engagement, parties for the bride and groom, and finally the wedding itself.

Engagement In the United States, if during the dating period a couple decides to take their relationship to another level, deciding that they will marry at some time in the future, they will typically end the formal and private dating phase of their relationship and move it to a more public expression of their relationship and intentions toward one another—the *engagement*. The engagement formalizes

the couple's commitment to marry, and, until recently, it has been a formal phase in the mate selection process whereby the man gives the woman an engagement ring, a public announcement is made in the media (newspapers and newsmagazines) either by the couple or the couple's family, and family and friends are invited to share the couple's happiness and commitment to marry (an engagement party). Ideally, at this juncture in the relationship, each member of the couple is emotionally committed to one another, are sexually monogamous, are getting to know each other's family (if they do not already know them), and are focused on planning the wedding.

Although the engagement functioned as a binding commitment to marry in the past, today it seems it is more symbolic and ritualistic than a binding commitment. This is evidenced today especially among celebrities who routinely announce simultaneously their engagements and the size of the intended bride's engagement ring (each newly engaged couple seemingly tries to outdo the prior one). Soon after, the couple often parts ways, and conflict over the oversized engagement ring—for example, who should get it—often ensues. In addition, given that more people are delaying first marriage until later ages, a growing number of people are remarrying, and an increasing number of single people are cohabiting, engagements also have become far less formal. The engagement phase of the mate selection process has changed in other ways as well. For instance, older couples may or may not go through a formal engagement period. Rather, they might forgo public announcements in the media and simply tell family and friends their intention to marry and then quietly do so. Sometimes, particularly if both partners work, they will buy an engagement and wedding ring jointly. Likewise, couples who have cohabited before making the decision to marry often do not announce an engagement. For example, a couple we know cohabited for 14 years prior to making the decision to marry. Once they made the decision, they announced it to their family and close friends and within a week they flew to Las Vegas and wed.

Although engagements no longer necessarily follow traditional customs, they continue to perform several key functions. For example, the engagement helps the couple define the goal of their relationship as marriage, and it lets the rest of those in the pool of eligibles know that each person is now "spoken for," that they have entered into a commitment with someone and are no longer available. Second, it provides the couple with an opportunity to seriously and systematically examine their relationship—that is, their expectations about the reality of marriage on a day-to-day basis, including appropriate gender roles, children, money, friendships, religion, in-laws, and family traditions. Third, it gives the couple a period of time to become better acquainted with their future in-laws and to become integrated into each other's family. Fourth, it provides the couple with a reason to get information about their respective medical histories. (Determining the Rh factor in each partner's blood, for instance, will be of major importance in any future pregnancy.) Finally, an important function of engagement is premarital counseling. It can be quite useful for a couple to discuss their ideas, expectations, and plans with an objective third person such as a member of the clergy or marriage counselor. (Historically, the Catholic Church has made premarital counseling a prerequisite for getting married in a Roman Catholic church.)

An increasing number of couples today are using the engagement period not only to define what their relationship with each other will be, but also to define their economic and social obligations

Although prenups are often criticized for their cold and unsentimental language, they serve to protect the assets of the persons involved. Celebrities such as Shaunie and Shaquille O'Neal (pictured) almost routinely negotiate prenuptial agreements prior to marrying. While the contents of their agreement was not made public, media reports indicated that Shaunie took more than a year after her filing before settling the divorce, trying to find evidence that her husband had an affair during the marriage. This led some people to speculate that perhaps their prenup included a steep financial penalty for infidelity.

to each other during their marriage. They are doing this by writing their own **personal marriage agreement**—a written agreement between a married couple in which issues of role responsibilities, obligations, and sharing are addressed in a manner that is tailored to their own personal preferences, desires, and expectations.

Prenuptial Agreements Today, the marriage plans of many couples include the use of a personal marriage agreement in one of two ways. One is as a **prenuptial agreement,** developed and worked out in consultation with an attorney and filed as a legal document. The purpose of drawing up a prenuptial agreement in this manner is to negotiate ahead of time the settlement of property, alimony, or other financial matters in the event of death or divorce. The prenuptial agreement can also serve as a personal agreement between the partners, drafted primarily for the purpose of helping the couple clarify their expectations concerning their marriage. Formal or legal marriage agreements such as prenuptial agreements are not new. Wealthy and celebrity members of society have long used these agreements to protect family and personal fortunes. Although most prenuptial agreements are not

very elaborate, they generally go far in protecting the assets of the persons involved as well as ensuring reasonable alimony and other financial payments agreed upon by the couple.

Few topics in the modern-day marriage arena inspire more attention, headlines, discussion, and fury than the mention of the words prenuptial agreement. Asking your future life partner to sign a contract that limits her or his rights to your assets flies in the face of love and romance. Some people look on prenuptial agreements as cold, unromantic, businesslike, and an expression of greed. They think that such contracts are an indication of distrust on the part of the couple—that they imply one or both partners do not have faith in the relationship and that they care more about their bank account than their soon-to-be spouse. However, most marriage advisers suggest that premarital contracting does not mean that a couple does not love or trust one another. Rather, in many ways, a prenuptial agreement can show how much two people really care about each other. Marriage today is an economic as well as an emotional partnership. Thus, contemporary couples are advised to think with their heads and not their hearts. A prenuptial agreement is not a bad idea, even for people who do not have a lot of money. They force couples to agree on how they want to handle their married life, including their money and other assets.

It is estimated that somewhere between 5 and 15 percent of altar-bound Americans enter into prenuptial agreements each year. Although most are people who have accumulated or inherited significant wealth, such agreements are gaining popularity among middle-class couples, elderly couples, and divorced people who are ensuring before the wedding that in case the marriage ends their assets will go or remain where they want them. According to the American Academy of Matrimonial Lawyers, couples of all income levels are hedging their bets before they say "I do" (Zaccaro, 2010; Willis, 2005; Potier, 2003). Those embarking upon a second marriage are particularly urged to consider a prenuptial agreement to protect the inheritances of children from a prior marriage. Rarely do couples break engagements because of disputes over prenuptial agreements. In almost every instance, the agreement is signed and the parties are married.

In addition to prenuptial agreements, some people enter into what are called *postmarital* or *antenuptial agreements*. And most recently, some people are buying divorce insurance. Postmarital contracts contain provisions similar to those in premarital contracts but are drafted after the marriage has taken place (as opposed to before) but before either party separates, divorces, leaves, or dies. A married couple may seek to enter into a postmarital agreement after a significant financial change or after a reunification subsequent to a separation. A *marital settlement agreement* is a particular form of postmarital agreement that specifies the distribution of property and responsibility for debt between the respective spouses as part of a divorce. For cohabiting couples, many of whom have some or all of the same issues, concerns, and considerations as legally married couples in terms of the division of property and other assets, financial planners suggest that they draw up a *cohabitation agreement*. Such agreements can contain simple provisions about shared expenses and the acquisition of property, including real estate, or can be more elaborate specifying a specific distribution of certain assets and protections for the couple in the event of disability or incapacity of one of the partners.

Perhaps a sign of the times, the market, including the Internet, is flooded with information and materials about prenuptial agreements. Couples planning to wed can go on the Internet, where they will find an array of information from lawyers who will describe what prenuptial agreements are, discuss their importance, offer their legal services, to what judges and courts will enforce and what they will not, to advice on how to discuss an agreement with a partner, to what topics need to be addressed in an agreement to make it valid, to books with titles such as *Prenups for Lovers: A Romantic Guide to Prenuptial Agreements*.

A law called the Uniform Pre-Marital Agreement Act provides legal guidelines for those wishing to make a prenuptial agreement. Some 27 states plus the District of Columbia have adopted this act, and those that have not have similar laws. A few states have their own unique laws in this regard. For example, some states, including California, do not allow premarital agreements to modify or eliminate the right of a spouse to receive court-ordered alimony at divorce. Other states, like Maine, void all premarital agreements 1 year after the parties to the contract become parents, unless the agreement is renewed (MedLawPlus.com, 2006). Although anyone can draw up a prenuptial agreement, for it to be upheld in court those involved must demonstrate that there was full, accurate, and fair disclosure of all assets at the time it was drawn up, that it was fair and reasonable when signed, and that it was signed voluntarily by both parties and entered into in good faith. To meet this criterion, parties should secure the services of an attorney familiar with state laws governing marriage and community property. Even then there is no guarantee that courts will uphold all of the agreement's provisions. The specifications in the agreement may be morally binding, but some, such as specifications concerning living arrangements, child custody, and/or the support of children, are not enforceable in court (CBS News, 2005).

Personal Contracts The most popular version of the personal marriage agreement among couples today is the personal contract, created by the couple without advice or counsel from an attorney. Although these contracts serve primarily as guides to future behavior, they are sometimes filed as legal contracts. As with the more formal and legal pre- and postnuptial agreements, personal contracts are not new. At different times in history couples have used the personal contract to satisfy a range of personal needs. For example, in the late seventeenth century, Eleanor Veazel and John French drafted a marriage contract in which the provisions included promises by John to not take any part of the estate that Elizabeth had inherited from her former husband, to let Elizabeth sell their apples, and a promise to leave Elizabeth 4 pounds a year after his death, which could be paid in any number of ways, including in corn, malt, pork, or beef (Scott and Wishy, 1982). In the nineteenth century, suffragist and feminist Lucy Stone and her husband-to-be, Henry Blackwell, a well-known abolitionist, wrote their own personal contract in protest against the inequality of women in marriage, which they read and signed as part of their wedding ceremony. In addition, Stone refused to take her husband's surname, preferring to be known instead as "Mrs. Stone" (Schneir, 1994).

Although there is a wide range of opinions about personal marriage agreements, many people find them to have several important benefits, including forcing a couple to communicate with each other their marital expectations, desires, and goals. A well publicized case in point was the 1995 premarital agreement drawn up by Rex and Teresa LeGalley of Albuquerque, New Mexico, that spelled out the rules of their life together in minute detail. Their 16-page, single-spaced premarital contract was a legally notarized document in which the LeGalleys attempted to cover almost every possible aspect of their lives. Examples from the agreement include the following:

- Healthy sex three to five times a week.
- Family leadership and decision making is Mr. LeGalley's responsibility. Ms. LeGalley will make decisions only in emergencies and when Mr. LeGalley is unavailable.
- Ms. LeGalley will be in charge of inside house chores, including laundry, while Mr. LeGalley will be responsible for inside repairs and will maintain the outside of the house, including the garage and cars.
- Ms. LeGalley will stay on birth control for 2 years after marriage, then the couple will try to get pregnant. When both are working, she can have only one child. When one parent is free, she can have another child. When both are free, she can have one more child. After the third pregnancy, both will get sterilized.

In an interview a year after they were married, the LeGalleys said that the contract was working well. According to Rex, "Things couldn't be better. We worked out so many things before we married that we didn't have that transition period that most couples do in their first year of marriage." Teresa commented: "Writing the prenup was one of the best things we ever did because we discussed everything and learned a lot about each other." The document is probably not legally binding, and the LeGalleys say they have no plans to enforce it. They said that it was simply "all about getting to know your partner" (Bojorquez, 1997). As far as our research could uncover, the LeGalleys are still together and abiding by their almost 20-year personal marital contract.

Personal agreements are not always this detailed, nor are they limited to couples planning to marry or to heterosexual couples. Any couple who is committed to each other or who lives together, as well as couples whom are legally prohibited from marrying, can benefit from such agreements. As the LeGalleys' agreement demonstrates, prenuptial or personal marriage agreements can include anything a couple considers appropriate, such as the division of roles and tasks in the marriage or living arrangement, how often they will engage in sexual activities, and whether they will have children. Several celebrities have included items such as penalties if the wife gains weight, requiring a spouse to undergo random drug tests with financial penalties for positive results, requiring a husband to pay $10,000 each time he is rude to his wife's parents, rules about football, and steep financial penalties for infidelity. At the end of this chapter, in the Writing Your Own Script box on page 269, we invite you to write your own personal marriage or relationship agreement.

THE WEDDING

Today's couples tend to prefer traditional weddings, but increasingly they are infusing the wedding ceremony with a touch of personal style—from unusual or ethnic wedding attire to male bridesmaids and female groomspersons to offbeat choices of locations for their wedding and receptions to elaborate reception menus. For instance, every Valentine's Day hundreds of couples are married in shopping malls around the country. These weddings are typically promoted by local radio stations. Recently, a Michigan couple took their wedding vows in the family-owned funeral home. Their reception, including dinner and dancing, also was held at the funeral home. In 2006, a bride and groom in the United Kingdom got married halfway through London's 26.2-mile marathon (Associated Press, 2008b; Dalton, 2006). Other couples have gotten married in a custom-built million-dollar public bathroom, while skydiving out of an airplane, and via satellite with one partner in absentia. Every year, for example, the Reverend Sun Myung Moon marries thousands of couples simultaneously by satellite hookups between Korea and hundreds of sites around the world. Brides and grooms who cannot be present are represented by a photo.

Cultural or ethnic weddings are also quite popular. For example, many African Americans who marry today have what is defined as an African-centered wedding. Such a ceremony varies according to the individuals but may include traditional African attire for the bride, groom, and other participants in the wedding made out of kente cloth, Guinea brocade, or other expensive African fabrics; African and other cultural cuisine at the reception; African drummers and dancers; a wedding cake baked by an African or Caribbean baker; a Yoruba priestess or priest to conduct the ceremony; and/or "jumping the broom," a tradition carried over from slavery.

Weddings are big business in the United States today. With the rise of a 40 billion plus wedding industry, getting married today is far more expensive than in the past. From a golden anniversary to a child's or grandchild's wedding, getting married has changed considerably in the last 50 years (see Figure 8.4 on page 252). For example, over the last 50 years, the average age of the bride and groom has risen. Because the average couple is older, they tend to have more money to spend on an elaborate wedding. The average bride is now 26, her groom is 28, they have an estimated combined household income of $74,886; will be engaged for a period of 14 months, and their wedding will have about 165 guests.

Over two million couples marry each year, spending anywhere from hundreds to tens of thousands of dollars on each ceremony. According to the experts, the average amount spent on weddings today is between $28,000 and $30,000, a far cry from an average of around $500 50 years ago (The Knot, 2011; CNNMoney.com, 2006).

The costs of a wedding, of course, will vary, depending on the quality and/or quantity of the items chosen for the wedding, the size and type of wedding, as well as where the couple marries. For example, weddings cost more in large urban areas. In contrast, a wedding in Las Vegas, Nevada, can cost as little as a $35 chapel fee to several hundred dollars for a chapel wedding package that includes any assortment or all of the following: chapel fee, wedding coordinator, organist or pianist, soloist, flowers, wedding photos, wedding album, professional video of the ceremony, custom marriage certificate holder, wedding garter, limousine service, bottle of champagne and champagne glasses, witnesses (if needed), and "Just Married" bumper sticker. At the other end of the continuum are the costs of the weddings for the

A growing number of couples today are infusing the wedding ceremony with a touch of personal style. For many African American couples, this includes mixing American and African dress styles in their wedding attire and a tradition of jumping the broom, which is said to be a tradition carried over from slavery.

The rising cost of weddings today is felt by couples around the world. For example, pictured here are grooms that took part in a mass wedding ceremony in Riyadh, Saudi Arabia in June 2008. The Governor of Riyadh Prince Salman and a local group organized the mass wedding for about 1,600 couples to help young Saudis who were unable to afford expensive ceremonies because of the rising cost of living.

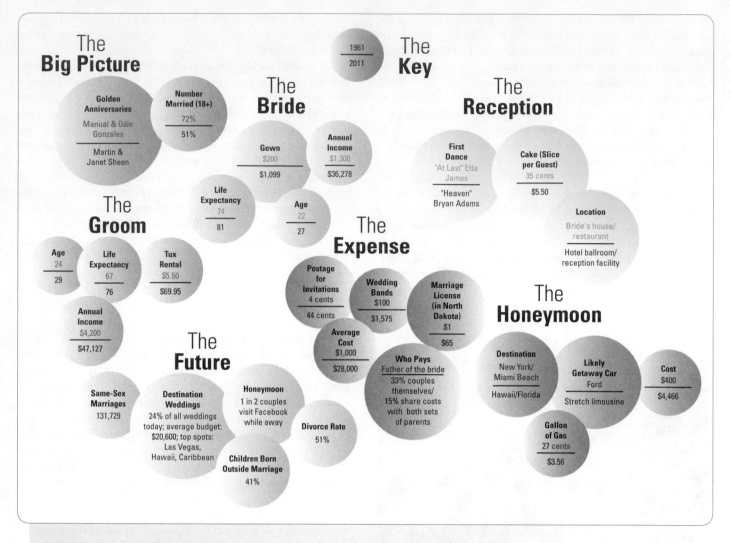

FIGURE 8.4 Wedding Changes over 50 Years: 1961–2011

Sources: Based on "Gonzaleses Celebrate 50 Years of Marriage." 2011. News-Bulletin.com. (Milestones-August 2011). www.news-bulletin.com/2011/08/27/milestones/gonzaleses-celebrate-50-years-of-marriage (15 December 2011). "Hawarden Independent." 1961. Newspaper Archive. www.newspaperarchive.com/SiteMap/FreePdfPreview.aspx?img+108078795 (15 December 2011). U.S. Census Bureau. 2012. Statistical Abstract. www.census.gov/compendia/statab/cats/income_expenditures_poverty_wealth/household (15 December 2011). "Fun Facts From 1961." 2011. www.woodstockcandy.com/fun-facts-from-1961.html (15 December 2011). "Women's Earnings and Income." 2011. *Catalyst* (August). www.catalyst.org/publication/217/womens-earnings-and-income (15 December 2011). Qualman, Eric. 2011. "Life Expectancy Study: 1 in 5 Will Live to be Over 100." www.socialnomics.net/2011/03/24/life-expectancy-study-1-in-5-will-live-to-be-over (15 December 2011). "Wedding and Honeymoon Statistics." 2011. www.honeymoons.about.com/cs/eurogen1/a/weddingstats.htm (15 December 2011). Jayson, Sharon. 2011. "Same-Sex Marriages: First Census Count Shows 131,729." *USA Today.* www.yourlife.usatoday.com/sex-relationships/story/2011-09-27/Same-sex-marriages-first (15 December 2011). Cohn, D'Vera, Passel, Jeffrey, Wang, Wendy, and Livingston, Gretchen. 2011. (December 14). "Barely Half of U.S. Adults are Married – A Record Low." www.pewsocialtrends.org/2011/12/14/barley-half-of-u-s-adults-are-married-a-record (15 December 2011). "First Dance Songs for Weddings." 2011. www.secretweddingsongs.com/first-dance-songs.html (15 December 2011). Fairchild Bridal Group. 2002. "The American Wedding." www.sellthebride.com/documents/americanweddingsurvey.pdf (15 December 2011). "Janet Sheen and Martin Sheen." 2011. Dating, Gossip, News. www.whodatedwho.com/tpx_1713928/janet-sheen-and-martin-sheen/ (15 December 2011). Weliver, David. 2011. "How Much Does an (Average) Wedding Cost?" www.moneyunder30.com/how-much-average-wedding-cost (15 December 2011). Ebon, Andy. 2011. "Brides Releases 2011 American Wedding Study: Are These Numbers Relevant to You?" (June 20). http://weddingmarketing.net/2011/06/20/brides-releases-2011-american-wedding-study-numbers-relevant/ (15 December 2011).

rich and famous, who often spare no expense, spending enough money in one day to buy the average couple two or three new homes. For example, the short-lived marriage of former Beatle star Paul McCartney and Heather Mills is reported to have cost $4.2 million. And one of the most expensive weddings thus far in the twenty-first century is reportedly the $78 million dollar wedding of Amit Bhatia, a London-based investor and Vanisha Mittal, the daughter of the owner of the largest steel company in the world. According to various sources, no money was spared for this six-day, multi-million dollar wedding, which included flying in 1,000 guests on 12 chartered Boeing jets. The wedding took place in Beirut, Lebanon, and featured 45 chefs,

APPLYING THE SOCIOLOGICAL IMAGINATION

WEDDING PLANNING: MATCHING YOUR PLANS WITH YOUR BUDGET

The skyrocketing increase in almost every item associated with weddings and getting married has spawned a subcategory of wedding industry vendors, ideas, and Web sites designed to assist brides in finding creative ways to spend less money on their weddings and/or to spend the money they have more wisely by discovering low-cost wedding ideas. Some examples from these various Web sites include the following:

- Instead of buying an expensive wedding gown for several thousand dollars, order one from a discount bridal store or rent one from a "rental salon."
- Cut down on the number of guests you invite; consider a smaller, more intimate wedding.
- Avoid a Saturday wedding (Saturdays are the most expensive days to rent an event space—Sundays are always cheaper).
- Hold your wedding during the Christmas season or immediately after Easter, when a church will already be decorated.

- Stay away from planning a wedding on popular holidays like Mother's Day and Valentine's Day, when the cost of flowers is inflated, or New Year's Day, when band rates are inflated.
- Hire a DJ instead of a band.
- Use only in-season and readily available flowers. Stick to your budget and use the most inexpensive flowers.
- Make your wedding reception a lunch instead of a dinner.
- Choose a buffet rather than a sit-down dinner.
- Choose foods that are in season; serve more vegetables and less meat (also, chicken is cheaper than beef).
- Eliminate champagne toasts.
- Hire a professional photographer to shoot only during the wedding ceremony. For the reception, leave disposable cameras at each table.

weddings.about.com/od/wedding flowers/a/cheapideas.htm
www/confetti.co.uk/weddings/ advice_ideas/wedding_you_want/

budget_ideas.aspstore.yahoo .net/nmcs/etiquette.html

Beginning with the Web sites listed above, find other Internet sources that help brides budget for the wedding as well as those that inform the bride of the proper protocol in terms of who pays for what wedding items, the types of wedding planners available and their costs, and different unique weddings and their cost. What other resources can you find that would aid someone planning her or his own wedding? You may also go to **www. costofwedding.com** and type in your zip code to find out the average cost of a wedding in your city.

After you have collected an ample amount of data, conduct a brief survey on your campus, asking questions of both married individuals and those who plan to marry. Your questions should include asking your respondents about their knowledge of Internet resources that assist brides and others in planning a wedding and if they plan to use such Internet resources.

10,000 flowers, a huge wedding cake, and luxurious gift bags for all female guests. In addition, nightclubs across the city were rented out so the couple could act out a specially written Bollywood story of how they met (Parker, 2011).

An interesting exercise, particularly for those planning a wedding now or in the near future, is to search the Internet to ascertain the costs for different types, sizes, and locales for weddings (see the Applying the Sociological Imagination box). After the wedding, for many couples there is the additional expense of the honeymoon. Today, couples planning a honeymoon will probably spend, on average, another $4,000 to $10,000, depending on whether they honeymoon within or outside the United States and how many days the honeymoon lasts.

Marriage Vows As more people change their views of marriage, they are also changing or at least modifying many of the rituals and traditions of weddings. For example, although some people continue to recite traditional wedding vows when they marry, others have modified or rewritten those vows to accommodate their preferences and to make their wedding romantic, meaningful, and unique. Perhaps as much a sign of the times as the Internet blitz of

prenuptial agreements and ways to save on wedding expenses is the wide range of Internet resources for writing your own wedding vows, from prewritten examples to custom wedding vows. Couples can add their own words or mix vows from different ceremonies. Even if they already have vows, they can find that one special line that adds an extra something to their wedding ceremony.

In Table 8.2 on page 254, we present three sets of wedding vows: (1) traditional wedding vows, (2) a set of vows written by a White middle-class couple (Mary and Richard) who married in the 1970s, and (3) a set of prewritten vows found on the Internet. For the fifth edition to this textbook, we asked Mary to reread the vows that she and Richard wrote in 1977 and tell us what meaning, if any, those vows had for her 29 years later (we first asked the question of Richard in 1999 for the third edition). In her response, Mary indicated that the couple renew their vows every five years, "not because we haven't followed them but because we live them. We know they work; they make the difficult times easier and they enhance the beauty and the joys we experience together. Love does grow deeper. Our love has" (Mary in 2006). The couple will celebrate 35 years of marriage and renew their vows for the seventh time in 2012. Although personalized wedding vows do not ensure a long and successful marriage,

TABLE 8.2 Telling Their Love: Marriage Vows for Different Preferences

Traditional Marriage Vows[1]

I, _____, take thee, _____, to be my lawful wedded wife [husband]. To have and to hold from this day forward; For better, for worse, for richer, for poorer; In sickness and in health; To love, honor, obey, and cherish; From this day forward; Till death do us part.

The Marriage Vows of Mary and Richard[2]

Mary [Richard], to manifest my deep love for you, I promise to cherish you, care for you, and to share with you the difficulties, the sorrows, and the hardships as well as the joys, the beauty, and the happiness that come our way.

I promise you a warm home and a dear and understanding heart in it, so that we may grow with and for each other. I promise to work together with you to build and to maintain this home and this love.

Internet: Prewritten Wedding Vows[3]

I, _____, take you as my husband [wife], and promise to walk by your side forever, as your best friend, your lover, and your soul mate. This day is the first day for the rest of our lives. As husband and wife, we will face many challenges that we will overcome with trust, commitment, and love. I pledge my love to you, _____, now and forever, with a hug and a kiss every day that we are married. I promise to laugh with you, love you, and honor you; to support you and your dreams, comfort you, always hold you in the highest regard, and to be there for you for all of our lives. I give you these things today, and all the days of my life. I will always cherish you in good times and those times that aren't so good. You are the love of my life. You put the sparkle in my eyes, and the smile on my face. I come to you today just as I am, and I take you just as you are, my cherished husband [wife]. Let's never change, but always love each other the way we do today.

[1]Most couples, even if they recite the traditional vows, no longer vow to obey their partner.
[2]In addition to writing their own vows, Mary chose to maintain her birth name.
[3]This set of vows was combined from the following two Internet sources: http://wedding-band-ring.com/weddingvowlist.html and http://www.weddingvowrings.com/customvows.html.

they very often serve as a guide or a set of goals that silently guides a couple's life together, as Mary's response suggests.

Although most women marrying today do not pledge to *obey* their husbands, the pendulum may be swinging back to vows of obedience, at least among the nation's Southern Baptists. At the close of the last decade, in response to what the leadership of the Southern Baptists viewed as a growing crisis in marriages and families, the nation's largest Protestant denomination (16 million members) issued a declaration on obedience to husbands. Those attending the Southern Baptists' 1998 national convention voted overwhelmingly to add a new article of faith, which declares that

marriage is a lifelong covenant between one man and one woman, and the husband has the "God given responsibility to provide for, to protect, and to lead his family. A wife is to submit herself graciously to the servant leadership of her husband." Critics of the Baptists' declaration argue that focusing on wifely submission implies that women are inferior to men and could even offer a religious excuse for some men to abuse their wives. Interestingly, the divorce rate for conservative Christians is significantly higher than for other faith groups and for atheists and agnostics. Research also shows that the divorce rate is highest in politically and religiously conservative Red states, especially in the Deep South, and actually lowest in politically and religiously liberal Blue states in the Northeast and Midwest (Cline, 2011; Family and Divorce News, 2011).

Personalizing the wedding vows, a personal marriage agreement, and the cost of weddings notwithstanding, what happens once a couple is married? What kinds of changes take place in their lives? Do women and men experience marriage in the same way? In the remaining sections of this chapter, we discuss marriage as it is experienced by women and men.

Marriage and Gender

In her now-classic book *The Future of Marriage* (1972), sociologist Jessie Bernard detailed the different experiential realities of wives and husbands. When asked identical questions about their marriage, husbands and wives answered so differently that Bernard called their marriages "her marriage" and "his marriage." Even when asked basic questions like how often they

☐▸⃞ Read the **Document**
The Two Marriages
on **myfamilylab.com**

had sexual relations or who made decisions, wives' and husbands' responses were so different it was as though they were talking about two different marriages. Though largely hidden, the female–male differences in the experience of marriage have a tremendous effect on the mental and physical well-being of wives and husbands.

"HER" MARRIAGE

Does it surprise you that Bernard found wives were much less happy in their marriages than their husbands? Some people believe that these are just a few disgruntled wives—that couples who love each other live in a kind of identical harmony and peace. Several of Bernard's findings challenge this assumption. For example, although wives reported being happier with their lives than did single women, when compared with husbands they reported being less happy. In addition, married women reported much higher rates of anxiety, phobia, and depression than any other group in society except single men, and wives had a higher rate of suicide than husbands.

Research continues to uncover women and men's different perceptions and experiences of marriage. For instance, husbands and wives differ dramatically in terms of how they evaluate their relationship. Men tend to rate almost everything as better than their wives. They have a much more positive perception of marital sex, family finances, ties with parents, listening to each other, tolerance of flaws, and romance. Wives, on the other hand, tend to complain more about their marriage than husbands do. Moreover, although married women experience better health than singles, they do not benefit in terms of health from marriage as much as men. For example, women in traditional marriages are especially prone to higher rates of illness than husbands (Kurdek, 2005; Whitehead and Popenoe, 2004).

Perhaps something about the nature or structure of marriage itself accounts for these gender differences. The structure of traditional marriage, particularly with regard to the housewife role, is revealing in this regard. For instance, the division of labor in traditional marriages leads to fewer sources of gratification for housewives than for husbands. The imbalance of power in traditional marriages further alienates the housewife from her wifely role. According to Bernard, the housewife role has a "pathogenic" effect on wives. Often when women marry they lose their legal and personal identity and become totally dependent on their husbands, which often leads to depression.

"HIS" MARRIAGE

Many of you have probably grown up on tales of men running from marriage, going to great lengths to avoid being "trapped." This folklore actually runs counter to the reality of women's and men's lives. In reality, men seem to prefer marriage to being single. For example, when asked if they would marry the same person again, they respond in the affirmative twice as often as their wives. In addition, most divorced and widowed men remarry, and the rate of marriage for these men at every age level is higher than the rate for single men. Furthermore, when compared with single men, married men live longer, have better mental and physical health, are less depressed, have a lower rate of suicide, are less likely to be incarcerated for a crime, earn higher incomes, and are more likely to define themselves as happy.

Although marriage is beneficial for men overall, it imposes certain costs. Bernard contends that a major cost of marriage for men is that they must give up their sexual freedom and take on the responsibility of supporting a wife and family. Whether or not this is a *cost* is debatable. Nonetheless, the provider role is costly in other respects, including the fact that it forces many men to work harder than they might otherwise. This, however, is changing, as women and men have become more sexually free both within and outside of marriage and as more married women work outside the home and contribute to the family income.

Transitions and Adjustments to Marriages

Getting married represents a significant change in the lives of a couple. The world of married couples is in many important ways different from the world of singles. As a married couple, two people must fit their lives together and meet and satisfy each other's needs. In simple terms, **marital adjustment** is the degree to which a couple get along with each other or have a good working relationship and are able to satisfy each other's needs over the marital life course. One major adjustment that a married couple must make involves being identified with a partner and thought of by the community as one unit, as opposed to the unique individual each was before the marriage. Another marital adjustment regards seeing and relating to a partner on a daily basis, and learning to live with that person and accommodate her or his wants, needs, expectations, and desires. Still other adjustments include sharing space, money, relatives, and friends with a partner; the division of tasks in the relationship; and adjustment to the partner's sexual attitudes and behaviors. Changing from a single to a married persona does not always run smoothly. Most couples, however, manage it with a minimum of problems.

Adjustment does not simply happen one day in a marriage; rather, it is an ongoing process. Research shows that couples must continuously make adjustments in marriage as they are confronted with new and different life course events.

A TYPOLOGY OF MARITAL RELATIONSHIPS

What makes a happy, well-adjusted marriage? Most contemporary studies have concluded that there is no single model for a well-adjusted marriage. Helpfulness, love, mutual respect, and selflessness are but a few of the many characteristics associated with successful marital adjustment. In a now-classic study of marital adjustment and happiness, researchers John Cuber and Peggy Harroff (1966) reported on 211 upper-middle-class couples who had been married for 10 or more years and who expressed commitment to each other. Cuber and Harroff concluded that satisfying, well-adjusted, enduring marital relationships can vary a great deal from each other and from societal ideals of a happy marriage. They identified five distinct types of marriages, representing a wide range of communication patterns and interaction styles: conflict-habituated, devitalized, passive-congenial, vital, and total.

The Conflict-Habituated Marriage The first type, the conflict-habituated marriage, is characterized by extensive tension and conflict, although for the most part the tension and conflict are managed or controlled. Channeling conflict and hostility is so important to these couples that it becomes a habitual part of their marriage. The couple engages in both verbal and physical arguments and fights, usually in private but sometimes in front of family and friends. They see their fighting as an acceptable way to solve problems and do not see it as a cause for separation or divorce. However, fighting seldom solves their problems.

The Devitalized Marriage The devitalized marriage involves very little conflict. Rather, it is characteristic of couples who were once deeply in love and had a satisfying sexual relationship but over time have lost their sense of excitement and passion. In this type of marriage, the partners pay very little attention to one another. There are occasional periods of sharing and time spent together, but this is done out of a sense of "duty" not joy. Although the marriage lacks visible vitality, these couples remain together believing that their marriage is the way most marriages are.

The Passive-Congenial Marriage The passive-congenial marriage is similar in many respects to the devitalized marriage. The primary difference is that the passivity that characterizes this marriage was there from the beginning. Couples in this type of marriage began the marriage with a low emotional investment and low expectations that do not change over the course of the marriage. Although there is little conflict in this type of marriage, there is also very little excitement. Passive-congenial couples share many common interests, but their fulfillment comes from involvements and relationships outside the marriage. In fact, they feel their type of marriage facilitates independence and security and allows them the time and freedom to pursue individual goals.

The Vital Marriage The vital marriage contrasts sharply with the previous three types. Vital couples are highly involved with each other; their sharing and togetherness provide the life force of the marriage. Despite their enjoyment of one another, the vital couple does not lose their sense of identity or monopolize each other's time; rather, they simply enjoy each other when they are together and make this time the focal point of their lives. The vital couple tries to avoid conflict; however, when it does occur, it is usually over a serious issue, and the couple makes every attempt to settle the disagreement as quickly as possible rather than let it drag on, as does the conflict-habituated couple.

The Total Marriage Finally, unlike the vital marriage in which the couple value their time together but maintain their individuality, the total marriage is characterized by constant togetherness and sharing of most, if not all, important life events. Couples in a total marriage often work together and share the same friends; the partners have few areas of tension or unresolved conflict primarily because tensions that do arise are dealt with as they occur. In fact, a defining characteristic of the total marriage is that when faced with tension, conflict, or differences, the couples deal with the issues without losing the feeling of unity and vitality paramount to their relationship.

Total relationships are rare, and the total couple is often aware of their exceptionality. Such relationships do exist, however. In fact, Cuber and Harroff report that they occasionally found relationships so total that every aspect of the relationship was mutually and enthusiastically shared. In a sense, it was as if these couples did not have an individual existence.

The researchers reported that the majority of the couples they studied fell into the first three categories. They labeled these marriages as *utilitarian*, because, in their view, the marriages appeared to be based upon convenience. They labeled the remaining two types of marriages *intrinsic* marriages, because these marriages appeared to be rewarding. One of several problems with this study and the categories used to describe types of marriages is the obvious bias in the choice of terms used to describe the marriages. For example, what criteria did the researchers use to determine if a marriage is intrinsic and thus rewarding? Could not a marriage be both convenient and rewarding? Do couples have an inferior or devitalized relationship simply because they are less passionate over time than at the beginning of their marriage? More recent research on marital adjustment and happiness has built upon the Cuber and Harroff typology, adding one or more new dimensions but essentially maintaining the typology elucidated by them (see, for example, Olson and Olson, 2000). However, like the Cuber and Harroff typology, much of this research is based on middle- or upper-class couples who are probably not representative of most marriages in the United States.

Do you think that you fit into one of these types of marriages or intimate relationships? Why or why not? Do you know couples who can be described in terms of one or more of these relationship types? What about your parents? Your grandparents? Where do they fit (if at all)? What are the problems with attempting to fit couples into such a typology?

It is clear that the meaning of marriage as well as what represents marital happiness and adjustment differ among human beings. Cuber and Harroff stress the point that each of these relationship types simply represents a particular type of interaction in and adjustment to the marital relationship. Thus, people living in any one of the relationships described by Cuber and Harroff may or may not be satisfied. In addition, the categories are not mutually exclusive. Rather, some couples are on the border, and others may move from one mode of interaction to another over the course of their relationship.

Heterogamous Marriages

In addition to types of relationships, social scientists often classify marriages in terms of social characteristics such as race, ethnicity, and religion. Although people tend to select partners with whom they share these characteristics, some couples do come from different backgrounds or traditions. Marriages between people who vary in certain social and demographic characteristics are referred to as **heterogamous marriages.** Such marriages have become more common in recent years. The following section focuses on two

"I don't hate him because he's black. I hate him because he's my husband."

The rate of divorce for interracial marriages is only slightly higher than for same-race couples. When conflicts occur, they are more likely to arise from cultural, gender, class, social, and personal differences than from racial ones.

major types of heterogamous marriage: interracial and interethnic marriages and interfaith marriages.

INTERRACIAL MARRIAGES

Race is only one of many characteristics that affect the choice of a marital partner; however, race has always been a divisive feature in most aspects of American life. Although many people interpret interracial marriage as referring to Black–White couples, interracial marriages actually involve a wide range of combinations, including not only Whites and African Americans, but also Native Americans, Asian Americans, and Latinos. Today, in fact, Black–White marriages make up only nine-tenths of 1 percent of all marriages in the United States (U.S. Census Bureau, 2011a). Interracial marriage is most common among college-educated, middle-income people of all races. However, the typical interracial married couple is a White person with a nonwhite spouse.

According to some estimates, there are about 600,000 interracial marriages annually in the United States; however, this country has a long history of intolerance of marriage across racial lines. For instance, a half-century ago, in 1958, a Gallup poll found just 4 percent of Whites approved of interracial marriage; Blacks and other racial groups were not even asked. That same year, two Black youths in North Carolina, a 7-year-old and a 9-year-old, were arrested after a White girl kissed the 9-year-old. Convicted of attempted rape, the 7-year-old was sentenced to 12 years in prison and the 9-year-old was sentenced to 14 years in prison. It was only after pressure from then-President Dwight D. Eisenhower that the two boys' release was secured (Kristof, 2005).

It was not until the 1967 landmark U.S. Supreme Court ruling in *Loving* v. *Virginia* that struck down state laws prohibiting interracial marriage that some interracial couples could legally marry. Prior to that Supreme Court decision, as many as 38 states had laws that specifically prohibited miscegenation, or the interracial marriage of Whites with other specific groups: Arizona, for example, prohibited marriage between Whites and Native Americans; California, Utah, Wyoming, and Idaho prohibited White and Mongolian marriages; and Nebraska and Montana prohibited marriages between Whites and Asian Americans. A year after the *Loving* decision, public disapproval of interracial marriage was still overwhelming—73 percent of Whites disapproved of such marriages. Some 40 plus years later, opposition to interracial marriage has decreased considerably, however it still lingers. For example, among religious groups, evangelicals remain the most opposed to interracial marriage. In response to the question posed in a recent Pew Research Center Poll—Is more people of different races marrying each other good or bad for society?—while only 9 percent of Americans said it was bad, 16 percent of White evangelicals said it was bad. Put another way, 27 percent of Americans said such marriages were good for society compared to 17 percent of White evangelicals. Although evangelicals have the most negative view of interracial marriages, there is opposition from other White Christians as well (for example, 13 percent of White mainline Protestants and 10 percent of White Catholics) (Grant, 2011).

Such a negative view of interracial marriage lingers in spite of its near universal acceptance among the general population today. For instance, the majority of Americans today are okay with the idea of interracial marriage and, in fact, a little more than one-third of Americans (35 percent) have a family member who is married interracially. In this context, one recent poll reported that two-thirds (66 percent) of Whites said they would not object if their own child or grandchild chose a Black spouse. Blacks (86 percent) and Hispanics (79 percent) were equally accepting about a child or grandchild's marrying someone of another race (Passel, Wang, and Taylor, 2010; Carroll, 2007; Price, 2006). As with interracial dating (see Chapter 5), younger Americans are much more accepting of interracial marriage than older adults. For example, 85 percent of Americans between the ages of 18 and 29 approve of interracial marriage compared to only 55 percent of those 50 to 64 years of age and older. And only 38 percent of Americans 65 and older approve of such marriages.

Moreover, a recent study by the Pew Research Center (Passel, Wang, and Taylor, 2010) found that one in seven new marriages in the United States is Interracial or Interethnic. The study grabbed headlines across the country with one writer after another heralding the blurring of racial barriers and the disappearance of racial taboos to interracial marriage, with some pundits claiming that America is now a colorblind society when it comes to saying "I do," second only to Brazil. Among the study's key findings about newlyweds in 2008:

- There was an increase in interracial marriage for four major racial groups with Asians topping the list with 31 percent married to someone of a different race or ethnicity from their own.
- Gender differences were obvious among Blacks and Asians with more Black men than Black women newlyweds married outside of their race. The reverse was true for Asians, with twice as many Asian women than Asian men married interracially.
- The rates of marrying out varied by group with the rate doubling for Whites, almost tripling for Blacks, but remaining pretty stable for Latinas/os and Asians.
- There was a strong regional pattern of interracial marriage with the West leading the way with 22 percent of all such marriages (see Figure 8.5 on page 258).

As we indicated in Chapter 5, sociologists and others have interpreted contemporary survey data such as this (reporting on interracial intimacy) as showing that despite a history of intolerance and opposition to interracial intimacy, dating and marriage, over the years Americans have grown increasingly tolerant and accepting of such relationships. Particularly since the election of Barack Obama to President of the United States, many scholars and non-scholars alike have used findings such as these to claim that we are now living in a post-racial America. However, we must be cautious with our interpretations of data such as these. As we have already pointed out there is still important opposition to such intimacy, particularly relative to African American–White marriages. Various surveys, including the 2010 Pew Survey, indicate that while there is growing acceptance to interracial marriage involving all racial groups, the least acceptance of such marriages is for those involving African Americans. In addition, some surveys have reported that as many as 10 percent of Whites still favor laws against marriage between African Americans and Whites (Lee and Edmonston, 2005).

The paradox of White Americans' attitudes and behavior relative to interracial marriage does not go unnoticed, however. In the face of a history of forced race-mixing vis-à-vis the sexual exploitation and rape of African women under slavery, Native American

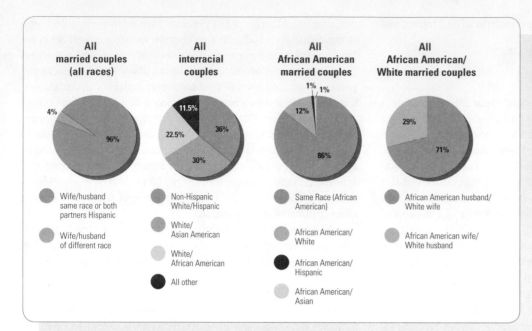

All married couples (all races)
- 96% Wife/husband same race or both partners Hispanic
- 4% Wife/husband of different race

All interracial couples
- 36% Non-Hispanic White/Hispanic
- 30% White/Asian American
- 22.5% White/African American
- 11.5% All other

All African American married couples
- 86% Same Race (African American)
- 12% African American/White
- 1% African American/Hispanic
- 1% African American/Asian

All African American/White married couples
- 71% African American husband/White wife
- 29% African American wife/White husband

FIGURE 8.5 Interracial Marriages in the United States, 2010

Source: U.S. Census Bureau, 2011. *America's Families and Living Arrangements: 2010. Statistical Abstract of the United States* (Washington, DC: U.S. Government Printing Office), Table FG4. http://www.census.gov/population/www/socdemo/hh-fam/cps2010.html

women during the European conquest and colonization, and other women of oppressed and exploited racial and ethnic groups in this country, it is indeed paradoxical that, through legal prohibitions against interracial marriage, White Americans have outlawed race mixing until recent times. Interestingly, some sociologists, historians, and geneticists have estimated that 75 percent of all African Americans have at least one White ancestor, and another 15 percent have predominant White ancestral lines as a result of the rape of their ancestors. Concomitantly, 95 percent of "White" Americans have widely varying degrees of African heritage. Yet miscegenation laws meant to separate the races by prohibiting interracial marriages between Whites and African Americans (and Whites and Native Americans) began as early as 1661 and lasted until 2000, and informal restrictions—sociocultural norms—concerning these marriages remain the most inflexible of all mate selection boundaries. It is well to note that even though the number of interracial couples has increased considerably over the past 40 or more years, they still remain rare proportionately, relative to marriages between people of the same race or ethnic group. For example, in 2010, 98 percent of Whites who were married were married to other Whites; 89 percent of Blacks who were married were married to other Blacks, and 86 percent of Asians who were married were married to other Asians (U.S. Census Bureau, 2010e). Given this type of racial endogamy, we cannot underestimate the power of informal social norms that operate in mate selection. For a better understanding, let us turn our attention to interracial marriages among various racial and ethnic groups in the United States.

African Americans Among various groups of color in the United States, African Americans have the highest rate of endogamous marriages and the lowest rate of exogamous marriages. When African American women and men do marry interracially, most often (four out of five such marriages) their mate is White. We can probably expect this trend to continue given that recent survey data indicate that African Americans are now three times

as likely to marry Whites than 30 years ago. Unlike any other race or ethnic group in the United States, African American men are more likely to marry outside the race than are African American women. For example, African American men are more than twice as likely as African American women to have a White mate. Even among newlyweds in 2008, 22 percent of African American men compared to just 9 percent of African American women married someone of a different race than their own.

In the past, most research indicated that in most cases of African American/White marriages, African American–White couples have been raised in racially sensitive homes; are more likely to have met through their jobs than in school, in their neighborhoods, in church, or through recreational activities; begin their courtship through repeated casual conversations rather than with immediate physical attraction, friendship over a period of time, or after close association with one another; are initially attracted to one another through their shared interests; and at least one partner in the marriage has been married previously. Some scholars have suggested that some African American–White couples might also belong to religions that encourage interracial unions, such as the Baha'i religion, which teaches that God is particularly pleased with interracial unions. Moreover, the couples usually live far from their families of orientation; mothers of daughters tend to be more supportive of the relationship than mothers of sons, and fathers of sons are more supportive of the relationship than fathers of daughters.

While these data continue to accurately reflect the factors associated with African American/White marriages, a number of scholars suggest that the increasing number of African Americans marrying out is due in large part today to higher educational attainment, a more racially integrated military and a rising Black middle class that provides more interaction with other races. This is particularly so for African American men who marry White women. These men are typically well educated, have a high income, and are usually older than their mate. In fact, African American men who have attended graduate school are the most likely to marry interracially (Associated Press, 2010; Lee and Edmonston, 2005; Zebroski, 1997). Although African American–White couples have similar educations, White women who marry African American men nonetheless, "marry up" more often than those who marry White men. This is especially notable given that the pool of highly educated White men greatly outnumbers the pool of highly educated African American men. More than half of African American husbands with White wives have at least some college education compared to only two-fifths of African American husbands with African American wives. In this sense, some researchers have suggested that White wives get more than their "share" of well-educated African American husbands. The growing tendency of African American men to marry outside their race, coupled with the overall decline in marriage rates among all racial and ethnic groups, compounds the problem of African American women finding a desired marriage partner (Curry, 2010; qian, 2005).

As the data on interracial marriage indicate, African American women are left out so to speak. For example, during the interracial marriage boom of 2008, only 9 percent of African American women married interracially making them the least likely of any race or gender to marry outside their race and the least likely to get married at all. As African American women see fewer African American men at the altar, the familiar lament among African American women continues to be: where are the "good" African American men to marry? The consensus among many African American women is that they want to get married, and their preference is to marry an African American man. But the pool of eligible bachelors continues to dwindle. When you add in the prison population, the pool is even smaller. And even though some African American women are willing to marry men of other races, as the data show, their options in this regard are also limited given that males in other races marry African American women the least often (Davis and Noll, 2010).

In response to the shrinking pool of potential marriage partners for African American women, several people have turned up the volume exhorting them to consider dating and marriage outside of their race. For example, writer Karen Folan (2010) has joined the broadening debate in recent years about whether or not African American women should date and marry interracially. Educated single African American women outnumber educated single African American men almost 3 to 1 in major urban areas. According to Folan, given this reality, African American women need to start looking elsewhere. African American women are in a failed market, and the remedy is to find a new market for their commodity—they are the commodity and the new market is men of other races. This is not to suggest that there aren't good, single African American men out there nor that all African American women are looking to get married. Rather, it is simply a reasonable solution to the shortage of available African American men. In this same vein, in a new and controversial book by Richard Banks (2011), the author also points out the glaring disparity between the marriage rates of African American women and men but his major concern is for successful African American women. He argues that African American women have been so disproportionately successful that they significantly outnumber successful African American men. The solution to this dilemma and the only realistic choice for African American women is to give up racial exclusivity

and marry outside their race. Critics of those who exhort African American women to marry outside their race argue that such suggestions presumes that African American women have control over access of men of other races, such as White males. This is again problematic given that White males, for instance display an overwhelming preference for whiteness and White beauty standards and are the least likely, in general, to marry outside their race. In addition, men in other racial categories marry African American women even less often than White males. Putting the onus on African American women who want to marry to embrace marrying outside their race is not where the focus should be some argue. Rather, the onus ought to be on men of all racial categories.

In the midst of such debates, interestingly, interracial marriage between African Americans and Whites (as well as between other racial and ethnic groups) has quietly grown in the Deep South shifting the image of both the South and interracial marriages. As a result of interracial marriages in the South, there has been an explosion of people identifying as mixed race, though it still ranks second to last in overall share of interracial marriages (Saulny, 2011b). Fifty-six years ago, interracial intimacy was one of the greatest taboos in the South, especially in Mississippi. Not only was marriage between African Americans and Whites illegal, such intimacy could and sometime was fatal. For example, the widely publicized and horrific murder in 1955 of 15-year-old Emmett Till, an African American teenager accused of whistling at a White woman in Mississippi, symbolized the historically deep-seated views of some Whites relative to the mere suggestion of Black–White racial mixing and intimacy. Although attitudes and behaviors have changed from such grotesque displays of disapproval, at least overtly, nonetheless, the FBI announced in 2005 that it had begun investigating the rising hate mail sent to prominent African American men married to White women.

So, although attitudes and behavior regarding racial intermarriages have changed somewhat, interracial couples, especially African American–White couples, are still frequently subjected to a range of societal reactions—forms of antagonism and indignities from stares to cross burnings to physical attacks and sometimes murder. According to some research, interracial couples say that the most pressing problem they face, both before and after marriage, is racism. The emotional wear and tear of social and cultural attitudes toward interracial couples is often enormous. For some of these couples, their way of coping with the indignities and nonacceptance of their relationship by family, friends, and/or the larger society is to not respond to the racism—to not let others make racism their problem. Others celebrate the cultural hybridity of their everyday lives while keenly aware of the differences in how they view themselves as family versus how they are viewed by the larger society (see, for example, the Schroeder family in the Family Profile box on page 260).

Reactions such as these reflect the importance that White Americans continue to attach to the preservation of racial segregation and the role of informal norms in shaping our behavior. Such statistics should not be taken to indicate that White Americans are the only group to oppose interracial marriage. There are those in almost every other racial group who also oppose such marriages. For example, many African Americans, especially women, oppose interracial marriages in the belief that it strains an already limited pool of eligible African American men. Others view such marriages as weakening cultural heritage and group solidarity.

Family Profile

CHRISTOPHER, RANIMARIE BUEN-SCHROEDER, MAHAL, AND MATEO SCHROEDER

Clockwise: Christopher, Ranimarie, Mahal, and Mateo Schroeder

Length of Marriage: 15 years

Christopher Schroeder is an associate professor of English at Northeastern Illinois University. Ranimarie Buen-Schroeder is an art therapist (ATR-BC, LCPC). Their children, Mahal and Mateo, are 12 and 11 years of age, respectively. Because they do not compartmentalize their lives based on how others respond or do not respond to them as an interracial family, Christopher and Ranimarie profiled their lives with what they describe as "a reflection of both how they see themselves (e.g., the cultural hybridity of their everyday lives) and how others view them."

Family Profile

In the United States, diversity seems disturbing. According to sociologist Robert Putnam, people who live in ethnically diverse communities tend to distrust their neighbors, no matter their skin color, and to withdraw from social life. The solution, he suggests, is not greater assimilation but more hybrid, or hyphenated identities, which lead to expanded social identities.

Hyphenation is life in our home. With their lolo and lola (grandparents) mga anak (our children) hear Tagalog, but with us, they speak mostly English. My asawa (spouse) understands Tagalog, and I catch enough to barely keep up. She says that she cannot keep up with me. I've learned to sit back when she speaks.

Outside of our home, our lives are different. Our community has its own official diversity statement reminding residents that interaction is the means to celebrate differences while establishing unity. Nonetheless, we can't help but wonder, whether we're talking to our neighbors or meeting with school administrators, if our diversity isn't a shadow in these interactions. The staff at my kids' school refers them to speech therapy, but no one can explain precisely why. I discover, after some research, that the standards are those of monolingual kids in Nebraska and Iowa from 20 years ago, but still, neither the speech therapist nor district administrators will see me. Then a colleague reports that according to a speech therapist who consults for the district, Filipino kids are referred more often than others.

At first glance, neither of our kids looks quite like us. Neither looks like the other. I was once asked, when they and I were walking through a park, how much I charge to care for children. These differences, though, are ones we want to see. Although for most I'm White, I too am mixed—German and Irish and Native American, all of whom have been criticized for their perceptions of the world and themselves. For example, Germans were condemned by Benjamin Franklin, in 1751, as aliens who would never acquire the English language, customs, or complexion, and many states, during World War I, prohibited the teaching and use of German. Nonetheless, these perceptions have social consequences.

Here in Illinois, the state declared, in 1923, that its official language was American. Even though it amended this legislation, in 1969, to English, the message is clear. More recently, an American President objected to the singing of the National Anthem in Spanish. However, he should have acknowledged the significance of solidarity regardless of the language used to express it.

At home, I am teaching Tagalog to my kids, which means that I must learn it too. Around the world, people are mixing languages—Taglish or Englog or Spanglish—in order to acknowledge who they are and how they see the world.

Mestiza, in the end, means more than one, not none. Among us, we have four hearts and four heads in bodies that span a spectrum.

In addition to racial attitudes and beliefs that shape the informal endogamous norms surrounding mate selection in the United States, various structural features of American society also affect the rate of interracial marriages. For instance, interracial marriage rates vary across geographic regions and are highest in regions where relatively large numbers of people of color live, where the population is racially diverse, and where attitudes toward interracial relationships are relatively more permissive and tolerant than in other areas of the country (Lee and Edmonston, 2005).

Native Americans If African Americans represent the most racially endogamous end of the marital continuum among people of color, Native Americans can be found at the other end of the continuum as they are the least likely to exhibit racial endogamy in marriage patterns. Native Americans are more likely than any other racial group to marry outside their group. They are more likely to marry a White American than another Native American and least likely to marry an African American. In fact, close to 60 percent of Native Americans are involved in interracial marriages. This trend of interracial marriage has increased steadily since the 1970s, and as with other racial groups, the rate of interracial marriages among Native Americans increases with education. However, although older Native Americans in the past had lower intermarriage rates than younger Native Americans, today such an age gradient is either small or absent. Moreover, unlike some other racial groups (for example, Asian Americans and African Americans), interracial marriage does not appear to be associated with gender; Native American women and men are almost equally likely to marry a non-Native American (Lee and Edmonston, 2005).

A number of explanations for this marital pattern have been proposed. The most common is related to the size of the Native American population. Only about 3.1 million (or one percent) Americans today identify themselves as being of native descent (U.S. Census Bureau, 2011a). Given the already small numbers of Native Americans, geographic areas with small Native American populations have significantly higher rates of interracial marriage than do those with large populations. The high rates of Native American interracial marriages are also linked to the increased migration of Native Americans to urban areas, expanding opportunities for education and employment in nonreservation settings, and a generally more favorable attitude about Native peoples and their cultures. In this context, interracial marriage is much higher for Native Americans living in urban areas than for those living on reservations and is more characteristic for those Native Americans who have left the reservation to pursue educational and occupational opportunities in cities. Researchers in the last decade found that approximately three-fourths of Native Americans living in 23 states were married to someone from another race.

Asian American Historically, social scientists have used the rates of interracial marriage with Whites as an indicator of the acculturation or assimilation of various groups of color into the American mainstream. If that is the case, then Asian American families have become increasingly acculturated. As we have learned, antimiscegenation laws were very common in the United States prior to 1967. Although the first such laws were passed to prevent freed Black slaves from marrying Whites, many people soon saw Asian intermarriage with Whites equally as threatening to American society and thus antimiscegenation laws were passed that prohibited Asians/Asian Americans from marrying Whites as well. These laws, part of the larger anti-Asian movement in this country, eventually led to the Chinese Exclusion Act in 1882 and other restrictive regulations against Asians that had an impact on the early interracial marital patterns that emerged, especially among Asian/Asian American men.

Today, Asian Americans in interracial marriages are very common. A little more than one-third of all Asian Americans who are married are in interracial marriages, primarily with Whites (40 percent). This trend is particularly prevalent among younger Asian Americans. In addition, their likelihood of marrying a foreign-born Asian tripled for men and increased five times for women to roughly 20 percent. Of the 3.8 million Americans who married in 2008, 31 percent of Asians married someone whose race or ethnicity was different from their own. Broken down by nativity, in 2008, 46 percent of native Asians married interracially compared to 26 percent of foreign-born Asians (Passel, Wang, and Taylor, 2010).

Of course, Asian Americans are not a monolithic group—thus rates of interracial marriage vary from group to group. For instance, among the six major Asian American ethnic groups in the U.S. (Asian Indian Americans, Chinese Americans, Filipina/o Americans, Japanese Americans, Korean Americans, and Vietnamese Americans), Japanese and Chinese Americans have the highest rates of interracial marriage. For example, Japanese Americans have the highest rate, with over 50 percent marrying outside the group. This fact notwithstanding, the most revealing data on interracial marriage patterns among Asian Americans are those that present rates by gender.

According to some observers of the interracial marriage scene, the topic of interracial marriage is one of the most explosive social issues within the Asian American community today. The issue of Asian Americans, especially Asian American women, marrying non-Asian Americans is said to be an emotionally divisive debate often loaded with charges of racism and sexism from within and without along gender lines due to the significantly higher numbers of interracial marriages among many Asian American women. For instance, in 2010, Asian American women married interracially almost three times more often than Asian American men. Indeed, for several ethnic groupings of Asian women, wives are twice as likely to have a non-Asian husband than an Asian husband. In contrast, U.S.-born Asian American men lag significantly behind in interracial marriages, giving rise to a so-called gender disparity (U.S. Census Bureau, 2011a; Le, 2006a, 2006b, 2008; Seraph, 2005). As Table 8.3 on page 262 shows, with the exception of Asian Indian Americans, Asian American women in each of the remaining five largest Asian ethnic groups have nearly or more than twice the outmarriage rate as Asian men in these groupings. Across Asian ethnic groups and gender, by far the majority of those married interracially are married to Whites. Although often overlooked by researchers focused on interracial marriage patterns, the Pan-Asian intermarriage rate has grown over the years. Currently, Japanese and Chinese American women and men are most likely to marry other Asian Americans (outside their own ethnic group) (Le, 2008).

Whether or not they are avoiding family complications as some researchers have suggested, the fact is that a large percentage of Asian Americans cohabit with an interracial partner. As with interracial marriage, a larger percentage of cohabiting Asian American women (55 percent) have a non-Asian partner compared to 37 percent of Asian American men. And, as with interracial marriage, the overwhelming majority of both cohabiting Asian American women and men live with a White partner, 40 and 27 percent, respectively (Le, 2006b). These patterns of interracial intimacy are believed to be causing a *marriage squeeze* for Asian American men, most of whom prefer to marry within their own race. The shrinking pool of eligible mates—the out-marriage of so many Asian American women—has caused deep resentments among some Asian American men. For example, it is reported that many Chinese men have strong feelings against interracial marriage and express a feeling of being betrayed and abandoned by Chinese women, who they believe should be committed only to Chinese men.

TABLE 8.3 Interracial Marriage Among the Six Largest Asian American Ethnic Groups by Race, Ethnicity, and Gender of Spouse

	Wives(%)	Husbands(%)		Wives(%)	Husbands(%)
Asian Indian Americans			**Japanese Americans**		
Asian Indians	93.6	91.9	Japanese Americans	47.4	63.9
Other Asians	0.7	0.9	Other Asians	6.4	9.9
Whites	4.3	5.5	Whites	38.2	19.7
Blacks	0.5	0.5	Blacks	1.6	0.4
Latinas/os	0.4	0.8	Latinas/os	2.8	2.8
Multiracial and all others	0.5	0.4	Multiracial and all others	3.7	3.2
Chinese Americans			**Korean Americans**		
Chinese	81.5	89.5	Korean Americans	69.4	90.7
Other Asians	2.7	4.5	Other Asians	3.7	2.6
Whites	13.9	5.3	Whites	23.7	5.5
Blacks	0.4	0.1	Blacks	1.0	0.3
Latinas/os	0.9	0.7	Latinas/os	1.1	0.5
Multiracial and all others	0.6	0.4	Multiracial and all others	1.1	0.4
Filipina/o Americans			**Vietnamese Americans**		
Filipinas/os	61.1	82.4	Vietnamese Americans	83.3	92.3
Other Asians	2.8	2.8	Other Asians	3.5	2.9
Whites	27.2	9.2	Whites	11.3	2.9
Blacks	2.8	0.3	Blacks	0.5	0.2
Latinas/os	3.6	2.9	Latinas/os	0.7	1.4
Multiracial and all others	2.5	2.3	Multiracial and all others	0.7	0.3

Source: Adapted from C. N. Le, 2008, "Interracial Dating and Marriage," *Asian Nation: The Landscape of Asian America*, www.asian-nation.org/interracial.shtml (2008, July 4). Reprinted by permission of C.N. Le, Ph.D.

High rates of out-marriages among Asian Americans have led sociologists and other social scientists to theorize about why Asian Americans choose to intermarry with Whites. A common theory emphasizes that marrying a White person is the ultimate form of assimilation and signifies full acceptance by White society. Thus, an Asian American may marry a White person because she or he (consciously or unconsciously) wants to be fully accepted in White society. A related theory of hypergamy also suggests that Asian Americans marry Whites to increase their social status because Whites generally occupy the highest sociocultural position in the U.S. racial hierarchy. As when applied to the higher rate of African American men than African American women marrying a White person, these theories are condescending in tone given the presumption that the only reason a nonwhite (in this case an Asian American) would marry (or cohabit with) a White person would be to fulfill a need for acceptance and an increase in social status (Le, 2006b).

Some Asian Americans argue that the cultural stereotype of or fetish for Asian women is a major reason why many males (particularly White males) are attracted to Asian women. In this context, Asian women are seen primarily as sexual objects that can be controlled and used by men. These critics point out that in most areas of American popular culture, rarely do you see the opposite happening—Asian males as the subject of infatuation or sexual desire by White women. Rather, Asian males have been and continue to be purposely portrayed as nonsexual martial arts experts, nerds and geeks, or evil villains—images that serve to eliminate them as potential rivals to White males for the affection of Asian women (Le, 2006b).

INTERETHNIC MARRIAGES

Latinas/os As we have already seen, like Asian Americans, Latinas/os represent a diverse group. Although inhibitions remain about marriages between African Americans and Whites, Latinas/os, like Asian Americans, increasingly marry outside of their racial or ethnic groups. Among all newlyweds in 2008, 26 percent of Latinas/os married someone of a different race or ethnicity than their own. Some Latina/o groups are much more likely to marry non-Latinas/os than others. For instance, Puerto Ricans are most likely to be intermarried, followed by Mexicans and Cubans. Although the rates of interracial marriage vary from one Latina/o group to another, overall the rates have increased rather dramatically in recent decades. Marriage between Latinas/os and non-Latinas/os is one of the most prevalent types of intergroup unions, as Figure 8.5 shows a little more than one-fourth (28 percent) of all married couples of Latina/o origin are married to a non-Latina/o (U.S. Census Bureau, 2011a). As with most every other nonwhite group, the majority of these marriages are between Latinas/os and Whites.

As we have pointed out for other groups, most Latina/o interracial or interethnic marriages occur among young, higher-income, and well-educated individuals. In this context, two-thirds of Latinas/os who have attended or graduated from college marry outside their ethnic or racial group, as do one-third of all Latinas/os in top-income brackets. Interracial marriage is uncommon among Latinas/os who have less than a high school education. Latinas/os with a substantial income are five times more likely to marry a non-Latina/o than those who did not finish high school or college or who live in poverty. Interracial marriage is also closely linked to youth among Latinas/os, though to a lesser extent than among Asian Americans. About one-third of all married Latinas/os under age 35 are involved in an interracial marriage. However, for most Latina/o groups, gender does not seem to be a factor in these marriages, as the rates are about the same for Latinas and Latinos. In addition, like Asian Americans, native-born Latinas/os are much more likely than immigrant Latinas/os to marry a White person, with interracial marriage rates for all native-born married couples approaching 30 percent. And the longer a Latina/o has been in this country, the greater the prevalence of interracial or interethnic marriage.

The rates of interracial marriage are far higher in the West—in states that have a large Latina/o population—than in the rest of the country. For example, non-Latina/o Whites and Latina/o marriages are approximately four to five times more common in California and Texas than in states that have relatively smaller Latina/o populations. On the other hand, Latina/o interracial marriages are uncommon in states with small Latina/o populations such as North and South Dakota, West Virginia, Kentucky, Vermont, Maine, Mississippi, and Alabama (Lee and Edmonston, 2005; suro, 2001). Some researchers have suggested that this pattern of interracial or interethnic marriage among various Latina/o groups indicates that there is perhaps less "social distance" between Latinas/os and non-Latinas/os than among people from different other groups. Others suggest that two demographic characteristics of Latinas/os appear to contribute importantly to their intermarriage with non-Latinas/os, especially non-Latina/o Whites. First, few Latinas/os identify as Black, which greatly minimizes the White–Black barrier to mate selection and marriage that historically kept interracial marriage rates low. Second, the rapid growth of the Latina/o population has likely contributed to the secular increase in racial and ethnic intermarriage (Lee and Edmonston, 2005).

Trends in racial and Latina/o intermarriage affect American society in a number of ways and will continue to do so. The increasing rate of interracial marriage among all racial and ethnic groups has contributed to the growing number of multiracial children and families in American society. In addition, as more people identify with more than one race, the debate over how we will

think about race in the future and how best to label and count the population by race and Latina/o status will be an important one.

Whites Interethnic marriage among non-Latina/o Whites is now so commonplace that most people do not pay much attention to it. Estimates are that three-fourths of U.S.-born Whites are married interethnically. As with other groups, ethnic intermarriage among Whites varies with age and region of residence. Although the data indicate that the rate of interracial marriage has been increasing and seems dramatic for some groups, we must be careful in drawing conclusions from them. Keep in mind that many of these statistics represent geographic- or age-specific groups and should not be generalized to a total population. We should not lose sight of the fact that, overall, interracial marriages are still an extremely low percentage of the total marriages in this country. In addition, we should remember that White Americans are the most racially endogamous group when it comes to marriage; they are statistically the least likely to marry interracially, though in absolute terms they are part of an interracial marriage more than any other racial group due to their sheer numbers. This should not be surprising given the advantages of White privilege in the United States. Further, we should also remember that race and intimacy are not experienced in a vacuum. As we learned in Chapter 5, race is interrelated with many other social factors that combine to have a significant effect on if and whom we meet, fall in love with, cohabit with, and/or marry.

Interfaith Marriages

Marrying within one's own religion was the social norm in the United States until recently. Summaries of studies of interfaith marriages have consistently found Americans to be much like their partners in terms of religion. In the 1980s, for example, 93 percent of Protestants were married to Protestants, 88 percent of Jews were married to Jews, and 82 percent of Catholics were married to Catholics (Glenn, 1982). Recent statistics on who marries whom suggest that Americans are much more willing to cross religious than racial boundaries in selecting a partner. For example, more than a quarter of married Americans have a spouse of a different faith. That statistic increases to 37 percent when Protestants from different denominations are included (for example, Protestants who are married to another Protestant from a different denominational family, such as a Baptist who is married to a Methodist). Religious intermarriage rates are much higher today than in the past among all religious groups except Fundamentalist Christians. Next to those who are unaffiliated with a religion, Buddhist have the highest interfaith marriages (55 percent) followed by Mainline Protestants, 46 percent of whom are married to someone of a different faith. Among other religious groups, 32 percent of Evangelical Protestants 31 percent of Jews, and 22 percent of Catholics are in interfaith marriages. Hindus and Mormons have the lowest rate of marriage outside their religion—10 percent and 17 percent, respectively (Pew Forum on Religion and Public Life, 2008). In recent years, Americans have been moving toward more religiously tolerant attitudes, which might account, at least in part, for the high interfaith marriage rate among some religious groups as well as the fact that in a recent study of attitudes toward interreligious marriage, only 27 percent of women and 15 percent of men indicated that they would not marry someone of a different religious background. Some scholars have suggested that the increase in religious intermarriage is because religion generally has lost some of its power and control over people's lives.

Like interracial marriages, interfaith marriages vary according to location and population. One researcher found, for example, that cities such as New York, whose population includes a large number of Catholics and Jews, have a higher than average incidence of cross-faith (Jewish–Catholic) marriages. Likewise, Catholics and Lutherans exhibit a higher than average rate of intermarriage in states such as Pennsylvania, Iowa, and Minnesota, where the population is almost evenly split between the two religious denominations. Gender is also a factor in some interfaith marriages. For instance, Jewish men are a bit more likely to marry outside their faith than Jewish women. This could be due primarily to the fact that the home is the focal point for the practice of Judaism, and women set the spiritual tone.

Most religions actively encourage same-faith marriages. One reason is the belief that cross-faith marriages tend to weaken people's religious beliefs, values, and behavior, leading to a loss of faith not to mention a loss of church membership. The pattern of interfaith marriage is particularly evident today among Jews. Since 1945, the percentage of Jews in America has declined from 4 to 2 percent. In 1945, only 1 in 10 Jews was married to a non-Jew, whereas one in 2 are today (Safire, 1995). Jewish rabbis, having long expressed a concern over the decline in the number of Jews, were so concerned about the high rate at which Jews were marrying non-Jews that in 1973 the Reform Judaism's Central Conference of American Rabbis denounced interfaith marriages, declaring that such marriages were contrary to Jewish tradition and discouraged rabbis from officiating at them. Consequently, many rabbis today will not officiate at an interfaith wedding.

Although interfaith couples are less often the victims of society's disapproval than are interracial couples, cross-faith marriages are not without difficulties. Deeply held religious beliefs are an important part of our core personality. If we believe very strongly in a particular religious ideology, to what extent will we compromise? Partners from different religions must confront a number of issues such as choosing a religion for their children and deciding which holidays to observe. These are not insurmountable barriers, of course, but they do require that a couple closely examine the ramifications of marrying across faith and find solutions that are mutually satisfying.

Although interfaith marriages are rising, according to some statistics it seems that they are failing fast as well. Some studies indicate that racially and religiously heterogamous marriages tend to be more stressful and less stable and, in general, are three times more likely to end in divorce or separation than are religiously homogamous marriages. In addition interfaith marriages have slightly lower levels of satisfaction than do homogamous marriages (Riley, 2010; Mahoney, 2005). Other researchers, however, have found no evidence that interreligious marriages are any less satisfying or successful than religiously and racially homogamous marriages (see, for example, Hughes and Dickson, 2005; Williams and Lawler, 2003). As with homogamous marriages, many factors affect the success of heterogamous marriages. Lack of familial, societal, and religious support; cultural hostility; and differences in background can often undermine the stability and success of these marriages. Two other critical factors in determining the success of all marriages, heterogamous and homogamous, are the ability to communicate openly and honestly and the ability to manage conflicts that arise within these relationships. The concluding section of this chapter focuses on the issues of marital satisfaction, communication, and conflict management and resolution in marriages.

Marital Satisfaction, Communication, and Conflict Resolution

Research has consistently found that married people, compared with unmarried people, report being happier, healthier, and generally more satisfied with their lives (although the "happiness gap" between married and unmarried individuals has closed considerably over the last several years). What is it about the quality of married life that makes it more satisfying than a single lifestyle? Researchers exploring the quality of married life have used a variety of terms, the most notable of which are marital success, marital happiness, and marital satisfaction. Because marital success is a relative concept—it depends on who is defining it—researchers have based much of their findings on marital satisfaction as reported by married couples and on the divorce rate.

SUCCESSFUL MARRIAGE

How successful are American marriages? On the one hand, although the divorce rate leveled off in the 1990s, almost two-thirds of the marriages entered into in recent years are expected to end in divorce or separation. According to some researchers, these statistics are a clear indication of a decline in marital success, the causes of which are attributed to a number of factors: for those who marry the motivation for marriage has become fairly selfish; individuals expect a lot from their partners in a marriage but are largely

There are likely to be times of disagreement, conflict, and fighting within a marriage or other intimate relationship. Rather than allow these conflicts to destroy their relationship, couples can use the skills of "fair fighting," whereby they agree to talk about their problems without shouting, blaming, finger-pointing, or name-calling. If the couple cannot resolve their issues, participation in marriage counseling or therapy may be an option to help the couple work through their issues by learning skills such as conflict resolution.

unwilling to give in order to get; the increased flexibility in marital roles has resulted in a breakdown in the consensus about what it means to be a wife or husband; the easing of moral, religious, and legal barriers to divorce has made people less willing and able to make needed commitments to and investments in marriage than they were in the past (Popenoe, 2008; The State of Our Unions 2007). On the other hand, general survey data repeatedly show that although the rate at which couples report marital happiness or satisfaction has declined in recent years, an overwhelming majority of married couples say that they are happy or very happy and describe their marriage as satisfying (Jones, 2007; Carroll, 2005a).

What are the factors that distinguish happily married couples from unhappy or dissatisfied couples? There is a vast literature on marital satisfaction, happiness, quality, and stability. Some of the more common factors elucidated in this literature are being in love; sharing aims, goals, and other important beliefs; sexual compatibility; financial security; having children; the amount of time spent together; family rituals; self-disclosure, open communication, and the ability to resolve conflict in a positive manner. In fact, most research in this area has found open and effective or positive communication and successful conflict resolution to be essential to the success of marriages and other intimate relationships (for example, Gottman, 2004).

EFFECTIVE COMMUNICATION

Indeed, effective and positive communication is essential to any relationship, married or unmarried. Two important components of communication are what is said and how it is said. You have probably heard the expression, "It's not what you say, it's how you say it." For instance, it is possible to say "I'm very happy in this relationship" several different ways. An individual could say it lovingly, sincerely, or sarcastically. In good communication, what we say should be consistent with how we say it. Also, communication involves not just words, but also gestures, actions, intonations, and sounds. Sometimes the messages that couples give to each other are misinterpreted, misread, or missed completely. Missed messages and misinterpretations can build on themselves and result in conflict and hostility in a relationship. Clinical psychologist Joel Block (1981) provides this example:

> A couple have just taken a moonlight walk by the ocean. They sit down by the water's edge. The woman says, "Let's go inside, I'm sleepy." The man responds, "It's nice out here. Why don't we lie

and rest here?" The woman, angry, storms into the house. The man, equally angry, gets dressed and drives off to a local bar.

What has happened here is miscommunication. When the woman suggested going inside because she was "sleepy," she was actually attempting to communicate to her partner that she wanted to make love in the house. Her partner, on the other hand, was attempting to communicate his wish to make love on the beach under the moonlight. According to Block, neither communicated her or his wishes directly; the evening thus ended with both partners feeling rejected and angry. When this type of miscommunication becomes a pattern of interaction in a relationship, a couple could find themselves continuously upset and irritated with each other. According to family therapist Joan Zientek, situations such as this could severely strain an already precarious line of communication and hamper the couple's ability to calmly and rationally generate options and select solutions that, at least in part, will meet each partner's needs (see the Strengthening Marriages and Families box on page 266). Because conflict is a natural and normal part of all relationships and the inability or failure to deal with it can be destructive, the field of family therapy has become an increasingly popular method by which couples seek to resolve relationship conflicts. It is estimated that close to one-half of American households seek some sort of counseling or therapy.

Despite our best desire to communicate, many of us fall short. Some of the most common communication problems identified by researchers and therapists include not listening, blaming, criticizing and/or nagging, not responding to issues as they emerge, using scapegoats, using the silent treatment, and using coercion or physical threats. One of the ways that couples can learn to communicate directly with each other is by conducting what Block calls "marital checkups." This involves identifying and appraising the assets and liabilities of the relationship. If done responsibly, the marital checkup can help the couple learn more about each other's needs, desires, and expectations.

SELF-DISCLOSURE

Self-disclosure is an important element in effective communication and higher levels of marital satisfaction. Self-disclosure commonly refers simply to telling another person about oneself; to honestly offer one's thoughts and feelings for the other's perusal, hoping that truly open communication will follow. Research on

Pros and Cons

YOU HAVE TO KEEP THE LINES OF COMMUNICATION OPEN.

THAT'S WHEN OUR PROBLEMS BEGAN.

IT WAS ONLY AFTER WE BEGAN COMMUNICATING WE REALIZED WE DIDN'T LIKE EACH OTHER.

TALKS WITH FAMILY THERAPIST JOAN ZIENTEK

Communication, Conflict Resolution, and Problem Solving in Marriages and Intimate Relationships

How Often Is Communication a Factor in Marital Satisfaction? Communication is one of the most powerful factors influencing the quality of the couple's relationship. Whether it is verbal or nonverbal, communication cuts through all aspects of a couple's life. Couples who exhibit effective communication skills are better equipped to deal with the inevitable conflicts and problems that accompany cohabitation and the construction of a life together. Although the communication of facts and ideas is necessary just to carry out the business of the day, it is not enough. Couples who share on this surface level will, in time, find themselves growing apart. On the other hand, true intimacy in a relationship comes from sharing on a more personal level. The sharing of feelings, goals, dreams, worries, fears, and so on, is the emotional glue that binds couples together and gets them through the rough spots. This kind of sharing, of course, demands a certain level of vulnerability and can only occur in an emotionally safe atmosphere. Being a good listener is the complement to emotional sharing. Each party needs to listen without judgment or interruption. They also need to be able to give and receive feedback about their partner's behavior without fear of reprisal, retaliation, or the demand for change. Patterns of communication in a marriage are influenced by the family background of each partner. This includes their parent's communication patterns and the emotional climate of the home in which they were raised. Were conflicts avoided or confronted? Was there a supportive and encouraging atmosphere, or were the parents depreciating, distant, or emotionally or physically absent? Each partner's birth order as well as their individual personality and level of maturity also play into the mix. Thus, the communication dyad is influenced by a multitude of factors.

What Kinds of Strategies Can Couples Adopt to Improve Communication? One of the most central communication skills is the ability to give and receive feedback from the other in a way that does not diminish either party. Speaking for yourself, giving messages that disclose the impact of the behavior of one person or the other is far more effective than using name-calling and negative labeling in an attempt to demonstrate displeasure. Being able to deal with feedback is also critical. Harville Hendrix, in his book, *Getting the Love You Want*, suggests a three-step process:

- *Mirroring:* Paraphrasing your partner's comment.
- *Validating:* Letting your partner know that what she or he says makes sense, at least, from her or his perspective.
- *Empathy:* Being able to imagine your partner's feelings.

Using this three-step process, though critical, can be difficult. It requires that the person hold on to her or his own feelings and perceptions, often intense anger, while truly hearing, understanding, and supporting her or his partners concerns. In addition, couples need to treat their marriage as an entity in itself that needs nurturing. They need to take time for each other on a daily, weekly, and monthly basis and not merely give half-hearted attention to their partner as they attend to the needs of children or wait for vacation time to catch up with each other. Simple things like having a cup of coffee after dinner (without interruption from the children or the phone), going for a walk, or sharing a hobby can keep the communication lines open. In addition, the planning of positive exchanges or little surprises, doing small favors, and sending cards or e-mails that show appreciation all make each party feel valued and appreciated and thus more open to the needs of the other.

Is All Conflict Bad for a Relationship? Conflict is a natural and normal part of all relationships. No two people will see a situation in the same way, have the exact same needs at the same time, or have the same priorities as they create a life together. The resolution of conflict in a positive manner can bring new life and direction to a relationship; it can prevent the storage of resentment on the part of one or both partners, thus allowing each problem its own day in court without the attachment of past unresolved issues. It can also bring a deeper understanding of the needs and vulnerabilities of each person and, many times, in the long run, lead to better decision making than if the decision in question were solely based on the views of only one of the partners.

What Strategies Can Couples Use to Resolve Conflicts? One of the main factors that impede the resolution of conflicts between partners is the lack of ability and/or skill to see a situation from another person's point of view. Couples waste much time demanding, convincing, and manipulating the other so they can get their way. This often results in anger, resentment, and the stifling of their creative energies that might, under more positive circumstances, stand them in good stead in resolving the conflict at hand. If they cannot control their emotions or if they are not able to express their feelings in such a way that they can be heard, they are not in a position to calmly and rationally generate options and select a solution that, at least in part, will meet the needs of both partners. Couples can learn the skills of "fair fighting," whereby they agree to talk about one problem at a time, refrain from interrupting, name-calling, counterattacking, blaming, and bringing third parties into the conflict. One or both parties may not be able to use these skills, not because they are incapable of learning them, but because they have a deep need to control the relationship. In these situations, therapy may be required to help each party work through personal fears so they can grow to truly be a partner in the relationship.

self-disclosure consistently shows that reciprocal self-disclosure (when both partners self-disclose) is positively related to marital satisfaction. When couples are open and self-disclosing, it creates togetherness and closeness and thus higher marital satisfaction. On the other hand, marital satisfaction is low when one partner is self-disclosing and the other is not, one is more self-disclosing than the other, or if neither partner is self-disclosing.

Some researchers have found that although marital satisfaction increases as the level of self-disclosure increases, there is a leveling off, whereby at the very highest levels of self-disclosure there is a decrease in marital satisfaction. One explanation for this phenomenon is that couples who exhibit high levels of self-disclosure tend to be more likely to express their opinions to and about each other more readily, whether positive or critical and disapproving. In turn, criticism and disapproval can become a problem in a relationship and can lead to lower relationship satisfaction. As in many other aspects of heterosexual relationships, women and men tend to differ in terms of disclosure, although the research findings are somewhat mixed. For example, some researchers have found women to be more disclosing than men, whereas others have found no major difference between the sexes. A major difference in female and male disclosure is in terms of the target person to whom they will disclose. Women tend to disclose more to same-sex friends, whereas men tend to disclose more to romantic partners. In contrast, research indicates that lesbians and gays are equally disclosing in their respective relationships. Perhaps one of the greatest consequences of self-disclosure for marital (or intimacy) satisfaction is that when it is done well, it takes much of the guesswork out of interpersonal communication.

In general, successful communication includes a number of other conditions and skills. Two basic conditions are a nonthreatening, noncoercive atmosphere and mutual commitment. In addition, a couple must be willing to change as the needs and demands of the relationship change. Some of the key skills that are important for successful communication are the ability to identify, accept responsibility for, and resolve problems, as well as a willingness to listen and negotiate conflict. Based on now 25-plus years of observing couples interact in the "Marriage Lab" at his Seattle Marital and Family Institute, research psychologist John Gottman (1994a,b) argues that most marriages and similar relationships fall into one of three categories: *validating partnerships,* which are dominated by affection and compromise; *volatile partnerships,* in which conflict is intense, but so is passion; and *others,* in which a pair of conflict-avoiders agree to disagree. All these relationships can work and all require conflict, both as fuel and as a venting mechanism. More importantly, however, to be successful they all require many more acts of positive reinforcement than of negative interaction. According to Gottman, the real reason marriages succeed or fail is really very simple: Couples who stay together are *nice* to each other more often than not. That is, Gottman claims that couples who are satisfied with their relationship maintain a five-to-one ratio of positive to negative moments in their relationship (they are five times as nice as they are nasty to each other). Couples who are unhappy and/or dissatisfied with their relationship have let the ratio slip below one-to-one. Couples can improve their relationship with some simple practices during moments of conflict, such as taking a deep breath, calming down, listening and speaking nondefensively, trying a morning leave-taking, a chat at the end of the day, or private time together without the children or other interferences. Gottman has found that successful relationships are not those that never have conflict, rather they are those in which the couple recognizes when there is a problem and tries to fix it.

CONFLICT AND CONFLICT RESOLUTION

Even when couples have positive and effective communication skills and high levels of self-disclosure, there are likely to be times of disagreement, conflict, and fighting. Several major areas of marriage and family life generally contribute to conflict in marriages: money, sex, children, power, loyalty, division of marital and family tasks, privacy, work, in-laws, friends, religion, and substance abuse. Gottman believes the four most destructive behaviors to marital happiness are criticism, contempt, defensiveness, and stonewalling:

- Criticism involves attacking one's partner's personality or character rather than complaining about a specific behavior. For example, a healthy and specific complaint might be "I wish you would spend more time with me." A generalizing and blaming attack on one's personality or character might be "There's something wrong with you. You never spend time with me."
- Contempt involves intense and intentional negative thoughts about a person and can be manifest in a number of ways, for example, subtle or not-so-subtle put-downs, hostile jokes, mocking facial expressions, or name-calling.
- Defensiveness is generally a response to being attacked or put down. It involves making excuses, tossing back counterattacks and insults, and denying responsibility.
- Stonewalling means that the couple has essentially stopped communicating. They have reached a point where they refuse to respond to one another even in self-defense. According to Gottman, when a couple reaches this stage, one or both of them are thinking negative thoughts about the other most of the time, and, if their behavior is unchecked, the marriage will likely end in divorce.

When conflict arises in a relationship, as it inevitably does, it does not have to be destructive. Researchers have found that some conflict can be constructive. Conflict management is the key. When conflict is managed or resolved through negotiation and compromise, it can strengthen the bonds of affection between partners. When it is dealt with ineffectively, it can lower satisfaction and even contribute to the dissolution of the relationship. Several researchers and marital therapists have suggested some of the following strategies to resolve marital conflict: Clearly define the problem, demonstrate a mutual respect for each other, agree to cooperate with each other, and agree to make decisions together.

Couples in successful marriages find ways to manage conflict so that each partner can maintain her or his differences while working collectively to find a negotiated solution that is satisfactory to both parties. According to Gottman (1994a, b), fighting, whether rare or frequent, does not have to be destructive. The important thing in a marriage is to find a compatible fighting style, not to stop fighting altogether. In fact, in many cases fighting can be one of the healthiest things a couple can do for their relationship. More important, the key to a happy and successful marriage or other intimate relationship is relatively simple: Learn to calm down, learn to speak and listen to one another nondefensively, validate one another, and practice the former steps over and over until they become routine, even in the heat of an argument.

Consider the intimate relationships in which you are or have been involved. Can you distinguish particular patterns of communication in these relationships? What are or were the major barriers to communication? What strategies of conflict resolution have you and your partners employed in these relationships? Did you learn anything about conflict resolution from your parents' relationship? How can you improve communication and conflict resolution in your close relationships?

Supporting Marriages and Families

Although those who advocate a return to how families *used to be* claim they support marriages and families, their critics accuse them of trying to legislate morality through a variety of laws, ordinances, constitutional changes and amendments, and state and federal legislative actions. Many of these actions are extreme, and rather than supporting marriages and families, critics argue that they penalize those who fall outside such narrow definitions of marriages and families (see, for instance, the Debating Social Issues box).

Debating Social Issues

UNWED AND UNWANTED: SHOULD CITIES LEGISLATE MORALITY?

Foundray Loving and Olivia Shelltrack

In 2006, a cohabiting couple, Olivia Shelltrack and Fondray Loving, purchased a five-bedroom three-bath house in Black Jack, Missouri, and moved into the home with their three children. However, the couple faced not only losing the house of their dreams but also being evicted from the city of Black Jack itself. It seems that Black Jack has a city ordinance that applies to unmarried couples with children. Under this Black Jack law, a home cannot be inhabited by three or more individuals not related by "blood, marriage or adoption." Unmarried and cohabiting for 13 years along with their three children, the couple was told that their household failed to meet Black Jack's definition of a *family*. Consequently, the couple was denied an occupancy permit for the house. According to Shelltrack, the law essentially means that you can have one child living in your house if you are not married, but more than that, you cannot. Shelltrack and Loving were engaged, but for financial reasons had delayed getting married so that they could buy a home and start a business (Kim, 2006; Goldstein, 2006).

The couple appealed the denial of an occupancy permit at a hearing before Black Jack's Board of Adjustment, where they were asked personal questions—about their relationship, such as why they didn't just get married; about their children; and about their previous home in another city—after which the board denied the couple's request. Shelltrack then filed an appeal with the Black Jack municipal court. A year later, the Missouri Court of Appeals upheld the ruling against the couple, who had lived in the home since 1981 (Kim, 2006; Goldstein, 2006).

Black Jack is not the only city with such an ordinance that defines what kind of family can live within its limits. Most municipalities in the St. Louis, Missouri, area have similar, if not identical, rules. The federal Fair Housing Act prohibits discrimination based on race, color, religion, national origin, gender, disability, and families with children. Most states include additional protected classes such as marital status. However, Missouri does not. Because some people believe the Black Jack ordinance crosses the line into discriminatory zoning, discrimination based on marital status and a denial of the right to live wherever one wants and can afford the ordinance has come under fire. In what seems to be one of the latest battlegrounds in the war on family values, various individuals and groups have drawn clear lines and as with most controversial issues, it has its supporters and detractors.

City officials such as the mayor of Black Jack and others defend the ordinance. They claim that the ordinance is about overcrowding and has nothing to do with defining family, family values, religion, marriage, or unwed cohabitation. Proponents of the ordinance claim that its sole purpose is to prevent overcrowding in houses and ultimately the schools of Black Jack—that it is designed to safeguard neighborhoods from everything from fraternities and group homes to crack houses (Goldstein, 2006).

On the other side of the issue, Shelltrack and others argue that the city is trying to regulate morality with the ordinance (Kim, 2006).

Given the history of the ordinance and its implementation, opponents contend that although the mayor and others deny it, the ordinance is indeed about marriage, family, and the city's attempt to legislate morality. Those against such ordinances argue that people should not be forced to marry just to live in their home. They also contend that Black Jack's definition of a family is too narrow and restrictive and is not compatible with the reality of intimacy and family life in twenty-first-century America. For instance, in Black Jack, family is defined as "an individual or two or more persons related by blood, marriage, or adoption, or a group of not more than three persons who need not be related by blood, marriage or adoption, living together as a single nonprofit housekeeping unit in a dwelling unit" (Kim, 2006:2). It also discriminates against lesbian and gay couples and immigrants who

often rely on living in larger groups to afford housing and who fall outside Black Jack's economically and heterosexually biased definition of family. Moreover, Shelltrack and others argue that a piece of paper—legal or otherwise—does not make a family. Shelltrack says that she, her fiancé, and their children are a family; their children are not children of an unmarried couple—rather they are children of two loving parents (Kim, 2006).

What do you think? On which side of the debate do you fall? Explain your position. Is the Black Jack ordinance essentially an attempt to regulate morality? Should cities and/or the state be in the business of regulating morality? If yes, why? Who gets to define what is a family, what are family values, and so forth? Whose definitions should prevail? What other groups beside the unmarried are discriminated against by the Black Jack ordinance?

If we as a society are serious about supporting marriages and families, we must make the concerns and issues of marriages and families a central national, local, and community priority and not work to undermine them. Rather than develop and implement policies, and programs that discourage some forms of marriages and families and reward others, we should develop and implement policies, programs, services, and resources that encourage and support the diversity of marriages and families in today's society. The provision of state and federal monies as well as that of private organizations should include support for skill-based marriage and parenting education, premarital education and counseling, marriage

education and counseling, and other services that would support marriages and families. Supporting marriages and families should be less about religious moralizing and more about providing tangible support such as marriage, family and couples or partner education courses, training, and other resources. Local communities can develop programs through various congregations and community organizations that help women and men in intimate relationships, whether legal marriage, cohabitation, or other, develop and maintain healthy and stable relationships. The divisiveness over which marriage and family structure is valid, in the long run, is detrimental to all marriage and family forms.

Writing Your Own Script

PREPARING YOUR RELATIONSHIP CONTRACT

The decision to marry or cohabit leads to a number of other related issues and areas of understanding that couples should consider, discuss, and resolve before establishing their living arrangement. Many couples have found it useful to write personal

contracts that clarify their feelings and expectations for the marriage or cohabitative relationship. To be most effective, this exercise should be done with your partner. It may be easier, however, if you and your partner write separate contracts

and then compare and discuss each other's contract before writing a final version that represents your collective view and consensus. Prenuptial and personal contracts include the

(continued on next page)

(continued from previous page)

expectations the couple bring to their relationship. In the exercise that follows, we present the items commonly included in marriage and personal contracts. It is not necessary that you cover every item simply because it is here. Concern yourself only with those areas relevant to your particular situation. Or feel free to add topics or issues relevant to you and your life. (Note: If you choose to remain single, either permanently or on a temporary basis, many of these items will apply to you as well. Although you do not need to consider a partner, reflecting on these items can help you get in touch with yourself as well as build a more satisfying lifestyle.) Under each topic, we present some questions to consider. These questions are not exhaustive.

Relevant History

Couples often assume they know all they need to know about each other without really discussing their past. However, a lack of knowledge can sometimes lead to problems later on.

Questions to Consider

Will we try to share all aspects of our history that might affect our intended relationship, for example, former marriages and our own and our families' health histories?

Division of Labor and Responsibilities

A source of difficulty for many couples is the perception of inequity in the performance of household tasks. Often partners have different assumptions about who should do these tasks. Some people believe household tasks should be allocated on the basis of gender even when both partners are employed full-time.

Questions to Consider

1. What rights do we each have as individuals, and what role expectations do we have for each other? How will we divide household responsibilities? Who will cook, clean, make the shopping lists,

shop, do laundry, make house and car repairs, do yard work, wash windows, plan entertainment, take out the trash, care for children, take care of finances, pay bills, and perform all the other tasks of daily living?
2. How will decisions be made— individually or jointly? How will we resolve differences of opinion?

Sexual Exclusiveness

One of the reasons some people give for dissolving their relationship is a partner's extramarital affairs. Such behavior can lead to feelings of betrayal, jealousy, insecurity, and anger. Often couples do not discuss their views on sexual matters until after they are married or cohabiting, and sometimes they find that they have conflicting values in this area.

Questions to Consider

Will our relationship be sexually exclusive? What is our understanding about sexual access to each other? How will we communicate our personal desires? What are our feelings about outside relationships, both sexual and nonsexual? Would we feel threatened by outside relationships?

Money Matters

Money matters are issues that all of us have to deal with regardless of our marital status. Couples may not always share the same values concerning money and the things it can buy. As a way of keeping money and money management from becoming problems, it is wise for couples to discuss their values and expectations. Agreement on financial planning, spending, and management is a key ingredient in marital or relationship satisfaction.

Questions to Consider

1. How will we handle the ownership, distribution, and management of property before and after marriage? How will we decide on the contribution of each person to the total family income and support? Will it matter if one of us earns more than the other?
2. As a couple, how compatible are our spending (including the use of credit cards) and savings patterns? Are we both comfortable with these patterns, or do we need to make changes in them? What are our financial goals? What plans can we make to achieve these goals? Should we have joint or separate savings and checking accounts? What are the advantages and disadvantages of each arrangement?
3. Who will manage the family finances? How will we decide on a family budget? How will we decide how family money will be spent? Who will pay the bills and make the investments? How will we decide this? If one of us assumes this responsibility, how will that one keep the other informed about our financial matters? Will each of us be able to manage if something happens to the other?

Family Surname

Names are important symbols of identity. In some cultures a newly married couple incorporates both family names into their surname. The cultural tradition in the United States is for a wife to take her husband's surname. Many couples, however, are questioning this practice.

Questions to Consider

Will we both carry the same surname? Will we hyphenate our name or use a new one? If we have children, what surname will they have?

Selecting a Place to Live

Where we live is an important decision that we make in adulthood. We spend a tremendous amount of time in the place we live. Thus, where and under what conditions we live is a major factor in how we perceive the quality of our lives.

Questions to Consider

What type of housing do we want? How will we decide on our place of residence? How important are each of these factors in our decision:

proximity to family, schools, work; convenience to community services and public transportation; the area's tax base; the overall safety and well-being of the neighborhood? What can we afford? Which is preferable for us, to buy or to rent?

Religion

Religion can be a source of comfort and support to couples, or it can be a source of conflict. If conflict occurs over religion, it may be because partners belong to different religions, have different values, or do not attach the same importance to religion.

Questions to Consider

What role will religion play in our relationship? Are we religiously compatible? Is this important to us? Will we attend services together? Separately? Will we raise our children in a specific religion?

Relationships with Others

In many marriages today, couples often experience difficulty in trying to manage work, marriage, and other social responsibilities. Finding time to spend together may require making adjustments in the time devoted to other relationships.

Questions to Consider

How do we feel about each other's relatives and friends? How much interaction do we want to have with them? How will we decide where to spend our holidays and vacations? How will relationships with others be determined? How will we manage to keep time for ourselves?

Conflict Resolution

Every couple will experience conflict in their relationship at one time or another. The critical factor in the relationship is not the experience of conflict but rather how the conflict is handled.

Questions to Consider

What will we do when things do not seem to be working out right? What mechanisms can we create for resolving disagreements? Will we be willing to get counseling if we are having problems? What are our attitudes regarding divorce?

Renewability, Change, and Termination of Contract

People and conditions change over time. An effective contract allows for these possibilities. Couples are well advised to have periodic reviews of how the contract is working and what changes, if any, should be made.

Questions to Consider

How will we provide for a periodic reevaluation and change (if necessary) in this contract? Under what conditions will we terminate this contract?

These are only a few of the many issues and decisions we all face in the course of our lives. For example, issues of work, jobs, or careers, or those concerning having or not having children are discussed in other chapters of this textbook. The decisions that are made will vary from one individual and family to the next. No single pattern can meet everyone's needs. Each individual and family must decide what arrangement is best for them. The most critical factor in all these areas is communication. All too frequently couples do not discuss these issues before becoming partners, with the result that they often begin a relationship with unrealistic expectations. Although communicating on these issues early in a relationship cannot by itself guarantee happiness or long-term stability, it can improve the probability of achieving these goals.

SUMMARY

Although we have witnessed some important changes in marriage and family patterns, most Americans will marry at least once in their lifetime. People marry for a number of reasons, such as having a committed relationship and someone to share life with. Marriage means different things to different people. For some people, the key to marriage is commitment. For others, marriage is a sacrament, a sacred union, or holy state under the direct authority of their God. Most people do not think of marriage as a legal contract. When two people marry, however, they are agreeing to abide by the terms of a marriage contract that they had no part in drafting. Although each individual state defines the rights and obligations of the marriage contract, all states specify who can marry whom and at what age they may do so. Marriage is a civil right that applies almost exclusively to heterosexual couples in U.S. society albeit that lesbians and gays can now legally marry in six states: Massachusetts, Connecticut, Iowa, Vermont New Hampshire, and New York as well as in the District of Columbia.

Historically, the marriage contract put women at a decided disadvantage. Although the process of marriage is different today, in many states women continue to lose legal rights when they marry. Marriage in the United States is imbued with rituals and traditions, many of which date back to ancient societies. Although many people continue to abide by tradition when they marry, an increasing number of people are modifying, changing, or creating their own personal marriage rituals.

Like other relationships, marriage is experienced differently depending on factors such as race, class, and gender. For example, researchers point out that women and men experience marriage differently. This has led several researchers to describe marriage as containing two marriages: hers and his. The female–male differences in the experience of marriage, though largely hidden, have a tremendous effect on the mental and physical health of wives and husbands.

Getting married represents a significant change in the lives of a couple. Marital adjustment is an important part of the marriage experience. Couples must continuously make adjustments over the life course of the marriage. The success of the relationship depends, in large part, on the degree to which both partners are able to adjust. Satisfying, well-adjusted marriages vary a great deal. A typology of marital relationships representing marital adjustment includes the conflict-habituated, the devitalized, the passive-congenial, the vital, and the total relationship.

Whenever two people live together over some period of time, some conflict is bound to occur. Conflict does not have to be destructive, however. Couples in successful marriages learn to manage or resolve conflict in such a way that is satisfactory to both parties. An essential element in managing or resolving conflict is open, honest, and direct communication. If couples are committed to the relationship, they will try to manage or resolve conflict in a constructive way. Moreover, whatever problem-solving style a couple uses, the relationship can be successful as long as positive feelings and interactions outweigh negative ones by a ratio of five to one.

KEY TERMS

principle of legitimacy	social marriage	fornication	conjugal rights	prenuptial agreement
sacrament	bigamy	affinal relatives	personal marriage	marital adjustment
legal marriage	adultery	coverture	agreement	heterogamous marriage

QUESTIONS FOR STUDY AND REFLECTION

1. Why do people marry? If you are married, why did you marry? If you are not married but plan to wed, why are you going to marry? Ask three different married couples—one in their 60s, one in their 40s, and one in their 20s—why they married and what were their expectations of marriage? Do the women and men differ in their appraisals of marriage? Are there generational differences across couples? If so, how do you explain these differences?

2. Thinking about yourself, your parents, or some couple you are close to, do you (they) have a successful marriage? What makes it successful? How important is communication to the success of the marriage? What communication skills does each partner possess?

3. As you have read in this chapter, important changes have taken place in marriage and family patterns. If you have computer access, locate Web sites pertaining to marriage. Classify the types of Web sites that you find on this topic. What are the most salient issues covered in these sites? How do these issues relate to the topics you have read in this chapter? Which of these issues seem to be Internet-specific? Gender-specific? Race/ethnicity- or class-specific? Are there issues that are different depending on one's sexual orientation? Explain.

4. Jessie Bernard's typology of marriages along gender lines is a classic in the field of sociology. Do you agree that marriages are experienced differently by women and men? Can you give evidence from your own experiences or the experiences of people you know to support or refute Bernard's argument?

ADDITIONAL RESOURCES

SOCIOLOGICAL STUDIES

ROOT, MARIA. 2001. *Love's Revolution: Interracial Marriage.* Philadelphia, PA: Temple University Press. At a time when race is much discussed yet less understood the author of this book presents an insightful social psychological study of people who are challenging the meaning of race in America today through the growing phenomenon of interracial marriage. The author traces the social changes that account for the growth of interracial marriage, the social and historical forces that both strain and strengthen such marriages as well as the lingering prejudices and false beliefs that oppress racially mixed families.

The book is based on more than 200 interviews of people from a wide spectrum of racial and ethnic backgrounds who speak out about their views and experiences; these partners, family members, and children of mixed race marriages confirm that the barriers are gradually eroding, but they also testify to the heartache caused by family opposition and disapproving strangers. Root traces race prejudice to the various institutions that were structured to maintain White privilege, but the heart of the book is her analysis of what happens when people of different races decide to marry.

LOUDEN, JENNIFER. 1994. *The Couple's Comfort Book: A Creative Guide for Renewing Passion, Pleasure, and Commitment.* San Francisco: Harper. A usable compendium of imaginative activities that couples can do together. It is cross-referenced so that you can skip around in the book and design your own program of relationship rebirth.

NOCK, STEVEN. L. 1998. *Marriage in Men's Lives.* New York: Oxford University Press. In this provocative book, the author uses surveys to examine how and why marriage affects men's lives so much, and to study marriage as a means for developing and sustaining masculinity. The author draws some interesting and far-reaching conclusions about the nature of marriage and presents an interesting and innovative model for a new marriage.

WAITE, LINDA, AND MAGGIE GALLAGHER. 2000. *The Case for Marriage.* Cambridge, MA: Harvard University Press. The authors focus on the benefits of marriage for all concerned: women, men, and children. It has an assortment of chapters covering a variety of relevant topics, including emotional well-being, sexuality, physical health, family violence, and children's outcomes.

FILM

Bee Season. 2005. Based on the best-selling novel by Myla Goldberg, this film is about a wife and mother who begins a downward emotional spiral as her husband avoids their collapsing marriage by immersing himself in his 11-year-old daughter's quest to become a spelling bee champion.

Monsoon Wedding. 2001. An insightful film about two young Punjabis from affluent Indian families coming together through an arranged marriage. The film consists of five intersecting stories, each dealing with different aspects of life and love as they cross boundaries of class, continent, and ideas of morality.

LITERARY WORKS

MCKINNEY-WHETSTONE, DIANE. 1996. *Tumbling.* New York: Scribner (paperback). A delightful novel and heartwarming story of a young couple in Philadelphia during the 1940s and 1950s who are unable to consummate their marriage because of a horrible secret in the wife's past. Despite their problems, the couple care deeply for one another and they struggle to keep their unconventional marriage and family whole. This novel is suspenseful, tragic, humorous, and, above all, useful for a sociological study and discussion of marriage, family, and intimacy.

AHERN, CECELIA. 2007. *P.S. I Love You.* New York: HarperCollins. Set in Ireland, this novel is about a woman (Holly) who married the love of her life (Gerry). When his life is taken by an illness, it takes the life out of Holly. The only one who can help her is the person who is no longer there. But Gerry planned ahead and before he died, he wrote Holly a series of 10 letters, each signed off with "P.S. I Love You," that will guide her, not only through her grief but in rediscovering herself. Holly's mother and best friends worry that Gerry's letters are keeping Holly tied to the past, but, in fact, each letter pushes her further into a new future. With Gerry's words as her guide, Holly embarks on a journey of rediscovery in this story about marriage, grief, family, friendship and how a love so strong can turn the finality of death into new beginning for life. (This novel was adapted for film in 2007).

INTERNET

www.couples-place.com Online since 1996, this site provides a learning community for solving marriage problems, improving relationship skills, celebrating marriage, and achieving happiness with your partner. The site includes practical articles about relationships, forums about marriage and couple life, bulletin boards, a relationship satisfaction quiz, and many other resources.

www.bridesandgrooms.com An interesting site that provides a free bookstore and newsletter and provides a variety of links to subjects ranging from guides and ideas for weddings and honeymoons, premarital counseling, wedding shopping, wedding attire, wedding styles, and wedding music to marriage encounters to surveys on sex and marriage.

http://www.gayweddings.com This site offers a range of wedding services and packages for a civil ceremony or a wedding event. The site offers ideas and planning for "Two Brides" or "Two Grooms" weddings, wedding etiquette, gay wedding and planning consultation, destination wedding packages, wedding invitations, discussion boards and forums, and access to wedding seminars.

http://www.covenantmarriage.com A Web site for conservative, Christian-based Covenant Marriage Movement members. The site provides a range of services, including a Covenant Marriage Online store, Sunday Promotion, Covenant Events, Covenant Legislation, Covenant Counselors, Cooperating Ministry, and Couple Support.

Succeed with MyFamilyLab®
www.myfamilylab.com

Watch. Explore. Read. The New MyFamilyLab is designed just for you. Each chapter features a pre-test and post-test to help you learn and review key concepts and terms. Experience Marriages and Families in action with dynamic visual activities, videos, and readings to enhance your learning experience.

Here are a few activities you will find for this chapter.

Watch on **myfamilylab.com**

Video clips feature important concepts in the study of Marriages and Families. Watch:
• Love and Marriage

Explore on **myfamilylab.com**

Social Explorer is an interactive application that allows you to explore Census data through interactive maps. Explore the Social Explorer Activity:
• Patterns Within the Married Population

Read on **myfamilylab.com**

MyFamilyLab includes primary source readings from classic and contemporary sociologists from around the world. Read:
• Bernard: "The Two Marriages"

9

Reproduction and Parenting

What Will You Learn?

- Define and understand the sociological meaning of key terms.
- Describe how and why fertility rates in the United States have changed over the past centuries.
- Apply the sociological imagination to examine how our concepts of fatherhood have changed over time.
- Assess the pro and con arguments for restricting abortion.
- Increase your awareness and understanding of the similarities and differences of parent-child relations among different social classes and across race and ethnic groups.
- Question the effectiveness of different parenting styles.

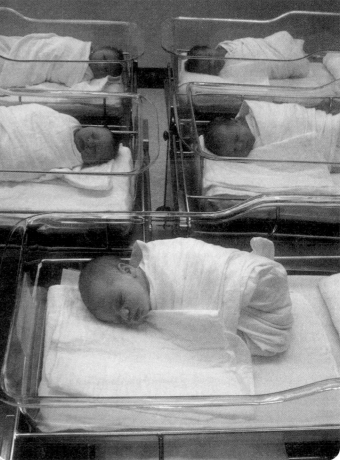

IN THE NEWS

Princeton, NJ

Having a child is one of the most exciting events in a person's life. But, sometimes it comes with strings attached. A recent Gallup poll asked Americans which sex they would prefer if they could have only one child. Forty percent responded that they would prefer a boy, 28 percent said they would prefer a girl and 26 percent said it didn't matter (Newport, 2011). This is not a recent development. When Gallup asked this question in 1941, the results were almost identical, 38 percent favored boys and only 24 percent favored girls. In the 10 times Gallup asked a similar question in the

(continued on next page)

(continued from previous page)

intervening 70 years, the results always tilted toward a male preference.

This preference is not uniform across all groups. Gender, age, and education all play a role. According to Gallup's findings, men drive the overall preference for a boy. In the latest poll, men favored a boy over a girl by a 49 percent to 22 percent margin while women were about equally divided (31 percent to 33 percent). Adults under age 30 were considerably more likely than their older counterparts to prefer a boy to a girl. Americans with less education were more likely to say they prefer a boy; those with postgraduate education broke even in their preferences.

The reasons for this preference in the United States are not as clear as in many East Asian countries where having boys can provide greater economic security, since in their old age parents are more likely to live with, and be financially supported by, their sons (Rampell, 2011). However, the impact of gender-preference attitudes can be profound now that advances in reproductive technology can increase the odds of having a child of the preferred sex. The preference for a male child has led to sex-selective abortions and female infanticide in countries such as China and India, where women feel pressured to conceive a son. According to a study in the British medical journal *Lancet,* as many as 10 million female fetuses may have been aborted over the last two decades (cited in Gentleman, 2006). The preference for a male child has serious consequences for marriage, family, and community life. Women may be forced to keep having children until they have a son or to abort the female fetus even though they want to keep the child.

WHAT WOULD YOU DO?

As a parent, would you use reproductive technology to determine the sex of your child? Explain. How do you account for this consistency in the preference for boys over the years? What are some of the likely implications of a preference for one sex over the other?

((●–[Listen to the **Chapter Audio** on **myfamilylab.com**

This chapter begins with a brief historical review of changing fertility patterns in the United States and then proceeds to look at the many factors that influence the decision whether to parent. The remaining sections examine some of the issues surrounding conception, pregnancy, and parenthood. As the In the News section makes clear, many factors, including new technology, influence decisions about reproduction and parenting.

Fertility—the actual number of live births in a population—is both a biological and a social phenomenon. In all societies, the timing and number of births are shaped by numerous social forces: the value attached to children and parenthood, marriage patterns and gender roles, political and economic structures, and knowledge about human reproduction, including reproductive technologies such as artificial insemination. Thus, fertility patterns vary greatly across cultures. For example, in some cultures children are highly valued as economic assets, and women are expected to have many children beginning at an early age. Other societies view children in terms of their emotional value. These societies promote small families and encourage women to delay childbearing until their middle or late 20s. In some societies, the birth of a first child precedes marriage; in others, a birth outside marriage is strongly condemned. Even within a given society fertility patterns may vary considerably across racial, ethnic, and class lines.

Historical Overview: Fertility Trends in the United States

Demographers use the term **fertility rate** to refer to the number of births per thousand women in their childbearing years (ages 15–44 in a given year). Evidence suggests that the fertility rate in early America was quite high. For example, the **total fertility rate** (the average number of children women would have over their lifetime if current birth rates were to remain constant) in 1790, when the first census was taken, is estimated to have been 7.7 (Gill, Glazer, and Thernstrom, 1992:41), in contrast to the estimated 2.06 in 2011 (CIA, 2011).

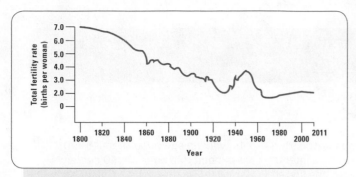

FIGURE 9.1 Total Fertility Rate in the United States, 1800–2011

Source: Adapted from Richard T. Gill, Nathan Glazer, and Stephan A. Thernstrom, 1992, *Our Changing Population* (Englewood Cliffs, NJ: Prentice Hall): 41. Reprinted by permission of Prentice Hall, Englewood Cliffs, NJ; J. A. Martin, B. E. Hamilton, and S. J. Ventura, 2001, "Preliminary Data for 2000," National Vital Statistics Reports 49, 5 (Hyattsville, MD: National Center for Health Statistics): 4. CIA, 2011, The World Fact Book, https://www.cia.gov/library/publications/the-world-factbook/geos/us.html (2011, September 1).

Figure 9.1 shows that by 1900 the total fertility rate had declined to half that of a century earlier. What happened to produce this dramatic decline? First, the transformation of the United States from a rural–agricultural society to an urban–industrial society lessened the economic value of children. Children are an economic asset in agricultural societies, where many hands are needed to cultivate the land. Second, the move to an urban–industrial society was accompanied by rapid advances in science and technology, leading to changes in people's views of the world. Couples came to believe that controlling family size would have economic benefits. By having fewer children, couples could reallocate their resources from the basic costs of providing for children to investing more in their future. The changing technology of an urban–industrial society required a more educated labor force. Thus, not only did the economic value of children decline, but it also became more costly to raise and educate them. Over time, a general pattern has emerged—the higher the income, the lower the fertility rate.

In the first decades of the twentieth century, the fertility rate continued to decline, particularly during the years of the Great Depression, when couples limited family size because of economic hardship. Demographers had predicted that the number of births would increase after World War II as couples put the depression and the war behind them. However, no one anticipated the dramatic rise in the total fertility rate from about 2.5 in 1945 to a high of 3.8 in 1957. Between 1946 and 1965, a period called the "baby boom," 74 million babies were born in the United States. Although demographers do not agree completely on the causes of the baby boom, two factors seem to have played a major role. First, the expanding postwar economy enabled unprecedented numbers of people to marry and have children at an early age. Second, a number of government policies were aimed at helping young families get started. The GI Bill helped veterans get an education and hence better-paying jobs. Federal housing loans and income tax deductions for children and interest on home mortgages encouraged people to buy houses and start families.

The baby boom was not to last, however. In 1957, the total fertility rate again began to decline, falling by more than 50 percent in less than 20 years to a low of 1.7 in 1976. This rate increased only slightly in the 1990s. This drastic decline, called the "baby bust," was not anticipated either. Among the factors thought responsible for this change was a slowing of the economy, the introduction of the birth control pill in the early 1960s, the legalization of abortion, the continuing increase in women's labor force participation, and increases in both the age at marriage and in the divorce rate. However, the most likely explanation is that the baby boom was simply a short-term deviation from the long-term decline begun in the nineteenth century. Whatever the reasons for the decline, another baby boom of this magnitude does not seem likely in the foreseeable future.

CURRENT FERTILITY PATTERNS

There were nearly 4.1 million births in 2009, 3 percent less than in 2008. The number of births and birth rates declined for all race and ethnic groups in 2009. The rate was not uniform across all race and ethnic groups. As Figure 9.2 shows, Native Americans/Alaska Natives and Whites had the lowest rates (1.77 and 1.78) and Latinas had the highest rate (2.73). Age, cultural norms, and class combine to explain these rate variations. Asian Americans tend to marry later than other groups and they are more likely than other groups to delay childbearing until their late 20s and 30s. Asian Americans have the lowest fertility rate of any group in the 15 to 19 age category and they have the highest fertility rate of any group in the 35 to 39 age category. In contrast, African Americans, Native Americans, and Latinas begin childbearing at early ages. African American and Native American women have lower fertility rates in their late 30s than other groups.

The United States has a higher fertility rate than every country in continental Europe, Australia, Canada, and Japan but considerably lower than many other countries (see the In Other Places box on page 278). For the first time in nearly four decades, the total fertility rate in the United States dropped below the theoretical level (2.1) required for the natural replacement of the population. Whether this recent decline in the birth rate is a blip or a trend is as yet too early to say. Many factors affect the decision to have children.

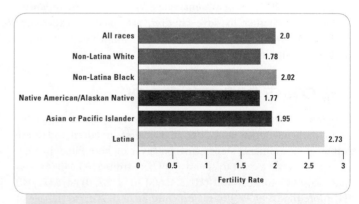

FIGURE 9.2 Total Fertility Rate by Racial or Ethnic Group, 2009

Adapted from B. E. Hamilton, J. A. Martin, and S. J. Ventura 2010. *Births: Preliminary Data for 2009.* National Vital Statistics Report 59, 3: Table 1.

THE DEMOGRAPHIC DIVIDE

Macau and Hong Kong have the lowest total fertility rates of any nation in the world (0.92 and 1.07, respectively), and Niger and Uganda have the highest (7.60 and 6.69) (CIA, 2011). Demographers refer to this vast range in birth and death rates among the world's countries as a "global demographic divide." On the one side of the divide are poor countries with high birth rates and low life expectancies. Among them are many African countries and some Middle Eastern countries like Yemen (4.63) and the Gaza Strip (4.73). The population structures of these countries have a "youth bulge" or a disproportionate concentration of young people. Without significant economic growth, these countries will remain poor. The limited ability of these countries to provide sufficient educational and economic opportunities for all its citizens makes integrating new generations into the social fabric problematic, thus increasing the potential for political instability in these societies (Helgerson, 2002).

On the other side of the divide are wealthy countries with high life expectancies and fertility rates so low that population decline is all but guaranteed, for example, Singapore (1.11) and Japan (1.21). Today in one country out of three, fertility is less than two children per woman, the level necessary to ensure a stable population or replacement of generations. In the absence of immigration, in a couple of generations, the population of these countries will shrink and age. For example, by 2050, Italy's population is expected to be 20 percent smaller than it is today and its working age population (15–64) is expected to be some 40 percent smaller (Chamie, 2004). Countries facing population decline are concerned about how it will affect their economies as they face economic strains of caring for an aging population with smaller numbers of workers. In addition, they worry about the loss of international prestige that may accompany population decline (Kent and Haub. 2005).

What do you think? Is the demographic divide a cause for concern? What, if anything, can countries on each side of the divide do to influence these different fertility rates? What do you see as the problems that families on each side of the divide are likely to experience as a result of the fertility rates in their countries?

To Parent or Not

Parenthood, like any other social activity, involves both costs and benefits that vary over the family life cycle and that people should consider before becoming parents. Even though people do sometimes change their mind after marriage, it is important to discuss the desire for children before marriage. Wives and husbands who disagree on whether to have children are likely to experience considerable marital conflict. If the issue cannot be satisfactorily resolved, the marriage may dissolve.

THE COSTS OF PARENTHOOD

In contrast to previous eras, when children worked at various jobs, particularly on farms and later in factories, children today are primarily consumers. Depending on level of household income (HI) parents can expect to spend anywhere from $163,440 (HI less than $57,600) to $226,930 (HI $57,600 to $99,730) to $377,040 (HI more than $99,730) to raise a child born in 2010 to the age of 17 (U.S. Department of Agriculture, 2011). These figures exclude college costs, expenditures by others outside the household such as grandparents and other relatives, and indirect costs such as a parent, usually the mother, foregoing earnings as a result of staying home or working part time because of the presence of children.

Time, Energy, and Emotional Costs Raising children involves more than financial outlays; it also requires a great investment of parental time and energy, resulting in high emotional demands (Evenson and Simon, 2005). Infants and toddlers are totally dependent on parents for meeting all their physical and psychological needs. As children enter school, parents are likely to find themselves enmeshed in rounds of school activities, organized sports, religious events, Scouts, music and dance lessons, family outings, and numerous other activities that compete for their time and attention. Raising children in today's environment also carries a high emotional cost in terms of parental worries over the easy accessibility of drugs, the lure of gangs, and random violence, all of which have taken a heavy toll on young people across all groups, but especially on the poor and children of color. An African American mother of two sons said, "I love my sons dearly, but if I had it all to do over again, I don't know if I would have children, especially boys. Every time my sons go out, my heart stops until they come home. Every day you read about some young African American male being shot or beaten up for being in the wrong place."

Lifestyle Disruptions The birth of a child can disrupt previously satisfying lifestyles. Not only do infants interrupt sleep and lovemaking and change household routines, they can alter a couple's social life and recreational pursuits. Babysitters are not always readily available, nor are babies easily compatible with work, hobbies, or leisure activities. Many parents find themselves in the position of having to forgo favorite pastimes at least until their children are much older. Although some parents find this a rather easy exchange to make, others are unprepared for the degree of change in their lives. Some parents become resentful and, as a result, both the marital relationship and the parent–child relationship may be negatively affected. Why, then, does anyone voluntarily become a parent? The answer to this question is twofold: Parenthood offers significant benefits to individuals, and society places enormous social pressure on its members to procreate.

THE BENEFITS OF PARENTHOOD

Although all parents experience the costs of having children to some degree, most parents believe the benefits of parenthood outweigh the costs.

Emotional Bonds Children are not only consumers and takers; they also give love and affection to parents. Furthermore, for many married couples their children are a tangible symbol of the love they share and the means for establishing "a real family life." Couples who recall happy childhoods and positive family life experiences are especially likely to want to reproduce those feelings through having children of their own. Children also enlarge the social interaction network of parents by providing connecting links to other family members (grandparents, aunts, uncles, cousins) and to the larger community via schools, churches, and neighborhoods.

Adult Status Many people see raising children as a means of achieving adult status, recognition, and personal fulfillment. From early on, girls are given dolls to play with to prepare them for the day they will become mothers themselves and affirm their womanhood to the larger community. Men, too, are socialized to affirm their manhood through procreation and financial support of their families. Beyond that, however, rearing children provides parents with a sense of purpose and gives their lives meaning.

Fun and Enjoyment Sometimes in the serious discussions of parenting another important benefit of having children is overlooked. Having children can be enormous fun. Through children, adults can reexperience some of the delights of their own childhood. They can recall their own sense of wonder of the world as they observe their children's new discoveries. The presence of children legitimizes many adult desires. Many parents delight in buying trains and other toys for their children so that they, too, can enjoy them. What adult has not at times looked wistfully on as children around them swing, swim, run, jump, and play games? Parents have the advantage of being able to do all these things with their children without needing to apologize or explain.

THE SOCIAL PRESSURES TO PROCREATE

Obviously, reproduction is necessary for the continuation of a society. Without a fertility rate approaching the replacement level and in the absence of immigration, a society would become, over time, extinct. Thus, it is in society's interest to promote a **pronatalist attitude,** one that encourages childbearing. Societies vary in their strategies for accomplishing this goal. For instance, France, worried

One of the benefits of having children is to be able to experience the world through children's eyes and to have fun doing it. This young couple clearly enjoys a day at the amusement park with their two children.

about its low birth rate, increased the monthly stipend for parents who take unsalaried leave to care for a third child (Leicester, 2005). In the United States, we celebrate parenthood by having special days to honor mothers and fathers. Federal and state governmental bodies show their support for childbearing by a tax structure that rewards earners with children through a system of tax deductions. Family members and friends often participate in encouraging childbearing by constantly dropping hints. "When are we going to be grandparents?" "Hurry up, our Jimmy wants a playmate [cousin]."

THE CHILD-FREE OPTION

Throughout most of U.S. history, having children was assumed to be the normal course of development for married couples. There were always some people who decided against childbearing, but until relatively recently a conscious rejection of parenthood was considered an unnatural and selfish act. About the only socially acceptable reason for not having children was biological incapacity. Those who were unable to have children were objects of pity and sympathy. Some psychoanalysts, like Sigmund Freud and Erik Erikson, believed that when couples decide not to parent, they are rejecting a major part of adult development that they may regret in later life.

However, researchers such as Marian Faux (1984) challenged this perspective. More recently, American writer Jennifer Shawne (2005), author of *Baby Not on Board: A Celebration of Life Without Kids*, and Britain-based writer Nicki Defago (2005), author of *Childfree and Loving It*, argued that many couples and women make conscious and rational decisions to remain child-free and do so without regrets. Among women ages 40–44 (who are nearing the completion of their childbearing years), the proportion that has never given birth, 18 percent in 2008, has grown by 80 percent since 1976, when it was 10 percent (Livingston and Cohn, 2010). The most educated women still are among the most likely to be child-free. However, in a notable exception to the overall rising trend, the rate among women with advanced degrees declined from 31 percent in 1994 to 24 percent in 2008. Although White women are the most likely to be childfree, over the past decade, childfree rates have risen more rapidly for Latinas and Black and Asian women. Women who have never married are most likely to be childfree, but their rates have declined over the past decade, while childfree rates have risen among women who are married or were at one time. Similar patterns exit in European countries as well.

Just as there are numerous reasons for having children, there are many reasons for not doing so. Among them are career and marital considerations, the desire for personal fulfillment, uncertainty about parenting skills, environmental concerns, and the influence of **antinatalist forces**—policies or practices that discourage people from having children, for example, China's one-child policy and here in the United States, the lack of a national system of child care. Finally, public attitudes toward being childfree have become more accepting. Most adults now disagree that people without children "lead empty lives," and a 2007 Pew Research Center survey found that only 41 percent of respondents said that children are very important for a successful marriage, a decline from 65 percent who said so in 1990 (Livingston and Cohn, 2010).

DELAYED PARENTING

Delayed parenting (having a first child at 30 or after) is a relatively new trend in the United States, increasing from only 4 percent of American women in the early 1970s to more than 26 percent in the late 1990s. Births to older women continue to increase. In 2009, the birth rate for women ages 40–44 increased by 3 percent from 2008, the only age group to have an increase. (Hamilton, Martin, and Ventura, 2010). Couples who delay parenting are more likely to be White, highly educated, work in professional occupations, and earn high incomes. They also tend to overestimate the age at which fertility begins to decline (Karimzadeh, and Ghandi, 2008; Madsen, 2003). Some in this later category seek help through assisted reproductive technology when it becomes clear that they have a reduced chance of conceiving, a topic we will turn to later. Western countries are not the only ones seeing an increase in delayed parenting. Japan is also experiencing a growing number of older first-time mothers. However, these mothers find less acceptance due in large part to traditional culture values that emphasize women's mother and homemaker roles as well as concern over Japan's low birth rate.

Several factors have contributed to the pattern of delayed parenting. Among them are a greater cultural acceptance of singlehood as a positive lifestyle, later age at marriage, men's and women's, but especially women's, desire to complete their education and establish themselves in a career before childbearing, improved contraception, and new reproductive technology that has made it possible for older women to bear children successfully. Although men can be fathers at almost any age, it is only recently that it became possible for menopausal women to become pregnant using donated eggs. In 2008, a 72-year-old Indian woman, Omkari Panwar, gave birth to twins. Omkari and her husband had two daughters and five grandchildren but always wanted a son. In 2009, in Spain 69-year-old Maria del Carmen Bousada died. She had given birth to twins almost three years earlier. Cases like these have led some governments to restrict access to reproductive technologies for women over age 50 and raised questions about the pros and cons of delayed parenting. Older parents may be more economically secure, more mature, and better prepared for the responsibilities of parenting than their younger counterparts, yet some older parents may lack the physical stamina needed to raise children. Children may benefit from having loving, involved older parents, yet some may find themselves caring for an ill or elderly parent while they are still in college.

> Would you want to become a parent after age 60? What would be the advantages and disadvantages? Explain.

It is becoming more common for parents to delay childbearing until their 30s or 40s. As this couple is discovering, parenting at a later stage in the life cycle has its advantages and disadvantages.

Controlling Fertility

Throughout history, many groups and societies have attempted to control the timing and number of births to ensure an adequate supply of food and other resources for the entire community. Early efforts to control fertility took many forms. Some groups tried creating contraceptive barriers made out of animal intestines and various roots and grasses; others ingested prepared herbs and potions thought to have preventive power. Over time, other techniques were also employed: celibacy, late marriages, abstinence for prolonged periods of time, prolonged breast-feeding, physical actions such as jumping to dislodge the semen, and abortion.

In contrast to these early methods, today efficient and safe methods of **contraception**—mechanisms for preventing fertilization—are readily available. Most of us take the availability of contraceptives for granted. However, the distribution and use of contraceptives in the United States were outlawed in the latter half of the nineteenth century and remained illegal in some states until 1965, when the Supreme Court, in *Griswold* v. *Connecticut*, invalidated laws prohibiting the use of contraceptives by married couples. Seven years later, in *Eisenstadt* v. *Baird*, the Court extended this principle to unmarried adults. In 1977, in *Carey* v. *Population Services International*, the Court extended the same constitutional right to privacy to minors, declaring that the state cannot deny them access to contraceptives.

Couples today can choose from a wide number of birth control methods. Each contraceptive method carries with it advantages as well as disadvantages. Some have health risks but are extremely convenient; others are safer but less convenient. Some have only a temporary effect; others are permanent. Some are costly, others are relatively inexpensive. Although a particular birth control device may prevent pregnancy, it does not necessarily provide protection against AIDS and other sexually transmitted infections. Thus, more than one form of contraception may be advisable at any given time. We will discuss each form of contraception and controversies surrounding them in Appendix D.

CONTRACEPTIVE USE

Of the 43 million sexually active women in their childbearing years (15–44) in the United States today, 7 percent are at risk for unintended pregnancy but are not using contraceptives (Guttmacher Institute, 2010). The most popular contraceptive method is the pill, followed by female sterilization, the male condom, and vasectomy. Other contraceptive choices ranged from injections, implants, abstinence, and other devices.

Contraceptive choices vary with age, education, marital status, race, and ethnicity. The pill is the method most widely used by women who have never married, women with a college degree or higher, and women under 30, especially those in their teens and 20s; by age 35, more women rely on sterilization. Sterilization is most commonly relied on by women with less than a college education and by women who are currently married or have previously been married. It is the leading method among African American women and Latinas, whereas White women prefer the pill (Mosher and Jones, 2010).

Almost half of all pregnancies in the United States that occur each year are unintended, the result of using unreliable or defective

Margaret Sanger, a public health nurse in New York City in the early 1900s, was alarmed at the high maternal and infant mortality rates associated with the large families of the working poor, who begged her for information about ways to prevent having more children. Sanger coined the term *birth control* as a positive description of family limitation and led the struggle to legalize contraceptive devices and to promote planned parenthood.

contraceptives, misusing contraceptives, or using no contraceptives at all (Finer and Henshaw, 2006). Nearly 80 million unintended pregnancies occur worldwide every year (Population Action International, 2005). Rates of unplanned births are particularly high in Latin America, Kenya, the Philippines, and Japan. Poor women in the United States and women in developing countries often do not have access to contraceptives or family planning services. Further, their ability to control whether and when to have children is related to gender roles within the family and society, their level of educational attainment, participation in the labor force, and the likelihood of being subjected to a domineering husband and even domestic violence. In many parts of the world, women's limited participation in reproductive decision making is a reflection of their second-class status in society. Given that there is a 2–4 percent chance of becoming pregnant after unprotected sex (which increases to 30–50 percent during ovulation), why do so many people risk the possibility of pregnancy by not using contraceptives?

REASONS FOR NOT USING CONTRACEPTIVES

As surprising as it might seem in this day and age, some young people believe they cannot get pregnant the first time they have intercourse. If they were lucky and pregnancy did not occur, they are likely to be tempted to have unprotected sex again, a pattern researchers Jerry Burger and Linda Burns (1988) call the "illusion of unique invulnerability." The reasons for not using contraceptives are the following:

- *Symbolism of sexual activity.* Being prepared with a contraceptive is a visible symbol of sexual activity, thus feelings of shame, guilt, fear, or anxiety may prohibit a person from using a contraceptive.
- *Role of peers.* Friends share information and tend to behave in similar fashion.
- *Role of parents.* Parents who have difficulty discussing sex with their children are more likely to have children who, if they become sexually active, will not use contraceptives.
- *Contraception is not romantic and/or not effective.* Some people complain that planning for and using contraceptives takes the spontaneity and romance out of a relationship.
- *The nature of the relationship.* People are more likely to use contraceptives in the context of an ongoing, steady relationship than when they begin a new relationship.

As indicated in the foregoing sections, contraceptive devices are not always used and, when used, are not always successful. Thus, many women faced with an unwanted pregnancy seek an abortion.

Abortion

Abortion refers to the premature termination of a pregnancy before the fetus can survive on its own. This can occur either spontaneously (a miscarriage) or can be induced through a variety of external methods (see Appendix C). Nearly half of all pregnancies among American women are unintended and about 4 in 10 of these are terminated by abortion (Finer and Zolna, 2011). In 2003, about 1 in 5 pregnancies worldwide ended in abortion (42 million, down from 46 million in 1995) (Sedgh, et al., 2007). Similarly, in the United States, slightly more than 1 in 5 pregnancies (22 percent) end in abortion. In 2008, 1.2 million abortions took place, down from an estimated 1.3 million in 2000 (Jones and Kooistra, 2011). The decline in the number of abortions is related to improved contraceptive use, particularly among teenagers, and to the use of the morning-after pill. Throughout the world, women give similar reasons for their decision to abort: they are too young or poor to raise a child; having a child would interfere with work, school, or other responsibilities; they are estranged from their sexual partner; and/or they do not want to be a single parent. Additionally, about 13,000 women have abortions each year following rape or incest ("Induced Abortion," 2005). Abortions are most common among young, White, unmarried women. White women account for 36 percent of abortions, African American women for 30 percent, Latinas for 25 percent, and women of other races for 9 percent. About 51 percent of women who have abortions are younger than 25, women aged 20–24 account for 33 percent of all abortions, and teenagers obtain the remaining 18 percent. Thirty-seven percent of women obtaining abortions identify themselves as Protestant and 28 percent identify themselves as Catholic. About 61 percent of abortions are obtained by women who have one or more children (Jones, Finer, and Singh, 2010).

Induced abortion has been a method of birth control throughout human history and for a major part of U.S. history as well. However, today induced abortions are the subject of an emotionally charged and highly politicized debate involving conflicting values regarding women's reproductive rights and the question of when life begins (see the Debating Social Issues box). In recent times, the struggle over the abortion issue has included violence against women's health clinics and the murder of several doctors and women who provided abortion services. Yet such polarized views of abortion were not always the case in the United States.

Debating Social Issues

SHOULD *ROE V. WADE* BE OVERTURNED?

Few issues in the United States are as contentious as the issue of abortion. Proponents of overturning *Roe v. Wade*, popularly referred to as the prolife movement, argue that life begins at conception and therefore, in their view, abortion is a form of murder, which should not be allowed. People who see themselves as prolife believe abortion demeans the value and dignity of life and robs society of the likely contributions of a significant number of potentially viable human beings. They further argue that abortion psychologically damages women who have abortions. They use, as an example of this position, the experience of Jane Roe (not her real name), the woman involved in the original court decision, who later regretted her decision and now supports the overturning of *Roe v. Wade*. Many who support Jane Roe's current position believe that as women get older, they will likely regret their decision and will probably always carry guilt for their action and will forever experience a feeling of loss for what might have been. Others who favor overturning *Roe v. Wade* do so because they believe some women are sexually careless and then use abortion as a means of birth control or they choose abortions because having a child would be inconvenient; they view such behaviors as morally objectionable. Many in the prolife

movement see abortion as a selfish act. Although they may agree that some women, especially young women, may not be ready to care for a child, they argue that there are many couples who are only too willing to adopt these infants. Many couples spend years trying unsuccessfully to adopt an infant or have to go outside the United States because there are so few infants available here. Rather than abort a fetus, they argue, women could help these couples by placing their babies up for adoption. The prolife movement is also concerned that *Roe v. Wade* allows minors, who are not yet emotionally, psychologically, and morally mature enough to make sound decisions, the means to have an abortion. Proponents of overturning *Roe v. Wade* also worry that if the law remains in place, advances in genetic testing may lead to more abortions if fetuses are identified as the wrong sex or less than ideal in some way. Finally, as taxpayers many people seeking to overturn *Roe v. Wade* do not want to see any of their tax dollars supporting a policy that they see as immoral.

On the other hand, proponents of keeping *Roe v. Wade*, those identifying themselves as prochoice, argue that abortion is not murder, that at conception there is potential life but the fetus is not a human being. They argue that women have a right to control their bodies, including deciding to abort a fetus that they are carrying, and that government does not have the right to interfere in this decision. Citing women's experiences before *Roe v. Wade*, prochoice people fear making abortion illegal would mean a return to "back alley" abortions, putting women's lives and well-being in jeopardy because the reasons women choose to abort would remain: incest, rape, the threat to a woman's emotional and physical health, poor economics, failure of contraceptives, inability to parent at that time, immaturity, birth defects, and a host of others. People in the prochoice movement agree that some women may suffer psychological damage as a result of having an abortion, but they believe that in most of those cases it is because of the stigma that some in society would put on them for choosing an abortion. Proponents of keeping abortion legal also point to data that show many young women have fared better academically, socially, and economically than their peers who gave birth and struggled to raise their children. They argue that one mistake can rob a woman of her childhood and limit opportunities for the rest of her life, not only at her expense, but of the child and the larger society as well. Prochoice advocates point out that giving a child up for adoption can be no less traumatic than abortion and women who do also suffer from regret, guilt, and a sense of loss that can last a lifetime. Finally, proponents of keeping abortion legal argue legal access is not the determining factor in abortion rates but rather it is the rate of unintended pregnancies. They point to research showing that abortion levels are high in countries where small families are desired but contraceptive use is low or ineffective. For example, in most of Eastern Europe and the former Soviet Union, where desired family size was small and modern contraceptives were not generally available until recently, women relied on legal abortions to control family size. In recent years, contraceptives have been easier to obtain, and abortion rates fell by as much as 50 percent in some countries between 1990 and 1996. And in the Netherlands, where abortion is legal and contraceptive use is widespread, both abortion and unintended pregnancy rates are low (Sedgh, et al. 2007; Dailard, 2000). Along these same lines, many in the prochoice movement echo former President Bill Clinton's desire to keep abortion legal, safe, and rare. To do this, proponents say, means providing programs for early and quality sex education, affordable and available contraception, affordable and quality child care, and living wages for women and their families.

What do you think? Should *Roe v. Wade* be overturned or retained? What would be the likely consequences of overturning the federal law? Is abortion a matter for individuals or government to decide? Are there social policies that, if implemented, could make abortion, legal, safe, and rare?

HISTORICAL PERSPECTIVES

Until the nineteenth century, American laws concerning abortion generally reflected the tradition in English common law that abortion is permissible until "quickening"—the time (generally between the 4th and 6th months) at which a pregnant woman could feel the fetus moving in her womb. Abortions were advertised in newspapers, and recipes for abortifacients (anything used to induce abortions) were provided in popular books of the day. Estimates are that by the middle of the nineteenth century, there was one induced abortion for every four live births (cited in Tribe, 1990:28). Connecticut was the first state to regulate abortion. It did so in 1821 not on any moral grounds but to protect women by prohibiting the inducement of abortion through the use of dangerous poisons. Over time, other restrictive measures followed, fueled in large measure by fears that the widespread use of abortion by White, married, middle-class women, coupled with the higher birth rates of ethnic immigrants, would upset the status quo. By 1900, abortion was illegal except when a physician judged it necessary to save a woman's life.

Criminalizing abortion did not end abortions. Rather, it drove them underground. Abortions became expensive, difficult to get, and often dangerous. Poor women who, unlike their wealthier counterparts, were unable to travel outside the country or have a physician diagnose the need for a therapeutic abortion suffered the most. Over time, stories about botched abortions resulting in permanent injury or death began to surface. Two events in the 1960s became a catalyst for a new debate on the abortion issue. The first involved Sherri Finkbine, a mother of four, who had taken the tranquilizer thalidomide while pregnant. When she discovered that the drug was associated with major birth defects, she elected to have an abortion rather than give birth to a seriously deformed child. After unsuccessful attempts to get an abortion in the United States, she went to Sweden, where she aborted a deformed fetus. The second event was a major outbreak of rubella (German measles) between 1962–1965. The occurrence of rubella during pregnancy causes major birth defects. During this period, some 15,000 babies were born with such defects. The medical profession, increasingly conscious of these tragedies, changed its position from one of opposition to abortion to one advocating easing abortion restrictions. In 1973, the Supreme Court, by a 7–2 vote in *Roe v. Wade*, struck down all anti-abortion laws as violations of a woman's right to privacy. Since that time, however, there have been renewed efforts to restrict this right.

Restrictions on Abortion Although still legal, abortion has become increasingly less accessible. In 1976, Congress passed the Hyde Amendment, which prohibited using federal Medicaid funds for abortions except in cases where the pregnancy threatens a woman's life. Over time, a majority of states followed the federal government's lead and prohibited state funding for abortions. In the late 1970s, the first laws were passed requiring that parents be notified or give parental consent when a minor seeks an abortion. Today, 35 states have such laws. An analysis of the impact of these laws in 6 states found that they had only a small impact on the number of abortions minors had in those states (Lehren and Leland, 2006). Supporters of parental involvement laws believe they bring parents and children closer together, allowing parents to play an important role in helping their children make important health care decisions. They also believe that in the long run, the law will result in fewer abortions. On the other hand, some abortion providers point out that it is often the case that the parents press their daughters to have an abortion rather than trying to stop them. Further, they say these laws often drive teenagers underground, sometimes with tragic consequences, as evidenced by the Becky Bell case. This Indiana teenager died as a consequence of an illegal abortion she had to prevent her parents from knowing about her pregnancy. Conversely, such restrictions may also result in forcing women to have a child they do not want.

The political struggle over abortion is ongoing. In 2011, about 70 restrictive measures were adopted in 14 states, ranging from a Kansas provision that requires abortion providers to describe the fetus to women as a "whole, separate, unique, living human being" to a South Dakota regulation compelling women who want an abortion to undergo counseling at pro-life pregnancy centers (Gee, 2011). Pro-choice groups have challenged many of these provisions. Given the current political climate in the United States, it is possible that some of these restrictive measures may provoke a legal challenge to *Roe v. Wade*.

PUBLIC ATTITUDES TOWARD ABORTION

According to a 2011 survey, a majority of Americans (54 percent) say abortion should be legal in all or most cases while 42 percent say abortion should be illegal in all or most cases. This represents a small but significant change from 2009 when opinions were almost evenly divided with 46 percent favoring and 44 percent opposing legal abortion in most or all cases ("Attitudes Toward Social Issues," 2011). These attitudes are strongly related to both religion and political preferences. Overall, evangelical Protestants remain the religious group most opposed to legal abortion with just 34 percent saying abortion should be legal and 64 percent saying it should be illegal in all or most cases. Support for legal abortion is higher among Democrats (65 percent) and independents (58 percent) than among Republicans (34 percent).

The abortion debate is not likely to end soon. The United States could benefit by examining the history of abortion in other countries like Hungary and Russia that have lowered their abortion rates by providing effective family planning services. To date, little of the abortion debate in the United States focuses on strategies to prevent abortion. Until the two sides in the debate can come to some agreement about the need for this kind of action, it is likely that the United States will continue to have the highest percentage of unplanned pregnancies of any developed country in the West and, as a result, whether abortion is legal or not, will continue to have a significant number of abortions.

Thus far, we have treated the decision of whether to have children as one of personal choice and control. However, personal choices are not always realized. Just as some couples experience unwanted pregnancies, others want children but find they cannot have them.

Infertility

The medical profession defines **infertility** as the inability to conceive after 12 months of unprotected intercourse or the inability to carry a pregnancy to live birth. Infertility affects approximately

10–15 percent of couples of reproductive age. Although infertility problems occur in all race and ethnic groups, research shows that women who pursue medical help for fertility problems are a highly selective group who are more likely to be White, married, older, more highly educated, and more affluent (Stephen and Chandra, 2006). Infertility treatments are costly. Most insurance companies do not offer coverage for treatment, thus further limiting access to such treatment.

CAUSES OF INFERTILITY

There is a tendency to view infertility, like birth control, as a woman's problem. This tendency is reinforced by a cultural tradition that has associated masculinity with fertility. For this reason, some men are unwilling to consider the idea that they could be infertile. However, men are as likely to experience infertility problems as women. About 40 percent of fertility problems are traced to the male partner and an equal percentage to the female; the causes for the remaining 20 percent are unknown. Thus, if a couple is unsuccessful in their efforts to have a child, both should be examined for any possible problems. Prolonged exposure to toxic chemicals can produce sterility in both women and men. So, too, can sexually transmitted infections. Other factors are specific to each gender.

The major causes of female infertility are failure to ovulate and blockage of the fallopian tubes. The major cause of male infertility is low sperm production. Additionally, the spermatozoa may not be sufficiently active (or motile), or the sperm-carrying ducts may be blocked. Regardless of the cause, however, infertility in either sex does not impede sexual performance.

CONSEQUENCES OF INFERTILITY

During the process of growing up, it is common for children to imagine themselves as future parents. Few, however, ever question the possibility of being unable to have children. Thus, for couples wanting to have children, the knowledge that they cannot comes as a shock. Many experience a "crisis of infertility," an emotional state characterized by a feeling of loss of control over their lives. As a result, they experience a wide range of emotions: depression, disbelief, denial, isolation, guilt, frustration, and grief, any of which can put damaging stress on the couple's relationship (Marcus, 2011).

For centuries, about the only available solution for infertile couples was adopting someone else's children. Today, however, there is a scarcity of adoptable infants, especially White infants. Currently, only about 2–3 percent of babies born out of wedlock are given up for adoption, compared to a high of almost 80 percent in the past (Dunkin, 2000). Although approximately 8 percent of women who are infertile adopt (Bachrach, 1986), many others who wish to have children seek medical help.

Historical records show that as early as the eighteenth century, women actively sought help from the developing medical profession in having a child. Outside of providing advice to relax or to adopt children, doctors had little knowledge to offer women who wanted to conceive. It was not until 1940 that researchers had developed a clear understanding of the relationship between ovulation and the menstrual cycle. This knowledge breakthrough was immediately applied to attempts to reduce unplanned pregnancies by regulating conception, pregnancy, and menopause. The result of these efforts was the mass production of an oral contraceptive. With fewer unwanted pregnancies, fewer children were available for adoption and pressure grew to find ways to overcome infertility. Artificial insemination and fertility drugs soon became common medical treatments. Another tool available today is **assisted reproductive technology (ART),** a general term that includes all treatments or procedures involving the handling of human eggs and sperm to establish a pregnancy.

Medical Treatments and Reproductive Technology: Implications for the Meaning of Parenthood

Considerable controversy has accompanied the development of medical and high tech means to treat infertility. As we shall see in the following section, artificial insemination and ART are challenging the traditional definitions of parenthood and family as well as raising numerous ethical and legal questions that are yet to be resolved.

ARTIFICIAL INSEMINATION

Artificial insemination (AI) involves the injection of fresh or frozen semen into the vagina or uterus of an ovulating woman. This process is one of the oldest and most successful of the reproductive technologies (20–25 percent when combined with fertility drugs) initially having been developed in the animal husbandry field several centuries ago. Although conception can occur after one insemination, two to five inseminations are more common. Compared with other reproductive technologies, the cost of AI is relatively modest, averaging around $500 to $1,000. Although there are no national statistics on live birth rates after using AI, it is estimated that 30,000 to 60,000 children are born annually using sperm donors (Mroz, 2011).

There is little controversy surrounding AI when the husband's sperm is used as the resulting offspring is biologically related to both husband and wife. However, legal and ethical concerns arise when AI donors (AID) are involved. When husbands agree to AID and willingly accept paternal responsibility for any resulting offspring, most state laws view these children as legitimate and recognize the father's obligations to support them. Similarly, the courts have held separated lesbian partners accountable for children conceived in this manner. Other problems may arise, however. If the donor's identity is known, conflicts can later develop over parental rights even when those rights were initially disavowed. Alternatively, an anonymous donor may be used for a number of different inseminations, thus creating the possibility that genes for rare diseases could be spread more widely through the population or increasing the odds of accidental incest between half siblings who may live in the same geographical area. Web-based registries make it possible to identify donors. One mother created an online group of half-siblings all conceived with sperm from one donor; the group numbers over 150 (Mroz, 2011). Although some countries (Britain, France, and Sweden) limit how many children a sperm donor can father, the United States does not.

ASSISTED REPRODUCTIVE TECHNOLOGY (ART)

In 2009, a total of 146,244 ART procedures were reported to the Centers for Disease Control and Prevention (2007), resulting in 45,870 live-birth deliveries and 60,190 infants—many were born in multiple birth deliveries. The most common ART procedure is in vitro fertilization.

In Vitro Fertilization Sometimes called "test-tube" fertilization, **in vitro fertilization (IVF)** involves surgically removing a woman's eggs, fertilizing them in a petri dish with the partner's or donor's sperm, and then implanting one or more of the fertilized eggs in the woman's uterus. The insertion of multiple eggs increases the chances of pregnancy, but it also increases the likelihood of multiple births and with them increased medical risks of premature birth and low birth weight (see later discussion).

Three million babies have been born worldwide using IVF and other assisted reproductive technologies since Louise Brown, the first in vitro baby, was born in England in 1978 (Horsey, 2006). IVF does not work for everyone. It is more successful for younger women and women who use their own eggs. The costs are high, ranging from $15,000 to $25,000 or more per procedure, out of the range of many couples.

Several objections have been raised to IVF. Some people question the "morality" of fertilizing more than one egg, given the possibility that the other fertilized eggs may be destroyed, a situation that they see as analogous to abortion. Sometimes the additional fertilized eggs are not destroyed but frozen with the idea that they will be implanted at a future date. This latter procedure, known as *cryopreservation,* has led to some complicated legal questions. For example, after an Australian couple died in a plane crash, the courts could not decide what to do with their frozen embryos. Who "owns" them? Do they have the right to exist, perhaps even inherit from their deceased "parents," or can someone (the doctor, a relative) decide to destroy them or implant them into an "adopting" party? These questions remain unanswered. In a recent case that went all the way to the U.S. Supreme Court, a divorced woman was denied custody of the frozen embryos she and her former husband had created and she now wanted to use. The ex-husband asked the court to prohibit any use of the embryos without his consent, arguing that he should not be forced to become a parent against his wishes. However, the court based its decision on the agreement the couple made with the fertility clinic that in the event of divorce the embryos would be destroyed ("Texas Frozen Embryo…, 2008).

Embryo Transplant The procedure whereby a fertilized egg from a woman donor is implanted into an infertile woman is called an **embryo transplant.** This procedure has been refined and is now available to postmenopausal women who want to become pregnant as well as to women who want to avoid passing on a known genetic defect to their children. Criticism of embryo transplants revolves around two central issues. One is the possible exploitation of women donors. Although a woman may donate ova out of a desire to assist an infertile couple, some women, especially poor women, may feel pressured to sell their ova to help support themselves or their families. Recently, an egg donor filed a class action lawsuit against two national reproductive-medicine groups alleging that

they have engaged in a price-fixing scheme to underpay female donors for their eggs. The organizations had set guidelines stating that paying more than $5,000 for an egg should only be done after careful consideration and paying more than $10,000 should not be done at all. The plaintiff said she was paid $3,500 in February 2008 for donating an egg to a Seattle clinic. About $85 million worth of human eggs are sold in the U.S. annually, according to the lawsuit (Jamison, 2011). College women are coveted donors. Ads in campus newspapers and Facebook solicit their eggs, often at rates higher than the recommended guidelines.

The second issue raises questions of what constitutes biological motherhood—the contribution of genetic material (via the ova) or pregnancy and childbirth. This question has become even more complicated with the development of surrogate motherhood.

Surrogacy In **surrogacy,** a woman agrees to be artificially inseminated with a man's sperm, carry the fetus to term, and relinquish all rights to the child after it is born. This is perhaps the most controversial of all the reproductive techniques, because, like AID, it involves a third party. Unlike AID, however, the donor is intimately involved in the reproductive process. Surrogate motherhood may develop in either of two situations. In the first, a third party is artificially inseminated with the husband's sperm (or donor sperm if he is also infertile). Here, the term *surrogate* is somewhat misleading because the woman who is inseminated is also the biological mother. In the second situation, the wife's uterus does not allow a fertilized egg to implant itself and develop. In such cases, the couple uses IVF, but the resulting embryo is then transplanted into a surrogate mother. The surrogate can be a relative or a stranger. In the latter case, the woman and the couple generally sign a contract. Generally, the provisions of the contract include a fee payment $20,000–$25,000 to the surrogate and coverage of all her medical expenses. Estimates are there are more than 1,000 surrogate births annually (Ali and Kelley, 2008).

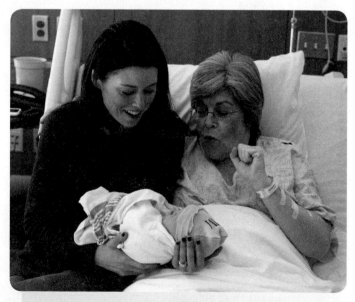

Sara Connell, left, and her mom Kristine Casey admire baby Finnean Connell at Prentice Women's Hospital in Chicago, Illinois. Casey, possibly the oldest women to give birth in Illinois, served as a surrogate for her daughter who had been unable to have a baby.

Questions inevitably arise regarding the motivations of the two parties in such an agreement. For the infertile couple there is a desire to have a child that is genetically related to at least one of them. Several motivational factors are probably involved in the decision to be a surrogate mother. Among them are altruism and money. Some surrogates desire to give the gift of a child to those who otherwise would not experience childrearing (Edelmann, 2004). Others are motivated more by their financial situation. *Newsweek* reporters Lorraine Ali and Raina Kelley (2008) found that an increasing number of military wives whose husbands are serving overseas supplement the family income by becoming surrogates. Some critics of surrogate motherhood see it as reproductive exploitation whereby poor women's reproductive capacity becomes a commodity that they are forced to sell to survive (Dworkin, 1987). Increasing numbers of infertile couples from the United States and England are going to India because of the lower cost of treatments and lighter regulations (Spring, 2006) as well as supportive cultural and religious attitudes. Indian women empathize with childless couples and believe doing a good deed in this life brings rewards in the next.

The legal issues surrounding surrogate motherhood are many. What if the surrogate mother changes her mind and decides to keep the child? Research shows this is relatively rare and that any emotional problems experienced by some surrogate mothers in the weeks following the birth lessen over time. After the birth of the child, positive relations continued, with the large majority of couples maintaining some level of contact with the surrogate mother (MacCallum et al. 2003; Jadva et al. 2003). Nevertheless, when a surrogate mother changes her mind, the results can be traumatic for all parties. One well-publicized example was the celebrated case of Baby M, whose biological mother, Mary Beth Whitehead, changed her mind after giving birth and wanted to keep the child. After a lengthy court battle, the contract was ruled invalid. Custody of the child went to the biological father and adoptive mother, who were seen as more stable and capable of parenting than the biological mother.

Other issues may also arise in surrogate cases. What happens if a child is born with a major physical problem? Can the contract then be rescinded? If so, does the responsibility for that child rest solely on the surrogate mother? What rights does each party have—the unborn child, the child's biological mother, the child's biological father, and the contractual parents? Do the contractual parents have a right to demand certain behaviors from the surrogate mother during her pregnancy—for example, maintaining a particular diet, refraining from drinking alcohol, or undergoing surgery to improve the life chances of the fetus? These questions have spurred considerable legislative activity. Some countries (Austria, Sweden, Norway, and Germany) ban surrogacy; others, like France, Denmark, and the Netherlands, ban payment to surrogates. To date, the United States has not developed a consistent legal view; some states regulate surrogacy under certain circumstances, others have no policy.

Another source of controversy has arisen with a relatively new ART procedure called **preimplantation genetic diagnosis (PGD)**, which allows physicians to identify chromosomal abnormalities such as Down syndrome or genetic diseases such as muscular dystrophy in the embryo before implantation. Thus, couples can avoid such "unhealthy" embryos. PGD can also be used to select an embryo that would be able to donate tissue to an existing sibling.

Public attitudes toward this technology are mixed. One survey found that 70 percent approved its used to avoid serious genetic disease and over 66 percent approved of using it to cure an existing sibling. However, less than 30 percent favored using the technology to choose a child's sex or other desirable characteristics such as strength or intelligence (Landhaus, 2004).

The Choice to Parent

"It's a girl." "It's a boy." Every year, millions of parents hear these words as they strain to get that first glimpse of the miraculous new life to which they have contributed. Whatever their feelings concerning marriage, pregnancy and childbirth, a majority of Americans have at least one child in their lifetime. This fact notwithstanding, an increasing number of women are without children. However, as we have seen, fertility rates vary considerably among different groups, and individual cases vary greatly as well. For instance, according to the *Guinness Book of World Records* (2001), the youngest female to conceive a child is recorded as a 5-and-a-half-year-old living in Peru. On the other hand, according to record books, the largest number of children born to one woman is 69. From 1725 to 1765, a Russian peasant woman from Shuva (150 miles east of Moscow) and the first of the two wives of Feodor Vassilvev, in 27 different confinements, gave birth to 16 sets of twins, 7 sets of triplets, and 4 sets of quadruplets. We might assume that this woman made a conscious choice to have 69 children. Although most people do not choose to have 69 children, millions of people do make a conscious choice to parent. However, we should also point out that many people *do not choose* to parent, but rather, they become parents as a result of unwanted pregnancies or taking on the responsibility of parenting children of family or friends. Still others consciously choose not to parent and they take the necessary measures to ensure that they will not have children.

However many children an individual or couple does have and no matter whether the choice is conscious or not, the process always begins with the fertilization of an egg by a sperm. The result can range from a single conception and birth, which is typical, to multiple conceptions and births.

MULTIPLE CONCEPTION AND BIRTHS

Multiple conceptions, in which two or more children are conceived at one time, used to be extremely rare. However, over the last two decades or more, the number of multiple births in the United States has skyrocketed. The most common form of multiple conception and birth is twins. Today, about 1 of every 31 births in the United States is twins. Worldwide, more than 100,000 multiple births occur each year, the majority of which are twins. Higher order births (three and above) constitute less than 3 percent of such births. For reasons not clearly understood, the frequency of naturally occurring multiple births varies across race and ethnicity. For example, African American women have had, in the past, the highest birth rate of twins, followed by White women and Latinas. Asian American women have the lowest birth rate of twins. However, in 2008, White women equaled Black women in the rate of twin births (36.6 and 36.8 respectively) due to a 60 percent increase in the birth of twins among White women (particularly older and more educated) since 1990. Although triplets and higher multiple births are still relatively rare, they have increased 200 percent over the last three decades. In 2008, about 1 in every 675 live births was triplets. Although triplets and larger sets of multiple conceptions, at each higher increment, occur less frequently there is still a fairly high rate of triplets and higher order births among non-Hispanic White women (198.1) and Black women (91.3) (Ogundipe, 2011; Martin et al., 2010).

Two related trends have been associated with the rise in multiple births, especially with the rise of higher order multiples: what some people call the *delayer boom*—educated women delaying childbearing until their mid-thirties or older age, and the more widespread use of fertility-enhancing therapies (women in their 30s are more likely than younger women to have a multiple birth, even without the use of fertility therapy). Older mothers are more likely to have twins, but they are also more likely to use some sort of reproductive technology to help them reproduce. But this is not the whole of the picture. Along with age, there is also an economic factor involved here. For instance, well-educated women tend to put off having children more often than the less-educated and they are also more able to afford fertility treatments which can run into several thousands of dollars. Given this, according to some observers, the rates of twins across the country should correspond with both the rates of educational attainment and average income.

Moreover, although two-thirds of the increase in multiple births is due to the delay of childbearing and to fertility treatments, according to some experts, where you live could also make a difference. For example, Massachusetts is currently the nation's most prolific producer of twins, triplets, and other multiple births, followed by New Jersey and Connecticut. On the other hand, the rate of multiple births in Hawaii is almost one-third below the overall U.S. rate (Tchou, 2011). Interestingly, Nigeria holds the world record for the birth of twins and other multiple births. Most of the multiple births occur among women of the Yoruba ethnic group in the western part of the country, who have the highest number of multiple births in the world (45 twins per 1,000 live births). The incidence of multiple birth in Nigeria is about 1 in 17 of all maternities, compared to the national average of 1 in 22. Nigerians attribute their population's consumption of a specific type of yam to the record high number of twins and multiple births. Scientists have found that the yams grown in Africa contain a high level of a substance similar to the hormone estrogen, which could bring on multiple ovulations (Ogundipe, 2011; March of Dimes PeriStats, 2008).

Sociologically speaking, while joyful, multiple births can present both multiple blessings and multiple problems. For instance, the high cost of raising multiples alone, can exert a tremendous financial burden on a family. Such births can also be detrimental to the health and well-being of a woman carrying multiple babies in terms of emotional strain as well as physical complications both for mother and babies. Multiples have an infant mortality rate that is 12 times higher than that of single births.

Media-highlighted cases of multiple births have contributed much to a growing public debate about the ethics of trying to carry an unprecedented six, seven, or eight children into the world, as well as the morality of such a decision. This debate was particularly sparked in the United States with the birth in 2009 of only the second full set of octuplets to be born in the United States. Born to 34-year-old Nadya Suleman, the octuplets were conceived through IVF and became Ms. Suleman's 7–14 children. That is, Ms. Suleman already had six other children (all of whom had also been conceived through IVF) when she had eight embryos implanted seeking what she said was a seventh child. The birth of the octuplets as well as the circumstances surrounding them and their mother (for example, the fact that she was unemployed and welfare dependent) led to controversy and debate in and outside the field of assisted reproductive technology as well as an investigation by the Medical Board of California of the fertility specialist that implanted Ms. Suleman. The Board ultimately stripped him of his medical license in 2011 (Rogers, 2009; "'Octomom' Doctor Stripped of Medical License," 2011).

One of the dangers of multiple births is that all the fetuses must share the nutrients and blood supply of one mother. And they do not share the nutrients equally—thus, one or more are shortchanged. Some people (including many doctors) believe that a woman should abort one or more of the fetuses to increase the chances of survival of some of the other fetuses. In London, the

Mother of only the second full set of octuplets to be born in the United States, 34-year-old Nadya Suleman, aka "Octomom," poses for photographs with her children in 2010 before being taken, via a tour bus, to Millions of Milkshakes in West Hollywood to create her own custom shake.

concern over multiple births following fertility treatments has caused fertility regulators to rule that doctors should normally transfer no more than two embryos at a time during IVF (Ross, 2001). There are no laws in the United States that prevent doctors from implanting multiple embryos. However, since the 2009 birth of the Suleman octuplets, national guidelines have been tightened limiting doctors' use of their discretion to increase the number of embryos implanted. Under the guidelines, no more than two embryos are recommended; according to the guidelines, the number should never be upped by more than one from the recommended limit for a patient, as determined by age and other factors (Mohajer, 2011).

> What do you think? Should the United States move beyond recommended guidelines for fertility treatments to impose stricter regulations on various reproduction technologies such as IVF procedures? Should transfers be limited to one embryo at a time?

Pregnancy

Pregnancy initiates many changes both physically and emotionally for a woman, her partner (if such a relationship exists), and the fetus. Major changes occur in the woman's hormone levels, body shape, and psychological state as the pregnancy develops. Pregnancy also brings about a variety of changes in the lives and relationship of the expectant parents. Their adjustment to the pregnancy is influenced to a large extent by whether the pregnancy was planned, their age at the time of pregnancy, their socioeconomic level, and their race and ethnicity.

PRENATAL DEVELOPMENT AND CARE

Pregnancy can be both a joyous occasion and one of concern. If the pregnancy is planned and/or wanted, the joy and excitement of impending parenthood can be tremendous. Pregnancy can bring a couple closer together as they adapt to this new stage in their lives and as they share common hopes and dreams for their future child. Pregnancy can also be a time of challenge. For example, a pregnancy can limit opportunities or it can place considerable strain on a relationship. Pregnancy can also be a time of discomfort, self-doubt, and low self-esteem. For instance, given the overwhelming emphasis we place on physical appearance in this society, it is no wonder that with the growth of a woman's body during pregnancy, some women feel ugly and unattractive. However, this is certainly not the case for all women. Some women are delighted with their appearance and believe they are more beautiful at this time than at any other time. This attitude is particularly apparent today among female celebrities, a number of whom have posed nude while pregnant. For some women, this is very controversial; others see these posed bare pregnant bodies as a beautiful art form and one-of-a-kind family keepsake as well as a sign of our changing culture.

Moreover, pregnancy can create anxieties and fears concerning a number of issues, some of which include the pregnancy's effect on the couple's relationship, whether one or both partners will be good parents, the probability of carrying a fetus to full term versus a pregnancy loss of one kind or another, as well as concerns about the health and well-being of both the mother and the unborn fetus. If there is concern about the health or well-being of the fetus, prenatal testing can provide the couple with specific information about the condition of the fetus.

Although maternal and infant health have been improving across the United States, according to the most recent data, the **infant mortality rate**—which is the rate at which babies die before their first birthday—is 6.4 deaths per 1,000 live births, higher than in 40 other countries. Although fewer newborns are dying worldwide, it is estimated that 2 million babies die within their first 24 hours each year worldwide; an additional 1 million die during days 2 through 7. Two million more babies die within their first month and another 4 million are stillborn. In total, almost 10 million children under the age of 5 die each year—more than 26,000 every day—accounting for 41 percent of all child deaths before the age of five. The overwhelming majority of these deaths (99 percent) occur in the developing world.

Ten countries account for more than two-thirds of all newborn deaths worldwide, with the highest number of deaths taking place in India (more than 1 million, accounting for roughly 28 percent of the global total). However, because of India's large population it does not have the highest rate of newborn deaths. Overall, the region of the world with the highest newborn death rates is sub-Saharan Africa where 1 out of 5 mothers have lost at least one baby in childbirth. Children in developing countries are ten times more likely to die before age five than children in developed countries. In fact, it has been reported that newborn deaths are so common in many parts of the developing world that parents put off naming their babies until they are a week to three months old (World Health Organization, 2011c; Sudan Vision Daily, 2011).

Almost three-fourths (70 percent) of infant deaths are due to conditions that could be prevented or treated with access to simple affordable interventions. In this context, three causes account for 77 percent of deaths in children under five: preterm delivery (29 percent), asphyxia—lack of breathing at birth (23 percent) and severe infections, such as measles, diarrhea, pneumonia, malaria, and HIV/AIDS (25 percent). Around 20 million children worldwide suffer from severe malnutrition (making children more vulnerable to severe disease), which is the underlying contributing factor in over one third of all child deaths. According to experts in the field, two-thirds or more of these deaths could be prevented by existing interventions if they reached those who need them (World Health Organization, 2009, 2011c).

In the United States, the leading causes of infant mortality are congenital anomalies, disorders related to premature birth and low birth weight, sudden infant death syndrome (SIDS), birth defects, and maternal complications. Despite the steady fall in the infant mortality rate over the last several decades, infant and child mortality rates in the United States are higher than in any other industrialized country, with the exception of Latvia, Lithuania, and Slovakia. American babies are three times more likely to die in their first month as children born in Japan, and newborn mortality is 2.5 times higher in the United States than in Finland, Iceland, or Norway. In addition, disparities in the United States remain high among racial and ethnic groups on many measures of maternal and child health. Although the trend in infant mortality rates among non-Hispanic Blacks and non-Hispanic Whites has been on an overall decline, the infant mortality rate among infants of non-Hispanic Black mothers is more than double that for non-Hispanic Whites. Babies born to African American mothers continue to have the highest rate of infant deaths at 12.7 per 1000 live births, while Asian/Pacific Islander Americans have the lowest rate at 3.8. The rate for Native Americans and Alaska Natives is 8.7 and for Whites it is 5.3. Infants born to Latina mothers, who can be of any race, have an infant mortality rate of 5.7 (Kochanek, 2011; Save the Children, 2011; The Annie E. Casey Foundation, 2008).

These facts notwithstanding, most often a pregnancy ends with the birth of a healthy baby. Nine out of 10 babies born in the United States are healthy. Although the chances of having a healthy baby are good, most parents want to do all they can to make this a reality.

Infant and Maternal Morbidity and Mortality Birth defects account for 20 percent of all infant deaths in the United States, more than from any other single cause. They include

In response to the high infant mortality rate in the United States, midwifery pioneer Ina May Gaskin initiated the Safe Motherhood Quilt Project, a national effort developed to draw attention to the current maternal death rates. The quilt is made up of individually designed squares, each one honoring a woman in the United States who has died of pregnancy-related causes since 1982. Each piece is personalized and may simply consist of the name of the woman or include the date and place of her death.

any condition that causes or leads to death or the lowering of the quality of life. Birth defects can usually be traced to one or more of the following factors: (1) the influence of the prenatal environment on the fetus—for example, exposure to toxic chemicals and the use of drugs, including alcohol and tobacco, by the mother; (2) heredity—that is, the parents' genes; and (3) injuries sustained at birth. Regardless of their causes, all defects present at birth are referred to as **congenital.** Only about one-fifth of birth defects can be traced to heredity. Research has shown repeatedly that experiences such as those of age, race, and class have important effects on **morbidity** (illness) and **mortality** (death). For example, although more women age 40 and older are having children today than in the past, it is believed that the optimum age for pregnancy is between ages 20 and 35. Thus, women younger than 20 and older than 35 are at greater risk of experiencing a miscarriage, a stillbirth, a premature birth, pregnancy-induced hypertension, high blood pressure, developing diabetes, placental separation, an underweight baby, prolonged and more difficult labor, or a child with a birth defect. Although the overall risks to maternal and fetal health for pregnant women over age 35 have lessened in some areas of health and well-being, these women are still more at risk than are younger women. Women over age 40, for example, have the highest rates of babies born with Down Syndrome. At the other end of the age spectrum, the maternal death rate from pregnancy and its complications is 60 percent higher for adolescents than for mothers in their early 20s (March of Dimes, 2009; Constable, 2008; March of Dimes, 2008).

Protecting the prenatal environment includes protecting the health of the mother. Every minute, at least one woman dies from complications related to pregnancy or childbirth—that translates to more than 500,000 women a year. In addition, for every woman who dies in childbirth, around 20 more suffer injury, infection or disease—approximately 10 million women each year. As in other areas of social life, race and class affect a woman's life chances when pregnant and/or delivering a baby. Countries and/or regions of the world that have high infant mortality rates also typically have high maternal mortality rates. For instance, in sub-Saharan Africa and South Asia, a woman has a 1 in 31 and 1 in 230 (respectively) lifetime chance of dying in childbirth compared to women in industrialized countries, where the risk drops dramatically to 1 in 3,600. Additionally, more than 50 million women suffer from a serious pregnancy-related illness or disability. In the United States, each year 30 percent of pregnant women have pregnancy-related complications before, during, or after delivery that often lead to long-term health problems. Approximately 1,000 of these women die each year. The United States has the highest maternal death rate of any industrialized nation (1 in 2,100) and lags behind 30 developed countries for mothers' well-being. An American woman is more than seven times as likely as one in Ireland to die from pregnancy-related causes and her maternal death risk is 15 times that in Greece (Save the Children, 2011; World Health Organization, 2010b).

In the United States, Latina, Asian/Pacific Islander, and Native American/Alaska Native women suffer a significantly higher risk of pregnancy-related mortality than non-Hispanic White women, while African American women, with the highest risk of all racial and ethnic groups, are four times more likely as White and other ethnic women to die in childbirth, with a maternal mortality rate as high as those seen in some developing countries. Additionally, Asian and Hispanic immigrant women also have a much greater risk of pregnancy-related deaths compared to White women. Further, as women age, as with other risk factors, the risk of dying in childbirth increases. Younger women are the least likely to die from pregnancy-related complications; White women under age 30 have the lowest risk of all groups (Save the Children, 2011; Miniño, et al., 2007).

PROTECTING THE PRENATAL ENVIRONMENT

The health of parents, particularly mothers before and during pregnancy, and the services available to them throughout their pregnancy, especially at delivery, are important determinants of the health status of their children. Infants whose health status is compromised at birth are more vulnerable to various health problems later in life. Although we cannot control heredity, we can to some degree control the prenatal environment. Some of the most prevalent prenatal concerns include nutrition, smoking, alcohol, drug use, and AIDS.

Nutrition Because nutrients pass from mother to fetus through the placenta, maternal malnutrition or an improper diet can have detrimental effects for the fetus—including congenital defects, small stature, and diseases such as rickets, cerebral palsy, and epilepsy; it can also cause a miscarriage or stillbirth. Various research studies show that girls who are inadequately fed in childhood may have impaired intellectual capacity, delayed puberty, and possibly impaired fertility and stunted growth, leading to higher risks of complications during childbirth. According to most authorities, maternal malnutrition is one of the leading causes of fetal death. The probability of malnutrition during pregnancy is highest among teen mothers and poor and working-class women regardless of age.

Smoking and Alcohol Consumption According to various reports on tobacco use, cigarette smoking continues to be the leading cause of preventable morbidity and mortality in the United States and the second leading cause of death in the world. Not only is smoking detrimental to the health of the smoker, it also has been shown to be detrimental to the health of the fetus. Although the extent of damage caused by cigarette smoking during pregnancy is still not fully known, since 1985 the U.S. surgeon general has cautioned that smoking during pregnancy increases the risk of miscarriage, premature birth, low birth weight, intrauterine growth retardation, stillbirth and infant mortality, probability of sickness, convulsions, or death in early infancy as well as negative consequences for child health and development. Breathing someone else's smoke is also harmful. Mothers who are exposed to second-hand smoke are also more likely to have lower weight babies, putting them at risk for many health problems. Infants whose mothers smoke during pregnancy are three times more likely to die from Sudden Infant Death Syndrome than babies whose mothers do not smoke during pregnancy. In addition, children born to mothers who smoked while pregnant, and possibly children whose grandmothers smoked while pregnant, have a higher risk of developing childhood asthma. Maternal smoking during pregnancy is also a risk factor for early childhood obesity and it is associated with later problem

behaviors for the child. For example, smoking by the mother during pregnancy has been found to be associated with substance abuse and criminal behavior in both male and female children when they reach adulthood (Child Trends, 2010a).

Smoking rates vary across age, race, and level of educational attainment. Women ages 20–24 have the highest rate of smoking during pregnancy followed by teens; women over age 40 have the lowest rate. Of all racial and ethnic groups, Native American and Alaska Native women have the highest rate of smoking during pregnancy, followed by non-Latina White mothers; African American mothers have lower rates and Latinas and Asian American and Pacific Islander women have the lowest rates of smoking of all groups. Smoking during pregnancy is also highly correlated with educational attainment. As the level of the mother's formal education increases, the likelihood that she will smoke during pregnancy decreases significantly. For instance college graduates have the lowest rate of smoking during pregnancy. However, pregnant women who smoke are not the only ones to put the developing fetus in jeopardy. Research studies suggest that smoking by fathers may have an indirect and negative effect on the fetus. Male smoking can harm or impair sperm, causing a miscarriage and passing on a slight but significant legacy of cancer, tumors, and leukemia to offspring, even if the mother does not smoke (Osterman, et al., 2011; March of Dimes, 2010; Matthews and MacDorman, 2006).

As with cigarette smoking, maternal alcohol consumption can have considerable negative effects, both for the mother and the fetus. Alcohol use during pregnancy is the leading cause of mental retardation in children. An alcoholic mother can give birth to a baby who is also dependent on alcohol. Heavy alcohol use during pregnancy, either alone or in conjunction with smoking, can cause a range of disorders known as *fetal alcohol spectrum disorders (FASD)*—an umbrella term describing the range of effects that can occur in an individual whose mother drank alcohol during pregnancy. One of the most serious effects of alcohol consumption during pregnancy is **fetal alcohol syndrome (FAS)** or *fetal alcohol effect (FAE)*, a lifelong condition that causes physical and mental disabilities characterized by growth deficiencies, skeletal deformities, facial abnormalities, organ deformities, and central nervous system handicaps.

FAS is one of the three leading known causes of birth defects in the United States. It is the leading cause of preventable mental retardation. Each year, between 4,000 and 12,000 American children are born with physical and cognitive disabilities attributed to FAS, and thousands more experience less severe abnormalities that persist through adulthood. The highest prevalence of FAS is found among Native American/Alaska Native newborns (30 per 10,000 live births) and is evidence of high rates of alcohol consumption during pregnancy. It is the leading cause of disability among these newborns. FAS occurs much less frequently among other groups of women: 6 percent of infants born to African American women have FAS, 1 percent of infants born to White women and Latinas have FAS, while fewer than 1 percent of the births to Asian American women have this condition. A child with FAS or FAE may have speech and language delays, poor reasoning and judgment skills, difficulty paying attention in school, various learning problems, and a lower IQ; this child may also be hyperactive ("Prevalence and Incidence of Fetal Alcohol Syndrome," 2008).

Experts have yet to agree on a safe level of alcohol consumption by pregnant women. Although many people believe an occasional glass of wine or beer is harmless for the fetus, most physicians recommend that a pregnant woman refrain from all alcohol consumption. FAS birth defects have no cure—thus, the effects never go away. However, FAS defects are 100 percent preventable if a woman does not drink alcohol while she is pregnant.

Drugs and Other Substance Abuse

The majority of drugs, whether street drugs, common drugs like caffeine and aspirin, or prescription and over-the-counter medications, contain chemicals that have been found to have some effect on the fetus. The fetus is particularly vulnerable to drugs in the first trimester, when the vital organs are forming. Because most pregnant women who use illicit drugs also use alcohol and tobacco, it often is difficult to determine which health problems are caused by a specific illicit drug. In any event, most research suggests that women who use cocaine during pregnancy, for example, increase the risk of hemorrhage and miscarriage; they have significantly higher rates of premature and low-birth-weight babies, and an increased risk of lifelong disabilities such as mental retardation and cerebral palsy. Cocaine and other illicit drugs can cause a baby to be born too small; have smaller heads; which generally reflect smaller brains or to have birth defects or learning or behavioral problems compared with babies of nonusers. Babies exposed to narcotics in the womb are frequently born addicted, and the misery they suffer from withdrawal makes them difficult to care for. These babies are also at greater risk of suffering strokes, seizures, heart attack, brain damage, mental retardation, and congenital abnormalities (March of Dimes, 2010).According to some observers, the overwhelming number of severely drug-damaged children is stretching to the limits the capabilities of most major societal institutions to provide assistance. What can society do? What, if anything, is the responsibility of parents? The state? The criminal justice system? These are questions of concern for a growing number of people in U.S. society who argue that the fetus has a right to be born with the best possible chance for a healthy and long life. Consequently, as the use and abuse of cocaine, particularly in the potent form of crack, has increased, drug-abusing women are being legally punished for the outcome of their pregnancies; they are being singled out and subjected to a sex-specific form of criminal prosecution for their drug use. Prosecutors in several states have brought cases against these women under statutes intended for other purposes. In 2000, the Ohio Supreme Court ruled that a baby born addicted to cocaine because of its mother's addiction is legally an abused child. And in 2001, in a landmark case, a 24-year-old mother of three gave birth to a stillborn infant and was charged with killing that child by smoking crack cocaine, making her the first woman in the nation to be convicted of homicide for killing an unborn child through drug abuse. Her sentence of 20 years, reduced to 12 years without the chance for parole, was the stiffest penalty yet for a woman who abused drugs while pregnant. This case rekindled the debate about fetal rights and opened the door to future prosecutions of women for smoking, alcohol use, or other behaviors that could harm a fetus. Apart from the constitutional issues they raise, critics of such policies and practices charge that such cases could affect abortion rights and open the door to the prosecution of mothers who smoke, fail to follow their obstetrician's diet, or take some other action that endangers a fetus (Sobey, 1997; Butler, 1999; Pressley, 2001).

AIDS and Pregnancy

Women who are HIV-positive face not only the probability that the infection will develop into full-blown AIDS but also face severe restrictions on their behavior, particularly their reproductive behavior. One of the biggest problems for these women, when or if they do become pregnant, is how to take care of their health and at the same time prevent transmitting the infection to their infant. Worldwide, some 2.1 million children are living with HIV. The major cause of HIV/AIDS among children is transmission of HIV during pregnancy, labor and delivery, and breast-feeding. This problem is more acute for pregnant HIV-infected women who do not receive preventive medication. For instance, if a mother living with HIV/AIDS receives no preventive drugs and breast-feeds, the chance of her baby becoming infected is between 20 and 45 percent. The availability of medications that can block the transmission of HIV during pregnancy, childbirth and the postnatal period has created new opportunities to slow the spread of the virus. However, fewer than 10 percent of HIV-positive women in developing countries get antiretroviral therapy during pregnancy and childbirth, despite the fact that overall access to the drugs has increased over the past several years. The term AIDS dysmorphic syndrome, or **HIV embryopathy,** has been used by some researchers to describe specific facial malformations in infants who acquired HIV infection from their mothers. However, more recent research suggests that there is a lack of evidence for such characteristic facial malformations in these babies (World Health Organization, 2011c; American Pregnancy Association, 2011).

In the United States, the problem of vertical transmission of HIV infection is exacerbated because most American women who are infected with HIV are not even aware that they carry the virus. Because of their limited access to drug treatment programs, medical information, and quality health care, poor communities and communities of color are especially at risk for HIV/AIDS babies. This is unfortunate given that, to date, most research and clinical study trials of pregnant women with HIV/AIDS have shown conclusively that medical therapy treatments with modern drugs are highly effective in preventing HIV transmission from mother to child, and when combined with other interventions, including formula feeding, a complete course of treatment can reduce the risk of transmission to 2 percent or less. Even where resources are limited, a single dose of medicine given to mother and baby can cut the risk in half (American Pregnancy Association, 2011; Kanabus, 2008).

We discuss other STIs such as syphilis and gonorrhea in Appendix A. These infections can also affect a fetus and can be contracted by the newborn. As with the AIDS virus, STIs in pregnant women can cause miscarriage, brain damage to the fetus, problems with eyesight, and other medical problems.

Expectant Fathers

Pregnant women are considered to be in a special condition, and we generally give them all of our attention and support. But what about the expectant father? Given that we expect men to play an increasingly active role in childbirth and childrearing, what do we know about their experiences through pregnancy and the birth of their children?

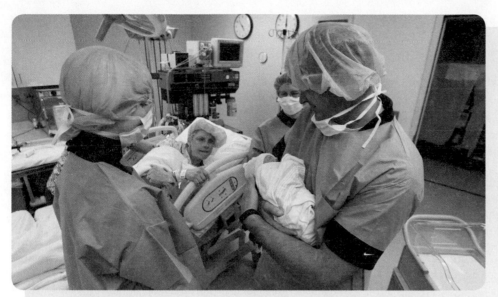

In the past, expectant fathers typically paced nervously in hospital waiting rooms, anxiously waiting to hear news of their child's birth. Today, however, a growing number of fathers are participating in every aspect of the pregnancy and childbirth experience. For example, many fathers like Tim Pearce, pictured holding his newborn son, are joining their pregnant partners in the delivery room where they participate in a range of behaviors from helping their partners with relaxation techniques to cutting the umbilical cord.

Historically, pregnancy has been viewed primarily as women's work. Expectant fathers were left in the background, unnoticed until the onset of labor. Few fathers participated in pregnancy and childbirth beyond offering general support to the mother. Today, however, a growing number of fathers are participating in the pregnancy and childbirth experience. Many prospective dads are joining their pregnant partners in prenatal classes and in the delivery room, where they help their partner with breathing and other relaxation techniques. Some fathers even assist in the delivery by cutting the unbiblical cord. Sometimes, it is the father who is the first of the two to hold the newborn, and a growing number of these men take some time off from work during the first few weeks after the baby is born to share in the caring for and bonding with the infant.

THE CULTURAL DOUBLE BIND

Research about expectant fathers conducted during the late 1980s and early 1990s suggested that expectant American fathers faced a cultural double bind. That is, they are encouraged to be part of a process about which they know little or nothing, and they have few role models because their fathers almost certainly did not participate actively in their mothers' pregnancies. Moreover, on the one hand, men are encouraged to participate in the pregnancy and birth of their children; but on the other hand, they are treated as outsiders by everyone concerned. At times, an expectant father might be as frightened, concerned, sad, and angry as his wife or partner. He needs to share these feelings and fears. But we allow only women to do this. The expectant father has neither the support systems nor the cultural sanctions for what he experiences during impending fatherhood (see, for example, Jerrold Lee Shapiro, 1987). While this was perhaps truer two or more decades ago, expectant fathers' role during pregnancy, labor and childbirth has become more participatory than it has ever been. During the 1960s and 1970s, men were encouraged to give support to their pregnant partners before, during and after childbirth by taking part in parent groups, participating during labor, and taking a more active role in caring for their infants. Today, that role has expanded; it is no longer simply for the support and benefit of the

mother and child but also for the benefit of the father himself and his potential to develop his identity as a parent as early as possible (Plantin, 2011).

A growing body of multidisciplinary research on men, masculinities, and fatherhood points out the importance of involving men as fathers early on in pregnancy and delivery. Many child psychologists, for instance, believe that the more involved a man is with the pregnancy and birth of his child, the more likely he is to be involved in childrearing. Sociological studies support this viewpoint. For example, various studies have found that fathers who were involved with their partner's pregnancy and were present at delivery showed more interest in looking at their infants and talking to them than did fathers who were not involved with the woman's pregnancy and were not present at the delivery. However, despite this research and the new more involved expectant father, many men still mainly act as financial providers for the family and remain only secondarily involved, if at all, during the pregnancy, labor and childbirth process. This is true in part because there is still a popular perception of men as bumbling and inept when it comes to children and the fact that there is still not widespread support for men and parenting (Plantin, 2011).

While some men still feel left out starting early on in the pregnancy others are speaking out and saying that they are more than simply sperm donors. Rather, they experience a wide range of emotions and there should be greater recognition that expectant fathers also experience things unique to that special time of life. The experience of pregnancy and childbirth is no less important or profound for men than it is for women. Expectant fathers often worry about what kind of father they will be, how they can afford to have a child, and if and how their relationship with their wife or partner will change. When men witness their babies entering the world, they almost always become active fathers, and it gives them a sense of self-worth and feeling of inclusion in the birth and life of their child.

At the end of pregnancy and the birthing process, parents embark on another set of experiences that often change their lives and their relationship with one another forever. In the last section of this chapter, we present a selective review of some of the experiences parents have after the birth of a child.

Parental Adjustments, Adaptations, and Patterns of Childrearing

Parenting is one of the most challenging roles that individuals and couples face in their lifetime. Research has shown repeatedly that the addition of children to a relationship increases stress and lowers relationship satisfaction, particularly when children are still young and dependent. The addition of a new and dependent person requires that the couple make major lifestyle adjustments. Either one or both parents, or someone acting on behalf of the parents, must constantly be available and responsible for the care of the child.

As in other areas of social life, experiences such as age, race, class, gender, and sexual orientation interact to make the experience of parenthood different for different individuals and groups. After the birth of a child, parents must develop a mother or father identity. Also, particularly in the early months after the baby is brought home, parents have to adjust their sleeping habits to coincide with those of the newborn. Getting up in the middle of the night can be disruptive and exhausting and can affect the parents' job performance. Financial obligations also increase with the birth of a child, as do household and child-care responsibilities. All of these changes can increase stress within the family unit.

For some women, these stresses can show up in **postnatal depression** (sometimes referred to as "the blues" or "postpartum blues"), a condition characterized by mood shifts, irritability, and fatigue. It is estimated that about 1 out of every 4 women who give birth experience a significant level of depression in the first 6 months that follow. It is the most common complication among women who have just had a baby. Until recently, postnatal depression had been considered a "woman thing." However, fathers are vulnerable to similar emotions, especially if they are in primary caregiver situations. For example, one study of postnatal depression in fathers found that about 1 in 10 fathers gets serious postnatal depression between the first trimester of their wives' or partners' pregnancy and their babies' first birthdays. That is a little more than twice the rate of depression among men, generally. Researchers believe a variety of factors contribute to male postnatal depression. The most common are fear of fatherhood, financial concerns, added responsibilities, and role anxieties (Wang, 2010).

Additionally, a couple often has to adjust their private and intimate time together to the schedule of a child. The sexual lifestyle of a couple may change drastically when a new child arrives. Childbirth does not preclude the early resumption of sexual activities. But, after childbirth, sexuality often loses its spontaneity as couples must now arrange sexual activities around working hours and at times when the newborn is asleep. Such adjustments can be long term in that as children get older, couples often continue to arrange sexual activities around times when the children are at school or otherwise away from home.

PARENTAL ROLES

Traditionally, U.S. culture has made a clear distinction between motherhood and fatherhood. Both of these concepts reflect our ideas about gender-appropriate behavior and heterosexuality:

Women are perceived as nurturant, caring, and supportive, and men as authoritative, strong, and protective. However, as we have emphasized repeatedly, this idealized notion of women, men, and parenting does not fit contemporary reality. As with other aspects of social life, a social constructionist perspective would direct us to view parenting as a social construction. The roles of women and men, mothers and fathers, are not innate; women and men are not "born" to perform certain roles. Rather, what seems natural or real in terms of parenting depends on time, place, and social location; the meaning of motherhood and fatherhood changes in response to different social, cultural, and historical circumstances. In this sense, parenting is socially constructed. This would help to explain why we give different meanings to the same or similar behavior depending on whether it is performed by women or men—mothers or fathers. For example, when women are nurturant, caring, and protective of their children, it is called *mothering* and considered women's duty or responsibility—it is not seen as out of the ordinary. On the other hand, when men are nurturant, caring, and protective of their children, it is not called *mothering* (for fear of de-masculinizing men). More importantly, we celebrate their actions as extraordinary and think that they are wonderful human beings. The attitudes and beliefs that people hold toward appropriate gender roles have a significant influence on how they parent. Researchers have found that, for many people, the transition to parenthood means taking on more traditional gender roles. For others, it means seeking an equitable balance in gender roles and parental responsibilities.

Motherhood As a social construct, traditional notions about motherhood are rooted in a middle-class ideology that emphasizes mothering as a woman's highest achievement and fulfillment in life. If we believe that motherhood is the only true and worthwhile role for women, then, by implication, those who consciously choose not to have children or who for various medical reasons cannot have children are less than complete women. Some researchers (for example, Hoffnung, 1998) have referred to traditional ideas about motherhood as the **motherhood mystique**—which proposes that (1) the ultimate achievement and fulfillment of womanhood is through motherhood; (2) work assigned to mothers—caring for children, home, husband—fits together in a noncontradictory manner; (3) to be a good mother, a woman has to enjoy being a mother and all the work that is defined as part of the mothering role; and (4) a woman's attitude about mothering will affect her children. The optimal situation for children is when women are devoted to mothering. According to Hoffnung, this social construction of motherhood and mothering is narrow and limiting, and it is harmful not only to women but also to men and children. For one thing, it conflicts with other important aspects of women's lives—productive work, companionate marriage, and economic independence. Although traditional motherhood has benefits, it has substantial material costs for women as well.

Some benefits of motherhood include the joy of intimate contact with a growing, developing infant, the sense of importance that nurturing holds for many women, and the personal growth that comes from facing and mastering a new developmental life stage. However, the pressures that push women to devote their major energies to the family and childrearing can also have negative economic consequences for women individually and for their families. For example, women who work often select jobs around the scheduling needs of their families rather than according to their own career development. The resulting part-time or intermittent employment patterns they develop contribute to the large wage differential between women and men and limit their economic contribution to their families.

In addition, the motherhood mystique also instills guilt in some women if they do not measure up to this ideal. Women who work outside the home, for instance, are often made to feel guilty for not giving their children their undivided attention. Significantly, no such expectation is made of fathers who work. The myth that children need their mother's exclusive and continuous attention also serves to make women the scapegoat for whatever happens to children and serves to support traditional gender roles that define women as subordinate to men. According to Hoffnung: "It is not enough for women to be able to do men's work as well as women's, it is necessary to reconsider the value of mothering and to reorder public priorities so that caring for children counts in and adds to the lives of women and men. Until children are valued members of society and child care is considered work important enough to be done by both women and men, the special burdens and benefits of motherhood will keep women in second place" (1998:278).

Evelyn Nakano Glenn (1994) reminds us that mothering is not just gendered but is also racialized in that the concept of mothering as universally women's work disguises the fact that it is further subdivided, so that different aspects of caring are assigned to different groups of women. For example, poor women of color are often employed to care for the children of middle-class White women. Furthermore, according to feminist sociologist Patricia Hill Collins (1991), the basic assumptions that underlie the traditional view of motherhood apply primarily to White middle-class families and most often do not reflect the realities of African American families and other families of color. As an alternative to the traditional view of motherhood, Collins has proposed a model of African American motherhood that consists of four basic themes:

- *Bloodmothers, othermothers, and women-centered networks.* Within some African American communities, the boundaries distinguishing biological mothers (bloodmothers) and other women (othermothers) are nebulous. In such communities, a network of bloodmothers and othermothers (mothers, grandmothers, sisters, aunts, cousins, and friends) shares responsibilities for the others' children. This responsibility includes temporary and long-term child-care arrangements that, when necessary, can turn into informal adoption.
- *Providing as part of mothering.* African American women make an essential economic *contribution to the financial* well-being of their families. They have long integrated economic activities into their mothering role, a combination that is looked on favorably in African American families.
- *Community othermothers and social activism.* African American women's experiences as othermothers in their extended family networks are generalized to the larger community, where these women feel accountable for all of the community's children.
- *Motherhood as a symbol of power.* Because mothers not only raise their own children but also serve as community othermothers, motherhood is a symbol of power in African American communities.

Among African American families, the adage *it takes a village to raise a child* is a carryover from their African heritage and, for many, it is an everyday lived reality. It is exemplified in sociologist Patricia Hill Collin's concepts *blood mothers* and *other mothers* (grandmothers, aunts, sisters, and sometimes community women) who continue a history of sharing the responsibilities of parenting.

In recent decades, the demographics of motherhood have changed considerably. Thus, contemporary women's views on motherhood can be seen as falling along a continuum identified by Collins. At one end of the continuum are traditionalists who want to retain the centrality of motherhood in women's lives; at the other end are those who want to eliminate what they perceive as a cultural mandate to mother. In the middle are large numbers of women who argue for an expanded but not essentially different role for women. In their view, women can be mothers as long as they are not just mothers. Many of these women are opting for both a career and motherhood. They continue to see motherhood as fulfilling but not as the only route to personal fulfillment. The motherhood mystique notwithstanding, the reality is that women can and do find satisfaction in a variety of roles. Not all women find motherhood fulfilling. In fact, not all women desire to mother. The best circumstance is one in which a woman has the freedom to choose or not choose this option.

Fatherhood As a social construct, the traditional notion of fatherhood emphasizes an instrumental role of father as breadwinner and authority figure: The father is expected to go out to earn money to support his family. He is expected to come home, play with the children a bit, but basically a traditional father must leave the nurturing, caring, and rearing of children to the mother. The father steps back in at later stages, disciplining, guiding, protecting, and exposing his children to the outside world. American culture perpetuates this traditional definition of fatherhood in a number of ways, one of them being the many messages we transmit to men about father-hood and fathering that say they are not up to the job—that we not only do not trust them to be parents, but also we do not really need them to be. A classic example can be seen in the fact that teachers and other professionals often treat fathers as if they are incapable of parenting. For example, when a father takes his child to the doctor's office, often the doctor will give him instructions about the child's care to pass on to his wife or partner, the assumed caretaker.

▶ Read the Document
Dilemmas of Involved Fatherhood
on **myfamilylab.com**

Critics of today's families claim that fatherhood has dimin-ished as a social role for men and they call for a return to the tra-ditional family structure with fathers as head of the family—the protector and breadwinner. David Blankenhorn (1998), president of the Institute for American Values, for example, claims that traditional fatherhood has become smaller, devalued, and decul-tured and a new fatherhood has emerged—caused by men being more devoted to their work than to their families, by women having increasing power within the home, and by high divorce rates and single parents. Most family researchers agree that the traditional concept of fatherhood is as limiting as the traditional concept of motherhood. However, until recently, public policy, societal sentiment, state and federal legislation, and family law all echoed a traditional view of fatherhood. Today, for a growing number of people, the word fathering, once a word that meant mainly to sire a child, now describes the life of a caring parent.

The increasing concern about child well-being, the push for fathers' rights by various individuals and groups, and the de-mand of some fathers—especially divorced fathers—to become more actively involved in their children's upbringing have pushed some social scientists to conceptualize, reconceptualize, measure, and gather information from and about men and fathering be-yond their traditional emphasis on nonmarital childbearing, child support, and child poverty (see the Applying the Sociological Imagination box). Consequently, amid the growing body of re-search on fatherhood and fathering has emerged research that has a primary emphasis on the quality and quantity of father involve-ment and its effect on children and families. Although fathers today define their roles in many different ways, many of today's fathers are far more tightly bonded to their children than were their fathers and grandfathers. Moreover, although there is ample evidence that the number of fathers defining their role in terms of the "new father" ideal is growing, the traditional view of father-hood remains the dominant view. According to some people, the "new father" is simply the latest adaptation of the nuclear family model. They suggest that people other than biological fathers can be and are equally beneficial to a child. For example, lesbian mothers who conceive children through artificial insemination or adopt; heterosexual mothers single by choice or necessity are legitimate alternatives to the "new father." Others point out the contradictions between the ideal of the "new father" and the real-ity of what fathers actually do. Nonetheless, it would be erroneous to assume that fathers do not play a significant role in childrearing

GENDER DIFFERENCES IN THE EXPERIENCE OF PARENTHOOD

Regardless of the division of labor before the birth of a child, after a child is born mothers are typically more involved in child-care activities than fathers are, with the possible exception of stay-at-home dads. New mothers find themselves with increased house-work expectations and responsibilities. There is little dispute that more and more fathers want to spend time with their children and desire a deeper emotional connection with their children. In a recent survey, 30 percent of fathers said they would take a pay cut to spend more time with their children (Belkin, 2009). However, their actions often lag behind their attitudes. Fathers may be bonding more with their children but they continue to be far less involved in the day-to-day care of their children than mothers. Indeed, surveys show that the world over, fathers spend only a small fraction of the time that mothers, even employed mothers, spend on child-care activities. The wife-to-husband ratio for child care is close to 5 to 1 (Belkin, 2008).

Current research points to a number of ways in which parent-ing in the United States continues to be gendered—even among those couples where fathers take on the "new father" role. For example, mothers clearly spend more time "doing" for children, including the emotional work of caring and worrying about them, than fathers. In addition, fathers across race, class, and religion tend to spend more time with sons than with daughters. Although children become just as attached to their fathers as to their moth-ers and fathers are just as sensitive to their infants as mothers, women and men interact with their children in different ways. For example, fathers tend to emphasize "play" over "caretaking"—they spend a larger proportion of their time together playing (40 versus 25 percent for mothers), and their play is more likely than mothers to involve physical and arousing play activities (Craig, 2006). In addition, children's views of their parents typically fall along gen-der lines as well. For instance, children often view their fathers as stricter and more likely to use punishment than mothers.

Some scholars claim that family organization is based on very real biological differences between women and men and that "parental androgyny" (mothers and fathers playing essentially the same social roles) is neither good for children nor marriage gener-ally (Popenoe, 1999; Glenn, 1997). Other scholars argue that such gender ideology is harmful and that equitable social arrangements within marriages and families is a must and a definite improvement over the traditional division of roles because such arrangements provide increased opportunities for adult self-fulfillment (Barnett and Rivers, 2004).

STYLES OF PARENTING

Just as every pregnancy and child is different, so too are parenting styles. However, sociologists have identified some common patterns of parenting among families in the United States, especially within particular social classes. Because one of the basic elements in socio-logical definitions of class is occupation, studies of parenting styles across class often examine the kinds of attitudes and values associ-ated with different occupations and how these attitudes and values are related to childrearing strategies. A classic statement using this approach is sociologist Melvin Kohn's (1977) discussion of parenting

APPLYING THE SOCIOLOGICAL IMAGINATION

HONORING FATHERS

The idea of Father's Day originated with Sonora Dodd of Spokane, Washington, while listening to a Mother's Day sermon in 1909. Dodd wanted to honor her father, William Smart, a widowed Civil War veteran who raised his six children by himself on a rural farm. June was chosen for the first Father's Day celebration—proclaimed in 1910 by Spokane's mayor—because it was the month of William Smart's birth. The first presidential proclamation honoring fathers was issued in 1966 when President Lyndon Johnson designated the third Sunday in June as Father's Day. It has been celebrated annually since 1972 (U.S. Census Bureau, 2011c).

Father's Day Facts

- An estimated 110 million Father's Day cards were given in 2010 in the United States, making Father's Day the fourth-largest card-sending occasion.
- Fifty percent of all Father's Day cards are purchased specifically by sons and/or daughters; nearly 20 percent are purchased by wives for their husbands; the remaining cards are bought for grandfathers, sons, brothers, uncles, and "someone special."
- In 2006, 73 percent of Americans said they planned to celebrate or acknowledge Father's Day.
- Neckties lead the list of Father's Day gifts. Sales at the nations nearly 11,000 men's U.S. clothing stores exceeded $800 million in 2005.

Facts About Fathers

- There are an estimated 70 million fathers across the United States. Approximately 25.3 million of these fathers are in married-couple families with their own children under age 18. One in 10 are raising their own infants under age 1; 22 percent are raising three or more children younger than 18. Four percent of married couple fathers are over age 55, and 22 percent have an annual family income of $50,000 or more.
- There was an estimated 154,000 stay-at-home dads in 2010. These married fathers with children younger than 15 have remained out of the labor force for at least one year primarily so that they can care for the family while their wives work outside the home. These fathers cared for 287,000 children.
- One in 5 single parents are men; about 46 percent are divorced, 30 percent have never married, 19 percent are separated, and 6 percent are widowed.
- Nine percent of single fathers are raising three or more children younger than age 18. Three in 10 children under 18 live with their single father and his unmarried partner. In contrast, only 1 in 10 children who live with their single mother share the home with mom's unmarried partner, and 39 percent of these fathers have an annual family income of $50,000 or more.
- Sixty-three percent of children under age 6 who live with married parents are praised by their fathers three or more times a day. The corresponding percentage for children living in unmarried single-father families is 57 percent.

www.census.gov/newsroom/
  releases/archives/facts_for_
  features_special_editions/cb
www.census.gov/Press-Release/
  www/releases/archives/
  facts_for_features_special_
  editions/006794.html;
http://www.census.gov/
  Press-Release/www/releases/
  archives/facts_for_features_
  special_editions/001792.html;
http://dadsandgrads.about.com/od/
  celebratingdad/a/aadadsday.htm

Begin an investigation of fatherhood in the United States starting with the Web sites listed above. Which aspects of the U.S. family system foster the gendered division of labor for mothers and fathers? What evidence is there to support the idea that there are gender-based inequalities in marriages and families? How involved are fathers in childrearing? What impact do fathers have on the successful socialization of young children? What, if anything, should be done to reduce or eliminate gender-based inequalities in parental responsibilities?

---

styles in terms of self-direction versus conformity parental-value orientations. According to Kohn, the *traditional* or *conformity value orientation* is more commonly found among working-class and lower-class parents who emphasize order, authority, obedience, and respectability. In contrast, the *developmental* or *self-direction orientation* most commonly found among middle-class parents, stresses the child's motives and the development of self-control. Emphasis is on internal qualities such as consideration, curiosity, and initiative rather than on external conformity.

Some social scientists, like Diane Baumrind (1968, 1979, 1991), have incorporated Kohn's findings into a model that divides parenting styles into four general categories: authoritarian, permissive, authoritative, and uninvolved, each varying along the dimensions of support (amount of affection, acceptance warmth, and caring) and control (expectations for behavior). The *authoritarian style* demands absolute obedience from children and often involves the use of physical punishment to control behavior. Although this style of parenting is commonly associated with working-class parents, variations do exist. Working-class fathers who experience autonomy at work and who have high self-esteem, for instance, are more accepting of their children and less likely to try to control them psychologically than are working-class fathers whose jobs carry less autonomy and who have lower self-esteem (Grimm and Perry-Jenkins, 1994). Parental exposure to economic disadvantages is associated with harsher parenting behavior (Scaramella et al. 2008). Some parents of color living in high-risk environments often use authoritarian parenting styles in an effort to protect their children from danger, realizing that if their children make a mistake, they are less likely than White children to be given a break by public authorities (Hill, 1995). Although numerous studies have found that authoritarian parenting is often associated with negative outcomes—a decrease in children's mastery of a situation (Moorman and Pomerantz, 2008) or in irritable, belligerent, hyperactive, and depressive behavior (Rothrauf, Cooney, and An, 2009)—it is not always the case. Researcher Amy Chua (2011), in *Battle Hymn of the Tiger Mother*, argues that her high level of parental control produced highly successful children. Her detailed account of some of her authoritarian practices ignited a heated debate about parenting styles in the United States.

The *permissive style* of parenting, more typical of middle-class parents, gives children autonomy and freedom to express themselves, and downplays conformity. Permissive parents generally have few rules and regulations, make few demands on their children to conform, and most often use reason instead of physical punishment to modify their children's behavior. However, permissive parents sometimes exercise too little control in conflict situations with their children and allow them to grow up with little self-control or discipline. This parenting style tends to be associated with low school performance, behavior problems, juvenile delinquency and high rates of teen sexuality and pregnancy (Aunola and Nurmi, 2005).

The *authoritative style* also encourages children to be autonomous and self-reliant but they also impose rules and standards of behavior. Authoritative parents generally rely on positive reinforcements, while avoiding, as much as possible, punitive and repressive methods of discipline. These parents are in control of their children's behavior while at the same time they allow the children much more freedom than do authoritarian parents. In contrast, the *uninvolved style* of parenting is mostly one of indifference. Parents make few demands on and offer little support to their children. A considerable body of research shows favorable outcomes for children raised with an authoritative parenting regardless of socioeconomic background, race/ethnicity, or family structure (Fivush, et al. 2009; DeVore and Ginsburg 2005; Shucksmith, Hendry, and Glendinning, 1995). For example, Nancy Hill (1995) found in her study of African American families that authoritative parenting was related to such positive family characteristics as cohesion, intellectual orientation, organization, and achievement. A more recent study of Korean American college students found similar results. Authoritative parenting styles and the number of years lived in the United States were predictive of higher academic competence whereas authoritarian and permissive parenting styles were predictive of lower self-reliance (Kim and Chung, 2003).

The fourth style of parenting, the *uninvolved style* of parenting is mostly one of indifference. Parents make few demands on and offer little support to their children. In general, these parents spend little time with their children and show little love and affection toward them, often to the point of ignoring or neglecting them. Many of these parents suffer from depression and have little energy left for parenting. Their children are often emotionally withdrawn and rebellious when confronted by authority figures (Pellerin, 2005).

As indicated above, styles of parenting have important consequences for children and the larger society. This notion is reinforced in Annette Lareau's (2003) research on middle- and working-class families, which found that middle-class families engage in practices of *concerted cultivation*, whereby parents actively foster and assess their children's talents, opinions, and skills and facilitate their children's activities, which are often quite extensive. The conversational style middle-class parents use with their children helps the children to learn negotiating skills with adults and the back-and-forth mode allows children to challenge adults and to engage in reasoning and problem solving. This pattern fosters a sense of entitlement that helps middle-class children navigate the educational system from elementary school to college. In contrast, working-class and poor families engage in childrearing practices that Lareau calls the *accomplishment of natural growth*, whereby parents provide their offspring with food, shelter, and clothing but development comes spontaneously and parents organize their children's lives so they spend time around the home. Children have more autonomy and initiate their own informal play activities with neighborhood peers, but there is less conversation and little emphasis on negotiating. Lareau concludes that both practices have benefits but she argues that the middle-class approach gives children advantages in terms of learning to assert themselves and to interact in a variety of settings with all kinds of people, behaviors that are rewarded in our economy. More research is needed to see if these patterns hold up across a wider spectrum of classes, races, and ethnic groups. It does suggest, however, that if all children are to have equal opportunities for social rewards, efforts must be made to help parents gain the tools they need to equip their children with the appropriate skills.

What style of parenting did you experience growing up? What did you like or dislike about it? Is it a style you wish to replicate if you have children? Given Professor Lareau's findings, what, if anything, do you think should be done to increase opportunities for working-class children?

Discipline A major issue for many parents is how to change their children's behavior when it is unacceptable. In the United States, it is commonly believed that physical punishment is sometimes necessary to discipline a child. In 2006, 75 percent of parents believed spanking was necessary (Ave, 2008). Experts on child care are somewhat divided on the efficacy of spanking. On the one hand, psychologist Diana Baumrind argues that many studies do not distinguish the effects of spanking as practiced by nonabusive parents from the impact of severe physical punishment and abuse. Her analysis of data from a 12-year study of more than 100 families found that mild to moderate spanking had no detrimental effects when such confounding influences were controlled (Goode, 2001). Similarly, a comparative study of child outcomes of corporal punishment versus alternative disciplinary tactics found that outcomes of corporal punishment compared unfavorably with alternatives only when used too severely or as the primary disciplinary method (Larzelere and Kuhn, 2005).

On the other hand, some researchers found that even minor forms of spanking increase the risk for increased child aggression (Taylor, et al. 2010). Murray Strauss (2007; 2001), a nationally recognized researcher on family violence, points out the harmful consequences of spanking:

- The more frequently a child is spanked, the more aggressive the child is likely to become.
- Spanking erodes the bond of affection between parent and child.
- Spanking teaches a child what not to do, not what is the right thing to do.
- Parents who were spanked as children are more likely to spank their own children.
- Spanking can get out of hand and escalate into physical abuse. Spouses who received harsh punishment as children are more likely to be abusive to their spouses and children.

To avoid these negative effects, child experts recommend alternative methods of discipline that include removing temptations that lead to misbehavior, establishing reasonable and consistent rules, modeling appropriate behavior, praising good behavior, treating children with respect, and providing emotional support by expressing love, warmth, and acceptance.

Given the obvious troubled nature of many of today's youth, an increasing number of people have expropriated the African proverb that so often served as a guiding principle in African American communities: "It takes a village to raise a child." Using this concept, they argue that parents, regardless of parenting style, need help from "the village"—a community or network of individuals and group support—to raise a child. A number of research studies support this notion of extended parenting. For example, various research shows that when teachers and parents work collaboratively and begin intervention early in children's lives, it has a significant long-term, positive effect on children's behavior and their academic achievement (Carter, 2002; Brody, 1999).

PARENTING ISSUES IN THE DIGITAL WORLD

A major challenge for parents today comes from new technology—cell phones, texting, and Internet chat rooms and social networking sites. Often their children are more adept at using these technologies than they are. According to a recent survey, some 75 percent of 12–17-year-olds now own cell phones that have become indispensable tools in teen communication patterns. Fully 72 percent of all teens (88 percent of teen cell phone users) are text messagers. Texting has overtaken the frequency of every other common form of interaction with their friends and may interfere with classroom performance. Sixty-four percent of teens with cell phones have texted in class; 25 percent have made or received a call during class time (Lenhart, 2010). For parents, the decision to give children a cell phone is a two-edged sword. On the one hand, they believe it improves the safety and security of their children, providing them with the means to stay in touch wherever they may be as well as providing an easy and fun way to share family experiences. On the other hand, their child's attachment to their phone is an area of conflict as well as one of potential risk.

Some of the sources of conflict are related to finances and distractions, others to potential risks. Teens tend to favor non-voice applications of their phones without understanding the costs involved and often run up huge bills that constrain family budgets. Teen texting is so pervasive that many a family meal is disrupted when a pocket buzz announces an incoming message that takes the child out of the present moment and focuses her/his attention elsewhere. Among the risks are texting and driving, harassment, and bullying. One in three (34 percent) of texting teens (ages 16–17) say they have texted while driving; 48 percent of all teens ages 12–17 say they have been in a car when the driver was texting. Twenty-six percent of teens have been bullied or harassed through text messages and phone calls. Fifteen percent of teens say they have received a sexually suggestive nude or nearly nude image of someone they know by text (Lenhart, 2010). Similar problems can arise when children become involved in social networks like Facebook.

To meet these challenges, parents must learn to use these technologies themselves. Asking their children to teach them can provide an opportunity to dialogue with them about the constructive use and abuse of various technologies. Beyond modeling appropriate behavior (no texting while driving or at the table), parents need to equip their children with strong critical thinking

Many studies have found that texting while driving distracts the driver's attention and often leads to serious car accidents. Texting is a problem not only for teens but also for their parents. Parents have a responsibility to provide their children with guidelines and personal examples of how to use information technologies in an appropriate way.

and decision-making skills—how to make wise choices when confronted with the wide array of options that technology offers and to set limits. How much time and what content is appropriate for them? Parents need to teach their children that there are dangers online and that bullying and harassment are never appropriate and that kindness and empathy are. They also need to teach their children what constitutes a safe situation and when it is and isn't appropriate to share personal information. Above all parents need to be aware of what their children are doing (Samland, 2008).

Married and heterosexual people are not the only ones who have children or face special challenges during pregnancy, childbearing, and childrearing. As we have emphasized often, the interrelationship of the axes of social structure such as race, class, gender, sexual orientation, and age shape the experiences of *all* people in this country. Thus, it is instructive to consider some of the ways in which these structures shape the reproductive and parenting experiences of a number of groups in U.S. society.

RACE AND CLASS

What is the significance of race/ethnicity and social class for our understanding of marriages and families? In this section, we provide a brief review and analysis of the intersections of race and class in the familial lives of various racial and ethnic groups.

SYSTEMIC RACISM AND ITS IMPACT ON AMERICAN FAMILIES

The idea that America is a post-racial society is clearly a debatable issue today. However, this debate notwithstanding, racism (both individual and institutional) continues to be a pervasive problem that impacts individual Americans and their families. That racism is alive and well in U.S. society is indicated in the responses of Americans (especially Americans of color) to questions about race, racism and race relations. For example, 43 percent of African Americans compared to 19 percent of Hispanics and 13 percent of Whites think that there is still a lot of discrimination against Blacks today. On the other hand, 33 percent of Blacks compared to 24 percent and 21 percent of Hispanics and Whites respectively think that there is a lot of discrimination against Hispanics. However, all three groups report that there is not a lot of discrimination against Asians (Pew Research Center, 2010a). Given that Blacks, Whites, and other racial groups view and experience race from different vantage points it is not surprising that their views about race vary (see Table 9.1).

Systemic racism is the belief that race is biologically determined and thus the primary determinant of human traits and capabilities. As such, racial differences produce an inherent or biological superiority of one race and the inherent or biological inferiority of other races. It is an ideology of domination and includes a wide assortment of social, economic, and political policies and practices that systematically deny the latter groups full access and participation in mainstream society, the unjustly gained economic and political power of those defined as superior, ongoing inequality in the distribution of wealth and other resources, and racist ideologies, attitudes, and institutions created to preserve advantage and power for those defined as superior (see, for example, Joe Feagin, 2010).

Systemic racism, discrimination, prejudice, and **xenophobia**—a fear or hatred of strangers or foreigners, or of anything foreign and/

or different—are powerful forces that have left Americans and their families across race and ethnic divisions victims of legal, social, and political systems that crush their hopes, dreams, and aspirations, not because they have committed a crime but rather because they were born into a particular racial or ethnic group or practice a particular religion. Individuals and whole families are unable to receive quality education, health care, housing, food, or clothing because they are trapped in a maze of unjust legal, social, and political practices that deny them access to the most basic human rights. In the United States, racism, prejudice, discrimination, violence, and inequality among racial and ethnic groups are deeply interwoven into the fabric of American society. The proliferation of hate groups—groups whose ideologies include tenets of racially based hatred and whose practices attack or malign an entire class of people, typically for their immutable racial characteristics—in the United States was again highlighted after the November 2008 election of Barack Obama as the nation's first African American President. Racism and racist actions against individuals and groups are often perpetrated by individuals either acting alone or in groups. However, wider societal and institutional racism perpetuates racist beliefs and ideologies that make it easier for individuals to commit racist acts. Research has consistently demonstrated that families, especially children, from racial and ethnic groups defined and treated as minorities suffer many forms of disadvantage because of individual and institutional racism, including poorer health, poverty, and educational underachievement.

AFRICAN AMERICAN FAMILIES

African American families have historically experienced issues that many other families have only recently become attentive to—combining work and family roles, single parenthood, and extended family relationships. Their experiences can be instructive for other families.

Family Structure African American families have in the past and continue today to represent a variety of household types and structures. Although African American families reflect the general American culture of families and structures, they have also formed some distinctive structures for surviving and getting ahead in response to a history of racism, discrimination, poverty, their own cultural heritage, and a variety of other social and political factors. Today, just under half of African American family households (47 percent) are married-couple families, 44 percent are female-headed families, and 9 percent are male-headed families. Like most other married-couple families, African American married-couple families are smaller than in the past; 89 percent of these families have two or fewer children living at home under age 18. Likewise, and contrary to the belief that African American female heads of household have large numbers of children, 95 percent of African American single-parent families have two or fewer children. Consistent with other racial groups, the average number of people per African American household is three. Finally, consistent with a cultural history of self-help and extended family households, almost one in five African American grandparents live in the home with their grandchildren (either their own home or that of their grandchildren), and one in four have full responsibility for their grandchildren (U.S. Census Bureau, 2010b).

TABLE 9.1 Black, White, and Latina/o Attitudes about Race and Racism in America

Survey research has shown historically that various racial groups differ in terms of their views about race, racism, discrimination, and race relations in the United States. Blacks and Whites, in particular, have had very divergent views about the prevalence or lack thereof of these phenomena. Have these two groups' views converged today? Do Blacks and Latinas/os more closely agree, or do Latinas/os and Whites more closely agree on these issues?

How pervasive is anti-Black discrimination?

	A Lot	Some	A Little	None
All	18%	51%	21%	6%
Blacks	43%	39%	14%	2%
Whites	13%	57%	21%	5%
Latinas/os	19%	35%	30%	13%

Has America done enough to give Blacks equal rights with Whites?

	The country has made the necessary changes.	More changes are needed to ensure that Blacks have equal rights with Whites.
All	47%	43%
Blacks	13%	81%
Whites	54%	36%
Hispanics	42%	47%

Is the situation of Blacks better, worse, or about the same compared to 5 years ago?

	Better	Worse	About the Same	Don't Know
All	48%	6%	41%	5%
Blacks	39%	12%	48%	1%
Whites	49%	6%	40%	5%
Latinas/os	47%	5%	43%	5%

Is race a factor in the opposition to President Barack Obama's policies?

His race is....	A Major Reason	A Minor Reason	Not a Reason
Blacks	52%	21%	19%
Whites	17%	33%	42%
Latinas/os	29%	34%	27%

Are Black and White values becoming more similar?

	Similar	Different	No Change	Don't Know
All	68%	20%	2%	9%
Blacks	60%	34%	2%	3%
Whites	70%	18%	2%	9%
Latinas/os	67%	22%	1%	10%

Source: Pew Research Center. 2010. "Blacks Upbeat about Black Progress, Prospects," (January 12). Washington, DC. http://pewsocialtrends.org/2010/01/12/blacks-upbeat-about-black-progress-prospects/

As a number of family sociologists have pointed out, there is nothing inherently pathological or dysfunctional in the structure of African American families. Most single mothers, for instance, have done a phenomenal job of raising their children in less than ideal circumstances. Rather than dysfunctionality, historically the structure of these families has been an adaptive response to a racist culture (see for example, Andrew Billingsley, 1968). Therefore, to understand African American families, scholars must take into account racism and inequality and a broad range of intersections, including race, class, gender, sexual orientation, age, and geographic location. Some policymakers and various African American scholars and researchers have suggested that we should be more interested in finding ways to constructively address the structural, social and political problems associated with all female-headed families rather that assigning blame to one group or another.

It is also important to keep in mind that although African American families share many commonalities, their experiences, opinions, beliefs are very diverse and there are important economic and social differences among African American families. For example, African American families differ by class, region of the country they live in, age, sex, gender, sexual orientation, gender of family head, and number of family members, to name but a few markers of difference. However, as we discussed in Chapter 1, the one thing that African American families typically are not is the stereotypic, mythical, and/or negative images commonly applied to them in both popular culture and in some scholarly research.

Dispelling African American Family Myths Contrary to popular myth, African Americans value family life and parenthood. According to some survey research, African Americans believe very strongly in the institution of the family, the majority (90 percent) reporting that they are satisfied with their spouse and/or family life. This is particularly true of the middle class, who report that family life is their greatest source of life satisfaction (Pew Research Center, 2010a). Other research has consistently shown that motherhood and childrearing are among the most important values in African American communities and that strong kinship bonds have had a significant impact on African American parents' ability to parent successfully in an environment that is so often negatively impacted by male sexism and White racism.

Since the 1960s, Americans' attitudes toward marriage and childbearing have become much more flexible, shifting substantially away from stigmatization of non-marital childbearing and toward greater acceptance of it. According to some observers, this attitudinal shift has been accepted more broadly among African Americans than among other racial and ethnic groups. However, recent survey research does not seem to support this viewpoint. Some of this research indicates that African Americans are actually more "traditional" or conservative in their views of marriage and family than most other racial groups. For example, various surveys report that three out of four African American report having "old-fashioned" values about marriage and family and about one-half believe that among the serious problems facing African American communities today is the high rate of unwed births. In addition, two-thirds believe that a child needs a home with both a mother and a father in order to grow up happily (Pew Research Center, 2010a, 2010b). Moreover, the value of family also can be seen in the fact that caring for kin is shared among female and male adults, elders, and children, so that single parents, for example, are not generally left alone to raise their children. They can often rely on the assistance of family members and/or fictive kin. Grandmothers, great grandmothers, and other mothers play an important role in the care of young and older family members. Furthermore, caring is often reciprocal, whereby members may be recruited to take care of other kin who cared for them earlier. Additionally, some researchers have reported that in two-parent families African American husbands are more likely than White husbands to share in household chores and child-care responsibilities. ("African American Families …," 2008; Hill, 2005; Willie & Reddick, 2003).

A number of scholars of African American families have noted that raising an African American child is not, and has never been, an easy task. Given the obstacles they face, however, African American parents have done a tremendous job in rearing their offspring, and they have generally done so with fewer resources than most other parents. African American parents face a dual responsibility in parenting: They must teach their children the folkways of their own culture and what it means to be "Black" in a racist society; at the same time, they must also socialize their children into the values of mainstream American culture to adapt successfully to mainstream group requirements and institutions. Given the poor social conditions under which many African American children are raised, it is not surprising that some of them fail in life. What is surprising is that so many more succeed given the adverse circumstances they encounter in the larger society ("African American Families …," 2008; Staples and Johnson, 2004; Staples, 1999).

The Myth of the Missing Black Father Perhaps one of most compelling myths about African American families and one closely tied to the myth of the Black matriarchy is the myth of the missing Black male. Myths and stereotypes abound about Black men in both academic and public opinion coverage and venues. African American men are often viewed synonymously in both venues as criminal, gang banger, illiterate, drug dealer, prison inmate, and the list goes on. Most important to this discussion is the fact that they have become the symbol of fatherlessness in America. Thus, to equate them with fatherhood is somewhat of an oxymoron. According to some scholarship on African American fatherhood, African American men are viewed as verbs but not nouns; that is, it is frequently assumed that they *father* children but seldom *are* fathers (Coles and Green, 2012).

Some of these assumptions about African American fathers did not arise from thin air. Statistics on the declining number African American married couple households, the increasing number of female-headed households, the increasing number of Black children living in mother-only households as well as that research that has shown that a large proportion of non-resident African American fathers are literally absent fathers has led many to assume that African American fathers in general are absentee fathers. Data such as these notwithstanding sociologist Patricia Hill Collins (1991) cautions against assuming that the centrality of women in childrearing is predicated on the absence of husbands and fathers, noting that men may indeed be physically present and/or have well-defined and culturally significant roles in the extended family. A considerable body of research supports Hill's contentions. For example, a variety of studies have found that while African American fathers are less likely than fathers in other racial groups to marry or cohabit with the mother, they nonetheless have the highest rate of visitation or provision of some care-taking or in-kind support and they tend to maintain their level of involvement over time longer than do White and Hispanic non-residential fathers (Coles and Green, 2012).

In addition, very often fictive or "*otherfathers*" (an extension of Patricia Hill Collins' concept of othermothers) step in for or supplement non-resident biological fathers. Although there has not been very much research on these non-biological or social fathers, what is known (see for example, Lempert, 1999) suggests that these *otherfathers* include relatives such as grandfathers, uncles, and other male extended family members; they also include friends, romantic partners, and new husbands of the mother as well as various community figures such as teachers, coaches, and community center staff. These men play central roles in the lives of African American children actively engaging themselves as providers, protectors, role models, and mentors in the lives of the children of other men: They may assume financial responsibility, in part or in whole, for these children, and serve as models of honesty, respectability, dignity, social wisdom, and race pride as they maintain a positive, interactive presence in the children's lives. Thus, while some African American children may be growing up without the care of their biological parents, they are not growing up without love and nurturing, protection, and provision from *otherfathers* (as well as *othermothers*).

Although these relationships are not and cannot be captured in census data and other statistics, research clearly shows that a large percentage of African American men act as social fathers of one sort or another. Yet little attention is paid to these dads. Rather, what we get is a relentless series of demeaning characterizations of African American men as deadbeat, absent, uninvolved and uncaring fathers. In addition to the invisibility of these fathers in scholarly research and the public arena, little attention is given to other fathers such as those in two-parent families or the nine percent of African American fathers who are full-time single parent fathers. Thus, by accepting popular myths and cultural stereotypical images of African American families as "matriarchal," where African American men are either absent or peripheral to the family, and by focusing research attention almost exclusively on female-headed African American families, researchers have all but ignored the significant role that African American men play in supporting their families and communities. From a sociological perspective, the issues surrounding African American fatherhood should not focus on who is or is not a good father or is or is not present in the household, but rather it should provide and understanding and recognition that fatherhood and fathering can and does come in many forms and many styles.

The Economics of African American Families Although the economic climate in America over the past several years has had devastating consequences for individuals and families, the intersection of race with class gives us a more intimate picture of how

⊙—|Watch the Video
Economics of the African-American Family on **myfamilylab.com**

some families have been more negatively impacted than others. Perhaps the most often used measures of the economic condition or well-being of families are median household income, employment rates, and home ownership rates. Although different groups have experienced the country's economic recession and setbacks over the past decade in different ways, relative to Whites, Blacks lost ground on all three major indicators of economic well-being. In 2010 dollars, the median household income for African Americans was $32,068. While African American median household income was above the 2010 poverty line of $22,314 for a family of four and $11,139 for an individual, it was nevertheless the lowest for all major racial categories

(U.S. Census Bureau, 2010b; Federal Register, 2010). In 2010, more than 46 million Americans were in poverty, an increase of almost 3 million people from the year before. And almost one-third of the poor lived in extreme poverty. Although the poverty rate for African Americans in 2000 was at its lowest since 1959, African American families today are still more likely than White families to live below the poverty level (27 and 10 percent, respectively, in 2010). In addition, African American children have a greater likelihood of growing up with only one parent (primarily mother-only) than children of other races and ethnicities. Such families tend to be disproportionately poor compared to two-parent African American families. However, contrary to popular myth, the majority of these families have a working head-of-household (U.S. Census Bureau, 2010b).

The flip side of these families consists of those African American families who, despite racism and discrimination and despite a culture of inequality, have managed to work their way into the middle class (albeit somewhat tenuous). In America, middle class typically refers to those who earn an annual income of between $35,000 and $100,000 per year. According to recent income data, almost one half of African Americans fall into the middle or upper middle class (38.4 and 8.1 respectively) though the majority fall at the lower end; a tiny 1.2 percent fall into the upper class while around 25.3 percent are working class and the rest are poor.

As with other measures of family economic well-being, African Americans are hardest hit by the loss of jobs and unemployment. In 2010, the unemployment rate was 17 percent compared to Asians who had the lowest rate of all groups at 7 percent. Eighteen percent of African American men and 13 percent of African American women were unemployed. Looking at home ownership as another indicator of economic well-being, in 2010 the rate for African Americans was 45.4. According to some experts, the economic recession of the past several years is erasing the slow but steady gains that African Americans had been making in recent decades. In terms of housing, the foreclosure crisis is having a particularly devastating impact on the racial progress African Americans have made. For example, recent data show that Blacks are losing their homes and their wealth at a much faster pace than most other groups, especially Whites.

While other indicators of economic well-being are important, household wealth is most important as it gives individuals and families choices and protection when times are good or bad. While the recession has caused families of all races and ethnicities to lose wealth because of a loss or reduction in the value of critical assets, such as their homes, some racial groups have been hit much harder than others with a consequent deeply widening wealth gap among the races. For example, a recent study by the Pew Research Center reported that the median wealth of a White family was 20 times greater than that of the average Black family ($113.00 and $5,700 respectively). This is of particular note given that African Americans typically have whatever wealth they have tied up in their homes (U.S. Census Bureau, 2011d; Bureau of Labor Statistics, 2011; Kellogg, 2011; Kochlhar, Fry and Taylor, 2011). While some of this gap can be explained in terms of inherited wealth, much of it also can be explained in terms of what some observers refer to as a culture of inequality. That is:

- Americans are typically segregated by race and often income.
- Jobs are low paid and scarce particularly so for the poor and racial minorities. This can lead to crime as a way of obtaining income and to unemployed men not willing to marry, which

can play a significant role in developing a cultural model of single parent families.

- The lack of income creates problems for individuals and families, including poor housing, lack of food, health problems, and inability to address needs of one's children.
- As a result of their situation, people living in poverty can themselves have patterns of behavior, such as alcoholism or a "life of crime" that are destructive to them, their families, and their communities (World Hunger Education Service, 2011).

Social Class Differences: Parents and Children Because most African Americans have encountered racism and discrimination in some form, African American childrearing practices and aspirations for their children tend to be similar across class boundaries. At the same time, however, they also exhibit class differences similar to those found among other groups in society. For example, African American middle-class families have a value orientation characterized by high achievement motivation, social striving, and a high regard for property ownership (Callis & Cavanaugh, 2008). African American middle-class families also have high educational and occupational expectations for their offspring. Thus, they try to teach their children positive attitudes toward work and thrift. These families tend to be more egalitarian than patriarchal. Parents stress conformity, chastity, and fidelity and are more inclined to use persuasive approaches to elicit obedience and conformity than to use coercion and physical punishment. Yet they demand a high degree of respect for parental authority. In addition, researchers have found that middle-class African American fathers are often integrally involved in parenting such as monitoring and supervising their children's behavior, teaching them life skills, stressing academic achievement, and generally being warm and loving and only moderately strict disciplinarians (McLoyd, Hill, and Dodge, 2005; Staples and Johnson, 2004).

African American working-class families hold similar attitudes concerning basic family goals, but their value orientation is much more affected by the constant struggle for survival, and they take great pride in the fact that they are self-supporting. The parenting style in working-class families includes an emphasis on respectability: Parents demand that their children behave well and not get into trouble with the police. Like their middle-class counterparts, they stress conformity and obedience. They typically make every attempt to buffer their children from exposure to the negative influences of drugs, gangs, and other problem behaviors by strictly monitoring their children's time and friendships. Like their middle-class counterparts, working-class parents socialize their children to exercise self-control and succeed in school.

Lower-class African American parents are often regarded as the most ineffective in their role as parents because of their reliance on physical punishment to control their children's behavior. However, what is missing from this assessment is the fact that most lower-class parents, across race, combine heavy doses of emotional nurturance with their physical measures of punishment. Some researchers suggest that this combination of childrearing practices may be more beneficial for a child's development than the middle-class practice of withholding love if the child does not behave correctly ("African American Families...," 2008; Boyd-Franklin, 2006; Newman, 2000).

Perhaps the greatest class differences in parental attitudes and parenting styles are those between the African American poor and middle class. Whether real or perceived, one in two African Americans believe that the values held by members of this group have become more and more divergent over the past years although they concede that they do still share some values with the poor (Pew Research Center, 2010a). In any case, the fact is that for good reason, many poor African Americans are disenchanted, disillusioned, and alienated and see little progress and even fewer possibilities for breaking out of their low economic status. As a consequence, according to some sociologists, many poor African American parents are generally limited in their ability to guide their children and often have little control over their children's behavior. Parental values and behaviors generally are those that are most expedient and offer hope of a livable or tolerable existence at the time. Although female-headed families make up a large proportion of the African American underclass, it is erroneous to assume that such families are synonymous with female-headed families or social problems, including a lack of family values. In fact, several scholars of African American families have suggested that single African American mothers may be particularly strong not only in terms of valuing and keeping their families together but also in protecting themselves and their offspring and coping in a world of chronic poverty, racism, sexism, and male violence ("African American Families...," 2008).

These facts notwithstanding, it is the widely publicized attitudes, actions, and behaviors of some of the members of this class (though such is not limited to this class) that is used to describe all African Americans. This might account for the attempt by middle-class Blacks to distance themselves from the realities as well as the stereotypes of poor African Americans. This distancing of African Americans along class lines was nowhere more visible and controversial than in 2004 when renowned African American comedian, actor and author, William (Bill) Cosby presented a scathing critique (in sometimes very harsh language) of African Americans, particularly poor African American children and their parents at an NAACP 50th anniversary celebration of the landmark Supreme Court decision in *Brown vs. the Topeka Board of Education*. Cosby lambasted poor African Americans for what, in his view, is their declining morality and bad behavior and he emphasized personal responsibility or the lack of it. He went on to accuse "lower economic (Black) people" of not parenting; single mothers of no longer being embarrassed because they are pregnant without a husband; single fathers of running away from being fathers; and having a high rate of criminal behavior and incarceration. Before he finished, he criticized the Black poor for their lack of education, their style of dress, the names they give their children, their poor speech, and their conspicuous consumption habits. He even suggested to the Black poor that "God is tired of you."

While some people across race and ethnicity agreed with Cosby, many others were very critical of his remarks, suggesting that it was nothing more than a vicious attack on the poor and most vulnerable members of African American communities. While it is acceptable to critique individual behaviors, Cosby's remarks went beyond that and were ahistorical and lacked a systematic grounding and understanding of the social forces that make it difficult for poor parents to do their best jobs and for poor children to prosper (see, for example, Michael Eric Dyson, 2005).

What do you think? Is Bill Cosby right or is much of the behavior he described a function of historical and contemporary factors beyond the control of the poor? Even so, should not such a critique be accompanied with recommended strategies or solutions to the problem(s)?

Family Strengths and Resiliency Historically, social science research on African American families has focused almost entirely on the so-called pathology of African American families and has almost completely ignored the diversity, strengths, and resilience of these families. Beginning in the 1970s, in response to this unbalanced depiction of African American families, a group of African American scholars across academic disciplines began to develop a corrective scholarship that debunked many of the pathology myths of traditional social science research on African American families. A pioneer in this regard, sociologist Robert Hill (1972) pointed out in his book *The Strengths of Black Families* that contrary to popular stereotypes, although some African American families experienced myriad social problems, the majority of them exhibited strong kinship bonds, a strong work orientation, a strong achievement orientation, a strong religious orientation, and flexible family roles. Twenty-five years after his pioneering work on the strengths of African American families, Hill (1997) revisited those strengths, suggesting that conventional depictions of African American families in the media and social science research continued to be unbalanced; the typical focus continued to be on the weaknesses or deficiencies of a disadvantaged minority of African American families, with little or no consideration of the majority. According to Hill, there continues to be a fixation on the nonworking poor (or underclass) that excludes an examination of the larger working class who often live in the same communities, or excessive attention is paid to the 2 out of 10 African American families on welfare or on the 1 out of 10 African American teenagers who had a baby outside of legal marriage. Little or no attention is paid to the majority of low-income African Americans who achieve against the odds. Despite economic adversity, the effects of continuing entrenched racism and discrimination, disproportionately high rates of unemployment, poverty, and incarceration of young African American males; and the street violence, as well as gang and criminal activities of a minority in the community, most African American families (whether married-couple or single-parent) are family-oriented, love their partners and their children, and teach their children to have self-respect, to be self-sufficient and achievement-oriented, and to be proud of their cultural heritage ("African American Families...," 2008).

NATIVE AMERICAN FAMILIES

Native American and Alaska Native families are perhaps the least studied families compared to other families living in the United States. Therefore, researchers often rely on aggregate data that yield a generalized picture of these individuals and families. As a group, for example, resulting from a history of legal and social domination, oppression, and, at times, total neglect, Native American families have among the highest rates of poverty, unemployment,

poor health, infant mortality, suicide, and alcoholism of any racial or ethnic group in the United States. Despite some important economic gains in recent years, the majority of Native Americans still remain in the bottom tenth of the economic hierarchy and at the bottom of the class hierarchy (Schwartz and Scott, 2010).

Family Structure Currently, approximately 1 percent of all households in the United States consists of Native American peoples. Of all Native American and Alaska Native households, 69 percent are family households. Among these family households, 57 percent are married-couple families, 32 percent are female-headed, and the remaining 11 percent are headed by males. Native American families typically consist of two children and are among the nation's youngest households. The average number of people in a Native American household is 3.5, larger than the national average size for all families. Moreover, with the increasingly large numbers of Native Americans marrying non-Native Americans, a growing number of children in these families are biracial. Those who marry other Native Americans tend to marry within their respective tribal groups. The extended family is an important characteristic of Native American family structure. More than one-half of all Native American families include a grandmother (56 percent) or other relatives. Within these families the elderly is particularly revered, not only because of their age and wisdom but also because of the care and support they provide in to the younger generation of parents. For instance, because parents often have to leave home to find employment, grandparents play a pivotal role in the raising of their grandchildren (U.S. Census Bureau, 2009).

The Economics of Native American Families Overcrowding and poverty are persistent and significant problems for Native Americans, particularly those who live on Native American lands. Two in five homes in tribal communities are overcrowded and have serious physical deficiencies and less than half of the housing is connected to a public sewer. Living conditions on some Native American lands have been described as comparable to the Third World. There has been a considerable migration of Native Americans from reservations since World War II. More than half of Native American families today live outside tribal lands, and although separated from their traditional tribal cultures, they typically fare a bit better economically and socially than those who remain on reservation (American Indian Relief Council, 2011; Housing Assistance Council, 2008).

There are a myriad of factors that contribute to the challenges that Native American families face but perhaps the most pressing are issues of economics, unemployment, housing, and health. In 2009, based on a three-year average, the median income of Native American households was $37,348. However, more than 20 percent of Native American households earn less than $5,000 annually and, according to some sources, the scarcity of jobs and lack of economic opportunity has led to extremely high unemployment rates (21 percent in 2010). Native American communities have fewer full-time employed individuals than any other high-poverty communities in the country. Only about one-third of Native American males in high-poverty Native American communities have full-time, year-round jobs. And, depending on the particular Native American land, anywhere from 4 to 8 out of 10 adults are unemployed. Native Americans also consistently have the highest rates of poverty among the major racial groups. Overall, about one in four Native Americans live below the federal poverty line. However, Native American lands are among the poorest in the United States with a rate of 39 percent. Depending on the Native American land, the poverty rate is as high as 63 percent. In addition, three out of five Native Americans who live outside of metropolitan areas live in communities characterized by persistent poverty as well (Rogers, 2011; American Indian and Alaska Native Heritage, 2009).

Despite the many challenges Native American families face, more than half of them (55 percent) own their own home with a median value of $129,800. This is compared to 66 percent and $185,200, respectively, for the general American population. However, like with African Americans, since the housing crisis, the rate of Native American home ownership has dropped nearly twice as much as for Whites, exacerbating an already huge racial wealth gap (Vissa, 2011; "U.S. Census Bureau Facts For Features…," 2010). Finally, while the life expectancy of Native Americans has improved, the health and well-being of Native Americans continues to be of serious concern. High rates of suicide, alcoholism, drug abuse, and domestic violence as well as high infant mortality rates and high rates of babies born with fetal alcohol syndrome are challenging health concerns among people who have limited health-care options; 29 percent of Native Americans do not have health insurance. These facts, as serious as they are, have not gone unchallenged. Native American leaders and groups have developed and implemented an array of policies and program designed to improve the economic, social and physical health of Native Americans.

Differences and Commonalities in Parenting Styles

Native Americans are a heterogeneous people, perhaps more heterogeneous than any group in the United States. There are, for instance, 562 federally recognized tribal governments. Specific social and economic characteristics, family structures, contents, and behaviors therefore vary considerably from group to group. Among the Navajo, for example, parents operate on the principle of the inviolability of the individual, which some researchers have translated as a principle of permissiveness. Navajo parents discipline their children through persuasion, ridicule, and shame rather than coercion and physical punishment. On the other hand, Native American groups such as the Hopi, Zunis, and various descendants of the ancient Anasazi continue today to be loyal to their matrilineal clan systems and religious ceremonies, and they emphasize sobriety and self-control (Coltrane and Collins, 2006).

Although there is considerable variation among different tribal groups, Native American families share a strong sense of tribalism, family identity, and pride, and parents of all backgrounds tend to stress to their children a sense of family unity, tribal identity, self-reliance, and respect for elders. Children are viewed as assets to both the family and the group. Some researchers have suggested that childrearing among Native Americans frequently is nonverbal: Parents communicate by giving stern looks or by ignoring inappropriate behavior. Furthermore, children are socialized by example and are expected to share with others, to be quiet and unassuming, to show deference to their elders, to control their emotions, to be self-reliant, and to make an economic contribution to the family from an early age. Interdependence and interfamily exchange are important family patterns, especially on reservations. In this context, extended families are significant. And elders typically hold a special place in Native American families. Not only are children taught to respect elders but also elders expect family members to take care of them when needed (AIMHAC, 2004; Yellowbird and Snipp, 2002).

Some of the recent literature on Native American families indicates that socialization practices among Native Americans have changed in recent times from "cohesive and structured" households characterized by high-dominance–high-support parent–child relations to "loosely structured" households with low-dominance–low-support parent–child relations. Today, rigid gender roles are loosening, and more Native American women are working outside the home.

Family Strengths and Resiliency Like every other group, Native American families exhibit important strengths. Although the problems, particularly as they are manifest on reservations, have yet to be resolved, the diversity and strengths of Native American families—extended family networks, interdependence and interfamily exchange, value of individuals and the group, group cooperation, tribal support systems, and preservation of culture and family traditions—promote a pan-Indian identity and facilitate the maintenance of strong tribal and family identities across the numerous tribes.

LATINA/O FAMILIES

Like Native Americans, Latinas/os are a highly diverse people whose marriage and family behaviors vary, sometimes considerably, from group to group. The following brief description of Latina/o family structure represents a generalized view of structural features that Latina/o families share.

✳️ **Explore** the **Concept** *Social Explorer Activity: Family Structure Among Hispanic Populations* on **myfamilylab.com**

Family Structure The structure of Latina/o families is more likely than African American families but less likely than Asian and White families to consist of two parents. About two-thirds (66 percent) of Latina/o family households consist of married-couple families and nearly one-fourth (24 percent) are female-headed. Forty-five percent of married-couple families have one to two children, and 18 percent have three or more children. Like most other groups in the United States, however, a growing number of Latina/o children are living in families with only one parent present. Currently, 29 percent of Latina/o children live in single-parent families, the majority (26 percent) of which are headed by a female. For some Latina/o groups such as Puerto Ricans, some of the increase in children living in single-parent households is due, as we noted earlier, to the increasing number of children born outside legal marriage. Generally, Latina/o family households consist not only of immediate but also extended family members (22 percent live in multi-generational households), an increasing number of mothers are working outside the home, and young children in these families are increasingly less likely to be under the exclusive care of their parents (U.S. Census Bureau, 2011d; Pew Research Center, 2010a).

The Economics of Latina/o Families According to some writers, race appears to be a fundamental factor in American economic situations as White and Asian families have significantly higher household incomes and lower poverty rates that all other racial groups. For instance, in 2010 dollars, the median Latina/o household income was $37,759 compared to $54,620 for Whites and $64,308 for Asians (Merco Press, 2011; Cauchon and Hansen, 2011). Consistent with the fact that Latinas/os are a diverse group, we find a considerable amount of variation in household income. For instance, among the three major Latina/o groups: Cubans, Puerto Ricans and Mexicans, the median household income falls above the median but is highest for Cuban families. Like other racial groups, especially those of color, Latina/s families have experienced the brunt of the bad U.S. economy. For instance, there are currently a little more than 6 million poor Latinas/os in this country under the age of 18, more than any other single group. The majority of these children are native born Latinas/os. The poverty rate for Latinas/os overall rose between 2009 and 2010 by two percent from 25 percent to 27 percent. On the other hand, although the unemployment rate among Latinas/os has decreased slightly recently, it is still very high at 12 percent, one and one half times that for Whites and Asians and the same as that for African Americans (Velasco, 2011; U.S. Census Bureau, 2011d).

On a somewhat brighter note, around 48 percent of Latinas/os own their own home, a rate slightly higher than that for African Americans but far below the rate of White homeownership (74 percent). As we have already pointed out, homeownership is an important measure of wealth, particularly for most groups of color whose wealth is tightly tied into their homes. Unfortunately for these groups, housing crisis of the last several years has had a devastating impact on their economic well-being, particularly in terms of the accumulation of wealth. In percentage terms, after the housing market bubble burst and the recession that followed, the median wealth for Latinas/os fell 66 percent compared with just 16 percent among Whites. As a result of these declines, the typical Latina/o household had only $6325 in wealth (assets minus debt) compared to the typical White household wealth of $113,149, 18 times that of Latinas/os. This wealth gap between White households and Latina/o as well as Black households is, according to the Pew Research Center, the largest since the government began collecting such data a quarter of a century ago (U.S. Census Bureau, 2011d; Pew Research Center, 2011c).

Parenting in Puerto Rican Families Although there is little research that focuses specifically on childrearing patterns among Latinas/os, one can glean from existing research that some Latina/o groups, such as Puerto Ricans, exhibit an emphasis on family interdependence and unity. Among Puerto Ricans, females are charged with the responsibility of creating and maintaining these values in offspring. In general, the Puerto Rican parenting style can be characterized as authoritarian. Children are rarely consulted on matters that directly affect them. They are viewed as passive people whose attitudes and behavior must be completely shaped by the parents. Good behavior is taken for granted, and reasons for punishment are seldom offered. Physical punishment is frequently used, especially by parents

with the least social mobility and status. However, for Puerto Rican parents, especially mothers, warm and supportive relationships characterized by high levels of parent–child interaction and sharing are important. Parents born in Puerto Rico, more so than those born or raised in the United States, tend to perpetuate, although with some modifications, a double standard of conduct between the sexes. Females are trained to be modest, and overt expressions of affection are more common with girls than boys. Furthermore, mothers tend to be warmer and more playful with children than fathers and interact more frequently with daughters than with sons (Guilamo-Ramos, et al., 2007; Carrasquillo, 2002).

Parenting in Mexican American Families Machismo, sex, and age grading characterize Mexican American families and childrearing patterns. For example, female children are socialized into the roles and skills of wife and mother early on because they will carry them out both in the absence of the mother and as a future wife and mother. In contrast, after puberty the eldest male has authority over the younger children as well as his older sisters because he is expected to take on the responsibility for the family in his father's absence and for his own family as a future father (Zin and Pok, 2002). Although Mexican American childrearing is mother-centered, some scholars have suggested that contemporary Mexican American fathers share more in child care than in the past as more Mexican American mothers enter the workforce (Sarmiento, 2002; Garcia, 2002).

Parenting in Cuban American Families Cubans, on the other hand, particularly second-generation Cubans raised in the United States, show a lesser inclination to embrace machismo or traditional sex roles. Because Cubans value lineality, children are expected to conform and to obey their parents and elders in general. In addition, Cubans have been found to endorse a "doing" orientation that emphasizes success-oriented activities, which are usually externally measurable. As a result, they tend to judge themselves and others by what the person achieves (Perez, 2002; Bevin, 2001). This value, no doubt, is transmitted to offspring during the socialization process.

Family Strengths and Resiliency Like other families of color who have experienced racism, prejudice, and within-group social problems such as gang membership and violence, male violence, drug abuse, a high school dropout rate, teenage pregnancy, and female-headed families, Latina/o families exhibit amazing strength and resiliency. They have maintained family values and ties and adapted positively to a variety of changing social, political, and economic circumstances. This is particularly true for Latina/o immigrants who must not only learn a new language but also adjust to a new and sometime hostile environment. Similar to Black families, Latina/o families across the ethnic spectrum also socialize their children to have a strong sense of ethnic pride and identity while also preparing them for life in the larger, diverse American culture. Some researchers have identified a number of family strengths characteristic of Latina/o families, including family unity and cohesion, extended family support networks, a strong family focus and ethnic identity, religious orientation, and flexibility of family roles (Berry, 2007; Zentella, 2005).

Although Latina/o families represent a diversity of family structures and cultural practices, in general, family, food, language, faith, and cultural pride are among the key cultural characteristics of Latina/o families. Family is the cornerstone of Latina/o culture; families, larger than those of most non-Latinas/os, tend to be close-knit, and social occasions tend to revolve around the family where immediate and extended members routinely share and honor family traditions such as parties on their children's birthday.

ASIAN AND PACIFIC ISLANDER AMERICANS

Although Asian Americans and Pacific Islanders are often lumped together, these two groups include people from a wide variety of countries (20 or more) whose cultures (representing more than 60 different ethnicities), including language (more than 100 different languages), religion, and customs, differ greatly. With this in mind, the following represents a brief discussion of Asian and Pacific Islander family structure in aggregate terms.

Family Structure Along with Whites, Asian and Pacific Islanders have the highest percentage of married-couple families (81 percent) and the lowest percentage of female-headed families (12 percent) than all other major racial or ethnic groups in the United States. The number of children in Asian and Pacific Islander families is in line with that of the larger society with 9 out of 10 Asian and Pacific Islander families having 2 or fewer children. The same percentage applies to both single-parent families and married-couple families as well. While the number of children in these homes is consistent with the national average, similar to Black and Latina/o households, roughly one-quarter of Asian and Pacific Islander households contain multi-generations. These households include not only parents and children, but often they also include unmarried siblings and grandparents. In most Asian and Pacific Islander families, a language other than English is spoken at home by both the younger and older generations. And in cities such as New York, one out of five Asian children in the public school system has limited English proficiency. About 20 percent of Asian American family households include at least three wage-earning workers, many of whom (particularly Asian immigrants) work in industries with low wages and long hours (U.S. Census Bureau, 2011d; Callis and Cavanaugh, 2008).

The Economics of Asian and Pacific Island Families

Like other groups we have described thus far, Asian and Asian American families have experienced a tremendous history of racism, prejudice and discrimination in the United States, including state sponsored acts of racism that at various points in time have restricted their right to immigration, citizenship, property, and family formation in the United States. The most memorable is the unwilling internment of Japanese Americans into government controlled camps during World War II while the United States was at war with Japan. During this dark period in American history, much of their property that was confiscated was never recovered. This history of discrimination not withstanding, Asian Americans as a group, have made some remarkable strides toward equal status in American society. For example, although since the housing crisis and the economic recession of the past few years, the median household income has fallen for all racial and ethnic groups, Asian American have a higher household income than any other racial group ($64,308). And, the Asian American unemployment rate is not only lower than all other groups at 7 percent, it is lower than the national average as well (U.S. Census Bureau, 2011d).

Despite faring better than other racial and ethnic groups, these figures should not lull us into thinking Asian Americans, unlike other Americans, were not hurt by the recent economic recession. The fact is that these figures and the limitation of data on various Asian ethnic groups mask the considerable variation among various populations of Asian and Pacific Islander Americans. For example, although the jobless rate for Asian Americans generally is low, young Asian Americans have a higher rate of unemployment (11 percent) than older Asian Americans (7 percent). Factors such as the country that the family migrated from, the era in which they migrated, and the education and skill levels of adult family members contribute to whether or not an Asian or Pacific Islander family will live at, below, or above the poverty level. For example, families consisting of less advantaged migrants from Southeast Asia (e.g., Laos, Cambodia) with low education and skill levels have very high levels of poverty and welfare dependency, whereas families consisting of Japanese and Taiwanese immigrants, as well as those consisting of second and third or more generations of Asian Americans, tend to have very low levels of poverty (McLoyd et al., 2001; U.S. Census Bureau, 2011d).

Finally, although Asian Americans have a recent history of faring better than Whites on most indicators of economic well-being, currently more than 3 percent more Asian Americans than White Americans live below the poverty line (12.1 and 9.4, respectively). In addition, a look at the wealth of Asian American and Pacific Island households in terms of home ownership reveals that despite a household income that exceeds that of Whites, and an unemployment rate that is lower, Asian Americans do not have a corresponding wealth status equal to or that surpass Whites today. For example, 59 percent of Asian American and Pacific Islanders own their own homes compared to 71 percent of Whites. Further, although Asian Americans had recently topped Whites in median household wealth, currently their household wealth is roughly only 69 percent of that of White households ($78,066 and $113,149 respectively). Like Latinas/os, Asian Americans are concentrated in states such as California that have been hit extremely hard by the housing downturn. In addition, newer arriving Asian immigrants who tend to be poor have also pushed down their median wealth (U.S. Census Bureau, 2011d; Yen, 2011; McLoyd et al., 2001).

Asian and Pacific Islander American Parenting Styles: Commonalities and Differences Parenting styles among Asian and Pacific Islanders vary according to the degree that parents are acculturated into U.S. society. Newly immigrated or first-generation parents typically use traditional approaches based on authoritarian methods. In general, family values and childrearing practices are similar across Asian and Pacific Islander families. Obedience and conformity, responsibility, obligation, and loyalty to the family as well as self-control and educational achievement are expected. Socialization practices are characterized by a strong parent–child bond; in traditional families, there is a rigid division of roles and tasks, and children are taught to defer to their parents' wishes and commands. Discipline is typically strict and involves physical punishment. In contrast, acculturated parents are generally more nurturing and verbal and give their children more autonomy (Kitano and Daniels, 2001; Min, 2002). Like Native American and other families in the United States, parenting styles and childrearing practices vary among Asian and Pacific Islander families by social class as well as degree of acculturation. For example, older Korean immigrant parents whose children were born in Korea are more authoritarian and controlling of their children's behavior than their younger middle-class counterparts. The more educated Korean parents are, the more liberal they are in their childrearing practices. Although somewhat moderated from practices in Korea, Korean American parents engage in very rigid, gender-based socialization practices for their daughters and sons. For example, Korean American mothers feel that certain chores, such as setting the table, should be done only by girls (Min, 2002).

Likewise, among Chinese Americans, some of the old traditional ways of childrearing have been maintained by recent immigrants. For example, parental authority, particularly the father's, is absolute. The extended family, if present, plays a much more significant role than typically is found in middle-class or more acculturated Chinese families. In upwardly mobile and middle-class Chinese families, the father maintains his authority and respect by means of a certain amount of emotional distance from his children. The mother does not interact with the children but commands and decides what is best for them, and the children are expected to obey. Although on the surface Chinese parents are seen as more indulgent with their young children than are parents in other racial and ethnic groups, discipline is much more strict than in the typical American home. Punishment is typically immediate and often involves removal from the social life of the family or the revocation of special privileges or objects rather than physical punishment. Moreover, Chinese parents stress independence and maturity in their children early on. Older children are expected to participate in the rearing of their younger siblings—serving as role models of adult behavior (Glenn and Yap, 2002; Kitano and Daniels, 2001).

Acculturation shapes socialization practices in a number of ways. For example, among the Issei, or first generation of Japanese Americans born in Japan, male dominance, a stronger parent–child than husband–wife bond, a rigid division of gender roles and discipline of children, and the precedence of family over the individual characterize childrearing in these families. By the Nisei, or second generation, husband–wife relations take precedence over parent–child relations, and parents are less rigid in their childrearing practices. The Sansei, or third-generation Japanese American families, are extremely likely to be interracial with biracial children. Because this generation marries, on average, later, parents tend to be, on average, older and increasingly less rigid in terms of gender role socialization and life expectations for their female and male children. However, for both the Nisei and Sansei generations of parents, close family ties and family loyalty, socialization for social control, including obligation and duty, continue to be part of the socialization practices of parents (Takagi, 2002; Kitano and Daniels, 2001).

Myths and Facts One of the greatest stereotypes that Asian American families face is that of the "model minority." This stereotype can be harmful in that it does not acknowledge the differences within Asian and Pacific Islander families and thus masks many of the unique problems and strains that some of these families face. Some researchers have pointed out that the model minority myth also creates and fuels tensions and conflicts within and across Asian American subgroups as well as across other racial and ethnic groups; it camouflages ongoing racism and discrimination in U.S. society (though more subtle today) by suggesting that the United States is a meritocracy in which Asian and Pacific Islanders are the model of unparalleled achievement and success—the model for pulling oneself up by the bootstraps that all other groups should emulate. In this context, other groups are judged by the myth of the model minority, and if they have not been as successful it is due to factors endemic of them as a race and not U.S. policies and ongoing structural and institutional racism (Aguirre and Turner, 2006; Saito, 2002).

Family Strengths and Resiliency Although they have experienced a history of prejudice and discrimination in terms of U.S. policies and practices, resilience marks the character of Asian and Pacific Islander families. Asian American families have managed to maintain strong family values and ties that are transmitted to each new generation and, in some cases, high economic and educational success. Characteristics such as family obligation and loyalty to family and culture, respect and care for the elderly, an extended family network of support, a high value on education, close family ties across generations, a low divorce rate (which is considered a hallmark of family stability), and a complex system of other positive values and behaviors have helped Asian and Pacific Islander families to successfully adapt to their environments in the United States and to counter some of the deleterious effects of racism and discrimination many experience.

LESBIAN AND GAY PARENTS

No one knows with any certainty how many lesbian and gay parents there are because many choose to keep their sexual orientation hidden in fear of discriminatory treatment. However, we do have some estimates based on census data. Of the 701,733 same-sex couples in 2003, 34 percent of female unmarried-partner households and 22 percent of male unmarried-partner households had at least one child under the age of 18 living with them. Sixty-two percent of the children are White, 17 percent are African American, and 25 percent of all children living with same-sex couples are Latina/o (Simmons and O'Connell, 2003; gaydemographics.org, 2003). Prior to the 1980s, the children of lesbians and gays were primarily the product of a heterosexual marriage that ended. From the 1980s on, many children were brought into a same-sex household through adoption or through use of AI or assisted reproductive technology, including surrogacy. In 2009, 19 percent of same-sex couples reported having an adopted child in the house, up from 8 percent in 2000. Lesbian and gay parents are raising approximately 65,000 adopted children, about 4 percent of all adopted children (Tavernise, 2011a).

Among the general population, there is still considerable controversy over lesbian and gay parenting. However, credible scientifically conducted studies have found no harmful effects on children who are raised by lesbian and gay parents. In fact, the American Academy of Pediatrics (Perrin, 2002), the American Psychological Association (Patterson, 1995), the American Academy of Family Physicians (2002, 2003), and the National Association of Social Workers (Vallianatos, 2002) have all concluded that lesbian and gay parents perform just as well as heterosexual parents. Jennifer Wainwright and her colleagues (2004) compared 44 adolescents being raised by female same-sex couples with 44 being raised by heterosexual couples and matched the children from the two groups on many traits. They found that across a wide range of assessment, the personal, family, and school adjustments of adolescents living with same-sex

parents did not differ from that of adolescents living with heterosexual parents. Similarly, a Canadian study concluded whether a child's parents are heterosexual or lesbian or gay has no significant discernable impact on that child's social competence (Hastings, et al., 2006). More recently, a longitudinal study found that adolescents raised by lesbian mothers demonstrated higher levels of social, school/academic, and total competence than children raised by heterosexual parents (Gartrell and Bos, 2010). A possible explanation for the differences in outcomes may well be the active involvement of lesbian mothers and their willingness to discuss issues of sexuality, diversity, and tolerance with their children from early on to prepare them for any discrimination and stigmatization they may experience, thus giving their children more confidence and self esteem. According to Charlotte Patterson (1992), there can be positive effects of being raised by lesbian or gay parents. For example, having a nontraditional adult role model gives children a greater appreciation of diversity. In addition, having a parent who is different can make it easier for a child to be different and independent. The child might be more tolerant, accepting, and less judgmental because she or he has been taught to accept social and personal differences in others. This seems to be true for the sons of gay men studied by clinical psychologist Orson Morrison. These men reported feeling more multifaceted and freer from rigid gender roles than children of heterosexual parents because their fathers provided an alternative model of masculinity (cited in Kuzma, 2005).

When problems do arise for children in nontraditional families, often it is due not to the sexual orientation of the parents but rather to outside influence and interference and the degree to which society accepts the negative stereotypes of lesbian and gay parents. As one young woman said, "It wasn't having a gay father that made growing up a challenge, it was navigating a society that did not accept him and, by extension, me" (Garner, 2002). Thus, it seems clear from most studies that quality parenting and not sexual orientation is the critical determinant of children's development (Biblarz and Stacey, 2010; Wainwright, Russell, and Patterson, 2004). Children who have a close relationship with their parents fare better than children who do not, regardless of family structure or their parents' sexual orientation.

Not all lesbian and gay parenting is "out" in the open. In the past and still today, some lesbian and gay parents have remained secretive and protective of their children, fearing that open disclosure might cost them custody of their children. For instance, gay parents Steven James and Todd Herrmann worry that their sons, Greg and Max, 4, might be taken away from them if they travel to visit Steven's parents in Oklahoma, one of 11 states that do not recognize adoptions by same-sex couples (Dingfelder, 2005). Thus, as long as homophobia continues to exist, getting a representative sample of children of lesbian and gay couples will remain problematic. Clearly, more research is needed if we are to understand the full range of lesbian and gay parenting.

SINGLE PARENTS

The number of single-parent families has increased dramatically over the past two decades as both the divorce rate and the number of children born outside of legal marriage have increased.

Approximately 40 percent of all births in the United States are now to single mothers (U.S. Census Bureau, 2011d). Although the percentage of single parents has increased most dramatically in the last 20 to 25 years, the fact is that the percentage of births to single women in this society has been steadily increasing since the 1950s. According to some experts, half the children born today will live in a single-parent family before they reach adulthood.

Although the majority of single mothers are poor or working class, poorly educated, and have few marketable skills, they are also both racially and ethnically diverse and are more frequently in their 20s and 30s. These families face many of the same challenges and rewards of parenting as other types of families. However, the situation of single parents, particularly for female single parents, carries a unique set of challenges, not the least of which is related to their economic position. A family's resources are strongly influenced by the number of parents and/or wage earners in the household.

Female-headed families are of concern not because they are inherently problematic but because people living in female-headed families typically have access to fewer economic or human resources than people in married-couple families. There are fewer potential earners in female-headed families, which partially explains their lower household income. Another part of the equation is the differential earning power of women and men in the American labor force (we discuss this issue in more detail in Chapter 10). In addition, delinquent child support payments from absent fathers also erode economic resources available to many female-headed families. Given this context, children living in female-headed families are particularly vulnerable to poverty. In 2009, for instance, 21 percent of American children lived in poverty (twice the rate for adult men), and close to one-half (44 percent) of them lived in extreme poverty. Poverty rates were particularly high for various groups of children. Families maintained by women with children were particularly poor, 38.5 percent compared to 23.7 percent for male-headed families with children and 8.3 percent for families with children headed by a married couple. Poverty rates approached one in two for Black, Latina, and Native American female-headed families and was about one in three for White female-headed families and lowest at around one in five for Asian female headed-families (see Figure 9.3). Furthermore, children in lower-income families (families with income below 200 percent of the official poverty level) are more likely to live with a single mother and less likely to live with two married parents than are higher-income children (U.S. Census Bureau, 2011d; National Women's Law Center, 2010).

Whether the single parent is divorced or never married seems an important indicator of the quality of life for children in these families. For example, children living with divorced single mothers typically have an economic advantage over children living with a mother who has never married. This might be accounted for, in part, because divorced parents are typically older, have higher levels of education, and have higher incomes than parents who never married. In terms of race and ethnicity, White single-mother families are more likely to be the result of a marital disruption (50 percent were divorced) than having never married (30 percent), whereas African American single mothers are the most likely to be never married (65 per-

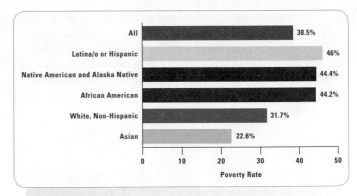

FIGURE 9.3 Poverty Rate of Female-Headed Households with Children by Race or Ethnicity, 2009

Source: National Women's Law Center. 2010. "Poverty Among Women and Families, 2000–2009: Great Recession Brings Highest Rate in 15 Years," (September): http://www.nwlc.org/sites/default/files/pdfs/povertyamongwomenandfamilies2009.pdf

cent) and the least likely to be divorced (17 percent). African American and Latina single mothers are also more likely than White single mothers to live in an extended family household (Fields and Casper, 2001).

These trends have important implications for the well-being of children and families and the programs and policies that relate to welfare, family leave, and other areas of work and family life. Studies show that children reared in these families tend to drop out of school, to become delinquent, to have emotional problems, to get pregnant as teenagers and give birth outside of legal marriage, to be at greater risk for drug and alcohol addiction, to end up on welfare, to be poor as adults, and to get divorced more often than children from two-parent families (Ambert, 2006).

Although these problems are typically attributed to the absence of a father, according to Andrew Cherlin (1992), the most detrimental aspect of the father's absence from female-headed families is not the lack of a male presence, but rather the lack of a male income. Recent research confirms that poverty and inadequate income are major threats to children's well-being and development regardless of how many parents are present. Although child poverty is much higher in the United States than in other Western countries, it is not an unalterable fact of nature that children born to single mothers have to grow up poor. According to some scholars, whereas social policies in the United States express disapproval of single parents, social policies in other Western countries support the well-being of the children.

Single Fathers As the number of married-couple families generally as well as those with children have decreased, as marital and relationship breakups and unmarried pregnancies have increased, there has been an explosion in the number of single-father homes. There are now 2.8 million single fathers raising children, up from 400,000 in 1970. And if we add to this those fathers who are sole caregivers to their children on a part-time basis, we have a formidable population, representing about 15 percent of all families (U.S. Census Bureau, 2011d). The increase in single-father parenting has occurred across all racial groups; however, White fathers are twice as likely as African American fathers to be the sole head of household. Nevertheless, a growing number of African American men who are divorced, widowed, or who have never married are confronting the economic and social challenges of single parenthood and are willingly providing a loving and nurturing environment for their children.

Some experts say that fathers' desire to be involved with their children is to the twenty-first century what women's desire to be in the workplace was to the twentieth century (Goldberg, 2001). These fathers are shattering the myth that fathers lack nurturing skills. Compared with single-parent mothers, single-parent fathers tend to be older, better off financially, have a higher level of education, hold full-time professional or higher-level jobs, and have a much higher median income than their female-headed counterparts (U.S. Census Bureau, 2011d). They also tend to be highly motivated parents. Some experts believe, however, that an important factor contributing to the increase in single fathers is not just more men wanting to be involved with their children, but rather a growing willingness on the part of mothers to cede primary custody. For example, fathers typically get custody of their children belatedly. That is, most courts in the United States are still more likely to award custody to mothers than fathers; thus, when a father does get custody, it is usually with the mother's consent.

A recent trend in unwed parenting is unmarried fathers who are fighting for babies placed for adoption by the birth mother. Although one in every three American babies has unwed parents, fathers' rights are an unsettled area. For example, what are the rights of unmarried fathers when the birth mother chooses adoption? In most states, unwed fathers who show a desire for involvement when the birth mother chooses adoption are required to put their names on a registry. In some states, an unwed father must actually claim paternity; in others, just the possibility of paternity. The deadlines range from 5 to 30 days after the birth of the child or any time before an adoption petition is filed. In most states, fewer than 100 men register each year, primarily because most have never heard of the registry.

The flip side of unwed fathers fighting to raise their babies is those unwed fathers who are unwilling to become fathers. Not long ago, for instance, a Michigan man, who says he was tricked into fatherhood, sued, he said, to establish his and other men's right to decide whether or not to have children. Supporters of the man are calling his case "*Roe v. Wade for Men*"—a precedent-setting case that could define a man's right to choose parenthood (Graham, 2006:3). The man, 25-year-old Matthew Dubay, claims that he told his girlfriend that he was not ready to have children. The girlfriend allegedly responded that she was infertile and on birth control pills just in case. However, when the woman became pregnant, she refused his request that she terminate the pregnancy. After the birth of the child, she obtained a court order requiring Dubay to pay child support. Subsequently, Dubay sued back, claiming that men have a constitutional right to "avoid" procreation. Dubay's case is the first to test the constitutional freedom to choose not to be a father under the equal protection clause of the U.S. Constitution. Dubay is one of a small number of men who argue they were duped into having children they never wanted and then forced to assume financial responsibilities for which they are unprepared. Dubay's case was dismissed as was his appeal ("Court Rejects...," 2007). The courts have been very clear on this matter, ruling that the child's interest

in receiving support overrides any interests the father may have. Many experts in this area of reproductive rights argue that if a man wants to avoid parenthood, there are many steps he can take beyond accepting the word of a woman or expecting a woman to take sole responsibility for the prevention of pregnancy (Graham, 2006).

> Do you think men should have the same right as women to decide whether or not to have children? Should such cases as outlined above be about the father and his rights, or should they be about the child and the child's rights and needs?

In any case, like single mothers, single fathers must balance the added demands of child care and maintain a satisfactory relationship with the noncustodial parent. Fathers who adapt well typically have higher incomes, had been involved in housework and child care during the time they were married, and actively sought custody of the children at the time of the break-up. They are also more likely to have the mother actively in the picture, sharing involvement with the children on a regular basis. This means that single fathers can often come very close to approximating an intact or nuclear family.

Although there is an increase in fathers parenting alone, for a significant number of families, fathers are absent. In addition, in whole neighborhoods fathers are scarce. About 1 in 4 children living in single-mother families were living in areas where single-mother families constituted more than one-half of all families. In Illinois, 1 in 8 children live in a neighborhood where fathers are scarce, compared with the national average of 1 in 14. The Illinois rate is surpassed in states such as Alabama, Maine, Massachusetts, Michigan, Mississippi, and New York. These data underscore the connection between poverty and family structure. One of the primary reasons that many fathers are absent from the home is unemployment and low wages. Many of these men lack the education and skills to successfully compete in today's labor force and thus to be able to contribute to the support of their children.

All too often the focus on single-parent families is on the problems they face. This gives the impression that single parenting is inherently problematic and that there is absolutely nothing positive about the experience. We know, however, that this is not the case. The amount of resources and availability of support systems available to single parents, like other parents, will determine the degree to which parenting will be more rewarding than challenging. Studies have identified many benefits of growing up in a single-parent family. One of these benefits is that there are more opportunities for the children to be androgynous—they experience less pressure to conform to rigid gender-appropriate roles and more opportunity to experience a wide range of social roles. Studies have also consistently shown that children raised by a single parent tend to be more mature and have a stronger sense of self than children in two-parent families (Lauer and Lauer, 2006).

TEENAGED PARENTS

As we have indicated, teenage pregnancy is particularly unsettling given that the majority of teen mothers live in or will live in poverty. Unfortunately, however, rather than develop programs that adequately address this issue, as a culture we blame unmarried teenaged parents, especially mothers, for the majority of family and societal problems. As in many other areas of life, teenage pregnancy is exacerbated by race and class. The typical teenaged mother in the United States today is White, in her late teens, and more likely to have a child outside of legal marriage than her counterparts in other industrialized countries. However, a disproportionately higher percentage of teenagers and young adults of color, particularly African Americans, Native Americans, and Latinas, are unmarried teenage mothers. In addition, a major factor impacting teenage mothers, particularly those of color, is a high unemployment rate and declining wages for both women and men. Some critics of teenage pregnancy and childbearing attribute its incidence to the availability of welfare. They suggest that welfare is a substitute for a husband's income and encourages teenage pregnancy, especially among poor teenagers. However, research studies show that the role of welfare is relatively small. There is very little evidence to support the conclusion that many unmarried teenagers deliberately allow themselves to become pregnant to collect welfare payments.

In any event, early motherhood places tremendous demands on teenaged mothers who, like their adult counterparts, are generally raising their children without much support (financial or emotional) from the fathers. Like older mothers, teenaged mothers are responsible for managing the developmental tasks of parenting. Many young mothers manage these tasks quite well. Continued education, as well as social and financial support from family and friends, appear to be some of the predictors of the unmarried teenager's ability to successfully meet the unique challenges of childbearing and childrearing. Most teenaged mothers are no less nurturant and caring than adult mothers. However, some early research found that some unmarried teenaged mothers interact less frequently and are less expressive with their children than many older mothers. According to this research, teen mothers are also much more likely

All too often, it is assumed that teenage fathers do not want to be involved in their children's lives. However, contrary to this popular belief, many teenage fathers—such as 18-year-old Andy Sydlar, pictured here with Nicole Terrio, also 18, and their son Cameron—find joy in participating in the rearing of their children. Although Andy and Nicole live in separate households, like many teenage fathers, Andy spends as much time as possible with Nicole and Cameron.

to have financial problems and other stresses and less likely to be able to control their emotions in the childrearing process.

As with single mothers generally, however, research shows that although a male role model in single-parent families may be needed to meet the challenges of parenting, their importance may be overrated. For instance, a national study by researchers at Ohio State University, comparing teens raised in single-parent households, found that children raised by single mothers were doing just as well as those raised by single fathers. These findings counter the notion that children in single-mother households are disadvantaged simply because there is no father present. What matters in children's well-being is the parent's economic and interpersonal investment in her or his children, not her or his gender (Parents Forever, 2001).

Teenaged Fathers Like adult unmarried fathers, teenaged unmarried fathers are all too often left out of the parenting equation, both in terms of our perspectives on parenting and their responsibilities in parenting. We continue to see teenaged fathers in terms of stereotypes and myths of them being streetwise, gangbangers, or potentially so—macho males who sexually exploit a long string of women; count their offspring as notches in their belt of armor of manliness; are often illiterate, unemotional, and incapable of caring about another person; have only a passing and casual relationship with the mother; do not support the child financially by choice; and do not want to be emotionally involved in the rearing of their children. Research on single fathers generally and teenaged fathers specifically is limited, and there are relatively few programs to help teenage fathers develop the skills they need to become involved and caring fathers. However, according to the research that does exist, contrary to these popular beliefs, many young teenage fathers acknowledge paternity of their children and actively seek to be involved in the rearing of their children (Bunting and McAuley, 2004b). Many are at the hospital at the time of the birth of their children, and many sign records indicating their paternity. And, many provide some child-care support as their financial situation allows. Other researchers report that fatherhood was often a "wake-up call" for some disadvantaged young men who gradually pulled their lives together afterward (Florsheim and Ngu, 2006).

Although our knowledge of parenting styles among teenaged unmarried fathers is limited, as we have already indicated, we do know that in general fathers who are involved in the socialization of their children—who are involved in child care—have a more positive impact on their children than fathers who do not and, in turn, these fathers experience a greater degree of emotional and psychological benefit and well-being from the parent–child interaction than traditional fathers. Research has shown consistently that children who are highly interactive with their fathers (whether teenaged or older adult) are characterized by higher levels of cognitive competence, increased empathy, and fewer sex-typed beliefs and behaviors.

Teenage childbirth affects many areas of social life and, as we have indicated, is deeply rooted in many of our society's social problems and cannot be understood simply on an individual level. From a sociological perspective, in analyzing teenage births and parenting, we must consider structural and institutional factors such as the continuing individual and structural racism, sexism, and class bias that is extant in U.S. society; the bleak economic picture for many individuals and families in the twenty-first century, especially teenagers of color; the proliferation of drugs in the United States, especially in those communities that are least able to fight them; and a mass media that continues to romanticize and popularize sexual themes and set standards about appropriate sexual behavior, often encouraging sexual intercourse and pregnancy, to name but a few. When we consider the link between individual experiences of unmarried childbirth and social structure, it helps us understand the socially constructed nature of teenage childbearing as a social phenomenon and directs us to seek remedies in terms of institutional and structural change.

Supporting Parents and Children

Clearly, today's marriages and families do not fit the mold forged by 1960s and 1970s family sitcoms. For instance, in 2003, a single gay father and his three adopted sons were honored as the National Adoption Center's Family of the Year. This recognition is not so earth-shattering in-and-of-itself, rather it is indicative of the profound changes in the structure and definition of family occurring in today's society.

Although many individuals and families receive sustained support from their families and friends, federal, state, local, and community policies are needed to supplement that support for those who need it. More community and private initiatives such as the Alternative to Marriage Project (AtMP)—a national nonprofit organization advocating equality and fairness for unmarried people, including people who choose not to marry, cannot marry,

or live together before marriage—are needed to embrace the diversity of American marriages and families and provide them support. Moreover, politicians must work to reverse or eliminate legislation that discriminates against and/or excludes marriages and families based on definitions biased by conservative politics. This would include granting same-sex partners the same rights and responsibilities as married heterosexual couples and not limiting their right to adopt children. In addition, there is a pressing need for federal, state, and local policies as well as various initiatives aimed at improving the health of mothers and reducing the increasingly high infant mortality rate in this country. We must also find ways to educate individuals, especially youth, to practice safe and responsible sexual behavior and, when pregnancy does occur, to provide the support that these parents (females and males) need to have healthy and sustaining lives.

That an overwhelming majority of parents today rate their parenting as fair or poor is indicative of the fact that parents across diversities are struggling with issues of parenting. A recent national survey revealed a significant gap between parents' efforts to teach their children *good* values and their perceived success in so doing. Most parents believe it is essential to the viability and strength of families to teach children self-discipline, self-control, and honesty. Yet most parents do not think that they have succeeded with these parental tasks. Interestingly, over one-half of today's parents think they are doing a worse job at parenting than their own parents (Pew Research Center, 2007). Data such as these suggest that despite parents' desires and efforts, they are having trouble parenting and they point all the more to the need for both internal and external support for families and children. Along with government policies and support, communities can play important roles in helping

Writing Your Own Script

TO PARENT OR NOT?

A major life choice many of us will make regardless of whether we choose to marry is whether we will parent. Choosing to parent will have significant consequences for us in terms of the time, energy, and resources required to perform this critical task. The parenting decision not only affects our personal lives, but also affects the life of the society. Fertility rates and the consequent size and composition of a nation's population have enormous social implications. In the past, it was almost a foregone conclusion that a woman would reproduce. Deciding whether or not to parent

today is much more a matter of choice than it was in the past.

Questions to Consider

1. Do you want children? For what reasons? What do you have to offer children? What do you expect to receive from the children you may have? How many children do you want? If you or your partner are infertile, will you consider alternatives for having children? Would you consider adoption? Any of the new reproductive technologies?
2. What advantages and disadvantages are there to being child-free?

What are your options if you or your partner have an unwanted pregnancy? Are there any conditions under which you would consider abortion? Putting a child up for adoption? If you do not want children now or in the future, will you use contraception? What kind? How will you reach agreement on this with your partner? Explain.
3. What kind of parenting style did you experience in your childhood? Looking back, are you satisfied with this parenting style? What parenting style do you think you would be most comfortable enacting with your own children? Why?

individuals, marriages, families, and parents succeed even in high-risk areas by providing programs for prenatal health care, parental education, job training, child abuse prevention, and other support services. It really does "take a village to raise a child."

Finally, for the most part, throughout most of our discussions of supporting marriages and families, we have stressed the role of social institutions and social policies that can help support marriages and families. There are, however, growing examples of how private enterprise is helping to support marriages and families by helping over-extended families. For example, a persistent complaint of working parents is the lack of time they have to spend with family members. Working, grocery shopping, and planning and preparing nutritious dinners can be overwhelming for many. More often than most parents would like, family meals end up being take-out pizza or other fast foods. Now there is another option.

Cook-and-carry companies, such as Dinners Together, Dream Dinners, and Dinner by Design, are springing up all across the country. They are taking over the tasks of menu planning, shopping, chopping, slicing, and clean-up so that families can spend their time enjoying a meal together without all the time and work usually required in preparation. Customers choose which menus they want and then, following the recipes, assemble dishes like cheesy chicken casserole and Salisbury steak from ingredients that have already been prepared for them. Among the several advantages of this kind of support is that spouses and children can easily help with getting dinner on the table. Of course, not all families can afford this service, but for many families the expenditure for two weeks of healthy meals prepared this way is less than what they spend at fast-food restaurants or for take-outs, and the time saved can be spent enjoying the companionship of all family members.

SUMMARY

At the beginning of the nineteenth century, the U.S. fertility rate was quite high. Since that time, it has steadily declined and now is slightly lower than the replacement level of 2.1, with the notable exception of the "baby boom" of the late 1940s and 1950s. Fertility rates vary across race and class; people of color and low-income groups have the highest rates.

Deciding whether to parent involves an evaluation of both the costs and benefits. Increasing numbers of people are deciding to be child-free or to delay parenting until their 30s or even 40s and beyond. During the mid-nineteenth century, the use of contraceptives and abortion became illegal. After a long struggle, the Supreme Court invalidated laws prohibiting contraceptives and, in 1973 in *Roe* v. *Wade,* it recognized a woman's right to an abortion. Since that time, many efforts have been made to restrict abortion, and abortion has become a major issue in national politics.

The decline in the fertility rate, the legalization of abortion, and the tendency for more unmarried mothers to keep their babies have led to a scarcity of infants available for adoption. New reproductive technologies have been developed to help infertile couples achieve their desire to have children. These new reproductive techniques present many legal, ethical, and social challenges and raise questions about the nature of parenthood and the meaning of families. Social policy is only slowly emerging to deal with these questions.

Conception, pregnancy, and childbirth have a tremendous effect on the lives of individuals and couples. Conception begins with the fertilization of an egg by a sperm. Once pregnancy is confirmed, the woman should get immediate and continuous prenatal care. Research indicates that a number of factors—especially age, race, and class—affect the prenatal attitudes and behaviors of pregnant women. Poor women and women of color are at a higher risk of receiving inadequate prenatal care because of a lack of economic resources. As a consequence, babies born to these women are at greater risk of birth defects, diseases, and other physical or medical problems. Some of the most common risks to the prenatal environment are poor nutrition, smoking, and drug and alcohol use. In addition, AIDS and other sexually transmitted diseases can harm the fetus.

In focusing on the pregnant woman, we often forget about the expectant father. Many expectant fathers now participate in their partner's pregnancy through a variety of actions, including taking a paternity leave for the birth of their child. Becoming a parent is a major transition in a person's life. Not all people experience parenthood in the same way. Rather, parenthood varies for individuals and groups within as well as across a number of important areas of experience: race, class, gender, age, sexual orientation, and marital status. Within all groups, however, females and males seem to experience parenting differently. Although many individuals and groups no longer adhere as strongly to the traditional gender division of labor, women nonetheless tend to spend far more time in childrearing and housework activities than men. In the final analysis, no matter who does the parenting, more support is needed for parenting and for those who parent.

KEY TERMS

fertility	abortion	embryo transplant	morbidity	motherhood
fertility rate	infertility	surrogacy	mortality	mystique
total fertility rate	assisted reproductive	preimplantation genetic	fetal alcohol	systemic racism
pronatalist attitude	technology	diagnosis	syndrome	xenophobia
antinatalist forces	artificial insemination	infant mortality rate	HIV embryopathy	
contraception	in vitro fertilization	congenital	postnatal depression	

QUESTIONS FOR STUDY AND REFLECTION

1. Trace and explain the changing fertility rates in the United States over the last three centuries. Project the patterns of fertility among various age, marital status, race, and class groupings that are most likely to develop in the first half of the twenty-first century. Explain the rationale for your projections. Discuss the implications of these changes for the society at large.

2. Discuss the legal and ethical issues surrounding assisted reproductive technology. How have these technologies affected our understanding of parenthood and families? Explain. U.S. bioethicist Daniel Callahan sees the open market in sperm as an acceptance of the systematic downgrading of fatherhood, in that men can now produce children and have no responsibility for them. Do you agree or disagree with Callahan's view? Explain. Overall, what guidelines would you recommend be established for each of the assisted reproductive technologies? Explain.

3. Hypothetically, you have been asked to join a blue ribbon panel to investigate the status and condition of children being raised in families living below the poverty level. The group's task is to develop some a set of social policies statements that will be given to the President of the United States. What are some social policies that you might develop that would benefit poor children and their families? How might you incorporate considerations of the intersections of race, class, gender, and sexual orientation into your policies?

4. What is your idea of a good mother? A good father? How do you rate yourself as a parent or prospective parent? What do you think are some of the important questions that people should ask themselves before they decide to become parents? Can men mother? Why? Why not? Does a person have to be legally married to be a good parent? Why? Why not?

ADDITIONAL RESOURCES

SOCIOLOGICAL

CAHN, NAOMI. 2009. *Test Tube Families: Why the Fertility Market Needs Legal Regulation.* New York: New York University Press. A lawyer who teaches family law at Georgetown University gives us insight into the multi-billion dollar industry by which "biology, medicine, human determination, and the law bring babies into being." As a new generation of "donor kids" comes of age, Cahn argues for better regulation to sustain the fertility industry while at the same time protecting the interests of donors, recipients, and the children that they produce.

DEFAGO, NICKI. 2005. *Childfree and Loving It.* London: Vision. Numerous people from around the world tell the author why they chose not to have children; others tell why they wish they had not had children and the reasons for their regrets.

LEV, ARLENE ISTAR. 2004. *The Complete Lesbian and Gay Parenting Guide.* New York: Berkley Books. Written by a family therapist, this book provides practical wisdom and advice as well as real-life stories of what it is like to be a gay or lesbian parent.

LEVINE, SUZANNE BRAUN. 2000. *Father Courage: What Happens When Men Put Family First.* New York: Harcourt. Based on interviews with fathers from various walks of life, the author illustrates how men, in their struggle to succeed at work and in parenthood, are reinventing what it means to be a father today. The fathers reported on explore new ways of childrearing, split time with their wives to cover household chores, and cope with sacrifice when it comes to their career, as they simultaneously discover and relish the pleasures of a dynamic relationship with their families. Drawing from social science, anthropology, media, psychology, and many other sources, the author not only highlights a current trend in male parenting but also recasts our understanding of the concept of fatherhood.

FILM

The Kids Are All Right. 2010. Two women, Nic and Jules, are in a long-term, committed relationship. They have each given birth to a child using the same sperm donor. One of the children seeks out and finds their donor father. The film highlights some of the emotional ups and downs affecting all members of this nontraditional family.

Mao's Last Dancer. 2009. Based on the autobiography by Li Cunxin, this film tells the moving story of an 11-year-old boy plucked from a poor Chinese village by Madame Mao's cultural delegates. He is taken from his family and sent to Beijing to study ballet where he and numerous other children must grow up and achieve success without the support of their families. Although he becomes a successful dancer, the question remains, at what cost?

LITERARY

ATWOOD, MARGARET. 1996. *The Handmaid's Tale.* New York: Fawcett Columbine. An interesting view is presented of a future society where women have lost their reproductive rights and no longer have control over their own bodies.

PARENT, MARC. 2001. *Believing It All: What My Children Taught Me about Trout Fishing, Jelly Toast & Life.* New York: Little, Brown. Wonderful poetic, contemplative, from-the-heart honest reflections of one man's journey of raising children through an incredible time and a unique view of life in the United States at the beginning of the twenty-first century.

INTERNET

http://www.childrensdefense.org The Children's Defense Fund is a nonprofit child advocacy organization and provides information on the status of America's children.

http://http:www.more4kids.info/549/best-parenting-websites/ A unique Web site that offers links to many different parenting sites. The sites provide information on health, toddlers, teenagers, media choices and much more.

http://www.childfree.net/index.html This Web site offers books and articles related to being child-free and provides links to resources and ways to contact others who are child-free.

www.childtrends.org Child Trends is a nonprofit, nonpartisan research organization that produces information about a number of marriage, family, and child-related issues in order to improve the decisions, programs, and policies that affect children and their families. The Web site includes a data bank indicator; press releases; a newsroom; and a variety of publications, projects, and research.

Succeed with MyFamilyLab®
www.myfamilylab.com

Watch. Explore. Read. The New MyFamilyLab is designed just for you. Each chapter features a pre-test and post-test to help you learn and review key concepts and terms. Experience Marriages and Families in action with dynamic visual activities, videos, and readings to enhance your learning experience.

Here are a few activities you will find for this chapter.

Watch on **myfamilylab.com**

Video clips feature important concepts in the study of Marriages and Families. Watch:
• Economics of the African-American Family

Explore on **myfamilylab.com**

Social Explorer is an interactive application that allows you to explore Census data through interactive maps. Explore the Social Explorer Activity:
• Family Structure Among Hispanic Populations

Read on **myfamilylab.com**

MyFamilyLab includes primary source readings from classic and contemporary sociologists from around the world. Read:
• Gerson: "Dilemmas of Involved Fatherhood"

Evolving Work and Family Structures

What Will You Learn?

- Define and understand the sociological meaning of key terms.
- Describe the relationship between work and family.
- Apply the sociological imagination to examine the extent and consequences of the growing inequality of income and wealth among families in the United States.
- Assess the pro and con arguments for increasing taxes on individuals and families in the wealthiest income bracket.
- Increase your awareness of how household tasks and childcare are divided among family members.
- Question how gender impacts employment, wages, working conditions, family relationships, and friendship patterns.

IN THE NEWS

Clarksville, TN

Josh Buchholz is a signal support systems specialist serving in Afghanistan. While he is fighting there, his wife, Tila Buchholz, a 29-year-old mother of two, is fighting to save their home from foreclosure. The Buchholz family had been living in Ludington, Michigan when Josh lost his construction job and enlisted in the military in order to support his family. He was sent to Fort Campbell, and his family followed so they could stay together. Since they were unable to sell their Michigan home, they rented it out, but the renter fell behind on his payments and eventually left. The Buchholz family couldn't afford to continue their mortgage payments while paying rent in Clarksville. Three months after Josh left for Afghanistan, the mortgage lender began foreclosure proceedings on the family home (Wadhwani, 2011).

They are not alone. More than 20,000 veterans, active-duty troops, and reservists who took out special government-backed mortgages lost their homes in 2010, the highest number since 2003. According to Realty Trac, a foreclosure research firm, the rate of foreclosure filings in 2010 among 163 Zip codes located near military bases rose 32 percent during 2008. This compares to a national rate increase of 23 percent for that same time period (Zoroya, 2011). Military families are particularly vulnerable to the current housing crisis because of loss of higher paid civilian jobs, transfers to new locations, and loss of income when spouses leave their jobs to take care of injured partners.

Some of the foreclosures, like that on Sgt. James Hurley's house, were improper and violated the Servicemembers Civil Relief Act, a law that provides consumer protection measures designed to protect military personnel from financial distress. Sgt. Hurley was serving in Iraq when Saxon Mortgage Services seized and sold his home. When he returned from Iraq, he sued the company. The Justice Department initiated an investigation of such foreclosures. Hurley and other service members who had been foreclosed on illegally received compensation for the loss of their homes. However, Hurley is still left with the question: "They took it illegally; why can't I get it back? I didn't want any money. All I wanted was my house back" (Kirkham, 2011).

Families who experience foreclosure experience more than the loss of their house. There is the stress of moving out and adjusting to new surroundings, depletion of savings, loss of credit, and the accompanying emotion toll—anger, shame, regret, grief, and loss of hope for the future.

WHAT WOULD YOU DO?

If you were facing a foreclosure on your home, what actions would you take to maintain the social fabric of your life? Have you or anyone you know experienced a foreclosure? What impact did it have on the adults? On the children?

((•—[Listen to the Chapter Audio on myfamilylab.com

I n our society, we frequently think of work and family life as separate spheres, but as we see in the situations of the Buchholz and Hurley families, changes in work and resulting income can have devastating and long-lasting consequences for families. As we shall see throughout this chapter, the availability and rewards of work are major factors in the structure and functioning of families.

The Work–Family Connection

Research shows that the worlds of work and family affect each other in significant ways. The quality and stability of family life are dependent to a large extent on the type of work available for family members. Work provides income that determines a family's standard of living. Because of changing economic and social conditions, a single income is no longer sufficient for most families. Many husbands remain major providers, but increasingly wives are sharing this role and, increasingly, wives are taking over this role due to their husbands' job loss. Additionally, growing numbers of families are headed by a single parent who must fulfill both the breadwinner and homemaker roles.

Work affects families in other ways as well. It can have *spillover effects*, either positive or negative, on family life. An example of positive spillover is the carryover of satisfaction and stimulation at work to a sense of satisfaction at home (Orbuch, 2011). Similarly, increases in marital satisfaction are related to increases in job satisfaction (Rogers, 2003). Negative spillover involves bringing home the problems and stresses experienced at work, making adequate participation in family life difficult (Voydanoff, 1987; Schulz et al., 2004). Family life can affect work in important ways as well. Family obligations can provide motivation for working hard, but problems at home, such as a child's illness, can hinder job performance.

This chapter focuses on the interconnection between families and work, beginning with a quick view of people's perceptions of the current economic climate followed by an examination of the changing composition of the labor force, notably the increasing participation of married women with small children and the impact of this change on marriage and family structures and functioning. We also examine today's growing inequalities of wealth and resources as manifested in low income, poverty, unemployment, and underemployment, all of which have contributed to a sense of unease and economic uncertainty among many working families. Despite government reports of a growing economy and some new job creation, recent polling data suggest that the majority of Americans are concerned about current economic conditions.

ECONOMIC CONCERNS ARE INCREASING IN THE UNITED STATES

In April 2011, only 19 percent of respondents rated the economic conditions in this country as good; 80 percent rated them as poor. Thirty-nine percent of respondents thought that economic conditions were getting worse (CBS/*New York Times*, 2011b). Similar concerns were observed in a recent Gallup poll that found that 58 percent of Americans were worried that they will not be able to maintain their standard of living, the highest response to this question to date. Respondents were even more concerned about their future. Sixty-six percent of respondents were worried about not having enough money for retirement. This was almost equally true for respondents with incomes of less than $30,000 and respondents with income of $75,000 or more, (69 to 68 percent) (Mendes, 2011). These attitudes contrast with more optimistic views exhibited in 2001 when 63 percent of respondents rated economic conditions as excellent or good ("Consumer Views of the Economy," 2006).

People's concerns about their economic future are not unfounded. In recent decades, both the U.S. and world economies have experienced major changes that have adversely affected many family budgets. According to the National Bureau of Economic Research (2010), the Great Recession that began in December 2007 and ended 18 months later in July 2009 was deeper than any recession since World War II. This recession was caused in large measure by the crash of a massive real estate bubble fueled by the packaging and selling of sub-prime mortgages during a period when many American consumers and investment banks were assuming large amounts of debt. During this period, Americans lost 21 percent of their net worth, the labor market shed some 7.3 million jobs, and 2.3 million homes were lost through foreclosure (Russell Sage Foundation, 2011). Although many economists agree that the economy is showing signs of some recovery, research on the impact of the recession on families shows it is deep, widespread, and likely to continue for many more years. Consider:

- More than half of all adults in the U.S. labor force (55 percent) had experienced some "work-related hardship"—a period of unemployment, a pay cut, a reduction in work hours, or an involuntary move to part-time employment—since the recession began.
- More than 70 percent of Americans age 40 and over felt they had been affected by the economic crisis.
- Long-term unemployment—joblessness lasting six months or more—is at its highest level since the 1940s.
- 20 percent of Americans have seen their available household income decline by 25 percent or more (quoted in Warner, 2010).

This process is not likely to end anytime soon. Forrester Research estimates that 3.4 million white-collar jobs will be sent overseas between 2003 and 2050 (Greenhouse, 2008). Millions of workers lost jobs because their plant or company closed (42,000 factories closed since 2001) or moved, there was insufficient work for them to do, or their positions or shifts were abolished. Although the majority of these workers eventually found other work, it was often at lower pay. During the last three decades, the real earnings of most male workers remained stagnant or fell. Other factors such as the rise in costs for gasoline, home heating, health care, food, and college education are contributing to the financial stress experienced by many families.

Not all families are affected equally by the experience of job loss. African Americans are more likely to be affected by job loss than White workers, and the consequences of job loss appear more severe for Blacks who, on average, have fewer economic resources to sustain them during periods of unemployment. In the past, white-collar workers and professionals were less likely to be affected by economic downturns. This is much less the case today. Financial struggles at companies like Ford and General Motors, United Airlines defaulting on its pensions, the collapse of Enron and WorldCom, and the need for a bank bailout led to the dislocation of thousands of workers and added to the anxiety among many employed workers. In a recent study, almost one out of three married Americans said the recession had brought financial stress to their marriage. Despite the stress, an equal number of married people said the recession has caused them to deepen their commitment to their marriage (Wilcox, 2011). Some couples deal with this anxiety by long-term planning (see the Family Profile box). We will discuss these trends in more detail throughout this chapter and conclude it with an assessment of the kinds of changes that need to be made in the organization of work and in social policies to help individuals maintain a decent standard of living while also maintaining a balance between the demands of work and family.

The Transformation of Work and Family Roles

The idealized images of men as providers and women as homemakers continued into the second half of the twentieth century, despite the fact that these roles were already being undermined. Figure 10.1 on page 322 traces the changes in women's and men's labor force participation rates from 1900 with projections to 2018. The **labor force participation rate** refers to the percentage

THE PARKINSON FAMILY

Karen, Brody, Craig, and Luke Parkinson

Length of Relationship: 15 ½ years

Length of Marriage: 10 years

Challenges in Parenting

Craig and I became parents again when our second son, Luke, was born on July 6, 2008. Luke joined his, at that time, almost 3-year-old brother, Brody. With Luke now 3 and Brody nearly turning 6, we are facing some new challenges. Craig is currently teaching in a large urban school district and has been for the previous 11 years. After a four year unpaid personal leave, I officially resigned from my teaching position in the same school district. I resigned from that position in an effort to remain home with the children through their early years. The plan at this point is for me to return to the teaching profession when both children are in school full time. As the economy stands in 2011, I am concerned about what type of full-time teaching positions will be available when the time comes to

return to work. The district my husband teaches in has experienced many budget cuts in recent years. Many teachers have been laid off based on seniority. With my husband having taught 11 years at the same school, it would be sad to see him have to start over in a different school. His current school is within walking distance of our home. It has been a challenge moving from two incomes down to just one. That being said, we have planned for this time of only one income since purchasing our house in 2003. Through long-term planning, we are able to afford our mortgage and many of the other necessities without having to worry about being a single-income family.

A second challenge at this point is teaching Luke that he may not be able to do all of the activities that Brody is able to do. For instance, Brody is currently playing summer T-ball and has practice two nights per week. As a family, we all attend but keeping Luke in the stands, sitting down, and watching is a

challenge. He wants to run out on the field and participate, too! We would like Luke to learn that some activities are for certain aged children and, therefore, he cannot participate. His turn will come.

Another challenge for me was the adjustment from having two children home to just one. Brody began all day K–4 in the fall of 2010, leaving Luke and me as the only ones home during the day. I was very concerned about how Luke would adjust to Brody being gone all day. Would he miss him, would he cry, be bored? It turns out I had nothing to worry about. Each morning, Luke happily waves good-bye in the window as Craig and Brody walk to work and school. I actually think he loves the one-on-one time he and I can spend together. I do, too! Which leads me to talk about the joys of parenting two boys.

Craig and I both love the fact that we have two sons who will grow up together and always have someone to play with. They may not always play well together, share, or talk kindly, but they have learned that they are brothers and will always have each other. It is looking like our children will only have one cousin, and she is 13 years old. Craig and I grew up with many cousins always around at family functions and we were concerned that our children would miss out on that experience. Having had two boys, it softened that concern a bit. They will have each other to play with as they grow up. We are a very active family and love to do things together outside, especially sports. As Luke approached two years old, we thought about whether or not we wanted to expand our family. We decided we love the fact that they were both more independent and didn't want to start all over with a newborn. Through thick and thin, we are happy to be a family of four!

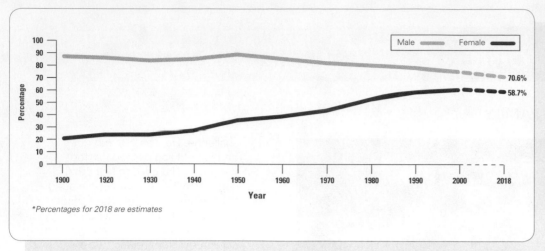

FIGURE 10.1 Civilian Labor Force Participation Rates, by Sex, 1900 to 2000 with Projections to 2018

Source: Adapted from U.S. Census Bureau, 1975, *Historical Statistics of the United States, Colonial Times to 1970*, bicentennial ed., part 1 (Washington, D.C: Government Printing Office): 131–132; U.S. Census Bureau 2011, *Statistical Abstract of the United States, 2011* (Washington, DC: Government Printing Office): Table 585; p. 377.

of workers in a particular group who are employed or who are actively seeking employment. If people are not employed and are not actively seeking work, they are not counted in the labor force. As the twentieth century opened, only 20 percent of women age 14 and older were in the labor force, compared with approximately 86 percent of men in that age category. The comparable rates 100 years later were 60 percent for women and 75 percent for men age 16 and over. Thus, during the twentieth century, the labor force participation rates for women and men have moved in opposite directions, with the result that women now constitute nearly 47 percent of all workers, up from 18 percent in 1900. This gap between the proportion of female and male workers is expected to narrow even further in the twenty-first century, as the percentage of women (58.7 percent) remains relatively stable but a lower percentage of men (70.8 percent) are expected to be in the labor force by 2018.

The decline in the male participation rate reflects a number of changes in the U.S. economy. On the one hand, improvements in pension and other retirement benefits have allowed older men to retire early; on the other hand, the labor market demands for better-educated workers have kept younger men in school longer and led to the displacement of workers with low levels of education and marginal skills, especially men of color.

VARIATIONS BY RACE, GENDER, AND MARITAL STATUS

Historically, labor force participation rates varied by race as well as by gender and marital status. In the past, White women were less likely than women of color to be in the labor force. As White women began to delay marriage and to divorce in greater numbers, however, their rates became similar to those of other groups of women. In 2009, the labor force participation rate for Black women was 60.3 percent, followed by White women with 59.1 percent, and Asian women with 58.2 percent. Latinas had the lowest rate of participation, 56.5 percent. For men, the differences in participation rates are more pronounced across race and ethnicity. Latinos lead with 78.8 percent, followed by Asian men with 74.6 percent, and White men with 72.8 percent. Black men have the lowest labor force participation rates, 65 percent (U.S. Census Bureau, 2011e).

The narrowing gap between women's and men's participation rates reveals only part of the story, however. According to historian Alice Kessler-Harris (1982), a marked shift occurred in the participation patterns of women. Prior to World War II, the majority of women workers were young, single, poor, and women of color. As Figure 10.2 shows as late as 1975, only 36.7 percent of all married mothers with children under age 6 were in the labor force. However, a much higher percentage of Black mothers (almost 55 percent) than White mothers (about 35 percent) were

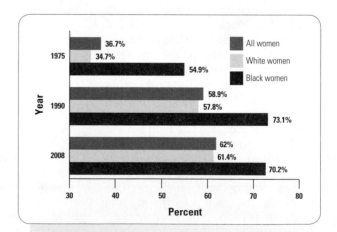

FIGURE 10.2 Labor Force Participation Rates for Wives, Husbands Present, with Children under Age 6, by Race, 1975–2008

Source: Adapted from U.S. Census Bureau, 2011, *Statistical Abstract of the United States, 2011* (Washington, DC: Government Printing Office): Table 599, p. 385.

working. More than three decades later, almost six out of 10 (62 percent) married mothers with preschool children were in the labor force. However, the gap between the percentages of working Black and White mothers narrowed somewhat, 70.2 to 61.4 percent. Latina mothers had the lowest rate (48.0 percent), and Asian mothers were next (59.3 percent). Even more noteworthy is that 58.9 percent of White married women and 61.2 percent of Black married women with children age 1 or younger were in the labor force, compared with 29.2 and 50.0 percent, respectively, in 1975. In 2008, comparable figures for Asia mothers were 57.8 percent and 43.7 percent for Latina mothers (U.S. Census Bureau, 2011e).

REASONS WOMEN WORK

Rarely do we ask men why they work—we assume they have no choice. They are expected to be family providers. But because the homemaker role was believed to be the traditional role for women, any departures from this role required explanation. Most women work for the same reasons men do—to support themselves or their family. Other reasons women give for working are interest and self-fulfillment. The recent Families and Work Institute's National Study of the Changing Workforce found that women under age 29 were just as likely as men to want jobs with greater responsibility (66 percent to 67 percent) compared to 54 percent to 61 percent in 1997 (Galinsky, Aumann, and Bond, 2009).

🕮 Read the Document
Detours on the Road to Equality: Women, Work, and Higher Education on **myfamilylab.com**

No single factor can explain the dramatic changes in women's labor force participation rates and aspirations. Rather, a complex interplay of demographic, economic, social, political, and personal factors have contributed to these changes. During the last 50 years, the economy underwent rapid change leading to an increased demand for women workers to fill the expanding number of jobs in the service sector such as teaching, health care, social services, government, and real estate. The women's movement and affirmative action legislation also enhanced employment opportunities for women and people of color. Additionally, in contrast to women in previous eras, women today are better educated, have fewer children, and live longer. Women who postpone marriage and childbearing to increase their level of education and to begin work are more likely to remain in the labor force after the birth of their children. Today, there is no difference between young women with and without children in their desire to move to jobs with more responsibility. Advanced education influences women in much the same way that it influences men. Not only does education offer better job possibilities, but it also raises awareness of personal options and creates a desire for self-expression and self-fulfillment. Women today also have more time in their total life span to pursue activities other than childrearing. All of these, changes as well as a desire for a higher standard of living for families, culminated in a change in social attitudes resulting in a greater acceptance of working women.

Work and Family Structures

The rapid entrance of married women with children into the labor force has altered family life in many ways. A variety of work and family structures have emerged as a response to these economic and social transformations, creating both opportunities and problems for family members.

TRADITIONAL NUCLEAR FAMILIES, INCLUDING STAY-AT-HOME DADS

The highly idealized family structure consisting of a working husband, a wife who is a full-time homemaker, and one or more children currently comprises only 22.6 percent of married couples with children under age 15, down from 23.7 percent in 2008. The number of stay-at-home moms was the lowest since 2001, also a period of recession (Yen, 2010). Smaller in numbers but similar in structure are households in which husbands and fathers (popularly called househusbands) stay home to care for home and family while their wives work. The exact number of stay-at-home dads

This stay-at-home dad keeps in touch while taking his children on an outing to the park.

is unknown. The U.S. Census Bureau puts the number at 154,000 (Facts for Features, 2011). Sociologist Beth Latshaw (2010) believes the number is much higher, arguing that the census figures are based on a narrow definition in which the wife must be in the labor force for the entire year and the husband outside the official labor force for the specifically cited reason of "taking care of home and family." She estimates that the share of fathers who stay at home to raise children is over 6 percent of all fathers. The United States is not the only country with stay-at-home dads. In Canada, one out of 8 stay-at-home parents are dads, up from 1 in 100 in 1976 (Jeong, 2011), and in the Republic of Korea the government data show that 177,00 men cited their main "job" as childrearing and housekeeping ("Korean Men Willing...," 2011).

Most men take this role on a temporary basis when they are unemployed, going to school, or able to do their work from home. In some cases, the comparative earning power of spouses dictates who stays at home. Today, one out of three wives earns more than her husband. If a wife's earnings are substantially higher than his, the family budget is improved if Dad is the one who stays home. Other stay-at-home men are retired; still others have remarried younger women and now want the opportunity to participate more fully in childrearing activities. Although most men find great personal satisfaction in caring for their children, many complain that they receive relatively little support from the larger society and often find their masculinity questioned by others. However, many moms, like Darla Stencavage, a captain in the U.S. Army, know better. When they leave for work, they go with the assurance that their children will be well carried for by active and loving stay-at-home dads. According to Darla, "He is a wonderful caregiver and nurturer for me and my daughter, and it really eases my mind. It was important for us to raise our own children, and I would have had to quit work if he had not been willing to stay home." Peter Stencavage not only assumed full-time parenting, he took on the role of the supportive spouse of an Army commander and participates in his wife's unit's family support group, often the only male in attendance ("Dad of the Month," 2006).

These men, like their female counterparts, engage in activities that some authors are now calling "home production," the non-market production of goods and services, usually for the family but occasionally on a volunteer basis for schools, churches, or other groups. According to sociologists Randy Hodson and Teresa Sullivan (1995), what is traditionally known as "housework" is only one aspect of home production, which also includes household budgeting, grocery shopping, care of dependents, and other tasks that go beyond cleaning and laundry. Consumer website Insure.com looked at the various tasks that a stay-at-home parent does and concluded that to replace that labor a family would have to spend $61,436 per year (Business Briefing, 2011).

Like all social roles, the role of home production worker (traditionally known as "housewife") has both costs and benefits (Oakley, 1974). On the positive side, it provides the possibility of scheduling activities to suit one's own priorities and the opportunity to watch children grow and develop on a daily basis. Many parents, including many women and men currently in the labor force, would prefer to stay home at least while their children are young. In a 2007 survey, 45 percent of women said they would prefer to stay home compared to 50 percent who said they would prefer to work. More men are reporting a preference to stay at home, 29 percent in 2007 compared with 24 percent in 2001 (Saad, 2007) and only 12 percent in 1985 (Moore, 2005).

Among the disadvantages of the home production role are the repetitive and sometimes boring nature of activities such as cleaning and doing laundry and the overall social devaluation of housework, often reflected in the phrase, "I'm just a housewife." Important financial costs as well become major burdens for families with only a single source of income and become particularly significant when divorce or death disrupts the family. This is particularly the case when the disruption is unexpected, as happens when accidents, natural disasters, or terrorist attacks result in the untimely death of the major breadwinner. Homemakers are economically dependent on their partners. Unlike homemakers in several European countries, U.S. homemakers are not covered by pensions, insurance, or social security. Thus, when a marriage is dissolved in the United States, the displaced homemaker frequently suffers downward social mobility (see Chapter 12).

THE TWO-PERSON SINGLE CAREER

One variation of the traditional nuclear family–work relationship is what some writers have called the "two-person career" (Papanek, 1973; Mortimer and London, 1984). This pattern, considered by Hanna Papanek to be a "structural part of the middle-class wife's role" (1973:857), incorporates the wife into her spouse's job through the expectation that she will be available to entertain his business associates, engage in volunteer activities that will enhance his organization's image, attend company parties and other events, socialize with her husband's coworkers off the job, and at the same time attend to the children and keep the household functioning smoothly. Much of the research on the two-person career focuses on middle- and upper-class occupations. Many business, professional, and political wives, for example, the first lady, are often viewed as typical examples of the two-person single career. Thus, men in these families symbolically bring two people to their jobs (Kanter, 1977). However, when women hold similar positions, husbands are rarely expected to perform these duties. One notable exception was Charles T. Hunt III, a stay-at-home dad and husband of former Massachusetts Acting Governor Jane Swift, who agreed to take on some of the responsibilities usually delegated to first ladies such as giving tours of the governor's mansion.

The two-person single career marriage, like all others, has advantages and disadvantages. On the positive side, employers benefit by having additional "workers" without having to pay for their efforts. Many husbands owe much of their career advancement to the social skills of their wives. Because the husband is away from home much of the time, the wife becomes the exclusive home manager. Fulfilling this role gives wives status and a sense of accomplishment, leaving their husbands free to devote most of their energy to work. Among middle- and upper-class wives, the financial rewards for taking on this responsibility may be significant—a secure lifestyle, travel, and opportunities for cultural enrichment. On the negative side, many wives experience unhappiness in this role. Like other nonemployed homemakers, these wives may believe their role is not appreciated or respected by the public. Wives may feel enormously limited in their behavior, constrained in their choice of friends, and restricted in their own occupational goals because of the demands of their husbands' careers (Papanek, 1973; Kanter, 1977). In addition, the husband's work often takes priority over family life, thus limiting the time spouses have to be together.

Economic shifts that require multiple family earners as well as the changing aspirations of women and men have led to a decline in the two-person single career strategy. The traditional nuclear family of working husband, homemaker wife, and children is being replaced by dual-earner families, or as some writers prefer, "two-paycheck couples."

DUAL-EARNER FAMILIES

Dual-earner families are not new; there have always been families where both spouses were employed outside the home. In the past, dual-earner families tended to be concentrated among the poor. However, by 2007, both parents worked in 62 percent of all married-couple families, cutting across all class, race, and ethnic lines (Bureau of Labor Statistics, 2008). However, this figure dropped to 47.8 percent in 2010 as a result of the recession that began in late 2007 (Bureau of Labor Statistics, 2011a). Women in dual earner families contributed an average of 44 percent of annual family income in 2008, up from 39 percent in 1997 (Galinsky, Aumann and Bond, 2009).

Dual-earner families do not all follow the same pattern. There is considerable variation in their commitment to work. At one end of the continuum are couples in which one of the spouses, usually the wife, works part time. At the other end is a small but growing number of couples in which both spouses are highly committed to work. These are what social scientists call dual-career couples. These households differ from other dual-earner households in their approach to work. Rather than simply having a job, these couples invest in careers, which have several identifying characteristics. First, they require extensive training, usually a college or professional degree. Second, careers are more structured than jobs, containing specific paths of upward mobility. Finally, careers involve commitment beyond a 9-to-5 workday.

COMMUTER MARRIAGES

Some couples work in different geographic locations and because of distance must maintain two separate places of residence. Social scientists refer to these arrangements as **commuter marriages.** Approximately 3.8 million Americans are currently in commuter marriages, a 30 percent increase since 2000 ("Love Tech Goes…," 2008). That figure is expected to increase as more couples find it necessary to accept jobs in distant locations (Kridel, 2009). Couples in other countries face similar challenges. Estimates are that in the central region of Thailand, 41 percent of all couples live apart after marriage due to economic, occupational, or educational needs (quoted in Schvaneveldt, Young, and Schvaneveldt, 2001). One form of commuter marriage has existed for a long time. Couples in which one spouse, most frequently the husband, is a politician, professional athlete, traveling salesperson, seasonal worker, prisoner, or serves in the military, have had some experience with living apart while maintaining a marital relationship. Today, however, 15 percent of active-duty military personnel are women who have entered military life for many of the same reasons men do—better job opportunities than in civilian life,

opportunities for education, travel, and adventure, patriotism, and a sense of duty. Many of these women are married; some have children who they have had to leave in the care of spouses, partners, or other relatives when called to serve in Afghanistan, Iraq, or other locations.

Dual-residency patterns were and continue to be common among low-income families around the world, where one spouse motivated by economic necessity migrates to another country, either making occasional visits home, such as many Latina/o migrants in the United States do, or works to reunite the family in her or his new location. Today, many commuter marriages develop because both spouses pursue careers but find that suitable jobs for each spouse are unavailable in the same location. Sometimes, too, the requirements of a job call for a transfer to a new area, and for whatever reason the other spouse cannot or will not relocate. A study examining corporate relocations found that families who opt for commuter marriage do so for specific reasons:

- Sixty percent do not want to disrupt their children's education.
- Forty-five percent want a spouse to continue her or his career track.
- Ten percent maintain homes in their old location so that a spouse and/or the children can continue to see familiar medical specialists and ensure continuity of care.
- Others did not want to move or could not sell their house (Worldwide ERC 2008 Family Issues Report, 2008).

When couples do commute, they are most likely to see their accommodations to their careers as a temporary lifestyle arrangement (Marszalek, 2010). Generally, the geographic distance involved determines the length of separation. Some couples are able to be together on weekends; others can manage only monthly reunions. These arrangements are more stressful for younger couples, especially those with children, those who have been married for only a short time, and those who feel insecure in their relationship.

Commuter couples, of necessity, have developed coping strategies for maintaining a sense of family. Many of these strategies require significant outlays of resources, particularly frequent telephone calls and travel to each other's place of residence. Through technologies like Skype, an Internet phone service, Twitter, Facebook, and e-mail couples can communicate in low-cost ways and have at least some virtual time together. Research comparing commuting and noncommuting dual-career couples found that commuters are more satisfied with their work life and the time they have for themselves but are more dissatisfied with family life, their relationship with their partner, and with life as a whole (Bunker et al., 1992). This finding appears constant across diverse racial and ethnic groups (Jackson, Brown, and Patterson-Stewart, 2000; Schvaneveldt, Young, and Schvaneveldt, 2001).

Would you be comfortable as a partner in a commuter marriage? Consider some of the unique problems you would face in such a relationship. How would you handle social events? Would you attend events alone or in the company of a same-sex or an other-sex friend? How would you convey emotional support and intimacy from a distance?

The Impact of Work on Family Relationships

Much of the research conducted in the past on the impact of work on family life has been sex-segregated—that is, based on the assumption that work has a different meaning for women than for men. For women, paid work was thought an option that had to be weighed against the disruption it would cause their families; for men, it was considered a given. Men might have choices in the type of work they selected but not in whether they would work. Therefore, outside of their earning power, there is "a dearth of empirical research on the effects of fathers' employment on father–child interactions and their children's behavior" (Barling, 1991:181).

Studies of working women, in contrast, focused on different questions. Recall from Chapter 2 Talcott Parsons's functionalist view that a woman's role in the family is expressive and a man's is instrumental. According to Parsons, stepping outside these roles leads to family instability. Thus, before 1960, researchers assumed that the entry of mothers into the labor force would have negative consequences for the family, leading, for example, to children getting into trouble at school or with the law.

These traditional role definitions no longer (if they ever did) adequately reflect the work and family experiences of women and men, especially those in dual-earner families. A new theoretical model is required that acknowledges the labor force participation of both women and men. Thus, sociologist Joan Spade (1989) called for a sex-integrated model to understand the impact of work on the family. Such a model asks how the type of work women and men do shapes their orientations and behaviors in the home.

Given the increasing number of dual-earner families, this question takes on major significance. The attempts by dual-earner couples to integrate work and family experiences affect many aspects of family life: power relationships and decision making, marital happiness, and the household division of labor. In short, by examining dual-earner couples, we can learn how gender roles in the family are changing in response to both spouses taking on paid employment.

MARITAL POWER AND DECISION MAKING

One of the most consistent findings relating to the impact of work on family life deals with the relationship between income and power in decision making. Money frequently translates into power. When both spouses work, the traditional pattern of male dominance in the marital relationship shifts to one of greater equality in terms of more joint decision making (Cherlin, 2009; Amato et al., 2007). Spouses, most frequently wives, who do not contribute financially in general, have little power in the relationship. The consequences of this may be severe. If the marriage is an unhappy one, the spouse without independent financial resources may feel compelled to stay in the relationship, whereas working may give an unhappy spouse the ability to leave the relationship. This relationship between independent resources and choice is illustrated by one of the respondents in a study of Chicana cannery workers: "It wasn't that my working hastened my divorce, in that it made my marriage worse, like Mario claims to this day. But rather it allowed me the freedom from a bad marriage" (Zavella, 1987:147). Examination of data from the National Survey of Families has provided empirical support for the observation that women's employment does not destabilize happy marriages but increases the risk of disruption in unhappy marriages (Schoen, 2002).

This pattern of wives gaining more power as a result of their economic contribution holds true across most racial and ethnic groups. Researchers Jose Szapocznik and Roberto Hernandez (1988), for example, observed that Cuban women who migrated to the United States often found jobs sooner than their husbands did. Their economic contributions were then translated into gains in family decision making, thereby weakening the traditional Cuban patriarchal family structure. For the first generation of Cuban Americans, these changes were often disruptive. Second-generation Cuban American couples who grew up in the United States are less troubled by the greater equality in decision making and have tended to construct family relationships that are less male-dominated than those of their parental generation (Boswell and Curtis, 1983; Szapocznik and Hernandez, 1988). Similar patterns have been observed among Chinese American and Korean American families (Min, 1988; Wong, 1988), among couples in Mexico (Attanasio and Lechene, 2002), and in Cameroon (Sikod, 2007). Furthermore, given the consistently high level of labor force participation of African American women, it is not surprising to find that egalitarian decision making is common in African American families as well (McAdoo, H.P., 2006).

There are significant exceptions to these patterns. Differences in economic power and decision making are often reinforced or offset by ideological considerations. In a study of women in second marriages, Karen Pyke (1994) found that some remarried women stopped working and became full-time homemakers, yet increased their power in the marital relationship. According to Pyke, the meaning couples give to women's paid employment or unpaid household labor is key to determining the woman's power in the relationship. Thus, if the working spouse values unpaid household labor, egalitarian power sharing between spouses is likely. Conversely, if couples believe men should be the primary breadwinners and, correspondingly, have the final say in most decisions, then the man will have more power in the relationship regardless of the earnings of either spouse (Benjamin and Sullivan, 1996).

MARITAL HAPPINESS AND SATISFACTION

Are couples with one earner happier than those with two? The results of research on this question are inconsistent. Some earlier studies have found homemakers to be happier than working wives (Stokes and Peyton, 1986; Saenz, Goudy, & Frederick, 1989). However, these researchers found that much of the dissatisfaction the working wives felt was attributable to the quality of the jobs they held—jobs with low pay, little status, and considerable stress. Later research also found a correlation between a stressful job and lower levels of marital adjustment (Sears and Galambos, 1992).

Other research found that working wives report higher levels of happiness than nonworking wives. Similarly, more recent research has consistently found that wives in dual-earner couples are healthier, less depressed, and less frustrated than their homemaker counterparts (Coontz, 1997; Amato et al., 2007). This finding is probably related to the fact that a wife's income contribution gives her more power within the family as well as being a source of satisfaction and self-esteem.

More important than work per se, however, is the couple's attitude toward work. If the couple disagrees about spousal employment or if the wife works only because of economic necessity, some tension and conflict are likely. Some wives who desire only a domestic role may be embittered about their need to work, whereas some husbands who adhere strongly to the good provider role might feel threatened or inadequate as a result of having a working wife. This is especially the case for some husbands whose wives earn more than they do (Minetor, 2002). However, if couples see themselves as a team, differences in income are less significant (Marshall, 2010). According to a recent study, only 39 percent of women and 42 percent of men agreed with the idea that men should earn the money and women should take care of the children and family. In 1977, 54 percent of men and 52 percent of women agreed with that statement (Galinsky, Aumann, and Bond, 2009). Figure 10.3 shows that this shift in attitudes about gender roles has occurred for all generations, but it is greatest among those in the older generations. For example, among employees age 28 and younger, the percentage agreeing with the statement fell from 55 percent in 1977 to 34 percent in 2008, a decline of 21 percentage points. However, among employees age 63 and older, there was a decline of 39 percentage points. These attitudinal shifts, no doubt, reflect the fact that a family's financial welfare is to a large degree dependent on women's contributions. In 2008, 27 percent of working wives whose husbands also worked earned more than their husbands, up from 18 percent in 1987. If we count working women married to men who are unemployed, the percentage increases to 34, up from 24 percent in 1987 (Bureau of Labor Statistics, 2010a).

The experience of marital happiness is related to another constraint confronting dual-earner families: finding time to be together, especially recreational time. "Couples with less time together express less satisfaction with their marriages" (Nock and Kingston, 1990:133). According to Ellen Galinsky (2004), President of the Families and Work Institute, the majority of employees (67 percent) say they don't have enough time with their children, while 63 percent say they don't have enough time with their spouses. Children reflect these views as well. A nationally representative group of children, ages 8–18, reported that their number one wish to improve their lives was that their parents were less tired and stressed.

Time is also related to two other important aspects of family living: household tasks and the care of children. Parsons's model of the family assumes that these are the wife's responsibilities and that they complement the husband's breadwinner role. Parsons did not anticipate the contemporary widespread need for two incomes, however. What happens to housework and child care when wives share the breadwinner function?

HUSBANDS AND THE DIVISION OF HOUSEHOLD LABOR

As more wives entered the labor force, social scientists began to investigate the degree to which husbands increased the amount of time they spent doing household work. Data collected from the 1960s to the mid-1970s show that family work remained almost exclusively the province of women, whether or not they were employed. For example, a study of 1296 New York State families found that husbands spent about 1.6 hours per day in family work compared with 8.1 hours per day for housewives and 4.8 hours per day for working wives (Walker and Woods, 1976). It is not surprising, then, that compared with their spouses, wives experienced more **role overload,** a situation in which a person's various roles carry more responsibilities than that person can reasonably manage. As a result of role overload, women have less free time and experience a diminished sense of well-being (Robinson, 1977; Hochschild, 1997). This pattern led sociologist Arlie Hochschild (1989) to describe women's dual role of worker and housewife as a "second shift."

Recent studies have documented a shift to a more equitable, albeit not equal, division of labor, with men doing slightly more work and women doing less work than was the case in the 1970s. According to a 2009 Time Use Study by the Bureau of Labor Statistics (2010b), on an average day, 85 percent of women but only 67 percent of men reported spending some time doing household activities such as housework, cooking, lawn care, or financial and other household management. Women reported spending 2.6 hours on such activities, while men spent 2.0 hours. However, only 20 percent of men reported doing cleaning or laundry compared to 51 percent of women. Men were somewhat more involved in food preparation and clean-up, with 40 percent of men and 68 percent of women reporting doing these activities. In households with the youngest child under age 6, women averaged 1.1 hours providing physical care (bathing, feeding) to household children while men averaged 0.5 hours.

Reviews of other national cross-time series of time-use diary studies found that from the 1960s to the twenty-first century, men's contribution to housework doubled, increasing from about 15 to over 30 percent of the total and that married women with children were doing, on average, two hours less housework per week than in 1965. Additionally, men's contribution to child care tripled during that same period of time (Fisher et al., 2006).

Data from a cross-national study of 13 countries reflect similar patterns to those in the United States. In only one country, Russia,

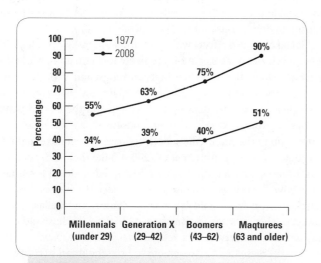

FIGURE 10.3 Changes in Gender Role Attitudes Across the Generations, 1977 to 2008

Source: Galinsky, E., K. Aumann, and J. T. Bond. 2009. *Times Are Changing: Gender and Generation at Work and at Home.* New York: Families and Work Institute Figure 9, p. 11.

did spouses say housework was shared about equally. In the other 12 countries, spouses reported that wives did more housework than husbands (Davis and Greenstein, 2004). Individuals' and couples' characteristics were found to influence the division of household labor. In households where wives were employed outside the home and/or had education levels equal to or above that of their husbands, husbands were reported to perform about half of the household labor. However, other research found that macro-level factors such as a country's level of economic development, female labor force participation, and gender ideology are equally important in the dynamics of how housework is divided between spouses. Overall, women in less egalitarian countries benefit less from their individual-level assets such as earning power and educational level than women in more egalitarian countries (Fuwa, 2004).

Similarly, gender equality in household work still eludes young girls. According to a study by the University of Michigan Institute for Social Research (2007), boys spend about 30 percent less time doing household chores than girls and more than twice as much time playing. Additionally, girls are less likely than boys to get paid for doing housework. Given that this gendered pattern is learned in childhood, it is not surprising that it is reproduced in adulthood.

Sharing the Load: Emergent Egalitarian Relationships Inequity in family work can affect marriage satisfaction. Among wives, there is a clear and positive connection between an equitable division of family work and marital and personal well-being (Rogers and Amato, 2000; Frisco and Williams, 2003; Wilcox and Nock, 2006). Lebanese wives, like their U.S. counterparts, are dissatisfied when their husbands' participation in household labor is only minimal (Khawaja and Habib, 2007). Data on couples in Moscow revealed similar patterns (Cubbins and Vannoy, 2004). Wives whose husbands do their share of family work are more satisfied with marriage than other wives. According to a 1990 national opinion poll, next to money, "how much my mate helps around the house" is the single biggest cause of resentment among women who are married or living as if married, with 52 percent of the respondents reporting this as a problem (Townsend and ONeil, 1990:28). Fifteen years later, wives still believe dads could do better. Forty-five percent of respondents wanted their husbands to provide more help with the kids and with household chores ("Voice of Mom Report," 2005). Similarly, a recent study found that a decline in marital satisfaction among new mothers was linked to their perceptions that the increases in housework associated with motherhood were inequitable (Dew and Wilcox, 2011).

Thus, there seems to be some consensus among both women and men for the need to alter traditional gender roles. That some of this is occurring, albeit slowly, is indicated by Audrey Smith and William Reid (1986) in their study of role-sharing marriages, by Rosanna Hertz (1986) in her study of dual-career marriages, by Pepper Schwartz (1999) in her study of peer marriages, by Shelley Haddock and her colleagues (2002) in their study of couples who perceive themselves as successful in balancing family and work, and by Suzanne Bianchi and her colleagues (2006) who examined how American parents are working together to ensure that they preserve their family time and provide adequately for their children. Hertz argues that dual-career couples generally do not start out with an ideology of equality in marital roles, but that it often emerges out of the opportunities and constraints they experience on a day-to-day basis. In contrast, the couples in Schwartz's

study had strong ideas about building a marriage based on equity and equality and made conscious efforts to achieve their goal—"marital intimacy that comes from being part of a well-matched, equally empowered, equally participatory team" (1999:162). Other couples have altered traditional gender roles in the family as well. However, as Francine Deutsch (1999) discovered in a study of 150 dual-career couples with children, most couples had a work-centered family in which work and career advancement, usually the husband's, was the priority. Nevertheless, 41 couples in her study (nearly 25 percent) had child-centered families in which their children's needs were the central focus for both parents. By fully sharing all responsibilities, these parents managed to have successful work lives and well-balanced family lives. More recent research indicates that couples who share household duties on an equitable basis have greater marital satisfaction and a lower incidence of divorce than couples who rely on more traditional gender role patterns (Hall and MacDermind, 2009; Coontz, 2007; Sullivan and Coltrane, 2008). Findings from a four-generational study by the Family and Work Institute (2004) seem to indicate that younger workers are moving away from a work-centric orientation to a dual-centric (those placing the same priority on their job and family) and family-centric (those placing a higher priority on family than work) orientations.

THE IMPACT OF GENDER IDEOLOGY, SOCIAL CLASS, AND RACE AND ETHNICITY

Research shows that gender expectations play a significant role in the division of household labor. For example, men in dual-earner families who see themselves as co-providers with their wives do more domestic tasks than men who still believe in the good provider role (Perry-Jenkins and Crouter, 1990). A recent study of men's household labor in 22 industrialized countries found a similar pattern. Men, who live in societies where breadwinning is strongly associated with masculinity, are more likely to feel considerable pressure to concentrate on work-related activities as opposed to doing household tasks (Thebaud, 2007).

Social class also affects who does domestic tasks. Spouses with higher levels of education are more likely to share domestic tasks, especially when the wife has high earnings and a professional status (Perry-Jenkins and Folk, 1994; Spain and Bianchi, 1996). Researchers examining data from Australia and the United States found that women decrease their housework as their earnings increase, up to the point where both spouses contribute equally to household income (Brittman et al., 2003). Like their U.S. counterparts, urban Chinese husbands with higher educational levels and whose wives' earnings are close to theirs have the highest rates of participation in household labor (Lu, Maume, and Bellas, 2000). However, when a wife's income is greater than the husband's, researchers have observed a mixed pattern. Some husbands in this situation decrease their involvement in household tasks (Hartwell-Walker, 2006; Brittman et al., 2003), while other husbands increase their involvement (Coontz, 2007). Additionally, the affluence of these dual-earner couples allows them to hire others to do their household tasks and/or child care. Although this solution may work well for them, it often creates problems for domestic workers who must sacrifice time with their own families to accommodate the family needs of their employers.

Race and ethnicity are also factors in how family work is divided. Research has found that African American husbands are more likely than White husbands to share in household tasks (Gerson, 2010). Lillian Rubin (1994) found that Latinos and Asian American men, especially those who live in ethnic neighborhoods where traditional gender roles remain strong despite women's employment, are less likely to share household work. However, other research on Mexican American couples found husbands participated more in domestic tasks if the wife's earnings equaled or surpassed that of her husband (Coltrane, 1996). In off-reservation Navajo Indian families, mothers invested significantly more time in cleaning, food, and child-related tasks than fathers, but mothers and fathers participated equally in household maintenance (Hossain, 2001). Such diverse findings underscore the complex nature of the work–family linkage. More research is needed to determine the various ways in which micro-level and macro-level forces interact to produce different patterns of work and family role tradeoffs.

Nevertheless, one dominant theme that cuts across all of these studies regards the expectations that women and men bring to their roles as partners, parents, and providers. If women and men are to share equally in home production work, then women must redefine the value of their jobs or careers as providers and men must redefine the meaning of domestic work as something beneficial, not demeaning (Lorber, 1994). Additionally, researchers have found a positive relationship between negotiation skills and both marital happiness and career satisfaction. Respondents reporting relatively effective negotiation skills indicated greater degrees of marital happiness and career satisfaction compared to respondents possessing less effective negotiation skill (Bartley, Judge, and Judge, 2007). Thus, it seems couples planning to marry would benefit by learning negotiating skills to assist them in achieving a satisfying work–family balance.

CHILD CARE

When a couple has their first child, their life changes dramatically. Workloads increase. Often without conscious planning, many couples move to a more traditional division of household tasks, with women taking on more tasks. One study found that the time devoted to work responsibilities increased by 64 percent for mothers and 37 percent for fathers after childbirth (Gjerdingen, 2004). To avoid conflict and marital dissatisfaction, it is important that parental spouses regularly evaluate and negotiate a division of labor that satisfies both their and their children's needs.

That some of this is happening is evidenced by the fact that fathers are spending more time with their children than fathers did 40 years ago (Aumann, 2011) and, as we saw earlier, a considerable number of fathers are stay-at-home dads. Although men's parenting activities appear to be increasing, women still take the major responsibility for child care in the United States. This situation puts working women at a competitive disadvantage with male colleagues, who are freed of this responsibility by their spouses. For women, having children constrains their labor market activities. Women with small children have lower labor force participation rates, and when they are employed, they are more likely to work part time. This is especially true of poor women with limited education and skills. Finding a job that pays an income sufficient to cover child-care costs is problematic for them. According to the National Association of Child Care Resource Referral Agencies (2010), the average cost of full-time child care for an infant in a child care center ranged from more than $4,550 in Mississippi to more than $18,750 in Massachusetts in 2009. The fee was slightly lower for infants being cared for in a family care home, $3,750 to $11,450.

Consider this:

- The average center-based child care fees for an infant exceeded the average annual amount that families spent on food in every region of the United States.
- Monthly child care fees for two children at any age exceeded the median monthly rent cost, and were nearly as high, or even higher than, the average monthly mortgage payment for most families.
- The cost of infant care in a child care center was higher than a year of tuition and fees at a four-year public college in 40 states (National Association of Child Care Resource Referral Agencies, 2010).

Some working parents, unable to meet these costs, reduce their hours of employment or drop out of the labor force completely. Other parents opt for split-shift employment and split-shift parenting, thereby enabling one parent to be home while the other is at work. Approximately one-third of dual-earner couples with children have one spouse working late or rotating shifts. Additionally, more than 66 percent of all dual-earner couples have at least one spouse working some time over the weekend. Both of these patterns are more common among low-income families and families with preschool children (Presser, 2003). These patterns also hold true for single mothers as well. Although a 24/7 economy provides a great deal of convenience for consumers and travelers, it creates serious problems for families whose members must work nonstandard hours. Often these hours mean that one parent is unavailable during dinnertime hours, a time that usually allows for meaningful family interaction. This lack of time together can cause tensions between spouses that can affect children as well. This is especially true for couples where one spouse works the late shift, as they have substantially less quality time together and experience more marital unhappiness. Although neither an evening shift nor weekend work seemed to affect the stability of marriages, couples with children where one spouse worked late night hours were more likely to separate or divorce than other couples.

Single working mothers and couples who work the same shift face a different set of problems, the most serious of which is finding alternative child care. Figure 10.4 on page 330 shows the distribution of primary-care arrangements for children ages 0 to 4 with employed mothers in 2010. Fathers cared for 18.6 percent of the preschool children, down from 20 percent in 1991; grandparents provided care for 19.4 percent of preschool children while siblings and other relatives cared for another 5.8 percent. Another 13.5 percent received care from a nonrelative and 23.7 percent were in center-based care, including day care centers, nursery schools, preschools and Head Start programs. Mothers cared for 4.4 percent either while working at home or on the job. These mothers were frequently employed as private household workers or were themselves child-care workers who took in other children while caring for their own at home. Another 14.1 percent of these children had some other or no regular arrangement, including self-care. The type of child-care arrangements available to parents depends heavily on their resources and family systems. When families are poor or on government assistance, they must rely on

A major concern of dual-earner families is finding adequate child care. In split-shift households one parent, like this father fixing dinner with his sons, takes primary responsibility for child care while the other parent is at work. In some cases, the child-care dilemma is resolved when one parent, like this executive, takes her child to work.

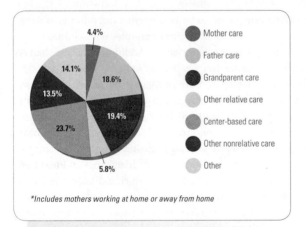

- 18.6% Mother care
- 19.4% Father care
- 5.8% Grandparent care
- 23.7% Other relative care
- 13.5% Center-based care
- 14.1% Other nonrelative care
- 4.4% Other

*Includes mothers working at home or away from home

FIGURE 10.4 Primary Child Care Arrangements of Children Age 0–4 with Employed Mothers, 2010

Source: Federal Interagency Forum on Child and Family Statistics. 2011. *America's Children: Key National Indicators of Well-Being.* Washington, DC.

relatives more so than other families. African American and Latina/o children are more likely to be cared for by grandparents and other nonparental relatives than White children.

Regardless of the type of child-care arrangement in use, the majority of families who need child care confronts two major problems: high cost and limited availability. These problems stem, in large measure, from cultural attitudes that see child care as primarily a private matter requiring a private solution. In other words, if couples have children, the reasoning goes, it is their responsibility to care for them. Some employers are reconsidering this attitude as many of the new entrants to the labor force are mothers. To attract and keep these employees, a number of companies (9 percent of employers nationwide) are providing on-site day or near-site care so that parents can visit their children during work or lunch breaks, thus relieving them of worry over how their children are

managing without them. A recent survey found that 31 percent of workers with employer-sponsored dependent benefits were less likely to report lost productivity due to stress than workers without such benefits. Workers without these benefits spent 20 percent more time dealing with childcare issues at work than workers with benefits ("Employer-sponsored...", 2010). Despite such findings, employer-sponsored child care in the United States is available to only 1 in 8 employees (13 percent), and even programs that offer tax savings for those able to pay for their own children are available only to 3 in 10 people (Heymann et al., 2004).

WORK–LIFE CONFLICT: THE "NEW MALE MYSTIQUE"

For decades, it has been a given that women bore the major responsibility for child care and household management regardless of their employment status. However, today's workplace is no longer the major province of men and the traditional gender role of men as breadwinners is being replaced with a more egalitarian role. Increasing numbers of men are now co-providers with their wives and caregivers for their children. Such transitions do not occur without some degree of difficulty. When more and more women entered the labor force and still assumed major responsibilities at home, they experienced work–family conflict at much higher rates than their male counterparts. Work–family conflict is typically measured by asking employees with family responsibilities how much their work and family responsibilities interfere with each other. Researchers at the Families and Work Institute analyzed data from a nationally representative study of the U.S. workforce and found that 60 percent of fathers in dual-earner couples reported work–family conflict in 2008, up from 35 percent in 1977, while that of mothers in dual-earner couples remained relatively stable (41 percent in 1977 and 47 percent in 2008 (Aumann, Galinsky, and Matos, 2011). These researchers suggest that the increase in work–family conflict is a symptom of the "new male mystique," today's version of the "feminine mystique" coined by Betty Friedan in 1963 to describe how assumptions about women finding fulfillment in traditional domestic roles created tension and conflict for many women. Applying Friedan's reasoning to men, these researchers suggest, would reflect the idea that men should seek fulfillment at work and strive to be successful breadwinners for their families and at the same time increase their participation at home. Since the workplace does not easily accommodate their new involvement at home, they are bound to experience conflicting demands. One benefit that would help working couples is parental leave. Yet, this benefit is rare in the United States, particularly for fathers.

PARENTAL LEAVE: A PARTIAL SOLUTION TO WORK–FAMILY CONFLICT

European fathers have access to more paid leave than their American counterparts and use it more readily, yet even then many men are still reluctant to take time off from work. Sweden is a good case study of some of the issues involved. Although Sweden long had one of the most generous parental leave policies in the world, less than half of all fathers (42 percent) took advantage of it, averaging 28 days or about 15 percent of the 16 months of paid parental leave (approximately 80 percent of their gross salary) offered to either mothers or fathers. In the Netherlands, approximately 16 percent of fathers take parental leave. In Italy, Denmark, and Germany, the rate is less than 10 percent (Anxo, et al., 2007). Why do so many European men reject what on the surface seems like a great opportunity to spend time with their infants and young children? The answer, according to some men, is found in the structure and culture of work. Overall, men earn more than women. Therefore, it makes sense for women, usually the lower income earner, to stay home. Steen Broust Nielsen, a 36-year-old marketing director in Denmark, was reluctant to take the leave to which, as a new father, he was entitled because, as he said, "We have an interim report coming up, so I can't possibly stay away too long, perhaps half a day here and half a day there when it's convenient." His reluctance was echoed by a 38-year-old Dortmund-based management assistant, who said, "When you are on your way up, you can't take a time out. That will set you back no end career-wise" (quoted in James, 2004).

In the United States, there is no federal paid parental leave program; only 13 percent of employers provide paid parental leave. Workers can, however, take leave under the Family and Medical Leave Act that requires employers with 50 or more employees to provide up to 12 weeks of unpaid leave to both female and male workers with a new child. However, most workers do not take advantage of that policy because they cannot afford to lose income for any period of time. Although the concept of parental leave is gaining greater public acceptance, many men who have access to such leave do not act on it for the same reasons given by European men. According to a survey by the U.S. Department of Labor (2000), 42.6 percent of men who were considering parental leave cited "fear of hurting career advancement" as the primary reason for not doing so; 31 percent feared they might lose their jobs if they took a leave. Their concerns are not unwarranted. Research shows that men who take advantage of family medical leave are considered less conscientious employees than those who do not (Wayne and Cordeiro, 2003).

Employers who do not promote leave policies to their employees communicate a silent message that, for men at least,

taking leave is not an appropriate career move. A recent survey in the United Kingdom found that only 18 percent of working men would take advantage of a proposed six-month parental leave. Although the primary reason given for not taking leave was concern about money (47 percent), 30 percent of respondents said they lacked the necessary support from their senior managers and colleagues (Clarke, 2010). Conversely, when employers actively promote parental leave for both genders, the results are quite different. For example, when New Jersey's XPMG Company sent e-mails at work and letters home explaining the company's parental leave policy and how to apply, 30 percent of eligible fathers took a leave in 2002. With those examples and the support of management, in the following year, 87 percent of eligible fathers took leave (Earls, 2003). Similarly, in Sweden, when the law was changed to reserve two months of the parental leave for fathers that were not transferrable to mothers and would be lost if not used, combined with more acceptance of the part of employers, the percentage of fathers taking leave rose to 80 percent of fathers now taking about a third of the total leave time (Bennhold, 2010). Other factors may influence a father's decision to take leave. If wives do not ask their husbands, or at least discuss the possibility with them, men may conclude they do not care or do not want them to take leave. As we saw in Chapter 9, men may experience more pressure to be a breadwinner with the birth of a first child or additional children. And if there is an economic downturn, men may be more apprehensive of taking any action that may jeopardize their current position.

In sum, the United States has not yet resolved the dilemma surrounding the gendered ideology of the family that assigns housekeeping and child rearing primarily to women and assumes that balancing work and family needs is a personal matter. Cultural myths, about the appropriate roles for each gender, internalized by both women and men, can harm relationships, children, work, and the larger society (Barnett and Rivers, 2004). To phrase this dilemma as one of individual choice ignores the reality that current employment structures prohibit many parents from making satisfying choices, thus preventing many women from exercising full partnership with men in economic and political arenas as well as precluding many men from full partnership with women in family life. We will consider some structural changes that can help to overcome this problem at the end of the chapter.

Inequities in the Workplace: Consequences For Families

Although the labor force participation rates of women and men are converging, women still confront issues of inequity in the labor market. These issues, in turn, can have a profound effect on women's sense of worth and their family's economic well-being. Three issues are of special significance: occupational distribution, the gender gap in earnings, and sexual harassment.

Read the Document
Detours on the Road to Equality: Women, Work, and Higher Education on **myfamilylab.com**

TABLE 10.1 Percentage of Work Force in Selected Occupations, by Sex, Race, and Ethnicity, 2009

	Women	African American	Asians	Latinas/os
All occupations	47.3	10.7	4.7	14.0
Aircraft pilots/flight engineers	1.3	2.3	1.6	3.9
Architecture and engineering occupations	13.8	5.5	9.9	7.2
Carpenters	1.6	4.5	1.5	24.2
Chefs and head cooks	20.7	12.6	13.8	20.6
Child-care workers	95.0	16.8	2.7	18.4
Clergy	17.0	12.4	4.0	5.3
Computer and mathematical occupations	24.8	6.7	15.7	5.4
Electricians	2.2	6.7	1.7	15.3
Lawyers	32.4	4.7	4.1	2.8
Librarians	81.8	5.3	3.0	6.8
Physicians/surgeons	32.2	5.7	16.4	6.3
Preschool/kindergarten teachers	97.8	14.2	2.6	10.3
Registered nurses	92.0	11.5	8.1	4.6
Social workers	80.7	22.5	2.5	9.6

Source: Adapted from U.S. Census Bureau, 2011, *Statistical Abstract of the United States, 2011.* Washington, DC: Table 615, pp. 393–396.

OCCUPATIONAL DISTRIBUTION

Occupational distribution refers to the location of workers in different occupations. Although the media like to highlight stories of women and men who are in nontraditional occupations, for example, women construction workers and male nurses, many occupations are still perceived as either women's work or men's work. Table 10.1 shows the percentage of the work force in selected occupations. Even work traditionally thought of as women's work such as cooking, when done outside the home and "professionalized," often becomes a male specialty. Only 20.7 percent of chefs and head cooks are women. Even though slightly more women than men are working in a management or professional specialty (51.4 percent), women tend to be working in the lower-paid professions such as nursing or elementary school education, whereas men are more concentrated in the higher-paid professions of law, medicine, architecture, and engineering. In 2009, only 32.4 percent of lawyers, 32.2 percent of physicians, and 13.8 percent of architects and engineers were women. Women and people of color are more heavily concentrated in low-paying clerical or service jobs, whereas men are concentrated in the higher-paying jobs of craft workers and operators.

The good news is that in the last three decades increasing numbers of women have entered many occupations traditionally thought to be exclusively male, for instance, computer and mathematical occupations (24.8%) and the clergy (17.0 percent). Women have been less successful in breaking other barriers; for example, only 1.6 percent of women are carpenters. An even smaller percentage of women are aircraft pilots and flight engineers (1.3 percent) and electricians (2.2 percent). Men, in contrast, have been more reluctant to enter "women's" occupations in any significant numbers. Thus, some job categories remain overwhelmingly female—for example, preschool and kindergarten teachers (97.8 percent) and nursing (92.0 percent)—although men have made gains as social workers (19.3 percent) and librarians (18.2 percent), once thought to be the domain of women. We can see that race and ethnicity also play a role in occupational distribution. Although African Americans make up 10.7 percent of all employed civilians, Latinas/os 14.0 percent, and Asians 4.7 percent, they often are underrepresented in the higher paying jobs and overrepresented in lower-paying jobs.

Women have fared even less well in business. Although women make up almost half of the U.S. labor force (46.7 percent), as Figure 10.5 clearly shows, in 2010 they constituted only 3.2% of *Fortune* 500 CEOs. And, despite gains since 1999, only 7.6 percent of the nation's top earners were women and only 15.7 percent of women held *Fortune* 500 seats; only 3 percent were Black women (Catalyst, 2011).

As Figure 10.6 shows, business women in the United States have not done as well as their counterparts in European countries. A recent survey of European companies with market capital of over 1 billion pounds found significantly higher percentages of women serving on corporate boards. Norway led with

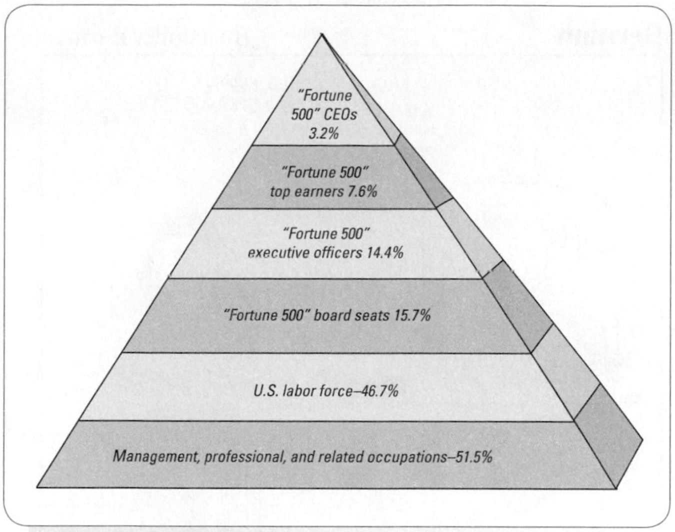
"Fortune 500" CEOs 3.2%
"Fortune 500" top earners 7.6%
"Fortune 500" executive officers 14.4%
"Fortune 500" board seats 15.7%
U.S. labor force–46.7%
Management, professional, and related occupations–51.5%

FIGURE 10.5 Women in the *Fortune* 500

Source: Catalyst. 2011. "The Catalyst Pyramid: U.S. Women in Business (May 2). www.catalyst.org/publication/132/us-women-in-business (2011, July 5).

37.9 percent; Sweden followed with 28.2 percent. Portugal had the lowest representation with just 3.4 percent. Norway's top position is not accidental. Gender equality is part of Nordic traditions. As long ago as Viking times, women ran farms and businesses while men were away at sea. In recent years, women have held approximately 40 percent of cabinet and parliamentary positions. In 2003, concerned with an underrepresentation of women in higher levels of business, Norway enacted a law requiring companies to fill 40 percent of corporate board seats with women by 2008 or face penalties. Many other European companies adopted corporate governance codes and/or legislation similar to Norway's, resulting in increased representation of women.

Women face many obstacles in reaching top positions. Among them is the fact that women are poorly represented in line positions, those jobs with profit-and-loss responsibilities that are the traditional route to executive promotion. Surveys of executives in the United States point to gender-based stereotyping as a major barrier to women's advancement (Prime, 2005).

As these data demonstrate, occupational segregation has consequences for the well-being of workers and their families. First, it restricts the options of both women and men. Men are less likely than women to enter a sex-atypical occupation. Second, when workers enter occupations that are not traditional for their race or gender, they often encounter prejudice and hostility, resulting in high levels of stress. For women and people of color, this hostility often takes the form of exclusion from the informal work groups so necessary to successful job performance and advancement. In contrast, men in nontraditional occupations experience prejudice from people outside their occupation, but are less likely than women to experience discrimination at work. Sociologist Christine Williams (1992) found that although women often encounter a "glass ceiling" that limits

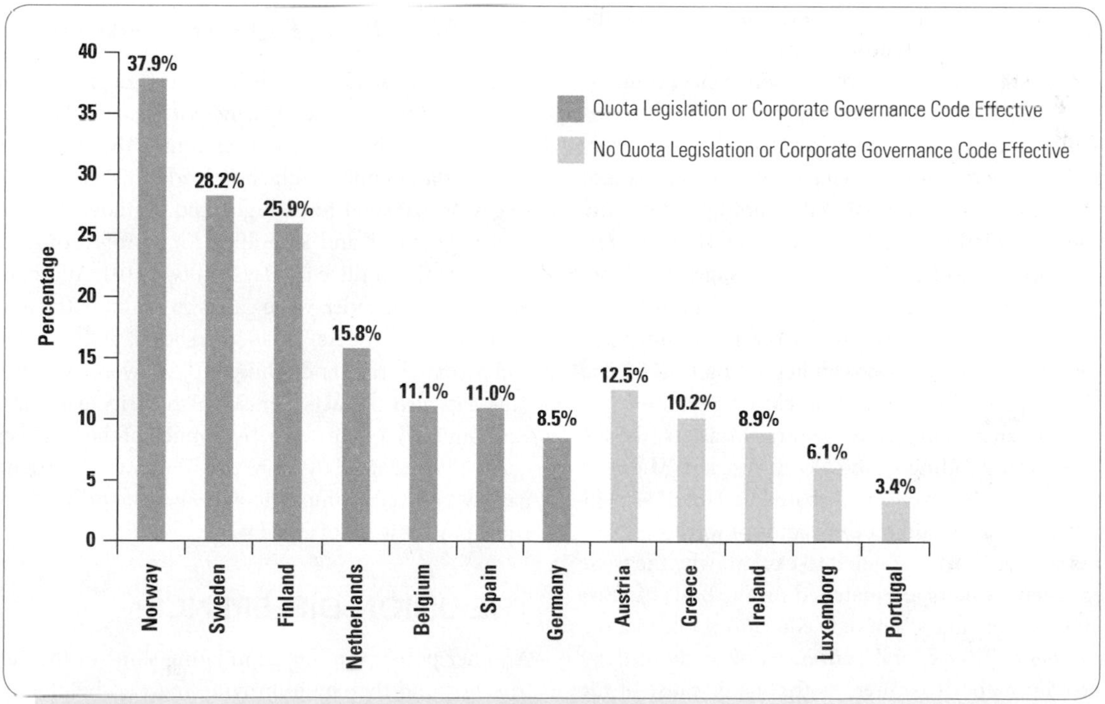
Quota Legislation or Corporate Governance Code Effective
No Quota Legislation or Corporate Governance Code Effective
Percentage
0
5
10
15
20
25
30
35
40
37.9%
28.2%
25.9%
15.8%
11.1%
11.0%
8.5%
12.5%
10.2%
8.9%
6.1%
3.4%
Norway
Sweden
Finland
Netherlands
Belgium
Spain
Germany
Austria
Greece
Ireland
Luxemborg
Portugal

FIGURE 10.6 Women in European Boardrooms

Source: Data from European Professional Women's Network.2010. EPWn Board Women Monitor, 2010, 4th Ed. www.europeanpwn.net/files/euroeanpwn_boardmonitor_2010.pdf (2011, July 5).

their advancement, men in sex-atypical occupations experience a "glass escalator" that propels them to higher positions in that field. Finally, occupational segregation results in an earnings gap between women and men and between Whites and people of color that limits the resources families receive when female members work.

THE RACE–GENDER GAP IN EARNINGS: GOOD NEWS AND BAD NEWS

No matter how earnings are measured, women's wages are lower than men's, regardless of race and ethnicity. Similarly, men of color are disadvantaged in comparison with their White counterparts. In the first quarter of 2011, the median weekly earnings for female full-time wage and salary workers were $683, nearly 82 percent of the $829 median for their male counterparts. In 1979, when comparable earnings data were first available, women earned only about 63 percent as much as men. However, White workers of either gender earned more than their Black or Latina/o colleagues. The differences among women were considerably smaller than those among men. White women earned $699, nearly 16 percent more than Black women ($590). In contrast, White men outearned their Black counterparts by 27 percent ($856 to $621). Asian men had the highest median weekly earnings (948); Asian women had median weekly earnings of $762 (U.S. Department of Labor, 2011).

Age, occupation, and education all impact wages. By and large, older workers (ages 45–64) earned more than younger workers. Persons employed in management, professional, and related occupations had the highest median weekly earnings, $1,266 for men and $939 for women. Full-time workers age 25 and over without a high school diploma had median weekly earnings of $444 compared with $633 for high school graduates and $1,150 for college graduates. Yet, even at the highest levels of education, the highest-earning 10 percent of male workers made $3,336 or more per week, compared with $2,291 or more for their female counterparts (U.S. Department of Labor, 2011).

The narrowing of the race–gender earnings gap in recent years can be attributed to a number of factors: women's increased investment in education and professional training, entry into higher-paying nontraditional occupations, fewer and shorter interruptions in their work lives, and a decline in men's wages. However, the gains many workers made in the 1990s as a result of low unemployment, low inflation, and the increase in the minimum wage started to erode in the economic downturn beginning in 2001 and the recession of 2007–2009. The terrorist attacks on September 11, 2001, the wars in Iraq and Afghanistan, natural disasters like the earthquake in Japan and flooding in the Northwest and Midwest, and state and local budget cuts have exacerbated this trend as public and private businesses alike laid off thousands of workers.

For years, researchers have struggled to explain why the wage gap persists even when workers are matched on the basis of years of experience, number of hours worked, education, occupation, and union membership. The general consensus of many of these studies is that discriminatory treatment is the major cause of the earnings gap between women and men and between Whites and people of color (Prime, 2005; Cherry, 2001). Discrimination takes many forms—lack of access, denial of promotions, assignment to lower-pay jobs, violations of equal pay laws, and devaluation of women's work. Additionally, researchers have found that family

Although the earning gap between women and men has narrowed in recent years, gender discrimination in employment still deprives women of many benefits enjoyed by their male colleagues.

responsibilities contribute to women's lower wages. For example, childbearing can lead to career interruptions that hinder women's overall advancement (Hewlett, 2007).

CONSEQUENCE OF THE EARNINGS GAP

Gender and racial inequalities in pay deprive families of greater purchasing power and this inequity accumulates over a lifetime. Economist Evelyn Murphy, president of the Wage Project, estimates that over a lifetime of full-time work, this gap amounts to a loss in wages of $700,000 for a high school graduate, $1.2 million for a college graduate, and $2 million for a professional school graduate (National Committee on Pay Equity, 2010). Another way to see the impact of the gender-wage gap is to examine the mean earnings of women and men. As Table 10.2 shows, at every educational level and across all race and ethnic groups, women earn less than men. This gap also impacts her social security benefits and pensions. Economists like Murphy believe much of the race–gender wage gap could be eliminated by more vigorous enforcement of current equal pay laws as well as implementation of the principle of pay equity—equal pay for work of equal value.

THE UNION DIFFERENCE

Another potent tool for eliminating some of the current disparity in wages and thereby improving the well-being of families would be to strengthening protections for workers' right to organize in unions and to bargain collectively with their employers. Data from the Bureau of Labor Statistics (2011d) show that in 2010, the median weekly earnings of union members were $917, considerably higher than the $717 earned by their nonunion counterparts. That

TABLE 10.2 Mean Earnings by Highest Degree Earned, 2011					
Characteristics	High School	Bachelor's	Master's	Professional	Doctorate
Total					
Male	36,753	72,868	88,450	147,518	116,574
Female	24,329	44,078	54,517	87,723	70,898
White					
Male	37,852	75,053	91,251	151,669	116,613
Female	24,610	43,848	54,308	85,545	71,702
Black					
Male	30,985	51,691	66,085	(B)	(B)
Female	23,195	42,858	52,919	(B)	(B)
Latino	30,618	56,980	92,644	99,804	(B)
Latina	21,725	39,231	54,385	(B)	(B)

(B) Base figure too small to meet statistical standards for reliability of a derived figure.

Source: Adapted from U.S. Census Bureau. 2011. *Statistical Abstract of the United States, 2011.* Washington, DC: Table 228, p. 150.

amounts to a yearly difference in salary of $10,400 for union vs. nonunion members. Figure 10.7 shows that union workers are more likely than their nonunion counterparts to be covered by health insurance and to receive pension and other benefits.

Despite these union advantages, union membership is at a historic low in the United States. In 2010, only 14.7 million workers (11.9% percent of all workers) belong to a union. Workers in the public sector are more than four times as likely to be union members as private-sector employees—36.2 percent to 6.9 percent (Bureau of Labor Statistics, 2011d). Men are more likely to belong to unions than women (12.6 percent to 11.1 percent). Union membership is highest among Black workers (13.4 percent), followed by White workers (11.7 percent), Asian workers (10.9 percent), and Latino workers (10.0 percent).

Several factors combined to produce a decline in union membership from its high of 35 percent in the mid-1950s to its current low level. For the last four decades, companies routinely outsourced many manufacturing jobs, which tend to have a high concentration of union workers, to other countries with lower labor costs. As new information technology developed, companies

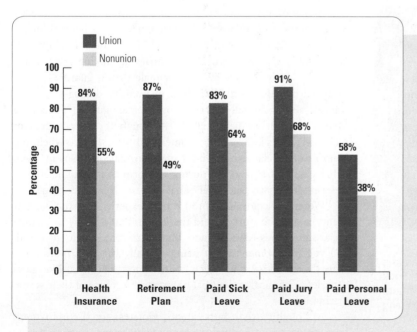

FIGURE 10.7 Health Insurance and Other Benefits by Union Membership

Source: Bureau of Labor Statistic. 2010. *National Compensation Survey: Employee Benefits in the U.S, March 2010.* Bulletin 2752. (September). www.bls.gov/ncs/ebs/benefits/2010/ebb10046.pdf (2011, July 7).

also began to outsource white collar and professional occupations to improve their bottom line. President Ronald Reagan's firing of striking air traffic controllers in 1981 encouraged many employers to develop more aggressive antiunion campaigns. The country's shift to a more conservative mood and some well-publicized corruption scandals involving union officials turned some people against unions. Additionally, unions lost members as a result of their success. As union members income increased, they sent their children to college and professional schools, traditionally not union strongholds. In the past when children followed their parents into the factory or other work settings, unions regenerated themselves. Whether under current economic conditions unions will be able to regenerate themselves is an empirical question. The recent financial crisis and the recession of 2007–2009 led to huge budget deficits for state and local governments. Public officials responded by asking public unions to agree to salary and benefit cuts and, in some cases, laying off union members. Following their election victories in 2010, several Republican governors and legislatures went further and passed legislation restricting traditional collective bargaining rights for public employees which led to mass protests in states like Wisconsin, Ohio, and Indiana. A *USA Today*/Gallup poll found that 61 percent of respondents opposed reducing collective bargaining rights (Saad, 2011b).

In an economy where higher-paying jobs are disappearing and are often being replaced with lower-paying jobs, the role of a union may be even more critical than in the past. According to a report by the Center for American Progress, there is a strong correlation between the presence of a strong labor movement and a vibrant middle class. The authors argue that as union membership has declined, income inequality has increased dramatically. Their research suggests that modest increase in unionization rates would help restore the broken link between productivity and wage gains adding billions of dollars more in wages and salaries to family budgets and the economy (Madland, Walter, and Bunker, 2011)

Demonstrators merge on the capital in Madison, Wisconsin, to protest anti–collective bargaining measures supported by Governor Scott Walker. Similar protests took place in other states. On November 8, 2011, Ohio voters repealed a controversial law limiting collective bargaining signed by Governor John Kasich earlier in the year.

SEXUAL HARASSMENT

Another problem workers may experience is some form of **sexual harassment,** unwanted leers, comments, suggestions, or physical contact of a sexual nature that the recipient finds offensive and causes discomfort or interferes with academic or job performance. Sexual harassment occurs in all types of educational and work settings. Because of the sensitive nature of sexual harassment, accurate data on its extent are difficult to collect. However, numerous studies both in and outside the United States indicate that it is an enormous problem (see the In Other Places box). Here in the United States the Equal Employment Opportunity Commission (EEOC), established by the passage of the Civil Rights Act of 1964, is charged with investigating alleged violations and enforcing the laws against sexual harassment. In 2010, the EEOC resolved 12,772 sexual harassment charges and recovered $48.4 million in monetary benefits for charging parties and other aggrieved individuals, not including monetary benefits obtained through litigation (Equal Employment Opportunity Commission, 2011b). Public and private employers that ignore the problem of sexual harassment can pay a high price. For example, Madison Square Garden and New York Knicks coach Isiah Thomas reached an $11.5 million settlement of a sexual harassment case brought by a former team executive (ESPN.com news services, 2007).

Sex, Race, Sexual Orientation, Age, and Marital Status Sexual harassment appears more prevalent in male-dominated occupations. For example, women soldiers, physicians, lawyers, coal miners, and investment bankers have all reported high levels of sexual harassment (Equal Employment Opportunity Commission, 2011a; Berdahl, 2007). One 29-year-old returning woman student provided a personal illustration of harassment at the job site: "I worked as a carpenter for 7 years. Many nights I came home and cried. I was the only woman on my first job. The men didn't want me there. They used to hide my tools and put obscene notes in my lunch bucket."

Although still quite low compared with that of females, sexual harassment of males may be increasing. Men's claims now account for 16 percent of all sexual harassment charges being brought to the EEOC, up from 9 percent in 1992 (Equal Employment Opportunity Commission, 2011a). Juries are taking men's complaints seriously. A jury awarded a male prison guard $750,000 in actual damages and $3 million in punitive damages after he claimed he was sexually harassed by a female guard ("Female on Male Sexual Harassment," 2004). Although the perpetrators in male complaints include both women and men, the overwhelming majority of the claims by men are male-on-male harassment. Men, either gay or straight, who do not conform to masculine stereotypes are frequently the target of harassment from other men.

Women of color are more likely to experience sexual harassment than White women, and the harassment is likely to include racial stereotypes (Berdahl and Moore, 2006).). Single, divorced, and younger women report being sexually harassed more often than then married and older counterparts. Lesbians, like gays, experience physical and verbal harassment because of their sexual orientation.

Although sexual harassment violates equal-employment laws, enforcement is difficult. Many victims are afraid to report

In Other Places

SEXUAL HARASSMENT

Sexual harassment as a legal concept is still unknown in many parts of the world. Even among the countries where it is recognized, there is still no universally agreed upon definition as to what constitutes sexual harassment. Therefore, it is difficult to compare the prevalence from one country to another. Nevertheless, there are movements in this direction. After a survey revealed that close to 50 percent of European women reported that they had been victims of sexual harassment at some point in their lives, the European Union Parliament called on its member states to investigate the extent of sexual harassment in their countries and to develop policies to remedy it (Moline, 2002). Although not strictly comparable, reports from various countries show that sexual harassment is a problem in all corners of the world.

- A joint Reuters/Ipsos global poll of 12,000 people in 24 countries found that 1 in 10 workers have been pressured to have sex by a senior employer. Workers in India were the most likely to report

sexual harassment (26 percent) followed by workers in China (18 percent, Saudi Arabia (16 percent), Mexico (13 percent), and South Africa (10 percent). ("Indians Most Likely…, 2010).
- According to the Egyptian Information and Decision Support Center, 44 percent of females in that country are subjected to sexual harassment. CBS Reporter Lara Logan was attacked by a group of men in Cairo's Tahrir Square where she was covering the reaction to the resignation of President Hosni.
- About 27 percent of Algerian female university students said that they were subjected to sexual harassment from their professors.
- In Qatar, 30 percent of working females reported being sexually abused by their bosses (Shalaby, 2011).
- In Japan, according to the Ministry of Health, Labor and Welfare, 8,120 women filed sexual harassment complaints with equal opportunity offices in 2008 (Silver, 2010).
- In Indonesia, after numerous complaints of groping by men, the rail system introduced train

cars for women only (Firdaus, 2010). Earlier, Japan and Korea made women-only cars available to prevent this type of harassment against women.
- In 2010, the Turkish ambassador to Rome was found guilty of sexual harassment (Adinah, 2010).
- In 2011, the biggest sexual harassment case in Australian history was settled for $850,000 from the country's oldest department store, David Jones (Malkin, 2011).
- A national telephone survey conducted by the Australian Human Rights commission found that 22 percent of females and 5 percent of males had experienced sexual harassment in the workplace (Sexual Harassment in Australia, 2009).

What do you think? Why does there appear to be such extensive patterns of sexual harassment in the United States and around the world? What strategies would you suggest for combating sexual harassment? Is the experience of sexual harassment the same or different for women and men?

---

the harassment for fear of losing their jobs, or being blamed for bringing it on themselves. All too often, victims do not believe anything can be done or they do not trust the organization to take any meaningful action to change the situation. Workers who are sexually harassed report a number of problems both physical (chronic neck and back pain, gastrointestinal disorders, sleeplessness, and loss of appetite) and psychological (feelings of humiliation, helplessness, and fear). Recent research suggests that experiences of sexual harassment may lead to use of alcohol and prescription drugs (sedatives and antidepressants) as a means to self-medicate the distress engendered by sexual harassment (Richman and Rospenda, 2005). Sexual harassment has other costly outcomes for employers as well, including high turnover and absentee rates (Merkin, 2008). Harassment victims frequently bring these problems home with them (recall the spillover effect discussed earlier), thereby adding tension to family relationships.

The Economic Well-Being of Families

Women's wages play an important part in the economic well-being of families. In families where both husband and wife work full-time throughout the year, the wife's wages account for 44 percent of family earnings. In 2008, the median income for all married-couple families was $72,743; half of those families had an income higher than that and half of those families had lower incomes.

Table 10.3 on page 338 reveals how important family structure has become to the economic well-being of families and the amount of money available to families to meet their ongoing needs. Dual-earner couples had incomes of $86,621, compared to the $48,502 of married couples where the husband was the sole breadwinner. Single

TABLE 10.3 Median Income of Families, by Type of Family, 2008	
Total married-couple families	$72,743
Wife in paid labor force	$86,621
Wife not in paid labor force	$48,502
Male householder, no wife present	$43,571
Female householder, no husband present	$30,129

Source: U.S. Census Bureau, 2011. *Statistical Abstract of the United States, 2022* (Washington, DC: Table 698, p. 457.)

householders, whether male or female, made less than their married counterparts even when the wife was not working. And, as we have seen before, female householders made considerably less than male householders. This aggregate figure, however, conceals important differences by race and ethnicity. For example, the median income for all White families in 2008 was $65,000, but only $39,879 for African American families, and $40,466 for Latinas/os families. Asian/Pacific Islanders had the highest medium income at $73,578. Their earning power and the fact that, in general, Asians Americans have higher levels of education than other groups, has led many observers to see them as a "model minority." However, this stereotype obscures the diversity within the Asian American population and the processes involved in reaching that income level. For example, Asian American household income generally reflects multiple wage earners, not necessarily high salaries per worker. Further, approximately half of the Asian American population is composed of the highly educated immigrants who came to the United States in the 1960s. Asian refugees who came to the United States after the Vietnam War were fleeing wartime persecution and had few resources. In 2009, 52.3 percent of Asian Americans age 25 or older had a college or professional degree compared to 29.9 percent of Whites, 19.3 percent of African Americans, and 13.2 percent of Latinas/os. However, there was considerable variation in educational levels within groups. For example, among Latinas/os, 27.9 percent of Cubans, 16.5 percent of Puerto Ricans, and 9.5 percent of Mexicans have college or professional degrees (U.S. Census Bureau, 2011e). Similarly, many within the Asian population were educationally disadvantaged. In 2000, almost 53 percent of Cambodian, Hmong, and Laotian adults did not have a high school education (Le, 2011).

These statistics take on even more significance when we look ahead to the future. In 2005, there were 15.7 million children in immigrant families residing in the United States. If current immigration levels continue, children in immigrant families will constitute 30 percent of the nation's school population in 2015. One in every five children in immigrant families (2.2 million) had difficulty speaking English in 2005. An even greater number, 4.3 million children, lived in linguistically isolated households in which no person 14 years or older speaks English very well. ("One Out of Five…," 2007). Although most immigrant parents have high educational expectations for their children, they often lack

the resources required to achieve this goal. Consequently, their children are likely to go to poor schools, live in unhealthy and even dangerous neighborhoods, and, when adults, are quite likely to be unemployed and even unemployable.

GROWING INEQUALITY AND THE DECLINE OF THE MIDDLE CLASS

The latter part of the 1990s saw real gains in income for most Americans. Inflation and unemployment were at their lowest in many years. However, many of these gains proved to be short-lived as the economy slowed in 2001 and moved into a recession in 2007. Many workers lost their jobs as companies reduced their labor costs by outsourcing jobs to other countries and introducing more automation in the workplace. Automation is not only changing the factory floor but it has made inroads into the service sector. Just as consumers learned to pump their own gas, they are now learning to check out and bag their own groceries, and cashiers are almost extinct in parking garages.

Automation and new technology have eliminated many service jobs. Like many other consumers, this woman is checking out and bagging her own groceries at her local supermarket.

At the same time that many families lost economic ground, there was a financial resurgence among the world's wealthy. According to the World Wealth Report (2011), there were an estimated 10.9 million high net worth individuals (HNWIs)—people with financial assets of at least $1 million, excluding primary residences and collectibles—at the end of 2010, an increase of 8.3 percent over 2009. The combined wealth of these individuals is estimated to be $42.7 trillion, an increase of 9.7 percent during 2009. The global HNWI population is still highly concentrated in only three countries—the United States, Germany, and Japan. Together, they account for 53 percent of that population. Despite the financial crisis of the last few years, the United States remains home to the single largest HNWI segment in the world with 3.1 million accounting for almost one-third (28.6 percent) of the global HNWI. The Asia-Pacific region, for the first-time is a close second with 3.3 million, followed by Europe with 3.1 million. India made it into the top 12 for the first time, and Australia edged up another notch to the number 9 spot.

In the United States, the disparity between rich and poor families grew ever wider during the last three decades. Figure 10.8 shows that in 1980, the richest fifth of all families received 44.1 percent of all aggregate income, compared to the 4.2 percent received by the poorest fifth of all families. By 2008, the gap had widened to 50.0 and 3.4 percent, respectively. Families at all other income levels, with the exception of the wealthiest families (the top 5 percent), who saw their share of income jump from 16.5–21.5 percent, experienced a decrease in their share of aggregate income.

Economists attribute this trend toward greater inequality to a number of factors: the loss of high-paid manufacturing jobs, the decline in union membership, the growth in low-paid service sector jobs, the increase in families with two high-wage earners, the higher salaries paid to people with higher education and technical skills, the increasingly popular practice of rewarding executives with stock options and bonuses and tax cuts for the wealthy. An analysis by the American Federation of Labor and Congress of Industrial Organizations of 299 companies in the Standard and Poor's Index found that in 2010, the Chief Executive Officers (CEOs) of the largest companies received, on average $11.4 million in total compensation. This pay average amounted to 343 times the workers' median pay, up from about 40 to 1 in the early 1980s ("Trends in CEO Pay," 2011). As the Applying the Sociological Imagination box on page 340 shows, Michael T. Duke, President and CEO of Wal-Mart, made more than $18.7 million dollars in 2011. By comparison, the median worker made $33,190 in 2010. Although Mr. Duke does not even make it to the top ten most highly paid CEOs, his pay is 563 times the median worker's pay. Wal-Mart is one of the largest employers in the United States and has been the subject of considerable controversy over the pay and benefits its employees receive.

WHO ARE THE POOR?

As we have just seen, all families do not share equitably in America's wealth. In 2008, more than 8.1 million families (10.3 percent of all families) were poor (U.S. Census Bureau, 2011e), a figure that has probably increased due to continuing high rates of unemployment. Each year, the federal government calculates the minimum level of income necessary to meet basic subsistence needs of families according to size and type. In 2011, the poverty level, as determined by the federal government, was $22,350 in annual income for a family of four in the 48 contiguous states and the District of Columbia. Hawaii and Alaska have slightly higher rates. Even so, many economists believe this overall threshold is too low because it does not take into account the variation in costs of living in different regions of the country nor the special needs some families have for elder or child care. A minimum-wage worker ($7.25) would have to work more almost 60 hours a week, 52 weeks per year, just to keep her or his family of four at the poverty line.

Poverty rates are not randomly distributed across the population. They vary by family type, race, and ethnicity. Married-couple families have a relatively low poverty rate (5.5 percent) compared

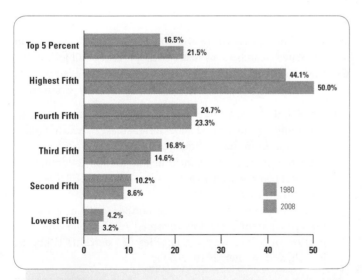

FIGURE 10.8 Share of Aggregate Income Received by Each Fifth and Top 5% of Households, 1980 and 2008

Source: U.S. Census Bureau, 2011. *Statistical Abstract of the United States, 2011.* Washington, DC: Table 693, p. 454.

Jim, left, Alice, and Rob Walton, children of the late Wal-Mart Stores, Inc. founder Sam Walton, are in the top 10 of Forbes 400 wealthiest people, each worth over $20 billion.

APPLYING THE SOCIOLOGICAL IMAGINATION

PAY WATCH FACT SHEET: MICHAEL T. DUKE, PRESIDENT AND CEO, WAL-MART STORES, INC.

Total 2011 Compensation (according to salary.com): $18,712,721

CEO-to-Worker Comparsons	Annual	Weekly	Daily	Hourly	Per Minute
Michael T. Duke	$18,712,721	$359,860	$71,972	$8,996	$149
Minimum-Wage Worker	15,080	290	58	7.25	0.12
Median Worker	33,190	638	127	15.96	0.27
President of the United States	400,000	7692	1538	192	3.21

How Many Years to Equal Michael T. Duke's 2011 Compensation

Minimum-Wage Worker	1,240 years	Completion Date 3251 A.D.
Average Worker	563 years	Completion Date 2574 A.D.
President of the United States	46 years	Completion Date 2057 A.D.

This information can be found at http://www.aflcio.org/corporatewatch/paywatch/paywatch/ceou/database.cfm?tkr=WMT&pg=6. Follow this and the related links to determine how your current income or your expected income after graduation compares with the CEO of your choice. Think for a moment about how your life would be different if you had the $33,190 income or the $18.7 million. Where would you live? What changes would you make in your lifestyle? What do you think about the growing income gap between top executives and rank-and-file workers? Is this trend something Americans should be concerned about? Explain. A growing number of shareholders and groups like Responsible Wealth have proposed that there be a maximum ratio between CEO and worker earnings. Do you agree or disagree with this concept? Explain.

to families with a female householder, no husband present (28.7 percent). Although families with a male householder, no wife present, fared better, their poverty rate was still high at 13.8 percent. More than 60 percent of the children born since 1980 will spend some part of their life in a single-parent household, and hence are vulnerable to the risk of being poor. This increase in the numbers of women and children who are poor is referred to as the **feminization of poverty.** In 2008, the overall poverty rate among children was 19 percent (14 million children). The poverty rates remains alarmingly high for African American and Latina/o children, 34.7 and 30.6 percent, respectively. Although in absolute numbers most poor children are White, White children had one of the lowest poverty rates overall (15.8 percent). Only Asian/Pacific Islander children had a lower rate (14.6 percent). Having immigrant parents increases a child's chance of being poor. Almost 18 percent of all the foreign born are poor, compared to 12.6 percent of the native born population (Census Bureau, 2011e).

Too often many people, including public officials, believe people are poor because they are lazy and do not want to work. However, the reality is that the majority of people living in poverty are in households where individuals work full-time but make very low wages. They are called the **working poor.** According to a team of Penn State researchers, as many as 25 percent of all jobs in the United States pay less than a poverty-level income. The rate reaches as high as 30 percent in some states (Glasmeier, 2005). Consider:

- In 2009, there were more than 10 million low-income working families in the United States, an increase of nearly a quarter million from the previous year.
- Forty-five million people, including 22 million children, lived in low-income working families, an increase of 1.7 million people from 2008.
- Forty-three percent of working families with at least one minority parent were low-income, nearly twice the proportion of White working families (22 percent) (Roberts, Povich, and Mather, 2010–2011).

Although the working poor live in every state of the union, in 17 states the majority of working poor totals more than 50 percent of the working age population. These states are concentrated in the Farm Belt, where economic decline has been going on for the last two decades, and in the West where, according to the Penn State researchers, population growth has helped to keep wages low.

Additionally, the South and Southwest, states traditionally with low union membership, have high concentrations of working-poor families with children.

Many jobs pay only the minimum wage and offer few, if any, benefits. Many are part-time or temporary jobs. Although educational and skill deficiencies contribute to the employment problems of some poor workers, two-thirds of poor workers have high school diplomas. Thus, for many, it is not a lack of basic skills but a scarcity of higher-paying positions that keeps them in poverty. In the future, workers with limited education will be even more disadvantaged. A recent national study predicts that 63 percent of all job openings occurring by 2018 will require workers with some postsecondary education (Carnevale, Smith, and Strohl, 2010).

Unemployment and Underemployment

To this point, we have discussed the complex connections between work and families. But what happens to families when this connection is broken or nonexistent? To date, the U.S. economy has been unable to provide jobs for everyone who wants to work. In June 2011, the U.S. unemployment rate was 9.2 percent (14.5 million people), double the rate of 4.6 percent in 2006. As Table 10.4 shows, other countries also experienced dramatic increases in their unemployment rates while rates in other countries either remained stable or declined. The level of unemployment in any country depends on a number of factors: structural transformations (economic growth or slowdowns, global competition, mergers, and new technologies), political events, governmental policies, as well as consumer confidence.

Any one set of figures, however, does not tell the full story of unemployment in this country. In any given year, hundreds of thousands of other people are not counted among the unemployed. Some cannot seek work at any given moment because of family responsibilities, illness, or disability, or because they are in school. The Bureau of Labor Statistics does not count these individuals in their monthly unemployment rate, and they are considered "marginally attached" to the labor force. These numbers rise and fall with business cycles as people withdraw from the labor force when job opportunities contract and they return when job opportunities expand. Others, unsuccessful in their job quest, give up looking for work altogether, convinced no one would hire them. The federal government calls these individuals "discouraged workers." In June 2011, the BLS estimated that there were 2.7 million marginally attached workers, with 982,000 listed as discouraged. If marginally attached workers were counted in Bureau of Labor Statistics calculations of the unemployment rate, it would increase by several percentage points.

Unemployment affects individuals and families in many ways. Clearly, the immediate result of becoming jobless is the loss of or at least a lowering of income. This loss of income puts a severe strain on family budgets and in extreme cases can lead to homelessness. Unemployment can also have a negative impact on family and social life. For example, things we take for granted—home entertaining, going out with friends for dinner or a movie, exchanging cards and presents—may no longer be possible. Children may feel isolated and rejected when they cannot participate in the activities of their friends.

To understand how devastating the experience of unemployment can be requires an appreciation of the role work plays in our lives. Paid employment is a means for earning a living, for providing food, clothing, shelter, and other basic necessities for ourselves and our families. Success or failure at this task is often the yardstick by which individual self-worth is measured. The unemployed repeatedly describe themselves as "being nothing," as "being looked down on," or as "having self-doubts." Some people who lack this ordering in their lives frequently feel psychologically adrift and may seek to escape these feelings through alcohol or other drugs. Other reactions to unemployment can be deadly. One researcher has statistically correlated the increase in the aggregate unemployment rate with increases in deaths, suicides, and homicides (Bender and Theodossiou, 2007).

TABLE 10.4 Unemployment Rates by Country, 2005–2009		
Country	**2005**	**2009**
Austria	5.1	4.8
Belgium	8.4	7.9
Canada	6.8	8.3
France	8.9	9.1
Germany	11.1	7.7
Ireland	4.3	11.7
Korea, South	3.7	3.7
Poland	17.8	8.2
Spain	9.2	18.0
Switzerland	4.3	4.2
United Kingdom	4.8	7.6

Source: Adapted from: U.S. Census Bureau. 2011. *Statistical Abstract of the United States, 2011.* Washington, DC: Table 1366, p. 857.

Have you ever been unemployed when you wanted to be working? If so, how did you feel about that experience? Do you know anyone who is currently unemployed? How does that person feel about being unemployed? How accurate is the argument made by some members of Congress that providing unemployment benefits do the unemployed only encourages people to not look for work? Many employers no longer consider people who are unemployed for any new positions in their company. What is the basis for such a policy? Is it fair? How are family relationships changed when one or more members are unemployed?

UNEMPLOYMENT AND MARITAL FUNCTIONING

In addition to causing distress for individual family members, unemployment can affect the functioning of the family as a unit. Many researchers have found that unemployment is associated with lower levels of marital satisfaction, marital adjustment and communication, harmony in family relations, and even divorce (Hetherington and Kelly, 2002; Kalil, 2005). Joblessness can also lead to a disruption in previously agreed-upon family roles, resulting in dissatisfaction for one or both partners. For example, Patrick Burman (1988), in his study of unemployment in Canada, found that when wives were unemployed, the egalitarian norms they had negotiated with their spouses disappeared. Consequently, the wives were forced back into the traditional role of housekeeper. Burman also found that when husbands were unemployed, they tended to do more housework, but not significantly more.

When parents are psychologically stressed by unstable work and unemployment, they may show less emotional warmth toward their children that, in turn, can lead to academic and emotional problems for their children. Additionally, parental unemployment can have intergenerational aspects. If children perceive their parents' labor market experiences in pessimistic ways, they may disengage from school and/or work and eventually be in the ranks of the unemployed themselves (Kalil, 2005).

Variations in Family Responses to Unemployment

As in other areas of family life, families differ in their ability to respond to a member's unemployment. In some cases, families can absorb the loss of income and provide emotional and physical support for their unemployed member until such time as new work is found. How family members react to unemployment depends a great deal on how the family functioned prior to the onset of unemployment as well as on the reasons for the unemployment. Patricia Voydanoff (1983) uses family stress theory to explain the conditions under which unemployment contributes to family crisis or disrupts family functioning. The model she uses is Reuben Hill's (1958) formulation of the A, B, C, X model of family crisis. A is the event (unemployment) that interacts with B (the family's crisis-meeting resources) that interacts with C (the definition the family gives to the event). This produces X (the crisis—the degree to which family functioning is affected).

Unemployment (A) hits some families harder than others. Families who receive unemployment compensation or severance pay or who anticipate new employment might experience fewer financial and psychological hardships than families lacking these benefits. Among the unemployed, women are least likely to have these benefits. Families also differ in the number and effectiveness of the resources (B) they have for coping with stressful events. Family savings, homeownership, additional sources of income, good communication, and problem-solving skills can minimize the problems associated with unemployment. Research shows that marriages based on a sharing model, in which both partners can perform economic and household labor competently, are more flexible and therefore better equipped to respond to the unemployment or loss of a partner than marriages based on strict gender specialization (Oppenheimer, 1997). Additionally, how the family defines unemployment (C) is critical to the outcome. "If the family perceives

the event as a crisis-producing situation, the likelihood of crisis is increased; if the family considers the event to be normal or manageable, family vulnerability to crisis is reduced" (Voydanoff, 1983:244).

Implicit in the family stress model are mechanisms for minimizing the negative consequences of unemployment. Leaving aside the need for more jobs, adequate financial assistance in the form of unemployment compensation and health insurance would help families get through a period of unemployment with fewer difficulties. In addition, educational or counseling programs aimed at improving family functioning would help families cope with the stresses of unemployment. Finally, knowledge about the structural causes of unemployment would help families define unemployment in a realistic way and lessen the tendency to blame individual members for the problem.

Age, Race, Ethnicity, and Unemployment

Table 10.5 shows that like social rewards, unemployment is unevenly distributed throughout the population. The recent recession has disproportionately affected America's youngest and most inexperienced workers. In June 2011, the unemployment rate for teenagers between the ages of 16 and 19 was 24.5 percent, compared with 9.2 percent for the adult population. Although this rate is at the highest level since the government started keeping track of it in 1948, it remains an underestimate since this figure does not take into account those teenagers who have given up looking for work. Including them would more than double the rate. The unemployment rate for Black teenagers was 39.9 percent, almost twice that of White teenagers (21.8 percent). Latinas/os had a rate of 35.4 percent. Comparable data were not available for Asians teens (Bureau of Labor Statistics, 2011b).

Youth unemployment is troubling for a number of reasons. First, a family may depend on income contributions from teenaged members for its economic wellbeing. Even when teenagers' earnings go directly toward meeting personal needs—clothing, books, and entertainment—this contribution is likely to relieve some of the pressure on household budgets. Second, research indicates that adolescents who have a job are less likely than their unemployed

TABLE 10.5 Unemployment Rates by Sex, Age, Race, and Ethnicity, June 2011

Workers	Unemployment Rate
All workers	9.2%
Adult men	9.1
Adult women	8.0
Teenagers	24.5
White workers	8.1
Black workers	16.2
Latinas/os	11.6

Source: Adapted from Bureau of Labor Statistics. 2011. Employment Situation—June 2011 (July 8). http://www.bls.gov/news.release/pdf.empsit.pdf (2011, July 11).

counterparts to become involved in illegal activities such as drug dealing and theft. Finally, if this high teen unemployment rate continues, the likelihood that these teenagers will establish stable marriages and make long-term commitments to the labor force will diminish. Research shows that those who do not work as teenagers have lower long-term wages and chances of employment even after 10 years (Graver, 2011).

Similarly, in adulthood the burden of unemployment continues to fall more heavily on people of color despite the progress in civil rights and affirmative action of the last three decades. Among the hardest hit by unemployment are Native Americans. Their unemployment rate is double the national average (Burke and Sikkema, 2007). However, this figure underrepresents the extent of the problem because large numbers of Native Americans live on reservations where few employment opportunities exist. On some reservations, as many as 50 to 80 percent of the tribe's adults may be unemployed and/or have given up looking for work. Blacks and Latinas/os also experience higher rates of unemployment than their White counterparts.

Additionally, significant numbers of people experience what economists call **underemployment,** a situation in which a worker is employed but not in the desired capacity, whether in terms of compensation, hours, or level of skills and experience. One form that underemployment takes is *involuntary part-time* employment, a person works part-time but desires full-time work. A recent Gallup survey found that nearly 1 in 5 Americans (19.3 percent) describe themselves as underemployed (either unemployed or involuntarily working part-time). The underemployed

©2011 Harry Bliss. Distributed by Tribune Media Services, Inc.   3/24

www.harrybliss.com

"Sean can say 'I'm unemployed' in <u>seven</u> languages."

In the past, unemployment was more likely to affect blue-collar workers. Today many college educated and professional workers are also experiencing high rates of unemployment.

respondents reported higher levels of stress, worry, sadness, and anger than did responders who were employed or voluntarily working part time (Mendes and Marlar, 2011). Damian Birkel was a marketing manager at Sarah Lee when he was downsized. Thereafter, he was laid off from three other jobs. He said, "I felt like I had 'loser' tattooed to my forehead, and 'will work for food' tattooed to my chest" (quoted in Roberts, 2011). For Birkel, the hardest part was telling his young daughter that there might not be enough money to pay the bills—among them, sending her to camp. He now teaches part time at a community college and founded Professionals in Transition, a non-profit that counsels the underemployed.

Janet Raiffa was a recruiting manager at a major law firm. She lost her job. Despite credentials from Dartmouth and Columbia, she was unable to find work that matched her skill set. "I got tremendously depressed. I had days where I couldn't get out of bed. It's difficult to motivate yourself," she said (quoted in Roberts, 2011). Like Birkel and Raiffa, other underemployed workers face serious problems; they are more likely than regular full-time workers to earn minimum wage and much less likely to receive health and pension benefits. In addition, such workers are likely to be dispirited. Like the unemployed, those who are underemployed worry about family finances and may experience low levels of marital and family satisfaction as a result.

This discussion of unemployment and underemployment illustrates C. Wright Mills's distinction between personal troubles and social issues (see Chapter 1). Unemployment of this magnitude is not simply a personal trouble of affected families; it is also a social problem. Thus, solving the problem of unemployment and underemployment requires action on the part of the larger society to create more jobs or to provide meaningful alternatives for those who cannot work.

HOMELESSNESS: OFTEN ONLY A PAYCHECK AWAY

As we have seen, millions of people live below or at the poverty level and, at any given time, millions of people lose their jobs. Thus, a missed paycheck, a medical emergency, or debt may push people out of their homes and in to homelessness. According to a survey of 27 cities by the U.S. Conference of Mayors (2010), the leading causes of homelessness among households with children are: unemployment (76 percent), lack of affordable housing (72 percent), poverty (56 percent), domestic violence (24 percent), and low-paying jobs (20 percent). The homeless inhabit every region of the country, from inner-city neighborhoods to the rural countryside. If you spend any time in parks or public facilities, be they bus or train stations, libraries, or airports, you will encounter the homeless. What you will observe if you look closely is a diverse population that includes the young and the old, every race and religion, as well as the unmarried and family groups. Additionally, 24 percent of homeless adults are mentally ill, 20 percent are physically disabled, 19 percent are employed, 14 percent are veterans, 14 percent are victims of domestic violence, and 3 percent are HIV positive (U.S. Conference of Mayors, 2010).

How many Americans are currently homeless? No one can answer this question with certainty because there is no agreement on how to define homelessness. Sociologist Peter Rossi (1989) distinguishes two kinds of homelessness. The "literally homeless" are those who already live on the streets. The "precariously housed" are those in danger of losing their homes or who have lost their homes but have found temporary shelter. Extended families often provide support by taking in homeless relatives, sometimes exhausting their own resources in the process. Therefore, if we use the first definition only, the number of homeless we count will be smaller than if we expand our definition to include those who are poorly or only temporarily housed. Most studies of the homeless have used the first definition, thereby understating the extent of the problem. That homeless people tend to move in and out of shelters and public view on a regular basis also makes counting them difficult. Finally, we can count people only if we can locate them. Not all homeless people are in shelters. Many live in parks, cars, cardboard boxes, doorways, or other places not readily accessible to researchers. Thus, any published figures on homelessness must be interpreted with caution. Estimates range from 600,00 to 3.5 million people.

If you suddenly found yourself homeless, where would you go? Who would you contact? What problems would you encounter on a daily basis? How would you attempt to solve them? What is your reaction when you meet a homeless person on the street? Do you think your attitude reflects that of most other people? To what extent is homelessness a personal problem or a structural problem? Do you think private efforts can solve the problem of homelessness? How is the structure and functioning of a family affected by homelessness? Whose responsibility is it to try to end homelessness?

The problems of poverty, unemployment, and homelessness are likely to grow in coming years unless the United States finds ways to create new good-paying jobs and to get its financial house in order. Thus far, government officials are divided on what policies would be most effective in this regard (see the Debating Social Issues box).

Debating Social Issues

SHOULD THE WEALTHY PAY MORE IN TAXES?

Occupy Wall Street demonstrations in New York and over 1500 other cities have put economic inequality on the political agenda.

No one doubts that the United States economy is in serious difficulty, but there is little agreement on what

should be done about it. A controversial and contentious debate has been going on in Congress for several years. Although both Democrats and Republicans agree that the federal government must reduce its spending, they don't agree on what should be cut or how deeply. The Democrats want to combine budget cuts with increases in tax revenues, including higher taxes on the wealthy, while the Republicans oppose any tax increases.

Those who favor increasing taxes on the wealthy argue that for decades, America's top earners have accumulated a larger and larger share of the nation's total income, from 10 percent in the 1960s to more than 20 percent today. During that same period, however, their tax rates have steadily declined. In the 1950s, the top marginal rate was 91 percent; today, it's 35 percent. When you include deductions and tax credits and the fact that as recently as the 1980s capital gains and dividends were taxed at 35 percent and not today's

15 percent, the wealthy are now paying a much lower portion of their incomes than any time since World War II (Reich, 2011).

Thus, they argue, fairness demands the wealthy pay more. Representative Jan Schakowsky, a member of President Obama's 18-member fiscal Commission introduced the Fairness in Taxation Act, which would create new tax brackets for millionaires (45 percent) and billionaires (49 percent) and would tax capital gains and dividend income as ordinary income for those taxpayers with incomes over $1 million. Such a change could raise an estimated $78 million dollars (Folbre, 2011). Increased revenue could then be invested in programs that would increase jobs and thus stimulate the economy. Raising taxes on the wealthy seems to resonate with the American public as well. A NBC News/*Wall Street Journal* poll found that 81 percent of respondents favor placing a surtax on federal income taxes for those who make more than $1 million a year. Other polls show that the majority of Americans favor some form of tax increases on the wealthy (Folbre, 2011). Finally, those favoring higher taxes for the rich point out that the United States is one of the least taxed countries in the developed world. In 2009, total federal, state, and local taxes in the United States were 22.6 percent of our gross domestic product, ranking 26th among the 28 Organization for Economic Cooperation and Development countries for which data are available (Citizens for Tax Justice, 2011).

Opponents of increasing taxes on the rich believe that such a tax increases would have a negative effect on the economy by providing less incentive for government to cut spending. At the same time, they argue higher taxes would lower potential profit and, therefore, create less incentive for business owners and the wealthy to invest, start new businesses, and create jobs. Additionally, they argue this would further divide Americans by turning the lower and middle classes against the rich who already pay more in income than the other classes. According to the Congressional Budget office, in 2007, the top 20 percent of households earned 55 percent of before-tax income and paid almost 70 percent of all federal taxes; for all other quintiles, the share of federal taxes was less than the share of income (Congressional Budget Office, 2010). Further, the poor and middle-income earners benefit as much or more from the tax code as do the wealthy (Dubay, 2009). Finally, opponents argue, if marginal rates are increased, it might motivate some of the richer people to move to another country, taking their potential tax dollars with them, or putting their money in "offshore tax havens." It is estimated that one-third of all wealth is currently held in such places.

This debate will not be resolved any time soon. However, there is no doubt, whatever its resolution, it will have a major impact on workers and their families.

What do you think? Who qualifies as wealthy and how are those decisions made? At what income threshold should households be expected to pay more in taxes? Do you think there is more or less to be gained by raising taxes on the wealthy? Explain.

BALANCING WORK AND FAMILY: RESTRUCTURING THE WORKPLACE

Throughout this chapter, we have seen how the relationship between work and families has changed drastically. However, a gap still exists between the current structures of families and the way other institutions continue to relate to them. For example, one of the major problems working parents face is getting children off to school in the morning and having a parent there to greet them when they come home. We are probably all familiar with stories of "latchkey children," children who return home after school to an empty house. According to the U.S. Census Bureau (2008), 6 percent of children ages 5–11 and 33 percent of children ages 12–14 regularly care for themselves after school. Children who are home alone confront many issues. For example, should they answer the doorbell? If they do, someone will know they are home alone. If they do not, someone will assume the house is empty. Both could lead to serious problems. Parents worry about

As this cartoon illustrates, balancing work and family is not an easy task.

this and other safety issues, so they use the telephone to keep in contact and to monitor their children's activities. Telephone companies report an increase in calls around 3 p.m. as children return from school.

Some school districts offer after school programs to assist working parents, but most do not. Without outside support, families frequently find they must solve this problem by having one parent, usually the wife, work part-time rather than full-time. The economic consequences of this approach include low pay, few benefits, and little or no mobility for the affected worker.

FAMILY-FRIENDLY POLICIES AND BENEFITS

Many employers are increasingly aware that they must institute organizational changes and provide family-friendly benefits to help employees balance work and family demands. One indication that this is happening is the increase in the number of companies identified and ranked as family-friendly businesses. In 1986, *Working Mother* magazine began compiling of list of family-friendly companies. Only 30 companies made the initial list; by 1992, 100 companies made the list, and each year since then the magazine has been able to run a list of the 100 best companies for working parents. To see which companies are family-friendly, go to www.workingmother.com. Among some of the most popular family-friendly benefits are child and dependent care, job sharing, flextime, and family leave. However, a word of caution is in order here. The Society for Human Resource Management conducts annual studies of the type of benefits employers offer their employees. In their 2010 report, the majority of companies surveyed said the U.S. and global recession have negatively affected them, and 72 percent reported that their benefit offerings have been affected in some way as a result. Consequently, some of these benefits may be at risk.

Child- and Dependent-Care Programs In the past, employers were reluctant to offer on-site day care because of cost. However, over time employers began to realize that employee concern about their children and other dependent relatives was a drain on productivity and morale. This growing realization was reinforced by a recent study that found a positive relationship between the availability of child-care centers, and employee's performance, attitudes, and retention rates (Connelly, DeGraff, and Willis. 2004). A majority of workers said they would be willing to contribute, on average, between $125 and $225 to subsidize on-site day care whether or not they used the benefit themselves. Respondents explained their willingness as both a concern for working parents and a concern to see their company stay profitable by reducing the rates of turnover and absenteeism and increasing worker productivity.

Job Sharing Another innovation allows workers more time for family matters through is **job sharing**, in which two workers split a single full-time job. Each job sharer gets paid for half-time work, although most usually contribute more than a half-time performance. Thus far, the existing evidence suggests that companies would benefit by getting more than half-time performances for half-time wages.

Flextime This represents yet another approach to meeting family scheduling needs. **Flextime** arrangements allow employees to choose when they arrive at and leave work within specified time limits. Flextime is especially helpful when one parent can start work early and arrive home early, while the other works a later shift. To date, only about 28 percent of U.S. workers have flextime, compared with more than 50 percent of the work force in Western European countries. However, this benefit is not evenly distributed among workers. Approximately 29 percent of White workers and 27 percent of Asian workers are on flexible schedules compared to 20 percent of African American workers and 18 percent of Latinas/os. Men are slightly more likely to have flexible schedules (28 percent) than women (27 percent) (U.S. Census Bureau, 2008).

Family Leave Until recently, the United States was one of the few industrialized countries that did not have a national family leave policy. Finally, in 1993, after two previous failed attempts, Congress passed the **Family and Medical Leave Act** (FMLA), which allows either parent to take up to 3 months of unpaid leave for births, adoptions, and family emergencies. The bill excludes workers in companies with fewer than 50 employees; thus, almost 41 million Americans, more than 40 percent of the private-sector work force, are not eligible. Because it provides only for unpaid leave, it is of little help to low-income workers. The benefits fall far short of those in other countries. A recent survey found that 169 countries offer mothers paid maternal leave and 66 offer new fathers paid leaves. Thirty-nine nations grant paid leave to workers whose children are ill and 23 offer it to employees to care for other family members (Heyman, Earle, and Hayes, 2007). The United States provides only unpaid leave for serious illnesses through the FMLA, which does not cover all workers. Congress is considering legislation to expand FMLA to provide up to 8 weeks of paid leave to workers for the birth or adoption of a child or to care for a family member with a serious illness.

Furthermore, unlike all other advanced industrialized countries, the United States has no statutory provision that guarantees a woman pregnancy leave, either paid or unpaid, or that guarantees that she can return to her job after childbirth. In the United States, pregnancy leaves are covered by the **Pregnancy Discrimination Act of 1978,** which requires that pregnant employees be treated the same as employees with any temporary disability. One obvious limitation to this law is that employers that do not offer disability insurance to their other employees are not required to provide pregnancy leaves to their workers. Family sociologist Joseph Pleck (1988) points to an additional problem with using disability as the mechanism for dealing with childbirth: It excludes fathers from parental leave.

Continuing Progress or Retrenchment?

Although the last three decades have brought considerable changes to the workplace, demographic trends (increases in number of dual-earner couples, in single parents, and in the

WORK–FAMILY DECISIONS

As we have seen in this chapter, the link between work and family is complex and constantly changing. Most families can no longer expect to survive with only the traditional male wage earner. Thus, partners in a relationship have to make considerable personal adjustments if both are working, especially if they have children.

Questions to Consider

1. Do my partner and I want jobs or careers? Will one of our jobs or careers take priority over the other? How will we make employment decisions that involve the other partner? How will we deal with career moves, including geographic relocation, especially if one of us does not want to relocate? If we both work, how will that affect our division of household labor? How will it affect our decision if and when to have children?

2. If our family does not need two wage earners, will we both work anyway? Can either of us consider staying home to take care of the children? Why or why not? If we both need to or want to work, what options do we have for quality child care? What can we do to reduce the stress of work–family conflicts? Some working parents have tried to resolve their work–family conflicts by working at home. Would one or both of us want to work at home? What would be the advantages and disadvantages of this for our personal and family relationships?

---

elderly) argue that more change is needed. Yet the volatility of the current economy may jeopardize existing benefits as companies struggle to contain costs and maximize profits. The Families and Work Institute's 2009 National Study of the impact of the recession on employers found that two-thirds of employers surveyed have suffered declining revenues with another 28 percent reporting that the revenues have held more or less steady. Only 6 percent have experienced growth. In response, 77 percent of employers have found ways to cut or control costs, most frequently decreasing or eliminating bonuses, eliminating salary increases, laying off employees, and instituting hiring freezes. Additionally, employers

- reduced health care costs or increased employee costs, (29 percent);
- instituted voluntary reductions in hours (29 percent); 28 percent instituted involuntary reductions in hours;
- allowed employees to compress their workweeks (22 percent); 19 percent increased telecommuting to save on occupancy costs;
- hired workers who earn less (13 percent); 11 percent outsourced work or moved employees into contract work;
- reduced sick time (8 percent), 7 percent reduced paid vacation time; and
- offered buyouts or other inducements for early retirement (7 percent); 7 percent encouraged phased retirement by working reduced hours (Galinsky and Bond, 2009).

Although most of these actions negatively impacted employees, some employers took actions to help those most adversely affected. Thirty-four to 44 percent of employers provided assistance to laid off employees in their new job search, helped employees to manage their own finances more effectively, and connected them to publicly funded benefits and services.

Supporting Marriages and Families

The United States lags behind most other countries in providing benefits that would help working families live less stress-filled lives. Overcoming this situation requires major efforts. Resolving work and family conflicts can no longer be seen as primarily a mother's issue, in which the solution puts the major responsibility on her, requiring her to reduce work hours or to leave the labor force entirely, thus becoming a low earner or even nonearner. However, to move to a more egalitarian culture requires women to share some of the more enjoyable aspects of parenting as well as their authority in the domestic sphere with men and it requires men to share power in the public square as well as to share more fully in family work. Nevertheless, changes in personal attitudes alone are insufficient. The larger society must more fully recognize and reward women's competence in the public spheres as well as men's competence in the private sphere of family life. In her book, *Restructuring Gender Relations and Employment: The Decline of the Male Breadwinner*, British sociologist Rosemary Crompton (1999) outlines a "dual-earn/dual-career" society in which women and men engage symmetrically in market work and in caregiving work. To achieve this does not require wives to become like husbands who work 40+ hours outside the home but rather that both wives and husbands equalize paid work hours and unpaid caregiving hours.

The ability for couples to implement more egalitarian attitudes and arrangements depends on structural changes in the workplace, including but not limited to the following:

- Revising work schedules that would allow for a shorter work week and allowing both female and male workers to request reduction in hours for a prorated reduction in wages and benefits as well as paid family leave for the birth or adoption of a child and for major family emergencies.
- Providing job opportunities for teenagers and education and skills development programs for low-skilled workers so they can obtain postsecondary credentials valued in the labor market.
- Providing a living wage for all workers and eliminating the existing discrimination in wages among different categories of the population.

- Providing a national system of affordable and quality day care.
- Ensuring a safety net for all workers and their families by providing universal health care and adequate retirement benefits.

Unquestionably, such policies would be expensive—thus, they are likely to be opposed by employers and even many taxpayers. However, implementing such benefits is not impossible. Many other countries have had similar benefits in place for many years (see, for example, Widener, 2007; Heymann, Earle, and Hayes, 2007). None of these countries rely on individual employers providing wage replacement for their own employees. Rather, paid leaves are funded through a variety of social insurance plans and/or general tax revenues. Because these proposals stand to benefit all segments of the population, the expenses should also be borne by all segments of the population.

SUMMARY

Although we frequently think of work and family life as discrete activities, research shows that the worlds of work and family affect each other in significant ways. The quality and stability of family life depend to a large extent on the type of work available to family members, and work can have spillover effects, both positive and negative, on family life.

In 1900, only 20 percent of women age 14 and older were in the labor force, compared with approximately 86 percent of men in that age category. One hundred years later, 60 percent of women and 75 percent of men age 16 and older were in the labor force. Before World War II, the majority of women workers were young, single, poor, and women of color. As late as 1975, only 36.7 percent of married women with children under age 6 were in the labor force. By 2008, the comparable figure was over 62 percent.

Women work for many of the same reasons men do, particularly to support themselves and their families. The rapid entrance of married women with children into the labor force has altered family life in many ways. The traditional nuclear family consisting of a working husband and a full-time homemaker with dependent children is in the minority today. The typical family today is a dual-earner, or "two-paycheck" family. The attempts by dual-earner couples to integrate work and family experiences affect many aspects of family life: decision making and power relationships, marital happiness, and the household division of labor. Working couples often experience role overload and role conflict as they struggle to balance the demands of work and family. Lack of affordable quality child care is particularly stressful for working parents of preschool children.

Although the labor force participation rates of women and men are converging, women still confront issues of inequity in the labor market. Among them are occupational segregation, a gender gap in earnings, and sexual harassment. Parents differ in their ability to provide a decent standard of living for themselves and their families. The disparity between rich and poor families grew even wider during the last three decades due to loss of high-paid manufacturing jobs, the decline in union membership, the growth in low-paid service sector jobs, the increase of in families with two-wage earners, tax cuts that primarily benefited the wealthy, and the increasingly popular practice of rewarding executives with stock options and other financial benefits. An increasing number of families are living in poverty. Being employed is not always sufficient to avoid poverty. Nearly two-thirds of all people living in poor families with children live in families with a worker.

The experience of unemployment or underemployment can have severe negative impacts on marital functioning and family life. Unemployment is unevenly distributed throughout the population. It is particularly high among teenagers and people of color.

The United States is one of the few countries that does not offer paid maternity leave for its workers. Although many employers are becoming more sensitive to the family needs of their employees, the volatility of the current economy has led to decreases in some family-friendly benefits. Some programs that have been introduced to help workers are job sharing and flextime. Given the widespread movement of mothers into the labor force and the growing number of workers caring for elderly parents, pressure will likely build for improved work–family policies. However, this is likely to come about only when work–family conflict is seen as a problem for both women and men.

labor force participation rate
commuter marriage
role overload

occupational distribution
pay equity
sexual harassment
feminization of poverty

working poor
underemployment
job sharing

flextime
Family and Medical Leave Act

Pregnancy Discrimination Act of 1978

QUESTIONS FOR STUDY AND REFLECTION

1. Describe the major changes in the characteristics of the U.S. labor force during the last six decades. How have these changes affected the quality of family life in the United States? Today, approximately 70 percent of families have two earners. For this reason, many people argue that the United States needs a national family policy. To what extent do you think the federal government and employers have a responsibility for resolving some of the problems confronting working parents? Would you be willing to see tax dollars subsidize all or a portion of child care for all working families? Explain.

2. How were household tasks divided in your family of orientation? What was the basis for this division of labor? Did family members perceive this division as equitable? Do you plan to replicate this division of labor in your family of procreation? Why or why not? How is the division of household labor related to marital functioning and satisfaction?

3. How have recent economic, social, and political trends, including the recent recession, impacted your lifestyle? Have they caused you to be optimistic, unenthused, or pessimistic about the future of the national economy? How has the evolution of a global economy affected the structure and functioning of families throughout the world? Discuss the pros and cons of the global economy that has developed in conjunction with the spread of capitalism. How do you feel about corporations relocating jobs to other parts of the country and to other countries to save on labor costs? Should corporations have an obligation to employees to pay living wage regardless of their geographic location? Explain.

4. In the section on Supporting Marriages and Families, we call for changing our cultural ideas about gender as a way to balance work and family. Do you agree or disagree? In your answer, consider the likely consequences of such a change, both positive and negative. Do you agree or disagree with the suggestions for changing the workplace environment? Are such proposals achievable? Under what conditions?

ADDITIONAL RESOURCES

SOCIOLOGICAL

DRAUT, TAMARA. 2006. *Strapped: Why America's 20- and 30-Somethings Can't Get Ahead.* New York: Doubleday. If you are feeling financial strapped, Draut provides statistical data to show that you are not alone. The author argues that depressed wages, inflated educational costs, and credit card debt are making it difficult for young adults to reach financial independence, and she advocates political action to reverse these trends.

GREENHOUSE, STEVEN. 2008. *The Big Squeeze: Tough Times for the American Worker.* New York: Knopf. A New York Times labor correspondent provides a sobering look and the stresses and strains faced by tens of millions of American workers as a result of globalization, the influx of immigrants, and the Wal-Mart effect.

LEWIS, JANE. 2009. *Work-Family Balance, Gender and Policy.* Camberley Surrey, UK: Edgar Elgar Publishing. The author presents a comparative analysis of the multiple dimensions and relationships involved in balancing family and paid work demands in European countries as well as the United States.

SMITH, JEREMEY A. 2009. *The Daddy Shift: How Stay-at-Home Dads, Breadwinning Moms and Shared Parenting Are Transforming the American Family.* Boston: Beacon Press. Scholarly research is coined with profiles of stay-at-home dads and their families to illustrate the many changes families have made in adapting to the uncertain global economy.

FILM

Capitalism: A Love Story. 2009. Filmmaker Michael Moore examines the impact of corporate dominance on the everyday lives of Americans with humor and outrage.

Larry Crowne. 2011. After losing his job, a middle-aged man reinvents himself by going back to college.

LITERARY

HICKMAN, CRAIG. 2009. *The Insiders.* BookSurge Publishing. This thriller captures some of the corporate financial malfeasance of recent years—insider trading and stock manipulation—that have resulted in the collapse of companies and left many families in serious economic difficulties.

SINCLAIR, UPTON. 1981. *The Jungle*. New York: Bantam. Sinclair provides one of the most important and moving works in the literature of social change as he tells the story of Jurgis Rudkus, a young Lithuanian immigrant who arrives in America with dreams of wealth, freedom, and opportunity, but instead encounters injustice and "wage slavery" in the turn-of-the-century meat-packing industry. This grim indictment led to government regulations of the food industry.

INTERNET

http://www.familiesandwork.org The Web site of the Families and Work Institute provides data to inform decision making on the changing work force, changing family, and changing community to improve working conditions and family lives.

http://www.mobiliyagenda.org The Mobility Agenda is a think tank that seeks to stimulate and shape a dialogue to build support for strengthening the labor market, the economy, workers, and communities.

http://www.studtentsagainsthunger.org The goal of the National Student Campaign Against Hunger and Homelessness is to end hunger and homelessness by educating, engaging, and training students to meet individuals' immediate needs while advocating for long-term systemic solutions. Their Web site provides information and links to many other resources and provides information for how you can get involved.

http://www.epi.org The Economic Policy Institute is a nonpartisan think tank that seeks to broaden public debate about strategies to achieve a prosperous and fair economy.

Succeed with MyFamilyLab®
www.myfamilylab.com

Watch. Explore. Read. The New MyFamilyLab is designed just for you. Each chapter features a pre-test and post-test to help you learn and review key concepts and terms. Experience Marriages and Families in action with dynamic visual activities, videos, and readings to enhance your learning experience.

Here are a few activities you will find for this chapter.

Watch on **myfamilylab.com**

Video clips feature important concepts in the study of Marriages and Families. Watch:
• Working Women and Childcare

Explore on **myfamilylab.com**

Social Explorer is an interactive application that allows you to explore Census data through interactive maps. Explore the Social Explorer Activity:
• Gender Breakdowns in the Different Employment Sectors

Read on **myfamilylab.com**

MyFamilyLab includes primary source readings from classic and contemporary sociologists from around the world. Read:
• Jacobs: "Detours on the Road to Equality: Women, Work and Higher Education"

11

Power, Abuse, and Violence in Intimate Relationships

What Will You Learn?

- Define and understand the sociological meaning of key terms.
- Describe the prevalence of power, abuse and violence in intimate relationships in a global context.
- Apply the sociological imagination to examine and analyze the intersections of race, class, gender, sexual orientation, and age in gender-based violence.
- Assess the pros and cons of men marching against violence against women as a strategy in the fight to eliminate violence against women.
- Increase your awareness and understanding of gender-based violence as a violation of human rights.
- Question the consequences of femicide for individuals, families, communities and societies.

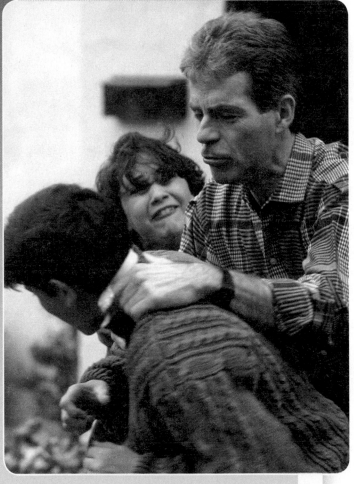

IN THE NEWS

Pittsburgh, PA

To date, most of what we have heard, read, or seen on television and the Internet about the economy and the American recession has focused on the financial cost. However, according to a recent study conducted by a physician at Children's Hospital of Pittsburgh (Berger, et al, 2011), the American recession has also had a punishing human cost. An increase in child abuse, mostly in infants, is linked with the recent American recession in a new study that some people say raises fresh new concerns about the impact

(continued on next page)

(continued from previous page)

of economic factors such as recessions on American marriage and family life.

Based on a small study of abused children primarily from lower-income families, known to be at greater risk of being abused, the author suggests that a decline in economic well-being is linked to violence. She found, for example, an increase in shaken baby cases and other forms of brain injury abuse during each of the recession years from 2007 through 2009 at her hospital. According to the author the number of such cases was almost double that of such annual cases prior to 2007. Although the sample was small (422 abused children from 74 counties and 4 states), the authors say that their results confirm anecdotal reports from many pediatricians who have witnessed an increase in the number of shaken baby cases and other forms of brain-injury abuse. While this type of abuse is still somewhat uncommon, the author found that the number of cases in the study areas increased sharply during the recession, rising from 9 cases per 100,000 children in pre-recession years to almost 15 per 100,000 children during the recession—a 65 percent increase. Linked to this child abuse finding is the increase in unemployment and the increase in the proportion of children on Medicaid in the study areas. According to a welfare professor at Washington University, combine the stress of raising a young child with wage cuts or lost of jobs and you get a sort of toxic mix in terms of thinking about possible physical violence.

Although government data do not support the author's conclusions, she suggests that this is so because government data on child abused is based on reports from child protective services, not medical diagnoses, and does not address brain injuries specifically. Though the research does not suggest a causal relationship between the recession and child abuse (that the increase in child abuse was caused by tough economic times), past research findings have linked violence with economic hardship. This research has consistently found that stress and poverty are risk factors for child abuse. In any case, some observers suggest that this study might be the first evidence of a hidden epidemic of child abuse caused by the recession. The latest statistics show that more than 46 million Americans are now living in poverty and the outlook for an improved economy anytime soon is grim. If concern about the economy and one's own and family economic situation is cause for stress, and if the results of this study are correct, then more and more families with babies will be at increased risk of abusing their children (Tanner, 2011).

WHAT WOULD YOU DO?

Do you know of any cases of child maltreatment, particularly for children under the age of one? If so, have you reported it? If not, why not? Would your action be different if it was a family member or close friend? Explain. In your opinion, is there a link between the recession and child abuse cases that you know of? If you were asked to be a part of a Blue Panel Group to develop strategies and interventions to prevent child maltreatment of all types where would you start?

((•—Listen to the Chapter Audio on myfamilylab.com

A father who wanted to avoid paying child support injected his infant son with HIV-tainted blood. The boy subsequently developed full-blown AIDS. Recently, a New York mother of seven children starved her 4-year-old to death, allegedly because she neither wanted nor loved her. A 33-year-old man was charged with attempted murder after beating his girl-friend's 14-month-old son into unconsciousness. A father killed his son by repeatedly punching him in the stomach because he was making too much noise during a televised football game. A mother of seven children was charged with manslaughter after her

15-year-old son, weighing only 23 pounds, died from pneumonia and apparent malnutrition. Until recently, most people in the United States probably would have shaken their heads in wonderment at these stories, thinking that they were isolated and unusual acts of cruelty that only the most deranged person could commit. Families, after all, are "havens in a heartless world" (Lasch, 1977:8).

Unfortunately, this picture of families as havens of nonviolence is inaccurate. Instead of havens into which we can retreat for comfort, safety, and nurturing, families are increasingly places of danger for many of us. Every year millions of Americans intentionally injure, abuse, assault, or murder members of their own families. Domestic or intrafamily violence is believed to be the most common yet least reported crime in this country. In no other U.S. institution or group is violence and abuse more of an everyday occurrence than it is within the family.

The Roots of Family Violence: A Historical Context

Many people think of family violence as a uniquely American phenomenon that has come into being only in recent decades. Records show, however, that as early as the 1640s Americans recognized the existence and seriousness of family violence and abuse and attempted to prevent or punish such behavior. However, we know very little about the history of violence in the United States or across cultures because the United States and most other cultures around the world have not officially recorded such historical data. Nonetheless, most social scientists today agree that family violence is not rare. Women are far more often the victims of violence and offenses against family members than are men with wife beating being the most common form of family violence. In fact, domestic violence is the single greatest cause of injury to women, exceeding rape, muggings, and auto accidents combined (Family Violence Prevention Fund, 2008).

The folkways and mores of various cultures show the universality of violence in women's lives. According to feminist philosopher Mary Daly (1978), such practices as the binding of young women's feet in China, the Indian suttee (the burning of Indian women on the funeral fires of their husbands), European and American witch burnings, the mutilation of African women's genitals through female circumcision, and past (and some present) gynecological practices in the United States such as unnecessary surgery and forced sterilization are all variations of the same thing: violence against women.

VIOLENCE AGAINST WOMEN

The historical subordination of women and children is linked to their experiences of violence and assault in the family. Historical accounts by colonists and missionaries as well as anthropological studies inform us of the extent to which violence against women

⟐ Read the Document
What Is Marriage For?
on **myfamilylab.com**

has been a part of the institutional structure of various societies throughout history. Consider for a moment the following historical facts about women and violence:

- Under Roman law, a husband could chastise, divorce, or kill his wife for adultery, public drunkenness, and other behaviors.
- According to the Decretum (ca. 1140), the first enduring systematization of Christian church law, women were "subjects to their men" and in need of punishment to correct their supposed inferiority and susceptibility to the influence of the devil.
- Well into the seventeenth century, in many European countries, including England, a man could legally kill his wife for certain behaviors.
- English common law held that men had a legal right to beat their wives as long as the stick they used was no thicker than the husband's thumb. (This law is the basis of the contemporary saying "rule of thumb.")
- The eighteenth-century Napoleonic Civil Code, which influenced Swiss, Italian, French, and German law, gave men absolute family power. Under this code, men could legally use violence against women up to the point of attempted murder.
- In the 1800s, in both Europe and the United States, men could use "reasonable" physical force against women, which included black eyes and broken noses.
- Sexual assault, as well as severe physical beatings, was an integral part of the female slave experience in the United States.
- A nineteenth-century Mississippi court declared that husbands could use corporal punishment on their wives. Not until 1883 was wife beating banned in the United States.

VIOLENCE AGAINST CHILDREN

Throughout history, children also have frequently been victims of violence and abuse, including sexual assault. Violence against children is linked to cultural values and attitudes that have defined children as the property of families. Historian Samuel Radbill (1980) reports that in ancient times, a father had the power to withhold the right to life from his child by abandoning the child to die. Although there are no clear records of the actual number of children

✳ Explore the Concept
*Social Explorer Activity:
Adolescent Violence and
Social Conditions*
on **myfamilylab.com**

who died as a result of such practice, **infanticide**—the killing of infants and young children—appears to have been widely practiced throughout much of history. Infanticide has been practiced by a wide range of groups, including some early Native American cultures, where newborns were thrown into a pool of water and declared fit to live only if they rose to the surface and cried. Even adult children did not escape the power of fathers. In France, for example, fathers had the legal right to kill an adult son or daughter under certain conditions.

Historically, girls and children born to unmarried parents have been the primary victims of child violence, abuse, and murder. Like their adult counterparts, girls have been far more vulnerable to family violence and abuse than have boys. Female infanticide continues even today in some societies, such as in parts of China, where male babies are preferred. In the past, much of the violence against children was socially acceptable. Although such treatment is not generally acceptable today, some level of violence against children by parents continues to be condoned (or certainly tolerated) in the United States.

VIOLENCE AGAINST THE ELDERLY

Little is known about the historical incidence of elder abuse. However, we do have examples of societal violence that has been directed against the elderly: Older women were the common targets of witchcraft trials, and older men were the most frequent murder victims. During the sixteenth, seventeenth, and eighteenth centuries, elders controlled the economic resources of the family, and independence for adult children came only with the parents' death. Elderly parents were thus frequently the targets of violence and abuse from adult children who sought to express their frustration or to take control of family resources. Following this period came the industrial era, during which adult children had opportunities to become independent of their parents. Parents often became financially dependent on their children rather than the other way around. This period seems to have witnessed relatively little reported elder abuse. The situation has not changed very much today. Many elderly continue to suffer neglect and abuse in silence out of fear or embarrassment. Therefore, many of these cases go undetected, unless, of course, the victim dies and the media picks up the story. (We will return to a more detailed discussion of contemporary elder abuse later in this chapter.)

VIOLENCE AGAINST SIBLINGS

To date, few systematic studies of nonfatal sibling violence in the United States have been conducted. One of the problems involved in documenting sibling violence and abuse is that historically parents have considered sibling conflict to be "normal" behavior and therefore have not generally reported it. Even today there is little information on or public awareness of sibling violence.

How much do you know about intimate violence? More likely than not, you probably know someone who is either a victim or perpetrator of such behavior. Moreover, it is possible that you have been or will be a victim of family violence yourself. Why is violence of all types so common among members of the most intimate of all human groups—the family? In the following pages, we explore this and other questions about family violence. To begin, we look at gender-based violence, a human rights and public health issue, in a global context.

Gender-Based Violence: A Human Rights and Public Health Issue

Violence is widespread around the world and, as in the past, women and girls continue to be overwhelmingly the victims. So much so that two decades ago, the United Nations General Assembly (UN) recognized the magnitude and patterns of violence perpetrated specifically against women worldwide and defined

Worldwide, gender-based violence against women, who represent half of the global community, is a pandemic and serious human rights violation. Individuals and communities have called attention to gender-based violence against women in a number of creative ways. For example, during a protest against violence against women in Georgetown, Guyana, South America, multi-colored handprints are applied to a poster (pictured) as a symbol of cooperation between people of various ethnic backgrounds and to call attention to the grave consequences of violence against women across the globe.

it as "any act of gender-based violence that results in, or is likely to result in, physical, sexual or psychological harm or suffering to women, including threats of such acts, coercion or arbitrary deprivation of liberty, whether occurring in public or in private life" (United Nations, 1993). Technically, gender-based violence includes any form of violence or abuse that targets women or men on the basis of their sex. However, as we have learned, women and girls have been in the past and continue today to be the primary victims. According to some observers, one of the most significant achievements in the last decade has been the recognition by the United Nations and a growing number of governments that violence against women is one of the most serious and widespread violations of human rights. Living free from violence is a human right, yet women and girls around the world suffer disproportionately from both during peace and times of war (UNFPA, 2008).

The United Nations defined violence against women as gender-based violence to both recognize and call attention to the fact that such violence is rooted in gender inequality; it is not only a manifestation of historically unequal power relations between women and men which have led to domination over and discrimination against women and has denied women full participation and advancement in their various societies, but also it often serves to enforce and maintain gender inequality and/or reinforce traditional gender roles for both women and men. Further, it is one of the most critical social mechanisms by which women are forced into a subordinate position compared to men and is all too often tolerated and condoned by laws, institutional, community and family norms (UN Women, 2011; Amnesty International, 2011; UNFPA, 2008).

Gender-based violence is a continuum of acts that cuts across boundaries of age, race, ethnicity, culture, community, wealth and geography. It may be perpetrated within families, in the home, within communities, on the streets, within institutions such as the schools and the workplace, in farm fields, refugee camps, during conflicts, wars, and crises and it can be perpetrated by governments. Gender-based violence comes in many forms throughout the life cycle and has many manifestations from the most universally prevalent forms of physical, sexual, psychological and economic abuse to specific practices such as battering, marital rape, sexual violence, abuse during pregnancy, acid burning, dowry-related violence including death, honor killings and other honor crimes, female infanticide, early marriage, forced marriage, female genital cutting, sexual harassment in the workplace and educational institutions, commercial sexual exploitation, trafficking of girls and women, violence based on actual or perceived sexual identity, violence against women in custody, and violence perpetrated against domestic workers (USAID, 2009; Bott, Morrison, and Ellsberg, 2005) (see the In Other Places box).

In Other Places

GLOBAL RESPONSES TO VIOLENCE AND SEXUAL ASSAULT AGAINST WOMEN

Nepal: Where the Consequences of Rape Result in Imprisonment of the Victim

In 1997, at age 13, Min Min Lama, a young girl from Nepal, was raped by her sister-in-law's brother and became pregnant. Scared and not knowing what else to do (given that in her society people would disapprove of her pregnant condition), she chose to have an abortion in a country where abortion is illegal. She was arrested and sentenced to 21 years in prison; her rapist went free. The International Planned Parenthood Federation (IPPF), in collaboration with other groups, worked actively for Min Min's welfare and release, including sending a mercy petition to the king of Nepal requesting him to grant Min Min amnesty for a crime she did not commit. Two years after her incarceration, at age 15, Min Min was officially released from Central Jail in Kathmandu (IPPF, 1999; Mandate the Future, 2002).

Ethiopia: Where Rape Is a Marriage Proposal

In some areas of Ethiopia, abducting and raping a woman is the customary way to procure a wife. If a man wants a wife, he kidnaps her and then rapes her until she becomes pregnant. According to tribal tradition, once the abducted girl is pregnant, the man can put his claim on her. Village elders then act as mediators between families and negotiate the bride's price. Recently, 14-year-old Aberash Bekele,

still a virgin, was abducted by seven men in southern Ethiopia, taken to a remote hut, and repeatedly beaten and raped by the gang's leader. On the second day of her kidnapping, taking with her a gun she found in the hut, the young girl tried to escape, but her rapist soon caught up with her. Frightened and trembling, Aberash fired three warning shots in the air, but the rapist kept advancing toward her. She lowered the gun and shot and killed him. Aberash was arrested for murder and brought to trial. The incident created a major rift between her parents and the abductor's family, who said, "Many people marry through abduction. He abducted her for marriage, not to be killed by her."

Although abduction is illegal in Ethiopia, it is a common practice and police typically turn a blind eye to it. It is almost always a matter left to the village elders to resolve. In Aberash's case, the village elders sent the young rape victim into exile in an orphanage and ordered her family to pay compensation for the abductor's death. With the assistance of the Ethiopian Women's Lawyers Association, Aberash became the first woman ever to challenge and resist this kind of violence. Although the village elders were furious, after two years of tedious legal proceedings, the judges hearing the case were convinced that Aberash acted in self-defense and she was acquitted. Unfortunately, Aberash was not completely free. Dissatisfied by the judges' decision, the village elders

decreed that Aberash remain in exile. Their ruling supersedes the power of the law. Meanwhile, the six men who participated in Aberash's abduction remained free ("Where Rape Is a Proposal of Marriage," 1999).

Batman, Turkey: Where Honor Killing Is Replaced with Honor Suicide

In Batman, Turkey, a small city of 250,000, when a woman (or girl) is suspected of engaging in sexual relations outside of wedlock, her male relatives convene a family council to decide her sentence. Female offenses can range from stealing a glance at a boy to wearing a short skirt, wanting to go to the movies, having consensual sex, or being raped by a stranger or relative. Once the family's shame, brought on by the woman's behavior, is known in the community, the family typically decides that the only way to restore family honor is to kill the woman. Hoping to join the European Union (EU), Turkey officials have been warned that its failure to make progress on women's rights (for example, putting a stop to honor killings) would impede its drive to enter the EU. In response, Turkey has tightened the punishment for attacks on women and girls by revamping its penal code and imposing life sentences for honor killings, regardless of the killer's age. But some families have taken other steps to achieve the same traditional

(continued on next page)

(continued from previous page)

goal such as forcing their daughters to commit suicide or killing them and disguising the deaths as suicides. In a 6-year period between 2000 and 2006, there were 165 suicides or suicide attempts in Batman, 102 of them by women. In the first 7 months of 2006 alone, some 36 women had killed themselves. A United Nations investigation of the suicides revealed that some few were authentic, but most appeared to be "honor killings" disguised as a suicide or accident. Thus, although the laws have been changed, tradition has not (Bilefsky, 2006).

Cape Town, South Africa: Where Men March against Rape

According to a number of sources, South Africa has one of the world's highest rates of rape and other crimes against women. Johannesburg, for example, has a reputation of being the world's "rape" capital. Fifty-two thousand rapes are reported each year in South Africa; many of the victims are young girls. Unreported cases would push this figure much higher. In 2000, led by the Anglican archbishop of Cape Town and other religious leaders, more than 2,000 men took part in a march to condemn South Africa's high rate of violence against women. The archbishop told the marchers that real men do not rape, and he urged the men to take a stand and act as role models for boys in the fight against violence against women. The men marched to parliament, where they gave the welfare minister a document stating that women were equal to men and that women and children were entitled to be safe and have their rights protected (BBC News, 2000).

What do you think? Do you think that antiabortion laws, even in the case of rape, are fair to women? Who do you think should have the right to develop legislation that affects women—their bodies, their reproduction, their lives? Using sociological concepts and analysis, how would you explain why Min Min is guilty of a crime but her rapist is not? That a Turkish female should die when she is raped but the rapist faces no penalty? How might women and other persons combat cultural traditions and practices such as those in some parts of Ethiopia that have institutionalized rape and violence against women? Do you think that men marching against violence against women is enough for men to do in the fight to eliminate violence against women? Tie your answer to this question to the exercise in the Applying the Sociological Imagination box on page 376.

Hundreds of thousands of women around the world carry the physical and mental wounds of gender-based violence. It is described by some as a global pandemic rooted in a global culture of discrimination which denies women equal rights with men and which legitimizes the appropriation of women's bodies for individual gratification or political ends. Worldwide, men experience higher levels of physical violence than women as a result of war, gang-related activity, street violence, and suicide, while women and girls are more likely to be assaulted or killed by someone they know, such as an intimate partner. It is estimated that up to six out of every ten women globally has been beaten, coerced into sex, or otherwise abused in their lifetime with rates reaching as high as 70 percent in some countries—most often by someone they know, including husbands or other male family members—and one in four women have been abused during pregnancy (Amnesty International, 2011; Bott, Morrison, and Ellsberg, 2004). In many Third World countries, 500,000 or more women a year die from pregnancy-related problems stemming from battering and abuse but also including botched abortions. In South Africa, every 83 seconds a woman is raped and in some countries, as many as one in three adolescent girls report forced sexual initiation and many of the sexual assault victims around the world are younger than 15 years of age (Family Violence Prevention Fund, 2008; George Mason University, 2008; Wallace, 2007).

Femicide—or female genocide; the systematic and mass murder of women simply because they are women, characterized by extreme viciousness, often involving rape, torture, mutilation, and dismemberment—is prevalent throughout Mexico and Central America. It is a term that has been coined in response to the violent murders of hundreds of young women (most between ages 17 and 22) on the U.S.–Mexico border in the city of Juarez, just across the border from El Paso, Texas, and in El Salvador, Honduras, and Guatemala City. In Ciudad Juarez, for instance, nearly 400 women have been murdered and many more have been abducted, and in Guatemala, over 3,800 women and girls have been murdered since the year 2000. Based on current statistics, on average, two Guatemalan women each day die a violent and often gruesome death. Although there does not appear to be a single cause for these murders, domestic violence ranks high among the causes which include singularly or in combination drug-and-gang-related crimes, and sometimes the abuse of power by authorities. Femicides are notable not only for their brutality but also for the impunity that exists for the perpetrators. Most cases of femicide have gone unsolved ("Femicide in Central America and Mexico," 2008; Center for Gender and Refugee Studies, 2008; Inter-American Commission on Human Rights, 2003).

Rape as a weapon during wartime is a particular insidious form of gender-based violence. Historically, wherever there has been conflict, violence against women, including violent rape and the forced impregnation of girls and women, has reached epidemic proportions, not just as a result of violent male opportunism, but rather consciously and maliciously as a weapon of war. This is particularly prevalent during ethnic conflicts, during which systematic rape is commonly used to destabilize populations and destroy community and family bonds. In many cases, men are forced to watch the rape of their wives, daughters, or other female family members (see Table 11.1).

Gender-based violence is not only an extreme human rights violation, it is also a serious public health epidemic that affects a

TABLE 11.1 The War Against Women: Domestic Violence Around the World

- In Europe, domestic violence is the major cause of death and disability for women aged 16 to 44 and accounts for more death and ill-health than cancer or traffic accidents. In Britain alone, approximately one-half of all women have been battered, sexually assaulted, or stalked by a male partner.

- Every day 36,000 women in the Russian Federation are beaten by their husbands or partners; every 40 minutes a woman is killed by domestic violence. Yet the law still does not recognize domestic violence as a specific crime.

- In Syria, one in four women is abused; in three-fourths of the cases, the abuser is her husband or father.

- In Bangladesh, 62 percent of ever-partnered women have experienced physical assault by a male partner. Throwing acid to disfigure a woman's face is so common in Bangladesh that it warrants its own section of the penal code.

- In Australia, 57 percent of women have experienced violence by a partner at some time during the relationship; Forty-two percent were pregnant at the time of the violence and 20 percent experienced violence for the first time during pregnancy. Aboriginal women and children are particularly vulnerable to domestic violence. For example, they are 45 times more likely than nonaboriginal women to be victims of domestic violence and 8 times more likely to be murdered.

- Studies in Canada, Israel, the United States, Australia, and South Africa found that 40 percent to 70 percent of female murder victims were killed by husbands or boyfriends.

- In a survey in the Kisii District of Kenya, 42 percent of women reported being "beaten regularly" by their partners.

- In Alexandria, Egypt, 47 percent of female homicides were "honor" killings of the victim after she had been raped.

- In Tanzania, approximately 500 elderly women accused of being witches are murdered each year. At the other end of the age spectrum, in Zambia, girls as young as 8 years of age are routinely sexually assaulted.

- In India, more than 5,000 women are killed each year because their dowries are inadequate—according to their husbands. Among children, 53 percent of those between the ages of 5 and 18 have been sexually abused, most by someone they knew.

- In Barbados, a national survey of women and men aged 20 to 45 found that 33 percent of women compared to 2 percent of men reported having been sexually abused during childhood.

- In a World Health Organization Multi-Country Study of Women's Health and Domestic Violence, the highest rates of violence against women by an intimate partner were found in Ethiopia (71 percent) and Peru (69 percent).

- In countries of the Middle East and Latin America, husbands are often exonerated from killing an unfaithful or disobedient wife.

Source: V-Day, 2008; Commonwealth of Australia, 2004; Amnesty International, 2004; World Health Organization, 2005; Bunch, 1999; "Abuse Spreads HIV among Zambian Girls," 2003; Morris, 2005.

woman's overall wellbeing and has particular consequences for her mental, sexual and reproductive health, including her ability to prevent unintended pregnancy and to protect herself from sexually transmitted infections such as HIV/AIDS. It also prevents women and girls from getting an education, working and earning an income needed to lift themselves and their families out of poverty. For women and girls 15–44 years old, violence is a major cause of death and disability. It kills and disables as many women between these ages as cancer, and its toll on women's health surpasses that of traffic accidents and malaria combined (Amnesty International, 2011).

According to the authors of a recent Australian study, there is a significant link between gender violence and key indicators of women's mental health, wellbeing and risk of suicide attempts. Said to be the most comprehensive ever undertaken of gender-based violence in a nationally representative sample of women, study investigators found that the four most common types of gender-based violence are strongly associated with a wide range of health problems for women including more severe current mental disorder, higher rates of three or more lifetime mental disorders, physical disability, mental disability, impaired quality of life, and overall disability. For example, for women exposed to two types of gender-based violence, the lifetime rate of mental disorder is 69 percent and for three or more types of gender-based violence, it is 89 percent compared to a rate of 28 percent for women who have not experienced violence (Nauert, 2011).

Violence against women and girls has far-reaching consequences beyond the individual, it harms communities, destabilizes countries, impedes economic progress and it prevents women from raising healthy children.

Intimate and Gender-Based Violence and U.S. Culture

Even a cursory look at any of the national and local media reveals that we live in an increasingly violent culture and world. Almost daily, for example, we hear about female celebrities who are or have been victims of gender-based violence. Women as diverse in celebrity as Rihanna, Oprah, Madonna, Halle Berry,

Tina Turner, Pamela Anderson, and Paris Hilton all share the experience of being a victim of gender-based violence perpetrated by a family member or an intimate partner, ranging from extreme physical battering by intimate partners to sexual assault as a child by male family members. Although these are the stories we are most familiar with, it would be a mistake to believe that only celebrities victimize or are victimized by intimate violence.

Today, one-fifth of all reported crimes are crimes of violence; a violent crime occurs every 25.3 seconds in the United States (U.S. Department of Justice, 2011). And despite our fears to the contrary, it is not a stranger, but a so-called loved one or an acquaintance who is most likely to assault, rape, or murder us. In fact, Americans are more likely to be hit, beaten up, sexually assaulted, and killed in their own homes by other family members than anywhere else or by anyone else. Forty-three percent of all murders in U.S. society are perpetrated by one family member or acquaintance against another, and violent assaults within families have been estimated to account for nearly one-fourth of all serious assaults. Every 5 years, the death toll of persons killed by relatives and acquaintances equals that of the entire Vietnam War (Fayette County Government, 2008). This non-stranger violence is often referred to as intimate partner violence or domestic violence. Intimate partner violence (IPV) is defined as a pattern of assaultive and coercive behaviors that may include inflicted physical injury, psychological abuse, sexual assault, progressive social isolation, stalking, deprivation, intimidation and threats. These behaviors are perpetrated by someone who is, was, or wishes to be involved in an intimate or dating relationship with an adult or adolescent, and are aimed at establishing control by one partner over the other (Understanding Intimate Partner Violence Fact Sheet, 2011). IPV exist along a continuum from a single episode of violence to ongoing violence.

The majority of intimate partner violence victims are females (85 percent); eight in ten are spousal abuse victims, nine in ten are victims at the hand of a boyfriend, and one third of women murdered in the U.S. are killed by an intimate partner. Nearly one-third of American women will experience domestic violence in her lifetime, and they are five to eight times more likely than men to be victimized by an intimate partner. As the leading cause of female homicides and injury-related deaths during pregnancy, IPV also accounts for a significant proportion of injuries and emergency room visits for women (U.S. Department of Justice, 2011; Understanding Intimate Partner Violence Fact Sheet, 2011; Devereaux, 2011). Contrary to popular beliefs about victims of violence and their perpetrators, victims do not ask for nor deserve the violence and the perpetrators are rarely insane or "sick" people who have simply lost control. Rather, their actions are deliberate (see Table 11.2).

Violence, abuse, and assault are deeply rooted in U.S. history and culture, beginning with the founding of this country. The early European American settlers subjected the native populations to widespread violence, abuse, and other atrocities, forcing

Watch the **Video**
Violence and Dating
on **myfamilylab.com**

them off their homelands and onto barren-land prisons called "reservations." Similarly, the American slave system was created and maintained through systematic violence, sexual assault, and oppression.

THE ROLE OF AMERICAN MEDIA

Today, violence pervades U.S. popular culture. Violence is standard fare in most of the media. For example, the most popular films are westerns, war movies, and crime dramas that contain (and sometimes romanticize) widespread death and destruction. Crime dramas in particular often center on violence perpetrated by males against females. In these films, women are almost routinely terrorized, physically and sexually assaulted, and murdered (Wallace, 2007). Television, like film, presents a constant stream of violent images. One of the largest content analysis of television violence to date found that nearly two out of three TV programs contained some violence, averaging about six violent acts per hour. Fewer than 5 percent of these programs featured an antiviolence theme or prosocial message emphasizing alternatives to or consequences of violence to the victim, perpetrator, and victim's family (Kaiser Family Foundation, 2003).

Violence is even more prevalent in children's programming. Although they portray killing less frequently than other programming, cartoons depict the highest number of violent acts and episodes of any kind of television program. On any given Saturday morning, the airwaves are filled with animated violence. The villains and superheroes in these cartoons routinely use violence as an acceptable and effective way to get what they want, and the perpetrators are valued for their violent combat abilities (Abelard, 2008; Kaiser Family Foundation, 2003).

Similar trends appear in contemporary music, particularly heavy metal rock and rap videos. Violence is a recurrent theme, as are rape, mock rapes, the implication of rape, and the anticipation of rape and conquest by males. According to those who study media violence, much of this music is misogynistic, defining women as sex objects and appropriate subjects of male fantasy, hatred, and violence. In addition to the visuals, the language itself is often violent and sexually explicit. The audience for these videos includes many teenagers and young adults, who are thus exposed to these attitudes and behaviors as they are growing up.

Added to the traditional media methods of transmitting violence are the new and changing technologies of the Internet and video games. Violence on the Internet, or its potential for violence, has increasingly become a concern, particularly as it relates to children and cyberspace seduction by pedophiles in which children have been lured by online predators into traveling to locations hundreds of miles from their homes where they are then sexually assaulted and sometimes murdered. In addition, video games, which constitute a multibillion-dollar industry in the United States, are increasingly violent, yet increasingly popular, particularly among America's youth. For example, more than 90 percent of children play video games, on average for about 30 minutes daily. Children no longer are merely passive witnesses to violence that happens in the media. Now they are actually

TABLE 11.2 Myths about Violence and Abuse

A number of oversimplifications, myths, and distortions continue to block our understanding of the nature and extent of marriage, family, and intimate violence. Although research has shown many of these beliefs to be overstated or blatantly false, many people continue to believe them. Consider the following.

Myth: **Family violence is rare.**

Fact: **Family violence occurs in epidemic proportions in the United States.**
Acts of family violence occur every 12 to 15 seconds, more frequently than any other crime in the United States (Clark County Prosecuting Attorney, 2006).

Myth: **Men are equally victims of domestic violence.**

Fact: **Approximately three in four victims of domestic violence are female. Females are 84 percent of spousal abuse victims and 86 percent of abuse victims at the hands of a boyfriend (National Coalition against Domestic Violence, 2007b).**
While it is acknowledged that men also suffer from abuse, women are five to eight times more likely than men to be victimized by an intimate partner and experience chronic domestic violence.

Myth: **Domestic violence occurs only in poor, poorly educated, minority, or "dysfunctional" families in urban inner-city communities.**

Fact: **Domestic violence occurs between people of all ages, races, and religions. It occurs regardless of sexual orientation, mental or physical ability, or geographical region. It happens to people of all educational and income levels. It happens in dating relationships, new marriages, and in long-term intimate partnerships. It happens in rural communities about as often as in cities or suburbs. A victim may be your neighbor, or a member of your family (Virginia Family Violence & Sexual Assault Hotline, 2008).**
- Educated, successful men, such as lawyers, doctors, ministers, politicians, and business executives, beat their wives as regularly and as brutally as do men in other classes (Clallam County Courts, 2006).
- Violence will occur at least once in two-thirds of all marriages. Violence is the reason stated for divorce in 22 percent of middle-class marriages.

Myth: **Domestic violence is a "loss of control" and only mentally ill or "sick" people abuse family members.**

Fact: **Domestic violence is rarely caused by mental illness, but mental illness is often used as an excuse for domestic violence (Coalition to End Family Violence, 2006).**
- Violent behavior is a *choice*. Perpetrators use it to control their victims. Domestic violence is about batterers *using* their control, not *losing* their control. Their actions are deliberate.
- Only a small percentage of abusers are actually mentally ill. Whatever we think of their behaviors, most abusers are "normal" in the psychological sense of the word.
- Most men who assault their partners are not violent outside the home. They do not assault or abuse their bosses, colleagues, or friends. Rather they target their intimate partners and children. In fact, some men, even those who drink alcohol until they are intoxicated, are in control enough to be selective about where they hit their partners so that the injuries will not show. If abusive men were truly mentally ill, they would not limit their violence in this way.
- Most people who suffer from various forms of mental illness do not engage in violent or aggressive behavior (Virginia Family Violence & Sexual Assault Hotline, 2008; Wallace, 2007).

Myth: **Domestic violence is more common in heterosexual than in same-sex relationships.**

Fact: **Domestic violence and abuse occurs in approximately 30 to 40 percent of LGBT relationships, which is the same percentage of violence that occurs in heterosexual relationships. It is a myth that same-sex couples do not batter each other—or if they do, they are just "fighting" or it is "mutual abuse."**
- Two in five gay and bisexual men experience abuse in intimate partner relationships, comparable to the rate for heterosexual women.
- Approximately one-half of lesbians have experienced or will experience domestic violence in their lifetimes.
- Many battered lesbians and gays fight back to defend themselves—it is yet another myth that same-sex battering and abuse is mutual (National Coalition Against Domestic Violence, 2008).

Myth: **Battered women are masochistic and provoke the abuse. They must like it or they would leave.**

Fact: **Victim provocation is no more common in domestic violence than in any other crime. Victims of domestic violence neither ask for nor like the abuse. Many victims stay in the relationship for any number of reasons, including fear. However, most victims eventually leave.**
- Violent behavior is solely the responsibility of the violent person. Perpetrators of violence choose violence; victims do not "provoke it."
- Almost all battering victims leave at least once. On average, battered women leave seven times before leaving permanently. However, leaving an abusive relationship is not easy. The decision to leave an abusive relationship places the victim at great risk. For example, 75 percent of women murdered by their abusive partners are killed in the attempt to leave or after they have left (Trauma Intervention Programs, 2006).

becoming involved in violent scenarios by way of video games and they are rewarded for their violence.

Although it is important to note that research linking media violence and the violent behavior of Americans is inconsistent, there is a consistency in the research suggesting that a constant diet of these kind of games, as well as media violence generally, desensitizes people, especially the young, who become immune to the constant images of violence and gradually come to view violence as an acceptable way to solve problems. A particularly compelling fact in this regard is the growing body of evidence indicating that exposure to sexual violence through the media is related to greater tolerance, acceptance, or even approval, of violence (Wood, 2008).

For example, one study of television violence on MTV found a strong relationship between women's viewing of sexual violence on MTV and their acceptance of sexual violence as part of *normal* intimate relationships; the more they viewed such violence the more likely they were to define violence as a natural part of female–male relationships and the less likely they were to object to violence perpetrated against them or to defend themselves from violent attacks. In essence, heavy exposure to violence in the media tends to normalize it such that violence and abuse come to be viewed as natural parts of love, sex, and romance. Nevertheless, detractors argue that there is no clear link between media content and actual behavior (see the Debating Social Issues box).

Debating Social Issues

VIOLENCE AND MISOGYNY IN THE MASS MEDIA: IS REGULATION THE ANSWER?

Violence against women—women as victims of men—has become a media mainstay, especially in TV crime dramas, as exemplified in this scene from the popular Showtime drama *Dexter*. Here, while investigating a murder for the Miami Metro Police Department, Dexter (played by Michael C. Hall) discovers one of dozens of trash cans filled with girls soaking in formaldehyde.

The media-saturated world in which we live is increasingly one in which sex, violence, brutality, and misogyny are common features. Media critics and the public at large have been long concerned about violence in the media, and its

impact on behavior. Today, however, that concern has intensified with what some view as an escalation of violence in the media, which all too often is sexualized, misogynistic, and sexist. Indeed, violence against women—women as the victim of men—has become a media mainstay. Despite the film industry's rating system, television's V-chip, and rap music's adult advisory indicating that a song has explicit lyrics, young people are exposed to a steady diet of violence, sex, misogyny, and homophobia in today's media. Rape and/or the threat of rape is a regular feature of films, no matter what their rating. Most often rape is presented as romantic, titillating, sexy, or justified because of some behavior on the part of a female (for instance, the way she walks, talks, or otherwise acts provocatively, or by leading a man on) instead of as a criminal act. These films perpetuate the "rape myth"—the idea that women enjoy sexual violence and that it leads to positive consequences—that the female victim is "turned on." The popular film *Swept Away*, for example, depicts a woman who falls in love with a man who rapes her (Neil Malamuth, cited in Center for Media Literacy, 2003). Other films, such as *Indecent*

Proposal, eroticize male domination expressed in the exchange of women, as well as the subjugation of other men, through brutal violence (hooks, 1994).

Likewise, much of contemporary music is misogynistic, defining women as whores and bitches and appropriate objects of male fantasy, hatred, and violence. Sodomy or reference to it has become commonplace in music videos, and teenagers and other viewers are fed a constant diet of women asking, sometimes begging, to be raped and sodomized. In his critical examination of MTV, the music industry, and music video representations of women, Sut Jhally (1995) argues that the images of women and girls in music videos are limited and have a negative effect on men's understanding of women and women's understandings of themselves.

In a recent analysis of television violence, Northwestern University Media Professor Jeffrey Sconce argues that television content increasingly presents a variety of images and depictions of women being raped, chained, butchered, or brutalized for the public's pleasure and entertainment. According to Sconce, *sadistic* is the only word to describe many of the prime-time television shows today. In his examination of the 2006 season, for instance, program content included gruesome shots of women being brutalized and terrorized in very graphic and extended ways. For example, the opening scene in Fox television's *Killer Instinct* shows a homicide of a woman paralyzed by venomous spiders, then raped while she is immobilized and powerless to do anything. In CBS's *Close to Home*, a woman's husband puts a dog collar on her as punishment (cited in Jones, 2005).

As with most issues in American society today, a line in the sand has been drawn separating two camps around the basic question of whether or not media violence actually causes real-life violence. On one side are those who link media violence to societal violence; they argue that constant exposure to the increasingly blatant violence, brutality, and misogyny in the media has a negative effect on both child and adult behavior. Therefore, the media should be regulated. Pro-regulation adherents argue that decades of research conclude that exposure to violence against women can lead to subsequent viewer aggression, especially among boys and younger children. Recent research, for example, has found that males who were heavy viewers of violence as children are twice as likely as other males to push, shove, or grab their spouse, and three times more likely to be convicted of criminal behavior by the time they are in

their early 20s (Swanbrow, 2003). Further, proponents of regulation argue that when people are exposed to violence and hatred toward women over a long period of time, they will come to be more accepting of the violence against women in the real world.

On the other side of the debate, those who oppose more media regulation argue that the data upon which those who call for more regulation is based are flawed, inconsistent, or incomplete. They see media regulation as simply a euphemism for more censorship or a smokescreen hiding the root causes of violence in society. More importantly, they see such regulation as an infringement upon First Amendment rights.

Increasingly, the focus of the debate is on the "culture of violence" and the normalization of aggression, violence, brutality, and hatred of women, and a lack of empathy, compassion, and respect for human life, especially that of women and girls. Those who call for more regulation of the media argue that media violence creates a climate in which violence is more acceptable in real life. Some proponents argue that media violence has become so embedded in the cultural environment that it is part of the "psychic air" that children and adults constantly breathe. Such an environment of violence, profanity, crudeness, misogyny, and brutality erodes civility in society by demeaning and displacing positive

social values (Media Awareness Network, 2006).

Those who are opposed argue just as strongly that just because a form of the media has a murder scene or sexual violence against women for that matter does not mean that people will go out and commit those same acts. They argue that proponents for media regulation overstate the power of the images and media content and underestimate the power of parents or adults to decide what to watch and what not to watch. Opponents of regulation argue that it is ultimately up to the viewer to decide what to watch. If a person does not like violence, misogyny, or sexual assault, they say, then turn off the TV or do not spend money on the movie or music video.

What do you think? In your opinion, should the media in all forms be regulated? If yes, by whom? If no, why not? Is there a difference between regulation and censorship? If yes, what is the difference? How do you feel about the content, images, and depictions of women in contemporary mass media? Do these viewpoints represent the reality that you live and experience? How so? How not? Is the problem simply one of the First Amendment right to free speech? Because women do not live in a vacuum, how, if at all, do media images and depictions of poor men and men of color parallel or are connected to those of women?

The popular depiction of the violation of women contributes to what has been called a **rape syndrome** or men's proclivity to rape—the group of factors that collectively characterize men's likelihood to rape. For example, the unwanted, unsolicited pinch on a woman's behind, the wolf whistles and lewd remarks directed at women when they walk down the street, and the unwelcome compliments about a woman's anatomy are all acceptable behaviors among various groups of men. When we tolerate these so-called minor acts, other acts of aggression and violation seem more acceptable. A brief examination of two of the most common forms of gender-based violence in America—physical assault and sexual assault—is informative.

Physical Assault: The Case of Battered Women

A spaniel, a woman, and a walnut tree. The more they're beaten the better they be.

—*Old English proverb*

In this section, we consider both the patterns of abuse and the strategies of resistance by victims of violence in the United States. Because 85–95 percent of all spousal or partner assaults are committed by men, we pay most attention here to woman assault or battering and

TABLE 11.3 | Got Flowers Today

I got flowers today. It wasn't my birthday or any other special day. We had our first argument last night, and he said a lot of cruel things that really hurt me. I know he is sorry and didn't mean the things he said, because he sent me flowers today.

I got flowers today. It wasn't our anniversary or any other special day. Last night, he threw me into a wall and started to choke me. It seemed like a nightmare. I couldn't believe it was real. I woke up this morning sore and bruised all over. I know he must be sorry, because he sent me flowers today.

Last night, he beat me up again. And it was much worse than all the other times. If I leave him, what will I do? How will I take care of my kids? What about money? I'm afraid of him and scared to leave. But I know he must be sorry, because he sent me flowers today.

I got flowers today. Today was a very special day. It was the day of my funeral. Last night, he finally killed me. He beat me to death.

If only I had gathered enough courage and strength to leave him, I would not have gotten flowers today.

Source: Reprinted with permission of Paulette Kelly.

later to sexual assault. All too often, the physical assault of women is accompanied by sexual assault, which sometimes ends in the murder of the victim. This point is nowhere more poignantly illustrated than in the anonymous letter featured in Table 11.3.

WHAT IS WOMAN BATTERING?

Within the context of family violence literature in the United States, the terms **woman battering** and woman assault are often used interchangeably to refer to a range of behaviors that includes hitting, kicking, choking, and the use or threatened use of objects and weapons such as guns and knives. Because many battered women are also sexually abused, some discussions of woman battering include **sexual assault**—violence in the form of forced sexual acts, including vaginal, oral, and anal penetration; bondage, beating; torture; mutilation; bestiality; and group or gang rape. Still other discussions include emotional as well as physical assault. In either case, domestic violence is always about power and control. One partner uses violence to intentionally establish and maintain power and authority over her or his partner (see Figure 11.1).

Most experts agree that woman battering is probably the most common and one of the most underreported crimes in this country. The lives, health, and well-being of more than one-half of women in the United States and their children are endangered on a daily basis due to brutal acts of violence committed by an intimate partner. Injuries that battered women receive are at least as serious as injuries suffered in 90 percent of violent felony crimes, yet under state laws, they are almost always classified as misdemeanors. Domestic violence affects one in every four women in the United States. A case is reported every minute in this country, and it is estimated that every 9 seconds a

woman in the United States is battered by her partner. While you are reading this paragraph, at least four women will be severely beaten.

Statistics also show that domestic violence is the main cause of injury to women—more than car accidents, muggings and rapes combined and it is the leading cause of death among women. It is estimated, for example, that an average of three women are murdered everyday by an intimate partner. And in 70 to 80 percent of these intimate partner homicides, no matter which partner was killed, the man physically abused the woman before the murder (Devereaux, 2011; National Institute of Justice, 2007). Perhaps because the issue of intimate violence was overlooked until recent times, early research on the topic often grouped all battering against women as "wife battering." In fact, violent treatment is not restricted to married women. Rather, women in all marital categories are battered by men they date, are related to, cohabit with, or simply know.

In general, the pattern of the battering experienced by women is referred to as the **battered-woman syndrome** and is defined in terms of frequency, severity, intent to harm, and the ability to demonstrate injury. Following a classification scheme presented in 1979 by social scientist Murray Straus, most researchers today define and classify battering in terms of severity. Battering is said to be severe if it has a high likelihood of causing injury, causes the victim to seek medical treatment, or is grounds for arrest. Certain forms of battering like slapping, pushing, shoving, grabbing, and throwing objects at the victim do not fit this category. Limiting battering or assault to discrete physical actions excludes a wide range of violence that women experience. For example, battering is often accompanied by verbal abuse, psychological abuse, and threats or actual violence toward children and other loved ones.

Children whose mothers are victims of battery in the home are twice as likely to be abused themselves as those children whose mothers are not victims of abuse. In fact, as violence against women becomes more severe and more frequent in the home, children experience a 300 percent increase in physical violence by the male batterer. Witnessing violence between one's parents or caretakers is the strongest risk factor of transmitting violent behavior from one generation to the next. Boys who witness domestic violence are twice as likely to abuse their own partners and children when they become adults. Moreover, when children witness violence in the home, they have been found to suffer many of the symptoms that are experienced by children who are directly abused. Ignoring "mild" or "less severe" violence overlooks the fact that any use of violence in a marriage or intimate relationship can have long-lasting detrimental effects on both the victim and the couple's relationship ("Domestic Violence Fact Sheet," 2010; Wallace, 2007). In the simplest language, the bottom line is that abuse is abuse whether or not it is severe (by someone else's definition). "The dynamics are the same—someone is misusing power and controlling someone else's life. It is a pattern of coercive control" (Linda Rudnick, quoted in Haddocks, 1995).

The Cycle of Domestic Violence Battering is generally cyclical in nature. Family violence researcher Lenore Walker (1984) proposed a *cycle of violence theory* that is still often cited today. The cycle of abuse includes three stages: (1) tension building, in which tension escalates gradually, making the woman increasingly uncomfortable in anticipation of the impending abuse—as the male becomes more violent, the female feels less able to defend herself; (2) acute battering, in which the woman is the victim of severe physical and verbal

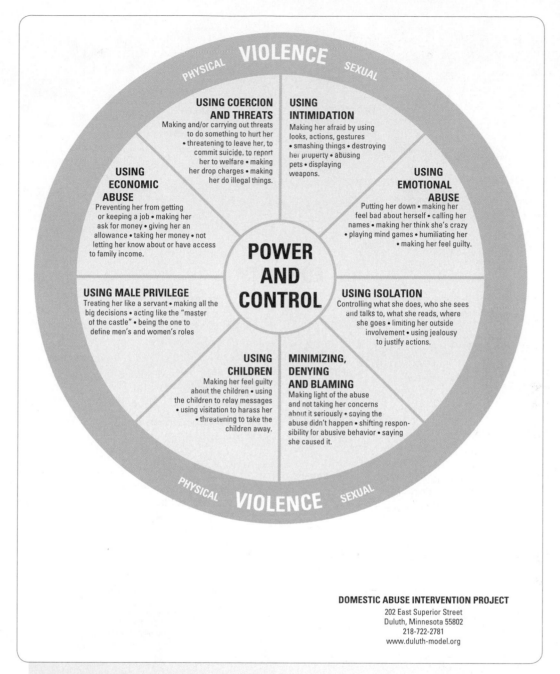

FIGURE 11.1 Power and Control Wheel

Source: Domestic Abuse Intervention Project, 202 E. Superior Street, Duluth, MN 55802, 218-722-2781, www.theduluthmodel.org, used with permission.

abuse; and (3) loving contrition, in which the man apologizes for his behavior, professes his love, and promises that he will never do it again. After a time, however, the remorse and contrition disappear, and the cycle starts all over again (Walker, 1978, 1984). In contrast to this cycle of violence and abuse, a group of battered women in Duluth, Minnesota developed an Equality Wheel to illustrate what nonviolence and equality in intimate relationships should look like (see Figure 11.2 on page 364). The green area of the wheel is the nonviolence that is or should be used in a relationship. The inner spokes are forms of nonviolent interactions and behaviors. These sections are held together by the use of respect, equality and nonviolence.

The Sexual Assault of Women

A man is always famous for his aggression toward a beautiful woman, and such aggression is sometimes considered rape. Although rape is not legally allowed, it is a fact that a woman likes a man who is very expert at rape.

—*Swami Prabhupada, founder of Hare Krishna:
Canto 4: Creation of the Fourth Order, Purport 4.25.41*

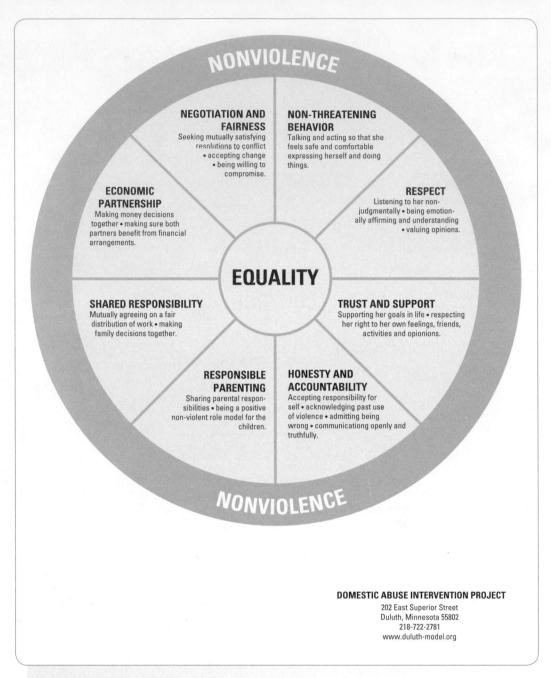

FIGURE 11.2 Equality Wheel

Source: Domestic Abuse Intervention Project, 202 E. Superior Street, Duluth, MN 55802, 218-722-2781, www.theduluthmodel.org, used with permission.

As we have already learned, the sexual assault of women is the second most common form of gender-based violence in the United States. Millions of women in the United States have suffered or will suffer some form of sexual assault in their lifetime. As with physical abuse, women and children represent the majority of the victims of sexual assault. In fact, over two decades ago, statisticians claimed that the average woman was as likely to suffer a sexual attack as she was to be diagnosed as having cancer or to be divorced. Looking at today's statistics on rape and the sexual assault of women, it seems that this statistic has changed little.

One of the most extreme forms of sexual assault is rape. Every 46 seconds, somewhere in the United States a woman is raped. Additionally, one out of every four girls and one out of every six boys will be sexually abused by the age of eighteen. Rape is legally defined as sexual assault in which a man uses his penis to vaginally penetrate a woman against her will, by force or threat of force, or when she is mentally or physically unable to give her consent. Because this definition overlooks the fact that men and boys are sometimes victims of rape as well, some states have broadened the legal definition of rape by removing sex-specific language to include males (who are almost always victimized by other males). According to recent statistics, 1 in every 10 rape and sexual assault victim is male and 1 in 33 (about 3 percent) men has experienced an attempted or completed rape in his lifetime, compared to 1 in 6 women. In addition, it is estimated that 1 woman in every 6 *will be* a victim of rape or attempted rape during her lifetime. As these figures reveal, the overwhelming majority (9 in every 10) of rape victims are female (U.S. Department of Justice, 2010; RAINN, 2009).

Contrary to what some people believe, rape is not about sexual arousal. Rather, it is about the violent abuse of power. As with physical assault, some observers have described rape as a terrorist tactic, a tangible and symbolic way for men to keep women in a subordinate position. A typical female rape victim, for instance, is raped nearly three times a year. More than one-half of all rapes/sexual assaults occur in the victim's own home or within one mile of where the victim lives. Another 20 percent take place in the home of a friend, relative, or neighbor. However, it is estimated that as many as two-thirds of rapes and sexual assaults are not reported to law enforcement officials (RAINN, 2009).

Estimates of rape would be even higher if they included assaults on young girls by their fathers, stepfathers, and other male relatives (usually categorized separately as incest; we will discuss incest later in this chapter), cases of statutory rape, and cases of male rape both within and outside of prison. Statistics on rape provided by the FBI do not include these categories, nor do they include date and marital rape.

RAPE MYTHS

As with battering, an enormous amount of myth surrounds rape. Two of the most persistent rape myths are that male sexual violence is caused by the attitudes and behaviors of female victims, and African American males are the primary perpetrators of rape. In the following discussion, we examine these two myths more closely.

Rape and Race Because of the relentless link of African American males to violence and crime, many people mistakenly believe the majority of rapists are African American males who are usually strangers to their victims. In fact, however, in most cases the rapist knows her or his victim. Statistics reveal that most rapes, especially those of White and young female victims, occur within the same race. That is, similar to other types of nonfatal violent victimization, sexual assault is primarily intraracial in nature. Therefore, the myth that African American men commit the majority of rapes is just that—a myth. Nevertheless, the myth of the African American male rapist, especially of White women, persists. As some scholars have pointed out, such a myth is dangerous in that it diverts the attention of White women away from the most likely sources of their sexual assault: White men. At the same time, it serves as a justification for negative attitudes toward and treatment of African American males.

Blaming the Victim Another common myth surrounding rape is that most (if not all) women secretly desire to be raped—that it is their greatest sexual fantasy. According to this belief, rape victims have generally acted in a manner that "invited" the rape; for example, they were a tease, had a sexy smile, were out too late, were too friendly, or were dressed seductively. Actually,

TABLE 11.4 Common Rape Myths

- A woman who gets raped deserves it, especially if she agreed to go to the man's house or ride in his car.
- It wasn't rape, it was just "rough sex." Some women like it that way. Other women simply enjoy rape.
- Women say "no" when they really mean "yes."
- Women provoke men by the way they dress, walk, talk, and behave, "leading men on." They thus deserve whatever happens to them.
- When men are sexually aroused, they must have sex. Once they are aroused, they can't control themselves.
- Rape happens only to certain kinds of women: women who are sexually active and promiscuous, women who are poor, women who take risks, women who like to party, women who have previously been abused.
- If a woman is not a virgin, she can't be raped.
- Women who don't fight back have not been raped. If they had resisted, they could have prevented it.
- If the man did not have a gun or knife, then the woman has not been raped.
- If there are no bruises, she must have consented.
- Sex is the proper repayment for a man who takes a woman out to dinner or pays for a movie or drinks.
- Women are asking to be raped when they go out alone at night.
- Women generally exaggerate about rape. Most times they make up rape stories to get revenge against a man who rejected them.
- Men who rape are mentally ill and out of control.
- When a husband rapes, it is because his wife withheld sex.

Source: Adapted from Robin Warshaw, 1988, *I Never Called It Rape* (New York: Harper & Row); Liz Kelly, 1988, *Surviving Sexual Violence* (Minneapolis: University of Minnesota Press): 35–36.

women fear rape—in fact, they fear it more than any other crime. Women must constantly act defensively; they must try not to be alone in public, especially at night. In one study, 40 percent of women said they avoid going out at night, while fewer than 1 in 10 men avoid doing so (North Carolina Coalition against Domestic Violence, 2002). Such fear acts to pressure some women into accepting their oppression and subordination. See Table 11.4 for a detailed list of some common rape myths. There are no scientific or systematic data to support any of the myths listed. The fact is, no matter how a woman dresses, walks, or talks, when she says no she means no—not yes or maybe. A man who has forced sexual intercourse with a woman who says no is exercising his power and ability to dominate her, and he is committing the violent crime of rape.

Intimate and Gender-Based Violence: Understanding the Intersections

As we know, violence against women affects all populations in the United States. However, some groups are more vulnerable to and experience higher rates of violence than others depending on their social location in the race/ethnicity, class, sex and age hierarchies in this society. Native Americans and Alaska Natives, African Americans, immigrants and refugees, women with disabilities, older women, children and youth, young adults, women on school campuses, and women living in rural areas are all groups who experience higher rates of victimization and often face unique challenges and barriers to receiving assistance and support to address victimization. In particular, experiences of IPV, domestic violence, sexual assault, dating violence, and stalking differ significantly for victims and survivors among various groups of color. The types of violence used or control exerted, the community supports available, strategies for help-seeking, gender roles, access to resources and the dictates of social norms also differ significantly across cultures and communities. Furthermore, victims may perceive, manage, and resist violence based on any number of factors including religious beliefs, ethnicity, language, race, immigration status, cultural and social norms, and economic opportunity (U.S. Department of Justice, 2010).

However, these facts are not always clear when reading mainstream literature on gender-based violence in the United States. For example, most often this literature fails to adequately represent the experiences of women of color and lesbians. Like other experiences, the experience of intimate violence is not the same for all women. How exactly it differs, however, is unclear from most research. Although some of the research indicates that social identities such as race, class, sexual orientation, age and marital status are important factors in the incidence and nature of intimate violence, seldom do such discussions provide clear documentation or focus specifically on how violence impacts women of color. Researchers have yet to investigate systematically, for example, whether there are any issues unique to women of color in violent relationships.

Much the same can be said about sexual orientation. Most of the research on intimate violence either fails to mention the sexual orientation of the people included in the sample or acknowledges that only heterosexuals were studied. And even less information is available on bisexual and transgendered victims of violence. The social pressures that contribute to family violence affect women and men of all sexual orientations and races. Because of the continued prejudice against lesbian, gay, bisexual, and transgendered people, much of the violence that occurs in these relationships goes unreported. Not only are many members of these communities reluctant to report intimate partner violence, but some in these communities actually deny the very existence of battering and other abuse. However, current statistics on same-sex violence show that LGBT individuals are not exempt from abusive relationships.

VIOLENCE BETWEEN SAME-SEX COUPLES

According to most sources, domestic violence and IPV affecting lesbian, gay, bisexual and transgendered (LGBT) individuals continues to be grossly underreported. When same-sex violence is considered, it seldom pays attention to the specificity and meaning of violence within the lives of LGBT people. Most agree that there is not only a lack of awareness but also a denial about the existence of this type of violence and its impact on LGBT individuals, couples, families and communities. Furthermore, various myths regarding gender roles perpetuate the silence surrounding these abusive relationships; for example, the belief that there aren't abusive lesbian relationships because women don't abuse each other. As a result of such beliefs, shelters are often unequipped to handle the needs of lesbians (as a women-only shelter isn't much defense against a female abuser), and transgendered individuals. Although there are few consistent national statistics regarding domestic violence against LGBT people, various regional studies indicate that domestic violence and IPV are much a problem within LGBT communities as they are among heterosexual ones, reporting that somewhere between 25–40 percent of same sex relationships involve abuse of one kind or another (NOW, 2011; Eastside Domestic Violence Program, 2011). One survey found that almost one in six same-sex cohabiting men report being raped, physically assaulted and/or stalked by a male partner. Another reported that of the same sex cases of domestic violence where race was recorded, the majority of couples were White (44 percent); 25 percent were Hispanic, 15 percent were of African descent, 5 percent were Asian/Pacific Islander, 4 percent were multicultural; 0.01 percent identified as Native Americans and the same negligible percent identified as Arab/ Middle Easterners, Jewish or other (cited by the American Bar Association, 2011).

When LGBT couples are reported on, most often it is said that domestic violence among these couples is largely the same as it is in heterosexual couples in the sense that one partner maintains control over the other person and limits her or his freedom to socialize; the abused partner becomes isolated and confused. There are others, however, while agreeing that there are similarities, also suggest that several aspects of LGBT intimate partner violence should be studied separately because domestic violence is often experienced differently by same sex/gender partners. Others argue more aggressively that this is an additive and homogenizing view that ignores key differences in experiences and socio-historical context that effect people's experiences (Davis and Glass, 2011). For example, while heterosexual women are more likely to be sexually assaulted by an intimate partner or someone they know, due to high amounts of homophobia, LGBT people are more likely to be sexually assaulted by a stranger who uses sexual assault as a way to punish and humiliate them. Some scholars have suggested that IPV among gay men of color, may be fueled by internalized homophobia, discrimination and stigma (Mendoza, 2011). In addition, it has been suggested that, unlike in some heterosexual communities, the complexities of IPV in LGBT communities is further complicated by: a greater degree of apprehension to report incidents of violence for fear of being ignored or stereotyped as promiscuous and that they invited the violence upon themselves or that their claims will be discounted if the attacker is a female because women are not socially seen as sexual perpetrators. Although homophobia and discrimination against LGBT people is still a serious issue, most Americans believe that IPV is an important issue that must be taken seriously no matter in what community it occurs (University of Minnesota, 2007).

GENDER, RACE AND ETHNICITY

A woman's relationship to the abuser is a key variable. Although more than two-thirds of violent victimizations against women were committed by someone known to them: husbands, boyfriends, acquaintances, or other relatives, in contrast, victimization by intimates and other relatives accounts for only 5 percent of all violence against men. Men are significantly more likely to be victimized by acquaintances (50 percent) or strangers (44 percent) than by intimates or other relatives. Research shows that women who are physically violated by intimates face a much higher risk of being recurring victims of violence than do women who are victims of a stranger's violence. Yet, ironically, women victimized by intimates are six times less likely than those victimized by strangers to report their violent victimization to police, because they are afraid of reprisal by the offender. Moreover, younger women (those aged 16 to 24) are the most vulnerable to nonfatal intimate violence, whereas women aged 35 to 49 are the most vulnerable to murder by an intimate partner (Family Violence Prevention Fund, 2010, 2008b; U.S. Department of Justice, 2010).

Intimate partner violence and domestic violence are problems with all racial and ethnic groups. However, according to some reports, because of differences in class, national origin, culture, a long history of systemic and pervasive racism and discrimination along with many other factors, the problem is more acute, more lasting and more devastating in communities of color. For example, Native American and Alaska Native women report higher rates of IPV than women from any other racial or ethnic group. Violence against Native American and Alaska Native women has reached such epidemic rates that in 2011, the U.S. Department of Justice placed a high priority on combating violence against women in tribal communities. Recent regional studies show that almost three out of five Native American women are assaulted by their husbands or intimate partners. Native women are 3.5 times more likely to experience sexual assault crimes compared to all other races, and one in three Native women reports having been raped during her lifetime. On some tribal lands, Native women are murdered at a rate more than ten times the national average (Weich, 2011; U.S. Department of Justice, 2010).

African American women are also disproportionately affected by violence. Behind Native women, they suffer IPV at higher rates than most other racial and ethnic groups in the United States, though research concerning violence for this group is considered by many to be woefully inadequate. For example, while the sensational incident of violence between popular singing stars Rihanna and Chris Brown grabbed national headlines and electrified airwaves and the Internet, the struggle against domestic violence among African American women is a serious but often silent battle. However, for the African American community, the statistics are staggering. For example, nearly 5 in every 1,000 African American women 12 years of age and older are victims of domestic violence and abuse. Approximately 40 percent of African American women report coercive sexual contact by age 18, and the lifetime rate of rape or attempted rate is 19 percent. Black women continue to be at greatest risk for lethal violence in intimate relationships. Homicide is the leading cause of death for African American women ages 15 to 45 (RAINN, 2009; Meeks, 2009).

Although Latinas/os are now the largest and fastest growing group of color in the U.S., there has been a lack of ethnic studies on violence against Latinas. Furthermore, it is difficult to find rates on domestic violence among Latinas/os as a whole or among Latina/o subgroups because in most national surveys, ethnicity is typically listed simply as White, Black or Other. Of the small number of studies that have been conducted, the results are not always consistent. For example, some studies indicate that Latinas/os have the highest rates of IPV though the rates vary according to Latina/o subgroups, while other studies report that the rates of IPV for Latinas/os are similar to those for non-Latinas/os. These conflicting reports notwithstanding, from the few studies that have focused on IPV and domestic violence among Latinas/os, it appears that domestic violence and IPV are just as serious and prevalent among Latinas/os as it is with other groups of color. For instance, according to a recent survey of domestic violence statistics, the rates of IPV among Latina/o couples is lower than among Black couples but 1.5 times higher than the rates for White couples. In addition, compared to White couples, Latina/o couples are at much greater risk for moderate to elevated risk when factors such as substance abuse/use, demographic and psychosocial factors are taken into account. Likewise, rates of IPV and domestic violence vary within Latina/o groups as well, with Mexicans having the highest rates (Burke, Oomen-Early and Rager, 2009; Cunradi, 2009; Gutiérrez and Zavella, 2009).

Like all other women, immigrant and refugee women are at high risk for domestic violence. However, due to their immigrant status (e.g., immigration laws, language barriers, social isolation, and lack of financial resources), it is often much harder for them to escape the abuse. Many immigrant and refugee victims of IPV are unaware of available services and among those who are aware, many are fearful of the stigma that may be associated with accessing services or fearful of deportation. In various studies and surveys almost one-half of Latinas and 60 percent of Korean women immigrants report being battered by their husbands or partners and that the violence against them increased since they immigrated to the United States. In contrast to married women who are U.S. citizens, married immigrant women experience higher levels of physical and sexual abuse than unmarried immigrant women. In addition, a little more than one-half (51 percent) of intimate partner homicide victims are foreign-born (U.S. Department of Justice, 2010; cited by American Bar Association, 2011).

Although Asian and Pacific Islanders report the lowest levels of IPV and domestic violence, it does not mean that it is any less a serious problem. In general, about one in five Asian and Pacific Islander women report having experienced pressure to have sex by an intimate partner without their consent, one in ten report that an intimate partner has hurt or attempted to hurt them by means of kicking, slapping, shoving, object throwing, or threatening their lives with a weapon, and three in ten have experienced emotional abuse at the hands of an intimate partner. When we examine specific Asian subgroups the rates of domestic violence and IPV varies. For example, some studies have found that the experience of domestic violence and IPV range from 61 percent among Japanese women, 20–54 percent among undocumented Filipinas, 44–47 percent among Cambodians to 18 percent among Chinese women.

It is difficult to find statistics specific to the prevalence of domestic violence and IPV for White women generally and/or various subcategories of this group. This is most likely the case because most studies tend to universalize women (to speak of women using White women's experiences) or they tend to give the rate of violence and abuse for White women and then focus on groups such as African American women. This situation is also due, in part, to the fact that domestic violence has been historically viewed and portrayed in American society as a "minority" problem or issue. As we have indicated elsewhere, this is particularly problematic for White women in that it masks the seriousness and prevalence of domestic violence and IPV among White women.

Every year more than 1 million women across racial and ethnic identities and sexual orientations seek medical assistance for potentially lethal injuries caused by battering. The overwhelming majority of these women will have additional or repeated injuries requiring treatment within the year (Family Violence Prevention Fund, 2010). In addition, for most battered women pregnancy does nothing to alter their abuse—they are at twice the risk of battery than non-pregnant women. Studies reveal that almost one-half of all assaults on women by their male partners begin during the first pregnancy. In addition, women are four times more likely to suffer increased abuse as a result of an unintended or unwanted pregnancy. Pregnant adolescents (ages 13 to 17) have a particularly high risk of violence from their partners. The results of this type of battering include hemorrhaging, fetal fractures, rupture of internal organs, placental separation, miscarriages, birth defects, low-birth-weight babies, and stillbirths (National Coalition against Domestic Violence, 2011, 2007b; Pan-American Health Organization, 2006). In all too many cases such battering is fatal. In fact, homicide is a leading injury-related cause of death among pregnant and post-partum women, second only to motor-vehicle accidents. African American women are especially vulnerable to being killed while pregnant. Being Black, under age 20 and receiving late or no pre-natal care increase a woman's chance of being a homicide victim while pregnant. The homicide rate for pregnant African American women is more than three times higher than that for White women. Added to these statistics is the fact that incidents of battering and abuse among women with disabilities may be as high as 85 percent (ABC News, 2007; Chang et al., 2005; St. George, 2004).

SOCIAL CLASS AND THE ECONOMY

Contrary to popular belief about gender-based violence and consistent with what domestic violence advocates have been emphasizing for more than 30 years, IPV affects individuals and families in all social classes and, as the increasing publicity around celebrity victims of domestic violence and IPV show, no one is protected by virtue of their race or class privilege. This fact notwithstanding, research over the years has consistently reported an inverse relationship between IPV and social class; as one moves up the class ladder, the rates of IPV decrease. Various large-scale national surveys report that women in homes with the lowest annual income are five times more likely to have experienced IPV than those living in homes in the highest income category and three times more likely than those women in the middle income category. Studies also show that poor women, homeless women, and women on welfare have the highest rates of IPV. In addition, studies consistently show, for instance, that 50–60 percent (some studies report as high as 82 percent) of women receiving some form of public assistance have experienced physical abuse by an intimate partner at some time in their lifetime. We should, however, keep

in mind that like other categories of identity, poor women, welfare women, and homeless women are not homogeneous groups, and there is a great degree of overlap between these groups. For example, many welfare recipients are poor; others, along with other poor women, work in low-paying jobs with no benefits; some are homeless, some live in shelters, and others are housed (cited in American Bar Association, 2011; Renzetti, 2009). Thus, we must be careful how we generalize about these populations. According to Claire Renzetti (2009), while attention given to IPV among economically well-to-do celebrities such as Rihanna and Chris Brown is important, the emphasis placed on their social class status and how IPV even happens among wealthy couples should not allow us to overlook the fact that the greatest burden of domestic violence and IPV falls on poor women. And as a direct result of racism, women of color are located disproportionately among the poor and have the fewest resources available to them to deal with violence in their lives.

Moreover, as we saw in the opening vignette to this chapter, researchers have suggested a link between financial stress (such as the recent failing American economy) and domestic violence. For example, in a recent survey of callers to the National Domestic Violence Hotline, callers were asked: "Has there been a change in your household's financial situation since last year?" and "Do you believe the abusive behavior has increased in the past year?" Fifty four percent and 64 percent of the respondents answered yes to each question respectively. According to the hotline pollsters, these results suggest a link between times of financial crisis and stress and domestic violence and that there is a greater chance that the amount of violence in households will increase during such times (Domestic Violence Hotline, 2009). Added to this type of violence is what some researchers have described as economic abuse—whereby the abuser

Pop star Rihanna and R & B singer Chris Brown made national and international headlines in 2009 amid charges that Brown had violently assaulted his lover. In what might have been a telltale sign that she was in an abusive relationship, Rihanna was seen with a large sore on her lip weeks before at an after party the two (pictured here) attended in Dublin, Ireland. After the attack that left her bruised and bloodied, Rihanna reportedly told police that Brown had abused her even before this incident.

uses someone's (usually a woman or an elderly person) lack of financial independence to keep them trapped in an abusive relationship. This kind of abuse is used to control relationships and maintain power by preventing the victim from having access to money and other financial resources such as credit cards, paychecks, and bank accounts. It also includes undermining victim's opportunities to become economically independent by not allowing them to work, calling and harassing them on their jobs to such an extent that they lose their jobs, refusing to pay spousal or child support to a survivor who has escaped an abusive partner, and forcing victim's to cash in, sell or sign over any financial assets or inheritances they might have (Allstate Foundation Domestic Violence Program, 2011).

MARITAL STATUS

When woman battering is compared across marital status, married women experience battering less often than single, separated, divorced, and never-married women. Marriage also reduces the likelihood of violent crime among men. Never-married men are more likely to commit assault, and they suffer most (60 percent) assaults. They are also five times more likely to rape and commit other violent crimes than are married men. In addition, women who cohabit are twice as likely to suffer severe battering or violence than married women. How might we account for this? Possible explanations are that cohabiting women may simply report battering more often, that violence against cohabiting women is more likely to be labeled as battering than is violence directed against married women, and that cohabiting women may be less willing to accept a battering situation because they are less dependent economically and may not have children. In any case, concern about cohabiting violence is becoming significantly more important as more and more couples choose this lifestyle (Catalano, 2007; U.S. Department of Justice, 2006; Ellis, 2006).

MARITAL RAPE

Marital rape is a taboo subject in countries around the world, including the United States. It is rarely acknowledged or discussed publicly. Yet it affects millions of women. Although it is the most underreported rape, according to some estimates, 25 percent of all reported rapes are from women who have been raped by their husbands. Many of these women have also been battered by their husbands.

Victims of marital rape are often referred to as "hidden victims" because they seldom report their experiences. The shame and intimidation associated with marital rape makes it extremely hard for a wife to come forward and report her husband's assault. Marital rape is typically not a random act; it generally occurs within the context of an abusive and exploitative relationship. Women who are raped by their husbands are likely to be raped many times. They experience not only vaginal rape, but also oral and anal rape. Marital rape has very little to do with sex and much more to do with anger, resentment, humiliation, and degradation. One of the most common myths about marital rape is that it happens when the wife withholds sex from her husband. However, that research that currently exists on the subject clearly demonstrates that a wife's withholding sex is not the cause of, and doesn't lead to, marital rape. Interviews with attackers and other evidence

have all shown that marital rape is a demonstration of control and power or an outlet for the attacker's rage and alcoholism ("Marital Rape," 2008). According to the Center for Constitutional Rights, every woman has the right to control her own body and to make decisions about having sex, using birth control, becoming pregnant, and having children. She does not suddenly lose these rights when she marries (Wellesley Centers for Women, 1998).

The impact of marital rape is no less serious and is sometimes more frightening, humiliating, and degrading than that of rape by strangers. Some researchers have found, for example, that the closer the association or prior association of the victim and the rapist, the more violent the rape tends to be. Consequently, wives who are raped suffer greater and longer trauma than other female rape victims. When a woman is raped by a stranger, she lives with a frightening memory, but when she is raped by her husband, she lives with the rapist. Marital rape can be classified in terms of the following categories: (1) *force-only rape,* wherein the husband controls the type and frequency of sexual activity within the marriage; (2) *battering rape,* in which a husband humiliates and degrades his wife; and (3) *obsessive/sadistic rape,* which involves sexual fetishes, sadism, and forcible anal intercourse—husbands use torture or perverse sexual acts (Finkelhor and Yllo, 1995). Whatever the classification, when a woman submits to sexual acts out of fear or coercion or implied harm based on prior assaults causing the woman to fear that physical force will be used, *it is rape* (Ghista, 2005). Researchers have identified several factors associated with marital rape. Among these factors, four have been most important: (1) the historical foundations of marriage in the United States, (2) the establishment of marital exemption in rape laws, (3) the socially and economically disadvantaged position of women, and (4) the violent nature of U.S. society and its "rape culture" (Pagelow, 1988).

Although it is perhaps difficult to conceive of today, in the past there was considerable resistance to the passage of laws that would allow a wife to charge her husband with rape. Until the mid-1970s, marital rape was legal in every state in the United States. It was not until 1993 that marital rape became a crime in all 50 states. However, 33 states consider marital rape a lesser crime than other types of rape and typically charge the marital rapist with spousal abuse or battery rather than rape. Marital rape is also now a crime under international law. However, cultural norms and the perceived social stigma attached to rape often discourage the reporting of marital rape and prosecution for marital rape is rare in most countries including the United States. In fact, a number of American states have actually broadened their marital rape exemptions to prevent the prosecution of a man who rapes the woman with whom he is living ("Marital Rape," 2008).

Theories of Spousal or Partner Abuse

What causes one human being to physically, emotionally, or otherwise violently abuse another human being that she or he professes to love? Various scholars across disciplines and professions have attempted to respond to this question. In this section, we present a brief and selective review of some explanations.

Social Stress Increasingly, life in the United States is characterized by high levels of stress, both for individuals and families. Various structural and environmental forces converge on us, causing an untold amount of stress. This increased level of stress, in turn, finds an outlet in the family or other intimate relationships. Very often, we respond to these stresses in our lives by using violence—all too often directed at the person closest to us, a partner, spouse, or child, and all too often in the form of physical assault. This explanation does not suggest that stress causes violence. Rather, it suggests that violence is one of many responses available to people who suffer from stress.

Patriarchy and the (Ab)use of Power The use and abuse of power and the imposition of one's will over another are major characteristics of spousal and partner abuse. Prominent characteristics of both the abuser and the abused are encapsulated in the concept of power. When dealing with intimate or family violence, feminist theories focus on the issue of power and gender inequality and encourage us to examine the influence of gender and gender-structured relations on the institution of the family and the violence and abuse within it. A key to comprehending this phenomenon using one of these perspectives is understanding the historical subordination of women to men. Although women have made significant historical contributions to society, men continue to control all major aspects of society (the patriarchal tradition). Thus, feminist perspectives encourage us to examine the social structure that is designed to condone, perhaps even encourage, and perpetuate the superordination (power) of men over women as well as encourage violence toward women.

Social Learning Theory This suggests that people learn from observing and modeling after others' behavior. With positive reinforcement, the behavior continues. If one observes violent behavior, one is more likely to imitate it. If there are no negative consequences (for example, the victim accepts the violence, with submission), then the behavior will likely continue. Often, violence is transmitted from generation to generation in a cyclical manner.

Dependency or Resource Theory Historically, the institution of marriage has fostered women's economic dependency on a husband. Women who are most dependent on the spouse for economic well-being (for example, homemakers/housewives, women with handicaps, the unemployed), and are the primary caregiver to their children, fear the increased financial burden if they leave their marriage. Dependency means that they have fewer options and few resources to help them cope with or change their spouse's behavior.

Although this is changing to some degree, many women still find themselves dependent on their partner not only for financial support, but also for emotional and other support as well. Accordingly, dependency makes a woman particularly vulnerable to physical abuse and increases her tolerance for it. Research on dependency and violence indicates that the more dependent a woman is, the more likely she is to suffer physical violence from her husband. Dependent wives or partners have fewer alternatives to marriage and fewer resources within the relationship with which to cope with or modify the abuser's behavior. According to Harvey Wallace, "This dependency is a pair of 'golden handcuffs' that binds the spouse to the abusive partner" (2002:186).

Alcohol "He had too much to drink." "He's not responsible." "He's really a nice quiet guy when he's not drinking." "When he's sober, he wouldn't hurt a fly." Sound familiar? People in this society typically associate violence with alcohol consumption. Various social scientists have suggested that there is indeed a link between the two but have been unable to establish a causal relationship. Disinhibition theorists suggest that alcohol releases our inhibitions and alters our judgment, making us capable of behavior that we would not otherwise engage in. Social-learning theorists suggest that violence is a learned behavior; we learn violence by observing people who drink and become violent. We rationalize that they are not responsible for their violence because they were drunk. Some social-learning theorists suggest that people use alcohol as a means of increasing their power and control over others. An integrated theoretical perspective suggests that it is not just the consumption of alcohol but the drinking mixed with a number of other factors that leads to violence—for example, conflict in the relationship and the cultural notion of drinking as an acceptable male behavior. The fact is, although alcohol can make it easier for a man to be violent, the real cause is not alcohol but the abuser's desire for power and control over his partner (Wallace, 2007).

Even from this cursory and selective review of theories of spousal or partner abuse, it is clear that much more study and research are needed before we can fully understand the determinants and dynamics of spousal and partner abuse and be able to predict the risk for women who enter into intimate relationships. Until such time as we are able to do this, it is instructive for all of us to recognize and understand some of the characteristics of this kind of abuse. Researchers have noted a number of variables that seem to be conducive to violence in intimate relationships including the following:

1. *A high level of family or intimate conflict.* Conflict is present for any number of reasons, including conflicting expectations, activities, or interests; gender-stereotypic role expectations; high levels of individual or family stress.
2. *A high level of societal violence.* As pointed out elsewhere, American society is characterized by a high level of violence. Violence within families and intimate relationships may simply be an extension of this external violence.
3. *Family socialization in violence.* Growing up in or living in a family that uses violence to resolve conflicts, release stress, or as a principal means of securing compliance teaches us that such behavior is acceptable.
4. *Cultural norms that legitimize family or intimate violence.* Although physical and sexual assault are illegal, various cultural norms including the historical rights of men in marriage tend to legitimize wife or woman battering and chastisement.
5. *Gender-stereotypic socialization and sexual inequality.* Many families continue to socialize females and males into rigid gender-stereotypic roles that reinforce a sexual double standard and inequality between the sexes. In marriage, this means that the husband is the family head and women and children are his subordinates. A husband's right to use physical force to "control" his wife and children for the most part remains unchallenged. This arrangement of roles and role expectations makes women and children particularly vulnerable to physical and emotional violence (Eshleman and Bulcroft, 2005).

6. *The privacy of the American family.* Because we believe that "what goes on behind closed doors" (especially if those doors are within the family residence) is not our concern, many people, including friends, relatives, and other family members, tend to ignore the signs or evidence of violence and abuse by rationalizing that it is a "private" matter between a husband and wife (or two intimate partners) and they have no right to interfere.

Researchers have found that these variables are interrelated and do not act alone in leading to family and intimate violence. Rather, they are mutually supporting and reinforcing in producing spousal or partner violence.

WHY DO WOMEN REMAIN IN ABUSIVE RELATIONSHIPS?

If the violence and abuse are so bad, why do women stay in these relationships? This question is often raised and is indicative of our lack of information concerning battered women. A more appropriate question would be "Why does he abuse her?" or "Why can't he be stopped from hurting his family?" Instead, the question—"Why does she stay?"—puts the responsibility on the victim, and is often followed with the statement, "She must like it" (ACADV, 2006). Battered women bear the brunt of considerable **victim blaming**— essentially, justifying the unequal treatment of an individual or group by finding defects in the victims rather than by examining the social and economic factors that contribute to their condition. Many people believe that female victims of domestic violence are somehow responsible for their mistreatment, or are masochists who enjoy being beaten, which explains their unwillingness to leave the relationship. However, as we have pointed out, there is no empirical evidence to support this anachronistic psychological viewpoint. The reasons women remain in violent relationships are far more complex than a simple statement about their strength of character. Victims of domestic violence desperately want the abuse to end and engage in a variety of survival strategies, including calling the police or seeking help from family members to protect themselves and their children. Enduring a beating to keep the batterer from attacking their children may be a coping strategy used by a victim, but it does not mean that the victim enjoys the battering.

Battered women often make repeated attempts to leave violent relationships but are prevented from doing so by increased violence and control tactics on the part of the abuser. Research and other scholarship in this area indicate that women remain in battering relationships for a variety of reasons. One of the most common is fear. Battered women may stay in a violent relationship because they think the situation is inescapable. They typically feel helpless about getting out of the relationship and fear that any action on their part will contribute to more violence, perhaps even their own death. A battered woman may also be concerned for the well-being of her children. She may fear that she will lose custody of her children or cause emotional or physical harm to them if she tries to leave. She may even fear that her abuser will kill himself if she leaves.

In addition to fear, a woman may have limited or no financial resources, access to alternative support, or skills to secure work. Economic dependence and a lack of viable options for housing and support can keep a woman in an abusive relationship. Even if a woman is financially secure, she may not perceive herself as being able to deal with economic matters outside of the relationship. And even if a woman leaves, economic necessity may force her back to her abusive partner, who might retaliate with even more severe violence and abuse. Or she may face the risk of becoming homeless. Nationally, 50 percent of all homeless women and children are fleeing abusive and violent households.

Sometimes women remain in battering relationships because of religious beliefs. They feel that their faith requires them to keep their marriage and family together at all costs and to honor and obey their husband, submitting to his will. And if she leaves or divorces her partner, her religious community may not support her. They not only believe that it is their responsibility to make the marriage or relationship work but also that leaving the abusive situation would be an admission of failure. In addition, some women stay because their family and friends may not support their leaving. Their partner or husband may have convinced their family and friends that everything is good in their relationship, that any problems are "her fault" or "in her head" (Wallace, 2007; Avon Foundation, 2006). They often come to believe that they caused or deserved the battering.

Other times women remain in such relationships because they sincerely believe in the notion of the "cult of domesticity" and family harmony. Even though their situation does not fit this ideal, they continue to believe that they can reach the ideal. They often feel physically and emotionally trapped by society's expectation of them: Society labels them stupid if they stay in the relationship and a failure if they leave. Still other women remain in battering relationships because they believe that children must be raised in a household with a father present. Thus, they endure physical and emotional abuse to keep the family together for the children's sake. Very often it is when the violence is directed at the children that a woman will take them and leave.

In some cases the fear of being alone keeps women in an abusive relationship. Often women in battering situations have no meaningful relationships outside their marriage or intimate relationship. The husband or lover may have systematically cut off all her ties to family, friends, and other supportive people. Having nowhere to go and no one to turn to, she remains with her abuser. In fact, being withdrawn and isolated is one of the primary telltale signs that a woman might be in an abusive relationship (see Table 11.5 on page 372). Other times, a woman may feel shame about being abused and reluctant to let anyone know that abuse is occurring in her relationship or it may be that she grew up with violence and abuse—so she may consider her own violent and abusive relationship normal. Sometimes women in abusive relationships do not know to whom to turn for help or where to get assistance or they may face language barriers to seeking help or independence, and may fear deportation. Although some people might not understand this, some women in abusive relationships remain because of pity—they feel sorry for their abuser. They believe he really loves them, but he simply cannot control himself. In other cases, low self-esteem keeps some women in an abusive relationship. As the battering continues, the abused loses confidence in herself, and her self-value and self-worth decline.

Finally, a common reason women remain in violent relationships is love. Most people enter a relationship for love, and that emotion does not magically disappear in an abusive relationship (Domestic Abuse Shelter, Inc., 2008). Many women want the violence to end but love their partner and want the relationship. They believe he loves them as well and their love will change the abuser. Each of these factors acts as a barrier to a woman trying to leave an

TABLE 11.5 Telltale Signs That a Woman Might Be in an Abusive Relationship

- She is withdrawn and isolated from her friends and family.

- Whereas she was once an active participant in social activities, she is no longer active.

- She displays poor self-esteem, poor self-concept. She speaks poorly of herself.

- She seems aloof and detached, and she will not make eye contact when talking.

- She appears nervous, especially when her partner is around, and she never accepts an invitation or a responsibility without getting his approval or okay first.

- She calls her partner frequently during the workday or whenever she is away from him.

- She is excluded from decision making at home and seldom has money of her own.

- Her husband or partner will not let her drive or learn to drive, go to school, or get a job.

- She has many "accidents," some of which seem illogical and suspicious.

- She has unexplained bruises, marks, scratches, or welts. She is often vague about how she got these injuries.

- She wears a lot of makeup or sunglasses, indoors as well as outdoors. She also wears a lot of turtlenecks, scarves, long sleeves, and slacks.

- She may complain of nonspecific aches and pains that are constant and recurring. These are stress-related problems.

CONFRONTING INTIMATE VIOLENCE

Do you know someone who is in an abusive relationship? Do you know what to look for?

Table 11.5 lists some of the factors that might indicate a woman is in an abusive relationship. If you know someone who is abused, have you tried to help? What have you done? Many individuals and groups are urging the public—relatives, friends, and neighbors—to intervene to help battered women and their children. For example, in a series of powerful public service announcements depicting the plight of abused women and children, begun in the mid-1990s, the San Francisco-based Family Violence Prevention Fund (FUND), has conducted a highly successful education campaign designed to prevent and reduce family violence. Using the theme There's No Excuse for Domestic Violence, the FUND has developed public service announcements such as the one shown on the next page. Another, designed to encourage intervention with batterers, reads: "It's Hard to Confront a Friend Who Abuses His Wife, But Not Nearly as Hard as Being His Wife." And, a radio announcement features a woman talking about her struggle to find the right words to say to her abused friend. The announcement concludes: "I just knew if I said the wrong thing, I'd lose her friendship. So I didn't say anything. And instead… I lost my friend." These public service announcements go to the heart of the problem of society's silence about intimate violence. Although we are increasingly aware of the devastation of intimate violence, too few of us know how to help battered women and children. Today, the FUND, along with a variety of other organizations and sources, regularly publicize domestic violence information and prevention strategies on the Internet with easy-to-read steps for simple, safe, and effective ways in which battered women can begin taking steps to leave their abusive relationships as well as how we, the public—family, friends, neighbors—can help battered women and children.

The Effects of Physical and Sexual Assault on Women

There is a growing recognition of battered women not only as "victims" but also as "survivors." The harm that men inflict on women takes many forms and has a wide range of effects. Research indicates that violent abuse exacts a tremendous toll on women: physically, mentally, psychologically, emotionally, and financially; it can have wide ranging long-and-short term effects for the victim as well as any children who witness the violence. The physical effects are perhaps the most obvious and can range from bruises and temporary pain to scars, permanently broken bones, disfigurement, and even death.

Victims of domestic violence are prone to health problems of all types. For example, victims of domestic violence or IPV often go untreated for their physical injuries because they feel too ashamed to seek help or are too afraid to do so. Some abusers coerce victims to forego treatment for injuries. As a consequence, untreated injuries may only partially heal resulting in long-term

abusive relationship. Although most battered women actively seek help from a variety of sources in ending the cycle of violence, very often the failure of various professionals and systems to provide adequate support keeps women in violent relationships. Those who make it beyond the barriers and do not go back are the fortunate ones who find support for their leaving the abuser, and most of them go on to lead healthy, happy, and productive lives.

Mentally put yourself in the shoes of a battered woman. Would you leave? Where would you go? How many services are available for women who are victims of courtship or marital violence at the college or university you are now attending? Are there offices you can go to? People you can talk to? Do you know women who are in battering relationships? What reasons, if any, do they give for remaining in such relationships?

WHILE YOU'RE TRYING TO
FIND THE RIGHT WORDS, YOUR FRIEND
MAY BE TRYING TO STAY ALIVE.

Talking with a friend who's being beaten up by her husband will never be easy. We understand that you want to say just the right thing, in just the right way. If you need help finding the right words, call 1-800-END ABUSE and we'll send you useful information and suggestions. Whatever you do, however, don't wait too long to offer her your help. At least one out of every three murdered women is killed by her husband or boyfriend. So your friend might not have the luxury of time.

THERE'S NO EXCUSE
for Domestic Violence.

Family Violence
Prevention Fund

Talking with a female relative or friend who we know or suspect is a victim of violence and abuse is never easy. We often remain silent for fear that we will not say the right thing in just the right way. Given that one out of every three murdered women is killed by her husband or boyfriend, our relative or friend may not have the luxury of waiting until we find the right words.

chronic problems such as back pain. Head injuries in particular can have chronic effects on the thinking, memory, mood, and behavior of the victim. In addition, they tend to have a lowered immune response leaving them vulnerable to respiratory ailments and other infections. If domestic violence involves sexual violence women are at risk for unwanted pregnancy, injury, and infection as is any victim of sexual assault.

Less visible but perhaps more damaging are the psychological and emotional scars brought on by abuse. Survivors of domestic violence and IPV are vulnerable to psychological and mental health disorders that are direct results of their victimization. Low self-esteem, self-hate, economic and emotional dependence on others (especially on those who perpetrate the violence), fear, self-destructive behavior such as alcohol and drug abuse, and suicide are common among abused women. Researchers have found that survivors of abuse often suffer conditions typically associated with prolonged and severe stress such as headaches and gastrointestinal problems, depression and severe anxiety long after escaping the abusive situation. Survivors may also develop Post-Traumatic Stress Disorder (PTSD)—a severe anxiety disorder that is brought on by exposure to extreme physical harm or danger. Near-death experiences, torture or extreme bodily harm, disaster, physical or sexual assault, or psychological damage and affliction can all lead to PTSD. People who directly lived through or were witnesses to such events can develop the disorder ("Effects of Domestic Violence on Women," 2010).

Given traditional gender role socialization, many abused women attribute the violence and abuse to something they did or did not do and therefore believe that they deserve to be treated violently. They frequently try to change themselves or the situations that they believe lead to the abuse. However, they usually come to realize that the abuse is unpredictable and could be triggered by almost anything they do or do not do. It is not surprising that women suffering under such conditions have a low sense of self-worth and a high sense of helplessness and hopelessness. Women who have been victims of incestuous assault as children report feelings of severe depression throughout their lives, often to the point of suicide. Probably the most extreme manifestation of battered women's self-blame and recrimination is their tendency toward self-destructive behavior as a method of coping with the persistent violence in their lives.

Coping and Survival Strategies

As with any stressful situation, coping with violence and abuse requires a variety of skills, survival tactics, and resources. Research shows that battered women have developed a wide range of strategies, both constructive (seeking help, leaving the violent situation) and destructive (substance abuse, suicide, murder). Although the ways individual women cope vary from situation to situation, their coping and survival strategies can be classified in the following ways: psychological and emotional, self-destructive, and fighting back.

PSYCHOLOGICAL AND EMOTIONAL STRATEGIES

One strategy employed by battered women is avoidance or prevention of violence. Victims of abuse sometimes develop plans to avoid future attacks. Sometimes they use sex (to the degree that they still have some control over their sexuality) in an attempt to change the batterer or to avoid further beatings. Some battered women cope by trying to make the relationship work in spite of the obstacles, and others manage to cope and survive by insisting that the violence is not serious enough to end the relationship. Some women resort to dreams or fantasies that can range from being in a violence-free relationship to killing their mates. Still other women block out or repress their experiences of violence, though these experiences often resurface at some future time.

SELF-DESTRUCTIVE STRATEGIES

Self-destructive behaviors such as alcohol and drug abuse, overeating, and suicide are all forms of coping, although most people would consider them unhealthy, unwise, and ineffective. Battering appears to be the single most important context for female alcoholism, suicide attempts, and a range of mental health problems. For example, battered women account for 42 percent of all attempted suicides; more than 25 percent of all female suicide attempts reported by hospitals are associated with battering. Of these women, 80 percent have a history of suicide attempts and have been seen in the hospital for at least one abusive injury prior to their first suicide attempt. For African American women, fully one-half of those who attempt suicide are abused (MSDVC, 2011; RAINN, 2008; University of Minnesota, 2008).

Battering is also closely associated with female alcohol and drug abuse. Some researchers caution that it is unclear whether substance abuse is the context or the consequence of stress precipitated by violence. That is, some researchers contend that alcohol abuse may contribute to a climate that makes abuse more likely. Other researchers respond that the rate of alcoholism among battered women is significantly greater than among nonbattered women. An examination of the recorded onset of alcoholism and of abusive injury among battered women reveals that three-fourths of the alcohol cases emerged only after the onset of abuse, suggesting that abuse leads to alcoholism among battered women, and not the reverse. Similarly, whereas drug abuse is no more common among battered women than nonbattered women before the onset of abuse, after abuse the risk of drug abuse is nine times greater than would normally be expected.

FIGHTING BACK

Some women who cannot escape abusive relationships cope by fighting back. Most often their self-defense takes the form of hitting or shoving the batterer. Only occasionally is women's self-defense more violent, such as pushing the batterer down a flight of stairs, biting him, kicking him in the groin, cutting him, or even shooting him. A small number of women who fight back eventually kill their abuser. Although a few of these women are acquitted by the courts on the grounds of self-defense, most are convicted and jailed. The majority of those convicted serve many years in prison despite their claims of self-defense and despite a large amount of evidence indicating that they had been severely abused by the men they killed. Some people consider women who respond to male violence by fighting back and who are then imprisoned to be political prisoners. Whatever term we use to describe these women, the fact is that killing an abuser is more the exception than the rule. Only a small percentage of battered women use this strategy to end the abuse they suffer. In fact, studies have shown that male batterers murder their victims four times more often than female victims murder their violent abuser.

Any discussion of domestic violence is necessarily depressing, given the high rate of victimization in the United States. However, many victims of violence are also survivors. As we have indicated, some victims fight back; others seek the assistance of family, friends, professionals, and institutions. Still others find ways, sometimes after years of victimization, to leave their abusive

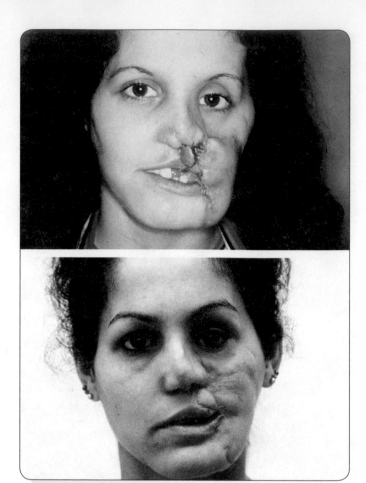

When seventeen-year-old Agnes Wilson tried to leave her abusive husband, he retaliated by shooting her in the face with a shotgun at close range. Through the National Domestic Violence Project, which provides free facial surgery to help lessen the physical scars of domestic abuse, she had several reconstructive operations over the course of almost a decade. Now, she shares her story so that other victims of domestic violence can learn about the program and receive help as well.

relationships, very often at great personal risk. Through individual and collective actions, they resist, challenge, and/or change the violent forces impacting their lives. Many victims of domestic violence have developed interesting and self-fulfilling methods by which to celebrate their survival. One such creative method is the *Clothesline Project,* which originated in Hyannis, Massachusetts, in 1990. The Clothesline consists of a clothesline hung with t-shirts designed by survivors of assault, rape, and incest using paint, magic markers, crayons, or elaborate embroidery to create their shirt. Families and friends of women who have died as a result of violence can and do make shirts to express their deep loss (Clothesline Project, 1995).

HAVE WE MADE PROGRESS IN THE ATTEMPT TO END DOMESTIC VIOLENCE AND IPV?

There is no clear-cut answer to the question of progress. The answer is both yes and no. One battered, violated, sexually assaulted

One of the tragedies of intimate partner violence is that often the perpetrator not only victimizes her/his partner but also sometimes turns the violence upon her/himself. For example, in 2010, Taylor Armstrong—known for her role on the reality TV program *The Real Housewives of Beverly Hills*—filed for divorce from her husband Russell (both pictured) after six years of marriage, claiming that he subjected her to a frightening life of physical and verbal abuse. Shortly after this, Russell hanged himself. Although before his death he acknowledged "problems" in their marriage and admitted to "pushing" his wife in the heat of the moment, he blamed the show for pushing the two of them to their limit.

among women in this age group is particularly acute (Biden, 2011). Moreover, the treatment of rape and battered victims has improved somewhat in recent years. Since the 1970s many state legislatures have changed their laws so that women no longer have to prove that they "fought back" or produce extensive evidence to corroborate their lived experience of rape or assault. Also, several states have passed "shield laws" that prevent the victim's previous sexual experiences from being used as evidence in a trial. In addition, most police officers now receive some type of training to sensitize them to the trauma of victims. Other indications of progress include the fact that more and more survivors are speaking out publicly, helping to lessen the stigma associated with battered women and rape victims; an increasing number of victim support and advocate services have appeared throughout the country; advocates, prosecutors, and survivors are finding ways to work together in states across the country to change laws and statutes; and more men are taking a public stand on domestic violence (U.S. Department of Justice, 2000, 2004, 2006a). Men challenging domestic violence has become an increasingly visible phenomenon both in the United States and in places such as South Africa, a country dubbed the *rape capital of the world* (go back to the In Other Places box on page 355; also see the Applying the Sociological Imagination box on page 376).

A Comparative Look at Battered Men

What evidence exists for female violence and male victimization? The suggestion that men are battered by women probably sounds implausible, if not silly, to some people. For others, the image of a skinny little henpecked man chased by a large, buxom wife with a rolling pin in her hand might immediately come to mind. In fact, some research during the 1970s and 1980s suggested that the phenomenon of battered husbands was as prevalent as that of battered wives. Studies based on national survey data in the 1980s found that in homes with couple violence, approximately one-fourth of the respondents indicated that men were victims and not perpetrators of violence, an additional one-fourth reported that women were victims and not offenders, and the remaining one-half reported that both wives and husbands were violent. Some recent studies suggest that there is a higher degree of female violence and aggression than previously thought (Wallace, 2007).

A major problem with claims that women use violence as often as men is that there is little or no clarification of how many of the women who use violence are actually acting in self-defense or retaliating against an abusive partner. Data from studies of violent relationships in which the police intervened clearly indicate that men are rarely the victims of battery. Research also clearly shows that men initiate violence in the majority of cases. This is especially true among married couples where husbands assault wives far more frequently than wives assault husbands. Moreover, men who kill their partner do so in self-defense far less frequently than do women who kill their partner. Further, rarely do battered women report initiating violence. The most frequent motive for violence in their self-reports is "fighting back," and the violent acts that they

or murdered woman is one too many. However, there are signs of progress. On the national level, due in part to the vigorous efforts of a variety of individuals and groups, as well as the support and efforts of Vice President Joseph Biden, author of the seventeen-year-old Violence against Women Act (a comprehensive approach to fighting domestic violence and violence against women, including improvement of official responses to violence against women by combining tough new penalties with programs to prosecute offenders and assist women victims of violence) it appears that violence against women has decreased over the past decade. A notable exception is women ages 16 to 24 who continue to suffer violence and abuse at extremely high rates. For instance, dating violence

APPLYING THE SOCIOLOGICAL IMAGINATION

MEN CHALLENGING WOMAN ABUSE AND VIOLENCE

Although we know that men are the primary perpetrators of violence against women and children and even against other men, most often our challenges of and activism against domestic violence is aimed at women—the victim. While it is certainly necessary for victims of violence to empower themselves and actively work to eliminate male violence, men must also be held accountable for their violence and abuse and to take responsibility in the fight to end domestic violence. The Texas Council on Family Violence (TCFV), one of the largest domestic violence coalitions in the United States, is doing just that. TCFV works to end violence against women through partnerships, advocacy, and direct services for women, children, and men. One of its major projects is the Men's Nonviolence Project, which pursues safety and justice for women, works to hold men accountable for their violence and abuse, and strives to eradicate the sexism from which violence against women grows. In addition, for more than ten years, women and children have marched along side men in high-heeled shoes in "Walk a Mile in Her Shoes" events held each year around the country. The brainchild of Frank Baird, a licensed marriage and family therapist, the march gives men the opportunity to publicly demonstrate their commitment to preventing sexualized and other violence against women. It also gives communities an opportunity to recognize and support men's commitment and it encourages people to talk more openly and publicly about these very important

"Walk a Mile in Her Shoes" events each year around the country, such as this one pictured at Ohio University in 2011, publicly urge an end to rape, sexual assault, and gender violence and help show that men can be part of the solution to the problem of gender violence.

issues. The walks raise hundreds of thousands of dollars each year to support local rape crisis services and domestic violence shelters. It seems that a growing number of men all over the world (see the In Other Places box on page 355) are choosing nonviolence and challenging other men to do the same. There is a plethora of Web sites for organizations and coalitions that focus on men's violence against women and challenge men to not only stop their own individual acts of violence toward women and children

but also to get involved with collective action against domestic violence. According to TCFV's Web site, a few separate actions are needed in order for violence against women to stop:

- Men as a group must make (and act on) the choice to stop gender-based violence. Women have always wanted violence against them to end.
- Changes must be made to American institutions so that they no longer inherently support violence against women.
- Addressing the symptoms of the violence against women through battering intervention projects alone will not work. The scale of the problem is too large to be fixed with the limited resources available. Rather, the root attitude leading to the violence must be changed worldwide.

www.tcfv.org/education/mnp.html
www.walkamileinhershoes.org
www.mensnonviolence.org/

Use these three Web sites as starting points and find other Web sites or links to organizations or coalitions led by men who are working to eliminate male violence and abuse. What kinds of programs, campaigns, and other actions are conducted by these groups? Can you ascertain their effectiveness in raising awareness about domestic violence? What kinds of men are involved in these efforts? Is there a comparable organization on your college campus? In your city? Would your campus benefit from such a group? Why? Why not?

---

report tend, most often, to be protective or self-defense actions (Felson and Cares, 2005).

Given that women are, on average, smaller and physically weaker than men, the abuse inflicted on them is far more severe and life-threatening than those instances of male or husband battering. In addition, not only are battered men less physically

injured than battered women, but they are also less trapped in an abusive relationship than women because men typically have greater economic resources and can more easily leave an abusive relationship as they usually do not have responsibility for children. Although some men are injured by a wife or lover, most women are unable to defend themselves effectively against male batterers.

Although gender-based violence is preponderantly inflicted by men on women and girls, this does not mean that men cannot be or have not also been victims of intimate partner violence. Gender-based violence and abuse of all kinds continues to be a pressing issue deserving of public attention.

In fact, most battered women find it far safer to submit to the battering than to fight back and risk being seriously injured or even killed (Anderson, 2002). In light of this fact, it seems inappropriate to generalize women's behavior in this regard as "husband abuse" or "battering." This is not meant, however, to trivialize male battering where it exists. And it does not alter the fact that domestic violence in all forms needs to be understood, investigated and prosecuted.

These facts notwithstanding, in response to those on either side of the debate about the sex of the primary perpetrator of domestic violence, sociologist Michael Johnson (2008) argues that there is more than one type of intimate partner violence. Most of our attention is directed toward domestic violence in which men are the primary perpetrators. However, there are also instances of violence that women are involved in. Johnson delineates three major, dramatically different, forms of partner violence: intimate terrorism, violent resistance, and situational couple violence. In the latter form of violence, both women and

men are perpetrators; the violence is most often a consequence of conflict that escalates into arguments, verbal abuse, and ultimately physical violence and abuse. Given that men are said to often be too embarrassed to report this kind of abuse when they are the victims, much of this kind of victimization goes unnoticed. Other scholars argue that a focus on males as equal victims of violence diminishes the fact that women are overwhelmingly the victim of domestic and IPV; they are ten times more likely than men to be injured as a consequence of battering or sexual assault. This is especially true among married couples where assaults by husbands against wives occur far more frequently than the reverse (Felson and Cares, 2005).

An interesting development in male abuse, and a fact that perhaps few people know, is that every year thousands of men turn to women's rape crisis agencies because there is no other place for men who have been sexually assaulted. Unlike in the case of female rape victims, however, the perpetrators of male rape are not the opposite sex. They are overwhelmingly other men, sometimes an intimate partner but more often a stranger. Although male rape occurs in non-institutional intimate relationships, it is estimated to occur most often within institutionalized settings such as prison. For example, more than one in five male inmates are raped at least once during their incarceration (Tjaden and Thoennes, 2006). Contrary to rape myths relative to male rape victims, regardless of size, shape, weight, age, race, ethnicity, social class, occupation, marital status, or sexual orientation, men can be and are sexually assaulted. According to some sources, about 3 percent of American men have experienced a rape at some point in their lifetime. One in every ten rape victims are male, almost three-fourths of whom were first raped before their eighteenth birthday. It can and does happen at home, work, outdoors, in a car, the military, prisons, locker rooms, rest rooms and public toilets ("Myths About Male Rape, the Rape of Men," 2011).

Nonetheless, this is an important form of violence that a growing number of men face. Many of the issues with male and female rape victims are the same. Both generally feel guilt, shame, and self-blame. Like women, men must also deal with "rape myths," which add to the emotional trauma of dealing with rape and prevents many men from reporting their rape. According to some authorities, in cases of rape, men's emotional needs are often ignored as cultural norms do not permit men to be victims. In an early study of male rape victims, a team of Memphis gynecologists found that in one free clinic for rape victims in Memphis, Tennessee, over a two-year period, six percent of the clients were male. More than one-half of these men had been abducted before the assault, and only two knew their attackers. Some observers have even suggested that there are more men raped in U.S. prisons than nonincarcerated women similarly assaulted. They estimate that young men are 5 times more likely to be attacked; and that the prison rape victims are 10 times more likely to contract HIV and other sexually transmitted infections (Stop Prisoner Rape, Inc., 2007). It goes without saying that most advocates for abused males believe the incidence of male rape is much higher because most male rapes go unreported and because the prison population is not included in rape figures.

Men are generally silent about their rape because they think most people will not believe them or because they think most people will think that they are gay. The fact is, although gay men are raped slightly more often than heterosexual men, 40 percent of men who are raped identify as exclusively heterosexual. In addition, the overwhelming majority of men who sexually assault other men identify themselves as heterosexual ("Myths About Male Rape, the Rape of Men," 2011). In the final analysis, men's silence about their victimization relative to rape contributes to the myth that rape affects only women and homosexuals. Research suggests that, as with women, most rapes of men are not prompted by sexual desire. Rather, it is an issue of power and control.

Gender-Based Violence: Both Ends of the Age Continuum

Today, hardly a day goes by without news of another child (or children) who has been severely abused, neglected, starved, or murdered, usually by a parent or close relative. The epidemic of violence against children is global. However, three out of four child killings in the industrialized world happen in the United States, and child suicide rates in this country are twice those of the rest of the industrialized world. As with woman victimization, the maltreatment of children takes many forms, including physical battering and abuse, child endangerment and neglect, sexual abuse and assault, psychological or emotional abuse, exploitation, murder, children thrown away, child runaways, and child abduction by parents and by strangers. Until recently, the greatest threat to children was believed to be stranger abductions. However, today a substantial body of research has documented that, of the thousands of children each year classified as missing or abducted, parents, not strangers, are responsible for the vast majority of these abductions—every day 559 children are kidnapped by a parent or other family member. In addition, the largest category of missing children today are runaway, thrown away, and homeless youth, a substantial number of whom have been victims of prior physical or sexual abuse in their homes. Their life on the streets continues this pattern of violence (Mignon, Larson, and Holmes, 2002).

Although child abuse has existed throughout human history, in the United States it attracted public interest only in the early 1960s when a published national survey described for the first time a series of behaviors known as the **battered-child syndrome**—a clinical condition in children who have received severe physical abuse, primarily from a parent or foster parent (Kempe et al., 1962). Even then, however, child abuse was not widely acknowledged to be a major issue until the 1980s, when expanded media coverage brought the problem to the attention of millions of Americans. Public opinion polls conducted in the 1970s revealed that only 1 in 10 Americans considered child abuse a serious problem. By the 1980s, the nation's awareness of the impact of crime and violence against children changed dramatically, as reflected in the change in that figure to 9 out of 10 (Childhelp, 2005; Gelles and Straus, 1987).

Moreover, new manifestations of child victimization have emerged over recent decades. For example, Munchausen syndrome by proxy is a rare form of abuse that is relatively new to public awareness and involves an adult, usually a White, middle-class mother with some knowledge or experience with medicine or nursing, who assumes the sick role indirectly (for example, by proxy) by feigning or inducing illness in her child (usually an infant or toddler). It can include making a child think that she or he is mentally ill, having the child committed to a mental hospital, claiming that the child suffers from depression or anxiety, inducing apnea (a cessation of breathing) by suffocating the child to the point of unconsciousness, scrubbing the child's skin with oven cleaner to produce a blistering rash, and various behavioral problems exhibited only in the presence of the perpetrator. The mother's motives range from a desire for attention from people—family, friends, and community—as the heroic caretaker of a tragically ill child, dislike or hatred for the child, to monetary returns from insurance. Because it takes many years of illness before the secret of Munchausen syndrome by proxy is discovered, the mortality rate for this form of child abuse is 9 percent (Asher-Meadow, 2001; Feldman, 2001).

Although not a new phenomenon, many Americans are only just beginning to recognize shaken-baby syndrome (SBS) as a form of child abuse. SBS is a form of child abuse in which the perpetrator, usually a parent or adult caretaker, shakes a child so violently that the brain sustains significant injury. Although the percentage of injuries to children as a result of SBS is not currently known, the syndrome is recognized as the most common cause of child maltreatment fatalities and accounts for the most long-term disability in infants and young children. Some of what we do know about SBS is that every year somewhere between 1,200 and 1,600 children in the United States are victims of SBS. About 25 percent to 30 percent of infant victims with SBS die from their injuries. Nonfatal consequences of SBS include varying degrees of visual impairment (e.g., blindness), motor impairment (e.g., cerebral palsy), and cognitive impairments (Barr, 2005).

Moreover, advances in technology now present serious threats and potential harm to children that we did not even imagine 10 or 20 years ago. Video cameras are increasingly used to produce homemade child pornography; personal computers with access to the Internet are used to instantly disseminate child pornography around the world and to solicit children for sexual encounters. Recently, a unique case of virtual rape of a child came to public attention when a 51-year-old New Jersey man acknowledged that he had made obscene phone calls to 12 girls, ranging in age from 8 to 14, and pleaded guilty to multiple counts of child endangerment. What made this case unique was that the man was also charged with aggravated sexual assault because he had persuaded one of his victims, a 10-year-old girl, to insert her finger into her vagina. The man never met his victim; his only contact was by phone. Nonetheless, he was convicted of aggravated sexual assault and given a 12-year sentence. The growing threat of telephone and online sexual predators notwithstanding, the overwhelming majority (90 percent) of juvenile sexual assault victims know their attacker—30 percent are family members and 60 percent are acquaintances (U.S. Department of Veteran Affairs, 2006; Kaminer, 2001).

GENDER-BASED CHILD ABUSE AND VIOLENCE

Just as for most types of violence and sexual assault, trying to determine the overall incidence of child abuse is a difficult task. However, the data do indicate, as we said earlier, that child victimization in the United States is an epidemic of national scope and importance and it involves children of all ages, races, classes, sexual orientations, and both sexes. Each year in the United States, it is estimated that millions of children directly experience or witness violence in their homes, neighborhoods, and schools. It is estimated that as many as 3.3 million children are exposed to violence against their mothers or female caretakers by family members alone (RAINN, 2008; American Psychological Association, 2001). Although there have been significant legislative changes relative to child victimization, children still have limited legal rights and are subject to the authority of their parents. Parents have a right and obligation to discipline their children, and few restrictions are placed on how they may do so. Perhaps more so than even woman abuse, parental violence against children historically has been considered a "family matter" with which the larger society should not interfere, except in extreme cases. In some ways, child abuse is even more difficult to deal with than woman abuse.

The Physical Assault of Children Because adults have great latitude in the methods they may use to discipline children, violence against children must be serious before it is labeled as abuse. (How many Americans recognize spanking as a form of violence? See Figure 11.3.) Of all the types of child abuse, physical abuse is probably the most likely to lead to intervention by outside forces because it most often leaves visible evidence (such as bruises, lacerations, and broken bones) that can be introduced into a court of law as evidence of maltreatment.

National surveys that ask Americans about violence in their homes have found considerable violence directed toward children. Most parents admit to using some kind of violence on their children, including beating up a child at least once, using severe forms of punishment, and threatening to use or actually using a gun or knife (Straus and Donnelly, 2001). National data show that of the most common forms of child abuse 78 percent of children suffered neglect, 18 percent physical abuse, 10 percent sex abuse, and 8 percent suffered from psychological maltreatment. Research results are mixed as to who receives more physical abuse, girls or boys. However, the most recent data show that 51 percent of abused children are female compared to 48 percent for males. Usually only one child in a family is abused. That child most often is the youngest, followed, in terms of frequency, by the oldest. Before the age of 10 or 11, boys are more frequently abused than girls. At that point, the incidence of abuse of girls becomes greater. Approximately 10 percent of the children in this country have a disability or chronic illness. The incidence of abuse and neglect among these children as well as children in foster care is twice as high as it is among the able-bodied child population. Almost 9 out of 10 child victims are of three racial or ethnic groups: Whites (44 percent), African Americans (22 percent), and Latinas/os (21 percent). For other groups, the percentages are 3 percent for multiple race victims, 1 percent for Native American and Alaska Natives, 1 percent for Asian and Pacific Islanders, and 8 percent unknown. However, in terms of the rate of victimization per 1,000 children within the population of their respective races, African American, Native American or Alaska Native, and multiple racial descent have the highest rates of victimization, 15.1, 11.6, and 12.4 respectively (Child Welfare Information Gateway, 2011; U.S. Department of Health and Human Services, 2009).

Each day in the United States, more than four children die as a result of child abuse in the home. Indeed, parental violence is among the five leading causes of death for children 18 years old and younger. More than three-fourths of the children who die due to child abuse and neglect are younger than 4 years old. However, child homicide risk is greater in the first year of life than in any other year of childhood with infant boys having the highest rate of fatalities in this age category. Infants are most likely to be killed by their mother during the first week of life but thereafter are more likely to be killed by a male, usually their father or stepfather or the mother's boyfriend. Maltreatment deaths are more associated with neglect (40 percent) than any other form of abuse. Boys have a slightly higher rate of death than girls, 2.4 compared to 2.1, and in terms of race and ethnicity, 39 percent are White, 29 percent are African American, and 17 percent are Hispanic. Native American, Alaska Native, Asian, Pacific Islander, and multiple race children account collectively for 4 percent of child abuse deaths. Eighty-five percent of these deaths are caused by one or more parents. One of the most striking differences between maltreatment fatalities and other types of maltreatment is that maltreatment fatalities are less frequently perpetrated by just one parent acting alone

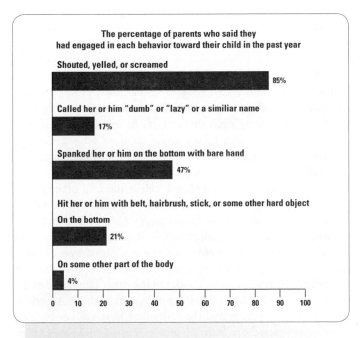

FIGURE 11.3 Is It Child Abuse?

Source: Adapted from Tamar Lewin, 1995, "Parents Poll Finds Child Abuse to Be More Common," *New York Times* (December 7). Copyright © 1995 by the New York Times Co. Reprinted by permission.

(U.S. Department of Health and Human Services, 2008, 2009; Childhelp, 2005).

It is estimated that as many as one-third of all abuse and neglect cases go unreported or undetected, especially if they involve middle-class or wealthy families. We can safely assume that like most other family violence, child abuse is often hidden in the privacy of the home, and most people do not admit to it. Furthermore, as with most statistics on violence, child assault statistics rely heavily on self-reports and on the reports of various professionals such as doctors, nurses, social workers, teachers, child-care workers, and police. The reporting of suspected child abuse has improved significantly in recent years because of increased training, awareness, and legislation. However, very often biases among professionals and others concerning race and class affect their decision on whether to report suspected cases of child assault. For example, research shows that doctors are twice as likely to label a Black child a victim of abuse as a White child. Similarly, they are twice as likely to miss abuse in two-parent families, compared with single-parent families, and they are more likely to label a case as abuse if the child is from a janitor's family than if the child is from a lawyer's family.

Current research indicates that certain characteristics predispose a child to being abused. Children born to unmarried parents; premature infants; children who are congenitally malformed or mentally retarded; twins; children born during a mother's depression illness, to parents with a history of domestic abuse, or into large families (with four or more children); children living in crowded home conditions and/or in isolated areas; and children whose parents are substance abusers are most vulnerable to abuse. It is estimated that 40 percent to 80 percent of the families who become child protective services cases have problems with alcohol or drugs (Baltimore County Police Department, 2007; Centers for Disease Control and Prevention, 2006; Childhelp, 2005). In addition, according to some studies, although child abuse and neglect occurs in all socioeconomic groups, children in low socioeconomic households have significantly higher maltreatment rates than other children; serious or fatal injuries to children are more prevalent among families whose annual income is below the poverty level; children in households with the lowest annual income (below $15,000) are more likely to be both emotionally and educationally neglected; children with no parent in the labor force or with a parent who is unemployed have higher rates of maltreatment than children with employed parents; compared to children living with married biological parents, children whose single parent have a live-in partner have more than 8 times the rate of maltreatment overall, over 10 times the rate of abuse, and more than 6 times the rate of neglect (Sedlak, et al., 2010; U.S. Department of Health and Human Services, 2009).

Because younger children are the most frequently reported victims of child abuse, until recently little attention was paid to abused adolescents. However, along with infants and toddlers, the highest rates of physical injury occur among adolescents (Barnett, Miller-Perrin, and Perrin, 2004; U.S. Department of Health and Human Services, 2009). Every year an unknown number of adolescents are abused. Many run away to someone or someplace, but most end up on the streets, unprotected and vulnerable to the abuse of a variety of unscrupulous people such as pimps, pornographers, and drug dealers. Sometimes adolescents fight back. Some researchers estimate that almost 2.5 million teenagers commit acts of violence against their parents every year. Approximately 2,000 parents die each year at the hands of a teenage son or daughter, often in self-defense or in retaliation against abuse. The killing of one's parents—known as parricide—is said to be most common during adolescence (Wallace, 2007). Almost all murders of parents are committed by sons. In the few cases that involve daughters, often a male accomplice is recruited. One common scenario of parricide involves a drunken, physically abusive father who is killed by a son who sees himself as the protector of the family. According to one source on parricide, 63 percent of boys aged 11 to 20 who commit homicide murder the man who was abusing their mother. Overall, however, teenagers are more likely to employ physical violence against mothers than against fathers (National Coalition Against Domestic Violence, 2007b; Wallace, 2007).

Abused children tend to have emotional scars and problems that they take into adulthood, such as low self-esteem and a tendency to abuse alcohol and other drugs. Moreover, children who grow up in abusive families, observing violence directed toward a parent, exhibit emotional problems and are likely to be "juvenile delinquents." In this context, nearly 2 million appear to have suffered (and more than 1 million still suffer) from posttraumatic stress disorder (PTSD) a long-term mental health condition often characterized by depression, anxiety, flashbacks, nightmares, and other behavioral and physiological symptoms (Family Violence Prevention Fund, 2006; U.S. Department of Health and Human Services, 2004b, 2008). Furthermore, of children who witness family violence, 60 percent of the boys eventually become batterers and 50 percent of the girls become victims; 73 percent of male abusers were abused as children and at least 80 percent of men in prison grew up in a violent home (National Coalition against Domestic Violence, 2007b; Childhelp, 2005; National CASA Association, 2000).

The Sexual Assault of Children Like child maltreatment and battering, child sexual abuse is also a major problem today, and public concern about this issue has been heightened by both numerous reports by adult survivors of its impact on their lives and the unfolding saga of sex abuse in the Catholic Church, the increasing incidents of sexual abuse associated with the Internet and the growing cases of child stranger abductions and child trafficking. On the one hand, celebrities and other public figures are calling attention increasingly to child sexual assault by sharing their childhood experiences of abuse. For example, the extremely successful talk show host Oprah Winfrey revealed that she was only 9 years old when she was raped by a 19-year-old cousin, the first of three family members to sexually assault her before she reached adulthood. On the other hand, one of the most public and controversial sex abuse scandals in American history involves priests and the Catholic Church. Over the past 25 or more years, more than 400 priests in the United States have been identified as child sexual abusers. The majority of their victims have been boys (many of whom served as altar boys). Studies of adult women and men estimate that as many as 20 million American adults have been victims of incest; 15 to 38 percent of women and about 10 percent of men were victims of sexual abuse as children, and almost half report that they kept the abuse to themselves ("Incest Sex Statistics in America," 2011; Kobbe, 2008). In addition, it is estimated that as many as 20 million American adults have been victims of incest, perpetrated by a father or mother figure.

In general, the term child sexual abuse refers to the use of a child for the sexual gratification of an adult. A central characteristic of any abuse is the dominant position of an adult, which allows him or her to use her or his power to force, coerce, or cajole compliance from a child who participates out of awe, fear, trust, respect, or love for the adult (Tower, 2007). Child sexual abuse or incestuous behavior is not confined to sexual intercourse. It may include nudity, disrobing, genital exposure, kissing, fondling a child's genitals and/or other body parts, masturbation, oral–genital contact, digital penetration, sodomy, as well as vaginal and anal intercourse. Child sexual abuse is not limited to physical contact; such abuse can include noncontact abuse, such as exhibitionism, voyeurism, child pornography, deliberately exposing a child to the act of sexual intercourse, and masturbating in front of a child. In addition, child sexual abuse can include sexual exploitation such as engaging a child or soliciting a child for the purposes of prostitution; using a child to film, photograph, or model pornography (American Humane Fact Sheets, 2008; American Psychological Association, 2001), and as we discussed earlier in the case of "virtual rape," it can include coercion via telephone. Moreover, one in five children are solicited sexually while on the Internet.

Child sexual abuse can be divided into two basic categories depending on who the abuser is: familial abuse and extrafamilial abuse. Familial abuse is generally referred to as **incest**—the sexual abuse by a blood relative who is assumed to be a part of the child's family. Most definitions of incest include stepfathers and live-in boyfriends. Because most child sexual abuse is perpetrated by family members, our discussion focuses on familial rather than extrafamilial abuse.

Prevalence Because of the extremely sensitive, embarrassing, and outrageous nature of incest, victims and perpetrators often keep it hidden. Family members and others outside the family cite personal reasons for not reporting known instances of child sexual abuse. The most common reason cited by adults is their reluctance to believe a child's claim of abuse and their hesitance to accuse an adult of such behavior. However, the reality is that children rarely lie about being abused. Thus, official reports of incest severely underestimate its actual occurrence. Despite the underestimation of the true magnitude of the problem, of all victims of sexual assault reported to law enforcement agencies it is estimated that 1 million or more children under the age of 18 are currently involved in incestuous relationships. Furthermore, 29 percent of all forcible rapes occurred when the victim was less than 11 years old. Research also indicates that 46 percent of children who are raped are victims of family members. Some studies have found that less than 2 percent of all allegations are false; in cases where children appear to have made false allegations, it was usually the result of adult manipulation. It is estimated that one in four girls are sexually abused before age 18. For boys, the figure is one in six. The sexual abuse of boys takes place less often in their homes and less often is the perpetrator a family member. Although most sexually abused children remain silent about their abuse, boys more often

Although the majority of children who are abducted each year are taken by a parent, in one of the most notorious cases of child stranger abduction in recent years, in 1991, 11-year-old Jaycee Dugard was abducted while walking from home to a school bus stop. Found in 2009, living with her abductors (Phillip Garrido and his wife Nancy), Dugard later reported that she lived in virtual solitary confinement in an area behind the Garridos' home, where she was repeatedly subjected to rape, manipulation, and verbal abuse. She gave birth to two daughters fathered by her abductor while in that backyard prison.

than girls say they did not talk to anyone about the abuse. ("Incest Statistics in America," 2011; Women's Web, 2008; Darkness to Light, 2008).

Approximately 93 percent of the offenders are known to the child. An estimated 77 percent of reported abusers are parents, 16 percent are other relatives, and only 6 percent are nonrelated or strangers. Typical child sex abusers—50 to 60 percent—are fathers, stepfathers, uncles, grandfathers, and brothers. The majority of incest cases involve stepfather and stepdaughter or father and daughter; only a small proportion of incest cases involve fathers and sons, and even more rare are cases that involve mother and son. For most victims, the abuse continues for years (National Coalition against Domestic Violence, 2007b; Childhelp, 2005). U.S. studies report that males are the abusers in up to 95 percent of reported cases of child sexual abuse, with many beginning to molest children by age 15 (e.g., about one-third of perpetrators are juveniles). However, the average age of perpetrators is 32. While up to 80 percent of perpetrators were themselves victims of sexual abuse as a child, more than 80 percent of sexually abused boys never become adult predators (Lutheran Family Services, 2008; Family and Children's Services of Central Maryland, 2006).

The underreporting of male child sexual abuse notwithstanding, we do know that, in general, boys, like girls, are most likely to be victimized by men. In addition, boys are more likely than girls to be one of a number of victims of the same perpetrator; boys are more likely than girls to be victims of both sexual and physical abuse; and boys are also more likely to be subjected to anal abuse than are girls (Mignon, Larson, and Holmes, 2002). Some researchers have pointed to a cycle of sexual abuse that they describe with the term **transmission of victimization**—abuse carried from one generation to the next. The cycle is as follows: Sexually abused girls often have mothers who were also sexually abused as a child. A significant proportion of women who were abused as a child grow up and marry or live with partners who abuse them and may also abuse their daughters, thus transmitting victimization from mother to daughter. Children who live with an abused mother are 12 times more likely to be sexually abused.

As with physical assault, White children are more likely than either African American or Latina/o children to be sexually assaulted by a family member within the household rather than someone outside the household. Among victims of child sexual abuse, 75 percent of White children are assaulted by a member of the household, as opposed to 13 percent of African American children and 9 percent of Latina/o children. In addition, the abuse of boys generally takes place for a shorter period of time. Furthermore, sexually abused boys are typically from poorer socioeconomic backgrounds than are sexually abused girls, and abused boys from families where the mother has less than a high school education are more than twice as likely as boys in families where the mother has higher education to report abuse. Moreover, Asian American boys are three times as likely as White boys to report sexual abuse (9 percent vs. 3 percent). Latinos also report higher rates of sexual abuse than White boys. The sexual abuse rates among African American and White boys are very similar.

The Effects of Child Abuse An estimated 39 million survivors of childhood sexual abuse exist in America today but researchers have only recently begun to focus on the long-term consequences of child abuse. A large percentage of sexually abused children become prostitutes or drug users, and sexually abused female runaways are more likely to be involved in deviant or criminal behavior than nonabused females (Andersen, 2008; Darkness to Light, 2008). In addition, victims frequently suffer any one or more of a wide range of ailments, which can include the following: (1) physical ailments, such as bruises, genital pain and bleeding, problems walking or sitting, eating disorders, headaches and stomachaches, sexually transmitted infections, brain injuries, infants and toddlers who have been shaken violently sometimes suffer bleeding within the brain; (2) emotional problems, such as anxiety, fear, guilt, nightmares, flashbacks, depression, low self-esteem, multiple personalities, temper tantrums, hostility, aggression, perfectionism, or phobias; (3) cognitive problems, including learning disabilities, poor attention and concentration, and declining grades in school; and (4) behavioral problems, such as social withdrawal,

aggression, sexualized behavior or sexual preoccupation, regression or immaturity, hyperactivity, and family or peer conflicts (Darkness to Light, 2008; Barnett, Miller-Perrin, and Perrin, 2004).

Food, sex, alcohol, and/or drugs deaden painful memories of the abuse and expel reality, at least temporarily. Bulimia and anorexia are also forms of self-punishment, eventually leading to the ultimate self-victimization, suicide. Seventy percent to 80 percent of sexual abuse survivors report excessive drug and alcohol use. Young female victims of sexual abuse are more likely to develop eating disorders as adolescents and three times more likely to develop psychiatric disorders or alcohol and drug abuse in adulthood, than girls who are not sexually abused. Promiscuity is often associated with child sexual abuse. For example, more than 75 percent of teenage prostitutes have been sexually assaulted and women who were raped in childhood are three times more likely to become pregnant before age 18. It is estimated that 60 percent of teen first pregnancies are preceded by experiences of molestation, rape, or attempted rape. The average age of these victims' offender is 27 (Darkness to Light, 2008).

Among male survivors, more than 70 percent seek psychological treatment for issues such as substance abuse, suicidal thoughts, and attempted suicide. Furthermore, males who have been sexually abused are more likely to violently victimize others. In addition, when child victims of sexual abuse become adults, they often have problems with their sexuality; many avoid intimacy and emotional bonding; and many become abusers themselves or victims of spousal battering and abuse (Women's Web, 2008; Darkness to Light, 2008). According to some researchers, one of the consequences for male victims is linked to the fact that definitions of masculinity in U.S. culture can compound the consequences of male sexual victimization. For example, some studies have found that the most common reaction of boys is to try to reassert their masculinity, often inappropriately. This can take the form of disobedience, hostility, aggression, fighting, violence, and destructiveness, or these boys may experience some confusion about their sexual identity (Mignon, Larson, and Holmes, 2002).

Finally, it should be pointed out that not all children who are sexually abused follow a deviant or self-victimization life course. With the support of parents, family members, friends, appropriate therapies, as well as individual interpersonal strength and resiliency, many of these children build healthy and constructive lives.

GENDER-BASED ELDER ABUSE AND VIOLENCE

As our earlier historical account of family violence illustrates, abuse of the elderly by their adult children (and sometimes grandchildren or other relatives) is not new, nor was it always viewed as a problem. Recently, however, elder abuse has gained widespread public attention and has been defined by some people as a major social problem. The term **elder abuse** is an umbrella term referring to any knowing, intentional, or negligent act by a caregiver or any other person that causes harm or a serious risk of harm to an older adult including physical, psychological, and material maltreatment and neglect. Although many older Americans are independent and in good health, the chances of poor health and dependency increase with age, as does the potential for victimization in any one or more of the following forms: physical violence (such as inflicting, or threatening to inflict, physical pain or injury, physical restraint, overmedication, or depriving them of a basic need—withholding medicine, food, or personal care); emotional or psychological abuse (such as verbal abuse, threats, intimidation, isolation, and neglect); sexual maltreatment (such as rape or other sexual assault); material abuse (such as theft or concealment or misuse of assets, money, or other personal property); neglect (such as the refusal or failure by those responsible to provide food, shelter, health care, or protection for an elder); abandonment (such as desertion by anyone who has assumed the responsibility for care or custody of an elder); and personal violation (such as placement in a nursing home against the person's will).

Each year in the United States, an estimated 2.1 million older Americans are victims of physical, psychological, or other forms of abuse and neglect. Roughly two-thirds of all elder abuse perpetrators are family members, most often the victim's adult child or spouse. Research has shown that the abusers in many instances are financially dependent on the elder's resources and have problems related to alcohol and drugs. According to some experts on elder abuse,

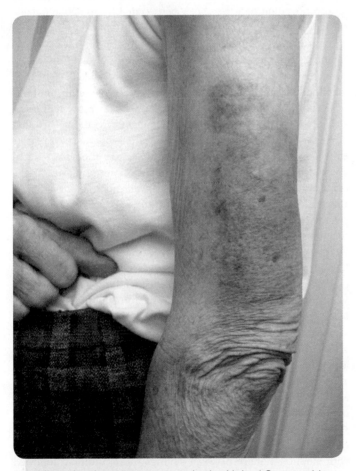

Like other low-status groups in the United States, older Americans are highly vulnerable to neglect and abuse. Although many older people are independent and healthy, as life expectancy increases more of the elderly population will spend some time in either a convalescent center or in their homes dependent on family members as caretakers. According to data on reported cases of elder abuse, family members are reported to be the perpetrators in 9 out of 10 cases.

these statistics may just be the tip of the iceberg because for every case of elder abuse and neglect reported to authorities, experts estimate that there may be as many as five cases not reported. Research suggests elders who have been abused tend to die earlier than those who are not abused, even in the absence of chronic conditions or life-threatening disease (they are three times more likely to die within 10 years than those who have not been abused). According to national statistics, elder abuse is grossly under reported because vulnerable older adults who are being abused find it very difficult to tell anyone due to shame and fear. The problem is exacerbated by the recent revelation that, although required by law to report suspected elder abuse of their patients, doctors seldom report such cases. Doctors report only 2 percent of the elder abuse and neglect cases recorded each year. According to a recent study the actual figure might be even lower (North Carolina Division of Aging and Adult Services, 2011; American Psychological Association, 2008b; Breton, 2008; National Center on Elder Abuse, 2005).

Who Are the Abused and the Abusers? As with women and children, some older adults run a greater risk of being abused than others: women, older people with physical or mental impairments, those who have problems with substance abuse, and those dependent on a caretaker to meet their basic needs. Although there is little current research that examines race- or ethnic-specific cases of elder abuse or the factors involved, we know that elder abuse affects men and women of all ethnic backgrounds and social status; it occurs in private residences and in facilities. Some observers have suggested that among specific racial or ethnic groups, African American elders might be at slightly higher risk than Whites, because, for example, African American seniors, especially grandmothers, are more likely than Whites to take in needy children, grandchildren, and even great-grandchildren (Wallace, 2007). Of the current research available relative to race and elder abuse, researchers suggest that over three-fourths (77 percent) of the victims of elder abuse and neglect are White, compared to 16 percent African American, 5 percent Latina/o, 0.7 percent Asian American/Pacific Islander, and 0.6 percent Native American. In addition, female elders, especially those 80 years of age and older (43 percent), are the most likely victims of elder abuse. In fact, older women are more likely than younger women to experience violence for a longer period of time, to be in current violent relationships, and to have health and mental health problems. Two out of every three (66 percent) elder abuse victims are females compared to 34 percent for males. Among married elderly couples, violence and abuse are typically perpetrated by the male spouse and are often a continuation of an earlier pattern of abuse. Elderly women who abuse their husbands may be enacting revenge for previous abuse by the husband. This probably reflects women's general lack of strength, their general lack of power, their devalued status, and the fact that they outnumber elderly men. Not everyone, however, agrees that elderly women run a greater risk of abuse than elderly men. One set of researchers, for example, found little difference in the victimization rates of older women and men, but the abuse inflicted by husbands was much more severe and serious than that inflicted by wives (Teaster et al., 2006; National Center on Elder Abuse, 2005, 2006; Wallace, 2007).

Studies repeatedly show that the overwhelming majority of confirmed cases of elder abuse (89 percent) occur in domestic settings. Although the picture is still inconclusive, family members alone are reported to be the perpetrators in 7 out of 10 substantiated cases of elder abuse and/or neglect. More specifically, the abuser is most often an adult child (33 percent), a spouse (11 percent), or some other family member (22 percent). Perpetrators of elder abuse are almost evenly female (53 percent) and male (47 percent) (Teaster et al., 2006). Among children who abuse their parents, sons are most likely to use physical violence whereas daughters are more likely to practice elderly neglect, and the most frequent offenders are adult daughters. This probably reflects the fact that because of gender role socialization, daughters most often have the responsibility of caring for an aging parent or other relative. Often, adult children who abuse their elderly parents were themselves abused and thus learned that violence toward intimates is acceptable behavior. In some cases, they may be acting in retaliation against an abusive parent (Wallace, 2007). In other cases, the abuser is financially dependent on the older person, and the abuse stems from this dependency and lack of power in the relationship.

The greatest amount of attention to domestic violence has been focused on heterosexual victims, primarily heterosexual women. Like their younger counterparts, lesbian, gay, bisexual, and transgender elder abuse victims have been frequently overlooked and/or ignored. Although the issues facing LGBT elders may be different than non-LGBT elders, nonetheless, as we have already reported, about one in four LGBT persons are battered by a partner. As with elder abuse in general, this omission is related to the devaluation and lack of respect for elder people as well as the negative cultural and societal attitudes toward LGBT individuals, including homophobia.

Although over two-thirds of U.S. states have focused enacted mandatory reporting laws to deal with elder abuse, some people question the effectiveness of these laws, given that they address the problem only after the fact. Critics have suggested that a more successful strategy might be to provide adult children with greater institutional assistance and support in caring for their elderly parents. We end this chapter with a brief discussion of, perhaps, the least known of all types of violence, namely sibling abuse.

SIBLING ABUSE

Given the enormity of the statistics we have presented in this chapter, who do you suppose most commonly abuses children? Perhaps surprisingly, the answer is not mothers or fathers or other adults, but siblings. Although the media, the public, researchers, social workers, and other relevant professionals have focused our attention on child and woman abuse, seldom have they discussed sibling violence and abuse. This fact notwithstanding, according to some authorities on the subject, it is perhaps the most common form of family violence. Indeed, it is probably even more common than child abuse (by parents) or spouse abuse. Like other forms of victimization, sibling abuse involves a number of forms of maltreatment including mental, emotional, and sexual abuse. It is estimated that 53 children in 100 are *dangerously violent* toward a brother or sister. It seems that when abusive acts occur between siblings, they are often not perceived as abuse.

However, siblings hit, slap, kick, and beat each other so frequently that few of us pay much attention to this behavior or

consider it to be a form of family violence. Indeed, such behavior is so commonplace that it is almost normative. For example, most of us have probably at one time or another during our childhood engaged in some type of altercation with a sibling: pulling hair, pushing, name-calling, biting, pinching, poking, scaring, and so on. Parents (and society at large) often do not take these behaviors seriously, viewing them as normal childhood behavior, labeling it sibling rivalry. In fact, critics agree with parents, arguing that much of the aggressive behavior between siblings is not really serious and thus should not be labeled as abusive. Although research confirms this argument, finding that the majority of violence between siblings could be classified as nonabusive, the fact remains that a high frequency of violence does occur between siblings that can definitely be classified as abusive (University of Michigan Health System, 2008). A complicating factor in sibling violence is that in some cases, siblings may switch back and forth between the roles of abuser and victim.

Research studies estimate that upward of 29 million siblings physically abuse each other every year. These acts are not minor acts of hitting. Rather, over half of them could have resulted in legal prosecution had they been perpetrated by someone outside the family. Added to this is the fact that 1 in 10 murders in families is committed by siblings. Coupled with physical violence between siblings, sibling sexual abuse or sibling incest is also seldom talked about but is perhaps a more common occurrence than parent–child incest. Sibling sexual assault is typically brother-to-sister initiated or coerced, but sometimes it occurs between same-sex siblings as well. Sibling victims are often much younger than the perpetrator. Sibling sexual abuse perpetrated by adolescents often occurs repeatedly and over a longer period of time than adolescent-perpetrated abuse against nonfamily members. This is due primarily to the ready availability of a sibling and the convenience of being at home. Even in old age, siblings often abuse one another. Some scholars suggest that it is often the case that, like elderly spouse abuse, sibling abuse in old age tends to be a continuation of earlier family violence (American Psychological Association, 2008b; Mignon, Larson, and Holmes, 2002).

The highest rates of sibling violence tend to occur in families with only male children. Families with all daughters have lower levels of sibling violence and, in fact, the presence of girls in the family reduces the level of sibling violence. Sibling violence is also higher among children in families in which child and spouse assault also occur. Sibling violence is more common during the youngest ages, when siblings are home together, and decreases as children get older and spend less time at home and with each other. Some children both physically and sexually abuse their younger siblings. Various research studies have reported a significant amount of overlap between the various forms of sibling abuse, with emotional abuse between siblings most common, followed by sexual abuse and then physical abuse (University of Michigan Health System, 2008; Wieche, 2002).

Little is known about the reasons for sibling violence. Some researchers have suggested that it is a learned response. Children raised in a violent environment learn that physical punishment is an appropriate way to deal with certain situations. In contrast, children raised in an environment free of violence learn other ways to resolve conflicts with siblings and later with other intimates.

Writing Your Own Script

RECOGNIZING ABUSIVE BEHAVIOR

As you have learned from reading this chapter as well as from simply being a member of contemporary U.S. society, violence and abuse in intimate relationships are of serious concern. Because they often occur in the privacy of our intimate relationships and in the privacy of our homes, we sometimes do not know what to do or where to go if we or someone we know is a victim of intimate violence.

If you are involved in an intimate relationship, consider your relationship for a moment. Is it a violence-free relationship, or is it bad for your health? Is it heading into dangerous territory? Has your partner ever been abusive? With the high incidence of verbal, physical, emotional, and sexual abuse in intimate relationships, it is very important to know as much as possible about our partners in terms of the likelihood that they could be or are abusive or violent. Although there is no specific profile of an abuser, the data presented in this chapter suggest certain characteristics or factors that are prevalent among abusers, such as poor self-esteem, rigidity, and excessive dependency. Are these characteristics familiar to you? If they are characteristic of you or your partner, they should alert you to the possibility that the person with such characteristics could become abusive or violent. (This is not to say that this will happen, but you should be alert for other signs of abusive behavior and seek help before violence occurs.)

Take the following test to find out if your relationship is violent or headed toward violence. Answer each of the following categories of questions. If you answer yes to more than two of the categories, you should seek help. Do you know or suspect that someone you know is in a violent relationship? Share these questions with that person and then help her or him get appropriate assistance.

Is Your Partner Someone Who…

1. Is obsessively jealous, aggressive, and possessive toward you; won't let you have friends; checks up on you; won't accept your leaving her or him?
2. Tries to control you by being very bossy, giving you orders and demanding that you follow her or him; makes all of the decisions; or doesn't take your opinion seriously or doesn't allow you to have an opinion at all?
3. Is threatening and whom you are afraid of? Do you worry about how this person will react to things you do or say? Does this person ever threaten you, or use or own weapons?
4. Is violent? Does this person have a history of violence: losing her or his temper, bragging about mistreating others? Has the person assaulted someone within or outside of the family or has the person committed some other violent crime?
5. Pressures you for sex, is forceful about sex? Accepts no when you say no? Thinks that women or girls are sex objects, attempts to manipulate you or make you feel guilty by saying things like, "If you really loved me, you would…?" Does the person get too serious about the relationship too fast for comfort?
6. Abuses alcohol or other drugs and/or pressures you to take them? Does the person use alcohol or other drugs as an excuse for aggression?
7. Mistreats you and then blames you for the mistreatment? Tells you that you provoked it, that you brought it on yourself?
8. Has a history of bad relationships and blames the other person for all of the problems?
9. Has very traditional views about women's and men's roles; believes that men should be in control and powerful and that women should be passive and submissive?
10. Has hit, pushed, slapped, choked, kicked, forced sex with you, or otherwise abused you?
11. Isolates you from your family, friends, neighbors, and the community? Makes your family and friends concerned about your safety?

Source: Adapted from: the Santa Clara Police Department Family Violence Center. www. scpd. org/crime/domestic_violence. html (2008, October 5).

Strengthening Marriages and Families

Based on all available data, family violence is of epidemic proportions globally. As we have shown, women and children are particularly vulnerable to this type of violence. According to Amnesty International, domestic and family violence is a fundamental violation of human rights and is not acceptable in any form. It cannot be justified by any political, religious, or cultural claims.

Systemic and systematic inequality and discrimination against women allow violence to occur daily and with impunity. If we are serious about strengthening marriages and families we must individually and collectively take responsibility and help eradicate violence against women and children so that they may achieve lives of equality and dignity. Individuals, national, state, and local government agencies, and community social service agencies must work to provide better and more comprehensive responses to domestic violence, no matter who the victim. The development of partnerships between advocacy and direct services for women, children, and men are needed. This would include providing more funds for additional shelters and more services within these shelters. Policies and programs are needed to provide parenting education and training to both women and men that address the batterer who is both a caretaker of the children and the person exposing them to violence and abuse. Additionally, changes in laws and the way the criminal justice system works are needed as well as the development of effective strategies to make batterers accountable for the well-being and safety of children in their families. These strategies should be built upon an accurate data collection system that allows decision makers to begin understanding the presence of violence in families. Given that much of societal and family violence is tied to sexism and male power, we must reconsider and reconceptualize our current thinking and practices in terms of women's and men's roles in marriages, families, and other intimate relationships to eradicate the sexism from which violence against women grows. A narrow devotion to traditional gender roles heightens, in our view, the potential vulnerability of women, children, and the elderly in marriages and families.

SUMMARY

Family and intimate relationship violence are deeply rooted in human history and widespread in contemporary societies around the world. The family is the major context within which most violence in this country occurs. A number of myths about family violence, ranging from the notion that it is a rare occurrence to the idea that women secretly desire to be raped, obscure our view of and knowledge about its pervasiveness. Although any family member can be abused, women and children are the most common victims. Woman battering is perhaps the most common and one of the most underreported crimes in this country. Its cyclic nature has been described in terms of the battered-woman syndrome. Although we do not know a lot about battering across race and sexual orientation, we know that it can be found among all groups. Family violence includes not only battering, but also sexual assault. Here, too, women and girls are the typical victims. Although information on the incidence and prevalence of marital rape is limited, there is a growing public awareness that husbands can and do rape their wives.

Some of the most visible effects of violence against women are low self-esteem, self-hate, economic and emotional dependence on others, fear, anxiety, and self-destructive behavior. Victims also develop a number of survival strategies, some of which, such as overeating and substance abuse, are self-destructive. In addition, a growing number of women are dealing with their violent situation by fighting back. Women sometimes use violence against men, although they most often do so in self-defense against a threatened or actual physical attack.

Men are also victims of violence. However, because men often do not report their abuse we cannot be sure of the prevalence of male abuse.

Women are not the only major victims of family violence: Somewhere around 2.1 million children are abused each year by parents or someone close to the family. We are only beginning to appreciate the extent of this problem today. Other, less visible victims of family violence include siblings, the elderly, and lesbians and gays.

KEY TERMS

infanticide	sexual assault	battered-child syndrome	transmission of	elder abuse
femicide	battered-woman	incest	victimization	
rape syndrome	syndrome			
woman battering				

QUESTIONS FOR STUDY AND REFLECTION

1. Do you have siblings? Same sex or different sex? Did or do you engage in behaviors that can be defined as abusive? When does behavior between siblings become abusive? What should we do about sibling abuse? Should sibling abusers be subject to the same penalties as other abusers? Why or why not? What if your 7-year-old son sexually assaulted your 3-year-old daughter? What would you do?
2. Which child-rearing philosophies and economic and social factors contribute to the prevalence of child abuse in the United States today? Should children be spanked? In your

opinion, is there a difference between spanking and child abuse? Have you ever hit a child with something other than your hand? Do you think your behavior constituted battering? Why or why not?

3. In your opinion, is it possible for a man to rape his wife? A woman to rape her husband? Why or why not? To what degree would you be willing to remain in a marriage if your spouse raped you or you raped your spouse?

4. What factors might explain why some societies are more likely than others to abuse their elderly members? What possible reasons do you think a person could have for battering an elderly parent? Have you ever been physically or psychologically abusive to one or both of your parents or grandparents? How might we deal with the problem of elder abuse?

ADDITIONAL RESOURCES

SOCIOLOGICAL STUDIES

BEATTIE, ELISABETH, AND MARY ANGELA SHAUGHNESSY. 2000. *Sisters in Pain: Battered Women Fight Back.* Lexington, KY: University Press of Kentucky. This book is based on interviews with 7 of 10 battered women in Kentucky who, in the 1980s and early 1990s, stood up to their brutally abusive husbands and boyfriends, and were subsequently convicted of killing, conspiring to kill, or assaulting the men who had abused them for years. The media began referring to them as the "Sisters in Pain," a name they embraced. In 1995, when Kentucky's Governor Brereton Jones learned of the Sisters in Pain and their stories, he became convinced the women had acted in self-defense. In a controversial move, Jones granted all of the women clemency on his last day in office. This was only the third mass clemency for battered women in U.S. history. Among the many topics of violence discussed, this book provides an example framework for students to address the relentless question: *Why don't abused women just leave?*

KIMMEL, MICHAEL S., AND MICHAEL A. MESSNER. 2010. *Men's Lives,* 8th ed. Boston: Allyn & Bacon. An excellent anthology focusing on the male experience. The book is organized around specific themes that define masculinity and the issues that men confront over their lifetime. Part 10 deals with men and violence, including some poignant articles on the American context of male violence and the rape of women.

MILLER, SUSAN. 2005. *Victims as Offenders: The Paradox of Women's Violence in Relationships.* New Jersey: Rutgers University Press. This timely book explores the "mutuality debate" (that women and men are equally perpetrators of intimate partner violence). The author demonstrates the seeming inability—or unwillingness—of the criminal legal system to recognize that gender (as well as race, class, and sexual orientation) matters in intimate partner violence, but even more importantly, she explores and attempts to answer a myriad of compelling questions raised by recent statistics that indicate that women's arrests for assault have increased 40 percent while male arrests for this offense have decreased by 1 percent. Miller argues that law enforcement strategies, designed to protect women, have often victimized women in different ways. She offers a critical analysis of the theoretical assumptions framing the study of violence and unveils a reality that looks very different from what current statistics on domestic violence imply.

RISTOCK, JANICE, L., ED. 2011. *Intimate Partner Violence in LGBTQ Relationships.* New York: Routledge. This edited volume brings together innovative research about intimate partner violence that is specific to the lives of LGBTQ people. It includes research of a global nature, including research conducted in the United States, the United Kingdom, Canada and Australia and it is framed around central themes: conceptualizing violence; exploring differing spaces and lived experiences of violence; and the ethical challenges of responding to violence. The contributors also consider issues of race, class, gender, sexuality and other social differences, moving beyond a simple gender lens to one involving a framework of intersectionality.

FILM

Domestic Violence 2. 2002. This documentary about domestic violence is long, painful, and sometimes difficult to watch. Educators should preview the film before using it and be prepared to deal with the emotions generated by viewing extreme violence. The film is based on filmmaker Frederick Wiseman's experiences following the Tampa, Florida, police as they responded to domestic violence calls, and spending time with women in a shelter for abused women. Although it does not offer solutions to the problem of domestic violence, it does provide an excellent framework for students to examine and come to understand the systemic nature of domestic violence—the system through which violence works and through which it is perpetuated.

Provoked: A True Story. 2006. This film is the true story of a Punjabi woman who leaves India and moves to London after marrying a London-based man. In the beginning, the marriage is fine, but soon the husband begins drinking and having affairs with numerous women. He also subjects his wife to spousal rape. After two children and experiencing 10 years of domestic violence, out of fear, she sets him on fire while he is sleeping, 2 hours after his last bout of domestic violence. She is sentenced to life imprisonment for murdering her abusive husband but is brought to justice through the campaigning of the Southall Black Sisters, an NGO that fights against domestic violence. After 3 1/2 years in jail, she is freed and reunites with her two children.

LITERARY WORKS

DRISCOLL, FRANCIS. 1997. *The Rape Poems.* New York: Pleasure Boat Studio. The author of this book of poetry believes that we are the stories we tell. The book includes poems that recount the author's experience with rape in a highly detailed way. In one poem, for example, the poet describes her postrape physical examination "inch by inch." In another, she describes a woman who was looking for someone to call to talk to about her rape. The book consists of a set of compelling poems that can be used to analyze the experiences and consequences of sexual assault against women.

HAULSEY, KUWAMA. 2001. *The Red Moon.* New York: Villard, a Division of Random House. Among the many sociologically relevant topics this novel deals with are the complex subjects of female circumcision, ritual circumcision, and routine domestic violence in a reclusive Samburu culture in rural Kenya. It is an excellent novel to help students understand the connection between women's subordinate status and violence.

INTERNET

www.nomsv.org Web site maintained by the National Organization on Male Sexual Victimization. This site is designed to meet the needs of adult male survivors of sexual abuse through the provision of a number of resources, including a chat room, a newsletter, books, news updates, and a directory of clinicians and therapists.

www.silcom.com/~paladin/madv/ Sponsored by the Paladin Group Grant Mentors, this is a practical research-oriented site that offers advocacy and information as well as a variety of other resources including addresses of shelters.

www.stopviolence.com/domviol/menagainst.htm This Web site offers a variety of resources to raise men's awareness about the problems of men's violence and to end their silence about it. Because the vast majority of violence against men is also committed by other men, some of the resources on this site explore problems with masculinity and how to find ways of "being a man" without being violent or homophobic. It is a good site for students to explore information about men who are working, both individually and collectively, to reduce the violence of men.

www.ojp.usdoj.gov/bjs The U.S. Department of Justice Web site provides statistics, data, and reports on crime and victims, criminal offenders, law enforcement, prosecution, courts and sentencing, expenditures, and other topics related to domestic violence and child abuse.

Succeed with MyFamilyLab®
www.myfamilylab.com

Watch. Explore. Read. The New MyFamilyLab is designed just for you. Each chapter features a pre-test and post-test to help you learn and review key concepts and terms. Experience Marriages and Families in action with dynamic visual activities, videos, and readings to enhance your learning experience.

Here are a few activities you will find for this chapter.

Watch on **myfamilylab.com**

Video clips feature important concepts in the study of Marriages and Families. Watch:
- Topeka, Kansas Decriminalizes Spousal Abuse

Explore on **myfamilylab.com**

Social Explorer is an interactive application that allows you to explore Census data through interactive maps. Explore the Social Explorer Activity:
- Adolescent Violence and Social Conditions

Read on **myfamilylab.com**

MyFamilyLab includes primary source readings from classic and contemporary sociologists from around the world. Read:
- Gelles: "Through a Sociological Lens: Social Structure and Family Violence"

12

The Process of Uncoupling: Divorce in the United States

What Will You Learn?

- Define and understand the sociological meaning of key terms.
- Describe the various stations of divorce.
- Apply the sociological imagination to examine the risk factors involved with divorce.
- Assess the pro and con arguments for eliminating no-fault divorce.
- Increase your awareness and understanding of how divorce affects the lives of all family members, especially children.
- Question how societal changes over time affect the divorce rate as well as how social policies can help strengthen marriages and families.

IN THE NEWS

Sioux County, IA

Located in northwest Iowa, Sioux Country is experiencing a major transformation in its pattern of family life. Only 40 years ago, this rural area looked more like America in the early 1900s. Divorce was largely unknown, few women were in the paid labor force, and most of it residents attended church services on a regular basis. Stores were closed on Sundays, and it was only in the late 1970s that its main city, Sioux Center, granted its first liquor license. In recent years, however, the divorce rate began to skyrocket, with a sevenfold increase since 1970, narrowing the gap between this rural part of the country and urban areas

(continued on next page)

(continued from previous page)

(Tavernise and Gebeloff, 2011). The ratio of married to divorced people moved from 18–1 in the 2000 census to 14–1 in 2009 census estimates. The number of divorced people living in Sioux County increased from 843 in 2000 to 1,088 in the 2009 estimate, for a 29 percent increase (Hayworth, 2011). Several other Iowa counties had similar jumps in their divorce rates: Buena Vista (31 percent), Dickson (32 percent), Monroe (30 percent), and Clay (13 percent).

It appears that changes that started in cities have spread to the rural areas—women going to work and college while at the same time the skill sets of blue-collar men have lost value in the marketplace. Such changes have put pressure on the institution of marriage. A 52-year-old female resident of Sioux County, Nancy Vermeer, tells her story. She married her high school sweetheart who came from a farming family and who never went further than high school. She went on to college and later earned a master's degree. He worked in a window factory; she became a music teacher. They grew apart; she grew more confident. They divorced in 2002. Ms. Vermeer, seemingly speaking for many women, said, "As we get more education, we get more confidence and more income. Women are saying, 'Look, she finally had the guts to stand up and walk out'" (Tavernise and Gebeloff, 2011). Family law scholars Naomi Cahn and June Carbone (2010), authors of *Red Families v. Blue Families,* observe that college-educated Americans are now more likely to get married as opposed to those with only a high school diploma. In rural America, only 1 in 6 residents have a college degree; in urban America, it is one in three.

WHAT WOULD YOU DO?

If you were a counselor, a teacher, or a public official in Sioux County, would you want to try to do something about the increasing divorce rate in your community? Explain. If so, what would be your approach?

((••—[Listen to the **Chapter Audio** on **myfamilylab.com**

The vast majority of people who promise to love, cherish, and comfort their spouse "until death do us part" really mean it. How, then, can we account for the fact that approximately 1 million married couples in the United States divorce each year as well as the fact that the gap in divorce rates between rural and urban areas is narrowing as our opening In the News indicates?

That divorce is so common today has led many to conclude that the family is a dying or at least a critically wounded institution. This thinking reflects the myths discussed in Chapter 1, that in the past, marriages were happier, families were more loving, and members treated each other with respect. People who feel this way tend to see divorce in a negative light, as a recent social problem that must be overcome. In contrast, some people see divorce as a solution to the problem of unhappy and sometimes abusive marriages. Both schools of thought find abundant evidence to support their positions. As with so many social phenomena, however, the reality concerning divorce lies somewhere in between. Regardless of the quality of the marriage they left, few people undergo separation or divorce without experiencing some pain. In fact, some divorced people never get over the trauma they experience with the break-up of their marriage. This is especially true for the spouses who did not want the divorce. Conversely, divorce allows people who were unhappy in their marriages to move on and build satisfying new relationships. To appreciate more fully these divergent outcomes of divorce, we need to see how the current institution of divorce came about. In this chapter, we examine the historical controversies surrounding divorce, with an eye to understanding current divorce laws and social policies. We also discuss how divorce rates vary from place to place, who divorces and why, and the consequences of divorce for family members, as well as its implications for the larger society.

Historical Perspectives

Contrary to popular belief, divorce is not a modern phenomenon. It has been a part of U.S. history since 1639, when a Puritan court in Massachusetts granted the first divorce decree in colonial America. This does not mean, however, that divorce was socially acceptable to all the early settlers. In fact, throughout U.S. history, conflict has existed between those who favor divorce and those who oppose it.

DIVORCE IN EARLY AMERICA

Although early in their history the New England colonies permitted divorce, divorces were often adversarial in nature—one partner was required to prove that the other was at fault and had violated the marriage contract. Thus, friends, relatives, and neighbors were called as witnesses and, in effect, were forced to choose sides in what often became an acrimonious procedure. The finding of fault became the basis for harsh punishments for the "offending" party: fines, whippings, incarceration in the stocks, prohibition from remarrying, and even banishment from the colony. This faultfinding also became the basis for **alimony,** a concept originating in England in the 1650s, whereby a husband deemed at fault for the dissolution of the marriage was required to provide his wife with a financial allowance. Conversely, if a wife was judged at fault, she lost any claim to financial support.

The population of the time included Native Americans and African Americans. Nevertheless, their marriages were rarely recorded in the White courts. Thus, it is likely that few Native or African Americans sought an official divorce. However, one researcher did uncover the record of a divorce granted in 1745 to a slave living in Massachusetts on the grounds of his wife's adultery. The same researcher also found that in 1768, Lucy Purnan, a free African American woman, received a divorce decree on the grounds of her husband's cruelty (cited in Riley, 1991:14).

Divorce was granted more infrequently in the middle section of the colonies than in the north. Most of the middle colonies did not enact explicit statutes regarding divorce, and records show that only a few divorces were granted in the colonies of New York, New Jersey, and Pennsylvania. For the most part, the southern colonies did not enact divorce legislation until after independence was achieved. The reluctance of these colonies to legalize divorce should not be interpreted to mean that marriages were happier and more tranquil there than in the rest of the country. Formal and informal separations seem to have been widespread in these colonies, including Native Americans and African Americans both free and enslaved.

Why did these early marriages dissolve? Historian Glenda Riley (1991) sees a variety of social and economic factors interacting to put strains on marriages and families. The growing mobility of the colonists, the movement west, and the emergence of a market economy along with new technology all combined to alter the role of the family as an economic unit, and thus to undercut to a degree a couple's sense of interdependency and common purpose. In addition, the resistance to British rule and the ideology of the Enlightenment, with its emphasis on liberty, justice, and equality, caused people to examine their own level of personal well-being. Whatever the causes, on the eve of the American Revolution, divorce was fairly well established in the social fabric of the nation.

DIVORCE IN NINETEENTH-CENTURY AMERICA

The period following the American Revolution was a time of rapid social, political, and economic change. Each state assumed jurisdiction for divorce. Although there were individual differences among the various states, the general trend was to liberalize divorce laws and expand the grounds for divorce. Two major exceptions to this rule were found in New York, where adultery remained the sole ground for divorce, and in South Carolina,

where divorce was not permitted. These restrictive laws led to "migratory" divorce, whereby residents of one state would travel to another with more liberal laws. To discourage people from coming into their state solely to obtain a divorce, many of the more liberal states instituted minimum-residency requirements.

Data on the number of divorces were not systematically collected until the end of the nineteenth century. Newspaper accounts and scattered divorce records, however, suggest that increasing numbers of people were using the liberalized divorce laws. Those opposing divorce, like newspaper editor Horace Greeley, saw it as immoral and responsible for most of the social ills of the day, and argued that restricting divorce would deter hasty or ill-advised marriages.

On the other side, social critics of the day argued that marriage, not divorce, needed reform. Women's groups spoke out against wife abuse, which had gained public visibility by the 1850s. Female divorce petitioners frequently cited cruelty, including sexual abuse, as the reason for wanting to end their marriage. Proponents of divorce, like Indiana legislator Robert Owen, saw personal happiness and fulfillment as the primary purpose of marriage; they believed that a marriage ought to end if these goals are frustrated.

In 1887, Congress responded to these public debates by authorizing Commissioner of Labor Carroll D. Wright to undertake a study of marriage and divorce in the United States. Wright found that 68,547 divorces were granted between 1872 and 1876, representing an almost 28 percent increase over the 53,574 divorces granted between 1867 and 1871 (cited in Riley, 1991:79). He noted several interesting patterns in these data: Women initiated two-thirds of the divorces (a pattern still evident today); desertion was the most common ground for divorce; and western states granted the most divorces and southern states the fewest. Although people in all classes and occupations sought divorces, more divorces occurred among the working class than among the middle and upper classes.

Although much of the public reaction to divorce focused on its frequency and availability, other problems connected with divorce were becoming evident. After divorce many women, especially those with custody of children, became impoverished. Although alimony was often granted by the courts, enforcement was difficult. Child custody was another problem area. The traditional view in colonial America was that children belong to the father; therefore, he should automatically get custody if a marriage was dissolved by either death or divorce. Thus, some women stayed in unhappy marriages rather than risk losing their children. With industrialization and the consequent notion of separate spheres for women and men, however, judges came to adopt the "tender years" principle that children under age 7 were better off with their mothers. This principle was based on the assumption that women are by nature more adept at nurturing than men.

Men did not always agree with this interpretation. Sometimes, heated custody battles ensued, especially if the mother was seen as the spouse at fault. Judges occasionally split siblings, giving girls or younger children over to the care of mothers and boys or older children to fathers. This decision, called **split custody,** is still made by some judges, albeit in a small number of cases. Americans were also troubled by the destructive consequences that often accompanied divorce. Most of the criticism, however, focused on the divergent laws and procedures that existed in the various states. Many sought a solution to these problems by proposing a uniform divorce law that would encompass the entire country.

TWENTIETH-CENTURY AMERICA: EFFORTS AT REFORM

Generally, those favoring a more restrictive and uniform approach to divorce saw it as a moral evil to be stopped. This moral–legal view was challenged by a group of scholars in the newly developing social sciences. These analysts believed divorce originates not in legislation but rather in the social and economic environment in which marriage is located. The changing patterns of divorce seemed to support this view. The divorce rate jumped considerably after World War I, when many marriages, some hastily conceived in the midst of war, floundered under the stress of economic and political uncertainty and the strains of separation and reunion. Industrialization, the decline in economic functions of the family, employment and financial independence of women, weakening of religious beliefs, and the declining social stigma of divorce were also viewed as causes of divorce.

By the 1960s, the focus of the divorce debate began to shift once again. Although still concerned with the high rate of divorce, public attention increasingly turned to the effects of divorce on spouses and children. Numerous voices were raised against the adversarial nature of divorce, and various proposals for divorce by mutual consent were put forth, culminating in California's

no-fault divorce bill signed into law by Governor Ronald Reagan (who was himself divorced) in 1969 (Jacob, 1988). Over the next 25 years, state after state adopted its own version of no-fault divorce, believing the most negative consequences of divorce would be eliminated by this measure. Spouses no longer had to accuse each other of wrongdoing; instead, they could apply for a divorce on grounds of "irretrievable breakdown" or "irreconcilable differences." Indeed, no-fault divorce removed much of the acrimony of divorce while also lowering its economic cost. As we shall see later in this chapter, however, after over four decades of experience with no-fault divorce, we know it is not the panacea its advocates anticipated. Issues of spousal support, division of marital property, and child custody remain problematic. Today, some critics of no-fault divorce are working to reform the process while others are working to eliminate it altogether (see the Debating Social Issues box).

What lessons are to be learned from an examination of the history of divorce in the United States? Perhaps the most important is that neither marriage nor divorce can be understood apart from its social context. The historical record also makes it abundantly clear that efforts to eliminate divorce will in all likelihood fail. Therefore, it is probably more effective to focus social efforts on strengthening marriages and creating compassionate and fair systems of helping people whose marriages have failed.

Debating Social Issues

IS IT TIME TO ABANDON NO-FAULT DIVORCE?

A new movement to toughen state divorce laws has emerged over the last several years in response to concerns over the impact of family break-ups on children and the high incidence of poverty in single-parent households. The principal target is the no-fault divorce statutes adopted by every state over the last 40 years. Supporters of abandoning no-fault divorce laws argue that the current rules encourage a casual attitude toward the dissolution of marriage and thereby have weakened the legal and social protections available to family members under more stringent laws. Thus, they argue, no-fault divorce empowers the spouse who wishes to leave, but wreaks havoc on the spouse being left behind. Those who want to end no-fault divorce believe it has contributed to an increase in the divorce rate and has lessened our

culture's commitment to marriage as a social institution and as a contract between two parties. They advocate legislation that would put pressure on couples to remain together and that would deny a divorce when one spouse opposes it unless the plaintiff can show that a spouse was physically or mentally abusive, had a problem with alcohol or drugs, had committed adultery, had deserted the home, or had been incarcerated. Those individuals who attend religious services regularly are more likely to favor stricter laws governing divorce (Stokes and Ellison, 2010).

On the other hand, those who oppose abandoning no-fault divorce fear that doing so could mean a return to the anger, lies, and distortions required to obtain a divorce before no-fault, resulting in more pain for children as parents engage in a legal blame game. Going back to establishing fault would be costly and hurt those who can least afford litigation. In addition, they believe that without no-fault divorce, couples would be discouraged from getting married in the first place, thereby increasing the incidence of nonmarital births, leaving more women and children economically and socially vulnerable. Family expert Barbara Dafoe Whitehead (1997) argues that the divorce revolution was a cultural rather than legal phenomenon, growing out of a complex set of social, economic, and cultural factors that created an ethic that emphasized individual well-being. In the process, divorce came to be seen as a healthy response to marital discontent. Thus, she cautions legal sanctions will not stop divorce and that the desire to do away with no-fault divorce is misplaced.

There is concern that making divorce more difficult to obtain would force people to stay in unhealthy and even abusive relationships. Rather than forcing people to stay together, those who oppose abandoning no-fault laws emphasize a focus on reducing the economic stresses that contribute to the high rate of break-up, including requiring absent parents to meet their child support obligations. Some opponents of divorce law reform argue that if you want to minimize divorce, make getting married more difficult and require couples to go through counseling before they get married.

What do you think? Does no-fault divorce increase the likelihood of divorce? Explain. Do you favor or oppose efforts to outlaw no-fault divorce? Explain. Should marriage laws be strengthened to make it more difficult to get married? Explain.

Current Trends: How Many Marriages End in Divorce?

If you have been paying attention to news-grabbing headlines, you may be tempted to say that one in every two marriages ends in divorce. This figure is based on a simple but flawed calculation: the ratio of divorces to the total number of marriages. For example, for many years there were approximately 2 million marriages and about 1 million divorces annually. Hence, we get a figure of 50 percent or one out of two marriages ending in divorce. This interpretation is problematic—a little bit like comparing apples and oranges—because this marriage statistic represents only couples married in a particular year, whereas the divorce statistic refers to all couples who divorce during that same year, regardless of when they married.

✳ **Explore** the **Concept**
Social Explorer Activity:
Divorce Rates Across the U.S.
on **myfamilylab.com**

A more meaningful and commonly used measure of divorce is the **crude divorce rate** (CDR), the number of divorces per 1,000 people in the population. In 2009, the rate was 3.5, the same as in 2008. This statistic has two advantages. It is easy to compute and it allows us to see whether the number of divorces is increasing or decreasing over time. Its disadvantage is its sensitivity to population characteristics. Since children are included as well as single people, this reduces the divorce rate because they are not eligible to divorce. And, even though more young and middle-aged adults may be divorcing, an increase in the number of elderly may mask what would otherwise be an increase in the divorce rate. Conversely, an increase in marriages in earlier years can raise the divorce rate in later years. The number of marriages increased dramatically in the 1970s as a large number of "baby boomers" took on adult roles. In subsequent years, many of these couples divorced. This pattern can be seen in Figure 12.1.

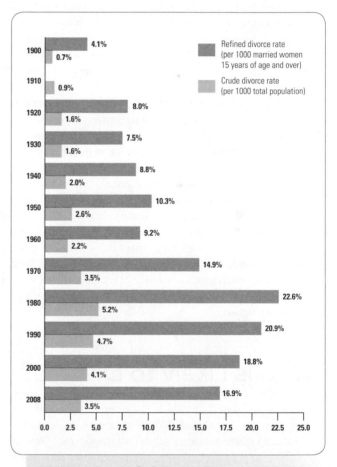

FIGURE 12.1 U.S. Divorce Rate, 1990–2008
Source: A. A. Platters, 1973, "100 Years of Marriage and Divorce Statistics: 1867–1967" (Rockville, MD: National Center for Health Statistics): 24, Table 4; National Center for Health Statistics, 2005, "Marriages and Divorces, 1900–2004," found at www.print.infoplease.com/ipa/AOOO544.html; W. Bradford Wilcox, ed., 2009. *The State of Our Unions.* Charlottesville, VA: University of Virginia, The National Marriage Project, Table 5, p. 75.

Another more accurate way to measure divorce is the **refined divorce rate** (RDR), the number of divorces per 1,000 married women age 15 and over. This statistic focuses on individuals who realistically are potential candidates for divorce. Figure 12.1 allows us to see the differences between the crude and refined divorce rates. Using the RDR allows us to examine changes over time and to investigate how the frequency of divorce is affected by economic and political events. For example, the divorce rate declined during the depression of the early 1930s, when couples simply could not afford to get divorced. The rate was 7.5 in 1930 and dropped to 6.1 by 1933. It increased dramatically during and immediately after World War II, because of an improved economy and because couples previously separated by the war had to readjust to living together. What accounts for some of these changes? No doubt, as we saw in Chapter 10, the increasing economic pressures that led many wives to enter the labor force in the 1970s and 1980s strained marital relationships, thus adding to the divorce rate. By the 1990s, cohabitation was well established. Many couples who otherwise would have married and then divorced broke up instead, remaining outside the official statistics. During the last two decades, considerable media attention has been given to the issue of divorce. This awareness may have encouraged couples to put more effort into making their marriages work. Finally, it is likely that the recession of 2007, led some couples contemplating divorce to abandon or, at least temporarily postpone that decision out of economic concerns (Roberts, 2009). The divorce rate fell from 18.8 in 2000 to 16.9 in 2008.

A third way of determining the divorce rate, one preferred by most demographers, is to calculate how many people who have ever married subsequently divorced. According to a recent study, the highest rate of divorce was 41 percent for women between ages 50 and 59 (Kreider and Ellis, 2011b). There is a tendency to use figures such as these to project into the future, that is, four out of ten marriages will end in divorce. However, such predictions assume that social conditions remain constant. In a rapidly changing society like ours, this is unlikely. For example, changes in marriage and/or divorce laws, may increase marital stability by making divorces more difficult to get and/or lead people to work harder to save a troubled marriage. Conversely, if we assume that we will return to the marriage patterns of the late 1970s; our divorce projections will be higher.

Who Is Likely to Divorce?

As Table 12.1 illustrates, divorce is not evenly distributed across all segments of the population. However, women are more likely to be divorced than are men across all major race and ethnic groups. This pattern is largely because men are more likely to remarry than are women. Keep in mind that this table reflects the percentage of people who were divorced in 2009. If we consider people who

TABLE 12.1 Percent of Divorce Population by Sex, Race, and Ethnicity, 2009			
	Total (%)	**Male (%)**	**Female (%)**
All Races	10.2	9.0	11.4
White	10.3	9.2	11.4
Black	11.4	10.0	12.6
Latina/o	8.0	6.8	9.4
Asian	4.4	3.4	5.4

Source: Adapted from U.S. Census Bureau, 2011, *Statistical Abstract of the United States,* 2011. Washington, DC: p. 52, Table 56.

were ever divorced, but who subsequently remarried, the percentages would be higher. A second pattern is also evident in this table: variations by race and ethnicity. African Americans have the highest percentage of divorced persons followed by Whites and Latinas/os, with Asians having the lowest rates. A somewhat similar pattern exists in the rate of marriage dissolution. Forty-nine percent of first marriages of African American women end within 7 years compared with 41 percent for White women, 34 percent for Latinas, and 22 percent for Asian women (Kreider and Ellis, 2011b).

DIVORCE AMONG AFRICAN AMERICANS

In the past, some analysts have viewed the higher rate of divorce among African Americans as the legacy of slavery (Frazier, 1939). Subsequent scholarship, however, has found that the increase in African American marital instability is a more recent development, accelerating in particular since 1960 and corresponding to a decline in the economic situation of large numbers of African Americans (Gutman, 1976; Cherlin, 1981; Teachman, Tedrow, and Crowder, 2000). Studies in other countries have also found a strong relationship between unemployment and marital dissolution (Lester, 1996; Blekesaume, 2008). In addition, as we saw in Chapter 9, there is a higher rate of teenage pregnancy and premarital pregnancies among African American women than in women in other groups, a factor that, in itself, increases the risk of marital dissolution across all groups. Finally, as we saw in Chapter 1, African Americans often rely on the extended family for social support. Thus armed with the knowledge that there will be help for them, couples may be less reluctant to divorce than others whose communities offer less support and acceptance for divorcing couples (Blake and Darling, 2000).

DIVORCE AMONG LATINAS/OS

Because Latinas/os also experience higher rates of poverty and unemployment as a result of discrimination, we might assume that the Latina/o divorce ratio would be closer to that of African

Americans than to that of Whites. In fact, as Table 12.1 indicates, Latinas/os rate of divorce was low in comparison to Whites and African Americans. Two factors are often cited to explain the relatively high level of marital stability among Latinas/os: a cultural tradition that emphasizes the importance of the family unit and a religion (Catholicism) that prohibits divorce.

Although these factors may contribute to the lower divorce rates found among Latinas/os, the Latina/o ratio itself presents several problems. It does not distinguish among the diverse categories of Latinas/os whose economic status and rates of marital stability might vary.

DIVORCE AMONG ASIAN AMERICANS

According to the U.S. Census Bureau (2011e), Asian Americans are less likely than the total population to be separated or divorced. In 2009, 10.42 percent of the population ages 18 and older were divorced, but only 4.4 percent of Asian Americans in that age category were. There are several factors that explain the lower rate of divorce among Asian Americans. First, both women and men tend to marry later than other groups. They are thus a bit older and likely to be more mature and settled at the onset of marriage. Second, Asian Americans tend to rank higher on numerous indicators of socioeconomic status, all of which can contribute to marital stability. For example, in 2009 a higher proportion of Asians (52.3 percent) than of the total population (29.5 percent) had earned at least a bachelor's degree. Similarly, Asians were more likely to be employed in management, professional, and related occupations than was the case for the total population. And, as we saw in Chapter 10, the median annual income of Asian American families was higher than that of families in other groups.

In addition, many Asian Americans are relative newcomers to the United States who brought cultural traditions of strong family ties with them, including living with or near extended and multigenerational families. However, as is the case with any racial or ethnic category that includes people with diverse languages, religions, customs, and countries of origin, a global figure obscures differences within the larger category. For example, Thai, Japanese, and Filipino divorce rates (7.4, 6.7, and 5.2 percent) are considerably higher than the 4.2 percent global rate for Asian Americans. Conversely, Pakistani, Hmong, and Asian Indian rates are considerably lower than the global rate (2.1, 2.3, and 2. 4 percent, respectively). Many Asian American community leaders are concerned that as Asian Americans become more assimilated into mainstream U.S. culture, their traditional family patterns will change and divorce rates will rise (Associated Press, 2003).

The need for further research is apparent if we are to understand the interactive effects of economic status, race, and ethnicity on marital stability. In particular, more data are needed on groups such as Native Americans who often are not included in major surveys. One of the few studies to examine marital stability among Native Americans found that in 1980, 48 percent of Native American women and 43 percent of their male counterparts were no longer in intact first marriages (Sweet and Bumpass, 1987). Again, it is likely that these high rates, in large part, were related to high rates of unemployment and poverty, but we lack recent comparable data to assess whether or not marital situations are improving for this segment of the population. In a similar vein, we have little systematic data concerning marital stability among other groups whose numbers are small and/or who are more recent arrivals to the United States, for example, people from the Middle East.

Race and ethnicity are, of course, not the only factors affecting divorce rates. The next section examines a variety of social and demographic factors that affect the likelihood of divorce.

Factors Affecting Marital Stability

Although no one can say with any degree of certainty which marriages will end in divorce, based on existing patterns, researchers can predict the statistical probabilities for different groups. The likelihood of any given couple getting divorced depends on a wide range of factors, including age at marriage, premarital childbearing, education, income, religion, parental divorce, cohabitation, and the presence of children. By understanding how these factors can influence a marital relationship, people contemplating marriage can better evaluate their chances of a successful marriage.

AGE AT FIRST MARRIAGE

Younger brides and grooms, especially those who are still in their teens when they marry, are more likely to divorce. Forty-eight percent of marriages of women who married under age 18 dissolved within 10 years compared with 24 percent of marriages of women at least 25 years of age at marriage (Bramlett and Mosher, 2002). The reasons for marital instability among the young come easily to mind: immaturity, lack of adequate financial resources, different rates of personal growth, and often the pressures of early parenthood, particularly if it involves premarital childbearing. Numerous studies document a negative relationship between premarital childbearing and the risk of divorce after first marriage (Norton and Miller, 1992; Teachman, 2002).

EDUCATION

Overall, individuals who graduate from college have more stable marriages than those with a high school education (Kreider and Ellis, 2011b). This pattern reflects a number of different factors. Individuals with only a high school education are more likely to marry at an early age and to hold low-paying jobs. Thus, financial pressures on the marriage are likely to be substantial. Moreover, those who persist in school tend to marry later, have higher incomes, and in general probably are better equipped to work out problems as they occur. This pattern holds for both women and men. Similarly, economists Adam Isen and Betsey Stevenson (2010) found that the group most likely to divorce were college drop-outs. They argue that the lack of stamina and/or resources that can stop an education short can also stop a marriage in its tracks.

INCOME/EMPLOYMENT

Income and spousal employment or their lack thereof can affect the likelihood of divorce in opposite ways. On the one hand, low income and its accompanying stresses are a major factor in the higher divorce rate found among some groups. The significance of income is shown, for example, in its impact on early marriages. Young couples with sufficient financial resources had more stable marriages than similar couples with inadequate resources (Spanier and Glick, 1981). Poverty and low incomes, regardless of age, are risk factors for divorce (Amato and Previti, 2003). Marital assets decrease the likelihood of divorce. One study showed that couples with no assets at the beginning of a 36-month period were 70 percent more likely to divorce than couples with $10,000 in assets (Dew, 2009). In their book, *For Better/For Worse,* E. Mavis Hetherington and John Kelly (2002) describe how the lack of money can corrode a marital relationship, particularly when the husband is unemployed and cannot find or hold a job. The husband may feel inadequate as a breadwinner, and if the wife complains, his self-esteem may decline even further. Both may become resentful and seek to dissolve their marriage.

On the other hand, however, a major downturn in the economy, such as the recession of 2007–2009, can make the cost of a divorce prohibitive. For example, when a house is the major marital asset, it often has to be sold or one spouse has to buy the other's share in order for each spouse to afford creating a separate household. In a weak housing market, they may not be able to sell or they may be unable to get sufficient income from the sale to finance the divorce (Sell, et al., 2010). In a recent survey, among the married respondents who said they were considering divorce or separation prior to the recession, 38 percent said the recession caused them to put aside that course of action (Wilcox, 2011).

RELIGION

Historically, many religions have either prohibited or tried to discourage divorce among their members. On this basis, we would predict that more religiously involved people would have lower rates of divorce, a view supported by a considerable body of research. Among Americans, those who attend church regularly and say they are religious report higher rates of marital happiness and have lower divorce rates than those who say they are not religious (Amato et al., 2007; Wilcox, 2005). Furthermore, couples who share the same religion are less likely than interfaith couples to divorce (Mullins et al., 2004). One possible explanation for this pattern is that religious homogamy increases the commonality spouses share in values and traditions. Membership in a religious organization also promotes social cohesion (Durkheim, 1951) and provides a source of support in times of difficulty. This support helps couples work through problems that otherwise might lead to divorce. A recent study found that couples who attend religious services regularly reported they deepened their commitment to marriage as a result of the recession compared to couples who do not regularly attend services (32 percent to 36 percent) (Wilcox, 2011).

Data from the General Social Survey showed a different tendency to divorce among various religious groups. Among U.S. adults, 53 percent of respondents identifying themselves as religiously unaffiliated were separated or divorced. Among the religiously affiliated, 53 percent of Black Protestants, 42 percent of Evangelicals, 39 percent of mainline Protestants, 36 percent of Jews, and 35 percent of Catholics were separated or divorced (Wilcox, 2005). Among the Protestant denominations there is also considerable variation, with Baptists and Pentecostals having higher divorce rates than Presbyterians and Episcopalians. Some caution is required in interpreting this last finding, however. The differences in rates may be the result of an interactive effect between religious membership and other factors such as education and income. Although religion continues to be a factor in people's willingness to divorce, there are indications that organized religions are no longer as effective in restricting divorce as they had been. For example, in the past, Catholic countries in Europe did not permit divorce. Now virtually all do. In 1995, voters in Ireland, where 95 percent of the population is Catholic, narrowly approved a constitutional amendment to allow couples to divorce if they have lived apart for at least 4 of the previous 5 years. Chile, another predominantly Catholic country, made divorce legal for the first time in 2004. When the law went into effect, more than 500,000 people were separated (Ross, 2004).

PARENTAL DIVORCE

Can the parents' divorce influence the outcome of their children's marriage? The answer apparently is yes. A recent student of 13 European countries, Canada, and the United States found that the divorce risk of children of divorced parents is on average about twice that of children of non-divorced parents (cited in Hong, Galher, and Bernhardt. 2006). Two factors may combine to produce this outcome. First, from their parents' example, children learn that divorce can be a solution to marital difficulties. They thus may be more ready than their peers from intact families to seek a divorce when problems start. Second, after a parental divorce children often experience downward social mobility, which in turn may limit college attendance and contribute to early marriage, putting them at increased risk of a divorce themselves. However, gender seems to play a role here. Daughters from both middle and lower socioeconomic families are at greater risk for divorce than sons from divorced parents of middle-class background. Parents are still more likely to encourage sons to go to college than daughters and therefore provide more resources for sons to continue their education (Feng et al., 1999).

Several other marital patterns have been observed in adult children whose parents were divorced. Parental divorce raises the likelihood of teenage marriage. However, if these children do not marry before age 20, they are likely to remain single or to cohabit. If they do cohabit, however, they are unlikely to marry their partner (Wolfinger, 2001, 2003). For the most part, research on the impact of parental divorce has been limited to their immediate offspring. A recent study suggests that the effects of parental divorce extend into the third generation. Sociologists Paul Amato and Jacob Cheadle (2005) examined data collected on divorced families covering a span of 20 years and found that the grandchildren of divorced couples had less education, more turbulent marriages, and more distant relationships with their parents than grandchildren of still married couples. This was especially true when the middle generation also experienced these divorce-related consequences.

IS DIVORCE CONTAGIOUS? SOCIAL NETWORK EFFECTS

A longitudinal study by the Social Science Research Network found the likelihood of divorce is influenced by the social network in which a person is involved. When divorce occurs among siblings, friends, and co-workers, the researchers found there is a fairly high probability that other couples in that social network will also divorce (McDermott, Fowler, and Christakis, 2009). This has led some people to see divorce as a contagious virus that spreads to other people. However, correlation is not causation. Just like friends influence each other regarding other behaviors such as smoking, drinking, and going to church, so, too, their behavior regarding divorce can lead others to reflect on their own lives. Couples who are happy and satisfied with their marriage are unlikely to contemplate divorcing because a friend or sibling did so. In fact, it may lead them to work on ways to strengthen their relationships. However, if couples are unhappy and dissatisfied with their relationship, the example of others may lead to them to evaluate their options and to decide if others divorce and move on with their lives, maybe they can as well.

COHABITATION

As we saw in Chapter 7, studies consistently show that people who live together before they marry are more likely to divorce. Attitudes and behaviors often interact to make premarital cohabitation risky. Cohabitation often involves less commitment than marriage, and when less committed couples drift into marriage, the experience of a less secure, committed, and even faithful cohabitation may shape their marital behavior (Dush, Cohan, and Amato, 2003). Additionally, cohabiting couples may bring into their marriage the attitude that relationships, including marriage, are temporary in and of themselves (Smock and Gupta, 2002). Other researchers report that, in the first two years of their marriage, couples who had cohabited had somewhat less positive problem-solving behaviors and were less supportive of each other on average than couples who had not cohabited (Cohan and Kleinbaum, 2002). Individuals who engage in serial cohabitation (living with different partners over time) were more likely to divorce than those who cohabited only with their eventual husbands (Jose, O'Leary, and Moyer, 2010; Lichter and Qian, 2008).

Although the weight of evidence continues to show that couples who cohabit before marriage are more likely to divorce than couples who do not cohabit, other recent research questions whether this divorce gap will narrow or even disappear in the future as cohabitation becomes more normative (Liefroer and Dourleijn, 2006; Reinhold, 2007). Clearly, more research is needed in this area to test the possibility that the experience of contemporary cohabitation has or will have different outcomes than that of cohabitation in earlier decades.

PRESENCE OF CHILDREN

A consistent research finding is that marital disruption is most likely when the marriage is child-free (Tilson and Larsen, 2000; Wineberg, 1988) and least likely when there are preschool children (Previti and Amato, 2003). This finding should not be construed to mean that marriages with children are happier than those without. In fact, couples with children still at home tend to be less happy than either childless couples or those whose children have left home (Twenge, Campbell, and Foster, 2003). Rather, parents who are having marital problems often delay divorce until all the children are in school. The likelihood of divorce increases when children reach their teens (AARP, 2004). Two plausible explanations for this behavior come readily to mind. Parents may believe that teenaged children are more capable of handling this family disruption, or it may be that coping with adolescent children puts additional strain on an already weakened relationship.

Increasingly, married couples are less likely to stay together because children are present in the home. More than 1 million children have been involved in divorce annually since 1972. Thus, increasing numbers of children are spending part of their childhood in a single-parent family.

Research has also found that a child's gender is a factor in divorce. Overall, parents of girls are more likely to divorce than parents of sons (Mammen, 2007; Bedard and Deschenes, 2005). Economists Gordon Dahl and Enrico Moretti (2004) found that parents of a girl are nearly 5 percent more likely to divorce than the parents of a boy, and the more daughters, the bigger the effect. Parents of three girls are almost 10 percent more likely to divorce than the parents of three boys. Dahl and Moretti also found this same relationship, although with much higher effects in Mexico, Columbia, Kenya, and Vietnam. Researchers attribute this to a greater preference of fathers for sons. In addition, they speculate that mothers of sons might resist a separation in the belief that raising sons without a father would be more difficult than raising daughters alone.

Thus far, we have examined a number of risk factors associated with divorce. Take a minute to see whether any of these risk factors apply to you (see the Applying the Sociological Imagination box on page 398).

The Process of Divorce

Divorce does not just happen. It is a complex social process in which a basic unit of social organization—marriage—breaks down over time, culminating in a legal termination of the relationship. Nonetheless, this process can vary significantly from culture to culture (see the In Other Places box on page 398).

APPLYING THE SOCIOLOGICAL IMAGINATION

ARE YOU AT RISK?

This exercise is designed to help you assess some of the risk factors of divorce that may be present in your life. Answer yes if the question accurately describes you or those close to you.

1. Did you marry or do you plan to marry before your 20th birthday?
2. Are your parents divorced?
3. Are any of your close friends divorced?
4. Do you attend religious services only occasionally?
5. Are you likely to drop out of college before graduating?

6. Did you or will you consider marrying someone who did not graduate from college?
7. Did you or will you want to cohabit with your partner before marriage?
8. Will both you and your spouse work?
9. Do you have difficulty managing money?

Scoring

Add up the number of times you answered *yes*. The higher the number of *yes* answers, the more risk factors you have for becoming divorced.

However, this does not automatically mean you will be divorced at some point in your life. Rather, it indicates that you have some of the characteristics that researchers have found to be associated with a tendency to divorce. Go to www.stateofourunions.org/2010/SOOu2010.pdf (pp. 73 and 74). What factors do the authors identify as marriage protectors? Why are they effective? How can knowledge of these factors be used by couples and by social institutions in attempts to develop strategies to lessen the likelihood of marital dissolution?

In Other Places

DIVORCE ON DEMAND TO NO DIVORCE PERIOD

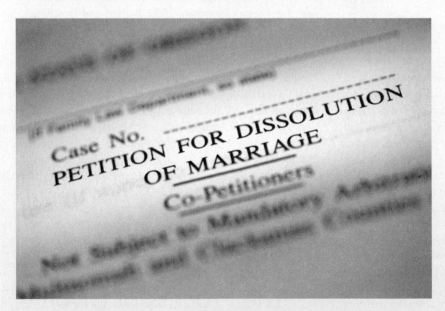

Cultures vary significantly in their degree of acceptance of divorce and the rules governing who can initiate a divorce. In some cultures, like the Hopi Native Americans of the Southwest, both women and men could initiate divorce. Among the Yoruba of West Africa, however, only women could initiate divorce; and for centuries among many Muslim and Asian cultures, only men could ask for a divorce.

Similarly, some cultures allow divorce on demand. For example, researchers who studied the matrilineal Hopi 50 years ago found a high divorce rate: about one out of three marriages. The divorce process was easy. A wife could initiate divorce simply by placing her husband's belongings outside their dwelling. A divorcing husband simply moved back into his mother's house. If the couple had children, they stayed with the mother (Queen, Habenstein, and Quadagno, 1985:49–50). In some countries, like India, a Muslim man can divorce his wife in a matter of minutes in a practice known as "triple talaq," or instant divorce, by saying three times in a row, "I divorce you." This can be done over the phone, by mail, or now through mobile phone text message. The husband does not have to give her reasons or have a face-to-face meeting with his wife (Pandey, 2004). The practice of instant divorce is banned in several Islamic countries including Pakistan, Bangladesh, and Indonesia and many scholars consider this practice un-Islamic and disapprove of its practice (Rahman, 2010).

Men in Egypt have a unilateral and unconditional right to divorce and they do not need to go to court to end their marriages. However, women who want a divorce must go to court to divorce their husbands, using one of two options. A woman can seek a fault-based divorce, which can provide financial rights, but to gain it, she must show harm inflicted by her husband during the course of their marriage, including eyewitness testimony in allegations of physical abuse. The second option is khoul' (Michael, 2008). This also requires a woman to petition the court, but here she must agree to forfeit her financial rights and repay the dowry given to her by her husband upon marriage. Court proceedings can take years and a noncooperative husband can appeal the court's decision, prolonging the process (Levinson, 2005).

Until recently, only two countries—the Philippines and Malta, both predominately Catholic—prohibited divorce. In May 2011, in a referendum Maltese voters approved a measure that would allow couples separated or living apart for four years to divorce. The measure is now awaiting action in Parliament. Maltese citizens who are married to foreigners and living abroad can obtain a divorce in the country in which they are living and have it registered in Malta if the marriage took place there (Ameen, 2006). The Family Code of the Philippines provides for a legal separation or annulment due to "psychological incapacity" of a marriage, but not divorce. Because the marriage is still valid under a legal separation, remarriage is not permitted. An annulment, which allows a couple to remarry, is difficult and costly to obtain.

What do you think? Do you think there is any merit to making divorce as easy as it is for the Hopi and Muslim males or as difficult as it is for the citizens of the Philippines and Malta? Explain.

STAGES IN THE DIVORCE PROCESS

Divorce involves more than a legal decree officially symbolizing the end of a marriage. Some researchers, like Constance Ahrons (1980) and George Levinger (1979), identify three stages in the divorce process: (1) a period of marital conflict and unhappiness, (2) the actual marital dissolution itself, and (3) a postdivorce period. James Ponzetti and Rodney Cate (1986) see divorce as a four-step process: (1) recognition by one or both spouses of serious marital problems; (2) discussion of these problems with the spouse and possibly with family, friends, or counselors; (3) initiation of legal action to dissolve the marriage; and (4) the postdissolution period, which involves adapting to a new status. Although both spouses go through the same stages, the timing may be different for each spouse, depending on who initiates the divorce.

Although these researchers propose different models, they all agree that the dissolution of a marriage occurs through a series of stages. The majority of separations and divorces follow a period of personal unhappiness, conflict, and deliberation, during which time individuals make decisions based on three types of criteria:

- An evaluation of the attractiveness of the relationship itself (the material, emotional, and symbolic rewards a spouse provides);
- An evaluation of the costs and benefits of a divorce (monetary, social, and psychological);
- An evaluation of the attractiveness of possible alternatives, including new relationships (Levinger, 1965).

For example, some parents anticipated that "divorce would worsen their economic situation and their abilities to fulfill their responsibilities of being a parent" (Poortman and Seltzer, 2007, p. 265). Such concerns may lead people to delay an intended divorce for many years. Similarly, the narratives of Israeli women and men who were married for 15 or more years show that divorce for these respondents was not a spontaneous or impulsive response to any immediate event but was rather the process of marital deterioration over time (Rokach, Cohen, and Dreman, 2004). Conversely, couples may find that over time their economic interests and friendship support networks increase and deepen, thus adding value to the marital relationship (Brown, Orbuch, and Maharaj, 2010).

THE SIX STATIONS OF DIVORCE

Anthropologist Paul Bohannan (1970) has identified not one but six divorces that couples experience in dissolving their marital relationship. These he calls the **stations of divorce**: emotional, legal, economic, coparental, community, and psychic divorce.

The **emotional divorce** can be present in the marriage for a long time before any legal action is taken to end the relationship. Here one spouse, or both, questions the viability or quality of the relationship and at some point shares this view with the other. There is often a period during which one or both partners withdraw emotionally from the relationship. A loss of mutual respect, trust, and affection follows. During this period both spouses may hurt or frustrate the other deliberately. Yet despite the deterioration of the relationship and talk of separation, one or both may not want a divorce for a variety of reasons. This process is well illustrated by Fran Welch, who divorced her alcoholic husband after 36 years of marriage. One evening during dinner with friends, her husband's obnoxious behavior pushed her to the edge. "I knew at that point that was it. I wasn't going to listen to or watch or see this kind of behavior anymore. I just couldn't do it. And that was the end," Welch said (quote in Smith, 2005). Thus, some marriages may remain intact in form but not in substance for extended periods of time. Other spouses take action to move to the next stage. This may involve one spouse walking out or a mutual decision to begin a period of separation.

Gender plays a role in the decision-making process. Women appear to take a more active role in preparing and planning for divorce or separation. They are more likely than men to think about divorce after a spousal argument, to make specific plans to discuss divorce or separation with their spouse or with others, and to initiate the divorce process itself (Amato et al., 2007).

The **legal divorce** officially ends the marriage and gives the former partners the right to remarry. Legal divorce generally follows a period of months or even years of deliberation. The divorce itself can be an adversarial process, especially when children and property are involved. In attempting to settle these issues, the divorcing couple may lose control of the process itself to lawyers who advocate their client's interest generally without regard to the needs of the other party. Legal divorce can be an expensive proposition. When lawyers are involved, the average cost of a divorce in the United States is around $27,000 and this only takes into account the legal costs and consequences. It does not include the emotional and familial costs, which are so much higher ("Average Cost…", 2011). For individuals who are able and willing to use the Internet, a "do-it-yourself" divorce can cost as little as $100.

Currently federal law defines marriage as being between a man and a woman, thus, the federal government does not extend many standard divorce benefits to same-sex couples. For example, federal law allows a pension to be divided during a divorce without triggering early-withdrawal penalties. Divorcing gay and lesbian couples must pay the penalties. Similarly divorced heterosexuals can deduct court-ordered alimony payments from federal income taxes but divorced gay and lesbians cannot (Horton, 2008). Courts in states that recognize same-sex civil unions and same-sex marriages are beginning to grant orders of separation to and make property arrangements for same-sex couples when their unions dissolve. In Massachusetts, more than 10,000 same-sex couples have married since 2004. Although the courts do not keep a breakdown of divorces by sexual orientation, it is estimated that more than 100 same-sex divorces have been granted. Vermont has dissolved 2 percent of the 8,666 civil unions performed there since they became legal in 2000 (Associated Press, 2008). Currently there is no way of knowing how extensive the real desire is for same-sex divorce is or how such rates compare to those of heterosexuals since many same-sex couples do not reside in states that will grant their petitions. For many couples establishing such residency is economically prohibitive. When a gay couple married in Massachusetts filed for divorce in Texas, a state which does not recognize same-sex marriage, a judge granted the divorce. Texas Attorney General Greg Abbott appealed to the 5th district court, which overturned the judge's decision. The lawyers for the couple have petitioned for a review by the Texas Supreme Court ("Gay Divorce Case…," 2011).

The **economic divorce** involves the settlement of property, a process that often involves considerable conflict. Most states now have laws specifying that both spouses are to receive an equitable share of the marital property. Equity is not always easy to determine, however. Tangible items like the house, the car, income, and bank accounts, whose values are easy to calculate, can be divided without great difficulty. But what about the current and future earning power of each individual? Spouses with advanced degrees or special labor market skills are at a real advantage after a divorce. Considerable controversy exists over what constitutes a fair return on an investment in human capital. This question arises in cases where one spouse (most frequently the husband) earned a degree or learned a skill while the other spouse (most frequently the wife) played a major supportive role in making that possible, earning the money to pay for the spouse's education. Future retirement funds also represent an important asset, the value of which changes dramatically over the years. The economic divorce can exist for years as former spouses return to court long after the divorce is final to try to renegotiate financial settlements, especially as children grow older and have more expensive needs.

The economic station of divorce is less often applicable than some of the other stations. It assumes that all couples have tangible assets to divide. Although this is certainly true for middle- and upper-class couples, it is generally not true for the poor and for many working-class couples who live in rental units and depend on public transportation. For some couples, there is little property to divide.

The **coparental divorce** involves decisions concerning child custody, visitation rights, and the financial and legal responsibilities of each parent. This station can also be a source of conflict, particularly when parents are engaged in a custody battle. We will return to the topic of child custody later in this chapter.

The **community divorce** involves changing social relationships. It can involve a loss of relatives and friends who were previously shared with the spouse. The withdrawal of former in-laws and friendship may occur for several reasons. Those who were friendly with both spouses may not want to be drawn into taking sides. Others may see the divorce as a threat to their own relationships. In this stage of divorce, people may feel lonely and isolated.

The **psychic divorce** involves a redefinition of self away from the mutuality of couplehood and back to a sense of singlehood. This process takes time and involves a distancing from and an acceptance of the break-up. Many people go through a mourning process similar to that experienced by people who lose a spouse to death (see Chapter 15). The time this takes and the degree of difficulty with which this station is passed through varies considerably from individual to individual.

Other Forms of Marital Disruption

Thus far, our discussion has focused on the legal concept of divorce. However, marriages can be disrupted by separation, desertion, annulment, and death.

Separation refers to the termination of marital cohabitation and can take a variety of forms. Sometimes one of the partners simply moves out. This can be the result of an individual or a mutual decision. Its goal may be to give one or both partners some space and time to think about the relationship, or it may be the first step toward divorce. Because this is an informal arrangement, the courts are not involved, and the couple remains legally married.

In other cases, when the couple does not want to divorce or to continue living together, the courts order legal separation with specific regulations governing the couple's interactions, including custody, visitation rights, and economic support. Such separation orders may also provide for counseling or therapy and give a stipulated time frame for the duration of the separation. Couples may reconcile or divorce at the end of the separation. Researchers have found that close to 10 percent of married couples have separated and reconciled (Wineberg and McCarthy, 1993). A study of African American women found that women who were separated after age 23 were more likely to reconcile than their younger peers. Greater maturity and a greater investment in the relationship were seen as key characteristics in the pattern of reconciliation (Wineberg, 1996). The desire to have day-to-day contact with children also provides an incentive for a couple's reconciliation. For some couples, however, a legal separation may become permanent. Some people reject divorce on religious grounds and therefore agree to live apart until the death of one spouse. Although either party may begin new relationships, neither is free to remarry.

Desertion refers to the abandonment of a spouse or family. The partner simply leaves, often without a word of warning. Desertion has sometimes been called the "poor people's divorce" because it frequently occurs when the family is experiencing economic hardship. However, desertion occurs among all classes, races, and ethnic groups. Although both women and men desert, men do so in greater numbers. This is perhaps the most difficult of all marital disruptions because the family is left without the financial and domestic support of the other spouse, and the courts cannot intervene unless the whereabouts of the deserting spouse are known. At the same time, the deserted spouse is not legally free to remarry until a specified number of years have passed. Thus, the family's life is overshadowed by uncertainty and ambiguity.

An annulment has quite a different meaning from the other forms of disruption we have been discussing. In divorce, separation, and desertion there is agreement that a legal marriage had existed. In contrast, a civil **annulment** legally states that the marriage never existed and thus the parties are free to marry at will. Generally, the basis for an annulment is that the couple did not meet the legal requirements for a marriage in the first place—they were underage, the degree of kinship was too close (first cousins, for example, are not legally permitted to marry in some states), the marriage was never consummated, or some form of fraud was involved. A civil annulment is distinct from the religious annulment granted by the Catholic Church. The church, after investigation, may decide that a religious marriage did not take place. In the eyes of the church, the individuals are free to marry, but to do so legally they must obtain a civil annulment or a divorce.

Finally, the death of a spouse brings an end to many marriages. Throughout much of U.S. history marital disruptions were generally caused by death, not divorce. This was due primarily to shorter life expectancies, harsher living conditions, and cultural patterns that discouraged divorce. Today widowhood most commonly occurs at later ages in the life cycle. We discuss the concept of widowhood in Chapter 14.

The Causes of Divorce

When couples divorce, others are prone to ask, "Why?" "What went wrong?" Such questions assume that some specific event or events disrupted the relationship and if only that hadn't happened, the marriage could survive. Yet, as our historical review made clear, divorce is a complex phenomenon that needs to be understood in the context in which it occurs. Thus, changes in social structures, economic relationships, demographic patterns, and cultural configurations all play a role in divorce.

SOCIETAL FACTORS

Several macro-level factors have contributed to the long-term trend of a rise in the divorce rate. Perhaps the most influential factor is a change in attitudes. Although divorce is still seen as an unfortunate occurrence, it has become far more socially acceptable than in the past. Today, 69 percent of Americans believe divorce is morally acceptable, up from 59 percent in 2001 (Saad, 2011a). Indeed, all major social institutions, including religion and the family, have become more tolerant of this behavior. These attitudinal factors have been reflected in more liberal divorce laws, which many people believe have made divorce more accessible to a wider share of the population. These changes in attitudes became possible as a result of transformations taking place in the organization and functioning of major social institutions. As we discussed in Chapter 1, the advent of industrialism weakened the family as an economic unit and placed more emphasis on the personal relationship between spouses. Spouses were less likely, under these new conditions, to remain in a union that was not personally fulfilling.

Similarly, as we saw in Chapter 10, changes in the economy led to major transformations in the relationship between work and family and in the gender roles of husbands and wives. Among the most striking changes in this regard is the increase in the labor participation of women, especially from 1970 on. Numerous studies show that marital instability has increased along with women's labor force participation (Cherlin and Furstenberg, 1988; Spitze, 1988). What is less clear, however, is why this relationship exists. One interpretation suggests that among marriages that are unsatisfactory for whatever reason, the costs of divorce are lowest for wives who are capable of self-support—the independence effect (Teachman, 2010; Hacker, 2003). Other explanations have been tied to changing gender role ideology. Some husbands find it difficult to adjust to a co-provider role, and some wives feel overburdened by working outside the home while still being expected to do the bulk of the housework (Springer, 2010; Rogers and Amato, 2000). In a nationally representative sample of individuals involved in dual-earner marriages, researchers found that unfair perceptions of the division of household labor not only decreases women's marital quality but also leads to role strain that makes them more likely to end unsatisfying marriages (Frisco and Williams, 2003). However, not all women respond to these inequities in the same way. Theodore Greenstein (1995) found that nontraditional women who saw marriage as an egalitarian partnership viewed such inequalities as unjust, whereas traditional women did not perceive these inequalities as inherently unfair.

Nevertheless, the relationship between the employment of women and divorce is not a simple cause-and-effect relationship. Other factors are at work here as well. For example, Greenstein (1990) found that the conditions under which wives work is the fundamental issue. He reported that divorce is less likely when the wife's earnings and her share of family income represent a significant part of a family's budget. Having two wage earners may relieve financial tensions that often contribute to divorce; thus, a wife's employment may contribute to greater marital stability. Under different circumstances, however, female employment can increase marital instability. As with men, for example, women in high-stress jobs frequently find that work-related pressures carry over into domestic situations and intensify marital difficulties.

The United States is not alone in experiencing these macro-level changes. Other countries confront similar changes and consequently they are also experiencing higher divorce rates. For example, a cross-cultural study found that 25 out of 27 countries saw divorce rates rise between 1950 and 1985 (Lester, 1996). Even in some of the more traditional societies in Asia, marital dissolution has increased in recent years. For example, in traditional Taiwanese society marriage was expected to last a lifetime. Divorce did occur, but historically divorce laws favored men with respect to property and child custody, leaving women reluctant to seek a divorce. However, as the economy changed, so, too, did gender role expectations. As women entered the labor force in large numbers, they became less accepting of unhappy relationships. Over two decades ago, just one in seventeen marriages ended in divorce (under 6 percent). Estimates are that in recent years 25–30 percent of marriages in Taiwan have ended in divorce (Warmack, 2004). Recent indications, however, are that the divorce rate is declining as more women are postponing marriage. Only one-third of Taiwan's women are married by age 30, in contrast to 20 years ago when the average age for marriage for women was 26 (Tso, 2009). Divorce rates have also doubled in mainland China over the last two decades as economic reforms put pressure on traditional marriages by giving women and men more personal freedom and life choices than they had previously known. It takes only 10 yuan (US$1.20) and less than 20 minutes to get a divorce at a local civil affairs department (Weihua, 2006).

Similarly, a cross-cultural study examining the reasons for divorce in a sample of 312 Muslim Arabs in Israel found a combination of modern and traditional sources of marital tension. On the traditional side, respondents complained of interference by relatives and male violence governed by a gender ideology giving husbands power over their wives. On the modern side, over two–thirds of both spouses reported communication problems and a failure to get along, problems commonly found in the United States and other Western countries (Cohen, 2003).

Although a discussion of these societal factors helps us to understand the context in which divorce takes place, it does not tell us what happens on the personal level. For that we have to look to the divorcing couples themselves or to the therapists who work with them.

FROM THE PERSPECTIVE OF DIVORCED PEOPLE

Paul Rasmussen and Kathleen Ferraro (1991) interviewed 32 divorced people, in most cases both husband and wife. Their findings raise questions about how we look at the causes of divorce. The behaviors most commonly cited as leading to divorce were poor communication, extramarital sex, constant fighting, emotional abuse, drug or alcohol problems, and financial mismanagement. Twelve years later, Paul Amato and Denise Previti (2003) classified 208 open-ended responses to a question on why respondents'

Watch the Video
Infidelity on **myfamilylab.com**

In the popular TV program *The Good Wife*, Chris Noth plays Peter Florrick, a current and former Cook County State's Attorney whose public sex and corruption scandal put a serious strain on his marriage to Alicia, played by Julianna Margulies.

marriages ended in divorce and found similar causes, with infidelity the most commonly reported cause, followed by incompatibility, drinking or drug use, and growing apart. In a national survey ex-husbands gave an average of 4.1 reasons for their divorce while ex-wives reported 5.1 reasons. The three most common reasons these ex-spouses gave for their divorces were lack of commitment, too much conflict and arguing and infidelity (Glenn, 2005).

Did these behaviors, however, actually "cause" the divorce? Many respondents in the Rasmussen and Ferraro study considered these activities to be after effects of crises or problems that derived from other sources. Other respondents reported that these behaviors had occurred prior to dating, during dating, and during the marriage. Many of the spouses had remained committed to marriages in which such offending behaviors were present and openly acknowledged. Rasmussen and Ferraro concluded that these behaviors may exist for years without leading to divorce or even creating any serious problems. Supporting evidence for this observation can be seen in a study of spouses' reactions to their partner's extramarital affair (EMA). The change in marital satisfaction because of the EMA increased the probability of divorce, but it was not the only determinant. The presence of dependent children in a family and good marital quality before the discovery of the EMA lowered the probability of divorce (Fan and Lui, 2004).

Thus, it appears that divorced people may not have a single reason for their divorce. Rather, a wide variety of "causes" are cited that pertain to a spouse's behavior, to perceived difficulties in the marital relationship, or to the impact of social and economic factors existing in the larger society.

FROM THE PERSPECTIVE OF FAMILY THERAPISTS AND MATRIMONIAL LAWYERS

A 1981 survey asked members of the American Association of Marriage and Family Therapists to rate the frequency, severity, and treatment difficulty of 29 problems frequently seen among couples experiencing marital difficulties (Geiss and O'Leary, 1981: 516–17).

The therapists were asked to rank the areas they considered most damaging to couple relationships and those most difficult to treat. The ten areas rated as most damaging were (1) communication, (2) unrealistic expectations of marriage or spouse, (3) power struggles, (4) serious individual problems, (5) role conflicts, (6) lack of loving feelings, (7) lack of demonstration of affection, (8) alcoholism, (9) extramarital affairs, and (10) sex. The ten areas rated as most difficult to treat successfully were (1) alcoholism, (2) lack of loving feelings, (3) serious individual problems, (4) power struggles, (5) addictive behavior other than alcoholism, (6) value conflicts, (7) physical abuse, (8) unrealistic expectations of marriage or spouse, (9) extramarital affairs, and (10) incest.

Although that survey was conducted over 30 years ago, its findings remain relevant. Recent surveys of matrimonial lawyers found many of the same problems in the clients they serve: extramarital affairs, family strains, emotional and family abuse, infidelity, addictions, and economic problems (Gornbein, 2011; Skul, 2005). New York psychotherapist Bonnie Eaker Weil (2008) sees financial infidelity as the number one problem in relationships. Although spouses may think they are not doing anything wrong, when their spouses discover their lies about money, savings, gambling and credit debt, the reaction is pain, distrust, and uncertainty, not unlike that experience after finding out a spouse is having an affair. According to a Harris Interactive survey of over 2,000 adults

- 58 percent of the respondents reporting hiding cash,
- 54 percent hid a minor purchase,
- 30 percent hid a bill,
- 16 percent hid a major purchase,
- 15 percent hid a bank account,
- 11 percent lied about debt, and
- 11 percent lied about earnings (Elejalde-Ruiz, 2011).

Even when spouses are honest about their finances, how they handle money can affect the quality and stability of marriage. When individuals feel that their spouse does not handle money well, they report lower levels of marital happiness (Brier, et al., 2008).

Do you agree with Dr. Weil that financial infidelity is a major problem for marital relationships? Why do you think spouses engage in this type of behavior? Why do you think people have difficulty talking about money? How should couples handle their financial affairs?

For more insight into how a therapist views the causes of divorce and the way therapy may help in resolving them, see the Strengthening Marriages and Families box on page 404.

DIVORCE AND THE INTERNET

Surveys of matrimonial lawyers and anecdotal reports of therapists and their clients suggest that the new informational technology may be putting serious strains on marital relationships and providing social networking evidence in an increasing number of divorces (American Academy of Matrimonial Lawyers, 2010). Some spouses engage in obsessive Internet use to the exclusion of meaningful family interaction and/or reconnect with "old flames" (or find potential new ones) that the other spouse views as a threat. Clinical psychologist Steven Kimmons describes the behavioral progression involved: "One spouse connects online with someone they knew from high school. The person is emotionally available, and they start communicating through Facebook. Within a short amount of time, the sharing of

Finances can become a source of conflict in a marital relationship. Spouses are well-advised to develop household budgets (like this couple is doing) and to openly discuss financial decisions.

The Internet is a useful tool, but it can also be a source of marital problems. One spouse may spend excessive amounts of time on the Internet and insufficient time on the marital relationship. In some cases, it can be a source of erotic fantasy, pornography, and cyber-affairs that can destroy the marriage.

TALKS WITH FAMILY THERAPIST JOAN ZIENTEK

Resolving Problems

In Your Practice, What Do You Find Are Some of the Problems that Lead to Divorce? A good percentage of divorcing couples come from families that lacked good models of spousal interaction. Thus, as children they did not learn the skills necessary to make a relationship work. Then when they grew up and married, they often selected a partner much like one of their parents, perhaps unconsciously using their marriage to work out their family of origin issues. If their partner comes with the same level of emotional health, the marriage lacks the resources to work out the natural conflicts that come from two people blending their lives together. When offspring are added to the mix, the picture becomes even more complex, resulting in three generations of issues living in one household.

Other problems can arise when a person marries without allowing time to get to know her or his partner. They can initially be drawn by the sexual energy that exists between them but when this wears out, they realize they little in common. Or they marry in a hurry because all of their friends are getting married, and they fear they will never find a suitable mate. In both these situations, as the years go by, often these couples grow in different directions and find they are strangers to each other.

Sometimes a couple faces a trauma, such as the death of a child, where one partner's grief is too intense for the other to bear as she or he is also struggling with grief. In situations like these, one party or the other may turn to someone outside the marriage for comfort and support; an affair may ensue, and in time the marriage may dissolve. This is especially true if, as psychologist John Gottman (1994b) suggests, they do not have an "emotional ecological balance," that is, engage in more acts of positive emotional interactions than of negative interaction.

Gottman found that couples who have a five-to-one ratio of positives to negatives have the greatest chance of marital success.

Are Some Problems More Difficult to Solve Than Others? Yes. One of the most difficult situations to manage is when one partner diagnoses the other as the source of the problem and refuses to see her or his contribution to the conflict in the marriage. It may take some time before the blaming person feels safe enough to begin to understand that feedback about her or his behavior need not be taken as harsh criticism, but instead as an opportunity to create changes that furthers closeness in the relationship. Another very difficult situation to confront occurs when one partner struggles with an addiction, whether it be alcoholism, gambling, or a sexual addiction. Addiction places enormous strain on the relationship. The resulting problems are often very intense and affect every aspect of family life, from lack of money to emotional withdrawal and even violence. The path to recovery is rarely smooth or easy. Even with the assistance of all the support groups that are now available, the impact is often more than the marriage can bear. An affair can also have a devastating affect on a marriage. Not only is the present condition of the relationship in question; an affair touches the meaning of the entire relationship—past, present, and future. The deception, the shattering of trust, the questioning of the relationship, and the loss of hope for a future together are all difficult issues to manage.

Can Counseling "Save" a Marriage? When a couple enters treatment, there are no guarantees about the outcome. Much depends on the strengths that each brings to the task. If, in therapy, each party is capable of observing her or his own behavior, if they speak directly to each other and not solely to the therapist, and if they refrain from placing the blame at their partner's feet, and if they

have a lot invested in the marriage, such as children, a shared history, financial investments, or friends, they have a good chance to work out their problems. These behaviors act as a cushion, absorbing the pain as well as providing the energy and support needed to resolve the problem. Also, couples need to have realistic expectations relative to the time it may take to resolve their issues without crying "divorce" when the road gets bumpy. They need to be willing to change their behaviors, to learn and practice new patterns of behavior as they relate to each other, and to sustain these changes after the therapy has ended. Some controlled studies of marital therapy outcomes have shown that only 50 percent of couples significantly improve their marriages, while 30–40 percent of those who do improve relapse within 2 years.

When Couples Decide to Divorce, Can Counseling or Mediation Help Make the Process Easier? When parties divorce, they can become involved with three types of professionals: a lawyer, a mediator, and a therapist. Rather than dealing with the expense of two lawyers, which often creates an adversarial situation, couples often seek the services of a mediator. The mediator serves as a guide to the parties as they define the issues in dispute and negotiate an agreement that includes the division of marital property and finances and decisions regarding child custody arrangements. Therapy, on the other hand, can help a couple resolve the emotional issues that may block the efforts of the mediation process. Having a third party involved in the dissolution of the marriage brings not only an objective point of view to the process, but it also provides a structure and sets limits that allow the couple a means for containing the anxiety and strong emotions that surround the situation. It also can prevent the children from becoming pawns in the process and ensure that their interests and well-being will be protected.

personal stories can lead to a deepened sense of intimacy, which in turn can point the couple in the direction of physical contact" ("Facebook and Divorce," 2011). The Internet provides an easy and inexpensive way to find alternative relationships. If spouses can't agree on alterations to this behavior, the marriage may be permanently ruptured.

How often do the members of your family use the Internet at home? Has your usage or that of other members of your family created any problems? What is it about the Internet that makes it so appealing? Should spouses establish any rules about their use of the Internet, particularly involving personal contacts? Explain.

The Impact of Divorce on Spouses

The consequences of divorce are many and varied. Although some of these are experienced by both spouses, a number of factors are gender-specific. We will begin this section by looking at those issues that commonly affect both spouses, and then we will isolate those features of divorce that affect women and men in distinctly different ways.

COMMON CONSEQUENCES OF DIVORCE

Charles Dickens could just as easily have been talking about divorce and its aftermath as about eighteenth-century London and Paris when he wrote, "It was the best of times; it was the worst of times." For most divorcing couples, both statements are true. On the positive side, divorce can free people from unhappy, conflict-ridden, or unsatisfactory relationships; it can also be a means to achieving personal growth. On the negative side, however, divorce can produce considerable pain, guilt, and uncertainty. This duality is clearly visible in Cheryl Buehler and Mary Langenbrunner's (1987) research. They asked 80 divorced people whose divorces had been finalized 6–12 months earlier to identify which of 140 items they had experienced since they separated from their spouses. The results showed that divorced people are almost equally likely to report both positive and negative outcomes. The most frequently reported items appear in Table 12.2. Although this research is 25 years old, the results are still valid today. A study of 1,147 people ages 40 to 79 who had divorced between the ages of 40 and 70 found they made similar assessments of their divorce experience (AARP, 2004).

Are you surprised to find that the most frequently occurring responses are positive? Many people are. However, this finding should not be interpreted to mean that the negative consequences are inconsequential. People in the process of divorce frequently encounter a number of problems. The most common problems experienced by both women and men are health problems (both physical and psychological), loneliness, the need for social and

TABLE 12.2 Most Frequently Reported Experiences of Divorced Persons	
I have felt worthwhile as a person.	96%
I have experienced personal growth and maturity.	94%
I have felt relieved.	92%
I have felt closer to my children.	89%
I have felt competent.	89%
The cost of maintaining the household has been difficult.	87%
I have felt angry toward my former spouse.	87%
I have felt insecure.	86%
My leisure activities have increased.	86%
I have been depressed.	86%
Household routines and daily patterns have changed.	85%

Source: Cheryl Buehler and Mary Langenbrunner, 1987, "Divorce-Related Stressors: Occurrence, Disruptiveness, and Area of Life Change." *Journal of Divorce and Remarriage* 11:35. Reprinted with permission of The Haworth Press, Inc., Binghamton, NY, 1987.

sexual readjustments, and financial changes in their lifestyles (AARP, 2004; Amato, 2000). This latter problem is more common to women than to men, so we will consider it later under gender-specific problems.

Health Problems Following divorce both women and men report feeling less healthy (Elwert and Christakis, 2008; Wu and Hart, 2002a). Additionally, many people experience depression and sometimes despair in the wake of a divorce. The process of divorce involves a number of major lifestyle alterations: loss of a major source of intimacy, the end of a set of daily routines, and a changed social status—going from a socially approved category (married) to a still somewhat disapproved category (divorced). Some divorced people believe they are excluded from social events, blamed for the marital breakup, and sometimes held in low regard. These feelings are especially true among members of various immigrant groups for whom a divorce is still seen as losing face for the whole family. A college student whose family is from India and whose parents divorced after a 24-year marriage said at a conference on Indian divorce stigmas, "Some people might think it's selfish. Marriage is a holy institution. Marriage is highly regarded, and to break that is taboo in itself" (Qamruzzaman, 2006:1). Hence, many divorced people respond to their new status with feelings of stress, guilt (especially for the initiator of divorce), and failure (especially for the partner who was asked for the divorce). Compared with their married peers, divorced people exhibit lower levels of psychological well-being, greater risk of mortality, more negative life events, greater levels of alcohol use, and lower levels of happiness and self-acceptance (Amato, 2000).

Loneliness Although people who live alone are not inherently more lonely than people who live together, a period of loneliness often accompanies the transition from being a part of a couple to being single again (the psychic divorce). This is especially true for childless couples and older couples whose children have already left home. However, divorce can involve more than the loss of a spouse. Relationships with former in-laws can be strained or broken off completely. Conversely, blood relatives might choose to retain contact with the ex-spouse even against the wishes of their own kin. The latter pattern often creates social distance among family members. Nevertheless, over time divorced individuals are able to compensate for their relationship losses (Terhell, 2004).

Social and Sexual Readjustments One of the major adjustments divorced people face is getting back into circulation. Dating is not easy at any age, but it is particularly problematic for older divorced people. Newly dating divorced people must deal with two key issues: how to explain their unmarried status and whether to be sexually active. Divorce does not lessen social or sexual needs. Studies from Alfred Kinsey, Wardell Pomeroy, and Clyde Martin (1948) through those of today show that most divorced people have sex within one year of being separated from their partner. Besides filling a physical need, providing intimacy, and exploring a new-found freedom, sex is often used to validate a sense of self-worth that may have been seriously eroded during the divorce process.

These needs are not always adequately met, however. Women in particular often feel exploited by men who assume that because they are divorced, they will automatically welcome any casual sexual relationship. Although both divorced women and men are sexually active, overall men have more sexual partners than women.

GENDER DIFFERENCES IN DIVORCE

In her study, *The Future of Marriage*, Jessie Bernard (1972) observed that every marital relationship contains two marriages that are often widely divergent. She called these "his" and "her" marriages. The same social structures and gender expectations that create differential marriage experiences for women and men also act to create differential divorces.

"Her" Divorce The most striking, even startling, difference between women and men following a divorce is a monetary one. Media headlines about the divorce settlements of the rich and famous, like Donald Trump, suggest that women are the recipients of huge alimony payments. Volumes of research over the last two decades reveal a markedly different pattern, however. The standard of living for children and their custodial parents (predominantly women) drops sharply after a divorce.

Downward Social Mobility In a pioneering study of the economic impact of California's no-fault divorce law (discussed earlier in this chapter) on divorcing spouses, sociologist Lenore Weitzman found a larger discrepancy. Weitzman analyzed 2,500 California court records covering a 10-year period, some before and some after the enactment of the law. She found that within a year of the final divorce decree, the standard of living of women and their children declined by an average of 73 percent, whereas that of

ex-husbands improved by an average of 42 percent (Weitzman, 1985:339). Other researchers have arrived at somewhat different numbers, but the general pattern they found is the same: downward social mobility for women and children, often to the point of impoverishment. This pattern holds across all racial–ethnic groups and can extend for long periods of time. One recent study found that 6 or more years after divorce, the family income of the average child whose custody parent remains unmarried is 45 percent lower than it would have been in the absence of a divorce (Page and Stevens, 2004). Another study examined an income-to-needs ratio and found that women and their children experience a decline of 20 to 36 percent in their income-to-needs ratio following a divorce (Sayer, 2006).

Women and children do not fare much better in other countries. Panel studies that included Belgium, Germany, Great Britain, Italy, and Sweden found that women may lose up to 80 percent of their income after a divorce, while the maximum loss for men was 23 percent (Andress, et al., 2006).

The decline in living standard following a divorce may push older women into poverty as well. In 1960, only 1.5 percent of women age 65 and older and 1.6 percent of men in that same age group were divorced. By 2006, the comparable figures were 10.6 and 8.3 (U.S. Census Bureau, 2011e). With first marriages lasting an average of 8 years (Kreider and Ellis, 2011b), the number of women who do not meet the 10-year marriage requirement that allows them to share in their husband's pension is increasing. Thus, it is expected that the proportion of economically vulnerable elderly women will increase when baby boomers retire.

Overall, this downward mobility for women and children is explained by two key factors: the earnings gap between women and men (see Chapter 10) and the failure of courts to award—and ex-husbands to pay—alimony and child support.

The Legal System and Women's Financial Well-Being According to sociologists Frank Furstenberg and Andrew Cherlin (1991:48–49), "When marriages dissolve, the shift in family responsibilities and family resources assumes a characteristic form. Women get the children and, accordingly, assume most of the economic responsibility for their support. Men become nonresidential parents and relinquish the principal responsibility for their support." These patterns are directly related to U.S. legal practices in granting alimony (also called "spousal support" or "spouse maintenance"), child custody, and child support.

Contrary to popular belief, courts today award alimony in only a small percentage of divorce cases. Both women and men are eligible to receive alimony from their former spouses. In practice, however, because men are usually the higher earner, they are less likely to be awarded alimony. Similar patterns exist in child support awards.

In spring 2008, an estimated 13.7 million parents had custody of 21.8 million children under 21 years of age whose other parent lived somewhere else. Almost 83 percent of custodial parents were mothers and slightly over 17 percent were fathers, proportions statistically unchanged from 1994. However, only 7.4 million of these parents (54 percent) had some type of support agreement or award for their children. Custodial mothers were more likely than custodial fathers to be awarded child support, 56.9 to 40.4 percent (Grall, 2009). However, as Table 12.3 shows, awards and receiving them may be two different things. Custodial mothers were more likely

TABLE 12.3 Child Support Awarded and Received, 2007

	%	Average Amount Due	Average Amount Received	% Receiving Full Amount	% Not Receiving Any Amount
Custodial Mothers	56.9	$5,366	$3,355	47.1	23.4
Custodial Fathers	40.4	5,239	3,343	45.0	25.8

Source: Adapted from T. Grall, 2009, *Custodial Mothers and Fathers and Their Child Support: 2007.* Current Population Reports, P60-237. (Washington, DC: U.S. Census Bureau), Table 2.

to receive awards than were fathers; White custodial parents had significantly higher award rates than African Americans or Latinas. The awards, in and of themselves, were not large and the majority of custodial parents worked. And although the poverty level of custodial mothers declined over the last decade, it was still significantly higher than the rate of custodial fathers (27 to 12.9 percent). Additionally, working full-time, year-round was not enough to keep 8.1 percent of custodial parents out of poverty.

Why do you think so many parents (both mothers and fathers) fail to make child support payments? Although there are laws allowing states to withhold child support payments from the noncustodial parent's paycheck, compliance remains a problem. What do you think could be done to get more noncustodial parents to pay child support? Many Internet sites now post photos of deadbeat parents. Do you think this is an effective technique to reach these parents? Explain.

Causes of Inequality between Divorced Women and Men What explains this economic discrepancy between divorced women and men? Weitzman (1985) attributes it to the provisions of the no-fault divorce laws, which require that husbands and wives be treated equally. In the abstract this sounds eminently fair. In reality, however, it overlooks the fact that women historically either were not in the labor force, or they received lower wages than did men if they were. Thus, simply dividing marital property equally without regard for the resources (professional degrees, skills) or the earning power of the respective spouses puts women at a real disadvantage vis-à-vis men. Women's advocates point out that by assuming responsibility for the majority of housework and child care, women sacrifice their own employment and earning power (see Chapter 10) and enhance that of their husband. Thus, these advocates argue that an equitable divorce settlement would take into account women's contributions to a husband's present and future earnings.

The Consequences of Divorce for Women What happens to women who experience this downward mobility? Many women, especially those in traditional marriages, suffer a loss of status, identity, and their domestic sphere—the home. Under the doctrine of equal division of property, homes are often sold so that both spouses can receive their share of the value of the house. The sale of the home often means moving out of a familiar and comfortable neighborhood into a smaller, less expensive place in a different neighborhood. Consequently, school, neighborhood, and friendship ties are often disrupted when they are most needed. Even when the house is not sold, financial strains may make maintenance and a comfortable style of living difficult.

Women with sole custody of children are often doubly burdened—they must be full-time parents as well as economic providers. In the process, they must watch their children do without many things that were taken for granted in the past. As the sole parent, divorced women may find little time for themselves or for social activities with peers.

Despite their economic stress, evidence suggests that women fare better in terms of divorce adjustment than do men. Numerous studies indicate that women improve the emotional and psychological quality of their lives more than men and are more likely than men to experience a sense of growth in self-esteem after a divorce (Demo and Fine, 2010; Braver, Shapiro, and Goodman, 2006). One explanation for women's and men's differing reactions may be that as women take on more instrumental roles, for example, becoming the sole provider and family head, they feel more confident about their abilities. Such changes were expressed by a female respondent: "I'm learning how to do things.... There's no mystery about it now, I can get out an electric drill.... I got satisfaction from putting a bookcase together" (quoted in Reisman, 1990:168). Men, on the other hand, lose some of those roles. The roles they add, such as housekeeper and cook, are not highly valued in this society. Many divorced men, especially those from traditional marriages, have trouble establishing a satisfying home environment and maintaining a household routine on their own. Because this was considered a wife's domain, many ex-husbands feel overwhelmed by shopping, laundry, cleaning, and cooking. This reaction is less likely for those husbands and fathers who participated more in household and child care tasks.

"His" Divorce Traditionally, men have been better off economically after a divorce than women. This is a result of many factors. Society has placed greater value on male workers and therefore paid them higher wages. Even when men pay child support, these payments often represent only a relatively small amount of their take-home pay. A combination of anger, emotional pain, irresponsibility, other debts, ongoing conflict with the former spouse, and remarriage often leads to noncompliance with court-ordered child support. Legal efforts to enforce compliance are often plagued by heavy caseloads, inadequate budgets, a shortage of personnel, and, until quite recently, a societal indifference to the plight of divorced women and children. Thus, a divorced husband typically has more discretionary income to support himself than his ex-wife has to support both herself and their children. Despite this finding, many divorced men feel they have been victimized by the divorce process and the aftermath of divorce (Lehr and MacMillan, 2001). Whether such patterns will continue to be as prominent is an empirical question. Today many men live in dual earner households and, in some cases, have wives who make higher incomes. Men who divorce under these circumstances may not enjoy monetary advantages over their former wives. Additionally, in the recession of 2007–2009 and its aftermath, men are experiencing higher rates of unemployment than women.

As we saw earlier, divorced people suffer more health problems and are more depressed than people who are married. In fact, divorce can be lethal, especially for men. An analysis of U.S. mortality data found that divorced men are two and one-half times more likely to commit suicide than married men. Additionally, men are more likely than women to respond to depression and isolation by abusing alcohol and drugs (Braver, Shapiro, and Goodman, 2006). Several factors are likely to contribute to this pattern. First, given that women tend to initiate divorce, men may feel more responsible for the breakup and/or were unprepared for it. Research suggests that the spouse who is left suffers more, at least initially (Sweeney, 2002). Second, because women are more likely to get custody of the children, men lose not only the husband role but a day-to-day father role as well. Third, norms of masculinity preclude many men from building effective social support networks that could help them during and after a divorce (Swiss and Le Bourdais, 2009).

Divorced men typically do not have custody of their children. Therefore, whether men desire it or not, divorce frees them from child care. Because they have more discretionary money, they are freer than their ex-wives to pursue social and leisure activities. Men's opportunities for remarriage are also greater than women's. Unencumbered by children, they are freer to date and to begin new relationships. Dating for divorced men is not problem-free, however. Divorced men may feel uncomfortable in this new role and may hold back because of a fear of rejection.

Although loneliness can be a problem for both women and men, divorced fathers without custody may feel it more intensely. Even with visitation rights, they miss out on the day-to-day contact with their children and may miss the ritual of family celebrations of special events and holidays. Dennis Meredith (1985) reports that some noncustodial fathers exhibit a child-absence syndrome, feeling depressed, anxious, and cut off from their children's lives. For some divorced fathers, this triggers negative reactions that erode the parent-child relationship. Visits with their children become more sporadic or stop completely. Researchers found that 42 percent of their male respondents, compared to 15 percent of their female respondents, said their worst fears after the divorce was that they would lose contact with their children (AARP, 2004). Their fears seem well founded. According to a recent study, 80 percent of children in the United States only live with their fathers for a maximum of 10–15 percent of the time after their parents' divorce. Almost half do not spend time with their father on a monthly basis and 25 percent do not spend any time at all with him. Less

Although many fathers lose contact with their children after divorce, other fathers find a way to build strong relationships with their children and share in childrearing tasks.

than 10 percent live with their father for more than 25 percent to 30 percent of the year (Kelly, 2007). Nonresidential mothers, on the other hand, visit their children more frequently and are less likely to stop contact with them (Kelly and Emery, 2003). This is a critical issue because when fathers do not maintain contact with children, they are less likely to pay child support (Maldonado, 2005).

Divorce also has a negative effect on men's contact with their adult children and on their perceptions of their children as potential sources of support in later life. When men relinquish ties to their children during childhood, even when they have provided child support, rarely do they resume those ties later in life (Connidis, 2009; de Graaf, 2007). For example, in one longitudinal study of divorced and married families, only one third of the adult sons and one quarter of the adult daughters were close to their divorced fathers (Hetherington and Kelly, 2002). A similar pattern exists for fathers who divorce later in life (Shapiro, 2003). Overall, the evidence suggests that divorced fathers are at greater risk for problematic relations with offspring regardless of the child's age. These studies raise questions about the degree to which family ties exist for divorced men as they age. Nevertheless, a word of caution is in order. Not all reports of relationship changes with fathers after divorce are negative and many adult children report improved relationships with their father over the years. Whether father–child relationships remain stable, improve or deteriorate depends on a number of both pre- and postdivorce factors (Ahrons, 2004a). Among the factors associated with worsening relationships over time are increased interparental conflict, early father remarriage, and low father involvement in the early postdivorce years, and poor quality relationships with stepfamily members (Ahrons and Tanner, 2003).

RECOVERING FROM DIVORCE

Given that the majority of divorcing couples face serious economic, social, and psychological problems, you may well wonder whether people ever recover from the trauma of divorce. Most do, although the process usually takes several years. For example, a study conducted over a period of 10 years by Judy Wallerstein and Sandra Blakeslee (1989) of 60 families disrupted by divorce found that women take an average of 3 to 3.5 years and men 2 to 2.5 years to reestablish a sense of external order after the separation. Not everyone recovers at the same speed, however. Wallerstein and Blakeslee found that some of their respondents had not recovered 15 years after their divorce. However, a more recent study found a gradual recovery usually begins by the end of the second year; 6 years after divorcing, 80 percent of both genders have moved on to build reasonably or exceptionally fulfilling lives (Hetherington, 2002). Similarly, a study of people who divorced at midlife or later found that three out of four respondents (75 percent) said they made the right decision and used words like freedom, self-identity, and fulfillment to describe their current situation (AARP, 2004).

Why do some people adjust more quickly than others? An emerging body of research has begun to identify certain factors that affect people's ability to adjust to divorce. Robert Lauer and Jeanette Lauer (1988) found that those who successfully coped with their divorce were able to redefine the divorce as an opportunity for growth. They did things like going back to school, building new social networks, becoming involved in community affairs, and learning to be more effective parents (Hetherington, 2002). Both women and men, but especially women, talked about gaining greater self-esteem and developing new competencies. Jane Burroughs, who married at 19 and divorced after more than 30 years of marriage, said, "After getting my divorce it was like going back and doing things I should have done when I was a teenager. I learned how to look within myself for happiness. It's a new experience, and I have found that I do it quite well" (quoted in Enright, 2004). Other researchers found that having higher income, getting remarried, having more positive attitudes about divorce, and being the party who initiated the divorce were associated with favorable postdivorce adjustment for both women and men (Wang and Amato, 2000).

The Impact of Divorce on Children

Writing in 1985, Sandra Hofferth estimated that 9 out of 10 African American children and 7 out of 10 White children (and most likely growing numbers of Native American and Asian American children) would spend part of their childhood in a single-parent household, mainly because of divorce and births to unmarried mothers. In 2009, 26.2 percent of all children under 18 lived with only one parent, up from 12 percent in 1970. Twenty-one percent of White children, nearly 54 percent of African American children, over 27 percent of Latina/o children, and almost 13 percent of Asian American children lived in one-parent families (U.S. Census Bureau, 2011e).

Some social theorists and many public and religious leaders argue that the intact, two-parent family is necessary for the normal development and well-being of children. This view is most evident in structural-functional, social-learning, developmental, and symbolic-interaction theories (see Chapter 2), all of which see the family as one of the primary agents of socialization and role modeling for children. However, these theoretical perspectives often ignore the fact that the effects of disrupted families on children might be short-lived, that the role of an absent parent might be filled by significant others (as was the case in much of human history), that the custodial parent might be warm and supportive (Ahrons, 2004b; Campbell, 2001; Kelly, 2000). Additionally, there is strong evidence to suggest that the degree of parental conflict is a good predictor of children's adjustment to divorce. Children have more emotional and behavioral problems when their parents are in conflict, either

A child's reaction to divorce can be similar to that of divorcing parents—it often includes feelings of denial, anger, sadness, rejection, despair, grief, and loneliness.

during marriage or following a divorce (McIntosh and Long, 2006; Grych, 2005; Kelly and Emery, 2003).

SHORT-TERM VERSUS LONG-TERM EFFECTS OF DIVORCE ON CHILDREN

For the most part, there is agreement about the short-term effects of divorce, some of which resemble those experienced by divorcing parents: rejection, anger, denial, sadness, despair, and grief (Kelly and Emery, 2003). Children frequently feel guilty, blaming themselves for the divorce, especially if their parents have quarreled over them. Children often entertain fantasies about reuniting their parents.

Just as with adults, these stresses can result in health problems, both psychological and physical. Research shows that the physical health ratings of children from divorced families are poorer than those of children from intact families (Amato, 2000). Children living with their mothers are more likely to lack health insurance, making timely and quality health care problematic. Children with divorced parents see themselves as less competent and exhibit more depression and withdrawal than children from intact families (Najman et al., 1997). The duration and intensity of these feelings depend in some measure on parental behavior. If parental conflict continues after the divorce, the adjustment process for children may be prolonged.

In contrast, many of the findings of long-term effects on children are not as clear-cut or consistent. On the one hand, some researchers like Judith Wallerstein and her colleagues (2000) conclude that the effects of divorce are long-lasting and interfere with normal social-emotional development. Twenty-five years after her 1971 study of 131 children whose parents divorced, Wallerstein interviewed 93 of the original subjects, now 33 years old on average. She found that in comparison to a control group of 44 adults similar in age and socioeconomic status but whose parents had not divorced, the adult children of divorced parents experienced greater anxieties and more failures in their interpersonal relationships. More recently, Elizabeth Marquardt (2005) drew a similar conclusion based on her study of adults whose parents divorced when they were children. On the other hand, sociologists like Andrew Cherlin (2000) have cautioned against reading too much into long-term effects without knowledge of the state of the parental home prior to the divorce. He points out that 50 percent of the fathers and close to half of the mothers in Wallerstein's study suffered from serious mental or addiction problems. Thus, it is possible that these adults would have had the same or similar problems even if their parents had not divorced. Other researchers have come to similar conclusions, noting that many of the estimated effects of divorce are not as strong as some researchers claim (Amato, 2003).

The fact that a number of longitudinal studies of children found that as many as half of the behavioral and academic problems of children in marriages whose parents later divorced were observed 4–12 years before the separation suggests that troubled families and not divorce, per se, may be more responsible for long-term negative effects (Cherlin, 2000; Kelly, 2000). Similarly, other research has found that marital conflict is a more important predictor of children's problems than is divorce itself (Buehler et al., 1998). Further, symptoms commonly found in children of

divorced parents (low self-esteem, depression, and school and behavioral problems) also are more often found in children of high-conflict marriages than in children of low-conflict marriages (Vandewater and Lansford, 1998).

Other family experts believe that although some children of divorced parents do have problems, the majority do not experience severe or long-term problems (Coontz, 1997; Barber and Demo, 2006). Accurate assessments of the long-term impact of divorce require more study and more precise controls for the complex variables that promote or hinder growth in children's lives.

How Does Divorce Affect Children's Behavior? Researchers report that children of divorce are absent from school more, do poorer schoolwork, are more likely to use alcohol, cigarettes, marijuana, and other drugs, and have a greater risk of dropping out of school and experiencing a premarital pregnancy than children from intact families (Coleman, Ganong, and Fine, 2000; Crowder and Teachman, 2004). College attendance is also affected by divorce. A government study found that 71 percent of the children from intact families went to college, compared with 54 percent of those whose parents were divorced (Mathews, 1996).

Again, however, these findings must be interpreted cautiously. The parental divorce is not the only factor affecting children's behavior. It is estimated that the declining economic status of disrupted households accounts for as much as half of the adjustment problems found in children of divorced parents (McLanahan, 1999). Other researchers found that the more transitions children experience in their family settings (divorce, remarriage, relocation), the more they are likely to exhibit behavioral problems (Fomby and Cherlin, 2007). However, this was true for White children, but not for Black children. A possible explanation for this finding is that the Black children included in that study were more likely to have extended families nearby that provided emotional support. In a similar vein, high levels of family cohesion and adaptability are likely to result in fewer behavior problems (Dremen, 2003).

Gender and Divorce Although both girls and boys are affected by parental divorce, researchers have found that, on average, divorce has a more negative effect on boys than girls; girls make a better adjustment to divorce than boys and they do so more quickly (Amato, 2001; Hetherington and Kelly, 2002; Hines III, 2007). However, it is well to keep in mind that in the population at large, school problems, run-ins with the police, and aggressive behaviors have been found to be more common among boys than girls regardless of family structure. Additionally, some of the general and assumed gender-specific problems attributed to divorce may instead be a result in a decrease in parental supervision (McLanahan, 1999). For example, when divorced fathers are more involved with their children, the children do better academically and have fewer school problems than children with less involved fathers and there are no significant differences in performance and achievement between them and children in intact families. Additionally, their children are more likely to adjust better and more quickly after the parental divorce (Nielsen, 2011; Fabricius, et al., 2010; Emery, 2004).

Not all research on the effects of divorce has found negative effects. In female-headed families, both mothers and children develop more androgynous behavior as they reorganize the household after the father has left. Additionally, assuming more responsibilities leads children to greater maturity and feelings of competence (Gately and Schwebel, 1992). Finally, of course, children may feel relief to be out of a conflictual and possibly abusive family situation. A study of 330 undergraduates at a large southeastern university found that almost a third (32.9 percent) reported a positive effect of their parents divorce (Knox, Zusman, and DeCuzzi, 2004). This study offers further evidence that children living in a stable single-parent family are emotionally better off than if they remain in a conflict-ridden two-parent family.

CHILDREN AND DIVORCE IN OTHER COUNTRIES

To date, most of the research on the effects of divorce on children has been conducted in the United States and other English-speaking countries, where the findings have been fairly consistent. However, in countries like China, divorce has traditionally been condemned and those who divorce are stigmatized. As globalization has increased, especially in countries where women's roles are changing, divorce tends to be increasing as well. Whether children in countries with diverse cultural and economic patterns will respond to parental divorce in the same way as children in Western countries is an intriguing empirical question.

Although there has been relatively little cross-cultural research on this topic, it does seem that there is at least some initial support for the belief that findings from the United States may be generalizable to other cultures. Researchers have found that Chinese children of divorced parents, like their U.S. counterparts, are more likely to be aggressive, to be withdrawn, and to have more behavioral and social problems than children from intact families. Also, divorced parents report more mental and physical health problems for their children than do nondivorced parents (Liu, Guo, and Okawa, 2000). Further support that there are at least some universal factors that affect children's reactions to family conflict and divorce comes from research on young Kuwaiti adults. Researchers found that children with divorced parents had low levels of contact with their fathers and more negative perceptions of marriage and greater openness to the idea of divorce than children from intact families (Alqashan and Alkandari, 2010). These findings are consistent with those of studies in the United States (see, for example, Amato, 2006; Nicholson, 2006). However, research in other countries, like China and Kuwait, suggest that there are culture-specific factors that also affect divorce outcomes.

Changing Patterns in Child Custody

In any marital disruption involving children, a question that must be resolved is, "Who gets the children?" We examine this difficult question by focusing specifically on the issues of sole custody, joint custody, and visitation rights.

In recent years, increasing public attention has focused on the high rate of divorce in the United States, particularly with respect to how divorce affects children. This young boy indicates his displeasure with the process by sticking out his tongue at his father during a custody hearing.
Source: Reprinted with permission of the Daily Breeze © 2002.

SOLE CUSTODY

In divorce cases, for much of U.S. history, courts have almost always awarded **sole custody,** in which one parent is given legal responsibility for raising the child. Earlier we noted that in colonial America, fathers were far more likely to get custody of their children following a divorce. Over the years, a cultural belief evolved that women are inherently better at nurturing than are men. The courts adopted the view that children, especially in their early years, need to be with their mothers. So entrenched did this view become by the mid-twentieth century that the only way a father could get custody was to prove his wife an unfit mother (Greif, 1985). Since then, however, a noticeable shift has occurred in child custody cases. Although most fathers still do not request custody, today those who do so have a good chance of being successful. In 2007, slightly more than 1 of 6 custodial parents (17.4 per cent) were fathers (Grall, 2009). Research shows that fathers increased their odds of receiving sole custody when they were the plaintiffs and when a friend of the court investigation was undertaken. Thus, fathers often have to exert extra legal efforts to strengthen their claims. The odds of fathers gaining custody are enhanced when they pay child support, when the children are older, and when the oldest child is male (Fox and Kelly, 1995).

Noncustodial Mothers According to the U.S. Census Bureau, there are 2.2 million mothers who lack custody of their children (Grall, 2009). Some of these mothers have voluntarily relinquished custody. Given the traditional view of women as nurturers and homemakers, women who agree to give custody to the father frequently are portrayed as unloving, uncaring, selfish, and un-womanly. However, studies show that these negative images have little to do with the woman's actual reasons for giving up custody: inadequate finances, child's preference for living with father, child's best interest, difficulty in controlling children, threats of legal custody fights, and physical or emotional problems experienced by the woman (Herrerias (2008; Bemiller, 2008). Although these women did not have custody, the vast majority of them actively maintained a relationship with their children.

Not all women who lose custody do so voluntarily. Some mothers are forced by the courts to give up custody due to their perceived inability to care for the children, either economically or emotionally, or they do so to avoid conflicts with their former spouse who may have been physically or emotionally abusive. Sometimes the women had poor legal representation and lost the custody battle (Herrerias, 2008). Using financial means as a criterion for child custody puts women at a real disadvantage because in the vast majority of cases fathers are better off economically.

Money is not the only issue over which custody battles are fought or decided. The sexual orientation of a parent can also be an issue. In the past, lesbian and gay parents' custody of their children was often challenged and threatened solely because of their sexual orientation. A 1995 decision in a child custody case in Tallahassee, Florida, is an especially eye-opening example of the prejudice and discrimination lesbians and gays faced, and sometimes still do, in child custody cases. In this case, a Florida judge took an 11-year-old girl from her mother simply because the mother was a lesbian and awarded custody to the father, a convicted murderer and accused child molester.

Such judicial decisions were often based on the mistaken belief that children raised in a lesbian or gay household would "naturally" adopt a gay or lesbian lifestyle or that they would suffer some psychological harm. Research findings have largely refuted these views and today most state courts require evidence of adverse impact before a parent's sexual orientation or involvement in a nonmarital relationship can be used to limit custody or visitation rights. This adverse impact test, also referred to as the *nexus test,* requires a clear connection between a parent's actions and harm to the child before a parent's sexual orientation can assume any relevance in the custody determination (National Center for Lesbian Rights, 2002).

When children are involved, divorcing couples must negotiate visitation rights for the noncustodial parent. If parents can cooperate with each other in this regard, children are less likely to feel caught in the middle and can benefit from a relationship with both of their parents.

JOINT CUSTODY

Spurred in part by fathers' rights advocates, who argued that the legal system discriminated against them, California passed the country's first joint-custody law in 1979. Currently, the vast majority of states allow for some form of joint custody (sometimes referred to as co-custody or shared parenting). **Joint custody** means that both parents are involved in childrearing and decision-making. Joint custody can take two forms: joint legal custody, in which both parents are to share decision making on such issues as education and health care, and joint physical custody, an arrangement in which children spend from one-third to one-half of their time with each parent. The increased role of fathers in child rearing has led to some creative joint-custody living arrangements, one form of which is known as *bird-nesting.* Here the children stay in the family home and the parents alternate living there,

with each parent having another place to stay on their off time (Navarro, 2005). However, full joint custody in this latter sense is still relatively rare. In practice, most joint custody involves shared legal custody, with physical custody remaining with one parent, usually the mother. In that sense, joint custody varies little from sole custody except for the assumption that decisions about the children's welfare will be made by both parents. About 18 percent of total custody cases presently involve joint custody (U.S. Census Bureau, 2005a).

WHICH IS BETTER, SOLE OR JOINT CUSTODY?

Earlier we examined the impact of divorce on children and found that raising a child as a single parent is extremely difficult. All things being equal, the evidence suggests that being raised in a loving, intact family provides the most beneficial arrangement for children. Thus, the motives behind the movement to increase joint custody are to provide children with continuing contact with both parents and to relieve one parent of the total burden of child care. A recent study comparing child adjustment in intact families with that in joint physical or joint legal custody and sole-custody settings indicate that some of these benefits are being realized. Children in joint-custody arrangements had less behavioral and emotional problems, had higher self-esteem, and had better family relations and school performance than children in sole-custody arrangements. In addition, these children were as well-adjusted as intact family children on the same measures, most likely because joint custody provides the child with an opportunity for continuing contact with both parents (Bauserman, 2002). Other research found that there was a higher compliance rate of paying child support in cases of joint custody compared to cases of solo custody (Sayer, 2006). In addition, families with joint custody had more frequent father-child visitation but lower maternal satisfaction with custody arrangements than families with sole maternal custody (Gunnoe and Braver, 2001). However, other earlier studies have found that outside the regular child support payments, there were few differences in adjustment between children in sole versus joint physical custody (Johnston, 1995; Pruett and Hoganbruen, 1998).

Because joint custody is relatively new, an evaluation of its effectiveness in minimizing the adjustment problems of children over time is still open to debate. Some experts, like Mary Ann Mason (1999), a professor of law and social welfare and author of *The Custody Wars,* are critical of the joint custody trend. Mason argues that the push for joint custody grew more out of a concern for the rights of parents, particularly fathers, rather than out of a concern for children's rights. Based on her years of experience practicing family law and her extensive research, she concludes that joint custody rarely works because it requires parents to cooperate, which she believes is more than most divorced couples can manage. Joint custody is not for everyone. It works successfully only in cases where divorcing couples have a fairly amicable relationship and desire a pattern of shared parenting. In the absence of these two characteristics, joint custody may simply perpetuate the conflict that led to the divorce in the first place. Additionally, joint custody is more likely to succeed when parents have stable job histories and other resources (Juby, Bourdais, and Marcil-Gratton, 2005). Problems with joint custody arise when one or the other parent decides to remarry, take a new job, or relocate.

Regardless of the form custody takes, provisions for visitation of the other parent must be agreed on. Noncustodial parents with visitation rights enter into a new set of interactions with their children. Often both the parent and the child are uncertain how to behave in this situation; thus, visitation itself becomes a source of stress. Logistics are a problem, too: Where to go? What to do? Whom to include? Often the spontaneity of parent–child relationships is transferred to a recreational relationship, with the time together being spent in a constant round of activities, for example, going to the movies or the zoo. Noncustodial fathers who engage in this pattern are referred to as "Disneyland dads."

Parents and children often perceive the visits in different ways. Parents may think that by engaging in recreational activities they are being loving, whereas children may feel rejected because the relationship seems artificial and as such does little to enhance children's sense of well-being (Stewart, 2003). Thus, in the best of circumstances problems can occur with visitation. The visits can become a source of real stress, especially in the period immediately after a divorce if parents have not worked through their own feelings. Visitation can then become a battleground through which ex-spouses carry on their conflict with each other. This takes many forms: The noncustodial parent often overindulges the children to look good in their eyes; both parents may grill the children about the other parent's new lifestyle or speak ill of the other parent; one or both parents may consistently violate the spirit of the visitation agreement by changing plans at the last minute, not having the children ready on time, or bringing them back late. Parents are more likely to avoid these behaviors if they reflect on the rights of children caught up in divorce situations as they have been identified by the judicial system. All children have the following rights:

- To have a continuing relationship with both parents;
- To be treated not as a piece of property, but as a human being with unique feelings, ideas, and desires;
- To receive continuing care and proper guidance from each parent;
- To not be unduly influenced by either parent to view the other parent negatively;
- To freely express love, friendship, and respect for both parents, without feeling shame or a necessity to hide those emotions;
- To be given an explanation that the parents' divorce was in no way caused by the child's actions; and
- To not be the subject and/or source of any arguments.

Noncustodial parents are not the only ones concerned about visitation rights. Grandparents can play an important role in helping their grandchildren adjust to a divorce. Grandparents symbolize stability and continuity. Because of the acrimony of some divorces or the geographic relocation of the custodial parent, however, grandparents may be unable to fulfill this role. Studies have revealed certain trends in relationships between grandparents and grandchildren following divorce. In general, the custodial grandparents (parents of the custodial parent) have an advantage in maintaining ties with their grandchildren. Because women are more likely to receive custody, relationships between maternal grandparents and grandchildren tend to be maintained and even strengthened, whereas ties with paternal grandparents frequently are weakened (Lussier et al., 2002).

Visitation rights are not the norm in all countries. In Japan, for example, joint custody is not legal. In the past, fathers got the children most of the time. Now that most women work and can support their children, mothers routinely get custody of their children. However, the usual pattern is that the other parent does not visit or is not allowed to visit her or his children. Although some parents engage in informal visitation, there is no legal mechanism to enforce visitation rights for the noncustodial parent ("Japan Fails...," 2008).

WHEN THINGS GO WRONG: FAMILY ABDUCTION

It should be clear by now that the process of divorce can involve ongoing conflict between the divorcing spouses. All too often children can end up in the middle of the fight. When this happens, a child might be abducted by a parent or other family member in an attempt to protect the child from abuse, to get back at the other parent, to gain control, or to use the child as a pawn in a divorce settlement. According to the U.S. Department of Justice, **family abduction** is the taking or keeping of a child by a family member in violation of a custody order, a decree, or other legitimate custodial rights, where the taking or keeping involved some element of concealment, flight, or intent to deprive a lawful custodian indefinitely of custodial privileges. It is estimated that 350,000 children are victims of family abduction each year in the United States. Fathers are significantly more likely than mothers to abduct children. Fortunately, in almost half of the cases, the children were gone for less than one week. However, some children are taken out of the country, presenting political as well as legal difficulties in getting them back. The Government Accountability Office has documented at least 6,966 cases of international parental adduction over the decade ending in 2009, mostly be foreign-born parents returning to their country of birth (Powell, 2011).

Reaching Accord: Counseling, Collaborative Law, and Mediation

Thus far, we have seen that divorce can cause a variety of problems, not only for the divorcing couple but also for their children, their extended family, and their friends. Because of the emotional content, most divorces can easily become bitter and acrimonious affairs, leaving deep emotional and psychological wounds. Therefore, a growing number of marriage counselors and other professionals have shifted some of their practice into **divorce counseling.** Essentially, their goal is to replace the adversarial and often destructive aspects that can accompany the legal divorce with a more cooperative spirit. At the same time, they try to help people withdraw and distance themselves from the relationship so that acceptance of the loss and subsequent healing can take place. When these goals are accomplished, people are better able to begin new relationships. Divorcing couples or individuals may seek such counseling during the process of the divorce or at a much later stage in their life. Some states, however, require **conciliation counseling** before the courts will consider granting a divorce. The purpose behind this kind of counseling is to see whether the marital problems can be resolved and the couple reconciled.

When reconciliation is not possible, couples often find themselves caught up in an adversarial divorce proceeding. Concerned by the destructive impact this causes, Stuart Webb, a prominent Minnesota divorce lawyer, instituted a practice called **collaborative law**—where the attorneys for both parties to a family dispute agree to assist in resolving the conflict using cooperative techniques rather than adversarial strategies and litigation with the goal of reaching an efficient, fair, and comprehensive out-of-court settlement of all issues. If the process fails and either party wishes to have the matter resolved in court, both attorneys withdraw and disqualify themselves from further representation except to assist in the orderly transfer of the case to adversarial counsel.

Divorce mediation has a related but somewhat different emphasis. It is a procedure designed to help divorcing couples negotiate a fair and mutually agreed-on resolution of such issues as marital property distribution, child custody, visitation rights, and financial support. Divorce mediators generally have backgrounds in law, social work, counseling, or psychology. In any given divorce, one or more mediators may be involved. For example, divorce lawyers may work with counselors or therapists to help the couple reach accord. Mediated settlements must be approved by the court to become legally binding on the parties involved.

Although divorce mediation is still relatively new, having emerged as a distinct practice only in the 1970s, evidence suggests that all parties benefit from the process (Shaw, 2010). Couples can learn negotiating skills that will help them deal with each other in the future. Children do not see their parents embroiled in a constant struggle over them. Having participated in drawing up the agreement, spouses are more likely to honor its terms, thereby reducing the likelihood of future conflicts. With divorce mediation, non-custodial fathers are more likely to feel they have more of a say in the decisions affecting their children than they would have had otherwise and, thus, are likely to stay more involved in their children's lives. Finally, mediated divorce agreements cost considerably less than adversarial divorces because less time and labor are required (Emery, 2004).

The Renewed Debate: Should Parents Stay Married for the Sake of Their Children?

In recent years, findings from a number of studies have revived this question. As Paul Amato (2001) observed, before the 1970s, divorce was viewed as catastrophic for children who were said to be from "broken homes," and at risk for a wide range of behavioral and emotional problems. People in unhappy marriages were expected to do the right thing and stick it out for the sake of the children. Then along came the 1970s, opening an era characterized by an emphasis on personal choice and self-fulfillment. Staying in an unhappy marriage, especially one marked with conflict, was viewed as bad for children. It was assumed that if parents were happy, so, too, would the children be. The divorce rate climbed. This liberalizing period was followed by a new wave of conservativism and religious renewal. Concern for the perceived breakdown of the family began to and continues to dominate public discourse, and with it a renewed concern about the negative impact divorce can have on children and society at large.

Studies finding long-term effects of divorce on children are a critical part of the current debate. For example, in her well-publicized book, *Between Two Worlds: The Inner Lives of Children of Divorce*, Elizabeth Marquardt (2005) found significant differences between children who grew up in intact families and children who experienced their parents' divorce and who said they felt like they grew up in two families, not one. However, what seems to be at the core of this question is the finding that many divorces involve low-conflict marriages, even marriages in which spouses say they were happy but perhaps experiencing a midlife crisis, were not feeling self-actualized, were bored, or were looking for new experiences. Thus, the question: Can these marriages be saved? And should saving these marriages become a goal of public policy?

These are not easy questions to answer. Much of the public discourse on this issue seems to pit the happiness and welfare of children against the happiness and welfare of adults. A recent longitudinal study tracking unhappy marriages over a 12-year period found that long-term, low-quality marriages have negative effects on overall well-being. Remaining unhappily married is associated with significant lower levels of overall happiness, life satisfaction, self-esteem, and health. The study also found evidence that staying unhappily married is more detrimental than divorcing as those who remained unhappily married scored lower on measures of well-being than people who divorced and remained unmarried (Hawkins, 2005). This finding notwithstanding, it is also likely that some divorces need not have happened. When asked in a recent survey "Do you wish you had worked harder to save the marriage?" only one-third of the respondents said "no." When asked do you wish your ex-spouse had worked harder to save the marriage, 62 percent of ex-wives and ex-husbands answered "yes" (DiCaro, 2005).

> What do you think? Should people in low-conflict (or unhappy) marriages be encouraged to stay married for the sake of the children? Would you? Under what conditions? How do you think staying married in these kinds of relationships would affect children? Explain.

Supporting Marriages and Families

The first step in formulating support for married couples and their families is to recognize that inevitably some marriages will not survive and that there are some relationships so abusive that for spouses and children to remain in them is a threat to health and even life itself. That being said, it is also reasonable to assume that other married couples could be helped to avoid divorce. There is considerable evidence that premarital and postmarital counseling, if undertaken early enough, can help couples to improve their communication and parenting skills and thus lesson sources of marital stress. Such counseling needs to be affordable and readily available in schools and in the community. Parents who make the decision to divorce should be encouraged to learn more about how divorce affects children and what they can do to lessen the risks their children face. If the goal of saving marriages is to improve the welfare of children, it will require strategies to create jobs that pay a decent wage so that household income will increase (see Chapter 10). Parent absence, particularly father absence, has been found to be a major factor in problems many children encounter after a divorce and in some ongoing marriages as well. A part of any program to foster and stabilize marriages and families needs to promote activities that keep parents and other adults connected with children at all ages.

Writing Your Own Script

EVALUATING RELATIONSHIPS

Although no one likes to consider the possibility that a loving relationship will come to an end, we do have to face the reality that more than 40 percent of first marriages will end in divorce. We also know that divorce is more common among certain groups and that every couple will experience problems and conflicts at one time or another. The critical factor in the relationship is not the experience of problems or conflicts in themselves but rather what resources and skills are available to help resolve them.

Questions to Consider

1. What will my partner and I do when things do not seem to be working out right? Can we create mechanisms for resolving disagreements before they occur? Will we be willing to get counseling if we are having problems?

2. Have our parents, siblings, or any of our friends been divorced? What are our attitudes regarding divorce?

3. What resources can we establish for meeting unexpected problems, such as unemployment, financial difficulties, or illness?

4. If we have children, what do we see as our responsibilities toward them should something happen to our marital relationship?

SUMMARY

Contrary to popular belief, divorce is not a modern phenomenon. It has been a part of U.S. history since 1639, when a Puritan court in Massachusetts granted the first divorce decree in colonial America. As public concern grew over the perceived consequences of divorce, reform efforts were debated.

Divorce rates vary from group to group and are associated with a wide range of factors. Among the most frequently cited factors are race and ethnicity, age at marriage, level of education and income, religion, cohabitation, parental divorce, and the presence of children.

Divorce does not just happen. It is a complex social process in which a basic unit of social organization, marriage, breaks down over time, culminating in a legal termination of the relationship. Researchers have identified several stages in this process: a period of marital conflict and unhappiness, the actual marital dissolution itself, and a period of adjustment following divorce. Both women and men in the process of divorce face some common problems: a decline in health, loneliness, and the need for social and sexual readjustment. However, there are also gender differences. Although women suffer more economic distress than men, they may fare better in terms of overall adjustment.

Increasing numbers of children are affected by divorce. Researchers generally agree that children experience some of the same short-term effects their divorcing parents do: rejection, anger, denial, sadness, despair, and grief. There is less agreement about the long-term effects. Some researchers believe that children gain equilibrium 1 or 2 years after the divorce; others feel that the effects are long-lasting and interfere with normal social-emotional development for a significant number of children.

Although the courts typically award one parent, generally the mother, sole custody of the children, more judges are awarding joint custody. It is still too early to assess the effectiveness of the latter approach for the welfare of children. Establishing fair and appropriate visitation rights for noncustodial parents (and increasingly for grandparents) is not an easy matter. Conflict over visitation rights can prolong the trauma of divorce. As a reaction to many of the problems associated with divorce, a number of legislatures across the country are debating proposals to change existing divorce laws. Divorce counseling, conciliation counseling, collaborative law, and divorce mediation are being used increasingly in an effort to reduce some of the conflicts in the divorce process.

KEY TERMS

alimony	stations of divorce	community divorce	annulment	divorce counseling
split custody	emotional divorce	psychic divorce	sole custody	conciliation counseling
no-fault divorce	legal divorce	separation	joint custody	collaborative law
crude divorce rate	economic divorce	desertion	family abduction	divorce mediation
refined divorce rate	coparental divorce			

QUESTIONS FOR STUDY AND REFLECTION

1. Historian Eric Sager, commenting on the growing ranks of singles, points out, "It is often said that divorce today performs the function that death did in the past. The promise to live together for better or worse, so long as you both shall live, means something very different if you anticipate a married life of 60 years, as opposed to a married life of 25 years." Do you agree or disagree with Sager? Is the goal of lifetime marriage realistic in today's society? What role, if any, does an increase in life expectancy play in marital stability? Explain.

2. Most marriages start out with many rituals. Among them are the engagement, the bridal shower, the bachelor party, the rehearsal dinner, and the wedding ceremony itself (often religious in nature). Friends and relatives offer their support by cards, gifts, and attendance at these events. Divorce, on the other hand, is often a solitary experience. In fact, the partners are not even required to be physically present when the divorce decree is issued. Yet divorce, like marriage, marks a new beginning in a person's life. Do you think society should initiate divorce rituals aimed at helping people move on with their lives? Marianne Williamson (1994) provides one example: At a ceremony, the divorcing couple can face each other and, in turn, say, "I bless you and release you. Please forgive me; I forgive you. Go in peace. You will remain in my heart." Other variations include readings and the return of wedding rings. What is your reaction to such rituals? Could they serve a useful purpose for the divorcing couple? Their children and other relatives? Society at large? Or do you think they would encourage more couples to divorce? Explain. Consider in your answer the benefits that rituals provide in many other aspects of our lives.

3. Consider both the positive and negative consequences of divorce. On balance, do you think restricting divorce through more stringent laws would be a wise public policy? Explain. Should couples who are experiencing marital difficulties be required to undergo counseling before being allowed to file for divorce? Should couples with children meet stricter standards for divorce than child-free couples? Conversely, should marriage licenses depend on receiving premarital counseling? Explain.

4. As we have seen, children suffer many consequences in the aftermath of a divorce. What steps could be taken to lessen the trauma of divorce for children? How and what should children be told about their parents' divorce? Who should tell them? What reactions should parents expect from children during and after the process of divorce? Would the trauma of divorce be lessened for children if parents followed the judicial guidelines covering children's rights? Explain.

ADDITIONAL RESOURCES

SOCIOLOGICAL STUDIES

BAIR, DEIRDRE. 2007. *Calling It Quits: Late-Life Divorce and Starting Over.* Following her divorce after 43 years of marriage, the author set out to explore the reasons for late-life splits by interviewing husbands, wives, and adult children to get at all sides of the stories.

CHERLIN, ANDREW J. 2009. *The Marriage-Go Round: The State of Marriage and the Family in America Today.* New York: Knopf. Sociologist Andrew Cherlin explores the tension between the Americana cultural ideal of commitment to marriage and the appeal of individual freedom and makes comparisons between U.S. values and those of Britain and France. He observes that American family life is a merry-go-round characterized by frequent marriage, frequent divorce, and short-term cohabiting relationships.

DEMO, DAVID H. AND MARK FINE. 2009. *Beyond the Average Divorce.* Thousand Oaks, CA: Sage Publications. This volume provides a rich depiction of how children and adults of all ages respond to diverse divorce experiences. Their emphasis is on variability and change over time in the pre-divorce, divorce, and post-divorce process.

FILM

The Squid and the Whale. 2005. Writer-director Noah Baumbach's semiautobiographical story provides a moving account of two teenage boys who struggle with the painful reality of their parents' divorce while at the same time facing the dilemmas of growing up and coming to terms with their emerging sexual selves.

It's Complicated. 2009. When attending their son's college graduation, a couple reignite the spark in their relationship, but the complicated fact is they're divorced and he's remarried.

LITERARY

CORMAN, AVERY. 2005. *A Perfect Divorce.* New York: St. Martin's Press. A fast-moving novel by the author *of Kramer vs. Kramer* that packs an emotional punch as it reveals the efforts of an urban, middle-class, dual-career couple who attempts to structure a "perfect divorce" for their son, only to find their expectations dashed when their son goes off the tracks.

GILBERT, ELIZABETH. 2006. *Eat, Pray, Love: One Woman's Search for Everything Across Italy, India and Indonesia.* New York: Viking. Feeling down after a nasty divorce, the author, in her early 30s, decides to reshape her life and travels the world in search of direction.

INTERNET

www.divorcehelpforparents.com/ This site is devoted to help divorced parents do what's best for their children. It provides resources on such topics as co-parenting, dealing with holidays, fair fighting, dating and many more.

www.divorceinfo.com/children.htm This Web site provides basic pointers to help parents make their children's lives easier when experiencing their parents' divorce.

www.divorcesupport.com This site provides divorce information on family law topics such as divorce, child custody, child support, visitations, property division, and state divorce laws.

www.prepare-enrich.com The mission of Life Innovation is designed to help build strong marriages and healthy relationships; it offers couples the opportunity to take a relationship assessment survey that identifies a couples's strength and growth areas.

Succeed with MyFamilyLab®
www.myfamilylab.com

Watch. Explore. Read. The New MyFamilyLab is designed just for you. Each chapter features a pre-test and post-test to help you learn and review key concepts and terms. Experience Marriages and Families in action with dynamic visual activities, videos, and readings to enhance your learning experience.

Here are a few activities you will find for this chapter.

Watch on **myfamilylab.com**

Video clips feature important concepts in the study of Marriages and Families. Watch:
- Infidelity

Explore on **myfamilylab.com**

Social Explorer is an interactive application that allows you to explore Census data through interactive maps. Explore the Social Explorer Activity:
- Divorce Rates Across the U.S.

Read on **myfamilylab.com**

MyFamilyLab includes primary source readings from classic and contemporary sociologists from around the world. Read:
- Lundquist: "A Comparison of Civilian and Enlisted Divorce Rates During the Early All Volunteer Force Era"

13

Remarriage and Remarried Families

What Will You Learn?

- Define and understand the sociological meaning of key terms.
- Describe the process of and various stages of remarriage.
- Apply the sociological imagination to assess how remarried families differ from intact nuclear families.
- Assess the pro and con arguments for extending legal parenting rights to stepparents.
- Increase your awareness and understanding of the role of children in remarried families.
- Question why remarriages are more likely to end in divorce than first marriages.

IN THE NEWS

Las Vegas, NV

Recently, singer Marie Osmond remarried her first husband, Steve Craig, a former pro-basketball player. The two initially married in 1982, had one child, Stephen, and divorced three years later in 1985. At that time the reason given for the divorce was "mental cruelty" (Larson, 2011). Marie Osmond married for a second time in 1986 to music producer Brian Blosil. Together they had two children and then adopted five more before divorcing in 2007. In 2010, Marie Osmond's 18-year old son from her second marriage committed suicide and Steve Craig provided sympathy and support. They started dating and remarried in 2011. Three of Marie's children from her second marriage are still young—15, 14, and 9.

(continued on next page)

(continued from previous page)

Osmond and Craig are not the only celebrities to remarry former spouses. Think Elizabeth Taylor and Richard Burton, Don Johnson and Melanie Griffith, Robert Wagner and Natalie Wood, Eminem (Marshall Mathers III) and Kimberley Scott to name a few. The extent of this pattern among the not-so-rich and famous is unknown since no official body keeps such statistics. However, some psychologists estimate the rate of former spouses reuniting might be as high as 6–10 percent (Larson, 2011). Anthropologist Helen Fisher, author of *Why Him? Why Her?* (2009) doesn't find such remarriages surprising. Her research suggest that the mechanisms that made a person fall in love the first time can often get triggered again.

WHAT WOULD YOU DO?

If in someway you reconnected with a former spouse/partner, would you consider remarriage or reestablishing an intimate relationship? What do you see as the advantages and disadvantages of doing so? What do you think the prospects for establishing a stable and satisfying remarriage are? Does it make a difference when children are present? Explain.

((•—**Listen** to the **Chapter Audio** on **myfamilylab.com**

In the previous chapter, we discussed the high divorce rate in the United States. Some writers have erroneously interpreted this high rate of marital dissolution to mean that marriage is no longer a popular institution among Americans. Remarriage statistics tell another story, however. The pattern of marriage, divorce, and remarriage has become well established in the United States today. Marie Osmond and Steve Craig are a good example of that process. About 40 percent of recent marriages involved a second marriage for at least one of the partners (Kreider and Ellis, 2011b). The United States is not alone in having a high rate of remarriage. Remarriage following divorce is becoming a common practice in many countries. For example, in England and Wales in 2006, only 61 percent of marriages were to first-time brides and groom; 18 percent of all ceremonies were remarriages for both parties, and another 21 percent were first marriages for one partner only (Batty, 2008). The number of remarriages is also increasing in more traditional societies (see the In Other Places box).

In Other Places

REMARRIAGE: A GROWING TREND IN ASIA

In the last chapter we discussed how divorce was on the increase in countries like Korea and China, in part because of more liberal divorce laws and changing social and economic conditions. The presence of a large number of divorced people, in turn, is eroding the stigma attached to marrying for a second or even third time, especially in Korea. According to Statistics Korea, the percentage of total marriages in which neither party has been married before fell from 89.3 in 1990 to 76.5 percent in 2009 while the percentage of total marriages in which both partners have been married before rose from 4.7 percent to 12.8 percent. Remarriages by women outpaced remarriages by men in terms of both the number of cases and the rate of increase (Se-ra, Jung, 2011). Remarriage has become so popular in Korea it is creating a whole set of new industries. In 2004, Petit Wedding, a wedding hall dedicated to second weddings, opened in southern Seoul and was quickly followed by others. Similarly, matchmaking firms dealing only with divorcees have been established. Wedding planners specializing in remarriages report that their clients tend to be financially more independent than younger

On April 26, 2009, a government-sponsored mass wedding of earthquake survivors was held in Sichuan, China. Family, friends, and government officials acted as matchmakers to help those who lost a spouse and children in the earthquake find the right new partner to help them and the larger community rebuild their lives.

couples marrying for the first time and they plan smaller but more elite weddings than was the case for their first marriages ("Remarriage Industry Sees Rapid Growth," 2006). Remarriage among the elderly, once considered taboo, is also increasing and finding wider acceptance. In 2009, there was an almost 2 percent increase in remarriage for men over 65 compared to a decade ago and an almost 3 percent increase for women in this age group. At the same time divorces were increasing even faster than remarriages ("Women Take Lead...," 2011).

Although remarriage rates are also increasing across all age groups in China, concern exists that there are still obstacles preventing many elderly from remarrying. This is causing consternation among government officials as they anticipate an aging society. In 2009, China had an elderly population (people 60 and over) of 167 million, or 12.5 percent of the total population ("Remarriage Hard Choice...,

2010); estimates are that it will reach 200 million by 2015 and increase to 400 million by 2040 ("China's Elderly Population," 2005). Many elderly people report being lonely and desirous of finding a companion. A nationwide survey by the Chinese Academy of Social Sciences found that 80 percent of widowed elderly wanted to remarry but most cohabited instead ("Remarriage Hard Choice...," 2011). Their reluctance to remarry is due to social tradition, the objection of children, and the fear of being ridiculed by others. Many older Chinese still believe that a person should marry only once and that to marry again is a betrayal of the deceased spouse. Some adult children share these traditional views, but they also oppose their parent's remarriage out of fear of losing their inheritance.

The government of China is taking steps to address these problems. In 2001, the National People's Congress added an amendment to its marriage laws, calling for children to respect their parents' right of marriage. Children are not allowed to interfere in the remarriage of their parents or their life after remarriage. Clauses protecting elderly marriage partners have been added to the local laws of 22 provinces and municipalities. Some children, responding to these new laws, have come to see the social, emotional, and health benefits that attach to a parent's finding a partner and are actively supporting their parents' efforts to do so. Recently, the Shanghai Women's Activities Center organized a matchmaking meeting for elderly singles in that city. Similar matchmaking programs are occurring in other parts of China as well. The government, too, has actively promoted community service aimed at the elderly, including matchmaking services for the widowed and divorced. Media programs are also dealing with this topic in an effort to reduce the stigma associated with remarriage in later life. Such efforts took on wider meaning after the devastating earthquake of May 12, 2008 when Sichuan province lost more than 87,000 of its inhabitants. In order to rebuild its society and to facilitate economic and social stability, the Chinese government, former-in-laws, neighbors, members of the local Communist work units all joined in matchmaking efforts to create instant families. By the end of 2008, thousands of earthquake survivors had remarried (Larmer, 2010).

What do you think? Should the Chinese government actively intervene to change the norms of remarriage in China? (Explain). What do the patterns of remarriage in Korea and China tell us about how social change occurs? How does the situation of the elderly in China and in the United States compare? Explain.

What Is a Remarried Family?

For purposes of our discussion in this chapter, we will use Esther Wald's (1981:2) definition of a **remarried family:** "A two-parent, two-generation unit that comes into being on the legal remarriage of a widowed or divorced person who has biological or adopted children from a prior union with whom he or she is regularly involved.... The children may or may not live with the remarried couple, but, in either case, they have ongoing and significant psychological, social, and legal ties with them." These two-parent, two-generation units are also referred to as stepfamilies.

Despite the large number of remarriages, however, social and legal changes have not kept pace with this new family form. The

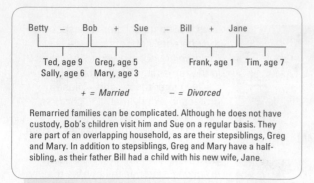

Betty — Bob + Sue — Bill + Jane

| Ted, age 9 | Greg, age 5 | | Frank, age 1 | Tim, age 7 |
| Sally, age 6 | Mary, age 3 | | | |

+ = Married   − = Divorced

Remarried families can be complicated. Although he does not have custody, Bob's children visit him and Sue on a regular basis. They are part of an overlapping household, as are their stepsiblings, Greg and Mary. In addition to stepsiblings, Greg and Mary have a half-sibling, as their father Bill had a child with his new wife, Jane.

FIGURE 13.1 Overlapping Households

general societal approach to these relationships is to view them in much the same way as first marriages. However, although all families share some of the same characteristics and face many of the same problems, families formed as a result of remarriage face additional problems that must be addressed if these relationships are to survive. Remarriages are less stable than first marriages. Unrealistic expectations are a contributing factor to this instability. To prepare themselves for the day-to-day reality of living in a remarried family, couples need to know about the structure and functioning of remarried families. Figure 13.1 illustrates some of the complexities of remarried families. William Beer (1989) identified ten fundamental ways in which the remarried family is different from the nuclear family:

1. *Complexity.* Remarried families take many forms: divorced individuals/single partners, divorced individuals/widowed partners, divorced individuals/divorced partners. The presence of children increases the families' complexity.

2. *A Changing Cast of Characters.* Remarried families may have shifting membership. Some of the stepchildren may live together permanently; others will come and go depending on visitation arrangements; still others may appear rarely, if at all.

3. *Unclear Boundaries.* Membership boundaries often are ambiguous in remarried families. For example, children may not include a noncustodial parent's new spouse in their definition of family. A stepparent's parents may or may not view themselves as stepgrandparents or be viewed that way by stepgrandchildren (or they themselves might have brought other people into the family as they themselves remarried).

4. *Undefined Rules.* Remarried couples often find it difficult to agree on rules regarding discipline, money, and parenting responsibilities.

5. *Unclear Laws.* Although the biological parent–child relationship is legally well defined, there still is considerable ambiguity regarding the legal rights and duties involved in stepparent–stepchild relationships.

6. *A Lack of Kinship Terms.* American culture has relatively few kinship terms, and in remarried families the same word is used to denote very different relationships. For example, the word *stepparent* applies to a person who has married either a custodial parent or a noncustodial parent. It also refers to a new spouse of an elderly parent, even though no parent–child relationship ever existed for this spouse. The new spouses of each biological parent may see each other frequently and join

in negotiations over stepchildren. Yet there are no kinship terms for their relationship to one another.

7. *Instant Families.* Remarried families come ready-made, often without appropriate time for members to establish emotional bonds with one another.

8. *Guilt.* New spouses may have unresolved feelings about their previous marriage. Children may feel guilty for showing affection to the stepparent, believing this to be disloyal to the noncustodial biological parent.

9. *Grieving.* Remarried families have undergone a loss before their formation, and some members may not have completed the grieving process. Children may be particularly affected because they must now relinquish the dream of reuniting parents.

10. *Myth of the Recreated Nuclear Family.* Stepfamilies are not like nuclear families. Complex stepfamilies often feel less like one family and more like two separate families than do first-married families (Banker and Gaertner, 1998, 2001).

These differences are being recognized, albeit rather slowly. Thus, there are as yet few clearly defined role models for stepfamilies to follow. Consequently, the participants generally lack preparation for the special complexities of remarried family life (Cartwright, 2010; Papernow, 1998, 2001). Members of stepfamilies often find themselves questioning their feelings and experiences, uncertain of how typical or "normal" their family situation is. In this chapter we will explore the history and cultural meanings of remarried families, their special characteristics and problems, and strategies for strengthening these families. Before beginning this examination, take the quiz in the Applying the Sociological Imagination box to see how many myths about stepfamilies you can dispel.

Read the **Document**
Stepfamilies in the United States: A Reconsideration on **myfamilylab.com**

Historical Perspective

In the previous chapter we discussed the fact that divorce has been a feature of American family life since 1639. Remarriage has also been a part of family life from this country's beginnings. During the seventeenth and eighteenth centuries, the proportion of remarriages among all marriages was approximately 20–30 percent (Ihinger-Tallman and Pasley, 1987). The circumstances leading to remarriage were quite different then, however. Whereas in early America the overwhelming majority of remarriages followed the death of a spouse, today remarriages typically involve divorced individuals. In the early colonies, the climate and harsh conditions as well as the lack of medical knowledge took a heavy toll on the inhabitants. For example, in Charles County, Maryland, marriages were likely to last an average of only 7 years and had only a 33 percent chance of lasting 10 years before one spouse died (Carr and Walsh, 1983).

Given the value attached to marriage in colonial America, remarriage following the death of a spouse was not only common

Explore the **Concept**
Social Explorer Activity: Divorce Rates by Age on **myfamilylab.com**

Indicate whether the following statements are **true** or **false**.

1. Attachment between stepparent and stepchildren needs to occur quickly.
2. Children ages 9 to 15 usually have the most difficult time adjusting to a new stepfamily.
3. Children of divorce and remarriage are forever damaged.
4. The stories and myths about wicked stepmothers do not affect today's stepfamilies.
5. It's not unusual for a stepfamily to take at least 4 years or more to feel like a solid family unit.

6. It helps stepfamily adjustment if the nonresidential parent withdraws.
7. Living in a stepfamily formed after a parent dies is easier than living in a stepfamily formed after a divorce.
8. Part-time stepparenting is easier than full-time stepparenting.
9. A strong couple relationship is an important part of forming a strong stepfamily.
10. A stepparent living with a stepchild has the same legal rights as the biological parent.

After completing this quiz, go to http://www.aces.edu/pubs/docs/H/HE-0829/HE-0829.pdf to find the Alabama Handbook on Marriage. Turn to Chapter 3, "Remarriages: Myths and Realities," pp. 31–32 to see how well you did. Where you surprised by any of the answers? Are you or is anyone you know living in a stepfamily? What problems are likely to occur in this type of family structure? What are the benefits of living in a stepfamily? Evaluate the effectiveness of the strategies suggested for successful stepparenting.

but socially expected for both women and men, especially for those with young children. Little is known about the nature and quality of early-remarried families. However, it is likely that remarriages, then as now, faced some problems not encountered in first marriages.

Cultural Images of Stepfamilies

One basic problem stepfamilies throughout history have had to contend with is their cultural image. The original meaning of the term *step* in *stepfamily* comes from Old German and Old English terms associated with the experiences of bereavement and deprivation. The earliest designations of *step* referred to a child who was orphaned. Later, the term was expanded to include the replacement parent, whether a stepmother or stepfather.

The terms *stepchild, stepparent,* and especially *stepmother* have conveyed negative connotations from earliest times. Most of these images derive from folklore and fairy tales that through the medium of storytelling sought to provide guidelines for daily living. An analysis of children's fairy tales found that stepmothers along with bears, wolves, giants, ogres, and witches were the most frequent representations of evil (Sutton-Smith, 1971). Other analyses confirm the consistent image of the stepmother as a cruel and evil person (Schrodt, 2008; Ganong and Coleman, 1997; Hetherington and Kelly, 2002). For centuries children have been entertained and/or frightened by *Hansel and Gretel, Snow White,* and *Cinderella* with their tales of maternal loss and cruel replacement.

Professionals and laypeople alike need to be aware of the fear and anxiety such images can create, especially for young children, who today increasingly live in stepfamilies. Such images also complicate

Throughout history, many nursery rhymes and children's stories have depicted stepmothers as wicked and cruel.

the stepmother role, making it difficult and ambiguous. Negative images also imply that "step is less," as conveyed in the metaphor that anything of lesser value is "like a stepchild" (Wald, 1981). Writer Jim Warda (2000), a stepfather, describes his pain at hearing a coworker say, "Jim, they're treating our department like a red-headed stepchild." Warda says that the comment implies that a stepchild is less than a biological child, someone whom a parent can like, and possibly love, but never to the same degree as his or her own biological child. Research on Asian remarried families has found similar stereotyping (Tan-Jacob, 2006; Yang and Rosenblatt, 2001).

Such images can affect the perceptions people have of stepfamilies and how they function (Fletcher, 2009; Jones and Galinsky, 2003). For example, counselors and teachers may be quick to assume that if students in remarried families are having difficulty, it is because of a faulty family structure. In an attempt to correct negative stereotypes, many stepparents, children's writers, and family professionals are publishing more accurate representations of today's stepfamilies. One result of this is an attempt to create more neutral terms to describe stepfamilies: *reconstituted, blended, merged, binuclear, bonus,* and *remarried families.* Some of these terms, however, create problems of their own. The notion of reconstituted, blended, or merged families implies that all members get along and fit comfortably into the new family structure. In fact, such a situation may never be achieved, or at least might not be achieved for a number of years. The pressure felt to measure up to such standards may add further stress to a remarriage. Thus, we prefer the term *remarried families.* Throughout this chapter we will use the term *remarried families* when referring to the family as a whole. However, because there are as yet no newly agreed-upon terms for relationships within remarried families, we will follow common practice and refer to them as steprelationships.

No one can say with certainty how many step relationships people have. The census bureau no longer compiles remarriage statistics. However, we can get some pretty accurate estimates from survey data using national random samples. According to a nationwide Pew Research Center survey, more than four-in-ten American adults (42 percent) have at least one step relative in their family (Parker, 2011). Table 13.1 shows the frequency of step relatives across a variety of demographic factors. Although stepfamilies can be found among all ages, races/ethnic groups, and educational levels, there is a distinct demographic pattern in the incidence of stepfamilies among adults. Young people, African Americans, and those without a college degree are more likely to have step relatives. Among those under 30, more than half (52 percent) reported that they have at least one step relative compared to 40 percent of those aged 30 to 49 and to 34 percent of those aged 65 and older. Marital histories play a role here. In this Pew study, 36 percent of the respondents younger than 30 said that during their growing up years, their parents were either divorced, separated, or never married while only 21 percent of those aged 30-49 and only 10 percent of those aged 50 and older reported similar patterns.

More African Americans (60 percent) have step family members than Whites (39 percent) with Latinas/os in the middle (46 percent). Socioeconomic status is also a factor in stepfamily formation. The highest number of step relatives is found among respondents with a high school education or less (47 percent) compared to 33 percent among those with college educations. Economic resources influence marital histories and, those, in turn, influence the extent of step relationships. Recall from previous chapters our discussions of the decline in the number of American married couples. This decline has been more dramatic among the demographic groups who today are more likely to live in stepfamilies or have step relatives.

TABLE 13.1 Demographics of Stepfamilies (in percent)

Demographic Characteristics	Any Step Relative	Step or Half Sibling	Stepparent	Stepchild
Men	40	27	17	15
Women	44	33	19	12
18-29	52	44	33	2
30-49	45	35	23	14
50-64	39	23	10	18
65+	34	16	2	22
White	39	26	18	14
Black	60	45	21	19
Latinas/Latinos	46	38	18	8
College	33	21	15	11
Some College	45	34	21	12
High School or Less	47	34	19	16

Source: Adapted from: Parker, K. 2011. "A Portrait of Stepfamilies." (January 13). http://pewsocialtrends.org/2011/01/13/a-portrait-of/stepfamilies/ (2011, July 28), p. 2.

The Process of Remarriage

Over time, most divorced and widowed persons are able to relinquish their strong emotional ties to the past and focus on the present and plan for the future. When this happens, the widowed or divorced individual confronts the issues of whether to date and perhaps whether to remarry.

DATING AND COURTSHIP PATTERNS

Are dating and courtship different the second time around? Older adults report many of the same anxieties about dating that adolescents do: appropriate behavior for the first date, what to talk about, who pays, whether to be sexually involved, and how to end the relationship if it is going nowhere. Adults with children may find dating even more complicated. Children often have difficulty accepting a parent's decision to date. When the parental loss was due to death, children may interpret the surviving parent's dating as an act of disloyalty to or betrayal of the deceased parent. When the loss was due to divorce, children may fantasize about their parents' getting back together again and thus react negatively to a parent's dating. In addition, children may feel displaced by the dating partner, so they may attempt to sabotage the relationship by behaving obnoxiously. Conversely, they may pressure parents by promoting the relationship in hopes of finding a new parent.

Children are not the only ones to react to the resumption of dating. Relatives of a deceased spouse may feel hurt or betrayed if they believe the surviving spouse is dating too soon following the death of their loved one. Ex-spouses may also be hostile to their former spouse's dating. They may be jealous themselves or fear someone else will replace them in their children's eyes. Thus, they may withdraw cooperation over visitation rights and delay or even end financial support.

We might assume that dealing with these complications would lengthen the courtship process. The opposite pattern seems to be the case, however. One study found that dating happens quickly and that many people resume dating even prior to the divorce decree (Anderson, et al, 2004). Divorced and widowed individuals who remarry tend to spend less time in dating and courtship than they did preceding their first marriage. Half of all women and men across all race and ethnic groups who remarry after divorcing from their first marriage do so within four years (Kreider and Ellis, 2011b). The style of dating among the divorced is more informal, and courtship often involves living together before marriage (Spearin, 2006). Couples often believe the experience of cohabitation will give remarriage a better chance to succeed. However, postdivorce cohabitation tends to be associated with higher levels of remarital instability (Xu, Husdpeth, and Bartkowski, 2006).

Some divorced people are reluctant to marry a second time and instead choose long-term cohabitation. These relationships may involve children from a previous marriage and/or children born to the cohabiting couple. The high prevalence of cohabitation after divorce has led some researchers to argue that the definition of stepfamilies should be expanded to include cohabiting couples with a child or children from previous relationships (Stewart, 2007; Tillman, 2007; Ganong and Coleman, 2004) and they are increasing not only in the United States but in Europe and Australia as well.

Beyond this cohabitation strategy, however, most individuals do little to prepare themselves for living in a remarried family and, thus, many people enter remarriage with nonverbalized expectations that, if not realized, become sources of conflict and disappointment (Carr-Gregg, 2011; Papernow, 2012).

THE DECISION TO REMARRY

Given the pain and trauma surrounding many divorces, and given the complications of resumed dating, why do so many Americans choose to remarry? First and foremost, marriage remains an important cultural value, and it is still perceived as the normal way to form an intimate connection with another person. Many of the reasons women and men give for remarriage are similar to those given for first marriages: desire for companionship, satisfaction of emotional needs, opportunities for legitimate sexual expression, yielding to family pressure, and desire to establish a two-parent home for children. Some divorced individuals want to alleviate the feelings of failure that accompanied the dissolution of their previous marriage and others may want to prove that they're still

attractive (Britsch and Olson, 2007). Furthermore, given the persistent economic inequalities between women and men and the downward mobility experienced by many divorced and widowed women, remarriage may also be a rational economic decision that results in an improved standard of living. Numerous studies show that women and children are almost always better off financially after remarriage (Dewilde and Uunk, 2008; Page and Stevens, 2004). Finally, divorced and widowed custodial parents may be motivated to remarry so they will have help raising their children.

PATTERNS OF REMARRIAGE

As we saw earlier, remarriages have always been quite common in the United States. In recent years between 75 and 80 percent of those who divorce, remarry, half of them within three to four years. About 12 percent of women and men, have married twice, and 3 percent have married three or more times. Of those 50 years and older, nearly 17 percent of women and almost 20 percent of men have been married three or more times (Kreider and Ellis, 2011b). A number of factors affect if and when people remarry: age, sex, marital status, social class, race and ethnicity, religion, and the presence of children.

Age, Sex and Marital Status As Figure 13.2 shows, 52 percent of men and 44 percent of women 25 years of age and older were remarried. A younger age at divorce, especially for women is associated with a higher likelihood of remarriage. The pool of potential partners declines as women get older. Data consistently show that groups remarry at different rates with widowed and divorced men having the highest rates and widowed women the lowest. As Figure 13.3 shows nearly 56 percent of men but only 40 percent of women ages 50 and over have remarried. Widows are less likely to remarry than divorced women, primarily for two reasons. First, widows, unlike most divorced women, may continue to hold a strong emotional attachment to the previous spouse. Thus, they may not be interested in establishing another relationship. Additionally, if women did the bulk of the household labor, they may be reluctant to take that on again, preferring their new-found

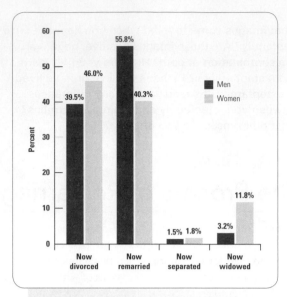

FIGURE 13.3 Current Marital Status for Men and Women 50 Years and Older, 2004

Source: www.remarriage.com/Remarriage-Facts/remarriage-after-divorce.html (2011, July 25).

independence to a second marriage. In contrast, widowers, with positive attitudes toward marriage, are more likely to miss the benefits of having a wife. Second, widowhood usually occurs at older ages than divorce. Although some widows might prefer to remarry, they may find themselves disadvantaged by norms that encourage men to marry younger woman.

Divorced men are considerably less likely than divorced women to have custody of children. Thus, men tend to have more resources and leisure time that allows them to reenter the dating scene more easily. The greater resources at men's command also make them more attractive in the marriage market. The median duration of second marriages that ended in divorce was approximately 8 years and did not differ from that for first marriages (Kreider and Ellis, 2011b).

Social Class For both women and men, however, age may be less of a factor in the decision to remarry than social class. Men with higher incomes are more likely to remarry than men with lower incomes. For men with low incomes the added burden of supporting two households may be prohibitive. Conversely, inadequate income may motivate some single mothers to remarry. As we saw in the previous chapter, divorce adversely affects women's and children's economic well-being. Remarriage, by adding another (often higher) wage earner, reverses this process (Dewilde and Uunk, 2008; Page and Stevens, 2004).

Race and Ethnicity As Table 13.2 shows, marital history varies across race and ethnic lines. For example, among people 50–59 years of age, Asian Americans are the most likely to marry only once, followed by Latinas/os. African Americans are the least likely to marry and Whites are the most likely to remarry and to remarry more often. The reasons for these differences are similar to our early discussion of first marriages. Asian Americans tend to marry later, thus,

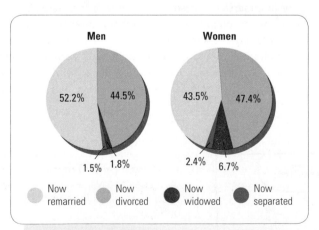

FIGURE 13.2 Current Marital Status for Men and Women 25 Years and Older Who Were Previously Divorced, 2004

Source: www.remarriage.com/Remarriage-Facts/remarriage-after-divorce.html (2011, July 25).

TABLE 13.2 Marital History for People 50–59 Years Old by Race and Ethnicity, 2004

Marital History	White	Black	Latinas/os	Asian
Never Married	7.2%	16.2%	8.3%	5.0%
Married Once	63.0	60.0	73.4	83.0
Married Twice	22.6	20.0	15.3	10.1
Married 3 or more time	7.2	3.3	3.0	1.9

Source: Adapted from Table 3. U.S. Census Bureau. Detailed Tables—Number, Timing and Duration of Marriages and Divorces: 2004. http://www.census.gov/population/www/socdemo/marr-div/2004detailded_tables.html (2008, August 10).

lowering their risk of divorce that still carries more of a stigma than among other groups. African Americans, especially women, have a smaller pool of eligible partners from which to draw because of higher rates of unemployment, incarceration, and mortality among Black males. This overall disadvantaged economic position has led many African Americans to see the marital relationship as less effective than the larger kin network in providing support.

Relatively little research has been done on remarried families of color. The reasons, then, for the varied patterns across racial and ethnic groups are not entirely clear. However, it is likely that part of the answer is to be found in the different economic positions of the various groups, the availability of support from kin members, and increased acceptability of cohabitation as an alternative to marriage (McNamee and Raley, 2011).

Religion As we saw in the last chapter, religion is one of the factors affecting patterns of divorce. Within 20 years of a first marriage, 48 percent of Catholics are divorced, compared with 49 percent of Jews, 56 percent of Protestants, and 59 percent of persons with no religious affiliation (Hout, 2000). Despite the Catholic Church's opposition to divorce and its ban on remarriage except in cases involving a church annulment (see Chapter 12), at least half of all divorced Catholics will eventually remarry. This pattern is similar to that for people of other faiths (Hornike, 2001). Divorced

Watch the **Video** *The Persistence of Religion in America* on **myfamilylab.com**

Catholics contemplating remarriage face the added dilemma that a decision to remarry can mean the loss of a beloved church and parish family. Seventeen to 20 percent of divorced Catholics leave the Catholic Church as a result of their remarriage (Hout, 2000). Despite the Catholic Church's official policy on remarriage, many members of the clergy have instituted a variety of programs to help remarried Catholics.

The Catholic Church is not alone in its objection to remarriage. Among other Christian religions, there are various views about under which conditions the Bible permits divorce and whether or not remarriage is permissible (see, for example, Goodman, 2006).

The Presence of Children Age and the presence of children affect the likelihood of remarriage for women and men in different ways. Divorced women without children remarried more frequently than women with children (Goldscheider, Kaufman, and Sassler, 2009). Similar patterns have been observed in Japan (Ono, 2010). Divorced fathers with coresident children were significantly more likely to marry women with children than were men without custody (Goldscheider and Sassler, 2006). Perhaps because they represented such a small minority and had not been socialized to be the primary caretaker, custodial fathers felt the need for a partner to assist them with child care. Among women, those with young children and those with fewer children were more likely to remarry than those with large families or older children (Glick and Lin, 1986; Coleman, Ganong, and Fine, 2000).). A logical explanation for this finding is that older children require less of a mother's time but may require more of a father's finances. More research is needed today to see to what extent the presence of children may lead more divorced parents to cohabit rather than to remarry.

Across all these factors, the decision to remarry begins a complicated series of adjustments that must be made if the new relationship is to survive.

THE STATIONS OF REMARRIAGE

In Chapter 12 we discussed the complex process of exiting from a marital relationship, using Paul Bohannan's (1970) six stations of divorce: emotional, psychic, community, parental, economic, and legal divorces. Ann Goetting (1982) found that there is a similarity between the developmental tasks that must be mastered in the divorce process and the many personal changes and adjustments that accompany the process of remarriage. Looking at remarriage this way makes it clear that remarriage requires individuals to adopt new roles, to unlearn old expectations from previous relationships, and to cope with an ambiguous legal status.

Goetting has identified six remarriages derived from Bohannan's stations of divorce. Each station of the remarriage process presents a challenge to the formation of a new couple and a new family identity. Keep in mind that, as is the case for the stations of divorce, the six stations of remarriage do not affect all remarrying people with the same intensity, nor do they occur in exactly the same order for everyone.

Emotional Remarriage The term **emotional remarriage** refers to the process of reestablishing a bond of attraction, love, commitment, and trust with another person. This can be a slow and difficult process for both the widowed and the divorced. The nature and quality of the previous marital experience affect the relationship with the new partner in different ways. On the one hand, people who were happily married and then widowed may idealize the deceased spouse and thus see the new partner in a less favorable light. Such people can become overly critical of the new partner's behavior if it does not measure up to this ideal. On the other hand, people who have been hurt and disappointed in previous relationships may be oversensitive to spousal criticism and may sense rejection by the new spouse when none is intended. For example, an intended compliment may be judged suspect because a former partner used similar comments as putdowns. Both the widowed and the divorced must be careful not to let the experiences of the first marriage unduly influence their new relationship.

Psychic Remarriage The process known as **psychic remarriage** requires moving back from the recently acquired identity of single person to a couple identity. This transition varies in intensity and perceived difficulty. For individuals who have accepted more traditional gender roles, regaining the status of husband or wife may be especially gratifying and their adjustments to couple identity may be relatively minor. Other people, however, especially women who experienced a new sense of autonomy and personal independence after widowhood or divorce, may feel constrained after taking on a marital role.

Community Remarriage Just as with a community divorce, a **community remarriage** involves changes in social relationships. Following the dissolution of a marriage, individuals often find that the nature and frequency of contact with relatives and friends is disrupted. As we have seen in Chapter 12, relationships with other married couples often suffer following a divorce. As a result, couple friends are often replaced with new, unmarried friends. Often these friendships are deeper and more intimate because they are selected on the basis of one's personal interests and needs, not those of a couple. Reentering the couple world may result in reverting back to less intimate and more couple-oriented relationships that can be shared more easily and "fit" more readily into a couple's lifestyle. Additionally, remarriage means that new in-laws must somehow be integrated into the family network.

Parental Remarriage Remarriage in which one or both spouses have children from a previous relationship is known as **parental remarriage.** More than half of all remarriages involve minor stepchildren living in the household. In 2009, 16 percent of children (11.7 million) lived in blended families. The U.S. Census Bureau defines *blended families* as families formed when couples remarry or live with new partners who bring children from previous unions, or who combine children from previous and current unions. Blended families include those that contain stepchildren and their stepparents, half siblings or stepsiblings. Nearly 48 percent of these children, 5.6 million, lived with at least one stepparent.

Individuals who plan to marry someone with children are well-advised to build a friendship with those children before assuming a stepparent role.

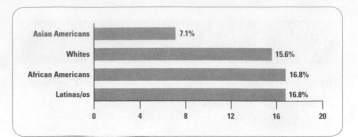

Asian Americans	7.1%
Whites	15.6%
African Americans	16.8%
Latinas/os	16.8%

FIGURE 13.4 Percentage of Children Living in Blended Families, by Race and Ethnicity, 2009

Source: Kreider, R. M. and R. Ellis. 2011 "Living Arrangements of Children: 2009." *Current Population Reports*, P70–126. Washington, DC: U.S. Census Bureau, 16, Table 6.

In blended families, stepparents were more commonly found living with White children (53 percent) than with Latina/o children (45 percent) or African American children (39 percent). This is not surprising since White women remarry more frequently than Latinas or African American women (Kreider and Ellis, 2011a).

As Figure 13.4 shows, African Americans and Latinas/os had the highest percentage of children living in blended families each with 16.8 percent, Whites had the second highest with 15.6 percent. Children of Asian Americans/Pacific Islanders were the least likely to live in blended families (7.1 percent). The lower rate among Asian Americans is generally attributed to the lower rates of nonmarital childbearing and divorce among Asian American adults compared to other groups.

Establishing good working relationships with stepchildren is perhaps the most challenging and emotionally trying aspect of remarriage. This process takes time and is primarily one of trial and error. Such adjustments are often confounded by the presence of the nonresidential biological parent. The attitudes and behavior of the ex-spouse, if hostile, jealous, or uncooperative, may slow the integration of the stepparent into the family unit.

Economic Remarriage An **economic remarriage** involves the establishment of a unit of economic productivity and consumption while at the same time working out mutually agreeable earning and spending habits. The presence of minor stepchildren can complicate the establishment of an economic plan for the new family unit in several ways. First, the remarried couple may be dependent, to a degree, on the economic behavior of people outside their immediate relationship. For example, when custodial parents remarry, they may be receiving alimony and child support from their ex-spouses. As we saw in the previous chapter, child support might become sporadic or stop entirely after remarriage. Second, new spouses may themselves be noncustodial divorced parents who are paying alimony and child support to their ex-spouses, thus diminishing the financial resources available to the new family unit. Friction may develop over resource distribution: Who should get how much of what is available?

Handling issues of financial equity, need, and flexibility may prove a daunting task. The nature of the financial arrangement may have an impact on the degree and speed of family integration. Some couples choose a common-pot approach, putting all wages and child support together and then allocating resources according to need rather than source of income. Others choose a two-pot arrangement, in which each spouse contributes a fixed amount to running the household but each biological parent is responsible for her or his children's expenses. Barbara Fishman (1983) found that the common-pot approach is more likely to unify the stepfamily, while the two-pot system tends to reinforce biological loyalties and individual autonomy. Couples who have used the "one-pot" method generally reported higher family satisfaction than those who kept their money separate (Bray and Kelly, 1998). More recently financial experts recommend a "three-pot" system—a "my" account, a "your" account, and an "our" account. This can work either of two ways:

- Pool all resources first for joint expenses, such as housing, food, household and car expenses, then withdraw money for individual accounts.
- Deposit paychecks into the individual accounts, then pay a percentage into the joint account (Beroset, 2011).

The critical factor in reducing conflict over financial matters is not which system is used but whether there is agreement on that system.

Other financial issues must be dealt with as well. If either partner has assets such as property, stocks, bonds, family heirlooms, insurance policies, the use and final disposition of those assets needs to be discussed. Each party may have different expectations about what happens to these assets in a remarriage, especially when the remarriage involves different sets of children.

Legal Remarriage Just as in a first marriage, a **legal remarriage** establishes a legally recognized marital relationship with all its responsibilities and privileges. However, it also requires people to make a number of adjustments. Taking on new responsibilities as a spouse does not absolve one from responsibilities that accompanied the first marriage. Court-awarded payments of alimony and child support remain in effect. Other responsibilities to the first family are not as clear-cut, however. For example, do nonresident biological children or an ex-spouse have a right to any health or life insurance, retirement benefits, or inheritance from a noncustodial parent or former partner? Because these issues are not clearly dealt with in most states, increasing numbers of couples sign a premarital agreement, declaring which assets belong to the remarried family and which should be directed toward the ex-spouse or nonresidential children.

Additionally troubling is the legal ambiguity surrounding stepchild–stepparent relationships. Only a few states have laws that obligate a stepparent to support a stepchild. This legal vacuum may create tension in several ways. On the one hand, some stepparents may resent being asked to assume responsibility for someone else's children. On the other hand, biological parents may feel guilty asking for help to support their children, or they may resent their new spouse's reluctance to help in this regard. A further complication for remarried families is stepparents' lack of legal rights concerning stepchildren. For example, in most states stepparents are not permitted to authorize medical treatment for stepchildren, nor do they have legal rights to custody and/or visitation of stepchildren who lived with them before the dissolution of their remarriage.

Another area in which the legal system has failed to provide adequate support and guidelines for remarried families is in the area of sexual relations. Although all 50 states prohibit marriage and sexual relations between persons closely related by blood, few make similar provisions for family members in a remarriage, for example, between a stepfather and stepdaughter or between stepsiblings. Although a sexual relation between a minor stepchild and a stepparent is considered a criminal offense, and although sexual relationships between stepsiblings are not socially condoned, neither behavior is defined as incest. This differential treatment of sexual relations in first marriages and remarriages can lead to tensions and even sexual exploitation in remarried families. All of these problems have led some people to argue for changes in the law that would prompt greater legal clarity for stepfamilies (see the Debating Social Issues box).

Debating Social Issues

SHOULD LAWS BE CHANGED TO MAKE STEPPARENTS LEGAL PARENTING PARTNERS IN STEPFAMILIES?

Today as many as one in three children will spend some part of their childhood years living with a stepparent. However, family law has been slow to recognize the many changes families have undergone over the past decades. For the most part only biological parents are legally and financially obligated to support their children, usually until the age of 18. However, with respect to stepparents, there is no uniform treatment regarding their financial responsibilities to stepchildren (Malia, 2005). Although marriage to a child's parent would seem to create a legal relationship to the child, it does not. Many employers do not recognize stepchildren as an employee's dependents. To date, about the only way to resolve the legal ambiguities of the stepparent role and establish a legal parent–child relationship is through stepchild adoption. However, for that to happen the noncustodial parent's

(continued on next page)

(continued from previous page)

Courts are increasingly being asked to settle complicated family issues.

legal rights must be terminated by court order or by voluntary consent. Few natural parents are likely to give this consent and a court order can be a traumatic step for all concerned.

The courts have not as yet readily accepted the position that it is in the child's best interest to have more than two legal parents. According to many family advocates, this norm of exclusivity does not serve the interests of children and it also denies recognition and respect to the adults who participate in their lives and who voluntarily contribute to their support without any legal rights. Thus, these advocates recommend that the courts recognize a contract establishing a legally recognized stepparent–stepchild relationship specifying rights and duties during marriage (and postmarriage in case of parental death or divorce), in effect creating a legal parenting partnership with the biological parent (see, for example, Malia, 2004). Such a contract would be negotiated between the custodial parent and the stepparent and could include such rights as giving stepparents access to school and medical records, the right to authorize permission for children to attend various events, the right to claim stepchildren as dependents for insurance and income tax purposes, the right to be named legal guardian if something happens to the custodial parent, and, in case of divorce, visitation rights as well as the obligations to provide financial support and care. Proponents of such a legal contract argue that this would strengthen stepfamilies by creating greater incentives for stepparents to become more involved in their stepchildren's lives and, hence, in the event of marital dissolution, it would also increase the likelihood that the stepparent would remain involved with her or his stepchildren.

Those who oppose such a contract are concerned that it would undermine the role of the noncustodial parent by putting her or him in competition with the stepparent. Other opponents see proposals such as these as further undermining the concepts of marriage and family by suggesting that children can have more than two legal parents. Some opponents fear that extending family law to include nontraditional family structures would open the door to same-sex marriages.

What do you think? How would giving stepparents legal rights and expecting certain obligations from them in return affect their roles and functions within the stepfamily? If you were a biological noncustodial parent, would you support or oppose such a contract? If you were a biological custodial parent, would you support or oppose such a contract?

REMARRYING A FORMER SPOUSE

You may recall that in Chapter 12, we discussed the fact that a number of former spouses wished they had tried harder to save their marriages. Overall that is what it remains, a wish. However, in a small number of cases, like singer Marie Osmond and Steve Craig who we discussed at the beginning of this chapter, some ex-spouses decide there was more to their relationship than they had thought and try again. According to Les Parrott, a clinical psychologist and coauthor of the book, *Saving Your Second Marriage Before It Starts*, "Most of the time these…are people who say, 'We've grown, we've learned new skills and we're ready to make a commitment again.' It's not done out of haste" (quoted in Hahn, 2006: Sec. 5, 1). This sentiment is echoed by author Helen Fisher who says, "Unless you part ways hating each other for some reason, that mechanism (initial attraction) could get triggered again. You can literally fall in love again" (quoted in Coffey, 2011). Amerah Henrene Shabazz-Bridges and B. C. Bridges who married in the early 1960s when they were both in their 20s, divorced four years later, went their separate ways for 31 years, married other people, and remarried in 2005, exemplify this process. The two met at his mother's funeral and then some time after B.C.'s wife died, they talked again and start reminiscing and laughing and realized they were still attracted to each other. During the course of dating, they dealt with the problems that led to their break-up. Each recognized their need to change and move toward the other.

Can these marriages work the second time around? According to relationship therapist John Gottman, it depends. In his 16 years of conducting couples workshops, he encountered about 20 couples who remarried each other after divorcing. For some, the events that led to divorce such as addictions were overcome; for others their perceptions of the incidents that led to the divorce changed. However, the couples he has encountered who remarry tended to have very little patience and when they sensed it wasn't working out the second time, they bailed. Conversely, others had developed new skills that helped them deal with their problems and stay together (Coffey, 2011). Clearly more research is needed before we can assess all of the factors that influence former spouses to remarry and, once remarried, to stay remarried.

The Development of Remarried Families

The process of remarriage takes time. According to James Bray and John Kelly (1998), all stepfamilies experience up and down patterns, with the first two years being the most difficult as they attempt to master the basic tasks of stepfamily life: parenting, managing change, separating a second marriage from a first, and dealing with the nonresidential parent. This stage is followed by a leveling off of the initial difficulties; the next three or four years become more tranquil as compromises are negotiated. However, a third cycle can see the reemergence of stress and conflict, as children and parents confront issues relevant to the adolescent years.

Remarried Families: Roles, Interactions, and Reactions

Children whose parents decide to remarry often experience fear and anxiety about what this means for their own place in the family. Thus, couples contemplating remarriage are well advised to consider including children from a previous marriage in the wedding ceremony.

CHILDREN AND THE REMARRIAGE SERVICE

Even though the wedding itself may take a simple form, planning for a remarriage ceremony when children are involved can be a delicate matter. Unlike a first marriage, which is usually a union between a woman and a man, a remarriage when children are

Increasing numbers of couples are including children from previous marriages in their wedding ceremony. Here the parent and stepparent are placing a family medallion around the daughter's neck to symbolize their commitment to building a strong family unit, inclusive of all parties.

involved is really a merging of families. Yet until recently, relatively little attention was given to how to include young children in the service itself except to have them stand next to or behind the couple during the ceremony, or if old enough, serve as bridesmaids or groomsmen. Today, as a result of the pioneering efforts of Dr. Roger Coleman, chaplain of Pilgrim Chapel in Kansas City, many religious bodies have modified their wedding rituals to include the children from previous marriages. Every year thousands of couples use Dr. Coleman's Family Medallion ceremony to help foster a new family bond between children, parents, and stepparents. Even a very young child can take part. After the couple exchanges wedding rings, their children join them for a special service focusing on the family nature of this remarriage. Each child is given a gold or silver family medallion with three interlocking circles, a symbol that represents family love in much the same way that wedding rings symbolize conjugal love. Just as the two individuals exchange vows with each other, as parents and stepparents they promise to care for all the children in the family.

A remarriage ceremony can be the basis for the first collective memory that the new family will share. However, for some children the prospect of a parent's remarriage may be painful, and some older children may decline an invitation to participate in the ceremony. They may even refuse to attend the wedding. Although couples may be hurt and disappointed by this reaction, it is generally best to let children decide this matter for themselves. Often when children know the decision is really theirs and that they will be welcome if they change their minds even at the last moment, they do decide to reverse their position and attend. Forcing children to attend against their wishes may set up a power struggle that will have a long-term negative impact on the quality of family life. On the other hand, even when they are present, they may feel excluded. When stepchildren at two Midwest colleges were asked to describe their parent's remarriage ceremony, many were critical of the ceremony, seeing it as empty ritual. A common theme in their responses was that they wanted greater involvement both prior to and during the ceremony (Baxter, et al., 2009).

Remarriages can also affect adult children who are celebrating their first marriage. Whether a biological father, a stepfather, or both should walk a bride down the aisle or whether a divorced parent's spouse should be an invited guest can be difficult and emotionally loaded issues even years after the parental divorce.

CHILDREN AND THE HONEYMOON

More parents are giving thought to how children should be integrated into the wedding ceremony but they sometimes overlook another area that can be equally problematic: the honeymoon. Sometimes, and often to their parents' surprise, children may assume that they will be included in the honeymoon trip. Travel agencies are beginning to acknowledge this issue and are helping couples to plan a "familymoon" where the whole family goes on the honeymoon (Greenberg, Kuchment, and Butler, 2006) in an effort to make the children feel like they are part of creating this new family.

Have you attended any remarriage ceremonies where children were included? If so, what was the ceremony like? What do you see as the advantages and/or disadvantages of including children in their parent's wedding ceremony? Should children be included in the honeymoon?

CHILDREN IN REMARRIED FAMILIES

Throughout this text we have emphasized that all families are influenced by persons and events outside the immediate family unit. This is particularly true for remarried families formed after a divorce. Although members of nuclear families generally share one household, divorce creates two separate but **overlapping households,** with children having membership in both households. Sometimes living in overlapping households leads children to feel as though they are "citizens of nowhere" (Lofas, 2009).

Despite those feelings this dual membership can have both positive and negative consequences for children. On the one hand, if one or both biological parents remarry, children have more adult role models to guide, love, and nurture them. Interacting in two households, each with distinct members, expectations, activities,

traditions, and family culture, can provide a richness of experience not found in any one household. On the other hand, this dual membership can be a source of conflict and confusion for children. Each household has a set of rules, so children must behave differently from one household to the next. For instance, one of the author's young friends who is involved in an overlapping household complained,

> When I'm at home, I can go to bed anytime I want. Mom doesn't care as long as I get up right away when she calls me in the morning. When I'm at Dad's house, they make me go to bed when the other kids do, around 9 o'clock. I don't think that's fair. I'm older than they are.

Adults in both households need to understand that adjusting to two sets of rules is not easy for children; there must be time and space to allow for the transition from one to the other. Mixed emotions in these circumstances are not unique to children. Both parents and stepparents may feel insecure and jealous when children visit the other household and they may communicate these feelings to their children who, in turn, may feel that to enjoy being in the other household is somehow disloyal to the other biological parent.

Whether overlapping households are beneficial to children depends, in large measure, on the attitude and behavior of the adults involved. If all parental adults cooperate in matters of visitation, refrain from criticizing each other in front of the children, and give children permission to care about and enjoy their other family household, the positive benefits of dual household membership are likely to outweigh the negative consequences for both children and other family members. For example, a study of adolescent family life satisfaction in remarried families found that adolescents who perceived their families to be more flexible reported greater satisfaction with both the overall remarried family household and the parent–stepparent subsystem (Henry and Lovelace, 1995).

Nevertheless, children, too, play a role in determining the nature and quality of overlapping households. They can cooperate or be a source of friction. A major factor in their behavior is the way in which they come to define family membership.

Who's In, Who's Out? Boundary Ambiguity in Stepfamilies When social scientists investigate who is in and who is out of the family system, they refer to this as **boundary ambiguity.** Initially most studies of boundary ambiguity relied on adult perceptions. Penny Gross (1987) conducted one of the first studies on children's perceptions of family membership involving 60 Canadian children, 30 females and 30 males between the ages of 16 and 18. Each had two living divorced parents, at least one of whom had remarried. Using a structured interview that focused on parent–child relationships, Gross asked the children who they considered family members. Four patterns emerged: retention, substitution, reduction, and augmentation.

Retention Twenty children (33 percent) defined the family in terms of its composition prior to the divorce—that is, with both biological parents but not the stepparent. Thus, some children lived with a stepparent but did not consider that person part of their family; nonresidential parents continued to play an important role in the lives of their children. Sons were more likely than daughters to include the nonresidential father as a family member.

Substitution Eight children (13 percent) excluded one biological parent and included at least one stepparent in their definition of family. This was most common when children lived with the remarried parent. For these children, the household membership and the family were synonymous.

Reduction Some children included fewer people than the original family. Fifteen children (25 percent) excluded their nonresidential biological parent as well as the stepparent, considering only the custodial parent as family. In most cases, the custodial parent's remarriage had occurred recently, and the children still had negative feelings about it. These children were the most dissatisfied with their lives and revealed emotional stress during the interview.

Augmentation Seventeen children (28 percent) added to their original family by including both biological parents and at least one stepparent as members. Most of these children lived with their biological fathers and their stepmothers but continued to have regular contact and a strong relationship with their biological mother. They felt free to move back and forth between the overlapping households without the fear of being disloyal to either biological parent.

A similar survey conducted in the United States also found variations in children's definitions of family membership. When asked, "When you think of your family, who specifically do you include?" Ten percent of the children did not list a biological parent, and 33 percent omitted a stepparent (Furstenberg and Spanier, 1987). Such research suggests that the realities for children involved in remarriages vary considerably. It also challenges definitions of the family that assume an overlap with household membership. More recent research finds that boundary ambiguity in stepfamilies can have a negative impact on the quality of a couple's relationship and the stability of the union itself (Stewart, 2007). Boundary ambiguity is even more likely in stepfamilies formed as a result of parental cohabitation, where children are even more likely to experience family instability. A study of boundary ambiguity in adolescent and mother reports of family structure found that the greater the family complexity, the more likely adolescent and mother reports of family structure were discrepant. Among mothers who reported living with a cohabiting partner, only one-third of their teenage children also reported residing in a cohabiting stepfamily. Conversely, for those adolescents who reported their family structure as a cohabiting stepfamily, just two-thirds of their mothers agreed. Levels of agreement between adolescents and mothers about residing in a two-biological-parent family, single-mother family, or married stepfamily were considerable higher (Brown and Manning, 2009).

Consequences of Parental Remarriage for Children How do children react to the remarriage of their parents? Do they experience more stress or behavioral problems than children in other family structures? To date, studies reveal no consistent and clear answer to these questions. A number of

studies found that stepchildren experience more stress, have more difficulty in school, and have higher rates of delinquency and emotional problems than children living in their original families (Heard, 2007; Amato, 2005; Wolfinger (2005). Yet at the same time other studies suggested that in the long run stepchildren are only slightly more troubled than children in original families and that the vast majority of divorced children and stepchildren eventually adapted and emerged as reasonably competent people who built productive and satisfied lives (Heatherington and Kelly, 2002).

Some researchers find fault with how some studies are done, arguing that they focus on the problems and stress in stepfamilies and ignore the positive behaviors that make them function effectively (Coleman et al., 2001). Closely related to this is the argument that many of the differences reported between children in stepfamilies and children in first-marriage families tend to be small and that, in fact, there are more similarities than differences among children from different family structures (Coleman, Ganong, and Fine, 2002). Other researchers have found that children in remarried families do quite well if conflict between parents is minimized and if stepfamilies build satisfactory relationships (Braithwaite et al., 2001). Thus, family structure per se may be less important than the kind of relationship that exists within it (Crawford and Novak, 2008; Doohan et al. 2009). Also, time may be a factor here. There is a growing body of evidence that men who became stepfathers more recently may be more involved with stepchildren than men in prior decades. This is significant because close bonds between stepfathers and stepchildren are associated with better child outcomes (Pryor and Rodgers, 2001). This pattern is enhanced when the child also has a close, non-conflictual relationship with the biological mother as well (Booth, Scot, and King, 2010; Yuan and Hamilton, 2006).

Stepfamilies, like all families, face many challenges and various factors are at work that influence whether the outcome will be positive or negative. The first step in trying to understand this process is to recognize the timing and complexity of divorce and subsequent remarriage. As one research team observed, "Empirical findings suggest that the age of the child at the time of parental divorce and remarriage, sex of the child, and sex of the stepparent are important factors for understanding and predicting the influence of family change on children" (Ihinger-Tallman and Pasley, 1991:461).

Age Studies suggest that if parental remarriage occurs early in the child's life, it has few adverse effects. In contrast, older children, especially adolescents, experience more stress after a residential parent remarries, and schoolwork and social behavior are frequently adversely affected (Amato, 2005). In comparison with younger children, older children find it more difficult to adjust to new people and new places, and they experience a complex set of emotions regarding both (Stoll, et al. 2005). As adolescents struggle to become more autonomous, the addition of another "parenting" adult in the household may be perceived as threatening (Skaggs and Jodl, 1999).

Sex Research has consistently shown that boys have more problems adjusting to divorce than girls. In contrast, in stepfamilies girls experience more adjustment problems and report poorer relationships with parents than boys (Ganong and Coleman, 1994; Isaacs, 2002). For example, after a parental divorce there is an upswing in drug use among boys but not among girls. However, the pattern is reversed following a remarriage; there is increased drug use by girls but reduced use by boys (Needle, Su, and Doherty, 1990). Recent research suggest that boys have closer relationships to stepfathers and nonresident fathers than girls (King, Harris, and Heard, 2004) and that close father–child relationships are predictive of less delinquency and substance use among adolescents, more so for sons than for daughters (Bronte-Tinkew et al., 2006).

Observational studies have found that compared with stepsons, stepdaughters are more sullen, withdrawn, and direct more negative problem-solving behavior toward stepfathers (Hetherington, 1989). Other researchers report similar findings, particularly in mother-custody stepfamilies (Vuchinich et al., 1991). Part of the explanation for this pattern lies in the nature of the relationships established after divorce. The most common structure in remarried families is a biological mother, her children, and a stepfather. Girls often become closer to the custodial parent after a divorce and view the stepfather as an intruder or the stepmother as competition. In fact, closer mother–stepfather relationships are associated with more behavior problems in girls. Additionally, the adolescent stepdaughter–stepfather relationship may be confusing for both parties. The emerging sexuality of adolescent girls may cause both to be uncertain about the appropriate way to express affection for each other. These tensions are reflected in the fact that girls in stepfamily households leave home to marry or live independently at an earlier age than those in either single- or two-parent households (Goldscheider and Goldscheider, 1993; Hetherington, 1999). Recent research supports an escape from stress perspective. Daughters living with remarried parents with a high-distress relationship were more likely to marry early and have early marital births (Amato and Kane, 2011).

Boys, on the other hand, are initially angry that dad was "sent away," but then they become comfortable with another male presence in the household. The presence of a stepfather often eases the mother–son problems that resulted from the divorce. Boys now find themselves with a source of support and companionship. Preadolescent boys who enjoy a close supportive stepfather–stepson relationship become less anxious and increase their self-esteem (Ganong and Coleman, 2004; Hetherington,1989).

Although stepparent–stepchild relationships can be troublesome, the majority of children in stepfamilies do not end up with major adjustments problems and they are able to adapt to their changed situations (Pinsof and Lebow, 2005). Additionally, many of these problems disappear by the third year into the remarriage. Perhaps the best advice for parents in such situations is to be patient.

Stepsibling Relationships: Rivalry or Solidarity? A

significant part of the tension in remarried families is centered on stepsibling relationships. Why is this the case? What is it like to be a stepsibling? How are stepsibling relationships different from sibling relationships in intact families?

William Beer (1989) reviewed the literature on remarried families and found only indirect references to the subject of stepsiblings. When stepsiblings were discussed, it was generally in relation to one of four themes: (1) stepsibling rivalry, (2) changes in age order, (3) stepsibling sexuality, and (4) the role of half-siblings. The following discussion relies heavily on his work.

Integrating children from two different families can be difficult. Nevertheless, remarriage can also provide emotionally satisfying relationships for stepsiblings over time.

Stepsibling Rivalry One of the main differences between siblings and stepsiblings is the origin of their relationships. In the idealized pattern, children arrive after the marital relationship has been solidified. They share two biological parents and hence a sense of belonging to the same family unit. This does not mean, however, that their relationships are always harmonious. In fact, siblings sometimes experience intense rivalry for parental love.

Stepsiblings, however, start out in a different place than children in intact families. They were part of a family unit disrupted by death or divorce. Since that disruption, they have formed close relationships with the custodial parent prior to a remarriage. Now they are asked to share this parent not only with another adult but with other children as well. Interviews with adolescents living in stepfamilies revealed their sense of a loss of intimacy and quality time that they had previously had with their custodial parent. A typical response was:

> There was kind of a space—because she had someone else to talk to about all this stuff. I guess I got kind of jealous of him (stepfather) because before they got married, I had all this time with my mom.
> *(cited in Stoll, et all, 2005, p. 183)*

In addition, children are asked to share living space, property, and other possessions that may be in short supply. Sharing space is less of a problem when the remarried family moves into new, neutral housing, where no one has yet established territorial claims. This option, however, requires a degree of affluence that is absent for many remarried families. Thus, the more common pattern is for one part of the remarried family to move into the residence of the other. When this occurs, the former are likely to be seen as intruders and to feel like unwelcome guests. As an 8-year-old stepdaughter reported:

> We feel like guests in Jim's house. We are careful of what we do. It is like we are intruders. And I feel very bad that we took Tommy's room. They fixed up a room for him in the basement, with posters and all, but he's still mad at us for taking his room.
> *(Cited in Fishman and Hamel, 1991:442)*

Several other factors contribute to stepsibling rivalry. First, there is often a feeling of "them" and "us." Children see their ties to their biological parent as giving them a greater claim in the competition for love and other resources: "She's my mom, not yours." Second, when the families were separate, both units had their own rules. After remarriage, stepparents may try to impose all the rules impartially on all stepchildren, both those living in the same household and those who only visit. This attempt at impartiality, however, may not be perceived as equitable by the stepchildren because the rules are often more familiar to one set of children than the other. Third, differential treatment by others can lead to feelings of rejection, hostility, and envy. For example, grandparents may provide generous gifts to their biological grandchildren and ignore their stepgrandchildren. Excluding some children in gift exchanges weakens the chances for establishing a sense of family integration as it reflects the image that some are "outsiders."

Changes in Age Order In intact families, the natural order of family births determines the age order and age interval of siblings that, in turn, provide a relatively stable ranking system for children. However, when two sets of siblings are combined through remarriage, some siblings may find their age order positions in the family altered. Some of these changes are easier to accept than others. For example, when an only child becomes the oldest child, a position of privilege is retained. To a degree, benefits also accompany the transition from being an only child to becoming the youngest child or "baby" of the family. The most difficult change is losing the position of being the oldest to another child, especially one of the same sex. Although these changes often cause tensions in the short run, over time children learn to adapt to the new sibling social structure.

Stepsibling Sexuality When the new sibling social structure includes adolescents of different sexes, drawing and maintaining sexual boundaries may become a critical task for remarried families. Sexual tension is usually a greater problem in remarried families than in first marriages. Several factors interact to create this atmosphere. First, the parent–stepparent union is relatively new. As a couple, they are still likely to be in a honeymoon stage, showing affection for each other, which may be sexually stimulating for adolescents. In first marriages, parents have already worked out patterns for privacy over the years. By the time their children reach adolescence, most parents no longer display sexuality overtly. Second, when a teenaged girl and boy who have not grown up together come to live in the same residence, they may become sexually attracted to each other. Parents may unintentionally contribute to this process by encouraging mutual activities as a way of bringing the children together. Third, stepsibling relationships are not covered by the same incest prohibitions as are sibling relationships. This lack of clear rules may cause confusion and uncertainty in remarried families. Given these conditions, it is not surprising that some sort of romantic or erotic attraction sometimes develops between stepsiblings. However, not all sexual feelings between

stepsiblings are acted out. A more likely pattern is for adolescents to convert this eroticism into expressions of hostility. Parents often report that stepsiblings seem to "hate each other." This anger can be temporary or long-term; if too severe, it can threaten family stability. A more positive outcome results when children can convert their erotic feelings into warm, supportive relationships. Which outcome is more likely depends, to a large extent, on parental reaction. Open and honest discussions with the involved stepsiblings, reassuring them of the normality of such feelings and making clear that there is a difference between feelings and acting on those feelings, can reduce the possibility of a negative outcome.

The Role of Half-Siblings As a result of tensions among siblings, it is often difficult for remarried family members to feel like a "real" family. One way in which remarried parents try to overcome this perception and create a cohesive family is by having a mutual child that will provide a blood tie among all members of the remarried family. The decision to have a mutual child is quite common and occurs soon after remarriage. According to Canadian family demographer Heather Juby (2003/2004), roughly half of stepfamily couples cement their union by having a child together. The youngest stepfamily couples are the ones most likely to decide to have a child together; an additional child is born to about two-thirds of stepfather families created when a young, unmarried mother marries (or moves in with) someone other than her child's father.

Stepchildren may have positive feelings about the birth of a half-sibling, believing that because they are now all related by a blood tie, they finally all belong to a "real" family. Some support for the beneficial role of having a mutual child comes from the pioneering research of Lucile Duberman (1973). Forty-four percent of her parent respondents who had a mutual child reported that relationships between the siblings were excellent, compared with 19 percent of those without mutual children. These relationships are likely to be strongest when the mutual child comes at a time when the remarriage is well established and when there is only one child from each of the two prior marriages.

However, the rapidity with which the birth of a mutual child takes place often causes confusion and adjustment problems for the other children. Although both adults may be biological parents in their own right, they are stepparents to each other's children, and they may or may not share responsibility for them. The birth of a mutual child adds a new role, a shared parental role.

Although this new role may help solidify the couple relationship, it is not problem free. A pattern may emerge whereby both parents exert authority over mutual children but only biological parents assert authority and take responsibility for their own children. This layering of authority and responsibility is a unique feature of remarried families and can produce problems, especially when disagreements over parenting styles arise and it may also result in reducing stepparents' participation in positive activities with their stepchildren (Stewart, 2005). Stepchildren may see the birth of a mutual child as adding yet another competitor for parental attention and may lessen their satisfaction in living in a stepfamily (Munroe, 2009; "Low Grades...," 2008). Additionally, there is some evidence that the presence of a half-sibling negatively impacts a child's personal development (Strow and Strow, 2008). This finding in and of itself does not mean remarried couples should forgo having a mutual child, but it does suggest that couples need to be aware of the mechanisms that lead to negative effects and to learn about ways to overcome negative influences.

In sum, we have seen that stepsibling and half-sibling relationships can be conflictual. However, that is only part of the story. The dynamics of living in a remarried family with stepsiblings and/or half-siblings can also have positive effects. Just as in first families, stepsibling rivalry can help children distinguish themselves from others in the family, thereby giving them a strong sense of personal identity. For example, if an older stepsibling is active in sports, a younger stepsibling may turn to music to express her or his individuality. Competition among stepsiblings in some areas does not prevent them from cooperating in other areas. Just as in intact families, solidarity among stepsiblings is a likely outcome of ongoing family dynamics (Ganong and Coleman, 1994).

Stepsibling Relationships over Time Sociologists Lynn White and Agnes Riedman (1992b) undertook the first empirical research on adult step/half-siblings, focusing on their relationships after they grow up and leave home. In general, they found evidence of continued contact and interaction. Although contact was more frequent among full siblings (one to three times a month) compared with the several times a year that step/half-siblings were seen, less than 1 percent of the respondents in that study were so estranged that they did not even know where their step/half-sibling lived. However, contact does not necessarily translate into feelings of obligation. In a recent study, 64 percent of respondents who have both biological siblings and step or half siblings said they would feel very obligated to help a sibling who was in serious trouble. Only 42 percent said they would feel very obligated to provide assistance to a step or half sibling (Parker, 2011). Contact among step/half-siblings was affected by three key factors: race, gender, and proximity. As true among full siblings, African Americans, females, and those who lived near one another had the most frequent contact.

Remarried families are complex. The members of this family include stepsiblings and a half-sibling. These parents have a shared parental role as well as a stepparent relationship with their spouse's biological child.

ADULT CHILDREN'S REACTION TO PARENTAL LATER-LIFE REMARRIAGES

It is not only younger children who get caught up in the dynamics of stepfamilies. As we saw in Chapter 12, the divorce rate is increasing among older adults. Thus, children who are independent adults can find themselves suddenly thrust into the world of adult stepfamilies. Estimates are that about 500,000 Americans over the age of 65 remarry each year; 266,600 were cohabiting in 2000 (cited in Cohn, 2005). In these situations, both parents and children are often surprised by the emotional reactions this process engenders. Parents often assume that since their children are grown and leading their own lives, a parental remarriage or cohabiting experience will be problem free. Yet, adult children may have some of the same fears as younger children—fear of being abandoned by their parents, displaced by the new spouse or partner, or losing an inheritance. They may express these fears by anger or by limiting their contact with the new couple. If the new spouse also has children, there may be jealousy, confusion, and perceived loyalty conflicts. Like in any stepfamily, boundaries need to be identified and expectations clarified. However, if adult children can come to terms with this new family form, they often find they have gained a friend and an ally who will be there as their parent gets older and needs more help. Conversely, stepparents acquired in later life may not be seen as family members and thus adult children may feel that norms of family obligations do not apply to them and they have little or no contact with stepparents after their biological parent dies (Ganong and Coleman, 2006).

Children are not the only players in determining how well remarried families function. Stepparents also play key parts. Let us first look at stepmotherhood. The most typical form of stepmothering in the United States is part-time, occasioned by the weekend and holiday visits of children to their remarried biological father.

STEPMOTHERS: A BAD RAP?

To what extent are the cultural images of the wicked stepmother valid? Although research does not substantiate the fairy tale image of the "wicked" stepmother, it does suggest that stepmothers have the most negative image of any family member and are often perceived as being less affectionate, good, fair, kind, loving, and likeable (Recker, 2001; Hetherington and Kelly, 2002; Campbell, 2007). Children who have negative images of stepmothers may not develop a positive relationship with their new stepmother. In turn, children's unpleasant behavior may cause stepmothers to be more critical of stepchildren (Schnieders and Schnieders, 2005).

Deciding how to approach the new stepmother role is not easy. Margaret Draughon (1975) suggests three possibilities: (1) "other mother," or second mother; (2) primary mother, who assumes major responsibility for day-to-day caregiving; and (3) friend, who is supportive and caring but does not try to be a substitute mother. According to Draughon, the choice of role should be based on the degree of emotional comfort the stepmother feels as well as on the child's emotional state at the time. Draughon believes if the child is still mourning the loss of the biological mother, whether through death or divorce, the role of friend works best. If, however, mourning has ended, the primary-mother role is probably more appropriate. This role, however, must be defined carefully. Generally speaking, defining it to mean primary caretaker instead of a replacement for the biological parent is likely to minimize stepparent–stepchild conflict. A more recent study of nonresidential stepmothers identified three roles enacted by stepmothers similar to Draughon's categories: mothering but not mother roles, other-focused roles, and outsider roles. The choice of role to enact depended on a variety of issues related to biological mothers, spouses, stepchildren, biological children, and the stepmother's own ideology of motherhood (Weaver and Coleman, 2005). Stepmothers, whether residential or not, face a difficult dilemma—doing mothering things but not being a mother.

Stepmothers and Mothering How do stepmothers fare in the mothering role? Much of the research on stepmother–stepchild relationships shows that these relationships are more tentative and difficult than are stepfather–stepchild relationships (Ward, Spitze, and Deane, 2009; Pryor, 2004). This is due, in large part, to the greater expectations placed on women in families (Martin, 2009). Women are expected to take primary responsibility for the well-being of the family, especially in the area of child care, regardless of whose children they "mother." Such expectations can be more distressing for a woman who chooses a marital role but not necessarily a parenting role when she marries a noncustodial father. After remarriage she may find that his children visit more frequently than anticipated or that child custody has shifted unexpectedly to him. Furthermore, the expectations for women regarding nurturing are so strong that stepmothers themselves often assume that "instant love" of stepchildren should be possible. For this reason, stepmothers frequently feel guilty when they do not as yet feel a strong attachment to their spouse's children. One stepmother writing in for advice said,

> I feel like a stereotypical wicked stepmother when I complain about my stepchildren because they are good kids. They really are. I understand that the irritating things they do are totally normal for kids their age and I think that maybe if I loved them then perhaps I wouldn't care so much about the stuff that bugs me. But I don't know how to make that happen....
>
> *(Quoted in Tennis, 2005)*

In addition, a stepmother's attempt to create a close-knit family structure may be misinterpreted. The biological mother may accuse her of trying to take her place. The stepchildren may also perceive her behavior as a threat to their mother's position. On the other hand, if the stepmother chooses a less involved approach toward her stepchildren, she may be accused by them and her spouse of not caring enough or not being a good mother. A common reaction to these situations is stress. Stepmothers report significantly greater role strain than stepfathers and biological mothers (Doodson, 2010; Nielsen, 1999). Melady Preece (2003/2004) suggests that this greater stress stems from traditional gender ideology. Many husbands view the caring for children as their wives' responsibility, even when the children are his, not hers. When stepchildren visit, the stepmothers, and not the fathers, usually acquire extra work, such as housecleaning and cooking.

We should remember, however, that not all stepparenting situations are alike. Research shows that having live-in stepchildren is less divisive than having children who live with the other parent come for visits (Ambert, 1986; Doodson and Morley, 2006). The former situation allows the couple more control over their lives. Wives feel more "appreciated" by their spouses because of their child-rearing contributions and feel less threatened by the biological mother. Stepmothers developed a closer and deeper relationship with their live-in stepchildren than with stepchildren living elsewhere. Some nonresidential stepmothers with biological children report that visiting stepchildren are bad influences on their own biological children (Henry and McCue, 2009). These research findings are significant in that they offer an explanation for why stepfathers seem to have fewer problems in their role. Most stepfathers, in contrast to most stepmothers, have live-in stepchildren. What role, then, do stepfathers play in remarried families?

STEPFATHERS: POLITE STRANGERS?

In an earlier section of this chapter, we discussed the cultural images of the "wicked" stepmother. Although no comparable image or body of folktales exists for stepfathers, they are often stereotyped as indifferent or even abusive. Newspaper accounts of lethal assaults on children by stepfathers as well as an extensive body of research on domestic violence involving stepfamilies (Daly and Wilson, 1994; Weekes-Shackelford and Shackelford, 2004) continues to contribute to a popular perception of a dysfunctional family structure. However, a considerable amount of social science research focused on stepfather families and the specific role of stepfathers in these families provides a substantially different view but, like the case of stepmothers, much depends on the living arrangement the stepfather shares with his stepchildren. Stepfathers come to their role in different ways—a man may have been single, divorced and childfree, divorced without custody of his children or divorced with custody (Pacey, 2005). He may cohabit with or marry the children' mother. If he cohabits, it may be for a brief period of time or for a long-time, perhaps culminating in a remarriage. If his involvement is the former, he may not develop much of a relationship with her children (Tach, Mincy and Edin, 2010). Conversely, if he adopts his stepchildren, he is likely to be more nurturing and involved and have closer relationships with them than those stepfathers who don't adopt (Schwartz and Finley, 2006).

Overall, stepfathers tend to be more positive and responsive and less negative and directive toward children than are biological fathers (Hetherington and Henderson, 1997). Samuel Vuchinich and his colleagues (1991) characterize such behaviors as the "sociable polite stranger" role. In studies of stepchildren's reports of stepfamily functioning, stepfathers tend to get higher marks than stepmothers (see, for example, Schrodt, 2008; Smith, 2004). However, this finding should not be interpreted to mean that stepfathers do not encounter problems in this role. They do. Elizabeth Einstein (1985) identified three areas of difficulty for stepfathers: sex, money, and discipline.

Sex Stepfathers may feel uncomfortable in the presence of sexually developing adolescent stepdaughters. To prevent any misinterpretation by the stepdaughter or her mother, stepfathers often remain emotionally distant from their stepdaughter, with the result that the stepdaughter may perceive him as uncaring.

Money Finances may be a source of conflict for stepfathers in a number of ways. If he is a noncustodial biological parent, he may feel guilty for not playing a more active role in his own children's lives (DeGreeff and Burnett, 2009). Thus, he may give his children money or expensive gifts to compensate for his absence, thereby creating envy among his stepchildren. This behavior may also cause friction with both his current spouse, who feels the money is needed elsewhere (Lofas, 2009), and with his ex-spouse, who fears he is buying his children's love by spoiling them (Hans and Coleman, 2009). Noncustodial fathers who remarried and have children often believe these new expenses should allow them to decrease support payments to the first family. Laws and public opinion disagree (Hans, 2009). However, if the economic demands of a second family seem severe noncustodial fathers may stop supporting their biological children. Despite these very real problems, many men invest significant financial resources in their stepchildren (Stewart, 2007; Hofferth and Anderson, 2003).

Discipline Issues involving discipline revolve around two key questions: Who should discipline? Under what conditions? The answers to these questions may be far from clear. The wife and mother in the remarried family may voice a desire to share authority with her new spouse, but when he takes her up on it, she may be emotionally unprepared to relinquish any of her authority over her children. Research suggests it may take as long as 5 to 7 years for stepfathers to form good relationships with their children (Cohn and Merkel, 2004). Rather than disciplining children from the outset, many stepfathers gradually slide into the role over time (Marsiglio, 2004).

Stepchildren, too, may hold contradictory views regarding discipline by a stepfather. They may resent his efforts to make them behave. Yet if he does not try to discipline them, they may perceive him as indifferent and uncaring, and respond angrily, "You don't care what I do; you don't love me." Researchers have found a correlation between stepchildren's perception of being loved by a stepparent and whether the stepparent makes them behave (Bohannan, 1985). The dilemma of discipline appears to be lessened in cases where children are young or where a friendship has been established first between the stepparent and the stepchild.

LESBIAN AND GAY STEPFAMILIES

Lesbian and gay parents who form same-sex unions confront the same challenges facing heterosexual stepfamilies. However, because of their sexual orientation, their very existence as a family unit is often questioned. Thus, lesbian and gay stepfamilies may lack the support given to heterosexual stepparents and often face prejudicial and discriminatory treatment (van Dam, 2004). In fact, Roni Berger (2001) considers lesbian and gay stepfamilies a triple stigmatized group. First, they are stigmatized because of their homosexuality, which is still regarded as deviant or a sin by many people. Second, gay parenthood is stigmatized because many people perceive lesbians and gay unfit to be parents and view their family structure of a stepfamily as deficient compared with nuclear families. Finally, within the homosexual community itself, lesbian and gay parents may suffer stigmatization from those who emphasize the primacy of the partner relationship and who perceive children as a threat to couple relationships. Interviews with adolescents and young adults from 15–29 years of age living in lesbian and gay stepfamilies show how the experience of this stigmatization impacted their lives (Robitallle and Saint-Jacques, 2009).

As we observed in previous chapters, studies on lesbian and gay lifestyles, particularly family lifestyle issues, are just beginning to emerge. One such study examined lesbian stepparent roles and found three distinct patterns: (1) the coparent family, in which the nonbiological mother takes the role of an active parent and committed family member by being a helper and supporter of and consultant to the biological mother; (2) the stepmother family, in which the lesbian stepparent fulfills many of the traditional mothering tasks while the biological mother functions as the decision maker, a pattern similar to the traditional heterosexual stepfamily model; and (3) the co-mother family, where both mothers share responsibilities in the day-to-day decision-making and child-rearing tasks (Wright, 1998). Similarly, other studies show that lesbian and gay stepfamilies are diverse and flexible in constructing family roles (see for example, Lynch, 2000).

EX-SPOUSES: DO THEY FADE AWAY?

Divorce ends a marriage, but it does not necessarily end the relationship between the former spouses. This is especially true for couples with children. How do couples come to view each other after divorce? One study of divorced fathers and their new wives found that most of these couples identified the children's mother as a major source of stress in their marriage. Both the ex-husband and their wives described the ex-wife in negative terms (Guisinger, Cowan, and Schuldberg, 1989). This finding seems to support the popular image of ex-spouses as warring factions (for a discussion of how stepfamily members manage tensions during interactions with nonresidential parents see, for example, DeGreeff and Burnett, 2009). In other studies, however, researchers found that only a fraction of the sample of divorced couples fit that description. Such couples were classified as either "angry associates," whose relationships are characterized by bitterness, resentment, and ongoing conflicts over visitation and support payments, or

In happier days, Bruce Willis, his former wife Demi Moore, and her husband Ashton Kutcher often attended social events together. Their behavior showed that former spouses can have positive relationships with each other. The Willis/Moore children referred to Kutcher as their MOD, My Other Dad. However, these relationships became strained amid rumors of Kutcher's infidelity. The six-year marriage of Moore and Kutcher is most likely over.

"fiery foes," whose relationships are extremely antagonistic. The lingering acrimony of their divorce made it impossible for them to cooperate with each other on any matter.

In contrast, a number of divorced couples maintained cordial relationships, with each other as "cooperative colleagues" who are friendly and mutually concerned about their children's' welfare. They managed to make decisions and celebrate their children's major life events together. A smaller number of ex-spouses remained "perfect pals." Their divorce was amiable; they continued to like and trust each other, and they worked cooperatively to maintain a positive environment for their children. Finally, there are the dissolved duos, ex-spouses who have little or no contact after the divorce (Ahrons, 1994). Some couples who have maintained cordial relationships tend to create family events for their children. One example of this is taking joint vacations together. According to one divorced father, "joint vacations are nice for the kids as well as the adults. Supervising and entertaining children is less stressful with two parents and you can enjoy adult interaction" (Schwartz, 2011).

A study of 1791 previously married women and men in the Netherlands found that 10 years after divorce, almost half of the respondents report contact with their former spouse and that the number of former couples with antagonistic contact decreases strongly over time. However, couples with joint children have both more friendly contact and more antagonistic contact than other couples (Fischer, de Graab, and Kalmijn, 2005). As we discussed previously, the nature of the relationship between former spouses is an important factor in how well their children adjust to a parent's remarriage and in the frequency and kind of contact children have with the nonresident parent.

As we saw in the last chapter, many divorced parents with children share in some form of joint custody. A stable coparenting relationship after divorce has been shown to combat negative effects on child development (Roberson, Sabo, and Wickel, 2011). One innovative study by Arizona State University researchers suggests a new norm may be emerging. Study participants were asked to imagine they were a judge deciding a series of hypothetical divorce scenerios. The most common decisions were to award equally shared custody arrangements (Braver, et al 2011). That such a norm might prove helpful to divorced parent is suggested by other research which found that parents who held positive perceptions of coparenting communicated more often with their former partner than did other parents as did those who perceived social encouragement to coparent (Ganong, et al. 2011).

Thus far, our discussion of remarried families has tended to focus on the numerous adjustment problems members face. This should in no way be interpreted to mean that there are few benefits to living in remarried families. Quite the opposite is true, as we will see in the next section.

The Strengths and Benefits of Remarried Families

Patricia Knaub and her colleagues (1984) were among the first to undertake an empirical study of what makes remarried families strong. They asked 80 randomly selected remarried families to indicate what strengths were most important to their families. Their respondents listed love and intimacy (caring, affection, closeness, acceptance, understanding), family unity (working together, shared goals, values, and activities), and positive patterns of communication (honesty, openness, receptiveness, and a sense of humor), characteristics important to all families.

Further insight into the strengths of remarried families comes from a study of remarried couples in central Pennsylvania (Furstenberg and Spanier, 1984). These couples felt their current marriage was stronger than their first marriage in three important ways. First, they had better communication skills. Second, they were more realistic about the existence of conflict in marriage, and perhaps as a result of having better communication skills, they reported having fewer conflicts in their second marriage. Third, the balance of power in decision making was more equal in the remarriage. A review of studies conducted in the 1990s supports the finding of equitable power sharing and decision making by spouses in stepfamilies (Coleman, Ganong, and Fine, 2002). A comparison of 111 remarried and 111 matched first-married spouses also found that remarried spouses endorsed more autonomous standards in child rearing and finances and remarried women endorsed greater autonomy regarding friendships and family. The division of household tasks also appeared to be less traditional in remarried families (Sandin et al., 2001).

In addition, John Visher and Emily Visher (1993), two therapists who work with remarried families, identified six behavior patterns associated with building successful stepfamilies: (1) developing realistic expectations, (2) allowing children to mourn their losses, (3) building and maintaining a strong couple relationship, (4) proceeding slowly in constructing the stepparent roles, (5) creating their own traditions and rituals, (6) developing satisfactory rules and arrangements for children living in overlapping households. Dawn Braithwaite and her colleagues (2001) found similar dynamics at work by which remarried families came to "feel like a family," and a review of 50 years of research on naturally occurring family routines and rituals found that the establishment of family routines and rituals contribute to parenting competence, child adjustment, and marital satisfaction (Fiese et al., 2002). Interview with parents, adolescents and stepparents from 51 families highlighted how relatively enjoyable shared family activities were critical to their efforts to jointly cope with immediate stressors and to maintain or rebuild a sense of family following changes in their family structure (Hutchinson, Afifi, and Krause, 2007).

More recently researchers followed more than 120 stepfamilies for three years to see what predicted success. They found four key elements. Couples who did better:

- Had shared and realistic expectations about how they shared the parenting roles,
- Worked to develop positive experiences shared by the whole family,
- Communicated effectively to their children about a joint couple position about parent and family life, and
- Gradually build a positive stepparent–child relationship ("Assistance in Managing a Stepfamily," 2011).

Finally, other researchers have also documented the importance that a strong couple relationship plays in the success of remarried families. When children see a stable and well-functioning relationship between their parent and stepparent, it reduces their fears about the possibility of another break-up and provides them with role models who can resolve problems in a rational and non-threatening manner (Kheshgi-Genovese and Genovese, 1997).

Remarriage offers a number of benefits to family members. A custodial parent gains a partner with whom to share family work as well as financial responsibility. In exchange, the new stepparent shares in the joys of family life. For the new spouses, remarriage restores the continuity of a sexual relationship and provides companionship and a sense of partnership. Additionally, although it might be viewed as a mixed blessing, the ambiguity of roles in remarried families offers family members the opportunity to create new ones that may prove more satisfying in the long run. For example, stepparents do not have to try to replace parents; instead, they can be friends, counselors, teachers, or companions to stepchildren.

The Quality of the Remarital Relationship

When remarried people are asked about the quality of their relationships, the results show a mixed picture. Despite all the problems we have just discussed, most remarried couples, overall, seem to find happiness in their new relationship. In reviewing the literature on remarriage, Coleman and Ganong (1991) found that there were very few differences between spouses in first marriages and those in remarriages. A more recent study comparing first-married and remarried military couples found that remarried couples reported lower marital satisfaction than first-married couples (Adler-Baeder, Taylor, and Pasley, 2005). However, like earlier studies, the difference between the two groups was small.

When gender is examined larger differences in levels of happiness and satisfaction emerge. In both first marriages and remarriages men report higher levels of satisfaction than women. For stepmothers, the perception of child-care inequities were the strongest predictor of marital dissatisfaction over time (Pasley, Dollahite, and Ihinger-Tallman, 1993). The help of the biological father in child-care and household tasks was associated with better adjustment to the stepparent role (Guisinger, Cowan, and Schuldberg, 1989).

Additionally, there seems to be a connection between family structure (whether stepchildren and/or biological children reside with the remarried couple) and remarital satisfaction (Stewart, 2005b). Role ambiguity and stress can lessen satisfaction. As is true with first marriages, the presence of children in stepfamilies can affect the quality of family happiness. Recent research on Turkish remarried families found that remarried individuals with residential stepchildren had lower marital satisfaction than those with nonresidential stepchildren and those without stepchildren (Bir-Akturk and Fisiloglu, 2009). Wives who felt that the demands of their husbands' first family negatively impacted their own family

were significantly more likely than those who did not have this view to report less marital happiness (Knox and Zusman, 2001). Remarried couples with children from previous marriages are more likely to divorce than are remarried couples without stepchildren (Pill, 1990).

Other studies reinforce the view that successful stepfamilies require partners who not only can cope with the usual stresses of stepfamily living but who can successfully relinquish traditional gendered parenthood roles (White, 1994). Discipline and primary nurturing are usually best done by the biological parent, not the stepparent, regardless of gender. When there is disagreement over discipline, house rules, and financial resources, remarried spouses are likely to express more marital dissatisfaction (Coleman et al., 2002). Conversely, predictors related to higher remarital quality include couple consensus on important topics, social support from family and friends and financial stability (Falke and Larson, 2007).

Other factors can also impact a remarried couple's relationship. Interviews with couples who have been together for more than five years revealed that being proactive in the family formation process, having widespread family acceptance of the new partner and marriage were conducive to successful remarriages and stepfamily relationships (Michaels, 2006).

In sum, then, what can couples do to facilitate happiness in remarriage? Remarried couples who accept their children's loyalties to noncustodial parents, accept their spouse's ongoing coparenting relationship with an ex-spouse, and resolve the problems raised by their prior marriage are likely to have a happy remarriage. However, as we shall see in the next section, happiness in the remarried couple relationship may not, in and of itself, be sufficient to ensure the stability of the remarriage.

STABILITY IN REMARRIAGE

Conventional wisdom would have us believe that second marriages should be more successful than first marriages. People often assume divorced people possess characteristics that should translate into more effective relationships. On average, the divorced are older and seemingly more mature and experienced than those entering marriages for the first time. Thus, the argument goes, they should make more intelligent choices, have more realistic expectations, and have more negotiating skills with which to handle the stresses and strains that arise in married life.

But do they? Overall, research shows that first marriages are somewhat more stable than remarriages. Approximately 60 percent of remarriages end in divorce (Campbell, 2011) compared to a divorce rate of between 40 and 50 percent for first marriages. Table 13.3 shows that the median duration of second marriages that end in divorce is about 8.5 years for men and 8.0 years for women.

Factors Affecting Stability Several factors combine to explain divorce among remarried couples. As we have already observed, remarriage is a complex process, requiring a number of adjustments that are outside the scope of first marriages and for which most remarried couples are not well prepared. Among them are kinship terms, outside support and pressures, attitudes toward divorce, the presence of children, and time.

TABLE 13.3 Median Duration of Second Marriages for People Age 15 and Older by Sex, Race, and Ethnicity, 2009					
Sex	Total	White	Black	Latinoas/os	All remaining races and combinations
Men	8.5	8.7	7.9	7.4	6.4
Women	8.0	7.9	8.3	9.0	8.1

Source: Adapted from Kreider, R. M. and R. Ellis. 2011. Number, Timing, and Duration of Marriages and Divorces, 2009. *Current Population Reports*, P70-114. Washington, DC: U.S. Census Bureau, p. 18, Table 8.

Kinship Terms and Interactions may be a sticky point for all those affected by remarriage. Because stepchildren already have biological parents they call "Mom" and "Dad," forms of address for stepparents must be worked out. A recent study of college students found that many respondents called their stepparents by their first names or referred to them as dad's wife (Kellas, LeClaire-Underberg and Normand, 2008). Such language can clarify relationships but also create emotional distance. On the other hand, familiar terms are used to convey a sense of closeness in the relationship. For example, when stepchildren refer to their fathers as "Dad" or "Daddy" it signifies to them a sense of genuine fatherhood and belonging (Marsiglio and Hinojosa, 2006).

Outside Support and Pressures The attitudes of relatives, friends, and community members can affect the stability of remarriages. Positive and supportive reactions from friends and relatives contribute to successful remarriages. Conversely, disapproval of the remarriage by significant others can put added stress on the relationship. Sometimes the announcement of a remarriage may be greeted with little enthusiasm on the part of relatives. As one stepmother said in an interview:

> My mother was thrilled for me when I told her I was going to marry, but her manner changed completely when I told her he had a child. She was wary for me, she wanted me to think about it. It was not the dream she had for my marriage.

> *(Smith, 1990:30)*

Sheer numbers add another challenge for remarried couples. A stepfamily can have an unusually large extended family. For example, a divorce and remarriage of a couple with three children could generate as many as 100 possible kin relationships. Stepfamilies need to think creatively about how to develop relationships with all their extended kin. Consider the Brunsons. Their son Blake has eight grandparents. Blake's maternal and paternal grandparents divorced before he was born. This pattern is no longer unusual. Today, nearly half of all American families have at least one set of grandparents who has been divorced, compared with just one-fifth in the mid-1980s (Harmon, 2005). This trend adds new complications to family structures and functions as a third generation is added to that part of the family tree. Each biological grandparent has step relationships with members of the new spouse's family. What happens to previous family customs and traditions? Sociologist Andrew Cherlin (1978) argues that "remarriage is an incomplete institution" that does not provide easy answers to these questions. Consequently, remarried families are left adrift to find their own solutions to these problems. Without institutionalized patterns of family behavior and support, family unity is likely to be precarious. The solution the Brunson family arrived at is to have independent celebrations with each biological grandparent and her or his spouse over a realistic period of time. At other times they all get together but must follow the rules set by Blake's parents. "If they want to be a part of his life then they need to get along with everybody" (quoted in Harmon, 2005).

If you were in Blake's parents' shoes, would you include all of the stepgrandparents in your children's lives? If so, how would you go about it? How would you handle a biological parent who might view such inclusion as a betrayal? What do you see as the advantages and disadvantages of this type of family formation?

As a result of the remarriages of both sets of grandparents, Blake Brunson finds his cheering section at basketball games has doubled.

Attitudes toward Divorce Moreover, the familiarity with the divorce process itself may remove some of the social barriers to a second divorce. Having survived a first divorce, some remarried people are less likely to stay in an unhappy or deteriorating relationship. Furthermore, because they have already dealt with the reactions of family and friends to their first divorce, they are likely to be less fearful of an adverse public reaction to their course of action.

The Presence of Children Disagreements regarding children often play a pivotal role in the parental decision to redivorce (Lofas, 2009). Women who have children at the time of remarriage are more likely to experience second marriage disruption than woman who do not have any children, and if the children were unwanted, the probability of disruption is even higher. After 10 years of remarriage, the probability of disruption is 32 percent for women with no children at remarriage. For women with children, but none of whom were reported as unwanted, the probability is 40 percent, and for women with children, any of whom were reported as unwanted, the probability is 44 percent (Bramlet and Mosher, 2002). On the other hand, stepfamily couples who have a mutual child together stay together longer than those who do not. Nevertheless, compared with other children, those born within most types of stepfamilies are more likely to experience their parents' separation before their 10th birthday (Juby, 2003/2004). Marilyn Ihinger-Tallman and Kay Pasley (1991) suggest three ways in which children can contribute to the dissolution of remarriages:

- *Personal Adjustments* Children limit a couple's privacy and their opportunities for intimacy. Couples may agree on aspects of their personal relationship but be at odds over what constitutes appropriate child behavior.
- *Discipline* Stepparents may feel that discipline was too lax in the "old" family and that new rules are in order. Stepchildren may resent such changes, and biological parents may feel caught in the middle. Consequently, all parties are likely to experience stress.
- *Disruptive Behavior* Children can manipulate the biological parent into taking sides against the stepparent or stepsiblings. If children refuse to cooperate in matters of daily family living, they can create a tense and hostile environment. Time is often required to resolve these issues.

Time Patricia Papernow (2012, 2001) cautions stepparents to be realistic about the time involved in solidifying stepfamily relationships. She divides the process of becoming a stepfamily into three major stages, each with its own set of developmental tasks. Tasks in the early stages involve becoming aware of fantasies such as "instant love" and letting go of or grieving for unrealistic hopes as well as learning about one's own and others' needs in the new family. In the middle stage members must actively confront differences between family cultures and generate new stepfamily rituals, customs, and codes of conduct in which all members of the family participate. The later stage, generally less conflictual, finds members enjoying the family's new boundaries and relationships and functioning well.

Here, too, however, the awareness process must continue as new issues arise. According to Papernow, families differ in the length of time it takes them to complete the stepfamily cycle. Fast-paced families move through the early stages quickly, and they take about 4 years to complete the cycle; average families take about 7 years; and slow families take about 9 years. These latter families get stuck in the early stages, taking longer to resolve their fantasies and grieve their previous losses. Some families never complete the cycle.

Researchers can gain a better understanding of how stepfamilies fare over time by using longitudinal studies, in which the same people are studied at different periods in time. Comparisons of stable remarried families with those that have dissolved should help us to identify ways to help remarried families cope with the unique aspects of remarriage. For example, the therapists' experiences show that it takes a minimum of 4 to 9 years for remarried families to begin to stabilize and develop their own customs, rituals, and history. Knowing that this is a normal pattern for remarried families, some remarried couples, who might otherwise contemplate divorce, may be able to stay together and wait for the "storms" to pass.

Research findings on stepfamilies suggest a number of ways in which social policy and enlightened individuals could be enlisted to help support the growing number of stepfamilies in the United States.

Supporting Remarriage and Remarried Families

Several steps can be taken immediately to help meet the needs of remarried families. First, legislators can modify state laws to include a form of legal guardianship, with the custodial parent's agreement, allowing stepparents to function more effectively in families. For instance, stepparents then could be allowed to sign school permission slips, view student records, sign emergency medical forms, and authorize driving permits.

Second, evidence shows that premarital counseling contributes to more stable marriages. Efforts should be made to offer (and to fund) premarital counseling for individuals contemplating remarriage, using remarried couples to share their experiences. Similarly, schools can do their part to recognize stepfamilies as one of a variety of families by including them in curricular materials and teacher preparation courses that reflect their organization and functioning. This process would minimize perceptions that stepfamilies are somehow "lesser" family structures. Popular media depictions of stepfamilies need to be more realistic than old TV program, *The Brady Bunch*, or the romantic comedy *Yours, Mine, and Ours*, where problems are resolved in short order and everyone lives happily ever after. In addition, more should be done to encourage the normalization of stepfamily relationships. For example, the exchange of greeting cards on special occasions has become an expected pattern of behavior in American culture. However, the greeting card industry, like many other businesses, has been slow to recognize the diversity of the

> There was a time
> when I was afraid—
> afraid that once you came
> into our family
> there would be less love,
> less understanding,
> less "family" than before.
> But you showed me how love can
> blossom in a caring relationship,
> how an understanding heart
> can smooth a painful transition,
> how a family can be more
> than a matter of birth.
>
> You have shown me
> so much friendship,
> so much caring,
> so much love
> that I want to thank you
> for being you—
> a wonderful stepparent,
> a wonderful person. *
>
> Joan L. Stone

* This is a condensed version of the original greeting card.

FIGURE 13.5

American population. In the past, it was difficult to find cards representing people of color outside of ethnic specialty shops. Today, most stores stock these cards. And even now, it is still difficult to find cards like the one depicted in Figure 13.5 that represent other than traditional family forms.

Visit your neighborhood card shop. Does it carry cards for stepfamilies? What does the selection of cards in the section marked "relatives" reveal about our culture's attitude regarding stepfamilies? Do you think there should be greeting cards specifically for stepfamilies? For other types of relationships? Why or why not?

Third, many stepchildren are members of overlapping households. Both households spend money on food, shelter, clothes, entertainment, travel, and many other items. Currently, however, dependent children can be claimed as a tax deduction for only one household. If the tax code were revised to allow stepparents to deduct more of their cost of shared child support, it would give them some financial assistance. Besides the obvious monetary benefit, this change would symbolize society's recognition of the contribution stepparents make to the well-being of children and hence to the community at large.

Writing Your Own Script

THINKING ABOUT REMARRIAGE

Consider these facts: One-third of all U.S. children under the age of 18 are connected to a stepfamily; approximately 43 percent of first marriages and more than 50 percent of remarriages will end in divorce. It is thus possible that you or someone you know will spend at least part of your life in a remarried-family household.

It is important to be aware of the complexities of remarried families and not to assume that they will be like intact nuclear families.

Questions to Consider

1. What factors would you take into account in determining whether to remarry?
   How would you go about preparing for a remarriage?

2. What expectations do you have for how a remarried family should function?
   How do you think each of the following roles should be constructed in a stepfamily: (a) the biological parent, (b) the stepparent, (c) stepchildren, (d) step-in-laws, (e) biological and stepgrandparents?

SUMMARY

The pattern of marriage, divorce, and remarriage has become well established in the United States. Today, however, most remarriages involve divorced individuals, whereas in previous eras most remarriages involved widowed people.

Despite the high rate of remarriage, relatively little is known about this family form, especially among different classes, races, and ethnic groups. Remarried families differ from nuclear families in fundamental ways: They are more complex, they have a changing cast of characters, their boundaries are unclear, and their rules are often undefined. Laws regarding remarried families are ambiguous, and there is a lack of kinship terms to cover all affected parties in a remarriage. Members of remarried families often feel guilty or are still grieving over previous relationships.

Divorced people who remarry tend to spend less time in dating and courtship than people who marry for the first time. Like couples marrying for the first time, divorced people spend little time discussing issues such as finances and children. The reasons for remarriage are similar to those for first marriage. Men remarry more frequently and sooner than women. Men with higher incomes are more likely to remarry than men with lower incomes. College-educated women are less likely to remarry than other women. Whites have the highest rate of remarriage of any racial and ethnic group in the United States.

Children of remarried or cohabiting parents often experience boundary ambiguity when defining who is inside and who is outside their family. Many children whose parents divorce and then cohabit or remarry find themselves living in overlapping households, having to adjust to two different sets of rules. Although stepchildren often have difficulties adjusting and may experience stepsibling rivalry, they also benefit from new extended families. A half-sibling may be yet another source of competition for a parent's attention, but may also help stepchildren feel they are now part of a "real" family.

Both stepmothers and stepfathers face difficulty in establishing relationships with stepchildren, although stepmothers experience more stress than do stepfathers. Remarried couples report levels of marital happiness similar to those reported by those in first marriages. However, due to the greater complexity of remarriages, especially those with children, the duration of remarriages is shorter than that of first marriages.

KEY TERMS

remarried family	psychic remarriage	parental remarriage	legal remarriage	boundary ambiguity
emotional remarriage	community remarriage	economic remarriage	overlapping households	

QUESTIONS FOR STUDY AND REFLECTION

1. Discuss the significance of viewing remarried families as entities that are distinct from nuclear families. In a similar vein, some sociologists have argued against referring to remarried families as reconstituted or blended families. How might these latter terms cause problems for individuals living in remarried families? Should biological parents who are cohabiting with a partner be considered stepfamilies? Explain.

2. Andrew Cherlin has referred to remarriage as an "incomplete institution." What did he mean by that? Do you agree or disagree? What would be necessary to make remarriage a complete institution? Explain.

3. The divorce rate is higher in second marriages than in first marriages and even higher in third marriages. What factors are involved in these lower rates of marital stability? Do you see any as more important than the others? Explain. What can individuals and the community do to help improve the duration of remarriages? Explain.

4. To what degree do you think remarried families are seen as a legitimate family form in the United States today? Be specific. Consider their relationships to other social institutions like schools, laws, government, and the media. What changes, if any, would you make in these institutions regarding remarried families? Explain.

ADDITIONAL RESOURCES

SOCIOLOGICAL STUDIES

ALLAN, GRAHAM, GRAHAM CROW, and SHEILA HAWKES. 2008. *Stepfamilies: A Sociological Review.* New York: Belgrave Macmillan. Combining published studies and original fieldwork this highly readable book focuses on the internal dynamics of stepfamily households as well as those outside the household.

MACDONALD, WILLIAM L. and SUSAN D. STEWART. 2006. *Brave New Stepfamilies: Diverse Paths Toward Stepfamily Living.* Thousand Oaks, CA: Sage. The authors present the latest scholarly research on stepfamilies and explore the diverse assortment of tradition and not so traditional stepfamilies, including multihousehold stepfamilies, stepfamily adoptions, stepfamilies with adult children and African American stepfamilies.

MARSIGLIO, WILLIAM. 2006. *Stepdads: Stories of Love, Hope, and Repair.* Lanham, MD: Rowman and Littlefield. Readers will enjoy the lively accounts of the real life experiences of men who take on the ambiguous role of stepfather. The author addresses provocative and timely questions confronting stepfamilies and offers down-to-earth advice for dealing with them.

MARTIN, WEDNESDAY. 2009. *Stepmonster: A New Look at Why Real Stepmothers Think, Feel, and Act the Way We Do.* New York: Houghton Mifflin Harcourt. Through an analysis of her own experiences and interviews with other stepmothers and stepchildren, the author provides insights into the myths and realities of stepmothering.

FILM

Yours, Mine and Ours. 2005. A widowed Coast Guard Admiral and a widowed handbag designer fall in love and marry much to the dismay of her 10 and his 8 children. Although hostile toward each other at first, the stepsiblings unite to try to break up their parents' remarriage.

Stepmom. 1998. Anna and Ben must cope with the divorce of their parents and learn to adjust to the new woman in their father's life. At the same time, their biological mother and new stepmother struggle to come to some kind of accommodation.

LITERARY WORKS

LOUIE, AL-LING. 1996. *Yeh-Shen: A Cinderella Story from China.* New York: Putnam Publishing Group. This Chinese version of the story Cinderella predates the European version by almost a thousand years and contains many familiar details—a poor overworked girl, a wicked stepmother and stepsister. But rather than being handed gifts from a fairy godmother, Yeh-Shen earns her good fortune through kindness to a magic fish.

WALDMAN, AYELET. 2006. *Love and Other Impossible Pursuits.* New York: Doubleday. Emellia Greenleaf marries her soulmate but he comes with a package, a know-it-all preschooler named William who will become her number one responsibility every Wednesday afternoon. Her time with him becomes almost impossible after she loses her newborn daughter.

INTERNET

www.rainbows.org This organization offers training and curricula for establishing peer support groups in churches, synagogues, schools, and social agencies for children and adults of all ages and denominations who are grieving a death, divorce, or other painful transition in their family.

www.secondwivesclub.com The Second Wives Club is an online support community for second wives and stepmothers. It provides practical advice for succeeding in these roles as well as relevant articles about a range of issues for people in remarried relationships.

www.stepfamilies.info The National Stepfamily Resource Center's primary objective is to serve as a clearinghouse of information, resources, and support for stepfamily members and the professionals who work with them.

www.Remarriage.com This Web site is dedicated to helping those who wish to marry again or who have remarried. It provides information and resources to help you navigate this journey.

Succeed with MyFamilyLab®
www.myfamilylab.com

Watch. Explore. Read. The New MyFamilyLab is designed just for you. Each chapter features a pre-test and post-test to help you learn and review key concepts and terms. Experience Marriages and Families in action with dynamic visual activities, videos, and readings to enhance your learning experience.

Here are a few activities you will find for this chapter.

Watch on **myfamilylab.com**

Video clips feature important concepts in the study of Marriages and Families. Watch:
- The Persistence of Religion in America

Explore on **myfamilylab.com**

Social Explorer is an interactive application that allows you to explore Census data through interactive maps. Explore the Social Explorer Activity:
- Divorce Rates by Age

Read on **myfamilylab.com**

MyFamilyLab includes primary source readings from classic and contemporary sociologists from around the world. Read:
- Cherlin and Furstenberg: "Stepfamilies in the United States: A Reconsideration"

14

Marriages and Families in Later Life

What Will You Learn?

- Define and understand the sociological meaning of key terms.
- Describe some of the characteristics of and issues connected with later-life families.
- Apply the sociological imagination to examine the economic and social implications of changing life expectancy in the United States and around the world.
- Assess the pro and con arguments for raising the age at which people would receive full Social Security benefits.
- Increase your awareness and understanding of the role and status of the elderly in the United States and around the world.
- Question the various factors that influence the frequency and quality of intergenerational interactions, especially family caregiving.

IN THE NEWS

Glencoe, IL

On July 7, 2011, Claire Blumenthal, age 86, and Bernard Miller, age 90, exchanged wedding vows at Am Shalom Synagogue before 200 family and friends who came from as far as Japan, London, and Korea to help celebrate the occasion. The newlyweds will honeymoon in Sweden. The groom, when asked about his proposal, responded with good humor: "I had to protect her reputation. People were beginning to talk" (quoted in Rubin, 2011). Claire and her new husband have known

(continued on next page)

(continued from previous page)

each other through mutual friends since the 1940s. Both married other people, raised children, and enjoyed numerous grandchildren. Claire's husband died 10 years ago and Bernard lost his wife in 2008. A mutual friend suggested they go out on a date. They did and, like many younger couples, found they had similar interests, had fun together, and were physically attracted to one another.

It is not clear if they're the oldest couple to marry in Illinois since the state doesn't keep records of marriages by age, but anecdotal evidence from senior communities and data from the Census Bureau suggests that the rate of older couple marriages is increasing, albeit slowly. In fact, in response to the news story about Claire and Bernard, a couple wrote in saying they married six months ago when the bride was 91 and the groom was 88. Their comment

was "we're lucky to have found each other" ("Voice of the People," 2011). According to the Census Bureau, in 2008, 3.3 percent of all marriages included a male age 65 years older, while women in the same age group accounted for 1.9 percent of all marriages, up from 2.6 percent and 1.3 percent in 2003 (Rubin, 2011). Given the greater longevity and rapid growth in the oldest part of our aging population (85+), it is likely that these numbers will grow.

WHAT WOULD YOU DO?

If you were single in your 80s or 90s, would you consider marriage? What are the advantages and disadvantages of late-in-life marriages? Do you think most adult children would encourage such marriages for their parents? Explain.

((•—[Listen to the **Chapter Audio** on **myfamilylab.com**

I n 1990, the United Nations General Assembly designated October 1 as the International Day for the Elderly, also known as the "International Day for Older Persons." The United Nations created this holiday to highlight the challenges and opportunities presented by the world's rapidly aging population. In 2009, one out of every nine persons (737 million) was 60 years of age or over. This population is expected to increase to 2 billion in 2050. According to the United Nations, today's rate of population ageing is unprecedented. A population ages when increases in the proportion of older persons (60 years of age or older) are accompanied by reductions in the proportion of children (under age 15) and then by declines in the proportions of persons in the working ages (15 to 59). Worldwide, the number of older persons is expected to exceed the number of children for the first time in 2050 (United Nations, 2009). As Figure 14.1 shows, the world's population is aging at an increasingly rapid rate, especially in the more developed countries. In 1950, only 8 percent of the world's population was 60 and over. By 2050, it is expected to jump to 22 percent. Japan is the world's oldest nation, with 30 percent of its population aged 60 or over. By contrast, the United Arab Emirates and Oman rank last (with only 2 percent of their populations in that age category). Asia, Latin

Explore the **Concept**
Social Explorer Activity: Patterns in Lifespan for Men and Women on **myfamilylab.com**

America, and the Caribbean are the world's fastest-aging regions, with the percent of elderly in these regions expected to double between 2000 and 2030.

At age 115, Besse Cooper, of Monroe, Gerorgia, is the oldest living person in the world. Cooper is one of approximately 400 supercentenarians (someone who has reached the age of 110) living today. By 2050, more than 600,000 Americans are expected to be 100 years of age or older.

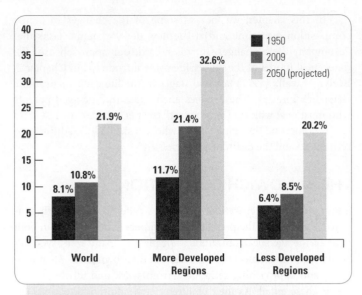

FIGURE 14.1 Proportion of World Population Age 60 and Over, 1950-2050 by World and Development Regions

Source: Adapted from United Nations. 2009. *Population Ageing and Development, 2009.* New York: Department of Economic and Social Affairs www.un.org/esa/population/publications/ageing/ageing2009chart.pdf (2011, August 8).

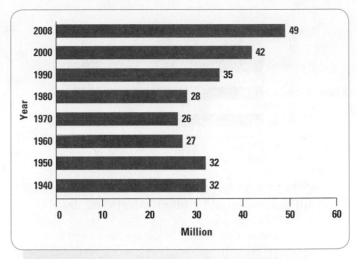

FIGURE 14.2 U.S. Population Living in Multigenerational Family Households, 1940–2008

Source: Pew Research Center. 2010. "The Return of the Multi-Generational Family Household." (March 18). http://pewsocialtrends.org/2010/03/18/the-return-of-the-multi-generational-family-household/ (2011, August 8).

A major concern of both developed and developing countries is how to meet the challenges of a growing elderly population at a time when traditional family support systems for elderly members are under considerable stress from a variety of quarters:

- Fewer children as caregivers because of earlier falling fertility rates;
- Higher divorce and remarriage rates both among the elderly and their offspring that disrupt existing kinship patterns;
- Geographical distance between family members;
- Changing norms of familial support with greater acceptance of institutional care for the elderly; and
- Increasing economic pressures.

Like these other nations, the United States is undergoing a major demographic transition. In 1900, only 3 million people in the United States were age 65 or over, representing just 4 percent of the total population. By 2010, more than 40 million people were in this age group, constituting 13 percent of the population. By 2050, the number of elderly is expected to climb to over 88 million, just over 20 percent of the population (U. S. Census Bureau, 2011e). If the demographic projections are correct, 1 in 5 persons in the United States will be 65 or over in 2050, compared with 1 in 25 in 1900.

These demographic changes have implications for how families are structured and on how they function. For the first time in recent history, middle-aged adults are dealing with the benefits and the burdens of being part of a multigenerational kinship structure. As Figure 14.2 shows, in 1940, 32 million Americans lived in multigenerational family households. Such arrangements fell out of fashion after World War II with the growth of nuclear family-centered suburbs and the dramatic increase in the health and economic well-being of older adults, making it possible for

them to live independently for longer periods of time. Cultural attitudes had also shifted and the nuclear family model became the idealized family form. By 1980, only 28 million Americans lived in multigenerational households. Recently, however, this downward trend reversed itself. By 2008, a record 49 million Americans (16.1 percent of the total U.S. population) lived in a family household that contained at least two adult generations or a grandparent and at least one other generation. Approximately one in five adults ages 25 to 34 and the same proportion of persons 65 and older now live in multigenerational households. Of the 49 million Americans living in a multigenerational family household, 47 percent live in a household made up of two adult generations of the same family (with the youngest adult at least 25 years of age); another 47 percent live in a household with three or more generations of family members; and 6 percent are in a "skipped" generation household made up of a grandparent and grandchild, but no parent (Pew Research Center, 2010c). As in the past, changing social and economic conditions are responsible for this reversal. An increasing number of young adult children are delaying marriage and remaining in the parental home longer; other young adults are part of a boomerang phenomenon—returning home because they can no longer afford to live independently. Not only has unemployment risen in the last few years so, too, have home foreclosures, forcing many families to double up.

GENDER, RACE, AND ETHNICITY

The gender profile of multigenerational families shows that in the 25–34 age group, there are significantly more men than women. The opposite is true among older age groups where women are more likely to live in a multigenerational setting. Part of the explanation for these differences is related to age at key life events. Men tend to marry at a later age than women and women are more likely to be widowed at an earlier age than men.

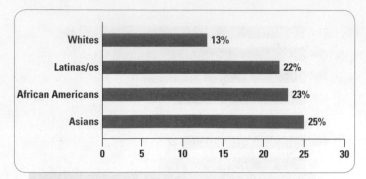

FIGURE 14.3 Percentage of Population in Multigenerational Family Households, by Race/Ethnicity, 2008

Source: Pew Research Center. 2010. "The Return of the Multi-Generational Family Household." (March 18). http://pewsocialtrends.org/2010/03/18/the-return-of-the-multi-generational-family-household/ (2011, August 8).

As Figure 14.3 shows, Asians, African Americans and Latinas/os are far more likely to live in multigenerational households than are Whites. These rates have increased during the recent recession as unemployment rates and foreclosures have increased. Immigration is a factor in these higher rates as well, especially for Asians and Latin Americans. Like immigrants from an earlier time, today's immigrants are more prone to share living space with other generations.

Since these living arrangements are relatively new for most participants, there are relatively few role models to guide them. Consequently, these households function with a great deal of confusion and uncertainty but they also provide excitement and joy. The primary focus of this chapter is on what family expert Timothy Brubaker (1990) has called "later-life families"—families beyond the childrearing years.

Characteristics of Later-Life Families

Later-life families exhibit three characteristics: (1) they are multigenerational, (2) they have a lengthy family history, and (3) they experience a number of new life events for which they may have little preparation, for example, grandparenthood, retirement, and widowhood.

In this chapter, we look at some of the changes in family composition over time and at the new developmental tasks that accompany these changes. In this regard, our approach uses the theoretical model of the family life cycle introduced in Chapter 2. Evelyn Duvall's (1977) last two stages in the life cycle incorporate "later-life families." These stages encompass middle-aged parents who must deal with the "empty nest," the period after the last child leaves home; and the aging family, whose tasks include adjusting to retirement and the death of a spouse.

THE SANDWICH GENERATION

The middle-aged generation, sometimes called the **sandwich generation** because of the pressures its members experience from both ends of the age spectrum, finds itself playing many roles. Middle-aged parents must meet the challenges of their own lives—their own aging and approaching retirement from work and all the adjustments these entail. As their children reach adulthood, parents expect to be free from major family responsibilities and to have more time to spend on their own pursuits. For many parents, however, the economic realities of recent decades have put some of these expectations on hold. As we saw in Chapter 7, many young adults find achieving financial independence difficult. Consequently, increasing numbers remain at or return to the parental home. Not only do middle-aged parents frequently have adult children living at home, but they often must care for elderly parents as well. Increasing life expectancy, combined with lower birth rates, has brought about a major shift in the amount of time people spend in various roles. The middle generation, for example, will spend on average more years with parents over 65 than with children under 18. According to a recent study, 72 percent of adults ages 52–58 find themselves still providing support for their children and grandchildren and 14 percent are providing care to older parents (MetLife Mature Market Institute, 2010). A similar study of Latino baby boomers (ages 45–64) found that 46 percent have helped a child pay bills or expenses and 28 percent are helping a parent pay for their expenses (Perron, 2010). Thus, the empty-nest stage is more a myth than a reality for increasing numbers of middle-aged parents. To commemorate the special needs of people caring for multiple generations, some state and local governments have proclaimed July as Sandwich Generation Month.

Although many middle-aged adults confront such changes, recent research indicates that popular images of a "midlife crisis"

For Better or For Worse®   **by Lynn Johnston**

To a degree, being old is a matter of self-definition. Some people may feel old at age 60; others may not feel old at age 80.

Source: For Better or For Worse © 2010 Lynn Johnston Productions. Dist. by Universal Press Syndicate. Reprinted with permission. All rights reserved.

are largely overdrawn. A 10-year study of nearly 8000 Americans aged 25–74 by the MacArthur Foundation Research Network on Successful Midlife Development, found that, for most respondents, the midlife years appear to be a time of good health, productive activity, psychic equanimity, and community involvement. Only 23 percent of the respondents reported having a "midlife crisis" and, of that group, the majority tied the crisis to a specific event in their lives, for example, a divorce. Only 8 percent described the crisis as a time of personal turmoil related to their realization that they were aging (Friedman, 2008)).

DIVERSITY IN THE FAMILY LIFE CYCLE

As we saw in Chapter 2, the family life cycle model has some inherent limitations that we will try to avoid. For example, our discussion of later-life families does not assume a nuclear family model. Child-free couples, single-parent families, and families that have taken in other kin or friends—a pattern common among families of color—must also make changes and confront new tasks as their members grow older. Additionally, like families at other stages of development, later-life families take diverse forms. They include couples in a first marriage, mothers who have never married, widows and divorced people who have not remarried, and people who have remarried, some more than once. Although these family patterns can be found in all social, economic, racial, and ethnic groups, much of the existing research is concentrated on White, middle-class families. Thus, our ideas concerning how the poor (and for that matter the rich) and people of color experience many of these later-life stages remain largely undocumented.

▶ Read the Document
Ageism in the Workplace
on **myfamilylab.com**

For much of the twentieth century, U.S. culture has emphasized youth. Consequently, many Americans have developed negative stereotypes of the elderly. Robert Butler, the former director of the National Institute of Aging and author of *Why Survive? Being Old in America* (1975), coined the term **ageism** to describe these stereotypes and the discriminatory treatment applied to the elderly. Coined over a quarter of a century ago, the concept is still relevant today. According to a recent poll, 62 percent of respondents say older persons face discrimination in today's society and fewer than half (46 percent) think older people are viewed with respect in America (Research! America, 2006). **Social gerontology,** the study of the impact of sociocultural conditions on the process and consequences of aging, shows us that the impact of aging on marriages and families is multifaceted. Some older family members are frail and in need of care, whereas others are living independent, healthy, active lives. Some of America's elderly live in isolation in single-room occupancy hotels, but many others enjoy happy lives, interacting with family and friends and engaging in numerous new and exciting activities. Our goal throughout this chapter is to present these differing realities of America's elderly and their families.

CHANGING AGE NORMS

In general, life course development tends to follow specific **age norms,** expectations of how one is to behave at any stage in life. These age norms currently show signs of being less restrictive than in the past. For example, today it is not unusual for people to marry for the first time in their 20s, 40s, or even 60s or to remarry in later life as illustrated in our In the News feature at the beginning of this chapter. Similarly, women are becoming mothers at both younger and older ages. Not only are teens giving birth but, due to new reproductive technologies, so too are menopausal women (see Chapter 9). Divorced and remarried men in their 40s and 50s are starting new families. As late as the 1960s, students typically attended college for 4 years, starting at age 18 and finishing at age 22. Today, your classmates may be 20, 30, 50, or even 70 years old, and they may take 4, 5, or even 8 years to complete their degrees. Although more people are opting for early retirement at age 55, others begin new careers at age 70. As these examples indicate, there has been an ongoing shift toward a loosening of age-appropriate standards of behavior. As a result of falling mortality rates, most of us can expect to experience many of these later-life events. By reflecting on the experiences of the generations ahead of us, we may better prepare ourselves to deal with these events. It is also useful to anticipate how long we can expect to live and to begin to prepare for our own aging experience (see the Applying the Sociological Imagination box).

APPLYING THE SOCIOLOGICAL IMAGINATION

HOW LONG CAN YOU EXPECT TO LIVE?

To answer this question, go to http://www.livingto100.com/calculator and use the Life Expectancy Calculator to determine your anticipated life expectancy. Were you surprised by that number? Are you satisfied with that number? Explain. Now that you have an estimate of how long you might live, reflect on the factors that influence the number of years you will likely live. What factors are due to your family background? What factors are due to your lifestyle choices? Is there anything in these factors that you should change to improve your chances for a longer life? Ask your friends and parents to use the calculator. Compare your findings. What patterns do you find? Would you like to live to be 100? Why or why not? What is your ideal of a normal life span? Explain.

This senior citizen, whose t-shirt reflects his sense of humor, participated in a New York marathon. His active lifestyle illustrates the reality of changing age norms.

The Demographics of Aging: Defining "Old"

Who are today's elderly? When does old age begin? One easy answer is at age 65, which was arbitrarily selected by government officials in 1935 as the age at which a worker could receive full social security retirement benefits. Defining old age is more complicated than this, however. According to a study by Charles Schwab, on average, respondents believed 'old age' doesn't begin until 75 or older (Business Wire, 2008). Similarly, an active 78-year-old friend of ours explained why she does not care to go to her local senior citizen center, "The people there are all so old." By that she meant they are in their 80s and 90s and less active than she is. Her experiences confirm what many researchers have come to call **functional age**—an individual's physical, intellectual, and social capacities and accomplishments. People grow old at different rates. One person may be "old" at 60, whereas another is "young" at 80.

AGE CATEGORIES OF THE ELDERLY

Including everyone over 65 in a single category called "the elderly" obscures significant differences in the social realities of older people. Recognizing the diversity among older people in terms of

physical and social functioning, gerontologists now speak of three distinct categories: the young–old (ages 65–74), the middle–old (ages 75–84), and the old–old (ages 85 and over). The older population itself is aging at a rapid rate. Figure 14.4 shows the projected changes expected in these age categories between 2010 and 2050. In 2010, only 14 percent of the elderly were expected to be 85 or older, but in only another 40 years, 22 percent of the elderly is expected to be that old. The oldest–old make up the most rapidly growing elderly age group. In 2010, the 65–74 age group (21.5 million) was ten times larger than in 1900, but the 75–84 group (13 million) was nearly 16 times larger and the 85+ group (5.7 million) was over 40 times larger. In 2010, 79,000 centenarians were living in the United States; their number is expected to grow to over 600,000 by 2050. These demographic changes present both opportunities and challenges. On the one hand, families and the society at large have much to gain by using the experience and wisdom of the older population. On the other hand, families and social planners must also prepare to meet the anticipated health care requirements and other service needs of an aging population.

GENDER AND MARITAL STATUS

Among the elderly population, especially those in the oldest category, women significantly outnumber men. This pattern has led some researchers to characterize old age as primarily a female experience (Longino, 1988). This, however, is a relatively recent development. Only around 1930 did women's life expectancy begin to increase more rapidly than men's as female deaths connected with pregnancy, childbirth, and infectious diseases declined dramatically. Although this trend is projected to continue over the next four decades, Table 14.1 shows that the gap between the number of women and men is expected to narrow. Among those 65 and older in 2050, 55 percent are expected to be female, down from 57 percent in 2010. This decline in the female share of the population is even more dramatic among the oldest old. Among those 85 years and over 61 percent are projected to be female in 2050, a decline of 6 percent from 2010. Women clearly have a longevity advantage over men. Why this should be the case is not fully understood.

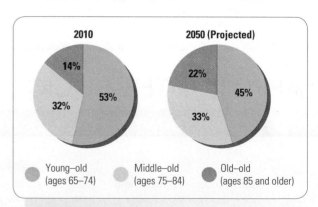

FIGURE 14.4 Percentage of Older Americans, by Age Group, 2010–2050

Source: Adapted from U.S. Census Bureau. 2011. *Statistical Abstract of the United States, 2011.* Washington, DC: Table 8, p. 12.

TABLE 14.1 Percent Female for the Older Population by Age, 2010 and 2050

Age Category	2010	2050
65+	57	55
65–74	54	52
75–84	58	55
85+	67	61

Source: Adapted from Vincent, G. H. and V. A. Velkoff. 2010. *The Next Four Decades, The Older Population in the United States: 2010 to 2050.* Current Population Reports, P25–1138, Washington, DC: U.S. Census Bureau, Figure 7, p. 8.

Science has not yet unraveled all of the reasons for the gender difference in mortality rates. Gerontologist Erdman Palmore (1980) attributes half of the difference to genetics and the other half to social roles and environmental factors.

Longevity for women, however, can be a mixed blessing. On the one hand, it allows for a rich and meaningful life, and it provides an opportunity to share in the socialization of new generations. On the other hand, it often means years alone, as husbands, male relatives, and friends die at earlier ages. As Table 14.2 shows, older women are much less likely to be married than older men—43.9 compared to 74.5 percent. Women are over three times as likely as men to be widowed (41.8 and 13.8 percent, respectively). Additionally, more elderly women are divorced than their male counterparts. Some of these patterns become more pronounced

TABLE 14.2 Marital Status, by Age Group and Sex, 2008

	65 and over	65–74	75–84	85 and over
Men				
Married	74.5	79.2	72.2	54.8
Widowed	13.8	6.9	18.7	37.7
Divorced	7.5	9.5	5.6	2.9
Never Married	4.2	4.4	3.6	4.7
Women				
Married	43.9	56.8	36.6	14.9
Widowed	41.8	25.1	52.5	76.2
Divorced	10.3	13.9	7.2	4.8
Never Married	4.0	4.2	3.7	4.1

Source: Adapted from Federal Interagency Forum on Aging-Related Statistics. 2010. *Older Americans 2010: Key Indicators of Well-Being.* Washington, DC: Table 3, p. 77.

at later ages. As we saw in Chapter 13, men are more likely than women to remarry after widowhood and divorce. By age 85 and over, the marriage rates decline for both women and men but they drop off more sharply for women. Only 14.9 percent of women but 54.8 percent of men are still married at 85.

These differences in marital status also vary significantly by race and ethnicity. Among males 65 and older, African Americans were the least likely to be married with spouse present (57 percent), compared with 73 percent of Whites, and 69 percent of Latinos and Asians. Similarly, among elderly women, 25 percent of African Americans, 43 percent of Whites and Asians, and 40 percent of Latinas were married with spouse present (He et al., 2005). These patterns are directly related to the different rates of marriage, divorce, and remarriage among the different racial and ethnic groups, as discussed in earlier chapters, as well as differences in mortality rates.

Gender differences in survivorship rates are significant because older women across all racial and ethnic groups have fewer financial resources and are more likely to experience poverty in old age than elderly men. To take just one example, the median income of older persons in 2009 was $15,282 for females and $25,877 for males (Administration on Aging, 2010).

RACE, ETHNICITY, AND CLASS

In 2010, the overall racial composition of the population 65 and older in the United States was 80.2 percent White, 8.5 percent African American, 7.1 percent Latinas/os, 3.3 percent Asian, and 1.4 percent all other races alone or in combination, including Native Amerians and Pacific Islanders (Figure 14.5). Together, people of color make up approximately 20 percent of the elderly population, and their numbers are increasing at a faster rate than those of the White elderly, primarily because of higher fertility and immigration rates. This trend is likely to continue well into the twenty-first century. Projections are that by 2050, people of color will constitute slightly over 40 percent of the population aged 65

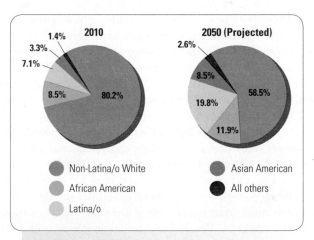

FIGURE 14.5 Population Age 65 and Over, By Race and Ethnicity, 2010 and 2050 (Projected)

Source: Vincent, G. K. and V. A. Velkoff. 2010. *The Next Four Decades, The Older Population in the United States: 2010 to 2050.* Current Population Reports, P25–1138. Washington, DC: U.S. Census Bureau, Table A-2, p. 12.

and over in the United States. Although all groups will experience change, the highest growth rates will be among Latinas/os and Asians. By 2050, nearly one in five elderly is likely to be Latina/o.

Although the gap in life expectancy rates for the White population and people of color is narrowing, these rates remain lower for people of color. In 2007, for example, life expectancy at birth was 80.8 for White females and 75.9 for White males. In contrast, it was only 76.8 for African American females and 70.0 for African American males. The gap narrows slightly at older ages. Life expectancy at 65 is 19.9 for White females and 17.3 for White males compared to 18.7 for Black females and 15.2 for Black males (U.S. Census Bureau, 2011e). Native Americans and Latinas/os also have lower life expectancies than Whites.

What accounts for these differences? One major factor, of course, is social class. In general, families of color have fewer economic resources in old age than do their White counterparts. This is mainly because of the disadvantages they faced in the labor market in earlier years: low-paying jobs, longer and more frequent terms of unemployment, and racial discrimination. Thus, they tend to have fewer health insurance or social security benefits than do the White elderly, and they are less likely to have supplementary retirement incomes from private pensions. In 2009, Asian American households containing families headed by person 65 had a median income of $47,319, followed closely by Whites with $45,400. African American and Latinas/os households had the lowest median income at $35,049 and $32,820 (Administration on Aging, 2011).

POVERTY AMONG THE ELDERLY

Although a smaller proportion of elderly is poor today than in the past, poverty remains a problem for millions of elderly, especially for the very old. In 1959, 35 percent of the elderly over 65 were poor; by 2009, only 9.7 percent were so identified, although many others had incomes only slightly above the poverty line. The initial decline in poverty rates was due to the nation's efforts to win the "War on Poverty" in the 1960s. Many new social programs were instituted for poor people of all age groups, including the elderly. Although many social welfare programs were reduced or eliminated during the last two decades, programs that benefit the elderly remained largely in place because of effective politically lobbying by groups such as the American Association of Retired Persons (AARP), which has over 35 million members. During this period, Social Security benefits were improved by providing for increases in the cost of living. Many companies instituted private pension plans for workers, thus providing workers with additional retirement income and numerous businesses instituted discount programs for senior citizens regardless of economic need. However, in recent years, the economy slowed and many companies struggling to remain competitive in an increasingly global economy cut many employee and retiree benefits. If these trends continue, it is likely that current poverty rates among the elderly will increase in the future.

Table 14.3 shows that the poverty rates vary from group to group and across different living arrangements. African Americans had the highest rate, 23.2 percent while Whites had the lowest rate at 7.4 percent; Latinas/os and Asians had rates in between these two groups (17.4 percent and 11.3 percent). Women had higher poverty rates (12.2 percent) than men (6.6 percent). Older people who live alone were more likely to be poor (17.8 percent) than were older married

TABLE 14.3 Percentage of the Population Age 65 and Over Living in Poverty, by Selected Charateristics, 2007

Selected characteristics	65 and over	65 and over Living Alone	65 and over Married Couples	75 and over
Both sexes	9.7%	17.8%	4.2%	10.6%
White	7.4	14.4	3.1	8.8
Black	23.2	33.5	9.6	22.8
Asian	11.3	31.3	7.4	14.1
Latinos	17.1	35.7	10.8	18.0
Men	6.6	11.8	4.3	6.7
White	4.7	8.9	3.1	5.5
Black	16.8	21.5	10.2	11.0
Asian	9.9	26.5	8.2	12.0
Latinos	13.3	24.1	11.8	13.6
Women	12.2	19.9	4.1	13.2
White	9.4	16.2	3.2	10.9
Black	27.3	39.0	8.7	29.2
Asian	12.4	33.0	6.4	15.4
Latinas	20.0	39.8	9.6	21.2

Sources: Adapted from Federal Interagency Forum on Aging-Related Statistics. 2010. *Older Americans 2010: Key Indicators of Well-Being.* Washington DC: Government Printing Office, Table 7b, p. 82.

couples (4.2 percent). Latinas living alone had the highest poverty rate (39.8 percent), followed closely by Black women (39 percent) while White women had the lowest at 16.2 percent. One of the key explanations for these differential rates has to do with discrimination in the workplace (see Chapter 10).

Living Arrangements

Disturbing stories of the plight of elderly in nursing homes frequently appear in the pages of newspapers. This may account for the widely believed myth that most aged persons end up institutionalized. In fact, only a small proportion of older Americans live in an institutional setting. In 2009, a relatively small number (1.6 million) and percentage (4.1 percent) of the 65 and over population lived in institutional settings such as nursing homes. However, the percentage increases dramatically with age, ranging from 0.9 percent for persons 65–74 years to 3.5 percent for persons 75–84 years and 14.3 percent for persons 85 and over (Federal Interagency Forum on Aging-Related Statistics, 2010). The majority of older nursing home residents are women. As we have seen earlier, women are more likely than men to be widowed and divorced at older ages and to live alone.

Americans are entering nursing homes at a later age than in the past and staying for shorter periods of time. It is likely that these changes reflect more use of home health care, assisted-living arrangements, and/or the use of nursing homes for short-term rehabilitation. Nevertheless, because the old–old are the fastest growing part of the elderly population, we can predict an increased need for quality nursing home care over the next several decades. Thus, many more families, perhaps yours included, will have to face the difficult decision of how to care for an elderly dependent relative. Some cultural groups have more problems making these decisions than others, however. Among U.S. Muslims, for example, there is a strong aversion to nursing homes. At the same time, however, like other immigrant groups before them, first- and second-generation adult siblings in Muslim families are often geographically separated and struggling to balance the demands of dual-income families with both children and elderly parents. To meet this need, some mosques are initiating plans to build assisted-living quarters for the elderly nearby so that their religious practices and cultural traditions can be maintained insofar as possible (Clemetson, 2006).

As Figure 14.6 shows, the vast majority of older people maintain their independence in the community, living alone or in a household with their spouse. Living arrangements show a clear gender and race/ethnic differences. Approximately 11.4 million men (72 percent) lived with their spouse compared to 8.7 million women (42 percent) in 2009. This pattern is true across all race and ethnic groups. However, living with other relatives is less common among Whites than among any other group. Latina, Black, and Asian women were most likely to live with their adult children and other relatives. Economic need and a cultural emphasis on the extended family are the most common explanations for these different patterns. Increasingly, however, even among these groups there is a trend away from coresidence with adult children. Greater numbers of women of color are now in the labor force, and today the younger generations are more likely to be in dual-earner families, leaving them less time and energy to care for elderly parents. Business is responding to this change. Several years ago Aegis Assisted Living, a company based in Redmond, Washington, opened Fremont Aegis Gardens, the first for-profit assisted-living community for Asians, offering ethnic foods and activities.

HOUSING PATTERNS

Of the elderly who live independently, the majority resides in their own homes. Homeownership offers a number of advantages: security and familiarity, lower cash outlays for shelter, a possible source of income when the home is sold, and a sense of control in one's life. In 2009, elderly householders were far more likely to own their own homes (80.5 percent) followed closely by householders aged 55–64 (79 percent) than other age groups. Married couples were more likely to own homes than were older persons who lived alone (U.S. Census Bureau, 2011e). Homeownership varies from group to group. Only 45 percent of African Americans and 47 percent of Latinas/os were homeowners compared to 67 percent of Whites.

Although overall today's elderly are less likely to be living in physically deficient housing than past generations, a significant portion of the housing occupied by the elderly is old and requires constant maintenance that is often too costly for people on fixed incomes. Because of these housing problems, the elderly are often exploited by unscrupulous individuals who promise to do home repairs but flee with the money without doing the work. There is concern that in the future, fewer elderly will own their homes because an increasing number of younger and middle-aged adults are unable to afford to purchase a home of their own or are losing them to foreclosures because they cannot afford the ballooning mortgages.

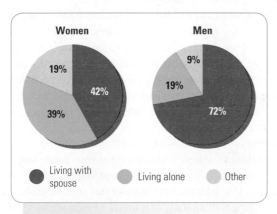

FIGURE 14.6 Living Arrangements of Persons 65+, 2009

Source: Administration on Aging. 2011. *A Profile of Older Americans: 2010.* Washington, DC: U.S. Department of Health and Human Services.

Today's families are smaller in size than in the past, resulting in fewer people to meet the needs of elderly members. Further, given that women live longer than men, increasing numbers of elderly women, like the woman above, are likely to spend their last years living alone.

The situation for elderly renters can be worse. Renters typically live in apartments, including public housing of varying quality. Some renters are boarders, and others live in residential hotels, including single-room occupancies (SROs). Increasingly, SROs, especially those that cater to low-income elderly men, have been demolished to make room for urban renewal projects. Not only does the destruction of SROs displace elderly residents, but, as we have seen in Chapter 10, it also contributes to homelessness.

Housing is more than a place to live. For many, it symbolizes continuity, independence, family history, and a sense of belonging. The majority of the elderly have lived in their current residence for 20 or more years. As the family life cycle changes, however, so, too, do housing needs. Houses can become too big, too isolated, too expensive, or too difficult to maintain for a retired couple or the widowed after children have left home. In addition, housing that once was satisfactory may become inadequate as a result of the resident's illness or disability. Sometimes, remodeling or the intervention of outside help can take care of these problems. In other cases, relocation to more suitable housing is the only alternative. When a change is voluntary, the personal and psychological disruption it causes is likely to be relatively minor because the perceived benefits outweigh the costs. When the elderly are forced to relocate, however, the result is often trauma, confusion, grief, and a sense of helplessness and isolation. When asked which living arrangements they prefer, the elderly consistently say they want to be independent and remain in their own homes.

AGING IN PLACE

Increasing longevity has given rise to an aging in place movement. A recent survey found that an overwhelming majority of people with disabilities age 50 and over (87 percent) want to receive long-term care services in their own homes. They want choice and control over everyday decisions and they want to live in a non-health care environment. Yet Medicaid and private insurance companies do not provide the range of choices people want and instead allocate a disproportionate share of resources for institutional services (Kassner, et al., 2008). However, this may be changing. About 80 communities nationwide are experimenting with an approach that uses a mix of government and philanthropic dollars, along with nominal membership fees, to create naturally occurring retirement communities (NORC) in neighborhoods or residential buildings where many residents are 60 or older. Typically, members of NORCs enjoy planned social outings, get together in their apartment buildings for activities and shared meals, and have use of transportation services for doctor visits and shopping. A nurse practitioner visits regularly to check on their health status and needs (Hannon, 2007).

In a similar vein, healthy people in their 50s, 60s, and 70s are anticipating the kinds of services they will need in the future to allow them to stay in their homes and neighborhoods and are becoming proactive in this regard. In 2001, a small group of residents living in Boston's Beacon Hill neighborhood came together and created a non-profit organization, a "virtual village." For a yearly member-

Watch the Video
Physical Challenges of Living Longer on **myfamilylab.com**

ship fee, older residents in the area who are in need of rides, home maintenance, social activities, meals, and other assistance can count on a community of volunteers and village-vetted service providers (generally at discounted prices) to assist them. Since Beacon Hill Village's virtual "doors" opened, similar villages have been developed in San Francisco, Washington, DC, Seattle, Cambridge, and Chicago and hundreds more are in the planning stages across the country.

Although only time will tell how effective these efforts will be, in an initial survey of 500 NORC residents, the vast majority of respondents reported that they were more socially involved, left the confines of their homes more often, and felt healthier than prior to their participation in the NORC demonstration projects. One resident summed it up this way: "You're involved with other people, so you don't get bored or depressed. It's wonderful. You come together and forget about what hurts you" (cited in Hannon, 2007).

Marriages in Later Life

Imagine being married to the same person for 50, 60, or even more years. Given current life expectancies, many married couples can expect to celebrate their golden wedding anniversary (6 percent) and beyond. What can we expect of a marital bond that endures this long? Does the quality of the relationship change over time?

MARITAL QUALITY AND SATISFACTION

Does marital quality improve with age? According to John and Amelia Rocchio, married for 83 years before passing away within a few months of each other in 2006, the answer was a definite yes. "Patience and understanding will get you a long way," said John. When asked what had kept them together so long, Amelia's answer was simple: "Love" (Associated Press, 2005). Nevertheless, to researchers, the answer is not so clear-cut. In an early review of more than 25 studies, no consensus was found on this question. Some studies reported little or no change in marital quality in later life. Couples who were happy in earlier years were likely to be happy in later years; early unhappiness remained in later years. Other studies found a gradual pattern of decline in marital love and companionship over the years. A third set of studies showing improvement in marital quality revealed a pattern whereby couples start out with high levels of satisfaction, "the honeymoon phase," followed by the childbearing and childrearing years, during which stress and anxiety levels may be heightened, leading to a decline in marital satisfaction. Once the children are grown and leave home, couples can concentrate on each other again and rediscover or develop common interests and interdependence, resulting in increased feelings of affection and companionship (Ade-Ridder and Brubaker, 1983). Later studies supported this curvilinear relationship between family stage and the perceived marital quality of both spouses (Story, et al., 2007; Vaillant and Vaillant, 1993). Further support for this relationship came from an 18-year longitudinal study that found women whose children left home were more satisfied with their marriage compared to women who still had children at home (Gorchoff, John, and Helson. 2008). However, research using a 17-year, 5-wave panel study did not find evidence of an increase in marital happiness following the launching of children or the transition to retirement (Van Laningham, Johnson, and Amato, 2001).

What are we to make of these different findings? Some of the differences may be related to the particular methodological techniques used in the studies themselves. Much of this research involved studies of small samples of older couples taken at only one point in time. Comparisons of changes are difficult to make unless the same couples are retested at different times and unless a standardized measure of marital quality is used. Outside events that may happen at any given point in a marriage also affect perceptions of satisfaction in a relationship. For example, in a study of mature marriages in which the ages of husbands and wives ranged from 55–75, daily stress was negatively related to marital quality (Harper, Sandberg, and Schaalje, 2000). Gender role ideology may also be a factor. Later-life couples who hold more egalitarian attitudes toward gender roles report higher levels of marital happiness than do those who hold more traditional attitudes (Walker and Luszcz, 2009; Kaufman and Taniguchi, 2006). Conversely when spouses feel their partners treat them unfairly, they are less likely to be satisfied with their relationship (Hagedoom, et al., 2006). Other research found that couples who have long-lasting marriages tend to characterize their marital relationship as based on trust, intimacy, shared values and belief systems, the ability to negotiate with each other, and a willingness to make adjustments (Arp and Arp, 2001; Hatch and Bulcroft, 2004). Jean and Harry Gottlieb, who have been married for 71 years, provide a good illustration of these dynamics (see the Family Profile box).

Throughout this text, we have examined a number of factors that influence a couple's level of marital satisfaction. For example, in Chapter 6 we discussed sexuality among the elderly. Marital satisfaction is positively related to sexual behavior among older couples who are still sexually active (Fisher, 2010). This does not mean, however, that couples no longer sexually active have poorquality marriages. Rather, for those still active, this intimate expression adds another satisfying dimension to their marital lives. Another important factor that affects later-life marriages is the way in which couples deal with retirement.

Family Profile

JEAN AND HARRY GOTTLIEB

Jean and Harry Gottlieb

Length of Relationship: 70 years

Challenges of Later Life:

The challenge is to maintain a real and caring interest in the world around us—in our children's and friends' lives as well as the more public events of the day—even though we are less in the mainstream and more like watchers on the riverbank. We must remain convinced that we can continue to make a real contribution to the world we live in. We have the long view and should be the all-important living link between a historic past and a still-mysterious future. We have fewer constraints on our own lifestyle and can do more things on impulse.

Relationship Philosophy:

We never take each other for granted. Our relationship has always been based on trust, a compatible sense of humor, close family ties, and good old romantic love. After 70 years of marriage, we love and respect each other more than ever. We are confidants, best friends, co-conspirators, and last—but not least—lovers. We spend more time together now, but we each have our own interests and activities as well as some mutual endeavors. When we have differences, we try not to go to bed mad. Although our life remains vibrant, we are saddened by the death of dear old friends and are aware of our own mortality.

ADJUSTMENT TO RETIREMENT

Retirement, as a distinct phase in the family life cycle, is a modern phenomenon. Before the twentieth century, American workers typically worked until they died or were physically unable to continue working. When they stopped working, there was no pension or Social Security for their later years, and their welfare most frequently depended on other family members. In the wake of the Great Depression, however, this situation changed. With the establishment of Social Security in 1935, the institution of retirement became part of the national culture. Nevertheless, not all elderly are retired, and those that do retire do so at different ages. In 2009, 21.9 percent of men and 13.6 percent of women 65 and over were working or actively seeking work (U. S. Census Bureau, 2011e). These numbers are projected to increase to 26.7 percent and 18.9 by 2018. A recent survey suggests the numbers many be higher than those projected. The non-profit Transamerica Center for Retirement Studies (2011) found in their survey of over 4,000 American workers that 40 percent of respondents expect to work longer and retire at an older age since the recession began. Of those who plan on working after retirement or age 65, the most frequently cited reason is necessity (44 percent). Additionally, about a third of the workers surveyed (31 percent) anticipate not just needing to provide for themselves in retirement, but for additional family members as well. Many economists see this as a positive trend, one that will ease the crunch of population aging (Maestas and Zissimopoulous, 2010). However, as the Debating Social Issues box suggests, raising the age of retirement is an emotional and controversial issue.

Like so much of social life in the United States, the experience of retirement is affected by an individual's gender, race, and class. Years ago it was common to hear housewives say, "I married him for better or worse, but not for lunch." Such a line usually produced chuckles in the listeners because they could easily envision a newly retired man who suddenly has time on his hands wandering aimlessly around the house, interfering with his wife's daily routines. However, today it can as easily be a retired wife who is disrupting the household system.

Types of Retirement Timothy Brubaker (1985) has identified four patterns of retirement among older couples:

- *Single or traditional retirement:* Here, one spouse, usually the husband, has been employed and thus only one spouse retires from paid employment.
- *Dissynchronized—husband initially:* In this situation, the husband retires before his wife. She continues to work because she is usually younger or started her career after his.
- *Dissynchronized—wife initially:* This pattern, in which the wife retires first, is rare. It may be that she has health problems or is needed to take care of an older relative.
- *Synchronized retirement:* In this situation, both the husband and wife were employed, and they retire at the same time.

Most of the studies conducted on retirement have not taken into account these variations, yet it is likely that marital satisfaction is affected in different ways not by retirement itself, but by the circumstances of retirement. For example, researchers found that synchronized retirement is most conducive to marital satisfaction while dissynchronized retirement is negatively related to marital happiness (Moen, Kim, and Hofmeister, 2001). Two possible explanations for these relationships come readily to mind. First, one partner is still employed, the time the couple has available to pursue joint social and recreational activities is limited. Second, if the husband retires first, a common practice because husbands tend to be older than their wives, he may only marginally increase his domestic labor.

Other factors also affect the quality of life after retirement. In 1986, Congress passed legislation ending mandatory retirement for most employees. Prior to that time, most workers were forced to retire at age 65 whether they wanted to or not. Despite the change in the law, 30 to 40 percent of early retirements are "forced," often the result of a company's downsizing, relocating, or going out of business or of an employee's or spouse's poor health (Taylor, 2009; Henkens and Van Dalen, 2003). Unanticipated and involuntary retirement is likely to produce stress and depression. In contrast, when people want to retire and make plans to do so, retirement is more likely to be a positive experience (Taylor, 2009: Van Solinge and Henkens, 2005). In general, when people control the timing of their retirement, they are more likely to feel satisfied with this stage in their lives. However, the degree to which workers have this control varies considerably. African American workers are less likely to experience voluntary retirement than are their White counterparts. Although financial readiness is a major factor in the decision to retire for Whites, poor health and disadvantaged labor force experiences are more likely to affect the retirement decision for African Americans. Compared with Whites, African Americans are more likely to retire at earlier ages, retire because of poor health, be forced to retire, be unemployed in the 12-month period before retirement, and report job dissatisfaction and job search discouragement prior to retirement (Weller and Fields, 2011; R. Gibson, 1996). Thus, it is not surprising to find that African American and Latino workers express less confidence about their retirement prospects and financial preparations than workers overall, and are more likely than other workers to say they will rely most heavily on Social Security for retirement income (Employee Benefit Research Institute, 2007).

The concept of retirement has little meaning for individuals whose jobs do not provide old-age benefits. They must keep working until they become physically incapacitated. This is particularly true for unskilled White workers and people of color, especially African American women, who often work to an advanced age. Finally, satisfaction during the retirement years also depends on the couple's financial status and health. If retirement income is sufficient to enable couples to pursue desired activities, retirement is likely to promote satisfaction. However, if couples have been unable to save much in the earlier years of married life or if their earnings have been so low that they receive only minimal Social Security benefits, they may experience considerable downward mobility with retirement.

Intergenerational Relationships: Contact and Social Exchanges

That most elderly live alone or with their spouse gave rise to a belief that most old people are neglected by their children. On the contrary, a recent national study found that 65 percent of

Debating Social Issues

SHOULD THE SOCIAL SECURITY RETIREMENT AGE BE RAISED?

The Great Depression of the 1930's and the ensuing economic crisis that followed led to the passage of the Social Security Act of 1935 which created a social insurance program designed to pay retired workers age 65 or older a continuing income. Since that time additional benefits were added to the program and reforms were made to ensure the solvency of the system, including a gradual increase in the normal retirement age to 67 in 2022. Today approximately 98 percent of all workers are in jobs covered by Social Security.

Those who believe it is time to raise the Social Security retirement age point out that when the first Social Security checks were mailed in 1940, the average life expectancy was less than 64 years. Thus, many Americans did not live long enough to receive benefits but with today's life expectancy rates nearing 80, increasing number of Americans will collect benefits for 15 years or more putting tremendous pressure on the system, increasing the nation's debt, and bankrupting the system. According to a recent CNN poll, 60 percent of

Americans under 60 and 70 percent of those under 50 believe that Social Security will not be able to pay them a benefit when they retire (Weisbrot, 2010). Proponents of increasing the retirement age argue that declining fertility rates over the last decades mean that there will be fewer younger workers in the future to support a rapidly growing population of older citizens. Thus, they conclude that as the source of new labor slows, so, too, will economic growth, leading to a decline in the nation's living standards. Thus, they believe it is necessary to abandon the statutory age of retirement and to recalibrate the ways we think about work, the work place and retirement to prevent a worsening economic and fiscal crisis.

Opponents of raising the retirement age believe such efforts are misguided and even deceitful. They argue that there is no basis for Americans to believe that Social Security will not be there for them. They point out that the United States can still afford retirement at age 65 and that the basic problem is a matter of willingness to pay for retirement, not the ability to do so. Social Security still has a surplus and it will remain solvent for years to come. Eliminating the cap on taxable income will ensure its solvency long into the future. According to these opponents, another major problem with raising the retirement age is the nature of work. Although many people do continue working after reaching age 65, for those in

physically demanding occupations like nurses, police officers, firefighters, construction workers, and teachers, this may not be possible. Research shows that increases in life expectancy in retirement are skewed in favor of those with less physically demanding jobs and those with higher incomes and more education (Cristia, 2009). For many others, there may no longer be a demand for their skills or they may experience age discrimination. According to the Equal Employment Opportunity Commission, there has been a 17 percent increase in age discrimination cases since the recession began in 2007, suggesting that many older workers will have difficulty in securing and maintaining good jobs. Additionally, there are currently not enough jobs for everyone who wants to and/or needs to work. With an unemployment rate of over 9%, the longer older workers stay in he workforce, the fewer jobs there will be for younger workers. Finally, a study released by the nonpartisan Employee Benefit Research Institute (2011) found that delaying retirement past 65 is no guarantee of households being able to afford retirement.

What do you think? Do you believe Social Security will be there when you retire? Explain. Which arguments concerning retirement age are most persuasive to you? How much is an appeal to fear used in the debates about Social Security? How should this debate be resolved? Explain.

respondents who have a living parent say they live within an hour's drive of that parent and 42 percent of adults say they see or talk with a parent (usually, it's Mom) every single day compared to just 32 percent of adults in 1989. Another 44 percent report seeing or talking to a parent at least once a week. There are some variations by race and ethnicity. More Blacks (59 percent) than Latinas/os (42 percent) or Whites (39 percent) are in daily contact with at least one parent, again usually Mom. Members of all three groups are equally likely to report a close relationship with their mother, but among those whose father is still living, Whites (78 percent) are more likely than Blacks (60 percent) to report a close relationship with their father (Pew Research Center, 2006). In another study, 68 percent of grandparents said they see a grandchild every one or two weeks; another 24 percent reported seeing a grandchild once a month to once every few months. Eighty percent of grandparents contact a grandchild by telephone at least once every couple weeks

(American Association of Retired Persons, 2002). A study of Asian Indian grandchildren in the United States found that 40 percent had weekly telephone conversations with their grandparents in India and another 33 percent called at least once a month (Saxena and Sanders, 2009). Some adult children go so far as to relocate to the area in which they grew up in order to be nearer to their aging parents and some retired grandparents move to be near their grandchildren (Lee, 2007). In 2008, a total of 6.6 million older adults lived in a household with one or more children. Of this group, 58 percent were themselves the household head, while in 42 percent of the cases, their grown child was the household head (Pew Research Center, 2010c).

Although there is considerable diversity, both around the world (see the In Other Places box) and within the United States, in the way different generations relate to one another, family interactions are shaped to a large degree by the norm of reciprocity or complementary exchanges. Contrary to popular belief, older people are not primarily dependent recipients of aid; in many cases, they are primarily donors. Older parents often remain a resource for their adult children, providing financial assistance, advice, and child-care services (Caputo, 2005). This is especially the case when adult children have stressful problems, for example, getting divorced or becoming widowed. In exchange, both generations expect that adult children will assist their parents in times of need (Ganong and Coleman, 2006). Social class, however, may influence the direction of tangible aid. For example, wealthier older people are likely to continue giving financial assistance to middle-aged children, whereas working-class parents are more likely to be receiving assistance.

Evidence suggests, however, that several decades of high divorce rates (see Chapter 12) are having negative effects on intergenerational exchange and contact. For example, research has found that widowed parents engage in more intergenerational transfers than divorced parents and that remarried parents are less likely to receive informal care from their children. Divorced men are particularly likely to lack intergenerational support in

later life as a result of weaker ties with their children. Although less common, mothers may find that the parental divorce weakens the bond with her adult children (Hans, Ganong, and Coleman, 2009). Families containing only stepchildren have lower rates of financial and time transfers and lower rates of intergenerational co-residence than families with biological children (Pezzin, Pollak, and Scone, 2008; Pezzin and Schone, 1999). Stepparents acquired later in life frequently are not perceived as family members and thus norms of family obligations are not applied to them (Ganong and Coleman, 2006).

QUALITY OF RELATIONSHIPS

Although we know a great deal about the frequency of intergenerational contact, we know less about the qualitative aspects of these relationships. Frequency of contact in and of itself does not ensure a strong emotional bond. Nevertheless, researchers have found that most adult children and their elderly parents like one another and express satisfaction with their relationships. Research indicates that this is also true for grandparent–grandchild relationships (Wiscott and Kopera-Frye, 2000). Gender seems to play an important role in this regard. For example, mother–daughter relationships tend to be particularly close and intimate during all phases of the life span (Pew Research Center, 2006).

Evolving Patterns of Kinship: Grandparenthood

Changing mortality and fertility rates can have enormous consequences for the kin network. As recently as 1900, families with grandparents were rare. An analysis by Peter Uhlenberg (1980) showed that families in which three or more grandparents are alive when a child reaches age 15 increased from 17 percent in 1900 to 55 percent in 1976. Further increases in life expectancy make it

Many older people remain active in their communities. These seniors are checking the accuracy of electronic voting machines at a Texas polling place.

THE ROLE AND STATUS OF THE ELDERLY: VARIED AND CHANGING

A considerable amount of mythology surrounds the role of the elderly in both industrial and nonindustrial societies. In industrialized countries, there is the myth that the elderly are isolated and alone. In nonindustrialized countries, there is the myth that the elderly are always respected and cared for by the next generation. What we find when we examine these and other myths is that the empirical reality is a lot more varied. In the United States, for example, although a significant minority of elderly struggle to survive, there is extensive intergenerational contact. Additionally, the government provides economic security and health care for many of its elderly citizens.

How do the elderly fare in other places? Nancy Foner (1993) examined ethnographic reports for a wide range of nonindustrial cultures and found in many cases a strong ethic of intergenerational caregiving. Let us look at some examples from her review. Among the Kirghiz herders of Afghanistan, the younger son (and his family) looks after aged parents, remaining in the parental household. In exchange, he inherits the family herd, tent, and camping ground. When traditional healers and health workers of the Akamba tribe of Kenya were asked to choose between a dying old man over 60 and a dying 25-year-old man when there was only enough medicine to cure one person, many favored saving the old man, even where the young man was first in line. A man from among the Gonja of West Africa said, "When you were weak (young) your mother fed you and cleaned up your messes, and your father picked you up and comforted you when you fell. When they are weak, will you not care for them?" Australian aborigines consider it callous and reprehensible for family members to desert an ailing elder. The Twareg pastoralists of Niger believe the elderly should be fed and served. In the 1980s, despite a severe 3-year drought and an inadequate supply of food, the Twareg daughters or granddaughters continued to feed and care for the physically weak elderly.

Unfortunately, in many of these societies today, limited resources combined with rapid social change are undermining the reciprocal relationships that have characterized intergenerational relationships, especially for elderly without children. These elderly are often neglected, since they have not been part of an exchange relationship. According to Foner, limited resources sometimes lead to extreme behavior—gerontocide or the abandoning or killing of the elderly. In some societies, there is an understanding by both generations that when the old are no longer productive and a drain on the community, it is time to go. Among the Mardudjara hunters and gatherers of Australia, when life was too difficult, some of the elderly asked to be left behind to die. The elderly Eskimos of northern Canada would go off by themselves onto the icy tundra to die.

In sum, a cross-cultural perspective helps us to understand that kinship structures and functioning are complex phenomena and that they can be understood only by examining cultural belief systems as well as social and economic factors.

What do you think? Which society would you prefer to live in as an elderly person? Explain. What obligations do you think the younger generation should have toward the older generation in the United States?

---

now common for grandchildren to have all four grandparents (or even more as a result of divorce and remarriage, as we saw in the case of Blake Brunson in Chapter 13) alive throughout childhood. According to a new report by the MetLife Mature Market Institute (2011a), more than one in every four adults is a grandparent; there are over 65 million grandparents in the United States, an increase from 40 million in 1980. About one in five grandparents are African American, Latina/o, or Asian compared to two in five young adults, indicating that grandparents will become more diverse in the future. The study finds that, in general, grandparents are younger (see Figure 14.7 on page 462), more financially comfortable, and bestowing a greater amount of their money on grandchildren than previous generations. At least half of all these grandparents will become great-grandparents and some will become great-great-grandparents. Nevertheless, the social role of grandparent, let alone great-grandparent, is a fairly recent one and one that is still evolving.

STYLES OF GRANDPARENTING

There is great diversity in the timing of grandparenthood. Given the incidence of teenage pregnancies, some parents become grandparents as early as their 30s. Other parents who had children later in life may not become grandparents until into their 60s or 70s. This diversity in ages of grandparents contributes to the ambiguity surrounding this role. Although a great deal of folklore is connected with grandparenting, there is little agreement on how to fulfill this role. Thus, most of us will construct our grandparenting role out of our own childhood memories of our grandparents, our perceptions of the way our parents acted as grandparents, and the attitudes we pick up about grandparenting from the media and from those around us, especially our adult children.

Over the years, researchers have investigated the role and meaning of grandparenthood and in the process have identified several styles of grandparenting. Bernice Neugarten and Karol

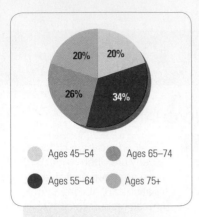

Ages 45–54   Ages 65–74
Ages 55–64   Ages 75+

20%   20%
26%   34%

FIGURE 14.7 U.S. Grandparents, by Age, 2010

Source: MetLife Mature Market Institute. 2011. *The MetLife Report on American Grandparents.* New York, Figure 2, p. 7.

Weinstein (1964) studied 70 middle-class grandparent couples and classified their interactions with their grandchildren into one of the following five categories:

- *Formal:* Grandparents follow what they see as a prescribed role for grandparents.
- *Fun seeker:* Grandparent–grandchild interaction is characterized by informality and playfulness.
- *Distant figure:* Interaction is limited to holidays and special occasions.
- *Surrogate parent:* Grandparents assume caretaking responsibilities for grandchild.
- *Reservoir of family wisdom:* Grandparents are the dispensers of special skills or resources.

One of the roles grandparents can fill is that of family historian. These grandparents show their grandchild where other family relatives live.

This study and other early descriptions of grandparent roles have been criticized for their unidimensional approach (Roberto, 1990). In Neugarten and Weinstein's study, each respondent was placed exclusively into one of the five categories. No provision was made for overlapping styles of grandparenting or changes in styles over time. Two decades after the Neugarten and Weinstein study was published, Andrew Cherlin and Frank Furstenberg (1986) analyzed telephone interviews with 510 grandparents (and personal interviews with 36 of them) and found three styles of grandparenting:

- *Remote:* Grandparents interacted infrequently and maintained a ritualistic or purely symbolic relationship with their grandchildren.
- *Companionate:* Grandparents had an easygoing, friendly style of interaction with their grandchildren.
- *Involved:* Grandparents took an active role in rearing their grandchildren, exerted substantial authority, and imposed definite and sometimes demanding expectations.

These three styles correspond roughly to Neugarten and Weinstein's grandparenting styles of distant figure, fun seeker, and surrogate parent. However, Cherlin and Furstenberg's analysis takes into account the dynamic quality of such relationships. They found that grandparent–grandchild relationships can change over time. For example, grandparents may have a fun-seeking relationship with young grandchildren, but when the children reach adolescence, the time spent together may decrease dramatically. Years later, the relationship may change again with the arrival of great-grandchildren. Also, the same grandparent may exhibit different grandparenting styles with different grandchildren. Numerous factors influence the kind of relationship grandparents have with their grandchildren: age, health, and employment status of grandparents, physical proximity, economic need, relationships between the grandparents and their adult children, number and ages of grandchildren, birth order, gender, and personality differences. Overall, grandparents are most actively involved with preadolescent, particularly preschoolers. As grandchildren become adolescents, they often are less interested in spending time with grandparents but this often reverses itself when they become adults (Mansson, Myers, and Turner, 2010; Davey et al. 2009).

Which style of grandparenting do you associate with your grandparents? If you become a grandparent, which style do you think you would adopt? What does this tell you about your view of grandparenthood? Should the role of grandparents be expanded? Explain.

BENEFITS AND CONFLICTS

The grandparent role has the potential to benefit all three generations. Grandchildren enrich their grandparent lives in many ways. Grandchildren contribute to a sense of immortality—something of the grandparent will continue after death. Playing the role of teacher, family historian, and resource person enhances the self-esteem of grandparents. Grandparents can take pride in the achievements of their grandchildren and boast about them to friends. Through social contact with grandchildren, grandparents can keep up-to-date on cultural and social changes and have great fun in the process. Later on, older grandchildren can provide assistance to grandparents—shopping, lawn care, and doing household chores.

In exchange, grandparents can provide grandchildren with love and guidance minus the intensity, responsibility, and tension that frequently exist in parent–child relationships. Grandparents can give children a sense of continuity, identity, belonging, and values as they share with the children stories about the family's history. In so doing, they often can help younger people understand their parents, and they frequently act as mediators between the two generations. Additionally, grandparents can be role models of successful aging for both their adult children and grandchildren. The parent generation can benefit by having someone they can trust assist them in their parenting role and, if necessary, act as surrogate parents in time of need. For example, research in the United States and England found that grandparents frequently play a prominent role in raising children as working mothers of young children increasingly rely on their own parents for childcare (Vandell et al., 2003: Doughty, 2008.). Finally, the current downturn in the economy finds that the income of many adult children has declined. Thus, grandparents are being called upon to provide economic support to their children and grandchildren.

Such benefits, however, can also produce tension and conflict. Parents and grandparents may disagree about child-rearing strategies. Parents may resent what they perceive as grandparental interference or be jealous of the child's affection for the grandparent. Older grandchildren may become preoccupied with their own lives and forget to call or visit grandparents. As a result, grandparents often feel hurt and ignored. These problems notwithstanding, much of the research on grandparenthood shows that both grandparents and grandchildren tend to be satisfied with their relationships.

Research also indicates that there is more contact with maternal grandparents; maternal grandmothers are consistently listed as the grandparent to whom grandchildren feel closest. The main factor contributing to this pattern is parental divorce. As we saw in Chapter 12, mothers are more likely to have sole custody of children than fathers, and many fathers lose contact with their children following a divorce. Thus, it is not surprising to find grandchildren losing contact with paternal grandparents. This pattern, however, may be a function of the timing of the divorce and the age of the grandchildren.

Earlier research suggested that grandmothers were more satisfied with the grandparenting role than were grandfathers (Thomas, 1986). However, today gender differences in satisfaction with the grandparenting role seem to be diminishing. Grandfathers who have frequent contact with grandchildren report similar levels of satisfaction with their role as grandmothers (Peterson, 1999). Recent studies found that many grandfathers attach great importance to the grandfather role, seeing it as an opportunity to experience the contact with babies and young children they missed out on with their own children (Cunningham-Burley, 2001; Wilton and Davey, 2006). Grandfathers make a difference,

especially when grandchildren live in a single-mother household. Grandchildren, especially boys, do better in school and have fewer behavioral problems when their grandfathers are involved in their lives (Zaslow, 2006).

Race and Ethnicity Many grandparents play a key role in providing care for children. In 2009, 7.8 million children (10 percent) lived in households with at least one grandparent present, a 64 percent increase since 1991. Among children living with a grandparent, 76 percent also were living with at least one parent. Table 14.4 shows that 9 percent of White, 17 percent of African American, and 14 percent of Latina/o children living with a grandparent had at least one parent living there as well. In addition, 3.1 million children lived with no parents. Over half (59 percent) of the children living with no parents were living with grandparents (Kreider and Ellis, 2011a). Sixty-four percent of African American, 61 percent of Latina/o, 55 percent of White, and 35 percent of Asian children without a parent present lived with grandparents. In addition, large proportions of Native American children are also living with grandparents—with some Native American tribes estimating up to 60 percent of their children in this living situation. Besides caring for grandchildren of working parents, Native American grandparents often ask their children to allow the grandchildren to live with them for a period of time so that they can teach their grandchildren about the Native American way of life (Weibel-Orlando, 2000). In particular, grandfathers are active in transmitting knowledge of tribal history and cultural practices through storytelling (Woods, 1996). Grandparents from other racial and ethnic groups, especially co-resident grandparents, play an important role as cultural transmitters of their group's traditions, language, and values to their grandchildren (see, for example, Saxena and Sanders, 2009; Tan, 2004).

UNPLANNED PARENTING

As indicated earlier, in a growing number of families grandparents have assumed sole responsibility for their grandchildren. In effect, they become surrogate parents. In 2008, 2.6 million grandparents were responsible for most of the basic needs (food, clothing,

TABLE 14.4 Percent of Children Living with Grandparents by Presence of Parents and Race and Ethnicity, 2009

Race/ Ethnicity	At Least One Parent Present	No Parents Present
White	9%	55%
Black	17%	64%
Latinas/os	14%	61%
Asian	NA	35%

Source: Adapted from: Kreider, R. M. and R. Ellis. 2011. *Living Arrangements of Children: 2009.* Current Population Reports, P70–126. Washington, DC: U.S. Census Bureau.

shelter) of one or more of the grandchildren who lived with them. Of these caregivers, 1.6 million were grandmothers, and 983,000 were grandfathers (U.S. Census Bureau, 2010b). Fifty-one percent of grandparents who have grandkids living with them are White (up from 46 percent in 2000), 24 percent are African American, and 19 percent are Latina/o (down from 20 percent in 2000). Additionally 1.9 million children (2.5 percent) live in households headed by other relatives, up from 1.5 million in 2000. Aunts, uncles, cousins and even siblings are stepping in to support America's children when needed (Goyer, 2010). As high as these numbers are in the United States, the numbers are even higher in Africa and other nations where grandparents and other relatives struggle to provide basic subsistence for their grandchildren. In the United States and these other countries, grandparents are increasingly taking on this parental role as a direct result of the incapacity of the middle generation to care for their children because of parental unemployment, death, poverty, disease, substance abuse, AIDS, incarceration, divorce, or increasingly today in the United States, military deployment.

Unplanned parenting produces both positive and negative outcomes for the caregivers. Interviews with custodial grandmothers found varied experiences. Some grandmothers find parenting their grandchildren easier and more enjoyable than was the case for parenting their own children. They see themselves as wiser, more experienced, more relaxed and having more time to spend with their grandchildren than they did with their own children. Others, however, found raising grandchildren to be more challenging because they had less energy and more physical limitations as a result of their own aging. Many worry about raising their grandchildren in a toxic environment where drugs, alcohol, sexual activity, gangs and violence all threaten their grandchildren's development (Dolbin-MacNab, 2006). Despite positive feelings about their involvement, the assumption of such responsibility is emotionally and financially exhausting for many grandparents. In some cases, the grandparents must abandon or fight their own children to provide their grandchildren with a healthy and stable environment. Retired grandparents on a fixed income may find their household budget severely strained by the unexpected expense of children. Custodial grandparents are more likely to live in poverty than noncustodial grandparents and they are more likely to be in poorer health and less educated than nonrelative foster parents (*Forging Connections,* 2004). Adequate housing, particularly a lack of space, is also a problem and the reality of unplanned parenting can be psychologically difficult to accept. The dreams these older couples have for spending time together, taking vacations, and pursuing other interests may be lost forever. Custodial grandparents may also experience profound changes in their friendship networks as their lifestyle is altered to fit the needs of children, babysitters, and finances.

Grandchildren, too, have ambivalent feelings about being raised by grandparents. On the one hand, they have strong emotional bonds with their grandparents and appreciate their providing them with a home instead of letting them fend for themselves or go into a foster care setting. At the same time, they believe their childhood experiences were often limited because of their grandparents' health or energy levels and/or generational conflicts over clothes, chores, dating, and leisure activities (Dolbin-MacNab and Keiley, 2009)

Although more communities are establishing programs to help these surrogate parents, many of these programs are underfunded, inadequately staffed, and are able to provide only minimal services. Additionally, some states deny benefits from Aid to Families with Dependent Children, the state welfare program, to any nonparent, even though grandparents should be eligible. Over the last several years support groups like Grandparents as Parents, Grandparents Raising Grandchildren, and Grandparents United for Children's Rights have been formed to assist these families. More recently, the first public housing development in the United States designed and built exclusively for grandparents raising grandchildren opened in the Bronx. The facility offers the services of a social worker and provides support groups, and parenting classes (Gordon, 2006).

THE GREAT-GRANDPARENT BOOM

Although no official statistics exist, Kevin Kinsella, head of the Aging Studies branch of the Census Bureau, believes we are in the midst of a great-grandparent boom. Demographer Kenneth Wachter estimates that by 2030, more than 70 percent of 8-year-olds will likely have a living great-grandparent (Rosenbloom, 2006). Despite the current tendency to delay marriage and have children later in life, the number of great-grandparents is expected to increase given our current elderly population. Nevertheless, we know little about what a great-grandparent's role in the family should be. A few researchers are beginning to examine the meaning of the great-grandparent role in later-life families. One study of great-grandparents found that the majority expressed positive feelings about the experience, reporting a renewed zeal for life and expressing satisfaction at the continuance of their families. Despite these positive reactions, most of the respondents reported having only a remote relationship with their great-grandchildren, interacting with them on a limited and mostly ritualistic basis (Barer, 2001).

The reasons for this kind of interaction pattern are not entirely clear. A partial explanation may be that because this is a new phenomenon, few cultural norms exist to guide individual behavior in these relationships, leaving it an ambiguous role. In one study asking respondents what they thought of themselves as parents, grandparents, and great-grandparents, the results indicated that there may be an ordered reduction in the importance of each role, that is, we tend to make most of our investment in generations that are closest to us (Drew and Silverstein, 2004). Additionally, the geographic dispersion of family members contributes to a physical and emotional distance between the youngest and oldest generations. As some great-grandmothers reported, "I got some but I don't know the names of them. They tell me I do have some greats, I ain't never seen them. I got pictures but I haven't seen none of them" (quoted in Barer, 2001). There is some indication, however, that at least among women of color, the great-grandparenting role is much the same as the grandparenting role—that is, it is simply a natural progression from that role (Scott, 1991). Further research is needed to study the costs and benefits of such relationships.

The Child-Free Elderly

Although the majority of today's elderly have surviving children, a substantial minority have none. Approximately 20 percent of Americans over age 65 have no children and that number is expected to increase to 30 percent with the aging of the baby boomer generation (Chang, Wilber, and Silverstein, 2010). A common assumption is that adult children provide a "natural" support system that elderly parents can rely on in old age. Thus, being without children is often regarded as a problematic state for older people (Wenger, 2009). Are the child-free elderly, then, without potential caregivers, as popularly believed?

An early examination of a national sample of the elderly population concluded that being child-free was a predictor of social isolation in later life. Compared with elderly parents, the child-free elderly had fewer social contacts. This was particularly true for those experiencing health problems (Bachrach, 1980). When marital status was controlled, however, an interesting pattern emerged. The unmarried child-free elderly interacted more frequently with friends and neighbors than did the married child-free elderly who tended to rely more on each other, thus limiting other social relationships. A recent study of nine countries, including the United States found similar patterns. Childfree older adults, regardless of marital status and gender were equally as likely as older parents to be active in the community and in voluntary organizations and to perform volunteer work. This was especially true for women. Married, child-free men were particularly dependent on their wives for social support. Thus, the authors conclude that in some countries, it appears that marriage rather than parenthood makes the difference in support networks (Wenger, et al., 2007).

In contrast to their married peers, the unmarried elderly realize that they may need help at some point in their lives and actively create a support network for themselves. An early study by Robert Rubinstein and his colleagues (1991) found that they their unmarried child-free elderly female respondents consciously developed strategies to overcome the cultural emphasis on "blood ties." Not only did these women cultivate relationships with existing kin (nieces, nephews, and siblings), but they also constructed ties, often becoming fictive kin, interacting in ways traditionally associated with those related by birth. Many of our families include people we call "aunt" or "uncle" who are not formally related to us. These relationships are characterized by strong affective bonds and shared activities. Rubinstein's respondents described key friendships with other women as being "sister like." More recent research confirms these patterns and also finds that childfree older people provide substantial help to other relatives outside the generational lineage and to nonrelatives (see, for example, Kohli and Albertini, 2009; Hurd, 2009; Wenger, et al. 2007)

Despite the fact that the unmarried childfree elderly are resourceful and have a fairly large social network, they have a greater chance of becoming institutionalized than do other categories of elderly (Span, 2011; Wenger, 2009). There are several reasons for this. At the point of needing residential care, they are often older and in poorer health than other elderly. Also, the social support networks they have built, particularly among siblings and friends, are aging along with them and, thus, unable to undertake caregiving tasks.

Additionally, friendship is not legally recognized in the way that blood ties are. For example, friends are not eligible to take time off to care for a sick friend under any equivalent of the Family and Medical Leave Act nor do friends have standing in the tax code which would allow them to take "friend care expenditures." Given that this segment of the population is going to increase, some scholars are advocating granting friendship legal recognition so that some of the legal rights granted to parents, children, spouses, and in some places, domestic partners could be invested in friends (Tuhus-Dubrow, 2008; Lott, 2008). Such a suggestion is controversial and not likely to be acted upon anytime soon but is worthy of consideration as more and more of the population will approach old age outside of nuclear families.

Sibling Relationships

The social relationships of the elderly are not restricted to the younger generations. Recent research on the elderly has pointed to the importance of siblings in later-life families. Sibling relationships are particularly valuable to the elderly for two reasons. First, elderly siblings share a similar family history. Second, the relationship is potentially the longest lasting one an individual will ever have, covering as it does the entire life course. Thus, siblings can help each other fill important needs in later life. They can reminisce about the past, be social companions, and provide emotional and other support during times of stress (Connidis and Campbell, 2001). Additionally, because of their prior experiences, older siblings can serve as role models for resolving the developmental tasks of later life.

Even those over 80 years old have and an average of one living sibling (Adult Sibling Relationships," 2011). Although much is made of sibling rivalry during childhood, it appears these conflicts are largely put aside in the desire to improve relationships in later adulthood. Researchers have consistently found that contact with

These two sisters, ages 93 and 90, enjoy spending time together and reminiscing about their lives.

siblings in later life is strongly related to feelings of social and psychological well-being. This seems particularly true of siblings who were close during childhood. During young adulthood and middle age, siblings may have had only limited contact because of the demands of their own families. As people age, however, they often renew or increase social contacts. These contacts may be triggered by a parent's illness or other needs. This is especially true for siblings who are in geographic proximity, are without partners, and/or have experienced a decrease in contemporaries who can share life review activities (White, 2001). Women are more likely than men to report feeling close to or getting along with their sibling. Sister pairs phone and exchange advice more often than do other sibling pairs (Spitze and Trent, 2006).

Sibling relationships vary by race and ethnicity. African American siblings are more likely to report closer emotional ties, living in closer proximity, and a greater frequency of exchange of various types of assistance than White siblings (Bedford and Diderich, 2009; Bedford, 1997). A plausible explanation offered for these differences is related to differences in cultural emphasis on family ties. Horizontal ties (siblings) are stronger among African Americans while vertical ties (parent–child, grandparent–grandchild) are stronger among Asian American, Latino, and Caucasian cultures, thus contributing to less emphasis on sibling relationships over the life span (White and Riedmann, 1992a; Connidis and Campbell, 2001).

It seems evident that developing positive relationships with siblings in earlier years is a good investment for the later years; siblings are likely to be a good source of support for the elderly well into the twenty-first century. This may not be the case for the elderly who follow them, however. Over the last several decades, life expectancy has increased and birth rates have decreased. Thus, families are becoming vertical in structure in that they cut across more generational lines but have fewer siblings and other age peers within each generation.

Health and Illness

A common fear about growing old is the loss of health and independence. Although health problems increase with age, the health status of today's elderly is varied and not as negative as is popularly portrayed.

PHYSICAL HEALTH

Figure 14.8 shows the results of a 2006–2008 National Health Interview Survey. Overall the majority of elderly rate their health as good to excellent. There was little difference between women's and men's reports but the proportion of people reporting good to excellent health decreased with age and varied by race and ethnicity. Among those 65 to 74, 80 percent of Whites but only 66 percent of Blacks and Latinas/os rated their health as good to excellent. Among those 85 and over Blacks and Latinas/os were again less likely to report their health as good to excellent compared to Whites. Not surprisingly, health reports vary by poverty status, with the poor reporting higher levels of fair or poor health compared to those not poor (Schoeborn, Vickerie, and Powell-Griner, 2006). Although self-ratings of health are subjective, they have

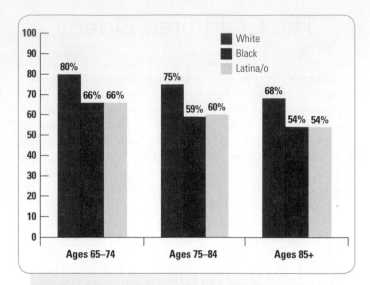

FIGURE 14.8 Percentage of People 65 and Over Who Reported Having Good to Excellent Health by Age Group, Race, and Ethnicity, 2006–2008

Source: Adapted from Federal Interagency Forum on Aging-Related Statistics. 2010. *Older Americans 2010; Key Indicators of Well-being.* Washington, DC: 29.

been correlated with higher risks of mortality. That is, older people who describe their health as poor are more likely to die sooner than those who report their health as good (DeSalvo, et al., 2006). Thus, these self-ratings reflect with some accuracy an individual's overall health status.

Longitudinal research that followed respondents for 60 years found that younger people can exert substantial control over their eventual physical and mental health after age 65. Those subjects who developed good health habits relatively early in life, such as regular exercise, a healthy diet, flexible coping styles, and social involvement, were healthier and happier in their later years than those subjects who had not developed such habits (Bower, 2001). Today's elderly are healthier than previous generations. Nevertheless, physical changes are a natural and inevitable part of aging and may lead to chronic conditions, long-term illnesses that are rarely cured, such as diabetes, arthritis, and heart disease. Limitations on activities because of chronic conditions increase with age. Twenty-five percent of 65- to 84-year-olds reported a limitation caused by a chronic condition compared to almost 51 percent of people 84 years and over (Kaiser Family Foundation, 2005).

MENTAL HEALTH

Chronic conditions, illness, and injury can impact mental health and lead to two of the most common mental health problems among the elderly: depression and dementia. The prevalence of depressive symptoms (deep feelings of sadness and worthlessness, loss of appetite and energy, difficulty in concentrating) is related to age. In 2006, the proportion of people ages 65 and over with clinically relevant symptoms was higher for people ages 85 and over (19 percent) than for people in any of the younger groups (13 to 16 percent). Women are more likely to report clinically-relevant depressive symptoms than men (Federal Interagency Forum on Aging-Related Statistics, 2010). Depression can result from many factors. Among them are family history of depression, stress brought on by life events (divorce, job loss, death of a loved one, and financial difficulties) and a side effect of medication.

Dementia is a clinical syndrome of loss or decline in memory and other cognitive abilities beyond what might be expected from normal aging. Dementia affects about 1–2 percent of people ages 60–64 but 30–50 percent of people ages 85 and older. The most well-known type of dementia is **Alzheimer's disease,** a progressive brain disorder that impairs memory, thinking, and behavior that leads to a decline in the ability to perform activities of daily living. Today it is the sixth leading cause of death in the United States. An estimated 5.4 million Americans are living with Alzheimer's disease, including 5.2 million people age 65 and over and 200,000 individuals with younger-onset Alzheimer's. Women are more likely to develop Alzheimer's disease than men. By 2050, as many as 16 million Americans will have the disease (Alzheimer's Association, 2011).

The cause or causes of Alzheimer's disease are not yet fully understood. People with Alzheimer's have abnormal clumps (amyloid plagues) and tangled bundles of fibers (neurofibrillary tangles) in their brains. Nerve cells are lost in areas of the brain that are vital to memory and other mental abilities. A growing body of research links the disease to lifestyle factors such as obesity, high blood pressure, high cholesterol, and diabetes. Maintaining strong social connections and keeping mentally active as we age may lower the risk of cognitive decline and Alzheimer's. In a recent study, researchers from the Harvard School of Public Health found evidence that elderly people who have an active social life have a slower rate of memory decline (Ertel, Glymoour, and Berkman, 2008). Although there is as yet no cure for dementia, research on a number of medications and treatments offers the hope that there may be a way to prevent or at least delay its onset.

We cannot talk about health issues without paying some attention to health care costs. A study by the Office of the Actuary of the Centers for Medicare and Medicaid Services found that people 65 or older account for four times more the amount of health care spending than those under that age (Black, 2006). Given that the elderly population is growing and living longer than in the past, there is concern that the aging of the population will put even more pressure on the country's health care system. Some people, like medical ethicist Daniel Callahan (2003), author of *Setting Limits: Medical Goals in an Aging Society,* argue that such a situation is not sustainable and offer as a solution rationing health care on the basis of age that would restrict coverage of life-extending treatments, such as organ transplants, bypass surgery, and kidney dialysis. Others argue that the health care system should be reformed to put more money into prevention that would eliminate the expenses involved in later treatments and to find ways to ease end-of-life situations without expensive medical treatments. Still others point out that a single-payer health care system would result in considerable savings, noting studies that show Medicare administrative costs are only 2 percent while those of private health insurance companies are about 15 percent (Black, 2006).

Should the United States ration health care on the basis of age? Explain. Is there any evidence of rationing health care in this country either age-based or other? Discuss. Who should be responsible for paying health care costs—individuals, families, employers, government, or some combination of these? Explain.

Family Caregiving

Do family members really help their needy elderly relatives, or do the government and taxpayers assume most of this responsibility? The weight of evidence in study after study indicates that families and friends, not the formal system, provide the bulk of care for the elderly across all cultural groups, providing as much as 80 percent of their long-term care at home. If the government and other health institutions delivered these services, the cost would be $350 billion dollars each year (AARP Public Policy Institute, 2008). In addition to providing direct care, caregivers often serve as mediators between institutional bureaucracies and the elderly, providing them with information on housing, pensions, insurance, and medical care.

A recent study by the National Alliance for Caregiving and the American Association of Retired Persons (2009) estimates that 19 percent of the U.S. population over age 18 (44 million people) provides unpaid care to friends and family age 50 years or older. According to this study, the average age of today's caregiver is 50, and the average age of today's care recipient is 77. At the broadest level, caregivers are:

- Female (67%), and 50 years of age, on average,
- White (76%),
- Married (59%),
- Caring for one person (70%) and currently providing care (69%),
- Assisting a relative (89%) who is most often the caregiver's mother (36%),
- Providing care for an average of four years,
- Providing 19 hours of care in an average week,
- Employed while caregiving (55%)
- Making workplace accommodation, such as going in late, leaving early or taking time off during the day to provide care (64%),
- Relatively healthy. One-quarter perceives their health as excellent (23%), very good (36%), good (25%), fair (13%), or poor (3%), and three fourths (75%) say caregiving has not affected their health.

In the United States, as well as around the world, women have traditionally provided the overwhelming majority of informal care for elderly relatives. Today, however, as all countries experience an increase in the number of older people, there is a growing recognition of the likelihood of a shortage of female caregivers because of demographic shifts and the increased participation of women in the labor force. Additionally, some African and Asian countries are seeing the caregiving generation being decimated by the AIDS epidemic, leaving the elderly not only to care for themselves but for the younger generation as well. Consequently, as some analysts point out (see, for example, Brewer, 2001), it is imperative that nations begin to develop strategies that enhance the ability of both women and men to share the responsibility of family caregiving. There are some positive signs that this may already be happening in the United States, at least among older men. The current female/male ratio involved in caregiving is more evenly split than in the past. Spouses are the first line of defense when illness strikes, followed by adult children. Compared with spouses, however, adult children provide care over a longer period of time.

THE SPOUSE AS CAREGIVER

The longer a couple lives together, the more likely one of the spouses will become ill. When this happens, the healthier spouse generally assumes the caregiver role. Because men have higher rates of morbidity and mortality, wives make up the majority of spousal caregivers. The degree to which this arrangement represents a satisfactory response to a changed living condition depends on the severity of the illness or disability and on the age and health of the spousal caregiver. Although spousal caregivers may have the greatest need for assistance in fulfilling this role, they receive less assistance from family and friends than other caregivers; they are also the least likely of any group of caregivers to use formal services, regardless of the degree of frailty (C. Cox, 1993). Without outside support, spouses can be physically overwhelmed by the demands of caregiving. If there is a need to have someone in attendance at all times, caregivers may find that they have little free time for themselves, with the result that they become isolated from friends. Alfred Fengler and Nancy Goodrich (1979) refer to such caregivers as "hidden patients."

Reactions to the caregiving role vary. Spouses who view caregiving as "reciprocity" for past affection and care experience a higher degree of gratification from their caregiving role than spouses who view it as a matter of responsibility. Providing care

When a spouse becomes ill, the other spouse generally assumes the caregiver role, as this wife is doing for her terminally ill husband.

can also enhance the caregiver's sense of self-worth and well-being. Despite the burdensome nature of their role, caregivers experience more positive emotions and fewer negative emotions when they engage in "active care" (feeding, bathing, and physically caring for the person). Conversely, passive care which requires the spouse to simply be nearby in case anything goes wrong, provokes negative emotions in the caregiver and leads to fewer positive emotions (Poulin, 2010).

Former Spouses as Caretakers In Chapter 13, we pointed out that the number of older Americans who are divorced has increased dramatically in recent years. In 2009, there were over 3 million divorced persons ages 65 and older compared with 1.7 million in 1994 (U.S. Census Bureau, 2008; 2011e). Many of these people have not remarried. When they become ill and need help, many are without an ongoing support system. Now, however, a new source of support appears to be emerging. Medical personnel and hospice workers are reporting more cases of former spouses stepping in as caregivers, most typically a woman caring for her former husband. According to J. Donald Schumacher, chief executive of the National Hospice and Palliative Care Organizaion, "They are acting more like a brother or sister, or cousin or extended family member, or sometimes they have the joy of being grandparents together" (quoted in Richtel, 2005:E2). This does not mean that the old emotions and conflicts disappear; rather, for most former spouses drawn together by illness and approaching death, they manage to get beyond any initial recrimination, realizing there is little to gain by rehashing the past. Divorced couples often remain in some form of contact because of their mutual children. When a serious illness strikes one parent, the former spouse is often motivated to become involved in caretaking to help their children through the process ("Women Caring for Ex-Husbands," 2011). Others are motivated by a sense of duty to complete their wedding vows. Many elderly do not have a spouse or former spouse to rely on for care, however, and they turn to their children for help.

ADULT CHILDREN AS CAREGIVERS

Although 30 states have filial responsibility laws requiring children who have the financial ability to do so to provide necessary food, clothing, shelter or medical attendance for their elderly parents who are unable to provide for themselves, these laws are rarely enforced (Ting and Woo, 2009). The reality is that when elderly parents need care, most can count on help from their adult children who are motivated to help out of a complex set of kinship norms (reciprocity in intergenerational relations) and emotions (gratitude, love, and respect). These motivations to help older parents are found in various degrees across many cultures (Lin and Yi, 2011; Katz, Gur-Yaish, and Lowenstein. 2010; Klaus, 2009; Lowenstein, Katz, and Nurit, 2007). Religiosity plays a significant role in shaping eldercare norms and behavior across countries. Adult children, who are highly religious, report higher levels of filial responsibility (Gans, Silverstein, and Lowenstein, 2009). According to a recent study by MetLife Mature Market Institute (2011b), nearly 10 million adult children over the age of 50 are caring for aging parents. Among the primary forms of assistance are emotional supports, financial aid, help with instrumental activities (transportation, meal preparation, shopping, housework), personal care (bathing, feeding, dressing), and mediating with agencies to obtain services. All children are not equally likely to assume this role. The degree of filial responsibility is related to proximity (the child living closest to the parent frequently assumes this responsibility) and gender.

A wide range of studies has consistently shown that across all racial and ethnic groups the role of caretaker is most frequently filled by daughters. In fact, some sociologists speak of a *daughter track*. Although daughters have always borne a disproportionate share of responsibility for elderly parent, in the past, the primary caregiver was generally an unmarried daughter still living at home. Today, many daughters are the leading-edge baby boomers who are lawyers, academics, media personalities, and businesswomen who choose to interrupt or give up careers to return home to care for ailing parents (Gross, 2005). Nonetheless, as we saw earlier, the gendered nature of caregiving is beginning to change. Researchers reported that in 1994 only 3 percent of men provided help with basic care (help with dressing, feeding, and bathing). By 2008, that figure had quintupled to 17 percent (MetLife Mature Market Institute, 2011b). Sometimes, men's contributions to parental care are overlooked in caregiving studies because of the gendered nature of their work. Qualitative interviews of paired female and male siblings found that women's and men's contributions to the care of their parents are divided much like household responsibilities among married couples. "Helper brothers" assumed a more traditional masculine role, taking limited responsibility for tasks such as car maintenance, lawn work, household repairs, and running errands, relying on their sister to tell them what needed to be done. In contrast, "co-provider brothers" expressed a willingness and desire to share more equitably in the care of their parents and participated in a wide range of helping tasks that crossed traditional gender lines such as providing personal hygiene and health-related assistance (using the bathroom or bedpan, bathing, and inserting or removing catheters) and providing emotional support. Co-provider brothers also took more initiative. If they saw something to be done, they did it without waiting to be asked. Nevertheless, women still assumed greater responsibility in coordinating overall care (Hequembourg and Brallier, 2005). An increase in male involvement in caring for the elderly is increasing in other cultures as well. A recent study shows that adult sons in Hong Kong actively participate in the care of their elderly parents, especially in financial and emotional support, in ways similar to their female siblings (Kwok, 2006).

Additionally, the kind of help that caregivers provide is often mediated by social class. Middle-class adult children provide more emotional support and financial aid, often assuming a "care manager" role whereby they identify needed services, help obtain them, and then supervise their delivery. Children from lower socioeconomic classes are more likely to provide the direct care themselves.

ADULT STEPCHILDREN AS CAREGIVERS

Additionally, unlike today's elderly, who preceded the period of high divorce rates, today's middle-aged population has an increasing number of stepchildren. Whether these stepchildren will be as likely as biological children to assume care for the elderly is as yet unknown, although, initial research on this population suggests that they will not (Pezzin and Schone, 1999). Overall, parent–adult child ties with stepchildren tend not to be as close as those with biological or adopted children (Ward, Spitze, and Deane, 2009). This is more likely to be the case when stepparents are acquired later in the adult child's life. Thus, adult stepchildren are less likely to feel the same obligations to aging stepparents that they feel towards their biological parent (Pezzin, Pollack, and Schone, 2008). Because remarried men are more likely than women to live with stepchildren than with biological children, men are seen as more at risk in this regard.

YOUNG CHILDREN AS CAREGIVERS

Discussions of caregivers generally evoke images of adults. Yet, according to a study by the National Alliance on Caregiving and the United Hospital Fund, as many as 1.4 million children in the United States between the ages of 8 and 18 provide care for an older adult, including approximately 400,000 children between the ages of 8 and 11. Some of the key findings from this study, the first of its kind in the United States, are as follows:

- Child caregivers are pretty evenly split by gender, with girls making up 51 percent of the total, and boys 49 percent.
- Child caregivers are more likely to live in households with lower incomes than their noncaregiver peers and they are less likely than noncaregivers to live in two-parent households.
- Seven in ten child caregivers (72 percent) are caring for a parent or grandparent; one in ten (11 percent) is helping a sibling.
- Over half (58 percent) of the child caregivers help their care recipient with at least one Activity of Daily Living (ADL) such as bathing, dressing, getting in and out of bed or chair, toileting, and feeding. Nearly all young caregivers help with shopping, household chores, and preparing meals. Nearly all also spend some time just "keeping the care recipient company." Almost a third (30 percent) help with medications and 17 percent help the care recipient communicate with doctors or nurses (Hunt, Levine, and Naiditch, 2005).

Although child caregivers are more likely to feel appreciated for their help than noncaregivers (64 to 53 percent) and are less likely to feel people expect too much from them (12 to 19 percent), 20 percent of caregivers say their caregiving has made them miss a school activity or an afterschool activity; 15 percent say it has kept them from doing schoolwork and 8 percent say it has made them miss homework. Further, according to parents' reports of their child's behavior, child caregivers tend to show anxious or depressed behavior more than noncaregivers and a larger share of caregivers ages 12–18 behave more antisocially than noncaregivers of the same age.

According to researchers, the effects of caregiving on a child appear stronger when one of three factors is present: when the child performs one or more personal care tasks, when the child lives in the same household as the care recipient, and when the child lives in a minority household. This latter fact is likely explained by the finding that smaller proportions of minority caregivers report that someone else helps them with caregiving tasks (Hunt, Levine, and Naiditch, 2005).

Given current economic and family dynamics—rising health care costs, stagnating or declining family income, more women in the labor force, high divorce rates, and an increasing number of single and multigenerational households—child caregiving is likely to increase. Support for these children is scarce. One exception to this pattern is The American Association of Caregiving Youth, founded by Dr. Connie Siskowski, to help child caregivers manage their personal and caregiving lives and feelings. The program provides youth support groups, tutoring, social activities, and, when needed, does home visits and helps arrange for special services, like respite care (Sederer, 2010).

THE STRESSES AND REWARDS OF ELDERLY CAREGIVING

Not only is caregiving physically and emotionally draining, it can be socially isolating, cause depression, and lead to declining health (Clark and Diamond, 2010). An analysis of hospitalizations and deaths from 1993 to 2002 among 518,240 married couples, ages 65–98, who were enrolled in Medicare found that a spouse's hospitalization for disabling conditions such as dementia, psychiatric illness, chronic obstructive pulmonary disease, and stroke raised the partner's likelihood of dying. According to the researchers, a spouse's illness or death may hasten a partner's demise by causing severe stress and removing a primary source of emotional, financial, or practical support. These effects can undermine the body's immune system and intensify preexisting health problems (Christakis and Allison, 2006). Providing care can affect the caregiver in a number of significant ways.

Caregivers are often so focused on meeting their loved one's needs that they neglect their own. Frequently, they are unaware of the resources that could help them manage their situation better. Studies show that caregivers experience high rates of sleeplessness, back pain, depression, anxiety, and stress-related problems from heart disease to gastrointestinal illnesses. This is especially the case when the illness is prolonged. According to Susan Mintz, co-founder and president of the National Family Caregivers Association, the average length of care is 8 years, with a third of caregivers providing care for a decade or more (Dang and Pitts, 2006).

For adult children, caring for an elderly parent can lead to financial hardship and can jeopardize the caregiver's sense of well-being. The most severe consequences, however, tend to be the psychological and emotional stress that comes from seeing formerly strong and independent parents become dependent as well as from the restrictions on the caregiver's time and freedom (see the Strengthening Marriages and Families box). The time demands of caring for a parent compete with other responsibilities and may result in conflict, particularly with regard to employment. Many caregivers juggle work with caregiving responsibilities. Nearly six in ten (57 percent) caregivers are currently employed. Male caregivers are more likely to be employed full-time than female caregivers. Those who are not working are most likely retired or are homemakers. Caregiving often has financial consequences for the caregiver, who may have to cut back on work hours or leave work entirely, resulting in loss of pay and reduced retirement income. According to one study, caregivers lose an average $303,880 over their lifetimes as a result of reductions in their salaries and retirement benefits (MetLife Mature Market Institute, 2011b).

The direct caregiver is not the only one affected by the pattern of caregiving. The family's lifestyle may be disrupted. Recreational activities and vacations may have to be postponed. If the elderly person is living with the caregiver's family, lack of privacy may become a problem. If spouses and other family members are supportive, however, the intensity of these strains is lessened. If, however, the strains become too great, caretakers or their families may resort to extreme behavior, for example, elder abuse (see Chapter 11). Despite these problems, many caregivers acknowledge that what they are doing is also rewarding. For many, it gives them a new purpose or direction. A daughter who gave up her career to help her mother take care of her father who has Alzheimer's spoke for many caregivers when she said, "Nobody asked me to do this, and it wasn't about guilt. I lived a very selfish life. I'd gotten plenty of recognition. But all I did was work, and it was getting old. I knew I could make a difference here. And it's expanded my heart and given me a chance to reclaim something I'd lost" (quoted in Gross, 2005:A1).

Certain situations arise, however, when regardless of the desires of the family, the ill spouse or parent can no longer be cared for at home. Institutionalization may be necessary in these circumstances. If this is to be done with a minimum of dislocation, both socially and psychologically, family, friends, and professionals must play a supportive role in the process.

The Experience of Widowhood

In Chapter 15, we will discuss issues related to death and dying. In this chapter we examine the many adjustments required in the transition from marital to widowed status. Not only have the widowed lost their main source of support, but they often find that their entire social network is disrupted to some degree. Social life may be curtailed as in-laws and friends brought into the relationship by the deceased spouse gradually grow distant. For example, in her classic study of widowhood, Helen Lopata (1973) found that only 25 percent of the respondents saw their husbands' families on a regular basis. Additionally, both widows and widowers may feel uncomfortable in social settings dominated by couples. Widows in particular may be perceived as a potential threat to friends' marriages. The role of the widowed itself is problematic. In the United States today there are few norms to guide the newly widowed person. In the past, the role was more clearly defined. There were rules about appropriate length of time for mourning, dress, behavior, and, in some cases, guidelines for when and if remarriage could occur.

TALKS WITH FAMILY THERAPIST JOAN ZIENTEK

Coping with the Caregiving Role

Why Is Caring for an Elderly Parent Such a Difficult Role? No longer can many in the 50–60 age group look forward to the fulfillment of their retirement dream of a life of travel, spending time with grandchildren, or the pursuit of a hobby or another leisure time activity; instead, it is likely that caring for an elderly parent will be central to their retirement years. This phenomenon requires a major shift in people's expectations as well as the learning of new skill sets that will be needed to meet the emotional and physical needs of aging parents. As the caregiver is confronted with this situation, she (most caregivers are women in their late 50s who work outside the home) must grieve the loss of a future that will never be; at the same time she is dealing with an aging parent who is also coping with loss—be it a home, health, friends, and/or economic independence. This can easily become an overwhelming situation.

Caring for an elderly parent places strain on the entire family system as it adjusts to this major shift in the family structure. The adult child now becomes the parent's parent and the parent slips into a childlike role of dependency. Conflict can emerge out of this role reversal concerning whose needs will be met first. Frequently, there is not enough time, energy, or resources to meet everyone's needs. There is often confusion about boundaries. What can Mom actually do for herself? With what tasks does she need assistance? When is it time for Dad to sell the house and enter an assisted-living situation? As adult children struggle to sort out the answers to these questions, the old unresolved issues rear their heads: Why do I get stuck with all the work when Mom has always favored him? Or, Dad never did like my husband or my career; and now I am expected to care for him! Once buried because either the feelings were too painful to face at the time or because the siblings were busy getting on with their lives, these feelings now erupt as anger, as shouting matches with siblings, as brusqueness with parents, or as fiery conversations with doctors.

How Can Families Provide Care for Elderly Members without Becoming Overwhelmed? First recognize what is happening and why. In previous generations, before the birth of the wonders of modern medicine, the elderly did not linger as long, most likely a few weeks or months before succumbing quickly to cancer, heart attacks, or strokes. Today the rising number of dementia and Alzheimer's in the elderly confronts families with a long-term illness, fraught with the sadness of watching a parent or spouse slowly disappear. These facts, coupled with the complexities and stresses of life today, mean that caregivers of the elderly burn out quite easily. In addition, because of the geographic mobility of some family members and the unwritten norms and expectations that family members have for one another, the caregiving all too frequently falls to just the spouse or to just one of the children, the one who is unmarried or who lives closer to the care recipient than other family members. To prevent burnout and resentment, it is essential that all family members communicate openly with one another, plan and cooperate in the caregiving, and provide periodic breaks for each caregiver, as well as set realistic expectations of what can and should be done. In many cases, the family by itself cannot provide all of the care needed for one of its aging members. Family members need to make themselves aware of the many elder care agencies and referral services now available. Generally, when a health care crisis arises, the medical personnel of the hospital, particularly the social worker, can be most helpful in putting the family in touch with the community resources available.

Individuals adjust to widowhood in different ways. Those whose marital relationships were particularly close may feel the loss more keenly than those with a more distant relationship. Socioeconomic status also plays a role. Those with greater personal resources, such as income, education, hobbies, and membership in formal and informal organizations, typically make better long-term adjustments to widowhood. For those with fewer personal resources, the degree of integration within a group can be an important factor in adjustment. This can be seen in some ethnic groups, which provide a definitive role for the widowed in the kin and community network (Gelfand and Barresi, 1987). Earlier research found African Americans, Mexican Americans, and Asian Americans seemed to adjust to widowhood more easily than their White counterparts did (Pitcher and Larson, 1989). However, more recent research found relatively little difference in psychological adjustment to spousal loss between Black and White older adults (Carr, 2004).

Finally, when death is expected, the period of adjustment may pass more quickly than when death is sudden. Anticipating widowhood and discussing key issues with a spouse before death occurs can facilitate successful adjustment. Robert Hansson and Jacqueline Remondet (1987) studied widows ages 60–90 and found that those who were more successful in resolving their grief and getting on with their lives had discussed with their spouse finances, family reactions, their own feelings, and how their lives might change as a result of the spouse's death.

GENDER, RACE/ETHNIC DIFFERENCES IN WIDOWHOOD

As Table 14.5 on page 472 shows, widowhood is largely a female experience. At ages 65 and older, women are three times as likely as men to be widowed (41.8 and 13.8 percent, respectively).

TABLE 14.5 Percent of Elderly Who Are Widowed, By Age Group and Sex, 2008			
Ages	Both Sexes	Male	Female
65+	29.8	13.8	41.8
65–74	16.8	6.9	25.1
75–84	38.6	18.7	36.6
85+	28.7	37.7	76.2

Source: Adapted from Federal Interagency Forum on Aging-Related Statistics, 2010, *Older Americans 2010: Key Indicators of Well-Being.* Washington, DC, p. 77.

Although the rates vary somewhat, there are pronounced sex differences across all race and ethnic groups. Among women ages 65 and over, 44 percent of Whites, 51 percent of African Americans, 40 percent of Latinas, and 40 percent of Asians are widowed. In contrast, the rates for men in the same age category are 14 percent of Whites, 19 percent of African Americans, 12 percent of Latinos, and 14 percent Asians (He et al., 2005). The probability of widowhood increases with age, and although the gender gap narrows, women are still more likely to be widowed than men. At ages 85 and over, 76.2 percent of women and 37.7 percent of men have lost a spouse through death. Although widowhood represents a major role change for both women and men, researchers have found some gender differences in how women and men experience widowhood.

Special Problems of Widows In addition to the adjustments associated with bereavement and grief, widows are likely to confront two major problems: changes in their self-identity and changes in their financial situation. For many women, especially those who are tradition-oriented, the experience of widowhood undermines the basis of their self-identity. The loss of the central role as wife may be psychologically devastating, and a widow may try to maintain her identity as "Mrs. John Smith" in her social and business interactions.

For other women, however, the role of wife is less central to their identity. These women place more emphasis on other roles such as mother, worker, or friend. Thus, they are less interested in preserving the wife role and more interested in being accepted in their own right. Some of these women find, however, that they must negotiate this new role with family and friends who still relate to them as "Mrs. John Smith."

Widows generally face a bleaker financial future than widowers do (Braniff, 2010; Weaver, 2010). Although widowhood can cause financial distress for all women, women of color are particularly hard hit by loss of their husband's financial contributions as well as their own lower wages and benefits during their working years (Angel et al., 2003). Inadequate income adversely affects the quality of life of the widowed. Widows with little money cannot afford to be active socially, which in turn increases their feelings of loneliness. Even widows with adequate income may experience problems related to finances. In many marriages, husbands control the family finances, not wanting to bother their wives with these matters. Thus, some women have no knowledge of their family's financial status, nor do they acquire the necessary financial skills to cope with the routine tasks of handling insurance premiums and claims, balancing a checkbook, paying bills, and making a budget. Having to learn to deal with these matters during their time of mourning may heighten their levels of anxiety and frustration and lower their self-esteem. It is likely that some of these problems will lessen for the new generation of elderly women who are better educated and have more extensive work experiences than the current generation of elderly women.

Special Problems of Widowers Widowers, too, face several problems related to traditional gender roles. Earlier studies like those conducted by Felix Berado (1968, 1970) concluded that many older widowers are ill-prepared to deal with day-to-day domestic matters like cooking, cleaning, and laundry. Researchers found that men do 6.8 more hours of housework after widowhood while widows do 3.5 fewer hours compared with their continuously married counterparts (Utz et al., 2004). For younger husbands today who share more of the household tasks with their wives than did previous generations, these problems are likely to be minimized.

In the social realm, widowers often experience a double bind. Not only do they lose their major source of intimacy but they also find it more difficult than widows to move in with their children and to find a useful place there. Researchers have found that compared with widows, widowers have fewer contacts with their families and receive less social support from them following the death of their spouse (Utz et al., 2004; Ha, 2005; Kalmijn, 2007). This may be a continuation of a pattern begun years ago. In many marriages, the wife is the primary initiator of family contacts; her death leaves a void in this area, lessening the interactions the widower is likely to have.

Earlier research found that widowers experience higher rates of mental illness and depression than widows (Gove, 1972) and that widowers have higher rates of death and suicide than widows during the first year following the death of their spouse (Smith, Mercy, and Conn, 1988). More recent studies, however, suggest that there are growing similarities between the experiences of widows and widowers on this measure (Lee et al., 2001). In fact, researchers Deborah Carr and Rebecca Utz (2002:67) found "a remarkable resilience of the widowed; at least 70 to 80 percent experience the widowhood transition without clinical depression."

BEYOND WIDOWHOOD

Widowhood is a difficult stage for both women and men. There is increasing evidence, however, that a successful transition to widowhood depends on the variety of roles that make up a person's self-identity. People whose identities are multifaceted—who are involved in several activities and relationships—appear to cope better. They are less likely to become depressed or ill than

The death of a spouse is a traumatic event. Yet after the period of grief and mourning passes, most widowed people are able to move on with their lives. Many people return to school, do volunteer work, learn new hobbies, exercise, and spend enjoyable time with friends. Some remarry.

are people with a more limited set of roles (DiGiulio, 1989). After the period of mourning and grief subsides, those who cared for an ill spouse may feel a sense of relief and freedom. For many people, widowhood may provide an opportunity for a reunion with friends or for making new friends. During marriage, family responsibilities often prevent people from participating in other activities. Many widowed people use their new time to return to school, take up a hobby, do volunteer work, travel, and in some cases remarry. Phyllis Silverman (1988) compared widows and widowers and found that in this phase both make changes in their lives, albeit in different directions. Women's changes tend to be more internal. The experience of coping with widowhood leads them to be more self-confident, assertive, independent, and willing to satisfy their own needs. Men, on the other hand, focus more externally, becoming more aware and appreciative of their friends and relationships. Nevertheless, both women and men are able to build satisfying new lives.

Lesbian, Gay, Bisexual, and Transgender Elderly

Few national surveys ask about sexual orientation and fewer still about gender identity. Thus, any assessment of the number of lesbian, gay, bisexual, and transgender elderly (LGBT) is, at best, an estimate. Current estimates are that there are 3 million LGBT elderly; that number will nearly double by 2030 (Grant, 2010). Until recently, their presence, especially among the oldest–old, was largely invisible and thus their special needs ignored. Their invisibility is attributable, in large part, to generational differences. Today's lesbians, gays, bisexuals, and transgender (LGBT) elderly lived through McCarthyism

and came of age before lesbian and gay rights were widely recognized. Fearing discrimination, many were reluctant to reveal their sexual orientation or to participate in LGBT organizations. Although only limited research is available on this population, what does exist suggests that older LGBT adults express the same kinds of concerns about aging voiced by their heterosexual peers. However, LGBT elderly confront additional problems not generally experienced by heterosexual elderly. For example, when a heterosexual spouse dies, the widow(er) receives Social Security survivor benefits, but a surviving lesbian or gay partner receives none. It is estimated that the LGBT community loses $124 million a year in survivor benefits because Social Security does not recognize same-sex unions (Friedman, 2006). As noted in Chapter 7, without careful estate planning or health directives, the death or disability of an unmarried partner may leave the other partner without legal protection regarding property inheritance or other benefits or without power to make medical decisions for their loved one. Medicaid regulations protect the assets and homes of married spouses but not those of same-sex partners.

Although many older LGBT adults have close ties to their families, some have little or no contact or support because of their sexual orientation. LGBT seniors are more likely to live alone, be child-free, and may experience poverty at higher rates than heterosexual seniors (Grant, 2010). When ill, they may face what Patricia Dunn, public policy director of the San Francisco–based Gay and Lesbian Medical Association, called "homophobia in medicine." Thus, they may feel uncomfortable accessing the system or in raising health care concerns with their doctors and, consequently, not get the preventive medical care they need (Roach, 2001; Brambila, 2009)). Additionally, LGBT elderly sometimes encounter homophopic attitudes among staff and/or residents in retirement communities, assisted-living facilities, and nursing homes. Often when lesbian or gay life partners enter assisted living or nursing homes, they are often barred from sharing a room together. Some of these concerns are being addressed. The Palms of Manasota in Palmetto, Florida, the first retirement community solely for graying gays opened in 2003. Others soon followed. There are now 25 clustered in Arizona, New Mexico, and Florida; other popular spots are Boston, Los Angeles, and New York. More housing projects for LGBT elderly are on drawing boards but have been stalled because of the recession (Hindman, 2010).

Supporting Families in Later Life

As we have seen throughout this chapter, we live in a world that is rapidly aging. This development affects all social, economic, cultural, and political aspects of our lives and requires us to respond in new ways. For example, many of today's elderly became poor after family illness, widowhood, or retirement. However, many of tomorrow's elderly, especially women and children and people of color, are already poor and uninsured. Thus, to prevent an increase in the number of elderly poor in the future, we need to see aging as a life-long process. Thus, while we need policies and programs to help the current generation of elderly, we need to create new policies and programs targeting the younger generations. Specifically, we need to help younger people learn healthy lifestyles and to become life-long learners so that they can constantly upgrade their skills to be marketable regardless of economic changes. Private and public savings and pension plans need to be more widely available at all income levels.

Because the kinship structure for many families now and in the foreseeable future will contain more elderly than younger members, there is a need for support models that combine both informal caregiving (family and friends) and formal caregiving at affordable prices (for example, adult day care, visiting nurses, housekeeping services). Many caregivers do not know where to turn for help, so a program to educate the public about services that are available is critically needed. Private and governmental agencies should be encouraged to publicize their programs via the mass media, churches, places of employment, and in local communities, especially in those areas with high rates of poverty and residents of color. Caregivers need to receive recognition for what they do as well as financial help when needed. Tax incentives for elder care would be a partial solution to this problem. Many elderly have difficulties living alone. They may be lonely or need some type of assistance. Alternatives to institutional living need to be expanded—group homes, intergenerational apartment complexes, and co-housing are just a few possibilities.

Finally, social support networks need not go in one direction only, however. The elderly represent a tremendous reservoir of skills and ability. Some public schools and universities have initiated intergenerational partnership projects where the elderly serve as tutors and teachers' aides. Other elderly serve as "foster" grandparents and as business, craft, and hobby mentors. More elderly should be encouraged to use their talents for the social good either through paid employment or volunteer work, thus enhancing their sense of purpose and self-esteem.

Writing Your Own Script

THINKING ABOUT LATER LIFE

Have you ever looked in the mirror and wondered what it would be like to be old? For most young people this is difficult to do. Old age seems such a long way off. Most of us have a good chance of living into our 80s and 90s, and perhaps some of us will celebrate a 100th birthday. Nevertheless, many of us do not plan very well for this stage of our life. News stories consistently report that the majority of Americans do not have realistic retirement plans with savings to match. One way to begin thinking about the experience of aging is to examine our current intergenerational relationships. It may be useful to discuss some of the following questions with elderly family members.

Questions to Consider

1. How many generations are in your kinship structure? Are your parents, grandparents, and/or great-grandparents still living? How healthy are they? How often do you see them? Do family members live in close proximity to one another? What kinds of services, if any, do family members exchange? In which generational direction do they flow? Are the patterns in your family typical of those for later-life families? How satisfied do you think the oldest members of your family are with the quality of their lives?

2. Are your parents or grandparents retired? How well are they managing economically? Did they have a financial plan for their retirement in place before they retired? What are the sources of their income?

3. What are your later-life goals? What age do you see as a desirable age to retire? What can you begin to do now that will contribute to your reaching your goals?

SUMMARY

Throughout this chapter, we have seen how family relationships have been altered by increased life expectancy and changing birth rates, resulting in multigenerational kinship structures. Additionally, social and demographic changes are altering the composition of elderly cohorts. In comparison with older people today, the elderly of the twenty-first century will be more heterogeneous. Future cohorts of the elderly will include a higher proportion of people of color, and more single, divorced, widowed, remarried, and child-free elderly, many of whom will be significantly older than current and past generations of elderly people.

Although most Americans fear ending their life in a nursing home, only a small minority do so. The majority of older people live alone or in a household with their spouse. Elderly women are more likely to live alone, whereas elderly men are more likely to live with their spouse. Elderly of color are more likely than White elderly to live with their adult children.

Studies of marital satisfaction in later-life families have shown diverse patterns. Some older couples experience higher levels of satisfaction than in the earlier years of their marriage, some show less, and still others show no change. Marital satisfaction is related to patterns of retirement and family income. Poverty remains a serious problem for many, especially widows and people of color. Later-life families are involved in reciprocal exchanges of services across the generations. Spouses and adult children provide the vast majority of care for elderly family members who become ill.

Later-life couples must eventually deal with bereavement and grief. The experience of widowhood requires many adjustments for both women and men.

An understanding of the strengths and the needs of later-life families is critical to social planning for the future. The multigenerational structure of families and the resulting interdependence among generations can provide a model for intergenerational cooperation and interdependence at the societal level.

KEY TERMS

sandwich generation

ageism

social gerontology

age norms

functional age

dementia

Alzheimer's disease

QUESTIONS FOR STUDY AND REFLECTION

1. Sharon Curtin wrote in her book, *Nobody Ever Died of Old Age*, "There is nothing to prepare you for the experience of growing old." Based on your attitudes toward aging and your experiences to date, do you agree or disagree with Curtin? How do your own ethnic and cultural experiences affect your attitudes toward aging? How would you advise today's families to approach the aging of their members?

2. Within the last decade, the world has experienced a number of severe political, economic, and social upheavals: terrorist attacks around the world, the growing AIDS epidemic in Africa and Asia, and ongoing armed conflict in the Middle East. Pick one of these problem areas and find demographic, economic, and social data to show how it is likely to affect the quality of life of the elderly and their families. Be specific.

3. How does the experience of aging differ for single, married, divorced, and widowed people?

   For heterosexual and homosexual elderly? For elderly with children and those without? What actions could communities take to improve the lives of their elderly citizens?

4. In Chapter 12, we asked whether the idea of a permanent marriage is a realistic option in today's society. In this chapter, we noted that 6 percent of all married couples celebrated golden wedding anniversaries. Can you imagine yourself married for 50 or more years? What do you think it takes to stay married that long? The longer people stay married, the more likely they are to experience widowhood. Can or should married couples prepare for this eventuality? Would this make a difference in the way they experience widowhood? What advice and support could you give to a couple when one spouse is terminally ill? Explain your position.

ADDITIONAL RESOURCES

SOCIOLOGICAL

BARUSCH, AMANDA SMITH. 2008. *Love Stories of Later Life: A Narrative Approach to Understanding Romance.* New York: Oxford University Press. Gerontologist Amanda Barusch presents original research on this long-neglected topic of what love and romance mean in seniors' lives.

CONNIDIS, INGRID ARNET. 2009. *Family Ties and Aging.* Thousand Oaks, CA: Pine Forge Press. The focus on single, divorced, and child-free older people and their family relationships, as well as sibling relationships among the elderly, live-in partnerships not formalized by marriage, and the kinds of family ties forged by gay and lesbian individuals over the life course provides an important tool for understanding the changes in the structure and functioning of today's families.

GROSS, JANE. 2011. *A Bittersweet Season: Caring for Our Aging Parents and Ourselves.* New York: Knopf Doubleday Publishing Group. Using her own experiences caring for her own aged and ailing mother, writer Jane Gross provides an essential guide for anyone navigating this psychologically demanding and powerfully emotional terrain.

RUSSO, FRANCINE. 2010. *They're Your Parents, Too: How Siblings Can Survive Their Parents' Aging Without Driving Each Other Crazy.* New York: Bantam. Dealing with the physical and/or mental decline and death of parents is an emotional experience. Often this is complicated when siblings have different views about what to do. Francine Russo shares her experiences and includes expert guidance from gerontologists, family therapists, elder-care attorneys, health care workers, financial planners as well as helpful family negotiation techniques that can help siblings work together to help their aging parents.

FILM

Young at Heart. 2008. This documentary follows a choir of rock n' roll seniors from Northampton, Massachusetts who go on tour to reinterpret pop songs. The film is fun, entertaining, and it challenges many of the popular stereotypes we have of people in their later years.

Another Harvest Moon. 2011. Four elderly Americans find themselves coping with life in a nursing home. Gathering each morning for a game of cards, they have become like family to one another, offering support, constant bickering and strong opinions about life, death and everything in between.

LITERARY

MILLER, SUE. 1999. *The Distinguished Guest.* New York: Harper Perennial. A famous writer, 72- year-old Lily Maynard, suffering from Parkinson's disease, moves in with her son and his wife. Her visit raises questions about their relationship, about life choices, and about the nature of love, disappointment, and grief.

MUNRO, ALICE. 2006. "The Bear Came Over the Mountain." In *Carried Away: A Selection of Stories*, 513. New York: Everyman's Library. This moving short story explores the obligations and pain felt by a husband after his wife suffers the loss of memory and sense of identity because of Alzheimer's. The 2007 film, *Away from Her,* was based on this story.

INTERNET RESOURCES

http://www.nia.nih.gov The National Institute on Aging provides links to caregiving sites as well as helpful publications on topics of aging and health.

http://www.aarp.org The American Association of Retired Persons provides information and resources on a variety of topics and activities.

http://www.seniorjournal.com The Senior Journal contains information and news on a variety of topics of interest to all ages—health, politics, finances, drugs, social security, recreation, and entertainment.

http://www.seniorlaw.com The SeniorLaw Home Page provides information for seniors and their advocates on numerous practical issues, including Medicare, Medicaid, estate planning, living wills, and the rights of the elderly and disabled.

Succeed with MyFamilyLab®
www.myfamilylab.com

Watch. Explore. Read. The New MyFamilyLab is designed just for you. Each chapter features a pre-test and post-test to help you learn and review key concepts and terms. Experience Marriages and Families in action with dynamic visual activities, videos, and readings to enhance your learning experience.

Here are a few activities you will find for this chapter.

Watch on **myfamilylab.com**

Video clips feature important concepts in the study of Marriages and Families. Watch:
- Physical Challenges of Living Longer

Explore on **myfamilylab.com**

Social Explorer is an interactive application that allows you to explore Census data through interactive maps. Explore the Social Explorer Activity:
- Patterns in Lifespan for Men and Women

Read on **myfamilylab.com**

MyFamilyLab includes primary source readings from classic and contemporary sociologists from around the world. Read:
- Roscigno: "Ageism in the American Workplace"

15

Issues Confronting Families at Home and Abroad

What Will You Learn?

- Define and understand the sociological meaning of key terms.
- Describe the process and implications of globalization for families.
- Apply the sociological imagination to assess the vulnerability of children around the world.
- Assess the pro and con arguments for legalizing marijuana for the health and well-being of families.
- Increase your awareness and understanding of how families in the United States and around the world are affected by inequality, racism, violence, terrorism, and war.
- Question the kind of social policies that could support families in the United States and around the world.

IN THE NEWS

The United States and the World

For more than 10 years, the United States has been involved in armed conflicts in Afghanistan and Iraq. Yet public awareness polls find that the majority of Americans have little understanding of how military deployment contributes to economic, social, and familial stress for the women and men who serve. Although less than 1 percent of Americans serve in the Armed Forces, many more are affected through direct relationship with service members who have been deployed ("New Poll Finds...," 2010). Over half of the military is married and over 40 percent of service members have children. According to recent studies, military children are more at risk for emotional and behavioral problems than their civilian peers due to the war time environment that so many of them have experienced. One study found that 30 percent of children of deployed parents had elevated symptoms of anxiety (feeling frightened or having difficulty sleeping), twice the rate found in other child studies. Older teens experienced more difficulties such as having to take on more household responsibilities, take care of siblings, missing school activities, and had trouble getting to know their deploying parent again and adjusting to the parent fitting back into the household routine. Girls reported more difficulties during the parent's reintegration into the family, including worrying about the parent's next deployment, dealing with the parent's mood changes, and worrying about how parents were getting along (Hosek, 2011).

An analysis of medical records of 307,520 children of active-duty Army personnel ages 5–17 found that almost 17 percent of them exhibited mental health problems. The children whose parents deployed at least once, for an average of 11 months, to war zones were especially likely to suffer from adjustment, behavioral, depressive or stress disorders compared with those whose parents never went to war. Boys were more likely to have mental health problems than were girls (Selyukh, 2011). The use of psychiatric medications by military children is on the rise. Overall, in 2009, more than 300,000 prescriptions for psychiatric drugs were provided to military children under 18 (Jowers and Tilghman, 2011).

Children in the United States are not the only ones affected by war. UNICEF has estimated that 1.5 million children have been killed in wars since 1980. Millions more have been housed in refugee camps, separated from their families, or suffer from **posttraumatic stress disorder (PTSD)** as a result of living in a wartime environment. Posttraumatic stress disorder is a common anxiety disorder that develops after exposure to a terrifying event or ordeal in which grave physical harm occurred or was threatened. In one study of school children in Afghanistan two-thirds of the children reported traumatic experiences due to accidents, medical treatment, domestic and community violence, and war-related events (Panter-Brick, et al. 2009). Another study of children in Kabul, Afghanistan found that 26 percent of boys and 14 percent of girls suffered from posttraumatic stress disorder (Catani, et al. 2009).

WHAT WILL YOU DO?

What steps can/will you take to learn more about how wars are affecting our nation's and the world's children? How might our society address the needs of these children? Be specific.

((•—[Listen to the Chapter Audio on myfamilylab.com

Most people probably agree that today's world is a more colorful, complicated, and perhaps more dangerous place than the one that existed when their parents' and grandparents' generations were coming of age. Not only is today's world shrinking in time and space, but the global milieu features new actors as people around the world struggle to cope with an array of global issues. Indeed, we are living in a new historical period that some have suggested is replacing the age of modernism that held sway over the last 500 years. This new age is variously referred to by scholars as postindustrialism, postmodernism, the information age, the computer age, and the global village. However, most scholars across academic disciplines use the term *globalization* to capture the diverse, and sometimes conflicting, trends occurring throughout the world today.

Joan Ferrante (1992) has defined globalization in terms of the concept **global interdependence**—a state in which the lives of people around the world are intertwined closely and in which any one nation's problems—unemployment, substance abuse, environmental pollution, disease, inequality, racism, sexism, inadequate resources, terrorism, and war, even for the noncombatants—increasingly cut across cultural and geographic boundaries. For example, as the opening vignette about the Afghanistan war implies, families from very different parts of the world and very different cultures are connected to one another and experiencing the impact of the same war regardless of on which land it is being fought. As more and more American parents are deployed to warzones leaving behind children and other family members, the impact on families left behind is not isolated from the impact of the war on Afghan children and their families. For example, Afghan children are also experiencing some of the same psychological, emotional and mental problems as American children exacerbated in many ways by the fact that the war is being fought right in their backyard. According to World Health Reports, about 20 percent of the Afghan population (children and adults) suffer from various forms of mental health problems, including depression. In addition, thousands of Afghan children demonstrate learning or behavioral problems that is the result of war-related trauma.

Globalization is not new. It began centuries ago when explorers left their home countries in pursuit of new sources of wealth and trade. These early international contacts produced new economic and political structures that are still evident today. What is different today, however, is the depth and breadth of this process. In polls conducted over the past decade, people surveyed in nations around the world have reported that globalization is a routine fact of their everyday lives, experiencing it through trade, finance, travel, communication, and culture. Majorities in every nation surveyed said growing business and trade ties are at least somewhat good for their country and themselves. However, at the same time, people in every country surveyed are deeply concerned about a range of worsening financial and social problems in their lives, related, in their view, to globalization—lack of good-paying jobs, deteriorating working conditions, and the growing gap between rich and poor. Many of these people also believe their traditional way of life is getting lost in the process (Pew Global Research Center, 2003; 2007). One poll, found that 46 percent of Americans had a favorable view of globalization; 36 percent of those polled had an unfavorable view and those that had a very unfavorable view (15 percent) were significantly greater than those who had a very favorable view ("Globalization," 2006). The most recent survey data in this regard, show that although people around the world today still broadly embrace key tenets of globalization, they continue to express deep fear of the disruptions and downsides of being a part of the global community. Most people express increasing concern about inequality, threats to their culture, threats to the environment and threats posed by immigration. According to the Pew Global Research Center (2011a), together these results reveal an evolving world view on globalization that is nuanced, ambivalent, and sometimes outright contradictory.

Regardless of geographic location or their country's level of development, today's children and their families are feeling the effects of a deepening globalization as new technological developments provide easier, cheaper, and faster means of communication and transportation. Although Americans have never experienced war the way that many other countries of the world have, the human costs of war, if nothing else, connects us.

In this final chapter, we discuss some of the marriage and family issues, particularly with regards to children, that are immersed in a global context. That is, we will examine marriage and family issues that confront families in the United States and in various countries around the world, paying particular attention to how these marriage and family issues are globally connected. Thus, wherever possible and or relevant, we make reference to both U.S. and global aspects of these issues. Our intent is to illuminate how the lives, welfare, and experiences of children and families around the world are influenced by globalization's reach, or as C. Wright Mills (1959) encouraged us to do, to grasp history and biography and the connections between the two (see Chapter 1). By understanding the forces shaping our lives and their global significance, we can respond in ways that improve our own lives and those of the larger communities we inhabit. We begin with a brief consideration of some global economic trends and challenges.

Globalization: Its Economic Impact on Children and Families

For the last three decades or so, global competition for new markets has intensified. Globalization was pushed forward in the aftermath of World War II as many nations increased their efforts to strengthen international relationships. The need for rebuilding the infrastructures of the countries devastated by the war also provided new opportunities for other countries seeking expanded markets for their goods and services. Additionally, advances in telecommunications, especially computers, the Internet, and cell phones, diminished the significance of national borders. At the same time, governments removed numerous protectionist barriers to the movement of capital across international boundaries, making it easier for businesses to open branches and production facilities in other countries. These *multinational corporations* or *transnational corporations,* as they are called, are not under the control of any one nation. Operating decisions are made on the basis of corporate goals, often without consideration of how these decisions will affect the people in the countries in which the corporation does business. One consequence of this is a "new international division of labor," in which the process of production is broken down and the various tasks dispersed to different parts of the world (Ehrenreich and Fuentes, 1992).Yet it is increasingly clear that the benefits and burdens of globalization are not shared evenly. Consider the following:

- About half of the world lives in poverty. Nearly 50 percent of the world's population (over 3 billion people) lives on less than two dollars a day (Population Reference Bureau, 2010).
- According to UNICEF (2011a), 21,000 children die each day from preventable causes.
- Approximately 66 million children of primary school age in the developing world were not in school in 2009; 35 million girls and 31 million boys (World Bank, 2011a).
- More than 80 percent of the world's population lives in countries where income differentials are widening, including the United States.
- Twenty percent of the population in the developed nations consumes 80 percent of the world's goods (cited in Shah, 2008).

Any one of these indicators has tremendous consequences for the well-being of the world's families. Obviously, income and wealth are related to a family's life chances. Families with a high income or substantial wealth have more control over their lives; they have greater access to the goods and services that are available in their societies. They can afford better housing, nutrition, education, and medical care. Families with limited income must devote what little resources they have to an ongoing struggle for survival. Just as in the United States, in many developing countries, married women who work are still responsible for domestic labor. However, one consequence of the long work hours for married women is the shifting of a substantial share of domestic labor to young girls, who are often forced to abandon school.

Increasingly, coalitions of environmentalists, antipoverty campaigners, trade unionists, and anticapitalist groups are demonstrating against globalization, alleging that industrialized countries have profited at the expense of developing countries. Other critics have linked the disparities that have developed along with globalization to growing resentment within impoverished nations where there are a lot of unemployed and angry people who have access to weapons and information technologies that give them the means to commit acts of terrorism at home and abroad. Even organizations like the World Bank and the United Nations are calling for what Nelson Mandela (2000) referred to as a globalization of responsibility—urgent global action to improve living conditions for people around the world by reducing the large inequities in income and wealth.

In contrast to Somalians, people living in developed countries consume a high percentage of the world's resources and can enjoy bountiful food buffets as these people are doing.

Inequities in Income and Wealth

As we saw in Chapter 10, recent studies have documented a widening income gap in the United States. The gap between rich and poor is growing in other industrialized countries as well, although

A parent in famine-stricken Somalia watches helplessly as her child dies from starvation.

to a lesser degree. A recent study in Britain found that income inequality is at its highest level since the late 1940s; the top 10 percent of individuals now receive 40 percent of all personal income, while the bottom 90 percent receive only 60 percent (Schifferes, 2008). Other studies have found growing inequality in Australia, Japan, Ireland, and New Zealand as well as in many developing countries including China and India and in most of the transitional postcommunist economies of the former Soviet Union and Central and Eastern Europe (see, for example, Toyama, 2011; Milanovic, 2010). Although there is no consensus on why inequality is increasing in developed countries, several plausible explanations have been proposed: falling wages, tax cuts favoring the rich, the decline in union membership, automation, outsourcing of jobs and global competition.

Figure 15.1 on page 482 provides insight into the income disparities that exist around the globe. The per capita gross national income (GNI) in international dollars of purchasing power parity of high-income countries was $37,183 compared with only $1,246 in low income countries and $6,780 in middle-income countries. Luxembourg had the highest GNI ($63,850); the United States ranked 18th, with a GNI of $47,020. The Democratic Republic of the Congo had the lowest GNI at $310. (World Bank, 2011b). This disparity illuminates another trend. The poorest 40 percent of the world population accounts for 5 percent of global income, while the richest 20 percent accounts for 75 percent (Watkins, 2007).

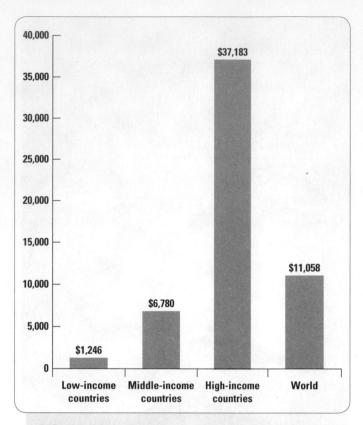

FIGURE 15.1 Per Capita Gross National Income, 2010

Source: Adapted from World Bank, 2011, "GNI Per Capita, 2010, Atlas Method and PPP," World Development Indicators Database (July 1) www.siteresources.worldbank.org/DATASTATISTICS/Resources/GNIPC.pdf). (2011, September 26).

Imagine trying to feed, clothe, and shelter yourself and your family on $2 a day. Women, children, and the elderly bear the major brunt of poverty. Poor children are hit by malnutrition and illness just when their brains and bodies are developing. Millions of children are moderately or severely malnourished; almost 9 million children in the developing world die before the age of 5 every year, mostly from preventable diseases. Many elderly, a growing group in all regions of the world, live out their last years in deprivation and neglect. Approximately one-half of the world's poor live in East Asia, about a third in Africa, and a substantial proportion live on the doorstep of the United States—in Mexico, and in Central and South America.

Health and Health Care

According to the World Health Organization, **health** is a state of complete physical, mental, and social well-being rather than merely the absence of physical disease or infirmity. Table 15.1 examines three commonly used indicators of well-being—infant mortality, life expectancy, and death rates. As we can see from the table, there is a wide gap between the low infant mortality rate in Monaco (1.79) and the high rate in Angola (175.90). Although infant mortality differences between developed and developing

countries declined in recent years, some countries have seen their rates increase. In India, for example, the infant mortality rate increased from 36.9 in 2008 to an estimated 47.57 in 2011. Improved nutrition, sanitation, and medical care as well as economic development all combined to lower infant mortality rates and to dramatically increase life expectancy in the developed countries during the past century. Life expectancy is also increasing in many developing countries due to improved economic and health conditions. Nevertheless, 24 countries still have life expectancy rates of 55 years or less; 23 of those are in Africa. (CIA, 2011). Poverty and disease, especially AIDS, are the major culprits. Some countries, like Angola, are seeing a reversal in the direction of life expectancy due to economic and political crises. Consequently, millions of children are now orphans, having lost one or both parents to disease or conflict. Without parents or other adult caregivers, the future for these children is bleak. Their very survival is in question. Not only are they experiencing emotional suffering and grief, but they are likely to lose access to basic necessities such as shelter, food, clothing, education, and health care.

ACCESS TO HEALTH CARE

One of the critical fallouts of global and national inequity is a differential access to health care for huge numbers of people. In many areas of the world, national health care systems are characterized by a lack of funds and other resources, particularly a shortage

TABLE 15.1 Indicators of Well-Being in Selected Countries, 2008 Estimates

Country	Infant Mortality Rate (per 1,000 Births)	Life Expectancy at Birth (Years)	Crude Death Rate (per 1,000 Population)
Afghanistan	149.20	45.02	17.39
Angola	175.90	38.76	23.40
Canada	4.92	81.38	7.98
China	16.06	74.68	7.03
France	3.29	81.19	8.16
India	47.57	66.80	7.48
Iran	42.26	70.06	5.94
Japan	2.78	82.25	10.09
Monaco	1.79	89.73	8.28
Singapore	2.30	82.14	4.95
Somalia	105.56	50.40	14.87
United States	6.06	78.37	8.38

Source: Adapted from CIA, 2011, "Guide to Country Comparisons. *The World FactBook 2011.* www.cia.gov/library/publications/the-world-factbook/rankorderrankorderguide.html (2011, September 26).

of trained health care professionals. The shortage is global, but the problem is greatest in countries overwhelmed by poverty and disease. For example, Africa has 2.3 healthcare workers per 1,000 population, compared with the Americas, which have 24.8 healthcare workers per 1,000 population. Only 1.3 percent of the world's health workers care for people who experience 25 percent of the global disease burden (Saraladevi, et al. 2009). A serious shortage of health workers in 57 countries is impairing provision of essential, life-saving interventions such as childhood immunization, safe pregnancy and delivery services for mothers, and access to treatment for HIV/AIDS, malaria, and tuberculosis as well as threats posed by relatively new diseases that could easily evolve into worldwide epidemics such as avian influenza. Infectious diseases and complications of pregnancy and delivery cause at least 10 million deaths each year. Better access to health workers could prevent many of those deaths. Statistics show that as the ratio of health workers to population increases; so in turn does infant, child, and maternal survival.

In some countries or regions of a country, health care systems have been destroyed by natural disasters such as the earthquakes in Japan, China, and Guatemala and hurricanes and tropical storms in Haiti, the United States, and the Philippine Islands. Additionally, health care systems have been destroyed and health care workers have been driven out by warring factions in countries such as Afghanistan, Iraq, Lebanon, and the Sudan. Compared to these situations, the health care system of the United States is quite robust. Nevertheless, many people throughout the country remain largely outside its reach, largely because they are without health insurance.

The Uninsured in the United States Although the United States has among the highest per capita health expenditures of the industrialized countries, it ranks considerably lower than many of its counterparts in terms of the percentage of its population covered by public health insurance. In contrast to most other industrialized countries, where comprehensive government-run national health programs exist, access to the American health care system is primarily through private insurance, with two major exceptions—Medicare, which covers over 99 percent of the elderly, and Medicaid for the poor. Those who have private insurance generally obtain it as a fringe benefit of their employment. However, as insurance premiums and health care costs increased, employer-sponsored health insurance decreased. The share of workers nationwide with employer-provided insurance from their own job fell from 64.1 percent in 1999 to 55.3 percent in 2010 (U.S. Department of Health and Human Services, 2011). During this same period, many employers shifted more of the insurance cost to their employees, especially the cost of insuring workers' families. Employers are not legally obligated to offer health insurance and workers can opt not to participate, as do many employees in low-paying jobs who must decide between paying for insurance or for other family needs. Additionally, when people lose their jobs, they often lose their health insurance as well. To cope with this problem, Congress passed the 1986 Consolidated Omnibus Budget Reconciliation Act (popularly known as COBRA) to bridge the insurance gap for workers who were between jobs. Although the law has been used by millions of workers (primarily middle class), it has some serious limitations. The law does not apply to

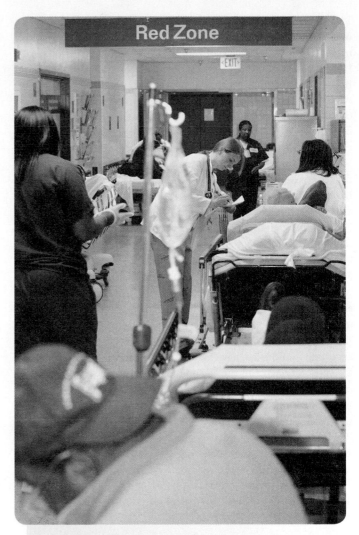

Emergency rooms like this one in Grady Hospital in Atlanta are being stretched to the breaking point with people being forced to be treated in hallways when rooms are not available. Millions of people without health insurance are seeking medical care at emergency rooms because they cannot get treatment at doctors' offices, thus contributing to this overcrowding.

people who work for businesses with fewer than 20 workers, and it requires workers to pay the full cost of their health insurance premiums plus some administrative costs, reaching as high as $400 to $1000 a month for family coverage. Thus, many unemployed workers cannot exercise their right to continued insurance coverage because the cost is prohibitive.

In 2010, 16.3 percent of the nonelderly population (49.9 million Americans) did not have health insurance, up from 15.3 percent (45.7 million Americans) in 2007. Those most likely to be uninsured are young adults age 18–24 (27.2 percent). Over 1 out of 4 persons (26.9 percent) of persons living in households with incomes under $25,000 did not have health insurance. Working does not guarantee you will have health insurance. Nearly 1 out of 5 workers age 18–64 (20.8 percent) are uninsured. The percentage of people without insurance varies across race and ethnic lines. Latinas/os are the most likely to be uninsured (30.7 percent), followed by Blacks (19.5 percent), and Asians (18.1 percent);

11.7 percent of Whites are without insurance (U.S. Department of Health and Human Services, 2011). Recent efforts to enroll more children in both Medicaid and the State Children's Health Insurance Program lowered the number of uninsured children from 12 percent in 1999 to 9.8 percent in 2010. Many other Americans, both adults and children are underinsured; any serious illness quickly would exhaust their benefits. Lack of insurance coverage can be deadly. Estimates are that having insurance could reduce mortality rates for the uninsured by 10 to 15 percent.

These statistics illuminate some of the problems related to the delivery of health care in the United States. In 2009, after a long and heated debate Congress passed the Patient Protection and Affordable Care Act (PPACA), and President Obama signed it in early 2010. Some of the reforms included in this act are providing coverage at the same premium to all applicants without regard to pre-existing condtions, expanded access to insurance to over 30 million Americans, an individual mandate that all persons not covered by any insurance programs purchase an approved insurance policy or pay a penalty, and a provision that allows children to remain on their parents' plans until age 26. Although this later provision is already responsible for an increase in the number of young adults covered by health insurance, critics of the law have filed actions in federal court challenging the constitutionality of the law and the 2012 Republican presidential candidates have all promised to repeal it if elected. A recent survey of medical students found that approximately, 95 percent believe the U.S. healthcare system needs to be reformed, 31 percent believe the PPACA will improve health care quality, while 21 percent disagree and almost have 48 percent are unsure. Two-thirds believe that the PPACA will increase access while 7 percent disagree (Huntoon, et al. 2011).

Regardless of the outcome of this renewed debate, issues of disability and trends in drug use and abuse are among the many issues that need to be addressed.

DISABILITIES

Disability is not an easy term to define. The International Classification of Functioning, Disability and Health (ICF) defines **disability** as an umbrella term for impairments, activity limitations and participation restrictions. Disability is the interaction between individuals with a health condition (e.g. cerebral palsy, Downs Syndrome, depression) and personal and environmental factors (e.g. negative attitudes, stigmatizing, inaccessible transportation and public buildings, and limited social supports) (World Health Organization and World Bank, 2011). Sociologically speaking, this definition points out that disability is not purely a medical problem to be treated by nurses and doctors, but rather it is also a social phenomenon best dealt with by enabling people with disabilities to lead independent lives free of prejudice and discrimination. Compatible with this kind of understanding and interpretation, disability is now understood to be a human rights issue; people are disabled by society, not just by their bodies.

Few people realize that the experience of disability is typical rather than rare. Disability affects hundreds of millions of families and communities around the world. For example, according to recent

✳ Explore the Concept
Social Explorer Activity:
Disability in the U.S.
on **myfamilylab.com**

Former army major Tammy Duckworth, walking with her husband, lost her legs after the Black Hawk helicopter she was piloting was hit by a missile. Over 30,000 veterans of the Iraq and Afghanistan wars have returned home with serious injuries. Their disabilities require prolonged care and assistance that can strain family relationships and erode family finances.

reports, more than one billion people, about 15 percent of the world's population, have some form of disability. Between 110 million and 190 million people age 15 and older have significant difficulties in functioning (World Health Organization and World Bank, 2011). In the United States, approximately 54 million people (representing 17 percent of the population) have some level of disability, making them the nation's largest minority group, and the only group that anyone—regardless of race, class, gender, sexual orientation, or age—can become a member of at any time. Around one-third of families include at least one member with a disability, and most families experience having a disabled member at some point in time. According to some sources, 65 to 70 percent of the U.S. population will become disabled simply by living to their full life expectancy. These statistics have important implications for marriage and family life and raise important questions for family members such as the following:

- Is the disability severe or mild, temporary, or permanent?
- If, and how, will disabilities be covered under their health insurance?
- Who will care for disabled family members?
- What kinds of disability-related assistance is available to them? (U.S. Census Bureau, 2011b; Disability Funders Network, 2009).

Many disabled people are forced to depend on family members and others in the community for physical and economic support. For those persons who are severely disabled and require prolonged care and assistance, such physical or mental requirements often severely strain family relationships and family finances; caretaking becomes a full-time occupation. Not only are many of the disabled persons unable to work, but those who can and want to, often face discriminatory practices that deny them access to work. For example, the unemployment rate for persons with disabilities is as high as 80 percent in some countries. Although the jobless rate is high for most groups in the United States, for disabled persons, it is ten times higher than the national average.

Military Service Individuals in the military and their families are especially hard hit with disabilities and their consequences. In 2009, for instance, 5.5 million veterans had some level of disability. Sixty percent (3.3 million) of these veterans suffered a disability as a result of injuries or illnesses sustained during, or as a result of, military service and received more than $35 billion dollars in compensation. Additionally, according to a 2011 report to the U.S. House Committee on Veterans' Affairs, an estimated 4 million veterans will receive disability benefits in 2012 totaling nearly $53 billion dollars in compensation (U.S. Census Bureau, 2010f; U.S. Department of Veterans' Affairs, 2011). Among veterans with disabilities the unemployment rate is almost twice that (41 percent) of their counterparts who have returned from war without a disability (27 percent). Additionally, many parents and spouses of wounded veterans have had to quit their jobs, uproot their families to be closer to hospitals, and rebuild their homes to accommodate the needs of their disabled loved one or relocate to another place. Because many of these disabilities have happened so early in life, families may have to cope for 20 or more years. However, no matter where individuals and families find themselves in the world today, they are connected by the similarity of the impact of global social and economic factors as well as the consequences of war for their family's stability and health. For example, families in war-torn societies such as Iraq and Afghanistan suffer similar extraordinarily high unemployment rates (15 percent and 35 percent respectively) high levels of stigmatizing, discrimination and poverty as American veterans and other groups (Schepp, 2011; Disability Funders Network, 2011; Index Mundi, 2011).

Poverty As alarming as these data are, the rates of disability are increasing, in part, due not only to ageing populations, an increase in chronic health conditions, and the ravages of war but also due to poverty. Researchers have consistently found a two-way link between poverty and disability. Poor people are at greater risk of acquiring a disability because of lack of access to good nutrition, health care, sanitation, as well as safe living and working conditions. In turn, after the onset of a disability, barriers to health and rehabilitation services, education, employment, and other aspects of economic and social life can trap people in a cycle of poverty. All over the world disabled people are among the poorest, most stigmatized and most marginalized groups in the world living lives of disadvantage and deprivation. People with disabilities have poorer health outcomes, lower education achievements, less economic participation and higher rates of poverty than people without disabilities. For example, 20 percent of the world's poorest people have disabilities and almost 80 percent of people with disabilities live in low-income countries. And in developed nations, a study in the United Kingdom, for instance, reported that when all factors were

considered, the poverty rate for disabled people was 47.4 percent compared to 17.9 percent for able-bodied people. In the United States, disabled people are the poorest and least educated of all citizens due largely to unequal opportunities, though this is slowly beginning to change as more disabled people are pursuing college degrees (World Health Organization, 2011a; Provost, 2011).

Age and Gender Disability is a normal part of life affecting individuals and families of all ages. Global statistics on the number of children with disabilities varies with estimates as high as 200 million children worldwide, with 80 percent living in developing countries. In the United States, 5 percent of children 5 to 17 years of age have disabilities; 10 percent of people 18 to 64 have disabilities; and 37 percent of adults 65 and older have disabilities. Sixty percent of people 25 to 64 with a non-severe disability live in married-couple families and 50 percent of people with severe disabilities live in married-couple families. Moreover, slightly more females (12.3 percent) than males (11.6) are living with a disability. In countries such as the United States with life expectancies over 70 years of age, people spend on average about 8 years, or 12 percent of their life living with disabilities (World Health Organization and World Bank, 2011; U.S. Census Bureau, 2011b).

Women An examination of the gender dimension of disability indicates that women are more prone to disability than men; they make up approximately three-fourths of disabled persons in low and middle income countries, primarily due to neglect in health care, poor workforce conditions, and/or gender-based violence. Women are particularly more vulnerable than men both economically and physically and they are recognized to be doubly disadvantaged, experiencing exclusion on account of both their gender and their disability. For example, when women work, they face a huge gender pay gap. In the United States, men with disabilities earn 55 percent more than their female counterparts. And when disabled women do not work, they are twice as unlikely to find work as disabled men (European Women's Lobby, 2011). Some other statistics pertaining to gender and disability include:

- 75 percent of women with disabilities and up to 100 percent in some developing countries are excluded from the workforce—though the majority contribute significantly to their families through cooking, cleaning, and caring for children and relatives.
- The literacy rate for people with disabilities is three percent, with the literacy rate for women and girls with disabilities as low as one percent.
- Women with disabilities are at much greater risk of being sicker, poorer, and more socially isolated than either men or able-bodied women.

Furthermore, disabled women are vulnerable to a host of other personal and societal problems. As we pointed out in Chapter 11, women in the United States are more likely to be abused and suffer violence when they are disabled. They are more likely to be victims of rape and are less likely to obtain police intervention, legal protection, or preventive care. This "feminization of vulnerability" is not unique to disabled women in the United States; rather, it is a recurring pattern that connects women living in countries around the world. A study in Orissa, India, for example, found that virtually all of the women and girls with disabilities in the sample were beaten at home, 25 percent of women with intellectual disabilities had been raped, and 6 percent of women with disabilities had been forcibly sterilized (Disabled World.com, 2011). Women in some developing countries are disabled due to the violence perpetrated against them through cultural practices such as female circumcision and infibulation. Although disabled women are particularly vulnerable in the developing world, the quality of life for disabled women is not much better in other parts of the world. In Canada, for example, Canadian girls and women with disabilities are 10 times more likely to be sexually assaulted or exploited than other girls and women. Overwhelmingly, their attackers are the people they trust most. In three out of four cases, the perpetrators are doctors, teachers, parents, and caregivers (Vancouver Sun, 2011). However, as we have shown repeatedly throughout this textbook, women are also active agents in changing, modifying, and adapting the social worlds in which they live. Thus, like their able-bodied counterparts, disabled women globally are active agents working to tear down the barriers that prevent them from full and equal participation in society; increasingly, they are forming their own self-help groups in their countries and internationally.

Children   Like women, children are extremely vulnerable to disability, and disabled children are extremely vulnerable to violence. Research indicates that violence against children with disabilities occurs at an annual rate almost twice greater than that for their able-bodied peers. Children at the greatest risk of disability tend to live in poor households, face discrimination and restricted access to social services, including education, are underweight and have stunted growth, and are subjected to severe physical punishment from their parents (World Health Organization and World Bank, 2011). In addition, superstitions, fear, stigmatization of and violence against people with a disability has sometimes led parents in some developing countries to abandon or kill a newborn suffering from a highly visible defect.

Over such a long period of time, even loved ones might tire of caring for a disabled family member and begin to resent the person or may themselves suffer declines in their own physical and mental health. Parents with disabled children are particularly vulnerable to stress, which is often produced by trying to meet the extra demands of caring for a disabled child without the necessary resources and support. Parental stress in turn can impact a disabled child's development. Thus, often it is not just the disabled who need services and support, but also parents and sometimes whole families (Beresford, Rabiee, and Sloper, 2005).

As with persons with disabilities generally, children with disabilities are marginalized in most major societal institutions. This is clearly the case in terms of education. According to a recent UNESCO Report (2010), 72 million children worldwide do not attend school; one-third of these children have one or more disabilities. Although children at risk of marginalization in education are found in all societies, an overwhelming majority are found in developing countries where 98 percent of children with disabilities do not attend school. And in almost every country, disabled girls are less likely to attend school compared to disabled boys. At first glance, the lives of these children around the world may appear poles apart. The daily experiences of slum dwellers in Kenya, ethnic minority children in Vietnam, a Roma child in Hungary, and children of color in the United States are perhaps very different. What they have in common, however, are missed opportunities to develop their potential, realize their hopes, and build a better future through education.

Furthermore, like women, girls and boys with disabilities, but especially girls, face extremely high risks of male violence and rape and consequently exposure to HIV/AIDS. Some studies suggest that between 39 and 68 percent of girls and 16 and 30 percent of boys with intellectual or developmental disabilities will be sexually abused before their 18th birthday. In some countries in Africa, the vulnerability of girls, like women, to sexual violence, rape, and HIV/AIDS is fueled by the myth that disabled females are virgins due to their disabilities and thus sex with a disabled person will cure AIDS (UNESCO, 2010).

Perhaps one of the greatest contributors to child death and disability is the explosive remnants of war (ERWs). According to UNICEF (2009), explosive remnants of war, including land mines and unexploded ordnance (for example, grenades and cluster bombs that did not explode on impact but can still detonate), pose an enormous threat to children and their families worldwide. Daily, civilians in dozens of countries around the world are injured or killed by landmines or other lethal leftovers of conflicts and wars, years after the conflicts or wars have ended. However, children and their families are not only living through the occupation of their homelands as a result of wars past and present but also, they are increasingly living through internal ethnic and other kinds of violent conflicts in their homeland which has greatly influenced childhood patterns of disabilities. This is perhaps nowhere more evident today than in Libya, a country whose civilian population in 2011 was beset by more than five months of civil war. A person was killed or maimed by mines and unexploded devices every two hours, and children represented a third of the victims (Yoon, 2011).

Children, particularly boys, are most likely to be harmed and account for almost one-third of all victims of landmines and ERWs, which they often mistake as toys. Injuries run the gamut and include loss of arms and legs, sight, or hearing and often cause lifelong disabilities that require urgent care and long-term support. Many of these children die before they can get medical attention. Of those that live, most of their families cannot afford life-saving reconstructive surgery or rehabilitative care for their disabilities even if it was available to them. However, many of these countries have limited rehabilitation capacity; health services are damaged, inadequate, and or underfunded which acts to further limit children's lives and puts tremendous strain on parents and or caretakers. When the reverse occurs, when parents are killed or maimed by landmines, the lives of children are also severely affected. Childhood without one or both parents may be plagued by inadequate nutrition or immunization, lack of protection from exploitation and abuse, or early withdrawal from school to supplement family income. In the final analysis, many of the problems facing mine-injured children and their families are similar to those facing all disabled children everywhere. All disabled children face the challenge of social reintegration, as well as the psychological problems that can arise from humiliation, rejection, and depression about the loss of life opportunities.

These facts notwithstanding, as a result of UNICEF and other individual and collective actions, a number of successful programs have been initiated to assist disabled children, their families, and their communities by providing them with the tools they need to break the cycle of poverty, illiteracy, violence, lack of health care, education, and livelihoods so that the world's children can have the optimum chances for growing up safe, healthy, educated, and happy (UNICEF, 2009; Save the Children Federation USA, 2011).

In the United States, increasingly, since the emergence of the disability rights movement in the 1970s, disabled persons are asserting their right to participate fully in schools, in the workplace, in businesses, in their families, and in community affairs. For example, they increasingly participate in their communities and the electoral process; they socialize with their friends, neighbors, and families members almost equal to that of able-bodied persons and have made small gains in securing employment and greater gains in increasing their education and skills levels. All of these factors have been shown to increase the life satisfaction of people with disabilities. For example, according to one poll, 43 percent of disabled persons who were working were very satisfied with their lives generally compared to 33 percent of their non-working counterparts (Abilities, 2011).

Although past negative attitudes toward disabled persons have abated some in the United States, contemporary attitudes toward the visibly disabled still tend to regard them as persons who are to be pitied, set apart, or avoided altogether. Common reactions to them continue to be condescension, ridicule, impatience, awkwardness, embarrassment, resentment, and even anger. The good news, however, is that there is some evidence of changing attitudes about disabled people, at least within some segments of the population.

TRENDS IN DRUG USE AND ASSOCIATED HEALTH PROBLEMS

Drug use is another global public health issue. The trend is toward an increase in the supply and the use of both legal and illegal drugs and an earlier initiation into their use, resulting in a broad spectrum of problems, including deteriorating health, social and family disruption, and economic exploitation. Problems related to drug use have traditionally affected males. However, the rapid social and economic changes discussed throughout this textbook have contributed to a dramatic increase in use among women. Because many women drug users are of childbearing age, their use can have profound negative effects on the next generation.

Thinking about drugs is complicated by the fact that almost daily the media send out mixed messages about drugs. In the same news hour we are likely to hear about the wonders of a new drug and the devastating effects other drugs have visited on individuals or whole communities. People are often surprised to discover that they are drug users. Until relatively recently, commonly used items such as coffee, tea, and cigarettes were not viewed as drugs.

▶ **Read** the **Document**
Association is Not Causation: Alcohol and Other Drugs Do Not Cause Violence on **myfamilylab.com**

Thus, it is important to clarify terms. A **drug** is any substance that alters the central nervous system and states of consciousness. Such alterations can enhance, inhibit, or distort the functioning of the body, in turn possibly affecting patterns of behavior and social functioning. The most commonly used and abused drugs are *narcotics* (opium, morphine, codeine, and heroin), *depressants* (barbiturates, benzodiazepines, and alcohol), *stimulants* (cocaine, amphetamines, methamphetamines, diet pills, caffeine, as in coffee or tea, and nicotine, as in tobacco), *hallucinogens* (LSD, mescaline, and peyote, psilocybin ("Shrooms"), PCP, DMT), *cannabis* (marijuana and hashish), *club and date rape drugs* (GHB, rohypnol ["roofies"], ecstasy, and ketamine) and *organic solvents* (inhalants such as gasoline, airplane glue, and paint thinner, as well as certain foods, herbs, and vitamins) ("Drug Use and Abuse," 2009; Hanson and Venturelli, 1995).

DRUG ABUSE: AN INTERNATIONAL CONCERN

Drug abuse is not unique to the United States. The illegal production, distribution, and use of drugs are global problems. The United Nations Office on Drugs and Crime (2011) estimates that, in 2009, between 149 and 272 million people (3.3 to 6.1 percent of the world population aged 15–64) used illicit substances at least once in the previous year. Cannabis remains by far the most widely used drug (125 to 203 million people), followed by amphetamine-type stimulants, opiates, and cocaine. Between 16 and 39 million people are problem drug users (10–15 percent of all who use drugs).

A recent survey by the World Health Organization of over 85,000 people in 17 countries found that the global distribution of drug use is unevenly distributed with the United States having the highest level of both legal and illegal drug use among all countries surveyed. The use of drugs varies across different socioeconomic groups within all the countries surveyed:

- Males are more likely than females to have used all drug types; however, this gender difference is narrowing among the younger age groups.
- Younger adults were more likely than older adults to have used drugs.
- Those with higher incomes are more likely than those with lower incomes to use drugs of all kinds.
- Marital status was found to be linked only to illegal drug use. People who had never married or were previously married were more likely than married people to use cocaine and cannabis.

The study found that drug use did not appear to be related to drug policy as countries with more stringent policies, like the United States, did not have lower levels of illegal drug use than countries with more liberal policies, like the Netherlands (Degenhardt, et al., 2008).

The consequences of the illegal traffic in drugs are many and varied. In the centers of production, like Colombia, it creates an economic problem, diverting money and energy that could be used for investment in legal economic activities. In the centers of consumption, like the United States, it creates a health problem, contributing to between 104,000 to 263,000 drug deaths occurring worldwide each year. More than half of the deaths are estimated to be fatal overdose cases. The United States has the highest number of drug-related deaths in the world followed by the Ukraine, the Russian Federation, Iran, Mexico, and the United Kingdom.

Considering the extent of drug use, we might well ask why people use drugs and when drug use becomes drug abuse. The reasons for drug use are as varied as the users themselves, but researchers have identified several common themes: to relieve pain and illness; for fun or curiosity; for pleasure; to fit in; to escape problems; and to relieve boredom, stress, and anxiety. The Food and Drug Administration defines **drug use** as the taking of a drug for its intended purpose and in an appropriate amount, frequency, strength, and manner, and **drug abuse** as the deliberate use of a substance for other than its intended purpose, in a manner that can damage health or ability to function.

Drug Use among the World's Children

It is illegal for children in the United States to purchase alcohol or tobacco products. Nevertheless, in 2010, 10.7 percent of children aged 12–17 used tobacco, down from 15.2 percent in 2002. About 10 million persons aged 12–20 (26.3 percent of this aged group) reported drinking alcohol in the past month, including 6.5 million binge drinkers (five or more drinks on the same occasion) and 2 million heavy drinkers. In this age group, more males than females reported current alcohol use (28.3 percent to 24.1 percent), binge drinking (19.8 percent to 14.0 percent), and heavy drinking (6.7 percent to 3.5 percent. Asian youths had the lowest alcohol use rates (14.4 percent), followed by Blacks (20.4 percent), American Indians/Alaska Natives (22.9 percent), and Latinas/Latinos (24.4 percent). White youth had the highest rate (29.2 percent).

At the same time, 10.1 percent of children ages 12–17 were current illicit drug users with 7.4 percent current users of marijuana, 3.0 percent current nonmedical users of psychotherapeutic drugs, 1.1 percent current users of inhalants, 0.9 percent current users of hallucinogens and 0.2 percent current users of cocaine (Substance Abuse and Mental Health Services Administration (2011). These substances are also popular among the world's "street children"—children made homeless because of family separations and conflicts associated with urbanization, economic crisis, political change, civil unrest, wars, epidemics, and natural disasters. Studies have found that between 25 and 98 percent of street children use substances of one kind or another. In Morocco, 98 percent of street children are thought to be dependent on glue. Cheap and easy to get, the children use glue to numb the feelings of cold, hunger, and rejection (Harter, 2004). The devastating consequences that follow such use include acute and chronic health and emotional problems, disruption of interpersonal relationships, school failure, social marginalization, and criminal behavior, including prostitution to pay for their habit.

One of the major factors in drug use among children is the absence of a supportive family. A study comparing Filipino street children with non-street children found that street children with little or no contact with their families were 2 times more likely to smoke tobacco, 1.3 times more likely to use alcohol, 36.7 times more likely to use inhalants and 5.5 times more likely to use illegal drugs (Njord, et al. 2010).

Drug Use among the College-Age Population

The rate of current use of illicit drugs among young adults ages 18–25 increased from 19.6 percent in 2008 to 21.5 percent in 2010, driven largely by an increase in marijuana use (from 16.5 percent in 2008 to 18.5 percent in 2010). The highest rate of current illicit drug use was among 18- to 20-year-olds (23.1 percent) with the next highest rate among 21- to 25-year-olds (20.5 percent). Among 18- to 25-year-olds, the rate of current nonmedical use of prescription-type drugs in 2010 was 5.9 percent, similar to the rates in the years from 2002 to 2009. During that same period, the use of cocaine declined from 2.0 to 1.5 percent, and methamphetamine use declined from 0.6 percent to 0.2 percent (Substance Abuse and Mental Health Services Administration, 2011). However, the rate of binge drinking and the rate of heaving drinking were high among this group (40.6 percent and 13.6 percent). The fact that alcohol use is legal and marijuana use is not has led to an ongoing and controversial debate over the possibility of legalizing this latter activity (see the Debating Social Issues box).

ALCOHOL USE AND ABUSE

Although the media pay far more attention to illegal drugs such as cocaine and heroin, alcohol abuse affects a much larger percentage of the population.

About 2 billion people worldwide consume alcoholic drinks. According to a national survey, an estimated 131 million Americans (51.8 percent) age 12 or older consume alcohol. The majority drinks in moderation and suffers little or any consequences from their use of alcohol; millions of others are not so fortunate. In 2010,

- An estimated 6.7 percent of the population age 12 and over (16.9 million people) were heavy drinkers; nearly one quarter (23.1 percent) participated in binge drinking at least once in the 30 days prior to the survey.
- An estimated 11.4 percent of persons age 12 or older (28.8 million persons) drove under the influence of alcohol at least once in the past year (Substance Abuse and Mental Health Services Administration (2011).

Worldwide, some 125 million people are affected by alcohol-use disorders, such as alcohol dependence and abuse (World Health Organization, 2011b). According to the National Institute on Alcohol Abuse and Alcoholism (NIAAA), **alcoholism,** also known as alcohol dependency, is a disease that includes four symptoms: craving—a strong need or urge to drink; loss of control—not being able to stop drinking once drinking has begun; physical dependency—withdrawal symptoms, such as nausea, sweating, shakiness, and anxiety after stopping drinking; and tolerance—the need to drink greater amounts of alcohol to get high. Annually across the globe, the harmful use of alcohol results in 2.5 million deaths. In the United States, excessive alcohol consumption is the third leading lifestyle-related cause of death. The Centers for Disease Control and Prevention (2011a) estimate that between 2001–2005, about 79,000 deaths were cause by excessive alcohol use annually.

SHOULD MARIJUANA USE BE LEGALIZED?

Over the years, numerous efforts have been made to legalize marijuana. Currently, 16 states and the District of Columbia allow the use of marijuana for medical purposes. Nevertheless, the public remains divided over whether the use of marijuana should be legal or not. In a 2011 survey, half of the respondents (50 percent) opposed legalization while nearly as many (45 percent) favored legalization. The comparable figures in 1990 were 81 percent and 16 percent. Younger people, men, the college educated, and Democrats are more likely to support legalization than older people, women, those with a high school education or less, and Republicans (Pew Research Center, 2011a).

Opponents of legalizing marijuana believe it is a stepping-stone drug, leading to heroin, cocaine, or other harder drugs. They also believe that using marijuana could easily lead to other problems such

as impaired driving, poor performance at work or school, and damages to a person's physical health. Additionally, they believe that more widespread use would increase the dangers of secondhand smoke-damage to non-users and increase the likelihood that more young people would experiment with marijuana. Those who oppose legalization argue that penalizing marijuana use deters others from using it and that drug arrests remove people from the street who have committed crimes or are likely to commit crimes. They further argue that legalization would become a slippery slope, leading to the legalization of harder, even more dangerous drugs. Finally, some oppose legalization for religious reasons. Many religious and moral codes prohibit the use of intoxicating substances, and they include marijuana in this category (Messerli, 2011).

Those who support legalization see the situation differently. Their arguments tend to center around issues of personal freedom and economics. They believe that marijuana isn't more harmful than tobacco or alcohol if used in moderation and that limiting its use derives people of pleasure. If marijuana were legalized, they argue, costs would go down, thus, reducing crimes like theft and putting some drug deal-

ers out of business. Police and the courts would be freed up to fight more serious crimes. And, as the economic situation grows worse, many supporters see legalization as a way to generate budgetary savings for states and the federal governments, both by eliminating expenditures on enforcement and by allowing taxation of legalized sales, much like what happened after the repeal of prohibition. Economist Jeffrey Miron (2010) estimates that the net impact of legalization would be a deficit reduction of about $20 million summed over all levels of government. Supporters point to the positive experiences of Portugal, the Netherlands, Spain, and Italy—countries that decriminalized the personal use and possession of marijuana and other drugs. In Portugal, for example, teen drug use declined, criminal justice resources targeted at vulnerable drug users were reduced and negative outcomes anticipated by opponents did not materialize (Szalavitz, 2010).

What do you think? Should marijuana use be legalized? Which arguments do you find the most persuasive? What do you see as the costs and benefits of legalizing marijuana on your campus, in your neighborhood, in the larger community?

The effects of alcohol—ranging from violence to traffic crashes to lost productivity to illnesses such as heart attacks, strokes, cirrhosis of the liver, pneumonia, mental illness, sexual dysfunctions, and premature death—cost the nation an estimated $220 billion in 2005. Problem drinking in the family is also a factor in many suicides, including adolescent suicide (About Alcohol Abuse, 2008).

ADDICTION: A FAMILY PROBLEM

Harold Doweiko (1996) identified a number of possible combinations between marriage, family, and addiction. Many people who are or who become addicted to chemicals are married. Some marry before

becoming addicted; others are already addicted, but their partners may be unaware of the addiction. Sometimes addicts marry each other in a marriage of convenience that brings with it an additional source of chemicals and money. Finally, nonaddicts may be aware of their partner's addiction but marry anyway in the hopes of "saving" the addict.

The problem of parental chemical use and abuse is a significant one. In 2007, more than 8 million children under age 18 (11.9 percent) lived with at least one parent who abused or was dependent on alcohol or an illicit drug, almost 7.3 percent (10.3 percent) lived with a parent who was dependent on or abused alcohol, and about 2.1 million (3 percent) lived with a parent who was dependent on or abused illicit drugs. More than 5 million children lived with a father and more than 3 million with a mother who met the criteria (Substance Abuse and Mental Health Services Administration, 2009). Most of what we know about the role addiction plays in families is based on studies involving alcohol abuse. Hence, our concentration here will be on families coping with alcohol addiction.

As we saw in Chapter 2, family systems theory explains how families function. It examines roles, rules, and communication processes that allow for predictable and consistent behavior. Whenever one part of the system is altered, all other parts are affected. This can readily be seen in the case of chronic alcoholism. When one member becomes chemically addicted, the remaining family members become enmeshed in the addiction process as they attempt to cope with the impact this behavior has on their lives. The spouse of an alcoholic is likely to deny the problem and cover up for her or his partner, taking on the role of an "enabler" who tries to help the alcoholic partner by engaging in behavior that allows the addiction to continue. For example, the nonaddicted spouse may report a partner as ill when in fact she or he is unable to go to work or attend a social function because of drunkenness.

Children also learn how to adapt to meet the demands of the addicted parent. In attempting to avoid a family crisis and as a means of coping with family stress, family roles and responsibilities are restructured as other family members take over the addicted parent's responsibilities. Many of these new patterns actually encourage the alcoholic to continue drinking and to become less involved in family life. For example, the oldest child often takes on the role of *hero*, looking after younger children and attempting to prevent the alcoholic parent from drinking. Conversely, a child may misbehave and in that way deflect attention away from the problems that the alcoholism creates. As a result, the child may become a *scapegoat*, receiving the anger that would otherwise be directed toward the alcoholic. Another child may react by becoming an independent loner, staying out of everyone's way. This *lost child* role is likely to lead to low self-esteem as this child receives little nurturing or attention during childhood. Finally, a child may take on the role of *mascot*, becoming entertaining and providing comic relief in an effort to distract the family's attention from its problems. The longer these behaviors continue, the more difficult it is to change them. There is widespread agreement among family therapists that alcoholism is one of the most difficult family problems to treat, partly because many people who need treatment do not want it, at least not at first.

Just as the onset of alcoholism leads to changes in the stability of the family system, recovery may also disrupt family functioning. Individual members may resist change because it may alter the roles with which they have become comfortable. For example, the enabler may have taken control over the family finances and may feel resentful if the recovering spouse now wants to resume this behavior. Children, too, may resist change. During the period when a parent was drinking, a child may have assumed the role of confidant to the nonalcoholic parent. In recovery, this role may be lost. Furthermore, family members often believe all problems will be over once the alcoholic member stops drinking. When they discover that problems remain and might even be exacerbated in the early stages of recovery, they may become discouraged and resentful.

Recovery is a time of great stress, and some families cannot cope; there is a high incidence of divorce within the first 3 to 5 years (Brown and Yalom, 1995). Nevertheless, with treatment many families are able to relinquish their previously unhealthy behaviors and thinking.

Children of Alcoholics (COAs) COAs most likely grow up in homes where there is considerable family stress and conflict that negatively impact the parent–child relationship. Further, children who live with an alcoholic parent are at greater risk for being physically abused and becoming abusers themselves (Freisthier, 2011; Widom and Hiller-Sturmhofel, 2001). Often, children of alcoholics (COAs) receive inconsistent parenting and inadequate parental support. This places these children at risk for many emotional and behavioral difficulties as they are growing up, including the probability of becoming alcoholics themselves. COAs may learn alcoholic behavior by modeling their behavior after that of an alcoholic parent, learning that drinking is an acceptable way to cope with life's problems. Researchers have established that genetic factors also play a role in the development of alcoholism, especially between fathers and sons (Wihelmsen Lab Elucidates the Genes, 2006).

Before leaving this section, it is important to note that not all COAs become maladjusted adults. Numerous studies comparing adult children of alcoholics and adults from nonalcoholic families found no clear differences in the grown children's emotional adjustment. Despite the difficulties of living in an alcoholic family, many children manage to cope and develop into happy, well-adjusted adults. This seems more likely when only one parent has a drinking problem and the other parent is able to provide support and guidance for their children (Schuckit and Smith, 2001), or when a parental surrogate such as an uncle, neighbor, or teacher is actively involved with the children (Whitehouse, 2000).

Differential Life Chances: Death and Disease

Nowhere can we so clearly see the differences in the well-being of families than by an examination of data on death and disease. A cursory glance back at Table 15.1 reveals the wide gulf between crude death rates (number of deaths during a year per 1,000 persons based on midyear population) in the developing and developed countries. For example, a poor country like Angola has a crude death rate of 24.4 compared to a rate of 4.95 for Singapore. Another indication of well-being is access to primary health resources such as safe drinking water and sanitation facilities. Figure 15.2 reveals major disparities among regions on these two indices. On one end of the scale, large numbers of families living in the least developed regions have little or no access to safe drinking water especially in rural areas. Although access to improved water supply and sanitation has increased since 1990, globally 40 percent of the population (more than 2.6 billion people) lack one of life's basic needs—an adequate sanitation facility, defined as one that hygienically separates sewage from human contact. For both water supply and sanitation,

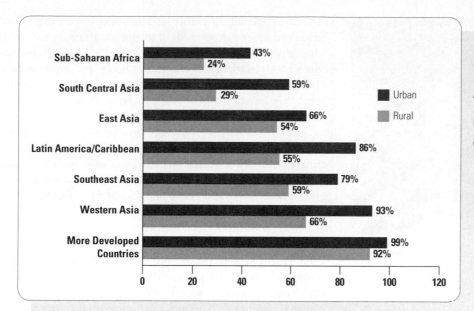

FIGURE 15.2 Percentage of Population Who Use Improved Sanitation by Area, 2008

Source: Population Reference Bureau. 2010. *2010 World Population Data Sheet.* Washington, DC: 5.

the vast majority of people without access live in Sub-Saharan Africa and South Central Asia. Every year millions of people die from water-related diseases; nearly 4000 children die each day from unsafe water and lack of basic sanitation facilities (UNICEF, 2011a).

Additionally, women and girls in many countries suffer health burdens brought on by their efforts to carry water from distant, often polluted, rivers and streams. Forty-four percent of women in rural Africa spend 30 minutes or more to fetch a single bucket of water for their family's needs. The level of water and sanitation services affect more than physical health. Children, especially girls, in countries with inadequate facilities often miss schools. Domestic chores and lack of separate school latrines force girls to stay home, thus impairing their and their family's chances to escape poverty. At the other end, families in North America and Europe have nearly universal access to basic health resources. The consequences of these differences can be seen in the different causes of death in developing and developed countries. People who live in developing countries are far more likely to die from infectious and communicable diseases than people who live in the developed countries. Epidemics of infectious diseases are common in some parts of the world. Although progress has been made in preventing malaria, in recent years there were still 225 infections and 782,000 malaria deaths mostly among African children in 2009 (World Health Organization, 2010c). This is a disease that is preventable, but because of the poverty in these regions, stocks of vaccine are too costly to maintain, and many areas are without medical services. Many of the diseases in developing countries are associated with extreme poverty. In contrast, many of the diseases in developed countries are associated with affluence and unhealthful lifestyles—little physical exercise combined with a diet high in fat. Thus, diseases of the circulatory system and cancer are far more common in developed countries than in developing countries. However, as the economies of developing countries grow, many are adopting Western lifestyles and their accompanying risk factors—smoking, high-fat diets, obesity, and lack of exercise. Deaths from cardiovascular diseases are rapidly increasing in the developing world.

The world's developed countries cannot afford to ignore infectious diseases in faraway countries. If not checked, they can easily pose a threat to the developed countries. As international travel increases, so, too, does the exposure to infectious diseases. Since the 1970s, some well-known diseases, including tuberculosis and malaria, have reemerged in the United States. During this same period, about 40 infectious diseases have been discovered, including SARS, Ebola, Avian flu, and swine flu. International trade provides another means for infectious diseases to cross borders. For example, in 1985, the tiger mosquito, which can transmit yellow fever, dengue, and other diseases, entered the United States inside a shipment of waterlogged used tires from Asia. Within 2 years, these mosquitoes were in 17 states (Heymann, 2000). It is thus in the interest of the developed countries to help eradicate infectious diseases in developing countries. Yet only 10 percent of global health research focuses on the illnesses that constitute 90 percent of the global disease burden.

Families Coping with Loss: Dying and Death

We have located the topic of death in this chapter because death is a universal experience for families everywhere. Every society constructs its own rules for handling the death and mourning the loss of their members. In recent years, televised reports of national disasters, war, and deadly terrorist attacks here and abroad have brought images of death and dying into our private spaces and exposed the resultant grief and mourning to a global audience. There is no way we can adequately address the scope of this phenomenon in this limited space. Thus, our discussion will focus on some general aspects of dying, death, and mourning as experienced in the United States.

Watch the **Video** *Planning for the End of Life* on **myfamilylab.com**

Thousands of plates bearing different numbers are prepared for use as burial markers in the Japanese city of Ishinomaki after 5,700 people were killed or remained missing as a result of the massive 2011 earthquake and tsunami.

THE PROCESS OF DYING

Dying is a complex process. For our purposes, we will use Robert Atchley's (1991) definition of a dying person, one identified as having a condition from which no recovery can be expected. Much has been written about how people react to the news that they are terminally ill. Psychiatrist Elizabeth Kübler-Ross (1969) invited dying patients to express their thoughts, fears, and anxieties about this last phase in their lives. On the basis of 200 interviews with dying patients of different ages, she identified five stages through which she believed the dying patient moves:

- Denial: "No, not me. It must be a mistake" is a common reaction.
- Anger: "Why me?" becomes the question.
- Bargaining: "Please let me live to see my daughter get married." "Please let me live to make amends for what I did." The appeal may be made to God or to one's doctors.
- Depression: This stage is characterized by generalized feelings of loss.
- Acceptance: The denial, anger, bargaining, and depression are replaced by contemplation of the approaching death with a quiet readiness.

In a later work, Kübler-Ross (1974) pointed out that patients may skip a stage, experience some or all of the stages simultaneously, or move through the stages in any order. Kübler-Ross's stages of dying have not received any empirical support; nevertheless, many practitioners as well as family members continue to use them in an effort to understand and respond appropriately to the behaviors of dying people.

THE NEEDS AND TASKS OF THE DYING

One of the needs that most dying people have is to know that they are dying, yet access to this information is not always available. Although in recent years the tendency in the medical community has been to tell the patient, some doctors are still reluctant to do so. This need is strongly related to the tasks that the dying person must

attend to—getting insurance and financial paperwork in order, making decisions about medical treatment, arranging for distribution of personal property, making a will, letting people know her or his wishes regarding funeral arrangements, and saying good-bye. Too often, these preparations are not made until the last minute, if ever, thus leaving the grief-stricken spouse or family to cope with them during a period of enormous stress.

In the nineteenth century, the overwhelming majority of Americans died at home, in the presence of family and friends. Information and skills for preparing the dead body were part of the common domestic knowledge of the day. The wake was held in the front parlor, and family and friends came there to pay their respects. By the twentieth century, in contrast, death had become culturally invisible (Aries, 1981). Physicians, hospitals, and nursing homes took control of the process. Today, few people ever see an untreated dead body. Instead, professional funeral directors quickly remove the body and prepare it out of sight of family members in an effort to make it appear "natural" or "sleeplike." Rather than say that someone died, we use a variety of euphemisms like *passed away, departed,* and *left us* (DeSpelder and Strickland, 2005). In the process, dying has become more depersonalized, and the rituals surrounding death have been shortened.

One of the consequences of these changes is that survivors experience greater difficulties in receiving support throughout their period of bereavement and in expressing their grief openly. **Bereavement** refers to the state of being deprived of a loved one by death; **grief** is the emotional response to this loss. Coping with a loved one's death involves a series of responses and adjustments. First is the painful process of bereavement. This typically involves a period of confusion; difficulty in concentrating; and intense feelings of loss, depression, and loneliness. There may also be physical manifestations of grief, for example, a loss of appetite, an inability to sleep, and deteriorating health. In her classic study of widows, sociologist Helen Lopata (1973) pointed out the necessity of doing "grief work," confronting and acknowledging the emotions brought about by death. Successful grief resolution involves four tasks: accepting the reality of the loss, experiencing the pain of grief, adjusting to an environment in which the deceased is missing, and withdrawing emotional energy and reinvesting it in another relationship (Worden, 1982).

Mourning refers to the outward expressions of grief, including a society's customs, rituals, and rules for coping with loss. Whatever the loss, be it an individual child, sibling, parent, spouse, or partner, or a national collective loss stemming from natural disasters like earthquakes, floods or from armed conflicts, people do not just get over it and move on with their lives. Rather, people reorganize their lives by finding ways to readjust to living in a world without the person or persons who died (Silverman, 2000). Mourning may be private or public, involving a few people or a whole country.

Do you remember your first wake or funeral? How did you feel? Were you uncomfortable in that setting? Were you uncertain about the proper way to behave? What funeral and mourning rituals does your family or religion practice? How helpful do you think they are? Explain.

NATIONAL MOURNING

Following the September 11 terrorist attacks that killed more than 3,000 people, President Bush declared Friday, September 14, 2001, as a day of national mourning. All schools, government departments and offices, and most businesses either closed or took time off from routine matters to pause and recall the tragic events of that day. Heads of major religious denominations and public officials at all levels arranged for memorial services around the country. At noon on that day, bells were rung, and in the evening candlelight, ceremonies were held in people's homes, places of worship, and public buildings to remember and honor those who died. Similar activities took place in other countries to show their sympathy for the United States. Such public expressions of grief occur whenever a nation or group of people experience a common loss, be it a political leader such as the assassination of President John F. Kennedy, or a celebrity figure who has touched the hearts of the people—for example, Princess Diana—or when many innocent people are suddenly and violently killed in natural disasters, sending shock waves through their communities. The rituals associated with national mourning help people make sense out of the loss, allow them to share their fears and insecurities, and create or reinforce people's feelings of collective solidarity.

DEATH OF A CHILD

In contrast to some of the developing countries with high infant mortality rates, here in the United States parents generally expect to live longer than their children. Because a child represents the past as well as future hopes and dreams, the death of a child is particularly devastating. Parents who have lost a child have consistently told researchers that they have never completely resolved their grief. The two main causes of death of children are accidents and malignant disease. The sudden, unexpected nature of an accidental death intensifies the grief experience, especially if one or the

Elle Jackman, 6, helps her mother Iris Jackman do a rubbing of her aunt's name, Brook Alexander Jackman, at the North Pool of the 9/11 Memorial during the tenth anniversary ceremonies at the site of the World Trade Center on September 11, 2011.

other parent was in any way involved—for instance, driving the car in which a child was killed or giving permission to go to the beach where the drowning occurred. The involved parent is likely to feel guilty. Blame from the other parent can compound such feelings. If parents are unable to forgive each other and to help each other mourn the death in appropriate ways, over time the marriage itself may dissolve. When death follows a lengthy illness, there is the added physical, emotional, and financial stress of caregiving. However, there may also be a process of gradual adaptation to the reality of the child's impending death.

DEATH OF A SIBLING

The well sibling of a terminally ill child faces many problems. The signs of sorrow, illness, and death are everywhere. A child sees the signs on a parent's face and recognizes them in the disruptions to household routines even when parents try to shield the child from what is going on. When a child is dying, the parents may be preoccupied with her or his care and the well sibling may feel excluded or deprived of parental attention. The well child may be struggling with conflicting emotions. She or he may love the ill sibling but resent the attention the sibling is getting. When death occurs, the well child may feel guilt for the death, especially if there was any sibling rivalry in the past.

A child takes its cues for coping with a sibling's death from parents. If the parents' response is dysfunctional, it can impede the surviving child's ability to cope. For example, sometimes parents resent a surviving child because she or he can be a painful reminder of the deceased child. This may compound the child's feeling of guilt. If, however, the parents listen to the surviving child, answer any questions the child has, and share their feelings of loss, giving the bereaved child opportunities to acknowledge and express grief too, chances are good that the child will cope successfully with this loss.

The death of an adult sibling is also traumatic for this is a loss of someone who was a part of a person's formative past, someone who shared common memories, important childhood experiences, and family history.

DEATH OF A PARENT

Reactions to the death of a parent vary depending on the age of the child. If the death occurs in childhood, the child's sense of loss may be accompanied by feelings of insecurity. The child may fear abandonment by the other parent as well. Just as we saw in the case of siblings, a child may assume responsibility for the parent's death and hence guilt. Often people assume that young children do not experience the depth of grief that adults do, or they assume that children will get over the death quickly. Yet children and adults grieve in similar ways. The surviving parent or other close relatives or friends need to be sensitive to the feelings of bereaved children, providing reassurance and helping them to work through their grief.

Even for adults, the death of parents can be very traumatic. No longer do they have the people in their lives that they could always turn to for guidance and acceptance. They have, in fact, become the older generation and thus much more aware of their own mortality.

DEATH OF A SPOUSE OR PARTNER

The death of a spouse has been identified as the most stressful event that can occur in a person's life (Holmes and Rahe, 1967). Spouses and partners provide an individual with a specific role, security, and many kinds of support—physical, emotional, financial, and social. All of these losses must be dealt with and a new role must be constructed. The intensity of the grief reaction depends on a number of factors—the quality of the marriage, whether the death was sudden or followed a long illness.

SUICIDE

In 2007, suicide was the 11th leading cause of death for all ages in the United States, with one suicide occurring on average every 15 minutes, and claimed about 34,000 lives (Centers for Disease Control and Prevention, 2010c). The United States has a moderate rate of suicide (10.1 per 100,000 population) compared with some other countries, for example, Lithuania (31.5), South Korea (31.0), and Japan (24.6) but higher when compared to others, for example Greece (3.0) and Italy (5.2) (Wikipedia, 2011). With the exception of some parts of China, the suicide rate for males is considerably higher than for their female counterparts. Risk factors are similar from country to country and include mental illness, substance abuse, hopelessness, recent loss of loved ones, unemployment, access to lethal means, and previous suicide attempts. The groups most at risk for suicide in the United States include the unmarried, males, Whites, adolescents, the elderly, and Native Americans.

Cultural attitudes toward suicide vary widely. In some societies, suicide was obligatory under certain conditions. Among the Japanese, a samurai warrior's ritual suicide called *hara-kiri* often followed disgrace in battle. In premodern India, the wife of a nobleman was expected to throw herself upon her husband's cremation pyre, a practice known as *suttee*. Other societies condemned suicide, viewing it as a crime or a sin. Acceptance or condemnation depends on many factors, such as religious beliefs, level of education, and the circumstances surrounding the suicide. Since the 1980s one particular form of suicide has been especially devastating and the source of much political and religious debate. Suicide bombings have become a staple of the ongoing conflict in the Middle East and elsewhere, including the September 11 attacks on the United States. Although suicide is prohibited in Islam as it is in Judaism and Christianity, some Islamic fundamentalist religious leaders approve and even encourage the practice, preferring to use the term *martyrdom,* or *shahid,* instead of suicide. Although the families and friends of these suicide bombers often see them as heroic figures, most cases of suicide are still met with dismay and disapproval.

All grief work is difficult, but suicide is particularly stressful for survivors. They constantly ask why and often blame themselves for not preventing the death. That someone they love has intentionally taken her or his life is difficult to accept. There is often anger and frustration. To many, a suicide conveys the ultimate rejection. Because others may also "blame" the survivors for the suicide, especially when the suicide involves children or young adults, they may not be able to provide the support needed in this situation.

AIDS

Just as in the case of suicide, grief work following the AIDS-related death of a loved one can be especially difficult, and survivors may not receive the support from others that is natural in times of bereavement. Several factors account for this. First of all, there is the issue of social disapproval. Some people may blame the victim for hastening her or his own death. For many, AIDS is viewed as a "dirty" disease brought on by illicit sexual behavior or intravenous drug use. Their compassion may be limited to people who are seen as "blameless," such as infants and transfusion recipients. Second, people who die from AIDS tend to be relatively young. This makes their deaths seem untimely and out of the natural order of life. Third, despite a heavy campaign of public education, many people still worry about the possibility of contracting the disease through any kind of contact with a person with AIDS. Finally, family members may be burdened by feelings of guilt if the relationship with the deceased had been estranged because of conflicts over lifestyle.

Suicide and AIDS are not the only situations where grief work is likely to be compounded by external factors. There are a number of situations where grief is, to a large extent, disenfranchised.

DISENFRANCHISED GRIEF

Gerontologists such as Kenneth Doka (1989) have called attention to **disenfranchised grief**—circumstances in which a person experiences a sense of loss but does not have a socially recognized right, role, or capacity to grieve. Societies construct norms, or "grieving rules," that tell us who can grieve, when, where, and how, and for how long and for whom. Only some relationships, primarily familial, are socially recognized and sanctioned. When the relationship between the bereaved and deceased is not based on recognizable kin ties, the depth of the relationship may not be understood, appreciated, or acknowledged by others. Yet the roles of friends, roommates, neighbors, colleagues, in-laws, and foster parents can be intense and long-lasting. Other relationships may not be socially sanctioned, for instance, homosexual relationships, cohabitation, and extramarital affairs. In still other cases the loss itself may not be defined as significant by others. Examples may include losses due to miscarriages or abortions and even the death of a pet. In other situations a person may not be thought of as being capable of grief, such as a child or a person with a mental disability. In these cases, the bereaved persons lack the supports that facilitate mourning. Although they have experienced a deep loss, they usually are not given time off from work. They may not have the opportunity to talk about their loss or to receive the expressions of sympathy and support that help people through this difficult time.

THE RIGHT-TO-DIE MOVEMENT

The discussion of death and dying would be incomplete without consideration of a major debate taking place in the United States and many other countries. With the advent of modern medical technology, it is possible to sustain life (from premature babies to the very old) under conditions that would have led to certain death in the past. People increasingly question such actions when any meaningful gain in the quality of life is unlikely. This issue is not new. For centuries people have debated the ethical issues surrounding euthanasia, or as it is popularly called, "mercy killing." The term *euthanasia* derives from Greek words meaning "good death," or dying without pain or suffering.

The 1976 landmark case involving Karen Ann Quinlan gave public impetus to the debate over the right to die with dignity. Karen, then 21, was admitted to a New Jersey hospital in a comatose state. Doctors held out no hope for her recovery. Karen's parents asked that the respirator artificially sustaining her life be disconnected. The hospital refused, and Karen's parents sued. After a lengthy legal battle, the respirator was disconnected. Karen continued in a vegetative state until her death in 1985.

Euthanasia can take two forms. In passive euthanasia, medical treatment is terminated, and nothing is done to prolong the patient's life artificially. Most states have laws that allow patients or their families to refuse treatment in the final stages of a terminal illness. This is usually done through what is called a living will, a legal document that stipulates a person's wishes in this regard. A more controversial form of euthanasia is active euthanasia, which refers to actions deliberately taken to end a person's life. The most recent debate on this issue relates to physician-assisted suicide. Proponents of physician-assisted suicide argue that it is cruel to prolong a terminally ill patient's suffering when she or he desires to die, that people are capable of making rational decisions about the quality of life they want and therefore should have the right to die in dignity with the help of a medically trained person. Opponents of physician-assisted suicide counter that this practice cheapens human life and puts society on a slippery slope that could lead to the killing of people considered a burden. They also argue that doctors are not always right and that hopeless cases have sometimes been reversed and that to assist someone in dying is contrary to the role of healer. Many health care professionals believe that increasing the availability and affordability of hospice care would eliminate the desire for physician-assisted suicide. A **hospice** is a physical environment within which supportive care is provided for terminally ill patients and their families that focuses on comfort, freedom from pain, and quality of life rather than cure. Hospice care can be provided in homes, hospitals, or nursing homes.

Thus far, only three states allow physician-assisted suicide (Oregon, Washington, and Montana). Since the 1994 passage of Oregon's Death with Dignity Act, 460 patients have opted to end their lives with a doctor's help. According to a state report, the first since Washington's law went into effect in 2009, 36 terminally ill people died after taking lethal medication prescribed by doctors (Yardley, 2010). Montana's law does not provide the state-regulatory mechanisms put into place in Oregon and Washington. Thus, Montana officials said it was unclear whether physicians there had been prescribing lethal medications.

> What do you think? Should physician-assisted suicide be legal? If so, under what conditions? Do you support or oppose this practice? Explain.

Issues and Challenges of Racism and Ethnic and Religious Discrimination in Family Life

Racism, racial discrimination, prejudice, and **xenophobia**—a fear or hatred of strangers or foreigners, or of anything foreign and/or different—are powerful forces that have stimulated migration, conflicts, wars, and subjugation throughout human history. Around the world millions of people find themselves the victims of legal, social, and political systems that crush their hopes, dreams, and aspirations, not because they have committed a crime but rather because they were born into a particular racial or ethnic group or practice a particular religion. Individuals and whole families are unable to receive quality education, health care, housing, food, or clothing because they are trapped in a maze of unjust legal, social, and political practices that deny them access to the most basic human rights. In the United States, racism, prejudice, discrimination, violence, and inequality among racial, ethnic, and religious groups are deeply interwoven into the fabric of American society. The proliferation of hate groups—groups whose ideologies include tenets of racially based hatred and whose practices attack or malign an entire class of people, typically for their immutable characteristics—in the United States was highlighted by the Southern Poverty Law Center (SPLC) (which keeps track of the actions of hate groups) in a 2010 intelligence report that listed 1,002 hate groups operating in the United States, up from 926 the previous year. This count includes only those groups that are active and does not include the hundreds of such hate groups that operate only via the Internet. In addition, according to SPLC, the election of America's first African American president in November 2008 triggered more than 200 hate-related incidents (beatings, effigy burnings, racist graffiti, threats and intimidations) across the country, a record for American presidential elections. Since his election, several White supremacists have been arrested for plotting to kill President Obama. In addition, hate crimes against Latinas/os have spiraled in the wake of ongoing political rhetoric and wrangling with regard to unauthorized immigrants. The hatred and violence of these groups extends beyond racial and ethnic categories and includes hateful rhetoric and crimes against LGBTQ persons and Muslims to name a few.

Racism and racist actions against individuals and groups are often perpetrated by individuals either acting alone or in groups. However, wider societal and institutional racism perpetuates racist beliefs and ideologies that make it easier for individuals to commit racist acts. Research has consistently demonstrated that families, especially children, from racial and ethnic groups defined and treated as minorities suffer many forms of disadvantage because of individual and institutional racism, including poorer health, poverty, and educational underachievement.

Although some people rushed to interpret the 2008 election of Barack Obama as evidence that America had moved beyond race and racism, others pointed to the unprecedented and ongoing racist rhetoric, actions, and attacks against the President as evidence that little has really changed. A typical example of the increasingly public racist rhetoric and behavior on the part of some Americans can be seen, for instance, in this 2010 protest on the U.S. Capitol lawn where protesters gathered with signs showing the President as the Joker, a witch doctor, Hitler, and a Muslim terrorist. While these are individual acts, we should keep in mind that such actions extend far beyond the individuals involved here.

RACISM AT HOME AND ABROAD

Racism is an ideology of domination and a set of social, economic, and political practices by which one or more groups define themselves as superior and other groups as inferior, then systematically deny the latter groups full access and participation in mainstream society. Racism can be both overt and covert. On the one hand, it can be manifested when individuals or groups, considering themselves superior, act against individuals or groups whom they define as inferior. According to Stokely Carmichael and Charles Hamilton in their now classic work, *Black Power: The Politics of Liberation in America* (1967), this behavior can be defined as **individual racism.** It is expressed through personal attitudes and behavior directed toward certain racial or ethnic groups by individual people. It can range from individual acts such as derogatory name calling, biased treatment during face-to-face contact, and avoidance, to overt acts by individuals that cause death, injury, or the violent destruction of property. This type of racism can be reached by television, cell phone, and other types of cameras and videocassette recorders; it can often be observed while it is taking place, such as the infamous Rodney King beating by five White Los Angeles policemen; or the brutal beating of Mexican immigrants in Los Angeles; or the brutality against an African American female motorist by a highway patrolman, videotaped by his own police camera. Today, this kind of racism is often replayed on the Internet and it is the kind that receives the most media attention. Because it focuses our attention on the individual perpetrator and the individual victim, we seldom realize that these actions extend far beyond the individuals involved.

On the other hand, racism can be manifested when a total community or whole society acts against another entire community. This behavior can be defined as **institutional racism.** Institutional racism is less overt, far more subtle, and far less easy to identify in terms of specific individuals committing the acts than is individual racism.

However, it is no less destructive to human life, marriages, families, communities and society. This kind of racism has its origins in the operation of established and respected forces in the society and thus receives far less public attention, scrutiny, and condemnation than individual acts of racism. Institutional racism consists of established laws, customs, and practices that systematically reflect and produce racial inequalities in a society, whether or not the individuals maintaining these practices have racist intentions (Newman, 2008). When a group of White students at the University of Connecticut spit at and taunt a small group of Asian American students who are on their way to a dance; when White Louisiana high school students hang nooses around their school campus, symbolic of the era of lynching experienced by African Americans during and after slavery; when a White female author co-opts Native American culture and artifacts for publication and profit; and when a Latina/o student is belittled by a teacher for not speaking "proper" English, these are individual acts of racism and condemned by many people. Although the impact of these acts extends beyond the individuals involved, they are nonetheless individual actions from which "respectable" members of society can divorce themselves. However, when in cities all across this country a highly disproportionate number of African American children are born into poverty or die because of a lack of adequate food, shelter, and medical facilities; when a disproportionate percentage of Latina/o students drop out of school; when the federal government evacuates over 100,000 persons of Japanese ancestry into concentration camps (described by the U.S. government as relocation camps), two-thirds of whom are American citizens; when a group of people are made wards of the government and forced to live on reservations and to assimilate; and when law enforcement agencies around the country (police, state troopers, and airport immigration officials) routinely use racial profiling against specific racial and ethnic groups—using race and or suspected religion as a basis to stop and search an individual—it is an example of institutional racism. Although both types of racism are insidious and damaging to marriages and families, our primary concern in this section is with the impact of institutional racism for various families in the United States and globally. It is worth noting, however, that individual racism does not operate in a vacuum. Wider societal and institutional norms, values, and practices maintain, perpetuate, and reinforce racist beliefs and ideologies that make it easier for individuals to commit and even justify their racist acts.

Racism, Ethnic and Religious Bigotry, and Discrimination at Home Historically, various groups of color in the United States have often been routinely victimized by the powerful force of institutional and individual acts of racism, discrimination, prejudice, and intolerance. Discrimination is no longer legal, but informal practices persist. A variety of studies (for example, Harris, 2003; Bussey and Trasviña, 2003; U.S. Department of Housing and Urban Development, 2005) show that African Americans and Whites are often treated differently when they shop, apply for jobs, attempt to rent or buy housing, and apply for mortgages. In addition, racist epithets, slurs, and actions have been increasingly perpetrated against Blacks as well as Middle Easterners and anyone suspected of being a Muslim on college campuses, and intolerance and racism are increasingly expressed by Whites on local and national talk radio, television, and the Internet. Likewise, the ongoing racism and hostility faced by Asian Americans such as the Chinese are said to be important factors that help explain Chinese poverty. Chicanos, whose families have lived in the United States for generations, find themselves blamed, along with new Latina/o immigrants, for many of the economic problems of this country. And the rights of Native American families continue to be subordinated to the rights of White Americans.

The increasing immigration of peoples into the United States has had and continues to have a significant impact on race and ethnic relations in this country; and racial and ethnic prejudice, discrimination, and violence have often been influenced by international relationships. A classic example occurred during the 1940s, when more than 100,000 Japanese Americans, many of whom were U.S. citizens, were interned for over 2 years in concentration camps. In addition to the racially inspired imprisonment of Japanese women, men, and children, many of these individuals and families lost most or all of their possessions, property, and businesses. When the war was over, many of these families were left homeless and destitute. In 2001, the September 11th terrorist attacks on the World Trade Center and the Pentagon, triggered a violent outbreak of American racism and religious intolerance—a proliferation of Anti-Muslim hate groups—targeted at people identified as or thought to be of Middle Eastern descent and Muslim that continues today (Southern Poverty Law Center Intelligence Report, 2001, 2010). And after a terrorist scare in the United Kingdom in 2006, racial profiling and other acts of racism against those identified or perceived to be Arabs and Muslims increased in several countries around the world. Many forces impinge on family life in the United States; however, racism continues to be one of the major challenges to the well-being of many families, particularly families of color and immigrant families. It is commonly believed that many, if not all, of the problems that these families experience are a function of either a lack of or decline in family values or their unauthorized (illegal) status. Nevertheless, because of the persistent racism and discrimination in major societal institutions such as education and the work force, these families are forced, structurally, to bear a disproportionately higher percentage of poverty, unemployment and underemployment, welfare dependency, dropping out of schools, infant mortality, illness, and early death.

Although families of color continually make serious efforts to defend the integrity of their cultures and their families and to advance their social position in the face of such persistent racism, prejudice, and discrimination from the wider society, many Whites continue to think of individuals and families of color in stereotypic terms. They believe, for example, that many people of color prefer welfare to jobs, and that they are lazy, violent, less intelligent, and less patriotic than Whites. In addition, many Whites believe that there is little or no racial inequality present in American society today. They generally believe that the American system is a fair one and that other groups have just as many if not more opportunities than Whites for success in American society. Thus, if these groups are disadvantaged, they are themselves responsible for that disadvantage (Pew Research Center, 2010a). However, even a cursory examination of statistics descriptive of the general quality of life of families of color contradicts this point of view.

Middle-class families of color have made some gains; nevertheless, among most of these groups, a number of their members are part of a growing underclass. This impoverished underclass, which outnumbers the middle class among all four major groups of color, is trapped in poverty and unable to move up. These families remain disadvantaged by racial and ethnic inequality on almost every measure of status and well-being in U.S. society. Numerous discriminatory processes exist that make it harder for many of these families to get ahead in American society than it is for White families. For many families of color, this means that life is a day-to-day struggle for survival. For all families of color, it means facing socially imposed disadvantages that they would not face if they were White. For instance, poor education, concentrated poverty, and rising unemployment in the country's predominantly African American and Latina/o inner cities are making it increasingly difficult for individuals and families that live there to develop the skills needed in today's high-tech economic environment. The effects of growing up in poverty are alone enough to greatly reduce the opportunities one has in life. Yet these families continue to be blamed for their victimization. For example, instead of addressing historical and contemporary structural barriers these families face, one politician (Newt Gingrich) in the 2011 presidential election cycle blamed the victims. He went so far as to charge that poor and inner city families have no work skills, work ethic, or values and that their children have no work habits and no one around them who works. Gingrich then suggested that these children should be taught work habits by mopping floors and cleaning bathrooms in their schools (ABC News, 2011).

Moreover, research shows that widespread economic inequality and marginality are perhaps the greatest threats today to the vitality and long-term survival of marriages and families of color. In the United States, for example, institutional racism and the pressure on immigrant cultures to assimilate have a particularly negative effect on children. And in Africa, children still suffer from the aftermath of apartheid and colonialism. The seriousness of the impact of racism on children is reflected in the fact that in 2002, the U.N. General Assembly hosted an international conference on children.

Some social scientists (such as Wilson, 1980) have argued that race has declined as a significant factor in the discriminatory treatment and unequal socioeconomic status of some racial groups, especially African Americans. If this is the case, then we would expect that middle- and upper-class members of these groups would face little, if any, discrimination. However, research shows that, in fact, middle- and upper-class members of various racial groups continue to face discrimination and prejudice, from a lack of respect and hostility to outright exclusion and sometimes even violence (see for example, Lois Benjamin, 1991). Not only are the quality of life and the well-being of individuals and families in the United States challenged by racism and prejudice, but so also is their physical well-being. This is especially true for people of color, LGBTQ persons, Muslims, and Jews. For example, according to the FBI Hate Crime Statistics Report, there were 8,152 hate crimes reported across the country; more than half (54 percent) were racial bias motivated, 18 percent were religious bias motivated, 16 percent were sexual orientation bias motivated, and 11 percent were ethnic bias oriented (see Table 15.2) (Uniform Crime Report, 2009). Many racially motivated crimes involve attacks made on families of color moving into a neighborhood where they are not welcome. Most such crimes are committed by young White males in their teens to 20s. These crimes should not be mistaken for youthful folly, however. These young perpetrators of hate and violence are acting out attitudes, values, opinions, and beliefs shared by their families, friends, and/or communities. Other hate crimes are even more serious and sometimes they are fatal. For example, in 2009, a Pennsylvania jury acquitted two teenagers of serious charges, including ethnic intimidation in the fatal beating of a 25-year-old Mexican immigrant. The teenagers were convicted of simple assault and sentenced to up to 23 months in prison. The acquittal on these charges, not surprisingly, sparked outrage from the civil rights community and others who pointed out the large body of evidence that the attack was racially motivated (The Leadership Conference, 2011). So, in these cases of hatred and hate crimes, what about family members left behind? The community?

Racism in a Global Context Racism, prejudice, and discrimination are not limited to the United States, and American individuals and families are far from the only victims of hatred, violence and intolerance. They are common throughout the world. Racial and ethnic pride and solidarity among some groups are on the rise, and racial and ethnic conflict around the world is increasing. Wherever racial and ethnic conflicts are played out, the consequences for marriages and families have been devastation and despair. Racism and anti-immigrant sentiment is on the rise in throughout much of Europe. In Western European countries, for example, the rise of neo-Nazism suggests that far from being a fringe activity, racism, violence, and neonationalism have become normal in many countries. In several of these countries, growing immigrant populations have been accompanied by high levels of prejudice and discrimination, sometimes mild and covert but increasingly overt and extremely violent. In this regard, the United Kingdom has one of the highest rates of racial violence in Western Europe. In Germany, hatred and violent attacks against "foreigners" escalated throughout the 1990s. Members of various right-wing White supremacist groups such as the neo-Nazis and the skinheads openly sported swastikas, dressed in a manner reminiscent of Nazi storm troopers, and called for "kicking the foreigners out" of Germany. These foreigners—Africans, Turks, Gypsies, and other immigrant groups identifiable by skin color—have suffered increasing violence, including death, at the hands of these groups. In France, extremist groups push for the ouster of North African immigrants (about 8 percent of the population) and Muslims, claiming that France must be made "racially pure"; in Italy, there is an increasing

TABLE 15.2 Percent of Hate Crimes by Victims and Bias Motivation for the Crime—2009	
Motivation	**%**
Anti-Race	
African American	71.5
White	16.5
American Indian/Alaska Native	2.1
Asian American/Pacific Islander	3.7
Groups consisting of more than one race	6.2
Anti-Ethnicity	
Hispanic	62.4
Other ethnicities/national origins	37.6
Anti-Religion	
Jewish	71.9
Islamic	8.4
Others	19.7
Anti-Sexual Orientation	
Gay	55.1
Lesbian	26.4
Bisexual	1.8
Homosexual Generic	26.4
Heterosexual	1.4
Anti-Disabled	
Physically Disabled	74 of 99 such crimes
Mentally Disabled	25 of 99 such crimes

Source: U.S. Department of Justice, Federal Bureau of Investigation. 2010. Hate Crime Statistics, 2009. Washington, DC. www2.fbi.gov/ucr/hc2009/index.html (2011, October 8).

racist reaction to the rise in undocumented immigrants from Tunisia. Spain is also experiencing an increase in racial violence. The growing Spanish economy invites immigrants from North African countries such as Morocco, but the poor conditions that immigrants have to endure in an already racially charged region have led to friction and racial confrontations. And in the Middle East, the most visible racism and violence occur between Palestinians and Israelis. Extreme views and religious intolerance within both groups have resulted in ongoing hostilities, racism, and violence perpetrated by people from both groups (Today's Views, 2010; Shah, 2010).

This glut of global racial and ethnic hatred and violence and its impact on marriages and families are perhaps nowhere more blatantly exemplified than in countries that have in the past or continue today to practice so-called **ethnic cleansing,** by which one category of people tries to rid the region of others who are different in some significant way. This policy has included the massive murder of thousands of Bosnians, Serbs, Croats, and Kosovars and their families. As in Europe, the collapse of totalitarian states in Africa and Asia has been accompanied by a resurgence of sometimes long-standing racial and ethnic hatred and conflict. The consequences of these conflicts have been devastating for individuals and families. For example, although apartheid has been dismantled in South Africa, deep racial tensions continue; in Zimbabwe, there has been increasing racism directed toward White farmers, due to poverty and a lack of landownership by Africans; the months of violence in Kenya following a recent presidential election have been described by many observers as a clear case of ethnic cleansing aimed at the Kikuyu peoples; in Somalia, the toll on individuals and families as a result of years of klan-based war/conflict has been devastating; and in India and other Asian nations, differences in color and culture frequently lead to prejudice, discrimination, violence, and death.

In far too many instances, racial or ethnic groups have been enslaved, impoverished, disenfranchised, and even exterminated in the name of power and ethnic purity. For instance, in just 100 days in 1994, up to a million men, women, and children were slaughtered and millions more were uprooted in the African nations of Burundi and Rwanda as the result of an ethnic war between the Hutus and the Tutsi (two groups who consider themselves distinct races). And in what has been described as the world's worst humanitarian crisis, in Darfur, Western Sudan, Arab-Muslim militia have targeted and murdered an untold thousands (or millions) of non-Muslim Black Sudanese in a systematic practice of ethnic cleansing. In 2011, voters

in southern Sudan voted to succeed from northern Sudan ending decades of ethnic and religious conflict and a horrific war that killed more than two million people. Children and families are just beginning to grapple with this new state of affairs in their lives ("Sudan Splitting Apart Peacefully," 2011).

It is generally cases such as these (some of the worst violations of human rights based on racism) that we hear about, but abuses based partially or entirely on racism take place every day around the world. And finally, in the wake of the terrorism committed in the United States on September 11, 2001, not only has there been an outpouring of violent racial hatred against people of Middle Eastern descent in this country but also in various countries around the globe. In addition, with the American-led attacks in Afghanistan and the Iraqi War (launched by the United States in 2003 and called the "War Against Terrorism") in retaliation for those terrorist attacks and the recent American military killing of high ranking al Qaeda leaders, including the infamous Osama bin Laden in 2011, there have been heightened attempts to retaliate against Americans on American soil as well as increasing violent street protests and racist acts against anyone and anything that appears to be Western, especially American (Shah, 2010).

So, then, individuals and families move in and out of countries fleeing prejudice, discrimination, racism, poverty, and political oppression only to face new prejudice, discrimination, and racism. Others remain and attempt to recover from and/or cope with the ongoing consequences of racism, discrimination, prejudice, oppression, and exclusion as well as violence and death. In either case, the resulting injury, humiliation, and destructiveness affect not only individual lives but also whole families and whole societies. For example, what of the mothers, fathers, siblings, and marital partners of the thousands of women, men, and children who have been slaughtered in Bosnia-Herzegovina? In Kosovo? In Burundi? In Rwanda? In Darfur? Somalia? What impact must the constant strife, violence, and ethnic wars have for family life and well-being? How do families cope with the reality of soldiers burning down their homes? Raping and/or murdering their loved ones, simply because of the racial, ethnic or religious group they happen to be born into or practice? What must it be like for the children of these families and societies?—children who are often forced to grow up long before they are ready; children who are sometimes forced to join armies, kill, maim, rape—sometimes their own family members; children who are vulnerable to becoming victims of trafficking and various other forms of exploitation?

These are compelling and challenging questions for the future well-being of individuals and groups and of marriages and families around the world. As racial discrimination and ethnic and religious violence grow in complexity and spiral in intensity, they become more and more a challenge for the global community.

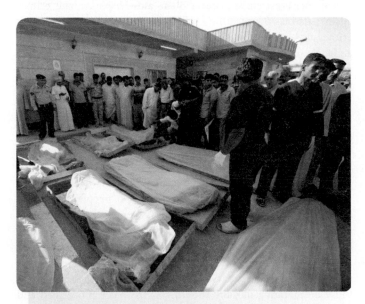

Violence, death, and destruction because of religious intolerance and hatred have become almost daily occurrences in many areas of the world. Often the perpetrators are neither apprehended nor prosecuted. For example, in 2011 unidentified gunmen killed 22 Iraqi Shi'ite pilgrims in an ambush in the Sunni heartland province of Anbar. The pilgrims were travelling from the southern Iraqi city of Kerbala to Syria when they were shot at a checkpoint set up by the gunmen. Pictured are dozens who gathered outside a hospital morgue in Kerbala to claim the bodies of their relatives killed by the gunmen.

Is life very different for poor, working-class, and families of color in the United States who are often caught in a web of violence, both directly and indirectly related to deep-rooted racism, bigotry, and discrimination from that of families in many of the countries in developed countries? In developing countries? How do any of these families cope with such violence? What impact does it have on the structure and stability of family and community life?

THE DOMESTIC AND GLOBAL CHALLENGE: IMMIGRATION, MIGRATION, AND MASS DISPLACEMENT

The international migration of people is largely driven by individuals and families who leave real or perceived poverty and poor living conditions in their own country in hope of acquiring a job and better living conditions in a new country. America has long been known as a land of immigrants. Because the United States is known as the land of opportunity, millions of people throughout this country's long history have migrated here looking for relief from poverty, misery, and oppression. Although the U.S. government has welcomed many new immigrants, that welcome has been highly selective. Historically, for instance, the majority of immigrants to the United States came from Europe. Because of immigration restrictions and racial and ethnic quotas, only a small number came from Asia, Africa, and Central and South America. However, since 1965, with a revision in the Immigration Act, this trend has been reversed; the majority of immigrants presently come primarily from Asian, Latin American, and Caribbean countries.

Today, 12.7 million Mexican immigrants reside in the United States accounting for the nation's largest single immigrant group (32 percent of all U.S. immigrants) and about 11 percent of the entire population born in Mexico. According to most estimates, a little more than one-half of these immigrants (55 percent) are unauthorized. In terms of the overall population of unauthorized persons in the United States, Mexicans are overwhelmingly the largest group comprising six-in-ten (59 percent) of the estimated 12 million unauthorized immigrants in the United States. When we take into account unauthorized immigrants from Central and South America, Hispanics make up three-fourths (76 percent) of the country's unauthorized immigrant population (see Figure 15.3) No other country in the world has as many total immigrants from all countries as the United States has immigrants from Mexico alone. The country with the next greatest number of immigrants is Russia with 12 million foreign born, many of whom are natives of countries that were part of the former Soviet Union (Pew Research Center, 2009).

Interestingly, unauthorized immigrants living in the United States are more likely than U.S. born residents or documented immigrants to live in a household with a spouse and children. Almost one-half (47 percent) of these households include a couple and their children, a greater percentage than that for U.S. born residents. In addition, an increasing number of the children of unauthorized immigrant parents (73 percent) were born in this country and thus are U.S. citizens. The fear of deportation among many of these families has led some parents to ask friends, relatives, co-workers, and acquaintances to take care of their children if they are arrested and or deported. Many of these families have low levels of education and job skills and about one-third live in poverty. Along with this, more than one-half have no health insurance, which adds to their vulnerability and threatens the health and stability of thousands of these families and their children (Fox News, 2011; Passel, 2009). Sometimes, racial and ethnic prejudice and violence accompany surges in immigration into the United States (both documented and undocumented). Most often, the targets of this discrimination and violence have been non-European immigrants of color. Researchers at the Southern Poverty Law Center report

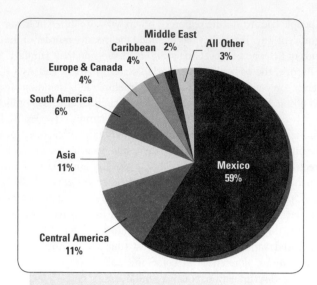

FIGURE 15.3 Origins of Estimated 12 Million Unauthorized Immigrants Living in the United States, 2009

Source: Roy Germano. 2011. "How Many Illegal Immigrants Live In The United States and Where Do they Come From?" (March 18). http://roygermano. wordpress.com/2011/03/18/how-many-illegal-immigrants-live-in-the-united-states-and-where-do-they-come-from/ (2011, October 7).

that the raging debate in the United States over immigration has fueled racist extremism and violent anti-Hispanic hate crimes against Latinas/os, regardless of their immigration status. Such crimes appear to be on the rise and include being beaten, burned, and even sodomized.

A growing number of Americans, whose ancestors themselves were immigrants, oppose immigration and are increasingly intolerant of immigrants. For example, national polls reveal that although a majority of Americans believed immigration was a good thing in the past, approximately one-third think it is a bad thing today. Furthermore, among those polled, there is considerably more opposition to immigration from Latin America, Africa, Asia, and the Caribbean than to immigration from Eastern Europe. Fully one-half, or one of every two people, polled believe immigration should be limited; 42 percent believe that the government's priority should be to tighten border security and more strictly enforce immigration laws but at the same time create a way for unauthorized immigrants to become citizens if they meet certain conditions; two of every three people believe that those immigrating illegally should be vigorously prosecuted and deported, and roughly six-in-ten approve of controversial laws that give police the power to stop and detain anyone they suspect of being in the country "illegally"; one in five believe immigration should be stopped immediately. Likewise, Americans are divided in their views about the overall effect of immigration. For instance, while many believe immigrants are a burden to the country, taking jobs and housing and creating strains on the already overworked health care system, many others believe immigrants strengthen the United States with their hard work and talents. However, what appears to be the public's greatest concern about immigration today, is the belief that unauthorized immigrants place a heavy burden on

Members of the "illegal" immigration movement, especially its student members, actively protest the stringent and punitive anti-immigration laws enacted in states such as Arizona and Alabama as well as the deportation of unauthorized immigrants, such as those pictured here waiting to be repatriated to their country of origin.

government services and they hurt American jobs. (Pew Research Center, 2011b; Polling Report, 2008).

Moreover, the American public continues to express conflicted views on Arabs and Islam. Particularly since September 11, 2001, a majority of Americans say they favor Arabs, even those who are U.S. citizens, being subjected to separate, more intensive security procedures at airports, and about half favor requiring Arabs, including those who are U.S. citizens, to carry special identification. Current surveys indicate that only about 30 percent of Americans have a favorable view of Islam compared to 38 percent who have an unfavorable view and 35 percent who believe that Islam is more likely than other religions to encourage violence. The public's ongoing conflicting views of Arabs and Muslims more generally is reflected in the recent controversy over the construction of an Islamic cultural center and mosque near the former site of the World Trade Center. A little more than one-half of the public was against the building of the center, yet 62 percent among the public believe that Muslims should have the same rights as other religious groups to build houses of worship in their local communities. It is noteworthy that the center was eventually built and opened without incidence (Pew Forum on Religion and Public Life, 2010).

These data reflect America's continuing and indeed growing quandary about immigration, particularly unauthorized immigration. The ongoing debate over this issue (both in Congress and the public) has also sparked a massive "illegal" immigration movement in this country. Throughout 2006, for instance, throngs of immigrants and their families as well as their advocates took to the streets in cities across the United States to protest proposed negative immigration laws (for example, tighter restrictions on immigration). Children skipped school, women and men walked off their jobs, and others did not even bother going to work. Businesses shut down for lack of patrons and/or employees. One such day of protest was dubbed "A Day Without Immigrants." Today, student members of the movement use civil rights-era strategies of civil disobedience, personal storytelling, sit-ins, boycotts of classes in protest of laws that target unauthorized immigrants. As during the civil rights era, advocates and participants are warned that their lives and that of their families could be in jeopardy. Nevertheless, student members of this movement continue to struggle against the deportation of unauthorized immigrants and the stringent and punitive anti-immigration laws enacted in states such as Arizona and Alabama. Many of these students consider themselves "culturally American" (because they have lived in this country most of their lives), yet they do not qualify for federal financial aid and cannot get in-state tuition rates in some states (*USA Today*, 2010).

Not unlike the United States, many countries around the world are dealing with the issue of immigration, especially unauthorized immigration. For example, in a poll on European opinions on immigration, 47 percent of Europeans said that immigration is more of a problem than an opportunity; 80 percent said controls at borders should be strengthened; 70 percent believe that unauthorized immigrants should be sent back to their country; and even when they are authorized immigrants, only 58 percent of Europeans think that they should have the same civil rights as non-immigrants (The German Marshall Fund of the United States, 2008). Immigration seems to be a particularly important and sometimes divisive issue in many countries in Europe. Germany and the United Kingdom, for example, have stringent rules around immigration. In Germany, it is extremely difficult for children of the foreign-born to obtain citizenship rights, thereby creating a population of people who are alienated from the German mainstream. Likewise, in the United Kingdom, all immigrants must demonstrate that they can speak English, even if they are a spouse of a British citizen. Britain also has a point system which sets educational and other restrictions on non-European Union (EU) immigrants. However, France is at the forefront of the battle over immigration in Europe. The president of France has pledged to reduce the flow of immigrants coming legally from Northern and Western Africa and he has vowed to deport 25,000 unauthorized immigrants (primarily Arabs and West Africans), per year. In his view, France is taking in people from the wrong countries. In his promotion of a French national identity, he has accused Arabs and African immigrants of not only being unwilling to assimilate, he has also suggested that they are incapable of doing so (Crabtree, 2011; Navarrette, 2008).

As in most countries, the children of unauthorized immigrants are targeted in order to uncover adults who are in the country unauthorized. For example, unlike the United States, France does not give children of unauthorized immigrants citizenship even if they were born in France. As a result, these families live in constant fear of deportation, many of whom hide or deny that they have children when they are arrested and deported. As in the United States, a network of parent and teacher activists (in this case, Education Without Borders) have launched a campaign to protect immigrant children (Núñez, 2009).

A World of Refugees: Mass Migration and Dislocation One of the most significant global demographic trends of the twentieth century was the massive immigration of people from one country to another all over the world. Exacerbated by ongoing and new wars and conflicts as well as international and domestic terrorism at the end of the twentieth century and throughout the opening decade of the twenty-first century, this trend continues today. Sometimes this immigration is voluntary, in that people leave their homelands seeking economic opportunities in other lands. All too often, however, the massive movement of people from one land to another has been and continues to be the result of communal violence and war; religious, political, racial, ethnic or other persecution; and most recently, violent and fatal environmental disasters.

According to the United Nations High Commissioner of Refugees Report (UNHCR, 2011), 43.7 million people are displaced worldwide, roughly equaling the entire populations of South Korea or Columbia. Within this total, 15.4 million are **refugees**—people who leave their country because of a well-founded fear of persecution for reasons of race, religion, nationality, social group, or political opinion. Many of these people (27.5 million) are displaced within their own country or on its borders as a result of war or other conflict. Almost one million displaced persons are asylum seekers, with nearly one-fifth of them in South Africa alone. Refugees are women, men, and children, from virtually every income level and living arrangement. As refugees they have often had to leave behind their livelihood, their families and other loved ones, their communities, and most, if not all, of their possessions. According to a number of reports, although a large number of refugees adjust well, many suffer significant psychological distress as a result of their exposure to traumatic events and the hardships associated with life as a refugee. Furthermore, prior to flight, many refugees have faced a wide variety of traumatic events, including witnessing fighting and mass destruction of life and property, violent acts perpetrated against loved ones, or were subjected to or witnessed sexual violence.

The mass movement of millions of refugees has transformed or is currently transforming the way of life in many countries throughout the world, the majority of which are in developing nations often already struggling to meet the needs of their own citizens. These populations are sometimes welcomed in the host countries; at other times they are met with resentment, hostility, and violence. For example, the terrorism of September 11 catapulted Afghanistan into the epicenter of fear and war, and millions of Afghan civilians, half a world away, became unintentional victims in the fallout, following history's worst single act of terrorism in the United States. However, the global refugee crisis affects every continent and almost every country in the world. Civil wars and revolutions in Central American countries such as Nicaragua, El Salvador, and Guatemala have contributed significantly to the migrant population of the United States. To escape ethnic cleansing carried out by Serb forces, more than 1 million people from the former Yugoslavia have fled to other European countries, most notably Germany. Some 2.4 million Rwandans left their central African homeland primarily for Zaire and Tanzania in an effort to escape the genocidal war that pitted Hutus and Tutsis against each other. In 2008, 100,000 refugees fled Georgia after Russian military forces divided the country into two. And hundreds of thousand civilians have fled the violence in the Democratic Republic of the Congo, southern Sudan, and Central African Republic.

Sometimes, refugees already established in a country are forced to flee in the face of internal conflicts and wars. For example, when conflict broke out in Libya in 2011, thousands of refugees and asylum-seekers living in the country were forced to

flee for their lives yet again. Many are said to be stranded in Egypt and Tunisia. They come from countries such as Cote d'Ivoire, Eritrea, Ethiopia, Iraq, Somalia, and Sudan. Paradoxically, they cannot go home, they cannot return to Libya, and they cannot stay where they are. Their only hope is to be resettled in a safe country. However, to date, host countries have been slow to respond to this crisis. In fact, Amnesty International has recently criticized European countries for their failure to help these refugees (Phillips, 2011; Coleman and Nowak, 2008).

Gender and age are important factors in communal war and violence. Women and children, for example, make up 75 to 80 percent of the world's refugees. Perhaps one of the more distressing aspects of the mass displacement of people is the fact that thousands of refugee children have been separated from their parents or families as a result of violent conflicts in their homelands. According to a recent UNHCR report (2011), the organization received more than 15,000 asylum applications in 2010 from unaccompanied or separated children, the majority Somali or Afghan. The massive number of displaced children is of immense concern as they are particularly vulnerable to threats to their safety and well-being. These include separation from families, sexual exploitation, HIV/AIDS infection, forced labor or slavery, abuse and violence, forcible recruitment into armed groups, trafficking, lack of access to education and basic assistance, detention, and denial of access to asylum or family-reunification procedures. Unaccompanied and separated refugee children are at greatest risk because they lack the protection, physical care, and emotional support provided by the family. In some countries, the statistics are staggering. For example, ten children die each day from malnutrition and disease in Ethiopia's Kobe refugee camp; Somali children are the biggest victims of the refugee crisis in the Horn of Africa; and recently, Australia was severely criticized by the UN Children's Aid Agency and Human Rights advocates for its plan to send unaccompanied child asylum seekers to Malaysia. Among the many dangers that await these children, especially girls, is the danger of being targeted by gangs for all types of exploitation (McGuirk, 2011; AlertNet, 2011; UNHCR, 2011).

Although the majority of refugees prefer to and do return home as soon as circumstances permit (generally, when a war or conflict has ended and a degree of stability has been restored), at any given time only about 6 percent of refugees return home. In any event, the magnitude of the mass movement of people can be fraught with challenges—both for the refugees and for the host country. There must be an adjustment on the part of the host society as well as at the individual level. For instance, on a societal level, large numbers of refugees into a society can impact its stability, particularly if the society is poor and already overcrowded. Newcomers to societies often intensify the competition for scarce resources—for jobs, education, housing, recreational activities, and sources of supplemental financial assistance.

On an individual and familial level, the first order of business for refugees is often the task of trying to piece together their families, who were shattered and separated by war, violence, and the exodus from their homelands. In addition, not only do refugees have to deal with the trauma of war and being separated from their cultural base, but they must also adjust and adapt to a new way of life. As we have indicated, their existence in foreign lands is sometimes complicated by racism, discrimination, and/ or intolerance. Some people believe that some of the cultural practices that refugees bring with them test the limits of tolerance on the part of the host society. People within host societies are often willing to accept cultural practices that seem to reinforce their own cultural values. However, those that differ are often met with intolerance, rejection, ridicule, and sometimes legal ramifications.

The Challenges of Safety and Security: Gangs, Street Violence, and Violence in America's Schools

The term *gang* strikes fear into the hearts of some people; disgust, resentment, and hatred in others. Still others use the term as a code word to describe inner-city neighborhoods and their residents as well as to rationalize the widening gap between rich and poor, people of color and Whites, and the alarming increase in police brutality and murder of people of color. Gangs are not new in the United States. Major cities across the country have long been the home of gangs, some of which have been around for 50 or more years. For example, in Chicago, the first street gangs appeared at the turn of the twentieth century, mostly in Irish communities (Macko, 1996). However, when most people think about gangs today, they picture African American and Latino/a youths. But White street gangs continue to exist. Gangs are usually composed of people of the same race or ethnicity. In Los Angeles, for instance, there are street gangs representing almost every racial and ethnic group living in the city.

GANGS

Gang violence is one of the most serious social problems in American Society today. An estimated 28,100 gangs with nearly 1 million members operate across the country today. According to the FBI, gangs in America include local neighborhood-based gangs, motorcycle gangs, prison gangs, gangs in the military, gangs on the Internet (recruiting, communicating, intimidating), and gangs on Native American reservations to name a few. In addition, there is an increasing number of women both joining gangs and leading their own subset of gangs. Contrary to popular belief, gangs are not confined to inner city communities. Rather, they can be found in suburbs and rural areas as well. And in many of these communities—urban, suburban, or rural—gangs of one kind or another are responsible for as much as 80 percent of all crimes. Over the last several decades, gang violence has escalated in cities across the country, and the attendant loss of life is staggering. Most authorities on the subject agree that gang violence has increased as guns on the streets have proliferated. Much of the violence, they say, is the direct result of the availability of firearms. Gang-related killings have become so common that police departments now use the term gang homicide to denote it as a separate

and unique category of criminal behavior (U.S. Department of Justice, 2009a).

The economic, physical, and psychological costs of gangs and their activities to individuals and their families are extremely high. Especially devastating to families and the community are the ongoing illegal activities and violence that often accompany gangs. These activities can be lucrative for gang members but can have a debilitating effect on family and community life. With substantial sums of money at stake, gang members often fight over dominance and control of these illegal activities. Not only do gang members kill each other, but as in contemporary wars and conflicts, innocent bystanders (civilians) are also increasingly the victims of gang violence. A growing number of these victims are children, murdered by stray bullets from drive-by shootings or the cross fire from open gang warfare on city streets. As a result, a growing number of parents fear for their children's safety even when they are playing in front of their own homes, walking to and from neighborhood schools, sitting on their front porch, or even sitting inside in their own living room. One of the consequences of living with this kind of fear for individuals and families is the separation of family members. For example, some parents, fearing gang recruitment and other activities, send their children to live with relatives in other cities. Parents worry about daughters as well as sons. Although seldom focused on, female gangs are often equally as violent as their male counterparts.

Gangs are not only a serious problem in the United States. Gang violence is now a global problem. Gangs can be found in Africa, North, South, and Central America, Europe, Asia, and Australia; however, no matter where they are found, they present complex dangers, fears, anxieties, and instabilities for children, their families, and their communities. The direct consequences are seen most visibly in the extremely high rates of violence in and between gangs. Gang homicide rates in the United States are said to be more than one hundred times higher than rates for the general population. The lack of a stable economy and political structure, coupled with the availability of high-power firearms in some global communities, fuels levels of gang violence that approximate or exceed those in the United States. These conditions are seen most clearly in Central America and several African countries. In Europe, however, where firearms are less available to gang members and other offenders, rates of lethal violence (though not other forms of assault) are considerably lower than in the United States. In countries that have experienced political turmoil, large-scale drug markets, and civil strife, gang violence is very high. Nowhere is this more evident than in Mexico where drug gangs and cartels have become increasingly aggressive, violent, and gruesome. Estimates are that upwards of 40,000 people were killed in Mexico nationwide over the 5-year period from 2006 to 2011. This violence included severed heads found in plastic bags and other decapitated heads impaled on posts; public hangings and hundreds of bodies buried in mass graves. Although the majority of the victims of this violence are gang and cartel members, Mexican citizens are also often the innocent victims as the gangs use them to show that they are in charge (BBC News, 2011; Small Arms Survey, 2010). Mexico's gang and cartel violence is not unrelated to the United States. According to some sources, the drug gangs in Mexico are fueled by the ongoing seemingly insatiable appetite

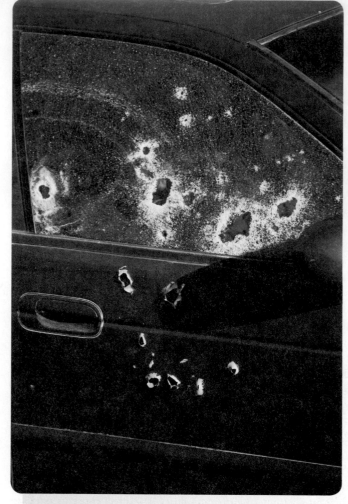

The body of an alleged hit man lies inside this bullet-riddled car after a clash between rival drug-related criminal gangs in the resort city of Acapulco, Guerrero state, Mexico in 2010. Nine alleged hit men and a civilian died in the shoot-out. Gang drug-related crime left more than 15,000 dead in Mexico between 2007 and 2010.

STREET VIOLENCE

Although the activities of street gangs constitute a high proportion of crime and violence in communities around the country, gangs are not the only source or victims of violence. More and more, individuals worry about how to protect themselves and family members in an increasingly criminal and violent atmosphere, where crime and violence are often random and pointless. Although street violence and crimes in the United States have continuously declined over the past decade, there is still considerable street violence in the United States. The rates of murder, robbery, rape, and aggravated assault in this country far exceed those in other industrialized countries.

Any discussion of crime and violence in the United States almost always raises the issue of race because many people link crime with certain racial or ethnic groups of color. In addition, most White Americans express fear of being victimized by African American strangers. In reality, however, two-thirds of the arrests police make for serious crimes involve White people. Furthermore, violent crime in the United States is primarily *intraracial*. That is, the overwhelming majority of single-offender violent crimes committed by African Americans are against African American victims. Similarly, the majority of such crimes committed by Whites involve White victims. In addition, more than one-half of all victims know their offender. Nonetheless, the link between race and criminal victimization and its differential impact across marriages and families in the United States is clear. Families living in big cities are especially affected by crime and random violence. Although the amount of crime varies throughout urban and rural areas, the greatest concentration of offenses occurs in poverty-stricken, inner-city communities of color. The poorest U.S. families are more likely than affluent families to be victimized by crime or violence. The problems generated by crime are worst in overwhelmingly African American urban neighborhoods. Despite some progress in the nation's fight against violent crime over the past decade, African American youth across all age groups are more likely to be victims of violent crime than their White counterparts (Children's Defense Fund, 2010; U.S. Department of Justice, 2009a). Similar to parents in war-torn Afghanistan who keep their children in the home in an attempt to shield them from the violence of war outside their doors, many parents in inner city neighborhoods try to shield their children from the organized as well as random violence on their streets by keeping their children in the house as well. As parents in both of these instances have found, sometimes this tactic works, but very often it does not.

YOUTH AND VIOLENCE

In general, as we have indicated, the amount of violence that impacts young people in the United States today is startling. With the proliferation of the ownership of handguns, families are losing members to handgun violence at a phenomenal rate, both as victims and as offenders. Children are particularly vulnerable to handgun violence and likely to be victims. The Children's Defense Fund reports that one child or teen every 3 hours, 8 every day, 58 every week is killed by a gun.

of Americans for drugs. Thus, sometimes their violence spills over into the United States and innocent as well as partners with the gangs pay the consequences of their actions. Moreover, many of the more powerful gangs in the United States have expanded their area of operations far beyond the local community; many have ties to drug-producing countries not only in Mexico but also around the world, from whom they secure their supplies, thus closing the circle of global connection.

It is worth noting that gangs do not occur in a vacuum. Gangs around the world have a number of common features. The strongest of these are the social and structural processes through which gang violence occurs. Key to understanding gang violence is the realization that it in addition to responding to daily triggers with violence, gang members also react to broader structural factors linked to their neighborhood, city, and country. Factors such as social exclusion, poverty, community and or societal disorganization, and immigration are key in the development and formation of gangs, especially youth gangs (Small Arms Survey, 2010).

A large number of American families have handguns or other types of firearms in the home for self-protection or for sport, such as hunting. However, almost two million children live homes with loaded and unlocked guns. Related to this is the fact that more than 500 children die each year from accidental gunshots. Some of these children shoot themselves, while others kill friends or siblings after discovering a gun in the home. Children and teens are not safe from gun violence at school, at home, or anywhere else in America. With over 280 million guns in civilian hands there is no place to hide from gun violence. For example, in 2007, a total of 3,042 children and teens died by gunfire—a number nearly equal to the total number of U.S. combat deaths in Iraq and four times the number of American combat fatalities in Afghanistan to date. Additionally, another 17,523 children and teens suffered non-fatal gun injuries and the emotional aftermath that followed for themselves and their family members. In each case it was a gun that ended or changed a young life forever (Children's Defense Fund, 2010).

Youthful violence is not confined to the United States. According to a recent report, 40 young Europeans are murdered every day. Interpersonal violence is the third leading cause of death in Europe among young people ages 10 to 29. Estimates are that for every young person that dies as a result of violence, 20 more are admitted to the hospital. Likewise, countries such as Japan have experienced a rise in youth violence which some observers attribute to the growing alienation among Japanese youth who are feeling increasingly disenfranchised by society (World Health Organization, 2010a).

VIOLENCE IN SCHOOLS

School violence is a many-faceted subset of youth violence but is not limited to youth as victims or perpetrators. It includes a variety of harmful behaviors such as slapping, bullying, punching, robbery, theft, weapon use, fatalities, homicide, and rape. Victims of this violence can suffer serious injury, significant social and emotional damage, and even death. During the 1990s, there was an incredible rise in the use of handguns to commit acts of violence, very often murder, in American schools. Despite a decrease in the percentage of students carrying weapons to school and a decrease in reports of fights, stolen property, and marijuana use on school property, school violence remains a public as well as family and community concern. For example, between 2001 and 2008, 116 school children were killed in 109 separate incidents—an average of 16.5 student homicides each year. Three out of four perpetrators of school violence are White males, 13 to 15 years of age (Centers for Disease Control and Prevention, 2008c; Ryan, 2007). Before White kids began killing White kids on school grounds, school violence was not an issue of national concern. However, over a period of time from the mid-1990s through the first two years of this century, of 19 violent incidents in U.S. schools reported in the media, 16 involved White male shooters, several of which resulted in multiple deaths. Perhaps the most violent and dramatic of these incidents, certainly the one with the greatest number of casualties to date, was the 1999 mass murders at Columbine High School in Littleton, Colorado (a suburb of Denver), where two male students initiated a gun and bomb assault that killed 15 people—14 students and a teacher before killing themselves. As this and other cases of school violence show, this type of violence does not limit itself to the student population. For instance, around 8 percent of teachers report being threatened with violence on school grounds at least once a month and another 2 percent report being physically attacked each year. In addition to fatal violence in schools, gang initiation and bullying are a growing problem for school children, incidents of which have increased dramatically over the past decade (Constitutional Rights Foundation, 2011).

As we indicated earlier in our discussion of gangs and gang violence, school violence also does not occur in a vacuum. A layering of social, structural, and demographic risk factors such as the proliferation of and easy access to weapons, media violence, cyber abuse, bullying, the impact of school, community, and family environments, and personal alienation, to name a few, provide a framework within which school violence develops and is implemented.

Although random mass shootings have generally been rare on college and university campuses, the world has changed. Today, violent tragedies such as this are occurring at alarming rates on college campuses across the nation and are extremely scary for parents and other family members who send their children off to college thinking it is a safe haven from street and neighborhood violence. In perhaps the deadliest college campus shooting in U.S. history, in 2007, a student gunman turned a gun on himself after killing 32 students and faculty and wounding 17 more in a dorm and a classroom at Virginia Tech University (Blacksburg, Virginia). Following right on the heels of this massacre, a former graduate of Northern Illinois University in DeKalb, Illinois, returned to the campus on Valentine's Day in 2008 dressed in all black, and opened fire in a lecture hall, shooting 22 students in 90 seconds, killing 5 of them before killing himself. This was the fifth college campus shooting between February 7–February 14 of that year and came only 10 months after the Virginia Tech massacre (MSNBC News, 2007; Reid, 2008).

Although random mass shootings are what grab public headlines and attention, the use of knives and cutting instruments is more widespread (two of three incidents) than firearms in campus violence and rape (Graves, 2007). In addition, other types of violence or potential violence such as bomb threats are also on the rise on college campuses. In addition to the various other arenas of crime in America, in 2008, families of victims of school violence and its survivors have devised an array of mechanisms for coping with the loss or victimization of a loved one, including traditional counseling, support groups, and student-run student-led campus organizations that provide mental health support, education, and advocacy in the university setting. Schools have also had to develop and implement new security methods and procedures to boost campus security including zero tolerance policies, metal detectors, lock downs, and campus sweeps. One school in Texas has gone so far as to implement a policy that allows some of its teachers to carry concealed weapons, a policy no other school in the country has followed. The intent of this decision is said to be to ward off a massacre like Columbine and others (McKinley, 2008).

Terrorism and War

Gangs, crime, violence, terrorism, and war are different faces of the same coin. In the not-too-distant past, when Americans thought of terrorism, they generally thought about faraway lands where governments practiced terrorism to sustain their power, and where individuals and groups within these countries practiced it in retaliation for oppressive governmental rule. Today, however, we are far more aware of terrorism in this country and recognize that it does not just occur in "foreign" or developing countries. Increasingly since the early 1990s and especially after the September 11, 2001, terrorist attacks on New York's World Trade Center and the Pentagon in Washington, DC, Americans are not only more aware of terrorism but also have experienced firsthand its consequences for individuals, marriages, and families as well as the terror that people in other countries around the world have, in the past and continue today, to experience on a daily basis. Technology has enabled terrorists to invade political arenas around the world and to make known their ideological views and goals; the end of colonial rule has been accelerated by terrorist actions carried out in the name of various oppressed racial and ethnic groups seeking self-rule.

Terrorism can be defined as the calculated use of unlawful violence or the threat of unlawful violence by individuals or groups intended to inculcate fear or to intimidate and/or coerce governments or societies as a political or revolutionary strategy to achieve political, religious, or ideological goals (Center for Defense Information, 2001). In today's world, we are witnessing an alarming rise in political terrorism—a form of warfare without any humanitarian constraints or rules. In general, the goal of such actions is to initiate a significant change in or the outright overthrow of existing governments. Often the goal is simply to intimidate. The Palestine Liberation Organization (PLO), the Irish Republican Army (IRA), the Red Brigades in Italy, the Basque separatists in Spain, and the al-Qaeda have all come to be household names in the vocabulary of political terrorism. Regional or domestic terrorism has existed throughout human history. However, terrorism as an international concern only emerged during the 1960s after a series of airplane hijackings became international news. There is no doubt that September 11 changed the world. Since that attack on the United States, terrorism has risen exponentially around the globe. Although the 9/11 terrorists were not the first to use an airplane as a weapon of terror, their actions ushered in a new phase of terrorism: terror in the skies. Contemporary terrorism can be felt most keenly at airports and not just through the interminable delays and difficulties in getting into and out of various cities or countries. Today's terrorism centers around plots to destroy human lives through the use of commercial airliners. In 2006, for example, British officials arrested 25 suspects in an alleged plot to blow up U.S.-bound jetliners using liquid bombs (MSNBC, 2006). Since that time, a number of would be airline hijackers have been caught in the U.S. and Britian.

To date, terrorists have been overwhelmingly male. However, there are women who have joined their ranks. Some observers claim that women terrorists are actually more effective because they are tougher, more fanatical, more loyal, and have a greater capacity for suffering than their male counterparts. For example, it is alleged that among those who plotted to blow up U.S.-bound

In 2011, two sequential terrorist attacks in Oslo, Norway—the bombing of government buildings and the subsequent shooting spree (less than two hours later) at a political youth camp on Utoya Island—were reported worldwide. The terrorism, described as the worst postwar terror attacks in Norway, claimed more than 90 lives. Anders Behring Breivik, the man accused of committing both attacks, is a 32-year-old Norwegian described as a right-wing extremist.

airliners departing from Britain in 2006 were women who planned to hide their liquid bombs in baby formula. Regardless of gender, terrorists and their leaders always profess that they seek to redress some political, social, or religious injustice and are fueled by a hatred that knows no bounds. An example can be seen in Hezbollah, a religious terrorist group perhaps best remembered in the United States for its 1983 bombings of the U.S. embassy and Marine barracks in Lebanon, which killed 258 Americans. Perhaps the group most recognizable by Americans in this regard is al-Qaeda. According to the Center for Defense Information (2004), at the heart of al-Qaeda terrorism is a fierce dual hatred of the present rulers of Saudi Arabia, considered to be apostates to Islam (secularists) and thus unworthy to rule, and of the United States, accused of defiling the holy land of Mecca and Medina. This new terrorism springs from an unswerving conviction that to destroy America is to do God's work.

TERRORISM IN THE UNITED STATES

In the past, American citizens were most vulnerable to terrorism and violence when traveling in foreign lands, particularly those openly hostile toward the American government.

Although American citizens continue to be prime targets of terrorism worldwide (targets in one in four terrorist acts), over the last decade not only individual citizens but also entire families have become increasingly vulnerable to and victims of terrorist actions at home. Terrorists in the United States are not always imported from other countries. Many are homegrown. For example, U.S. citizen Timothy McVeigh was convicted of perpetrating one of the single-most destructive terrorist act ever committed on U.S. soil: the bombing of a federal building in 1995, in Oklahoma. One hundred sixty-eight people died and another 467 were injured as a result of the blast. The loss of life and the devastation of this terrorist act for individuals and families will last a lifetime and beyond. Even so, the September 11 attacks struck at the very heart and soul of the American people and have been described as the worst acts of terrorism in modern history, leaving Americans feeling stunned and extremely vulnerable. For more facts and figures about terrorism in the United States, see Table 15.3.

WAR

Most experts on war agree that the intensity and frequency of wars increased in the twentieth century. For example, as the twentieth century came to a close, there had been 250 wars and 109,746,000 war-related deaths. Since the mid-twentieth century, wars have become more frequent and much more deadly. Since the mid-1940s alone, more than 23 million people have died as a result of war and another 20 million have died as a result of war-related factors. Today, wars are fought not on some distant battlefield, but deep within the homeland of the warring factions. Even when civilians are not purposefully targeted, they end up the major casualties. In the 1980s, for example, 74 percent of wartime casualties were civilians. By 1990, civilians constituted 90 percent of such casualties (Sivard et al., 1996). After nearly 5 weeks of war between Israel and Lebanon in 2006, an estimated 5,000 Lebanese civilians were killed or wounded and 1 million Lebanese were displaced. By comparison, 157 Israelis died, the

TABLE 15.3 Facts and Figures about Terrorism within U.S. Borders

1920	**September 16—New York City:** A TNT bomb planted in an unattended horse-drawn wagon exploded on Wall Street opposite the House of Morgan, killing 35 people and injuring hundreds more. Bolshevist or anarchist terrorists were believed responsible.
1975	**January 24—New York City:** A bomb set off in historic Fraunces Tavern killed 4 and injured more than 50 people. FLAN (a Puerto Rican nationalist group) claimed responsibility and the police tied 13 other bombings in the United States to the group.
1993	**February 26—New York City:** A bomb exploded in the basement garage of the World Trade Center killing 6 and injuring at least 1,040 others. Al-Qaeda involvement is suspected.
1995	**April 19—Oklahoma City:** A car bomb exploded outside the federal office building, collapsing walls and floors. One hundred sixty-eight people were killed, including 19 children. Another 467 people were injured. Timothy McVeigh and Terry Nichols were later convicted in the antigovernment plot to avenge the Branch Davidian standoff that occurred in Waco, Texas, exactly 2 years earlier.
2001	**September 11—New York City, Arlington, Virginia, and Shanksville, Pennsylvania:** Hijackers crashed two commercial jets into the twin towers of the World Trade Center; two more hijacked jets were crashed into the Pentagon and a field in rural Pennsylvania. The total estimated loss of life and missing people is estimated to be between 3,000 and 5,000 people. The Islamic al-Qaeda terrorist group was blamed.
2010	**May 1—New York City:** A car bomb is discovered in Times Square, New York City after smoke is seen coming from a vehicle. The bomb was ignited, but failed to detonate and was disarmed before it could cause any harm. Times Square was evacuated as a safety precaution. Faisal Shahzad pled guilty to placing the bomb as well as to 10 terrorism and weapons charges.
	May 10—Jacksonville, Florida: A pipe bomb explodes while approximately 60 Muslims are praying in a mosque. The attack caused no injuries.
	October 29—Two packages are found on separate cargo planes. Each package contains a bomb consisting of 300 to 400 grams (11–14 oz.) of plastic explosives and a detonating mechanism. The bombs are discovered as a result of intelligence received from Saudi Arabia's security chief. The packages, bound from Yemen to the United States, are discovered at en route stop-overs, one in England and one in Dubai in the United Arab Emirates.
2011	**January 17—Spokane, Washington:** A pipe bomb is discovered along the route of the Martin Luther King, Jr. memorial march. The bomb, a "viable device" set up to spray marchers with shrapnel and to cause multiple casualties, is defused without any injuries.

Source: Center for Defense Information, 2001b, "The International Islamic Terrorist Network," Terrorism Project (September 14): www.cdi.org/terrorism/terrorist-network-pr.cfm (2002, January 18); "Terrorists Attack in the U.S. or Against Americans." 2011. Infoplease, Pearson Education, Inc. www.infoplease.com/ipa/A0001454.html (2011, October 11).

The death, destruction, and impact of war on civilians and their families as primary victims of war is no better seen than in this picture of a Lebanese family passing by a damaged area in the southern Beirut suburb of Dayeh that was heavily bombed by Israel during the month-long conflict between Hezbollah and the Israeli Army in 2006. The stench of death and heavy dust from the clean-up permeates the area, forcing many people to don masks or to cover their faces.

majority of whom were soldiers. And by 2011, 4,683 Americans had been killed in Iraq and Afghanistan since the launch of Operation Enduring Freedom (Afghanistan) in 2001. In Iraq and Afghanistan, the casualties of war are far more numerous. Some reports place civilian deaths in Iraq between 103,000 and 112,000 since 2003; citing the rising death toll of Afghani civilians, the UN Assistance Mission in Afghanistan indicated that since 2007, 8,832 Afghani civilians had been killed (UN News Center, 2011; Reid, 2010; Iraq Body Count, 2008; Human Rights Watch, 2006a).

As these statistics suggest, the consequences of war for individuals, marriages, and families extended far beyond the borders of any one country. War causes many dire consequences for the civilian population even if they are not directly killed or injured in military strikes. They may suffer long-term injury or illness (as a result, for instance, of radiation, postconflict contact with unexploded munitions, pollution from spillage of toxic materials). People may suffer deep psychological trauma, miscarriage, bereavement, dislocation, and loss of home and property (Amnesty International, 2006) (see Strengthening Marriages and Family box).

STRENGTHENING MARRIAGES AND FAMILIES

TALKS WITH FAMILY THERAPIST JOAN ZIENTEK

Talking about Military Families

What Are the Problems That Confront Military Personnel Returning from Deployments? Many service personnel return home with profound physical, emotional, and spiritual wounds that affect their ability to reenter civilian life. Their fantasy of homecoming, of being united with their families after a long absence, is often destroyed as they struggle with the effects of posttraumatic stress disorder (PTSD), major depression, traumatic brain injury (TBI), substance abuse, and physical injuries. Trauma results when the automatic nervous system's responses of fight, flee, freeze are activated by the trauma, but are never fully released after the traumatic situation is over. During combat there is not time to stop and think, to process what is happening. Instead intense feelings have to be put aside, only later to be manifested indirectly through the symptoms of PTSD: sleep difficulties, hyper vigilance, irritability or outbursts of anger, difficulty concentrating, exaggerated startle response, and the avoidance of places, activities, or people that arouse memories of the trauma.

Many veterans suffer TBI after being hit by a roadside bomb or other explosive devices. Injuries range from mild concussions

to loss of limbs and chronic pain. These veterans need to grieve the lost part[s] of themselves as well as to grieve the other losses that ripple out, such as not being able to take a long walk on a sandy beach or participate in sports with their children. The required adjustment to these injuries is overwhelming. Such trauma affects a person's ability to absorb, control, and use sensory data. As a result our warriors come back changed persons, strangers to their families who do not know what to make of these new behaviors. The war has left them with intrusive thoughts and images, nightmares, and feelings of panic and anxiety. Riddled with guilt, anger, and confusion, they come home and feel like they do not fit in with others who haven't done and experienced the places, activities or people that arouse memories of the trauma.

What Are the Effects of War on Families? The deployment of young men and women places great challenges on families. Initially deployment demands a redistribution of roles. Parenting, previously shared by two people, now falls on the shoulders of one. The parent left behind struggles to fulfill both the role of mom and dad. Additionally, the family faces a reduced income. The emotional toll is great. Families may not hear from

loved ones for stretches at a time and they fear the worst. Young children are particularly vulnerable. They miss their mom or dad on a daily basis and do not understand where they are. Older children are fearful when they see scenes of war on the nightly news. Consequently, in addition to their own stress, the non-deployed parent has to help their children cope with their scary and confusing feelings. Since children generally take their cues from adults about how to handle a situation, parents or other caretakers must manage their own feelings as well as those of their children. It is not so much what the parent says, but what the parent does.

When the deployed parent returns home, the inevitable conflicts that come with family life, even small issues over toys scattered about the house, can evoke disproportionate responses. When spouses and children see the veteran become enraged at the sight of the child running into the street or "hitting the dirt" at a loud noise, family members react to these new behaviors by changing their own behavior. They begin to "walk on eggshells" in an attempt to reduce the triggers that the veteran fears and that cause feelings of panic and anxiety. They try to keep the house quiet, avoid

TV news programs, or family gatherings. Over time, instead of the veteran being reintegrated into the family, the family begins to take on the fragile and isolating life of the vet. The experience of war has put veterans in a very vulnerable state. Facing life and death day after day takes its toll. Now at home, veterans may find themselves avoiding situations that elicit feelings of vulnerability. A tender moment with a child or a romantic encounter with a spouse can end with an angry response. This not only confuses the child or spouse but also begins to erode the relationships, further isolating veterans and confirming their own fears and mistrust. Thus, the anger that was protection at war now jeopardizes reentry into civilian life.

Veterans also need to reenter the job market. Finding a job into today's economy is difficult in and of itself; keeping a job may present other problems. The same struggles with anger management can spill over into the workplace.

Can Therapy Help? Yes, but obstacles to getting treatment must be overcome first. Many veterans use drugs and alcohol to numb their pain and to forget the trauma. They may resist seeking help out of a fear of being labeled weak or crazy and fear talking about experiences that seem unsafe to disclose. Any therapy that is to be helpful must be premised on the idea that the veterans' behaviors are normal reactions to an unusually horrific situation. Even though there is a diagno-

sis of PTSD, made for the purposes of the mental health system, these veterans do not have a disease. They have been affected by their experiences, but they are not flawed, defective human beings. Their behaviors are a defense against experiences and feelings that were more than any human being could take in at one time. These defensive behaviors, the PTSD symptoms, were the body/mind's natural way of helping them survive. With the therapist as their guide, they can gradually let go of the defenses that they no longer need. In a nonjudgmental, safe environment where the therapist respects and values the person and all that they have experienced, the tragic effect of the war can be greatly diminished, but perhaps never "cured."

Terrorism as a weapon of war is not new. It has been used historically in domestic, regional, and international disputes. However, as Americans have found since September 11, the weapons of war are no longer just the traditional bombs and warheads of the past but increasingly include chemical and biological weapons as well. And as we have discussed, the weapons of war often have an impact on individuals and families well after the war is officially over. For example, America's use of cluster bombs in Afghanistan has a consequence similar to land mines. According to experts on the subject, at least 5 percent of such bombs do not explode on impact, becoming de facto land mines and remaining a threat to people, including civilians, who come into contact with them (Amnesty International, 2001). Moreover, during the Persian Gulf War, U.S. soldiers (women and men) were exposed to chemical warfare that has affected not only their own health but also that of their partners and children. Testifying before a Senate committee about the symptoms they suffer as a result of chemical attacks in the Persian Gulf, hundreds of soldiers reported that their spouses and children displayed the same symptoms as they do, raising the possibility that exposure to debilitating chemicals can be passed on (Soroka and Bryjak, 2000). Most often, the majority of civilian casualties of war are women and children. In addition to deaths resulting from air strikes and bombing, huge numbers of civilians have died as a result of the collapse of their country's public health system, destroyed during bombings.

Perhaps the most heinous war-related behavior, to date, is the mass rape of women and girls. For example, the Serbs not only brutalized and murdered thousands of Muslim men but they also conducted mass rapes of Muslim women and girls. Some eyewitness accounts of these atrocities as well as first-person accounts by survivors tell how women and girls (sometimes as young as age 6) were often assaulted in their own homes in front of their families, while others were taken to hotels or camps where they were locked up and raped repeatedly by soldiers. Entire villages became "rape camps," where women were raped and sodomized by as many as 20 men per night, every night. The attacks were so violent and vicious that many of the victims died. Added to this horror is that many of the women and girls who survived this assault to their humanity were held captive until impregnated by their rapists (*Ms.* magazine, 1993; Post,

1993; Bryjak and Soroka, 1994; Gelles and Levine, 1995). Mass rape as a tool of war is not unique to Bosnia. Women fleeing Kosovo also reported stories of systematic rape by Serb forces. The pattern was the same and echoed the rape horror stories that emerged from the Bosnian war: Young Albanian girls and women were separated from their families and brutally sexually assaulted (ABC News, 1999).

Historically, the sexual assault of women has been an integral part of war and conquest. What better way to conquer an enemy than to destroy families, and what better way to destroy families than to attack its most vulnerable members—women and girls. When a girl or woman is raped, she, her family, and her community are all victims. Rape is and has been used historically as a means of subduing enemies and civilians. In concert with the physical and psychological damage to individuals and whole families, faced with rape, many civilians flee their homes leaving their land and property to their attackers. Table 15.4 on page 510 presents a brief snapshot of some of the documented cases of war and mass rape in recent human history. The damage done to families as a result of the rape and impregnation of thousands of women is manifold. Women and girls who survive the physical assault of rape often are so psychologically traumatized that they never completely recover. Many of these women never marry or reproduce because of the lingering psychological damage or because they are considered damaged goods (no matter that they were raped) and are ostracized when the war is over.

Children, Terrorism, and War Children around the world bear a disproportionately high cost of war. Millions of children are caught up in conflicts in which they are not merely bystanders, but targets. Some are victims of a general onslaught against civilians; others die as part of a calculated genocide. Other children suffer the effects of sexual violence or the multiple deprivations of armed conflict that expose them to hunger or disease. Still other young people are exploited and often die as combatants in grown-up wars. It is estimated that more than 20 million children have been uprooted from their homes due to war. In the past decade alone, wars in countries such as Rwanda, Bosnia-Herzegovina, Kosovo, Mozambique, Angola, Somalia, Sudan, Zimbabwe, Afghanistan, Cambodia, and Haiti have claimed the lives of more than 2 million children; millions more

TABLE 15.4 A World of Rape: Women, War, and Rape

In ancient history, the kidnapping and rape of women were the spoils of war. In more modern times, random as well as systematic, organized rape by soldiers during armed conflict has been a common phenomenon and has occurred from Bosnia and Herzegovina to Peru to Rwanda, Bangladesh, Cambodia; Cyprus, Haiti, Liberia, Somalia, Germany, Japan, and Uganda. Women and girls have been singled out for rape, imprisonment, torture, and execution. Some examples follow.

Rape During World War I

- Rape was a weapon of terror as the German Hun marched through Belgium.
- German soldiers raped thousands of Belgian women.

Rape During World War II

- From 1937 to 1938, during the infamous "Rape of Nanking," Japanese soldiers slaughtered more than a quarter of a million people and raped 20,000 or more Chinese women, many of whom died after repeated sexual assaults. Some 200,000 sex slaves were then provided for the Japanese Army.
- Three million Polish Jews and an untold number of Russian women were raped and murdered by Nazi soldiers.
- As many as 250,000 Korean, Chinese, Manchurian, and Filipino girls and women (age 13 and up) were forcibly abducted and raped for extended periods of time by Japanese soldiers. In the waning days of World War II, Soviet soldiers brutalized and raped 2 million German women.

Rape During Recent Wars

- During the 1971 civil war between Bangladesh and Pakistan, Pakistani soldiers raped more than 280,000 Bangali girls and women.
- During the U.S. and Vietnamese War, American soldiers gang-raped Vietnamese women and girls.
- More than 20,000 Muslim girls and women were raped during the conflict in the former Yugoslavia in Bosnia primarily as part of an organized Serbian program of cultural genocide.
- It is estimated that Iraqi soldiers raped at least 5,000 Kuwaiti women during Iraq's invasion of Kuwait.
- During the civil war in Rwanda, as many as 500,000 women and girls suffered brutal forms of sexual violence, including gang-rape and sexual mutilation, after which many of them were killed.
- During the Sierra Leone civil war (1991–2002), more than 50,000 women and girls were raped.
- In Algeria, the women of entire villages have been raped and killed. It is estimated that approximately 1,600 girls and young women have been kidnapped and held as sexual slaves.
- In ongoing conflicts in various countries in Sub-Saharan Africa, an untold number of women and girls have been raped and many were killed afterward. For example, as the Congo's army and myriad of militias do battle, the rape of women and girls has become a defining feature of the conflict. In one year alone (2009), almost 18,000 women were raped.

Source: George J. Bryjak and Michael P. Soroka, 1994, *Sociology: Cultural Diversity in a Changing World* (Needham Heights, MA: Allyn and Bacon): 300–301; Michael P. Soroka and George J. Bryjak, 1999, *Social Problems: A World at Risk* (Needham Heights, MA: Allyn and Bacon); B. A. Robinson, 2008, "Rape of Women During Wartime: Before, During, and Since World War II," Religious Tolerance. (May 3): www.religioustolerance.org/war_rape.htm (2008, September 11); The Economist. 2011. "Violence Against Women: War's Overlooked Victims." (January 13). *The Economist.* www.economist.com/node/17900482 (2011, October 10).

have died from war-induced malnutrition and disease, and about 6 million have been seriously injured or permanently disabled. A million or more children have been orphaned or separated from their families; some 10 million suffer psychological trauma and countless other children have been forced to witness or even to take part in horrifying acts of violence (UNICEF, 2011b).

Children are the victims of war in many ways. Thousands are killed in the indiscriminate bombing and shelling of their homes, schools, or playing fields; thousands are or have been subject to deliberate and arbitrary killings at the hands of armed political groups. And many children have been killed or maimed by the millions of landmines (1 for every 20 children around the world) and cluster munitions that litter their countries (UNICEF, 2011b). Sometimes children are deliberately used or targeted in war. In 2006, for example, Hezbollah militia were accused of using children (and women) as human shields in the war with Israel. Not only are children driven from their homes, killed, maimed, sexually abused, or exploited in other ways during wars and ethnic conflicts but also, in many conflict situations, children are used as soldiers to supplement adult armies and militias. In recent years, in more than 40 countries, including in Latin America, the Middle East, Asia, and Africa, thousands of children under age 18, some as young as 7, have been routinely used in this way. According to a published report on child soldiers produced by a coalition of groups against the use of children as soldiers, more than 500,000 children, girls and boys, under age 18 are in government armies or guerrilla groups around the world; at any one time, more than one-half (300,000) of them are in actual combat. In Uganda, for example, during more than 20 years of civil war, an estimated 35,000 Ugandan children have been abducted by the army and trained as soldiers to kill on behalf of the army rebels. Children are considered a cheap and expendable commodity, and the lighter weight of today's weapons makes it easier to arm them.

The dangers these children face are not only on the frontlines of war but also in myriad other situations. For example, children are routinely used as spies, messengers, sentries, porters, servants, and sexual slaves; they are often used to lay and clear land mines or are conditioned to commit atrocities even against their own families and communities (UNICEF, 2010; Coalition to Stop the Use of Child Soldiers, 2001).

The good news (if there can be good news about children in armed conflict and the abuse of children) is that, due in part to the work of UNICEF and human rights organizations and groups around the world, 73 countries to date have adopted legislation that prohibits the recruitment of children under the age of 18. In addition, 80 countries, including the United States, have signed an international agreement barring children in armed conflict. On the other side of this coin, however, thousands of children are still being recruited or forced to fight in armies in various African countries. In Colombia, at least 14,000 children are fighting with both guerrilla groups and antirebel paramilitaries, and in Sri Lanka, a guerrilla army is still recruiting or drafting girls and boys into the army, some of whom are drafted specifically to undertake suicide missions (UNICEF, 2010; 2011b).

The psychological trauma experienced by children under conditions of war is unprecedented. For example, a UNICEF survey of 3,000 Rwandan children in 1995 found that during the genocidal massacres in their country in 1994, 95 percent of these children had witnessed massacres, over one-third had seen the murders of family members, almost all of the children believed they would die, almost two-thirds were threatened with death,

and over 80 percent of them said they had had to hide to protect themselves, sometimes up to 8 weeks or longer (UNICEF, 2002). In the United States, the terrorist attacks of September 11 left many children with questions about things that many small children in this country typically had not had to face in the past. Buildings on fire, buildings falling down, daddy or mommy or both suddenly yanked from their lives—either missing or dead. The parallels, thus, between children around the world in the face of war is unprecedented.

This discussion of the well-being of children has focused on the impact of war, violence, and terrorism, but they are not the only threats to children. Although there are vast cultural differences around the world, cross-culturally it is generally assumed that families have the primary responsibility for protecting and caring for their children. However, as the Applying the Sociological Imagination box shows, reality is often quite different. As this chapter makes clear, around the world natural disasters, economic disruptions, diseases, substance abuse, racism, terrorism, and armed conflict are disrupting the lives of millions of children every day. In many places in the world, children find themselves in environments made dangerous as a result of these events. Additionally, some children are at risk because their parents are unwilling or unable to care for them properly, often due to problems with drugs and alcohol. Creating policies and structures that ensure that orphans and children at risk have a safe and permanent home is an issue that challenges government officials and child advocates everywhere. Foster care and adoption are two common responses to this need.

APPLYING THE SOCIOLOGICAL IMAGINATION

THE VULNERABILITY OF CHILDREN AROUND THE WORLD

Moments in America for Children

- Every second a public school student is suspended.
- Every 20 seconds a child is arrested.
- Every 35 seconds a child is confirmed as abused or neglected.
- Every 35 seconds a baby is born into poverty.

For more of these moments, go to www.childrensdefense.org/site/pageserver?pagename=Research_National_Data_Moments.

Facts on Children around the World

- More than 1 billion children suffer from a lack of proper nutrition,

safe drinking water, decent sanitation facilities, health care services, shelter, education, and information.

- The exact number of street children is impossible to count, but estimates are that tens of millions exist across the world.
- It is estimated that trafficking affects about 1.2 million children each year.

For more facts on the world's children, go to www.unicef.org/voy/explore/sowc06/explore_2463.html

As you visit these sites and reflect on the status of millions of children in the United States and

around the world, what is your reaction? How is it that so many children are uncared for and unprotected? What are the consequences for the children and for their societies, if these trends continue? Are these inevitable problems, or can the situations for these children be improved? To help you answer this last question, visit the United Nations Web site (www.mdgs.un.org/unsd/mdg/Default.aspx) to assess to what degree millennium development goals are being reached and to find out what various countries, including the United States, are doing to meet these goals.

Meeting the Needs of Children: Foster Care and Adoption

The idea behind foster care is that substitute families will provide short-term care until the children can be adopted or returned to their biological parents. Foster care is practiced in many different ways throughout the world, depending on the culture and the structures in place. Although kinship or informal fostering by family or friends occurs to some degree in all societies, it is especially normative in developing countries.

Here in the United States, in 2010, 408,425 children were without permanent homes and living in foster care, 48 percent female and 52 percent male, drawn from major racial and ethnic groups: African Americans (29 percent), White (41 percent), Latina/o (21 percent), Native American/Alaskan Native (2 percent), Asian (1 percent), multiple races, unknown/unable to determine (7 percent) (Administration for Children and Families, 2011). Many of these children were removed from their homes as a result of being neglected, abused, or abandoned. Many children remain in foster care for extended periods of time; others move in and out of the system several times over. This is especially true for older children, those with behavioral or emotional problems, and children of color. In 2010, the median length of stay in foster care was 14 months; the average length of stay was 25 months. Children move out of foster care in a variety of ways. Of those leaving foster care in 2010, 51 percent were reunited with their parents, 21 percent were adopted, 8 percent were living with other relatives, and 11 percent were emancipated (Administration for Children and Families, 2011).

PROBLEMS CONFRONTING FOSTER CARE

Whether it is the United States or some other country, the foster care system is plagued by similar problems. The needs of children in care are becoming increasingly complex and specialized at a time when there are limited resources available to meet their needs. Welfare workers continue to turn over at a high rate, and many are underpaid, poorly trained, overworked, and demoralized. The pool of foster families is inadequate, especially the kind qualified to care for children with multiple problems. Permanent adoptive homes for older, handicapped, and healthy children of color are in short supply. For example, there is a shortage of at least 10,000 foster parents across the United Kingdom (Tapsfield and Collier, 2005). And, in sub-Sahara Africa the number of available adult caregivers has been drastically reduced through illness and disease.

Numerous studies show a variety of outcomes for children in foster care. On the positive side, many children benefit by being placed in a safe environment where they receive the medical and mental health services they need. Many find adults they can trust and who are good role models for later life (Whiting and Lee, 2003). On the negative side, however, studies have found poor school outcomes among foster children compared to the general population (Christian, 2003) and higher levels of mental impairment (Landsverk and Garland, 2000). Additionally, the prospects for many children who remain in foster care long-term are not good. After aging out of foster care, one in four will be incarcerated within two years of leaving foster care, one in five will become homeless after 18, only half will graduate from high school, and less than 3 percent over the age of 25 earn a college degree (Casey, 2007).

Prior to 1975, agencies discouraged foster parents from adopting the children in their care but reversed themselves later as they recognized the benefits of continuity for children who could not be returned to their birth parents. Foster parent adoptions have increased dramatically over the last decade. In 2010, 26,308 (or 53 percent) of the children adopted from foster care that year were adopted by their foster parents (Administration for Children and Families, 2011).

BECOMING PARENTS THROUGH ADOPTION

There are several important differences between foster care and adoption. In adoption, parents assume full legal, financial, and decision-making responsibility for a child and incorporate the child as a permanent member of their own family. Adoption has a long history. The early Greeks, Romans, Egyptians, and Babylonians had adoption systems. Informal adoptions whereby orphaned children were taken into the homes of others existed in early America as well. However, it was not until the mid-nineteenth century that it became enshrined in our legal system. Adoption is highly regarded in the United States. In a 2002 survey, 94 percent of Americans had very or somewhat favorable opinions regarding adoption, up from 90 percent in 1997. Thirty-nine percent had very or somewhat seriously considered adopting a child, up from 36 percent in 1997, and 64 percent said that a family member or close friend was adopted, had adopted, or put a child up for adoption, up from 57 percent 5 years earlier (National Adoption Attitudes Survey, 2002). According to census data there were 1.8 million adopted children (about 2 percent of all children) in 2007; of those, 37 percent were White, 23 percent Black, 16 percent Asian, 15 percent Lainas/os and 9 percent other races (Vandivere, Malm, and McKlindon, 2010).

Individuals and couples wishing to adopt have several options. In *public adoptions* children in the public child welfare system are placed in permanent homes by government-operated agencies. *Private adoptions* involve the placement of children in nonrelatives' homes through the services of a licensed nonprofit or for-profit agency. In *independent adoptions*, children are placed in the homes of either relatives or nonrelatives directly by the birth parents or through services of a medical doctor, a member of the clergy, an attorney, or a licensed or unlicensed facilitator. Independent adoptions are illegal in some states. In *kinship* adoptions, children are placed in relatives' homes with or without the services of a public agency. In *stepparent adoptions,* children are adopted by the spouse of

ent. Today adoptions can be open or closed. In a
_on,_ the adoptive parents and the birth parents do
open adoptions, however, the two parties meet and
rk out the process of adoption. The birth mother
ake an active role in selecting the adoptive parents.
ases, the adoptive parents will invite the birth mother
th them during her pregnancy. Some open adoptions
acterized by ongoing contact with the birth mother.
nt of the contact may vary from periodic reports of the
rogress to the birth mother's integration into the family
end or **fictive kin,** in which kinship terms are attributed
onrelatives.

WHO CAN ADOPT?

In the past, adoption agencies considered only married couples as suitable candidates to adopt children. Around 1978, however, single-parent adoptions became possible. Since then there has been a steady increase in such adoptions, especially of children with special needs. In 2010, 28 percent of adoptions of children in foster care were single women; 3 percent were single men; 67 percent were married couples; and 2 percent were unmarried couples (Administration for Children and Families, 2011).

In recent years, lesbian and gay singles have been able to adopt. However, the situation remains more complicated for same-sex couples. Although only two states explicitly prohibit same-sex couples from adopting (Utah and Mississippi), they still face many obstacles. Chief among them is the prohibition of same-sex marriage. In many states like Ohio where same-sex marriage is not allowed, second-parent adoptions by unmarried couples is not allowed unless the first parent renounces her or his right to the child. Thus, children being raised by same-sex parents often lack the rights and protections enjoyed by children of heterosexual parents. Nevertheless, the number of adoptions among same-sex couples is growing. In 2009, approximately 19 percent of same-sex couples reported having an adopted child, up from 8 percent in 2000 (Tavernise, 2011b). Public support, at least in one state (Virginia), is on their side. A recent poll found that 55 percent of respondents said it should be legal for same-sex couples to adopt Waldman, 2011).

INTERNATIONAL ADOPTIONS

Because of a shortage of available healthy babies in the United States, many people have turned to international adoptions. In 2009, approximately 15,000 foreign children were adopted by Americans. The majority of international adoptions involve infants of color from economically disadvantaged countries. The most common countries of origin for internationally adopted children were, in order, China, Ethiopia, Russia, South Korea, Guatemala, Ukraine, Vietnam, Haiti, India, and Kazakhstan (Howard and John, 2011).

Although the vast majority of international adoptions are successfully completed and bring great joy to the adopting parents and children (see the Family Profile box on page 514), they can be risky. There have been allegations of baby selling

in a number of countries, so prospective adopting parents are advised to be well informed about the agency and/or individuals they are dealing with and to seek appropriate legal guidance throughout the process. In general, there are many bureaucratic regulations (both in the United States and abroad) that must be met before the proceedings are finalized and the child is allowed to leave the country. These adoption proceedings are costly, ranging from $15,000 to $35,000, depending on the country. The cost includes legal fees in both countries and sometimes the payment of "contributions" or bribes to various agencies and officials, putting international adoptions beyond the reach of many people. Some agencies are not up front in revealing important information about the children being placed for adoption. For example, in the past some of the international children available for adoption have been institutionalized for extensive periods of time and, as a result, their emotional development has been stunted, making it difficult for them to bond with their new parents; others may have acute illnesses that are not disclosed to the adoptive parents.

Adoptions may be terminated either through disruption, an adoption process that ends after the child is placed in an adoptive home but before the adoption is legally finalized, or dissolution, an adoption that ends after it is legally finalized. In both cases the child is returned to (or enters into) foster care or placement with new adoptive parents. Parents who make this decision do not do so lightly and they suffer pain, guilt, embarrassment, grief, and a sense of failure. Children suffer, too. They may become even more emotionally withdrawn and, as a result, become more difficult to place with another family. Although figures are not available for disruptions or dissolutions involving international adoptions, social workers do report seeing an increase. They attribute this pattern to the increased number of children coming from institutionalized settings after being abused, neglected, or abandoned, as well as an increase in the number of older children placed for adoption. Adoptions of children with special needs are more likely to be disrupted than children without special needs. Often a major contributing factor to the difficulties parents face is their lack of information about where to go for services and/or inadequate resources to pay for them when available. The older the child and the more emotional and physical problems the child has, the higher the disruption rate.

TRANSRACIAL (INTERRACIAL) ADOPTIONS

Race is also a factor in the politics and policies of the adoption process. With the exception of Native American children, transracial adoption was largely unheard until the 1950s. The prevailing policy and practice of adoption agencies was race-matching in the belief that this was in the best interest of the child and the community. However, this began to change in the 1960s with the civil rights movement. Increased attention began to focus on children of color who were placed in foster care. During the 1960s and early 1970s there was a rapid growth in transracial adoptions. Between 1969 and 1974 more than 80 percent of the Native American children adopted were placed with White families. By 1972, approximately 10,000 African American children had been

THE WILLIS AND WOLF FAMILIES

Nina and Reid Willis; Orin, Shiri, and Nomi Wolf

Length of Relationship: 19 years

Challenges in Parenting

Orna and I have been married for 19 years and have two children, Shiri (age 31) and Nina (age 10). I like to say that we have two only children because neither of them has known what it's like to live in the same household with a sibling. When Orna and I married, my biggest challenge was trying to figure out my role as a new parent to my then 13-year-old stepdaughter. Through trial and error, I discovered my best chance of success with Shiri was not to try to force my will upon her but rather to make myself worthy of her trust. One of the first things I asked of Shiri is that she give me permission to refer to her as my daughter, not stepdaughter, although I did not expect that she refer to me as her dad. I also hit on the idea of never referring to Orna as "your mom"; I always used Mom. In kind, Shiri started saying Mom, not my mom. If these distinctions sound minor, they are not. They had a huge impact on our relationship, which was rocky for

a year or two. Through patience and persistence we grew to appreciate each other and to build a loving relationship, which had a predictably positive impact on the marriage.

When Shiri was 21 years old, a time when most middle-aged couples are feeling a little guilty about enjoying their freedom from their children, Orna and I decided to adopt a baby. Because of our age, we looked into international adoptions. We discovered an orphanage in Cambodia founded by a wonderful pediatrician. The process of adoption was arduous, but patience and persistence again served us well. A few months into the adoption process we got the call informing us of the arrival of a baby girl that was ours if we wanted her. We said "yes" and when we received her picture the following week, we fell in love with her on the spot. From that moment, Nina was our second daughter.

We live in a highly diverse neighborhood in Philadelphia. Nina's friends are Jewish and Christian, Black, White, Asian, and ethnically mixed. Their parents range in age from the

twenties to late fifties. Although Nina has experienced some taunting by other children because of the color of her skin, thankfully, those incidents are rare. A challenge that is particularly common with international adoptions is the capacity to instill into the child the uniqueness of her or his culture of origin. We want Nina to be proud of her Cambodian heritage. We filled her room with pictures, books, and mementos from Cambodia and we read and told her stories about her native land. We enrolled her in a Cambodian dance class so she could meet and play with other Cambodian children, receive instruction from a Cambodian teacher, and become more closely connected with her Cambodian heritage. Nina is a proud Cambodian-Jewish-American; we are already making plans to return to Cambodia in celebration of Nina's Bat Mitzvah in 2014.

Shiri and Nina are surprisingly close given their 21+-year age difference. Shiri lives in Brooklyn with her husband Orin and their beautiful baby, Nomi. It is only a 2-hour drive, but we simply don't see each other as much as we would like. When I was a child, I developed a very close connection with my grandmother because we spent so much time together. I ask myself what can I do to bridge this distance, to ensure a strong connection with my granddaughter. A friend suggested that I start writing letters to Nomi. Of course, the letter writing will be a trifle one-sided for a time.

Just as we are new grandparents, and Shiri and Orin are new parents, Nina is a new aunt. She is proud of her awesome title. Along with Nina's ascent into aunthood, we have seen other signs of maturity. For one, she has begun to perceive Orna and me as older parents. We hope that it will not be a source of embarrassment for her. Nina has also become keenly aware of her Asian heritage and her adopted by White couples (cited in McRoy, 1989). Alarmed by this trend, the National Association of Black Social Workers and some Native American organizations came out against transracial adoptions, raising concerns about the possible adjustment problems these children might have and the loss of these children to their original communities—what they saw as "cultural genocide." This controversy led many agencies to revert to race matching for adoption placements; in the 1980s only about 8 percent of adoptions were interracial (Bachrach et al., 1990).

In the 1990s, however, the controversy took another turn. Some public officials, believing that race-matching practices deny thousands of children of color a stable and permanent home, pushed for legislation to limit the practice and to reduce the length of time children wait to be adopted or placed in foster care. In response to these pressures, Congress passed the Multiethnic Placement Act of 1994. The law prohibits any agency that receives federal funds from denying a foster care or adoption placement solely on the basis of race, color, or national origin. Since the passage of that legislation, the rates of transracial adoptions began to move upward. In 2008, 21.5 percent of adopted children were of a different race than their adoptive parent (Federal Interagency Forum on Child and Family Statistics, 2011a). Besides this legislation, several other factors contributed to this increase. Attitudes became more accepting of multicultural families as the number of international adoptions grew.

Most of the objections to transracial adoptions center on the possible adjustment these children might have as well as issues of identity. The first concern has not materialized. Research shows that adopted children raised in interracial homes generally adjust quite well (Morrison, 2004). However, research findings on identity issues are more mixed. A study of transracially and intraracially adopted young adults found no statistical difference in problem behaviors between the two groups. However, transracial adoptees living in mostly White neighborhoods were more likely to feel discomfort about their appearance than transracial adoptees who lived in more racially mixed neighborhoods, and those young adults who felt discomfort and experienced discrimination were more likely to have behavioral problems (Feigelman, 2000). Similarly, other researchers have found that when adoptive families encourage the adoptive child's participation in multicultural and multiracial activities, identify issues are not a significant problem (Simon

and Altstein, 2000). Yet anecdotal evidence suggests it may be more complicated than that. For example, Rodney Williams, age 29, was adopted by a White couple when he was 3 days old. He is still searching for where he belongs. He said, "Black people think I'm arrogant, because I talk 'proper.' White people? 'You're not like most Black people.' That's what I get" (quoted in Gammage, 2006).

As we saw earlier, racism is still a major problem in the United States and there is concern that transracial adoptees may not be as fully prepared to cope with it as children of color raised in same-race homes. Until more progress is made in improving race relations, transracial adoptions are likely to remain controversial and one-sided. With rare exception have people of color been able to adopt White children. With an increasing number of children living in biracial or multiracial families, either as a result of adoption or birth, racial identity is fast becoming one of the most urgent and controversial issues facing marriages, families, schools, the work

Regina Bush hugs her two adopted daughters after Stacey's adoption became final in Flint, Michigan, in 1998. Bush's adoption of 9-year-old Stacy (right) followed months of legal struggle. Stacey's adoption attracted media because it is one of the relatively rare cases involving the adoption of a white child by an African American parent.

force, and society at large today. Given the nature of U.S. race relations and the demographic changes that ushered in the twenty-first century, it is imperative that we reexamine the manner in which people are categorized racially and ethnically and then treated on the basis of these categories.

Supporting Children and Families Here and Abroad

Finally, as we have seen, families everywhere are experiencing the challenges of living in a global world. After reading this chapter, you may be tempted to think that the world is out of control, that the challenges humans face are so complex and overwhelming that positive change is not only improbable but next to impossible. This kind of thinking can give rise to feelings of depression and hopelessness. However, history teaches us that problems can be solved; that concerned people can and do meet a wide variety of human challenges. An example from the past comes quickly to mind. Legalized discrimination—for instance, the apartheid system in South Africa or the "Jim Crow" system of racial segregation in the southern United States—has been abolished. Clearly this has not eliminated racism, but it is a major step forward and an example of people working individually and collectively to find solutions.

Although we have pointed out some horrific problems that exist locally, nationally, and globally, there are movements to alleviate many of them. In 2000, world leaders adopted 8 Millennium Development Goals to be achieved by 2015: eradicate extreme poverty and hunger, achieve universal primary education, promote greater gender equality and empower women, reduce child mortality, improve maternal health, combat HIV/AIDS, malaria and other diseases, ensure environmental sustainability, and develop a global partnership for development (United Nations Development Programme, 2010). These problems are complex and multifaceted; thus, resolutions will not be easy or accomplished fully by 2015 but progress is being made. Many of the factors contributing to these problems are structural in nature and require structural changes to solve them. Space permits only a quick example of how lives are being improved by international efforts. It is estimated that malaria costs Africa over $12 billion a year in terms of costs of health care, working days lost to sickness, days lost in education, and loss of investment and tourism dollars not to mention the pain and grief of families who lose loved ones to the disease. Additionally, African parents compensate for high child mortality by having large families that limits

Writing Your Own Script

THINKING GLOBALLY

At the end of one century and well into a new one, we find ourselves living in a world filled with contradictions. On the one hand, there are deep conflicts, tensions, and forms of extreme inequality. On the other hand, technological innovations provide us with amazing power to improve our lives for the better. One thing is certain, however. Human beings everywhere are, for better or worse, part of a common future. The choices we make as individuals and in groups will shape the quality of life we all experience.

Questions to Consider

1. Given the rate of change taking place around the world, what are you doing and can you do in the future to prepare yourself for living in a global society? Do you think any new political structures are warranted in terms of global interdependence? If so, what kind of structures can you envision?

2. What do you think the advantages and disadvantages are of the worldwide migration currently taking place? Would you consider migrating to another country? Why or why not? If you did migrate to another country, what problems do you think you and your family might encounter as "outsiders?" How do you think you would feel in such a situation?

3. Have you or any one in your family ever been discriminated against? What do you think the basis of that discrimination was? What was your reaction? Did you ever, consciously or unconsciously, discriminate against someone else? Why or why not? Can you as an individual or can your family do anything to eliminate discrimination in your communities or in the larger society? Explain. Do societies have a moral responsibility to end all forms of discrimination?

4. What do you think of the movement to allow transracial adoptions? Would you consider adopting a child from another racial or ethnic group? Why or why not? Do you think transracial adoptions are good for the adopted child? If you were raising a child from another race or ethnic group, how would you prepare her or him to live in a society that frequently undervalues her or his group?

5. If you could change anything about the society (or the world) in which we live today, what would it be? How would you want things changed? Why? Do you think any other people share your view? What could you begin to do now to help bring this change about?

their ability to accumulate household savings. The international community provided funding, personnel, and expertise to help local officials develop awareness and educational programs in their countries. Such help enabled 11 countries in Africa to slash their malaria cases and deaths by more than 50 percent through the distribution of insecticide-treated nets, interventions with indoor residual spraying programs, the expansion of rapid diagnostic tests allowing clearer detection of malaria cases and faster and more appropriate treatment (Roll Back Malaria, 2011). Governments at all levels need to involve both professional and laypeople alike in meaningful dialogue and action to confront the problems facing families around the globe.

SUMMARY

Increasingly, the lives of people around the world are intertwined. Any one nation's problems—unemployment, substance abuse, disease, inequality, racism, sexism, inadequate resources, terrorism, war, and displacement—cut across cultural and geographic boundaries. The process of globalization is not new. What is different today is the depth and breadth of the process. For the past three decades or so, global competition for new markets has intensified. Families in wealthy and poor countries alike are hearing that they must adapt to this increased competition, yet the benefits and the burdens of adapting are not shared evenly.

These inequities are apparent in the health of a population as well as in its access to health care. Infant mortality rates tend to be higher and life expectancy rates tend to be lower in developing countries than they are in developed countries. Even today billions of people are without clean water or adequate sanitation services, leaving them vulnerable to diseases and early death. Even in the United States, where per capita health expenditures are the highest of any of the industrialized countries, 16.3 percent of the population (49.9 million people) do not have health insurance.

Few people realize that the experience of disability is typical rather than rare. Disability is a normal part of life affecting people of all ages. More than one billion people, about 15 percent of the world's population, have some form of disability, almost one-third of whom are children. In the United States, approximately 54 million people (representing 17 percent of the population) have some level of disability.

Another challenge that many families face is coping with members who are addicted to alcohol or other drugs. The abuse of alcohol and other drugs creates numerous economic and health problems and often causes major restructuring of family roles, in some cases leading to the death of a family member or to the dissolution of the family.

All families must cope with the loss of loved ones. People need to be able to express their sorrow and to receive social support as they do their grief work. Because some social relationships are either unrecognized or socially disapproved, many individuals experience disenfranchised grief.

Although many forces impinge on family life in the United States, racism continues to be one of the major challenges to the well-being of many families, particularly families of color. Despite improvements in the life conditions of some families of color, the majority remain disadvantaged by racism and discrimination. Because of the persistence of racism and discrimination in major U.S. institutions such as education and the work force, families of color are forced to bear a disproportionately higher amount of poverty, unemployment and underemployment, welfare dependency, dropping out of school, infant mortality, illness, and death.

Racism, prejudice, ethnic discrimination racism, xenophobia, hate, and violence are not limited to the United States but can be found in a number of countries around the world. Wherever racial and ethnic conflicts are played out, the consequences for marriages and families have been devastation and despair.

Although America is known as a land of immigrants, the increasing number of unauthorized immigrants into the country, especially unauthorized Mexican immigrants, have spawn both a spirited public and legislative debate about unauthorized immigrants as well as a growing "illegal immigrant" movement to keep unauthorized immigrants in the country.

One of the most significant global demographic trends of the twentieth century was the massive immigration of people from one country to another all over the world. Sometimes this immigration is voluntary, in that people leave their homelands seeking economic opportunities in other lands. All too often, however, the massive movement of people from one land to another has been and continues to be the result of communal violence and war. Current statistic indicate that 43.7 million people are displaced worldwide.

In addition to the challenge of racism and discrimination, families around the world are confronted with gangs and gang violence. Although street violence and crime decreased in the United States in the mid-1990s, the rate of juvenile or youth violence and criminal behavior has increased at an alarming rate. In addition, of increasing concern to parents is the violence that occurs inside the nation's schools. Over the last decade, there have been a number of highly publicized violent crimes committed on American school grounds, the overwhelming majority of which involved White male student shooters.

Terrorism, war, and displacement also take a tremendous toll on family life. The terrorist events of September 11, 2001, dramatically demonstrated Americans' increasing vulnerability to terrorist acts at home.

More than 408,000 children are currently without permanent homes in this country alone. Many of these children were removed from their homes as a result of being neglected or abused as a result of parental addiction and escalating poverty. Only a small percentage of children currently in foster care are eligible for adoption. There are many controversies surrounding adoption today. Adoption costs are high, thus prohibiting many poor and working-class families, especially those of color, from being able to adopt.

Although these challenges sometimes seem insurmountable, history teaches us that problems can be solved and that concerned people can and do meet a variety of challenges.

KEY TERMS

post traumatic stress disorder	drug	grief	racism	refugees
global interdependence	drug use	mourning	individual racism	fictive kin
health	drug abuse	disenfranchised grief	institutional racism	
disability	alcoholism	hospice	ethnic cleansing	
	bereavement	xenophobia	terrorism	

QUESTIONS FOR STUDY AND REFLECTION

1. Throughout this chapter, we have examined a number of international issues (globalization, worldwide inequalities, health issues, substance abuse, death and dying, racism, street violence, terrorism, war, foster care, and adoption). How appropriate is it to consider these issues in a marriages and families text? Would you add to this list or eliminate any issues? Explain. Does the United States—and, by extension, its citizens—have a responsibility to be involved in what happens to families in other parts of the world? Explain.

2. Search the Internet for sites pertaining to either disabilities or the status and welfare of children. What do these sites tell us about disabilities? The status of children? Compare the information of different countries around the globe. Write an essay on either topic that includes a comparative analysis of data you find and that ends with a policy statement on the subject.

3. It is often said that the United States is a death-denying society, that we remove the dying to hospitals and nursing homes and use euphemisms for death—she has "passed on," he has "gone to a better place"—and that, consequently, Americans are not well prepared for this last stage of life. Do you agree or disagree? Explain. Do you think that televised reports of death in the Middle East and elsewhere are changing attitudes towards death and dying? Explain. How much experience have you had with death or dying? Should there be death education in the schools? What should people do to prepare for their own death or that of a loved one? Explain.

4. Hypothetically, you and a number of college students from across the country are asked to develop and implement a youth summit on the health and well-being of the world's children. What are some of the issues or themes you would suggest for the summit? Who would you suggest should be involved? Are there people who should not be involved? Explain.

ADDITIONAL RESOURCES

SOCIOLOGICAL

BONILLA-SILVA, EDUARDO. 2003. *Racism Without Racists: Color-Blind Racism and the Persistence of Racial Inequality in the United States.* Lanham, MD: Rowman and Littlefield. A probing analysis of White racial attitudes that challenges the persistent individualistic interpretations of race and racism by leading survey researchers. The author presents compelling evidence of persistent prejudice and discrimination in American society and the often subtle, but no less compelling, everyday racism faced by various groups of color.

MILANOVIC, BRANCO. 2010. *The Haves and the Have Nots.* New York: Basic Books. Using history, literature and today's news stories, economist Branko Milanovic discusses why inequality matters, how it damages our economic prospects, and how it can threaten the foundations of the social order that we take for granted. Entertaining and serious at the same time, he teaches us not only how to think about inequality, but why we should.

STEINBERG, GAIL, and BETH HALL. 2000. *Inside Transracial Adoption.* Indianapolis, IN: Perspective Press. The authors, both adoptive moms, tackle the challenges, emotions, responsibilities, and joys of transracial adoptions and insist that adoptive parents face the realities of racism in the United States.

TRASH, BAHIRA SHERIF. 2009. *Globalization and Families: Accelerated Systemic Social Change.* New York: Springer. According to Professor Trask, globalization has profound implications for how families make major decisions about work, care, movement, and identity. She examines the linkages between globalization and gender identities, work-family relationships and conceptualizations of children, youth and the elderly.

FILM

Sin Nombre (Nameless). 2009. A young Honduran woman, Sayra, joins her father on a dangerous journey across the Latin American countryside to seek a new life in America. Along the way she crosses paths with a teenaged Mexican gang member (El Casper) who is maneuvering to outrun his violent past. This film is an eye-opening look at the brutal real world that people experience when traveling across Mexico to enter the United States.

The Help. 2011. Set in Jackson, Mississippi in the turbulent 1960s, the film focuses on the fascinating and complex relationships between women from vastly different social worlds. Skeeter Phelan, daughter of a well-connected family, returns from college determined to be a writer. She slowly recognizes inequities in the social interactions between her country club friends and the Black maids on whom they both rely and mistrust. Skeeter writes the stories of the Black women trusted to raise White children but not trusted to handle the household silver or use the family bathroom.

LITERARY

Pausch, Randy. 2008. *The Last Lecture*. New York: Hyperion. Diagnosed with terminal cancer, a computer science professor gives his last lecture but it wasn't about dying—it was about living.

De Rosnay, Tattiana. 2007. *Sarah's Key*. In July 1942, Sarah, age 10, is about to be arrested with her Jewish family by the French police in the Vel' d'Hiv section of Paris. She locks her younger brother in a closet to keep him safe, believing she will return in a few hours to release him. Sixty years later, an American journalist living in Paris is asked to write an article about the mass removal of Jews from their homes and discovers a trail of long-hidden family secrets that connects her to Sarah and the tragedies and injustices of that time.

INTERNET

www.who.int/en The World Health Organization site contains excellent information on environmental, health, and human rights issues around the world and offers links to many governmental and nongovernmental sites that also deal with these issues.

www.globalissues.org This Web site looks into global issues that affect everyone and attempts to show how most of them are interrelated. It provides links to news articles and Web sites on a variety of social issues such as human rights, geopolitics, poverty and globalization, the economy, and the environment.

www.un.org/en/ The United Nations is an international organization founded after World War II. It is committed to maintaining international peace and security and improving living standards and human rights for people across the world.

www.worldfamilyorganization.org The World Family Organization's goal is to promote policies to bring about better life conditions for all families. It is now part of the United Nations; it provides resources and links to other international organizations.

Succeed with MyFamilyLab®
www.myfamilylab.com

Watch. Explore. Read. The New MyFamilyLab is designed just for you. Each chapter features a pre-test and post-test to help you learn and review key concepts and terms. Experience Marriages and Families in action with dynamic visual activities, videos, and readings to enhance your learning experience.

Here are a few activities you will find for this chapter.

Watch on **myfamilylab.com**

Video clips feature important concepts in the study of Marriages and Families. Watch:
- Planning for the End of Life

Explore on **myfamilylab.com**

Social Explorer is an interactive application that allows you to explore Census data through interactive maps. Explore the Social Explorer Activity:
- Disability in the U.S.

Read on **myfamilylab.com**

MyFamilyLab includes primary source readings from classic and contemporary sociologists from around the world. Read:
- Gelles and Cavanaugh: "Association is Not Causation: Alcohol and Other Drugs Do Not Cause Violence"

Sexual Dysfunctions and Sexually Transmitted Infections

SEXUAL DYSFUNCTIONS

Sexual dysfunction is a broad term that includes a number of specific problems. We describe the most common sexual dysfunctions found among women and men, distinguishing them as much as possible along gender lines.

SEXUAL DYSFUNCTIONS IN WOMEN

The most common sexual dysfunctions found among women are related to penetration and orgasm.

Inhibited sexual excitement refers to a lack of erotic response or feeling during sexual activity. A woman who experiences inhibited sexual excitement does not show any of the physiological manifestations of arousal such as expansion of the vagina, nipple erection, or vaginal lubrication. Consequently, sexual intercourse might be uncomfortable or even painful. In some cases a woman may never have experienced arousal (*a primary* dysfunction). In other cases a woman may have experienced arousal in the past but is not currently experiencing it (a *secondary* dysfunction).

Anorgasmia refers to the inability of a woman to reach orgasm. Prior to 1970, this dysfunction along with several others was lumped under the term *frigidity*. There are many forms of anorgasmia. In *primary anorgasmia*, no matter what type of stimulation has been tried, a woman has never experienced orgasm. In *secondary anorgasmia*, a woman has been regularly orgasmic in the past but is not currently orgasmic. A third category, *situational anorgasmia*, describes a woman who experiences orgasm only under certain specific circumstances, such as in a hotel room but not in her own bedroom. Finally, *random anorgasmia* refers to a woman who has experienced orgasm in a variety of sexual activities but only on an infrequent basis.

The immediate cause of anorgasmia is an involuntary inhibition of the natural orgasmic reflex, but other factors can contribute to this condition, such as severe chronic illness, drug and alcohol abuse, hormonal deficiencies, diabetes, and various medications such as tranquilizers and blood pressure medications. In addition, social factors such as the double standard regarding the acceptability of sexual feelings in women and men can also contribute to anorgasmia. Some anorgasmic women find sexual activities pleasurable and satisfying even though they do not experience orgasm; others experience depression, a lack of self-esteem, or a sense of futility.

About 2 to 3 percent of adult women experience pain during penetration. *Vaginismus* is a condition in which the muscles around the outer part of the vagina contract involuntarily during penetration, closing the vagina almost totally. In most cases, vaginismus is specific to vaginal penetration and does not necessarily affect other aspects of a woman's sexual responsiveness. In some women, however, the same involuntary muscle spasms may occur in response to any attempt to enter the vagina. Therefore, foreplay, such as the insertion of a finger, or even gynecological exams will produce the involuntary spasms and vaginal closure.

Vaginismus may be caused by factors such as poor vaginal lubrication, the use of various drugs, some illnesses, vaginal infections, and pelvic disorders. Most often, however, it seems to be a result of psychological factors, for example, a strict religious upbringing, having been taught that sex is unpleasant and painful, fear of or hostility toward men, and psychological reactions to rape. Reactions by partners of a woman with vaginismus range from self-blame or passivity about sex to impatience, resentment, and open hostility. Sometimes vaginismus can be treated with simple relaxation exercises.

Another sexual dysfunction of women is *dyspareunia*, or painful intercourse, which can occur at any point during or immediately following intercourse. The pain of dyspareunia can range from burning sensations to sharp, searing pain or cramps and can occur in the vagina or in the pelvic region or abdomen. Although the exact incidence of dyspareunia is not known, it is estimated that approximately 15 percent of adult women experience painful intercourse a few times each year, and 1 to 2 percent experience it on a regular basis. The anxiety about the pain associated with intercourse can make a woman tense and decrease her sexual enjoyment or cause her to abstain altogether either from sexual intercourse or from all forms of sexual activity.

Finally, a very small number of women experience *rapid orgasm*, a condition in which a woman reaches orgasm too quickly. A minority of women who experience rapid orgasm lose interest in further sexual activity and may even find further activity to be physically uncomfortable. Most of these women, however, remain sexually aroused and interested, sometimes going on to have multiple orgasms. These women frequently view this condition as an asset rather than a liability. Sometimes the woman's partner will view this condition in personal terms, taking it to be symbolic of her or his unique lovemaking ability.

SEXUAL DYSFUNCTIONS IN MEN

The most common sexual dysfunctions among males are related to erection and ejaculation.

Erectile dysfunction refers to the condition in which a male cannot have or maintain an erection that is firm enough for coitus. Erectile dysfunction is sometimes referred to as *impotence* and can be classified as either *primary,* in which case a male has never experienced an erection that has been adequate enough to have sexual intercourse, or *secondary,* in which case a male has previously experienced one or more erections. Of the two, secondary erectile dysfunction is more common. Erectile dysfunction can occur at any age, and it takes many forms. In only a few cases is the man totally unable to have an erection. Usually the man has partial erections, but they are not firm enough for vaginal or anal insertion. In some cases, a man may be able to have an erection but only under certain conditions, such as during masturbation. Because losing or not having erections is so common among men, isolated incidents do *not* constitute a sexual dysfunction. Only when such incidents occur in at least 25 percent of a man's sexual activities is the man said to be experiencing secondary impotence.

Although some physical conditions can cause primary erectile dysfunction, most cases are caused by psychological conditions such as a high level of anxiety or stress, a highly religious upbringing, early homosexual experiences that led to feelings of guilt and confusion, or a single traumatic sexual intercourse experience. Secondary erectile dysfunction is also caused by a number of factors. In most cases it is brought on by some precipitating event such as fatigue, work pressure, financial problems, drug or alcohol abuse, depression, or arguments. Men react to erectile dysfunction in a number of ways, the most common of which is a feeling of dismay. The partner of a male with erectile dysfunction may blame herself or himself, thinking that she or he is not skilled enough to arouse the man's passion.

Premature ejaculation, or *rapid ejaculation,* is a common dysfunction in which a male reaches orgasm too quickly. In most cases, the male ejaculates just before or immediately after entering his partner. Because ejaculation is so rapid, stimulation of his partner does not occur. As a result, both partners are often dissatisfied. Some men are not bothered by ejaculating quickly, whereas others become embarrassed or frustrated, develop low self-esteem, or question their masculinity.

Premature ejaculation is believed to be the most common male sexual dysfunction, affecting an estimated 15 to 20 percent of men on a regular basis. Less than 20 percent of these men consider this condition to be problematic enough to seek therapy. The primary causes of premature ejaculation are psychological factors such as anxiety or early experiences with rushing through intercourse or other sexual activity for fear of being caught (for example, having sex in the backseat of a car).

Another sexual dysfunction for men is *inhibited male orgasm,* sometimes referred to as *retarded ejaculation,* in which a man is unable to ejaculate during sexual intercourse despite a firm erection. Although the muscle contractions of orgasm do not occur, fluid containing sperm may leave the penis and enter the vagina; thus, pregnancy is possible. As with erectile dysfunction, inhibited orgasm can be *primary,* in which a man has never ejaculated during coitus, or *secondary,* in which a man who has experienced ejaculation and orgasm in the past suddenly develops a problem. In both instances, ejaculation is often possible by masturbation or some other noncoital stimulation. Drug and alcohol use accounts for about 10 percent of cases of inhibited male orgasm. Inhibited male orgasm should be distinguished from *retrograde ejaculation,* a condition in which the bladder neck does not close off properly during orgasm, causing the semen to spurt backward into the bladder.

Another male dysfunction, *priapism,* is a condition in which the penis remains erect for prolonged periods of time. Priapism results from damage to valves that are supposed to regulate penile blood flow. Under this condition, erection can last for days, but it is generally not accompanied by a desire for sex. Prolonged erection can be painful as well as embarrassing for most men.

Finally, men, like women, can suffer from *painful intercourse,* or *dyspareunia.* Typically, the pain is felt in the penis. Some men, however, experience the pain in the testes or even internally, where it might be related to a problem with the prostate or seminal vesicles. Both physical and psychological factors can contribute to dyspareunia. Physical factors include inflammation or infection of the penis, testes, urethra, foreskin, or prostate. A few men experience pain if the tip of the penis is irritated by vaginal contraceptive foams or creams.

SEXUALLY TRANSMITTED INFECTIONS

Sexually transmitted infections (STIs) is a broad term used to describe a variety of bacterial, viral, yeast, and protozoan infections that are almost always transmitted by sexual contact and to refer to various other infections that are sometimes transmitted in nonsexual ways. In the past, many of these infectons were referred to as *venereal diseases.* Most STIs are transmitted through genital–genital, oral–genital, and anal–genital contact. Some STIs, such as AIDS and hepatitis B, however, can be transmitted through blood transfusions or the use of infected needles. In addition, as we pointed out in Chapter 9, some STIs can also be passed from the mother to the fetus through the placenta and from the mother to the newborn as it passes through the birth canal.

STIs vary greatly in terms of their symptoms, progressions, treatments, seriousness, and outcomes. Most STIs can be prevented with proper care and can be cured with drugs. Being cured does not mean that a person cannot contract the same STI again at a later time. In addition, it is possible for a person to contract more than one STI at a time. In this appendix we present some of the most common STIs: chlamydia, gonorrhea, syphilis, genital herpes, papilloma, hepatitis B, tricho moniasis, moniliasis, lymphogranuloma venereum, and chancroid. A full discussion of AIDS appears in Chapter 6.

Chlamydia is probably the most common sexually transmitted infection in this country. It affects between 3 million and 4 million people every year. Chlamydial infections are caused by a bacterium (*Chlamydia trachomatis*) that attacks the reproductive system. The majority of infected females and about one-third of infected males experience no symptoms. In the other two-thirds of males, symptoms include a whitish discharge from the penis. Sometimes infected females or males experience a mild irritation of the genitals and an itching or burning sensation during urination. Because chlamydia has symptoms similar to gonorrhea, it sometimes goes undetected. Untreated, it can result in sterility in both females and males, pelvic inflammatory disease (PID), infection of the uterus and tubes, infections in newborns, miscarriages, and stillbirths (Allgeier and Allgeier, 1988). Chlamydia can be cured with antibiotics such as tetracycline.

Gonorrhea is a highly infectious disease that can affect the genitourinary tract, tissues of the genitals, fallopian tubes, rectum, and cervix. It can also occur in other areas of the body such as the mouth, throat, and eyes. Gonorrhea is caused by the bacterium *Neisseria gonorrhoeae*. It can be transmitted by any form of sexual contact ranging from sexual intercourse to fellatio, anal intercourse, and, in rare cases, cunnilingus and kissing. It is almost always transmitted through sexual intercourse, however, because the bacterium cannot live more than a few seconds outside the human body. It generally takes from 2 to 7 days after contact with an infected person for symptoms to appear. A woman who has intercourse once with an infected male runs a 50 percent risk of contracting gonorrhea, whereas a man who has intercourse once with an infected female runs only about a 20 to 25 percent risk of contracting the disease.

Symptoms in women include a yellowish green vaginal discharge, pain in the abdominal area, burning during urination, fever, abnormal menstrual bleeding, and pain in the stomach. In males, symptoms include a thick yellowish green discharge from the penis, inflammation of the tip of the penis, burning during urination, and the appearance of pus or blood in the urine. As with chlamydia, many males and the majority of females show no symptoms during the early stages of the infection. When left untreated, gonorrhea can cause considerable damage to a person's reproductive capabilities, possibly causing sterility. It can also cause PID, heart disease, arthritis, and blindness. Gonorrhea can be cured with antibiotics, the most effective of which is penicillin G.

Syphilis is a chronic infection caused by a type of bacterium known as a spirochete. Because the bacterium generally dies within seconds outside the body, it is usually transmitted through sexual intercourse, but it can also be contracted from a blood transfusion, or it can be transmitted from a mother to the fetus. Syphilis progresses through three stages of increasing severity: the primary, secondary, and tertiary stages. If allowed to run its full course, syphilis can cause paralysis, blindness, heart disease, nervous disorders, insanity, and even death. The incubation period for syphilis is 10 to 90 days.

Primary stage Between 2 and 4 weeks after infection a hard, crusty, painless oval sore called a *chancre* appears on the vaginal wall, cervix, penis, scrotum, anus, tongue, lips, or throat. It begins as a dull red spot that develops first into a pimple and then into the chancre. If immediate attention is not given to these symptoms, they may disappear, but this does not mean that the syphilis has cured itself. The syphilis remains, and after several months the symptoms of the secondary stage appear.

Secondary stage The secondary stage begins anywhere from 1 week to 6 months after the chancre heals if it has been untreated. In this phase, a person may experience reddish patches in the mouth and around the genitals that emit a clear liquid and are highly infectious. Other symptoms include a nonitching rash, sore throat, fever, headaches, and weight and hair loss. These symptoms can last from 3 to 6 months, but, as in the primary stage, they may disappear if they are not treated. For some people, these symptoms will appear and disappear many times if untreated. Between 50 and 70 percent of people with untreated syphilis remain in this stage for the rest of their lives. In the remaining cases, syphilis resurfaces after a latency period that can last for many years.

Tertiary stage In this stage a number of more serious symptoms appear. Some people develop ulcers in the eyes, liver, lungs, or digestive tract. A few people suffer damage to the brain and spinal cord, which can result in paralysis, dementia, or fatal heart damage. Pregnant women with syphilis almost always pass it on to their offspring, who may be born blind, deaf, or deformed, or may die soon after birth.

Penicillin is the best treatment for syphilis and is effective at all stages of the infection. Although existing damage cannot be reversed, penicillin can prevent further damage.

The term *herpes* refers to any one of several viral infections characterized by the eruption of blisters of the skin or mucous membrane. One type, *genital herpes*, received widespread attention in the 1980s as a result of its epidemic spread. Genital herpes is caused by the herpes simplex virus types 1 and 2. Genital herpes is usually transmitted by sexual contact but can also be transmitted by kissing or by touching your genitals after putting your fingers in your mouth. The incubation period for genital herpes is 2 to 6 days after being infected. Symptoms of the infection are similar for women and men. The first signs are itching, irritation, and a rash at the site of the infection. Other fairly common symptoms include pain or burning during urination, discharge from the urethra or vagina, soreness and swelling of lymph nodes in the groin, fever, weakness, and fatigue. Symptomatic blisters usually occur on the penis, scrotum, anus, vulva, clitoris, cervix, or mouth. These blisters are extremely painful and, over time, will rupture and eventually heal themselves even without treatment.

As with syphilis, the disappearance of the blisters does not mean that the virus is no longer in the body. Instead, the virus is still present, and blistering can recur at any time. Untreated, genital herpes can increase the risk of cervical cancer in women and can spread to women's and men's eyes from the hands. Women, more often than men, also develop aseptic meningitis, an inflammation of the covering of the brain. Pregnant women with herpes are likely to pass it on to their offspring, who might suffer blindness, brain damage, or even death. There is no cure for genital herpes, nor is there a single effective treatment. A drug called acyclovir is useful in lessening the severity of the symptoms. People with herpes should avoid having sexual contact during periods when the blisters are apparent.

Papilloma, or venereal warts, is one of the fastest growing STIs. Venereal warts are dry, often painless, grayish white warts with a cauliflowerlike surface that grow inside, or near the genitals or anus. These warts are caused by a sexually transmitted virus and are not always visible. There may be one or a cluster of warts, and they may coexist with other STIs. Venereal warts may cause pain during sex and may multiply during pregnancy. If untreated, venereal warts increase the risk of cervical cancer in women and penile cancer in men. There is no known cure for venereal warts. They can, however, be treated with liquid nitrogen or podophyllin ointment, or they can be burned off surgically.

Hepatitis B is one of three main types of viral hepatitis (the other two are hepatitis A, and non-A, non-B hepatitis). It is a viral infection of the liver and varies in terms of seriousness from mild symptoms such as poor appetite or indigestion, to diarrhea, vomiting, fever, and fatigue; to more serious medical problems such as jaundiced skin and eyes. Although hepatitis B is generally transmitted through blood or blood products, many Americans contract the disease through sexual contact. Hepatitis B can also be spread by saliva, vaginal secretions, seminal fluid, and other body fluids. Many people with hepatitis B remain in a carrier state for years or even a lifetime. Hepatitis B increases the risk of liver cancer and other liver diseases.

Trichomoniasis is caused by a one-celled protozoan, *Trichomonas vaginalis,* that thrives and grows rapidly in moist, warm tissues such as the vagina and the urethra. The infection is most common among women. As many as 25 percent of women will probably contract trichomoniasis at some point. Trichomoniasis has probably received the least attention of all STIs. In fact, because it can be transmitted in many different ways besides sexual contact, some experts in the field do not consider it an STI.

Among women symptoms are generally a foul-smelling, foamy, yellowish green vaginal discharge accompanied by vaginal itching and irritation. In addition, sexual intercourse may be painful. Men experience itching, pain in the urethra, and a slight discharge similar to that caused by gonorrhea. Most infected people do not exhibit symptoms, however. Although lack of treatment does not carry any serious consequences, it does make control of the spread of trichomoniasis difficult. Trichomoniasis is commonly treated with the drug metronidazole, which is about 80 percent effective in both women and men.

Moniliasis, like trichomoniasis, is an infection that can be contracted through both sexual and nonsexual contact. Sometimes referred to as a *yeast infection,* moniliasis is caused by the fungus *Candida albicans.* Women and men seldom exhibit symptoms of this infection. When it invades the vaginal area of women, however, it sometimes produces a lumpy, white discharge that resembles cottage cheese. There is also itching and inflammation of the vaginal area, and intercourse becomes extremely painful. If untreated, moniliasis does not produce any serious complications, but it is extremely uncomfortable and severely limits sexual activity. It is generally treated with vaginal creams or suppositories that contain the drug nyastatin, but the infection can and does recur repeatedly with some women.

Lymphogranuloma venereum (LGV) is a bacterial infection caused by *Chlamydia trachomatis,* which invades the lymph system, a network of vessels in close contact with blood vessels. Of Asian origin, this infection was almost nonexistent in the United States before the Vietnam War. The first symptom of LGV is a small blister that usually appears on the external genitals between 5 and 21 days after contact. Sometimes, however, the blister appears inside the vagina or the urethra. The blister usually heals itself within a few days, but the infection moves on and settles in the lymph glands nearest the infected site. The glands swell and form a painful sausage- shaped mass that settles within the fold of the groin. Other symptoms are similar to those of the flu, including chills, fever, headache, pain in the joints, and upset stomach. If untreated, LGV can produce serious effects, including swelling of the inguinal (groin) lymph nodes, penis, labia or clitoris, and closure of the rectum. Although the infection is curable, treatment is often difficult because the infection responds very slowly to antibiotics. The most effective forms of treatment seem to be tetracycline and sulfa drugs.

Chancroid, like LGV, is a tropical bacterial infection that is usually transmitted by sexual intercourse, although it also can be contracted through less intimate contact. Chancroid is caused by the bacterium *Haemophilus ducreyi* and is particularly contagious if there are breaks or cuts in the skin. The primary symptom of chancroid is one or more ulcerated sores that appear on the genitals 3 to 7 days after exposure. In the beginning the sores appear as pimplelike bumps, that eventually burst into very painful and open sores that bleed easily. The lymph glands in the groin area may also become swollen, and in some cases the sores may spread over the entire genital area. If the infection is left untreated, chancroid gangrene can occur. Chancroid can be cured within a short period of time with tetracycline or sulfa drugs.

Human Anatomy and Reproduction

FEMALE INTERNAL ANATOMY AND PHYSIOLOGY

The parts of a woman's anatomy that are critical to reproduction are internal and include the vagina, ovaries, paired fallopian tubes, uterus, and cervix. Figure B.1 shows the female reproductive system and the major structures of the uterus.

Leading from the vaginal opening to inside the woman's body is the *vagina,* a thin-walled elastic structure 3 to 4 inches long. The vagina functions in a number of ways: It receives the penis during heterosexual intercourse and serves as a depository for sperm during intercourse, as a passageway for menstrual flow, and as the birth canal.

The female body contains two *ovaries,* almond-shaped structures that lie on each side of the uterus. The ovaries produce ova (eggs) and the hormones estrogen and progesterone. Ova are embedded in follicles near the surfaces of ovaries; each follicle contains one ovum. A female is born with about 400,000 immature eggs. Only about 400 of these eggs mature and are released over the course of a woman's fertile years, however. More specifically, each month during a woman's reproductive years one or the other ovary releases one (or infrequently more than one) *egg* on a day approximately midway between the menstrual periods into the abdominal cavity, a process known as *ovulation.*

Following ovulation the egg begins to migrate toward the *fallopian tubes,* small structures extending 4 inches laterally from each side of the uterus to the ovaries. Hairlike projections called *fimbria* at the end of the fallopian tubes create currents with lashing movements that draw eggs into and down through the tube. Fertilization generally occurs inside the fallopian tubes at the end closest to the ovaries.

Once fertilized, the egg continues its journey through the fallopian tube and into the *uterus,* or *womb.* The uterus is a hollow, pear-shaped organ, approximately 3 inches long and 3 inches wide, composed of three alternating layers of muscle: endometrium, myometrium, and perimetrium. The endometrium—the innermost layer—is rich in blood vessels after ovulation. If fertilization does not occur, the endometrium sloughs off and is discharged from the body during menstruation. If the egg is fertilized, it implants in the endometrium, where it develops, is nourished, and grows for approximately 9 months.

At the lower end of the uterus is the *cervix,* a narrow opening leading into the vagina. At birth, the baby forces itself through the cervix and the vagina to the outside world.

MALE INTERNAL ANATOMY AND PHYSIOLOGY

Male reproductive organs can be found both within and outside the body (see Figure B.2). The external organs (testes, scrotum, penis) are important in both sexual arousal and gratification as well as reproduction. The internal reproductive system includes the seminal vesicles, prostate gland, vas deferens, seminiferous tubules, Cowper's glands, urethra, epididymis, and interstitial cells.

The *testes (testicles),* the primary reproductive organs in males, produce both the spermatozoa necessary for reproduction and male hormones, primarily testosterone. Each testicle consists of three sets of tissue that come together to form a tube: seminiferous tubules, where sperm are produced; epididymis, where sperm are stored; and interstitial cells, where the male sex hormones are produced. From the testes the sperm travel through a duct system (epididymis, vas deferens, ejaculatory duct, and urethra) until they are expelled from the penis during ejaculation.

If ejaculation occurs, sperm leave the testes through the second part of the duct, two small tubes called the *vas deferens,* which lead from the testes to the prostate gland, where they form the urethra. Contractions during ejaculation send the sperm into the two *ejaculatory ducts* that run through the prostate gland. After mixing with seminal fluid to form semen, sperm are propelled through the *urethra,* the tube through which males urinate and through which sperm leave the body.

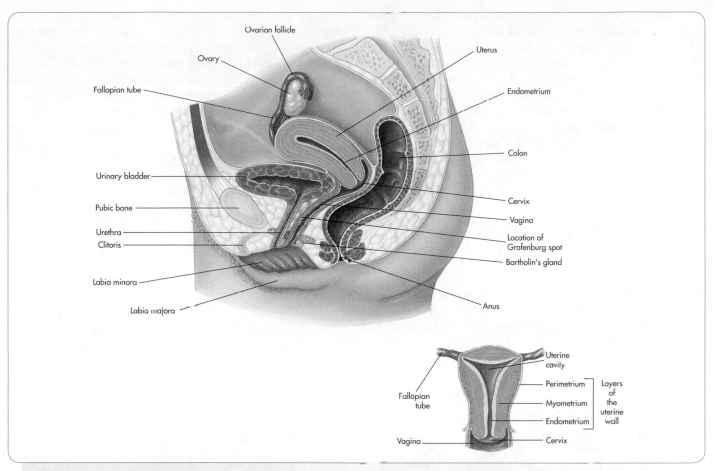

FIGURE B.1 Female Reproductive System (Above) and Major Structures of the Uterus (Right)

Source: Adapted from Frederic Martini, *Fundamentals of Anatomy and Physiology*, 2nd ed., Englewood Cliffs, NJ: Prentice Hall, 1992. Drawings by William C. Ober, M.D., and Claire W. Garrison, R.N.

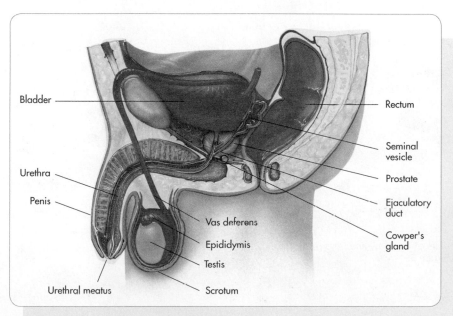

FIGURE B.2 Male Reproductive System and Structures of the Scrotum

Source: Adapted from Frederic Martini, *Fundamentals of Anatomy and Physiology*, 2nd ed., Englewood Cliffs, NJ: Prentice Hall, 1992. Drawing by Craig Luce.

Three male organs play key roles in helping the sperm move through the reproductive system to the penis and outside the body: the seminal vesicles, the prostate gland, and the Cowper's glands. The *seminal vesicles,* two small organs located behind the bladder, secrete fluids, many of which come from the prostate gland. These fluids add volume to the semen. The *prostate gland,* located under the bladder, where the vas deferens meet, adds an alkaline fluid to semen that protects the sperm. During orgasm it contracts, helping the semen to move out of the urethra. Located just below the prostate gland are two glands called *Cowper's glands,* or *bulbourethral glands.* These tiny glands produce an alkaline fluid that prolongs the life of sperm.

CONCEPTION, PREGNANCY, AND CHILDBIRTH

Conception, pregnancy, and childbirth are profound events. When female ovum and male sperm unite, conception occurs, marking the beginning of pregnancy. During the course of a pregnancy a woman's body experiences a number of internal and external changes as she carries a developing embryo and later fetus within her uterus. By the end of the fourth month of pregnancy, most women begin to "show" (their stomach swells as the fetus develops and grows) and can feel the fetus moving. Once the fetus is ready for birth it will turn its body so that its head is downward toward the cervix. Figure B.3 illustrates the various stages of labor and delivery. In most cases, the fetus is expelled from the uterus without complications.

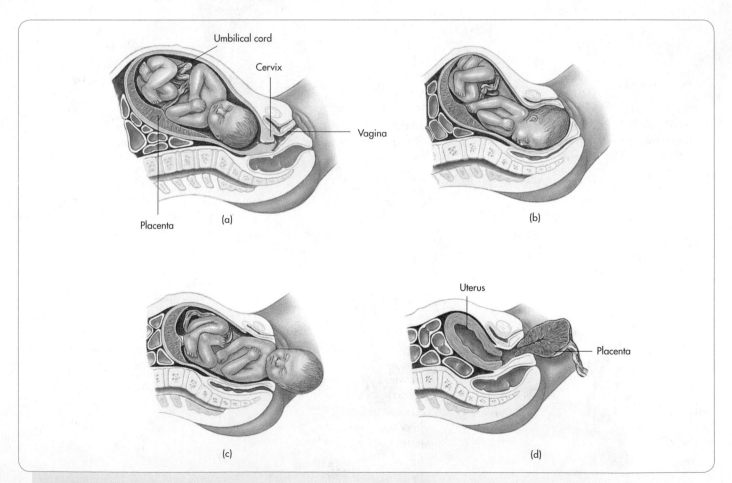

FIGURE B.3 Labor and Delivery

Source: Adapted from Frederic Martini, *Fundamentals of Anatomy and Physiology,* 2nd ed. Englewood Cliffs, NJ: Prentice Hall, 1992, p. 977, Figure 29–14.

Methods of Abortion

Approximately one-third of all reported abortions are spontaneous (miscarriages), whereby the developing embryo or fetus is expelled from the uterus naturally. Spontaneous abortions are triggered by many factors: emotional shock, abnormal development of the fetus, wearing an intrauterine device (IUD) while pregnant, and other problems that prevent further development of the fetus. Abortions can also be induced through medication or surgery.

MEDICATION-INDUCED ABORTIONS

Medication abortion (also called medical abortion, pharmacological abortion, RU-486, and the abortion pill) uses pharmacological agents, such as mifepristone and misoprostol, usually during the first 9 weeks of pregnancy. Used in combination, these medications stimulate uterine contractions and cause expulsion of the pregnancy. RU-486, developed in France, has been used successfully by millions of women worldwide. Protests against the drug by antiabortion groups delayed its testing in the United States until 1993. Although approved by the Food and Drug Administration in 2000, the drug remains controversial and its use has been greatly restricted. Most women undergoing medication abortion experience some amount of abdominal cramping and bleeding. Other possible side effects, depending on dosage and route of administration, include vomiting, nausea, diarrhea, chills, and fever.

SURGERY-INDUCED ABORTION

Abortion in the early stages of pregnancy is a relatively simple and safe procedure, although any surgical procedure runs some risk and can have varying degrees of discomfort. The most common surgical methods of abortion in the first trimester are dilation and curettage and vacuum aspiration. Dilation and evacuation and hysterotomy are the methods used in second-trimester abortions.

Vacuum Aspiration Used early in a pregnancy, this procedure, also known as suction curettage, is performed under local anesthesia, often in a doctor's office. The cervix is dilated (made larger) with a series of instruments. A tube is inserted into the uterus connected to a strong vacuum. The embryo is removed by suction. Over the next few days the woman may experience some cramping and bleeding. She is advised not to use tampons or have sexual intercourse for a week or two after the procedure.

Dilation and Curettage (D&C) This procedure is used later in the first trimester; it is the same technique used after miscarriages. The cervix is dilated, after which a curette (a spoon-shaped surgical instrument) is used to scrape the uterine wall. This procedure is usually done in a hospital, with the woman under local or general anesthesia. Some women experience pain and bleeding after this procedure, but full recovery occurs within 10 to 14 days; women are advised to abstain from sexual intercourse for several weeks.

Dilation and Evacuation (D&E) Similar to a D&C, this procedure is performed later in the pregnancy, usually between the thirteenth and sixteenth weeks. Local or general anesthesia is used. Because the pregnancy is more advanced and the fetus is larger, the cervix requires more dilation, and the uterine contents are removed through a combination of suction equipment, special forceps, and scraping with a curette. Women may experience cramping and blood loss after undergoing a D&E.

Hysterotomy Performed in the second trimester, this procedure is similar to a Cesarean section; an incision is made into the woman's abdomen and the fetus is removed. Hospitalization is required. Hysterotomy carries the most risk and therefore is rarely used.

Intact Dilation and Extraction (D&X) The most controversial method of abortion, usually performed in the fifth or sixth month, involves removing the fetus intact by dilating a pregnant woman's cervix, then pulling the entire body out through the birth canal. The National Right to Life Committee coined the term "partial-birth" abortion and lobbied Congress to pass legislation outlawing the procedure, which it did in 2003. President Bush signed the bill, which was immediately appealed. Opponents of prohibition argued that there are times when the procedure is necessary to safeguard the health of the mother; proponents of prohibition argued that it amounts to killing the fetus. Three different appeals courts at the federal level ruled the prohibition unconstitutional. However, in 2007 the Supreme Court upheld its constitutionality in the case of *Gonzales* v. *Carhart*.

Methods of Birth Control

Avoiding sexual intercourse is the surest, safest, and most cost-effective way to prevent pregnancy. Many sex education programs aimed at adolescents stress abstinence as a way to avoid both pregnancy and sexually transmitted infections, including AIDS. However, abstinence is not a popular choice with people who desire a mutually satisfying sexual relationship but do not want children. The following section examines the birth control techniques that are legally available to couples living in the United States.

STERILIZATION

Surgical sterilization runs a close second to abstinence in both reliability and, if a long-term view is taken, cost-effectiveness. This is now the most popular form of birth control among married couples in the United States. Traditional female sterilization, called *tubal ligation*, is the procedure by which a woman's fallopian tubes are cut and tied, thus preventing passage of the egg, which disintegrates and is discharged during menstruation. The procedure is performed by laparoscopy, whereby a laparoscope (a thin instrument with a viewing lens) is inserted through a small incision in the abdomen. Using this incision or a tiny second one, the surgeon inserts another small instrument that cauterizes the interior of the fallopian tubes. A new procedure, *Essure*, provides an alternative to tubal ligation and surgery. Approved by the Federal Drug Administration in 2002 after being used successfully in other countries, Essure is made of a flexible device called a micro-insert that is inserted into the fallopian tubes, where body tissue will then grow into it, causing blockage in the fallopian tubes. This prevents fertilization by blocking the sperm from reaching an egg. Most women can return to normal activities within 24 to 48 hours after undergoing the procedure. It has been found to be more than 99 percent effective in preventing pregnancy in the first 3 years of use. The most common side effects are light bleeding, mild cramping, nausea, and vomiting following the insertion procedure. It is not reversible.

Male sterilization is called a *vasectomy*. During the procedure small incisions are made on each side of the scrotum, and then the vas deferens is tied off and cut, preventing passage of sperm through the male's reproductive tract. This procedure does not prevent sperm production. Rather, when sperm are produced, instead of being ejaculated they are absorbed in the man's body. Discomfort is minimal. However, live sperm remain in parts of the reproductive system for several weeks after the vasectomy, so to be safe a couple should use an additional form of contraception. This other form of contraception can be eliminated once the semen is examined and found to be sperm free. Many insurance policies cover both female and male sterilization. Sterilization has several clear advantages. Once it is done, no further thought need be given to the task of prevention. It is 100 percent effective, except in rare instances when the procedures have not been performed properly. Most women and men who have undergone sterilization report little or no decrease in sexual desire or sexual pleasure. Some even report more enjoyment after the fear of pregnancy is removed. Sterilization has the added advantage of not interfering with sexual spontaneity. Sterilization has certain drawbacks, however. A small percentage of women and men experience some psychological problems after sterilization, equating their loss of fertility with diminished feelings of femininity and masculinity.

ORAL CONTRACEPTIVES ("THE PILL")

The birth control pill, available since the early 1960s, is the most popular type of contraceptive. Pills come in packs of 21 or 28 pills. There are two basic types—combination pills (synthetic estrogen and progestin) and progestin-only pills. Combination pills work by preventing a woman's ovaries from releasing eggs and by thickening the cervical mucus, which inhibits sperm from joining with an egg. Progestin-only pills work by thickening the cervical mucus. Taking the pill daily maintains the level of hormone needed to prevent pregnancy. The advantages of the pill are its convenience, its noninterference with spontaneity during intercourse, and its high rate of effectiveness (95 to 98 percent) when used correctly. Additionally,

528

many women report reduced premenstrual tension and cramps and lighter blood flows during menstruation. Birth control pills are available only with a doctor's prescription. A woman's medical history may rule out use of the Pill. Women suffering from hypertension, poor blood circulation, and other risk factors should not take the Pill because of the danger of blood clots and high blood pressure. Side effects may include nausea, breast tenderness, weight gains due to water retention, migraine headaches, mood changes, and an increased tendency to develop yeast infections.

EMERGENCY CONTRACEPTION (EC)

Also known as emergency birth control, the morning after pill, and by the brand name Plan B, EC is a safe and effective way to prevent pregnancy after unprotected intercourse. It can be started up to 5 days after unprotected intercourse. However, the sooner it is started, the more effective it is. EC is composed of the same hormones found in birth control pills and works by keeping a woman's ovaries from releasing eggs (ovulation). Pregnancy cannot happen if there is no egg to join with sperm. The hormones in the morning after pill also prevent pregnancy by thickening a woman's cervical mucus, thus blocking sperm and keeping it from joining with an egg. Although some critics of EC believe that the morning after pill causes an abortion, that is not the case. EC is birth control, not abortion ("Emergency Contraception," 2008).

EC does not protect against sexually transmitted infections. Although many women use EC without any problems, there may be side effects such as nausea and vomiting. Other side effects may include breast tenderness, irregular bleeding, dizziness, and headaches. EC should not be used as a form of ongoing birth control because it is less effective than most of the other forms of birth control.

HORMONAL METHODS: IMPLANTS, PATCHES, AND INJECTIONS

Implanon is a matchstick-size device that health care providers inject into the underside of a woman's arm, where it releases a continuous dosage of the synthetic hormone progestin over a 3-year period. It stops ovaries from releasing eggs and thickens cervical mucus, preventing sperm from fertilizing any released egg. It is 99 percent effective. Its major side effect is irregular menstrual cycles. Implanon does not affect long-term fertility. When the implant is removed, pregnancy can result within a month. Used successfully in Europe since 1998, Implanon was approved for use in the United States in 2006. It replaces Norplant, which was removed from the U.S. market in 2002 after numerous lawsuits were filed against the manufacturer. The *Ortho Evra Contraceptive Patch* is a new hormonal alternative to the birth control pill. This thin patch is placed on the body once a week for 3 weeks and then removed for 1 week to allow for a menstrual period. Hormones are continuously released through the skin into the bloodstream, thereby preventing pregnancy. It has a 99 percent effective rate but requires a prescription. The side effects are similar to the birth control pill.

Depo-Provera injection, popularly known as "the Shot," contains synthetic progesterone that blocks ovulation. It is injected into the buttocks every 3 months and it is 99 percent effective. Although some women experience irregular bleeding during the first year of use, most women stop menstruating entirely after a year. Depo-Provera has a number of beneficial effects: It relieves some of the discomfort associated with premenstrual syndrome and decreases the risk of inflammatory disease and yeast infections. Side effects include menstrual irregularities, fatigue, dizziness, and headaches. A similar injection, *Lunelle,* is given once a month, every 28 to 30 days. The shot must be given in a physician's office. Like Depo-Provera, Lunelle is 99 percent effective. It may cause spotting and bleeding.

INTRAUTERINE DEVICE

An IUD is a T-shaped device made of flexible plastic that is inserted into the uterus through the cervical opening. If inserted improperly, it can pierce the uterine wall and cause serious injury. For this reason, an IUD should be inserted only by a medical practitioner. Two types of IUDs are currently available in the United States. *Para Gard* contains copper and can be left in place for 12 years. *Mirena* releases a low dose of progesterone into the uterus, causing the lining to thin, and is effective for up to five years. Both work by preventing sperm from joining with an egg. This process is seen by some critics as equivalent to abortion and therefore morally objectionable. Small strings are left in the vagina to allow women to check to see if the IUD is still in place. Spontaneous expulsions occur in about 10 percent of users, primarily during menstruation, so periodic checking is important. The IUD is 99 percent effective, requires little care, is reversible, and does not interfere with sexual spontaneity. Side effects include spotting, backaches, and infection.

BARRIER DEVICES

Male condoms have been around since the early Romans used a condom made of animal intestine and bladder. The condoms used today consist of a thin cover of latex rubber (recommended) or processed sheep's intestine (not recommended because they are porous and can be penetrated by HIV and other viruses) that is placed over the erect penis by either partner to prevent the sperm from entering the vagina. Condoms come in different sizes and colors. They are convenient (can be carried in a wallet or purse) and can be purchased over the counter in drugstores and supermarkets. Condoms are about 90 to 98 percent effective, depending on use. Latex condoms protect against various sexually transmitted infections, including AIDS. The drawback to the condom is that it is put on after the man is aroused but before he enters his partner. Because sexual activity must be interrupted to do this, some couples neglect or forget to put it on. Some men complain that condoms interfere with sensation and spontaneity. Also, condoms can tear or slip off when in use and must be carefully removed after intercourse to avoid spilling the ejaculate.

The *female condom* is a 7-inch-long lubricated, thin, polyurethane pouch with an inner and outer ring. The inner ring fits over the cervix, like a diaphragm; the outer ring covers part of the vulva. The female condom has several advantages over the male condom.

It tears less, and there is less chance of exposure to semen. Like the latex male condom, it can prevent the spread of sexually transmitted infections, including AIDS. However, some couples find the pouch less spontaneous and somewhat comical. It is 85 to 95 percent effective. It may cause vaginal irritation.

Another barrier device, the *diaphragm*, originated in Western Europe as early as 1600 when women used scooped-out halves of lemons and pomegranates to prevent pregnancy. The modern diaphragm is a flexible, dome-shaped rubber cup inserted into the vagina to cover the mouth of the cervix. A *cervical cap* is a thimble-shaped device, similar to a diaphragm in appearance and function but considerably smaller. Either method can be inserted up to 6 hours before intercourse and must not be removed until at least 6 hours after ejaculation. It is recommended that both of these methods be used with contraceptive creams and jellies. Both methods block sperm from entering the uterus and fertilizing the egg. Both methods require a prescription after an internal pelvic examination. To be effective both must be properly fitted to conform to a woman's vaginal opening, and to ensure proper fit they should be checked every 2 years or after childbirth, an abortion, or significant weight changes. A woman (or her partner) inserts

Birth control devices include IUDs, male and female condoms, oral contraceptives, and diaphragms.

the diaphragm or cervical cap before having sex. The diaphragm is about 81 to 95 percent effective and the cervical cap is 82 to 94 percent effective. Both are reversible methods and neither interferes with a woman's hormonal system. Although there are few side effects, some women develop bladder infections or experience a mild allergic reaction to the rubber, cream, or jelly. Some women see these methods as messy, and some feel that the required preparation takes away from spontaneity.

The newest entry to barrier methods is the *Lea Shield,* which is similar to the diaphragm and cervical cap. This dome-shaped, reusable silicone device covers the cervix and prevents the sperm and egg from joining. It can be inserted hours before intercourse and is to be left in place for at least 8 hours after ejaculation. When used with spermicide, it is 79 to 92 percent effective. Women do not need to have the Lea's contraceptive fitted by a doctor as one size fits all and it can be bought over the counter at most pharmacies. Some women have found it uncomfortable to insert and some men complain they can feel it during intercourse.

A *contraceptive sponge* is a small disposable polyurethane device, containing spermicide. The sponge fits over the cervix, blocking and killing sperm. It can be inserted hours before intercourse and needs to be left in at least 6 hours after intercourse (for a maximum of up to 12 hours after being inserted). It is 72 to 82 percent effective, easily available (no prescription is needed), and convenient. The sponge cannot be used during menstruation. If left in for more than 12 hours, women can develop toxic shock syndrome; some women are allergic to the spermicide contained in the sponge.

SPERMICIDES

A variety of chemical sperm-killing agents called spermicides (foams, creams, jellies, suppositories, tablets, and contraceptive film) can be purchased over the counter. They are more effective when used with a barrier method, but they can be used alone. They are inserted into the vagina and when used alone have an effectiveness of 79 percent. They are safe, simple to use, and reversible. However, some users complain of irritation and burning sensations, and some find them messy. Because they must be used shortly before intercourse, couples sometimes feel they interrupt the sexual mood.

FERTILITY AWARENESS

Fertility awareness, also called natural family planning because it uses no mechanical or hormonal barriers to conception, makes use of the recurring pattern of fertile and infertile phases of a woman's body during the menstrual cycle. The goal of fertility awareness methods is to predict these phases so that couples can abstain from sexual activity during the fertile period. To determine the "safe" days, it is necessary to determine the time of ovulation. This can be done in several ways: (1) The rhythm method uses a calendar calculation of unsafe days based on the length of a woman's menstrual cycle. (2) The basal body temperature (BBT) method calculates temperature change. A woman's temperature dips slightly just before ovulation and increases after ovulation. (3) The cervical mucus method, also called the Billings or ovulation method, examines the change in appearance and consistency of cervical mucus. The general pattern moves from no visible mucus for several days after menstruation to whitish, sticky mucus, then to clear and slippery mucus during ovulation, and then back to a cloudy discharge when ovulation ends. (4) The symptothermal method is a combination of the BBT and mucus methods. This method is the most successful because it uses two indicators of fertility rather than one.

All these methods are designed to help women check changing body signs so that they will know when ovulation occurs. The effectiveness of these methods thus depends on a woman's knowledge of her reproductive cycle as well as the couple's self-control (abstinence) during fertile periods. Although it is difficult to ascertain exactly when ovulation occurs, when these methods are used diligently, they have a high effectiveness rate. However, risk taking during the fertile phase contributes to a fairly high failure rate. These methods are acceptable to most religious groups. There are no side effects. However, couples may experience frustration during periods of abstinence, which can last from 7 to 14 days.

WITHDRAWAL (COITUS INTERRUPTUS)

The withdrawal of the penis from the vagina prior to ejaculation can be an attractive form of contraception because it is simple, it does not require any devices, and it is free. Unfortunately, it also does not work very well. Withdrawal requires great control by the man, and it may limit sexual gratification for one or both partners. In addition, leakage of semen can occur prior to ejaculation.

DOUCHING

Douching, or washing out the vagina, is another old but unreliable method of birth control. Douching after intercourse may actually push some sperm toward the cervix. In addition, douching can lead to pelvic inflammatory disease.

FUTURE CONTRACEPTIVE STRATEGIES

Research to find safer, more effective, and less expensive methods of birth control is underway in many countries. For example, doctors in India are developing a birth control vaccine for women that would be effective for a year. Preliminary testing is encouraging, but the vaccine will not be available for several years. Most contraceptive research remains centered on the woman's reproductive system. However, some researchers are now investigating a male contraceptive pill that would inhibit sperm production as well as a testosterone gel combined with the female contraceptive Depo-Provera. Other promising areas of research include "heating" the testes with high frequency sound waves, which, in some cases, stops sperm production for months and a gel injected into the scrotum which would inhibit sperm but would be reversible (DeNinno, 2011).

Whether these promising developments become reality depends on the willingness of drug companies to invest money into bringing them to the market. Thus far, major pharmaceutical companies have not viewed male contraceptives as a profitable enterprise. However, a recent survey of 9,000 men on four continents might give them reason to reconsider their attitude. More than half of the respondents said they would use male hormonal birth control (Columbia News Service, 2008).

Caution Most of these contraceptive devices, when used alone, do not protect against sexually transmitted infections. Therefore, it is a good idea to use a latex condom in conjunction with these other devices.

Glossary

abortion The termination of a pregnancy before the fetus can survive on its own. This can occur either spontaneously (miscarriage) or be induced through a variety of external methods.

achieved status A position we hold in society by virtue of our own efforts, for example, that of teacher or mother.

acquaintance rape Sexual assault by a person with whom the victim is familiar.

acquired immune deficiency syndrome (AIDS) A viral syndrome that destroys the body's immune system.

adultery Extramarital sexual intercourse.

affinal relatives People related by marriage and not by blood, for example, a brother- or sister-in-law.

agape (pronounced "ah GAH pay") A style of loving that combines eros and storge, is selfless and giving, expecting nothing in return.

ageism The application of negative stereotypes and discriminatory treatment to elderly people.

age norms The expectations of how one is to behave at specific ages in the life cycle.

agents of socialization Individuals, groups, and institutions that help form an individual's attitudes, behaviors, and self-concepts.

alcoholism A chronic behavioral disorder manifested by repeated drinking of alcoholic beverages in excess of the dietary and social uses of the community and to the extent that it interferes with the drinker's health or social and economic functioning.

alimony Court-ordered financial support paid to a former spouse following a divorce.

Alzheimer's disease A progressive brain disorder that impairs memory, thinking, and behavior that leads to a decline in the ability to perform activities of daily living.

androgynous Sharing feminine and masculine traits.

annulment A legal declaration that a marriage never existed, leaving both parties free to marry.

anticipatory socialization Socialization directed toward learning future roles.

antinatalist forces Policies or practices that discourage people from having children.

artificial insemination The injection of sperm into the vagina or uterus of an ovulating woman.

ascribed status A position we hold in society because we were born into it, for example, that of being female or male.

assisted reproductive technology (ART) A general term that includes all treatments or procedures involving the handling of human eggs and sperm to establish a pregnancy.

autoeroticism Sexual activities involving only the self, for example, masturbation, sexual fantasy, and erotic dreams.

battered-child syndrome A group of symptoms that collectively describe a clinical condition in children who have received severe physical abuse.

battered-woman syndrome A group of symptoms that collectively describe a general pattern of physical battering experienced by women. It is defined in terms of frequency, severity, deliberateness, and ability to demonstrate injury.

bereavement The state of being deprived of a loved one by death.

bigamy The act of marrying one person while still being legally married to another person.

bisexuality A person who has partners of both sexes either simultaneously or at different times.

boundary ambiguity Who is in and who is out of the family system.

case study A detailed and in-depth examination of a single unit or instance of some phenomenon.

cenogamy (group marriage) A situation in which the women and men in a group are simultaneously married to one another.

cognitive-development theory A theory that asserts that children take an active role in organizing their world, including learning gender identity.

coitus Penile–vaginal intercourse.

collaborative law A way of practicing law in which the attorneys for both parties to a family dispute agree to assist in resolving the conflict by using cooperative techniques rather than adversarial strategies and litigation, with the goal of reaching an efficient, fair, and comprehensive out-of-court settlement of all issues.

common-law marriage A cohabitive relationship that is based on the mutual consent of the persons involved, is not solemnized by a ceremony, and is recognized as valid by the state.

commune A group of people (single or married, with or without children) who live together, sharing many aspects of their lives.

community divorce The changes in social relationships that often accompany a divorce—the loss of relatives and friends who were previously shared with a spouse and their replacement with new friends.

community remarriage The changes in social relationships that often accompany a remarriage—the integration of new in-laws and "couple-oriented" relationships, and sometimes the loss of unmarried friends.

commuter marriage A marriage in which each partner works in a different geographic location and therefore maintains a separate place of residence.

conciliation counseling Counseling intended to determine whether marital problems can be resolved and the couple reconciled. Some states require conciliation counseling before the courts will consider granting a divorce.

conflict theory A theoretical perspective that focuses on conflicting interests among various groups and institutions in society.

congenital Existing at birth but not hereditary.

conjugal rights A set of rights pertaining to the marriage relationship.

content analysis A research technique used to examine the content of books, documents, and programs.

contraception Mechanisms for preventing fertilization.

coparental divorce The arrangements divorcing couples work out concerning child custody, visitation rights, and the financial and legal responsibilities of each parent.

courtship The process of selecting a mate and developing an intimate relationship.

coverture The traditional belief that a wife is under the protection and influence of her husband.

crude divorce rate (CDR) The number of divorces per 1,000 people in the population.

cunnilingus Oral stimulation of the female genitals.

date rape Sexual assault by a person with whom the victim had gone on a date.

dating A process of pairing off that involves the open choice of mates and engagement in activities that allow people to get to know one another and progress toward mate selection.

dating violence The perpetration or threat of an act of violence by at least one member of an unmarried couple on the other member within the context of dating or courtship, encompassing any form of sexual assault, physical violence, and verbal or emotional abuse.

dementia A clinical syndrome of loss or decline in memory and other cognitive abilities beyond what might be expected from normal aging.

desertion The abandonment of a spouse or family.

developmental family life cycle theory A theory that explains family life in terms of a process that unfolds over the life course of families.

disability A physical or mental condition that often stigmatizes or causes discrimination.

disenfranchised grief Circumstances in which a person experiences a sense of loss but does not have a socially recognized right, role, or capacity to grieve.

divorce counseling Counseling intended to help couples replace the adversarial and often destructive aspects that frequently accompany divorce with a more cooperative spirit and to help them distance themselves from the relationship so that acceptance of the loss and subsequent healing can take place.

divorce mediation A procedure in which trained professionals help divorcing couples negotiate a fair and mutually agreed-upon resolution of such issues as marital property distribution, child custody, visitation rights, and financial support.

domestic partnership A category of relationships consisting of unmarried couples who live together and share housing and financial responsibilities. Some communities and businesses allow unmarried couples who register as domestic partners to receive certain legal rights similar to those of married couples.

drug Any substance that alters the central nervous system and states of consciousness.

drug abuse The deliberate use of a substance for other than its intended purpose, in a manner that can damage health or ability to function.

drug use The taking of a drug for its intended purpose and in an appropriate amount, frequency, strength, and manner.

dysfunctional Having a negative consequence or performing a negative service by hampering the achievement of group goals or disrupting the balance of the system.

economic divorce The division of marital property and assets between the two former partners.

economic remarriage The establishment of a new marital household as an economically productive unit.

elder abuse Physical, psychological, or material maltreatment and neglect of older people.

embryo transplant A procedure whereby a fertilized egg from a donor is implanted into an infertile woman.

emotional divorce A period during which one or both partners withdraw emotionally from a marriage.

emotional remarriage The process of reestablishing a bond of attraction, love, commitment, and trust with another person.

empirical evidence Data or evidence that can be confirmed by the use of one or more of the human senses.

enculturated-lens theory A theory of gender role acquisition that argues that hidden cultural assumptions about how societal members should look, behave, and feel are so deeply embedded in social institutions and cultural discourse, and hence individual psyches, that these behaviors and ways of thinking are systematically reproduced from one generation to the next.

endogamy The practice of requiring people to marry within a particular social group.

eros A style of loving characterized by an immediate, powerful attraction to the physical appearance of another.

ethnic cleansing A term euphemistically applied to the process whereby one group of people tries to rid the region of others who are different in some significant way.

ethnography A research technique of describing a social group from the group's point of view.

exogamy The practice of requiring people to marry outside particular groups.

expressive traits Personality traits that encourage nurturing, emotionality, sensitivity, and warmth.

extended or multigenerational family A family consisting of one or both parents, siblings, if any, and other relatives, such as grandparents, aunts, uncles, or cousins.

family Any relatively stable group of people who are related to one another through blood, marriage, or adoption, or who simply live together, and who provide one another with economic and emotional support.

family abduction The taking or keeping of a child by a family member in violation of a custody order, a decree, or other legitimate custodial rights, where the taking or keeping involved some element of concealment, flight, or intent to deprive a lawful custodian indefinitely of custodial privileges.

family household At least two persons related by birth, marriage, and/or adoption—one of whom is the householder.

family and medical leave act A law that allows either parent to take up to 3 months of unpaid leave for births, adoptions, and family emergencies.

family of orientation The family into which a person is born and raised.

family of procreation A family that is created when two people marry or enter into an intimate relationship and have or adopt children of their own.

fellatio Oral stimulation of the male genitals.

feminization of poverty The increase in the proportion of poor people who are women or children.

fertility The actual number of live births in a population.

fertility rate The number of births per 1,000 women in their childbearing years (ages 15 to 44).

fetal alcohol syndrome A condition caused by a mother's consumption of alcohol during pregnancy and characterized by physical deformities in the fetus.

fictive kin The attribution of kinship terms to nonrelatives.

flextime An arrangement that allows employees to choose within specified time limits when they arrive at and leave work.

fornication Sexual intercourse outside legal marriage.

functional Having a positive consequence or performing a positive service by promoting the achievement of group goals or helping maintain a system in a balanced state.

functional age The use of an individual's physical, intellectual, and social capacities and accomplishments as a measurement of age rather than the number of years lived.

gender The socially learned behaviors, attitudes, and expectations associated with being female or male; what we call femininity and masculinity.

gender identity A person's awareness of being female or male.

gender role socialization The process whereby people learn and adopt the gender roles that their culture deems appropriate for them.

gender role stereotypes The oversimplified expectations of what it means to be a woman or a man.

gender similarity hypothesis The idea that girls and boys, women and men are more alike than different.

generalized others The viewpoints of society at large—widespread cultural norms and values that individuals use as a reference when evaluating themselves.

getting together A pattern of dating that involves women and men meeting in groups, playing similar roles in initiating dates, and sharing equally in the cost of activities.

global interdependence A state in which the lives of people around the world are intertwined closely and in which any one nation's problems increasingly cut across cultural and geographic boundaries.

going steady An exclusive dating relationship with one partner.

grief The emotional response to the loss of a loved one.

group marriage A marriage of at least four people, two female and two male, in which each partner is married to all partners of the opposite sex.

Hawthorne effect The distortion of research results that occurs when people modify their behaviors, either deliberately or subconsciously, because they are aware they are being studied.

health A state of complete physical, mental, and social well-being, not merely the absence of physical disease or infirmity.

heterogamous marriage Marriage in which the partners are unlike each other in terms of various social and demographic characteristics, such as race, age, religious background, social class, and education.

heterosexism The notion that heterosexuality is the only right, natural, and acceptable sexual orientation.

heterosexuality Both identity and behavior; includes a preference for sexual activities with a person of the other sex.

HIV embryopathy Used by some researchers to describe specific facial malformations (for example, small heads, slanted eyes that sit far apart from each other, a square forehead, a wide and flat nose, loosely shaped lips, and a growth deficiency).

homogamy The attraction of people who are alike in terms of various social and demographic characteristics such as race, age, religious background, social class, and education.

homophobia An extreme and irrational fear or hatred of homosexuals.

homosexuality Both identity and behavior; includes preference for sexual activities with a person of the same sex.

hooking up A casual sexual encounter that can range from meeting with a friend, kissing, making out, touching, and oral stimulation to sexual intercourse, with no expectation of future emotional commitment.

hospice A physical environment within which supportive care is provided for terminally ill patients and their families that focuses on comfort, freedom from pain, and quality of life rather than cure.

households All persons who occupy a housing unit, such as a house, apartment, single room, or other space intended to be living quarters.

human sexuality The feelings, thoughts, and behaviors of humans who have learned a set of cues that evoke a sexual or an erotic response.

hypergamy Marrying upward in social status.

hypogamy Marrying downward in social status.

hypothesis Statement of a relationship between two or more variables.

ideology A set of ideas and beliefs that support the interests of a group in society.

incest Sexual abuse by a blood relative or someone who is thought of as a part of a person's family.

individual racism Behavior by individuals or groups who define themselves as superior toward individuals whom they define as inferior.

infant mortality rate The rate at which babies die before their first birthday.

infanticide Killing of infants and young children.

infatuation A strong attraction to another person based on an idealized picture of that person.

infertility The inability to conceive after 12 months of unprotected intercourse or the inability to carry a pregnancy to live birth.

institution Patterns of ideas, beliefs, values, and behavior that are built around the basic needs of individuals and society and that persist over time.

institutional racism Established laws, customs, and practices that systematically reflect and produce racial inequalities in a society, whether or not the individuals maintaining these practices have racist intentions.

instrumental traits Personality traits that encourage self-confidence, rationality, competition, and coolness; for example, an orientation to action, achievement, and leadership.

intersexuality Condition where an infant's genitalia are ambiguous in appearance and whose sexual anatomy cannot clearly be differentiated at birth.

interview A method of collecting data in which a researcher asks subjects a series of questions and records the answers.

in vitro fertilization A reproductive technique that involves surgically removing a woman's eggs, fertilizing them in a petri dish with the partner's or donor's sperm, and then implanting one or more of the fertilized eggs in the woman's uterus.

jealousy Thoughts and feelings of envy, resentment, and insecurity directed toward someone a person is fearful of losing.

job sharing An employment pattern in which two workers split a single full-time job.

joint custody A situation in which both divorced parents are given legal responsibility for raising their children.

kinship Relationships resulting from blood, marriage, or adoption, or among people who consider one another family.

labor force participation rate The percentage of workers in a particular group who are employed or who are actively seeking employment.

latent functions Unintended, unrecognized consequences or effects of any part of a social system or the system as a whole for the maintenance and stability of that system.

legal divorce The official dissolution of a marriage by the state, leaving both former partners legally free to remarry.

legal marriage A legally binding agreement or contractual relationship between two people that is defined and regulated by the state.

legal remarriage The establishment of a new legally recognized relationship.

limerence A style of love characterized by a complete absorption or obsessive preoccupation with and attachment to another person. It is accompanied by extreme emotional highs when the love is reciprocated and lows when it is not.

love map A group of physical, psychological, and behavioral traits that one finds attractive in a mate.

ludus A style of loving that is playful, nonpossessive—a challenging love, without a deep commitment or lasting emotional involvement.

manic A style of loving that combines eros and ludus, is characterized by obsession and possessiveness. It is a jealous and stressful love that demands constant displays of attention, caring, and affection from the partner.

manifest functions Intended, overt consequences or effects of any part of a social system or the system as a whole for the maintenance and stability of that system.

marital adjustment The process by which marital partners change or adapt their behavior, attitudes, and interactions to develop a good working relationship and to satisfy each other's needs over the marital life course.

marriage A union between people that unites them sexually, socially, and economically, that is relatively consistent over time, and that accords each person certain agreed-upon rights.

marriage gradient Phenomenon by which women marry upward in social status and men marry downward in social status. As a result, women at the top and men at the bottom of the social class ladder have a smaller pool of eligible mates to choose from than do members of the other classes.

marriage market Analogy of the commercial marketplace to explain how individuals choose the people they date, mate, live with, and marry by "comparison shopping" and "bargaining for" the mate with the most desirable characteristics.

marriage squeeze A condition in which one sex has a more limited pool of eligibles from which to choose than the other does. Sociologists use the concept to describe the phenomenon of an excess of baby boom women who had reached marriageable age during the 1960s compared with marriage-aged men.

master (key) status A position we hold that affects all aspects of our lives, for example, being female or male.

masturbation Erotic stimulation of self through caressing or otherwise stimulating the genitals for the purpose of sexual pleasure.

mate selection The wide range of behaviors and social relationships individuals engage in prior to marriage and that lead to long- or short-term pairing or coupling.

matrilineal Kinship or family lineage (descent) and inheritance come through the mother and her blood relatives.

menopause A period in the female life cycle (typically between ages 45 and 50) characterized by the cessation of ovulation, the menstrual cycle, and fertility.

midwife Most often a woman who is trained either to deliver a baby or to assist a woman in childbirth. Most midwives today are professionals who practice in birth centers or who deliver babies at home.

modeling A process of learning through imitation of others.

modified extended family Family in which a variety of relatives live, not necessarily in the same household, but in very close proximity to one another, interact on a frequent basis, and provide emotional and economic support to each other.

monogamy Exclusivity in an intimate relationship. In marriage, it means marriage to only one person at a time.

morbidity The rate of occurrence of illness or disease in a population.

mortality The rate of occurrence of death in a population.

motherhood mystique The traditional belief that the ultimate achievement and fulfillment of womanhood is through motherhood.

mourning The outward expression of grief, including a society's customs, rituals, and rules for coping with loss.

myth A false, fictitious, imaginary, or exaggerated belief about someone or something.

nocturnal emissions (wet dreams) Erotic dreams that lead to orgasm during sleep.

no-fault divorce The dissolution of a marriage on the basis of irreconcilable differences; neither party is judged at fault for the divorce.

nonfamily household A person living alone or a householder who shares the housing unit only with nonrelatives.

norms Cultural guidelines or rules of conduct that direct people to behave in particular ways.

nuclear family A family consisting of a mother and father and their natural or adopted offspring.

occupational distribution The location of workers in different occupations; for example, women are more heavily concentrated in lower-paying clerical or service jobs, whereas men are concentrated in the higher-paying jobs of craft workers and operators.

overlapping households The dual membership of children in the separate households of their divorced (and frequently remarried) parents.

palimony A payment similar to alimony made to a former unmarried live-in partner and based on the existence of a contract (written or implied) between the partners regarding aspects of their relationship.

parental remarriage A process that involves the establishment of relationships with the children of the new spouse.

parricide The killing of one's parents.

patriarchal family A family organized around the principle of male dominance, wherein the male (husband or father) is head of the family and exercises authority and decision-making power over other family members, especially his wife and children.

patrilineal Kinship or family lineage (descent) and inheritance come through the father and his blood relatives.

pay equity Equal pay for work of equal value.

personal marriage agreement A written agreement between a married couple in which issues of role responsibility, obligation, and sharing are addressed in a manner tailored to their own personal preferences, desires, and expectations.

petting Various types of physical contact and activities for the purpose of sexual arousal and pleasure without engaging in penile–vaginal intercourse. It is common among adolescent girls and boys.

pleasuring Engaging in activities during a sexual encounter that feel good; giving and receiving pleasurable feelings without the necessity of intercourse.

polyandry A form of marriage in which one female is married to two or more males.

polygamy A broad category applied to forms of marriage that involve multiple partners. In heterosexual marriage, polygamy involves a person of one sex being married to two or more people of the other sex (either polyandry or polygyny).

polygyny A form of marriage in which one male is married to two or more females.

pool of eligibles People who are potential mates by virtue of birth and societal definition as appropriate or acceptable partners.

postnatal depression A condition experienced after the birth of a child and characterized by mood shifts, irritability, and fatigue.

posttraumatic stress disorder (PTSD) A common anxiety disorder that develops after exposure to a terrifying event or ordeal in which grave physical harm occurred or was threatened.

Pregnancy Discrimination Act of 1978 Requires that pregnant employees be treated the same as employees with any temporary disability.

preimplantation genetic diagnosis Allows physicians to identify abnormalities such as Down syndrome or genetic diseases such as muscular dystrophy in the embryo before implantation.

prenuptial agreement An agreement developed and worked out in consultation with an attorney and filed as a legal document prior to marriage.

principle of legitimacy The notion that all children ought to have a socially and legally recognized father.

pronatalist attitude A cultural attitude that encourages childbearing.

propinquity Proximity, or closeness in time, place, and space; an important factor in mate selection.

psychic divorce A redefinition of self away from the mutuality of couplehood and back to a sense of singularity and autonomy.

psychic remarriage A process in which a remarried individual moves from the recently acquired identity of a single person to a couple identity.

push/pull factors Negative and positive factors in a current situation that influence our decision making.

qualitative analysis Focuses on specific or distinct qualities within the data that show patterns of similarity or differences among the research subjects.

quantitative analysis A processs in which data can be analyzed using numerical categories and statistical techniques (for example, determining the percentage who report certain attitudes or behaviors numerically).

questionnaire A research method of collecting data in which research subjects read and respond to a set of printed questions.

racism An ideology of domination and a set of social, economic, and political practices by which one or more groups define themselves as superior and other groups as inferior, and then systematically deny these groups full access to and participation in mainstream society.

rape Sexual intercourse forced by one person upon another against the person's will; usually perpetrated by a male against a female.

rape syndrome Men's proclivity to rape—the group of factors that collectively characterize men's likelihood to rape.

refined divorce rate The number of divorces per 1,000 married women age 15 and over.

refugee A person who leaves his country because of a fear of persecution for reason of race, religion, nationality, social group, or political opinion.

remarried family A two-parent, two-generation unit that comes into being on the legal remarriage of a widowed or divorced person who is regularly involved with biological or adopted children from a prior union. The children may or may not live with the remarried couple, but in either case, they have ongoing and significant psychological, social, and legal ties with them.

role A set of socially prescribed behaviors associated with a particular status or position in society.

role conflict A situation in which a person occupies two different roles that involve contradictory expectations of what should be done at a given time.

role overload A situation in which a person's various roles carry more responsibilities than that person can reasonably manage.

romantic love A deeply tender or highly intense set of feelings, emotions, and thoughts coupled with sexual passion and erotic expression directed by one person toward another.

sacrament A sacred union or rite.

safe sex Protection from AIDS and other sexually transmitted diseases through abstinence or use of protective methods such as condoms.

sandwich generation The middle-aged adults who find themselves pressured by responsibilities for both their children and their elderly parents.

scientific method A set of procedures intended to ensure accuracy and honesty throughout the research process.

scientific research Research that provides empirical evidence as a basis for knowledge or theories.

self-esteem The overall feelings, positive and negative, that a person has about her- or himself.

separation The termination of marital cohabitation; the couple remains legally married, and neither party is free to remarry.

serial monogamy A system in which an individual marries several times but only after each prior marriage is ended by death or divorce.

sex The physiological characteristics that differentiate females from males. These include external genitalia (vulva and penis), gonads (ovaries and testes), sex chromosomes, and hormones.

sex ratio The number of men to every 100 women in a society or group.

sexual assault Violence in the form of forced sexual acts that include vaginal, oral, or anal penetration; bondage; beating; mutilation; beastiality; and group or gang rape.

sexual double standard Differing sets of norms based on gender.

sexual dysfunction A psychological or physical condition in which a person is unable to engage in or enjoy sexual activities.

sexual harassment Unwanted leers, comments, suggestions, or physical contact of a sexual nature, as well as unwelcome requests for sexual favors.

sexual identity Refers to how a person describes her or his sexuality and how that person expressed that self to others.

sexual orientation The ways in which people understand and identify themselves sexually.

sexual script Societal or cultural guidelines for defining and engaging in sexual behaviors.

significant others People who play an important role in a person's life, such as parents, friends, relatives, and religious figures.

singlism The negative stereotypes and discrimination faced by singles.

social constructionism A perspective that focuses on the processes by which human beings give meaning to their own behavior and the behavior of others.

social construction of reality The process by which individuals shape or determine reality as they interact with other human beings.

social exchange theory A theoretical perspective that adopts an economic model of human behavior based on cost, benefit, and the expectation of reciprocity and that focuses on how people bargain and exchange one thing for another in social relationships.

social gerontology The study of the impact of sociocultural conditions on the process and consequences of aging.

socialization The lifelong process of social interaction through which people learn knowledge, skills, patterns of thinking and behaving, and other elements of a culture that are essential for effective participation in social life.

social learning theory A theory that asserts that gender roles and gender identity are learned directly through a system of positive reinforcement (rewards) and negative reinforcement (punishments).

social marriage A relationship between people who cohabit and engage in behavior that is essentially the same as that within legal marriages except that the couple has not engaged in a marriage ceremony that is validated or defined as legally binding by the state.

social structure Recurrent, stable, and patterned ways that people relate to one another in a society or group.

sociological imagination A way of looking at the world whereby one sees the relations between history and biography within society.

sole custody A situation in which one divorced parent is given legal responsibility for raising children.

split custody A situation whereby siblings are split up between their two biological parents following a divorce. A typical pattern is for mothers to have custody of daughters and fathers to have custody of sons.

stations of divorce The multiple types of divorces that couples experience in dissolving their marital relationship: emotional, legal, economic, coparental, community, and psychic.

status A social position that a person occupies within a group or society.

storge (pronounced "stor gay") A style of loving that is said to be unexciting and uneventful; an affectionate style of love with an emphasis on companionship.

structural functionalism A theoretical perspective that views society as an organized system, analogous to the human system, that is made up of a variety of interrelated parts or structures that work together to generate social stability and maintain society.

surrogacy The process whereby a woman agrees to be artificially inseminated with a man's sperm, carry the fetus to term, and relinquish all rights to the child after it is born.

survey A research method in which researchers collect data by asking people questions, for example, using questionnaires or face-to-face interviews.

symbolic interactionism A theoretical perspective that focuses on micropatterns (small-scale) of face-to-face interactions among people in specific settings, such as in marriages and families.

symbols Objects, words, sounds, or events that are given particular meaning and are recognized by members of a culture.

systemic racism A belief that race is biologically determined and thus the primary determinant of human traits and capabilities.

terrorism The employment or threat of violence, fear, or intimidation by individuals or groups as a political or revolutionary strategy to achieve political goals.

theory A set of interrelated statements or propositions constructed to explain some phenomenon.

theory model A minitheory; a set of propositions intended to account for a limited set of facts.

total fertility rate The average number of children women have over their lifetime if current birth rates were to remain constant.

transgender Refers to living life as the opposite sex.

transmission of victimization Abuse carried from one generation to the next.

transsexuals Persons who believe they were born with the body of the wrong sex.

trust Feelings of confidence and belief in another person; reliance upon another person to provide for or meet one's needs.

underemployment A concept that refers to several patterns of employment: part-time workers who want to work full-time, full-time workers who make very low wages, and workers with skills higher than those required by their current job.

variables A factor or concept whose value changes from one case or observation to another.

wet dreams Erotic dreams that lead to orgasm during sleep.

wheel theory of love A perspective of love developed by social scientist Ira Reiss in which love is viewed in terms of a four-stage, circular progression from rapport through self-revelation, mutual dependence, and personality need-fulfillment as a couple interacts over time.

woman battering A range of behaviors that includes hitting, kicking, choking, and the use or threatened use of weapons, such as guns and knives.

working poor Underemployed individuals who work full time but make very low wages.

xenophobia A fear or hatred of strangers or foreigners or of anything foreign or different.

References

AARP Public Policy Institute. 2008. "Valuing the Invaluable: A New Look at State Estimates of the Economic Value of Family Caregiving (Data Update)." www.caregiving.org/data/AARPDataUpdate-StateEstimatesofEconomicValue.pdf (2008, August 25).

AARP. 2004. *The Divorce Experience: A Study of Divorce at Midlife and Beyond.* Washington, DC: The American Association of Retired Persons.

ABC News. 1999. "Accusations of Rape: Women Say They Were Attacked by Serb Forces." (April 13). abcnews.go.com/sections/world/DailyNews/Kosovo990413-refugees.html (June 10) (2005, January 27).

———. 2007. "Homicide: A Top Cause of Death among Pregnant Women." (June 24).

Abelard. 2008. "Children and Television Violence." http://www.abelard.org/tv/tv.htm (2008, August 8).

Abilities. 2011. "August Disability Employment Report." www.abilitiesinc.org/index.aspx (2011, October 1).

About Alcohol Abuse. 2008. www.about-alcohol-abuse.com/Alcohol_Abuse-Statistics.html

Abrahamy, M., E. B. Finkelson, C. Lydon, and K. Murray. 2003. "Caregivers' Socialization of Gender Roles in a Children's Museum." *Perspectives in Psychology* (Spring): 19–25.

"Abuse Spreads HIV among Zambian Girls." 2003. BBC. (January 28). news.bbc.co.uk (2008, August 8).

ACADV. 2006. "Barriers to Leaving." www.acadv.org/barriers.html (2006, July 14).

Adams, G. 2011. "Legal Victory for Supporters of Gay Marriage in California." (June 15). www.independent.couk/new/world/americas/legal-victory-for-supporters-of gay-marriage-in-california-2297348.html (2011, June 15).

Adams, J. 2011. "Hand Gun Control Debate." www.awesomelibrary.org/guncontrol.html. (2011, May 24).

Ade-Ridder, L., and T. H. Brubaker. 1983. "The Quality of Long-Term Marriages." In T. H. Brubaker, ed., *Family Relationships in Later Life,* 19–30. Beverly Hills, CA: Sage.

Adelman, G. 2011. "Where Is the Honor?" (February 2) www.weeklyblitz.net/1263/where-is-the-honor (2011, February 5).

Adinah, 2010. "Italy: Turkish Ambassador Guilty of Sexual Harassment." (February 17). http://islamwatch2010.wordpress.com/2010/02/17/ital-turkish-ambassador-guilty-of-sexual-harassment/ (2011, July 8).

Adler-Baeder, F., L. Taylor, and K. Pasley. 2005. *Marital Transitions in Military Families: Their Relevance for Adaption to Military Life.* Final Report. (March). Lafayette, IN: The Military Family Research Institute.

Administration for Children and Families, 2011. " The AFCARS Report." (June). www.acf.hhs.gov/programs/cb/stats_research/afcars/tar/ report18.pdf (2011, September 20).

Administration on Aging. 2010. *A Profile of Older Americans: 2010.* Washington, DC: U.S. Department of Health and Human Services.

"Adult Sibling Relationships." 2011. (June 3). www.extension.org/pages/9057/adult-sibling-relationships (2011, August 19).

AFL-CIO, 2009. *Young Workers: A Lost Decade.* Washington, DC.

"African American Families—African American Families in the New Millennium." 2008. http://family.jrank.org/pages/60/African-American-Families-African-American-Families-in-New-Millennium.html (2008, July 26).

Agosto, D. 2004. "Girls and Gaming: A Summary of the Research with Implications for Practice." Teacher Librarian 31, 3: 8–14.

Aguirre, A., and J. Turner. 2006. *American Ethnicity: The Dynamics and Consequences of Discrimination.* Boston: McGraw-Hill.

Ahrons, C. 1980. "Crises in Family Transitions." *Family Relations* 29: 533–40.

———. 1994. *The Good Divorce: Keeping Your Family Together When Your Marriage Comes Apart.* New York: HarperCollins.

———. 2004a. *Family Ties: Adult Children Speak Out About the Long-term Effects of Divorce and Remarriage.* New York: HarperCollins.

———. 2004b. *We're Still Family: What Grown Children Have to Say About Their Parents' Divorce.* New York: Harper Collins.

———, and J. L. Tanner. 2003. "Adult Children and Their Fathers: Relationship Changes 20 Years After Parental Divorce." *Family Relations* 52: 340–351.

AIMHAC (American Indian Mental Health Advisory Council). 2004. Cultural competency guidelines for the provision of clinical mental health services to American Indians in the state of Minnesota. (March) http://edocs.dhs.state.mn.us/lfserver/Legacy/DHS-4086-ENG

Albas, D., and C. M. Albas. 1987. "The Pulley Alternative for the Wheel Theory of the Development of Love." *International Journal of Comparative Sociology* 28 (3–4): 223–227.

Albelda, R., M. V. Badgett, A. Schneebaum, and G. J. Gates. 2009. *Poverty in the Lesbian, Gay, and Bisexual Community.* Los Angeles: UCLA, The Williams Institute.

Alford, A. L. 2009. "Communal Living May Be Answer for Confusing Times." (July 23). www.associatedcontent.com/article/1976212?communal_living_may_be_answer_for_confusing.html?cat=3 (2011, May 11).

Ali, L., and R. Kelley. 2008. "The Curious Lives of Surrogates." (March 29). http://www.newsweek.com/id/129594 (2008, July 24).

Allen, K. 1989. *Single Women/Family Ties.* Newbury Park, CA: Sage.

Allstate Foundation Domestic Violence Program. 2011. "The Allstate Foundation Economics Against Abuse Program, Financial Empowerment Curriculum Fact Sheet." www.clicktoempower.org/domestic-violence-facts.aspx (2011, September 7).

Alqashan, H., and H. Alkandari. 2010. "Attitudes of Kuwaiti Young Adults Toward Marriage and Divorce: A Comparative Study Between Young Adults from Intact and Divorced Families." *Advances in Social Work* 11, 1: 33–47.

Alternet. 2011. "Children Bear Brunt of Somali Refugee Crisis." (September 6). www.trust.org/alternet/news/children-bear-brunt-of-somali-refugee-crisis/ (2011, October 8).

Alzheimer's Association. 2011. *Alzheimer's Disease Facts and Figures Report.* Washington, DC.

Amato, P. R. 2000. "The Consequences of Divorce for Adults and Children." *Journal of Marriage and the Family* 62, 4: 1269–87.

———. 2001. "Children and Divorce in the 1990s: An Update of the Amato and Keith (1991) Meta-Analysis." *Journal of Family Psychology* 15: 355–370.

———. 2003. "Reconciling Divergent Perspectives: Judith Wallerstein, Quantitative Family Research, and Children of Divorce." *Family Relations* 52, 4 (October): 332–339.

———. 2005. "The Impact of Family Formation Change on the Cognitive, Social and Emotional Well-being of the Next Generation." *The Future of Children* 15, 2: 75–96.

———. 2006. "Marital Discord, Divorce and Children's Well-being: Results from a 20-Year Longitudinal Study of Two Generations." In A. Clarke-Stewart & J F. Dudd, eds., *Families Count: Effects on Child and Adolescent Development,* 179–202, New York: CambridgeUniversity Press.

———., and A. Booth. 1997. *A Generation at Risk.* MA: Harvard University Press.

———, A. Booth, D. R. Johnson, and S. J. Rogers. 2007. *Alone Together: How Marriage in America Is Changing.* Cambridge, MA: Harvard University Press.

Amato, P., and J. Cheadle. 2005. "The Long Reach of Divorce: Divorce and Child Well-Being Across Three Generations." *Journal of Marriage and Family* 67, 1 (February): 191–206.

539

Amato, P. R., and J. B. Kane. 2011. "Parents' Marital Distress, Divorce, and Remarriage: Link with Daughters' Early Family Formation Transitions." (April 2008). http://jfi.saagepub.com/content/early/2011/04/08/019251 3X11404363.full.pdf (2011, July 30).

Amato, P., and D. Previti. 2003. "People's Reasons for Divorcing: Gender, Social Class, the Life Course, and Adjustment." *Journal of Family Issues* 24: 602–626.

Ambert, A. 1986. "Being a Stepparent: Live-in and Visiting Children." *Journal of Marriage and the Family* 48: 795–804.

Ambert, A. M. 2006. "One-Parent Families: Characteristics, Causes, Consequences, and Issues." (March). http://www.vifamily.ca/library/cft/oneparent.html (2008, July 27).

Ameen, J. 2006. "Divorce in Malta." *The Malta Independent Online* (February 19). http://2117.145.4.56/ind/news2.asp?artid=28483 (2006, March 21).

American Academy of Family Physicians. 2002, 2003. "Children's Health." http://www.aafp.org/x16320.xml?printxml (2006, April 28).

American Academy of Matrimonial Lawyers. 2010. "Facebook is Primary Source for Compromising Information." (February 10). www.aaml .org/about-the-academ/press/press-release/e-sisscovery/big-surge-social-networking-evidence-says-survey (2011, July 23).

American Association of Retired Persons. 2002. *The Grandparent Study 2002 Report*. Washington, DC: AARP.

American Bar Association. 2011. "Survey of Recent Statistics." www .americanbar.org/groups/domestic_violence/resources/statistics .html (2011, September 19).

American Civil Liberties Union, 2006. "911 Dispatcher Lost Her Job Because She Lived With Her Boyfriend 'Out of Wedlock.'" (July 20). http://www.aclu.org/womensrights/discrim/26197prs20060720. html (2008, April 20).

American Humane Fact Sheets. 2008. "Child Sexual Abuse." Child Fact Sheets. www.americanhumane.org/site/PageServer?pagename=nr_ fact_sheets_childsexabuse (2008, August 26).

American Indian Relief Council. 2008. "Living Conditions." www .nrcprograms.org/site/PageServer?pagename=airc_livingconditions (2011, September 7).

American Pregnancy Association. 2011. "HIV/AIDS During Pregnancy." www .americanpregnancy.org/womenshealth/hiv.html (2011, September 7).

American Psychological Association. 2001. "Understanding Child Sexual Abuse: Education, Prevention, and Recovery." Office of Public Communications, Washington, DC. PsycNET. www.apa.org/releases/sexabuse/homepage.html (2002, January 19).

———. 2008a. "Answers to your Questions About Sexual Orientation and Homosexuality." http://www.aoa.irg/topics/orientation.html# cantherapychange (2008, April 15).

———. 2008b. "Elder Abuse and Neglect:In Search of Solutions." www .apa.org/pi/aging/eldabuse.html (2008, August 26).

———. 2010. *Report of the Task Force on the Sexualization of Girls*. Washington, DC.

———. 2011. "Answers to Your Questions About Transgender People, Gender Identity, and Gender Expression." www.apa.org/topics/sexuality/ transgender.aspx (2011, June 18).

Amnesty Internationl. 2001. "Afghanistan: Accountability for Civilian Deaths." (October 26). http://www.amnesty.org/en/library/asset/ ASA11/022/2001/en/e20451ea-d8ca-11dd-ad8c-f3d4445c118e/ asa110222001en.html (2002, February 3).

———. 2004. "Making Violence Against Women Count: Facts and Figures." web.amnesty.org/library/Index/ENGACT770362004 (2004, July 8).

———. 2006. "Israel/Lebanon: Deliberate Destruction or 'Collateral Damage'? Israel Attacks on Civilian Infrastructure." (August 23). web .amnesty.org/ library/index/ENGMDE/180072006 (2006, August 24).

———. 2011. "Violence Against Women Information." www.amnestyusa .org/our-work/issues/women-s-rights/violence-against-women/ violence-against-women-information (2011, September 19).

Andersen, M. 2005. *Thinking About Women: Sociological Perspectives in Sex and Gender*. 7th ed. Boston: Allyn & Bacon.

———. 2008. *Thinking About Women: Sociological Perspectives in Sex and Gender*, 8th ed. Boston: Allyn & Bacon.

———., and P. H. Collins. 1992. *Race, Class, and Gender: An Anthology*. Belmont, CA: Wadsworth.

Anderson, D. A., and M. C. Hamilton. 2005. "Gender Role Stereotyping of Parents in Children's Picture Books: The Invisible Father." *Sex Roles* 52: 145–151.

Anderson, E. R., et al. 2004. "Ready to Take a Chance Again: Transitions into Dating Among Divorced Parents." *Journal of Divorce and Remarriage* 40, 3/4: 61–75.

Anderson, K. 2002. Perpetrator or Victim? Relationships Between Intimate Partner Violence and Well-Being." *Journal of Marriage and Family* 64 (November): 851–863.

Anderson, M. L., and P. H. Collins. 2007. "Why Race, Class and Gender Still Matter." In M. L. Anderson and P. H. Collins, eds., *Race, Class, and Gender: An Anthology*, 6th ed., 1–6. Belmont, CA: Wadsworth.

Andress, H. J., B. Borgloh, M. Brockel, M. Giesselmann, and D. Hummelsheim. 2006. "The Economic Consequences of Partnership Dissolution: A Comparative Analysis of Panel Studies from Five European Countries." *European Sociological Review* 22, 5: 533–560.

Angel, J. L., C. J. Buckley, R. J. Angel, and M. A. Jimenez. 2003. "The Economic Consequences of Marital Disruption for Pre-Retirement Age African American, Hispanic, and Non-Hispanic White Women." A paper presented at the Population Association of America Annual Meeting. (May 2). Minneapolis, MN

Antonovics, K. and R. Town. 2004. "Are All the Good Men Married? Uncovering the Sources of the Marital Wage Premium." *American Economic Review* 94: 317–321.

Anxo, D., C. Fagan, and M. Smith. 2007. *Parental Leave in European Countries*. Dublin: European Foundation for the Improvement of Living and Working Conditions.

Arber, S. 2004. "Gender, Marital Status, and Aging." Linking Material, Health, and Social Resources." *Journal of Aging Studies* 18, 1(February): 91–108.

———, K. Perren, and K. Davidson. 2002. "Involvement in Social Organizations in Later Life: Variations by Gender and Class." In L. Anderson, ed., *Cultural Gerontology,* 77–93. Westport, CT: Greenwood.

Aries, P. 1981. *The Hour of Our Death*. New York: Knopf.

Armstrong, S. C. 2009. *Not All Black Girls Know How to Eat: A Story of Bulimia*. Chicago: Lawrence Hill Books.

Arnett, J. 2003. *Adolescence and Emerging Adulthood: A Cultural Approach*, rev. 2d ed. Upper Saddle River, NJ: Prentice Hall.

Arnold, D. 2007. "Decline in the Traditional Family." Yahoo Contributor Network. http://www.associatedcontent.com/article/234244/decline_in_the_ traditional_family.html (2011, March 14).

Arp, C., and D. Arp. 2001. "The Magic of Older Love: Stoking Your Marital Fires Through the Years." In J. R. Levine and H. J. Markman, eds., *Why Do Fools Fall in Love? Experiencing the Magic, Mystery, and Meaning of Successful Relationships,* 117–122. San Francisco, CA: Jossey-Bass.

Artacoz, L., J. Benach, C. Borrell, and I. Cortes. 2004. "Unemployment and Mental Health: Understanding the Interactions Among Gender, Family Roles and Social Class." *American Journal of Public Health* 94, 1: 82–88.

Asher-Meadow. 2001. "The Many Faces of MSP." *MSP Magazine*. www .ashermeadow.com/amm/notes2.htm (2002, January 24).

"Assistance in Managing a Stepfamily." 2011. (June 24.) www.stepfamily .org.au/?p=1093 (2011, August 1).

Associated Press. 2003. "Asian-American Divorce Rate Up, Census Shows." *Starbulletin.com* (May 29). http://starbulletin.com/2003/05/29/new/ story5.html (2006, March 9).

———. 2005. "You Couldn't Ask for a More Perfect Union." *Chicago Tribune* (June 30).

———. 2008a. "Gay Couples Having Trouble Obtaining Divorces." (April 15). www.msnbc.msn.com/id/24132681/ns/us_news-life/t/gay-couples-having-trouble-obtaining-divorces/ (2011, July 20).

———. 2008b. "Michigan Couple Takes Vows at Family Funeral Home." *FoxNews.com* (September 1) www.foxnews.com/story/0,2933,414401,00 .html (2008, September 17).

———. 2010."Interracial Marriage Rising but Not As Fast." www.cbsnews .com/8301-201_162-6520098.html (2011, August 15).

———. 2011. Associated Press-Lifegoesstrong.com Boomers Survey, June 2011. Palo Alto, CA: Knowledge Networks. www.knowledgenetworks .com (2011, July 5).

Atchley, R. 1991. *Social Forces and Aging,* 6th ed. Belmont, CA: Wadsworth.

Attanasio, O., and V. Lechene. 2002. "Tests of Income Pooling in Household Decisions." *Review of Economic Dynamics* 5, 4: 720–748.

"Attitude Toward Social Issues." 2011 (March 3). http://people-presss .org/2011/03/03/section-3-attitudes-toward-social-issues/ (2011, September 9).

Atwater, L. 1982. *The Extramarital Connection: Sex, Intimacy, Identity.* New York: Irvington.

Aumann, K., E. Galinsky, and K. Matos. 2011. *The New Male Mystique.* New York: Families and Work Institute.

Aunola, K., and J. E. Nurmi. 2005. "The Role of Parenting Styles in Children's Problem Behavior." *Child Development* 76 (November/ December): 1144–1159.

Ave, M. 2008. "Parents Waiver Over Wisdom of Spanking. (February 6).

"Average Cost of Divorce." 2011. (May 31). http://thedivoreinsider.com/ average-cost-of-divorce/ (2011, July 20).

Avon Foundation. 2006. "Speak Out Against Domestic Violence." www .avoncompany.com/women/speakout/informational_materials/pa (2006, July 16).

Bachrach, C. A. 1980. "Childlessness and Social Isolation among the Elderly." *Journal of Marriage and the Family* 42: 627–37.

———. 1986. "Adoption Plans, Adopted Children, and Adoptive Mothers." *Journal of Marriage and the Family* 48: 243–53.

———, P. F. Adams, S. Sambrano, and K. A. London. 1990. *Adoption in the 1980s.* U.S. National Center for Health Statistics, Advance Data no. 181 (January 5).

Baker, K., and A. A. Raney. 2007. "Equally Super? Gender-Role Stereotyping of Superheroes in Children's Animated Programs." *Mass Communication & Society* 10, 1: 25–41.

Baltimore County Police Department. 2007. "Facts About Child Abuse." www.baltimorecountymd.gov/Agencies/police/community/abuse .html (2008, August 23).

Baltimore Sun. 2011. "Is Dating Dead? Hook-Ups, Hang-Outs Changing Romance." (February 14). http://mobile.baltimoresun.com/p.p?m=b&a =rp&id=13508&postId=13508&postUserId=46&sessionToken= (2011, July 8).

Bandura, A., and R. H. Walters. 1963. *Social Learning and Personality Development.* New York: Holt, Rinehart & Winston.

Banis, R., ed. 2006. *Sexually Transmitted Diseases: Symptoms, Diagnosis, Treatment, Prevention.* 2nd ed. Science and Humanities Press.

Banker, B. S., and S. L. Gaertner. 1998. "Achieving Stepfamily Harmony: An Intergroup-Relations Approach." *Journal of Family Psychology* 12, 3 (September): 310–25.

———. 2001. *Intergroup Relations in Stepfamilies: In Search of Processes Involved in the Attainment of Stepfamily Harmony.* Paper presented at the annual meeting of the Society for the Study of Social Problems, Anaheim, CA.

Banks, R. 2011. *Is Marriage for White People? How the African American Marriage Decline Affects Everyone.* New York: Dutton Adult.

Barber, B. L., and D. H. Demo. 2006. "The Kids Are Alright (at Least Most of Them): Links between Divorce and Dissolution and Child Well-being." In M. A. Fine and J. H. Harvey (eds) *Handbook of Divorce and Relationship Dissolution,* 289–311. Mahwah, NJ: Erlbaum.

Barcus, E. F. 1983. *Images of Life on Children's Television: Sex Roles, Minorities and Families.* New York: Praeger.

Bardasi, E., and M. Taylor. 2005. "Marriages and Wages." Working Papers of the Institute for Social and Economic Research. Paper 2005–1. Colchester: University of Essex.

Barer, B. M. 2001. "The 'Grands and Greats' of Very Old Black Grandmothers." *Journal of Aging Studies* 15, 1 (March): 1–11.

Barker, O. 2005. "Never-Married Singles Face Negative Reaction." *USA Today* (February 22): E1.

Barling, J. 1991. "Father's Employment: A Neglected Influence on Children." In J. V. Lerner and N. L. Galambos, eds., *Employed Mothers and Their Children,* 181–209. New York: Garland.

Barnett, O. W., C. L. Miller-Perrin, and R. D. Perrin. 2004. *Family Violence across the Lifespan.* Thousand Oaks, CA: Sage.

Barnett, R., and C. Rivers. 2004. *Same Difference: How Gender Myths Are Hurting Our Relationships, Our Children, and Our Jobs.* New York: Basic Books.

———. 2006. "The Boy Crisis—Fact or Myth?' (Publication ID Number 12750, October 2). www.tcrecord.org (2011, April 10).

Barr, M. 2005. "Shaken Baby Syndrome Is Real and Based on Medical Evidence." National Center on Shaken Baby Syndrome. www.dontshake .com (2006, July 19).

Bartkowski, J. 1999. "One Step Forward, One Step Back: Progressive Traditionalism and the Negotiation of Domestic Labor in Evangelical Families." *Gender Issues* 17, 4 (Fall): 37–61.

Bartkowski, J. P., and J. G. Read. 2003. "Veiled Submission: Gender, Power, and Identity Among Evangelical and Muslim Women in the United States." *Qualitative Sociology* 26, 1: 71–92.

Bartley, S. J., W. Judge, and S. Judge, 2007. "Antecedents of Marital Happiness and Career Satisfaction: An Empirical Study of Dual-Career Marriages." *Journal of Management,* 1, 1. http:/www.scientificjournals.org/ journals2007/articles/1059.htm (2008, July 1).

Barton, J. 2010. "Who Should Pay for a Wedding? Fewer Parents Are Footing the Bill." (September 14). www.lemondrop.com/2010/09/14/who-should-pay-for-a-wedding/4 (2011, July 4).

Basow, S. 1992. *Gender: Stereotypes and Roles,* 3rd. ed. Belmont, CA: Brooks/Cole.

Batalova, J., and M. McHugh. 2010. "Dream vs. Reality: An Analysis of Potential DREAM Act Beneficiaries." *Insight.* (July). Migration Policy Institute.

Battle, J., C. Cohen, D. Warren, G. Fergerson, and S. Audam. 2002. *Say It Loud, I'm Black and I'm Proud: Black Pride Survey.* 2000. New York: The National Gay and Lesbian Task Force Policy Institute.

Batty, D. 2008. "Marriage Rates Fall to Lowest-ever Level." (March 26).

Baumrind, D. 1968. "Authoritarian versus Authoritative Parental Control." *Adolescence* 3: 255–72.

———. 1979. "Current Patterns of Parental Authority." *Developmental Psychology Monographs* 41: 255.

———. 1991. "Effective Parenting during the Early Adolescent Transition." In P. Cowan and E. M. Hetherington, eds., *Advances in Family Research:* vol. 2, Family Transition, 111–63. Hillsdale, NJ: Erlbaum.

Bauserman, R. 2002. "Child Adjustment in Joint-Custody Versus Sole-Custody Arrangements: A Meta-Analytic Review." *Journal of Family Psychology* 16, 1: 91–162.

Bauza, V. 2008. "New to American, but Old and Lonely." *Chicago Tribune* (January 8): 1, 13.

Baxter, J. 2001. "Marital Status and the Division of Household Labour." *Family Matters* 58 (Autumn): 16–21.

Baxter, L. A., D. O. Braithwaite, J. K. Kellas, C. LeClair-Underberg, E. L. Normand, T. Routsong, and M. Thatcher. 2009. "Empty Ritual: Young-adult Stepchildren's Perceptions of the Remarriage Ceremony." *Journal of Social and Personal Relationships* 26, 4: 467–487.

BBC News. 2000. "Globalisation: What on Earth Is It All About?" (September 14). ncws.bbc.co.uk/hi/english/special_report/1999/02/99/e-cyclopedia/ newsid_711000/711906.stm (2002, January 18).

———. 2005. "Call for More Male Primary Teachers." (October 13). http://news.bbc.co.uk/go/pr/fr/-/2/hi/uk_news/education/4336092 .sm (2011, April 6).

———. 2009. "Call for More Male Nursery Staff." (January 20). http:// news.bbc.co.uk/go/pr/fr/-/2/hi/uk_news/eduction/7838273.stm (2011, April 6).

———. 2011. "Mexico's Drug-Related Violence." (August 26). www.bbc.co .uk/news/world-latin-america-10681249. (October 8).

Bean, F., R. Curtis, Jr., and J. Marcum. 1977. "Familism and Marital Satisfaction among Mexican Americans: The Effects of Family Size, Wife's Labor Force Participation."

Beauboeuf-Lafontant, T. 2005. "Keeping Up Appearances. Getting Fed Up: The Embodiment of Strength among African American Women." *Meridias* 5, 2 (Spring): 104–123.

———. 2009. *Behind the Mask of the Strong Black Woman.* Philadelphia: Temple University Press.

Becker, H. 1967. "Whose Side Are We On?" *Social Problems*, 14 (Winter) 239–247.

Beckman, J. 2010. "Can a Breakup Be Good for Your Health?" www.sheknows.com/health-and-wellness/articles/815830/can-a-breakup-be-good-for-your-health-1 (2011, July 8).

Bedard, K., and O. Deschenes. 2005. "Sex Preferences, Marital Dissolution, and the Economic Status of Women." *The Journal of Human Resources* 40, 2 (Spring): 411–434.

Bedford, V. H. 1997. "Sibling Relationships in Middle Adulthood and Old Age." In R. M. Blieszner and V. H. Bedford, eds. 1995. *Handbook on Aging and The Family*, 201–222, Westport, CT: Greenwood.

———, and M. Diderich. 2009. *Encyclopedia of Human Relations*. SAGE Publications.

Beer, W. R. 1989. *Strangers in the House: The World of Stepsiblings and Half-Siblings*. New Brunswick, NJ: Transaction.

Belkin, L. 2008. "When Mom and Dad Share it All." *New York Times*. (June 15) http://www.nytimes.com/2008/06/15/magazine/15parenting-t.html (July 26 2008).

———. 2009. "Father's Day Facts." *New York Times* (June 19). http://parenting.blogs.nytimes.com/2009/06/19/fathers-day-facts/ (2011, September 9).

Bell, A. P., and M. Weinberg. 1978. *Homosexualities: A Study of Diversities among Men*. New York: Simon & Schuster.

Bem, S. L. 1983. "Gender Schema Theory and Its Implications for Child Development: Raising Gender-Schematic Children in a Gender-Schematic Society." *Signs* 8: 598–616.

———. 1993. *The Lenses of Gender: Transforming the Debate on Social Inequality*. New Haven, CT: Yale University Press.

Bemiller, M. 2008. "Non-custodial Mothers: Thematic Trends and Future Directions." *Sociology Compas* 2, 3: 910–924.

Bender, K. A., and I. Theodossiou. 2007. "Your Job or Your Life? The Uncertain Relationship of Unemployment and Mortality (July). http://ssrn.com/abstract=1003356 (2008, July 15).

Benjamin, L. 1991. *The Black Elite: Facing the Color Line in the Twilight of the Twentieth Century*. Chicago: Nelson-Hall.

Benjamin, O., and O. Sullivan. 1996. "The Importance of Difference." *Sociological Review* 44, 2: 225–51.

Bennhold, K. 2010. "The Female Factor: Paternity Leave Law Helps to Redefine Masculinity in Sweden. (June 15). http://query.nytimes.com/gst/fullpage.html?res=9FOCES5DD1338F936A25755COA9669D8863 (2011, July 4).

Berado, F. M. 1968. "Widowhood Status in the U.S.: Perspectives on a Neglected Aspect of the Family Life Cycle." *Family Coordinator* 17: 191–203.

———. 1970. "Survivorship and Social Isolation: The Case of the Aged Widower." *Family Coordinator* 19: 11–15.

Berdahl, J. L. 2007. "The Sexual Harassment of Uppity Women." *Journal of Applied Psychology* 92, 2: 425–437.

———, and C. Moore. 2006. "Workplace Harassment: Double Jeopardy for Minority Women." *Journal of Applied Psychology* 91, 2: 426–436.

Beresford, B., P. Rabiee, and T. Sloper. 2005. "Priorities and Perceptions of Disabled Children and Young People and their Families Regarding Outcomes of Social Care." The University of York, Social Policy Research Center. www.york.ac.uk/inst/spru/research/summs/priorpercep.htm (2006, August 17).

Berger, R. 2001. "Gay Stepfamilies: A Triple-Stigmatized Group." In J. M. Lehmann, ed., *The Gay and Lesbian Marriage and Family Reader*, 171–194. Lincoln: University of Nebraska Press.

Berger, R., J. Fromkin, H. Stutz, K. Makoroff, P. Scribano, K. Feldman, L. Tu, and A. Fabio. 2011. "Abusive Head Trauma During a Time of Increased Unemployment: A Multicenter Analysis." *Pediatrics* (September 19). http://pediatrics.aappublications.org/content/early/2011/09/15/peds.2010-2185 (September 19).

Bergman, M. 2006. "Americans Marrying Older, Living Alone More." In "Households Shrinking, Census Bureau Reports." Press Release CB06-83, May 25. Washington, DC: U.S. Census Bureau.

Berkofsky, J. 2001. "By Numbers, NJPS Paints Portrait of American Jewry." *Jewish Community Federation*. (September 10). www.sfjcf.org/news/archive/story.asp?ArticleID=84299 (2006, February 10).

Berland, G., et al. 2001. "Health Information on the Internet: Accessibility, Quality and Readability in English and Spanish." *Journal of the American Medical Association* 285 (May 23/30): 2612–2621.

Berman, L. 2011. "10 Sexual Fantasies for Women." *Everyday Health*. www.everydayhealth.com/sexual-health/better-sex/10-sexual-fantasies-for-women.aspx.

Bernard, J. 1972. *The Future of Marriage*. New York: World.

———. 1984. "The Good-Provider Role: Its Rise and Fall." In P. Voydanoff, ed., *Work and Family: Changing Roles of Men and Women*, 43–60. Palo Alto, CA: Mayfield.

Bernstein, E. 2007. "Men, Boys Lack Options to Treat Eating Disorders." *The Wall Street Journal Online*. http://www.online.wsj.com/public/article_print/5b117676525698871913_QhQj40rCTnk_ljyPof6Tnj_PNrQ_20080416.html (2008, March 20).

Beroset, D. 2011. "Finance Tips for Second Marriages." www.bhg.com/health-family/finances/work-insurance-wills/whats-yours-mine-and-ours-in-a-second-marriage/ (August 5).

Berry, J. 2007. "Acculturation Strategies and Adaptation." In J. Lansford, K. Deater-Deckard, and M. Bornstein, eds., *Immigrant Families in Contemporary Society*. New York: The Guilford Press.

Best, J., ed. 1995. *Images of Issues: Typifying Contemporary Social Problems*. New York: Aldine de Gruyter.

Bevin, T. 2001. "Parenting in Cuban American Families." In Webb, N. B., ed., *Culturally Diverse Parent-Child and Family Relationships*. New York: Columbia University Press.

Bhalla, V. 2008. "Couch Potatoes and Super-Women: Gender Migration and the Emerging Discourse on Housework among Asia Indian Immigrants." *Journal of American Ethnic History* 27 (4): 71–99.

Bhanot, R., and J. Jovanovic. 2005. "Do Parental Academic Stereotypes Influence Whether They Intrude on Their Children's Homework?" *Sex Roles* 52, 9/10 (May): 597–607.

Bianchi, S. M., J. P. Robinson, and M. A. Milkie. 2006. *Changing Rhythms of American Family Life*. New York: Russell Sage Foundation.

Biblarz, T. J., and J. Stacey. 2010. "How Does the Gender of Parents Matter?" *Journal of Marriage and Family* 72, 13–22.

Biden, J. 2011. "Biden on 17th Anniversary of the Violence Against Women Act." (September 27): *ABC Television, The View*.

Bilefsky, D. 2006. "How to Avoid Honor Killing in Turkey? Honor Suicide." *New York Times* (July 16): 3.

Billingsley, A. 1968. *Black Families in White America*. Englewood Cliffs, NJ: Prentice Hall.

Bingham, J. 2009. "One in Five of 'Boomerang Generation' Graduates Now Living at Home." (December 8). www.telegraph.co.uk/earth/greenpolitics/population/6762298/One-in-five-of-boomerang-generation-graduates-now-living-at-home.html (2011, April 25).

Bir-Akturk, E. and H. Fisiloglu. 2009. "Marital Satisfaction in Turkish Remarried Families: Marital Status, Stepchildren, and Contributing Factors." *Journal of Divorce and Remarriage* 50, 2: 119–147.

Black, H. 2006. "Weighing Age, Care: Elderly Are Target of Calls for Ration of Health Care." *Milwaukee Journal Sentinel*. (April 9). http://www.jsonline.com/story/index.aspx?id=414101 (2006, June 26).

Blackless, M., A. Charuvastra, A. Derryck, A. Fausto-Sterling, K. Lauzanne, and E. Lee. 2000. "How Sexually Dimorphic Are We? Review and Synthesis." *American Journal of Human Biology* 12: 151–166.

Blake, W. M., and C. A. Darling. 2000. "Quality of Life: Perceptions of African Americans." *Journal of Black Studies* 30 (January): 411–427.

Blankenhorn, D. 1998. "The Diminishment of American Fatherhood." In S. J. Ferguson, ed., *Shifting the Center: Understanding Contemporary Families*, 337–35. Mountain View, CA: Mayfield.

Blau, P. 1964. *Exchange and Power in Social Life*. New York: Wiley.

Blekesaune, M. 2008. "Unemployment and Partnership Dissolution." (May). http://iser.essex.ac.uk/pubs/workpapers/pdf/2008-21.pdf (2008, July 31).

Block, J. 1981. "Your Marriage Survival Kit." *Parents* (April): 61+.

Blow, C. 2008. "The Demise of Dating." *New York Times*. (December 13). www.nytimes.com/2008/12/13/opinion/13blow.html?pagewanted=print (2011, July 8).

Blumstein, P., and P. Schwartz. 1983. *American Couples: Money, Work, Sex*. New York: Morrow.

Bohannan, P. 1970. *Divorce and After*. New York: Doubleday.
———. 1985. *All the Happy Families*. New York: McGraw-Hill.

Bojorquez, J. 1997. "Line by Line, Their Marriage Is Working." *Sacramento Bee* (February 10). www.sacbee.com/static/archive/news/projects/lessons/linebyline.html (2001, November 11).

Booth, A., M. E. Scott, and V. King. 2010. "Father Residence and Adolescent Problem Behavior: Are Youth Always Better Off in Two-Parent Families?" *Journal of Family Issues* 31, 5: 585–605.

Borland, D. 1975. "An Alternative Model of the Wheel Theory." *Family Coordinator* 24 (July): 289–292.

Boston Women's Health Book Collective. 2011. (9th ed.) *Our Bodies, Ourselves*. New York: Touchstone Publishing.

Boswell, T. D., and J. R. Curtis. 1983. *The Cuban-American Experience: Culture, Images and Perspectives*. Totowa, NJ: Rowman and Allanheld.

Bott, S., A. Morrison, and A. Ellsberg. 2005. "Preventing and Responding to Gender-Based Violence in Middle and Low-Income Countries: A Global Review and Analysis." World Bank Policy Research Working Paper 3618, (June). World Bank. Washington, DC.

Boushey, H., J. Arons, and L. Smith. 2010. "Families Can't Afford the Gender Wage Gap." (April 20). www.americanprogress.org/issues/2010/04/equal_pay.html (2011, July 5).

Bower, B. 2001. "Healthy Aging May Depend on Past Habits." *Science News* 159, 24 (June 16): 373.

Boyd-Franklin, N. 2006. *Black Families in Therapy: Understanding the African American Experience*. New York: Guilford Press.

Bradsher, K. 1989. "Employers Urge Men to Wed for Success." *News and Observer* (December 23): 3D.

Braithwaite, D. O., L. N. Olson, T. D. Golish, C. Soukup, and P. Turnman. 2001. "Becoming a Family: Developmental Processes Represented in Blended Family Discourse." *Journal of Applied Communication Research* 29: 221–247.

Brambila, N. C. 2009. "Gay Seniors Lack Social Safety Net." (July 6). www.sageusa.org/about/news_item.cfm?new=136 (2011, August 26).

Bramford, G. 2005. "Cohousing of Older People: Housing Innovations in the Netherlands and Denmark." *Australasian Journal of Aging* 24, 1: 44–46.

Bramlett, M. D., and W. D. Mosher. 2002 *Cohabitation, Marriage, Divorce, and Remarriage in the United States*. Series 23, No. 22. Hyattsville, MD: National Center for Health Statistics.

Braniff, D. 2010. "Widow's Tax." (May 20). www.50plus.com/money/widows-tax/528/ (2011, August 27).

Braver, S. L., I. M. Ellman, A. M. Votruba, and W. V. Fabricius. 2011. "Lay Judgments About Child Custody after Divorce." *Psychology, Public Policy, and Law* 17, 2: 212–240.

Braver, S., J. R. Shapiro, and M. R. Goodman. 2006. "Consequences of Divorce for Parents." In M. A. Fine and J. H. Harvey, eds., *Handbook of Divorce and Relationship Dissolution*, 313–337. Mahwah, NJ: Erlbaum.

Bray, J., and J. Kelly. 1998. *Stepfamilies: Love, Marriage and Parenting in the First Decade*. New York: Broadway Books.

Breton, T. 2008. "Most Doctors Don't Report Elder Abuse." *The Providence Journal*. (August 18), San Angelo, TX: Scripts Interactive Newspaper Group.

Brewer, L. 2001. "Gender Socialization and the Cultural Construction of Elder Caregivers." *Journal of Aging Studies* 15, 3 (September): 217–35.

Bricheno, P., and M. Thorton. 2007. "Role Model, Hero or Champion? Children's Views Concerning Role Models. *Educational Research* 49 (4): 383–396.

Brier, S., J. E. Grable, B. S. N. Goff, and M. White. 2008. "The Influence of Perceived Spending Behaviors on Relationship Satisfaction." *Financial Counseling and Planning* 19: 31–43.

Britsch, R. Lanier, and T. D. Olson. 2007. "Remarriage and Combined Families." *Counseling: A Guide to Helping Others* 2 (April 22): 172–186.

Brittman, M., P. England, L. Sayer, N. Folbre, and G. Matheson. 2003. "When Does Gender Trump Money? Bargaining and Time in Household Work." *American Journal of Sociology* 109, 1 (July): 186–214.

Brod, H., ed. 1987. *The Making of Masculinities: The New Men's Studies*. Boston: Allen & Unwin.

Brody, J. 2006. "Children, Media and Sex: A Big Book of Blank Pages." *New York Times* (January 31): Sec. F, 7.

Brody, J. E. 1999. "Earlier Work with Children Steers Them from Crime." *New York Times* (March 15): A16.

Bronte-Tinkew, J., K. A. Moore, R. C. Capps, and J. Zaff. 2006. *The Influence of Father Involvement on Youth Risk Behaviors Among Adolescents: A Comparison of Native-born and Immigrant Families*. Social Science Research 35: 181–209.

Broverman, I., D. M. Broverman, F. E. Clarkson, P. S. Rosenkrantz, and S. R. Vogel. 1970. "Sex-Role Stereotypes and Clinical Judgments of Mental Health." *Journal of Consulting and Clinical Psychology* 34: 1–7.

Brown, D. 2010. "Single Black Women Being Urged to Date Outside Race." (February 25). *Washington Post*. www.washingtonpost.com/wp-dyn/content/article/2010/02/24/AR2010022405727.html (2011, October 8).

Brown, E. T., L. Orbush, and A. Maharaj. 2010. "Social Networks and Marital Stability among Black American and White American Couples." In K. T. Sullivan and J. Davila, eds., *Support Processes in Intimate Relationships*, 318–34, New York: Oxford University Press.

Brown, J., and S. Keller. 2000. "Can the Mass Media Be Healthy Sex Educators?" *Family Planning Perspectives* 32, 5 (September/October): 255–256.

Brown, J., K. L'Engle, C. Pardun, G. Guo, K. Kenneavy, and C. Jackson, 2006. "Sexy Media Matter: Exposure to Sexual Content in Music, Movies, Television, and Magazines Predicts Black and White Adolescents' Sexual Behavior." *Pediatrics*. (117): 1018–1027.

Brown, S. L., and W. D. Manning. 2009. "Family Boundary Ambiguity and the Measurement of Family Structure: The Significance of Cohabitation." *Demography* 46, 1: 85–101.

Brown, S., and I. D. Yalom. 1995. *Treating Alcoholism*. San Francisco: Jossey-Bass.

Browning, A. 2011. "First Valentine: Lasting Legacy of 500-Year-Old Love." BBC News. (February 13) www.bbc.co.uk/news/uk-12419712 (2011, May 29).

Brownsworth, V. 1996. "Tying the Knot or the Hangman's Noose: The Case against Marriage." *Journal of Gay, Lesbian, and Bisexual Identity* 1 (January): 91–98.

Brubaker, T. H. 1985. *Later Life Families*. Beverly Hills, CA: Sage.
———. 1990. *Family Relationships in Later Life*. 2nd ed. Newbury Park, CA: Sage.

Bryjak, G. J., and M. P. Soroka. 1994. *Sociology: Cultural Diversity in a Changing World*. Needham Heights, MA: Allyn & Bacon.

Buchler, C., A. Krishnakuman, G. Stone, C. Anthony, S. Pemerton, and J. Gerard. 1998. "Interparental Conflict Styles and Youth Problem Behaviors: A Two-Sample Replication Study." *Journal of Marriage and the Family* 60: 119–32.

Buckley, C. 2007. "Gays Living in Shadows in New Iraq." *New York Times* (December 18): A8.

Buehler, C., and M. Langenbrunner. 1987. "Divorce-Related Stressors: Occurrence, Disruptiveness, and Area of Life Change." *Journal of Divorce* 11: 25–50.

Bukhari, A. 2004. *Muslims' Place in the American Public Square: Hope, Fears, and Aspirations*. Walnut Creek, CA: Alta Mira.

Bumpass, L., and H. Lu. 2000. "Trends in Cohabitation and Implications for Children's Family Contexts in the United States." *Population Studies* 54 (March): 29–41.

Bunch, C. 1999. "Violence against Women and Girls: The Intolerable Status Quo." In C. Albers, *Sociology of Families: Readings* 296–298. Thousand Oaks, CA: Pine Forge Press.

Bunker, B. B., J. M. Zubek, V. J. Vanderslice, and R. W. Rice. 1992. "Quality of Life in Dual-Career Families: Commuting versus Single-Residence Couples." *Journal of Marriage and the Family* 54: 399–407.

Bunting, L., and C. McAuley. 2004a. "Teenage Pregnancy and Motherhood: The Contribution of Support." *Child and Family Social Work* 9 (2): 2007–2015.
———. 2004b. "Teenage Pregnancy and Parenthood: The Role of Fathers." *Child and Family Social Work* 9, 3: 295–303.

Bureau of Labor Statistics. 2008. "Employment Characteristics of Families in 2007." *News* (May 30). Washington, DC: U.S. Department of Labor.

——. 2010a. *American Time Use Survey*. Washington, DC: U.S. Department of Labor.

——. 2010b. "Percent of Men and Women Engaged in Household Activities, 2009." (June 29). http://data.bls.gov/cgi-bin/print.pl/opub/ted/2010/ted_20100629.html (2011, March 30).

——. 2010c. *Women in the Labor Force: A Databook 2010*. Washington, DC, Table 25.

——. 2011a. "Employment Characteristics of Families—2010." (March 24). www.bls.gov/news.release/famee.nr0.htm (2011, June 25).

——. 2011b. "Employment Situation—June 2011." (July 8). www.bls.gov/news/release/pdf/empsit.pdf (2011, July 11).

——. 2011c. "Labor Force Characteristics by Race and Ethnicity, 2010." U.S. Department of Labor (August). Report 1032. www.bls.gov/cps/demographics.htm (September 7).

——. 2011d. "Union Members Summary." (January 21). www.bls.gov/news.release/union2.nr0.htm (2011, July 7).

Burger, J. M., and L. Burns. 1988. "The Illusion of Unique Invulnerability and the Use of Effective Contraception." *Personality and Social Psychology Bulletin* 14: 264–70.

Burgess, E. W. 1926. "The Family as a Unity of Interacting Personalities." *Family* 7: 3–9.

Buri, J. 2010. "Love at First Sight." (February 16). www.psychologytoday.com/blog/love-bytes/201002/love-first-sight (2011, May 29).

Burke, K., and L. Sikkema. 2007. *Native American Power*. State Legislatures (June): 32–35.

Burke, S., J. Oomen-Early, and R. Rager. 2009. "Latina Women's Experiences with Intimate Partner Violence: A Grounded Theory Approach." *Family Violence Prevention & Health Practice*. (February 2). www.endabuse.org/health/ejournal/2009/02/latina-womens-experiences-with-intimate-pa (2011, September 7).

Burman, P. 1988. *Killing Time, Losing Ground: Experiences of Unemployment*. Toronto: Wall and Thompson.

Burns, A. L., G. Mitchell, and S. Obradovich. 1989. "Of Sex Roles and Strollers: Female and Male Attention to Toddlers at the Zoo." *Sex Roles* 20: 309–15.

Burst Media. 2007. "Online, The Doctor Is Always In." Burst Media Online Insights. (August). *Burst Media, Inc.*

Business Briefing. 2011. "Hey, Mom's Worth $61,436." *Chicago Tribune* (May 6): 35.

Business Wire. 2008. "Schwab Study Finds Four Generations of American Adults Fundamentally Rethinking Planning for and Living in Retirement." (July 15). http://findarticles.com/p/article/mi_m)EIN/is_2008_July_15/ae_n27912973 (2008, August 20).

Buss, D. 2000. *The Dangerous Passion: Why Jealousy Is as Necessary as Love and Sex*. New York: Free Press.

Bussey, J., and J. Trasviña. 2003. "Racial Preferences: The Treatment of White and African American Job Applicants by Temporary Employment Agencies in California." Berkeley, CA: Discrimination Research Center.

Butler, D. 1999. "Healthy Ideas: Pregnant and Prosecuted." http://healthyideas.com/poll/980825/html (1999, May 19).

Butler, R. 1975. *Why Survive? Being Old in America*. New York: Harper & Row.

Cahn, N., and J. Carbone. 2010. *Red Families v. Blue Families*. New York: Oxford University Press, USA.

Calhoun, A. W. 1917. *A Social History of the American Family: From Colonial Times to the Present*, vol. 1. Cleveland: Arthur H. Clark.

Callahan, D. 2003. *Setting Limits: Medical Goals in an Aging Society*. Washington, DC, Georgetown University Press.

Callis, R., and L. Cavanaugh. 2008. "Census Bureau Reports on Residential Vacancies and Home Ownership." *U.S. Census Bureau News* (July 24). Washington, DC: U.S. Department of Commerce.

Campbell, G. 2011. "Stepfamily Fact Sheet" (March 16). http://support|forstepdads.com/2011/03/stepfamily-fact-sheet/ (2011, August 1).

Campbell, L. 2007. "What Maintains the Myth of the Wicked Stepmother?" *Journal of Child and Adolescent Psychiatric*, 8, 4 (August 23): 17–22. http://www3.interscience.wiley.com/journal/119965555/abstract (2008, August 15).

Campbell, S. 2001. "Moving On: Parental Breakups May Not Always Be Bad for Kids." *Psychology Today* 34, 4 (July/August):16.

Canada, G. 1998. *Reaching Up for Manhood: Transforming the Lives of Boys in America*. Boston: Beacon Press.

Cancian, F. 1993. "Gender Politics: Love and Power in the Private and Public Spheres." In B. J. Fox, ed., *Family Patterns, Gender Relations*, 204–212. Toronto: Oxford University Press.

Cano, A., and K. O'Leary. 1997. "Romantic Jealousy and Affairs: Research and Implications for Couple Therapy." *Journal of Sex and Marital Therapy* 23 (4): 249–275.

Capps, R., R. M. Castanada, A. Chaudry, and R. Santos. 2007. *Paying the Price: The Impact of Immigration on America's Children*. Washington, DC: The National Council of La Raza and the Urban Institute.

Caputo, R. K. 2005. "Editor's Introduction: Challenges of Aging on U.S. Families: Policy and Practice Implications." *Marriage and Family Reviews* 37, 1/2: 3–6.

Carbon, S. 2010. "Message From the Director." Washington, DC: U.S. Department of Justice, Office of Violence Against Women. www.ovw.usdoj.gov/director-sept2010msg.htm (2011, July 5).

Careerbuilder.com. 2011. "Nearly One-in-Five Workers Have Dated Co-Workers At Least Twice During Their Career." (February 10). www.careerbuilder.com/share/aboutus/pressreleasesdetail.aspx? (2011, October 8).

Carmichael, S., and C. Hamilton. 1967. *Black Power: The Politics of Liberation in America*. New York: Vintage Books/Random House.

Carnevale, A., N. Smith, and J. Strohl. 2010. *Help Wanted: Projections of Jobs and Education Requirements Through 2018*. Washington, DC: Georgetown University Center of Education and the Workforce.

Carr, D. S. 2004. "Black/White Differences in Psychological Adjustment to Spousal Loss Among Older Adults." *Research on Aging* 26, 6: 591–622.

——, and R. Utz. 2002. "Later-Life Widowhood in the United States: New Directions in Research and Theory." *Aging International* 27, 1: 65–88.

Carr, L. G., and L. S. Walsh. 1983. "The Planter's Wife: The Experience of White Women in 17th Century Maryland." In M. Gordon, ed., *The American Family in Social-Historical Perspective*, 263–88. New York: St. Martin's Press.

Carr-Gregg, M. 2011. *Surviving Step-families*. Penguin Group Australia.

Carrasquiullo, H. 2002. "The Puerto Rican Family." In R. Taylor (ed.), *Minority Families in the United States*. Upper Saddle River, NJ: Prentice Hall.

Carroll, J. 2005a. "Americans' Personal Satisfaction." The Gallup Organization (January 4) www.gallup.com/poll/14506/Americans-Personal-Satisfaction.aspx? (2008, July 4).

——. 2005b. "Who's Worried About Their Weight?" The Gallup Organization (August 9). www.gallup.com/poll/content/print.aspx?ci= 17752 (2005, August 16).

——. 2007. "Most Americans Approve of Interracial Marriages." The Gallup Organization www.gallup.com/poll/2841//Most-Americans-Approve (2008, July 4).

Carter, S. 2002. *The Impact of Parent/Family Involvement on Student Outcomes: An Annotated Bibliography of Research from the Past Decade*. Eugene, OR: Consortium for Appropriate Dispute Resolution in Special Education.

Cartwright, C. 2010. "Preparing to Repartner and Live in a Stepfamily: An Exploratory Investigation." *Journal of Family Studies* 16, 3: 237-250.

Casey, J. 2007. "Time for Reform: Aging Out and On Their Own." (May 27). www.docuticker.com/?p=13579 (2008, August 31).

Castleman, M. 2009. "How Common Is Masturbation Really?" *Psychology Today*, (March 30). www.psychologytoday.com/blog/all-about-sex-200903/how-common-is-masturbation (2011, August 1).

Catalano, S. 2007. "Intimate Partner Violence in the United States." U.S. Department of Justice, Office of Justice Programs, Bureau of Justice Statistics (December 19). www.ojp.usdoj.gov/bjs/ (2008, August 8).

Catalyst. 2011. "The Catalyst Pyramid: U.S. Women in Business." (May 2). www.catalyst.org/publication/132/us-women-in-business (2011, July 5).

Catani, C., E. Schauer, T. Elbert, I. Missmahl, J. P. Bette, and E. Neuner. 2009. "War Trauma, Child Labor, and Family Violence: Life Adversities and PTSD in a Sample of School Children in Kabul." *Journal of Traumatic Stress* 22, 3: 163–171.

Cauchon, D., and B. Hansen, 2011. "Typical U.S. Family Got Poorer During the Past 10 Years." *USA Today*. (September 14). www.usatoday.com/news/nation/story/2011-09-13/census-household-income/50383882/1 (2011, September 14).

CBS News. 2005. "Celeb Prenups Rule Hollywood." (December 14) www.palmbeachpost.com/accent/content/accent/epaper/2005/01/21/a1e_new_TRUMP_PRENUP_0121.html (2006, April 24).

———. 2011. "Is Internet Sex Cheating? Many People Say Yes." (June 8). www.cbsnews.com/2101-201_162-20069942.html?tag=content Main;contentBody (July 31).

CBS/New York Times Poll. 2011a. "The Economy, The Budget Deficit and Gun Control." (January 15-19). www.cbsnews.com/htdocs/pdf/Jan11_Econ.pdf (2011, May 24).

———. 2011b (April 21). www.cbsnews.com/stories/2011/04/21/politics/main/20056282.shtml (2011, June 24).

Celio, A. A., M. F. Zabinski, and D. E. Wilfley. 2002. "African American Body Images." In T. F. Cash and T. Pruzinsky, eds., *Body Image*, 234–242. New York: Guilford Press.

Center for Advancing Health. 2011. "Parents Want to Talk With Teens, But Fear Advice Falls on Deaf Ears." (February 6). www.cfah.org/hbns/archives/getDocument.cfm?documentID=22346 (2011, June 8).

Center for Defense Information. 2001. "On Terror and Terrorism." Terrorism Project. (December 3). www.cdi.org/terrorism/onterror-pr/cfm (2002, January 18).

———. 2004. "Explaining Religious Terrorism Part 1: The Axis of Good and Evil." (May 20). http://www.cdi.org/program/issue/document.cfm?DocumentID=2381&IssueID=138&StartRow=1&ListRows=10&appendURL=&Orderby=DateLastUpdated&ProgramID=39&issueID=138 (2009, February 10).

Center for Gender and Refugee Studies. 2008. cgrs.uchastings.edu/campaigns/femicide.php (2008, August 5).

Center for Media Literacy. 2003. "Media's New Mood: Sexual Violence, an Interview with UCLA Media Researcher Neil Malamuth." http://www.medialit.org/reading_room/article443 (2006, July 22).

Centers for Disease Control and Prevention. 2002. Fact Sheet "Young People at Risk: HIV/AIDS Among America's Youth." *National Center for HIV, STD and TB Prevention* (March).

———. 2006. *Child Maltreatment: Fact Sheet*. Washington, DC: National Center for Injury Prevention and Control. www.cdc.gov/ncipc/factsheets/cmfacts.htm (2006, July 14).

———. 2007. "CDC Health Survey System Meets the Cell Phone Challenge." CDC In the News. www.cdc.gov/news/2007/07/SurveySystem.html (2008, February 29).

———. 2008a. "Dating Violence Fact Sheet." Centers for Disease Control and Prevention, National Center for Injury Prevention and Control. www.cdc.gov/ncipc/dvp/DatingViolence.htm (2008, August 20).

———. 2008b. HIV/AIDS Surveillance Report, Vol. 18. 2006. Atlanta: U.S. Department of Health and Human Services, Centers for Disease Control and Prevention: 1–55. www.cdc.gov/hiv/topics/surveillance/resources/reports/

———. 2008c. "School-Associated Student Homicides—United States, 1992–2006." MMWR 2008; 57(02): 33–36.

———. 2009a. "Assisted Reproductive Technology." www.cdc.gov/reproductivehealth/data_stats/index.htm#ART (2011, September 9).

———. 2009b. *HIV/AIDS Surveillance Report*, 2009, Vol. 21. Atlanta: U.S. Department of Health and Human Services, Centers for Disease Control and Prevention. www.cdc.gov/hiv/topics/surveillance/resources/reports/. Published February 2011.

———. 2010a. "Choose Respect." www.cdc.gov/chooserespect/ (2011, July 5).

———. 2010b. "HIV/AIDS." Department of Health and Human Services. www.cdc.gov/hiv/default.htm (2012, January 10).

———. 2010c. "Suicide." (Summer). www.cdc.gov/ViolencePrevention/pdf/Suicide_DataSheeet-a.pdf (2011, October 1).

———. 2011a. "Healthy Communities." (April 6). www.cdc.gov/chronicdisease/resources/publications/aag/healthy_communities.htm (September 28).

———. 2011b. Centers for Disease Control and Prevention. *HIV Surveillance Report, 2009*; vol. 21. www.cdc.gov/hiv/topics/surveillance/resources/reports/ (August 8).

Chafetz, J. S. 1988. *Feminist Sociology: An Overview of Contemporary Theories*. Itasca, IL: Peacock.

Chambers-Schiller, L. V. 1984. *Liberty, a Better Husband: Single Women in America, the Generations of 1780–1840*. New Haven, CT: Yale University Press.

Chamie, J. 2004. "Coping with World Population Boom and Bust: Part II." (August 24). http://yaleglobal.yale.edu/display.article?id=4413 (2008, July 27).

Chandra A., A. S. Lara-Cinisomo, L. H. Jaycox, T. Tanielian, B. Han, R. M. Burns, and T. Ruder. 2011. *Views from the Home Front: The Experiences of Youth and Spouses from Military Families*. Santa Monica, CA: Rand Corporation, TR-913-NMFA. www.rand.org/pubs/technical_reports/TR913 (2011, February 7).

Chandra, A., C. S. Minkovitz. 2006. "Stigma Starts Early: Gender Differences in Teen Willingness to Use Mental Health Services." *Journal of Adolescent Health* 38, 6, Online Exclusive, June, 754. e1-754. e8.

Chandra, A., W. Mosher, C. Copen, and C. Sionean. 2011. "Sexual Behavior, Sexual Attraction, and Sexual Identity in the United States: Data From the 2006–2008 National Survey of Family Growth." Centers for Disease Control *National Health Statistics Report* 36 (March 3).

Chang, D. F., and S. Sue. 2003. *Journal of Consulting and Clinical Psychology* 71 (2): 235–242.

Chang, E., K. H. Wilber, and M. Silverstein. 2010. "The Effects of Childlessness on the Care and Psychological Well-being of Older Adults with Disabilities." *Aging and Mental Health* 14, 6: 712–719.

Chang, J., C. Berg, L. Saltzman, and J. Herndon. 2005. "Homicide: A Leading Cause of Injury Deaths Among Pregnant and Postpartum Women in the United States, 1991–1999." *American Journal of Public Health* 95, 3: 471–477.

Charles, M., and K. Bradley. 2005. "A Matter of Degrees: Female Underrepresentation in Computer Science Programs Cross-Nationally." In J. McGrath Cohoon & W. C. Aspray, eds., *Women and Information Technology: Reasons for Underrepresentation*. Cambridge: MIT Press.

Cherlin, A. 1978. "Remarriage as An Incomplete Institution." *American Journal of Sociology* 84, 3: 634–650.

———. 1981. *Marriage, Divorce, Remarriage*. Cambridge, MA: Harvard University Press.

———. 1992. *Marriage, Divorce, Remarriage*, rev. ed. Cambridge, MA: Harvard University Press.

———. 2000. "The Unexpected Legacy of Divorce" (book review). *The Nation* 271, 19 (December 11): 62–68.

———. 2009. *The Marriage-Go-Round: The State of Marriage and the Family in America Today*. New York: Knopf.

———, and F. F. Furstenberg, Jr. 1986. *The New American Grandparent: A Place in the Family Apart*. New York: Basic Books.

———. 1988. "The Changing European Family." *Journal of Family Issues* 9: 291–97.

Cherry, K. 2002. *Womansword: What Japanese Words Say about Women*. Tokyo/New York: Kodansha International.

Cherry, R. 2001. *Who Gets the Good Jobs? Combating Race and Gender Disparities*. New Brunswick, NJ: Rutgers University Press.

Chicago Tribune. 2011. "Timing, Meaning of 'I Love You' Differs by Gender." (April 24): Sec. 6, p. 31.

Child Trends. 2010a. "Mothers Who Smoke While Pregnant." www.childrentrendsdatabank.org/?q=node/51 (2011, September 7).

———. 2010b. "Teen Births." www.chilodtrendsdatabank.org/?q=node/311 (2011, August 1).

———. 2011. "Teen Homicide, Suicide, and Firearm Deaths." www.childtrendsdatabank.org/?q=node/124 (2011, May 24).

Child Welfare Information Gateway. 2010. Foster Care Statistics 2008. Washington, DC: U.S. Department of Health and Human Services, Children's Bureau.

Childhelp. 2005. "National Child Abuse Statistics." www.childhelpusa.org/resources/learningcenter/statistics (2006, July 15).

———. 2011. "National Child Abuse Statistics Child Abuse in America." www.childhelp.org/pages.statistics (2011, September 19).

Children Now. 2004. *Fall Colors 2003-04: Prime Time Diversity Report*. Oakland, CA.

Children's Defense Fund. 2010. "Protect Children, Not Guns." www.childrensdefensefund.org/child-research-data-publications/data/protect-children-not-guns-2010-report.pdf (2011, May 24).

CHINAdaily. 2005. "Parents Explore Dating Scene for Choosy Children." (November 11). www/chinadaily.com.cn/English/doc/2005-11/11/content_493925.htm (2011, July 4).

———. 2007. "Nigeria's 'Land of Twins' Baffles Fertility Experts." www.chinadaily.net/world/2007-11/13/content_6249808.htm (2008, July 14).

"China's Elderly Population to Reach 400 Million by 2040." 2005. *China Knowledge* (October 11). http://www.chinaknowledge.com/news_print.asp?ID=292&cat=economy (2006, April 10).

Christakis, N. A., and P. D. Allison. 2006. "Mortality After the Hospitalization of a Spouse." *New England Journal of Medicine* 354 (February 16): 719–730.

Christian, S. 2003. *Educating Children in Foster Care.* Washington, DC: National Conference of State Legislatures.

Christopher, S., and S. Sprecher. 2000. "Sexuality in Marriage, Dating, and Other Relationships: A Decade Review." *Journal of Marriage and the Family* 62, 4 (November): 999–1018.

Chua, A. 2011. *Battle Hymn of the Tiger Mother.* New York: Penguin Press.

Chudowsky, N., and V. Chudowsky. 2011. *State Test Scores Trends Through 2008-09, Part 3: Student Achievement at 8th Grade.* Washington, DC: Center on Education Policy.

Chun, H., and I. Lee. 2001. "Why Do Married Men Earn More? Productivity or Marriage Selection." *Economic Inquiry* 39, 2: 307–319.

CIA. 2011. *The World Factbook.* http://www.cia.gov/library/publications/the-world-factbook/rankorder/2127rank.html (2011, September 1).

CitizenLink. 2008. "ABC Takes a Bow for Gay-Affirming Television Programming." www.citizenlink.org/CLNews/A000006352.cfm (2008, June 4).

Citizens for Tax Justice. 2011. "U.S. Is One of the Least Taxed Developed Countries." (June 30). www.ctj.org/pdf/oecd201106.pdf (2011, July 15).

Clallam County Courts. 2006. "Domestic Violence." www.clallam.net/Courts/ html/court_domesticviolence.htm (2006, July 12).

Clark County Prosecuting Attorney. 2006. "Domestic Violence: Myths and Facts About Domestic Violence." www.clarkprosecutor.org/html/domviol/myths.htm (2008, August 8).

Clark, C., P. Shaver, and M. Abrahams. 1999. "Strategic Behaviors in Romantic Relationship Initiation." *Personality and Social Psychology Bulletin* 25, 6: 707–720.

Clark, J. 1999. *Doing the Work of Love: Men and Commitment in Same-Sex Couples.* Harriman, TN: Men's Studies Press.

Clark, M. C., and P. M. Diamond. 2010. "Depression in Family Caregivers of Elders: A Theoretical Model of Caregiver Burden, Sociotropy, and Autonomy." *Research in Nursing and Health* 33: 20–34.

Clarke, J. 2010. "Independent.co.uk Poll shows '18% of Male Workers Would Take Paternity Leave.'" (March 17). www.indepent.coluk/lifestyle/health-and-families/health-new-poll-shows-18-of-would-take-paternity-leave-1922579.html (2011, July 15).

Clearfield, M. W., and N. M. Nelson. 2006. "Sex Difference in Mothers' Speech and Play Behavior with 6-, 9-, and 14-Month-old Infants. *Sex Roles* 54 (January): 127–137.

Clemetson, L. 2006. "For U.S. Muslims, an Aversion to Nursing Homes." *New York Times* (June 13): A1, A18.

Clemmitt, M. 2008. "Internet Accuracy." *CQ Researcher,* 18, 27 (August 1): 627-634. www.library.cqpress.com/cqresearcher (2011, May 24).

Cline, A. 2011. "Southern Baptists and the Role of Women: Wives Must Submit to Husbands." www.atheism.about.com/od/baptistssouthernbaptists/a/baptistwomen.htm (2011, August 27).

Clothesline Project, The. 1995. "Bearing Witness to Violence against Women." (August 26). home.cybergrrl.com/dv/orgs/cp.html (1999, June 4).

Clunis, D., and G. Green. 2010. *Lesbian Couples.* Berkeley, CA: Seal Press.

CNNMoney.com. 2006. "Wedding $eason: Bridal Spending Has Increased 100% Over Last 15 Years, the Average Cost of a Wedding Now Tops $27,000." (February 10). money.cnn.com/2006/02/10/pf/weddings_costs/ index.htm (2006, April 24).

Coalition for Asian American Children and Families. 1999. http://www.cacf.org/ (2002, January 5).

Coalition to End Family Violence. 2006. "Myths and Reality." www.thecoalition.org/education/myths.html (2006, July 11).

Coalition to Stop the Use of Child Soldiers. 2001. "Child Soldiers: Global Report." www.child-soldiers.org/report2001/global_report_contents.html (2002, February 3).

Coats, P. P., and S. J. Overman. 1992. "Childhood Play Experiences of Women in Traditional and Nontraditional Professions." *Sex Roles* 26: 261–71.

Coffey, L. T. 2011. "This Divorce Just Isn't Working Out: Will You (Re) marry Me?" (June 27) http://today.msnbc.msn.com/id/43500616/ns/today-relationships/t/divorce-just-isnt-working-out-will-you-remarry-me/#Tjhyi8016Ko (2011, August 2).

Cohan, C. I., and S. Kleinbaum. 2002. "Toward a Greater Understanding of the Cohabitation Effect: Premarital Cohabitation and Marital Communication." *Journal of Marriage and the Family* 64 (February): 180–192.

Cohen, O. 2003. "Reasons for Divorce Among Muslim Arabs in Israel: An Exploratory Study." *European Societies* 5, 3: 303–326.

Cohn, D., J. Passel, W. Wang, and G. Livingston. 2011. (December 14). "Barely Half of U.S. Adults are Married—A Record Low." www.pewsocialtrends.org/2011/12/14/barely-half-of-u-s-adults-are-married-a-record (2011, December 15).

Cohn, L. 2005. "Remarriage After Retirement." *Christian Science Monitor* (June 9): 11.

———, and W. Merkel. 2004. *One Family, Two Family, New Family: Stories and Advice for Stepfamilies.* Edmonton, Alberta: RiverWood Books.

Cohoon, J. M. 2001. "Toward Improving Female Retention in the Computer Science Major." *Communications of the ACM* 44, 5: 108–114.

Coker, D. R. 1984. "The Relationship among Concepts and Cognitive Maturity in Preschool Children." *Sex Roles* 10: 19–31.

Colapinto, J. 2000. *As Nature Made Him: The Boy Who Was Raised as a Girl.* New York: HarperCollins.

———. 2004. "What Were the Real Reasons Behind David Reimer's Suicide?" (June 3). http://slate.msn.com/id2101678 (2005, May 16).

Coleman, J. 2003. *Imperfect Harmony.* New York: St. Martin's Press.

Coleman, M., M. A. Fine, L. H. Ganong, K. Downs, and N. Pauk. 2001. "When You're Not the Brady Bunch: Identifying Perceived Conflicts and Resolution Strategies in Stepfamilies." *Personal Relationships* 8: 55–73.

Coleman, M., and L. H. Ganong. 1991. "Remarriage and Stepfamily Research in the 1980s." In A. Booth, ed., *Contemporary Families: Looking Forward, Looking Back,* 192–207. Minneapolis: National Council on Family Relations.

———, and M. Fine. 2000. "Reinvestigating Remarriage: Another Decade of Progress." *Journal of Marriage and the Family* 62, 4: 1288–1307.

———. 2002. "Reinvestigating Remarriage: Another Decade of Progress." In R. M. Milardo (ed.), *Understanding Families Into the New Milennium: A Decade in Review,* 507–526. Minneapolis: National Council on Family Relations.

Coleman, N., and Novak, D. 2008. "100,000 Refugees Flee Conflict." (August 13) www.theage.com.au/world/100000-refugees-flee-conflict-20080812-3u5k.html (2008, September 7).

Coles, R., and C. Green. 2012. In M. Andersen, K. Logio, and H. Taylor, *Understanding Society: An Introductory Reader* (4th ed.), Belmont, CA: Wadsworth, 362–370.

"College Dating Violence." 2009. Dating Violence on College Campuses. www.thesafespace.org/tje-basics/in-your-community/domestic-and-dating-violence (2011, July 5).

Collins, P. H. 1991. "The Meaning of Motherhood in Black Culture." In R. Staples, ed., *The Black Family: Essays and Studies,* 4th ed., 169–78. Belmont, CA: Wadsworth.

———. 2004. *Black Sexual Politics: African Americans, Gender, and the New Racism.* New York: Routledge.

Coltrane, S. 1996. *Family Man: Fatherhood, Housework, and Gender Equality.* New York: Oxford University Press.

———. 1998. *Gender and Families.* Thousand Oaks, CA: Pine Forge Press.

———, and R. Collins. 2006. *Sociology of Marriage and the Family.* Belmont, CA: Wadsworth/Thompson Learning.

Coltrane, S., and M. Messineo. 2000. "The Perpetuation of Subtle Prejudice: Race and Gender Imagery in 1990s Television Advertising." *Sex Roles* 42, 5/6 (March): 363–80.

Columbia News Service. 2008. "Male Fertility Options Growing." *Chicago Tribune* (July 13): Sec. 13, 7.

Commonwealth of Australia. 2004. "Women in Australia 2004," Australian Government, Department of the Prime Minister and Cabinet, Office of the Status of Women. ofw.facs.gov.au/womens_safety_agenda/index .htm (2006, July 8.).

Congressional Budget Office. 2010. "Trends in Federal Tax Revenues and Rates." (December 2). www.cbo.gov/doc.cfm?index=11976&zzz=41410 (2011, July 15).

Connelly, R., D. DeGraff, and R. Willis. 2004. *Kids at Work: The Value of Employer-Sponsored On-Site Child Care Centers*. Kalamazoo, MI: Upjohn Institute for Employment Research.

Conner, S. 2009. "The Fantasy Sex Lives of Men and Women." www.lifewise .canoe.ca/SexRomance/Lovewise/2009/03/10/8697436.html.

Connidis, I. A. 2009. *Family Ties and Aging*. 2nd ed. Thousand Oaks, CA: Pine Forge Press.

———, and L. D. Campbell. 2001. "Closeness, Confiding, and Contact Among Siblings in Middle and Late Adulthood." In A. J. Walker, M. Manoogian-O'Dell, L. A. McGraw, and D. L. G. White, eds., *Families in Later Life: Connections and Transitions*, 149–155. Thousand Oaks, CA: Pine Forge Press.

Constable, A. 2008. "Births to Women Over Age 40 Soaring, and So Is Birth Rate." *Las Cruces Sun-News.com*. http://www.lcsun-news.com/ci_9303163 (Accessed 21 July, 2008).

Constantine, L., and J. Constantine. 1973. *Group Marriage*. New York: Collier.

Constitutional Rights Foundation. 2011. "Causes of School Violence." www. crf-usa.org/school-violence/causes-of-school-violence.html (2011, October 7).

"Consumer Views of the Economy." 2006. *The Gallup Poll* http://poll .gallup.com/content/defaultaspx?ci=1609 (2006, January 10).

Cool Nurse. 2005. "Teen Dating Violence." www.coolnurse.com/dating_ violence.htm (2006, February 20).

Coontz, S. 1988. *The Social Origins of Private Life*. New York: Verso.

———. 1997. *The Way We Really Are: Coming to Terms with America's Changing Families*. New York: Basic Books.

———. 2000. *The Way We Never Were: American Families and the Nostalgia Trap*. New York: Basic Books.

———. 2005. *Marriage, A History*. New York: Viking.

———. 2006. "A Pop Quiz on Marriage." *New York Times* (February 19): Sec. 4, 12.

———. 2007. "The Romantic Life of Brainiacs." (February 18). www .stephaniecoontz.com/articles/article36.htm (2011, July 4).

Corbett, C., C. Hill, and A. St. Rose. 2008. *Where the Girls Are: The Facts About Gender Equity in Education*. Washington, DC: American Association of University Women.

Cornfield, N. 1983. "The Success of Urban Communes." *Journal of Marriage and the Family* 45, 1: 115–26.

Costa, Jr., P. T., A. Terracciano, and R. R. McCrae. 2001. "Gender Differences in Personality Traits Across Cultures: Robust and Surprising Findings." *Journal of Personality and Social Psychology* 81, 2 (August): 322–331.

"Cougars on the Hunt for the Younger Man," 2010. (September 18). www .romanicallyimpaired.com/blog/2010/09/18/cougars-on-the-hunt-for-the-younger-men/ (2011, July 4).

"Court Rejects 'Roe v Wade for Men' Suit." 2007. (November 6) http://www .usatoday.com/new/nation/2007-11-06-roe-wade-men_N.htm?csp==34 (2008, July 27).

"Courtship in America...," 2011. Courtship in America: Dating in the 20th Century. www.digitalhistory.uh.edu/do_history/courtship/flapper.html (2011, June 8).

Covel, S. 2003a. "Cheating Hearts." *American Demographics* 25 (July/ August): 16.

———. 2003b. "The Heart Never Forgets." *American Demographics* (July 1).

Cowdery, R. S., N. Scarborough, C. Knudson-Martin, G. Seshadri, M. E. Lewis, and A. R. Mahoney. 2009. "Gendered Power in Cultural Contexts: Part II. Middle Class African American Heterosexual Couples with Young Children." *Family Process* 48 (1): 25–39.

Cox, C. 1993. *The Frail Elderly: Problems, Needs, and Community Responses*. Westport, CT: Auburn House.

Crabtree, V. 2011. "UK Immigration, Economics and Pensions." (May 31). www.vexen.co.uk/UK/immigration.html (2011, October 7).

Craig, L. 2006. "Does Father Care Mean Fathers Share? A Comparison of How Mothers and Fathers in Intact Families Spend Time with Children." *Gender and Society* 20, 2: 259–281.

Crary, D. 2010. "Sex Study by National Survey of Sexual Health and Behavior Is Biggest Since 1994." (October 4). www.huffingtonpost. com/2010/10/04/sex-study-by-national-sur_n_748751.html (2011, August 2).

Crawford, L. A., and K. B. Novak. 2008. "Parent-child Relations and Peer Associations as Mediators of the Family Structure-Substance Use Relationship." *Journal of Family Issues* 29, 2: 155–184.

Cristia, J. P. 2009. "Rising Mortality and Life Expectancy Differentials by Lifetime Earnings in the United States." *Journal of Health Economics* 28, 5: 984–995.

Cromer, K. 2005. "Building Blocks for Gender Equity." *Chicago Tribune* (May 25): Sec. 8, p. 3.

Crompton, R. 1999. *Restructuring Gender Relations and Employment: The Decline of the Male Breadwinner*. Cambridge: Oxford University Press.

Croskey, M. 2007. "How the Factors of Age, Marital Status, and Race Are Reflected in Educated Women's Attitudes Toward Heterosexual Never-Married Women Over Forty." *Dissertation Abstracts International: Section B: The Sciences and Engineering* 67 (9-B): 5394.

Cross, S., and B. Bagilhole, 2002. "Girls' Jobs for the Boys? Men, Masculinity and Non-traditional Occupations." *Gender, Work and Organization* 9, 2: 204–226.

Crouse, J. S. 2004. "Cohabitation: Consequences for Mothers and Children." Paper Presented at the Asia Pacific Dialogue, Kuala Lumpur, Malaysia, October 11–14.

Crowder, K., and J. Teachman. 2004. "Do Residential Conditions Explain the Relationship Between Living Arrangements and Adolescent Behavior?" *Journal of Marriage and Family* 68: 721–738.

Crowley, K., M. A. Callanan, H. R. Tenenbaum, and E. Allen. 2001. "Parents Explain More Often to Boys Than to Girls During Shared Scientific Thinking." *Psychological Science* 12, 3: 258–261.

Cubbins, L. A., and D. Vannoy. 2004. "Division of Household Labor as a Source of Contention for Married and Cohabiting Couples in Metropolitan Moscow." *Journal of Family Issues* 25, 2: 182–215.

Cuber, J. F., and P. B. Harroff. 1966. *The Significant Americans*. New York: Random House. (Published also as "Five Types of Marriage." In A. S. Skolnick and J. H. Skolnick, eds., *Family in Transition*, 7th ed., 177–88. New York: HarperCollins, 1992.)

Cullen, L., and C. Masters. 2008. "We Just Clicked." *Time* (January 28): 86–89.

Cunningham-Burley, S. 2001. "The Experience of Grandfatherhood." In A. J. Walker, M. Manoogian-O'Dell, L. A. McGraw, and D. White (eds.). *Families in Later Life: Connections and Transitions*, 92–96. Thousand Oaks, CA: Pine Forge Press.

Cunradi, C. 2009. "Intimate Partner Violence Among Hispanic Men and Women: The Role of Drinking, Neighborhood Disorder, and Acculturation-Related Factors." *Violence and Victims*, 24, (1), (November 1): 83–97.

Cuomo, C., and S. Netter. 2009. "Face-Shaven Chaz Bono: 'I'm Living the Life That I Always Wanted.'" (November 19). http//abcnews.go.com/GMAC/ chaz-bono-gender-reassignment-best-decision-made/story?id=9124302 (2011, March 3).

Curezone. 2009. "Top 10 Sex Fantasies for Men." www.curezone.com/forums/ fm.asp?i=1418020.

Curry, G. 2010. "Interracial Marriages: Blacks Are Last Choice of Other Groups." (June 16). www.themadisontimes.com/news_details.php?news (2011, September 7).

Cwikel, J., H. Gramotnev, and C. Lee. 2006. "Never-Married Childless Women in Australia: Health and Social Circumstances in Older Age." *Social Science and Medicine* 62 (8): 1991–2001.

D'Augelli, A. R., S. L. Hershberger, and N. W. Pilkington. 1998. "Lesbian, Gay, and Bisexual Youth and Their Families: Disclosure of Sexual Orientation and Its Consequences." *American Journal of Orthopsychiatry* 68, 3: 361–71.

"Dad of the Month." 2006. *iParenting* (January 4). http://iparenting.com/ dad/1000.php (2006, January 4).

Dahl, G. B., and E. Moretti. 2004. "The Demand for Sons: Evidence from Divorce, Fertility, and Shotgun Marriage." NBER Web site http://www .nber.org/papers/w10281 (2006, March 13).

Dailard, C. 2000. "Abortion in Context: United States and Worldwide." New York: The Alan Guttmacher Institute. http://www.guttmacher.org/pubs/ ib_0599.html (2001, December 17).

Daily News Brief. 2011. "Ninety Percent of Americans Believe in True Love Says New Survey." (February 11). www.dailynewsbrief.net/2011/02/ninety-percent-of-americans-believe-in.html (2011, May 29).

Dalton, A. 2006. "Couple Take Their Vows After 13-Mile Run to Arrive at Ceremony." *The Scotsman* (April 24). news.scotsman.com/uk.cfm?id=612072006 (2006, April 24).

Daly, E. 2005. "DNA Test Gives Students Ethnic Shocks." *The New York Times* (April 13): A18.

Daly, M., 1978. *Gyn/Ecology: The Metaethics of Radical Feminism.* Boston: Beacon Press.

———, and M. Wilson. 1994. "Some Differential Attributes of Lethal Assaults on Small Children by Stepfathers vs. Genetic Fathers." *Ethology and Sociobiology* 15: 207–17.

Dang, A., and S. Frazer. 2005. *Black Same-Sex Households in the United States: A Report From the 2000 Census,* 2nd ed. (December 2005). New York: National Gay and Lesbian Task Force Policy Institute.

Dang, D. T., and J. Pitts. 2006. "Caregivers Feel Love's Anguish." *Chicago Tribune* (March 8): 1, 6.

Daniels, R. 1990. *Coming to America: A History of Immigration and Ethnicity in American Life.* New York: HarperCollins.

Dao, J. 2011. "A Deadly Mixture." *New York Times* (February 13): 1, 25.

Darkness to Light. 2008. "Statistics Surrounding Child Sexual Abuse." www.darkness2light.org/KnowAbout/statistics_2.asp (2008, August 26).

Darling, C., D. J. Kallen, and J. E. VanDusen. 1989. "Sex in Transition: 1900–1980." In A. S. Skolnick and J. H. Skolnick, eds., *Family in Transition,* 6th ed., 236–78. New York: Scott, Foresman.

"Date Rape and Dating Violence." 2011. www.vsofbigspring.com/sexualAssault/dateRape.php (2011, July 5).

Dating Sites Reviews.com. 2011. "Current Online Dating and Dating Services Facts & Statistics." www.datingsitesreviews.com/staticpages/index.php?page=online-dating-industry-facts-statistics (2011, July 5).

Davey, A. J. Savla, M. Janke, and S. Anderson. 2009. "Grandparent-Grandchild Relationships: From Families in Context to Families As Contexts." *Aging and Human Development* 69, 4: 311–325.

Davidson, K., T. Daly, and S. Arber. 2003. "Older Men, Social Integration and Organizational Activities." *Social Policy and Society,* 2: 81–89.

Davis, K. 2004. *Love's Many Faces Apprehended.* Washington, DC: American Psychological Association.

———, and Glass, N. 2011. "Reframing the Heteronormative Constructions of Lesbian Partner Violence: An Australian Case Study." In Janice L. Ristock (ed.), *Intimate Partner Violence in LGBTQ Lives.* London:Routledge, 13–36.

Davis, K., and M. Todd. 1985. "Assessing Friendship: Prototypes, Paradigm Cases and Relationship Description." In S. Duck and D. Perlman, eds., *Understanding Personal Relationships: An Interdisciplinary Approach,* 17–38. London: Sage.

Davis, L., and H. Karar. 2009. "Single, Black, Female—and Plenty of Company." (December 22). http://abcnews.go.com/Nightline/single-black-female/story?id=9395275 (2011, April 29).

Davis, L., and E. Noll. 2010. "Interracial Marriage More Common Than Ever, but Black Women Still Lag." (June 4). www.abcnews.go.com/WN/Media/black-women-marry-interracial-marriage-common/story (2011, September 7).

Davis, S. N., and T. N. Greenstein. 2004. "Cross-National Variations in the Division of Household Labor." *Journal of Marriage and Family* 66 (December): 1260–1271.

———, and J. P. Gerteisen Marks. 2007. "Effects of Union Type on Division of Household Labor: Do Cohabiting Men Really Perform More Housework?" *Journal of Family Issues* 28, 9: 1246–1272.

Davison, P. 2010. "Conquering Game Development's Gender Divide." (September 28). www.thebigpixels.com/musings/2010/9/28/conquering-game-developments-gender-divide.html (2011, March 27).

de Graaf, P. M. 2007. "Contacts Between Divorced and Non-divorced Parents and Their Adult Children in the Netherlands: An Investment Perspective." *European Sociological Review* 23, 2: 267–277.

De Vaus, D., L. Qu, and R. Weston. 2005. "The Disappearing Link Between Premarital Cohabitation and Subsequent Marital Stability, 1970-2001." *Journal of Population Research* 22, 2: 99–118.

Dee, T. 2004. " Teachers, Race and Student Achievement in a Randomized Experiment." *The Review of Economics and Statistics* 86 (1): 195–210.

———. 2006. "Teachers and the Gender Gaps in Student Achievement." *Journal of Human Resources* 42 (3): 529–554.

Defago, N. 2005. *Childfree and Loving It.* London: Vision Paperbacks.

Degenhardt, L., W. T. Chiu, N. Sampson, R. C. Kessler, J.C. Anthony, et al. 2008. "Toward a Global View of Alcohol, Tobacco, Cannabis, and Cocaine Use: Findings from the WHO World Mental Health Surveys." http://medicine.plosjournals.org/archive/1549-1676/5/7/pdf/10.1371_journal.pmed.0050141-L.pdf (2008, September 1).

Degler, C. 1980. *At Odds: Women and the Family in America from the Revolution to the Present.* New York: Oxford University Press.

DeGreeff, B. L., and A. Burnett. 2009. "Weekend Warrior: Autonomy-Connection, Openness-Closedness, and Coping Strategies of Marital Partners in Nonresidential Stepfamilies." *The Qualitative Report* 14, 4: 604–628.

Demasi, L. 2007. "Older Women—Younger Men Relationships." *EzineArticles* (September 24) ezinearticles.com/?Older-Women—Younger-Men Relationships&id=748067 (2008, April 6).

Demo, D. H,. and M. A. Fine. 2010. *Beyond the Average Divorce.* Thousand Oaks, CA: Sage Publications.

DeMont, J. 2000. "I Am Single." *Maclean's* 113, 9 (May 8): 36–40.

Demos, J. 1970. *A Little Commonwealth: Family Life in Plymouth Colony.* New York: Oxford University Press.

———. 1974. "The American Family in Past Time." *American Scholar* 43: 422–446.

DeNinno, N. 2011. "Male Birth Control? New Contraceptive Alternative Underway." (July 25). www.ibtimes.com/articles/185955/20110724/male-birth-control-contraceptive.htm (2011, October 18).

DePaulo, B. M., and W. L. Morris. 2006. "The Unrecognized Stereotyping and Discrimination Against Singles." *Current Directions in Psychological Science* 15, 5: 251–254.

DeSalvo, K. B., N. Bloser, K. Reynolds, H. Jiang, and P. Muntner. 2006. "Mortality Prediction with a Single General Self-Rated Health Question. A Meta-Analysis." *Journal of General Internal Medicine* 21, 3 (March): 267–275.

DeSpelder, L. A., and A. L. Strickland. 2005. *The Last Dance: Encountering Death and Dyinge.* 7th ed. New York: McGraw-Hill.

Deutsch, F. M. 1999. *Halving It All: How Equally Shared Parenting Works.* Cambridge, MA: Harvard University Press.

DeVault, M. L. 1990. "What Counts as Feminist Ethnography?" Paper presented at Exploring New Frontiers: Qualitative Research Conference, York University, Toronto.

Devereaux, R. 2011. "Characteristics of Battered Women From the American Psychiatric Association." www.ehow.com/list_6952812_characteristics-women-american-psychiatric-association.html (2011, September 19).

DeVore, E. R., and K. R. Ginsburg. 2005. "The Protective Effects of Good Parenting on Adolescents." *Current Opinion in Pediatrics* 17: 460–465.

Dew, J., and W. B. Wilcox. 2011. "If Momma Ain't Happy Explaining Declines in Marital Satisfaction Among New Mothers." *Journal of Marriage and Family* 73, 1: 1–12.

Dew, J. P. 2009. "The Gendered Meaning of Assets for Divorce." *Journal of Family and Economic Issues* 30: 20–32.

Dewilde, C., and W. Uunk. 2008. "Remarriage As a Way to Overcome the Financial Consequences of Divorce—A Test of the Economic Need Hypothesis for European Women." *European Sociological Review* 24, 3: 393–407.

Di Clemente, R., J. McDermott, F. Danner, and R. Crosby. 2011. "Association Between Sexually Transmitted Diseases and Young Adults' Self-reported Abstinence." *Pediatrics,* Online (January 3). DOI: 10.1542/peds.2009-0892. www.pediatrics.aappublications.org/content/early/2011/01/03/peds.2009-0892 (2011, June 28).

Diamond, M., and H. K. Sigmundson. 1997. "Sex Reassignment at Birth: Long-Term Review and Clinical Implication." *Archives of Pediatric and Adolescent Medicine* 151: 298–304.

DiCaro, V. 2005. "NFI Releases Report on National Marriage Survey." *Fatherhood Today* 10, 3 (Summer): 4–5.

Dicky, C., and D. McGinn. 2001. "Meet the bin Ladens." *Newsweek* (October 15): 55–56.

Diener, E., C. L. Gohm, E. Suh, and S. Oishi. 2000. "Similarity of the Relations Between Marital Status and Subjective Well-being Across Cultures." *Journal of Cross-Cultural Psychology* 31: 419–436.

DiGiulio, R. C. 1989. *Beyond Widowhood: From Bereavement to Emergence and Hope.* New York: Free Press.

Dingfelder, S. F. 2005. "The Kids Are All Right." *Monitor* 36, 11 (December): 66.

Dion, K. K., and K. L. Dion. 1998. "Individualistic and Collectivistic Perspectives on Gender and the Cultural Context of Love and Intimacy." In D. L. Anselmi and A. L. Law, eds., *Questions of Gender: Perspectives and Paradoxes*, 520–531. New York: McGraw-Hill

Disability Funders Network. 2009. "Disability Stats and Facts." www.disabilityfunders.org/disability-stats-and-facts. (2011, September 30).

Disabled World.com. 2011. "World Facts and Statistics on Disabilities and Disability Issues." www.disabled-world.com/disability/statistics/(2011, September 30).

DiscoveryHealth.com. 2011. "Speed Dating: A New Form of Matchmaking." www.health.howstuffworks.com/relationships/dating/speed-dating-a-new-form-of-matchmaking.htm (2011, July 5).

Dittman, L. 2011. "New Online Dating Site Designed for College Students, And College Students Only." *The Huffington Post* (June 22) www.huffingtonpost.com/2011/06/22/new-online-dating-site-de_n_882504.html (2011, July 4).

Doka, K., ed. 1989. *Disenfranchised Grief: Recognizing Hidden Sorrow.* Lexington, MA: Lexington Books.

Dolbin-MacNab, M. L. 2006. "Just Like Raising Your Own? Grandmothers' Perceptions of Parenting a Second Time Around." *Family Relations* 55 (December): 564–575.

———., and M. K. Keiley. 2009. "Navigating Interdependence: How Adolescents Raised Solely by Grandparents Experience Their Family Relationships." *Family Relations* 58, 2: 162–175.

Domestic Abuse Shelter, Inc. 2008. "Information on Domestic Violence." www.domesticabuseshelter.org (2008, August 8).

Domestic Violence Fact Sheet. 2010. *Healthier You.* www.healthieryou.com/dv.html (2011, September 19).

Domestic Violence Hotline. 2009. "Increased Financial Stress Affects Domestic Violence Victims." www.thehotline.org/2009/01/increased-financial-stress-affects-domestic-violence-vi (2011, September 7).

Domrose, C. 2008. "Massachusetts Groups Reach Out to Gay and Lesbian Elderly Population" (March 10). http://include.nurse.com/apps/pbcs.dll/article?AID=20080310/NE02/103/0/00028 (2008, April 12).

Doodson, L. 2010. *How to Be a Happy Stepmum.* London: Vermilion.

———, and D. Morley. 2006. "Understanding the Roles of Non-residential Stepmothers." *Journal of Divorce and Remarriage* 45, 3/4: 109–130.

Doohan, E. M., S. Carrere, C. Siler, and C. Beardslee. 2009. "The Link Between the Marital Bond and Future Triadic Family Interactions." *Journal of Marriage and Family* 71, 4: 892–904.

Dougherty, C. 2010. "New Vow: I Don't Take Thee." (September 29). http://online.wsj.com/article/SB10001424052748703882404575519871444705214.html?mof=e2fb (2011, May 5).

Doughty, S. 2008. "Great Grandparents: Their Wisdom Helps Children Handle Problems and Plan for the Future." (June 3). www.dailymail.co.uk/new/article-1024001/Great-grandparents-Their-wisdom-hlps-children-handle-problems-plan-duture.html (2008, August 24).

Dow, B. J. 1996. *Prime-Time Feminism.* Philadelphia: University of Pennsylvania Press.

Doweiko, H. E. 1996. *Concepts of Chemical Dependency.* Boston: Brooks/Cole.

Draughon, M. 1975. "Stepmother's Model of Identification in Relation to Mourning in the Child." *Psychological Reports* 36: 183–89.

Dreger, A. D. 1998. "'Ambiguous Sex'—Or Ambivalent Medicine? Ethical Issues in the Treatment of Intersexuality." *The Hastings Center Report* 28, 3: 23–36.

Dremen, S. 2003. "Family Cohesiveness, Flexibility and Maternal Anger: Boon or Detriment to Children's Adjustment?" *Journal of Divorce and Remarriage* 39, 1–2: 65–87.

Dressel, P. L., and B. B. Hess. 1983. "Alternatives for the Elderly." In E. D. Macklin and R. Rubin, eds., *Contemporary Families and Alternative Lifestyles: Handbook on Research and Theory.* Beverly Hills, CA: Sage.

Drew. L. M., and M. Silverstein. 2004. "Inter-Role Investments of Great-Grandparents: Consequences for Psychological Well-Being." *Aging and Society* 24: 95–111.

Driessen, G. 2007. "The Feminization of Primary Education: Effects of Teachers' Sex on Pupil Achievement, Attitudes and Behavior." *International Review of Education* 53 (20) 183–203.

"Drug Use and Abuse." 2009. (March). www.pamf.org/teen/risk/drugs/ (2011, September 26).

Dubay, C. 2009. "Seven Myths About Taxing the Rich." (August 3). www.heritage.org/research/reports/2009/08/seven-myths-about-taxing-the-rich (2011, July 15).

Duberman, L. 1973. "Stepkin Relationships." *Journal of Marriage and the Family* 35: 283–92.

Dunkin, A. 2000. "Adopting? You Deserve Benefits, Too." *Business Week* (February 21): 160.

Dunn, K., P. Croft, and G. Hackett. 2000. "Satisfaction in the Sex Life of a General Population Sample." *Journal of Sex and Marital Therapy* 26: 141–151.

Dunwald, S. 2005. "15-Year-Old Weds 37-Year-Old." WGRZ Channel 2 News. File://C:/MyFiles/woman weds 15 year old_files\redir.htm (2005, December 18).

Durex, 2005. "Global Sex Survey, 2005." www.durex.com/uk/globalsexsurvey/index.asp (2005, March 17).

———, 2007. "Durex Global Sex Survey, 2007." www.durex.com/uk/globalsexsurvey/index.asp (2007, April 18).

———, 2010. "The Face of Global Sex 2010." Durex Network. www.durex.com/en-GB/SexualLifestyle/durex-explores/Pages/Face-of-global-sex-s (2011, July 31).

———, 2011. "Sexual Well-being Global Survey." www.durex.com/en-US/SexualWellbeingSurvey/pages/default.aspx (2011, July 31).

Durkheim, E. 1951/1897. *Suicide, A Study in Sociology.* New York: Free Press.

Dush, C., C. L. Cohan, and P. R. Amato. 2003. "The Relationship Between Cohabitation and Marital Quality and Stability: Change Across Cohorts?" *Journal of Marriage and Family* 65: 539–549.

Duvall, E. M. 1977. *Marriage and Family Development*, 5th ed. Philadelphia: Lippincott.

Dworkin, A. 1987. *Intercourse.* New York: Free Press.

Dye, J. L. 2005. Fertility of American Women: June 2004. *Current Population Reports*, P20-555. Washington, DC: U.S. Census Bureau.

Dyson, M. 2005. *Is Bill Cosby Right? Or Has the Black Middle Class Lost Its Mind?* Westminster London: Basic Civitas Books.

Earle, A. M. 1893. *Customs and Fashions in Old New England.* New York: Scribner's.

Earls, A. 2003. "Men Still Worry About Taking Time to Be Dads." *Boston Globe* (November 23). http://bostonworks.boston.com/globe/articles/112303-dads.html (2006, February 8).

Earls, M. 2005. "GLBTQ Youth." Washington, DC: Advocates for Youth. www.advocatesforyouth.org/publications/factsheet/fsglbt.htm (2008, August 20).

Eastside Domestic Violence Program. 2011. "LGBT & Domestic Violence." www.edvp.org/GetInformed/lgbt.aspx (September 7).

Eastwick, P., and E. Finkel. 2008. "Sex Differences in Male Preferences Revisited: Do People Know What They Initially Desire in a Romantic Partner?" *Journal of Personality and Social Psychology* 94 (February 2): 245–64.

Ebon, A. 2011. "Brides Releases 2011 American Wedding Study: Are These Numbers Relevant to You?" (June 20). http://weddingmarketing.net/2011/06/20/brides-releases-2011-american-wedding-study-numbers-relevant/ (2011, December 15).

Eckholm, E. 2010. "Saying No to 'I Do' With the Economy in Mind." *The New York Times* (September 29). www.nytimes.com/2020/09/29/us/29marriage.html (2011, April 20).

———. 2011. "With Few Jobs, A Single Pastor Points to a Bias." *The New York Times* (March 22): A1, A3.

Edelmann, R. J. 2004. "Surrogacy, the Psychological Issues." *Journal of Reproductive and Infant Psychology* 22, 2 (May): 123–136.

Edl, H. M., M. H. Jones, and D. B. Estell. 2008. "Ethnicity and English Proficiency: Teacher Perceptions of Academic and Interpersonal Competence in European American and Latino Students." *School Psychology Review* 37 (1): 38–45.

Edwards, H. 2008. "All-Male Gatherings Making a Comeback." *Chicago Tribune* (February 21): Sec. 5, 5B.

"Effects of Domestic Violence on Women." 2010. Post-Traumatic Stress Disorder Information. www.ptsdtraumaqtreatment.org/trauma-effects/effects-domestic-violence (2011, September 15).

Ehrenreich, B., and A. Fuentes. 1992. "Life on the Global Assembly Line." In H. F. Lena, W. B. Helmreich, and W. McCord, eds. *Contemporary Issues in Society*, 104–11. New York: McGraw-Hill.

Ehrensaft, D. 2011. *Gender Born, Gender Made: Raising Healthy Gender-Nonconforming Children*. New York: The Experiment.

Eiland, D. A. 2008. "Considering Race and Gender in the Classroom: The Role of Teacher Perception in Referral for Special Education." Unpublished dissertation, Michigan State University.

Einstein, E. 1985. *The Stepfamily: Living, Loving, and Learning*. Boston: Shambhala.

Elejalde-Ruiz, A. 2011. "Financial Infidelity." *Chicago Tribune* (February 13): p. 1, sec. 7.

Elias, M. 2007. "Gay Teens Coming Out Earlier to Peers and Family" (February 11). http://www.usatoday.com/news/nation/2007-02-07-gay-teens-cover_x.htm(2008, April 12).

Eliot, L. 2009. *Pink Brain, Blue Brain: How Small Differences Grow into Troublesome Gaps and What We Can Do About It*. Boston: Houghton Mifflin Harcourt.

Ellis, D. 2006. "Male Abuse of a Married or Cohabiting Female Partner: The Application of Sociological Theory to Research Findings." *Violence and Victims* 4: 235–55.

Elmslie, B., and E. Tebaldi. 2007. "Sexual Orientation and Labor Market Discrimination." *Journal of Labor Research* 28, 3: 436–453.

Elwert, F., and N. A. Christakis. 2008. "Wives and Ex-wives: A New Homogamy Bias in the Widower Effect." *Demography* 45, 4: 851–873.

"Emergency Contraception (Morning After Pill)." 2008. (February 12). www.plannedparenthood.org/health-topics/emergency-contraception-morning-after-pill-4363.htm (2012, January 3).

Emery, R. 2004. *The Truth About Children and Divorce: Dealing with the Emotions So You and Your Children Can Thrive*. New York: Viking.

Emory Health Sciences Press Release. 2004. "Black Men Who Have Sex With Men Often Share Common Experiences." whsc.emory.edu/press_releases.cfm?show=2004 (2004, January 27).

Employee Benefit Research Institute. 2007. "Minority Workers Expectations About Retirement Income." (July 12). www.ebri.org/pdf/publications/facts/fastfacts/fastfact071207.pdf (2008, August 23).

———. 2011. "The Impact of Deferring Retirement Age on Retirement Income Adequacy." (June). www.ebri.org (2011, August 19).

"Employer-sponsored Child Care Benefits = Better Health?" 2010. (June 23). http://weblogs.baltimoresun.com/features/baltimoreomblog/2010/06/employersponsored_child_care_b.html (2011, July 5).

Eng, H. 2005. "Grads Coming Home and Staying: 'Boomerang' Generation Moving Back." *Boston Herald*. www.findarticles.com/p/articles/me_qn4154/is_20050823/ai_n14914229/print (2005, October 15).

Eng, P. 2005. "Cell Phones That Literally Locate Love." ABC News. (July 28) abcnews.go.com/Print?id=982335 (2008, March 20).

Enright, E. 2004. "A House Divided." *AARP Magazine* (July/August). Accessed March 2, 2006. http://www.aarpmagazine.org/family/Articles/a2004-05-26-mag-divorce.html/?print

Entertainment Software Association. 2010. "Essential Facts About the Computer and Video Game Industry." www.theesaa.com/facts/pdfs/ESA_Essential_Facts_2010.PDF (2011, March 27).

Equal Employment Opportunity Commission. 2011a. "Fisher Sand & Gravel to Pay $150,000 to Settle EEOC Sex Discrimination and Retaliation Suit." (May 16). www.eeoc.gov/eeoc/newsroom/release/5-16-11a.cfm (2011, July 8).

———. 2011b. "Sexual Harassment Charges." http://www.eeoc.gov/statistics/enforcement/sexual_harassment.cfm (2011, July 7).

"Equal Pay for Working Families: National and State Data." 1999. AFL-CIO. http://www.aflcio.org/women/exec99.htm (2001, October 20).

Ertel, K.A., M. M. Glymour, and L. F. Berkman. 2008. "Effects of Social Integration in Preserving Memory Functions in a Nationally Representative U.S. Elderly Population." *American Journal of Public Health* 98, 7 (July): 1215–1220.

Escobar-Chaves, S., S. Tortolero, C. Markhan, and B. Low. 2004. "Impact of the Media on Adolescent Sexual Attitudes and Behaviors." Atlanta, GA: Centers for Disease Control and Prevention. Grant #H75/ CCH623007-01-1.

Eshleman, J., and R. Bulcroft. 2005. *The Family*, 11th ed. Boston: Allyn & Bacon.

ESPN.com news services. 2007. "MSG, Thomas Settle Lawsuit with Compensatory Damages Looming." (December 11). http://sports.espn.go.com/nba/news/story?id=3149371 (2008, July 14).

Essley, L. 2011. "12 Percent of Seniors Got the Ring." (April 28). www.hillsdalecollegian.com/12-percent-of-seniors-got-the-ring-1.2211432 (2011, July 5).

Estioko-Griffin, A. 1986. "Daughters of the Forest." *Natural History* 95 (May): 5.

European Women's Lobby. 2011. "Women Are More Prone to Disability Than Men, and Particularly Vulnerable to Discrimination and Violence." (May 17). www.womenlobby.org/spip.php?article1664 (2011, October 1).

Evans, L. 2000. "No Sissy Boys Here: A Content Analysis of the Representation of Masculinity in Elementary School Reading Textbooks." *Sex Roles* 42, 3/4: 255–70.

Evenson, R. J., and R. W. Simon. 2005. "Clarifying the Relationship Between Parenthood and Depression." *Journal of Health and Social Behavior* 46 (December): 341–358.

Fabricius, W., S. Braver, P. Diaz, and C. Scheck. 2010. Custody and Parenting Time: Links to Family Relationships and Well-being After Divorce." In M. Lamb, ed., *The Role of the Father in Child Development*, 201–240, New York: Wiley.

"Facebook and Divorce." 2011. (March 25). http://mybroadband.co.za/news/gneral/19311-facebook-and-divorce.html (2011, July 23).

"Facts and Statistics About Infidelity." 2011. www.truthaboutdeception.com/cheating-and-infidelity/stats-about-inflidelity.html (2011, July 31).

Faderman, L. 1989. "A History of Romantic Friendship and Lesbian Love." In B. Risman and P. Schwartz, eds., *Gender and Intimate Relationships*, 26–31. Belmont, CA: Wadsworth.

Fairchild Bridal Group. 2002. "The American Wedding." www.sellthebride.com/documents/americanweddingsurvey.pdf (2011, December 15).

Falk, C. 1990. *Love, Anarchy, and Emma Goldman*, rev. ed. Piscataway, NJ: Rutgers University Press.

Falke, S. I., and J. Larson. 2007. "Premarital Preditors of Remarital Quality: Implications for Clinicians." *Contemporary Family Therapy* 29: 9–23.

Families and Work Institute. 2004. *Gender and Generation in the Workplace*. Boston: American Business Collaboration.

Family and Children's Services of Central Maryland. 2006. "Facts About Child Sexual Abuse." www.fcsmd.org/issues/sexualabuse.htm (2008, August 26).

Family and Divorce News. 2011. "Study Finds Higher Divorce Rates Among Conservative Christians." (January 27). www.newsfamilylaw.wordpress.com/2011/01/27/study-finds-Higher-divorce-rates-among (2011, August 15).

Family Violence Prevention Fund. 2008. "Domestic Violence Is a Serious, Widespread Social Problem in America: The Facts." www.endabuse.org/resources/facts/ (2008, August 8).

———. 2009. "The Facts on Teens and Dating Violence." www.futureswithoutviolence.org/userfiles/file/Teens/teens_facts.pdf (2011, July 4).

———. 2010. "Intimate Partner Violence and Healthy People 2010 Fact Sheet." www.futureswithoutviolence.org/userfiles/file/Children...Families/ipv.pdf (2011, September 7).

Fan, C. S., and H. Lui, 2004. "Extramarital Affairs, Marital Satisfaction, and Divorce: Evidence from Hong Kong." *Contemporary Economic Policy* 22, 4 (October): 442–452.

Farrell, D. 1997. "Jealousy and Desire." In Roger E. Lamb, ed., *Love Analyzed*, 165–188. Boulder, CO: Westview.

Fausto-Sterling, A. 1985. *Myths of Gender*. New York: Basic Books.

———. 2000. "The Five Sexes, Revisited." *Sciences* 40, 4 (July/August).

Faux, M. 1984. *Childless by Choice: Choosing Childlessness in the 80s*. Garden City, NY: Anchor Press/Doubleday.

Fayette County Government. 2008. "Domestic Violence." www.admin.co.fayette.ga.us/courts/solicitor/domestic_violence.htm (2008, August 8).

Feagin, J. 2010. (2nd ed.). *Racist America*. New York: Routledge.

Federal Interagency Forum on Aging-Related Statistics. 2010. *Older Americans 2010: Key Indicators of Well-Being*. Washington, DC.

Federal Interagency Forum on Child and Family Statistics. 2011a. "Adoption." www.childstats.gov/americaschildren/special1.asp#155 (2011, October 5).

———. 2011b. *America's Children: Key National Indicators of Well-Being*. 2011. Washington, DC.

Federal Register. 2010. "Delayed Update of the HHS Poverty Guidelines for the Remainder of 2010." Department of Health and Human Services (August 3). www.federalregister.gov/2010/08/03/2010-19129/delayed-update-of-the-hhs-poverty-guidelines-for-the-remainder-of-2010 (2011, September 7).

Feigelman, W. 2000. "Adjustments of Transracially and Inracially Adopted Young Adults." *Child and Adolescent Social Work Journal* 17, 3 (June): 165–184.

Feldman, M. 2001. "Parenthood Betrayed: The Dilemma of Munchausen Syndrome by Proxy." www.shpm.com/articles/parenting/hsmun.html (2002, January 24).

Felson, R., and A. Cares. 2005. "Gender and the Seriousness of Assaults on Intimate Partners and Other Victims." *Journal of Marriage and the Family* 67 (December): 1182–1195.

"Female on Male Sexual Harassment." 2004. http://www.fightsexual harassment.com/facts/female_on_male_sexual_harassment.htm (2006, January 12).

"Femicide in Central America and Mexico." 2008. www.unfpa.org/16days/documents/pl_femicide_factsheet.doc (2008, August 15).

Feng, D., R. Giarruso, V. L. Bengston, and N. Frye. 1999. "Intergenerational Transmission of Marital Quality and Marital Instability." *Journal of Marriage and the Family* 61 (May): 451–63.

Fengler, A., and N. Goodrich. 1979. "Wives of Elderly Men: The Hidden Patients." *Gerontologist* 19 (April): 175–83.

Ferguson, S. 2000. "Challenging Traditional Marriage: Never-Married Chinese American and Japanese American Women." *Gender and Society* 14 (1): 136–159.

———, ed. 2005. *Shifting the Center: Understanding Contemporary Families*, 3rd ed., 129–39. Mountain View, CA: Mayfield.

Ferrante, J. 1992. *Sociology: A Global Perspective*. Belmont, CA: Wadsworth.

———. 1995. *Sociology: A Global Perspective*. Belmont, CA: Wadsworth.

———. 2007. *Sociology: A Global Perspective*. Belmont, CA: Wadsworth.

Fetto, J. 2003. "Love Stinks." *American Demographics*. 25 (February): 10–11.

Fields, J., and L. M. Casper. 2001. *America's Families and Living Arrangements: March 2000*. Current Population Reports, P20–537. Washington, DC: U.S. Census Bureau.

Fiese, B. H., T. Tomcho, M. Douglas, K. Josephs, S. Poltrock, and T. Baker. 2002. "A Review of 50 Years of Research on Naturally Occurring Family Routines and Rituals: Cause for Celebration?" *Journal of Family Psychology* 16, 4: 381–390.

Finer, L. 2007. "Trends in Premarital Sex in the United States, 1954–2003." *Public Health Reports* (January/February): 122.

———. and S. K. Henshaw. 2006. "Disparities in Rates of Unintended Pregnancy in the United States, 1994 and 2001." *Perspectives on Sexual and Reproductive Health*, 38, 2: 90–96.

Finer, L. B., and M. R. Zolna. 2011. "Unintended Pregnancy in the United States: Incidence and Disparities, 2006." (July 13). www.guttmacher.org/pubs/journals/j.contraception.2011.07.13.pdf (2011, September 3).

Finkelhor, D., and K. Yllo. 1995. "Types of Marital Rape." In Patricia Searles and Ronald Berger, eds., *Rape and Society: Readings on the Problem of Sexual Assault*, 152–159. Boulder, CO: Westview Press.

Finkelman, P., ed. 1989. *Women and the Family in a Slave Society*. New York: Garland.

Firdaus, I. 2010. "Women-Only Train Carriages Introduced in Indonesia." (August 20). www.huffingtonpost.com/2010/08/20/womanoly-trains-introduc_n_688856.html (2011, July 8).

Firebaugh, G., and L. Tach. 2005. "Relative Income and Happiness: Are Americans on a Hedonistic Treadmill?" Paper presented at the American Sociological Association Centennial Annual Meeting, Philadelphia, August 14.

"First Dance Songs for Weddings." 2011. www.secretweddingsongs.com/first-dance-songs.html (2011, December 15).

Fischer, A. H. 2000. *Gender and Emotion: Social Psychological Perspectives*. New York: Cambridge University Press.

Fischer, J., and M. Heesacker. 1995. "Men's and Women's Preferences Regarding Sex-Related and Nurturing Traits in Dating Partners." *Journal of College Student Development* 36, 3: 258–268.

Fischer, T. F., P. M. de Graaf, and M. Kalmijn. 2005. "Friendly and Antagonistic Contact Between Former Spouses After Divorce." *Journal of Family Issues* 26, 8: 1131–1163.

Fisher, H. 1999. "The Origin of Romantic Love and Human Family Life." In L. H. Stone, ed., *Selected Readings in Marriage and Family*, 65–68. San Diego, CA: Greenhaven Press.

———. 2009. *Why Him? Why Her? Finding Real Love By Understanding Your Personality Type*. New York: Henry Holt and Company.

Fisher, K., M. Egerton, J. I. Gershuny, and J. P. Robinson. 2006. "Gender Convergence in the American Heritage Time Use Study (AHTUS)." ISER Working Paper. 2006–25. Colchester: University of Essex.

Fisher, L. 2010. *Sex, Romance, and Relationships: ARRP Survey of Midlife and Older Adults*. Washington, DC: American Association of Retired Persons.

Fisher, T., Z. Moore, and M. J. Pittenger, 2011. "Sex on the Brain? An Examination of Frequency of Sexual Cognitions as a Function of Gender, Erotophiloia, and Social Desirability." *Journal of Sex Research, Online* (April 19). www.tandfonline.com/doi/abs/10.1080/00224499.2011.5654 29 (2011, August 5).

Fishman, B. 1983. "The Economic Behavior of Stepfamilies." *Family Relations* 32: 359–66.

———. and B. Hamel. 1991. "From Nuclear to Stepfamily Ideology: A Stressful Change." In J. N. Edwards and D. H. Demo, eds., *Marriage and Families in Transition*, 436–52. Boston: Allyn & Bacon.

Fisk, R. 2010. "The Crimewave That Shames the World." (September 7) www.independent.co.uk/opinion/commentators/fisk/the-crimewave-that-shames-the-world-207201.html. (2011, February 7).

Fisman, R., S. Iyengar, E. Kamenica, and I. Simonson, 2006. "Gender Differences in Mate Selection: Evidence From a Speed Dating Experiment." *The Quarterly Journal of Economics* (May).

Fivush, R., L. J. Berlin, J. M. Sales, J. Mennuti-Washburn, and J. Cassidy. 2003. "Functions of Parent-child Reminiscing About Emotionally Negative Events." *MEMORY* 11 (2): 179–192.

Fivush, R., K. Martin, K. McWilliams, and J. Bohanek. 2009. "Family Reminiscing Style: Parent Gender and Emotional Focus in Relation to Child Well-being." *Journal of Cognition and Development* 10, 3: 210–235.

Flanigan, C., R. Huffman, and J. Smith. 2005. "Teens Attitudes Toward Marriage, Cohabitation, and Divorce, 2002." *Science Says*, 14. Washington, DC: The National Campaign to Prevent Teen Pregnancy.

Fletcher, J. B. 2009. "What's in a Name?" (May 21). http://becominastep-mom.wordpress.com/2009/05/21/whats-in-a-name/ (2011, July 26).

Flood, M. 2008. *The Men's Bibliography: A Comprehensive Bibliography of Writing on Men, Masculinities, Gender, and Sexualities* (19th ed.).Canberra, Australia. www.mensbiblio.xyonline.nte/ (2011, May 24).

Florsheim, P., and L. Ngu, 2006. "Differential Outcomes Among Adolescent Fathers: Understanding Fatherhood as a Transformative Process." In Lori Kowaleski-Jones and Nick Wolfinger (eds.), *Fragile Families and the Marriage Agenda*. Springer, 226–248.

Fogarty, K., and Wyatt, C. 2009. "Communicating With Teens About Sex: Facts, Findings, and Suggestions." Gainesville, FL: University of Florida, IFAS Extension. Publication #FCS2251. www.edis.ifas.ufl.edu/fy852.

Folan, K. 2010. "Black Women Should Diversify Their Dating Pool This Valentine's Day." www.thegriot.com/opinion/black-women-should-diversify-their-dating-pool-this-valentines-(2011, September 7).

Folbre, N. 2011. "Taxing the Rich." (April 11). http://economix.blogs.nytimes.com/2011/04/11/taxing-the-rich/ (2011, July 15).

Fomby, P., and A. J. Cherlin. 2007. "Family Instability and Child Well-Being." *American Sociological Review* 72, 2: 181–204.

Foner, N. 1993. "When the Contract Fails: Care for the Elderly in Nonindustrial Cultures." In V. L. Bengtson and A. Achenbaum, eds., *The Changing Contract across Generations*. New York: Aldine de Gruyter.

Ford-Mitchell, D. 2008. "Patricia W. Arthur Carries on Her Husband's Legacy As Pastor of God's Harvest Center in Saginaw." (March 19). http://blog.mlive.com/saginawliving/2008/03/patricia_w_arthur_carries_on_h.html (2008, March 22).

Foreign Press Center Japan. 2005. "Concern Deepens Over Continuing Slide of Birth Rate in Japan; No Halt in Sight." http://www.fpcj.jp/e/mres/japanbrief/jb_534.html (2006, April 7).

Foreman, J. 2005. "A Web of Information Untangled." (November 28). www.myhealthsense.com/F051128_healthWebSites.html (2008, February 29).

Forging Connections: *Challenges and Opportunities of Older Caregivers Raising Children*. 2004. New York: New York: Council on Adoptable Children, Inc.

Fornek, S. 2007. "Samuel Hinckley and Sarah Soole." http://www.suntimes.com/news/politics/obama/familytree/545460,BSX-News-wotreep09.article#

Fox News. 2011. "Families Fear Deportation Amid Alabama Immigration Crackdown." (October 9). www.foxnews.com/us/2011/10/09/families-fear-deportation-amid-alabama-immigration-crackdown (2011, October 7).

Fox, G. L., and R. F. Kelly. 1995. "Determinants of Child Custody Arrangements at Divorce." *Journal of Marriage and the Family* 57 (August): 693–708.

FoxNews.com. 2005. "Saudi's 58 Marriages Angers Some." (January 1). http://www.foxnews.com/story/0,2933,143074,00.html (2011, March 14).

———. FoxNews.com. 2008. "All Texas Polygamist Sect Children Reunited With Parents." (June 4). http://www.foxnews.com/story/0.2933,362816,00.html (2011, March 14).

Francis, B. 2010. "Gender, Toys, and Learning." *Oxford Review of Education* 36 (30: 325–344).

Frazier, E. F. 1939. *The Negro Family in the United States*. Chicago: University of Chicago Press.

Freeman, R., and P. Klaus. 1984. "Blessed or Not: The New Spinster in England and the United States in the Late Nineteenth and Early Twentieth Centuries." *Journal of Family History* 9: 394–414.

Freisthier, B. 2011. "Alcohol Use, Drinking Venue Utilization, and Child Physical Abuse: Results from a Pilot Study." *Journal of Family Violence* 26, 3: 185–193.

Friedman, R. A. 2008. "Crisis? Maybe He's a Narcisstic Jerk." (January 15). www.nytimes.com/2008/01/15/health/15mind.html?_r=1&oref=slogin (2008, August 20).

Friedman, S. 2006. "Time to Recognize Gay Seniors." (June 3). http://www.newsday.com/news/columnists/nybzsaul4766895jun03,0,7094119.column?coll-ny-rightrail-columnist (2006, June 28).

Frisco, M., and K. Williams. 2003. "Perceived Housework, Equity, Marital Happiness, and Divorce in Dual-Earner Households." *Journal of Family Issues* 24, 1 (January): 51–73.

Fromm, E. 1956. *The Art of Loving*. New York: Bantam.

Fuchs, V. 2010. "Shy Guys Switching on to Text Message Courtship—and Girls Say It's OK." (June 16). www.couriermail.com.au/lifestyle/shy-guys-switching-on-to-text-message-courtship-and-girls-say-its-ok/story-e6frer4f-1225880329000 (2011, July 4).

"Fun Facts From 1961." 2011. www.woodstockcandy.com/fun-facts-from-1961.html (2011, December 15).

Furman, E. 2005. *Boomerang Nation: How to Survive Living with Your Parents*. New York: Fireside.

Furstenberg, F., Jr., and A. Cherlin. 1991. *Divided Families: What Happens to Children*

Furstenberg, F., Jr., and G. B. Spanier. 1987. *Recycling the Family: Remarriage after Divorce*. Newbury Park, CA: Sage.

Fuwa, M. 2004. "Macro-Level Gender Inequality and the Division of Household Labor in 22 Countries." *American Sociological Review* 69 (December): 751–767.

Galinsky, E. 2004. "Testimony: Subcommittee on Children and Families." http://familiesandwork.org/3w/testimony.html (2006, January 17).

———, K. Aumann, and J. T. Bond. 2009. *Times Are Changing: Gender and Generation at Work and at Home*. New York: Families and Work Institute.

Galinsky, E., and J. T. Bond. 2009. *The Impact of the Recession on Employers*. New York: Families and Work Institute.

Gallagher, S. K. 2003. *Evangelical Identity and Gendered Family Life*. New Brunswick, NJ: Rutgers University Press.

Gallup. 2011. "Doctor-Assisted Suicide Is Moral Issue Dividing Americans Most." (May 31). www.gallup.com/poll/147842/doctor-assisted-suicide-moral-issue-dividing-american (2011, June 18).

Gammage, J. 2006. "For Adoptees, Racial Divide Still Wide." (May 8) http://www.philly.com/mld/inquirer/new/local/14525508.htm (2006, August 17).

Gamory, W. 2010. "Male Teachers Impact on Male Student Behavior and Achievement in Mathematics: An Action Research Project." (Fall). earlyactionresearch.wikispaces.com/file/view/Powerpoint+blank.ppfx (2011, April 6).

Ganong, L. H., and M. Coleman. 1994. *Remarried Family Relationships*. Thousand Oaks, CA: Sage.

———. 1997. "How Society Views Stepfamilies." *Marriage & Family Review* 26, 1/2: 85–106.

———. 2004. *Stepfamily Relationships: Development, Dynamics, and Interventions*. New York: Kluwer Academic/Plenum Publishers.

———. 2006. "Obligations to Stepparents Acquired in Later Life: Relationship Quality and Acuity of Needs." *The Journals of Gerontology Series B: Psychological Sciences and Social Sciences* 61:S80–S88.

———, M. Markham, and T. Rothrauff. 2011. "Predicting Postdivorce Coparental Communication." *Journal of Divorce and Remarriage* 52, 1: 1-18.

Gans, D., M. Silverstein, and A. Lowenstein. 2009. "Do Religious Children Care More and Provide More Care for Older Parents? A Study of Filial Norms and Behaviors Across Five Nations." *Journal of Comparative Family Studies* 40, 2: 187–201.

Garcia, A. 2002. *The Mexican Americans*. Westport, CT: Greenwood Press.

Garner, A. 2002. "Don't 'Protect' Me; Give Me Your Respect." *Newsweek* (February 11).

Gartrell, N., and H. Bos. 2010. "U.S. National Longitudinal Lesbian Family Study: Psychological Adjustment of 17-Year-Old Adolescents." *Pediatrics* 126, 1: 28–36.

Gately, S., and A. I. Schwebel. 1992. "Favorable Outcomes in Children after Parental Divorce." In E. Everett, ed., *Effects on Young Adults' Patterns of Intimacy and Expectations for Marriage*, 57–78. New York: Haworth Press.

Gates, Gary. 2011. "How Many People are Lesbian, Gay, Bisexual and Transgendered?" Los Angeles, CA: The Williams Institute.

"Gay Divorce Case Appealed to TX Supreme Court." 2011. (March 2). www.dallasvoice.com/jb-takes-2year-battle-gay-divorce-texas-supreme-court-1067191.html (2011, July 20).

Gaydemographics.org. 2003. "Percent of Households with Children Under 18 Years" (Accessed April 25, 2006 http://gaydemographics.org/USA/SF1/_children.htm).

Gee, A. 2011. "Anti-abortion Laws Gain More Ground in the USA." (June 17). http://europeanprochoicenetwork.wordpress.com/2011/06/17/anti-abortion-laws-gain-ground-in-the-usa/ (2011, September 6).

Geiss, S. K., and K. D. O'Leary. 1981. "Therapists' Ratings of Frequency and Severity of Marital Problems: Implications for Research." *Journal of Marital and Family Therapy* 7: 515–20.

Gelfand, D. E., and C. M. Barresi, eds. 1987. *Ethnic Dimensions of Aging*. New York: Springer.

Gelles, R. J., and M. Straus, 1987. "Is Violence toward Children Increasing? A Comparison of 1975 and 1985 National Survey Rates." *Journal of Interpersonal Violence* 2: 212–222.

Gelles, R., and A. Levine. 1999. *Sociology*, 6th ed. New York: McGraw-Hill.

"Gender Pay Gap Starts with Pocket Money, Find Survey." 2009. *The Telegraph* (August 28). www.telegraph.co.uk/finance/personalfinance/6105603/Gender-pay-gap-starts-with-pocket-money-finds-survey.html (2011, March 30).

General Characteristics. 2005. http://www.utexas.edu/depts/ic2/et/learner/general.html (2005, January 27).

Genovese, E. D. 1974. *Roll, Jordan, Roll*. New York: Pantheon.

Gentleman, A. 2006. "Millions of Abortions of Female Fetuses Reported in India." *The New York Times* (January 10): A10.

Genuis, S., and S. Genuis. 2006. "Parental Guidance: Talking to Your Teens About Sex." www.christianwomentoday.com/parenting/teensex.html (2006, March 23).

Gershaw, D. A. 1997. "Our Androcentric Language" (June 15). http://virgil.azwestern.edu/-dag/lol/Androcentric.htm (2011, April 7).

George Mason University. 2005. "Worldwide Sexual Assault Statistics." Fairfax, VA: George Mason University Sexual Assault Services. www.gmu.edu/facstaff/sexual/brochures/WorldStats2005 (2008, August 15).

———. 2008. "Updated Statistics, Redeem the Silence." www.redeem thesilence.com/?p=388. (2011, September 7).

Gerson, K. 2010. *The Unfinished Revolution: How a New Generation Is Reshaping Family, Work, and Gender in America.* New York: Oxford University Press.

Ghista, G. 2005. "Marital Rape." World Prout Assembly. www.worldproutassembly.org/archives/2005/05/marital_rape.html (2006, July 17).

Gibson, R. 1996. "The Black American Retirement Experience." In J. Quadagno and D. Street, eds., *Aging for the Twenty-First Century: Readings in Social Gerontology,* 309–26. New York: St. Martin's Press.

Gilbert, L. A., and M. Scher. 1999. *Gender and Sex in Counseling and Psychotherapy.* Boston: Allyn & Bacon.

Gill, R. T., N. Glazer, and S. A. Thernstrom. 1992. *Our Changing Population.* Englewood Cliffs, NJ: Prentice Hall.

Gilmore, D. 1990. *Masculinity in the Making: Cultural Concepts of Masculinity.* New Haven, CT: Yale University Press.

Giordano, P., M. Longmore, and W. Manning. 2006. "Gender and the Meanings of Adolescent Romantic Relationships: A Focus on Boys." *American Sociological Review,* 71 (April): 260–87.

Giuliano, T. A., and K. E. Popp. 2000. "Footballs versus Barbies: Childhood Play Activities as Predictors of Sports Participation by Women." *Sex Roles* 42, 3 (February): 159–82.

Gjerdingen, D. 2004. "The Effects of Domestic Work Responsibilities On Parents' Marital Satisfaction and Mental Health." A paper presented at a Conference and Signature Study of the Hubert H. Humphrey Institute of Public Affairs Conducted in Collaboration with the School of Public Health, University of Minnesota (October 1).

Glasmeier, A. 2005. *An Atlas of Poverty in America: One Nation Pulling Apart, 1960–2003.* Routledge.

Glenn, E. N. 1983. "Split Household, Small Producer and Dual Wage Earner: An Analysis of Chinese American Family Strategies." *Journal of Marriage and the Family* 45 (February): 35–46.

———. 1994. "Social Constructions of Mothering: A Thematic Overview." In E. N. Glenn, G. Chang, and L. R. Forcey, eds., *Mothering: Ideology, Experience, and Agency,* 1–29. New York: Routledge.

———, and S. Yap. 2002. "Chinese American Families." In R. Taylor, ed., *Minority Families in the United States.* Upper Saddle River, NJ: Prentice Hall.

Glenn, N. D. 1982. "Interreligious Marriage in the United States: Patterns and Recent Trends." *Journal of Marriage and the Family* 44 (August): 555–566.

———. 1997. *Closed Hearts, Closed Minds, A Report from the Council on Families.* New York: Institute for American Values.

———. 2005. "With This Ring A National Survey on Marriage in America." National Fatherhood Initiative. www.fatherhood.org/doclibrary/nms.pdf (2008, August 3).

Glick, P., and S. Lin. 1986. "Recent Changes in Divorce and Remarriage." *Journal of Marriage and the Family* 48: 737–47.

Glick, P., and R. Parke. 1965. "New Approaches in Studying the Life Cycle of the Family." *Demography* 2: 187–202.

Global Health Council. 2008. "At Risk Groups—Women & Youth." http://www.globalhealth.org/hiv_aids/risk_groups1 (2008, June 9).

"Globalization." 2006. www.americans-world.org/digest/global_issues/globalization/general.cfm (2006, July 18).

Goetting, A. 1982. "The Six Stations of Remarriage: Developmental Task of Remarriage after Divorce." *Family Relations* 31: 213–22.

Goldberg, C. 2001. "Quiet Anniversary for Civil Unions." *New York Times* (July 31): A14.

Goldblatt, J. 2004. "Cheaper by the Half-Dozen? Hardly." *The New York Times* (October 17): C8.

Goldscheider, F. K., and C. Goldscheider. 1993. *Leaving Home before Marriage: Ethnicity, Familism, and Generational Relationships.* Madison: University of Wisconsin Press.

Goldscheider, F., G. Kaufman, and S. Sassler. 2009. "Navigating the 'New' Marriage Market: How Attitudes Toward Partner Characteristics Shape Union Formation." *Journal of Family Issues* 30, 6: 719–737.

Goldscheider, F., and S. Sassler. 2006. "Creating Stepfamilies: Integrating Children into the Study of Union Formation." *Journal of Marriage and Family* 68 (May): 275–291.

Goldstein, S. 2006. "We Are Family." Broadsheet (March 23). www.letters.salon.com/mwt/broadsheet/2006/03/23/shelltrack/view?order=asc (2006, April 3).

Goleman, D. 1996. *Emotional Intelligence.* New York: Bantam Books.

"Gonzaleses Celebrate 50 Years of Marriage." 2011. News-Bulletin.com. (Milestones-August 2011). www.newsbulletin.com/2011/08/27/milestones/gonzaleses-celebrate-50-years-of-marriage (2011, December 15).

Goode, E. 2001. "Findings Give Some Support to Advocates of Spanking." *New York Times* (August 25): A6.

Goode, W. 1959. "The Theoretical Importance of Love." *American Sociological Review* 24, 1 (February): 38–47.

Goodman, B. 2006. "Remarriage Issue Gives Denomination an Identity Crisis." (August 26). http://www.NYTimes.com/2006/08/26/us/26religion.html (2008, August 10).

Gorchoff, S. M., O. P. John, and R. Helson. 2008. "Contextualizing Change in Marital Satisfaction During Middle Age: An 18-Year Longitudinal Study." *Psychological Science* 19, 11: 194–200.

Gordon, P. 2006. "Grandparents Raising Grandchildren." *Gotham Gazette* (April 12). http://www.gothamgazette.com/print/1816 (2006, June 20).

Gornbein, H. S. 2011. "Top 11 Reasons for Divorce." (July 19). www.simpledivorceadvice.com-divorce-questions-answered/reasons-for-divorce (2011, July 23).

Gottman, J. 1994a. "What Makes Marriage Work?" *Psychology Today* (March/April): 38–43, 68.

———. 1994b. *What Predicts Divorce? The Relationship between Marital Processes and Marital Outcomes.* Hillsdale, NJ: Erlbaum.

———. 2004. "Gottman's Marriage Tips 101." The Gottman Institute www.gottman.com/marriage/self_help/index.php? (2008, July 4).

Gottman, J. M., R. W. Levenson, C. Swanson, K. Swanson, R. Tyson, and D. Yoshimoto. 2003. "Observing Gay, Lesbian and Heterosexual Couples' Relationships: Mathematical Modeling of Conflict Interaction." Journal of *Homosexuality* 45, 1: 65–91.

Gove, W. 1972. "The Relationship between Sex Roles, Marital Status, and Mental Illness." *Social Forces* 51: 34–44.

Goyer, A. 2010. "More Grandparents Raising Grandkids." (December). www.aarp.org/relationships/grandparenting/info-12-2010/more_grandparents_raising-grandchildren.html (2011, August 19).

Graham, J. 2006. "Unwilling Father Tests Men's Rights." *Chicago Tribune* (March 10): Sec 1, p. 3.

Grall, T. 2009. "Custodial Mothers and Fathers ad Their Child Support: 2007." *Current Population Reports,* P60-237. Washington, DC: U.S. Census Bureau.

Grant, J. M. 2010. *Outing Age 2010: Public Policy Issues Affecting LGBT Elders.* Washington, DCL National Gay and Lesbian Task Force Policy Institute.

Grant, T. 2011. "Opposition to Interracial Marriage Lingers Among Evangelicals." *Christainity Today.* (June 24). www.christianitytoday.com/ct-politics/2011/06/opposition_to_i.html (2011, August 15).

Graver, H. 2011. "The Looming Teen Unemployment Crisis." (June 20). www.frumforum.com/solving-teen-unemployment-problem (2011, July 11).

Graves, L. 2007. "The Weapon of Choice for School Violence." *U.S. News and World Report.* (November 9). www.usnews.com/articles/education/2007/11/09/the-weapon-of-choice-for-school-violence.html (2008, September 11).

Gray, R. 2011. "Sexting Today: Teenagers Are Awful, the Times Reports." (March 27). www.blogs.villagevoice.com/runninscared/2011/03/sexting_today_t.php (2011, June 21).

Green, B., and N. Boyd-Franklin. 1996. "African American Lesbians: Issues in Couple Therapy." In J. Laird and R. Green, eds., *Lesbians and Gays in Couples and Families,* 251–71. San Francisco: Jossey-Bass.

Greenberg Quinlan Rosner Research. 2005. "Faith and Family in America." Washington, DC: Greenberg Quinlan Rosner Research, Inc. (October 19).

Greenberg, B. S., M. Eastin, L. Hofschire, K. Lachlan, and K. D. Brownell. 2003. "Portrayals of Overweight and Obese Individuals on Commercial Television." *American Journal of Public Health* 93, 8 (August): 1342–1348.

Greenberg, S. H., A. Kuchment, and S. Butler. 2006. "The 'Familymoon.'" *Newsweek* 47, 2 (January 9): 46–47.

Greenhouse, S. 2008. *The Big Squeeze: Tough Times for the American Worker.* New York: Random House.

Greenstein, T. N. 1990. "Marital Disruption and the Employment of Married Women." *Journal of Marriage and the Family* 52: 657–76.

———. 1995. "Gender Ideology, Marital Disruption and the Employment of Married Women." *Journal of Marriage and the Family* 57 (February): 31–32.

Greif, G. L. 1985. *Single Fathers*. Lexington, MA: Lexington Books.

Greven, P. 1970. *Four Generations: Population, Land and Family in Colonial Andover, Mass*. Ithaca, NY: Cornell University Press.

Grieco, E. M., and E. N. Trevelyan. 2010. *Place of Birth of the Foreign-Born Population: 2009*. U.S. Census Bureau: Washington, DC.

Grimm, T. K., and M. Perry-Jenkins. 1994. "All in a Day's Work: Job Experience, Self-Esteem, and Fathering in Working-Class Families." *Family Relations* 43, 2 (April): 174–81.

Griswold del Castillo, R. 1984. *La Familia*. Notre Dame, IN: University of Notre Dame Press.

Gross, J. 2005. "Forget the Career: My Parents Need Me at Home." *The New York Times* (November 24): A1, A20.

———. 2007. "Aging and Gay, and Facing Prejudice in Twilight." *New York Times* October 10: A1.

Gross, P. 1987. "Defining Post-divorce Remarriage Families: A Typology Based on the Subjective Perceptions of Children." *Journal of Divorce* 10, 1/2: 205–17.

Grossman, C., and I. Yoo. 2003. "Civil Marriage on the Rise Across USA." *USA Today* (October 7): A, 01.

Grossman, H., and S. H. Grossman. 1994. *Gender Issues in Education*. Boston: Allyn & Bacon.

Grusec, J. E., and M. Davidov. 2007. "Socialization in the Family: The Role of Parents." In J. E. Grusec and P. D. Hastigs, eds., *Handbook of Socialization*, 284–308, New York: Guilford.

Grych, J. H. 2005. "Interparental Conflict as a Risk Factor for Child Maladjustment: Implications for the Development of Prevention Programs." *Family Court Review* 42: 97–108.

Gubrium, J. F. 1975. "Being Single in Old Age." *Aging and Human Development* 6: 29–41.

———. 1976. *Time, Roles, and Self in Old Age*. New York: Human Science Press.

Guess, A. 2008. "The Sociology of 'Hooking Up.'" (January 29). *Inside Higher Education*. www.insidehighered.com/news/2008/01/29/hookups (2011, July 4).

Guilamo-Ramos, V., P. Dittus, J. Jaccard, M. Johansson, A. Bouris, and N. Acosta. 2007. "Parenting Practices Among Dominican and Puerto Rican Mothers." *Soc Work*. January: 52(1): 17–30.

Guillory, K. S. 2007. "Assessment of Social Support and Peer Influence as Factors Contributing to High School Completion Among African Americans." Doctoral Dissertation, University of Texas at Arlington. https://dspace.uta.edu/bitstream/handle/10106/747/umi-uta-1940.pdf?sequence=1 (2011, April 5).

Guisinger, S., P. A. Cowan, and D. Schuldberg. 1989. "Changing Parent and Spouse Relations in the First Years of Remarriage of Divorced Fathers." *Journal of Marriage and the Family* 51: 445–56.

Gun Violence in America. 2008. "Gun Violence In America: Proposals for the Obama Administration." Brady Campaign to Prevent Gun Violence, (December 18). www.bradycampaign.org (2011, May 24).

Gunn, C. 2003. "Dominant or Different? Gender Issues in Computer Supported Learning." *Journal of Asynchronous Learning Networks* 7, 1: 14–30.

Gunnoe, M. L., and S. L. Braver. 2001. "The Effects of Joint Legal Custody on Mothers, Fathers, and Children Controlling for Factors that Predispose a Sole Maternal versus Joint Legal Award." *Law and Human Behavior*, 25, 1 (February): 25–43.

Gutiérrez, R., and Zavella, P. (Eds.) 2009. *Mexicans in California: Transformations and Challenges*. Champaign, IL: University of Illinois Press.

Gutman, H. G. 1976. *The Black Family in Slavery and Freedom: 1750–1925*. New York: Vintage Books.

Guttmacher Institute. 2010. "Facts on Contraceptive Use in the United States." (June). www.guttmacher.org/pubs/fb_contr_use.html (2011, September 3).

———. 2011. "Facts On American Teens' Sexual and Reproductive Health." (January).www.guttmacher.org/pubs/FB-ATSRH.html (2011, August 1).

Gwartney-Gibbs, P. A. 1986. "The Institutionalization of Premarital Cohabitation: Estimates from Marriage License Applications, 1970 and 1980." *Journal of Marriage and the Family* 48: 423–34.

Ha, J. 2005. "Gender Difference in Social Contact after Spousal Loss." http://paa2005.princeton.edu/download.aspx?submissionId=51340 (2006, June 28).

Hacker, A. 2003. *Mismatch: The Growing Gulf Between Women and Men*. New York: Scribner.

Haddad, Y. Y. 1985. "Islam, Women and Revolution in Twentieth-Century Arab Thought." In Y.Y. Haddad and E. B. Findley (eds). *Women, Religion and Social Change*, 275–306, Albany, NY: State University of New York Press.

Haddock, S., T. S. Zimmerman, L. R. Current, and A. Harvey. 2002. "The Parenting Practice of Dual-Earner Couples Who Successfully Balance Family and Work." *Journal of Feminist Family Therapy* 14, 3/4: 37–55.

Haddock, S. A., T. S. Zimmerman, S. J. Ziemba, and L. R. Current. 2001. "Ten Adaptive Strategies for Work and Family Balance: Advice From Successful Families." *Journal of Marital and Family Therapy* 27: 445–458.

Haddocks, R. 1995. "Live-in Relationships More Prone to Violence." *Standard-Times* [online]: 3.

Hagedoom, M., N. W. Van Yperen, J. C. Coyne, C. van Jaarsweld, A. Ranchor, E. van Sonderen, and R. Sanderman. 2006. "Does Marriage Protect Older People from Distress? The Role of Equity and Recency of Bereavement." *Psychology and Aging* 21, 3: 611–620.

Hahn, L. 2006. "Couples Remarrying Their Ex-spouses, What Are they Thinking?" *Chicago Tribune* (January 24): Sec. 5, 1, 7.

Haili, J. 2004."The Fastest Way to Fall in Love." (September 16). www.edu.sina.com.cn/en/2004-09-16/25857.html (2011, July 4).

Hailparn, R. 2005. In Tim Warstall, "Cosmetic Gynecology." timworstall.typepad. com/timworstall/2005/05/cosmetic_gyneco.html (2006, March 21).

Halberstadt, A. G., and M. B. Saitta. 1987. "Gender, Nonverbal Behavior, and Perceived Dominance: A Test of the Theory." *Journal of Personality and Social Psychology* 53: 257–72.

Hale-Benson, J. 1986. *Black Children: Their Roots, Culture, and Learning Styles*, rev. ed. Provo, UT: Brigham Young University Press.

Hall, S. S., and S. M. MacDermid. 2009. "A Typology of Dual Earner Marriages Based on Work and Family Arrangements." *Journal of Family and Economic Issues* 30, 3: 215–225.

Hamilton B., J. Martin, and S. Ventura. 2006. "Births: Preliminary Data for 2005." Health E-Stats. (November 21). Hyattsville, MD: U.S. Department of Health and Human Services, Centers for Disease Control and Prevention, National Center for Health Statistics.

———. 2010. "Births: Preliminary Data for 2009." U.S. Department of Health and Human Services, Centers for Disease Control and Prevention, National Center for Health Statistics, National Vital Statistics Reports. 59(3) (December 21).

Hamilton, M. 2008. "Prosecuting Polygamy in El Dorado." (April 8). http://www.huffingtonpost.com/marci-hamilton/prosecuting-polygamy-in-e_b_95674.html (2011, March 14).

Hamilton, M. C., D. Anderson, M. Broaddus, and K. Young. 2007. "Gender Stereotyping and Under-representation of Female Characters in 200 Popular Children's Picture Books: A 21st Century Update." (February 19). www.centre.edu/web/news/2007/2/gender.html (2011, March 17).

Hangum, C. 2009. "Toys "R" Us Gets Schooled on Sex Roles." (October 12). www.advocate.com/printArticle.aspx?id=99901 (2011, March 27).

Hannon, K. 2007. "Aging at Home with Government Help." (November 5). http://health.usnews.com/articles/health/2007/11/05/aging-at-home-with-government-help.html (2008, August 27).

Hans, J. D. 2009. "Beliefs about Child Support Modification Following Remarriage and Subsequent Childbirth." *Family Relations* 58 (February): 65–78.

———, and M. Coleman. 2009. "The Experiences of Remarried Stepfathers Who Pay Child Support." *Personal Relationships* 16, 4: 597–618.

Hans, J. D., L. H. Ganong, and M. Coleman. 2009. "Financial Responsibilities Toward Older Parents and Stepparents Following Divorce and Remarriage." *Journal of Family Economic Issues* 30 :55–66.

Hanson, G., and P. Venturelli. 1995. *Drugs and Society*. Boston: Jones and Bartlett.

Hansson, R. O., and J. H. Remondet. 1987. "Relationships and Aging Family: A Social Psychological Analysis." In S. Oskamp, ed., *Family Processes and Problems: Social Psychological Aspects*. Beverly Hills, CA: Sage.

Harding, A. 2011. "Report: Women Should Be Allowed to Serve in Combat." (January 15). http:articles.cnn.com/2011-01-15/politics/military.women_1_combat-units-direct-combat-roles-iraq-and-afghanistan?_s=PM-Politics (2011, February 28).

Harmatz, M. G., and M. A. Novak. 1983. *Human Sexuality*. New York: Harper & Row.

Harmon, A. 2005. "Ask Them (All 8 of Them) About Their Grandson." *The New York Times* (March 20): 1, 18.

Harney, A. 2010. "The Rise of the Parasite Singles." (August 13). www.slate .com/id/2263805/ (2011, April 27).

Harper, J. M., J. G. Sandberg, and B. G. Schaalje. 2000. "Daily Hassles, Intimacy, and Marital Quality in Later Life Marriages." *American Journal of Family Therapy* 28, 1 (January): 1–18.

Harper, S. R. 2006. "Peer Support for African American Male College Achievement: Beyond Internalized Racism and the Burden of 'Acting White.'" *Journal of Men's Studies* 14 (3): 337–358.

Harris Poll. 2010. "Cyberchondriacs" on the Rise?" *Harris Interactive*. www .harrisinteractive.com. (2011, May 14).

Harris, A. 2003. "Shopping While Black: Applying 42 U.S.C. § 1981 to Cases of Consumer Racial Profiling." *Boston College Third World Law Journal* (Winter, 2003): 1–55.

Harrison, L. 2008. "Scenes from a Group Marriage." (June 4). www.salon .com/life/features/2008/06/04/open-marriage

Harry, J. 1984. *Gay Couples*. New York: Praeger.

Harter, P. 2004. "Child Glue Sniffing Rises in Morocco." BBC News (December 21). http://news.bbc.co.uk/2/hi/africa/4113441.stm (2006, August 8).

Hartwell-Walker, M. 2006. "When Women Earn More Than Men." http://psychcentral.com/lib/2006/when-women-earn-more-than-men (2008, June 25).

Harvey, D. 1992. "The Psychologists Who Changed Our Minds." *San Francisco Chronicle*, Datebook (June 14): 31–32.

Hastings, P., J. Vyncke, C. Sullivan, K. E. McShane, M. Benibgui, and W. Utendale. 2006. *Children's Development of Social Competence Across Family Types*. Canada: Department of Justice.

Hatch, L. R., and K. Bulcroft. 2004. "Does Long-term Marriage Bring Less Frequent Disagreements?" *Journal of Family Issues* 25, 4: 465–495.

Hauser, D. 2004. "Five Years of Abstinence-Only-Until-Marriage Education: Assessing the Impact." *Advocates for Youth* (September). www .advocatesforyouth.org (2005, January 27).

"Hawarden Independent." 1961. Newspaper Archive. www.newspaperarchive .com/SiteMap/FreePdfPreview.aspx?img+108078795 (2011, December 15).

Hawkins, D. N. 2005. "Unhappily Ever After: Effects of Long-Term, Low-Quality Marriages on Well-Being." *Social Forces* 84, 1(September): 451–471.

Hawkins, K. 2010. "World's Longest-Married Couple Share Relationship Advice on Twitter." www.gimundo.com/news.article/worlds-longest-married-couple-share-relationship-advice (2011, August 15).

Hayworth, B. 2011. "Rising Divorce Rate Worries Northwest Iowa." (March 27). www.siouxcityjournal.com/news/local/article_0d650292-4ecl-5c-9865-67eaaa22ec91.html (2011, July 19).

He, W., M. Sengupta, V. A. Velkoff, and K. A. DeBarros. 2005. *65+in the United States: 2005*. Current Population Reports, Series P23-209. Washington, DC: U.S. Census Bureau.

Heimdal, K. R., and S. K. Houseknecht. 2003. "Cohabiting and Married Couples' Income Organization: Approaches in Sweden and the United States." *Journal of Marriage and the Family* 65: 525–538.

Helgerson, J. L. 2002. "National Security Implications of Global Demographic Changes." (April 30). http://www.au.af/mil/au/awc/awcgate/cia/helgerson2.htm (2008, July 27).

Hendrick, S., and C. Hendrick. 1983. *Liking, Loving, and Relating*. Monterey, CA: Brooks Cole.

———. 1987. "Love and Sexual Attitudes, Self-Disclosure and Sensation Seeking." *Journal of Social and Personal Relationships* 4: 281–297.

———. 1995. "Gender Differences and Similarities in Sex and Love." *Personal Relationships* 2: 55–65.

———. 1996. "Gender and the Experience of Heterosexual Love." In Julia T. Wood, ed., *Gendered Relationships*, 131–148. Mountain View, CA: Mayfield.

———. 2002. "Linking Romantic Love with Sex: Development of the Perceptions of Love and Sex Scale. *Journal of Social and Personal Relationships*, 19 (June): 361–376.

Hendricks, C. 2011. "86 Years of 'I Do.'" *AARP Bulletin*. (February 14). www .aarp.org/relationships/love-sex/info-08-2009/couple-maintains-world-record-for-longest-marriage.2.html (2011, August 15).

Henkens, K., and H. Van Dalen. 2003. "Early Retirement Systems and Behavior in an International Perspective." In G. A. Adams and T. A. Beehr, eds., *Retirement: Reasons, Processes and Results,* 242–263. New York: Springer.

Henry, C. S., and S. G. Lovelace. 1995. "Family Resources and Adolescent Family Life Satisfaction in Remarried Family Households." *Journal of Family Issues* 16, 6 (November): 765–86

Henry, P. J. and J. McCue. 2009. "The Experience of Nonresidential Stepmothers." *Journal of Divorce and Remarriage* 50: 185-205.

Hequembourg, A., and S. Brallier. 2005. "Gendered Stories of Parental Caregiving Among Siblings." *Journal of Aging Studies* 19: 53-71.

Herbert, B. 2001. "A Black AIDS Epidemic." *New York Times* (June 4): A21.

Herek, G. M. 2000. "Homosexuality." www.psychology.ucdavis.edu/rainbow/html/eop_2000.pdf (2005, December 6).

Herrerias, C. 2008. "Inequities Faced by Noncustodial Mothers." *Journal of Interdisciplinary Feminist Thought* 3, 1. http//escholar.sale.edu/jift/vol3/iss1/3 (2011, July 24).

Hertz, R. 1986. *More Equal Than Others: Women and Men in Dual-Couples*. Berkeley: University of California Press.

Hetherington, E. M. 1989. "Coping with Family Transitions: Winners, Losers, and Survivors." *Child Development* 60: 1–18.

———, ed. 1999. *Coping with Divorce, Single Parenting, and Remarriage: A Risk and Resiliency Perspective*. Mahwah, NJ: Erlbaum.

———. 2002. "Marriage and Divorce American Style." *American Prospect* 13, 7(April 8): 62–63.

———, and S. H. Henderson. 1997. "Fathers in Stepfamilies." In M. E. Lamb, ed., *The Role of the Father in Child Development,* 212–26. New York: Wiley.

Hetherington, M. E., and J. Kelly. 2002. *For Better or Worse: Divorce Reconsidered*. New York: W. W. Norton.

Hetherington, E. M., R. Parke, and V. Locke. 2006. *Child Psychology: A Contemporary Viewpoint*, 6th ed. Boston: McGraw-Hill.

Hewlett, S. A. 2007. *Off-Ramps and On Ramps: Keeping Talented Women on the Road to Success*. Boston: Harvard University Press.

Heymann, D. L. 2000. "The Urgency of a Massive Effort against Infectious Diseases." Statement presented to the Committee on International Relations of the U.S. House of Representatives, June 29. Washington, DC.

Heymann, J., A. Earle, J. Hayes. 2007 *The Work, Family, and Equity Index: Where Does the United States Stand Globally?* Boston, MA and Montreal, QC: The Project on Global Working Families and The Institute for Health and Social Policy.

Heymann, J., A. Earle, S. Simmons, S. M. Breslow, and A. Kuehnhoff. 2004. *The Work, Family, and Equity Index: Where Does the United States Stand Globally?* Cambridge, MA: The Project on Global Working Families, Harvard School of Public Health.

Higgins, L. T., M. Zheng, Y. Liu, and C. H. Sun (2002). Attitudes to marriage and sexual behaviors: A survey of gender and culture differences in China and United Kingdom. *Sexual Roles* 46, 75–89.

Hill, N. 1995. "The Relationship between Family Environment and Parenting Style: A Preliminary Study of African American Families." *Journal of Black Psychology* 31, 4 (November): 408–23.

Hill, R. 1958. "Generic Features of Families under Stress." *Social Casework* 39 (February/March): 139–50.

———. 1972. *The Strengths of Black Families*. New York: Emerson Hall.

———. 1997. *The Strengths of African American Families: Twenty-Five Years Later*. Washington, DC: R & B Publishers.

———. 1998. "Understanding Black Family Functioning: A Holistic Perspective." *Journal of Comparative Family Studies* 29 (Spring): 15–25.

Hill, S. 2005. *Black Intimacies: A Gender Perspective on Families and Relationships*. (The Gender Lens Series). Walnut Creek, CA: AltaMira Press.

Hindman, S. 2010. "Gay Seniors Gaining More Options for Retirement Communities." (January 27). www.silverplanet.com/housing/gay-seniors-gaining-more-options-retirement-communities/56300 (2011, August 26).

Hines III, M. T. 2007. "Adolescent Adjustment to the Middle School Transition: The Intersection of Divorce and Gender in Review." *RMLEOnline* 31, 2 http://www.nmsa.org/portels/0/pdf/publications/RMLE/rmle_vol31_no2.pdf (2008, August 7).

Hite, S. 1976. *The Hite Report: A Nationwide Study of Female Sexuality*. New York: Macmillan.

Hochschild, A. R. 1989. *The Second Shift: Working Parents and the Revolution at Home.* New York: Viking.

———. 1997. *The Time Bind: When Work Becomes Home and Home Becomes Work.* New York: Metropolitan Books.

Hodson, R., and T. Sullivan. 1995. *The Social Organization of Work.* Belmont, CA: Wadsworth.

Hofferth, S. 1985. "Updating Children's Life Course." *Journal of Marriage and the Family* 47: 93–115.

———, and K. Anderson. 2003. "Are All Dads Equal? Biology vs. Marriage as Basis for Parental Investment." *Journal of Marriage and Family* 65: 213–232.

Hoffman, J. 2011a. "A Girl's Nude Photo, and Altered Lives." *New York Times.* (March 27): 3, 18, 19.

———. 2011b. "Toddling Past Gender Lines." (June 12): 3, 8.

Hoffnung, M. 1998. "Motherhood: Contemporary Conflict for Women." In S. J. Ferguson, ed., *Shifting the Center: Understanding Contemporary Families,* 277–91. Mountain View, CA: Mayfield.

Holmes, T., and R. Rahe. 1967. "The Social Readjustment Rating Scale." *Journal of Psychosomatic Research* 11: 213–18.

Holmlund, H., and K. Sund. 2005. "Is the Gender Gap in School Performance Affected by the Sex of the Teacher?" Working Paper Series 5/2005, Swedish Institute for Social Research.

Homans, G. 1961. *Social Behavior in Elementary Forms.* New York: Harcourt, Brace and World.

Hondagneu-Sotelo, P. 1996. "Overcoming Patriarchal Constraints: The Reconstruction of Gender Relations among Mexican Immigrant Women and Men." In E. Ngan-Ling Chow, D. Wilkinson, An M. Baca Zinn, eds., *Race, Class, and Gender,* 184–205. Newbury Park, CA: Sage Publications.

Hong, Y., M. Gahler, and E. Bernhardt. 2006. "Parental Divorce and Union Disruption Among Young Adults in Sweden." (June). http://epc2006.princeton.edu./download.aspx?submissionID=60154 (2008, August 1).

"'Honour' Killing: It's a Global Phenomenon." 2010 (July 2011) www.timesofindia.indiatimes.com/India/Honour-killing-Its-a-global-phenomenon/articleshow/6154172.cms (2011, February 7).

"Hooking Up, Hanging Out, and Hoping for Mr. Right: College Women on Dating and Mating Today." 2001. Independent Women's Forum. http://www.iwf.org/news/010727.shtml (2001, October 20).

hooks, b. 1994. "Sexism, Misogyny: Who Takes the Rap? Misogyny, Gangsta Rap, and the Piano." Race and Ethnicity. http://www.race.eserver.org/misogyny.html (2006, July 22).

Hopper, B. 2010. "Did Facebook Lead to a Jealous Rage?" (August 31). www.cbs47.tv/news/local/story/Did-Facebook-Lead-to-a-Jealous-Rage/1qDJQSNJNEKPNbfn4IZZkg.cspx (2011, July 4).

Hornike, D. 2001. "Can the Church Get in Step with Stepfamilies?" *U.S. Catholic* 66, 7 (July): 33–34.

Horrigan, J., and Rainie, L. 2002. "Counting on the Internet: Most Find the Information They Seek, Expect." (December 29). www.pewinternet.org/Reports/2002/Counting-on-the-Internet-Most-find-the-information-they-seek-expect.aspx (2011, May 24).

Horsey, K. 2006. "Three Million IVF Babies Born Worldwide." (June 28) www.ivf.net/ivf/three_million_babies_born_worldwide-02105-en.html (2008, July 26).

Horton, S. 2008. "For Gay Couples, Divorcing Is as Challenging as Getting Married." *Chicago Tribune* (July 27): 8.

Hosek, J. 2011. "Insights from Early Rand Research on Deployment: Effects on U.S. Service Members and Their Families." (July 27). www.rand.org/content/dam/rand/pubs/testimonies/2011/RAND_CT367.pdf (2011, September 24).

Hossain, Z. 2001. "Division of Household Labor and Family Functioning in Off-Reservation Navajo Indian Families." *Family Relations* 50, 3 (July): 255–261.

Houseknecht, S. K., and S. K. Lewis. 2005. "Explaining Teen Childbearing and Cohabitation: Community Embeddedness and Primary Ties." *Family Relations* 54, 5: 607–620.

Housing Assistance Council. 2008. "Housing on Native American Lands." Washington, DC: Housing Assistance Council. (June): www.ruralhome.org/manager/uploads/NativeAmerInfoSheet.pdf (2008, July 27).

Hout, M. 2000. "Angry and Alienated: Divorced and Remarried Catholics in the United States." *America* 183, 20 (December 16): 10–12.

Howard, C. R., and C. C. John. 2011. "International Adoption." (July 1). wwwnc.cdc.gov/travel/yellowbook/2012/chapter-7-international-travel-infants-children/international-adoption.htm (2011, October 7).

Huber, B. R., and J. W. Schofield. 1998. "I Like Computers, But Many Girls Don't: Gender and the Sociocultural Context of Computing." In H. Bromley and M. W. Apple, eds., *Education/Technology/Power: Educational Computing as a Social Practice,* 103–131. Albany: State University of New York Press.

Huffington Post. 2011. "Teens Becoming Pregnant to Get On 'Teen Mom?'" (February 6). www.huffingtonpost.com/2010/12/07/teems-becoming-pregnant-t_n_793063.html (2010, August 1).

Hughes, P., and F. Dickson. 2005. "Communication, Marital Satisfaction, and Religious Orientation in Interfaith Marriages." *Journal of Family Communication,* 5 (1): 25–41.

Hughes, Z. 2001. "How to Get What You Want from the Man in Your Life." *Ebony* (March): 124–128.

Human Rights Campaign, 2010. (January 13). "Statewide Marriage Prohibitions." http://www.hrc.org/state_laws. (2011, August 15).

———. 2011. (July 6). "Marriage Equality and Other Relationship Recognition Laws." www.hrc.org/state_laws (2011, August 15).

Human Rights Watch. 2006. "U.N.: Open Independent Inquiry into Civilian Deaths." www.hrw.org/english/docs/2006/08/08/lebano13939.htm (2006, August 24).

Hunt, G., C. Levine, and L. Naiditch. 2005. *Young Caregivers in the U.S.* Bethesda, MD: National Alliance for Caregiving and the United Hospital Fund.

Hunt, M. 1974. *Sexual Behavior in the 1970s.* Chicago: Playboy Press.

Huntoon, K. M., C. J. McCluney, C. A. Scannell, E. A. Wiley, R. Bruno, A. Andrews, and P. Gorman. 2011. "Healthcare Reform and the Next Generation: United States Medical Student Attitudes toward the Patient Protection and Affordable Care Act." www.ncbi.nim.nih.gov/pmc/articles/PMC3172206/pdf/pone.0023557.pdf (2011, September 26).

Hupka, R. 1991. "The Motive for the Arousal of Romantic Jealousy: Its Cultural Origin." In P. Salovey, ed., *The Psychology of Jealousy and Envy.* New York: Guilford.

Hurd, M. 2009. "*Inter-vivos* Giving by Older People in the United States of America: Who Received Financial Gifts from the Childless?" *Aging & Society* 29, 8: 1205–1224.

Huston, M., and P. Schwartz. 1996. "Gendered Dynamics in the Romantic Relationships of Lesbians and Gay Men." In J. T. Wood, ed., *Gendered Relationships,* 163–176. Mountain View, CA: Mayfield.

Hutcherson, H. 2010. "Women's Top 5 Sexual Fantasies—and What They Mean." *Redbook.* www.redbookmag.com/love-sex/advice/erotic-fantasy-meaning.

Hutchinson, S. L., T. Afifi, and S. Krause. 2007. "The Family that Plays Together Fares Better: Examining the Contribution of Shared Family Time to Family Resilience Following Divorce." *Journal of Divorce and Remarriage* 46, 3/4: 21–28.

Hyde, J. S. 1984. "Children's Understanding of Sexist Language." *Developmental Psychology* 20, 4: 697–706.

Hyde, J. 2005. "The Gender Similarities Hypothesis." *American Psychologist* 60, 6: 581–592.

Hymowitz, K. S. 2003. "The Cohabitation Blues." *Commentary* 116 (Marlgbtmap.org/file/improving-the-lives-of-lgch): 66–69.

Ibrahim, R., and Z. Hassan. 2009. "Understanding Singlehood from the Experiences of Never-Married Malay Muslim Women in Malaysia: Some Preliminary Findings." *European Journal of Social Sciences* 8 (3): 395–405.

IHC Research Activities. 2005. "Pre-Impact Preparedness and Post-Impact Restoration Activities Following Hurricane Andrew." *International Hurricane Research Center, Florida International University,* http://www.ihc.fiu.edu/ (Accessed 2005, January 27).

Ihinger-Tallman, M. 1987. "Sibling and Stepfamily Bonding in Stepfamilies." In K. Pasley and M. Ihinger-Tallman, eds., *Remarriage and Stepparenting: Current Research and Theory,* 164–82. New York: Guilford Press.

———, and K. Pasley. 1991. "Children in Stepfamilies." In J. N. Edwards and D. H. Demo, eds., *Marriage and Family in Transition,* 453–69. Boston: Allyn & Bacon.

"Improving the Lives of LGBT Older Adults." 2010. (March). www.lgbtmap.org/file/improving-the-lives-of-lgbt-older-adults.pdf (2011, June 15).

"Incest Sex Statistics In America." 2011. www.articlebrain.com/Article/Incest-Sex-Statistics-in-America/6134 (2011, September 19).

Index Mundi. 2011. "Afghanistan Unemployment Rate." www.indexmundi.com/afghanistan/unemployment_rate.html (2011, September 30).

"Indians Most Likely to Report Sexual Harassment at Work—Poll." 2011. (August 12). http://in.reuters.com/article/2010/08/12idNIndia-5080312010812-India (2011, July 8).

"Induced Abortion in the United States." 2005. *Facts in Brief* (May 5). New York: The Alan Guttmacher Institute.

Infidelity Statistics. 2011. www.womansavers.com/infidelity-statistics.asp (2011, June 18).

Inglehart, R., and P. Norris. 2003. *Rising Tide—Gender Equality and Cultural Change Around the World.* Cambridge: Cambridge University Press.

Inman, C. 1996. "Friendships among Men: Closeness in the Doing." In J. T. Wood, ed., *Gendered Relationships,* 95–110. Mountain View, CA: Mayfield.

Inter-American Commission of Human Rights. 2003. "The Situation of the Rights of Women in Ciudad Juarez, Mexico: The Right to be Free from Violence and Discrimination." (March 7): www.cidh.org/annualrep/2002eng/chap.vi.juarez.htm (2008, August 15).

Interparliamentary Union. 2011. "Women in National Parliaments." (March 31). www.ipu.org/wmn-e/world.htm (2011, April 14).

IPPF. 1999. "15-Year-Old Girl Jailed for Abortion in Nepal Released from Prison This Week." (October 4). www.ippf.org/newsinfo/pressreleases/nepal9910.htm (2002, January 21).

Iraq Body Count. 2008. "Civilian Deaths from Violence in 2007." (January 1). www.iraqbodycount.org/analysis/numbers/2007/ (2008, September 13).

"Is High School Ready for Girls' Wrestling?" 2011 (February 18) www.womentalksports.com/items/read/85771 (2011, February 28).

Isaacs, R. 2002. "Children's Adjustment to Their Divorced Parents' New Relationships." *Journal of Paediatrics and Child Health* 38, 4: 329–331.

Isen, A., and B. Stevenson. 2010. "Women's Education and Family Behavior: Trends in Marriage, Divorce and Fertility." (February). www.nber.org/papers/Wi5725.pdf. (2011, July 19).

Jackson, A. P., R. P. Brown, and K. E. Patterson-Stewart. 2000. "African Americans in Dual-Career Commuter Marriages: An Investigation of Their Experiences." *Family Journal: Counseling and Therapy for Couples and Families* 8: 22–36.

Jacob, H. 1988. *Silent Revolution: The Transformation of Divorce Law in the United States.* Chicago: University of Chicago Press.

Jacob, M. 2009. "History Lesson: 10 Things You Might Not Know About Marriage." *Chicago Tribune* (April 19): Section 1, p. 25.

Jacobs, S., W. Thomas, S. Lang. 1997. *Two Spirit People: Native American Gender Identity, Sexuality, and Spirituality.* Champaign, IL: University of Illinois Press.

Jadva, V., C. Murray, E. Lycett, F. MacCallum, and S. Golombok. 2003. "Surrogacy: The Experiences of Surrogate Mothers." Human Reproduction 18, 10 (October): 2196–2204.

James, J. 2004. "And What About the Dads?" Time Europe 163, 19 (May 10). http://www.time.com/time/europe/magazine/printout/0,13155,901040510-631996m00.html (2006, February 8).

James, S. 2010. "Many Successful Gay Marriages Share an Open Secret." (January 29). *New York Times.* www.nytimes.com/2010/01/29/us/29sfmetro.html (2011, August 1).

Jamison, P. 2011. "Donors Allege Price-Fixing Scheme by Fertility Clinics for Human Eggs." (August 5) http://blogs.sfweekly.com/thesnitch/2011/08/human_egg_price_fixing.php (2011, September 9).

"Janet Sheen and Martin Sheen." 2011. Dating, Gossip, News. www.whodatedwho.com/tpx_1713928/janet-sheen-and-martin-sheen/ (2011, December 15).

Jankowiak, W., and Fischer, E. 1992. "A Cross-Cultural Perspective on Romantic Love." *Ethnology* 31, 2 (April): 149–155.

Janofsky, M. 2001. "Polygamy Case Raises Thorny Issues." *Chicago Tribune* (May 15): Sec. 1, 9.

———. 2003. "Young Brides Stir New Outcry on Utah Polygamy." *New York Times* (February28). www.nytimes.com/2003/02/28/us/young-brides-stir-new-outcry-on-utah-polygamy.html (2011, March 14).

Jansz, J., and R. G. Martis. 2007. "The Laura Phenomenon: Powerful Female Characters in Video Games. *Sex Roles* 56: 141–148.

"Japan Fails to Safeguard Parental Rights in Divorce." 2008. (July 14). www.taipeitimes.com/News/world/archieves/2008/07/14/2003417391 (2008, August 6).

Jayson, S. 2005. "Dating Game Changes After 40." *USA Today* (December 1): D4.

———. 2006. "New Generation Doesn't Blink at Interracial Relationships." *USA Today* (February).

———. 2008. "Living Together No Longer Playing House." (July 28) www.usatoday.com/news/2008-07-28-cohabitation-research_N.htm# (2011, May 5).

———. 2010. "What Does A 'Family' Look Like Nowadays?" *USA Today.* www.usatoday.com/yourlife/sex-relationships/marriage/2010-11-18-pew18_ST_N.htm (2011, March 14).

———. 2011. "Men, Women Flip the Script in Gender Expectation." *USA Today,* (February 2). http://yourlife.usatoday.com/sex-relationships/dating/story/2011/02/Men-women-flip-the-script-in-gender-expectation/43219110/1 (2011, July 4).

———. 2011. "Same-Sex Marriages: First Census Count Shows 131,729." *USA Today.* www.yourlife.usatoday.com/sex-relationships/story/2011-09-27/Same-sex-marriages-first-Census-count-shows-131729/50571788/1 (2011, December 15).

Jelinek, P. 2011. "Airman Discharged Under 'Don't Ask, Don't Tell.'" (June 2). http://news.yahoo.com/s/ap/us_gays_in_military (2011, June 15).

Jenkins, M. 2005. "Black Woman's Quandary." *Chicago Sun Times* (December 7): 64–65.

Jeong, M. 2011. "Number of Stay-At-Home Dads on the Rise." (June 17). http://boards.askmen.com/showthread.php?123091-Number-of-stay-at-home-dads-on-the-rise (2011, June 25).

Jerome, R., J. Fowler, D. Stuart, J. Blonka, P. Grout, and J. Bane. 2004. "The Cyberporn Generation." *People* 61(16): 72, 5p, 8c.

Jhally, S. 1995. *Dreamworlds II: Gender/Sex/Power in Music Video.* (55 Minute Video Documentary). Northhampton, MA· Media Education Foundation.

Johnson, F. L. 1996. "Friendships among Women: Closeness in Dialogue." In J. T. Wood, ed., *Gendered Relationships,* 79–93. Mountain View, CA: Mayfield.

Johnson, L. A. 2005. "Experts: Girls Using Steroids for 'Weight Control.'" *Chicago Tribune* April 26): 10.

Johnson, M. 2008. *A Typology of Domestic Violence: Intimate Terrorism, Violent Resistance, and Situational Couple Violence.* Boston, MA: Northeastern University Press.

Johnson, S. M. 2003. "The Revolution in Couple Therapy: A Practitioner-Scientist Perspective." *Journal of Marital and Family Therapy* 29: 365–384.

Jones, A. J., and M. Galinsky. 2003. "Restructuring the Stepfamily: Old Myths, New Stories." *Social Work* 48, 2: 228–237.

Jones, G. W. 2010. "Changing Marriage Patterns in Asia." Asia Research Institute Working Paper No. 131 (January 15). http://papers.ssrn.com/sol3/papers.cfm (2011, April 26).

———, and B. Gubhaju. 2009. "Trends in Marriage in Low Fertility Countries of East and South East Asia." *Asian Population Studies* 5 (3): 237–265.

Jones, J. 2006. "Marriage Is for White People." *Washington Post* (March 26): B, O1.

———. 2007. "More Than Half of Americans Are 'Very Satisfied' with Personal Life." The Gallup Organization. (January 3). www.gallup.com/poll/26032/More-Than-Half-Americans-Very-Satisfied-Personal-Life (2008, July 4).

Jones, J. M. 2005. "Gender Differences in Views of Job Opportunity." *The Gallup Organization* (August 2). www.gallup.com/poll/content/print.aspx?ci+17614P (2005, August 2).

Jones, P. 2005. "TV Terror." *Chicago Tribune* (October 18): Sec. 5, p. 1, 5.

Jones, R. K., L. B. Finer, and S. Singh. 2010. "Characteristics of U.S. Abortion Patients, 2008." New York: Guttmacher Institute.

Jones, R. K., and K. Kooistra. 2011. "Abortion Incidence and Access in the United States, 2008." *Perspective on Sexual and Reproductive Health* 43, 1: 41–50.

Jones, S. M., and K. Dindia. 2004. "A Meta-analytic Perspective on Sex Equity in the Classroom." *Review of Educational Research* 74 (4): 443–471.

Jose, A. K., D. O'Leary, and A. Moyer. 2010. "Does Premarital Cohabitation Predict Subsequent Marital Stability and Marital Quality? A Meta-Analysis." *Journal of Marriage and Family* 72 (1): 105–116.

Jowers, K., and A. Tilghman. 2011. "Children in Military Families Taking More Psychiatric Drugs." (January 2). www.courier-journal.com/fdcp/?1296171693734 (2011, August 20).

Joyce, K. 2009. *Quiverfull: Inside the Christian Patriarchy Movement.* Boston: Beacon Press.

Juby, H. 2003/2004. "Yours, Mine, and Ours: New Boundaries for the Modern Stepfamily." *Transition Magazine* 33, 4 (Winter): 2–6.

———, C. Le Bourdais, and N. Marcil-Gratton. 2005. "Sharing Roles, Sharing Custody? Couples' Characteristics and Children's Living Arrangements at Separation." *Journal of Marriage and Family* 67, 1: 157–171.

Kaestle, C., C. Halpern, and J. Brown. 2007."Music Videos, Pro-Wrestling, and Acceptance of Date Rape Among Middle School Males and Females: An Exploratory Analysis." *Journal of Adolescent Health*, 40, 185–187.

Kain, E. 1990. *The Myth of Family Decline: Understanding Families in a World of Rapid Social Change.* Lexington, MA: D. C. Heath.

Kaiser Family Foundation. 2003. "Key Facts: TV Violence." (Spring), Menlo Park, CA: The Henry J. Kaiser Family Foundation, www.kff.org (2006, June 2).

———. *Medicare Chart Book 2005.* http://www.kff.org/medicare/7284.cfm (2006, June 27).

———. 2006. "Sexual Health Statistics for Teenagers and Young Adults in the United States." (September). www.kff.org.(2006, February 4).

———. 2007. "Health Challenges for the People of New Orleans: The Kaiser Post-Katrina Baseline Survey," www.kff.org/kaiserpolls/7659.cfm (2008, February 27).

———. 2008. "HIV/AIDS Policy Fact Sheet: Black Americans and HIV/AIDS." (May). www.kff.org (2008, June 4).

Kalajian, B. 2006. "Making Love Last: Communication, Commitment and Giving More Than 50 Percent Among Secrets to Marital Longevity." *The Record Eagle.* (February 12) www.record-eagle.com/2006/feb/12marr.htm (2006, April 14).

Kalata, J. 2006. "Looking at Act II of Women's Lives: Thriving & Striving from 45 On."

Kalil, A. 2005. "Unemployment and Job Displacement: The Impact on Families and Children." *Ivey Business Journal* (July/August): 1–5.

Kalmijn, M. 2007. "Gender Differences in the Effects of Divorce, widowhood and Remarriage on Intergenerational Support: Does Marriage Protect Fathers?" *Social Forces* 85, 3 (March): 1079–1104.

Kaminer, W. 2001. "Virtual Rape." *The New York Times Magazine* (November 25): 70–73.

Kanabus, A. 2008. "HIV, Pregnancy, Mothers and Babies." (July 21) http://www.avert.org/pregnancy.htm (Accessed July 24 2008).

Kanter, R. M. 1977. *Work and Family in the United States.* New York: Russell Sage Foundation.

———. 2005. *Commitment and Community: Communes and Utopias in Sociological Perspective.* Cambridge, MA: Harvard University Press.

Karbo, K. 2009. "Men, Women, and Friendship." *Psychology Today* (January 8). www.psychologytoday.com/articles/200612/men-women-and-friendship (2011, April 11).

Karimzaeh, M. A., and S. Ghandi. 2008. "Early Marriage: A Policy for Infertility Prevention." *Journal of Family and Reproductive Health* 2, 2: 61–64.

Karp, D. A., W. Yoels, and B. Vann, 2003. *Sociology in Everyday Life.* Long Grove, IL: Waveland Press.

Kassner, E., S. Reinhard, W. Fox-Grage, A. N. Houser, and J. C. Accius. 2008. "In Brief: A Balancing Act: State Long-Term Care Reform." (August 26). www.aarp.org/research/longtermcare/programfunding/inb/61_ltc.html (2008, August 27).

Katz, E., N. Gur-Yaish, and A. Lowenstein. 2010. "Motivation to Provide Help to Older Parents in Norway, Spain, and Israel." *International Journal of Aging and Human Development* 71, 4: 283–303.

Kaufman, G., and H. Taniguchi. 2006. "Gender and Marital Happiness in Later Life." *Journal of Family Issues* 27, 6: 735–757.

Keith, P. 1986. "Isolation of the Unmarried in Later Life." *Family Relations* 35: 389–96.

Kellas, J. K., C. LeClair-Underberg, and E. L. Normad. 2008. "Stepfamily Address Terms: 'Sometimes They Mean Something and Sometimes They Don't.'" *Journal of Family Communication* 8: 238–263.

Kellogg, A. 2011. "Racial Gap in Home Ownership Widens in U.S. Slump." (August 24). www.npr.org/2011/08/24/139877687/racial-gap-in-home-ownership-widens-in-u-s-slump (2011, September 7).

Kelly, G. F. 2007. *Sexuality Today.* 9th ed. New York: McGraw-Hill.

Kelly, J. 2007. "Children's Living Arrangement Following Divorce." *Family Process* 46: 35–52.

Kelly, J. B. 2000. "Children's Adjustment in Conflicted Marriage and Divorce: A Decade Review of Research." *Journal of the American Academy of Child and Adolescent Psychiatry* 39, 8 (August): 963–73.

———, and R. E. Emery. 2003. "Children's Adjustment Following Divorce: Risk and Resilience Perspectives." *Family Relations* 52: 352–362.

Kelly, L. 1988. *Surviving Sexual Violence.* Minneapolis: University of Minnesota Press.

Kelty, R., M. Kleykamp, and D. Segal. 2010. The Military and the Transition to Adulthood." *Transition to Adulthood* 1 (Spring) 181–207.

Kempe, C. H., F. N. Silverman, B. Steele, W. Droegemueller, and H. K. Silver. 1962. "The Battered Child Syndrome." *Journal of the American Medical Association* 181: 17–24.

Kennedy, J. 1999. "Romantic Attachment Style and Ego Identity, Attributional Style, and Family of Origin in First-Year College Students." *College Student Journal* 33(2), 171–180.

Kennedy, P. 2007. *The First Man-Made Man: The Story of Two-Sex Changes, One Love Affair, and a Twentieth Century Medical Revolution.* London: Bloomsbury Publishers.

Kennedy, S., and L. Bumpass. 2008. "Cohabitation and Children's Living Arrangements: New Estimates from the United States." *Demographic Research* 19: 1663–1692.

Kenney, C. T., and S. S. McLanahan. 2006. "Why Are Cohabiting Relationships More Violent Than Marriages?" *Demography* 43, 1 (February): 127–140.

Kent, M. M., and C. Haub. 2005. "Global Demographic Divide." *Population Bulletin* 60, 4.

Kephart, W. M. 1988. "The Oneida Community." In N. D. Glenn and M. Tolbert, eds., *Family Relations: A Reader,* 17–24. Belmont, CA: Wadsworth.

Kessler-Harris, A. 1982. *Out to Work: A History of Wage-Earning Women in the United States.* New York: Oxford University Press.

Khawaja, M., and R. R. Habib. 2007. "Husbands' Involvement in Housework and Women's Psychosocial Health: Findings From a Population-Based Study in Lebanon." *American Journal of Public Health.* 97, 5: 860–866.

Kheshgi-Genovese, S., and T. A. Genovese. 1997. "Developing the Spousal Relationship within Stepfamilies." *Families in Society: The Journal of Contemporary Human Services* 78 (May–June): 255–64.

Kiefer, H. 2004. "Teens: Sometimes Love Just Ain't Enough." (September 28). The Gallup Organization www.gallup.com (2006, April 14).

Kiernan, K. 2002. "Cohabitation in Western Europe: Trends, Issues, and Implications."

Kilborn, P. 2004. "Alive, Well and on the Prowl, It's the Geriatric Mating Game." *New York Times* (March 7): online, P.1.

Kim, E. K. 2006. "Black Jack's Rule on Unwed Parents is Unusual Here." *STLtoday.com* (February 23). www.stltoday.com/stltoday/news/special/srlinks.nsf/0/ F9FCE3731F7C4BD 38625712300801F1B?OpenDocument (2006, April 3).

Kim, H., and R. Chung. 2003. "Relationship of Recalled Parenting Styles to Self-Perception in Korean American College Students." *Journal of Genetic Psychology* http:www.alternet.org/module/printversion/22199 (2006, April 25).

Kimmel, M.2001. "Manhood and Violence: The Deadliest Equation." *Newsday* (March 8): A-41.

King, D. K. 1990. "Multiple Jeopardy, Multiple Consciousness." In M. R. Malson, E. Mudimbe-Boyi, J. F. O'Barr, and M. Wyer, eds., *Black Women in America*, 265–295. Chicago: University of Chicago Press.

King, V., K. M. Harris, and H. E. Heard. 2004. Racial and Ethnic Diversity in Nonresident Father Involvement. *Journal of Marriage and Family* 66: 1–21.

Kinnon, J. 2003. "The Shocking State of Black Marriage." *Ebony*, no. 1 (November): 59.

Kinsey, A., W. B. Pomeroy, and C. E. Martin. 1948. *Sexual Behavior in the Human Male.* Philadelphia: Saunders.

Kirkham, C. 2011. "Improper Military Foreclosures: U.S. Settles with Two Firms." (May 26). www.huffingtonpost.com/2011/05/26/improper-military-foreclosures-justice-department-settles_n_867804.html (June 24).

Kitano, H., and R. Daniels. 2001. *Asian Americans: Emerging Minorities*, 3rd ed. Upper Saddle River, NJ: Prentice Hall.

Klaus, D. 2009. "Why Do Adult Children Support Their Parents?" *Journal of Comparative Family Studies* 40, 2: 227–241.

Kleinfeld, J., and M. Reyes. 2007. "Boys Left Behind: Gender Role Disintegration in the Arctic." *THYMOS Journal of Boyhood Studies* I (2): 179–190.

Klimek, D. 1979. *Beneath Mate Selection in Marriage: The Unconscious Motives in Human Pairing*. New York: Van Nostrand Reinhold.

Knaub, P., S. L. Hanna, and N. Stinnett. 1984. "Strengths of Remarried Families." *Journal of Divorce* 7, 3: 41–55.

Knox, D., M. Kaluzny, and C. Cooper. 2000. "College Student Recovery from a Broken Heart." *College Student Journal*, 34, 3 (September): 322–324.

Knox, D., and M. Zusman. 2001. "Marrying a Man with 'Baggage': Implications for Second Wives." *Journal of Divorce and Remarriage* 35, 3/4: 67–79.

———, and A. DeCuzzi. 2004. "The Effect of Parental Divorce on Relationships with Parents and Romantic Partners of College Students." *College Student Journal* 38, 4: 597–601.

Knudson-Martin, C., and A. R. Mahoney. 2005. "Moving Beyond Gender: Processes That Create Relationship Equality." *Journal of Marital and Family Therapy* (April).

Kobbe, A. 2008. "Preventing Sexual Abuse of Children." The University of Tennessee Institute of Agriculture. www.utextension.utk.edu/publications/wfiles/W021 (August 26).

Koch, Wendy. 2008. "2nd Arrest Made at Texas Polygamist Ranch." *USA Today* (April 9). http://www.usatoday.com/news/nation/2008-04-07-polygamist-compound_N.htm (2011, March 14).

Kochanek, K., J. Xu, S. Murphy, A. Miniño, and H. Kung. 2011. "Deaths: Preliminary Data for 2009." *National Vital Statistics Report*, 59, 4 (March 16). Washington, DC: U.S. Department of Human Services, Centers for Disease Control and Prevention.

Kochhar, R., R. Fry, and P. Taylor. 2011. "Wealth Gap Rise to Record Highs Between Whites, Blacks and Hispanics." (July 26). www.pewresearch.org/pubs/2069/housing-bubble-subprime-mortgages-hispanics-blacks-household-wealth-disparity (September 7).

Kogan, T. S. 2004. "Transsexuals, Intersexuals, and Same-Sex Marriages." *BYU Journal of Public Law* 18, 2: 371–418.

Kohlberg, L. 1966. "A Cognitive-Developmental Analysis of Children's Sex-Role Concepts and Attitudes." In E. Maccoby, ed., *The Development of Sex Differences*, 82–173. Stanford, CA: Stanford University Press.

Kohli, M., and M. Albertini. 2009. "Childlessness and Intergenerational Transfers: What Is At Stake?" *Aging & Society* 29: 1171–1183.

Kohn, M. 1977. *Class and Conformity*. Chicago: University of Chicago Press.

Kong, C. 1998. "Sometimes Love Hurts: When Romance Turns Rocky." *Summer Romance*: Special issue. http://enterprise.sjme...talhigh/love/abuse.html (March 19).

"Korean Men Willing to Tend Home, Survey Finds." 2011. (April 25). http://blogs.ws/com/korearealtime/2011/korean-men-willing-to-tend-home-survey-finds/ (2011, June 25).

Kotz, D. 2009. "Bristol Palin: Poster Child for Teen Pregnancy Prevention." (May 6). www.health.usnews.com/health-news/blogs/on-women/2009/05/06/bristol-palin-poster-child-for-teen-pregnancy-prevention (2011, July 31).

Kovacs, J. 2005. "U.S. Teacher Sexpidemic Spreading Across Planet." WorldNetDaily. www.worldnetdaily.com (2005, December 18).

Krebs, C., C. Lindquist, T. Warner, B. Fisher, and S. Martin. 2007. "Campus Sexual Assault (CSA) Study, Final Report." Washington, DC: U.S. Department of Justice, Office of Justice Programs. www.ncjrs.gov/App/Publications/abstract.aspx?ID=243011 (2011, July 4).

Kreider, R. M. 2010. Housing and Household Economic Statistics Division Working Paper (September 15). www.ccnsus.gov/population/www/socdemo/Inc-Opp-Sex-2009-t0-2010.pdf (2011, May 8).

———, and D. B. Elliot. 2009. America's Families and Living Arrangements: 2007. Current Population Reports, P20-56. U. S. Census Bureau. Washington, DC.

———, and R. Ellis. 2011a. "Living Arrangements of Children: 2009." *Current Population Reports*, P70-114. Washington, DC: U.S. Census Bureau.

———. 2011b. *Number, Timing, and Duration of Marriages and Divorces, 2009*. Current Population Reports, P70-125. Washington, DC: U.S. Census Bureau.

Kridel, K. 2009. "Going the Distance for Love and Marriage." (March 9). http://articles.latimes.com/2009/mar/09/nation/na-commuter-marriage9 (2011, June 25).

Kristof, N. 1996. "Who Needs Love? In Japan Many Couples Don't." *New York Times* (February 11): A6.

———. 2005. "Blacks, Whites and Love in America." *New York Times* (April 24): Sec. 4, 13.

Kroszner, R. S. 2007. "The Challenges Facing B&C Mortgage Borrowers." New York, NY: National Mortgage News. http://www.nationalmortgagenews.com/plus/?show+oforum453.htm (2008, February 20).

Kübler-Ross, E. 1969. *On Death and Dying*. New York: Macmillan.

———. 1974. *Questions and Answers on Death and Dying*. New York: Macmillan

Kulik, L. 2002. "The Impact of Social Background on Gender-Role Ideology." *Journal of Family Issues* 23, 1: 53–73.

Kurdek, L. A. 1998. "Relationship Outcomes and Their Predictors: Longitudinal Evidence From Heterosexual, Married, Gay, Cohabiting, and Lesbian Cohabiting Couples." *Journal of Marriage and the Family* 60: 553–568.

———. 2005. "Gender and Marital Satisfaction Early in Marriage: A Growth Curve Approach." *Journal of Marriage and Family* 67: 68–84.

———. 2006. "Differences Between Partners from Heterosexual, Gay, and Lesbian Cohabiting Couples." *Journal of Marriage and Family* 68, 2: 509–528.

———. 2007. "The Allocation of Household Labor by Partners in Gay and Lesbian Couples." *Journal of Family Issues*. 28, 1: 132–148.

Kuzma, C. 2005. "The Kids Are Alright." *AlterNet* (June 9). http://www.alternet.org/module/printversion/22199 (2006, April 25).

Kvale, A. 2006. "Wedding Traditions: Legends & Stories." http://voices.yahoo.com/wedding-traditions-42119.html?cat=23 (2011, December 8).

Kwok, H. 2006. "The Son Also Acts as Major Caregiver to Elderly Parents." *Current Sociology* 54, 2: 257–272.

La Ferla, R. 2000. "The Once and Future Virgins." *New York Times*. (July 23). www.nytimes.qpass.com/qpass-archives (2001, December 4).

Lacey, M. 2008. "Attacks Show Easygoing Jamaica Is Dire Place for Gays." *New York Times* (February 24): 4.

LaFraniere, S. 2011. "China Might Force Visits to Mom and Dad." *New York Times* (January 30): 8.

Lai, T. 1992. "Asian American Women: Not for Sale." In M. Anderson and P. H. Collins, eds., *Race, Class, and Gender*, 163–71. Belmont, CA: Wadsworth.

Lakoff, R. 1975. *Language and Woman's Place*. New York: Colophon.

Lamm, S. 2008. "Threesomes are Every Man's Fantasy." *Psychology Today*. www.psychologytoday.com/blog/great-sex/200806/threesomes-are-every-mans-fantasy.

Lampman, J. 2006. "Women Clergy Bring a New Sensibility to an Old Calling." (July 19). http://www.csmonitor.com/2006/0719/p14s01-lire.html (2008, March 22).

Landhaus, E. 2004. "Pre-implantation Genetic Diagnosis Offers Hope But Prompts Ethical Concerns." *Stanford Report* (March 3). http://newservice.stanford.edu/news/2004/march3/invitro-33.html (2004, April 24).

Landsverk, J., and A. F. Garland. 2000. "Foster Care and Pathways to Mental Health Services." In P. A. Curtis et al., eds., *The Foster Care Crisis: Translating Research into Policy and Practice*, 193–210. Lincoln: The University of Nebraska Press.

Langer, G., C. Arndt, and D. Sussman. 2004. "Primetime Live Poll: American Sex Survey: A Peek Beneath the Sheets." ABC News. abcnews.go.com/ Primetime/News/story?id=174461&page=1 (2006, March 20).

Langford, B. Y. 2011. "Closing the Gender Gap: Communication Styles of Women and Men. (February 1). www.womenetics.com/my-careerlife/1727-closing-the-gender-communication-gp (2011, April 11).

Lapidos, J. 2010. "Epilogue: Till Love Do Us Part: What Will Happen to My Friendship with Jeff in the Years to Come?" *Slate* (October 1). www.slate.com/articles/life/strictly_plantonic/2010/09epilogue_til_love_do_us_part.html (2011, April 11).

Lareau, A. 2003. *Unequal Childhoods: Class, Race, and Family Life.* Berkeley, CA: University of California Press.

Larmer, B. 2010. "China's Arranged Remarriages." (May 7). www.nytimes.com/2010/05/09/magazine/09widows-t.html?partner=rss&emc=rss (2011, July 25).

Larson, S. 2010. Susan's Place: Transgender Resources. www.susans.org/reference/index.html (2011, June 18).

Larson, V. 2011. "Would Your Remarry Your Ex?" (May 13). www.huffingtonpost.com/vicki-larson/would-you-remarry-your-ex_b_859906.html (2011, July 25).

Larzelere, R. E., and B. R. Kuhn. 2005. "Comparing Child Outcomes of Physical Punishment and Alternative Disciplinary Tactics: A Meta-analysis." *Clinical Child and Family Psychology Review* 8, 1: 1–37.

Lasch, C. 1977. *Haven in a Heartless World: The Family Besieged.* New York: Basic Books.

———. 1978. *The Culture of Narcissism.* New York: W. W. Norton.

Laslett, P. 1971. *The World We Have Lost,* 2nd ed. New York: Scribner's.

"Latest Dating Trends…," 2011. Latest Dating Trends: Today's Dating Scene—What You Need to Know to Find Love by Online Dating. (January 2). www.latinonlinedating.net/137/latest-dating-trends-todays-dating-scene-what-you-need-to-know-to-find-love-by-online-dating/ (2011, July 5).

Latshaw, B. A. 2010. "What Makes Men Mother and Mop?—Constancy and Change in the Care Work Performed by American Men." Dissertation, Chapel Hill: The University of North Carolina.

Lauer, R., and J. Lauer. 1988. *Watersheds: Mastering Life's Unpredictable Crises.* New York: Little, Brown.

———. 2006. *The Quest for Intimacy.* Dubuque, IA: Brown.

Laumann, E. O., J. H. Gagnon, R. T. Michael, and S. Michaels. 1994. *The Social Organization of Sexuality: Sexual Practices in the United States.* Chicago: University of Chicago Press.

Lauzen, M. M., D. M. Dozier, and N. Horan. 2008. "Constructing Gender Stereotypes Through Social Roles in Prime-Time Television." *Journal of Broadcasting & Electronic Media* 52 (2): 200–214.

Lawrence, A. A. 2003. "Factors Associated with Satisfaction or Regret Following Male-to-Female Sex Reassignment Surgery." *Archives of Sexual Behavior* 32, 4: 299–315.

Le, C. N. 2006a. "By the Numbers: Dating, Marriage, and Race in Asian America." *Asian Nation.* IMDiversity. www.imdiversity.com/villages/asian/family_lifestyle_traditions/le_interracial_dating.asp (2006, April 24).

———. 2006b. "Multiracial/Hapa Asian Americans." *Asian-Nation: The Landscape of Asian America.* www.asian-nation.org/multiracial.shtml (2006, April 24).

———. 2008. "Interracial Dating & Marriage." *Asian Nation: The Landscape of Asian America.* www.asian-nation.org/interracial.shtml (2008, July 4).

———. 2011. "Socioeconomic Statistics and Demographics." *Asian Nation: The Landscape of Asian America.* www.asian-nation.org/demographics.shtml (2011, July 8).

Leaper, C. 2002. "Parenting Girls and Boys." In M. H. Bornstein, ed., *Handbook of Parenting,* 2nd ed., 189–215. Mahwah, NJ. Erlbaum.

Lee, D. 2011. "Saudi Arabian Woman Challenges Male Guardianship Laws." (June 29). www.bbc.co.uk/news/world-middle-east-13932287 (2011, July 4).

Lee, E. 2008. "Attitudes Predict Interracial Dating Behaviors and Vice Versa." (December 15). http://www.eharmony.com/labs/2008/12/attitudes-predict-interracial-dating-behaviors-and-vice-versa/ (2011, July 4).

Lee, G. R., A. DeMaris, S. Bavin, and R. Sullivan. 2001. "Gendered Differences in the Depression Effect of Widowhood in Later Life." *Journal of Gerontology B: Psychological Sciences and Social Sciences* 56B, 1: S56–S61.

Lee, G. R., K. Seccombe, and C. L. Shehan. 1991. "Marital Status and Personal Happiness: An Analysis of Trends and Data." *Journal of Marriage and the Family* 53: 839–44.

Lee, J. 1974. "The Styles of Loving." *Psychology Today* 8, 5 (October): 46–51.

———. 2007. "The Incredible Flying Granny Nanny." *New York Times* (May 10).

Lee, S., and B. Edmonston. 2005. "New Marriages, New Families: U.S. Racial and Hispanic Intermarriage." *Population Bulletin* 60(2). Washington, DC: Population Reference Bureau.

Leeder, E. 2004. *The Family in Global Perspective: A Gendered Journey.* Thousand Oaks, CA: Sage.

Lefkowitz, E. S., and P. B. Zeldow. 2006. "Masculinity and Femininity Predict Optimal Mental Health: A Belated Test of the Androgyny Hypothesis." *Journal of Personality Assessment* 87 (1): 95–101.

Legal Community Against Violence. 2011. "Major Victories in California: Governor Brown Signs Three Crucial Bills to Prevent Gun Violence." www.lcav.org/ (2011, May 24).

Lehman, K. 2004. "Hook-Ups." Families.Com. www.recreation.families.com/hook-ups-451-452-erla (2006, January 18).

Lehr, R., and P. MacMillan. 2001. "The Psychological and Emotional Impact of Divorce: The Noncustodial Fathers' Perspective." *Families in Society* 82, 4 (July/August): 273–382.

Lehren, A., and J. Leland. 2006. "Scant Drop Seen in Abortions if Parents Are Told." *The New York Times* (March 6): A1, A19.

Leicester, J. 2005. "France Eyes More Aid to Foster Baby Boom." *Chicago Tribune* (September 22): 3.

Leland, J. 2001. "Gays Seeking Asylum Find Familiar Prejudices in U.S." *New York Times* (August 1): A10.

LeMasters, E. 1957. *Modern Courtship and Marriage.* New York: Macmillan.

Lemmon, K. 2006. "Wedding Traditions and Their Origins." http://voices.yahoo.com/wedding-traditions-their-origins-124665.html (2011, December 8).

Lemmons, E. 2011. "Interfaith Marriages." www.foryourmarriage.org/catholic-marriage/church-teachings/interfaith-marriages/ (2011, July 4).

Lempert, L. B. 1999. "Other Fathers: An Alternative Perspective on African American Community Caring." In R. Staples, ed., *The Black Family: Essays and Studies,* 6th ed., 189–201. Belmont, CA: Wadsworth.

Lengermann, P. M., and J. N. Brantley. 2004. "Feminist Theory." In G. Ritzer, ed., *Sociological Theory,* 400–443. New York: Knopf.

Lenhart, A. 2009. "Teens and Sexting." *Pew Research Center Publications.* (December 15). www.pewresearch.org/pubs/1440/teens-sexting-text-messages (2011, June 18).

———. 2010. "Teen, Cell Phones and Texting." (April 20). http://pewresearch.org/pubs/1572/teens-cell-phones-text-messages (2011, September 9).

"Lesbians, Gays Gaining Acceptance." 2005. *China Daily* (October 10). www.chinadaily.com.cn/english/doc/2005–10/10/content_483531.htm (2005, October 10).

Leshnoff, J. 2011. "Sexting Not Just for Kids." (June). www.aarp.org/relationships/love-sex/info-11-2009/sexting_not_just_for_kids.print.html (2011, June 18).

Lessinger, J. 2002. "Asian Indian Marriages—Arranged, Semi-Arranged, or Based on Love?" In Nijole Benokraitis, ed., *Contemporary Ethnic Families in the United States,* 101–104, Upper Saddle River, NJ: Prentice Hall.

Lester, D. 1996. "The Impact of Unemployment on Marriage and Divorce." *Journal of Divorce and Remarriage* 25, 3/4: 151–53.

Levine, B. 2005. "Back to the Nest." *Chicago Tribune* (October 8): Sec. 5, 1, 8, and 9.

Levine, M. P., and L. Smolak. 2002. "Body Image Development in Adolescence." In T. F. Cash & T. Pruzinsky, eds., *Body Image,* 74–82. New York: Guilford Press.

Levinger, G. 1965. "Marital Cohesiveness and Dissolution: An Integrative Review." *Journal of Marriage and the Family* 27: 19–28.

———. 1979. "A Social Psychological Perspective on Marital Dissolution." In G. Levinger and O. Moles, eds., *Divorce and Separation,* 37–60. New York: Basic Books.

Levinson, C. 2005. "Egyptian Women See Divorce as a Religious Right." *Womens News* (January 9). http://www.womensenews.org/article.cfm/ dyn/aid/2139/context/archieve (2006, March 21).

Lewin, T. 1995. "Parents Poll Finds Child Abuse to Be More Common." *New York Times* (December 7).

Lewis, T., F. Amini, and R. Lannon. 2000. *General Theory of Love.* New York: Random House.

"LGBTQ Teens and Dating Abuse." 2011. www.dosomething.org/tipsandtools/lgbtq-teens-and-dating-abuse (2011, July 4).

Lichter, D. T., and Z. C. Qian. 2004. *Marriage and Family in a Multiracial Society.* Washington, DC: Russell Sage Foundation and the Population Reference Bureau.

———. 2008. "Serial Cohabitation and the Marital Life Course. *Journal of Marriage and Family* 70 (4): 861–878.

———, and L. M. Mellott. 2006. "Marriage or Dissolution? Union Transitions Among Poor Cohabiting Women." *Demography* 43, 2 (May): 223–240.

Liefbroer, A. C., and E. Dourleijn. 2006. "Unmarried Cohabitation and Union Stability: Testing the Role of Diffusion Using Data from 16 European Countries." *Demograph* 43, 2 (May): 203–221.

Light, D., S. Keller, and C. Calhoun. 2000. *Understanding Sociology: Guide to Critical Thinking.* Glencoe: McGraw-Hill.

Ligutom-Kimura, D. 1995. "The Invisible Women." *The Journal of Physical Education, Recreation and Dance* 66, 7:34–41.

Lin, J-P., and C-C. Yi. 2011. "Filial Norms and Intergenerational Support to Aging Parents in China and Taiwan." *International Journal of Social Welfare.*

Lindberg, L., and S. Singh. 2008. "Sexual Behavior of Single Adult American Women." *Perspectives on Sexual and Reproductive Health* 40 (March): 27–33.

Lindsey, E., P. R. Cremeens, and Y. M. Caldera. 2010. "Gender Differences in Mother-Toddler and Father-Toddler Verbal Initiations and Responses During a Caregiving and Play Context." *Sex Roles* (June 2). http:/ts-si .org/files/doi101007s1119901098035.pdf (2011, March 27).

Lindsey, L. 2005. *Gender Roles: A Sociological Perspective*, 4th ed. Upper Saddle River, NJ: Prentice Hall.

Lips, H. 1993. *Sex and Gender: An Introduction.* Mountain View, CA: Mayfield.

———. 1995. "Gender-Role Socialization: Lessons in Femininity." In J. Freeman, ed., *Women: A Feminist Perspective*, 5th ed., 128–148. Mountain View, CA: Mayfield.

Liptak, A. 2008. "California Court Overturns A Ban on Gay Marriage." *New York Times* (May 16): A1, A19.

Liu, P., and C. S. Chan. 1996. "Bisexual Asian Americans and Their Families." In J. Laird and R. Green, eds., *Lesbians and Gays in Couples and Families*, 137–152. San Francisco: Jossey-Bass.

Liu, X., C. Guo, and M. Okawa. 2000. "Behavioral and Emotional Problems in Chinese Children of Divorced Parents." *Journal of the American Academy of Child Adolescent Psychiatry* 39, 7: 896–903.

Livingston, G., and D. Cohn. 2010. "More Women Without Children" (June 25). http://pewresearch.org/pubs/1642/more-women-without-children (2011, September 1).

Liz Claiborne, Inc. 2008. "Tween and Teen Dating Violence and Abuse Study." (July). www.loveisnotabuse.com/web/guest/search/-/journal_content/56/10123/83545

———. 2009. "Impact of the Economy and Parent/Teen dialogue on Dating Relationships and Abuse." *Teen Dating Abuse Report 2009.* (June). www.loveisnotabuse.com/web/guest/search/-/journal_content/56/10123/81382 (2011, July 4).

Lofas, J. 2009. "The Dynamics of Step." www.stepfamily.org/dynamics. (2011, August 1).

Loh, E. S. 1996. "Productivity Differences and the Marriage Wage Premium for White Males." *Journal of Human Resources* 31, 3: 566–589.

Longino, C. F., Jr. 1988. "A Population Profile of Very Old Men and Women in the United States." *Sociological Quarterly* 29: 559–64.

Longman, J. 2011. "On Mat, Girls Still Face Uphill Struggle." *New York Times* (February 28): D1, D7.

Lopata, H. Z. 1973. *Widowhood in an American City.* Cambridge, MA: Schenkman.

Lorber, J. 1994. *Paradoxes of Gender.* New Haven, CT: Yale University Press.

Lott, J. 2008. "Single, Childless and 'Downright Terrified.'" (July 29). http://newoldage.blogs.nytimes.com/2008/07/29/single-childless-and-down-right-terrified/ (2011, August 19).

"Love at First Sight." 2011. www.peoplerelationships.syl.com/loverelationships/loveatfirstsight (2011, May 29).

"Love Tech Goes Long Distance." 2008. (February 6). http://www.forbes .com/technology/2008/02/06/love-gadgets-valentine-tech-lovebiz08-cx_ag_0206distance.html (2008, June 24).

"Low Grades, Bad Behavior? Siblings May Be To Blame, Study Says." 2008. (April 22). http://www.sciencedaily.com/releases/2008/04/080422120304 .htm (2008, August 15).

Lowenstein, A., R. Katz, and N. Gur-Yaish. 2007. "Reciprocity in Parent-Child Exchange and Life Satisfaction among the Elderly: A Cross-National Perspective." *Journal of Social Issues* 63, 4: 865–883.

Lu, Z., D. J. Maume, and M. L. Bellas. 2000. "Chinese Husbands' Participation in Household Labor." *Journal of Comparative Family Studies* 31, 2 (Spring): 191–215.

Luscombe, B. 2010. "Marriage: What's it Good For?" *Time.* 176, 22 (November 29): 48–54.

Lussier, G., K. Deater-Deckard, J. Dunn, and L. Davies. 2002. "Support across Two Generations: Children's Closeness to Grandparents Following Parental Divorce and Remarriage." *Journal of Family Psychology* 16: 363–376.

Lutheran Family Services. 2008. "Myths and Facts About Childhood Sexual Abuse." www.lfsneb.org/behavioralhealth/sexualabuse/myths.asp (2008, August 26).

Lynch, J. M. 2000. "Considerations of Family Structure and Gender Composition: The Lesbian and Gay Stepfamily." *Journal of Homosexuality* 40, 2: 81–95.

Lynn, D. 1966. "The Process of Learning Parental and Sex-Role Identification." *Journal of Marriage and the Family* 28: 466–70.

MacCallum, F. E., C. Murray Lycett, V. Jadva, and S. Golombok. 2003. "Surrogacy: The Experience of Commissioning Couples." *Human Reproduction* 18, 6 (June): 1334–1342.

Maccoby, E., and C. Jacklin. 1987. "Gender Segregation in Childhood." *Advances in Child Development and Behavior* 20: 239–87.

Macionis, J. 1991. *Sociology*, 3d ed. Englewood Cliffs, NJ: Prentice Hall.

Macklin, E. D. 1972. "Heterosexual Cohabitation among Unmarried Students." *Family Coordinator* 21: 463–472.

Macko, S. 1996. "Street Gangs Come to a Quiet Chicago Neighborhood." *Emergency Net News Service*, vol. 2, no. 30. http://www.emergency .com/swcjgng.htm (2002, February 5).

Madden, M., and S. Fox. 2006. "Finding Answers Online in Sickness and in Health." *Pew Research Center Publications.* (May 2). www.pewresearch .org/pubs/220/finding-answers-online-in-sickness-and-in-health. (2011, May 24).

Madden, M., and A. Lenhart. 2006. "Online Dating." Washington, DC: Pew Internet and American Life Project (March 5): 202–419–450. www .pewinternet.org/ (2008, March 21).

Madland, D., K. Walter, and N. Bunker. 2011. "Unions Make the Middle Class: Without Unions, the Middle Class Withers." Washington, DC: Center for American Progress.

Madsen, P. 2003. "Just the Facts Ma'am: Coming Clean about Fertility." *Sexuality, Reproduction and Menopause* 1, 1: 27–29.

Madsen, W. 1964. *The Mexican American of South Texas.* New York: Holt, Rinehart & Winston.

Maestas, N., and J. Zissimopoulos. 2010. "How Longer Work Lives Ease the Crunch of Population Aging." *Journal of Economic Perspectives* 24, 1: 139–160.

Magdol, L., T. E. Moffitt, and A. Caspi. 1998. "Hitting without a License: Testing Explanations for Differences in Partner Abuse between Young Adult Daters and Cohabitants." *Journal of Marriage and the Family* 60, 1 (February): 41–55.

Maheshwari, N., and V. Kumar. 2008. "Personal Effectiveness as a Function of Psychological Androgyny." *Industrial Psychiatry Journal* 17 (1): 39–45.

Mahoney, A. 2005. "Religion and Conflict in Marital and Parent-Child Relationships." *Journal of Social Issues*, 64 (4): 689–717.

Majors, R. 1995. "Cool Pose: The Proud Signature of Black Survival." In M. S. Kimmel and M. A. Messner, eds., *Men's Lives*, 82–85. Boston: Allyn & Bacon.

Maldonado, S. 2005. "Beyond Economic Fatherhood: Encouraging Divorced Fathers to Parent." *University of Pennsylvania Law Review* 153: 1–84.

Malia, S. E. 2004. "Stepparent Policy Reforms." *Policy Brief.* (September): Columbia, MO: Center for Family Policy Research.

———. 2005. "Balancing Family Members' Interests Regarding Stepparent Rights and Obligations: A Social Policy Challenge." *Family Relations* 54, 2: 298–319.

Malinowski, B. 1929. *The Sexual Life of Savages in North Western Melanesia.* New York: Harcourt Brace.

Malkin, B. 2011. "Australia's Biggest Sexual Harassment Case Settled for 500,000." (July 8). www.telegraph.co.uk/new/worldnews/australiaand thepacific/australia/8070721/Australias-biggest-sexual-harassent-cae-settled-for-500000. (2011, July 8)

Malone-Colon, L. 2007. "Responding to the Black Marriage Crisis: A New Vision of Change." New York: Institute for American Values: Center for Marriages and Families, (June): Research Brief No. 6.

Mammen, K. 2007. "The Effect of Children Gender on Divorce and Child Support." (April). http://client.norc.org/jole/soleweb/7226.pdf

Mandate the Future. 2002. "13-Year-Old Rape Victim Sentenced to 21 Years in Prison!!" (February 5). www.ctrkaktesc,irg/abortion/01/02/02/0656200 .shtml (2002, January 21).

Mandela, N. 2000. "Globalizing Responsibility." *Boston Globe* (January 4). http://www.igc.apc.org/globalpolicy/socecon/inequal/nelson.htm (2002, January 18).

Manis, R., ed. 2001. *The Marriage and Family Workbook: An Interactive Reader, Text and Workbook*. Boston: Allyn & Bacon.

Manlove, J., E. Terry, L. Gitelson, A. Papillo, and S. Russell. 2000. "Explaining Demographic Trends in Teenage Fertility, 1980–1995." *Family Planning Perspectives* 32 (July-August): 166–175.

Manning, W. D., and P. J. Smock. 2005. "Measuring and Modeling Cohabitation: New Perspectives from Qualitative Data." *Journal of Marriage and Family* 67 (November): 989–1002.

Manolith Team. 2010. "Sex: By the Numbers," *Manolith Men's Magazine*. (February 15). www.manolith.com/2010/02/15/sex-by-the-numbers/ (2011, July 23).

Mansson, D. H., S. A. Myers, and L. H. Turner. 2010. "Relational Maintenance Behaviors in the Grandchildren-Grandparent Relationship." *Communication Research Reports* 27, 1: 68–79.

March of Dimes. 2008. "Teenage Pregnancy." http://www.marchofdimes .com/professionals/14332_1159.asp (2008, July 21).

———. 2009. "Teenage Pregnancy." www.marchofdimes.com/medicalre-sources–teenpregnancy.html (2011, September 7).

———. 2010. "Alcohol and Drugs." www.marchofdimes.com/alcohol_ smoking.html (2011, September 7).

March of Dimes PeriStats. 2008. "Multiple Deliveries: 1995–2005." http:// www.marchofdimes.com/peristats/level1.aspx?dv=ls&reg=99&top=7& stop=81&lev=1&slev=1&obj=1 (2008, July 14).

Marcotte, A. 2011. "Why Are Americans Still Giant Hypocrites About Sex?" *Sex &Relationships*. AlterNet:www.alternet.org/sex/151699/why_ are_americans_still_giant_hypocrites_about_sex? (2011, July 23).

Marcus, D. 2011. "The Counseling Needs of Infertile Couples." (June 19). www,ivf-infertility.com/infertility/counseling3.php (2011, September 9).

"Marital Rape." 2008. www.wordpress.com. (2011, September 15).

Marketwire. 2007. "It's Official: Men Are More Romantic Than Women." (February 12). www.marketwire.com/press-release/its-official-men-are-more-romantic-than-women-as-study-21000-test-takers-on-queendomcom-717393.htm (2011, June 8).

Marquardt, E. 2005. *Between Two Worlds: The Inner Lives of Children of Divorce*. New York: Crown.

"Marriage on the Rocks in Britain." 2005 (September 30). http://news.yahoo .com/s/afp/20050930/ts_afp/afplifestylebritain_050930140708 printer. (2005, October 19).

Marriott, N. 2001. "What's Love Got to Do with It?" In Robert Manis, ed., *Marriage and Family: An Interactive Reader, Text, and Workbook*, 79–81. Boston: Allyn & Bacon.

Marsh, H. W., A. J. Martin, and J.H.S. Cheng. 2008. "A Multilevel Perspective on Gender in Classroom Motivation and Climate: Potential Benefits of Male Teachers for Boys?" *Journal of Educational Psychology* 100 (1): 78–95.

Marshall, B. 2010. "How Do Couples Cope When a Wife Makes More than a Husband?" (February 22). www.palmbeachpost.com/money/how-do-couples-cope-when-a-wife-makes-254522.html (2011, June 26).

Marsiglio, W. 2004. *Stepdads: Stories of Love, Hope and Repair*. Lanham, MD: Rowman and Littlefield.

———, and R. Hinojosa. 2006. "Stepfathers and the Family Dance." In J. E. Gubrium and J. A. Holstein (eds.). *Couples, Kids, and Family Life*, 178-196, New York: Oxford University Press.

Marszalek, D. 2010. "Commuter Marriages Can Work…in the Short Run." (October 13). www.gazettenet.com/print/287761 92011, (June 25).

Martin, C. L., and R. A. Fabes. 2001. "The Stability and Consequences of Young Children's Same-Sex Peer Interaction. *Developmental Psychology* 37 (May): 431–466.

Martin, J., B. Hamilton, P. Sutton, S. Ventura, T.J. Mathews, and M. Osterman. 2010. Births: Final Data for 2008 *National Vital Statistics Report* 59, 1 (December 8). Washington, DC: U.S. Department of Human Services, Centers for Disease Control and Prevention.

Martin, W. 2009. "What Makes Stepmothering a Feminist Issue?" (November 3). www.psychologytoday.com/blog/stepmonster/200911/ what-makes-stepmothering-feminist-issue (2011, July 30).

Masci, D. 2008. "An Overview of the Same-Sex Marriage Debate." (April 10). http://pewresearch.org/pubs/795/gay-marriage (2008, April 15).

Mason, D. 2010. "The Cold Hard Facts About Internet Dating." (March 10). www.chinadaily.com.cn/life/2010-03/10/content_9566320.htm (2011, July 4).

Mason, M. A. 1999. *The Custody Wars*. New York: Basic Books.

Mastekaasa, A. 1992. "Marriage and Psychological Well-Being: Some Evidence on Selection into Marriage." *Journal of Marriage and the Family* 54: 901–11.

Masters, W., V. Johnson, and Kolodny. 1992. *Human Sexual Response*, 4th ed. Boston: Little, Brown.

Mather, M., and D. Lavery. 2010. "In U.S., Proportion Married at Lowest Recorded Levels." *Population Reference Bureau*. (September). www.prb .org/Articles/2010/usmarriagedecline.aspx (2011, August 15).

Mathews, L. 1996. "Who Pays?" *Chicago Tribune* (January 21): sec. 3.

Mathur, I. 2006. "First Comes Marriage, Then Comes Love." www.geocities. com/Wellesley/3321/win4a.htm (2006, January 16).

Matthews, T., and M. MacDorman. 2006. "Infant Mortality Statistics From the 2003 Period Linked Birth/Infant Death Data Set." *National Vital Statistics Reports* 54, 16 (May 3). Washington, DC: U.S. Department of Health and Human Services, Centers for Disease Control and Prevention National Center for Health Statistics.

Mattocks, C., M. Hines, A. Ness, S. Leary, A. Griffiths, K. Tilling, S. N. Blair, and C. Riddoch. 2010. "Associations Between Sex-typed Behavior at Age 3½ and Levels and Patterns of Physical Activity at Age 12: The Avon Longitudinal Study of Parents and Children." *Archives of Disease in Childhood* 95: 509–512.

Mays, V. M., and S. D. Cochran. 2001. "Mental Health Correlates of Perceived Discrimination Among Lesbian, Gay, and Bisexual Adults in the United States." *American Journal of Public Health* 91: 1869–1876.

Mazur, F. 1989. "Predicting Gender Differences in Same-Sex Friendships from Affiliation Motive and Value." *Psychology of Women Quarterly* 13: 277–91.

McAdoo, H. P. 2006. *Black Families*, 4th ed. Thousand Oaks, CA: Sage.

McCabe, M. P., and L. A. Ricciardelli. 2003. "Sociocultural Influences on Body Image and Body Changes Among Adolescent Boys and Girls." *Journal of Social Psychology* 14: 5–26.

McCoy, L. P., and T. L. Heafner. 2004. "Effect of Gender on Computer Use and Attitudes of College Seniors." *Journal of Women and Minorities in Science and Engineering* 10, 1: 55–66.

McCurry, J. 2005. "Japan's Virgin Wives Turn to Sex Volunteers." *Guardian Unlimited*. (April 4). www.guardian.co.uk/print/0,,5162349-108018,00 .html (2006, April 7).

———, and R. Allison. 2004. "40m Bachelors and No Women." *The Guardian*. (March 9). http://www.guardian.co.uk/china/story/ 0,7369,1165129,00. html (2006, January 16).

McDermott, R., J. H. Fowler, and N. A. Christakis. 2009. "Breaking Up is Hard to Do, Unless Everyone Else is Doing It Too: Social Network Effects on Divorce in A Longitudinal Sample Followed for 32 Years." (October 18). http://jhfowler.ucsd.ed/social_network_effects_on_ divorce.pdf (2011, July 19).

McDill, T., K. Sharon, and S. Turell. 2006. "Aging and Creating Families: Never-Married Heterosexual Women Over Forty." *Journal of Women and Aging* 18 (3): 37–50.

McGalliard, G. 2010. "What is the Evangelical 'Stay-at-Home Daughter Movement?'" (November). http://churchand state.org.uk/2010/12/what-is-the-stay-at-home-daughtermovement/ (2011, April 11).

McGrath, E. 2002. "The Power of Love." *Psychology Today Magazine* (December 1).

McGuirk, R. 2011. "Australia to Deport Lone Children in Refugee Plan." (June 3). www.msnbc.msn.com/id/43262662/ns/world_news-asia_pacific/ t/australia-deport-1 (2011, October 8).

McHale, S. M., A. C. Crouter, and S. D. Whiteman. 2003. "The Family Contexts of Gender Development in Childhood and Adolescence." *Review of Social Development* 12: 125–151.

McIntosh, J. E., and C. M. Long. 2006. *Children Beyond Dispute: A Prospective Study of Outcomes from Child Focused and Child Inclusive*

Post-separation Family Dispute Resolution. Final Report. Canberra: Australian Government Attorney General's Department.

McIntyre, M. H., and S.C. P. Edwards. 2009. "The Early Development of Gender Differences." *Annual Review of Anthropology* 38 (1): 83–97.

McKeon, B. 2006. "Effective Sex Education." Washington, DC: Advocates for Youth. www.advocatesforyouth.org/publications/factsheet/fssexcur. htm (2008, February 24).

McKinley Jr., J. 2008. "In Texas School, Teachers Carry Books and Guns." *New York Times* (August 29): A1.

McLanahan, S. S. 1999. "Father Absence and Children's Welfare." In E. M. Hetherington, ed., *Coping with Divorce, Single Parenting, and Remarriage: A Risk and Resiliency Perspective.* Mahwah, NJ: Erlbaum.

McLoyd, V., A. Cauce, D. Takeuchi, and I. Wilson. 2001. "Marital Processes and Parental Socialization in Families of Color: A Decade Review of Research." In R.M. Milardo, ed., Minneapolis: National Council on Family Relations, 289–312.

McLoyd, V., N. Hill, and K. Dodge. 2005. *African American Family Life: Ecological and Cultural Diversity.* New York: Guilford Press.

McNamee, C. B,. and R. K. Raley. 2011. "A Note on Race, Ethnicity and Nativity Differentials in Remarriage in the United States." (February 15). www.demographic-research.org/Volumes/Vol24/13/24-13.pdf (2011, July 28).

McRoy, R. G. 1989. "An Organizational Dilemma: The Case of Transracial Adoptions." *Journal of Applied Behavioral Science* 25, 2: 145–60.

McShane, L. 2011. "Interracial Marriage Should be Illegal, Say 46% of Mississippi Republicans in New Poll." *New York Daily News.* (April 8). http://articles.nydailynews.com/2011-04-08/news/29415165_1_new-poll-respondents-public-policy-polling (2011, July 5).

Mead, M. 1935. *Sex and Temperament in Three Primitive Societies.* New York: Morrow.

———. 1970. "Communes: A Challenge to All of Us." *Redbook* 35 (August): 51–52.

Mead, S. 2006. *The Evidence Suggests Otherwise.* Washington, DC: Education Sector.

Media Awareness Network. 2005. "Ethnic and Visible Minorities in Entertainment Media." www.media-awareness.ca/english/issues/ stereotyping/ethnics_and_minorities/minorities_entertainment.cfm (2005, August 27).

———. 2006. "Media Violence Debates." http://www.media-awareness.ca/english/issues/ (2006, July 22).

MedLawPlus.com. 2006. "Premarital Agreement: State Law." www .medlawplus.com/legalforms/instruct/statelaw.tpl (2006, April 24).

Meeks, N. 2009."Black Women Bear Brunt of Domestic Violence." (October 22). www.blackamericaweb.com/?q=articles/news/moving_america_news/13144/1 (2011, September 7).

Melwani, L. 2007. "The Mating Game." *Little India.* (September 3). www .littleindia.com/nri/1871-the-mating-game.html (2011, July 5).

Mendes, E. 2011. "Lack of Retirement Funds Is Americans' Biggest Financial Worry." (June 15). www.gallup.com/poll/148058/lack-retirement-funds-americans-biggest-financial-worry.aspx (2011, June 24).

———, and J. Marlar. 2011. "Underemployed Americans' Wellbeing Continues to Suffer." (June 8). www.gallup.com/poll/147962/Underemployed-Americans-Wellbeing-Continues-Suffer.aspx (2011, July 12).

Mendoza, J. 2011. "The Impact of Minority Stress on Gay Male Partner Abuse." In Janice L. Ristock, ed., *Intimate Partner Violence in LGBTQ Lives.* London: Routledge, 169–181.

Men's Health. 2008. "Make Her 5 Fantasies Come True." www.menshealth.com/sex-women/her-sexual-fantasies.

Merco Press. 2011. "One Out of Every Four U.S. Hispanics Is Living in Poverty, Shows 2010 Census." (September 15). www.en.mercopress .com/2011/09/15/one-out-of-every-four-hispanics-is-living-in-poverty-shows-2010-census (2011, September 7).

Meredith, D. 1985. "Mom, Dad, and the Kids." *Psychology Today* (June): 62–67.

Merighi, J. R., and M. D. Grimes. 2000. "Coming Out to Families in a Multicultural Context." *Families in Society* 81, 1 (January/February): 32–41.

Merkin, R. S. 2008. "The Impact of Sexual Harassment on Turnover Intentions, Absenteeism, and Job Satisfaction: Findings from Argentina, Brazil, and Chile." *Journal of International Women's Studies* 10, 2: 73–91.

Messerli, H. 2011. "Should Marijuana Be Legalized Under Any Circumstances?' (August 6). www.balancedpolitics.org/marijuana_legalization.htm (2011, September 26).

Meston, C., and D. Buss. 2007. "Why Humans Have Sex." *Archives of Sexual Behavior.* (August). New York: Springer. 36, 477–507.

Meteyer, K. B., and M. Perry-Jenkins. 2009. "Dyadic Parenting and Children's Externalizing Symptoms." *Family Relations* 58, 3: 289–302.

MetLife Mature Market Institute. 2010. *The MetLife Study of Boomers in the Middle: An In-Depth Look at Americans Born 1952–58.* Westport, CT.

———. 2011a. *The MetLife Report on American Grandparents.* New York.

———. 2011b. *The MetLife Study of Caregiving Costs to Working Caregivers: Double Jeopardy for Baby Boomers Caring for Their Parents.* Westport, CT.

Meyer, I. H. 2003. "Prejudice, Social Stress, and Mental Health in Lesbian, Gay, and Bisexual Populations: Conceptual Issues and Research Evidence." *Psychological Bulletin* 129: 674–697.

Michael, M. 2008. "Divorced Women Receive Worse Treatment than Other Woman, Says Study." (July 14). http://www.thedailynewsegypt.com/article/aspx?ArticleID=15068 (2008, August 2).

Michaels, M. L. 2006. "Factors That Contribute to Stepfamily Success: A Qualitative Analysis." *Journal of Divorce and Remarriage* 44, 3/4: 53–66.

Miet, H. 2011. "Serendipity Is No Algorithm on College Dating Site." (February 25). *New York Times.* www.nytimes.com/2011/02/27/fashion/27DATEMYSCHOOL.html (2011, July 4).

Mignon, S., C. Larson, and W. Holmes. 2002. *Family Abuse: Consequences, Theories, and Responses.* Boston: Allyn & Bacon.

Milanovic, B. 2010. *The Haves and the Have-Nots.* New York: Basic Books.

Miller, B. 2001. "Life-Styles of Gay Husbands and Fathers." In M. Kimmel and M. Messner, eds., *Men's Lives,* 443–450. Needham Heights, MA: Allyn & Bacon.

Miller, M. K., and A. Summers. 2007. "Gender Differences in Video Game Characters' Roles, Appearances and Attire as Portrayed in Video Game Magazines." *Sex Roles* 57, 9–10 (November): 733–742.

Miller, R. 2011. "Speed Dating Ideas." www.ehow.com/way_5242509_speed-dating-ideas.html. (2011, July 5).

———, D. Perlman, and S. Brehm. 2007. *Intimate Relationships.* 4th ed. New York: McGraw-Hill.

Mills, C. W. 1959. *The Sociological Imagination.* New York: Oxford University Press.

Min-seok, K. 2009. "Changing View on Cohabitation." (March 4). http://joongangdaily.joins.com/article/view.asp?aid=2901766 (2011, May 5).

Min, P. 2002. "Korean American Families." In R. Taylor, ed., *Minority Families in the United States.* Upper Saddle River, NJ: Prentice Hall.

Min, P. G. 1988. "The Korean American Family." In C. H. Mindel, R. W. Habenstein, and R. Wright, Jr., eds., *Ethnic Families in America,* 199–229. New York: Elsevier.

Minetor, R. 2002. *Breadwinner Wives and the Men They Marry: How to Have a Successful Marriage While Outearning Your Husband.* Far Hills, NJ: New Horizon Press.

Minino, A., M. Heron, S. Murphy, and K. Kochanek. 2007. "Deaths: Final Data for 2004." Centers for Disease Control and Prevention, National Vital Statistics Reports, (August 21): Vol. 55, No. 19.

Mintz, S., and S. Kellog. 1988. *Domestic Revolution: A Social History of American Family Life* New York: Free Press.

Mirande, A. 1985. *The Chicano Experience: An Alternative Perspective.* Notre Dame, IN: University of Notre Dame Press.

Miron, J. A. 2010. "Marijuana Legalization in California." (May 27). www .cato.org/pub_display.php?pub_id=11850 (2011, September 28).

Moen, P., J. E. Kim, and H. Hofmeister. 2001. "Couple's Work/Retirement Transitions, Gender, and Marital Quality." *Social Psychology Quarterly* 64: 55–71.

Mohajer, S. T. 2011. "Octomom Case Rattled Fertility Medicine." *Associated Press.* (June 3). www.abcnews.go.com/Health/wireStory?id=13754500 (2011, September 7).

Moline, A. 2002. "European Union Tells Members to Bar Sexual Harassment." Women's E News (July 22). www.womensenews.org/articlecfm/dyn/aid/980/ (2006, January 12).

Monsour, M. 2002. *Women and Men as Friends: Relationships Across the Life Span in the 21st Century.* Mahwah, NJ: Erlbaum.

Monster.com. 2010. 2010 State of the College Workplace. (Spring). http://media.monster.com/a/i/intelligence/2010State oftheCollegeWorkplace_Spring2010.pdf (2011, April 26).

Moore, D. W. 2005. "Gender Stereotypes Prevail on Working Outside Home." *The Gallup Poll* (August 17). http://poll.gallup.com/content/default.aspx?ci=17896 (2006, January 18).

Moore, F. 1995. "Girls Shortchanged by TV, Seek More Diverse Shows." *Chicago Tribune* (October 1):sec. 13.

Moore, M. 2010. "Thirty Years of China's One-child Policy." (September 25) www.tellegraph.co.uk/news/worldnews/asia/china/8024862/thirty-years-of-chinas-one-child-policy.html (February 5).

Moore, S., and C. Leung, 2002. "Young People's Romantic Attachment Styles and Their Association with Well-Being." *Journal of Adolescence*, 25: 243–255.

Moorman, E. A. and E. M. Pomerantz. 2008. "The Role of Mothers' Control in Children's Mastery Orientation: A Time Frame Analysis." *Journal of Family Psychology* 22, 5L 734–741.

Morales, E. 1996. "Gender Roles among Latino Gay and Bisexual Men: Implications for Family and Couple Relationships." In J. Laird and R. Green, eds., *Lesbians and Gays in Couples and Families*, 272–97. San Francisco: Jossey-Bass.

Morin, R., and M. Rosenfeld. 1998. "With More Equity, More Sweat." *Washington Post* (March 22): A1.

Morris, E. 2005. "From 'Middle Class' to 'Trailer Trash:' Teachers' Perceptions of White Students in Predominately Minority School." *Sociology of Education* 75 (2) (April): 99–121.

Morris, N. 2005. "Violence against Women at Crisis Level in Britain." *The Independent.* (November 24). news.independent.co.uk (2006, June 30).

Morrison, A. 2004. "Transracial Adoption: The Pros and Cons and the Parents' Perspective." *Harvard BlackLetter Law Journal* 20: 163–202.

Mortimer, J. T., and J. London. 1984. "The Varying Linkages of Work and Family." In P. Voydanoff, ed., *Work and Family: Changing Roles of Men and Women*, 20–35. Palo Alto, CA: Mayfield.

Mosher, W.D., and J. Jones. 2010. "Use of Contraceptives in the United States: 1982–2008." *Vital and Health Statistics*, Series 23, No. 29.

Moynihan, D. P. 1965. *The Negro Family: The Case for National Action*. U.S. Department of Labor, Office of Policy Planning and Research. Washington, DC: U.S. Government Printing Office.

Mroz, J. 2011. "From One Sperm Donor, 150 Children." *New York Times* (September 9): D1, D6.

Ms. magazine. 1993. "Action Alert: International News." (January/ February): 12–13.

MSDVC. 2011. "The Correlation Between Domestic Violence, Dating Violence, Sexual Assault and Suicide." www.missourishores.com/correlation.html (2011, September 7).

MSNBC News. 2007. "Worst U.S. Shooting Ever Kills 33 on VA. Campus." (April 17). www.msnbc.msn.com/id/18134671/ (2008, September 11).

MSNBC. 2006. "11 of 23 Held in UK Plot Charged." www.msnbc.msn.com/ id/14287289/ (2006, August 23).

Mulick, M. 2011. "Green Mile Actor, 51, Marries 16-Year-Old Aspiring Country Singer; Says 'True Love Can Be Ageless.'" (June 20). www.eonline.com/uberblog/b248227green_mile_actor_51_marries_16-year-old.html (2011, July 4).

Mullins, L. C., K. P. Brackett, D. W. Bogie, and D. Pruett. 2004. "The Impact of Religious Homogeneity on the Rate of Divorce in the United States." *Sociological Inquiry* 74, 3: 338–354.

Munroe, E. A. 2009. *The Everything Guide of Stepparenting*. Avon, MA: Adams Media.

Munroe, R. L., and A. K. Romney. 2006. "Gender and Age Differences in Same-sex Aggregation and Social Behavior." *Journal of Cross-cultural Psychology* 37 (1): 3–19.

Murphy, D. 2002. "Need a Mate? In Singapore, Ask the Government." *Christian Science Monitor* (July 16): 1, 10.

Murray, B., and B. Duffy. 1998. "Jefferson's Secret Life." *U.S. News & World Report* (November 9).

Murstein, B. I. 1980. "Mate Selection in the 1970's." *Journal of Marriage and the Family* 42: 777–792.

———. 1987. "A Classification and Extension of the SVR Theory of Dyadic Pairing." *Journal of Marriage and the Family* 42: 777–792.

Muwakkil, S. 2001. "AIDS and the State of Denial." *Chicago Tribune* (June 18): 11.

Myers, D. J., and K. B. Dugan. 1996. "Sexism in Graduate School Classrooms: Consequences for Students and Faculty." *Gender & Society* 10: 330–50.

"Myths About Male Rape, the Rape of Men." 2011. www.aest.org.uk/ survivors/male/myths_about_male_rape.html (2011, September 19).

Najman, J. M., B. C. Behrens, M. Anderson, W. Bor, M. O'Callaghan, and G. M. Williams. 1997. "Impact of Family Type and Family Quality on Child Behavior Problems: A Longitudinal Study." *Journal of the American Academy of Child and Adolescent Psychiatry* 36: 1357–65.

Nakosteen, R. A., O. Westerlund, and M. A. Zimmer. 2004. "Marital Matching and Earnings: Evidence from the Unmarried Population in Sweden." *Journal of Human Resources* 39, 4: 1033–1044.

Nardi, P. 1999. *Gay Men's Friendships: Invincible Communities*. Chicago, IL: University of Chicago Press.

———. 2001. "The Politics of Gay Men's Friendships." In M. Kimmel and M. Messner. *Men's Lives*, 5th ed., 380–383. Needham Heights, MA: Allyn & Bacon.

National Adoption Attitudes Survey. 2002. (June). http://www.adoptioninstitute.org/survey/Adoption_Attitudes_Survey.pdf (2006, August 16).

National Alliance for Caregiving. 2009. *Caregiving in the United States: A Focused Look at Those Caring for Someone Age 50 and Older, Executive Summary.* (November) www.caregiving.org/data/FINALRegularEXSum50plus.pdf (2011, August 23).

National Association for Girls and Women in Sport. 2005. "Fact Sheet: Title IX in Athletics." www.aahperd.org/advocacy/fact_titleix.pdf (2005, August 23).

National Association of Child Care Resource Referral Agencies. 2010. *Parents and the High Cost of Child Care: 2010 Update.* Arlington, VA.

National Bureau of Economic Research. 2010. (September). www.nber.org/cycle/Sept2010.html (2011, June 21).

National CASA Association. 2000. "Statistics on Child Abuse and Neglect, Foster Care, Adoption and CASA Programs." www.casanet.org/library/abuse/ abuse-stats98.htm (2002, January 26).

National Center for Lesbian Rights. 2002. "Fact Sheet: Custody Cases." http://www.nclrights.org/publications/pubs_custody.html (2002, January 31).

National Center on Elder Abuse, 2005. "Fact Sheet: Elder Abuse and Prevalence." Washington, DC: National Center on Elder Abuse.

National Clearinghouse on Marital and Date Rape. 2005. members.aol.com/ ncmdr/state_law_chart.htm (2006, April 19).

National Coalition Against Domestic Violence. 2007a. "Dating Violence." Washington, DC: NCADV Public Policy Office. http://www.ncadv.org/publicpolicy/ThePublicPolicyOffice.php.

———. 2007b. "Domestic Violence Facts." Washington, DC: NCADV Policy Office. http://www.ncadv.org/publicpolicy/ThePublicPolicyOffice .php (2008, August 8).

———. 2008. "Domestic Violence and Lesbian, Gay, Bisexual and Transgender Relationships." Washington, DC: National Coalition Against Domestic Violence Policy Office. publicpolicy@ncadv.org (2008, August 8).

———. 2011. "Pregnancy and Domestic Violence Facts." www.sc.edu/ healthycarolina/pdf/facstaffstu/safety/PregnancyandDomesticViolence.pdf (2011, September 7).

National Coalition of Anti-Violence Programs. 2007. *Annual Report on Anti-LGBT Violence in 2006: A Report of the National Coalition of Anti-violence Programs.* New York.

National Committee on Pay Equity. 2010. "The Wage Gap Over Time: In Real Dollars, Women See a Continuing Gap." http://www.pay-equity.org/info-time.html (2011, July 5).

National Conference of State Legislatures. 2008. "Same Sex Marriage, Civil Unions and Domestic Partnerships." (March). http://www.ncsl.org/programs/cyf/same sex.htm (2008, April 14).

National Crime Victimization Survey. 2009. Washington, DC: U.S. Department of Justice, Office of Justice Programs, Bureau of Justice Statistics. www.ojp.usdoj.gov/bjs/

National Institute of Child Health and Human Development. 2001. "Bullying Widespread in U.S. Schools, Survey Finds." NIH News Release

(April 24).Washington, DC: National Institute of Health, National Institute of Child Health & Human Development. www.nichd.hin.gov/news/releases/bullying.cfm (2011, May 24).

National Institute of Justice. 2007. "How Widespread is Intimate Partner Violence?" U.S. Department of Justice, Office of Justice Programs. www.nij.gov/nij/topics/crime/intimate-partner-violence/extent.htm (2011, September 19).

National Transgender Advocacy Center. 2011. "Transgender Basics." www.ntac.org/transgender-basics (2011, June 18).

National Women's Health Information Center. 2005. "Sexually Transmitted Diseases: Overview." U.S. Department of Health and Human Services, Office on Women's Health. www.4woman.gov/faq/stdsgen.htm (2006, April 3).

National Women's Law Center. 2010. "Poverty Among Women and Families, 2000–2009: Great Recession Brings Highest Rates in 15 Years." http://www.nwlc.org/resource/poverty-among-women-and-families-2000-2009-great-recession-brings-highest-rate-15-years (2011, September 15).

Nature. 1998. "Scientific Correspondence." 36, 5 (November): 27–28.

Nauert, R. 2011. "Gender-Based Violence Increases Women's Risk of Mental Disorders." (August 3). www.psychcentral.com/news/2011/08/03/gender-based-violence-increases-womens-risk-of-mental-disorders/28325.html (2011, September 19).

Navarrette, Jr., R. 2008. "France's Immigration Problem." *Sign On San Diego*. (April 27). http://www.signonsandiego.com/uniontrib/20080427/news_lz1e27navarre.html (2011, October 7).

Navarro, M. 1996. "Teen-Age Mothers Viewed as Abused Prey of Older Men." *New York Times* (May 19): 1.

———. 2005. "More Options to Answer 'What About the Kids?'" *New York Times* (November 27): C13.

NBC Sports. 2011. "Should Girls Be Allowed to Wrestle Boys?" (February 17) www.nbcsports.newsvine.com/_question/2011/02/17/6074430-should-girls-be-allowed-to-wrestlw-boys#vine-t (2011, February 28).

Needle, R. H., S. S. Su, and W. J. Doherty. 1990. "Divorce, Remarriage and Adolescent Substance Use." *Journal of Marriage and the Family* 52: 157–70.

Neiman, S. 2011. *Crime, Violence, Discipline, and Safety in U.S. Public Schools: Findings From the School Survey on Crime and Safety: 2009–10* (NCES 2011-320). U.S. Department of Education, National Center for Education Statistics. Washington, DC: U.S. Government Printing Office.

"Nepal May Be First Nation to Recognize 'Third Gender' in Census." 2011. *The Chicago Tribune*. (June 6): 14.

Neugarten, B., and K. Weinstein. 1964. "The Changing American Grandparent." *Journal of Marriage and the Family* 26: 199–204.

Neumark-Sztainer, D., and P. J. Hannan. 2000. "Weight-Related Behaviors among Adolescent Girls and Boys." *Archives Pediatrics & Adolescent Medicine* 154: 569–77.

"New Poll Find Majority of Americans Are Unaware of Issues Facing Iraq/Afghanistan Veterans and Troops." 2010. (May 11). www.prweb.com/releases/iraq_afghanistan/veterans/prweb3984134.htm (2011, September 24).

"New Zealand Attracting Young Female Immigrants." 2005. Workpermit.com (July 27). www.workpermit.com/news/2005_07_27/australia/nz_attracts_females.htm (2006, February 10).

Newberry, C. 2010. *The Hands-on Guide to Surviving Adult Children Living at Home*. Christiana Newberry.

Newman, D. M. 2008. *Sociology: Exploring the Architecture of Everyday Life*, 7th ed. Thousand Oaks, CA: Pine Forge Press.

Newman, K. 2000. *No Shame in my Game: The Working Poor in the Inner City*. New York: Vintage.

Newport, F. 2001. "Americans See Women as Emotional and Affectionate, Men as More Aggressive." http://www.gallup.com/poll/release/pr010221.asp (2001, July 12).

———. 2011. "Americans Prefer Boys to Girls, Just as They Did in 1941." (June 23). www.gallup.com/poll/148187/Americans-Prefer-Boys-Girls-1941.aspx (2011, August 25).

"Newsweek Poll: Obama and Race in America." 2007. http://www.psral.com/news.jsp?op=detail8ed=1661 (2008, March 20).

Nicholas, M., and K. Milewski. 1999. "Downloading Love: A Content Analysis of Internet Personal Advertisements Placed by College Students." *College Student Journal* (March). www.findarticles.com/cf_0/mOFCR/1_33/62894065/p1/article.jhtml?term=Research (2001, October 26).

Nichols, H. 2008. "The Advantages of Communal Living." (May 18). www.suite101.com/content/the-advantages-of-communal-living-a54208 (2011, May 11).

Nicholson, K. 2006. "Quality of Parent-child Relationship, Self-esteem, and the Marital Attitudes of African American and Hispanic Young Adults from Divorced and Intact Families." Ph.D. Thesis. University of Hartford.

Niebur, S. 2011. "Gender-Neutral Language Matters." (February 24). http://womeninplanetaryscience.wordpress.com/2011/02/24/gender-neutral-lnguage-matters/ (2011, April 7).

Nielsen, L. 1999. "Stepmothers: Why So Much Stress: A Review of the Literature." *Journal of Divorce and Remarriage* 30: 115–148.

———. 2011. "Divorced Fathers and Their Daughters: A Review of Recent Research." *Journal of Divorce and Remarriage* 52, 2: 77–93.

Njord, I., R. M. Merrill, R. Njord, R. Lindsay, and J. D. R. Pachano. 2010. "Drug Use Among Street Children and Non-Street Children in the Philippines." *Asia-Pacific Journal of Public Health* 22, 2: 203–211.

Nock, S. L., and P. W. Kingston. 1990. *The Sociology of Public Issues*. Belmont, CA: Wadsworth.

North Carolina Coalition against Domestic Violence. 2002. "A Fact Sheet on Sexual Assault." www.nccadv.org/Handouts/Sexual_Assault.htm (2002, January 8).

North Carolina Division of Aging and Adult Services. 2011. "North Carolina Observes Vulnerable Adult and Elder Abuse Awareness Month." www.ncdhhs.gov/aging/eaday/ (2011, September 19).

Norton, A. J., and L. F. Miller. 1992. "Marriage, Divorce, and Remarriage in the 1990's." In U.S. Census Bureau, Current Population Reports, P23–180. Washington, DC: U.S. Government Printing Office.

Noveck, J. 2011. "Many Think Flirting on Internet Is Still Cheating."(June 8). www.azcentral.com/news/articles/2011/06/08/20110608cheating-on-internet-poll.html. (2011, July 4).

NOW. 2011. "Violence Against Women in the United States: Statistics." www.now.org/issues/violence/stats.html (2011, September 19).

Nowinski, J. 1980. *Becoming Satisfied: A Man's Guide to Sexual Fulfillment*. Englewood Cliffs, NJ: Prentice Hall.

———. 1989. *A Lifelong Love Affair: Keeping Sexual Desire Alive in Your Relationship*. New York City: W. W. Norton & Company.

NPR. 2005. "Speed Dating With Yaacov and Sue Deyo." www.npr.org/templates/story/story.php?storyId=4803880 (2011, July 5).

Núñez, C. 2009. "France Deports Children of Undocumented Immigrants." (December 1). www.news.newanericamedia.org/news/view_article.html?article_id=043c72df4d3a00d4 (2011, October 7).

O'Dougherty, M., M. Story, and J. Stang. 2006. "Observations of Parent-Child Co-Shoppers in Supermarkets: Children's Involvement in Food Selections, Parental Yielding, and Refusal Strategies." *Journal of Nutrition Education and Behavior* .38: 183–188.

Oakley, A. 1974. *The Sociology of Housework*. New York: Pantheon.

"'Octomom Doctor' Stripped of Medical License." 2011. (June 2). www.physorg.com/news/2011-06-octomom-doctor-medical.html (2011, September 7).

Ogletree, S. M., and R. Drake. 2007. "College Students' Video Game Participation and Perceptions: Gender Differences and Implications." *Sex Roles* 56, 7–8 (April): 537–542.

Ogundipe, S. 2011. "Multiple Birth: Reactions From Medical Experts." (June 17). www.vanguardngr.com/2011/06/multiple-birth-reactions-from-medical-experts/ (2011, September 7).

Olson, D., and A. Olson. 2000. *Empowering Couples: Building on Your Strengths*. Minneapolis, MN: Life Innovations.

"One Out of Five U.S. Children is Living in an Immigrant Family." 2007. www.kidscount.org/datacenter/smasjpt_immigrant.pdf (2008, July 8).

"Online Dating Industry…" 2010. Online Dating Industry 2010—Statistics & Facts. www.bizopedia.biz/2010/04/online-dating-industry-2010-statistics.html (2011, July 5).

"Online Dating Statistics." 2010. *Online Dating Magazine*. www.onlinedat-ingmagazine.com/onlinedatingstatistics.html (2011, July 4).

Ono, H. 2010. "The Socioeconomic Status of Women and Children in Japan: Comparisons with the USA." *International Journal of Law, Policy and the Family* 24, 2: 151–176.

Ooms, T. 2002. "Strengthening Couples and Marriage in Low-income Communities." In A. J. Hawkins, L. D. Wardle, and D. O. Coolige, eds., *Revitalizing the Institution of Marriage for the Twenty-first Century*, 79–100. Westport, CT: Praeger.

Oppenheimer, V. K. 1997. "Women's Employment and the Gain to Marriage: The Specialization and Trading Model." *Annual Review of Sociology* 23: 431–53.

———. 2003. "Cohabiting and Marriage During Young Men's Career-Development Process." *Demography* 40, 1: 127–149.

Orbuch, T. 2011. "How Being Happy at Work Could Improve Your Marital Satisfaction, Too." (May 18). www.huffingtonpost.com/dr-terri-orbuch/job-satisfacion_b_859855.html (2011, June 24).

Orenstein, P. 1994. *School Girls: Young Women, Self-Esteem, and the Confidence Gap*. New York: Anchor Press.

Ornish, D. 1998. *Love and Survival, The Scientific Basis for the Healing Power of Intimacy*. New York: HarperCollins.

———. 2005. "Love is Real Medicine." *Newsweek*, (October 3): 56.

Ortigue, S., F. Bianchi-Demicheli, N. Patel, C. Frum, and J. Lewis. 2010. "Neuroimaging of Love: MRI Meta-Analysis Evidence toward New Perspectives in Sexual Medicine." *The Journal of Sexual Medicine*.

Osterman, M., J. Martin, T. J. Mathews, and B. Hamilton. 2011. "Expanded Data from the New Birth Certificate 2008." *National Vital Statistics Report*, 59, 7 (July 27). Washington, DC: U.S. Department of Human Services, Centers for Disease Control and Prevention.

Pacey, S. 2005. "Step Change: The Interplay of Sexual and Parenting Problems When Couples Form Stepfamilies." *Social and Relationship Therapy* 20, 3: 359–369.

Packer-Williams, C. 2009. "Understanding the Impact of Maternal Messages Given to Single, Educated African American Women About Relationships." *Black Women, Gender and Families* 3 (2): 48–67.

Page, M. E., and A. H. Stevens. 2004. "The Economic Consequences of Absent Parents." *The Journal of Human Resources* 39, 1(Winter): 80–107.

Pagelow, M. 1988. "Marital Rape." In V. B. Van Hasselt, R. L. Morrison, A. S. Bellack, and M. Hersen, eds., *Handbook of Family Violence*, 207–232. New York: Plenum.

Palmore, E. 1980. "The Facts on Aging Quiz: A Review of Findings." *Gerontologist* 20: 669–72.

Palo Alto Medical Foundation. 2001. "For Parents—Teens and Sex." www.pamf.org/teen/parent/sex/sex.html (2006, March 22).

Pan-American Health Organization. 2006. "Domestic Violence During Pregnancy." www.paho.org/English/AD/GE/VAWPregnancy.pdf (2006, July 13).

Pandey, G. 2004. "Muslim Women Fight Instant Divorce." BBC News (August 4). http://newsvote.bbc.co.uk/mpapps/pagetools/print/news.bbc.co.uk/2/hi/south_asia/3530608.stm (2006, March 21).

———. 2010. "Indian Community Torn Apart by 'Honour Killing.'" (June 16) www/bbc.co.uk/new/10334529 (2011, February 5).

Panter-Brick, C., M. Eggerman, V. Gonzalez, and S. Safdar. 2009. "Violence, Suffering, and Mental Health in Afghanistan: A School-based Survey." *Lancet*. 374: 807–816.

Papanek, H. 1973. "Men, Women, and Work: Reflections on the Two-Person Career." *American Journal of Sociology* 78, 4 (January): 852–72.

Papernow, P. 1998. *Becoming a Stepfamily: Patterns of Development in Remarried Families*. Hillsdale, NJ: Analytic Press.

———. 2001. "What Works (and What Doesn't) in Building Healthy Step-families." Paper presented at the First Annual Ohio State University Extension Family Live Electronic In-Service: A Systemic Examination of Stepfamily Relationships. Columbus, OH, May 8–10.

———. 2012. *Surviving and Thriving in Stepfamily Relationships*. New York; Routledge.

Parents Forever. 2001. "Gender Differences in Parenting." The University of Minnesota Extension Service. http://www.extension.umn.edu/parentsforever/unit1/unit1=3a.asp (2001, December 30).

Parke, R. D. 2002. "Fathers and Families." In M. H. Bornstein, ed., *Handbook of Parenting: Being and Becoming a Parent*, Vol. 3, 27–73. Hillsdale, NJ: Erlb.

Parker, B. 2009. "Top 10 Male Sexual Fantasies." www.foreverpleasure.com/catalog/male-sexual-fantasies-a-105.html.

Parker, K. 2011. "A Portrait of Stepfamilies." (January 13). http://pewsocialtrends.org/2011/01/13/a-portrait-of-stepfamilies/ (2011, July 29).

Parker, T. 2011. "Top 5 Most Expensive Celebrity Weddings." (July 28). www.financialedge.investopedia.com/financial-edge/0711/Top-5-Most-Expensive-Celebrity (2011, August 15).

Parsons, T. 1955. "The American Family." In T. Parsons and R. Bales, eds., *Family, Socialization and Interaction Process*, 3–34. Glencoe, IL: Free Press.

———. 1964. *Social Structure and Personality*. New York: The Free Press.

Pasley, K., D. C. Dollahite, and M. Ihinger-Tallman. 1993. "Clinical Applications of Research Findings on the Spouse and Stepparent Roles in Remarriage." *Family Relations* 42: 315–22.

Passel, J. 2009. "A Portrait of Unauthorized Immigrants in the United States." (April 14). www.pewresearch.org/pubs/1190/portrait-unauthorized-immigrants-states (2011, October 7).

———, W. Wang, and P. Taylor. 2010. "Marrying Out: One-In-Seven New U.S. Marriages Is Interracial or Interethnic." (June 4). www.pewsocialtrends.org/2010/06/04/marrying-out (2011, August 15).

Paton, G. 2007. "White Boys Let Down by Education System." http://www.telegraph.co.uk/news/main.jhtml?xml=news/2007/06/22/nschools322.xml2008, (March 17).

Patterson, C. J. 1992. "Children of Lesbian and Gay Parents." *Child Development* 63 (October): 1025–42.

———. 1995. *Lesbian and Gay Parenting: A Resource for Psychologists*. Washington, DC: American Psychological Association.

Patterson, J., and P. Kim. 1991. *The Day America Told the Truth: What People Really Believe about Everything That Really Matters*. Englewood Cliffs, NJ: Prentice Hall.

Paul, P. 2011. "He Sexts, She Sexts More, Report Says." *New York Times*. (July 15). www.nytimes.com/2011/07/17/fashion/women-are-more-likely-to-sext-than-men-stu (2011, July 31).

Paulson, M. 2007. "Preaching Fashion" (February 18). http://www.boston.com/yourlife/fashion/articles/2007/02/18/preaching_fashion/ (2008, March 22).

Pellerin, L. A. 2005. "Applying Baumrind's Parenting Typology to High Schools: Toward a Middle-range Theory of Authoritative Socialization." *Social Science Research* 34 (June): 282–303.

Penha-Lopes, V. 2006. "To Cook, Sew, to Be a Man": The Socialization for Competence and Black Men's Involvement in Housework." *Sex Roles* 54 (3/4): 261–274.

Peplau, L. A., and S. L. Gordon. 1983. "The Intimate Relationships of Lesbians and Gay Men." In E. R. Allgeier and N. McCormick, eds., *Changing Boundaries: Gender Roles and Sexual Behavior*, 1–14. Mountain View, CA: Mayfield.

Perez, L. 2002. "Cuban American Families." In R. Taylor, ed., *Minority Families in the United States*. Upper Saddle River, NJ: Prentice Hall.

Perrin, E. C., and the Committee on Psychosocial Aspects of Child and Family Health. 2002. "Technical Report: Co-Parent or Second-Parent Adoption by Same-Sex Parents." *Pediatrics* 109, 2: 341–344.

Perron, R. 2010. "Recession Takes Toll on Hispanics 45+: Boomers Particularly Hard Hit." (March). www.aaro.org/money/budgeting-saving/info-03-201d0/hispeconomy.html (2011, August 10).

Perry-Jenkins, M., and A. C. Crouter. 1990. "Men's Provider Role Attitudes: Implications for Household Work and Marital Satisfaction." *Journal of Family Issues* 11: 136–56.

Perry-Jenkins, M., and K. Folk. 1994. "Class, Couples, and Conflict: Effects of the Division of Labor on Assessments of Marriage in Dual-Earner Families." *Journal of Marriage and the Family* 56 (February): 165–80.

Perry, I. 1995. "It's My Thang and I'll Swing It the Way That I Feel." In Gail Dines and Jean Humez, eds., *Gender, Race and Class in Media*, 524–30. Thousand Oaks, CA: Sage.

Perry, T., C. Steele, and A. Hilliard III. 2003. *Young, Gifted and Black: Promoting High Achievement Among African American Students*. New York: Beacon.

Pesek, W. 2006. "Durex Offers Japan a Population Wake-Up Call." Bloomberg.com. www.bloomberg.com/apps/news?pid=71000001refer=columnis (2006, April 7).

Peters, G. 2009. "The Dangerous Side of Online Dating." (June 8). www.thenational.ae/news/worldwide/americas/the-dangerous-side-of-online-dating (2011, July 5).

Peterson, C. C. 1999. "Grandfathers' and Grandmothers' Satisfaction with the Grandparenting Role: Seeking New Answers to Old Questions." *International Journal of Aging and Human Development* 49, 1: 61–78.

Peterson, K. 2001. "College Women Can't Find Mr. Right." *Chicago Sun-Times* (July 27): 1, 2.

Pew Forum on Religion and Public Life, 2008. U.S. Religious Landscape Survey, Religious Affiliation: Diverse and Dynamic. February 2008. www.religions.pewforum.org/reports (2011, August 15).

———. 2010. "Public Remains Conflicted Over Islam." (August 24). www/pewforum.org/Muslim/Public-Remains-Conflicted-Over-Islam.aspx (2011, October 7).

Pew Global Research Center. 2003. "Globalization with Few Discontents?" (June 3). yaleglobal.yale.edu/display.article?id=1764 (2006, July 27).

———. 2007. "World Publics Welcome Global Trade—But Not Immigration." 47-Nation Pew Global Attitudes Survey. www.pewglobal.org/files/pdf/258.pdf (2011, September 29).

Pew Internet and American Life Project. 2010. "Teens, Adults & Sexting: Data on Sending & Receipt of Sexually Suggestive Nude or Nearly Nude Images by American Adolescents & Adults." (October 23). www.slideshare.net/PewInternet/teens-adults-sexting (2011, June 8).

Pew Research Center. 2006. *Families Drawn Together By Communication Revolution.* Washington, DC.

———. 2007. "Motherhood Today: Tougher Challenges, Less Success." (May 2). www.pewsocialtrends.org/2007/05/02/motherhood-today-tougher-challenges-less-success/ (2011, September 7).

———. 2008. "Men or Women: Who's the Better Leader?" (August 25). http://pewresearch.org/pubs/932d/men-or-women-whos-the-better-leader (2011, April 2)

———. 2009. "Mexican Immigrants in the United States, 2008." (April 15). www.pewresearch.org/pubs/1191/mexican-immigrants-in-america-largest-group (2011, October 7).

———. 2010a. "Blacks Upbeat About Black Progress, Prospects." (January 12). Washington, DC: http://pewsocialtrends.org/2010/01/12/blacks-upbeat-about-black-progress-prospects/ (2011, September 7).

———. 2010b. "The Decline of Marriage and Rise of New Families," (November 18). www.pewresearch.org/pubs/1802/declinemarriage-rise-new-families (2011, March 14).

———. 2010c. *The Return of the Multi-Generational Family Household.* Washington, DC.

———. 2010d. "Support for Same-Sex Marriage Edges Upward." (October 6). http://people-press.org/2010/10/06/support-for-same-sex-marriage-edges-upward/ (2011, May 10).

———. 2011a. "Fewer Are Angry at Government, But Discontent Remains High." (March 3). http://people-press.org/2011/03/03/section-3-attitudes-toward-social-issues/ (2011, September 26).

———. 2011b. "Public Favors Tougher Border Controls and Path to Citizenship." (February 24). www.people-press.org/2011/02/24/public-favors-tougher-border-controls-and-path-to-citizenship (2011, October 7).

———. 2011c. "The Toll of the Great Recession: Hispanic Household Wealth Fell by 66% From 2005 to 2009." (July 26). www.pewhispanic.org/reports/report.php?Reportid=145 (2011, September 14).

Pezzin, L. E., R. Pollak, and B. S. Steinberg Schone. 2008. "Parental Marital Disruption, Family Type, and Transfers to Disabled Elderly Parents." *Journal of Gerontology: Social Sciences* 638, 6: S349–S358.

Pezzin, L. E., and B. S. Schone. 1999. "Parental Marital Disruption and Intergenerational Transfers: An Analysis of Lone Elderly Parents and Their Children." *Demography* 36, 3 (August): 287–97.

Pflum, M. 2011. "Safer Sex? Some Parents Allow Their Teens to Have Sex Inside Family Home." *ABC News,* (June 22). www.abcnews.go.com/US/parents-teens-sex-family-home/story?id=13898548 (2011, July 31).

Phillips, C. 2011. "Refugees and Migrants." *Amnesty International.* www.amnesty.org/en/refugees-and-migrants (2011, October 8).

Pichierri, M., and C. Corcoran. 2005. "Respect for Individuals that Engage in Premarital Sexual Intercourse: The Influence of Gender and Family Structure." *FSC Journal of Behavioral Sciences,* vol. 9.

Pill, C. J. 1990. "Stepfamilies: Redefining the Family." *Family Relations* 39: 186–93.

Pinkerton, S., L. Bogart, H. Cecil, and P. Abramson. 2002. "Factors Associated with Masturbation in a Collegiate Sample." *Journal of Psychology and Human Sexuality* 14(2/3): 103–121.

Pinsof, W. F., and J. Lebow (eds.). 2005. *Family Psychology: The Art of the Science.* New York: Oxford University Press.

Pinto, K., and S. Coltrane. 2008. "Division and Labor in Mexican Origin and Anglo Families: Structure and Culture." *Sex Roles* 60 (7/8)): 482–95.

Pitcher, B. L., and D. C. Larson. 1989. "Early Widowhood." In S. J. Bahr and E. T. Peterson, eds., *Aging and the Family,* 59–81. Lexington, MA: Lexington Books.

Plantin, L. 2011. "Positive Health Outcomes of Fathers' Involvement in Pregnancy and Childbirth Paternal Support: A Scope Study Literature Review." (January 1). http://periodicals.faqs.org/201101/2297562821.html (2011, September 7).

Pleck, J. H. 1988. "Fathers and Infant Care Leave." In E. F. Zigler and M. Franks, eds., *The Parental Leave Crisis,* 177–94. New Haven, CT: Yale University Press.

Poisson, J. 2011. "Parents Keep Child's Gender Secret." (May 21). www.parentcentral.ca/parent/articlePrint/995112 (2011, June 13).

Polling Report, 2008. "Immigration." www.pollingreport.com/immigration.htm (2008, September 7).

Pollmann-Schult, M. 2011. "Marriage and Earnings: Why Do Married Men Earn More Than Single Men?" *European Social Review* 27 (2): 147–163.

Ponzetti, J., Jr., and R. M. Cate. 1986. "The Development Course of Conflict in the Marital Dissolution Process" *Journal of Divorce* 10: 1–15.

Poortman, A., and J. Seltzer. 2007. "Parents' Expectations about Children after Divorce: Does Anticipating Difficulty Deter Divorce?" *Journal of Marriage and Family* 69, 1: 254–69.

Popenoe, D. 1999. "Parental Androgyny." In C. Albers, ed., *Sociology of Families: Readings,* 187–94. Thousand Oaks, CA: Pine Forge.

———. 2008. "Cohabitation, Marriage, and Child Well-Being: A Cross-National Perspective." Piscataway, NJ: The National Marriage Project: Rutgers, the State University of New Jersey.

———, and B. Whitehead. 2002. *Sex Without Strings: Relationships Without Rings.* Piscataway, NJ: The National Marriage Project, Rutgers.

Population Action International. 2005. "Contraceptive Use Helps Reduce the Incidence of Abortion." (August 1) http://www.populationaction.org/Publications/Fact_Sheets/F529/Summary.shtml (2008, July 21).

Population Reference Bureau. 2010. *2010 World Population Data Sheet.* Washington, DC.

Post, T. 1993. "A Pattern of Rape." *Newsweek* (January 4): 32–36.

Potier, B. 2003. "For Many, Prenups Seem to Predict Doom." *Harvard University Gazette.* (October 16). www.news.harvard.edu/gazette/2003/10.16/01-prenup.html (2006, April 24).

Poulin M. J., S. L. Brown, P. A. Ubel, D. M. Smith, A. Janovic, and K. M. Langa. 2010. "Does a Helping Hand Mean a Heavy Heart? Helping Behavior and Well-being Among Spouse Caregivers." *Psychology and Aging* 25, 1: 108-117.

Powdthavee, N. 2005. "Life Satisfaction, Income, and Friendship: Evidence From Panel Data." (July). http://www2.warwick.ac.uk/fac/ soc/economics/research/phds/n.powdthavee/friends2005.pdf (2005, October 25).

Powell, K. A., and L. Abels. 2002. "Sex-Role Stereotypes in TV Programs Aimed at the Preschool Audience: An Analysis of Teletubbies and Barney & Friends." *Urbana* 25, 1:14–27.

Powell, S. M. 2011. "What Happens If Your Ex Abducts Your Child?" (July 4). www.chron.com/disp/story.mpl/chronicle/7638140.html (2011, July 24).

Preece, M. 2003/2004. "When Lone Parents Marry: The Challenge of Stepfamily Relationships." *Transition Magazine* 33, 4(Winter): 7–15.

President's Council on Physical Fitness and Sports. 1997. *Physical Activity and Sport in the Lives of Girls.* Minneapolis: Center for Research on Girls and Women in Sport, University of Minnesota.

Presser, H. B. 2003. *Working in a 24/7 Economy: Challenges for American Families.* New York: Russell Sage Foundation.

Pressley, S. 2001. "S.C. Verdict Fuels Debate Over Rights of the Unborn: Jury Finds Mother Guilty of Homicide in Stillbirth." *Washington Post* (May 27): A03.

Preston, J. 2011. "Judge Gives Immigrant in Same-Sex Marriage a Reprieve from Deportation." *New York Times* (May 7): A11.

Prevalence and Incidence of Fetal Alcohol Syndrome. 2008. (July 9): http://www.wrongdiagnosis.com/f/fetal_alcohol_syndrome/prevalence .htm. (2008, July 22).

Previti, D., and P. R. Amato. 2003. "Why Stay Married? Rewards, Barriers, and Marital Stability. *Journal of Marriage and Family* 65 (August): 561–563.

Price, D. 2006. "Americans More Accepting Despite Culture Wars." (March 20). *The Detroit News*, detnews.com, www.detnews.com/apps/pbcs.dll/ article?AID=/20060320/OPINION03/603200308/1272 (2006, April 19).

Primack, B., E. Douglas, M. Fine, and M. Dalton. 2009. "Exposure to Sexual Lyrics and Sexual Experience Among Urban Adolescents." *American Journal of Preventive Medicine* (2009): (36) 317–23.

Prime, J. 2005. "Women 'Take Care,' Men 'Take Charge:' Stereotyping of U.S. Business Leaders Exposed." *Catalyst*. www.catalyst.org (2006, January 12).

Provost, C. 2011. "Disability Must Be Seen As A Development Issue, Says Report." *The Guardian*, (June 9). www.guardian.co.uk/global-devel- opment/2011/june/09/world-disability-Report-development=issue. (2011, September 29).

Pruett, M. K., and K. Hoganbruen. 1998. "Joint Custody and Shared Parenting: Research and Interventions." *Child Adolescent Psychiatric Clinic North America* 7: 273–94.

Pryor, J. 2004. "Parenting in Reconstituted and Surrogate Families." In M. Hoghughi and N. Long (eds.), 110–129. *Handbook of Parenting: Theory and Research for Practice*, 110–129, Thousand Oaks, CA: Sage.

———, B. Rodgers. 2001. *Children in Changing Families: Life After Parental Separation*. Maulden, MA: Blackwell.

"Psychological Impact of Infertility and Its Treatment." 2009. *Harvard Mental Health Letter* 24, 11: 1–3.

Public Policy Polling. 2011. "Arizonans Want More Gun Control." (February 3). www.publicpolicypolling.com (2011, May 24).

Punke, H. H. 1940. "Marriage Rate among Women Teachers." *American Sociological Review* 5, 4: 505–511.

Purcell, P., and L. Stewart. 1990. "Dick and Jane in 1989." *Sex Roles* 22: 177–85.

Pyke, K. D. 1994. "Women's Employment as Gift or Burden?" *Gender and Society* 8: 73–91.

Qamruzzaman, M. 2006. "Conference Explores Indian Divorce Stigmas." *Michigan Daily* (February 6). www.michigandaily.com/news/2006/ 02/06/ (2006, March 2).

qian, z. 2005. "Breaking the Last Taboo: Interracial Marriage in America." *Contexts* 4, 4: 33–37.

Qualman, E. 2011. "Life Expectancy Study: 1 in 5 Will Live to be Over 100." www.socialnomics.net/2011/03/24/life-expectancy-study-1-in-5-will- live-to-be-over (2011, December 15).

Queen, S. A., R. W. Habenstein, and J. S. Quadagno. 1985. *The Family in Various Cultures*. New York: Harper & Row.

"Quick Facts on Single Moms and Educational Attainment." 2011. www .elearners.com/projectworkingmom/quick-facts-on-single-moms-and- education (2011, August 3).

Radbill, S. 1980. *A History of Child Abuse and Infanticide*. Chicago, IL: University of Chicago Press.

Raffaelli, M., and L. Ontai, 2004. "Gender Socialization in Latino/a Families: Results from Two Retrospective Studies." *Sex Roles: A Journal of Research*. (March), 50:5/6, 287–299.

Rahman, V. M. 2010. "Triple Talaq—Instant Divorce." (October 31). http:// vmkhaleelurrahman.blogspot.com/2010/10/separation-in-one-go .html (2011, July 20).

Rainie, L., and M. Madden 2006. "Not Looking for Love: The State of Romance in America." (Pew Internet & American Life Project). www .pewinternet.org (2008, March 21).

RAINN. 2008. "The Rapist Isn't a Masked Stranger." www.rainn.org/ get-information/statistics/sexual-assault-offenders (2011, September 19).

———. 2009. "Who Are The Victims? Breakdown by Gender and Age." www.rainn.org/get-information/statostocs/sexual-assault-victims (2011, September 19).

Ramos, C. 2009. "Breaking Down Stereotypes: Asian Women Speak Out on Speaking Up." (October). www.Toastmasters.org/ToaststersMagazine/ ToastmasterArchieve/2009/October/Articles (2011, March 23).

Ramos, J. 2002. "'For Adults Only' Maybe Not, as Marketing of Sexy Products Reaches Kids." ABCNEWS Internet Ventures. www.abcnews.go.com/ setions/ business/DailyNews/Ramos_adultproduct_020612.hmtl (2004, May 28).

Ramos-Sanchez, L., and D. R. Atkinson. 2009. "The Relationship Between Mexican American Acculturation, Cultural Values, Gender, and Help- Seeking Intervention." *Journal of Counseling & Development* 87 (1): 62–71.

Rampell, C. 2011. "Preferring Boys to Girls." (June 24). http://economix .blogs.nytimes.com/2011/06/24/preferring-boys-to-girls/ (2011, Sep- tember 3).

Ramu, G. N. 1989. "Patterns of Mate Selection." In K. Ishwaran, ed., *Family and Marriage: Cross-Cultural Perspectives*, 165–178. Toronto: Wall and Thompson.

Rand, M. 2009. "Criminal Victimization, 2008." *Bureau of Justice Statistics Bulletin, National Crime Victimization Survey*. Washington, DC: U.S. Department of Justice, Office of Justice Programs. www.ojp.usdoj.gov/ bjs/pub/pdf/cv08.pdf (2011, July 4).

Rankin, B. 2004. "Transexual vs. Transgender: Explaining the Intricacies." http://fusion.kent.edu/archives/spring04/trans/trans.html (2011, June 6).

Rasmussen, P. K., and K. J. Ferraro. 1991. "The Divorce Process." In J. N. Edwards and D. H. Demo, eds., *Marriage and Family in Transition*, 376–88. Boston: Allyn & Bacon.

Rathus, S., J. Nevid, and L. Fichner-Rathus. 2008. *Human Sexuality in a World of Diversity*. Boston: Allyn & Bacon.

Raybeck, D., S. Dorenbosch, M. Sarapata, and D. Herrman. 2000. "The Quest for Love and Meaning in the Personals." Unpublished paper.

Real Sex Education Facts. 2010. "Pressure From Peers." www.realsexedfacts .com/facts/peer-pressure (2011, August 1).

Reay, D. 2001. "'Spice Girls,' 'Nice Girls,' 'Girlies' and 'Tomboys': Gender Discourses. Girls Cultures and Femininities in the Primary Classroom." *Gender and Education* 13 (2): 153–67.

Recker, N. K. 2001. "The Wicked Stepmother Myth." *Family Tapestries*. The Ohio State University Extension.

Reece, M., D. Herbenick, V. Schick, S. Sanders, B. Dodge, and D. Fortenberry. 2010. Findings from the National Survey of Sexual Health and Behavior. *The Journal of Sexual Medicine*. Plymouth, MA: Wiley-Blackwell, Vol. 7, Supplement 5.

Reich, R. 2011. "Raise Taxes on the Rich. (April 6) http://marketplace .publicradio.org/display/web/2011/04/06/pm-raise-taxes-on-the- rich/?refid=) (2011, July 15).

Reid, R. 2010. "Afghanistan War Death Toll: 1000 U.S. Military Dead." *Huff Post World*. (May 28). www.huffingtonpost.com/2010/05/28/afghani- stan-death-toll-100_n_593087(2011, October 14).

Reid, T. 2008. "Police Baffled by Deadly Rampage of a 'Normal, Unstressed' Student." *The Times* Online. www.timesonline.co.uk/tol/news/world/ us_and_americas/article3374287.ece (2008, September 11).

Reinhold, S. 2007. "Reassessing the Link Between Premarital Cohabita- tion and Marital Instability." (December 20). http://client.norc.org/jole/ SOLEweb/8197.pdf (2008, May 10).

Reisman, J. M. 1990. "Intimacy in Same-Sex Friendships." *Sex Roles* 23: 65–82.

Reiss, I. L. 1960. "Toward a Sociology of Heterosexual Love Relationship." *Marriage and Family Living* 22, 2 (May): 139–145.

———. 1971. *The Family System in America*. New York: Holt, Rinehart & Winston.

ReligiousTolerance.org. 2003. "Longitudinal U.S. Public Opinion Polls: Same-Sex Marriage and Civil Unions." www.religioustolerance.org/ hom_poll5.html (2005, December 13).

"Remarriage Industry Sees Rapid Growth." 2006. *Digital Chosunilb*. (March 20). http://english.chosun.com/cgi-bin/printNews?id=200603200024 (2006, March 26).

Rempel, J., and J. Holmes. 1986. "How Do I Love Thee?" *Psychology Today* (February): 30–31.

Renout, F. 2005. "Immigrants' Second Wives Find Few Rights." *Christian Science Monitor* (May 25) 17.

Renzetti, C. 2009. "Social Class, Race, and Intimate Partner Violence." (March 14). www.racismreview.com/blog/2009/03/14/social-class-race-and-intimate-partner-violence (2011, September 7).

Renzetti, C. M., and D. J. Curran. 1995. *Women, Men, and Society*, 3rd ed. Boston: Allyn & Bacon.

———. 2002. *Women, Men, and Society*, 5th ed. Boston: Allyn & Bacon.

Research America. 2006. "Health and Longevity." http://www. researchamerica .org/polldata/2006/Longevity_fullresults.pdf (2006, June 26).

Rhoades, G. K., S. M. Stanley, and H. J. Markman. 2009. "The Pre-engagement Cohabitation Effect: A Replication and Extension of Previous Findings." *Journal of Family Psychology* 23: 107–111.

Riccardi, N. 2007. "Leader of Polygamous Sect Convicted of Abetting Rape." *Chicago Tribune* (September 26): 1,18.

Rich, A. 1980. "Compulsory Heterosexuality and Lesbian Existence." *Signs* 5: 631–660.

Richman, J. A., and K. M. Rospenda. 2005. "Sexual Harassment and Alcohol Use." *Psychiatric Times* 22, 2 (February). www.psychiatrictimes .com/showArticle.jhtml?articleId=60403927 (2006, January 12).

Richtel, M. 2005. "Past Divorce, Compassion at the End." *New York Times* (May 19): E1, E2.

Rideout, V. J., U. G. Foehr, and D. F. Roberts. 2010. *Generation M2: Media in the Lives of 8- to 18-Year-Olds*. Menlo Park, CA: Kaiser Family Foundation.

Riley, G. 1987. *Investing the American Woman: A Perspective on Women's History*. Arlington Heights, IL: Harlan Davidson.

———. 1991. *Divorce: An American Tradition*. New York: Oxford University Press.

Riley, N. 2010. "Interfaith Marriages are Rising Fast, but They're Falling Fast Too." (June 6). www.washingtonpost.com/wp-dyn/content/ article/2010/06/04/AR2010060402011.ht (2011, August 15).

Risman, B., and P. Schwartz. 2002. "After the Sexual Revolution: Gender Politics in Teen Dating." *Contexts* 1, 1 (Spring): 16–24.

Ritter, J. 2001. "AIDS Experts Say U.S. Ignores Africa." *Chicago Sun-Times* (February 5): 8.

Roach, M. 2001. "New Challenges Ahead as Gay Population Ages." *Chicago Tribune* (October 24): 7.

Robbins, R. 2005. *Cultural Anthropology: A Problem-Based Approach*. 3rd ed. Belmont, CA: Wadsworth.

Roberson, P. N, M. Sabo, and K. Wickel. 2011. "Internal Working Models of Attachment and Post Divorce Coparent Relationships." *Journal of Divorce and Remarriage* 52, 3: 187–201.

Roberto, K. A. 1990. "Grandparent and Grandchild Relationships." In T. H. Brubaker, ed. *Family Relationships in Later Life*, 100-112. Newberry Park, CA: Sage.

Roberts, A. 2009. "Marriage and the Great Recession," in W. B. Wilcox, ed. *The State of Our Unions*, 31–48. Charlottsville, VA: University of Virginia, the National Marriage Project.

Roberts, B., D. Povich, and M. Mather. 2010–2011. *Great Recession Hit Hard at America's Working Poor: Nearly 1 in 3 Working Families in United States are Low Income*. Washington, DC: The Working Poor Families Project.

Roberts, J. 2011. "The Underemployed: The New Reality of the American Job Market." (July 6). www.foxnews.com/us/2011/07/06/underemployed-new-reality-american-job-market/ (2011, July 12).

Roberts, L. 2009. "Are People Attracted to People Who Look Like Them?" www.whyfiles.org/2009/are-people-attracted-to-people-who-look-like-them/ (2011, July 4).

Roberts, S. 2006. "To Be Married Means to Be Outnumbered." *New York Times*. (October 15). www.nytimes.com/2006/10/15/us/census/htm (2008, June 27).

Robinson, B. A. 2008. "Rape of Women During Wartime: Before, During, and Since World War II." *Religious Tolerance*. (May 3): www.religioustolerance.org/war_rape.htm (2008, September 11).

Robinson, J. P. 1977. *How Americans Use Time*. New York: Praeger.

Robison, J. 2002. "The Future of Marriage: Part III." *The Gallup Poll* (August 13). http://poll.gallup.com/content/default.aspx?ci=6592&VERSION=p (2006, August 13).

Robitalle, C. and M. C. Saint-Jacques. 2009. "Social Stigma and the Situation of Young People in Lesbian and Gay Stepfamilies." *Journal of Homosexuality* 56, 4: 421–442.

Robnett, R., and J. Susskind. 2010. "Who Cares About Being Gentle? The Impact of Social Identity and the Gender of One's Friends on Children's Display of Same-Gender Favoritism." *Sex Roles* 63 (11/12): 820–832.

Rochlin, M. 1992. "The Heterosexual Questionnaire." In M. Kimmel and M. A. Messner, *Men's Lives*, 2nd ed., 482–83. New York: Macmillan.

Rodriguez, N. 2006. "What to Expect When You Find Out Your Teen is Having Sex." *The Desert Sun* www.thedesertsun.com/apps/pbcs.dll/ article?AID=/20060221/LIFESTYLES12/602210308/ (2006, March 22). (2008, February 21).

Rogers, J. 2009. "Octomom is on the Receiving End of a Historic Backlash." *Associated Press*. (February 24). www.seattlepi.com/lifestyle/ article/Octomom-is-on-the-receiving-end-of-a-historic-1300978 .php (2011, September 7).

Rogers, S. J. 2003. "Spillover Between Marital Quality and Job Satisfaction: Long-Term Patterns and Gender Differences." *Journal of Marriage and Family* 65 (May): 482–495.

———, and P. R. Amato. 2000. "Have Changes in Gender Relations Affected Marital Quality?" *Social Forces* 79, 2: 731–53.

Rogers, T. 2011. "Native American Poverty."www.spotlightonpoverty.org/ Exclusive_Commentary.aspx?id=Ofe5c04e-fdbf-4718-980c-0373ba-823da7 (2011, September 7).

Roisman, G. I., E. Clausell, A. Holland, K. Fortuna, and C. Elieff. 2008. "Adult Romantic Relationships as Contexts of Human Development: A Multimethod Comparison of Same-Sex Couples with Opposite-Sex Dating, Engaged, and Married Dyads." *Developmental Psychology* 44, 1: 91–101.

Rokach, R., O. Cohen, and S. Dreman. 2004. "Triggers and Fuses in Late Divorce: The Role of Short Term Crises vs. Ongoing Frustration on Marital Break-Up." *Journal of Divorce and Remarriage* 40, 3/4: 41–61.

Roll Back Malaria. 2011. "RBM Partnership Marks a Decade of Progress on World Malaria Day 2011 and Sets Its Sights on Near Zero Deaths by 2015." (April 21). www.rbm.who.int/globaladvocacy/pr2011-04-21-2 .html (2011, October 10).

Rollins, J. 1986. "Single Men and Women: Differences and Similarities." *Family Perspectives* 20: 117–25.

Romero, M. 1992. *Maid in the USA: Perspectives on Gender*. New York: Routledge.

———. 2002. *Maid in the USA: 10th Anniversary Edition—Perspectives on Gender*. 2nd ed. New York: Routledge.

Rose, S., and Zand, D. 2000. "Lesbian Dating and Courtship From Young Adulthood to Midlife." *Journal of Lesbian Studies*, 6(1), 85–109.

Rosenbloom, S. 2006. "Here Come the Great-Grandparents." *New York Times* (November 2) www.nytimes.com/2006/11/02/fashion/02parents .html?fta=y (2008, August, 24).

Rosenblum, K. E., and T. C. Travis. 1996. *The Meaning of Difference*. New York: McGraw-Hill.

Rosenfeld, M. 1998. "Little Boys Blue: Reexamining the Plight of Young Males." *Washington Post* (March 26): A1.

Rosenfield, S., J. Phillips, and H. White. 2006. "Gender, Race, and the Self in Mental Health and Crime." *Social Problems* 53, 2: 161–185.

Rosenthal, C. S., J. Jones, and J. A. Rosenthal. 2003. "Gendered Discourse in the Political Behavior of Adolescents." *Political Research Quarterly* 56, 1(March): 97–104.

Ross, E. 2001. "British Put Limits on Embryo Transfers." *Chicago Tribune* (August 15): sec. 8, 5.

Ross, J. 2004. "Chilean Women Celebrate Gaining Right to Divorce." *Womens eNews* (December 3). http://www.womensnews.org/article .cfm/dyn/aid/2095/context/archieve (2006, March 20).

Rossi, P. H. 1989. *Down and Out in America*. Chicago: University of Chicago Press.

Rothrauff, T. C., T. M. Cooney, and J. S. An. 2009. "Remembered Parenting Styles and Adjustment in Middle and Late Adulthood." *Journal of Gerontology Series B: Psychological Sciences and Social Sciences* 64B, 1: 137–146.

Ruane, J. M., and K. A. Cerulo. 1997. *Second Thoughts: Seeing Conventional Wisdom through the Sociological Eye*. Thousand Oaks, CA: Pine Forge Press.

Rubin, B. M. 2011. "In Love, Later in Life." *Chicago Tribune* (July 6): 1, 5, sec. 5.

Rubin, L. B. 1985. *Just Friends: The Role of Friendship in Our Lives*. New York: Harper & Row.

———. 1994. *Families on the Fault Line: America's Working Class Speaks about the Family, the Economy, Race, and Ethnicity*. New York: HarperCollins.

Rubinstein, R. L. 1986. *Singular Paths: Old Men Living Alone*. New York: Columbia University Press.

———, B. B. Alexander, M. Goodman, and M. Luborsky. 1991. "Key Relationships of Never-Married Childless Older Women: A Cultural Analysis." *Journal of Gerontology* 46, 5 (September): 270–77.

Russell Sage Foundation. 2011. "The Social Effects of the Great Depression." www.russellsage.org/research/social-and-economic-impact-great-recession (2011, June 21).

Rust, J., S. Golombok, M. Hines, K. Johnston, and G. Golding. 2000. "The Role of Brothers and Sisters in the Gender Development of Preschool Children." *Journal of Experimental Child Psychology* 77 (4): 292–303.

Ryan, J. 2007. "FBI Report on School Violence an Eye Opener." ABC News. www.abcnews.go.com/The:aw/story?id=3806725&page=1 (2008, September 7).

Saad, L. 2001. "Majority Considers Sex before Marriage Morally Okay." *Gallup News Service* (May 24). http://www.gallup.com/poll/ releases/ pr010524.asp (2000, July 24).

———. 2003. "Pessimism About Crime Is Up Despite Declining Crime Rate." (October 23). www.poll.gallup.com/9559/pessimism-about-crime-up-despite-declining-crime-rate.aspx (2005, October 25).

———. 2006. "Americans Have Complex Relationship with Marriage." The Gallup Poll. May 31. www.poll.gallup.com (2008, June 27).

———. 2007. "Women Slightly More Likely to Prefer Working to Homemaking." *Gallup News Service* (August 31). www.gallup.xom/poll/28567/Women-Slightly-More-Likely-prefer-Working-Homemaking.aspx? (2011, March 22).

———. 2008. "Cultural Tolerance for Divorce Grows to 70%." (May 19). www.gallup.com/poll/107380/cultural-tolerance-divorce-grows-70.aspx (2008, August 2).

———. 2011a. "Doctor-Assisted Suicide Is Moral Issue Dividing Americans Most." May 31). www.gallup.com/poll/147842/Doctor-Assisted-Suicide-Moral-Issue-Dividing-Americans.aspx (2011, July 22).

———. 2011b. "Scaling Back State Program is Least of Three Fiscal Evils." (February 22). www.gallup.com/poll/146276/Scaling-Back-State-Programs-Least-Three-Fiscal-Evils.aspx (2011, July 7).

Sadker, M., and D. Sadker. 1994. *Failing at Fairness: How America's Schools Cheat Girls*. New York: Scribner's.

Saenz, R., W. J. Goudy, and L. Frederick. 1989. "The Effects of Employment and Marital Relations on Depression among Mexican American Women." *Journal of Marriage and the Family* 51: 239–51.

"Safe Sex." 2011. www.health.nsw.gov.au/publichealth/sexualhealth/sex_safesex/asp (2011, August 1).

Safire, W. 1995. "News about Jews." *New York Times* (July 17). http://www.nytimes.com/1995/07/17/opinion/essay-news-about-jews.html (2008, September 17).

Saito, L. 2002. *"Ethnic Identity and Motivation: Socio-Cultural Factors in the Educational Achievement of Vietnamese American Students.* New York: LFB Scholarly Publishing.

Salovey, P., and J. Rodin. 1989. "Envy and Jealousy in Close Relationships." In C. Hendrick, ed., *Close Relationships*, 221–246. Newbury Park, CA: Sage.

Saluter, A. F. 1994. "Marital Status and Living Arrangements: March 1993." U.S. Census Bureau, Current Population Reports, Series P20–478. Washington, DC: U.S. Government Printing Office.

Samland, V. 2008. "Parent Challenges and New Technology." (November 4). http://conflictcenter.org/wordpress/?p=97 (2011, September 10).

Sampson, R. 2003. Acquaintance Rape of College Students. U.S. Department of Justice, Office of Community Oriented Policing Services. Problem-oriented Guide for Police Series, No. 17. www.cops.usdoj.gov (2008, April 8).

Sanders, J. 2005. "Gender and Technology in Education: A Research Review." www.josanders.com/pdf/gendertech0705.pdf (2005, August 21).

Sandin, E. A., D. H. Baucom, C. K. Burnett, N. Epstein, and L. A. Rankin-Esquer. 2001. "Decision-Making Power, Autonomy, and Communication in Remarried Spouses Compared with First-Married Spouses." *Family Relations.* 50, 4(October): 326–336.

Santa Clara Police Department Family Violence Center 2009. www.scpd.org/crime/domestic_violence.html (2011, October 10).

Sapiro, V. 1990. *Women in American Society,* 2nd ed. Mountain View, CA: Mayfield.

Saralaadeve, N., J. Plange-Rhule, R. C. Tutt, and J. B. Eastwood. 2009. "Shortage of Healthcare Workers in Developing Countries—Africa." *Ethnicity & Diseases* (Spring): Sl-60–Sl64.

Sarmiento, S. 2002. *Making Ends Meet: Income-Generating Strategies among Mexican Immigrants*. New York: LFB Scholarly Publishing.

Sassler, S., and J. McNally. 2003. "Cohabiting Couple's Economic Circumstances and Union Transitions: A Re-Examination Using Multiple Imputation Techniques." *Social Science Research.* 32, 4: 553–578.

Saulny, 2011a. "Black? White? Asian? More Young Americans Choose All of the Above." *New York Times National* (January 30): 1, 20.

———. 2011b. "Black and White and Married in the Deep South: A Shifting Image." *New York Times.* (March 20): 1, 4.

Save the Children. 2011. "State of the World's Mothers 2011 Statistics and Facts." www.savethechildren.org/site/c.8rKLIXMGIp14E/b.6748295/k.BE47/State_of_the_Worlds_Mothers_2011_Statistics_and_Facts.htm (2011, September 7).

Save The Children Federation USA. 2011. "Background Statement." www2.guidestar.org/organizations/06-0726487/save-children-federation.aspx (2011, October 1).

Saxena, D., and G. F. Sanders. 2009. "Quality of Grandparent-Grandchild Relation in Asian-Indian Immigrant Families." *International Journal of Aging and Human Development* 68, 4: 321–327.

Sayer, L. 2006. "Economics of Divorce and Relationship Dissolution." In M. A. Fine and J. H. Harvey, eds., *Handbook of Divorce and Relationship Dissolution,* 385–406. Mahwah, NJ: Erlbaum.

Scanzoni, J. 1980. "Contemporary Marriage Types." *Journal of Family Issues* 1: 125–140.

Scaramella, L. V., T. K. Neppi, L. L. Ontal, and R. D. Conger. 2008. "Consequences of Socioeconomic Disadvantage Across Three Generations: Parenting Behavior and Child Externalizing Problems." *Journal of Family Psychology* 22, 5: 725–733.

Schepp, D. 2011. "People @Work: The Tough Job of Getting Disabled Veterans Back to Work." (February 14), *DailyFinance,* www.dailyfinance.com/2011/02/14/tough-job-of-getting-disabled-veterans-back-to-work (2011, September 30).

Scher, A., and R. Sharabany. 2005. "Parenting Anxiety and Stress: Does Gender Play a Part at 3 Months of Age? *The Journal of Genetic Psychology* 166, 2: 203–213.

Schifferes, S. 2008. "Wealth Rise Boosts Unequal Britain." (January 18). http://news.bbc.co.uk/1/hi/business/7193904.stm (2008, August 29).

Schneir, M., ed. 1972. *Feminism: The Essential Historical Writing,* 104–5. New York: Vintage Books/Random House.

———, ed. 1994. *Feminism: The Essential Historical Writing,* 104–105. New York: Books/Random House.

Schoen, R. 2002. "Women's Employment, Marital Happiness, and Divorce." *Social Forces 81,* 2 (December): 643–662.

Schoenborn, C. A., J. L. Vickerie, and E. Powell-Griner. 2006. *Health Characteristics of Adults 55 Years of Age and Over: United States, 2000–2003.* Advance Data from Vital and Health Statistics, No. 370 (April 11). Hyattsville, MD: National Center for Health Statistics.

Schrodt, P. 2008. "Sex Differences in Stepchildren's Reports of Stepfamily Functioning." *Communication Reports* 21, 1: 46–58.

Schuckit, M. A., and T. L. Smith. 2001. "Correlates of Unpredicted Outcomes in Sons of Alcoholics and Controls." *Journal of Studies on Alcohol* 62, 4 (July): 477–85.

Schulz, M. S., P. A. Cowan, C. P. Cowan, and R. T. Brennan. 2004. "Coming Home Upset: Gender, Marital Satisfaction, and the Daily Spillover of Workday Experience Into Couple Interactions." *Journal of Family Psychology*. 18, 1: 250–263.

Schvaneveldt, P. L., M. H. Young, and J. D. Schvaneveldt. 2001. "Dual-Resident Marriages in Thailand: A Comparison of Two Cultural Groups of Women." *Journal of Comparative Family Studies* 32, 3 (Summer): 347–60.

Schwartz, K. 2011. "Divorced Former Spouses Choose to Travel As a Family." (March 16) www.huffingtonpost.com/2011/03/17/divorced-families-travel_n_836821.html (2011, August 1).

Schwartz, M. A., and B. M. Scott. 2010. *Marriages and Families: Diversity and Change*. Upper Saddle River, NJ: Prentice Hall.

Schwartz, M. A., and P. Wolf. 1976. "Singlehood and the American Experience: Prospectives for a Changing Status." *Humboldt Journal of Social Relations* 4, 1 (Fall/Winter): 17–24.

Schwartz, P. 1999. "Peer Marriage: What Does It Take to Create a Truly Egalitarian Relationship?" In A. S. Skolnick and J. H. Skolnick, *Family in Transition,* 154–63. New York: Addison Wesley Longman.

Schwartz, S. J.. and G. E. Finley. 2006. "Father Involvement, Nurturant Fathering, and Young Adult Psychosocial Functioning: Differences Among Adoptive, Adoptive Stepfather and Nonadoptive Stepfamilies." *Journal of Family Issues* 27, 5: 712–731.

Schworm, P., and M. Carroll. 2011. "More Listed in State as Same-Sex Couples." (February 8). http://articles.boston.com/2011-02-08/news/29343648_1_gay-couples-gay-marriage-gay-rights-group (2011, May 11).

Science Daily. 2002. "Closeness to Mother Can Delay First Instance of Sexual Intercourse Among Younger Teens." www.sciencedaily.com/releases/2002/09/020911073512.htm (2006, March 22).

———. 2007. "Sex Education Linked To Delayed Teen Intercourse, New Study Says." (December 23). www.sciencedaily.com/releases/2007/12/071220231428.htm (2008, February 24).

Scott, B. M. 1991. Unpublished interviews with African American women.

Scott, B., and M. A. Schwartz. 2006. *Sociology: Making Sense of the Social World*. Boston: Pearson/Allyn & Bacon.

Scott, D., and B. Wishy, eds., 1982. *America's Families: A Documentary History*. New York: Harper & Row.

Scott, M. 2009. "Multitaskers Say One Online Dating Site Won't Do." (February 5). www.heraldnews.com/lifestyle/x545172880/Multitaskers-say-one-online-dating-site (2011, July 5).

Scott, M. E., E. Schelar, J. Manlove, and C. Cui. 2009. *Young Adult Attitudes About Relationships and Marriage: Times May Have Changed, But Expectations Remain High*. Washington, DC: Child Trends Research Brief.

Se-ra, Jung. 2011. "Fewer Weddings Overall, With Remarriages on the Rise." (January 1). http://english.hani.co.kr/arti/english_edition/e_national/40714.html (2011, July 25).

Sealey, G. 2002. "No More Big Man on Campus? College Gender Gap Could Mean Women Lose Mating Game." (July 18). ABCNews.com (2006, February 10).

Sears, H. A., and N. L. Galambos. 1992. "Women's Work Condition and Marital Adjustment in Two-Career Couples: A Structural Model." *Journal of Marriage and the Family* 54: 789–97.

Sears, R. B., G. Gates, and W. B. Rubenstein. 2005. *Same-Sex Couples and Same-Sex Couples Raising Children in the United States: Data from Census 2000*. Los Angeles: UCLA School of Law.

Sederer, L. I. 2010. "Children as Caregivers: Saving the Saviors." (October 20). www.huffingtonpost.com/lloyd-i-sederer-md/children-as-caregivers-sa_b_768916.html (2011, August 24).

Sedgh, G., S. Henshaw, S. Singh, E. Ahman, and I. H. Shah. 2007. "Induced Abortion: Rates and Trends Worldwide." *Lancet* 370: 1338–1345.

Sedlak, A., J. Mettenburg, M. Basena, I. Petta, K. McPherson, A. Greene, and S. Li. 2010. *Fourth National Incidence Study of Child Abuse and Neglect (NIS-4): Report to Congress*. Washington, DC: U.S. Department of Health and Human Services, Administration for Children and Families.

Segura, D. A. 1994. "Working at Motherhood: Chicana and Mexicana Immigrant Mothers and Employment," In Evelyn Nakano Glenn, Grace Chang, and Linda Rennie Forcey, eds., *Mothering: Ideology, Experience, and Agency*. New York: Routledge.

Sell, K., S. Zlotnik, K. Noonan, and D. Rubin. 2010. "The Effect of Recession on Child Well-Being: A Synthesis of the Evidence." Philadelphia: Policy Lab, The Children's Hospital of Philadelphia.

Seltzer, J. 2000. "Families Formed Outside of Marriage." *Journal of Marriage and the Family* 62, 4: 1247–69.

Selvaraj, R. 2005. "The Challenges of Being Different: The Perspective of an Asian Immigrant on Cultural Diversity in the Workplace." Ramond. Selvaraj@WaitemataDHB.govt.nz

Selyukh, A. 2011. "Wars Take Mental Toll on GIs' Kids, Study Says." *Chicago Tribune* (July 10): Sec. 1, 29.

Senior Journal. 2005. "Primetime Live Sex Survey Has Interesting Findings About Senior Citizens." *Senior Journal*. (October 31). www.seniorjournal.com/NEWS/Sex/4-10-22SexSurvey.htm (2006, March 21).

Seraph. 2005. "Interracial Marriages Decrease Among Asian Americans." Fighting 44s.com. (November 24). www.thefighting44s.com/article.php?id_art=43 (2006, April 26).

"Sex By The Numbers." 2010. *Manolith.com*. (February 15). www.manolith.com/2010/02/15/Sex-by-the-numbers/

Sexinfo. 2006. "Sexuality in the Mass Media: How to View the Media Critically." University of California at Santa Barbara. www/soc.ucsb.edu/sexinfo/?article (2006, March 24).

"Sexual Harassment in Australia." 2009. www.hreoc.gov.au/sex_discrimination/programs/sexual_harassment.html (2011, July 8).

Sexualityandu. ca. 2010. "Teenage Sex: Can You Influence Your Teens Decisions About Sex?" www.sexualityandu.ca/parents/talking-to-your-child-about-sexuality/influencing-teen-decision-about-sex (2011, July 31).

Shah, A. 2008. "Poverty Facts and Stats." (March 4). www.globalissues.org/article/26/poverty-facts-and-stats (2008, August 26).

———. 2010. "Racism." (August 8). www.globalissues.org/print/article/165 (2011, October 7).

Shalaby, E. 2011. "Study Says 44% of Egypt's Females Are Subjected to Sexual Harassment." (February 24). http://eternian.wordprss.com/2011/02/04/sexual-harassment-by-muslim-men-common-in-egypt/ (2011, July 8).

Shanshan, W. 2006. "Dating on Singles' Day." (November 11). www.chinadaily.com.cn/china/2006-11/11/content_730393.htm (2011, July 4).

Shapiro, A. 2003. "Later-Life Divorce and Parent-Adult Child Contact and Proximity." *Journal of Family Issues* 24, 2 (March): 264–285.

Shapiro, J. L. 1987. "The Expectant Father." *Psychology Today* (January): 36–9, 42.

Shaw, L. 2010. "Divorce Mediation Outcome Results." *Conflict Resolution Quarterly* 27, 4: 447–467.

Shawne, J. 2005. *Baby Not on Board: A Celebration of Life Without Kids*. San Francisco: Chronicle Books.

Sheehy, S. 2000. *Connecting the Enduring Power of Female Friendship*. New York: HarperCollins.

Shellenbarger, S., 2006. "Boys Mow Lawns, Girls Do Dishes: Are Parents Perpetuating the Chore Wars?" *The Wall Street Journal* (December 7). http://onlinewsj.com/public/article/58116545148742855-7bcmSOwQycM2rMyGHnK_yvwD9CY-20071206.html (2011, March 30).

Sherkat, D. E. 2000. "That They Be Keepers of the Home: The Effect of Conservative Religion on Early and Late Transitions into Housewifery." *Review of Religious Research* 41, 3: 344–358.

Shostak, A. 1987. "Singlehood." In M. Sussman and S. Steinmetz, eds., *Handbook of Marriage and the Family*, 355–66. New York: Plenum.

Shriver, S., C. Byer, L. Shanberg, and G. Galliano. 2002. *Dimensions of Human Sexuality*, 6th ed. New York: McGraw-Hill.

Shucksmith, J. L., B. Hendry, and A. Glendinning. 1995. "Models of Parenting: Implications for Adolescent Well-Being within Different Types of Family Contexts." *Journal of Adolescence* 18: 253–70.

Shurtleff, N. B., ed. 1853/1854. *Records of the Governor and Company of Massachusetts Bay in New England: Vol. 1, December 13, 1636*. Boston: w. White, Printer to the Common-wealth.

Sigler, E. 2005. "Latinos & Love." *Hispanic* 18, 1/2 (January/February): 44–46.

Signorielli, M., and I. H. Frieze. 2008. "Interrelations of Gender Schemas in Children and Adolescents: Attitudes, Preferences, and Self Perceptions." *Social Behavior and Personality* 36 (7): 941–54.

Signorielli, N. 2001. "Television's Gender Role Images and Contribution to Stereotyping: Past, Present, Future." In D. G. Singer and J. L. Singer, eds. *Handbook of Children and the Media,* 341-58. Thousand Oaks, CA: Sage.

Sikod, F. 2007. "Gender Division of Labor and Women's Decision-Making Power in Rural Households in Ameroon." *African Development* 32, 3: 58–71.

Silver, S. 2010. "Foreigners Victims, Perpetrators of Sekuhara." (October 26). http://search.co.jp/cgi-bin/fl20101026zg.html (2011, July 8).

Silverman, P. 1988. "Research as a Process: Exploring the Meaning of Widowhood." In S. Reinharz and G. Rowles, eds., *Qualitative Gerontology,* 217–40. New York: Springer.

———. 2000. *Never Too Young to Know: Death in Children's Lives.* New York: Oxford University Press.

Simmons, T., and M. O'Connell. 2003. "Married-Couple and Unmarried-Partner Households: 2000. *Census 2000 Special Reports.* (February). Washington, DC: U.S. Census Bureau.

Simon, R. J., and H. Altstein. 2000. *Adoption Across Borders: Serving the Children in Transracial and Intercountry Adoptions.* Lanham, MD: Rowman and Littlefield.

Singh, J. 2005. "The Contemporary Indian Family." In B. N. Adams and A. J. Trost, eds. *Handbook of World Families,* 129–166. Thousands Oak, CA: Sage.

Situmorang, A. 2007. "Staying Single in a Married World: The Life of Never Married Women in Yogyakarta and Medan." *Asian Population Studies* 3, 3 (November): 287–304.

Sivard, R., A. Brauer, L. Lumpe, and P. Walker. 1996. *World Military and Social Expenditures 1996.* Washington, DC: World Priorities.

Skaggs, M. J. and K. M. Jodl. 1999. "Adolescent Adjustment in Nonstepfamilies and Stepfamilies." *Monographs of the Society for Research in Child Development* 64: 144–160.

Skolnick, A. S., and J. H. Skolnick, eds. 1999. *Family in Transition,* 10th ed. New York: Longman.

Skul, D. 2005. "Divorce Is So Final: Have You Really Thought It Through?" (December 17). http://www.articlealley.com/article_19963_27.html (2006, March 3).

Small Arms Survey. 2010. www.smallarmssurvey.org/publications/by-type/yearbook/small-arms-survey-2010 (2011, October 8).

Smith, A. D., and W. J. Reid. 1986. *Role-Sharing Marriage.* New York: Columbia University Press.

Smith, D. 2005. "Fed-up Wives Bailing Out of Longtime Marriages." *Chicago Tribune* (June 8): Sec 8, p.1.

Smith, J., J. Mercy, and J. Conn. 1988. "Marital Status and the Risk of Suicide." *American Journal of Public Health* 78, 1: 78–80.

Smith, J., V. Waldorf, and D. Trembath. 1990. "Single White Male Looking for Thin, Very Attractive…." *Sex Roles* 23: 675–85.

Smith, L., and Clanton, G. 1987. *Jealousy.* Lanham, MD: University Press of America.

Smith, M. 2004. "Relationships of Children in Stepfamilies with Their Non-resident Fathers." *Family Matters* 67: 28–35.

Smith, S. L., and M. Choueiti. 2010. "Gender Disparity On Screen and Behind the Camera in Family Films." www.thegeenadavisinstituteorg/dowloads/FullStudy_GenderDisparityFamilyFilms.pdf (2011, April 10).

Smock, P. J., and S. Gupta. 2002. "Cohabitiation in Contemporary North American." In A. Booth and A. C. Crouter, eds. *Just Living Together,* 53–84. Mahwah, NJ: Erlbaum.

Smock, P. J., and W. D. Manning. 2004. "Living Together Unmarried in the United States: Demographic Perspectives and Implications for Family Policy." *Law and Policy* 26, 1: 87–114.

Sobey, A. R. 1997. "Alert: All Pregnant Women Avoid South Carolina." http://kubby.com/pr/971031.html (1999, October 31).

Sommers, C. H. 2000. *The War Against Boys.* New York. Simon & Schuster.

Sorenson, S. B., and K. A. Thomas. 2009. "Views of Intimate Partner Violence in Same-and Opposite-Sex Relationships." *Journal of Marriage and Family* 71 (2): 337–352.

Soroka, M. P., and G. J. Bryjak. 2000. *Social Problems: A World at Risk.* Boston: Allyn & Bacon.

Southern Poverty Law Center (SPLC). 2001. Intelligence Report. "Raging against the Other." www.splcenter.org/intelligenceproject/ip-4t6.html (2002, February 2).

———. 2010. "Rage on the Right." *Intelligence Report.* (Spring) 137. www.splcenter.org/get-informed/intelligence-report/browse-all-issues/2010/spring/rage-on-the-right (2011, October 7).

———. 2011. "The Year in Hate & Extremism, 2010." *Intelligence Report.* (Spring) 141. www.splcenter.org/what-we-do/hate-and-extremism (2011, October 7).

Spade, J. 1989. "Bringing Home the Bacon: A Sex-Integrated Approach to the Impact of Work on the Family." In B. Risman and P. Schwartz, eds., *Gender in Intimate Relationships,* 184–92. Belmont, CA: Wadsworth.

Spain, D., and S. M. Bianchi. 1996. *Balancing Act.* New York: Russell Sage Foundation.

Span, P. 2011. "Aging Without Children." (March 25). http://newoldage.blogs.nytimes.com/2011/03/25/aging-without-children/ (2011, August 15).

Spanier, G. B., and P. C. Glick. 1981. "Marital Instability in the United States: Some Correlates and Recent Changes." *Family Relations* 31 (July): 329–38.

Spearin, C. E. 2006. "Forming a Union Plus Kids: The Role of Children in Stepfamily Formation." http://paa2006.princeton.edu/download.aspx?submissionld=60477 (2006, March 31).

Spitze, G. 1988. "Women's Employment and Family Relations: A Review." *Journal of Marriage and the Family* 50: 585–618.

———, and K. Trent. 2006. "Gender Differences in Adult Sibling Relations in Two-Child Families." *Journal of Marriage and Family* 68, 4: 977–992.

Spohn, R. 2004. "Research Shows Link Between Family Type, Abuse, and Delinquency." (September 30) http://ww.k-state.edu/media/WEB/NewsReleases?familylink93004.html (2008, May 2).

Sprecher, S., and M. Toro-Morn. 2002. "A Study of Men and Women from Different Sides of Earth to Determine if Men Are from Mars and Women Are from Venus in Their Beliefs About Love and Romantic Relationships." *Sex Roles* 46, 5–6 (March): 131–147.

Spring, S. 2006. "The Trade in Fertility." *Newsweek* (April 12). (Accessed April 24) http://www.msnbc.msn.com/id/12289078/site/newsweek/print/1/displaymode/1098/

Springer, K. W. 2010. "Economic Dependence in Marriage and Husband's Midlife Health." *Gender & Society* 24, 3: 378–401.

Spruill, J. C. 1938. *Women's Life and Work in the Southern Colonies.* New York: Russell and Russell.

St. George, D. 2004. "Pregnant Women Murdered at an Alarming Rate." *The Washington Post* (December 19).

Stacey, J. 2003. "Gay and Lesbian Families: Queer Like Us." In M. A. Mason, A. Skolnik, and D. Sugarman, eds., *All Our Families: New Policies for a New Century,* 144–169, New York: Oxford University Press.

Stanley, S. 2005. *The Power of Commitment: A Guide to Active, Lifelong Love.* Jossey-Bass.

———, and G. K. Rhoades. 2009. "Sliding vs. Deciding: Understanding a Mystery." National Council on Family Relations newsletter. *Family Focus* (Summer): F1–F4.

Staples, R. 1988. "The Black American Family." In C. H. Mindel, R. Habenstein, and R. Wright, Jr., eds., *Ethnic Families in America: Patterns and Variations,* 303–24. New York: Elsevier.

———. 1999. *The Black Family: Essays and Studies,* 6th ed. Belmont, CA: Wadsworth.

———, & Johnson, L. 2004. *Black Families at the Crossroads: Challenges and Prospects.* Revised Edition. Somerset, NJ: Jossey-Bass.

Stein, P. 1976. *Single.* Englewood Cliffs, NJ: Prentice Hall.

———, ed. 1981. *Single Life: Unmarried Adults in Social Context.* New York: St. Martin's Press.

Steinfirst, S., and B. B. Moran. 1989. "The New Mating Game: Matchmaking via the Personal Columns in the 1980's." *Journal of Popular Culture* 22, 4: 129–140.

Stephen, E. H., and A. Chandra. 2006. "Infertility Service Utilization Among Women Aged 15–44 in the United States: 2002." A poster paper presented at the 2006 annual meeting of the Population Association of America, March 30–April 1, Los Angeles, CA.

Stephens, E. 2011. "Adolescent Romantic Relationships." www.cedu.niu.edu/~shumow/iit/AdolRomanticRelationships.pdf (2011, July 4).

Sternberg, R. J. 1986. "A Triangular Theory of Love." *Psychological Review* 93, 2: 119–135.

———. 1988. *The Triangle of Love: Intimacy, Passion, and Commitment.* New York: Basic Books.

———. 1998. *Love Is a Story.* London: Oxford University Press.

———. 2001. *What's Your Love Story?* In Kathleen R. Gilbert, ed., *Annual Editions: The Family.* Guilford, CT: McGraw-Hill/Duskin.

Sternberg, S., and Gillum, J. 2011. "Poverty, HIV Link Strongest in South." *USA Today.* (July 11): 1A, 4A.

Stevenson, B. 2010. "Beyond the Classroom: Using Title IX to Measure the Return to High School Sports." *The Review of Economics and Statistics* 92 (2): 284–301.

Stewart, S. D. 2003. "Nonresident Parenting and Adolescent Adjustment." *Journal of Family Issues* 24 (March): 217–244.

———. 2005. "How the Birth of a Child Affects Involvement with Stepchildren." *Journal of Marriage and Family* 67 (May): 461–473.

———. 2007. *Brave New Stepfamilies: Diverse Paths Toward Stepfamily Living.* Thousand Oaks, CA: Sage.

Stinnet, N., and C. Birdsong. 1978. *The Family and Alternative Life Styles.* Chicago: Nelson-Hall.

Stokes, C. E., and C. G. Ellison. 2010. "Religion and Attitudes Toward Divorce Laws Among U.S. Adults." *Journal of Family Issues* 31, 10: 1279–1304.

Stokes, J. P., and J. S. Peyton. 1986. "Attitudinal Differences between Full-Time Homemakers and Women Who Work Outside the Home." *Sex Roles* 15: 299–310.

Stoll, B. M., G. L. Arnaut, D. K. Fromme, J. A. Felker-Thayer. 2005. "Adolescents in Stepfamilies: A Qualitative Analysis." *Journal of Divorce and Remarriage* 44, 1/2: 177–189.

Stop Prisoner Rape, Inc. 2007. "Fact Sheets." Los Angeles, CA: Stop Prisoner Rape, Inc. www.spr.org/en/fact_sheets.asp (2008, August 23).

Story, T. N., C. A. Berg, T. W. Smith, R. Beveridge, N. Henry, and G. Pearce. 2007. "Age, Marital Satisfaction, and Optimism As Predictors of Positive Sentiment Override in Middle-aged and Older Married Couples." *Psychology and Aging* 22, 4: 719–727.

Strasburger, V. 2005. "Adolescents, Sex, and the Media: oooo, Baby, Baby—a Q & A." *Adolescent Medicine Clinic,* 16 (2): 269–288.

Straus, M. A. 2001. *Beating the Devil Out of Them: Corporal Punishment in American Families and Its Effects on Children,* 2nd ed. Somerset, NJ: Transaction Publishers.

———. 2007. "Do We Need A Law to Prohibit Spanking?" *Family Focus* (June): FF34: F7.

———, and D. Donnelly. 2001. *Beating the Devil Out of Them: Corporal Punishment in American Families and Its Effects on Children,* 2nd ed. New Brunswick, NJ: Transaction Publishers.

Streb, M. J., et al. 2007. "Social Desirability Effects and Support for a Female American President." http://poq.oxfordjournals.org/cgi/content/full/nfm035v1 (2008, March 21).

Strong, B., C. DeVault, B. Sayad, and W. Yarber. 2004. *Human Sexuality: Diversity in Contemporary America.* New York: McGraw-Hill.

Strow, C. W., and B. K. Strow. 2008. "Evidence That the Presence of a Half-sibling Negatively Impacts a Child's Personal Development." *American Journal of Economics and Sociology* 67, 2: 177–206.

Stutzer, A., and B. S. Frey. 2003. "Does Marriage Make People Happy or Do Happy People Get Married?" Working Paper Series, Paper 143, Institute for Empirical Research in Economics, University of Zurich.

Substance Abuse and Mental Health Services Administration. 2009. *The National Household Survey on Drug Abuse Report: Children Living with Substance-Abusing or Substance-Dependent Parents: 2002–2007.* (April 16). Rockville, MD.

———. 2011. *Results from the 2010 National Survey on Drug Use and Health: National Findings,* NSDUH Series H-341, HHS Publication No. (SMA) 11-4658. Rockville, MD.

"Sudan Splitting Apart Peacefully." 2011. *San Francisco Chronicle.* (January 9). www.articles.sfgate.com/2011-01-09/opinion/27018669_1_oil-fields-abyei-oil-sales (2011, October 7).

Sudan Vision Daily. 2011. "First 24 Hours of Life Most Dangerous Time for Children in Developing World." May 20. www.sidamvosopmdao;u/com/modules.php?name=News&file=print&sid=12940 (2011, September 7).

Sullivan, O., and S. Coltrane. 2008. "Men's Changing Contribution to Housework and Childcare." Prepared for the 11th Annual Conference on Contemporary Families, April 25–26.

Supporting Family Values. 2005. www.ronrolheisercom/arc052905.html (2005, July 21).

suro, r. 2001. "Mixed Doubles." *American Demographics.* www.inside.com/product/product_print.asp?pf_id (2001, November 14).

Sutton-Smith, B. 1971. "The Expressive Profile." In A. Paredes and R. Bauman, eds., *Toward New Perspectives in Folklore,* 80–92. Austin: University of Texas Press.

Swanbrow, D. 2003. "Childhood Viewing of TV Violence Affects Women as Well as Men." (March 10). http://www.umich.edu/news/releases/2003/mar03/r031003a.html (2006, July 22).

Sweeney, M. M. 2002. "Remarriage and the Nature of Divorce: Does It Matter Which Spouse Chooses to Leave?" *Journal of Family Issues* 23: 410–440.

Sweet, J. A., and L. L. Bumpass. 1987. *American Families and Households.* New York: Russell Sage Foundation.

Swiss, L. and C. Le Bourdais. 2009. "Father-Child Contact After Separation: The Influence of Living Arrangements." *Journal of Family Issues* 30, 5: 623–652.

Szalavitz, M. 2010. "Portugal's Drug Experience: New Study Confirms Decriminalization Was a Success." (November 23). http://helthland.time.com/2011/11/23/portugals-drug-experience-new-study-confirms-decriminalization-was-a-success/ (2011, September 28).

Szapocznik, J., and R. Hernandez. 1988. "The Cuban American Family." In C. H. Mindel, R. W. Habenstein, and R. H. Wright, Jr., eds., *Ethnic Families in America: Patterns and Variations,* 160–72. New York: Elsevier.

T.E.A.R. 2007. "Teens Experiencing Abusive Relationships:Statistics." www.teensagainstabuse.org/index.php?q=statistics (2011, July 5).

Tach, L., R. Mincy, and K. Edin. 2010. "Parenting As a 'Package Deal': Relationships, Fertility, and Nonresident Father Involvement among Unmarried Parents." *Demograph* 47, 1: 181–204.

Tagorda, R. 2005. "Trends in Interracial Dating." *Outside the Beltway* (June 25).

Takagi, D. 2002. "Japanese American Families." In R. Taylor, ed., *Minority Families in the United States.* Upper Saddle River, NJ: Prentice Hall.

Tan, A. L. 2004. *Chinese American Children and Families: A Guide for Educators and Service Providers.* Olney, MD: Association for Childhood Educational International.

Tan-Jacob, I. L. 2006. "A Qualitative Analysis of Stepfamily Formation in Singapore." Master's Thesis, Department of Social Work, National University of Singapore.

Tannen, D. 1990. *You Just Don't Understand: Women and Men in Conversation.* New York: Ballantine.

———. 1994. *Talking from 9 to 5. Women and Men in the Workplace: Language, Sex and Power.* New York: Avon Books.

———. 2002. *I Only Say This Because I Love You: Talking to Your Parents, Partner, Sibs, and Kids When You're All Adults.* New York: Ballantine Books.

Tanner, L. 2011. "Child Abuse Rose During Recession, Research Says." (September 19). www.thesouthern.com/news/local/article_4c87da56-e23b-11e0-9ae3-001cc4c002e0.html (2011, September 19).

Tapsfield, R., and F. Collier. 2005. "The Cost of Foster Care: Investing in Our Children's Future." http://www.crin.org/bcn/details.asp?id=9769 themeID=1002 topicID=1013 (2006, August 15).

Tausug Marriages. 2008. "Wedding Customs Around the Muslim World: Philippine Muslim (Tausug) Marriages on Jolo Island." www.zawaj.com/weddingways/tausag/tausag2.html (2008, 21 March).

Tavernise, S. 2011a. "Adoptions by Gay Couples Rise, Despite Barriers." (June 13). www.nytimes.com/2011/0614/us/14adoption.html?pagewanted=all (2011, September 10).

———. 2011b. "Adoptions Rise by Same-Sex Couples, Despite Legal Barriers." *New York Times* (June 14): A10, A15.

———, and R. Gebeloff. 2011. "Once Rare in Rural America, Divorce Is Changing the Face of Its Families." *New York Times.* March 24: A18, A21.

Tavris, C. 2000. "Women as Love's Experts and Love's Victims." In N. Benokraitis, ed., *Feuds about Families*, 123–130. Upper Saddle River, NJ: Prentice Hall.

Taylor, C. A., J. A. Manganello, S. J. Lee, and J. C. Rice. 2010. "Mothers' Spanking of 3-Year-Old Children and Subsequent Risk of Children's Aggressive Behavior." *Pediatrics* 125, 5: e1057-e1065.

Taylor, P. 2009. *America's Changing Workforce: Recession Turns a Graying Office Grayer.* Washington, DC: Pew Research Center.

———, ed. 2010. *The Decline of Marriage and Rise of New Families.* Washington, DC: Pew Research Center.

Taylor, R. L. 2002. *Minority Families in the United States: A Multicultural Perspective.* 3rd ed. Upper Saddle River, NJ: Prentice Hall.

Tchou, A. 2011. "Are Twins Taking Over? Making Sense of the Dramatic Rise in Multiple Births." (August 23). www.slate.com/articles/life/twins/2011/08/are_twins_taking_over.html. (2011, September 7).

Teachman, J. 2002. "Stability Across Cohorts in Divorce Risk Factors." *Demography* 39: 331–351.

———. 2003. "Premarital Sex, Premarital Cohabitation, and the Risk of Subsequent Marital Dissolution Among Women." *Journal of Marriage and the Family* 65 (May): 444–455.

———. 2010. "Wives' Economic Resources and Risk of Divorce." *Journal of Family Issues* 31, 4: 1–19.

———, L. M. Tedrow, and K. D. Crowder. 2000. "The Changing Demography of America's Families." *Journal of Marriage and the Family* 62, 4: 1234–46.

Teaster, P., T. Dugar, M. Mendiondo, E. Abner, and K. Cecil. 2006. *The 2004 Survey of State Adult Protective Services: Abuse of Adults 60 Years of Age and Older.* Washington, DC: National Center on Elder Abuse.

Teeple, A., and Craig, B. 2011. "Where Do Lesbians [Really] Meet?" www.thelavenderlens.com/Vfest.html (2011, July 4).

Telecomworldwire. 2001. "Both Men and Women Turn to SMS to Find New Partners—Study." (September 19). http://findarticles.com/p/articles/mi_m0ECZ/is_2001_Sept_19/ai_78408573/ (2001, October 24).

Tenenbaum, H. R., S. For, and B. Alkhedairy. 2010. "Telling Stories: Gender Differences in Peers' Emotion Talk and Communication Style." *British Journal of Developmental Psychology*, no. doi: 10.1348/2044-835x.00203.

Tenenbaum, H. R., and C. Leper. 2003. "Parent-Child Conversations About Science: The Socialization of Gender Inequities?" *Developmental Psychology* 39 (January): 34–47.

Tennis, C. 2005. "I Wish My Stepchildren Would Go Away." (Dec. 1). http://dir.salon.com/story/mwt/col/tenn/2005/12/01/stepmon/index.html (2006, March 27).

Tennov, D. [1979] 1999. *Love and Limerence: The Experience of Being in Love.* 2nd ed. New York: Scarborough House.

Terhell, E. L. 2004. "Changes in the Personal Network After Divorce." (Jan. 22). http://dare.ubvu.vu.n/handle/1871/10453 (2008, August 3).

"Terrorists Attack in the U.S. or Against Americans." 2011. Infoplease, Pearson Education, Inc. www.infoplease.com/ipa/A0001454 .html (2011, October 11).

"Texas Frozen Embryo Case of Roman v. Roman Finally Over." 2008 (May 13). http://texasfamilylawblog.wordpress.com/2008/05/13/texas-frozen-embryo/ (2008, July 24).

The 8 Minute Matchmaker. 2002. Tufts e-News. (June 13). www.8minutedating .com/press/pdfs/Tufts.htm (2006, February 17).

The Annie E. Casey Foundation. 2008. "Infant Mortality by Race." The Annie E. Casey Kids CountDataCenter, http://www.kidscount.org/datacemter/compare_results.jsp?i=71 (2008, July 20).

The Community Board, 2010. "Entertainment Assessment: The Portrayal of Race, Gender, and Social Class on Sesame Street and the Electric Company." (July 15). www.good.is/post/entertainment-assessment-the-portrayal-of-race-gender-and-social-class-on-sesame-street-and-the-eletric-company/ (2011, April 11).

"The Dos and Don'ts of Office Romance." 2011. www.ilstv.com/the-dos-and-donts-of-office-romance/ (2011, July 5).

The Economist. 2011. "Violence Against Women: War's Overlooked Victims." (January 13). *The Economist.* www.economist.com/node/17900482 (2011, October 10).

The German Marshall Fund of the United States. 2008. "Transatlantic Trends: Immigration 2008 Partners." November 18.

The Knot, 2011. "Wedding Money: What Does the Average Wedding Cost?" www.wedding.theknot.com/wedding-planning/wedding-budget/qa/what-does-the-average-wedding-cost.aspx (2011, November 12).

The Leadership Conference. 2011. "Hate Crimes in the United States." The Leadership Conference on Civil and Human Rights. www.civilrights .org/hatecrimes/united-states/ (2011, October 7).

The Media Project. 2011. "Teen Sexual Behavior." www.themediaproject .com/facts/behavior/index.htm (2011, August 1).

"The Reality of Women at War." 2011 *The New York Times* (April 14): A22.

"The State of Our Unions 2007: The Social Health of Marriage in America." 2007. Piscataway, NJ: The National Marriage Project: Rutgers, the State University of New Jersey.

The Urban Institute. 2001. "Characteristics of Recent Welfare Population Dispel Some But Not All Concerns as Time Limits Approach." (April 27). www.urban.org/url.cfm?ID=900400 (2008, February 26).

"The Wage Gap…," 2007. The National Committee on Pay Equity. http://www.pay-equity.org/PDFs/coupon.pdf (March 11).

The Washington Informer, 2010. "African Americans Twice as Likely as Whites to Go Hungry." (November 17). www.washingtoninformer.com/index.php?option=com_content&view=article&id= (2011, March 14).

The Williams Institute. 2011. "United States Census Snapshot: 2010." (September). www.williamsinstitute.law.ucla.edu/research/census-lgbt-demographics-studies/us-census (2011, September 7).

The Working Group on Girls. 2011. "Girls With Differing Abilities: Fact Sheet." http://girlsrights.org/wp/wp-content/uploads/2011/10/WGG-Girl-Child-with-disabilities-fact-sheet-with-addendum1.pdf (2011, September 29).

"The World Communal Scene." 2005. www.communa.org.il/world.htm (2005, December 7).

Thebaud, S. 2007. "Masculinity, Bargaining and Breadwinning: A Study of Men's Household Labor in 22 Countries." Paper presented at the annual meeting of the American Sociological Association. New York, August 11.

"There's No Place Like Home . . . for Sex Education." 2011. www.noplacelike-home.org (2011, July).

Thies, C. F. 2000. "The Success of American Communes." *Southern Economic Journal* 67, 1: 186–199.

Thomas, J. L. 1986. "Gender Differences in Satisfaction with Grandparenting." *Psychology and Aging* 1: 215–19.

Thomsen, S. R., M. Weber, and L. B. Brown. 2001. "Health and Fitness Magazine Reading and Eating-disordered Diet Practices Among High School Girls." *American Journal of Health Education* 32, 3 (May/June): 130–135.

Tiefenbrun, S., and Edwards, C. 2008. "Gendercide and the Cultural Context of Sex Trafficking in China." *The Berkeley Electronic Press.* www .works.bepress.com/susan_tiefenbrun/2/ (2011, July 4).

Tillman, K. 2007. "Family Structure, Pathways and Academic Disadvantage among Adolescent in Stepfamilies." *Sociological Inquiry* 77, 3: 383–424.

Tilly, L., and J. W. Scott. 1978. *Women, Work and Family.* New York: Holt.

Tilson, D., and U. Larsen. 2000. "Divorce in Ethiopia: The Impact of Early Marriage and Childlessness." *Journal of Biosocial Science* 32, 3(July): 355–372.

Ting, G., and J. Woo. 2009. "Elder Care: Is Legislation of Family Responsibility the Solution?" *Asian Journal of Gerontology and Geriatrics* 4, 2: 72–75.

Tjaden, P., and Thoennes, N. 2006. *Extent, Nature, and Consequences of Rape Victimization: Findings From the National Violence Against Women Survey.* Washington, DC: U.S. Department of Justice, Office of Justice Programs.

Today's Views. 2010. "Fourth Reich: Rising Neo-Nazis in Europe." (October 8). www.todaysviews.com/2010/10/08/fourth-reich-rising-neo-nazis-in-europe/ (2011, October 7).

"Top Ten Dating Sites for 2011." 2011. www.dating-online-today.com /top-10-dating-sites-for-2011. (2011, July 5).

Tower, C. 2007. *Understanding Child Abuse and Neglect*, 7th ed. Boston: Allyn & Bacon.

Towner, B. 2008. "Something Old Something New." *AARP Bulletin*, 49 No. 5, (June) 35.

Townsend, A. 2007. "Woman Describes Childhood in Polygamous Household." (July 31) *CNN U.S.* http://articles.cnn.com/2007-0731/us/fleeing.polygamy_1_warren-jeffs-flds-polygamous-sect-leader?_s=PM:US (2011, March 14).

Townsend, B., and K. O'Neil. 1990. "American Women Get Mad." *American Demographics* (August): 26–29, 32.

Toyama, K. 2011. "Income Inequality Around the World Is a Failure of Capitalism." (May 13). www.theatlantic.com/business/archive/2011/05/income-ineqquality-around-the-world-is-a-failure-of-capitalism/238837/ (2011, September 25).

Transamerica Center for Retirement Studies. 2011. "Transamerica Study Reveals the New Retirement: Working." (May 17). www .transamericacenter.org/resources/tc_center_research.html (2011, August 15).

Trauma Intervention Programs. 2006. "Facts About Domestic Violence." www.tipnational.org/node/262 (2006, July 13).

Treas, J., and D. Giesen. 2000. "Sexual Infidelity Among Married and Cohabiting Americans." *Journal of Marriage and the Family* 62 (February): 48–60.

"Trends in CEO Pay." 2011. www.aflcio.org/courporatewatch/paywatch/ceopay.cfm (2011, July 8).

Tribe, L. H. 1990. *Abortion: The Clash of Absolutes.* New York: W. W. Norton.

Trojan 2010 U.S. Sex Census. 2010. *Trojan Condoms.com.* www.trojancondoms.com/ ArticleDetails.aspx?ArticleId=25 (2011, July 31).

Tso, N. 2009. "Why Has Taiwan's Birthrate Dropped So Low?" (December 7). www.time.com/time/world/article/0,8599,1945937,00.html (2011, July 22).

Tuhus-Dubrow, R. 2008. "I Now Pronounce You…Friend and Friend." (June 8). www.boston.com/bostonglobe/ideas/articles/2008/06/08/I_now_pronounce_you_friend_and_friend? (2011, August 19).

Twenge, J. M. ,W. K. Campbell, and C. A. Foster. 2003. "Parenthood and Marital Satisfaction: A Meta-Analytic Review." *Journal of Marriage and Family* 65, 3: 574–583.

Twitter.com. 2010. "Longest Married @ longestmarried." www.twitter.com/#!/longestmarried (2011, August 15).

UCLA Center for Labor Research and Education. 2007. *Undocumented Students, Unfulfilled Dreams.* California, Los Angeles.

Uhlenberg, P. 1980. "Death and the Family." *Journal of Family History* (Fall): 313–21.

UIC Campus Advocacy Network. 2008. University of Illinois Chicago. Chicago www.uic.edu/depts./owa/dvtoc.html.

UN News Centre. 2011. "Citing Rising Death Toll, UN Urges Better Protection of Afghan Civilians." (March 9). www.un.org/apps/news/story.asp?NewsID=37715&Cr=Afghan&Cr1 (2011, October 14).

UN Women. 2011. "Violence Against Women." www.unifem.org/gender_issues/violence_against_womcn/ (2011, September 19).

UNAIDS/WHO. 2008. *2008 Report on the Global AIDS Epidemic. Joint United Nations Programme on HIV/AIDS (UNAIDS).* www.data.unaids .org/pub/ GlobalReport/2008/JC1511_GR08_Exec (2008, August 20).

Understanding Intimate Partner Violence Fact Sheet. 2011. Centers for Disease Control and Prevention, National Center for Injury Prevention and Control, Division of Violence Prevention. www.cdc.gov/violenceprevention/pdf/ipv_factsheet-a.pdf (2011, September 7).

UNESCO. 2010. Education For All Global Monitoring Report, Reaching the Marginalized. UNESCO Press and Oxford University Press.

UNFPA. 2008. "Putting Rights Into Practice: Addressing Gender-Based Violence." www.unfpa.org/rights/violence.htm (2011, September 19).

UNHCR. 2011. "Global Trends 2010." *The UN Refugee Agency.* www.unhcr .org/statistics.html (2011, October 7).

UNIAIDS. 2008. "2008 Progress Reports Submitted by Countries." http:// www.unaids.org/en/dataanalysis/monitoringcountryprogress/2010 progressreportssubmittedbycountries/2008progressreportssubmitted bycountries/ (2008, June 9).

UNICEF. 2002. "Children and War." Voices of Youth. www/imocef/prg/voy/meeting/war-exp2.hmtl (February 18).

———. 2009. "Landmines and Explosive Remnants of War Continue to Threaten Children." (April 3). www.unicef.org/media/media_49079. html (2011, October 1).

———. 2010. "Child Soldiers in Uganda Chronicled in 'Children of War' Documentary." (October 15). www.unicefusa.org/news/news-from-the-field/award-winning-documentary-child-soldiers-uganda.html (2011, October 1).

———. 2011a. "12,000 Fewer Children Perish Daily in 2010 than in 1990." (September 15). www.unicefusa.org/news/releases/uicef-believes=in-zero.html (September 25).

———. 2011b. "Child Protection From Violence, Exploitation, and Abuse." www.unicef.org/protection/index_armedconflict.html (2011, October 10).

Uniform Crime Report. 2009. "Hate Crime Statistics, 2009." www2.fbi.gov/ucr/hc2009/index.html (2011, October 1).

United Nations. 1993. "48/104. Declaration on the Elimination of Violence Against Women." Resolution Adopted by the General Assembly. (December 20). www.un-documents.net/a48r104.html (2011, September 19).

———. 2009. *Population Aging and Development, 2009.* New York: Department of Economic and Social Affairs. www.un.org/esa/population/publications/ageing/ageing2009chart.pdf (2011, August 8).

United Nations Children's Fund. 2006. *The State of the World's Children 2007.* New York: Author.

United Nations Development Programme. 2005. *Human Development Report 2005.* New York: Oxford University Press.

———. 2010. *Human Development Report 2010.* New York: Oxford University Press.

United Nations Office on Drugs and Crime. 2011. *World Drug Report 2011.* New York: United Nations.

U.S. Census Bureau. 2005a. "Child Custody Statistics 2004." *America's Families and Living Arrangements, 2004.* Current Population Survey, March 2005. Table FG-6. www.gocrc.com/research/custody-stats .html (2006, March 23).

———. 2005b. *Statistical Abstract of the United States, 2004–2005.* Washington, DC: U.S. Government Printing Office.

———. 2006. "Facts for Features: Special Edition." Newsroom News Release, CB06-FFSE.06, (August 9): http://www.census.gov/PressRelease/www/Releases/archives/facts_for_features_special_editions/ (2008, February 15).

———. 2007. *Statistical Abstract of the United States, 2007.*

———. 2008. *Statistical Abstract of the United States, 2008.* Washington, DC.

———. 2009. "American Indian and Alaska Native Heritage Month: November 2009." Profile America: Facts for Features (October 15). www.census.gov/newsroom/releases/archives/facts_for_features_special_editions/cb09-ff20.html (2011, September 7).

———. 2010a. "American Indian and Alaska Native Heritage Month: November 2010." Profile America: Facts for Features (November 2). www.census.gov/newsroom/releases/archives/facts_for_features_special editions/cb10ff22.html (2011, September 7).

———. 2010b. "America's Families and Living Arrangements 2010." www.census.gov/population/www/socdemo/hh-fa,/cps2010 .html (2011, September 7).

———. 2010c. Current Population Survey, 2010 Annual Social and Economic Supplement. www.census.gov/population/www/socdemo/hh-fam.html (2011, March 14).

———. 2010d. "Grandparents Day 2010: Sept 12." (July 12) www.census.gov/newsroom/releases/archives/facts_for_features_special_editions/cb10-ff16.html (2011, August 10).

———. 2010e. *Statistical Abstract of the United States.* Washington, DC: Government Printing Office. www.census.gov/population/www/socdemo/hh-fam/cps2010.html (2011, August 15).

———. 2010f. "Veterans Day 2010: Nov. 11." *Profile America: Facts for Features.* (October 27). http://www.census.gov/newsroom/

releases/archives/facts_for_features_special_editions/cb10-ff21
.html (2011, September 30).

———. 2011a. America's Families and Living Arrangements: 2010. *Statistical Abstract of the United States, 2011.* Washington, DC: Government Printing Office. www.census.gov/compedia/statab/cats/population.html (2011, August 15).

———. 2011b. "Anniversary of Americans with Disabilities Act: July 26." *Profile America: Facts for Features.* (May 31). www.census.gov/newsroom/releases/archives/facts_for_features_special_editions/cb11-ff14.html (2011, September 30).

———. 2011c. "Father's Day: June 19, 2011." Profile America: Facts for Features. www.census.gov/newsroom/releases/archives/facts_for_features_special_editions/cb11-ff11.html (2011, September 7).

———. 2011d. "Income, Poverty, and Health Insurance Coverage in the United States: 2010." (September). *Current Population Reports.* Washington, DC: U.S. Department of Commerce, Economics and Statistics Administration.

———. 2011e. *Statistical Abstract of the United States, 2011.* Washington, DC: Government Printing Office.

———. 2012. *Statistical Abstract.* www.census.gov/compedia/statab/cats/income_expenditures_poverty_wealth/household (2011, December 15).

U.S. Conference of Mayors. 2010. *2010 Status Report on Hunger and Homelessness.* (December). Washington, DC.

U.S. Department of Agriculture. 2011. "A Child Born in 2010 Will Cost $226,920 to Raise According to USDA Report." (June 9) www.cnpp.cusa.gov/Publications/CRC/2010CRCPPressRelease.pdf (2011, September 1).

U.S. Department of Commerce, Economics and Statistics Administration. 2010. *Women in America: Indicators of Social and Economic Well-Being* (March). Washington, DC.

U.S. Department of Education Office for Civil Rights. 2011. "Dear Colleague Letter: Sexual Violence Background, Summary, and Fast Facts." (April 4). www2.ed.gov/about/offices/list/ocr/index.html (2011, July 4).

U.S. Department of Health and Human Services. 2011. "Overview of the Uninsured in the United States: A Summary of the 2011 Current Population Survey." (September). http://aspe.hhs.gov/health/reports/2011/CPSHealthins2011/ib.shtml (2011, September 26).

U.S. Department of Health and Human Services, Administration for Children, Youth, and Families. 2008. *Child Maltreatment 2006.* Washington, DC: U.S. Government Printing Office. www.acf.hhs.gov/programs/cb/pubs/cm06/index.htm (2008, August 23).

———. 2009. *Child Maltreatment 2009.* www.acf.hhs.gov/programs/cb/stats_research/index.htm#can (2011, September 7).

U.S. Department of Housing and Urban Development. 2005. *Housing Discrimination Study 2000.* Washington, DC: U.S. Government Printing Office.

U.S. Department of Justice. 2000. "Sexual Assault of Young Children as Reported to Law Enforcement: Victim, Incident, and Offender Characteristics." Bureau of Justice Statistics. www.ojp.usdoj.gov/bjs/abstract/saycrle.htm (2002, January 7).

———. 2004. "Criminal Victimization in the United States." Office of Justice Programs, Bureau of Justice Statistics. www.ojp.usdoj.gov/bjs/cvict.htm (2006, July 15).

———. 2006. Crime Victimization in the United States, 2005 Statistical Tables. U.S. Department of Justice, Office of Justice Programs, Bureau of Justice Statistics (December): NCJ215244.

———. 2009a. National Gang Threat Assessment 2009. (January). Bureau of Justice Statistics: Document ID: 2009-MO335-001. www.justice.gov/ndic/pubs32/32146/index.htm (2011, October 8).

———. 2009b. "Victims and Perpetrators." Washington, DC: U.S. Department of Justice, Office of Justice Programs. www.nij.gov/topics/crime/rape-sexual-violence/victims-perpetrators.htm (2011, July 4).

———. 2010. Criminal Victimization in the United States, 2008 Statistical Tables. Bureau of Justice Statistics: Document ID: NCJ 227669.

———. 2011. "Criminal Victimization, 2010." *National Crime Victimization Survey.* Office of Justice Programs. Bureau of Justice Statistics. (September). NCJ 235508.

U.S. Department of Labor. 2000. *Balancing the Needs of Families and Employers: The Family and Medical Leave Surveys 2000 Update.* Washington, DC.

———. 2006. "Highlights of Women's Earnings in 2005." Report 995. Washington, DC: Government Printing Office.

———. 2011. "Usual Weekly Earnings of Wage and Salary Workers: First Quarter 2011." (April 17). http://www.bls.gov/news.release/wkyeng/nr0.htm (2011, July 5).

U.S. Department of Veteran Affairs. 2006. "Child Sexual Abuse." www.ncptsd.va.gov/facts/specific/fs_child_sexual_abuse.html (2006, July 19).

———. 2011. "Statement of Mike Walcoff, Acting Under Secretary for Benefits Department of Veterans' Affairs…" www.va.gov/OCA/testimony/hvac/sdama/VBA03172011.asp (2011, September 30).

U.S. Equal Employment Opportunity Commission. 2011. "Age Discrimination in Employment Act (Includes Concurrent Charges with Title VII, ADA and EPA) FY 1997-FY 2010. www.eeoc.gov/eeoc/statistics/enforcement/adea.cfm (2011, August 19).

University of Michigan. 2007. "How Dads Influence Their Daughters' Interest in Math." *Science Daily* (June 25). www.sciencedaily.com/releases/2007/06/070624143002.htm (2011, March 26).

University of Michigan Health System. 2008. "Sibling Abuse." www.med.umich.edu/libr/yourchild/sibabuse.html (2008, August 26).

University of Michigan Institute for Social Research. 2007. "Time, Money and Who Does the Laundry." *Research Update.* 4 (January): 1–2.

University of Minnesota. 2007. "LGBT—Sexual Violence, Relationship Violence and/or Stalking." University of Minnesota, Morris. www.morris.umn.edu/services/ViolencePrevention/lgbt.html (2011, September 7).

USA Today. 2008. "Presidential Candidates on Immigration." USA Today.com: http://content.usatoday.com/news/politcs/election2008/issues.aspx?i=2 (19 February).

———. 2010. "Student Immigrants Use Civil Rights-Era Strategies." (June 2). www.usatoday.com/news/education/2010-06-02-immigration-students_N.htm (2011, October 7).

USAID. 2009. "Women in Development: Gender-Based Violence." www.usaid.gov/our_work/cross-cutting_programs/wid/gbv/index.html (2011, September 19).

Utz, R. L., E. B. Reidy, D. H. Carr, R. Nesse, and C. Wortman. 2004. "The Daily Consequences of Widowhood: The Role of Gender and Intergenerational Transfers on Subsequent Housework Performance." *Journal of Family Issues* 25, 5 (July): 683–712.

V-Day. 2008. "Get the Facts: Violence against Women Statistics." v10.vday.org/take-action/violence-against-women/battery-abuse (2008, August 8).

Vaillant, C. O., and G. E. Vaillant. 1993. "Is the V-Curve of Marital Satisfaction an Illusion? A 40-Year Study of Marriage." *Journal of Marriage and the Family* 55, 1: 230–39.

Vallianatos, C. 2002. "Gay Parents' Rights Backed: Parents' Sexual Orientation 'Appears to be Irrelevant.'" *NASW News.* Washington, DC: National Association of Social Workers.

Van Dam, M. A. 2004. "Mothers in Two Types of Lesbian Families: Stigma Experiences, Supports, and Burdens." *Journal of Family Nursing* 10, 4: 450–484.

Van Laningham, J., D. R. Johnson, and P. R. Amato. 2001. "Marital Happiness, Marital Duration, and the U-Shaped Curve: Evidence from a Five-Wave Panel Study." *Social Forces* 79, 4 (June): 1313–1341.

Van Solinge, H., and K. Henkens. 2005. "Couples' Adjustment to Retirement: A Multi-Actor Panel Study." *The Journals of Gerontology Series B: Psychological Sciences and Social Sciences* 60: S11–S20.

Vancouver Sun. 2011. "Evidence Rules Leave Disabled Canadian Girls Open to Sex Abuse." (May 30). www.canada.com/vancouversun/news/editorial/story.html (2011, October 1).

Vandell, D. L., K. McCartney, M. T. Owen, C. Booth, and A. Clarke-Stewart. 2003. "Variations in Child Care by Grandparents During the First Three Years." *Journal of Marriage and Family* 65 (May): 375–381.

Vandewater, E., and J. Lansford. 1998. "Influences of Family Structure and Parental Conflict on Children's Well-Being." *Family Relations* 47: 323–30.

Vandivere, S., K. Malm, and A. McKlindon. 2010. *Adoption USA: Summary and Highlights of a Chartbook on the National Survey of Adoptive Parents.* Alexandria, VA: National Council For Adoption.

VanGoethem, J. 2005. *Living Together: A Guide to Counseling Unmarried Couples.* Kregel Publications.

Vazquez-Nuttall, E., I. Romero-Garcia, and B. DeLeon. 1987. "Sex Roles and Perceptions of Femininity and Masculinity of Hispanic Women: A Review of the Literature." *Psychology of Women Quarterly* 11: 409–25.

Velasco, S. 2011. "Poverty Rate Rises, Especially For Hispanics." (September 13). www.csmonitor.com/Business/2011/0913/Poverty-rate-rises-especially-for-Hispanics. (2011, September 14).

Vincent, G. K., and V. A. Velkoff. 2010. *The Next Four Decades, The Older Population in the United States: 2010 to 2050.* Current Population Reports, P25–1138. Washington, DC: U.S. Census Bureau.

Virginia Family Violence and Sexual Assault Hotline. 2008. "Cut Out Domestic Violence Fact Sheet." www.vaag.com (2008, August 8).

Visher, E. B. 2001. "Strengthening the Couple Relationship in Stepfamilies." Paper presented at the First Annual Ohio State University Extension Family Life Electronic In-Service: A Systemic Examination of Stepfamily Relationships. Columbus, OH, May 8–10.

Visher, J., and E. Visher. 1993. "Remarriage, Families, and Stepparenting." In F. Walsh, ed., *Normal Family Processes,* 2nd ed., 235–53. New York: Guilford Press.

Vissa, P. 2011. "New Data, Old Worries on Homeownership." (February 3). www.greenlining.org/news/in-the-news/2011/new-data-old-worries-on-homeownership (2011, September 7).

"Voice of Mom Report 2005." 2005. Club Mom. http://www.clubmom.com/display/202659 (2006, January 4).

"Voice of the People." 2011. *Chicago Tribune* (July 15).

Voo, J. 2007. "Older Women and Younger Men: Can It Work?" (September 7). http://articles.cnn.com/2007-09-07/living/olderwomen_1_younger-men-older-women-older-men?_s=PM:LIVING (2011, July 4).

Voydanoff, P. 1983. "Unemployment and Family Stress." In H. Z. Lopata and J. H. Pleck, eds., *Research in the Interweave of Social Roles: Families and Jobs,* 239–50. Greenwich, CT: JAI Press.

———. 1987. *Work and Family.* Beverly Hills, CA: Sage.

Vuchinich, S., E. M. Hetherington, R. Vuchinich, and W. G. Clingempeel. 1991. "Parent-Child Interaction and Gender Differences in Early Adolescents' Adaptation to Stepfamilies." *Developmental Psychology* 27, 4: 618–26.

Wade, C., and S. Cirese. 1991. *Human Sexuality,* 2nd ed. New York: Harcourt Brace Jovanovich.

Wadhwani, A. 2011. "Military Families Fight Battle at Home Against Foreclosure." (February 6). www.wbir.com/cleanprint/?unique=1308933924674 (2011, June 24).

Wainwright, J. L., S. T. Russell, and C. J. Patterson. 2004. "Psychosocial Adjustment, School Outcomes, and Romantic Relationships of Adolescents with Same-Sex Parents." *Child Development* 75, 6 (December): 186–1898.

Waite, L., and M. Gallagher. 2000. *The Case for Marriage: Why Married People are Happier, Healthier and Better Off Financially.* New York: Doubleday.

Waite, L., and K. Joyner. 2001. "Emotional Satisfaction and Physical Pleasure in Sexual Unions: Time Horizon, Sexual Behavior, and Sexual Exclusivity." *Journal of Marriage and Family,* 63 (Feb): 247–264.

Wald, E. 1981. *The Remarried Family: Challenge and Promise.* New York: Family Service Association of America.

Waldman, P. 2011. "Adoption by Gays Gaining Support." (May 10). http://prospect.org/csnc/blogs/tapped_archieve?month=05&year=2011&base_name=adoption_by_gays_gaining_suppo (2011, October 5).

Walker, D. 2007. "More Black Women Reassess 'Dating Out.'" *The Post & Courier* (August 6) charleston.net/news/2007/.../more_black_women_reassess_dating_out12334 (2008, 28 April).

Walker, K. 1994. "Men, Women, and Friendship: What They Say, What They Do." *Gender and Society* 8: 246–265.

———. 1995. "Always There for Me: Friendship Patterns and Expectations among Middle and Working Class Men and Women." *Sociological Forum* 10 (2): 273–296.

———. 2001. "I'm Not Friends the Way She's Friends: Ideological and Behavioral Constructions of Masculinity in Men's Friendships." In M. Kimmel and M. Messner, *Men's Lives,* 5th ed., 367–379. Needham Heights, MA: Allyn & Bacon.

Walker, K., F. Dickson, and P. Hughes. 2005. "An Exploratory Investigation into Dating Among Later-Life Women." *Western Journal of Communication.* (January 1).

Walker, K. E., and M. Woods. 1976. *Time Use: A Measure of Household Production of Goods and Services.* Washington, DC: American Home Economics Association.

Walker, L. 1978. "Treatment Alternatives for Battered Women." In J. R. Chapman and M. Gates, eds., *The Victimization of Women,* 143–74. Beverly Hills, CA: Sage.

———. 1984. *The Battered Woman Syndrome.* New York: Springer.

Walker, R. B. and M. A. Luszcz. 2009. "The Health of Relationship Dynamics of Later-Life Couples: A Systematic Review of the Literature." *Aging and Society* 29: 455–480.

Wallace, H. 2002. *Family Violence: Legal, Medical, and Social Perspective,* 3rd ed. Boston: Allyn & Bacon.

———. 2007. *Family Violence: Legal, Medical, and Social Perspectives,* 5th ed. Boston: Allyn & Bacon.

Wallace, R. A., and A. Wolf. 2005. *Contemporary Sociological Theory.* Englewood Cliffs, NJ: Prentice Hall.

Wallace, S. P., S. D Cochran, E. M. Durazo, and C. I. Ford. 2011. *The Health of Aging Lesbian, Gay and Bisexual Adults in California.* Los Angeles: UCLA Center for Health Policy Research.

Waller, W. 1937. "The Rating and Dating Complex." *American Sociological Review* 2: 727–35.

Wallerstein, J. S. 1986. "Women after Divorce: Preliminary Report from a Ten-Year Follow-Up." *American Journal of Orthopsychiatry* 56: 65–77.

———, and S. Blakeslee. 1989. *Second Chances: Men, Women, and Children a Decade after Divorce.* New York: Ticknor and Fields.

Wallerstein, J. S., J. M. Lewis, and S. Blakeslee. 2000. *The Unexpected Legacy of Divorce: A 25 Year Landmark Study.* New York: Hyperion.

Wang, F., and Cai Yong. 2011. "China's One Child Policy at 30." (January 26). www.brookings.edu/opinion/2010/0924_china_one_child_policy_wang.aspx (February 7).

Wang, H., and P. R. Amato. 2000. "Predictors of Divorce Adjustments: Stressors, Resources, and Definitions." *Journal of Marriage and Family* 62: 655–668.

Wang, S. 2010. "New Dads Too, Can Suffer Depression." *The Wall Street Journal.* www.online.wsj.com/article/SB10001424052748703957904575252263501070290.html (2011, September 7).

Wang, W., and R. Morin. 2009. "Home for the Holidays and Every Other Day." Pew Research Center (November 24). http://pewsocialtrends.org/2009/11/24/home-for-the-holidays-and-every-other-day/ (2011, April 26).

Wang, W., and P. Taylor. 2011. "For Millennials, Parenthood Trumps Marriage." (March 9). http://pewresearch.org/pubs/1920/millennials-value-parenthood-over-marriage (2011, April 26).

Ward, R. A., G. Spitze, and G. Deane. 2009. "The More the Merrier? Multiple Parent-Adult Child Relations." *Journal of Marriage and Family* 71: 161–173.

Warda, J. 2000. "Stepping Up to Protect a Son's Feelings." *Chicago Tribune* (July 30): sec. 13, 2.

Warmack, L. F. 2004. "Women in Taiwan Find Marriage Is No Fairy Tale." *The Mercury News* (February 22). www.international-divorce.com/d-taiwan.htm. (2006, March 26, 2006

Warner, J. 2010. "What the Great Recession Has Done to Family Life." (August 6). www.nytimes.com/2010/0808/magazine/08F08-wwin-t.html

Warshaw, R. 1988. *I Never Called It Rape.* New York: Harper & Row.

Washington Post-ABC News Poll. 2003. "Washington Post-ABC News Poll: The Pope and the Catholic Church." (October 15). www.washingtonpost.com (2005, September 30).

Watkins, K. 2007. *Human Development Report 2007/2008.* New York: United Nations Development Programme.

Watson, A., M. Kehler, and W. Martino. 2010. "The Problem of Boys' Literacy Underachievement: Raising Some Questions." *Journal of Adolescent & Adult Literacy* 53 (5): 356–361.

Watson, R., and P. DeMeo. 1987. "Premarital Cohabitation vs. Traditional Courtship: Their Effects on Subsequent Marital Adjustment: A Replication and Follow Up." *Family Relations* 36: 193–97.

Watters, E. 2003. *Urban Tribes: A Generation Redefines Friendship, Family, and Commitment*. New York: Bloomsbury USA.

Wayne, J. H., and B. L. Cordeiro. 2003. "Who is a Good Organizational Citizen? Social Perception of Male and Female Employees Who Use Family Leave." *Vocational Behavior* 49, 5/6: 233–247.

"We Need More Women in Games." 2009. www.guardian.co.uk/technology/gamesblog/2009/jul31/videogames-gender-balance (2011, March 27).

Weale, S. 2010. "It Was an Amazing Way to Grow Up." (July 17).www.guardian.co.uk/lifeandstyle/2010/jul17/geetie-singh-organiz-pub-commune (2011, June 8).

Weaver, D. A. 2010. "Widows and Social Security." *Social Security Bulletin* 70, 3: 89–109.

Weaver, S. W., and M. Coleman. 2005. "A Mothering But Not a Mother Role: A Grounded Theory Study of the Nonresidential Stepmother Role." *Journal of Social and Personal Relationships* 22, 4: 477–497.

WebMD. 2010. "Your Guide to Masturbation." www.webmd.com/sex-relationships/guide/masturbation-guide. (2011, August 1)."

"Wedding and Honeymoon Statistics." 2011. www.honeymoons.about.com/cs/eurogen1/a/weddingstats.htm (2011, December 15).

Wedell, K. 2010. "Advice for Living with the Boomerang Generation." (December 25). www.daytondailynews.com/lifestyle/advice-for-living-with-the-boomerang-generation-1038432.html (2011, April 26).

Weekes-Shackelford, V. A., and T. K. Shackelford. 2004. "Methods of Filicide: Stepparents and Genetic Parents Kill Differently." *Violence and Victims* 19: 75–81.

Weibel-Orlando, J. 2000. "Grandparenting Styles: Native American Perspectives." In E. P. Stoller and R. C. Gibson, eds., *Worlds of Difference*, 249–251. Thousand Oaks, CA: Pine Forge Press.

Weich, R. 2011. "Legislative Proposal: Violence Against Native Women." (July 21). www.justice.gov/.../legislative-proposal-violence-against-native-women.pdf. (2011, September 7).

Weihua, C. 2006. "Divorce Rate Surges Across China." *China Daily* (February 15). http://www.chinadaily.com.cn/english/doc/2006-02/15/content_520204.htm (2006, March 6).

Weil, B. E. 2008.*Financial Infidelity*. New York: Hudson Street Press.

Weisbrot, M. 2010. "No: Life Expectancy Is Not Rising for the Poor; Later Retirement Is Unjust." (December 6). www.ajc.com/opinion/pro-con-cut-benefits-768832.html (2011, August 19).

Weitzman, L. 1977. "To Love, Honor, and Obey: Traditional Legal Marriage and Alternative Family Forms." In A. S. Skolnick and J. H. Skolnick, eds., *Family in Transition*, 2nd ed., 288–313. Boston: Little, Brown.

———. 1985. *The Divorce Revolution: The Unexpected Social and Economic Consequences for Women and Children in America*. New York: Free Press.

Weitzman, N., B. Birns, and R. Friend. 1985. "Traditional and Nontraditional Mothers' Communication with Their Daughters and Sons." *Child Development* 56: 894–96.

Weliver, D. 2011. "How Much Does an (Average) Wedding Cost?" www.moneyunder30.com/how-much-average-wedding-cost (2011, December 15).

Weller, C. E., and J. Fields. 2011. "The Black and White Labor Gap in America: Why African Americans Struggle to Find Jobs and Remain Employed Compared to Whites." (July 25). www.americanprogress.org/issues/2011/07/black_unemployment.html (2011, August 19).

Wellesley Centers for Women. 1998. "The Wife Rape Information Page." www.wellesley.edu/wcw/projects/mrape.html (2006, July 17).

Wellman, B. 1992. "Men in Networks: Private Communities, Domestic Friendships." In P. Nardi, ed., *Men's Friendships*, 74–114. Newbury Park, CA: Sage.

Wellner, A. S. 2005. (June). "U.S. Attitudes Toward Interracial Dating Are Liberalizing." Washington, DC: *Population Reference Bureau*. www.prb.org.

Welter, B. 1978. "The Cult of True Womanhood: 1820–1860." In M. Gordon, ed., *The American Family in Social-Historical Perspective,* 313–33. New York: St. Martin's Press.

Wenger, G. C. 2009. "Childlessness at the End of Life: Evidence from Rural Wales." *Aging and Society* 29: 1243–1259.

———, P. A. Dykstra, T. Melkas, and C.P. M. Knipscheer. 2007. "Social Embeddedness and Late-Life Parenthood: Community Activity, Close Ties, and Support Networks." *Journal of Family Issues* 28, 7: 1419–1456.

Weston, K. 1997. *Families We Choose: Lesbians, Gays, Kinship*. New York: Columbia University Press.

Weston, R., and L. Qu. 2006. "Trends in Couple Formation." *Family Relationships Quarterly* 1: 12-15.

"Where Rape Is a Proposal of Marriage." 1999. (June 18). www.sn.apc.org/wmail/issues/990618/NEWS47.HTML (2002, January 21).

White Paper. 2011. "Is There a Crisis in Boy's Achievement?" http://teachingboyswhostruggle.com/Products-Resoures/Articles—Downloads/WHITE-PAPER-NO-1-IS-THERE-A-CRISIS.ASPX (2011, April 4).

White, J. 1987. "Premarital Cohabitation and Marital Stability in Canada." *Journal of Marriage and the Family* 49: 641–47.

White, L. K. 1981. "A Note on Racial Differences in the Effect of Female Opportunity on Marriage Rates." *Demography* 18: 349–54.

White, L. K. 1994. "Growing Up with Single Parents and Stepparents: Long-Term Effects on Family Solidarity." *Journal of Marriage and the Family* 56 (November): 935–48.

White, L. K. 2001. "Sibling Relationships Over the Life Course: A Panel Analysis." *Journal of Marriage and the Family* 63: 555–568.

White, L. K., and A. Riedman. 1992a. "Ties Among Adult Siblings." *Social Forces* 71: 85–102.

———. 1992b. "When the Brady Bunch Grows Up: Step-/ Half- and Full-Sibling Relationships in Adulthood." *Journal of Marriage and the Family* 54: 197–208.

Whitehead, B. D. 1997. *The Divorce Culture*. New York: Knopf.

———, and D. Popenoe. 2004. "The State of Our Unions: The Social Health of Marriage in America." *The National Marriage Project Report*. Piscataway, NJ: Rutgers, the State University of New Jersey. (June). marriage.rutgers.edu/Publications/SOOU/TEXTSOOU2004.htm (2006, April 14).

Whitehouse, B. 2000. "Alcohol and the Family." *Parenting* 14, 5 (June/July):154–62.

Whiting, B., and C. P. Edwards. 1988. *Children of Different Worlds: The Formation of Social Behavior*. Cambridge, MA: Harvard University Press.

Whiting, J. B., and R. E. Lee III. 2003. "Voices from the System: A Qualitative Study of Foster Children's Stories." *Family Relations* 52 (July): 288–295.

Whitmire R. 2010. *Why Boys Fail*. New York: AMACOM 1.

Whyte, M. K. 2001. "Choosing Mates—The American Way." In S. Ferguson, ed., *Shifting the Center: Understanding Contemporary Families*, 2nd ed., 129–39. Mountain View, CA: Mayfield.

Widener, A. J. 2007. "Family Friendly Policy: Lessons From Europe—Part I." *The Public Manager* 9 (Fall): 57–61.

Widom, C. S., and S. Hiller-Sturmhofel. 2001. "Alcohol Abuse as a Risk Factor for and Consequence of Child Abuse." *Alcohol Research and Health* 25, 1:52–57.

Wieche, V. 2002. *What Parents Need to Know About Sibling Abuse: Breaking the Cycle of Violence*. Bel Air, CA: Bonneville Books Publisher.

Wikipedia. 2011. "List of Countries by Suicide Rates." http://en.wikipedia.org/wiki/List_of_Countries_by_Suicide_rate.wikipedia.org/wiki/List_of_Countries_by_Suicide_rate (2011, October 3).

Wilcox, B., and S. Nock. 2006. "What's Love Got to do With It? Equality, Equity, Commitment, and Women's Marital Quality." *Social Forces* 84, 3 (March): 1321–1345.

Wilcox, W. B. 2004. *Soft Patriarchs, New Men: How Christianity Shapes Fathers and Husbands*. Chicago: University of Chicago Press.

———. 2005. "Analysis: Religion, Family and the General Social Survey." (October 19). www.pbs.org/wnet/religionandethics/week/908/Wilcox_Data.pdf (2006, March 11).

———. 2011. *The Great Recession and Marriage. National Marriage Project Report Web Release*. Charlottesville, VA: National Marriage Project.

———, and M. Gonsoulin. 2003. "Domestic Rites and Enchanted Relations: Religion, Ideology and Household Labor." Paper presented at the Annual Meeting of the American Sociological Association, Atlanta Hilton Hotel, Atlanta, Georgia.

Wilgoren, J. 2005. "Rape Charge Follows Marriage to a 14-Year-Old." *New York Times* (August 30): A1, A16.

"Wilhelmsen Lab Elucidates the Genes That Underlie Hereditary Aspects of Alcoholism." 2006. *Center Line*, Bowles Center for Alcohol Studies 17, 3 (March): 1–2.

Wilkins, D., and M. Kemple. 2011. *Delivering Male: Effective Practice in Male Mental Health.* London. Men's Health Forum.

Willetts, M. C. 2006. "Union Quality Comparisons between Long-term Heterosexual Cohabitation and Legal Marriage." *Journal of Family Issues* 27, 1: 110–127.

Williams, C. 1992. "The Glass Escalator: Hidden Advantages for Men in the 'Female' Professions." *Social Problems* 39, 3 (August): 253–67.

Williams, D., N. Martins, M. Consalvo, and J. D. Ivory. 2009. "The Virtual Census: Representations of Gender, Race and Age in Video Games." *New Media and Society* 11 (5): 815–34.

Williams, L., and M. Lawler. 2003. "Marital Satisfaction and Religious Heterogamy." *Journal of Family Issues*, 24 (8): 1070–1092.

Williams, R. 2010. "People Coming Out as Gay at Younger Age, Research Shows." (November 15). www.guardian.co.uk/world/2010/nov/15/gay-people-coming-out-younger-age (2011, June 15).

Williamson, M. 1994. *Thoughts, Prayer, Rites of Passage.* New York: Random House

Willie, C., and Reddick, R. 2003. *A New Look at Black Families.* Walnut Creek, CA: AltaMira Press.

Willis, G. 2005. "Are Prenups For You?" CNNMoney.com. money.cnn.com/2005/06/01/pr/saving/ (2008, June 27).

Willmsen, C., and O'Hagan, M. 2003. "Coaches Continue Working For Schools and Private Teams After Being Caught for Sexual Misconduct." *The Seattle Times,* (December 14). www.seattletimes.nwsource.com/news/local/coaches/news/dayone.html (2011, July 4).

Wilson, B. 2009. "Sex without Intimacy: No Dating, No Relationships." www.npr.org/templates/story/story.php?storyId=105008712 (2011, July 4).

Wilson, E. D. 1975. *Sociology: The New Synthesis.* Cambridge, MA: Harvard University.

Wilson, J. Q. 2002. *The Marriage Problem: How Our Culture Has Weakened Families.* New York: HarperCollins.

Wilson, W. 1980. *The Declining Significance of Race.* Chicago: University of Chicago Press.

Wilton, V., and J. A. Davey. 2006. *Grandfathers—Their Changing Family Roles and Contributions.* Wellington, New Zealand: New Zealand Institute for Research on Aging.

Wineberg, H. 1988. "Duration between Marriage and First Birth and Marital Stability." *Social Biology* 35: 91–102.

———. 1996. "The Prevalence and Characteristics of Blacks Having a Successful Marital Reconciliation." *Journal of Divorce and Remarriage* 25, 1/2: 75–86.

———, and J. McCarthy. 1993. "Separation and Reconciliation in American Marriages." *Journal of Divorce and Remarriage* 20: 21–42.

Wiscott, R., and K. Kopera-Frye. 2000. "Sharing of Culture: Adult Grandchildren's Perceptions of Intergenerational Relations." *International Journal of Aging and Human Development* 51, 3: 199–215.

Wiseman, P. 2004. "No Sex Please—We're Japanese." *USA Today.* (June 2). www.usatoday.com/news/world/2004-06-02-japan-women-usat_x.htm (2006, April 3).

Wjote, T. 2008. "Supporting Seniors in their Own Homes: A Growing Elderly Population Is Turning to a Network of Caregivers and Volunteers to Retain Independence." *The Baltimore Sun* (March 24): 1.

Wolcott, J. 2004. "Is Dating Dated on College Campuses?" *Christian Science Monitor.* (March 2, 2004). www.csmonitor.com/2004/0302/p11s01-legn.html (2006, January 18).

Wolfinger, N. H. 2000. "Beyond the Intergenerational Transmission of Divorce: Do People Replicate the Pattern of Marital Instability They Grew Up With?" *Journal of Family Issues* 21: 1061–1086.

———. 2001. "The Effects of Family Structure of Origin on Offspring Cohabitation Duration." *Sociological Inquiry* 71: 293–313.

———. 2003. "Parental Divorce and Offspring Marriage: Early or Late?" *Social Forces* 82, 1(September): 337–353.

———. 2005. *Understanding the Divorce Cycle.* New York: Cambridge.

"Woman Convicted of Killing Ex-Bear's Girlfriend Sentenced to Life." 2011. *CBS Sports* (May 20). www.cbssports.com/nfl/story/15084185/woman-convicted-of-killing-exbears-girlfriend-sentenced-to-life/rss (2011, June 8).

"Women Caring for Ex-Husbands." 2011. (February 10) www.sciencedaily.com/releases/2011/02/110210184338.htm (2011, August 23).

"Women in Development." 2011. www.isaod.gov/pir_work/crlss-cutting_programs.wid/gbv/index.html (2011, September 19).

"Women Take Lead in Late-Life Divorce, Remarriage." 2011. (January 12). http://english.chosun.com/site/data/html_dir/2011/01/12/12011011200435.html (2011, July 25).

"Women-Only Communal Housing Helping Newcomers to Tokyo Follow Dreams." 2010. www.japantoday.com/category/lifestyle/view/women-only-housing-helping-newcomers-to-Tokyo-to-Follow-Dreams (2011, May 11).

"Women's Earnings and Income." 2011. *Catalyst* (August). www.catalyst.org/publication/217/womens-earnings-and-income (2011, December 15).

Women's Sports Foundation. 2004. "Athlete's Earnings Gap Index." www.womenssportsfoundation.org/cgibin/iowa/issues/business/article.html?record=866) (2005, August 22).

"Women's Top 10 Sexual Fantasies." 2009. www.healthyplace.com/sex/psychology-of-sex/womens-top-ten-sexual-fantasies/menu-id-1482/.

Women's Web. "Child Sexual Abuse/Incest." www.womensweb.ca/violence/incest/ (2008, August 26).

Wong, M. G. 1998. "The Chinese-American Family." In C. H. Mindel, R. W. Habenstein, and R. Wright, Jr. *Ethnic Families in America: Patterns and Variations,* 284–310. Upper Saddle River, NJ: Prentice Hall.

Wong, W. 2010. "Women Missing from Video Game Development Work Force." *Chicago Tribune* (August 5). http://articles.chicagotribune.com/2010-08-05/business/sc-biz-0806 (2011, March 27).

Wood, J. T., ed. 1996. *Gendered Relationships.* Mountain View, CA: Mayfield.

———. 2004. *Gendered Lives: Communication, Gender, and Culture.* Belmont, CA: Wadsworth.

———. 2008. *Gendered Lives: Communication, Gender, and Culture,* 8th edition. Belmont, CA: Wadsworth.

Wood, R. G., S. Avellar, and B. Goesling. 2008. *Pathways to Adulthood and Marriage: Teenagers' Attitudes, Expectations, and Relationship Patterns.* ASPE Research Brief. Washington, DC: Department of Health and Human Services.

Woods, R. D. 1996. "Grandmother Roles: A Cross-Cultural View." *Journal of Instructional Psychology* 23 (December): 286–92.

Worden, J. W. 1982. *Grief Counseling and Grief Therapy: A Handbook for the Mental Health Practitioner.* New York: Springer.

World Bank. 2011a. "Girls' Education: A World Bank Priority." (August 18). http://worldbank.org/WEBSITE/EXTERNAL/TOPICS/EXTEDUCATION/0,,CONTENTMDK:20298916-MENUPK:617572-PAGEPK:148956-THESITE (2011, September 25).

———. 2011b. "GNI Per Capita, 2007, Atlas Method and PPP." World Development Indicators Database (July 1). www.siteresources.worldbank.org/DATASTATISTICS/Resources/GNIPC.pdf (2011, August 26).

World Health Organization. 2005. WHO Multi-Country Study on Women's Health and Domestic Violence against Women: Summary Report of Initial Results on Prevalence, Health Outcomes and Women's Responses. Geneva, Switzerland: World Health Organization.

———. 2008. "Gender and Women's Mental Health." http://www.who.int/mental_health/prevention/genderwomen/in/print.html (2008, March 22).

———. 2009. "Children: Reducing Mortality." (November). www.who.int/mediacentre/factsheets/fs178/en/index.html (2011, September 7).

———. 2010a. "Forty Young Europeans Murdered Every Day: New WHO Report Shows These Deaths Can Be Avoided." (September 21). www.euro.who.int/en/what-we-publish/information-for-the-media/scctions/latest-press-releases/forty-young-europeans-murdered-every-day-new-who-report-shows-these-deaths-can-be-avoided (2011, October 8).

———. 2010b. Trends in Maternal Mortality: 1990 to 2008. Geneva, Switzerland: WHO Press.

———. 2010c. *World Malaria Report* 2010. Geneva, Switzerland: World Health Organization, 2011.

———. 2011a. "Disability and Health." Fact Sheet, (June). www.who.int/mediacentre/Factsheets/fs352/en/index.html (2011, September 29).

———. 2011b. mhGAP Newsletter. (January). www.who.int/mental_health/mhGAP_newsletter_jan2011.pdf (2011, September 28).

———. 2011c. "Newborn Deaths Decrease but Account For Higher Share of Global Child Deaths." (August 30). www.who.int/mediacentre/news/releases/2011/newborn_deaths_20110830/en/index.html (2011, September 7).

———. 2011d. "Sexually Transmitted Infections." (August). www.who.int/mediacentre/factsheets/fs110/en (2011, July 31).

———, and World Bank. 2011. World Report on Disability. (June, 2011). World Health Organization: Geneva, Switzerland. www.who.int/mediacentre/factsheets/fs352/en/index.html (2011, September 29).

World Hunger Education Service. 2011. "Hunger in America: 2011 United States Hunger and Poverty Facts." www.worldhunger.org/articles/Learn/us_hunger_facts.htm(2011, September 7).

World Wealth Report 2011. (June 22). www.us.capgemini.com/new-and-events/new/merrill=lynch-global-wealth-management-and-capgemini-release-15th-annual-world-wealth-report/ (2011, July 8).

Worldwide ERC. 2008. Family Issues 2008. Washington, DC.

Wright, J. M. 1998. Lesbian Step Families: An Ethnography of Love. New York: Haworth Press

Wu, Z., and R. Hart. 2002a. "The Effects of Marital and Nonmarital Union Transition on Health. Journal of Marriage and Family 64: 420–432.

———. 2002b. "The Mental Health of the Childless Elderly." Sociological Inquiry 72, 1: 21–42.

Xu, X., C. D. Hudspeth, and J. P. Bartkowski. 2006. "The Role of Cohabitation in Remarriage." Journal of Marriage and Family 68, 2: 261–274.

Yang, S., and P. Rosenblatt. 2001. "Shame in Korean Families." Journal of Comparative Family Studies 32, 3: 361–376.

Yardley, J. 2010. "India Tries Using Cash Bonuses to Slow Birthrates." (August 21) www.nytimes.com/2010/08/22/world/asia/22india.html (2011, February 5).

Yardley, W. 2010. "Report finds 36 Died Under Assisted Suicide Law." (March 4). www.nytimes.com/2010/03/05/us/05suicide.html (2011, September 28).

Ybarra, M., and Mitchell, K. 2005. "Exposure to Internet Pornography Among Children and Adolescents: A National Survey." CyberPsychology & Behavior. (November 5), 8 (5): 473–486.

Yellowbird, M., and Snipp, M. 2002. "American Indian Families." In R. Taylor, ed., Minority Families in the United States. Upper Saddle River, NJ: Prentice Hall.

Yen, H. 2010. "Census Finds More Stay-at-Home Dads." (January 15). www.manufacturing.net/News-Census-Finds-More-Stay-At-Home-Dads-011510.aspx (2011, June 25).

———. 2011. "Wealth Gap Widens Between Whites, Minorities." (July 26). www.amren.com/mtnews/archives/2011/07/wealth_gap_wide.php (2011, September 14).

Yoon, E. 2011. "Educational Approaches to Tackling Disability in War-Torn Countries." (July 21). www.mediaglobal.org/?p=688. (2011, October 1).

Young, A. 2000. Women Who Become Men: Albania's Sworn Virgins. Oxford, UK: Berg Publishers.

Young, Jr., A., and Holcomb, P. 2007. "Voices of Young Fathers: The Partners for Fragile Families Demonstration Projects." Washington, DC: The Urban Institute, Center on Labor, Human Services, and Populations.

Yuan, A., S. Vogt, and H. A. Hamilton. 2006. "Stepfather Involvement and Adolescent Well-being." Journal of Family Issues 27, 9: 1191–1213.

Zablocki, B. 1980. Alienation and Charisma: A Study of Contemporary Communes. New York: Free Press.

Zaccaro, L. 2010. "More Middle Class Couples Are Getting Prenuptial Agreements, According to a Lawyer's Association." (September 30). www.abcbews,gi,cin.GMA/MelodyHobson/prenups-101-couples-married/story (2011, September 7).

Zaslow, J. 2006. "Mr. Moms Grow Up: A New Generation of Granddads Is Helping to Raise the Kids." Wall Street Journal (June 8): D1.

———. 2010. "Friendship for Guys (No Tears!)." Wall Street Journal (April 7). http://online.wsj.com/article/SB1000142527023046203045751660909048 2912.html (2011, April 11).

Zavella, P. 1987. Women's Work and Chicano Families: Cannery Workers of the Santa Clara Valley. Ithaca, NY: Cornell University Press.

Zebroski, S. 1997. "Findings for Research on Interracial Marriages." Interrace: SoftLine Information, Inc. http://www.sistahspace.com/nommo/ir13.html (2001, November 14).

Zentella, A. 2005. Building on Strengths: Language and Literacy in Latino Families and Communities. New York: Teachers College Press.

Zhou, Z., M. A. Bray, T. J. Kehle, and T. Xin. 2001. "Similarity of Deleterious Effects of Divorce on Chinese and American Children." School Psychology International 22, 3 (August): 357–363.

Zimmerman, J., and G. Reavill. 1998. Raising Our Athletic Daughters: How Sports Can Build Self-Esteem and Save Girls' Lives. New York: Doubleday.

Zinn, M. B., and Pok, A. 2002. "Tradition and Transition in Mexican-Origin Families." In R. Taylor, ed., Minority Families in the United States. Upper Saddle River, NJ: Prentice Hall.

Zoosk. 2011. "Global Survey." Press Release. (May 25). www.zoosk.com/release.php?key=16 (2011, July 31).

Zoroyaa, G. 2011. "20,000 Military Members, Vets Faced Foreclosure in 2010." (February 4). www.usatoday.com/clearprint/?unique=130893396562 (2011, June 24).

Zuckerman, D. M., and D. H. Sayre. 1982. "Cultural Sex-Role Expectations and Children's Sex-Role Concepts." Sex Roles 8: 853–62.

Zuger, A. 1998. "Girls and Women Are as Aggressive as Males, Studies Show." Chicago Tribune (December 27): sec. 13, 2.

Zumbrun, J. 2007. "Albania's Sworn Virgins." Chicago Tribune. (August 22): 1, 9.

Photo Credits

Name Index

Subject Index

Females. *See also* Gender roles; Gender role socialization
in abusive relationships, 371–372
career trends for, 81
data on unmarried, 141
dating by older, 132
delayed childbearing in, 280, 288
discrimination against, 386
divorce and, 406–407
earnings gap and, 334
eating disorders in, 79
economic role of, 69
in higher education, 75–76
HIV/AIDS and, 198–199
household labor division and, 47, 80, 220, 225, 327–329
in labor force, 68, 320, 322–323, 331–337
love and, 107–109
mental health issues and, 83–84
in military, 62
never-married, 215–216
in nineteenth century, 19, 20
in nontraditional jobs, 83
occupational distribution and, 332–334
in politics, 81, 82
as refugees, 502
in religious institutions, 81–83
sexual assault of, 363–365 (*See also* Violence; Violence against females)
sexuality and, 174–175, 192, 193
sexually transmitted infections and, 195
in sports, 75
as terrorists, 506
unemployment among, 342
union membership among, 335
union membership and, 334–336
view of marriage by, 254–255
violence against, 353–375 (*See also* Violence; Violence against females)
work-family conflict for, 330–331
workplace sexual harassment and, 336–337
Femicide, 356
Feminine mystique, 330–331
Femininity

cross-cultural perspective on, 67
explanation of, 63
traditional meaning of, 66–67
Feminist perspective
on families, 53
on marriage, 236
scientific methodologies and, 41–42
Feminist theories, 52–53
Feminization of poverty, 340
Fertility awareness, 530–531
Fertility rates. *See also* Infertility
abortion and, 282–284
contraception and, 281–282
explanation of, 276, 277
trends in, 276–277
Fertility treatments
artificial insemination as, 285
assisted reproductive technology as, 286–287
multiple births and, 288–289
Fetal alcohol effect (FAE), 291
Fetal alcohol syndrome (FAS), 291–292
Films
sex in, 183
violence and, 358, 360–361
Filter theories, 138–139
Fimbria, 524
Firearms. *See* Gun control
Flextime, 346
Foster care, 512
Friendships
cross-sex, 84–85
gender differences in, 84
love vs., 101–103
Frigidity, 520
Functional, 46–47
Fundamentalist Church of Jesus Christ of Latter Day Saints (FLDS), 3, 4
Fundamentalist religions, spousal roles in, 80
The Future of Marriage (Bernard), 254

Gang violence, 503–504
Gay and Lesbian Alliance Against Defamation (GLAAD), 183
Gay bars, 137, 148
Gays. *See also* Homosexuals/homosexuality; Lesbians; Same-sex marriage; Same-sex relationships
adoption by, 513
African American, 137
attitudes about, 165, 222–224
child custody and, 412

cohabitation among, 216, 222, 224, 225
dating and mate selection by, 124
HIV/AIDS and, 196, 198
love relationships for, 109
marriage and, 10, 26, 136, 221–224, 241–243
older, 226–227, 473
as parents, 310
partner abuse and, 366
research on, 43–44
sexuality and, 176, 187–188
stepfamilies and, 438
Gender-based violence. *See also* Violence; Violence against females
battered women as, 361–363
against children, 378–382
against elderly, 382–384
explanation of, 354–355
as human rights and public health issue, 354–357, 385
intersections in, 366–369
physical assault as, 361–363
sexual assault as, 363–365, 380–381
against siblings, 384
in U. S. culture, 357–361
Gender dysphoria, 64
Gender/gender differences. *See also* Females; Males
in attitudes toward sex, 174–175
in child's adjustment to parent's divorce, 433–434
in cohabitation satisfaction, 219–220
in dating and mate selection, 134–135
disabilities and, 485–486
in divorce, 406–409
explanation of, 63
as factor in research, 43
friendships and, 102–103
HIV/AIDS and, 198–199
household labor division and, 47, 80
in jealousy, 115
in love, 101, 107–109
mental health and, 83–84
in multigeneration families, 449
nature–nurture debate and, 63, 65
occupational distribution, 332–334
of older adults, 452–453
in parenthood experience, 296

remarriage and, 426, 440
sexuality and, 167–168, 174–175, 180, 192–193
social experience and, 6–7
toys and, 72–73
in views of marriage, 254–255
Gender/gender roles, child care and, 329
Gender identity
explanation of, 63, 69
teachers and, 75–76
variations in, 63–65
Gender identity disorder, 64–65
Gender polarization, 71
Gender roles
cross-cultural perspective on, 67
dating and, 134–135
household labor division and, 47, 80, 220, 225, 327–329
nature-nurture debate and, 63, 65
resolving issues related to, 69–70
traditional, 66–67
in transition, 67–71
Gender role socialization
agents of, 72
boys and, 76–77
cognitive-development theory and, 71
encultured-lens theory and, 71
explanation of, 65
language and, 74
love and, 111
mass media and, 77–80
methods to modify, 87
organized sports and, 74–75
parents and, 72–74
peers and, 74
religion and, 80
social-learning theory and, 70–71
teachers and school organization and, 75–76
violence to females and, 373
Gender/sex variations, 63–65
Gender similarities hypothesis, 63
Gender stereotypes
career and lifestyle choices and, 81–83
communication patterns and, 85–86
consequences of, 80–81
in curricular materials, 75
dating and, 134–135
explanation of, 61
friendships and, 84–85

Social Purity Movement, 169
Social Security, 458, 459, 473
Social Security Act of 1935, 459
Social stress, violence and, 370
Social structure, 9
Sociological imagination, 27
Sociology
    critical look at, 42–44
    link between research and
        theory, 34–35
    role of, 34
    theoretical perspectives in,
        44, 46
Sole custody, 411–413
South Africa
    HIV/AIDS and, 200
    interracial dating in, 144
    rape in, 356
South America, HIV/AIDS in,
    199, 200
Southern Poverty Law Center
    (SPLC), 495
Spain, 498
Speed dating, 151
Spermicides, 530
Spillover effects, work-family,
    319–320
Split custody, 391
Sports, gender identity and,
    74–75
Spousal roles, 80
Spouses
    as caregivers, 68
    death of, 494
    remarriage and role of
        former, 438–439
    remarriage to former,
        430–431
Status grading and
    achievement, 123–124
Stay-at-home fathers, 323–324
Stepchildren
    as caregivers, 469
    relationship between
        stepfathers and,
        433, 442
    stepsibling relationships
        and, 434–436
Stepfamilies. See also Remarried
    families
    boundary ambiguity in,
        432–433
    children and, 431–436
    cultural images of, 423–424,
        436, 437
    demographics of, 424
    gay and lesbian, 438
Stepfathers
    cultural images of,
        423–424, 437
    discipline and, 438

economic issues, 437–438
    as legal parenting partners,
        429–430
    relationship between
        stepchildren and, 433, 442
    sex and, 437
Stepmothers
    cultural images of,
        423–424, 436
    as legal parenting partners,
        429–430
    in mothering role, 437
    role of, 436–437
    tasks for, 442
Stereotypes, 11–15. See also
        Gender stereotypes
Sterilization, 528
Stimulus-value-role theory, 138
Storge, 100
Street violence, 504
Structural functionalism, 46–47
Sub-Saharan Africa
    HIV/AIDS and, 199, 200
    infant death rate in, 289
Substance abuse
    global issues related to,
        487–490
    HIV/AIDS and, 199, 200
    in victims of violence,
        374, 382
    violence and, 155
Suicide, 494
Support networks
    for cohabiting couples, 219
    for nonmarried individuals,
        214–216
    for remarried families,
        441, 442
Surrogacy, 286–287
Surveys, 38–39
Sweden
    occupational distribution
        in, 333
    parental leave in, 331
Sworn virgins (Albania), 65
Symbolic interactionism, 49
Symbols, 49
Syphilis, 522
Systemic racism, 300

Tahitians, 67
Talk shows, 183
Taxation, of wealthy
    individuals, 344
Tchambuli, 49
Teachers, gender identity and
    influence of, 75–76
Technology/technology use. See
    also Internet
    child abuse and, 378
    divorce and, 403, 405

gender differences in, 73
    parenting issues related to,
        299–300
    service job elimination due
        to, 338–339
Teenagers. See Adolescents
Teletubbies, 77
Television
    children's shows on, 77–78
    gender messages transmitted
        by, 77–80
    political talk shows on, 78
    sex on, 182–183
    violence and, 358, 360–361
Terrorism. See also War
    children and, 509–511
    explanation of, 506
    family life and, 23
    in United States, 506–507
    as weapon of war, 509–511
Testes, 524
Text messaging, 149, 170–171
Theories
    explanation of, 34
    feminist, 52–53
    link between research and,
        34–35
Tibet, 5
Tiwi of Australia, 246–247
Tobacco use. See Smoking
Toda, 4–5
Tornados, 56
Total fertility rate, 276–278
Total marriage, 256
Toys, gender stereotypical, 72–73
Traditional family, 11, 13–14
Transgendered individuals
    African American, 137
    dating and mate selection
        by, 136–137
    explanation of, 63, 65,
        166–167
    older, 473
Transracial adoptions, 513,
    515–516
Transsexuals, 64–65, 167
Transvestites, 167
Triangular theory of
    love, 105
The Triangular Theory of Love
    (Sternberg), 105
Trichomoniasis, 523
Trust, 113–114
Tubal ligation, 528
Turkey, 355–356
Twin Oaks, 227
Two-person single career
    families, 324–325

Uganda, 278, 510
Underemployment, 343

Unemployment
    African Americans and,
        303, 320
    among adolescent
        parents, 313
    date and intimate partner
        violence and, 155
    Great Recession of
        2007–2009 and, 320
    issues related to, 341
    marital functioning and,
        342–343
    poverty and, 339
    statistics for, 341
UNICEF, 486, 511
Uninvolved parenting style, 298
United Nations, 2, 354, 448, 487
Upper class, 135
Urethra, 524
Uterus, 524

Vacuum aspiration, 527
Vagina, 524
Vaginismus, 520
Valentines, 90–91
Valentine's Day, 99
Validating partnerships, 267
Variables, 34
Vas deferens, 524
Vasectomy, 528
Venereal diseases, 521
Victim blaming, 371
Victorians, 169
Video games
    gender differences and, 73
    violence and, 358, 360
Violence
    alcohol consumption
        and, 155
    against children, 353–354,
        378–382
    in cohabitation
        situations, 220
    coping and survival
        strategies for victims
        of, 373–375
    dating, 152–157, 220
    disabilities and, 485–486
    against elderly, 354, 382–384
    family, 155
    gang, 503–504
    against gays and lesbians, 226
    gun, 35–36
    intimate partner, 358
    against males, 364–365
    media and, 358, 360–361
    myths about, 359
    in same-sex relationships,
        153, 366–367
    in schools, 505
    against siblings, 354, 384